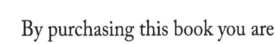

English
Français
Deutsche
Italiano
Español
Português

www.forgottenbooks.com

Mythology Photography **Fiction**
Fishing Christianity **Art** Cooking
Essays Buddhism Freemasonry
Medicine **Biology** Music **Ancient
Egypt** Evolution Carpentry Physics
Dance Geology **Mathematics** Fitness
Shakespeare **Folklore** Yoga Marketing
Confidence Immortality Biographies
Poetry **Psychology** Witchcraft
Electronics Chemistry History **Law**
Accounting **Philosophy** Anthropology
Alchemy Drama Quantum Mechanics
Atheism Sexual Health **Ancient History**
Entrepreneurship Languages Sport
Paleontology Needlework Islam
Metaphysics Investment Archaeology
Parenting Statistics Criminology
Motivational

DIOCESE OF ALBANY.

Convention Journal.

A. D. 1890.

JOURNAL OF THE PROCEEDINGS

OF THE

TWENTY-SECOND ANNUAL CONVENTION

OF THE

Protestant Episcopal Church

IN THE

DIOCESE OF ALBANY,

WHICH ASSEMBLED IN

ALL SAINTS' CATHEDRAL, ALBANY, N. Y.

TUESDAY, NOVEMBER 11,

A. D., 1890.

——— ——

ALBANY, N. Y.:
WEED, PARSONS & COMPANY, PRINTERS.
1890.

LIST OF THE CLERGY

IN THE

DIOCESE OF ALBANY

IN THE ORDER OF CANONICAL RESIDENCE

NOVEMBER 11, 1890.

Showing the dates of becoming resident, and in case of those not gaining residence by Ordination, the name of the Diocese from which each was received.

Date of Reception.	Diocese from which received.	Name.
1868. Nov. 15.	At Primary Convention.	The Rt. Rev. WILLIAM CROSWELL DOANE S. T. D., LL. D., Bishop.
" "	" "	The Rev. JOSEPH CAREY, S. T. D.
" "	" "	The Rev. EDGAR T. CHAPMAN.
" "	" "	The Rev. WILLIAM H. COOK.
" · "	" "	The Rev. JOSEPH N. MULFORD.
" "	" "	The Rev. GEORGE H. NICHOLLS, S. T. D.
" "	" "	The Rev. WILLIAM M. OGDEN.
" "	" "	The Rev. WILLIAM PAYNE, D. D.
" "	" "	The Rev. J. LIVINGSTON REESE, D. D.
" "	" "	The Rev. WILLIAM S. ROWE.
" "	" "	The Rev. DAVID L. SCHWARTZ.
" "	" "	The Rev. EDWARD SELKIRK.
" "	" "	The Rev. JOHN B. TIBBITS, Deacon.
" "	" "	The Rev. J. IRELAND TUCKER, S. T. D.
" "	" "	The Rev. ROBERT WASHBON.
" Dec. 1.	New York	The Rev. JAMES WILKINS STEWART.
1869. Sept. 22.	Montreal	The Rev. CHARLES H. LANCASTER.
1870. Mar. 7.	Massachusetts	The Rev. FENWICK M. COOKSON.
" June 12.	-	The Rev. WILLIAM CURTIS PROUT.
" Dec. 6.	Pennsylvania	The Rev. JAMES CAIRD.
1871. April 12.	Montreal	The Rev. J. D. MORRISON, D. D., LL. D.
" July 12.	Vermont	The Rev. J. W. McILWAINE.
" Sept. 27.	New York	The Rev. ERASTUS WEBSTER.
" Nov. 21.	Massachusetts	The Rev. WILLIAM R. WOODBRIDGE.
1872. July 14.	-	The Rev. JOHN H. HOUGHTON.
1873. Nov. 26.	Massachusetts	The Rev. ROBERT T. S. LOWELL, D. D.
1874. May 13.	New York	The Rev. WILLIAM CHARLES GRUBBE.

Date of Reception.	Diocese from which received.	Name.
1874. Aug. 3.	Western New York -	The Rev. WALTON W. BATTERSHALL, D. D.
" Sept. 17. - - - - -		The Rev. THEODORE A. SNYDER.
" Sept. 29.	Central New York -	The Rev. MOSES E. WILSON.
" Oct. 7.	Pennsylvania -	The Rev. R. J. ADLER.
" Nov. 1. - - - - -		The Rev. HENRY M. SMYTH.
1875. Nov. 5.	New York - - -	The Rev. CHARLES C. EDMUNDS.
" Dec. 16.	New York - - -	The Rev. ROBERT G. HAMILTON.
1876. Mar. 12. - - - - -		The Rev. WILLIAM B. REYNOLDS, Deacon.
" Mar. 18.	New York - - -	The Rev. RICHARD TEMPLE.
" Aug. 22.	Central New York	The Rev. WILLIAM N. IRISH.
" Sept. 26.	North Carolina - -	The Rev. WILLIAM W. LORD, D. D.
" Dec. 11.	New York - - .	The Rev. CHARLES S. OLMSTED.
1877. Jan. 24. - - - - -		The Rev. CHAS. EDWARD CRAGG, Deacon.
" Mar. 1.	Newark - - -	The Rev. ERNEST A. HARTMANN.
" May 31. - - - - -		The Rev. SCOTT B. RATHBUN.
1878. Feb. 27.	Montana - - -	The Rev. EUGENE L. TOY.
1879. Jan. 1.	Long Island - -	The Rev. THOMAS B. FULCHER.
" July 13. - - - - -		The Rev. JOHN N. MARVIN.
" July 15.	Massachusetts -	The Rev. SILAS M. ROGERS.
1880. Mar. 29.	Connecticut - -	The Rev. HEMAN R. TIMLOW
" May 23. - - - - -		The Rev. JOHN BREWSTER HUBBS.
" May 23. - - - - -		The Rev. JOHN PROUT.
" June 1. - - - - -		The Rev. CHARLES C. EDMUNDS, Jr.
" Oct. 18.	Massachusetts -	The Rev. FREDERICK H. T. HORSFIELD.
1881. Jan. 8.	Western New York -	The Rev. CHARLES M. NICKERSON.
" Mar. 1.	Massachusetts -	The Rev. THADDEUS A. SNIVELY.
" Mar. 14.	Central New York -	The Rev. ROBERT GRANGER.
" Dec. 19.	New York - - -	The Rev. GEORGE DENT SILLIMAN.
1882. Jan. 9.	Newark - - -	The Rev. WILLIAM HENRY HARISON, D.D.
" Feb. 23,	Utah - - - -	The Rev. R. M. KIRBY
" Nov. 7.	Connecticut - -	The Rev. HOBART COOKE.
" Dec. 28.	Rhode Island - -	The Rev. CLEMENT J WHIPPLE.
1883. Feb. 12.	Central New York -	The Rev. E. BAYARD SMITH.
" May 5.	Delaware - - -	The Rev. W. G. W. LEWIS.
" Oct. 31.	New York - - -	The Rev. C. P. A. BURNETT.
1884. Jan. 8.	Western New York -	The Rev. W. D. U. SHEARMAN.
" Jan. 20. - - - - -		The Rev. JAMES A. DICKSON.
" Feb. 13.	Fredericton - - -	The Rev. F S. SILL.
" Mar. 4.	Ohio - - - - -	The Rev. SAMUEL T STREET.
" May 27.	Newark - - - -	The Rev. CHARLES PELLETREAU.
" June 3. - - - - -		The Rev. EDWARD S. DeG. TOMPKINS.
" June 4. - - - - -		The Rev. DAVID SPRAGUE.
" July 12. - - - - -		The Rev. RUSSELL WOODMAN.
1885. Jan. 10.	Springfield - - -	The Rev. JAMES E. HALL.
" Mar. 16.	Exeter, England -	The Rev. THOMAS H. R. LUNEY.
" May 1.	Central Pennsylvania -	The Rev. J. PHILIP B. PENDLETON.
" May 30. - - - - -		The Rev. CHARLES TEMPLE.
" May 31. - - - - -		The Rev. SHELDON M. GRISWOLD.
" Aug. 6.	Maine - - - -	The Rev. RICHMOND SHREVE, D. D.
" Oct. 10. - - - - -		The Rev. EDWARD DUDLEY TIBBITS.
" Nov. 5.	Wisconsin - - -	The Rev. LOUIS HECTOR SCHUBERT.
" Dec. 18.	Connecticut - - -	The Rev. EATON W. MAXCY, D. D.
1886. Jan. 14.	Michigan - - - -	The Rev. MILTON C. DOTTEN.
" Mar. 8.	Western New York -	The Rev. WILLIAM B. BOLMER.
" June 7.	Massachusetts -	The Rev. JAMES O. LINCOLN.
" Aug. 2.	Iowa - - - -	The Rev. NASSAU W. STEPHENS.
" Sept. 24.	Yedo - - - -	The Rev. CLEMENT THEOPHILUS BLANCHET.
" Nov. 13.	Central Pennsylvania	The Rev. DANIEL WASHBURN.
1887. Jan. 15.	Connecticut - - -	The Rev. FRANK B. REAZOR.
" Feb. 12. - - - - -		The Rev. JOSEPH T. ZORN.
" May 19.	Connecticut - - -	The Rev. EDGAR A. ENOS.

Date of Reception.	Diocese from which received.	Name.
1887. Aug. 1.	New York - - -	The Rev. CHARLES E. FREEMAN.
" Aug. 1.	New York - - -	The Rev. WILLIAM ROLLINS WEBB.
" Aug. 4.	Virginia - - -	The Rev. J. A. FARRAR.
" Sept. 24.	New York - - -	The Rev. J. FREDERICK ESCH.
" Nov. 1.	New York - - -	The Rev. GEORGE H. NORTON, Deacon.
" Nov. 5.	Massachusetts - -	The Rev. WILFORD LASH ROBBINS.
1888. Jan. 20.	Southern Ohio -	The Rev. HENRY T. GREGORY.
" Jan. 23.	New Hampshire -	The Rev. FREDERICK MORLAND GRAY.
" May 18.	Pittsburgh - - -	The Rev. WILLIAM MASON COOK, S. T. B.
" May 20.	- - - -	The Rev. GEORGE MERIWETHER IRISH.
" May 22.	Springfield - -	The Rev. THOMAS WHITE.
" Sept. 3.	Tennessee - - -	The Rev. ALFRED TAYLOR.
" Oct. 7.	- - - - -	The Rev. WALTER CHARLES STEWART.
" Nov. 20.	Nova Scotia - -	The Rev. ANGUS C. MACDONALD.
" Nov. 20.	Pennsylvania - -	The Rev. CHARLES W. BOYD, Deacon.
" Dec. 8.	New Jersey - -	The Rev. SAMUEL B. MOORE.
" Dec. 21.	- - - - - } -	The Rev. FREDERICK G. RAINEY.
1889. Jan. 14.	New Hampshire -	The Rev. ISAAC PECK.
" Jan. 21.	New Jersey - - -	The Rev. THOMAS DICKINSON.
" Mar. 8.	Maine - - -	The Rev. WILLIAM DICKINSON MARTIN.
" April 15.	Maine - - - -	The Rev. ROBERT N. PARKE, D. D.
" April 30.	New York - - -	The Rev. PHILIP W. MOSHER.
" June 16.	- - - - -	The Rev. ROBERT MORRIS KEMP.
" June 16.	- - - - -	The Rev. ELMER PLINY MILLER.
" June 16.	- - - - -	The Rev. MEREDITH OGDEN SMITH, Deacon.
" Sept. 23.	New York - - -	The Rev. JOHN McCARTHY WINDSOR.
" Sept. 23.	Springfield - -	The Rev. HOWARD McDOUGALL.
" Oct. 31.	Missouri - - -	The Rev. E. W. FLOWER.
" Nov. 1.	New York - - -	The Rev. WALTER HASKINS LAROM.
" Dec. 27.	Easton - - -	The Rev. A. T. DeLEARSY.
1890. Jan. 10.	East Carolina -	The Rev. FREDERICK NASH SKINNER.
" Feb. 5.	Western New York -	The Rev. E. RUTHVEN ARMSTRONG.
" Mar. 14.	Massachusetts - -	The Rev. ERNEST MARIETT.
" April 25.	New Jersey - -	The Rev. HARRIS COX RUSH.
" May 8.	Rochester, England	The Rev. S. C. THOMPSON.
" June 4.	- - - - -	The Rev. ASA SPRAGUE ASHLEY, Deacon.
" June 7.	- - - - -	The Rev. FREDERICK STIRLING GRIFFIN, Deacon.
" June 7.	Central New York -	The Rev. CHAUNCEY VIBBARD, Jr.
" July 20.	Fredericton - -	The Rev. CHARLES H. HATHEWAY.
" Sept. 24.	Vermont - - -	The Rev. FREDERICK SHUBALL FISHER.
" Oct. 10.	New York - - -	The Rev. WILLIAM GEORGE IVIE.
" Oct. 13.	New York - - -	The Rev. WILLIAM HENRY BOWN.
" Nov. 1.	Durham, England -	The Rev. REYNER EDWARD WILLIAM COSENS.
" Nov. 8.	Colorado - - -	The Rev. PHINEAS DURYEA.

AN ALPHABETICAL LIST OF THE CLERGY.

The Right Rev. WILLIAM CROSWELL DOANE, S. T. D., LL. D., Bishop, Albany.

The Rev. R. J. ADLER, Rector, St. Mark's Church, Green Island, Albany county.

The Rev. E. RUTHVEN ARMSTRONG, Rector, Zion Church, Sandy Hill, Washington county.

The Rev. ASA SPRAGUE ASHLEY, Missionary, Immanuel Church, Otego, Otsego county.

* The Rev. WALTON W. BATTERSHALL, D. D., Rector, St. Peter's Church, Albany, Albany county.

The Rev. CLEMENT T. BLANCHET, Missionary, St. Sacrament Church, Bolton, Warren county.

The Rev. W. B. BOLMER, Rector. St. Luke's Church, Troy, Rensselaer county.

The Rev. WILLIAM HENRY BOWN, Rector, Grace Church, Albany, Albany county.

The Rev. CHARLES W. BOYD, Head Master, St. Paul's Hall, Salem, Washington county.

* The Rev. *C. P. A. Burnett*, Missionary, Christ Church, Gloversville, Fulton county.

The Rev. JAMES CAIRD, Rector, Free Church of the Ascension, Troy, Rensselaer county.

* The Rev. JOSEPH CAREY, S. T. D., Rector, Bethesda Church, Saratoga Springs, Saratoga county.

* The Rev. EDGAR T. CHAPMAN, Canon and Treasurer, Cathedral of All Saints, Priest in charge, St. Margaret's Mission, Menands Station. P. O., Troy road, Albany.

The Rev. *William H. Cook*, Missionary, St. John's Church, East Line, and Grace Mission, Jonesville, Saratoga county.

* The Rev. WILLIAM MASON COOK, S. T. B., Rector, St. Augustine's Church, Ilion, Herkimer county.

The Rev. HOBART COOKE, Rector, Trinity Church, Plattsburgh, Clinton county.

* The Rev. FENWICK M. COOKSON, Rector, Church of the Messiah, Glen's Falls, Warren county.

The Rev. *Reyner Edward William Cosens*, Rector, Trinity Church, Whitehall, Washington county.

The Rev. CHARLES EDWARD CRAGG, Assistant Minister, Christ Church, Port Henry, Essex county.

* The Rev. *A. T. DeLearsy*, Missionary, Grace Chapel, Stamford, Delaware county.

The Rev. *Thomas Dickinson*, Missionary, Trinity Church, Schaghticoke, Rensselaer county.

The Rev. JAMES A. DICKSON, Rector, Trinity Church, Gouverneur, and Missionary, St. Lawrence county.

* The Rev. *Milton C. Dotten*.

* The Rev. *Phineas Duryea*, Missionary, Santa Clara, St. Regis Falls, Brandon and Tupper Lake, Franklin county.

* The Rev. *Charles C. Edmunds*, Missionary, Zion Church, Fonda, Montgomery county. P. O., Johnstown, Fulton county.

* The Rev. CHARLES C. EDMUNDS, Jr., Rector, Christ Church, Herkimer, Herkimer county.

The Rev. EDGAR A. ENOS, Rector, St. Paul's Church, Troy, Rensselaer county.

The Rev. JOHN FREDERICK ESCH, Rector, St. Stephen's Church, Schuylerville, Saratoga county.

The Rev. *J. A. Farrar*, Rector, St. Peter's Church, Hobart, and Missionary, Bloomville, Delaware county.

* The Rev. FREDERICK S. FISHER, Rector, Christ Church, Deposit, and Missionary, Delaware county.

The Rev. E. W. FLOWER, Rector, Christ Church, Duanesburgh, Schenectady county.

* The Rev. CHARLES E. FREEMAN, Rector, Grace Church, Waterford, Saratoga county.

* The Rev. THOMAS B. FULCHER, Canon and Precentor, Cathedral of All Saints, Albany, Albany county, and Rector, Church of the Messiah, Greenbush, Rensselaer county.

The Rev. ROBERT GRANGER, Rector, St. John's Church, Richfield Springs, Otsego county.

The Rev. FREDERICK MORLAND GRAY, Honorary Canon, Cathedral of All Saints, and Chaplain, St. Agnes' School, Albany, Albany county.

The Rev. HENRY T. GREGROY, Rector, Church of the Cross, Ticonderoga, and Missionary, Essex county.

* The Rev. FREDERICK STIRLING GRIFFIN, Missionary, St. Paul's Church, Sidney, Delaware county, Christ Church, West Burlington, and at Edmeston, Otsego county.

* The Rev. SHELDON M. GRISWOLD, Rector, Christ Church, Hudson, Columbia county.

The Rev. WILLIAM CHARLES GRUBBE, Rector, Gloria Dei Church, Palenville, and Missionary, Greene county.

* The Rev. JAMES E. HALL, Rector, Grace Church, Cherry Valley, Otsego county.

The Rev. R. G. HAMILTON, Rector, Grace Church, Canton, and Missionary, Trinity Chapel, Morley, St. Lawrence county.

* The Rev. *William Henry Harison*, D. D., Ogdensburgh, N. Y.

* The Rev. ERNEST A. HARTMANN, Rector, St. James' Church, Oneonta, and Missionary, Immanuel Church, Otego, Otsego county.

, The Rev. CHARLES H. HATHEWAY, Honorary Canon, Cathedral of All Saints, Albany, also Missionary, St. Andrew's Church, West Troy, Albany county, and St. Giles', Castleton, Rensselaer county.

* The Rev. FREDERICK H. T. HORSFIELD, Rector, St. Luke's Church, Cambridge, Washington county.

* The Rev. JOHN H. HOUGHTON, Rector, St. Paul's Church, Salem, and Missionary, Washington county.

* The Rev. JOHN BREWSTER HUBBS, Rector, St. John's Church, Johnstown, Fulton county.

* The Rev. GEORGE M. IRISH, Rector, Zion Church, Colton, St. Lawrence county.

The Rev. WILLIAM N. IRISH, Rector, St. John's Church, Essex, and Missionary, Essex county.

* The Rev. WILLIAM GEORGE IVIE, Assistant Minister, All Saints' Church, Hoosac, and Missionary, Church of the Holy Name, Boyntonville, Rensselaer county.

The Rev. *Robert Morris Kemp*, New York city.

* The Rev. R. M. KIRBY, Rector, Trinity Church, Potsdam, St. Lawrence county.

The Rev. *Charles H. Lancaster*, Rector, St. James' Church, Caldwell, and Missionary, French Mountain, Warren county. P. O., Lake George.

The Rev. WALTER HASKINS LAROM, Missionary, Church of St. Luke the Beloved Physician, Saranac Lake, and St. John's in the Wilderness, St. Regis Lake, Franklin county, and Good Shepherd, Bloomingdale, Essex county.

The Rev. WILLIAM G. W. LEWIS, Rector, St. Luke's Church, Mechanicville, and St. John's Church, Stillwater, Saratoga county.

The Rev. *James O. Lincoln*.

The Rev. *William W. Lord*, D. D., Cooperstown, Otsego county.

The Rev. *Robert T. S. Lowell*, D. D., Schenectady, Schenectady county.

The Rev. THOMAS H. R. LUNEY, Officiating, All Saints' Church, Hoosac, Rensselaer county.

The Rev. ANGUS C. MACDONALD, Rector, St. Paul's Church, Waddington, and Missionary, St. Luke's Church, Lisbon, St, Lawrence county.

* The Rev. HOWARD McDOUGALL, Missionary, St. John's Church, Massena, and Grace Church, Louisville Landing, St. Lawrence county, and St. James', Hogansburgh, Franklin county.

The Rev. J. W. McILWAINE.

The Rev. ERNEST MARIETT, Rector, Emmanuel Church, Little Falls, Herkimer county.

The Rev. *William Dickinson Martin*, Priest in charge, St. Barnabas' Church, Troy, Rensselaer county.

The Rev. JOHN N. MARVIN, Missionary, Church of the Good Shepherd, Canajoharie, and Holy Cross Church, Fort Plain, Montgomery county.

The Rev. EATON W. MAXCY, D. D., Rector, Christ Church, Troy, Rensselaer county.

* The Rev. ELMER P. MILLER, Missionary, All Saints' Church, Hudson, and Trinity Church, Claverack, Columbia county.

The Rev. *Samuel B. Moore.*

The Rev. J. D. MORRISON, D. D., LL. D., Rector, St. John's Church, Ogdensburgh, St. Lawrence county.

* The Rev. PHILIP W. MOSHER, Assistant Minister, St. Paul's Church, Troy, Rensselaer county.

The Rev. *Joseph N. Mulford*, Lake Worth, Florida.

The Rev. *George H. Nicholls*, S. T. D., Rector Emeritus, St. Mark's Church, Hoosick Falls, Rensselaer county.

* The Rev. CHARLES M. NICKERSON, Rector, Trinity Church, Lansingburgh, Rensselaer county.

The Rev. GEORGE H. NORTON, Missionary, St. James' Church, Ausable Forks, Essex county.

* The Rev. WILLIAM M. OGDEN, Rector, Church of the Holy Cross, Warrensburgh, Warren county.

* The Rev. CHARLES S. OLMSTED, Rector, Christ Church, Cooperstown, Otsego county.

* The Rev. ROBERT N. PARKE, D. D., Rector, St. Matthew's Church, Unadilla, Otsego county.

* The Rev. WILLIAM PAYNE, D. D., Rector Emeritus, St. George's Church, Schenectady, Schenectady county.

The Rev. ISAAC PECK, Rector, St. Paul's Church, Kinderhook, and Missionary, St. Luke's Mission, Chatham, Columbia county.

* The Rev. *Charles Pelletreau*, Rector, Christ Church, Ballston Spa, Saratoga county.

* The Rev. J. PHILIP B. PENDLETON, Rector, St. George's Church, Schenectady, Schenectady county,

* The Rev. JOHN PROUT, Rector, St. Paul's Church, East Springfield, and Missionary, Otsego county.

* The Rev. WILLIAM C. PROUT, Rector, Trinity Church, Granville, and Missionary, North Granville, Washington county.

The Rev. FREDERICK G. RAINEY, Rector, St. Barnabas' Church, Stottville, Columbia county.

* The Rev. SCOTT B. RATHBUN, Rector, Christ Church, Walton, Delaware county.

* The Rev. FRANK B. REAZOR, Rector, St. John's Church, Delhi, Delaware county.

The Rev. J. LIVINGSTON REESE, D. D., Rector, St. Paul's Church, Albany, Albany county.

The Rev. WILLIAM B. REYNOLDS, Assistant Minister, Church of St. John the Evangelist, Stockport, Columbia county.

The Rev. WILFORD LASH ROBBINS, Dean, Cathedral of All Saints, Albany, Albany county.

The Rev. *Silas M. Rogers*, Rector, St. Peter's Church, Ellenburgh, and St. Paul's Church, Ellenburgh Centre, and Missionary, Clinton county.

The Rev. *William S. Rowe.*

* The Rev. HARRIS COX RUSH, Associate Rector, St. Paul's Church, Salem, Washington county.

The Rev. LOUIS H. SCHUBERT, Rector, Christ Church, Coxsackie, Greene county.

* The Rev. *David L. Schwartz*, Paris, France.

* The Rev. EDWARD SELKIRK, Rector Emeritus, Trinity Church, and Honorary Canon, Cathedral of All Saints, Albany, Albany county.

* The Rev. W. D. U. SHEARMAN, Rector, St. John's Church, Champlain, and Missionary, Christ Church, Rouse's Point, Clinton county.

The Rev. RICHMOND SHREVE, D. D., Rector, Church of the Holy Innocents, Albany, Albany county.

* The Rev. FREDERICK S. SILL, Rector, St. John's Church, Cohoes, Albany county.

* The Rev. GEORGE D. SILLIMAN, Rector, St. Mark's Church, Hoosick Falls, Rensselaer county.

* The Rev. FREDERICK NASH SKINNER, Rector, St. James' Church, Fort Edward, Washington county.

* The Rev. E. BAYARD SMITH, Rector, Trinity Church, West Troy, Albany county.

* The Rev. *Meredith Ogden Smith*, Nashville, Tennessee.

The Rev. *Henry M. Smyth.*

The Rev. THADDEUS A. SNIVELY, Rector, St. John's Church, Troy, Rensselaer county.

The Rev. *Theodore A. Snyder*, Rector, Christ Church, Greenville, and St. Paul's Church, Oak Hill, Greene county.

* The Rev. DAVID SPRAGUE, Rector. St. Ann's Church, Amsterdam, Montgomery county.

The Rev. *Nassau W. Stephens*, Missionary, Church of the Good Shepherd, Chestertown, and St. Paul's, Bartonville, Warren county.

* The Rev. JAMES WILKINS STEWART, Rector, Trinity Church, Athens, and Missionary, Greene county.

The Rev. WALTER CHARLES STEWART, Rector, Zion Church, Morris, Otsego county.

The Rev. *Samuel T. Street.*

The Rev. ALFRED TAYLOR, Rector, Grace Church, Mohawk, and St. Alban's, Frankfort, Herkimer county.

* The Rev. CHARLES TEMPLE, S. T. B., Rector, St. Mark's Church, Malone, Franklin county.

The Rev. RICHARD TEMPLE, Honorary Canon, Cathedral of All Saints, Albany, Albany county.

The Rev. S. C. THOMPSON, Assistant Minister, Trinity Church, Rensselaerville, Albany county.

* The Rev. EDWARD DUDLEY TIBBITS, Rector, All Saints' Church, Hoosac, Priest in charge, Church of the Holy Name, Boyntonville, Rensselaer county, Honorary Canon, Cathedral of All Saints.

The Rev. *John B. Tibbits*, Officiating, All Saints' Church, Hoosac, Rensselaer county.

The Rev. HEMAN R. TIMLOW, Rector, Calvary Church, Burnt Hills, and St. Paul's Church, Charlton, and Missionary, Saratoga county.

The Rev. EDWARD S. DEG. TOMPKINS, Kinderhook, Columbia county.

* The Rev. EUGENE L. TOY, Rector, Christ Church, Schenectady, Schenectady county.

* The Rev. JOHN IRELAND TUCKER, S. T. D., Pastor, Church of the Holy Cross, and Principal of the Warren Free Institute, Troy, Rensselaer county.

The Rev. *Chauncey Vibbard, Jr.*, Rector, Calvary Church, Cairo, Greene county.

* The Rev. *Robert Washbon*, Rector, Trinity Church, Rensselaerville, and Missionary, Berne and Westerlo, Albany county.

The Rev. DANIEL WASHBURN, West Burlington, Otsego county.

* The Rev. *William Rollins Webb.*

The Rev. *Erastus Webster*, Acra, Greene county.

* The Rev. CLEMENT J. WHIPPLE, Rector, St. Mary's Church, Luzerne, Warren county, and Missionary, St. John's Church, Conklingville, Saratoga county.

* The Rev. THOMAS WHITE, Missionary, Church of the Epiphany, Bath, Rensselaer county.

The Rev. *Moses E. Wilson*, Rector, St. Luke's Church, Clermont, and Missionary, Columbia county.

The Rev. *John M. Windsor*, Rector, Trinity Church, Sharon Springs, Schoharie county.

The Rev. WILLIAM R. WOODBRIDGE, Rector, Christ Church, Port Henry, and Missionary, Emmanuel Mission, Mineville, Essex county.

The Rev. RUSSELL WOODMAN, Rector, Trinity Church, Albany, Albany county.

The Rev. *Joseph T. Zorn*, Missionary, Christ Church, Morristown, St. Lawrence county.

I certify the above to be a correct list of the clergy canonically resident in the Diocese of Albany.

WM. CROSWELL DOANE,

ALBANY, *November* 11, 1890.   *Bishop of Albany.*

2

LIST OF LAY DEPUTIES.

The names of those who were not known to be present are printed in *italics*.

County.	Church.	Deputies.
Albany..................	Cathedral of All Saints....	*Melvil Dewey.*
		Wm. Bayard Van Rensselaer.
		James Bell.
	St. Peter's, Albany........	*George S. Weaver.*
		Henry T. Martin.
		Charles L. Pruyn.
	Trinity, Rensselaerville...	*John L. Rice.*
		Nathaniel Teed.
		J. B. Washburn, M. D.
	St. Paul's, Albany	Charles L. Blakeslee.
		Harvey J. Cady.
		Andrew B. Jones.
	St. John's, Cohoes.... ...	Michael Andrae.
		John Horrocks.
		P. Remsen Chadwick.
	Trinity, West Troy.	William Hollands.
		John H. Hulsapple.
		Thomas Rath.
	Trinity, Albany..........	George T. Granger.
		William Little.
		Richard Norris.
	Grace, Albany.......	Benjamin F. Hinman.
		Charles W. White.
		Frank J. Smith.
	Holy Innocents, Albany. ..	Samuel M. Van Santvoord.
		Henry S. McCall, Jr.
		James Oswald.
	St. Mark's, Green Island ..	*Henry Stowell.*
		Richard Leonard.
		W. W. Butler.
Clinton	Trinity, Plattsburgh......	Hon *S. A. Kellogg.*
		Charles H. Moore.
Columbia...............	Christ, Hudson.	John M. Pearson.
		Clarence L. Crofts.
		Frank T. Punderson.
	St. John's, Stockport......	Joshua Reynolds.
		William H. Van de Carr.
		Frank M. Snyder.
	St. Paul's, Kinderhook....	H. S. Wynkoop.
		E. P. Van Alstyne.
		Dr. T. Floyd Woodworth.
	Trinity. Claverack.... ...	*Frank P. Studley.*
		Cornelius Shaw.
		Robert F. Ludlow.
	Our Saviour, Lebanon Spg.	*William H. Babcock.*
		Charles E. Wackerhagen.

County.	Church.	Deputies.
Columbia	All Saints', Hudson	William H. Cookson.
		Richard A. Aitkin.
		Carroll Hankes.
	St. Barnabas', Stottville...	*Richard H. Harder, Jr.*
		Francis H. Stott.
		John J. Plass.
Delaware	St. John's, Delhi	*John A. Kemp.*
		Robert G. Hughston.
		Herbert A. Pitcher.
	Christ, Walton	David H. Gay.
		Joseph Harby.
		Horace E. North.
	St. Paul's, Franklin	*Henry S. Edwards.*
		Alfred Barnes.
		Jay W. Cook.
	Christ, Deposit	*William H. Gregory.*
		T. M. Bixby.
Essex	St. John's, Essex	*Anthony J. B. Ross.*
		William N. Knowlton.
		Stephen D. Derby.
	St. Paul's, Keeseville	Henry Dundas.
		Francis Cassidy.
		Fred. W. Cramphorn.
	Christ, Port Henry..	*Francis S. Atwell.*
		Charles W. Woodford.
		Charles A. Neide.
Fulton	St. John's, Johnstown	*Abiram S. Van Voast.*
..		Thomas E. Ricketts.
		Frederic L. Carroll.
Greene	St. Luke's, Catskill	William L. Dubois.
		William H. H. Schofield.
		Walton Van Loan.
	Christ, Coxsackie	*Dr. N. Clute.*
		N. H. Vosburgh.
		J. E. Brown.
	Trinity, Athens	*George S. Nichols.*
		Robert Cleet.
		Samuel H. Nichols.
	St. Paul's, Oak Hill	*John H. Cheritree.*
		Walter S. Cheritree.
		Byron Hall.
	Christ, Greenville	*George W. Robbins.*
		Byron Waldron.
		Winfield S. Rundel.
Herkimer	Emmanuel, Little Falls ...	*Eben B. Waite.*
		Lawrence A. La Rue.
		Merrick Freeman.
	Christ, Herkimer..	*Robert Earl.*
		J. D. Henderson.
		W. C. Prescott.
	St. Augustine's, Ilion	*F. C. Shepard.*
		George Rix.
		George H. Dyett.
Montgomery	St. Ann's, Amsterdam	Le Grand S. Strang.
		Thomas Mansfield.
		Herbert Trent.
	Zion, Fonda	Richard H. Cushney.
		Henry T. E. Brower.
		Edward B. Cushney.
Otsego	Zion, Morris....	Isaac Mansfield.
		L. S. Pearsall.
		T. O. Duroe.
	St. Matthew's, Unadilla...	*William J. Thompson.*
		George B. Fellows.

County.	Church.	Deputies.
Otsego	St. Matthew's, Unadilla...	*Clark I. Hayes.*
	Christ, Cooperstown	Horace M. Hooker.
		G. Pomeroy Keese.
		S. E. Crittenden.
	Immanuel, Otego..	*Charles Blake.*
		J. H. Cossart, M. D.
		George W. Sherman, Jr.
	Grace, Cherry Valley.....	A. B. Cox.
		William C. Roseboom.
		F. P. Harriott.
	St. John's, Richfield Spg's.	Myron D. Jewell.
		De Witt W. Harrington.
		Ira D. Peckham.
	St. Paul's, E. Springfield..	*James H. Cooke.*
		Leslie Pell-Clarke.
		G. Hyde Clarke.
	St. James', Oneonta.......	R. M. Townsend.
		James Stewart.
		Richard S. Downes.
Rensselaer................	St. Paul's, Troy	Joseph J. Tillinghast.
		John I. Thompson.
		Charles E. Patterson.
	Trinity, Lansingburgh....	James McQuide.
		Edward H. Leonard.
		George F. Nichols.
	St. John's, Troy	Norman B. Squires.
		Benjamin H. Hall.
		Francis N. Mann.
	Christ, Troy........	Hon. William Kemp.
		Washington Akin, M. D.
		J. W. Alfred Cluett.
	St. Mark's, Hoosick Falls.	*George B. Pattison.*
		James Russell Parsons, Jr.
		John G. Darroch.
	Trinity, Schaghticoke.....	Edward Searles.
		Thomas L. Doremus.
		William H. Hawkins.
	Messiah, Greenbush.....	*Benjamin F. Allen.*
		Harry E. Cole.
		Richard W. Stevens.
	St. Luke's, Troy.........	*James Wood,*
		Thomas B. Iler.
		Henry E. Darby.
St. Lawrence.............	St. John's, Ogdensburgh ..	Levi Hasbrouck.
		Louis Hasbrouck.
		Charles Ashley.
	Trinity, Potsdam........	T. Streatfeild Clarkson.
		E. W. Foster.
		W. A. Dart.
	Trinity, Gouverneur......	*Duncan G. Wood.*
		Aaron B. Cutting.
	Zion, Colton.............	*Thomas S. Clarkson.*
		Myron E. Howard.
		Frederick Horton.
Saratoga.................	Christ, Ballston Spa	John H. Westcot.
		Andrew S. Booth.
		Charles M. Brown.
	St. John's, Stillwater.	Joseph Moll.
		John Bradley, Jr.
		Charles Greene.
	St. Paul's, Charlton.......	*William Taylor.*
		George H. Valentine.
		John Marvin.
	Grace, Waterford	*Henry Stoughton Tracy.*

County.	Church.	Deputies.
Saratoga	Grace, Waterford	*John Higgins.*
		Roland Henshall Stubbs.
	St. Luke's, Mechanicville	*M. W. Hart.*
		S. H. Hall.
		H. O. Bailey.
	Bethesda, Saratoga Spg's	*Spencer Trask.*
		William A. Sackett.
		Windsor B. French.
	St. Stephen's, Schuylerville	Malcolm S. Potter.
		Thomas E. Bullard.
		Thomas B. Aitcheson.
	Calvary, Burnt Hills	*Edwin Mead.*
		Frederick German.
		Charles H. Upham.
Schenectady	Christ, Duanesburgh	Ralph W. McDougall.
		George Matthews.
		Wesley Van Pelt.
	St. George's, Schenectady	A. A. Van Vorst.
		John Keyes Paige.
		Charles S. Washburn.
	Christ, Schenectady	Prof. Sidney G. Ashmore.
		Edward E. Kriegsman.
		Rufus W. Lampman.
Warren	Messiah, Glen's Falls	L. G. McDonald.
		Nelson La Salle.
		H. W. Coffin.
	Holy Cross, Warrensburgh	*Frederick O. Burhans.*
		Henry Griffin.
		John Hayes.
	St. Mary's, Luzerne	*C. W. Trumbull.*
		William Beardmore.
		John Burneson.
Washington	Zion, Sandy Hill	*Dr. Albert Mott.*
		Byron G. Knapp.
		Orson R. Howe.
	St. James', Fort Edward	*Francis B. Davis.*
		Benjamin M. Tasker.
		Robert O. Bascom.
	St. Paul's, Salem	James Gibson.
		George B. McCartee.
		George B. Martin.
	Trinity, Whitehall	*Fred. H. MacFarran.*
		Jeremiah Adams.
		Hon. William H. Teft.
	St. Luke's, Cambridge	*Henry C. Day.*
		Thomas Le Grys.
		Robert Davis, Jr.

DIOCESE OF ALBANY.

RULES OF ORDER.

1. After the administration of the Holy Communion, the President shall take the chair, and call the Convention to order.

2. If the President *ex officio* is not present at the opening of the Convention, the Secretary of the last Convention shall call the Convention to order, when the Presbyter, senior by ordination, present, shall take the chair; and, in such case, immediately after the organisation of the Convention, a President shall be elected from among the clergy.

3. When the President takes the chair, no member shall [continue standing, or hall afterward stand, unless to address the Chair.

ORDER OF BUSINESS.
FIRST DAY.

4. After the Convention is called to order, the roll of the clergy and of the parishes entitled to representation shall be called by the Secretary of the last Convention; the certificates of the lay deputies, as presented, being referred to a committee consisting of the Secretary and two members appointed by the President. If a quorum of twenty clergy and a representation of twenty parishes be present, the President shall declare the Convention duly organized.

5. The first business shall be the election of a Secretary, a Treasurer, and a Registrar. The Secretary may appoint one or more Assistant Secretaries, announcing their names to the Convention.

6. Notices, resolutions, motions and other miscellaneous business shall then be in order.

7. The following committees shall be appointed by the President:
    A. On the Admission of Parishes into Union with the Convention.
    B. On the Constitution and Canons.
    C. On the Treasurer's Accounts.
    D. On the Diocesan Fund and Mileage of the Clergy.
    E. On Diocesan Missions.
    F. On the Bishop's Salary and the Episcopal Fund.
    G. On the Fund for the Widows and Orphans of Deceased Clergymen.
    H. On the Aged and Infirm Clergy Fund.
    I. On the General Theological Seminary.
    J. On the Society for Promoting Religion and Learning.
    K. On unfinished business.
    L. On non-reporting Clergy and Parishes.

8. Business for these committees shall be received in the following order:
    A. Report of the Treasurer.
    B. Report of the Board of Diocesan Missions.

C. Report of the Trustees of the Episcopal Fund and of the Bishop's salary.

D. Report of the Trustees of the Fund for the Widows and Orphans of Deceased Clergymen, and the Treasurer of the same.

E. Report of the Trustees of the Aged and Infirm Clergy Fund, and the Treasurer of the same.

F. Report of the Society for Promoting Religion and Learning.

These reports, and those mentioned in the next rule, shall be referred to the appropriate committees, and shall not be read until such committees be ready to report upon them.

9. A. Report of the Committee on Applications of Parishes for Admission.

B. Report of the Secretary of the Convention.

C. Report of the Standing Committee of the Diocese.

D. Report of the Registrar of the Diocese.

E. Report of the Secretary and Treasurer of the Bible and Prayer Book Society of Albany and its Vicinity.

F. Reports from the Orphan House of the Holy Saviour, Cooperstown.

G. Reports of Special Committees appointed at the last Convention.

H. Miscellaneous business.

SECOND DAY.

10. On the second and each succeeding day of the session, after Daily Morning Prayer, the order of business, which shall not be departed from without the consent of two-thirds of the members present, or a special order of the day previously voted, shall be as follows:

A. Reading, correcting and approving the minutes of the previous day.

B. Calling the roll of members absent on the previous day.

C. Reports from the Regular Committees of the House, in the order of their appointment.

D. Reports from Special Committees, in the order of their appointment.

E. Unfinished business.

F. Miscellaneous business.

11. The Bishop's Address is in order at any time.

12. The annual elections shall be held at noon on the second day, and continued at the order of the House until completed.

13. All reports embodying long statements of accounts shall be accompanied with a brief abstract of them, and such abstract only shall be printed in the Journal.

GENERAL.

14. When any member is about to speak, he shall rise from his seat, and shall, with due respect, address himself in an audible tone of voice to the President, confining himself strictly to the point in debate.

15. No member shall speak more than twice in the same debate without leave of the House; nor more than once, until every other member wishing to speak shall have spoken.

16. No motion shall be considered as before the House unless it be seconded, and reduced to writing when required, and announced by the Chair.

17. The mover may withdraw a motion or resolution at any time before amend_ment or decision, with the consent of the Convention; in which case it shall not be entered upon the minutes.

18. When a question is under consideration, it shall be in order to move to lay it upon the table, to postpone it indefinitely, to postpone it to a time certain, to com_mit it, to amend it, or to divide it; and motions for any of these purposes shall have precedence in the order here named.

19. If the question under debate contains several distinct propositions, the same shall be divided at the request of any member, and a vote taken separately; except that a motion to strike out and insert shall be indivisible.

20. All amendments shall be considered in the order in which they are moved. When a proposed amendment is under consideration, a motion to amend the same may be made. No after amendment to such second amendment shall be in order; but a substitute for such second amendment, or a substitute for the whole matter, may be received. No proposition on a subject different from that under consideration shall be received under colour of a substitute.

21. A motion to lay upon the table shall be decided without debate.

22. A motion to adjourn shall always be in order when no member is speaking; and, if unqualified, shall be decided without debate. If negatived, it shall not be renewed until some other business has intervened.

23. When a question is put by the President, it shall be determined by the sound of voices, for or against it; but any three members may require a count of the votes, and tellers for that purpose shall then be appointed by the Chair; or any five votes may require that the decision be by yeas and nays and by orders, which shall be done by calling the roll of the clerical members and parishes represented, and the votes shall be entered on the Journal.

24. When the President is putting any question, the members shall continue in their seats, and shall not hold any private discourse.

25. Every member present shall vote when a question is put, unless excused by a vote of the House.

26. A motion once determined, whether in the affirmative or the negative, shall stand as the judgment of the Convention, and shall not again be considered during the same session, unless the motion to reconsider be made by one of the majority on the first decision, and be carried by a vote of two-thirds of the members present.

27. All questions of order shall be decided by the President, subject to an appeal to the House; and on such appeal no member shall speak more than once, without leave of the Convention.

28. All committees shall be appointed by the President, unless otherwise ordered by the Convention.

29. The reports of all committees shall be in writing; and unless recommitted, shall be received of course, without motion for acceptance. They shall be entered on the minutes, unless otherwise ordered. If recommending or requiring any action or expression of opinion by the Convention, they shall be a accompanied by a resolution or resolutions for its consideration.

30. No rule of order shall be suspended, unless by a vote of two-thirds of the members present; nor shall any be changed or rescinded without one day's previous notice.

31. No member shall absent himself from the session of the Convention without leave of the President.

32. Before the final adjournment of the Convention, the minutes of the last day's proceedings shall be read, corrected and approved.

33. When the Convention is about to rise, every member shall keep his seat until the President leaves the chair.

3

STANDING ORDER.

OF THE CONDUCT OF ELECTIONS.

WHEREAS, it is expedient to provide by a standing order, for the manner of conducting all elections by ballot in the Convention of the Diocese of Albany, it is hereby ordered as follows:

1. The President of the Convention shall appoint one clergyman and one layman to be tellers of the clerical vote, and one clergyman and one layman to be tellers of the lay vote, for each office that is to be filled, except that all the members of any committee, board or delegation shall be voted for upon one ticket, and only one set of tellers shall be appointed therefor. Vacancies, arising from temporary absence or otherwise, shall be supplied by the President.

2. When the election is to be held, the tellers for the clerical vote shall take their places, together, on one side of the house or place of meeting, and the tellers for the lay vote, together, upon the other side; and the Secretary shall supply them with the necessary boxes, and also with lists of the clergy entitled to seats in the Convention, and of the parishes entitled to representation, on which lists, as each vote is deposited, they shall make a mark against the name of the clergyman or parish voting; and these lists, signed by the tellers, shall be returned with their reports to the Convention. The names of the clergy and of the parishes shall be called by the Secretaries, and the votes shall be received by the tellers.

3. So soon as voting shall appear to have ceased, the President shall announce that the polls are about to be closed, and not less than ten minutes after such announcement, he may direct the tellers to count the votes, for which purpose they shall have leave to retire. The tellers shall then proceed to count the votes, and shall make written reports, stating the whole number of votes cast, and the number cast for each person, except that when less than five votes are cast for any one person, it shall suffice to include all such votes under the head of scattering. These reports shall be signed by the tellers respectively, and shall be entered upon the Journal, and the President shall announce the result.

4. In case of any contest arising as to the right of any person to cast a vote, the tellers shall submit the question to the Convention before the closing of the polls.

5. If in regard to any office there shall not be a majority of votes, either in the clerical or in the lay order, for any one person, or if there shall not be a concurrence of the two orders, the Convention shall forthwith proceed to another ballot, for such and so many offices as have not been filled at the first ballot; and such second and all other ballots shall be conducted in the same manner as above provided. In case there shall still remain any vacancy to be supplied after such second ballot, further ballots may be held at the order of the Convention.

6. Immediately before any ballot, it shall be in order for the nomination of any person to be made and seconded; but no speech or debate shall be allowed upon such nomination, or while the Convention is holding an election.

Resolved, That the Secretary be directed at each Convention to prepare ballots for the offices to be then filled, containing the names of the persons holding those offices and who have not desired to be excused from service, with a note indicating the whole number to be chosen. (Adopted, 1880.)

Resolved, That the resolution at present governing the printing of nominations for offices in the gift of the Convention, so far as it includes the members of the Standing Committee and the Deputies and Provisional Deputies to the General Convention, be and is hereby rescinded. (Adopted, 1889.)

Resolved, That all nominations for the Standing Committee and for the Deputies and Provisional Deputies to the General Convention be made on the first day of the session of the Convention, and that the Secretary be directed to have all such nominations printed and ready for the use of the Convention on the second day when such elections shall take place. (Adopted, 1889.)

JOURNAL.

All Saints' Cathedral Church, Albany, N. Y.,
Tuesday, November 11, A. D., 1890.

This being the place designated by the Bishop of the Diocese and the day appointed by the Constitution, for the meeting of the Twenty-second Annual Convention of the Diocese of Albany, the Bishop, and a number of the Clergy and Lay Deputies assembled in All Saints' Cathedral Church at half-past ten o'clock in the morning.

The Bishop of the Diocese administered the Holy Communion, being assisted in the service by the Rev. Archdeacons Carey, Morrison and Olmsted, the Rev. J. Ireland Tucker, S. T. D., and the Dean of the Cathedral.

In place of the sermon, the Bishop delivered a portion of his Annual Address.

THE BISHOP'S ADDRESS.

My well beloved brethren of the Clergy and Laity:

I combine with my accustomed Address to you this year, rather more formally than usual, what may be counted as a Charge, after the suggestion of the Canon as to the propriety of such a deliverance; for however one may hesitate and shrink from the attempt to deal with the grave matters of present interest and enquiry in the religious world, in the brief limits of an Episcopal Address, it yet seems right that those who are set on the watch tower of the episcopate should give the word of warning, from time to time as to the outlook of the hour.

And no one will question but that to-day the interest of students in all classes of thought is centred upon the Old Testament Scriptures. I am abundantly sure that the spirit of the study is largely reverent and real. In many instances, no doubt, the spirit that is behind and underneath what has come to be called the higher criticism is not the spirit of an earnest desire for the discovery of truth, nearly so much as it is a determination to dethrone the Holy Scriptures from their position of authority and power. But whatever the spirit may be, *the fact is* the thing which

presses upon you and me; and it is a fact that we have no right to shirk
or dodge or deal with in any way, except by intelligent and competent
argument. A good deal of stir has been made in the religious world, and
especially among us, by the publication of the book called Lux Mundi, and
curiously enough, nine-tenths of the criticism of that book has turned
upon the single essay on the inspiration of the Holy Scriptures.

I have no intention of entering upon any criticism, either of that particular essay or of the book itself, but I do want to call the attention of
the clergy to two things. In the first place, I believe that the true attitude of the Christian believer and still more of the Christian teacher is
the attitude of simple and unquestioning confidence and courage; the
confidence and courage that not only do not fear, but court most thorough
investigation.

And we have abundant warrant for this confidence, and sufficient
reason for this courage, in the fact that to us the Canon of Scripture
comes, first, bearing the seal of the Historic Church with the same
certainty with which Abraham said to Dives in the parable, "They
have Moses and the prophets;" with the same confidence with which our
Lord said: "Ye search the Scriptures, and they are they which testify of
me;" with the same assurance with which Saint Paul counted it first
among the honours of the Jewish Church, that unto them were "committed
the oracles of God." You and I have the authoritative witness of those to
whom the Lord gave power to try the spirits, that the Bible, as we have
it to-day, *is* the WORD OF GOD. It is no blind acceptance. It rests upon
the decision of no special Council remote from the times of the written
books. It is simply the handing on and down, from age to age, of certain
books until the Canon was complete, by the contemporaneous and continuous testimony of the Church of God, Jewish and Christian. Whatever
beside this may have been given to us, in the personal experience of our
religious lives, as the Holy Spirit witnesses to our spirit, is so much added
evidence. And beside all that, as putting nerve into the cowardice of the
faint-hearted, is the outcome of what is called the Tübingen school of
criticism, which, after bringing to bear every conceivable kind of de-
structive missile upon the books of the New Testament, has closed its
doors, dismissed its scholars, retired its professors, and given up its claim.
They were men of infinite ability and absolute honesty. They verily
thought within themselves, I have no doubt, that they were set to expose a gigantic fraud. But it was a case of gnawing a file; and out of the
whole of those years of careful and critical study nothing has come, except a growing confidence, in the Church and in the world, in the authority
and authenticity of the New Testament Scriptures; *and*, the discovery
that God had so wonderfully guarded the story of the Incarnation, as to
have written it from beginning to end in the four undisputed Epistles of
St. Paul, as plainly as in the four once disputed Gospels.

What attitude then ought we to take toward this enquiry into the Old Testament Scriptures, their date and authorship; or into this still subtler study of the full reach of our Lord's references to the authors of the Old Testament Scriptures, and to the marvellous events which sometimes they record ? I may as well confess at the outset that I absolutely believe that to all intents and purposes Moses wrote the Pentateuch, and David, the Psalms, and Daniel, the Prophecy which bears his name; by which I mean to say that there are some Psalms that David plainly did not write, some portions of the Pentateuch, like the description of his death, which, of course, Moses did not write; and that it is quite consistent with the Mosaic authorship of the Pentateuch, that he should have had recourse to earlier records in regard to certain earlier facts. And I may as well go on to confess, that I have not the slightest difficulty in accepting the story of a human speech passing through the vocal organs of Balaam's ass, or the story of the great fish that could swallow the prophet Jonah, and cast him out at God's command. If I am to be a Christian at all, I must accept, in the humanity of God, in the Divinity of Man, in the Incarnation, the Crucifixion, the Resurrection of our Lord, miracles which so infinitely surpass these small wonders, that they make no impression whatever in the way of difficulty upon my mind. But, outside of my own convictions comes the question, how we shall deal with the difficulties, the doubts, and the denials of other people, and I merely suggest in outline two or three things. For instance, take the question of the authorship of the first five books of the Bible. There are nearly thirty, I think, different theories, each one of which is vigorously contended for by most intelligent critics. It seems to me that we can afford to stand aside and let those combatants, after the manner of the frogs and mice, dispose of each other. A good many battles have been won by the soldiers of one side mistaking each other for soldiers of the other side, and having sufficiently slaughtered each other, leaving an easy victory to the army that never even drew sword nor fired gun. As for the question of the authorship of the Psalms, or of the Prophecy of Daniel, I think the wise counsel is that we should discriminate between wholesale assertions and wholesale denials. There is very much of wise counsel and timely caution in the able critique of Mr. Gore's paper, on the side of sympathy with his position, in the late charge of the Bishop of Carlisle. Perhaps it is not wise, as he says, to quote our Lord's words describing a certain document as the work of Moses, and another as the work of David, as *meant* to decide a modern controversy as to authorship; because one needs to be chary of any straining of the Master's speech beyond its first and evident intention, and that intention plainly was to show in Himself the fulfilment of prophecy.

But, on the other hand, it must, I think, be noted ; first, that the implication of authorship in one or two cases is very important to the force of the application of the passage.   For instance, if David did not write the one hundred and tenth psalm, the evidential value of "The Lord said unto *my* Lord," is gone, for the whole point turns on the question how *David* could call his son his Lord.   And so the references to the Pentateuch, while it certainly is unjust to argue from them that Moses wrote every word of all the five books, are yet chiefly valuable as claiming, to those who looked up to Moses as their great legislator, his personal testimony to Christ.   And secondly, it must be noted that it is impossible to escape the pointedness of the things to which our Lord chose to give the emphasis of His endorsement.   Why should He have singled out Daniel, the prophet, to quote by name, unless he had foreseen the attempt from Porphyry down, to discredit that particular prophecy by the assignment of a later date; or why should He with that strong expression, "even so," καθὼς-οὕτως, ὥσπερ-ουτως, have chosen the brazen serpent and Jonah, the manna and the Rock, the days of Noe and the days of Lot to be the special subjects of selected types and prophecies; but that He foresaw and would forestall the tendency of merely intellectual criticism to deny and to deride the reality of these miracles?   Certainly the stamp of our Lord's assimilation into Himself of the great accepted characters, events, and facts in what the Jews of His time acknowledged as authentic Scripture, is a mighty vindication and verification of the canon of the Old Testament, as it stood then and stands now, authors and dates and all.

I should say, therefore, that we may safely claim an *a priori* probability of the strongest kind, to the Law and the Prophets and the Psalms being what they claim to be; but I should also say that it is unwise to press the argument too far, or to feel that every thing hangs on it.   Still more, I think, that we may not count as impugners and impairers of our Lord's inevitable and infallible truthfulness, those who out of very reverence and regard to his Prophetic office, are needlessly, it seems to me, proposing suggested reconciliations between a *possible* discovery of a different view of portions of the Bible and the *impossible* detection of any falsehood in His words.   In the defense of any earthly position they may be wise who are forecasting means of holding the inner citadel *when*, and *if* the enemy shall have carried the outworks by storm.   True courage will do this, rather than think of a capitulation.   But the higher Christian position, I think, is rather the fearless confidence that no inch of foothold can be gained by the enemy, in any portion of God's stronghold of truth.

Meanwhile there are two things which you and I are bound to bear in mind.   First, that the changeless, dogmatic position of the Church does not mean, that we are not quite likely to be called upon, in the varying approaches of those who attack it, to look at the old truths in new lights, and to use new means and methods of defense.   The same flag flies from the modern cruiser which waved alike in battle and in victory from the old frigate, but it would be simple madness to maintain the methods of defensive warfare of the days of Nelson and Perry. I believe it most important that striplings should not put on the armour of grown men. David can fight better with the sling and the stones than with the armour of Saul; but he had no difficulty in using the sword of Goliath. We can turn, that is to say, the weapons of the enemy against themselves. We can use the familiar weapons of faith and prayer. We shall be wise to let alone the weapons of the world's warfare. But I am abundantly sure that no man is qualified to-day to preach the everlasting Gospel who is not familiar with the best modern writings of men like Lightfoot and Westcott in text and criticism; and with the great writers on the evidences of revealed religion, up to the very moment of the latest discoveries or imaginations of science. And it is for this that I commend most earnestly the use of the lending library, which will put in the hands of the clergy of this Diocese the freshest results of the study of theology.

I am glad to adopt the wise warning of the Address of the Bishop of Argyle and the Isles as admirably expressing my own thought:

And further let us remember that we have a duty to Christ's faithful disciples as well as to sceptical inquirers. We have to take into consideration the sensitive loyalty of those men and women who, through the power of the Holy Ghost, have "become as little children," who hear Christ's voice and follow Him. Concerning such the Lord Himself has said, "Whoso shall offend one of these little ones which believe in Me, it were better for him that a mill-stone were hanged about his neck and that he were drowned in the depth of the sea."

For the precious faith of Christ's humble servants we are surely bound to show more tender consideration than for the unbelief of carping critics. Among such we do not hear of many returning into the way of life and light. *Some* are brought to repentance and faith, but very few, if we may judge from past experience, and those few *not by compromises.* The path of sceptics is mostly a downward path, as with advancing age the shadows of the eternal night creep slowly on.

I think we are sometimes apt to be too anxious about our most holy faith, and too ready to take an apologetic tone in dealing with unbelievers. We must not forget that Christ's religion is built upon a foundation which cannot be shaken, because it is divine. Our great Lord and Master has no need of our feeble apologies, still less of our weak compromises with the wisdom of this world — with that wisdom which is ever changing, and which in its very nature can never bring us to the knowledge of God.

It seems to me that one of the gravest needs, is to guard against that curious attitude of mind, which expects and demands the clearing up of all difficulties, and the explanation of all obscurities in the Holy Scriptures, as a condition precedent to their acceptance. It is quite against the common habit of our lives. The dullest of all unthinking people, who move about with absolute incomprehension of the mysteries and marvels of all human life, is not readier than the keenest of all critical examiners, to receive and act upon principles unintelligible and inexplicable at every turn. But in religion (the highest and in a sense, the farthest away of all the things that touch life closely) there is a looking after clearer conception, which grows to constant desire,—sometimes by denial, sometimes by attempts at reconciliation, sometimes by curious and almost ludicrous suggestions — to explain or to explain away the difficulties of revelation. Surely we do not deal so with nature, with providence, with life.

The attitude, which courts enquiry and invites investigation, is a different attitude from that which proposes solutions and seems ready to surrender whatever is insoluble. What Mr. Wilfred Ward says in his paper in the *Nineteenth Century* for June, is well worth quoting. " It is perhaps worth while to remind ourselves that truths may be lost as well as gained; that there are old truths to preserve as well as new truths to learn; that scientific discovery is concerned only with new truth; that though all truth is intrinsically consistent, it may not always appear so in the course of its attainment; and that at a given stage a too exclusive concentration on steps toward new truth may obscure for the individual mind its perception of truths already possessed. The truest discoveries may come upon an individual, or even upon a nation, accompanied by all the peculiarities of a new fashion; and it is of the essence of the new fashion, to neglect and undervalue the old; to develop a pet tendency out of due proportion; to pass over as of no account that which is out of harmony with itself; to absorb the attention of its votaries for the moment as though it were all-sufficient; to discourage and expel by its sneer that which is unlike itself. These are characteristics of all fashions, intellectual or social, artistic or religious. The question then may be asked, whether qualified sympathy with a particular scientific movement may not sometimes be due to suspicion of its form as a fashion, its surroundings and exaggerations, rather than to want of love for the truth to which it is leading; to an attachment to old truth rather than indifference to new — nay, to love of truth itself measured by the quantity and importance of the knowledge preserved rather than by its novelty alone."

Before we enter on the attempt to solve all difficulties, I cannot but think that we are mistaken in not using the element of mysteriousness, as in itself an evidence of highest truth. I recall as an illustration our Lord's dealing with the multitude, in the wonderful discourse at Jerusalem, on the great day of the feast of Tabernacles. Plainly in word and act, His method is *not* to reveal Himself with clearness which compels instant and universal acceptance. He does not, even when His disciples and His unbelieving brethren beg Him to do it, "show Himself openly unto the world."

That is to say, neither the intense desire, of those who have come to know Him, to make that knowledge universal, nor the sneers of unbelievers, induced Him to force, as though it was a material thing, the moral act of faith. When He goes up to the feast, He goes "not openly, but as it were in secret;" and I think we may safely take Saint Augustine's paraphrase of the mysterious cry in the Temple — " Ye both know Me and ye know whence I am " to mean — " Ye both know Me, and ye do not know Me."

And what is the result ? The Pharisees were embittered into more violent antagonism, *but* "many of the people believed in Him." And I think it is true to-day. ' The preaching of the mystery, of the naturalness in the spiritual world, of supernaturalness, offends many, excites opposition, provokes antagonism; but this is better than the listless acquiescence and indifferent indolence of assent. And to the simple mind of average humanity, the very element of wonder is attractive: not in the stupid superstitious way of besotted ignorance; but in the child's ready reverence before the mind is poisoned by false impressions, or perverted by an alienated will. Let me illustrate what I mean. There is a tendency in modern teachings to present only the barest and baldest upper side and surface of truth. The Christ is presented as a man of marvellous beauty of character and consecration to good works: but His eternal Deity is withheld as a sort of Eleusinian mystery for the initiated only. The Church is held up as a great society of men, banded together for purposes of moral elevation, of vague religious teaching, and of mutual fellowship among men; but the splendid mystery, like a mountain whose top is behind clouds, with which she is enshrouded, as the Mystical Body of Christ, having nourishment ministered and knit together by living bands, with a living circulation, by which she is one with her Divine Head, is not insisted upon. The blessed Eucharist is a thoughtful and tender reminder of the great act of the Divine love, that dared even to die; but the God Man, Who pleads in it for us and gives Himself in it to us, is lost out of sight. And whatever may seem to be the advantage of avoided antagonism in this degraded and diluted presentation of the truth, it is against the Divine method and against reasoning experience, as well. For what excites no opposition equally excites no active and earnest assimilation of truth.

Wholeness in declaring the counsel of God is the plain duty of the teacher of truth, and say what we will of plausible propositions, to avoid the points of difference in the proclamation of truth, no one can study the Saviour's dealing with individuals as at the Well at Sychar; or with the multitude as in Jerusalem, at the feast of Tabernacles, and not feel the force and fulness, of His unhesitating presentation of the very doctrine, which went, if we may so say, against the grain of concealed sin, of national pride or of religious prejudice. I am not sure, either, that the discourse recorded by Saint John, in the seventh chapter of his Gospel, does not throw some light upon the very question of the day. Think out two points in outline, and then run the line out and fill it in yourselves, dear brethren of the Clergy, in other ways. "How knoweth this man letters, having never learned," they said, and He answered "My doctrine is not mine, but His, that sent me." They did more than recognize, they exaggerated, what we hear so much of now, the limitation of knowledge which He, as God put upon Himself, in His human capacity. He had learned γράμματα, writings, τὰ γράμματα, *the* writings, the Holy Scrip-

4

tures, in boyhood, from His mother, and in the Temple, when He heard
and questioned the Doctors of the Law. But He lifts the whole
question about His human knowledge, limited or unlimited, out beyond the farthest verge of any human horizon, and up above the
reach of any human enquiry. "My doctrine, My teaching, is not
Mine, but His that sent Me." It is heavenly truth, revelation, the
knowledge that He had with the Father before the world was, so far as
earthly speech could hold, or finite mind receive it. That is its only
limitation. The truth is from heaven. He *is* the Word of God.

And then He tells us what the limitation to *our* knowledge is, and
whence it comes. It is the will to do the will of God, that paves the way
to the knowledge of His doctrine. It is unwillingness to do His will which
hinders us from recognizing and receiving the truth; because of the instinct in us, conscious or unconscious, that religious truth requires certain moral results, which we have not the will to submit to.

But I am bound, while I press upon you the need to keep abreast with all
the study and research of the day, to add my urgent counsel for wise caution in the matter of preaching. We are dealing in our ordinary congregations with believing Christian people, and to a large extent with the
immature and impressible minds of children and young people. And
there is for the first no need, and for the second real danger, in the perpetual proving of things which the elders believe in already; and which
the young people may come to think doubtful, if the necessity of constant
evidence is pressed upon them. That men in the outer world are so un-
ceasingly questioning religion, antagonizing revelation, and examining
with hostile eye the Holy Scriptures, shows plainly their realization, growing from year to year, of the authority and value of the Bible and of its
elevated position in the intelligent thought of the world. I do not think
we ought, because I do not think we have need, to accord to any one of
all the constantly changing theories of this or that school, the same consequence, by constantly attacking them. The mere fact of their un-per-
manence, of their mutual contradictions, puts them upon another footing
altogether. And in our public dealing with all questions of truth or of
error, I am abundantly sure that we must avoid the danger of suggesting
doubt which we are aiming to suppress; or of conveying the appearance
of uneasiness and uncertainty in ourselves; as one casts doubt upon
his innocence when he protests too much. And on the other hand I am
amazed at the recklessness with which men make free to ventilate, often
upon the thin air of poor and pointless joking, their own rejection of portions of God's word. There is a discourtesy, an irreverence, and often a
vulgarity which cannot be too strongly deprecated, in the way in which
slurs are cast upon a miracle, a character or an event in the Old Testament times. And this word fills up a child's ear to whom the old story
in all its fulness is familiar, and one of the little ones is offended;

a scandal is put in the way in which their feet were walking fearlessly and faithfully in the light of truth; a rude shock is given to the whole fabric of their faith. "The false in one false in all" suggests itself. And while *you* are holding fast to the great verities, and only regarding these things as outside and unimportant, *they* are cut loose, and drift and drift, till a denial of the three days of Jonah takes away their faith in the three days of Jesus; and the frank honesty of a young mind, taught to think that the speeches of Moses and the prophecies of Daniel are afterthoughts of an idealizing dramatist or of an unscrupulous nationalist among the Jews, argues most reasonably that conscious deception destroys the trustworthiness of the whole Book; and either that authority must be refused to Books whose authorship and authenticity are so discredited if not denied; or that the Church can no longer be trusted in her witness to the Canon, if she has in the ignorance of wilfulness or of carelessness, allowed such things to be.

Let me close what I have to say with the strong words of Canon Lidden, who, "being dead, yet speaks" to us, in this late testimony to the blessed Word of God. Preaching, last Advent, from St. Paul's words, "Whatsoever things were written aforetime were written for our learning," he says: "It implies, first of all, the trustworthiness of the Old Testament. I say its trustworthiness; I do not go so far, for the moment, as to say its inspiration. Unless a book or a man be trustworthy it is impossible to feel confidence in it or in him, and confidence in an instructor is a first condition of receiving instruction to any good purpose. Now, if this be so, it shows that the Apostle would have had nothing to do with any estimate of the books of the Old Testament which is fatal to belief in their trustworthiness. We may have noticed that, when estimates of this kind are put forward, they are commonly prefaced by the observation that the Church has never defined what inspiration is; and it is left to be inferred that a book may still be in some singular sense inspired, although the statements which it contains are held by the critic to be opposed to the truth of history or to the truth of morals. It is doubtless true that no authoritative definition of the Inspiration of the Holy Scriptures, of what it does and does not permit or imply, has been propounded by the Church of Christ, just as she has propounded no definition of the manner and measure of the action of the Holy Spirit on the soul of man. "The wind bloweth where it listeth, and thou hearest the sound thereof, but canst not tell whence it cometh and whither it goeth." Our Lord's words apply to an inspired book no less than to a sanctified soul, but at the same time, both in the case of the soul, and of the book we can see that there are certain things inconsistent with the Holy Spirit's agency. Just as wilful sin is incompatible with the indwelling of the Holy Spirit in the soul, so inveracity is incompatible with the claim of a book to have been inspired by the Author of all truth."

It is almost impossible as I look about the Cathedral which holds, this once at least in every year, its most legitimate congregation, not to speak *first* of those whom we miss from our annual gatherings from year to year. This year, the word of exhortation which I have felt bound to speak, brings the mention of their names nearer to our commemoration of them at the Altar (where they were wont to come in person to join in our Communion), which is the only way in which we can be one with those who have died in the Lord.

For the first time in many a year, the list includes the name of one of the oldest Priests of the Diocese, one of the few surviving clergy of our Primary Convention held twenty-two years ago. The Rev. William Ross Johnson, who filled both Parochial and Missionary positions in the Diocese, departed this life on the 17th of April, in the Insane Asylum at Utica, where he had been withdrawn, of course, from work for nearly twenty years. His insanity was not very marked, and yet it was necessary for him to be under the wise and careful treatment of that most admirable Institution. He said himself to some one who asked him what brought him there — the questioner being a victim to drink — "It was brains that brought *me*:" and that was perfectly true; the intense energy and activity of his mind producing an undue excitement of the brain. In many ways his intellect was unclouded, and his spiritual insight and religious interest never failed him to the very last; when his faithful friend and brother, the Rev. Dr. Gibson, whose ministrations have been an untold comfort to many a one in that asylum, commended his peaceful soul to God. Dr. Gibson writes me "he was very bright on all questions of the day, and especially all Church questions; an omnivorous reader, from whom I drew much intellectual stimulus and companionship. On his dying bed he expressed much satisfaction at the part he was allowed to take in your election as Bishop and the great blessing of God upon your administration." "He was a brave Christian and remarkably acute in his perceptions of religious truth. What a glorious legacy he and his heroic wife have left to the Church — three sons for the ministry, and such sons!" The message, I confess, was most grateful to me. I had received a very loving note from him in February, when I wrote him of my sympathy at the death of his wife. "The dear soul," he said, "rests from her labours; we toil and suffer and sorrow on. hoping to reap the reward of the faithful together, when our labours for our dear Lord are ended. As you and yours, have always been in my prayers, so are you now, and let me have a place in your love, with my wife of whom you speak so affectionately."

The **Rev.** Mr. Toy writes me, "His body was placed in the Choir of Christ's Church, with the head towards the Altar. At 8 A. M., on the 17th, I celebrated. There were present, his brother, the Rev. J. E. Johnson of Syracuse, the Rev. W. E. Johnson and Rev. E. C. Johnson, Priests, Mr. Irving P. Johnson, student in the General Theological Seminary — the last three being his sons. At 3 P. M., I said the Burial office, assisted by Rev. Dr. Payne and the Rev. Mr. Pendleton. Dr. Payne said the committal, and I the prayers, at the grave, in Vale Cemetery. The Rev. Dr. Lowell was present, but took no part in the service."

So he was laid at last, to rest, and so his soul entered where no clouds come in to mar the clearness of the soul's sight, of Him who is the Lux Mundorum.

Among the prominent Lay people, certainly the greatest loss in many ways in Albany and in the State, has come from the death of Judge Parker. He has been most generously interested in the Church and in every thing to which I have put my hand, helping with counsel and confidence and sympathy and generous gifts. I felt always strong in the sense of his friendship, because he was a man who did not give his confidence on any grounds of personal favor or from any merely personal feelings, unless his judgment commended it. He was the head of the home, which in all its branches has given to me my closest and dearest friends; and in all ways that benefit manhood, in his look, in his voice, in his public interests, in the noble record of service to the city, which must always, I trust, put his name and Mr. Pruyn's by the side of Harmanus Bleecker's, he was a most honorable and valuable citizen of this old city; and one is thankful that such a stock and such a name survive, and are handed down with all their traditions behind them to serve the State, the City and the Church.

Mr. Roland Smyth was a man whom few people in Albany knew at his real worth, for he was very retired and very humble in all matters that concerned himself, but those of us who knew him recognized always, what I think was the most marked characteristic of his nature, his absolute loyalty in the largest sense of the word, to God and to man, which kept him patient and full of trust under all the sorrows and disciplines of his life, which steadied him in all the years of patient plodding about his lowly work, which attached him with an unfailing and an unfaltering devotion to his family and friends, and which made him, what to the very latest hour of his life he was, rich in lavish and generous devotion to the Cathedral.

Mr. Henry C. Lockwood had been more or less withdrawn, owing to illness, from the active service which he rendered to the Diocese in its earlier history, but he had lost no love, no interest, no will. He was a very ideal Christian gentleman in look and speech and manner, and in the really elegant cultivation of his mind. What the French people call "beautiful letters" were a great delight to him, and he had in more than usual ways the afflatus of a poet. But after all we loved him best who knew him most, for his sweet, refined, delightful nature, for the high and noble standards of his character and life, and for the warmth of his affectionate and generous heart. It was a great grief to me that I was hindered from being present at his burial.

One of the staunchest and most devoted Laymen whom I ever knew in this or in any other Diocese, Mr. Calvin S. Wheeler, died in Burnt Hills in the early part of the year. He was a Churchman and a Church-worker by inheritance and instinct. Of the family his father was the first Warden, his brother has been Warden twenty years, and his nephew in the Vestry, either in Burnt Hills or Ballston Spa.

Dr. Timlow says of him what I know to be true: "That he gave all that he could of time, strength and means for the Church." No warmer welcome ever came to me than his in my visitations, and no one was more welcome than he in our Diocesan Conventions, which he very constantly attended; and I shall always remember him as a fine specimen of what I have come greatly to value — a simple-hearted, clear-headed country Churchman, to whom, perhaps, because there were fewer things to distract him than come into a city life, the Church comes always first. Since writing this, the death of his brother William, has been notified to me. "Par nobile fratrum," the strongest words that could be said of either would be true of both.

Full of years and honours Judge Palmer has passed away, leaving a gracious memory behind him in the Parish of Trinity, Plattsburgh. He had received, during his life, almost every public token of confidence that his fellow citizens could give him, and he had been faithful and capable to the duties of every office that he filled. Besides which he always had closely at heart the best interests of the Church, to whose service he gave his time and means and influence, and, better still, the example of his consistent, Christian life.

We have been greatly bereaved this year too, by the death of very noble and very earnest women. Mrs. Tillinghast of Troy, delicate as she was in physical health, had an untiring capacity for work. She had passed long ago out of the sunshine of her life, but she walked most sweetly and graciously in its shadow; and many and many an interest of Church and City, of Parish and Diocese, will sorely miss her service. To an unusual degree I think, we may say of her that she was happy in the opportunity of her death, and I hardly recall more blessed words than her own Nunc Dimittis, "rest and peace, when they do come, come through our Lord Jesus Christ."

Mrs. Mary Brevoort Cushney, who died in Fonda, was a true mother, not in Israel, but in the Kingdom of Christ. I have never had, it seems to me, in all my going in and out of the homes that make me welcome in the Diocese, a more assured sense of loving and ready hospitality than I had in her home. She had been married to one of our truest and noblest Laymen for sixty-one years, and had lived nearly all that time in Fonda, and while her active kindliness reached out to every place and person in the community, she was intensely and *first* devoted to the duties and delights of home and to the interest of the Church, which exists in Fonda, only because of Judge Cushney and his wife.

Mrs. Alexander Hemsley, the founder of the Church in Tannersville, passed away from the midst of the beautiful surroundings of her mountain home in the mid-summer of this year. Only those who knew intimately as I did the story of her life since early girlhood, can possibly appreciate the nobility and dignity of her Christian character. Most loyal and loving to Christ and His Church, most devoted in her domestic duties, most patient under every variety of pain and sorrow, never losing hope nor cheer nor trust, there are not many characters, that I have known, which rise up before my recollection in more real and rounded beauty than hers.

It was my privilege to minister, by what we call an accident, at the death bed of Miss Meads, whose passing in great age was very peaceful and full of trust in Him whom she had always served, and recalled one of the great losses of the Church and my life, when her beloved brother died and left so many places, public and personal, empty and never to be filled.

Mrs. Annie Fulton Evans died in the early winter. She is associated to me with my earliest work in the Diocese, and with the generous interest which built and maintains the Church in Hogansburgh and with the kindly hospitality of her father's most delightful home. And last, up to the moment of my writing at least, has come the death of Mrs. Robert Lowber of Bald Mountain, a strong, fine woman of the best birth and highest breeding, chastened by much of suffering and sorrow yet full of cheer and courage to the last, with large and loving interest in the Church and most gracious hospitality. Nobody knows, nobody can know, it seems to me, what true loyalty to the Church is until they have seen it in such characters as Mrs. Cushney's, Mrs. Hemsley's, the Fultons' and Mrs. Lowber's, holding fast against all odds of opposing communities, infrequent services, and often unappreciated service, with a wealth of love and faith and patience and courage which shames so many of us, on whom all privileges are showered with such unstinted and unsparing hand.

Passing for a moment into our sphere of duty as citizens I have the right to ask the Laymen of the Diocese to consider the example of such a man as Walter Howe, so sadly and suddenly taken away this Summer from his faithful and fearless discharge of the service to which he was called. He had every temptation to the sort of elegant leisure, so called, — it ought to be called unpardonable laziness, — which lies

behind so much of the emasculated and enervated manhood of our century.
Possessed of abundant means, most satisfying personal surroundings,
cultivated tastes, exuberant enjoyment of the beautiful, the material,
the sensual in the world, he set himself to higher things. My own association with him was not only here — in connection with his official place
in the New York Legislature, where he stood always for the largest idea
of *politics,* namely the common weal, the good of the State — but in the
High License Commission, where he was an invaluable counsellor and
helper, with keen insight, quick and sound judgment, wise counsel, unreserved readiness to give time, pains and money to advance the cause of
just and sound legislation in regard to the Excise Laws. And I am still
more impressed with the fact and force of his example, to young men especially, in his unofficial life. Public office in America is not the aim or
the opportunity of many men or of the best. The more is the pity.
And the reason is not far to find. When parties hold their offices for sale,
the payment to be in money or in votes, or in subservience, the men who
will not pay or cringe or sell their consciences, do not get office. But
Walter Howe set the example of two things; first, of the fearless discharge of public office, when he held it, as a trust, and as a matter of
individual responsibility; and, secondly, of unofficial service, of doing
what he could as a private citizen to purify and advance the city and the
State. Mr. Roosevelt's tribute to him is worth emphasizing and impress-
ing, all the more because it lifts the question of citizenship, out of paid
office and elevated positions to the dignity and duty of the individual
man.

" He was for three years a member of the State Legislature, during most of which
time I was his colleague; and for the last three years he had been a member of the
very important Aqueduct Commission. But this by no means represents the sum
total of his public life. He was one of those men, by far too few in our city, who
understand that a good American citizen is in honor bound to keep at all times actively interested in our politics. Whether in or out of office he was always a power
for good in the primaries and conventions which settle beforehand, in so many cases,
what can be done at the polls. He never shirked his work because it was disagree-
able, because he had to leave his own attractive home in order to do it, or because
he could often see no immediate result from his labor and self-sacrifice. It would
be hard to overestimate the effect such a man, when strong, earnest and sincere,
and with Walter Howe's wise common sense, exerts in elevating and purifying the
tone of public life wherever his influence extends."

Now and then a cloud of sorrow in the sense of loss falls, and shuts
down not the narrow horizon of the Diocese, or the ecclesiastical outlook
of our chief interest, but even the wider horizon of the Church at large.
And I cannot stand here to-day and not recall, and ask you to realize
and recognize with me how the Church is poorer and weaker in the world
to-day for the loss of Henry Parry Liddon.

Canon Liddon's service to the Church cannot, it seems to me, be overestimated. That he was the great Preacher of this century every body knew, not only those who came under the spell of the living voice that filled the greatest preaching-place of the world to-day, with the mighty power of persuasive argument and penetrating appeal, but to those to whom his books have become mines of gold to be moulded into new forms of truth, or stamped and made current with the coinage of new images and superscriptions in the Kingdom of Christ. To me the loss of Liddon seems the more irreparable, because of other qualities than those which go to make up the subtle and very inexplicable power of the Preacher. Golden mouthed he was, indeed. But he was far more. Clear as crystal and pure as crystal in his heart and brain, he was quick to discern the needs and demands of the day; fearless to speak out for truth and righteousness; furnished absolutely in theology, and true to the inspirations of the Holy Ghost, to the instruction of the Church Catholic, and to the instincts of his Priestly Order. He never swerved a hair's breadth from the τύπον διδάχης. No apparent possibility of temporary advantage ever tempted him to yield an inch of ground to the questions of the absolute Catholicity of the Church of England; the final conclusiveness of the Catholic Creeds; or the infallible inspiration of the Word of God. And his last service to the Church when in grief of spirit and gentleness of speech, he stood his ground against the men who in all friendliness seemed to incline towards a dis-integration of the Canon of the Scripture, as this Church had received it, was almost the noblest and most heroic service of his life; not less so be-cause it cost him the pain of differing from those who were associated with him by the closest ties. There has been much vulgar criticism and ques-tion about the lack of appreciation of Canon Liddon's power in the Church of England, because he was never elevated to the Episcopate. I am the last man to derogate in any degree from the dignity and honour of the highest office that a human being can hold — the office of a Bishop in the Church of God. But the Episcopate is degraded when it is thought of, or spoken of, or used. as a reward of eloquence, or learning, or holiness; and I have faith enough in the goodness of God to believe that the Holy Spirit still rules in the administration of His kingdom, making some to be Apostles, and some to be Evangelists, and so on through the roll of honourable service to the King. And no man had in his gift, nor could God, it seems to me, have given to this man, a place of honour so high, or post of service so suited to his unequalled power, as the position of Preacher in St. Paul's Cathedral, London, the very heart and centre of the thinking and believing world, where he spoke to the great nation of the world, in the world's greatest language, truths that are greater than the greatest speech, in the interest of the world eternal, and the life to come.

The Rev. Dr. Sawyer's tribute to him in the *Evangelist*, will recall a scene which they can never forget who ever saw it:

5

Four thousand people often were gathered under the dome of St. Paul's to hear this greatest English Preacher. It was worth a journey over sea to be there, even for a single service. Such another study for any preacher, it would be impossible to find. The place, the audience, the Preacher, all were great; each seemed suited to the other, and the sublimest truth finding such conditions, taught you the meaning of the word so sadly misunderstood: 'It pleased God by the foolishness of preaching, to save them that believe.' It was the highest praise, an unconscious tribute to the Preacher of St. Paul's, that such silences fell over the great assembly. Not more than two-thirds were seated, or could be within reasonable distance, so there was a constant murmur of feet on the pavement, a sigh, a surge of the world afar, as if its jar and roar beat up against the temple walls, and fell like waves on a distant shore. Over it all sounded the voice that spoke for God, for right, for Heaven. The mastership of the speaker never faltered. You could follow his discourse and mark its strong points by the pulsations of sound out there in the distance. When the thought rested, the murmur rose; when the thought rose, the murmur fell. Again and again there would be a hush, as if even the wind and seas listened and were still.

Thank God, though that strong, sweet, stirring, sonorous voice is stilled on earth, the Word which it uttered, ringing on in convinced minds, convicted consciences, and converted souls, has free course and is glorified. Think of him to-day, and pray for him, that more and more he may rejoice in the beatific vision which he has brought near to so many souls; and thank God for the manifestation of truth and power which He vouchsafed in this great Preacher of righteousness, this mighty witness of the Faith. And let us recall and realize these his own solemn words:

*" We, its ministers of the hour, appear one after another in quick succession, each doing his work, speaking his message, and then passing to his account. But the great Church remains, an image in the realm of sense and time of the eternal realities as were the hills which stood about Jerusalem."

If any thing could increase the sorrow of his death, it would be the fact that England and the Christian world have lost in the same year its ripest scholar in †Bishop Lightfoot, its keenest controversialist in Dr. Littledale, and its rarest student of God's Revelation in Nature and in Religion in Canon Aubrey Moore, whose paper in Lux Mundi, on the Christian doctrine of God, is, I think, *the* jewel of that brilliant book.

On Tuesday, Nov. 12, the twenty-first Annual Convention met in the Cathedral. I delivered a portion of my Address in the place of the sermon, and celebrated the Holy Communion, assisted by the Rt. Reverend the Missionary Bishops of Nevada and Utah, and New Mexico and Arizona, and by the Archdeacons of Albany and Troy, the Dean of the Cathedral and the Secretary of the Convention. The arrangements for the business meeting in the gymnasium of St. Agnes School were satisfactory, although perhaps not quite sufficient in room ; but the business

---

* Liddon's Christmastide Sermons, preached January, 1871.

† I add in the appendix the words of reverent affection for the Bishop of Durham, which I sent you at the time of his death.

was never more promptly or more thoroughly attended to, as was proved, I think, by the adjournment at 4·o'clock on the second afternoon. We succeeded in this way in keeping a full attendance to the end, which seems impossible to do when the session reaches over into the evening. And the two addresses that were made in the Cathedral at night at the Missionary meeting, by the Rector of St. Paul's, Troy, and the Archdeacon of Ogdensburgh were models as missionary speeches; while the third address, which Mr. Houghton made, in presenting the claim of St. Paul's Hall in Salem, told upon all who heard it, as any message will that comes from a man, clear and strong in his own sense of a special vocation from God.

I was glad that we were able to report the Mission Stations almost all filled, and the Missionary expectations from the different Parishes almost all fulfilled; so that at our meeting of the new Board on the night of Wednesday, the 13th, we were able to make the new appointments with some very slight addition to the number and some still more slight addition to the stipends of the Missionaries. We have not yet reached the point, I am sorry to say, when the Board has felt free to take up the appointment of an itinerant missionary for the Diocese at large. I believe in it and hope for it, but it can only be done when the Convocations are willing to make extra efforts and pledges for his support. The question of a Missionary itinerant in the separate Convocations hangs fire, partly for lack of means, and partly because the Parishes have got in the way of expecting that they shall either each have a particular clergyman, or at any rate each have services every Lord's day. But I believe the time has come, when this sort of expectation must be broken up and some larger groups made, even at the cost of local disappointment. And I say this fully recognizing the consideration that ought to be given to the little places, where a few people are faithful and generous and intensely in earnest to maintain the Church. It is a sort of trial which every body knows it is difficult to accept or provide for; like diminishing one's establishment when the income that supported it is reduced.

On Monday, Nov. 25th, I confirmed in private in Saratoga two persons for Bethesda Parish.

On Monday, Dec. 2d, I made an inspection of the bit of land since then actually acquired for the Diocesan Boys' School, at Salem, about which I shall have something to say later on.

On Wednesday, Dec. 4th, I admitted Harriet Fry a probationer in the Sisterhood of the Holy Child Jesus.

On Tuesday, Dec. 10th, I baptized in New York in private the child of two old friends, presided at the meeting of the Board of Managers, (having been elected President,) and at a meeting of the Society for the Home Study of Holy Scripture and Church History.

On Sunday, Dec. 15th, in the new and very nicely ordered room for St. Giles' Mission, Castleton, I preached and confirmed eight persons.

On Monday, Dec. 16th, I organized Grace Mission, Stamford, in Delaware county, and on Friday, Dec. 20th, I organized, with the consent of the Rector of Trinity Church, St. Andrew's Mission, West Troy.

On Thursday, Dec. 21st, in All Saints, Chapel, Hudson, I ordained Priest the Rev. Elmer P. Miller, the Rev. Mr. Cookson presenting him and the Rev. Messrs. Tebbetts and McDougal assisting in the laying on of hands. I preached and celebrated the Holy Communion.

On Tuesday, Dec. 24th, I blessed the new Sanctuary of the Church of the Holy Cross, Troy, and made the address. It was hard to believe that any thing could add to the beauty of this exquisite building, the first of its kind in America, and in its peculiar character still unsurpassed. But this addition admirably well done, not only enlarges the convenience of the building for the accommodation of the school and for the rendering of the Choral service, but really enhances the dignity of the Church itself. The place is always, and was never more so than on this Christmas Eve, rich to me in its associations with dear friends living, and in the sacred memories of the beloved dead.

Wednesday, Jan. 8th, in private, I confirmed one person for the Parish of the Holy Innocents, Albany.

Monday, Jan. 13th, I blessed the Chapel with its Altar, and the Parish School-house of All Saints, Hoosac. There is most thorough earnestness and entire devotion in this Mission, and both in the constant outreaching of its missionary enterprise and the thorough laying of the foundation of the "first principles of the doctrine of Christ," there is an outlook for the future of this neighborhood, it seems to me, full of encouragement.

On Wednesday, Jan. 15th, in St. John's Church. Troy, I preached and celebrated the Holy Communion, at a meeting of the Convocation of Troy, and afterward I blessed the new Parish house. This valuable addition to the working capacity of the Parish has been done in excellent taste and is complete in every detail. It has in it at once the evidence and the promise of earnest life; and the three buildings together, the Church, the Parish House and the Rectory, and I am glad to say, an open space of land in the quad and on the other side of the Rectory, make this one of the most attractive Church properties in the Diocese.

From the twentieth to the twenty-fourth I was in New York in attendance upon meetings of the Board of Regents of the Church University, the High License Committee and the Commission on the New Hymnal. Of the first, I desire to say, that although our progress may seem slow and slight, I believe we are moving as rapidly as wisdom allows, and in directions which are sure to bring about valuable results. Of the second, I bound to say that the measure which the Commission introduced this year, and which passed the Senate, failed of final adoption, because the party that had been supposed to favour it shirked the issue. It was a new evidence of the fact that this great moral question cannot safely be handled either as a platform for the victory of one party, or the war cry for the defeat of another. And until the citizens of this State recognize this fact, and send men to Albany pledged to their party on party issues, but with enough courage and conviction to vote for moral questions upon moral grounds, we shall be left, not to the tender mercies, but to the odious cruelties of the unlimited and irresponsible sale of liquor. The Commission on the Hymnal asks nothing of the Church but a candid examination of its work. It has had no choice given it of proposing the authorization of the present Hymnal *with* Hymns Ancient and Modern. It was charged with the duty of improving the Hymnal, and of setting forth the best collection of hymns that can be gathered in the present greatly improved condition of what is called hymnology. And it has undertaken this work in good faith at the bidding of the General Convention, pledged to no existing collection, but earnestly trying to make what the Greek poets used to call an Anthology; a collection of the fairest flowers, in the garden of the great hymn writers of the world.

January 28th, in the Crypt of the Cathedral, I made an address to the women of St. Mary's Guild.

On Sunday, February 2d, in the Cathedral I preached and celebrated keeping the twenty-first anniversary of my consecration to the Episcopate. Always a very solemn day, to me the solemnity increases as the years go on with their reminder that the majority of them are in the past and not in the future. It was a great comfort to me to have not only the presence of so many in the Cathedral at the Holy Communion, but to realize that the coincidence this year of the Feast of the Presentation with the first Sunday in the month, made possible and certain the intercessions of the Clergy and people, at every Altar in the Diocese.

Tuesday, February 4th, I presided at the meeting of the Diocesan Board of Missions.

Friday, February 7th, I confirmed one person in the Cathedral.

Friday, February 21st, I made an address before the young men and women of the Albany Business College, and have rarely faced a more interesting and intelligent gathering.

Sunday, February 23d, in the evening at Grace Church, Albany, I preached, and confirmed twenty-three persons.

Wednesday, February 26th, in St. James' Church, Oneonta, in the evening I preached, and confirmed twenty persons. There is a very abundant evidence here of growth in all best ways. By far the most important town between Albany and Binghamton, Oneonta is coming to be as vigorous in its Church life as in its material growth.

Wednesday, March 5th, I was most glad to use a service of benediction in a private house in Albany, recognizing what I wish we realized more often than we do, the family element in religion, and how much meaning there is, and how much blessing there ought to be, in the Apostolic thought, "the Church which is in their house."

Tuesday, March 11th, I presided at the meeting of the Board of Managers in New York.

Thursday, March 13th, I made my visitation of the Church Home in Troy, preaching and celebrating the Holy Communion.

Sunday, March 23d, in the evening in St. John's Church, Troy, I preached and confirmed twenty-five persons.

Tuesday, March 25th, the Feast of the Annunciation, in the evening, in the Cathedral, I preached and confirmed seventy-two persons; making, with later confirmations, seventy-nine this year.

Sunday, March 30th, in the morning, in St. Peter's Church, Albany, I preached and confirmed fifty-six persons and celebrated the Holy Communion, and in the evening in St. Paul's Church, Albany, I preached and confirmed thirty-seven persons.

On Monday, the 31st, in the House of Refuge in Hudson, I preached after a most interesting service and with a sense of the intense mercy of the Gospel Message, such as I have rarely felt before. So far as I could see it, the administration of the house is admirable in every way; a very deep sense of personal responsibility combined with, and controlled by, the calm dignity of a well-balanced judgment, making the residence of the unfortunate women who are gathered there, rich with every opportunity for reform. The whole atmosphere of the influence was most impressive.

Tuesday, April 1st, in the evening, in the Church of the Holy Innocents, Albany, I preached and confirmed ten persons, and in the evening, in Trinity Church, Albany, I preached and confirmed thirty-nine persons, two of them presented by the Rev. Mr. Bevington from St. Peter's Church. There is great evidence of rooting and grounding and growth of the new life in this old Parish.

On Thursday, April 3rd, Maundy Thursday, I confirmed one person in the Cathedral. On Good Friday I preached the three hours' service in the Cathedral, and on Saturday, Easter Even, after the Even song, I said a collect and we sang a hymn, and then unveiled the great west window — the gracious gift of the Misses Clarkson of Potsdam, all the more gracious because it was unasked. The glory of this window in its place is certainly unsurpassed. It tells the story — as the angelic faces look upward in adoration, surrounding the central panel in which are the two figures of forgiven penitents — of "the joy in the presence of the Angels of God over one sinner that repenteth." And as it catches the accordant of the sinking sun, and floods the nave with the gorgeous colours of the western sky, it shows forth that Love of God which never sets; whose fruition shall be in the land where there is no night, and where also they have no need of the sun because the Lamb is the light thereof.

Our Easter celebration in the Cathedral, with more than five hundred communicants at the three celebrations, tested the size and attested the dignity of the Cathedral, and was full of beauty and thankfulness.

Monday, April 7th, in the evening in Trinity Church, West Troy, I preached and confirmed twenty-six persons.

On Tuesday, the 8th, I presided at the Board of Managers at New York.

Wednesday, the 9th, after a long and tedious drive through mud that was only not impassable but is impossible to describe, I came late to the little Church at Chestertown, where I preached and confirmed five persons.

On Thursday morning, I consecrated St. Paul's Chapel, Bartonville — a pretty and convenient Church, largely due, as is the Mission itself, to the energy and interest of the Rev. Mr. Taylor; and a great comfort to me as indicating what we ought to have more of; aggressive growth and advancement in the Diocese. I preached and confirmed eight persons and celebrated the Holy Communion. The Rev. Mr. Taylor read the Instrument of Donation, and the Rev. Mr. Ogden the Sentence of Consecration.

In the evening in the Church of the Holy Cross, Warrensburgh, I preached and confirmed three persons.

Friday, the 11th, in St. Sacrament Church, Bolton, I preached and confirmed eleven persons, and celebrated the Holy Communion, and in the evening in St. James' Church, Lake George, I preached and confirmed five persons. I ask your prayers for the faithful and beloved Rector of Lake George, not unmingled with thanksgiving that God has given him partial and promising relief from the total blindness which threatened.

Sunday, April 13th, in the morning in St. Paul's Church, Troy, I preached, confirmed forty-six persons and celebrated the Holy Communion.

In the afternoon in the Church of the Holy Cross, Troy, I preached and confirmed twenty persons; and in the evening at St. Barnabas' Church, Troy, at a second confirmation, I preached and confirmed eight persons.

Tuesday, April 15th, in the morning in Zion Church, Fonda, I preached and celebrated the Holy Communion, sadly missing for the first time the cordial greeting of my dear old friend Mrs. Cushney.

In the afternoon, in Christ Church, Gloversville, I preached and confirmed fourteen persons. In the evening in St. John's Church, Johnstown, I preached and confirmed eighteen persons. I was thankful to find the Rector in his new Rectory, whose hospitality I greatly enjoyed.

Wednesday, April 16th, in the morning in the Church of the Holy Cross, Fort Plain, I preached and confirmed nine persons and celebrated the Holy Communion.

In the afternoon, in the Church of the Good Shepherd, Canajoharie,

I preached and confirmed four persons, and in the evening in St. Ann's Church, Amsterdam, I preached and confirmed sixteen persons.

Thursday, 17th, in the morning, in Christ Church, Herkimer, I preached and confirmed twenty-three persons and celebrated the Holy Communion.

In the afternoon, in a hall used for the Mission, which we organized that day, of St. Columba, in St. Johnsville, I preached and confirmed seven persons. Mr. Marvin's energetic devotion has created this Mission, built the Church in Fort Plain and serves the three places, after the manner of the successors of the great Saint of Iona.

In the evening in St. Augustine's Church, Ilion, I preached and confirmed twelve persons.

On Friday morning, the 18th, in Grace Church, Mohawk, I preached, confirmed one person and celebrated the Holy Communion. In the afternoon, in St. Alban's, Frankfort, I preached and confirmed four persons, and in the evening, in Emmanuel Church, Little Falls, I preached and confirmed eleven persons.

On Sunday, April 20th, in the afternoon, in Christ Church, Schenectady, I preached and confirmed ten persons, and in the evening at St. George's, I preached and confirmed twenty persons. The visitation of the Mohawk Valley is always one of the most pleasant and satisfactory that I make. Nowhere in the Diocese has the Church gained and grown in twenty years more than here; and from one end to the other now it is astir with the life and energy of first-rate young men, with new tokens this year, not only of spiritual results; but with the new rectories at Johnstown and Schenectady (for Christ Church) the boy choirs at St. George's, Schenectady, and in Herkimer, and the admirable new buildings — the Church and the Rectory and the Parish-House at Herkimer. And it is growth in tough soil and against bitter odds: nowhere more than in Gloversville, where, nevertheless, it seems to me the faithful and persistent patience of Mr. Burnett, is beginning at last to tell.

Tuesday, April 22d, in the morning at St. Luke's, Mechanicville, I preached, confirmed two persons, and celebrated the Holy Communion.

In the afternoon in St. John's, Stillwater, I preached. In the evening in Bethesda Church, Saratoga, I preached and confirmed sixty-two persons, one in private. The life spiritual here, like the wonderful gifts of the Mineral Springs, seems to have a perennial and perpetual flow.

Wednesday, 23rd, in the morning in St. Mary's, Luzerne, I preached and confirmed three persons and celebrated the Holy Communion.

Thursday, the 24th, in St. Peter's Church, Albany, I took part in the service at the burial of Miss Meads, and attended the meeting of the Diocesan Board of Missions.

On Monday, the 28th, in the Cathedral, I confirmed four persons, making in all seventy-eight confirmed this spring.

On Sunday, May 4th, I preached and celebrated in the morning, and preached again in the evening in St. John's Church, Ithaca, and in the afternoon I preached one of the University sermons in the Sage Chapel.

The marked advance in every best way in the University and the increased hold and attention which the Church is gaining there, are most satisfactory to know.

On Monday, May 5th, in St. John's Church, Richfield Springs, I preached and confirmed thirty persons.

On Wednesday, May 7th, in Trinity Church, New York, I said the burial office over the body of Mr. Alfred Davenport — my friend and the son of my friends, a young man whose brilliant promise had so far fulfilled itself before the prime of his life came, that its harvest ripened early for the sickle, and left many mourning the sorrow, but patient before the mystery, of his death.

In the evening, in St. Luke's Church, Catskill, I preached and confirmed fifty-three persons, after a service, short, but full of the tokens of the earnest life to which such unusual results are due.

On Thursday, the 8th, in the Cathedral, I preached and celebrated the Holy Communion at one of our very best meetings of the Diocesan Branch of the Woman's Auxiliary. There were about two hundred women present and a good many Clergy ; the addresses and reports were both interesting and encouraging, and we inaugurated there what must, I think, be a means of most valuable help and cheer to the Clergy, a Diocesan Lending Library, from which every Clergyman in the Diocese will be enabled and entitled to borrow. We begin with the Cathedral Library of about six hundred volumes, the gift of the children of Judge Forsyth, and a most valuable collection of the best theological books. Mr. Snively with his accustomed thoughtfulness has secured the gift of $100, from what is known as the Mann bequest. Dean Hoffman most kindly sent his check for $100, and about the same amount was pledged at the meeting, and a staunch and generous church woman of St. John's, Johnstown, gave $25 on All Saints day, to be offered in the Cathedral.

More even than money, we have the volunteer service of Mr. Melvil Dewey, the State Librarian, and of several of the corps of his assistants, in arranging and cataloguing the books. And as I realize the immense need and value of fresh and free reading for the Clergy and the paucity of their Libraries, because of the poverty of their lives, I believe this to be one of the most important agencies for the strengthening and establishing the Church in the Diocese. I very earnestly commend it to the generous interest of the people, that it may be kept stocked with the best books from time to time, because while it is true, that theology like all fixed truth, is changeless in its principles, it is also true that no science in the world has so large, so fresh and so increasing a literature.

6

In the evening, in St. John's Church, Cohoes, I preached and confirmed nineteen persons.

May 9th, in the morning, at Trinity Church, Athens, I preached, confirmed six persons, and celebrated the Holy Communion.

In the afternoon, in Trinity Church, Claverack, I preached and confirmed seven persons; and in the evening, in All Saints' Chapel, Hudson, I preached and confirmed nine persons.

May 10th, in the morning, in St. John's Church, Stockport, I preached, confirmed five persons and celebrated the Holy Communion.

In the afternoon, in St. Barnabas', Stottville, I preached and confirmed thirty-eight persons. The result of the division of this Parish has evidently been good. The only marvel is that Mr. Fisher, to whose careful work much undoubtedly of this large result is due, could have accomplished what he did, when his work included the three places with so many miles between. The very earnest devotion of Mr. Rainey, concentrated upon this point, is already bringing forth remarkable fruits; and the enlargement of the Chapel is called for and is to be begun at once.

Sunday, May 11th, in the afternoon, in Trinity Church, Lansingburgh, I preached and confirmed eighteen persons; and in the evening, in Christ Church, Troy, I preached and confirmed twenty persons.

The next four days I was in New York at meetings of the Committees on the Standard Prayer Book and the Missionary Council, and of the Board of Managers; and on Thursday, the feast of the Ascension, I had the privilege of being with the Bishops of New York and Mississippi, and celebrating the Holy Communion in Trinity Church, New York.

In the evening, in the Free Church of the Ascension, in Troy, I preached and confirmed six persons.

On the 16th, in St. Peter's Church, Albany, I took part in the service for the burial of my old and revered friend, Judge Parker.

May 17th, I presided at a meeting for the formation of the Charity Organization for the city of Albany.

Sunday, the 18th, in the Cathedral, I admitted Miss Monell into the Sisterhood of the Holy Child Jesus, to be Sister Pamela.

In the afternoon, in the Church of the Epiphany, Bath, I preached and confirmed ten persons; and in the evening, in the Church of the Messiah, Greenbush, I preached and confirmed ten persons.

May 19th, in the evening, in St. Mark's Church, Hoosick Falls, I preached and confirmed twenty-five persons.

May 20th, I assisted in a marriage service in Stockbridge, Mass., in the morning; and in the evening, in Trinity Church, Granville, I preached and confirmed two persons.

May 21st, in the afternoon, in St. Luke's Church, Cambridge, I preached and confirmed three persons.

May 23d, in St. John's Church, Delhi, I preached and confirmed ten persons, and afterward, I dedicated the exquisite Memorial Chapel of this Church, built by Mr. Edwin Sheldon in memory of his parents, and consecrated the Sanctuary and Altar, making an address and celebrating the Holy Communion. It is one of the most lovely memorials that I know, both as a token of the deep reverence of filial love and for all its lavish expenditure of exquisite taste; and greatly as we missed the presence of the builder of the Chapel, it was a pleasure to have a share in the dedication of his gift to God, and afterward to see him. In the evening, in Christ Church, Walton, I preached and confirmed fifteen persons.

May 24th, I confirmed in private one person for the Cathedral.

Sunday, May 25th, in the afternoon, in Grace Church, Waterford, I preached and confirmed seventeen persons, and in the evening, in St. Mark's Church, Green Island, I preached and confirmed seventeen persons.

May 26th, in the morning, in St. Mark's Church. Philmont, I preached, confirmed three persons and celebrated the Holy Communion.

In the afternoon, in the room occupied by the congregation of St. Luke's Church, Chatham, I preached, having confirmed one person before in private; and in the evening, in St. Paul's Church, Kinderhook, I preached and confirmed eight persons.

May 27th, in New York, I presided at the meeting of the Trustees of the General Theological Seminary with a feeling of thankful pride in the admirable condition, scholastic and spiritual as well as material, to which this central institution of the Church has been brought under the administration of the present Dean.

May 29th, I had the great pleasure of preaching the sermon on Founders' day in the Chapel of St. Paul's School, Concord. To be associated in any way with my dear old friend Dr. Shattuck is an honour and delight; and to be in any way connected with this noble Institution, is one of the things for which American Churchmen ought to be most thankful. The very atmosphere of the place is a charm; and all its influences, academic and athletic; as well as religious, are certainly unrivalled in America.

May 31st, I confirmed, in private, one person for Trinity Church, Albany.

Sunday, June 1st, I had the pleasure of being present in the Cathedral at the festival of the united Choirs of the Cathedral and St. Paul's Church, Troy, and afterward, in St. Margaret's Chapel, Menands, I preached, and confirmed five persons.

June 2d, I confirmed, in the Cathedral, one person.

June 3d, I confirmed, in the Cathedral, one person.

The next three days I was occupied with the closing examinations and exercises of St. Agnes' School, giving the diplomas, with my blessing, to the graduates on the 5th of June, in the Cathedral.

That evening and the next day, I was with the candidates for Holy Orders, partly for their examination and partly for their spiritual preparation; and, on the 7th of June, in the Cathedral, I ordered Deacon, Mr. Frederick Stirling Griffin, and advanced to the Priesthood, the Rev. Walter Charles Stewart and the Rev. Robert Morris Kemp. The Rev. Archdeacon Olmsted preached the sermon, and I celebrated the Holy Communion, the Clergy present being the Dean, the Precentor, the Rev. Canons Chapman, Temple and Gray, the Rev. Drs. Battershall, Mulcahey and Maxcy, and Messrs. Mulford, Snively, Schwartz, Beattie and Greer.

June 9th, in the evening, in St. Andrew's Mission, West Troy, I preached and confirmed five persons. The setting off of this Mission from the parish Church has plainly, I think, deepened the interest of the people and increased the efficiency of the work.

June 10th, I presided at the meeting of the Board of Managers, in New York.

June 11th, in the morning, in St. Paul's Church, Salem, I preached, confirmed eighteen persons and celebrated the Holy Communion. The service was full of beauty and interest, as always, here, and at its close I presented the prizes to the boys. In the afternoon we went out to the grounds of the new School. Every arrangement had been made for a pleasant and delightful afternoon, but the rain fell in such persistent torrents that much of the pleasure of course was spoiled, and the possibility of an out-door service entirely taken away. I made the address, however, and we sang some hymns, and I read the office of Benediction of the Land, suggesting that we might accept the visitation of God as His own baptizing of the place with its new name — Rexleigh or the King's Meadow. One result at any rate was beyond all peradventure, and that was the cheerful ardour of the Rector which nothing can damp, and the really pleasant patience of the large number of persons who were gathered there that day; and the readiness with which our good hosts bore the disappointment and adapted themselves to the difficulties of the situation.

June 12th, in the evening, in the Church of the Cross, Ticonderoga, I preached and confirmed three persons.

June 13th, in the morning, in Christ Church, Port Henry, I preached and confirmed two persons, and celebrated the Holy Communion ; and in the evening, in St. John's Church, Essex, I preached and confirmed four persons.

June 14th, in the morning, in St. James' Church, Ausable Forks, I preached, confirmed eight persons and celebrated the Holy Communion, and in the afternoon, in St. Paul's Church, Keeseville, I preached and confirmed five persons. I was not sorry to find myself at ten o'clock at night in the delightful home, that makes me welcome at Champlain, after a day of work and travel which had been nineteen hours long.

June 15th, in the morning, in St. John's Church, Champlain, I preached and confirmed two persons, and in the afternoon, I preached in Christ Church, Rouse's Point.

June 16th, in the morning, in St. Paul's Church, Ellenburgh Centre, I preached and celebrated the Holy Communion. In the afternoon, in St. Peter's Church, Ellenburgh, I baptized an adult, preached and confirmed four persons, one of whom came from the Centre; and in the evening, at Trinity Church, Plattsburg, I preached and confirmed eleven persons. The circumstances connected with the vacancy of this Parish have been personally very painful to me, and the loss from active work in the Diocese of the Rev. Henry Mason Smyth is a great personal grief. Mr. McIlwaine's temporary service has been most useful and acceptable, and I am thankful to say that the Parish has since been filled most wisely, I think, by the election of the Rev. Hobart Cooke.

June 18th. I preached the sermon at the graduation of the class from the Episcopal Theological School in Cambridge. There were two days of great enjoyment here; of the gracious hospitality of the Dean; of a most pleasant impression of the work done in the School, and of great satisfaction in the wisdom and courage of those who planted under the shadow of this great University, an institution of sound religious teaching according to the Creeds of the Catholic Church. Nothing, it seems to me, can be wiser, than in a place like Cambridge, where the spirit of investigation and inquiry is carried out in the most thorough way into every thing to show how the Church courts just this most radical examination of all that she holds in trust for God. The buildings are very delightful, and the whole property, nestled among the older buildings, and the still older trees, is a beautiful memorial of the faith and liberality of the men who founded the School; and to those of us who knew and loved Dean Gray, it is most gratifying to feel that his best memorial is here, and that his work has been handed down to such wise and able hands.

June 21st. In Bethesda Church, Saratoga Springs, I had the pleasure of baptizing the young son of the Rector, and of sharing the pleasure, which I am sure he must have felt, in the large gathering of people who showed their love for him by their presence in the Church that day.

Sunday, June 22d. In the morning, in the Church of the Messiah, Glens Falls, I preached, confirmed twenty-nine persons and celebrated the Holy Communion. In the afternoon, in Zion Church, Sandy Hill, I preached, and confirmed sixteen persons; and in the evening in St. James' Church, Fort Edward, I preached, and confirmed seven persons. The day was full of the great pleasure which I always find in my visit to these three Churches, with all the tokens that are in them of earnest religious life.

June 24th, in the Church of the Memorial, Middleville, I preached, confirmed twelve persons, and celebrated the Holy Communion. It was a hurried visit made after two disappointments, under difficulties which I only overcame by the kindness of Mr. Burns, who put the railroad virtually at my disposal; but I was glad to find good encouragement here for Mr. Lylburn's work, and very much pleased with the new Rectory which has been built, in carrying out Mrs. Varney's purpose, by her descendants here.

On Wednesday, the 25th, I was most graciously surprised to find that under the kindly inspiration of the President, nine of the St. Agnes' girls were gathered to greet me in the College library at Geneva. He made the address to which with very grateful feeling, I replied; and they gave me a little compass with a suitable inscription, and a kindly reference to my North East Harbour Summer Seas, and to my wintry duty in the Churches across the sea.

June 26th, I was present at the commencement of Hobart College, and delivered the Chancellor's oration. The exercises were, it seemed to me, of unusual interest, and the essays riper in thought than I remember such papers ordinarily to be ; and I had an added personal satisfaction in seeing on every hand tokens of the success of Dr. Potter's administration of the College, and in the fact that the son of my very dear friend Dr. Nelson graduated as valedictorian *"summa cum laude."*

The situation of the College in Geneva is so beautiful, the influences about it are so refined and elevating, and the character of the faculty is so high, that one wonders in some ways, why there are not more students there. It is proposed, and I trust it will be successful, to add to the efficiency of the College by establishing a fuller scientific course. When this is done and when Churchmen realize, more than they do now what the great Universities are learning from the smaller Colleges, that where there are few students, each one comes in direct contact with the first-class professors, there will be more boys, I think, to take advantage of the great advantages of Hobart College.

June 28th, in the morning, in Grace Church, Norfolk, I preached and celebrated the Holy Communion. In the afternoon, in St. Andrew's Church, Norwood, I preached and confirmed two persons. We owe more than I can tell to Dr. Kirby's unfailing and self-sacrificing service which has maintained services here.

June 29th, in the morning, in Trinity Church, Potsdam, I preached, confirmed twelve persons and celebrated the Holy Communion. In the afternoon, in Zion Church, Colton, I preached and confirmed five persons.

June 30th, in the morning, in St. John's Church, Massena, I preached, confirmed one person and celebrated the Holy Communion. In the evening, in Trinity Chapel, Morley, I preached and confirmed two persons.

July 1st, in the morning, in Grace Church, Canton, I preached, confirmed four persons and celebrated the Holy Communion. In the afternoon, in Trinity Church, Gouverneur, I preached and confirmed six persons.

July 2d, in the morning, in the Hall occupied by the Mission in Santa Clara, I preached, confirmed two persons and celebrated the Holy Communion; and, in the evening, in the Church of St. Luke the Beloved Physician, at Saranac Lake, I preached and confirmed twelve persons.

July 3d, in the morning, in the Church of the Good Shepherd, Bloomingdale, I preached, confirmed seven persons and celebrated the Holy Communion.

I am delighted with the whole look of the Adirondack Mission. Mr. Larom has thrown himself into it with enthusiastic earnestness, and his layreader, Mr. Thompson, is an invaluable helper. The work grows in all best ways and is reaching out in new directions, as his report will show. The stations are increasing in number and interest, and the excellent arrangements made by the missionary, have sustained services in more places than ever this year, thanks to the helpfulness of the visiting clergy. I am most anxious that the Clergy-house at Saranac Lake, the Winter centre of the work, should be secured.

July 4th, I made a short address at the Fourth of July service at St. John's Church, Ogdensburgh, which, among many other good works, the Rector here has instituted and sustains.

July 5th, in the afternoon, in Christ Church, Morristown, I preached and confirmed five persons.

Sunday, July 6th, in the morning, in St. John's Church, Ogdensburgh, I preached, confirmed twenty-nine persons and celebrated the Holy Communion.

In the afternoon, in St. Luke's Church, Lisbon, I preached and confirmed eight persons, four of whom had come from Waddington by the kindness of the Missionary, as I had been compelled to give up my visitations to Waddington and Hogansburgh. In the evening, I preached again in St. John's Church.

July 7th, in the morning, in St. Peter's Church, Brushton, I preached and celebrated the Holy Communion, and in the evening, in St. Mark's Church, Malone, I preached and confirmed eighteen persons. This northern visitation always impresses me with the possibilities of the work in this remote, impoverished and scattered region, and with the great power that comes into it, partly personal and partly official, from the Rectors of Ogdensburgh and Potsdam. Mr. John Hurd's work at Santa Clara continues to be full of zeal and energy; and the condition of things at Gouverneur is more satisfactory than it has been for many a year.

I went from my Northern Visitations to my Summer home and work. It was never more beautiful than this year. And although I was disabled by illness, almost the whole Summer from the enjoyment of my work and of my pleasure, the work went on, and had its own blessing with it, in the strange and unexpected way which marks so much of the ministration there. And I passed out of it, through the great rest and refreshment of the Retreat in the Cathedral, to my Autumn Visitations, strengthened in soul at least, and better physically for what lies ahead.

On Monday, September 8th, Mr. Reazor, acting for me, laid the Corner-stone of the Chapel at Griffin's Corners. He writes me: "The service was very impressive; the Rev. Mr. Butler, of the Epiphany, New York, and the Rev. L. T. Wattson, of Kingston, were present, vested. The latter contributed immensely to the dignity and beauty of the function, by bringing his surpliced Choir and about fifteen singers from his Auxiliary Choir. There was a large Congregation and the impression made was most favourable. The box contained a Bible, a Prayer Book and the Appendices, a copy of our last Diocesan Convention Journal, and a copy of the Diocesan Canons. At the Even-song (7:30 o'clock) I baptized four children — the ἀπαρχή of Challen's noble work there. Yesterday morning, at 8:30, I celebrated the Holy Eucharist and administered it to Challen and Woodruff, and James Lasher, the last two about to start that morning for St. Stephen's."

In Christ Church, Cooperstown, on the evening of September 19th, I preached and confirmed twelve persons, and the next day I presided at the annual meeting of the Trustees of the Orphan House of the Holy Saviour. In all ways but one, the review of the year and the appearance of the Orphanage were admirable. The enlargement of the building, giving room most needed for health and convenience, and the condition of the children, never more in number and never more satisfactorily taught and trained, were all that one could ask. But the old story still holds true; of debt incurred in the building, of very small endowment which does not grow, and of difficulty of support which is discreditable and inexplicable. But for the economics of management which are extraordinary, and for the income from the maintenance of the county children, the work could not go on. The appeal is to be made to wipe out the debt, which I hope will be promptly responded to, at this meeting of the Convention. And I again appeal most earnestly to the Clergy to see that the annual canonical collection for the Orphan House is made, and is made not merely as a formal and perfunctory act of obedience. If you would inform yourselves, my brethren, as to the importance and blessedness of the work; if you would make it real to your Congregations; if you would impress upon them the fact that this is really one of the two only works of charity and mercy that the Church in this Diocese is to be judged by, I think the response would be generous and adequate to the need. Passing by the higher motives of service and duty to the Lord, I confess I am ashamed, when I think how, to-day and for all time, Miss Cooper's life and work is almost our chiefest honour, that we should show such poor appreciation of her service, as not to lift from her the burthen of anxiety about the support of that to which she has given her life.

I was delighted to find the Rector and his family at home in the beautiful new Rectory; in which I was glad to say a prayer of benediction before I left the Parish.

Sunday, September 21st, St. Matthew's Day, I consecrated St. Mary's Church, Springfield Centre. The request to consecrate was read by Mr. Leslie Pell-Clarke, and the sentence of consecration, by the Rev. W. C. Prout, and I preached and celebrated the Holy Communion, and confirmed four persons, presented by the Missionary, the Rev. John Prout. The Church, in itself beautiful, and beautifully placed between the lovely hill-sides and the lovelier lake, was quite ideal that day. Infinite pains and thought and cultivated taste were visible in it everywhere, and the coloring of glass and leaves and flowers and embroideries was a perfect harmony. It stands a witness to the power of a strong and earnest purpose which utters itself in prayer, and asserts itself in the sacrifice and service of personal effort; and while the Building crowns past years of loving thought and hope and work, it means, I trust, for the future the growth of the Church, and the in-gathering of the people to whom it is a great blessing. The very many who shared it that day will not soon forget the gracious hospitality of Swanswick. And I rejoice to feel that in the rehabilitation of such old homes, as Swanswick and Hyde Hall, and the building up by Church people of summer homes near the upper end of the Lake, the Church is to be strengthened in the neighbourhood.

In the evening, in Grace Church, Cherry Valley, I preached, and confirmed one person, one having been previously confirmed in private (two in all).

September 22d, A. M. In St. Paul's Church, East Springfield, I preached, confirmed three persons and celebrated.

St. Agnes School re-opened on the 24th, I was in the Cathedral for the morning Celebration; and at the Even-song; which really began the new year, our twenty-first, with every promise of fulness of blessing, which may God fulfil. It is an old story to many; but, to us each year brings its new store of fresh interest, as other lives come to be moulded by the influence and discipline of the School.

Sept. 25th. In the morning in St. Paul's Church, Greenwich, I preached, confirmed eight persons and celebrated. The Rev. Mr. Horsfield kindly assisted me and presented the candidates, who had been prepared by Mr. David Clarkson, a student of St. Stephen's, Annandale, who has been acting as Lay Reader during the summer with marked acceptance and success. One of the candidates was from St. Luke's Church, Cambridge. In the afternoon, in St. Stephen's Church, Schuylerville, I

7

preached, and confirmed five persons, presented by the Rector, tho Rev. Mr. Esch.

September 30th. In the afternoon, in the Church of the Holy Spirit, Schenevus, I preached, and confirmed two persons; and in the evening, in Immanuel Church, Otego, I preached, and confirmed six persons.

October 1st. In St. Matthew's, Unadilla, I preached, confirmed nine persons, and celebrated the Holy Communion; and in the afternoon, in St. Paul's, Franklin, I preached, and confirmed five persons. I am very sorry that Mr. Moore feels compelled to give up his work here.

October 2d, P. M. In Christ Church, Deposit, I preached, and confirmed fifteen persons. This remote corner of the Diocese abundantly repaid the journey, really two nights and a day, which the visitation involved. My welcome from old friends and from the new Rector was most delightful, and the promise of this work was never, I think, so good as under Mr. Fisher, who came last May. The great need is of a new Church building, large enough and prominent enough to assert and to assume its proper influence in the town.

October 3d, A. M. In the little room most admirably fitted for its use, in Sidney, I preached, confirmed six persons and celebrated the Holy Communion. Here, too, the Church is needed and must be undertaken, and there is real hope of a strong Mission. In the afternoon, in a disused Universalist Meeting-house, at Edmeston, I preached and confirmed two persons (one from Cooperstown).

I failed to reach West Burlington, owing to a mistake about the time-table of the trains. But some were present from the Parish there, and I was pleased to find the people in both places accepting cordially the very imperfect provision made for services. It is largely due, as is the renewed hope at Sidney, to the Missionary. the Rev. Mr. Griffin, who has thrown himself, with entire devotion and excellent good sense, into his work. But the time is coming when Sidney must be served apart, and Edmeston and Burlington be alone together; just as I think it will be necessary, when we can, to divide Schenevus from Otego. Oh, for the means and the men to do the work of the Diocese as it ought to be done.

In the evening, in Zion Church, Morris, after a hearty and reverent service I preached and confirmed three persons.

October 5th. In St. Thomas Church, New York, I confirmed one person, a Candidate for Orders in this Diocese. And on this same Sunday, the Bishop of Springfield most kindly acting for me, confirmed five persons in the Union Chapel in Sabbath Day Point. The candidates were presented as they had been prepared by the venerable Lay-reader, Mr. Chamberlain: and the Rev. Mr. Blanchet assisted in the service.

Oct. 7th, Tuesday, in the evening in the Chapel at Stamford, I preached.

Oct. 8th. In the afternoon, in Christ Church, Coxsackie, I preached and confirmed two persons. And in the evening in Gloria Dei Church, at Palenville, I preached and confirmed seven persons. This is the result of the separation of Palenville into a separate mission and is very encouraging. The Church, which has grown by slow degrees into completeness, is very nearly finished now; and while the *new* adds to its beauty — especially the reredos, which has just been put in by the Rector in memory of his boy — the old portion of the building keeps its new look, so that the whole is in entire harmony and very attractive.

October 9th. In Calvary Church, Cairo, I preached and confirmed three persons and celebrated the Holy Communion. In the afternoon, at Christ Church, Greenville, I preached; and in the evening in St. Paul's Church, Oak Hill, I preached and confirmed two persons.

October 10th. I the morning in Trinity Church, Rensselaerville, I preached and celebrated the Holy Communion.

October 14th. I confirmed one person in Brooklyn; and also performed the marriage ceremony at a private house.

October 15th. In Christ Church, Ballston, in the evening, I preached and confirmed ten persons.

October 16th. In the morning in Calvary, Burnt Hills, I preached; confirmed two persons and celebrated the Holy Communion. In the afternoon, in St. Paul's, Charlton, I preached; and in the evening in Trinity Church, Whitehall, I preached and confirmed ten persons. The service was tinctured with the double sense of sorrow and of thankfulness. The sorrowful element was the very unwelcome and unexpected resignation of the rectorship, by the Rev. Mr. Lincoln; whose work here, short as it has been, has been attended with very unusual success, both in spiritual and material returns. The number of persons confirmed, the character of the services and the size of the congregation gave proof of the first; and the fact that the debt of the Parish was absolutely cleared up, and enough money left in the treasury to paint and repair the Church, is evidence of the second.

October 17th. In the morning, in Grace Chapel, Jonesville, I preached, confirmed two persons and celebrated the Holy Communion. And in the afternoon, in St. John's, East Line, I preached. The venerable missionary here, past four score years, was unable to be with me in the morning, so that he was represented by his son. And in the afternoon, we were all three together in the little Chapel at East Line. Mr. Cook is preparing to lay aside his active labours for such rest as may make him readier, when the time shall come to enter into the perfect rest of Paradise. The work that has been done here, quiet and withdrawn from public view, has been full of great faithfulness, most self-denying labor in season and out of season, and constant intellectual and spiritual zeal; and considering the material, the results have been very striking; in Jonesville especially, where the intelligent interest of the men, who are staunch and strong in their support of the Church is very satisfactory. It takes one back to the foundation which Mr. Delafield laid at East Line, upon which, that which he designed was never built, but which I think has more than fulfilled its purpose; first in the active earnestness of the few Church people, who have been gathered in, next in the provision which has been made for the little children of St. Margaret's House, who have here their summer home; and last and no means least in the provision that it has made for the last years of service of the Rev. Mr. Cook, who leaves behind a very fragrant memory in many hearts.

October 18th, being the Feast of St. Luke, after the celebration in the Cathedral, I laid the corner-stone of the new building of the Child's Hospital. It is one of those events which naturally recalls the story of this blessed work; and I hope its appeal will not go unheeded. The hospital began March 21st, 1875, in a small building on Lafayette street, with three beds. In six months it occupied a large building on Elk street, with sixteen beds. In February, 1877, the present hospital building was completed and used, in which the children are at present. An addition to it was built in 1882. During these years 1,277 children have been cared for, of whom a very large proportion have been discharged cured, and the deaths have been unusually few. It is hoped that the new building will be completed and occupied next Spring, with provision for one hundred children. The managers have money enough to finish it, but not to put in the plumbing, or to furnish it, which will call for at least $5,000 more. The work is commended again to the generous interest of old and new friends. It depends almost entirely upon freewill gifts for its support. And that interest will, it is hoped, secure, before long, money to add proper accommodations for the Sisters, and to put up, where the present hospital stands, a permanent building for St. Margaret's House for the care of little babies.

October 21, 22, 23, I was in my place at the meeting of the Missionary Council and of the House of Bishops in Pittsburgh.

October 27 and 28, I was in New York at meetings of the Church University Board of Regents, and of the Hymnal Commission.

October 31, I lighted the Hallowe'en fire on the hearth of the great school-room in St. Agnes School.

November 1, All Saints' Day, I celebrated the Holy Communion at the second service in the Cathedral, and preached.

The Dedication Anniversary had much in it of encouragement this year. More than $200 were in the offertory for the Woman's Diocesan League. A faithful churchwoman from the old Johnstown Parish sent her offerings, towards various objects to be offered on the Cathedral Altar. And the four children of Judge Parker and Mrs. Parker offered that day their purpose of filling the tympana of the four great arches on the north and south sides of the Choir and Sanctuary, with stone mosaics; as memorials of their father and mother.

I am constrained out of the fulness, at once of thankfulness and of
anxiety, to speak of the Cathedral to the people of the Diocese. And I
am thankful to find in a recent Pastoral of the Bishop of Missouri, words
in regard to his own work in St. Louis, which he will pardon me for
adopting as my own.

*"To the Church People of the Diocese of Missouri, and the friends of
Christ Church Cathedral:*

I may be pardoned for saying that it is borne in upon my own soul more and more,
that I ought to do all that lies in me to secure the maintenance of the Cathedral
structure where it is, and the continuance of the Cathedral work, before I go hence
and am no more seen.

To the eye of man, what other safe recourse is there than to have an endowment
fund for partial support?

To care for the revered edifice as we ought, to make the Church Home for the
Bishop that is suitable, to exhibit the norm of edifying and reverent worship that
may rightfully be expected, and to discharge pressing spiritual duty to the thousands
of poor souls, in the midst of whom we are placed, will imperatively demand a yearly
outlay of not less than $12,000.

It seems clear, therefore, that we need at least $100,000 for endowment, to furnish
$5,000 of this annual outlay.

I earnestly appeal:

1. To all the Diocese. The Cathedral is the Bishop's home. It is the home for
the Diocese. You all have a part and lot in it. It stands for rights and privileges
in which you are sharers. We shall be glad and grateful for your help to our need.

2. To those making their wills. Suffer a word of exhortation. By the way you
distribute your estate you may, under God's blessing, secure that in more ways than
one the good you do shall not die with you. A clause inserted of a bequest for the
use and benefit of Christ Church Cathedral would be twice blessed.

3. To friends, especially for an immediate All Saints' Day gift.

I well know that the Church's needs press claims upon you.

But, dear brethren, I honestly believe that if God blesses us in basket and in store,
the oftener and the more we give, so much the oftener and the more we will like to
give. Giving for God's work is a blessing. God's smile is upon it. Affliction is
less bitter for it. Death is less dreadful after it. Therefore I have no hesitation in
the midst of your doing many things to ask you to do one more.

Faithfully and affectionately,

Your bishop,

DAN'L S. TUTTLE."

I have neither need nor desire to ask the Diocese to aid in carrying on
the Cathedral services. Each year it has been self-supporting. But I
do want the work to be rooted and grounded for all time. More
and more, day by day and year by year, I know what this Cathedral
is as a source and centre of spiritual life. Its daily Celebrations, and the
daily Morning and Evening Prayer; its dignified services; its constant
preaching; its great congregations; and the known and unknown results of
its work, in the large number of Baptisms, Confirmations and Communions, and in the souls reached by its ministries; its care for vacant par-

ishes and missionary stations near by; all these are of infinite value. And it will not be forgotten that, like the palm trees which spring up about wells in a wilderness, St. Agnes' School, the Sisterhood, the Child's Hospital, St. Margaret's House, besides its own Cathedral guilds and the Diocesan Library derive and draw their life from this central source. I am infinitely thankful for the blessing of God upon it; for its generous offerings to Diocesan Missions; for the fact, which faults so many prophecies, of the support of its services by its offerings. But I am intensely anxious that the Church people of the Diocese in their gifts from time to time, and in their wills, should do what ought to be done to secure permanence and perpetuity for the Cathedral and its surrounding works of mercy and Christian education. Everywhere but here, there are endowments, given sometimes in large and sometimes in smaller sums. Chicago has its endowed Church School for girls, thank God; endowed before the School was even undertaken. And after twenty-one years of work St. Agnes' School has no endowment, but its reputation. The Cathedral of New York, not even yet on paper, receives from the daughter of the Bishop of another Diocese $100,000, and again I say, thank God for it. And we stand to-day complete as an Institution, with records of work done and of opportunities for more; with our debt unpaid, our building unfinished and the offertory of the constant congregation our only reliance for support. I am not pressing a favorite theory of my own. The whole work has grown beyond the time of dreams or of dislike of the dreamer. It is. It has vindicated its right to be. But I long, while I am living,—whether or not God shall grant me the sight of any added stone to the building as it stands,—I long for some generous gifts in the way of endowment to perpetuate the work of the Diocese in its centre. And I beg the men and women to take it into their hearts and minds, to give if they will while they live, or to leave by their will at their death, sums of money to endow Scholarships at St. Agnes' School, and beds in the Hospital; to sustain and carry on the Sisterhood; to create and carry on the Choir School; to make a permanent fund by which the offerings of the continual worshippers may be in part set free from the support of the services of the Cathedral to advance the general work of the Church, and to enable it to do missionary work in the city and the neighbourhood.

November 5th, in the evening, in All Saints' Chapel, Hoosac, I preached and confirmed six persons.

November 6th, in the morning, in the Chapel at Esperance, I preached, confirmed two persons and celebrated the Holy Communion; and in the afternoon, in Christ Church, Duanesburgh, I preached and confirmed three persons.

November 7th, in the morning, I consecrated St. James' Church, Oneonta. I preached, confirmed fifteen persons (thirty-five in all this year) and celebrated the Holy Communion.   The Instrument of Donation was read by the Rev. E. A. Hartmann, the Rector, and the Sentence of Consecration by the Rev. Canon Fulcher.   The other Clergy present were the Archdeacon, the Rev. Dr. Parke and the Rev. Messrs. Reazor, Stuart, Washburn, E. B. Russell and Griffin.   It was a service of great rejoicing. The debt which has long oppressed the Parish is lifted off.   The growth of the Church is manifest in all best ways.   And the people who have come generously up to their duty know as I do, how much is due to the inspiration of the Rector's devoted energy.

The Retreat of the Clergy this year, held in the Cathedral in the September Ember Season was infinitely helpful to those who were there.   I wonder that it does not appeal more and to more of the Clergy.   The very small expense and the comparatively short time required bring it within the reach of almost all the Clergy.   And apart from the individual, spiritual advantage there is a knitting together in the closest and holiest of bonds of those who are associated in the Communions, and devotions and instructions of the three days, which I prize very greatly.   It is not a mere indolent religious luxury.   It involves strong and positive effort of the very deepest powers of the soul.   It has in it the brace of high mountain air — air upon the mountain top with the Master.   And I count it one of the best and richest uses of the Cathedral, which certainly must have, as one of the Clergy expressed it this year, a home-feeling about it, to any who have used and enjoyed its atmosphere at such a time.

The Convention will, I am sure, share with me the sense of satisfaction that comes from the settlement by the Diocese of New York, of what has long been known as the Albany claim.   My peculiar gratification is that through the long discussion, only the most cordial feeling between the Dioceses has prevailed ; that Albany has both made and met all propositions with a very generous readiness to secure even less than what we felt were our rights, and that now in the increase of the capital of the Episcopal Fund there will be a somewhat lessened assessment on the Parishes for the Episcopal Income.   I very earnestly ask that this may not be considered as money saved from giving, but that you will see to it that by so much as you diminish your assessment for the support of the Bishop, you will increase voluntarily your gifts to the Missionary work of the Diocese.   It is pain and grief to me as to the Board, that year by year we are crippled in two ways, at least, in the apportionment of the Missionary means.   Give us the means to increase the stations and to enlarge the stipends, so that more work may be done and the workers be less meanly paid.

I cannot dismiss the subject without saying that among those who are living now, in whose hands this matter has rested so long, the honor of the result is due among us chiefly to the Rev. Dr. Reese, the Chairman of our Committee, and in New York to Bishop Potter and the Rev. Clarence Buel.

And I am bound not merely for myself, but for the credit of the Diocese, the convenience of the Bishop and the relief of the Treasurer, to call the attention of the Diocese to the fact that some authority ought to be given to the Committee on the Bishop's Salary to provide for the regular payment of the salary. It is not a matter I think for discussion here, but it ought to be considered and arranged somewhere; for while the income is sufficient, the irregularity of its receipt by the Treasurer is a matter of annoyance and inconvenience to all concerned.

You are undoubtedly aware that I have received from the Presiding Bishop his commission to act for him, as Bishop in charge of our foreign Churches.

Honour and pleasure are, of course, involved in this appointment, and in the travelling to which it calls me; and I hope to find in it such rest and refreshment as may make me better able than I have been during the last few months, to discharge the duties of the Diocese. But I am very free to say that I undertake it under a sense of duty; to accede to the Bishop's wish, and to take my share of the anxiety and burden which the position involves. Personally I should far rather be about my home work.

It is my purpose to sail in early February, for an absence of three months, during which I shall, of course, put the Diocese in charge of the Standing Committee to act, so far as the Canon directs, as the Ecclesiastical Authority. My dear and faithful Chaplain and Secretary, Canon Fulcher, will receive for me, and forward any personal or official correspondence, other than shall be sent to the care of Messrs. Drexel, Morgan & Co., London.

It will be unwise and impossible for me, I think, to undertake any large amount of visiting in the Diocese after my return. The Trinity Ordination I shall hope to hold in the Cathedral, and to be here in time for the graduating exercises in St. Agnes' School. Such visitations as can be undertaken before I sail and after my return in June, and then later in the Autumn, I shall hope to arrange; and my Rt. Rev. Brother, the Bishop of Delaware, has kindly and generously offered to do any necessary Episcopal duty in the Diocese.

I should be glad, before the 1st of January, to hear from the Clergy who desire visitations during my absence. They will, I am sure, understand me when I say that I very greatly prefer to retain the privilege of giving the Confirmations myself, unless higher interests make the postponement of the visitation impossible. And, of course, the Standing Committee will be quite free to call in the services of any Bishop whom they can secure. Meanwhile the very thorough visitation of the Diocese during the last two years, and, indeed, I think, I may say, during the twenty-two years that we have been together, seems to me to make it safe to forego, in most of the Parishes, the usual annual confirmation.

That you will have me in your prayers, and that my constant thoughts and prayers will be with you, my well-beloved, you and I may be sure of without request or promise.

The summary of my acts is as follows:

Confirmations, 1,401; *Celebrations of Holy Communion, 50; *Sermons, 130; Addresses, 10; Clergy dismissed, 11; Received, 14; Added by ordination, 2; Present number of Clergy: Bishop, 1; Priests, 123; Deacons, 8; Total, 132; Priests ordained, 3; Deacons ordained, 2; Total ordinations, 5; Postulants admitted, 7; Total Postulants, 15; Candidates for Deacon's order admitted, 6; Total Candidates for Deacon's order, 16; Candidates for Priest's order admitted, 2; Total Candidates for Priest's order, 9; Total Candidates for Holy orders, 18; Lay-Readers Licensed, 18; Lay-Reader's Licenses renewed, 3; Total Lay-Readers, 21; Probationer admitted, 1; Sister admitted, 1; Missions organized, 3; Churches consecrated, 3; Corner-Stones laid, 2; Buildings, etc., blessed, 7; *Baptisms: Infants, 2; Adults, 1; Total, 3; *Burials, 3; *Marriages, 2; Notices of deposition, 6.

I have attended the regular meetings of the Board of Missions; the Cathedral Chapter; the Trustees of the Corning Foundation; the Managers of the Child's Hospital; and of St. Margaret's House; the Trustees of the Orphan House of the Holy Saviour; the Diocesan Branch of the Woman's Auxiliary; the Woman's Diocesan League; the Trustees of the various Diocesan Funds; the Bible and Prayer Book Society, and two of the Convocations. I have also attended meetings of the House of Bishops, the Trustees of the General Theological Seminary; the Board of Managers of the Missionary Society; the Missionary Council; the Committees on the Prayer Book and the Hymnal; the Board of Regents of the Church University; the High License Committee; the Society for the Home Study of Holy Scripture, and the meeting for Charity Organization in the City of Albany.

ORDINATIONS.

December 21, 1889. The Rev. Elmer Pliny Miller, to the Priesthood, in All Saints' Church, Hudson.

June 4, 1890. Asa Sprague Ashley, to the Diaconate, by Bishop Williams, in the Church of the Holy Trinity, Middletown, Connecticut.

June 7, 1890. Frederick Stirling Griffin, to the Diaconate, in the Cathedral.

June 7, 1890. The Rev. Walter Charles Stewart, to the Priesthood, in the Cathedral.

8

* Not included in the Cathedral report.

June 7, 1890. The Rev. Robert Morris Kemp, to the Priesthood, in the Cathedral.

CLERGYMEN RECEIVED FROM OTHER DIOCESES.

1889.

November 1. The Rev. Walter Haskins Larom, from the Diocese of New York.

December 27. The Rev. A. T. de Learsy, from the Diocese of Easton.

1890.

January 10. The Rev. Frederick Nash Skinner, from the Diocese of East Carolina.

February 5. The Rev. E. Ruthven Armstrong, from the Diocese of Western New York.

March 14. The Rev. Ernest Mariett, from the Diocese of Massachusetts.

April 25. The Rev. Harris Cox Rush, from the Diocese of New Jersey.

May 8. The Rev. S. C. Thompson. from England.

June 7. The Rev. Chauncey Vibbard, Jr., from the Diocese of Central New York.

July 20. The Rev. Charles H. Hatheway, from the Diocese of Fredericton.

September 24. The Rev. Frederick S. Fisher, from the Diocese of Vermont.

October 10. The Rev. William George Ivie, from the Diocese of New York.

October 13. The Rev. William Henry Bown, from the Diocese of New York.

November 1. The Rev. Reyner Edward William Cosens, from the Diocese of Durham.

November 8. The Rev. Phineas Duryea, from the Diocese of Colorado.

CLERGYMEN DISMISSED TO OTHER DIOCESES.

1889.

November 20. The Rev. George H. S. Somerville, to the Diocese of Central New York.

November 26. The Rev. R. W. Rhames, to the Diocese of Kansas.

December 13. The Rev. George Fisher, to the Diocese of Massachusetts.

1890.

January 18. The Rev. John McKinney, to the Diocese of Massachusetts.

January 21. The Rev. S. T. Brewster, to the Diocese of Missouri.

March 21. The Rev. Horatio Gates, to the Diocese of Colorado.

April 21. The Rev. W. E. Wilson, to the Diocese of New York.

May 30. The Rev. Lawson Carter Rich, to the Diocese of Maryland.

July 12. The Rev. Alexander McMillan, to the Diocese of New York.

September 29. The Rev. John C. Tebbetts, to the Diocese of Massachusetts.

October 7. The Rev. Robert G. Osborn, to the Jurisdiction of the Platte.

CANDIDATES FOR PRIEST'S ORDER.

September 29, 1886. Mr. Alvin J. Vandebogart.

December 23, 1886. The Rev. Meredith O. Smith.

April 26, 1888. The Rev. Frederick S. Griffin.

May 19, 1888. Mr. John C. Woodworth.

October 18, 1888. Mr. James F. Olmsted.

April 29, 1889. Mr. George Lynde Richardson.

June 10, 1889. Mr. George Kilpatrick McNaught.

December 2, 1889. Mr. Freeborn Garrettson Jewett, Jr.

October 10, 1890. Mr. Marvin Hill Dana.

CANDIDATES FOR DEACON'S ORDER.

April 26, 1883. Mr. Gulian V. P. Lansing.

December 17, 1885. Mr. Alvin J. Vandebogart.

June 4, 1887. Mr. George K. McNaught.

October 3, 1887. Mr. George H. Rhames.

October 3, 1887. Mr. Charles H. Moore.

December 1, 1887. Mr. John C. Woodworth.

September 26, 1888. Mr. James F. Olmsted.

November 19, 1888. Mr. Keble Dean.

November 19, 1888. Mr. George Lynde Richardson.

November 19, 1888. Mr. Freeborn Garrettson Jewett, Jr.

January 1, 1889. Mr. John Montgomery Rich.

September 15, 1890. Mr. William Anderson Stirling.

September 15, 1890. Mr. Marvin Hill Dana.

September 15, 1890. Mr. Eugene Griggs.

November 8, 1890. Mr. Frank N. Bouck.

November 8, 1890, Mr. Edward T. Carroll.

POSTULANTS.

August 10, 1883. William Beach Olmsted.

February 16, 1885. Robert Perine.

May 12, 1885. Isaac Borts, M. D.

January 29, 1886.   Harry Sherman Longley.
March 22, 1887.   Charles Hegamin, Jr.
March 3, 1888.   E. Townsend Jones, M. D.
May 1, 1889.   George Henry Chase.
May 27, 1889.   William Croswell Doane Willson.
June 24, 1890.   George William Farrar.
June 24, 1890.   Frederic Henry Farrar.
September 1, 1890.   Eugene Griggs.
September 9, 1890.   Frank Norwood Bouck.
October 31, 1890.   Edward T. Carroll.
November 8, 1890.   Gouverneur T. Mosher.
November 10, 1890.   George Arthur Ingalls.

CORNER-STONES LAID.

September 8, 1890.   Emmanuel Chapel, Griffin's Corners.
October 18, 1890.   Child's Hospital, Albany.

CHURCHES CONSECRATED.

April 10, 1890.   St. Paul's Chapel, Bartonville.
September 21, 1890.   St. Mary's Church, Springfield Centre.
November 7, 1890.   St. James' Church, Oneonta.

BENEDICTIONS.

December 24, 1889.   Sanctuary of the Church of the Holy Cross, Troy.
January 13, 1890.   Chapel and Altar, and Parish School House, Hoosac.
January 15, 1890.   Parish House, St. John's Church, Troy.
May 23, 1890.   Sanctuary and Altar, and Memorial Chapel, Delhi.
June 11, 1890.   Rexleigh.
September 8, 1890.   Rectory, Christ Church, Cooperstown.

MISSIONS ORGANIZED.

December 16, 1889.   Grace Mission, Stamford.
December 16, 1889.   St. Andrew's Mission, West Troy.
April 17, 1889.   St. Columba's Mission, St. Johnsville.

LAY-READERS LICENSED.

November 15, 1889.   William J. Calhoun, St. Peter's Church, Hobart.
November 18, 1889.   J. R. P. Shackelford, Bethesda Church, Saratoga Springs.
December 7, 1889.   Lewis Collins Boyle, All Saints' Church, Hoosac.

January 7, 1890. R. W. Alban Thompson, St. Luke's Church, Saranac.

January 7, 1890. Halsey Joslyn Spencer, for Edmeston and West Burlington.

February 4, 1890. Philip Monson, Christ Church, Deposit.

February 7, 1890. Joseph Walker, Christ Church, Hudson.

March 25, 1890. H. M. C. Vedder, St. Luke's Church, Catskill.

April 10, 1890. George W. Farrar, St. Peter's Church, Hobart.

April 18, 1890. John A. Howe, Trinity Church, Albany. (Renewal.)

April 29, 1890. Alvin J. Vandebogart, for the Diocese.

May 14, 1890. Thurston W. Challen, St. John's Church, Delhi, Griffin's Corners, Grand Hotel. (Renewal.)

May 22, 1890. Frederick St. George McLean, St. Mark's Church, Hoosick Falls.

May 26, 1890. A. E. Heard, St. John's Church, Stockport.

June 9, 1890. David Henry Clarkson, St. Paul's Church, Greenwich.

June 21, 1890. Joseph R. Norwood, St. Luke's Church, Catskill.

July 7, 1890. Charles J. Wills, Zion Church, Morris.

October 13, 1890. Elias P. Howe, St. Paul's Church, Franklin. (Renewal.)

October 13, 1890. Ernest E. Smith, St. Paul's Church, Franklin.

October 19, 1890. George W. Farrar, for the Diocese.

November 8, 1890. Gouverneur T. Mosher, for St. George's Church, Schenectady.

NOTICES OF CLERGY DEPOSED.

October 20, 1889. John M. Leavitt, D. D., Priest, by the Bishop of New York.

December 4, 1889. Myron S. Robinson, Deacon, by the Bishop of South Dakota.

March 2, 1890. Daniel D. Hefter, Priest, by the Bishop of Central Pennsylvania.

April 24, 1890. Thomas Hood, Priest, by the Bishop of Colorado.

June 11, 1890. W. H. Milnes, Priest, by the Bishop of Florida.

July 2, 1890. Frank O. Osborne, Priest, by the Bishop of Fond du Lac.

APPENDIX TO THE BISHOP'S ADDRESS.

PASTORAL LETTERS.

To the Clergy and Laity of the Diocese of Albany:

It will be twenty-one years on Sunday since the hands were laid upon me that set me apart to the solemn duties of a Bishop's office and sealed my life to your service, dear brethren and friends in the Diocese of Albany. They have been years of increasing labour and of deepening love, of faithfulness in my desire of service and of great fruitfulness, by God's blessing, in spite of all my failures and of all my faults. Coming, as it were, of age in the Episcopate, you will, I trust, join with me in the earnest asking, to-morrow, that God will deepen the one and continue the other, while He accepts the mingled thanksgivings and confessions which fill my heart to-day. I am very earnestly moved not to recount what has been, but rather "forgetting the things that are behind to press on to the things that are before," for whatever length of time we may be spared to work together. I plead with you, dear brethren and friends, that we may have a more earnest consecration of ourselves to the high honour of His dear service, who permits us, Clergy and Laity alike, to carry on the work which He began and to which He received to-day one of the three great consecrations of His life. "Presented in the temple in the substance of our flesh," He permits us to present ourselves to Him that we may "prepare His way before Him," in the hope that when He comes again we may be presented unto Him with pure and clean hearts."

What we need, it seems to me, first of all in this Diocese, is a more earnest consecration to that which, certainly as much as in any other Diocese in the American Church, is our characteristic feature, namely, our Diocesan Missionary work. I most earnestly beg that, both in prayers and alms, you will remember that work this year; that we may not only better support the men who are labouring in the field, but may increase and extend God's kingdom in the desert places, of which there are too many in the Diocese. Give us the means, dear friends, as your representatives in the Board of Missions, to send out "more laborers into the harvest," and to give them promptly the "hire" of which they are so worthy.

I ask with deep and earnest anxiety for a general and generous support, in every Parish in this Diocese, of the Orphan House of the Holy Saviour at Cooperstown. Its benefactions hitherto have been too much confined to the immediate neighborhood of the place in which it is, or to a few Parishes which have been faithful and constant in its care. There ought to be no Parish in the Diocese that does not send something toward the maintenance of that most gracious and good work. I greatly hope that this year will be signalized by such gifts as will entirely wipe out the debt which the new and greatly needed buildings have involved, and that moneys may be sent from *every* Parish for the annual support of the children gathered there.

I commend also, with a keen sense of its value and importance, the Child's Hospital to your gracious consideration. Gathering in the suffering children from every quarter of the Diocese and of the State, I think it has a right to ask that it shall also gather in the means for its support. It is of the utmost importance to us, this year, to put up a new building, which shall be larger and better suited for this work, and I entreat you, in His name who makes, on this festival of His childhood, a very special plea for the little children in whom we minister to Him, to enable us to carry out our purpose of building and to carry on our work.

And lastly, not to Parishes or to Clergymen, but to individuals, I beg to present, as in my judgment in every way worthy of your generous gifts, the Cathedral of the Diocese, your common central home, for which we greatly need: first of all, help to pay off the debt of $50,000 which still remains upon it; secondly, to complete such of the interior decorations as are yet unfinished, especially in the filling of the five windows in the transepts with glass; and thirdly, to make provision, by bequests and gifts, for the carrying out of the building by and by to its final finishing.

Commending you to God's special favour and blessing and asking your prayers, that in the years to come the holy and helpful unity of thought and feeling and practice, which has so long existed among us, may continue, and that we may be, in such unity and love, faithful fellow-labourers unto the Kingdom of God,

I am, your very faithful brother and Bishop,

WM. CROSWELL DOANE.

Eve of the Feast of the Presentation of Christ in the Temple, A. D. 1890.

ALBANY, N. Y., *February 8th*, 1890.

My Dear Brethren of the Clergy :

In sending out the proposed list, for the Twenty-Second Annual Visitation of the Diocese, I beg to add a few words, as to this yearly personal share, which it is my privilege to have, in your constant labours. As the places rise up before me, one by one, in the somewhat anxious and difficult task of consulting the various demands of distances and conveyances on my part, and of convenience and advantage on yours,— I look back, with infinite thankfulness, on the enjoyment of the companionship and hospitality in all parts of the Diocese, and realize the goodness of God, which has so enabled me to keep, with accuracy, the successive appointments, from place to place and from year to year. I beg to say, that I shall be glad of such occasions as may offer of meeting the members of the Congregations, after the services, in the Church or in the Rectory, and of the opportunity to examine the Registers of Parishes and Missions. Then I want to say a word, not of excuse but of explanation, as to the plan and theory of my visitations.

It constantly seems to those who speak to me of my appointments, that they are not arranged in what would seem to be the natural order; but it must be borne in mind, that a 'mere following in order of the places on a railway time-table is the least element of consideration. To give Sundays, where the larger number of people are to be reached; to arrange services, in manufacturing towns for the evening; to consult the wishes of the Clergy as to the season of the year; to avoid the many months of mud and storm, when appointments could not be kept with certainty; require careful study and the adjustment of many interests. Over and above this lie all the demands of outside duties to the Church at large, which a Bishop must consider of paramount claim, and which naturally increase as one goes on in his Episcopal life ; the work of General Committees and the duties to the Board of Missions, and the demands of our Church Institutions, and, these are for me, this year increased, by my acceptance, under a very positive sense of duty, of the unexpected appointment from the Presiding Bishop, which puts me in charge of our Church Organizations on the Continent of Europe.

Glad as I am of criticism and suggestions, I have generally found, that, in the main, after I have carefully studied the whole sphere of work and duty, it is easier to criticise than to improve.

I think it right in connection with this list of appointments to make you sharers in the satisfaction with which I recognize the reported results of our year's work together, as they contrast themselves with the condition of things in the Diocese twenty-one years ago.

Then there were 1,167 Baptisms reported and last year 1,999.

Then there were 795 persons confirmed and last year 1,588.

The Communicants have increased from 6,561 to 16,507, and the offerings have grown from $118,000 to $350,000.

The Parishes have increased from 98 to 116 with 63 Missions, making a total of 179, and the Clergy have grown from 68 to 129, so that we stand to-day among our fifty-one Dioceses:

Seventh in the number of Clergy and Baptisms.

Sixth in the number of Parishes and Confirmations.

Fifth in the number of Missions and Candidates for Holy Orders.

Eighth in the number of Communicants and the amount of Offerings.

I think it wise to add one or two suggestions consequent upon what is to all intents and purpose I believe the final action in regard to the Book of Common Prayer. I do not believe that we have a right, even if we had before, when there was hope of change, to keep up any of the practices whose sanction has been distinctly refused by the General Convention ; such as the use of the English Te Deum, the utterance of " the thanks " after the Gospel, the saying of the General Thanksgiving, or of the opening petitions of the Litany, by the Priest and people together. In honest loyalty these ought to be discontinued ; so also I think should be the posture of kneeling during the Hymn *Gloria in Excelsis* in the Common Office ; or any shortening of the services, or introduction into our public worship of any thing not provided for, by the recent changes in the Book of Common Prayer. And, in answer to a question which has been asked me more than once, I beg leave to say, that the following " Collect, Epistle or Gospel," which have the warrant of early English use, are authorized to be used in this Diocese, where the Holy Communion is celebrated at a burial. You will recognize, that the " directions concerning the Services of the Church " allow the Bishop to " set forth such form or forms as he shall think fit for special occasions for which no service or prayer hath been provided in the Prayer Book." And while of course the *invariable* portions of the Liturgy must always be used and *only those*, at any Celebration ; the permission, which gives authority to appoint a special Collect, Epistle and Gospel for a Harvest Home or a National Festival, or for a special occasion of any sort, allows the Bishop in this *variable* part of "the Liturgy " to authorize that which fits it for a service, demanded, as I believe this is, by the instincts of human hearts, seeking in their sorrow, consolation, from the closest communion with our dear Lord, in whom the living and dead are one.

Giving and asking the blessing of God Almighty, Father, Son and Holy Ghost.

I am your brother and fellow-servant in Christ,

WM. CROSWELL DOANE.

AT A BURIAL.

The Collect.

O MERCIFUL God, the Father of our Lord Jesus Christ, who is the resurrection and the life; in whom whosoever believeth shall live, though he die ; and whosoever liveth, and believeth in Him, shall not die eternally; who also hath taught us, by His holy Apostle St. Paul, not to be sorry, as men without hope, for those who sleep in Him ; We humbly beseech thee, O Father, to raise us from the death of sin unto the life of righteousness, that, when we shall depart this life, we may rest in Him, as our hope is this our brother doth, and that, at the general Resurrection in the last day, we may be found acceptable in Thy sight ; and receive that blessing, which Thy well-beloved Son shall then pronounce to all who love and fear Thee, saying, Come, ye blessed children of My Father, receive the kingdom prepared for you from the beginning of the world. Grant this, we beseech Thee, O merciful Father, through Jesus Christ our Mediator and Redeemer. *Amen.*

The Epistle, 1 Thess. IV, 18.

I would not have you to be ignorant, brethren, concerning them which are asleep that ye sorrow not, even as others which have no hope. For if we believe that Jesus died and rose again, even so, them also which sleep in Jesus will God bring with Him. For this we say unto you by the word of the Lord, that we which are alive and remain unto the coming of the Lord shall not prevent them which are asleep. For the Lord Himself shall descend from Heaven with a shout, with the voice of the Archangel, and with the trump of God : and the dead in Christ shall rise first. Then we which are alive and remain shall be caught up together with them in the clouds, to meet the Lord in the air: and so shall we ever be with the Lord. Wherefore comfort one another with these words.

The Gospel, St. John VI, 37.

All that the Father giveth Me shall come to Me ; and him that cometh to Me I will in no wise cast out. For I came down from Heaven, not to do My own will, but the will of Him that sent Me. And this is the Father's will which hath sent Me, that of all which He hath given Me I should lose nothing, but should raise it up again at the last day. And this is the will of Him that sent Me, that every one which seeth the Son, and believeth on Him, may have everlasting life : and I will raise him up at the last day.

The following prayer is also authorized for use:

A PRAYER FOR SEASONABLE WEATHER.

O Gracious Father, who makest Thy sun to rise on the evil and on the good, and sendest rain on the just and on the unjust, we beseech Thee, of Thy infinite mercy, to hear us who make our prayers and supplications unto Thee. Remember not our sins, but Thy promises of mercy ; and grant unto us such seasonable weather, That our land may give her increase, and Thy servants rejoice in Thy goodness, through Jesus Christ our Lord. *Amen.*

REPRINTED MEMORIALS.

MARGARET SCOTT TILLINGHAST.

Margaret Scott Tillinghast, daughter of Griffith P. Griffith, and widow of the late Thomas A. Tillinghast, of Troy. Born in Troy, December 10, 1827; died in Dorchester April 14, 1890.

Mrs. Thomas Tillinghast's death, in the parsonage at Dorchester, is a surprise and shock, chiefly because she had been so often near the border-land before and had come back again. And yet she had lived with so much of her heart upon the other side that those who loved her best hoped least to keep her here so long. The end came, as she would have wished, quietly and gently, with the Church's ministrations from the hands of the Priest of her own household, and with all that were dearest to her here near her to speed her way, where they waited to make her welcome, whom she "had loved and lost awhile."

She was a woman of rare power of service to God and man. Not less intelligent in planning and directing than intense in love, she accomplished, with a frail and

9

delicate body, an amount of work to which few strong and well people have been equal. In her Parish of St. John's, Troy, she was indefatigable and invaluable in the Sunday-school and the Industrial Society, and to every interest of the Diocese of Albany she was loyal and loving in her prayers and sympathies and gifts.

Her husband was one of the noblest of the noble laymen which the city of Troy has given from the beginning to the Diocese of Albany, alas! so lessened now in number as the years have gone on. And the first falling of the sorrow of his death, healed now for her, comes back so vividly and seems so recent, that one almost realizes how short all partings must seem to the souls in Paradise who wait their perfecting till the better thing is secured, which God hath " provided for us."

She was a true Christian lady, rich in labours of love, gracious, patient, reverent, and in her widowhood, which was widowhood indeed, and desolate, " she trusted in God; she continued in supplications and prayers;" and she "diligently followed every good work." She was a true daughter of the Church, "instructed unto the kingdom of Heaven." Her soul was refreshed here from the deep fountains of the hidden life, which are beneath the unrest of storms and beyond the reach of drought. Eminently a holy woman in the loveliest and most attractive guise of holiness, she was to her household a very " bond of peace and of all virtues."

When she was dying, looking back upon the toil and sorrow and on to the quiet and joy, she said, bowing her head in its last weakness at the Holy Name : " Rest and peace, when they do come, come through our Lord Jesus Christ." And we borrow her own words, in the prayer in which we commend and commemorate her pure soul before the Altar: " Rest and peace, through our Lord Jesus Christ." Amen.

W. C. D.

AMASA J. PARKER.

With characteristic simplicity Judge Parker wrote last March a private note, found among his papers after his death, expressing his desire that no display should mark, and no eulogy mar the dignity of his burial. " The beautiful service of the Episcopal Church," he wrote, " is all that I desire." But there are desires of our own that *will* be gratified, and that may be now, since he has been laid at rest by the side of his beloved wife, under the shadow of the massive Celtic cross of pure New Hampshire granite, which admirably typified the upright dignity of his character, and bears upon its face the legend of his own crest, so largely the law of his life and so full of his realized hope, " *Fideli certa merces,*" " the reward to the faithful is sure."

My knowledge of Judge Parker lies outside his political and professional life, to which his brethren have already paid their eloquent and affectionate tributes. For twenty years I have known him in his daily walk and conversation as a man not only constantly occupied with his duties as a lawyer, but closely concerned with all that could advance the interests of the city in which he had lived for nearly half a century. I knew him also in his home where his old-time dignity lent itself with very gracious kindness to its delightful hospitality; where he realized and illustrated Jeremy Taylor's exquisite description of married life, " as doubling joy and halving care;" and where with patriarchal pride, he gathered children and grandchildren who love and reverence his memory as a heritage of honour in the blood and in the name.

His early interest in education gave him the foundation of an elegant scholarship; and, in spite of the constant pressure of his professional life, he was a man of literary accomplishments and large information. He was permitted, in the completion of Harmanus Bleecker Hall, to fulfil that sacred and honourable trust which links in the name of Mr. Bleecker and Mr. J. V. L. Pruyn with his own to illustrate, in a degenerate age, how honor, integrity and faithfulness are jewels in the crown of character. And he died, like the old leader of Israel, with unabated natural force, and with his undimmed eye, looking back upon a record of distinguished public service, of success achieved by devotion to his calling, of an unblemished reputation in private life: and looking forward to "the morn" in which "the angel faces smile" of those "whom he had loved long since and lost awhile."

Most pleasant to his host of friends is the recollection of his life in Albany. Young in his old age, because of the freshness of good sympathies and kindly interests in life, keeping pace with progress in all best ways, he had been, I fancy, old in his youth, in the habits of carefulness, and thoroughness and thoughtfulness, which marked his mind. And he was what we call old-fashioned, always since I knew him, in his courteousness and dignity of speech and bearing.

He will be greatly missed in Albany, for long as he has lived, rounding out more than the circle of most completed lives, he had the will and ability, if God had pleased, to work still longer here. But he had amply earned his rest, and they who love him most cannot grudge him the happiness of dying, as he would have wished, with all his native powers passing through no painful process of decay, into their fuller completeness and their larger service.

An old landmark has gone from the city. A home is empty here whose atmosphere was fragrant with all that graces human life. But the city is richer and better for the memory which will live on, as will the home life passing into other spheres in the heritage of his influence and his name.   W. C. D.

J. ROLAND SMYTH.

The news of the death of Mr. Roland Smyth comes to me just when and where I cannot possibly come, to render in person my tribute of real and reverent regard for him. There are some people in Albany who well remember a meeting at the Bishop's House ten or fifteen years ago, called to consider the possibility of beginning the effort to build a suitable Cathedral building. The friends who had cast their lot in with the humble and ugly beginning were there, and a good many felt and said that something ought to be done, and toward the close of a rather dull meeting Mr. Smyth got up, with the eloquence of a man of strong convictions, clear faith and what people call dead earnest, which I suppose means earnestness to death, and in a few word of fire he kindled in all the life of a new hope and purpose. It was one of the events in the long waiting time, and he was the man from which I have always dated and o whom I have felt always that I owed the impulse which started the Cathedral building. From that time on, in gifts that were gracious and generous, not of much money, but of collections and accumulations of interesting things, and in continuous interest and earnest words, and faithful prayers, he helped the work on And his happiness when the corner-stone was laid, and his joy on the dedication day fou. I their completeness and crown, when he went, last Sunday morning, from the Cath- dral Altar, "strengthened with the bread of life," to meet the summons — s. 'h. : , us — which called him home. May God rest his patient and faithful soul, and re- fresh him with the multitude of peace.

Mr. Smyth was a man of singularly straight-forward simplicity, earnest purp e, strong faith, most loyal love to God and man. Quiet and retiring, constant to his work, content with his l. position (which was below his education and deserving, few people knew him at he real worth For more than twenty years he has been my friend, and I have been his And the leading trait of his character was his loyalty to his friends. No truer, stauncher, more grateful, more generous friend ever lived He had gone through deep waters of sorrow and suffering; he fought a good fight of which few people knew; and he bore the discipline, which had been sharp and long, not with patience only, but with the cheerfulness of true courage. Steadfast to duty, true to his home life, faithful to his friends, he was a loving servant of Jesus Christ. His highest happiness was in his religious life. And his pride and delight in the Cathedral building and services was a passion to him. His face was an inspiration to the preacher, and there are none of us who have for twenty years worked with him for the completion of the Cathedral, who will not sadly miss his kindly and reverent presence with us in its worship. I thank God for my belief that in the perfect worship of Paradise he will remember us, as we remember him. And *there*, far more even than *here*, the words of the Psalmist shall describe him, "Lord, I have loved the habitation of Thy house and the place where Thine honour dwelleth."

W. C. D.

Northeast Harbour, *July 28*, 1890.

LIGHTFOOT MEMORIAL.

Albany, N. Y., *April 30th*, 1890.

My Dear Mr. Archdeacon :

I take advantage of the meeting of your Convocation to call the attention of yourself and the Clergy to an appeal just received from the Committee on the Bishop Lightfoot Memorial. It is proposed to restore the Chapter House in Durham in his memory and to erect an effigy of the Bishop; and American Churchmen are, not so much asked, as offered the opportunity, to have a part in this Memorial. It is a privilege, which some of us, I am sure, would be glad to take advantage of; to show our sense of deep and loving obligation to the foremost Christian scholar of this century. I should only insult the intelligence of the Clergy, if I attempted to state in detail, the debt which we owe to this most candid and complete scholar; to whose Scriptural commentaries and to whose contributions to the history of the Church, as well as to the defence of the faith, we have turned for renewed confidence in our belief, and stronger assurance of our Catholic position as a Church.

We may not, for our poverty and for the pressure of claims of nearer duty, be able to add much money to this Memorial Fund, but we may gratify our desire to honour the memory of this great Bishop, and to have a share in the material design which perpetuates his name whose true memorial "*aere perennius*" is in the reverent affection of all Christian English-speaking men.

I shall be glad, when I have added my own gift to any you may send to me, to forward an Albany contribution to "the Bishop Lightfoot Memorial," soon after Whitsunday.

Faithfully your Brother,
W. C. Doane.

After the service, the Convention was called to order by the Bishop of the Diocese, in the gymnasium of St. Agnes' School.

In accordance with Section 1, Canon I, of the Diocese, the Bishop presented a List of Clergy canonically resident in the Diocese.

The Secretary called the roll of the Clergy, and eighty-five were found to be present.*

* See List of Clergy, page 6.

The roll of Parishes entitled to representation was called, and the Bishop appointed the Rev. R. G. Hamilton and Mr. William Hollands as a committee, with the Secretary, to examine the credentials of the Lay Deputies.

The Committee presented the credentials of seventy-two Parishes as correct.

The Secretary then called the names of the Deputies, and fifty Parishes were found to be represented.*

A constitutional quorum being present, the Rt. Rev. President declared the Convention organized and ready for business.

The election of officers being in order, on motion of the Rev. James E. Hall, the ballot was unanimously dispensed with.

The Rev. William C. Prout was elected Secretary, Mr. Selden E. Marvin, Treasurer, and the Rev. Frederick S. Sill, Registrar.

The Secretary appointed the Rev. Thomas B. Fulcher as the Assistant Secretary.

On motion of the Rev. W. C. Prout, it was

Resolved, That Clergymen of other Dioceses, Professors and Students of Theology in this Church, and all persons holding any office or trust under the Convention, if not members thereof, being present, be invited to seats in the Convention.

The Rt. Rev. President having announced the invitation, the Rev. Charles M. Niles of the Diocese of Vermont, and Gen. Selden E. Marvin, Treasurer of the Diocese, took seats in the Convention.

On motion of the Secretary, it was

Resolved, That the order of services and sessions for this Convention be as follows: That a recess be taken from five to eight o'clock this evening; that at eight o'clock the Convention assemble in the Cathedral for the annual Missionary service and meeting; that to-morrow the Holy Communion be celebrated at eight o'clock in the morning, and the Morning Prayer and Litany said at ten o'clock, in the Cathedral; the business session shall be resumed in this place at half-past ten with the usual recesses from one to two and from five to eight o'clock.

On motion of the Rev. William M. Ogden, it was

Resolved, That the Trustees of the Episcopal Fund be requested to report to this Convention, at the earliest possible moment, whether, in their judgment, the probable large increase of the fund this year does not justify and warrant the minimum increase of $1,000 per annum of the Episcopal salary, and if so, that they recommend the same.

The Committee on the Certificates of Lay Deputies reported the certificates of St. Luke's Church, Mechanicville, †St. Matthew's Church, Unadilla, and Church of Our Saviour, Lebanon Springs, defective.

On motion of the Rev. W. G. W. Lewis, it was

Resolved, That the certificate from St. Luke's Church, Mechanicville, be accepted, and the Deputies admitted to seats in the Convention.

---

* See List of Lay Deputies, page 10.

† A corrected certificate from St. Matthew's Church, Unadilla, was subsequently presented, under which Deputies from that Parish took their seats.

On motion of the Rev. Thaddeus A. Snively, it was

Resolved, That the Deputies from Parishes presenting defective certificates be admitted to seats on the floor of the House, with the right to speak, but not the right to vote.

Under which resolution, Mr. Charles E. Wackerhagen, of the Church of Our Saviour, Lebanon Springs, took a seat in the Convention.

The Rev. Frederick S. Sill, gave notice of the following amendment to Canon XIV, which, on his motion, was referred to the Committee on the Constitution and Canons.

Resolved, That Canon XIV, section 6, be amended by striking out after the words Secretary and Treasurer, in line four, the words " who shall make annual reports to the Convention," so that the sentence affected shall simply read, " Each Convocation, moreover, shall annually elect a Secretary and Treasurer."

The Rev. Charles S. Olmsted presented verbally the request that the Convention would authorize and advocate a change in the act by which the Orphan House of the Holy Saviour, at Cooperstown, is incorporated, which, on his motion, was referred to the Committee on the Orphan House.

ACT OF INCORPORATION OF THE ORPHAN HOUSE OF THE HOLY SAVIOUR.

SECTION 1. David H. Buel, George W. Ernst, G. Pomeroy Keese, David A. Avery and Susan Fenimore Cooper of Cooperstown, and their associates and successors duly elected and appointed in the manner hereinafter provided, are hereby constituted a body corporate, by the name of " The Trustees of the Orphan House and Industrial School of the Holy Saviour, at or near Cooperstown," and by that name shall have perpetual succession, and be capable of taking and holding by purchase, gift, grant, devise and bequest (subject to all provisions of law relating to devises and bequests by last will and testament), any and all such estate, both real and personal, as may be necessary for the purposes and objects of such corporation, provided the yearly value or income of the same shall not exceed the sum of twenty thousand dollars.

§ 2. The objects of the said corporation shall be charitable and religious, and the care, management, and distribution of the property and funds now provided, together with such property and funds as may be hereafter provided, contributed to, collected for, or acquired by said corporation, by purchase, gift, grant, devise or bequest, and any accumulations thereof, in trust or otherwise, for the support and maintenance of the Orphan House and Industrial School of the Holy Saviour, at or near Cooperstown, a home for orphans, half orphans, and destitute children, and inmates of the same. And to take and receive orphans, half orphans and destitute children generally under its charge, and to care for, aid, maintain and educate the same according to such rules and regulations as the said trustees, with the approbation of the Convention of the Protestant Episcopal Church in the Diocese of Albany shall, from time to time adopt. All property and funds not required for current use may be invested and held in trust by said trustees.

§ 3. The said trustees shall consist of the Bishop of the Protestant Episcopal Church in the Diocese of Albany, who shall be *ex-officio* president of the same, and ten other persons, as follows, viz.: David H. Buel, George W. Ernst, G. Pomeroy Keese, David A. Avery and Susan Fenimore Cooper of Cooperstown, J. H. Hobart Brown of Cohoes, William Payne of Schenectady, John Tweddle of Albany, F. W. Farnham of Troy, and William J. Averell of Ogdensburgh, who shall constitute the first board of trustees, and shall hold their offices for one year and until others are elected to fill their places. The said trustees shall appoint a secretary and a treasurer, and cause a record to be kept of their proceedings in a book or books which shall be open to the inspection of the said convention, or any committee of the same. And a report shall be made annually to the said convention, signed by at least a majority of the said trustees, showing in detail their proceedings, the condition of the property and funds intrusted to their charge, and also their receipts and expenditures. All vacancies in said board may be filled by the remaining trustees. The said trustees shall conform to any instructions or directions of the said convention touching the management and care of said orphanage, and the property and funds of the same, provided the same shall be in writing and entered on the journals of said convention.

§ 4. It shall be lawful for the board of supervisors of any county, or the overseers of the poor of any town within the state to arrange and contract with the said trustees for the reception, care, maintenance and education of orphans, half orphans and destitute children, in said orphan house from their respective towns and counties, subject to such rules and regulations as the said trustees may adopt in regard to the same.

§ 5. This act shall take effect immediately.

PROPOSED ACT OF INCORPORATION OF THE ORPHAN HOUSE OF THE HOLY SAVIOUR.

AN ACT to amend chapter one hundred and five of the laws of eighteen hundred and seventy, entitled "An act to incorporate the trustees of the Orphan House and Industrial School of the Holy Saviour, near Cooperstown, New York."

The People of the State of New York, represented in Senate and Assembly, do enact as follows :

SECTION 1. Section three of chapter one hundred and five of the laws of eighteen hundred and seventy, entitled " An act to incorporate the trustees of the Orphan House and Industrial School of the Holy Saviour, near Cooperstown, New York," is hereby amended so as to read as follows:

§ 3. The corporation shall be managed by a board of trustees, which shall consist of the Bishop of the Protestant Episcopal Church in the Diocese of Albany, who shall be *ex-officio* president of the same, the rector of Christ church, Cooperstown, Miss Susan Fenimore Cooper, and nine other persons. Said nine trustees shall be elected by the annual diocesan convention of said diocese. At the first annual election held after the passage of this act, nine trustees shall be elected, who shall divide themselves by lot into three classes, three of whom shall hold office for one year, three for two years, and three for three years. At each annual election thereafter, three trustees only shall be elected to hold office for three years. The board of trustees may fill any vacancy in the office of trustee by appointment to serve until the next annual election, at which time a trustee shall be elected to fill such vacancy for the unexpired term. By their corporate name said trustees shall be persons in law capable of suing and being sued, and they and their successors may have and use a common seal, and the same may alter and change at pleasure; may make by-laws for the management of the affairs of said corporation not inconsistent with the Constitution and laws of this State or the United States; may appoint servants and teachers for the institution under their charge, and allow them a suitable compensation for their services; may appoint a secretary and treasurer, and cause a record to be kept of the proceedings of the board of trustees in a book or books which shall be open to the inspection of the said convention, or any committee of the same; shall make an annual report to the said convention, showing in detail their proceedings, the condition of

the property and funds intrusted to their charge, and their receipts and expenditi
shall conform to any instructions or directions of the said convention touching
management and care of said orphanage, and the property and funds of the s
provided the same shall be in writing and entered on the journals of the said
vention. The trustees of said corporation who shall be in office at the date of
passage of this act shall hold the same until the annual election herein provided
and until their successors are elected.

§ 2. Section five of said act is hereby amended so as to read as follows:

§ 5. The personal estate of said corporation shall be exempt from taxation, and
provisions of chapter four hundred and eighty-three of the laws of eighteen hun
and eighty-five, entitled " An act to tax gifts, legacies and collateral inheritanc
certain cases," and the acts amendatory thereof and supplementary thereto, shal
apply to this corporation, nor to any gifts to said corporation by grant, beque
otherwise.

§ 3. This act shall take effect immediately.

The Right Rev. President appointed the regular committees.

On the Incorporation and Admission of Churches.

The Rev. J. Philip B. Pendleton.   Mr. Richard H. Cushney.
                                     Mr. Harvey J. Cady.

On the Constitution and Canons.

The Rev. J. W. Stewart.   Mr. James Gibson.
The Rev. R. M. Kirby, D. D.   Mr. T. S. Clarkson.
The Rev. James Caird.   Mr. J. D. Henderson.
The Rev. Wilford L. Robbins.

On the Accounts of the Treasurer.

Mr. Ralph W. McDougall.   Mr. LeGrand S. Strang.

On the Diocesan Fund and Mileage of the Clergy.

The Rev. Sheldon M. Griswold.   Mr. Benjamin F. Hinman.
The Rev. Russell Woodman.   Mr. J. D. Henderson.
                                      Mr. Myron D. Jewell.

On Diocesan Missions.

The Rev. Charles S. Olmsted.   Mr. Thomas Mansfield.
The Rev. Ernest Mariett.   Mr. Andrew S. Booth.
                                      Mr. Samuel M. Van Santvoord.

On the Bishop's Salary and the Episcopal Fund.

The Rev. Fenwick M. Cookson.   Mr. Edward B. Cushney.
The Rev. John N. Marvin.   Mr. Francis N. Mann.
                                      Mr. James McQuide.

On the Fund for the Widows and Orphans of Deceased Clergymen

The Rev. Eaton W. Maxcy, D. D.   Mr. Robert M. Townsend.
                                      Mr. Windsor B. French.

On the Aged and Infirm Clergy Fund.

The Rev. William M. Ogden.   Mr. G. Hyde Clarke.
                                      Mr. George F. Granger.

On the General Theological Seminary.

The Rev. Charles Temple.
The Rev. Frederick N. Skinner.
The Rev. Frederick S. Griffin.

Mr. T. Streatfeild Clarkson.
Mr. Frederick German.

On the Society for Promoting Religion and Learning.

The Rev. David Sprague.

Mr. A. B. Cox.
Mr. Michael Andrae.

On Unfinished Business.

The Rev. Walter C. Stewart.

Mr. Nelson La Salle.
Mr. Thomas E. Ricketts.

On Non-Reporting Clergy and Parishes.

The Rev. James A. Dickson.

Mr. John Horrocks.
Dr. T. Floyd Woodworth.

On the Registrar's Report.

The Rev. Richmond Shreve, D. D.

Mr. James Bell.
Mr. Joseph Moll.

On the Orphan House at Cooperstown.

The Rev. Frank B. Reazor.
The Rev. E. Ruthven Armstrong.

Mr. William Kemp.
Mr. S. E. Crittenden.

On the Salary of the Bishop.

The Rev. Joseph Carey, S. T. D.
The Rev. W. W. Battershall, D. D.

Mr. J. J. Tillinghast.
Mr. Erastus Corning.
Mr. Walter A. Wood.
Mr. J. W. Tillinghast.
Mr. John I. Thompson.
Mr. Spencer Trask.

On the Society for the Home Study of Holy Scripture.

The Rev. Heman R. Timlow.
The Rev. Edgar A. Enos.
The Rev. John B. Hubbs.

Mr. Levi Hasbrouck.
Mr. James Russell Parsons, Jr.
Mr. William L. Du Bois.

On the Woman's Diocesan League.

The Rev. Ernest A. Hartmann.
The Rev. Edward Dudley Tibbits.

Mr. John Keyes Paige.
Mr. Walton Van Loan.
Mr. David H. Gay.

On the Bible and Prayer Book Society.

The Rev. John H. Houghton.
The Rev. William Mason Cook.
The Rev. Walter H. Larom.

Mr. John H. Hulsapple.
Mr. Edward Searles.
Mr. George B. McCartee.

10

The following named reports were received and referred to the appropriate committees: of the Treasurer of the Diocese; of the Board of Diocesan Missions; of the Trustees of the Episcopal Fund and of the Committee on the Salary of the Bishop; of the Trustees of the Fund for the Widows and Orphans of Deceased Clergymen, and of the Treasurer of the same; of the Trustees of the Aged and Infirm Clergy Fund, and of the Treasurer of the same; of the Registrar of the Diocese; of the Superintendent and of the Treasurer of the Orphan House of the Holy Saviour, Cooperstown; of the Society for Promoting Religion and Learning; of the Bible and Common Prayer Book Society.

The Rev. R. G. Hamilton nominated for election as members of the Standing Committee, the Rev. William Payne, D. D., the Rev. J. Livingston Reese, D. D., the Rev. J. Ireland Tucker, S. T. D., the Rev. Fenwick M. Cookson, Mr. Norman B. Squires, Mr. Henry S. Wynkoop, Mr. John I. Thompson and Mr. John H. Van Antwerp; for Lay Deputy to General Convention, Mr. John Hobart Warren; for Provisional Lay Deputy to General Convention, Mr. Thomas L. Harison.

The Secretary of the last Convention presented and read the following

REPORT OF THE SECRETARY OF THE CONVENTION.

ALBANY, *November* 11, 1890.

To the Convention of the Diocese of Albany:

The Secretary of the Diocese respectfully presents the following report:

Twelve hundred copies of the Bishop's Address and 1,250 copies of the Journal of the Convention were printed and distributed.

Letters were sent to the Clergy who failed to report to the Convention of 1888. Three replies were received.

Application for admission into union with the Convention was duly received from St. Barnabas' Church, Stottville, Columbia county, and forwarded to the chairman of the Committee on the Incorporation and Admission of Churches.

Efforts were made, as for the past two years, to secure from the railroads leading to Albany reduced rates for members attending the Convention, without success, except so far as concerns the Delaware and Hudson Canal Company's railroad, which forwarded to the Secretary certificates entitling members of the Convention, who have paid full fare to Albany, to return for one-third fare. The other railroads refused to grant the request of the Secretary, because the number who availed themselves of the reduction was so small last year, as not to justify the making of any reduction this year, unless the Secretary would guarantee that one hundred persons would avail themselves of the privilege.

Appended to this report is a notification from the Secretary of the House of Deputies of the General Convention in regard to a Canon for the support of Aged and Infirm Clergy.

The Secretary has also received from the Secretary of the House of Deputies of the General Convention, notification of proposed changes in the Prayer Book, adopted at the General Convention of 1889, and to be finally acted upon at the General Convention of 1892, also of changes finally adopted at the General Convention of 1889.

Letters have been received from the Rev. Dr. Payson of the Presbyterian Synod of New York State, in regard to a conference to be held in the city of New York on the 17th and 18th of the current month, to discuss the matter of securing "better moral training in our public schools;" to which conference this Convention is invited and requested to send a committee.

Nominations for members of the Board of Missions have been received: For the Convocation of Albany, the Rev. Walton W. Battershall, D. D., and Mr. John H. Van Antwerp; for the Convocation of Troy, the Rev. Fenwick M. Cookson and Mr. George A. Wells; for the Convocation of the Susquehanna, the Rev. F. B. Reazor and Mr. Robert M. Townsend; for the Convocation of Ogdensburgh, the Rev. R. M. Kirby, D. D., and Mr. T. Streatfeild Clarkson.

A large number of Journals of other Dioceses and other documents have been received and forwarded to the Registrar.

Respectfully submitted,

WM. C. PROUT,
Secretary of the Convention.

COMMUNICATION FROM THE SECRETARY OF THE GENERAL CONVENTION.

CONCORD, MASS., *May* 3, 1890.

DEAR SIR — I beg to communicate through you to the Convention of the Diocese of Albany the following resolutions adopted by the House of Deputies of the General Convention, October 24, 1889:

Resolved, That the Clergymen's Retiring Fund Society is heartily approved in its principles and methods, and is commended to the support of the Clergy and Laity of the Church

Resolved, That every Diocese of this Church be asked to pass a Canon similar to that of the Diocese of Newark, on the subject of a Clergy Pension Fund.

Resolved, That the Secretary of this House be instructed to transmit these resolutions, together with copies of the Report of the Clergymen's Retiring Fund Society, and of the aforesaid Canon of the Diocese of Newark to the Convention of each Diocese.

Appended hereto you will find the Canon referred to in the foregoing resolutions.

I am, dear sir, your obedient servant,

CHARLES L. HUTCHINS,
Secretary.

CANON OF THE DIOCESE OF NEWARK.

Of the Fund for Aged and Infirm Clergymen.

SECTION 1. It shall be the duty of every Minister having charge of a congregation of this Diocese, to make at least one annual collection for the relief of Clergymen disabled by age or disease.

§ 2. All contributions and donations for this object shall be transmitted to the treasurer of "The Trustees of the Fund for Aged and Infirm Clergymen "

§ 3. All collections and all donations not limited by the donor, received during the Conventional year, shall be subject to the order of "The Trustees of the Fund for Aged and Infirm Clergymen," and may be appropriated by said Trustees for the relief of Clergymen disabled by age, accident or disease, who have been canonically connected with the Diocese for the two years immediately preceding their application for relief, and have spent at least two successive years within the limits of the Diocese in the active discharge of the duties of the Ministry, or in the work of Christian education. Clergymen to whom appropriations are made under this section shall be known as "Special Annuitants," and shall not receive more than three hundred dollars in any one year.

§ 4. The Trustees shall have power to appropriate, from the collections received during the year, a sum not exceeding seventy-five dollars toward defraying the funeral expenses of any Clergyman of the Church.

§ 5. All appropriations (unless otherwise ordered) shall be payable semi-annually, on the first day of May and November, and all moneys unappropriated at the end of each Conventional year shall be paid into a fund, which shall be known as the "Permanent Fund," and shall be kept safely invested. The interest accruing on the existing capital fund, now in the hands of the Treasurer of the Convention, shall be permitted to accumulate. All accumulations shall be safely invested by the Trustees of the Fund for Aged and Infirm Clergymen, and added to the Permanent Fund until the same shall, with the existing capital fund, reach the sum of thirty thousand dollars.

§ 6. All legacies and all donations limited by the donor, paid to the Trustees, shall be used and applied by them agreeably to the terms and provisions under which the money is received; and when not otherwise directed by the donor, the legacy or donation shall be added to the "Permanent Fund," and the income thereof alone used.

As soon as said funds shall together reach the sum of thirty thousand dollars, the Trustees shall grant an annuity to every Clergyman who, (1) has reached the age of sixty-five years, and (2) has been canonically connected with the Diocese for the five years immediately preceding his application for an annuity, and (3) has been for at least five years of his last term] of canonical residence a settled Minister of the Diocese, or a Missionary duly appointed by the Ecclesiastical Authority.

The interest received from said funds shall be divided equally among the Clergymen entitled to receive an annuity under the terms and provisions of the previous paragraph of this section, and if this interest shall not be sufficient to give to each Clergyman the sum of three hundred dollars, then the balance of collections and donations remaining after the "Special Annuitants" are provided for, shall be used to increase the annuity to said sum.

Clergymen receiving an annuity under this section, which shall in no case exceed one thousand dollars, shall be known as "Regular Annuitants."

On motion of the Secretary, it was

Resolved, That the communication from the Secretary of the House of Deputies of General Convention in regard to a Canon on the support of Aged and Infirm Clergy be referred to the Committee on the Constitution and Canons.

Resolved, That receipt of the notification of proposed changes in the Prayer Book, adopted at the General Convention of 1889, and to be finally acted upon at the General Convention of 1892, as mentioned in the Report of the Secretary of the Convention, is hereby acknowledged by this Convention.

Resolved, That the letters of the Rev. Dr. Payson in regard to securing better moral training in the public schools, as mentioned in the Report of the Secretary of the Convention, be referred to a special committee.

The Rt. Rev. President appointed as the Committee on the correspondence from the Presbyterian Synod of New York, the Rev. John H. Houghton, the Rev. Frederick S. Sill, and Mr. T. O. Duroe.

The Rev. R. J. Adler presented and read the following report, which, on his motion, was referred to the Committee on the Constitution and Canons:

REPORT OF THE COMMITTEE ON THE DUTIES AND POWERS OF THE ARCHDEACONS.

The Committee appointed under the following resolution: "*Resolved,* That a Committee of two Presbyters and two Laymen be appointed, to report at the next Convention, upon the duties and powers of the Archdeacons and the Archdeaconries, and their relations to the Board of Missions," beg leave to report:

First. That the duties and powers of the Archdeacons as defined by section 6 of Canon XIV, are "To be the executive officer of the Convocation; to visit the Mission stations and vacant Parishes, and with the consent of the Clergy in charge, the other Parishes receiving missionary aid; to ascertain their condition, and to give such advice as may be required; to report the result of his inquiries to the Bishop; to stir up an increased missionary interest and zeal and to urge to more liberal offerings; and as a member of an advisory committee to the Board, to counsel as to the amount which should be expended in, and raised by his Convocation, and to use their best efforts to secure the same."

All these duties, it will be seen, except the last, relate to the Convocation; but as there is no relationship defined nor existing between the Convocation and the Board of Missions, his duties to the Convocation are ineffective to the Board, except indirectly. Such duties are also ineffective to the Convocation; the Convocation being absolutely powerless in relation to the Missions or Missionaries within its limits, or to the Board in its requirements. In short, nearly all his duties to the Convocation are in a great measure ineffective ,since the Convocation is objectless except in an altogether undefined interest in the general subject of Diocesan Missions, and in "promoting the fraternal intercourse and spiritual and intellectual life of its Clergy." He is like a chairman tied hand and foot to the chair and almost gagged.

The Committee feel that his duties to the Convocation as its executive officer should be commensurate with his duties to the Bishop as his Archdeacon. That the dignity, authority and power of the Bishop's representative should clothe his duties with directness and effectiveness. The Archdeacon's relation to the Bishop and the Convocation should be that of the ideal Deacon to the Parish Priest and the Parish. In the service of the Bishop he cometh and goeth and doeth, and receives a glad welcome among those to whom he ministers with his delegated authority in the Convocation. Therefore, as the Bishop is the chief itinerant Missionary in the Convocation, and his authority is unquestioned by it, his duties definite and effective to and in it, so unquestioned and definite and effective must be the authoritatively delegated duties of the Archdeacon.

Second. What has above been said of the duties and powers of the executive of the Convocation, equally applies to the Convocation itself. Its duties must be definitely defined. Its authority must be authoritatively authorized in order to powerfully exert its power. What has it ever done for the Board? It leads now, except indirectly, an objectless, powerless, lifeless life. Therefore, the Committee desires to give directness to its objective existence by defining its duties, clothing its power with delegated Episcopal authority; and

Third. Establishing its relationship to the Board of Missions in the exercise of those duties and the acknowledged obligations which they impose. It shall be the right hand — the executive — with the delegated authority of the Board, through its head, the Bishop, increasingly multiplying its effectiveness by the many-sided contact of its Missions and Missionaries with the members of the Archdeaconry. The Spirit of Missions is abroad — itinerant — riding the circuit of every Diocese in the land—given the rein in some till its attenuated form leaves but a shadow of infinitesimal results; whilst in others reined well in hand of the Bishop's Archdeacon, till it results in an ideal Archdeaconry, orderly, progressive, powerful.

To give force to the necessity of establishing orderly relationship between the Board of Missions, the Archdeaconry, and the Missionaries and their work, we need but cite a few of the methods pursued in various Dioceses.

In *New Hampshire*, the creation of the office and defining the duties of the Archdeacon was at the last Convention referred to the Board of Missions, evidently looking toward establishing such a relationship that would supersede the office and title of General Missionary, and abolish its inherent uncontrollable roving character.

In *Massachusetts*, action was taken at the last Convention, " that the Board of Missions shall apportion to each Convocation the amount considered its proportional part of the whole sum to be raised for Missionary purposes, shall receive all funds raised by the Convocations, and shall then allot to each Convocation according to its needs the amounts to be spent within its limits. That the sum allotted to each shall be administered by the Convocation as it may see fit; that there shall be no necessary proportion between the amount contributed by it and the amount received by it for administration." To put this briefly, each Convocation raises funds for the whole work. The Board allots and the Convocation administers its allotted portion. The relationship of the Bishop to this plan does not appear, though this is very nearly working out the original purpose of Convocational existence.

In *Connecticut*, there are *six* Archdeaconries, and the Canons give to the Archdeacons great power. He appoints all Missionaries with the approval of the Bishop. He has authority to visit the Parishes, and to look up new fields for work. May appoint Lay helpers to aid in temporal matters. All this is tending, according to reports, to increased efficiency of the work.

In *New York* there are *five* Archdeaconries. "The Diocesan Board of Missions conducts its work through the Archdeaconries, the Archdeacon being nominated by the Bishop and confirmed by the Archdeaconry." It nominates to the Bishop all its Missionaries. It has full management of all its funds. New York has by far the most systematic, efficient Archdeaconal organization of any on this continent. It is after it that most of the features of the following recommendations are modeled, modified by our local corporate necessities.

In *Central New York*, it is proposed to have the two Archdeacons superintend the whole Missionary work of the Diocese under the Bishop.

In *New Jersey*, the two Convocations have at their head a rural Dean, to be appointed by the Bishop from three Clergymen nominated by ballot of the Convocation. He is to superintend all Missionary work, and visit Mission stations at least once a year, also all Parishes, with the consent of their Rectors, in the interest of the work.

In *Central Pennsylvania*, the diffusive method of an itinerant Missionary is still further diffused by the appointment recently of a second itinerant Missionary.

In *Virginia*, there is no Convocational system, only a Diocesan Missionary Society. Three Evangelists work solely under the direction of the Bishop.

In *North Carolina* the Dean of Convocation " shall visit once or twice each year all Missions within the bounds of the Convocation, search out the scattered members of the Church, and examine promising points to start Missions, and also visit the regular Parishes, to give information about the work and field, and to make an effort to procure Lay preachers to preach the Gospel in school-houses and private houses, and wherever else they can get a hearing."

In the *Florida* Convention it was resolved that the duties of the Archdeacons (for work among coloured people) be defined by the Bishop, and that " whatever power or dignity is given by the Bishop to the Archdeacon, when he goes into a Parish or Mission, whether for a day or six months, he shall be considered only as an Assistant, Associate or Missioner."

Lastly, in *Chicago* the Archdeacon shall represent the Episcopal authority and that of the Board of Missions, and shall devote himself exclusively to the interest of the same. He shall have supervisory power in the erection of houses of worship for the use of Missions, and the maintenance or improvement of the same. He was voted a salary of $2,000 out of the General Missionary Fund.

The Committee have quoted at such length to show the heterogeneous methods in use of the various Dioceses. They recommend an unhasty, careful consideration of the subject as set forth in the proposed amendment of Canon XIV, and if necessary, a gradual conformity to its provisions — as for instance, the Canon does not necessitate an immediate salarying of all the Archdeacons — for they believe that the right man and the right time will come first to one Archdeaconry, and then another and so on. They believe that then and thus the increased interest and funds will demonstrate the feasibility of its working in each of the Archdeaconries. They believe that it is not possible that the comparatively little interest and small stationary amount that has been raised for years shall be the measure for years to come. Where $10,000 has been raised annually, and not increased with the growth of the Diocese— there must be a growth when agencies are multiplied, knowledge of the work and its needs disseminated and brought into closer contact with the heart of the Church, that is charged of our Lord with this work.

The Committee recommend the following amendments to Canon XIV:

Sec. 4, line 2, by inserting after the word "Treasurer:"

"And shall determine what proportion of the whole sum voted by the Board should be raised by, and expended within each Archdeaconry."

And add to the end of the section:

"including the following points:

"(1.) The names of all Missionaries and stations and the appropriation to each.

"(2.) All resources and liabilities of each station.

"(3) An estimate of the funds needed for the ensuing year; and an apportionment of same to be raised by each Archdeaconry."

Sec. 6, that it shall read:

SEC. 6. The Bishop shall be *ex-officio* President of each Archdeaconry. The other members shall be the canonical members of the Diocesan Convention residing within the limits of the Archdeaconry. It shall be the duty of each Archdeaconry:

(1.) To submit to the Bishop, when there is a vacancy, the names of three Clergymen, one of whom the Bishop may appoint to be its Archdeacon, who shall hold his office until his successor is appointed.

(2.) To elect a Secretary and a Treasurer.

(3.) To adopt its own by-laws.

(4.) To meet, and to report at least quarterly to the Board of Missions.

(5.) To nominate to the Bishop for his appointment all its Missionaries and to fix their salaries.

(6.) To search out its religious needs and to conduct the Missionary work within its own limits.

(7) To collect and preserve careful statistics of its work, and of the needs of the communities within its limits.

Sec. 7, that it shall read.

SEC. 7. The Archdeacon shall be, in the absence of the Bishop, the President of the Archdeaconry. His services shall be, at all times, at the command of the Bishop. He may be present, but without a vote, at the meetings of the Board of Missions. It shall be his duty

(1.) To superintend all Missionary work conducted by the Archdeaconry.

(2.) To visit each Parish and Mission, as the Bishop's acknowledged representative.

at least once each year, to disseminate knowledge of the work and its needs, and to stimulate offerings for the same.

(3.) To exercise a general supervision of the material affairs of each Mission; to examine its financial ability; to promote its self-help; to advise with the laity of the station as to the buildings, repairs, etc.; to obtain where possible grants of land for site of future church, chapel or rectory; to appeal to the wealthy churchmen for loans, and to invest them in land and buildings, especially where there is a church or chapel, in a rectory for the Missionary.

(4.) He shall make a full report of all his acts to the Bishop; and to the Archdeaconry at each meeting. And shall make an annual report to the Board of Missions.

(5.) His salary, voted by the Board, shall be paid as the salaries of all the other Missionaries, out of the appropriations to the Archdeaconry by the Treasurer of the Board.

Sec. 8, that it shall read:

Sec. 8. The Treasurer of each Archdeaconry shall receive all Missionary offerings within its limits, and remit the same to the Treasurer of the Board at least quarterly. He shall report the same to the Archdeaconry at each meeting.

The Committee recommend the adoption of the following resolution:

Resolved, That the foregoing amendments to Canon XIV, with this report be referred to the Committee on Constitution and Canons.

R. J. Adler,

Henry S. Wynkoop,

Fenwick M. Cookson,

F. N. Mann,

Committee.

The Rev. J. Philip B. Pendleton presented and read

THE REPORT OF THE COMMITTEE ON THE INCORPORATION AND ADMISSION OF CHURCHES.

The Committee on the Incorporation and Admission of Churches report that they have received through the Secretary of the Convention, an application to be admitted into union with the Convention of the Diocese of Albany, from St. Barnabas' Church, Stottville, Columbia county.

They have examined the Articles of Incorporation and other papers accompanying the said application, and find them, after giving the provisions of the Canon a free interpretation, to be in accordance with the requirements of Canon IV, and therefore recommend the adoption of the following resolution:

Resolved, That the Church of St. Barnabas, Stottville, Columbia county, be admitted into union with the Convention.

Respectfully submitted,

J. Philip B. Pendleton,

Chairman.

Albany, N. Y., *November* 11, 1890.

On motion of the Rev. J. Philip B. Pendleton, the resolution contained in the above report was adopted. St. Barnabas' Church, Stottville, Columbia county, was admitted into union with the Convention; a certificate of Lay Deputies from that Parish was presented, referred to the Committee on Credentials of Lay Deputies, and by them reported correct, and the names of the Deputies were called by the Secretary.

The Rev. Thaddeus A. Snively read

THE REPORT OF THE BIBLE AND COMMON PRAYER BOOK SOCIETY OF ALBANY AND ITS VICINITY,

OFFICE OF THE CORRESPONDING SECRETARY, ST. JOHN'S RECTORY, TROY, N. Y.

The Corresponding Secretary of the Bible and Common Prayer Book Society of Albany and its Vicinity begs leave to present the following report on behalf of the Society:

During the Conventional year, November, 1889, to November, 1890, grants have been made to the amount of more than 6,000 volumes.

From the Society itself, as follows: 600 Bibles, 2,500 Prayer Books (including 30 12mo and Chancel copies), 925 Hymnals (of which 90 were editions with music): a total for the Society proper of 4,025 books. From the Mann Bequest, auxiliary to the Society, but under the direction of the authorities of St. John's Church, Troy, there were distributed, as follows: 88 Bibles (including 5 for Lectern use), 128 Prayer Books (of which 22 were 12mo), 1,477 Hymnals (of which 77 were musical editions), 285 volumes for Sunday School and Parish libraries: a total for the Francis N. Mann Bequest of 1,978 volumes. A grand total for the Society's work of 6,003 books.

By far the largest year in the history of the Society, both as to number of books distributed and expenditures for the same. Probably the demand will not be much less this year, although it will be impossible to grant the books asked for, unless there is a decided increase in the amounts contributed by the Parishes of the Diocese.

In addition to this ordinary demand upon the Society's treasury, by direction of the Board of Managers, your Secretary had printed and distributed 20,000 copies of a leaflet of eight pages, containing the amendments made to the Prayer Book which appear in the Morning and Evening Prayer, the Litany and the Holy Communion.

At the same time the Clergy of the Diocese received from the Mann Bequest for Parish use, 2,000 copies of the 12mo edition of these offices as amended, 1,000 copies of the notifications of changes proposed and of those adopted, and 500 lectionaries.

We have great pleasure in announcing that arrangements have been made for a special edition of the Prayer Book for our Society. The first edition of this year contained the Society's imprint on the title page. Then later we had the gratification of getting an edition with the further improvement of the seal of the Society embossed on the outer cover of the books, and the certificate signed within by our own Bishop, and dated upon the twenty-first anniversary of his consecration, and therefore of his presidency of this Society.

As we have had a special edition of the Hymnal in use for the Mann Bequest for some time past, it will be seen that the Society now practically issues its own publications

These special editions cost the Society no more than before, the only condition being that they must be ordered from the English publishers in editions of a thousand each.

An abstract of the report of the Treasurer, Mr. H. B. Dauchy of Troy (to whom offerings should be sent), is here given:

The Permanent Fund amounts to.............. ... . $13,385 42

Summary of Receipts and Expenditures for the Year.

Receipts from thirty-seven Parishes $252 18

11

Income from Permanent Fund including an extra and unusual dividend
of $250.. $1,143 00
From Mann Bequest (including part of next year's income from same)...   780 00

Total receipts during the year........................... .... $2,175 18
Cash balance from last year... ....   426 20

Total receipts, including balance.................... .... $2,601 38

Total payments for year... $2,406 19
Cash carried to new account......... ....   195 19

Total................................. .... $2,601 38

The attention of the Convention is called to the very small amount of offerings
from the Parishes of the Diocese. There is an impression abroad that we have no
need of funds. This is manifestly unjust and injurious.

It is little short of humiliating that out of an expenditure of $2,406.19, only $252.18
(barely one-tenth) came from the Parishes.

This is exclusive of the large amount from the Mann Bequest ($780), which is
really the income of two years from this fund. Next year the amount from this
source will be very much smaller, as by a happy arrangement we were enabled to
have its funds advanced for the coming year to save us from a glaring deficiency at
this time. Without the help of this generous bequest, the Society's Treasurer to-day
would have come to us with a difference between the outlay and the receipts of $600
on the wrong side of the account. This is the case after we make all allowance for the
special gifts made through its help. When to this fact we add the other one to be noted
above, that in the income from the Permanent Fund for the year as given by the Treasurer, there is a special dividend of $250, which of course will not be repeated, it
shows that the Society for the proper performance of its work must depend upon the
Parishes for largely increased offerings. This is all the clearer, too, when it is remembered that of necessity the marvellously high rate which our funds are now
earning must suffer gradual diminution.

It will not be considered amiss, we hope, to state that a sample of the neglect of
the Parishes to do for this Society, will be seen from the fact that of the Albany
Parishes, Grace Church is the only one that is recorded as having sent an offering
during the past two years, while only three of the Troy churches are thus recorded,
although almost all of the Parishes in both of these leading cities of the Diocese have
applied for, and received, grants of books from the Society. Indeed, it is worthy of
mention that the offerings are in the larger proportion from the smaller Parishes and
Mission stations, many of the larger Parishes forgetting the Society entirely except
when in need of more books.

The excuse for the Secretary's venturing to make these statements is to be found
in the further fact that he has not been able to answer fully all the appeals which
have come to him for grants during the past year.

There is a constant need of Hymnals with music for use in the Mission Parishes.
This is not in the line of luxury, but of necessity. What is the service of the Church
without the proper aid of music? And how is a Missionary to teach his people to
sing the Church hymns and canticles without proper books? And how shall these
costly books be furnished by men, whose living is measured by a standard that
makes even some of the necessities of life almost hopelessly beyond their reach? The

best way seems to be that the brethren in Parishes to whom God has given the ability, should come forward and by offerings to this Society, enable it to supply the Missionary with these and other kindred helps deeply needed in their work.

The Society has funds sufficient to supply with a cramped hand the smaller grants of Prayer Books and Hymnals, but if the other needs are to be met, it is absolutely necessary that the Parishes should come forward and give more generous help to this very useful agency.

Respectfully submitted,
THADDEUS ALEXANDER SNIVELY,
Corresponding Secretary.

The Rev. William M. Ogden read the report of the Trustees of the Fund for Aged and Infirm Clergymen, and of the Committee on the same.

REPORT OF THE TRUSTEES OF THE FUND FOR AGED AND INFIRM CLERGYMEN.

DIOCESE OF ALBANY,
ALBANY, *November* 11, A. D., 1890. }

The undersigned, Trustees of the Fund for the Support of Aged and Infirm Clergymen, respectfully report that the receipts and disbursements for the year have been, as reported in detail by the Treasurer, and are as follows:

Receipts.

From Parishes.........	$507 15
From interest on investments...........	841 62
From individuals..................	1 00
Total......	$1,849 77

Disbursements.

Balance due Treasurer as per report to last Convention	$16 38
For Stipends	1,025 00
Total..............	$1,041 38
Balance on hand	$308 39

The Trustees have the following securities which constitute the Permanent Fund:

Bond and mortgage, Bishop's house............................ ...	$3,600 00
Perry judgment, Bishop's house.	6,565 86
Learned bond and mortgage...........	4,000 00
Burnett bond and mortgage....	1,700 00
Troy and Lansingburgh railroad bond.	1,000 00
U. S. registered 4 per cent bond.....	1,000 00
New York, Lake Erie and Western railroad bond	1,000 00
Cash on hand	700 00
Total...	$19,565 86

Which represents the following receipts:

Diocese of New York.. .	$10,000 00
St. Paul's Church, Albany......................................	2,000 00
Miss Burr legacy, Diocese of New York.....................	2,000 00
Total..................	$14,000 00

WM. CROSWELL DOANE,

SELDEN E. MARVIN,

Treasurer.

REPORT OF THE COMMITTEE ON THE AGED AND INFIRM CLERGY FUND.

Your Committee to whom was referred the report of the Trustees of the Aged and Infirm Clergy Fund observe with pleasure that there stands to the credit of the Fund a cash balance of $308.39. Thirty-nine Parishes contributed $507.15 in the past year, against a debit of last year of $16.88.

Your Committee would suggest for the consideration of the Trustees of the Fund the advisability of using a part of this balance of three hundred and odd dollars in buying an interest in the Clergymen's Retiring Fund Society for the benefit of some of the elder Clergy of the Diocese. They have examined the report of the Treasurer of the Fund and found it correct.

They append the following resolution :

That the Trustees of the Fund report to the next Convention as to the advisability of purchasing an interest for some of the more aged of the Clergy in the Clergymen's Retiring Fund.

WM. M. OGDEN,

G. HYDE CLARKE,

G. F. GRANGER.

The resolution recommended in the report was adopted, after having been amended on motion of the Rev. R. G. Hamilton, so as to read as follows :

Resolved, That the Trustees of the Fund be requested to report to the next Convention as to the advisability of purchasing an interest for some of the more aged of the Clergy in the Clergymen's Retiring Fund Society, unless in their judgment the balance ought in whole or in part to be distributed among the beneficiaries.

The Rev. Charles Temple presented and read the

REPORT OF THE COMMITTEE ON THE GENERAL THEOLOGICAL SEMINARY.

The Committee on the General Theological Seminary beg leave to report their satisfaction at the continued prosperity of this great center of churchly learning as evidenced by the large class just matriculated — by far the largest class in the history of the institution — and also by the recent completion of Jarvis Hall and the building of two new dormitories. The Committee beg leave to call the attention of the Convention to the appeal of the Special Committee of the Trustees for the erection of a new refectory and also for a gymnasium, of both of which the Seminary stands in great need. A Trustee of the Seminary to serve for three years is to be elected by this Convention. Your Committee nominate the Rev. Joseph Carey, S. T. D., for that position.

CHARLES TEMPLE,

F. N. SKINNER,

F. S. GRIFFEN,

FRED. E. GERMAN.

On motion of the Secretary of the Convention, the recommendation of the Committee was adopted, and the Rev. Joseph Carey, S. T. D., was elected a Trustee of the General Theological Seminary for three years from November 15, 1890.

On motion of the Rev. R. G. Hamilton, the following preambles and resolution were unanimously adopted by a rising vote of the Convention:

WHEREAS, The Rev. John Henry Hopkins, S. T. D., for many years an honoured Priest in the Diocese of Albany, is now in the providence of God seriously ill in the city of Troy, and with little hope of recovery; and

WHEREAS, Besides the debt which the whole American Church owes to the fearless champion of the Catholic Faith and Order, this Diocese enjoyed the benefit of his advice in its organization, and of his service in work and counsels during the earlier years of its existence.

Be it resolved, That the tenderest sympathy of this Convention be and is hereby conveyed to our Reverend Brother, and that he be assured of our earnest prayers to Almighty God in his behalf.

The Rev. Frederick S. Sill, Registrar, presented and read the

REGISTRAR'S REPORT, 1890.

The Registrar would respectfully report that he has completed the files of all the Diocesan Journals for 1888 and 1889, and has received forty-three of the Journals published up to this date. Six of the fifty-two Dioceses of the United States hold their Conventions as late as September, November or December, and their Journals are not ready for distribution until the following year. No Journals from the Missionary Jurisdictions have come to hand. Of Journals reported as wanting last year, we have now a full set of East Carolina. The Registrar has obtained a complete set of the Journals of the Provincial Synod of Canada, through the kind help of the Rev. Dr. Norman, its Secretary. They date from 1861 to 1889, and have been bound in two volumes. The Journal of the General Convention for 1889 has been received.

The Registrar is also happy to report that he has had two sets of the Bishop's Annual Addresses bound in two volumes each. With the first volume is Bishop Horatio Potter's sermon at the Primary Convention, and with the second Bishop H. C. Potter's sermon at the Dedication of the Cathedral. As some of the annual addresses have already become scarce, these bound sets of all the Bishop's Addresses from 1869 to 1889, the first twenty-one years of his Episcopate, are a valuable addition to our Archives, containing as they do a rich store of that eloquent and graceful diction, and that fearlessness in discussing every living question of the times, for which our Bishop is deservedly distinguished.

The Registrar's Scrap Book of circulars, pastoral letters, newspaper cuttings, programmes and other materials of Diocesan history, likely to be lost sight of unless collected at once, has received some additions during the year.

The Rev. II. T. Gregory has presented to the Diocese a collection of documents containing sermons, both bound in several volumes, and in pamphlet form, addresses, almanacs, journals, the *Spirit of Missions* for several years, as also the *Churchman,* and the Magazine. Among the sermons are a number of valuable ones by the older Bishops of the Church, now deceased, some preached before the General Convention. Among the Journals are those of Connecticut from 1850 to 1870.

Miss Whittingham of Baltimore has also sent some sermons and charges by Bishops Whittingham, Doane of New Jersey, Coxe and others.

In this line we have received fifty-eight pamphlets; of historical and controversial matters we have added fifty pamphlets; of commemorative sermons, eight pamphlets. Besides a number of Reports of Institutions and catalogues of the Seminary. The Registrar has a full set of the Catalogues of St. Agnes' School, together with the Addresses of the Bishop to the Graduating Class. He would like to have the Reports of the Child's Hospital previous to the year 1884.

Mrs. Twing has given four bound volumes of the *Church Work*, edited by herself.

The Registrar gratefully acknowledges contributions from the Rev. H. T. Gregory, the Rev. Dr. Battershall, the Rev. Dr. Carey, the Rev. Dr. Drowne of Long Island, the Rev. O. E. Ostensen of Colorado, the Rev. J. B. Shepherd of Ohio, the Rev. William Dudley Powers of Georgia, the Rev. L. D. Hopkins of Fond du Lac, Dr. A. J. Rosset of East Carolina, the Rev. Secretary of this Diocese, Miss Whittingham of Maryland, Mrs. Twing of New York, and Miss Boyd of Albany.

The Registrar has great pleasure in presenting to the Diocese an Historical Index containing nearly seven hundred items that relate to the history of the Diocese, the Bishop's commemorations and discussions, the reports of important committees, and the action taken by the Convention on canonical legislation and other matters. It has been compiled from the Journals of the General Convention, and of the Dioceses of New York and Albany. It is hoped that it may some time prove of value to the future historian of the Diocese as a guide and reference. An alphabetical index to the Historical Index is in course of preparation, so that any matter referred to may be readily found. The latter, though in manuscript, has been substantially bound in half morocco, and space is allowed for items that may have been overlooked.

As suggested by the Registrar in his last report, he has had glass plates put in the panels of the doors of his cases, which now protect the shelves from dust, and also considerably improve their appearance.

The Registrar acknowledges the receipt of $15 from the Treasurer of the Diocesan Fund, together with a balance from last year of $2.74. His expenses have been: For panels, $10; scrap book, $2; binding, $2.70; expressage, $1.90; cleaning cases, $1; fares and stationary, $3.25. Total, $20.85. Account overdrawn, $3.11.

For the coming year he would respectfully ask that the sum of $10 be appropriated from the Diocesan Fund for the expenses of his office. This is needed especially for binding Journals, which have increased sufficiently to form new volumes.

FREDERICK S. SILL,

COHOES, N. Y., *November* 10, 1890. *Registrar.*

The Rev. Richmond Shreve, D. D., presented and read the following report of the Committee on the Registrar's Report, the resolution presented in which was adopted :

REPORT OF THE COMMITTEE ON THE REGISTRAR'S REPORT.

The Committee to whom was referred the Report of the Registrar, congratulate the Convention upon their good fortune and wisdom in the election to that position of a gentleman who gives such continued proof of his special fitness for the duties of the office. They desire to put on record their appreciation of the labor involved in the compilation of the Historical Index to which he refers, and to express the belief that it will be a most useful document to all who desire to keep themselves acquainted with the history of the Diocese.

The Committee recommend the adoption of the following resolution:

Resolved, That the sum of $10 be appropriated from the Diocesan Fund for the expenses of the Registrar's office for the ensuing year.

RICHMOND SHREVE,
JAMES BELL,
JOSEPH MOLL.

The Rev. Fenwick M. Cookson presented the following reports:

REPORT OF THE TRUSTEES OF THE EPISCOPAL FUND.

To the Convention:

The undersigned, Trustees of the Episcopal Fund of the Diocese, respectfully report, that they hold the following investments for the Fund:

Bond of Grace Church, Waterford.................................	$500 00
Bond of St. John's Church, Cohoes...............................	800 00
Bond and mortgage of J. Judge, 6 per cent........................	1,500 00
Bond and mortgage of D. McElveney, 5 per cent...................	5,000 00
Bond and mortgage of L. Sautter, 6 per cent.....................	6,000 00
Bond and mortgage of J. Kennah, 6 per cent......................	6,000 00
Bond and mortgage of E. A. Clark, 5 per cent....................	8,000 00
Bond and mortgage of Smead & Northcott, 4½ per cent.............	8,500 00
Deposit in Savings Bank, 4 per cent.............................	2,541 02
Total	$38,841 02

No contribution has been made to the Fund during the past year, and no change made in the principal or interest of the securities. The interest has been promptly paid on all of them.   Respectfully submitted,

JOHN H. VAN ANTWERP,
W. B. VAN RENSSELAER,
THEODORE TOWNSEND,
A. P. PALMER,
ALBANY, *November* 10, 1890.   C. WHITNEY TILLINGHAST, 2d.

REPORT OF THE TREASURER OF THE EPISCOPAL INCOME FUND.

J. H. Van Antwerp, Treasurer, in account with the Episcopal Income Fund:
Dr.

November 10, 1890.

To 1 year's interest, bond, Grace Church, Waterford....	$35 00
To 1 year's interest, bond, St. John's Church, Cohoes..................	56 00
To 1 year's interest, Judge mortgage, 6 per cent......................	90 00
To 1 year's interest, McElveney mortgage, 5 per cent..................	250 00
To 1 year's interest, Sautter mortgage, 6 per cent....................	360 00
To 1 year's interest, Kennah mortgage, 6 per cent....................	360 00
To 1 year's interest, Clark mortgage, 5 per cent.....................	400 00
To 1 year's interest, Northcott mortgage, 4½ per cent.................	382 50
To 1 year's interest on bank deposits, 4 per cent....................	101 64
To 4 dividends on 10 shares Missouri Pacific Railroad stock in name of Bishop, in trust	40 00
Remittance received from W. W. Rousseau, Secretary of Bishop's Salary Committee, inclusive of $300 borrowed March 20, on note of members of the Committee (yet unpaid)......................................	2,960 00
Balance due me...	3 28
Total..	$5,038 42

Cr.

November 10, 1890.
By balance due November 12, 1889.... .... $288 42
By payments to Bishop on salary account 4,750 00
  (Leaving due him $250 on October 1, and still unpaid)

  Total $5,038 43

E. & O. E., ALBANY, *November* 10, 1890.

J. H. VAN ANTWERP,
Treasurer Episcopal Fund.

REPORT OF THE COMMITTEE ON THE BISHOP'S SALARY * AND THE EPISCOPAL FUND.

The Committee to whom was referred the Report of the Treasurer of the Episcopal Fund and Bishop's Salary, respectfully report that they have examined the reports of the Trustees of the Episcopal Fund and of the Treasurer of the same, and found them to be correct.

The Committee regret that several Parishes of the Diocese have not paid their assessments, and recommend that the names of those in arrears at the next Convention be read to the Convention.

FENWICK M. COOKSON,
J. N. MARVIN,
FRANCIS N. MANN,
JAMES McQUIDE.

The Rev. Eaton W. Maxcy, D. D., presented and read the following reports:

REPORT OF THE TRUSTEES OF THE FUND FOR THE SUPPORT OF WIDOWS AND ORPHANS OF DECEASED CLERGYMEN.

DIOCESE OF ALBANY,
ALBANY, *November* 11, 1890. }

The Trustees of the Fund for the Support of the Widows and Orphans of Deceased Clergymen present herewith the report of the Treasurer showing the receipts and disbursements for the year.

Receipts.

Balance on hand as reported to last Convention......... .... $1,840 92
From Parishes... .... 219 14
From Investments 145 00

  Total.. .... $2,205 06

Disbursements.

Special................................ .... 50 00

  Balance on hand.... .... $2,155 06

The Trustees hold the following securities contributed by St. Paul's Church, Albany:
One United States registered 4 per cent bond................ .... $1,000 00

---

* For the Report of the Committee on the Salary of the Bishop, see Appendix D.

Two Chicago, Burlington and Quincy Railroad, Nebraska extension bonds,
4 per cent... $2,000 00
One Chicago, Burlington and Quincy Railroad bond, 4 per cent........ .. 1,000 00
One Wabash Railway bond, 5 per cent. 1,000 00

Total $5,000 00

WM. CROSWELL DOANE,
SELDEN E. MARVIN,
Treasurer.

REPORT OF THE COMMITTEE ON THE REPORT OF THE TRUSTEES OF THE FUND FOR THE SUPPORT OF THE WIDOWS AND ORPHANS OF DECEASED CLERGYMEN.

The Committee on the Report of the Trustees of the Fund for the Support of the Widows and Orphans of Deceased Clergymen respectfully report that they have examined the same and find it correct, and most earnestly commend this worthy object to the sympathy of the Churchmen of the Diocese.

EATON W. MAXCY,
WINSOR B. FRENCH,
R. M. TOWNSEND.

November 11, 1890.

The reports of the Treasurer of the Diocese and of the Committee on same, and of the Committee on the Diocesan Fund were presented and read.

REPORT OF THE TREASURER OF THE DIOCESE.

ALBANY, *November* 11, 1890.

Herewith find statement of receipts and disbursements on account of the Diocesan Fund for the year, showing as follows:

Receipts.

Received from Parishes..... .... $2,496 29
Received from individuals................ .... 275 00

Total... .... $2,771 29

Disbursements.

Balance due Treasurer............. .... $93 95
For mileage.... ... . 226 45
For Secretary's expenses....... .... 84 42
For Secretary's salary................ .... 250 00
For taxes and repairs, Bishop's house. 665 24
For assessment, General Convention. 125 00
For Bishop's traveling expenses 300 00
For printing......... .... 669 44
For Registrar................................. .... 15 00

Total $2,429 50
Balance on hand 341 79

$2,771 29

12

Cr.

... ... 10, 1890.

by balance due November 12, 1889.... .... $288 42

by payments to Bishop on salary account 4,750 00

(Leaving due him $950 on October 1, and still unpaid)

Total $5,038 42

E. & O. E , ALBANY, *November* 10, 1890.

J. H. VAN ANTWERP,
Treasurer Episcopal Fund.

REPORT OF THE COMMITTEE ON THE BISHOP'S SALARY * AND THE EPISCOPAL FUND.

The Committee to whom was referred the Report of the Treasurer of the Episcopal Fund and Bishop's Salary, respectfully report that they have examined the reports of the Trustees of the Episcopal Fund and of the Treasurer of the same, and found them to be correct.

The Committee regret that several Parishes of the Diocese have not paid their assessments, and recommend that the names of those in arrears at the next Convention be read to the Convention.

FENWICK M. COOKSON,
J. N. MARVIN,
FRANCIS N. MANN,
JAMES McQUIDE.

The Rev. Eaton W. Maxey, D. D., presented and read the following reports :

REPORT OF THE TRUSTEES OF THE FUND FOR THE SUPPORT OF WIDOWS AND ORPHANS OF DECEASED CLERGYMEN.

DIOCESE OF ALBANY,
ALBANY, *November* 11, 1890.

The Trustees of the Fund for the Support of the Widows and Orphans of Deceased Clergymen present herewith the report of the Treasurer showing the receipts and disbursements for the year.

Receipts.

Balance on hand as reported to last Convention $1,846 92

From Parishes 219 14

From investments 145 00

Total.... ... . $2 205 06

Disbursements.

Special 50 00

Balance on hand. $2 155 06

The Trustees hold the following securities contributed by St. Paul's Church, Albany:

One United States registered 4 per cent bond $1,000 00

Two Chicago, Burlington and Quincy Railroad, Nebraska extension bonds,
4 per cent.. ..... $2,000 00
One Chicago, Burlington and Quincy Railroad bond, 4 per cent........ .. 1,000 00
One Wabash Railway bond, 5 per cent. 1,000 00

Total $5,000 00

WM. CROSWELL DOANE,
SELDEN E. MARVIN,
Treasurer.

REPORT OF THE COMMITTEE ON THE REPORT OF THE TRUSTEES OF THE FUND FOR THE SUPPORT OF THE WIDOWS AND ORPHANS OF DECEASED CLERGYMEN.

The Committee on the Report of the Trustees of the Fund for the Support of the Widows and Orphans of Deceased Clergymen respectfully report that they have examined the same and find it correct, and most earnestly commend this worthy object to the sympathy of the Churchmen of the Diocese.

EATON W. MAXCY,
WINSOR B. FRENCH,
November 11, 1890. R. M. TOWNSEND.

The reports of the Treasurer of the Diocese and of the Committee on same, and of the Committee on the Diocesan Fund were presented and read.

REPORT OF THE TREASURER OF THE DIOCESE.

ALBANY, *November* 11, 1890.

Herewith find statement of receipts and disbursements on account of the Diocesan Fund for the year, showing as follows:

Receipts.

Received from Parishes..... .... $2,496 29
Received from individuals............... .... 275 00

Total... .... $2,771 29

Disbursements.

Balance due Treasurer............. .... $93 95
For mileage.... .... 226 45
For Secretary's expenses....... .... 84 42
For Secretary's salary....... .... 250 00
For taxes and repairs, Bishop's house. 665 24
For assessment, General Convention. 125 00
For Bishop's traveling expenses 300 00
For printing........ .... 669 44
For Registrar........................ .... 15 00

Total $2,429 50
Balance on hand 341 79

$2,771 29

12

It will be necessary for the Convention at this meeting to provide for the following objects:

Mileage to Clergymen in attendance upon Convention ; printing the Journal of the Convention; taxes and repairs, Bishop's house; sundry current expenses; one-third dues to General Convention; salary of the Secretary; traveling expenses of the Bishop.

For the above purposes I suggest the following estimate of the sums that will be required:

For mileage..........	$250 00
For printing ....,.....................	700 00
For taxes and repairs, Bishop's house	600 00
For sundry current expenses...............	150 00
For one-third dues, General Convention....	125 00
For salary of the Secretary........................	250 00
For Bishop's traveling expenses	300 00

To provide the above amount I recommend the Convention order an assessment of three (3) per centum upon the salaries paid or pledged the Clergymen by the Parishes and Mission stations, one-half payable April 1, and one-half payable October 1, 1891.

I further recommend that the Treasurer be directed to pay to each Clergyman in attendance upon the Convention and belonging to this Diocese, residing a distance of thirty miles from Albany, his actual traveling expenses, provided that in no case shall he pay to exceed seven cents a mile.

I desire to express my thanks to those individuals who so willingly and generously responded to my special appeal for aid to this fund.

SELDEN E. MARVIN,
Treasurer.

REPORT OF THE COMMITTEE ON THE ACCOUNTS OF THE TREASURER.

Examined and found correct by

R. W. McDOUGALL,
LE GRAND S. STRANG.

REPORT OF THE COMMITTEE ON THE DIOCESAN FUND AND MILEAGE OF THE CLERGY.

The Committee on the Diocesan Fund recommend the adoption of the following resolution:

Resolved, That the recommendations of the Treasurer of the Diocese be adopted by this Convention as follows: 1st, that an assessment of three *per centum* be levied on the salaries paid or pledged the Clergy by the Parishes and Mission stations, one-half payable April 1, the other half October 1, 1891; and, 2d, that the Treasurer be directed to pay to each Clergyman, in attendance upon this Convention and belonging thereto, residing a distance of twenty miles from Albany, his actual traveling expenses ;·provided, that in no case shall he pay to exceed seven (7) cents per mile.

SHELDON M. GRISWOLD,
Chairman.

On motion of the Secretary, the resolution presented in the above report was adopted.

The Rev. William M. Ogden offered the following resolution :

Resolved, That as soon as this Diocese shall be in possession of, and in receipt of income from, the $25,000 to be paid, or already paid, to this Diocese by the Diocese of New York toward the Episcopal Fund, the Bishop's salary shall be increased from $5,000 to $6,000 per annum.

Pending action in regard it, the Right Rev. President called the Rev. J. D. Morrison, D. D., LL. D., to the chair, and withdrew from the Convention.

After discussion, on motion of Mr. J. D. Henderson, Lay Deputy from Christ Church, Herkimer, the resolution of the Rev. Mr. Ogden was laid on the table.

On motion of Mr. Benjamin H. Hall, Lay Deputy from St. John's Church, Troy, it was

Resolved, That the laying on the table of the resolution, that has just now been laid on the table, is not to be considered as an expression of this Convention on the question of raising the salary of the Bishop.

The Rev. J. D. Morrison, D. D., LL. D., for the Committee on a Clergy Reserve Fund (the Secretary of the Convention speaking in his stead, Dr. Morrison being in the chair), gave notice of a proposed Canon on a Clergy Reserve Fund, which, on his motion, was referred to the Committee on the Constitution and Canons.

PROPOSED CANON OF THE CLERGY RESERVE FUND.

SECTION 1. A fund shall be established to be known as the Clergy Reserve Fund of the Diocese of Albany.

§ 2. It shall be the duty of each Parish and Mission station in the Diocese to contribute an offering annually in behalf of this fund.

§ 3. The fund thus formed shall be permitted to accumulate until it shall amount to $20,000, and the income shall then be divided into annuities of $300, which shall be paid to the beneficiaries of the fund.

§ 4. The beneficiaries of the fund shall be the Clergy of the Diocese according to the seniority of their canonical residence.

§ 5. No Clergyman shall be a beneficiary of the fund whose salary or stipend exceeds $1,000 per annum. Nor shall any Clergyman receive the annuity who has allowed the Parish or Mission under his charge to neglect its annual contribution to the fund.

ERRATUM.

On page 91, 3d line from the bottom, for " provisions of *the* Canon," read " provisions of *this* Canon."

The Convention took a recess.

HALF PAST FIVE O'CLOCK IN THE AFTERNOON.

The Evening Prayer was said in the Cathedral, the Dean and the Precentor officiating.

EIGHT O'CLOCK IN THE EVENING.

The Convention reassembled in the Cathedral.

A special Missionary Service, set forth by the Bishop, was said, the Rev. the Precentor of the Cathedral, and the Rev. W. H. Bown officiating.

After the service the Right Rev. President took the chair and called the Convention to order.

The Rev. W. R. Woodbridge, Secretary of the Board of Missions, read the

REPORT OF THE BOARD OF MISSIONS.

The Board of Missions respectfully reports, that it has held four meetings during the past year, at which the Missionary work of the Diocese has been provided for to the best of its ability with the means at hand. Eighty-eight stations have been under its care. A list of the stations, Missionaries and stipends is herewith submitted. During the year three new stations have been added, viz.: St. Paul's Church, Bartonville, Grace Church, Stamford, and St. Andrew's Mission, West Troy.

There are now forty-six Missionaries at work, and the following stations and groups of stations are at present vacant.

In the Convocation of Albany: Trinity Church, Fairfield; Grace Church, Norway; Memorial Church, Middleville; St. Mark's Church, Philmont; Church of Our Saviour, Lebanon Springs.

In the Convocation of Troy: St. John's Church, East Line; Grace Church, Jonesville, St Paul's Church, Greenwich.

In the Convocation of the Susquehanna: St. Paul's Church, Franklin.

In the Convocation of Ogdensburgh: St. Mark's Church, West Bangor; St. Peter's Church, Brushton; St. Thomas' Church, Lawrenceville; Grace Church, Norfolk; St. Andrew's Church, Norwood.

The Board, while sincerely thankful that it is not compelled to report a debt, assures the Convention that this is not due to the increased offerings of the people.

The full amount of $10,000 is needed for the work as now carried on, besides the added and aggressive work which should be encouraged and provided for.

The Board has received from the Convocation of Albany a memorial urging the appointment of an itinerant Missionary for the Diocese, with a salary of not less than $1,500, and that Convocation engaging to do its share toward providing the amount.

The Board resolved that this memorial be referred to the Convention for its action.

The Rev. W. H. Cook having resigned as Missionary at East Line and Jonesville, the Board requested the Rev. Archdeacon Carey to prepare a Minute, and ordered it to be incorporated in this report. It is as follows

MINUTE.

This Board, in view of the retirement of Rev. William H. Cook from East Line and Jonesville, owing to his great age, would put on record this expression of their high estimate of his character and his unremitting labours during a long life as a Priest in the Church of God He has always been in his place, in season and out of season, diligent in the study of the Holy Scriptures, and earnest in proclaiming the message of the Gospel.

Through his maintenance of the Faith once delivered to the Saints, his loyalty to the Church, his wise counsels, his loving ministrations, and his unspotted life, he has advanced the best interests of the Kingdom of Christ, and has furnished an example worthy the imitation of his brethren in the sacred ministry. The prayers of the Church which he has so loved, and for which he has toiled so unselfishly, will still follow him, while she will ever point to his ministry with gratitude. May our Divine Master shed on him and his family His abundant blessing and grant him at last to see the felicity of His chosen.

In conclusion the Board recommend the adoption of the following resolutions:

I. *Resolved,* That the Board of Missions be authorized to appropriate from the offerings of the people the amount of $10,000 for the support of the Missions in the Diocese during the ensuing year, and that it be requested to increase the stipends whenever needed and practicable, and to enlarge the sphere of their work.

II. *Resolved,* That the Board of Missions be requested to consider and act on the Memorial of the Convocation of Albany on the subject of an itinerant Missionary.

All of which is respectfully submitted,

By order of the Board,

WILLIAM R. WOODBRIDGE,

Secretary.

MISSIONS IN THE DIOCESE OF ALBANY, NOVEMBER 10. 1890.

CONVOCATION OF ALBANY.

County.	Church.	Place	Missionary.	Stipend.
Albany........	Trinity........	Rensselaerville..	Rev. R. Washbon and Rev. S. C. Thompson	$150
	St. Andrew's...	West Troy........	Rev.C. H. Hatheway	50
Greene........	Gloria Dei	Palenville..........	Rev. W. C. Grubbe.	250
	Grace.........	Prattsville......	....	100
	Trinity	Ashland.		
	Trinity	Athens	Rev. J. W. Stewart.	
	Christ	Coxsackie.........	Rev. L. H. Schubert	300
Herkimer.....	Trinity	Fairfield.........		
	Grace.	Norway	....	400
	Memorial.. ...	Middleville		
	St. Alban's	Frankfort......	Rev. Alfred Taylor..	200
	Grace	Mohawk		
	St. Augustine's.	Ilion	Rev. W. M. Cook...	200
Fulton	Christ...	Gloversville.	Rev. C. P.A.Burnett	600
Montgomery ..	Zion...........	Fonda....	Rev. C. C. Edmunds	300
	Good Shepherd.	Canajoharie	Rev. J. N. Marvin..	250
	Holy Cross....	Fort Plain.....		
Columbia.....	St. Luke's......	Clermont	Rev. M. E. Wilson.	100
	All Saints'	Hudson..... ..	Rev. E. P. Miller...	250
	Trinity	Claverack.		
	St. Luke's. ...	Chatham	Rev. Isaac Peck....	100
	St Mark's.	Philmont......	....	250
	Our Saviour....	New Lebanon ...	.. ..	300
		Lebanon Springs .		
				$3,800

CONVOCATION OF TROY.

County.	Church.	Place.	Missionary.	Stipend.
Rensselaer...	Trinity	Schaghticoke........	Rev. T. Dickinson..	$350
	St. Giles'	Castleton	Rev. C. H. Hatheway	200
Saratoga....	St. John's......	Stillwater ... ... }	Rev. W. G. W. Lewis	225
	Luke's	Mechanicville.... }		
	St. Paul's	Charlton.... .... }	Rev. H. R. Timlow.	100
		West Charlton ... }		
	St. John's.....	East Line .... }		
	Grace....... ..	Jonesville........ }	....	
	St. John's	Conklingville .... }	Rev. C. J. Whipple.	300
Warren ......'	St. Mary's	Luzerne .... }		
	Good Shepherd .	Chestertown .... }	Rev. Nassau Wm.	200
	St. Paul's	Bartonville....... }	Stephens........	100
	St. Sacrament..	Bolton.......... ...	Rev. C. T. Blanchet.	100
Washington...	St. Luke's....	Cambridge........	Rev.F.H.T.Horsfield	100
	St. Paul's..	Greenwich....... }	....	150
Saratoga	St. Stephen's...	Schuylerville.... }		
Washington...	Trinity........	Granville........ }	Rev. W. C. Prout.	200
		North Granville.. }		
	St. Paul's	Salem	....	100
Essex.........	Of the Cross....	Ticonderoga........	Rev. H. T. Gregory.	300
	Christ	Port Henry..... }	Rev. W. R. Wood-	350
	Emmanuel.....	Mineville........ }	bridge..........	
	St. John's	Essex............	Rev. W. N. Irish...	200
	St. James'. ...	Ausable Forks....	Rev. Geo. H. Norton	250
	St. Paul's...	Keeseville........	Rev. J. W. Gill....	300
Clinton.	Christ.	Rouse's Point ... }	Rev. W. D. U.	250
	St. John's......	Champlain ..... }	Shearman	
	St. Peter's....	Ellenburgh ...... }	Rev. S. M. Rogers..	200
	St. Paul's	Ellenburgh Center }		
	St. John's.....	Salmon River.....		
				$3,975

CONVOCATION OF THE SUSQUEHANNA.

County.	Church.	Place.	Missionary.	Stipend.
Delaware......	St. Paul's......	Franklin	....	$300
		Bloomville........	Rev. J. A. Farrar ..	100
	Christ.	Deposit....	Rev. F. S. Fisher...	300
	St. Paul's	Sidney...... .. }	Rev. F. S. Griffin...	300
Otsego	Christ....	W. Burlington.. }		
	St. James'	Oneonta. .... }	Rev. E. A. Hartmann	300
	Immanuel....	Otego .... }		50
	Holy Spirit.....	Schenevus.... ... }	Rev. A. S. Ashley..	300
	St. John's......	Portlandville..... }		
	Christ........	Gilbertaville .. }	Rev. David McDon-	125
		Maple Grove... }	ald	100
	St. Paul's..	East Springfield.. }	Rev. John Prout...	200
	St. Mary's.....	Springfield Centre }		
	St. Timothy's ..	Westford	Rev. J. E. Hall.....	
	Grace..........	Stamford.	Rev.A. T. DeLearsy.	200
Schoharie ...	St. Luke's.....	Middleburgh.......	....	50
				$2,325

CONVOCATION OF OGDENSBURGH.

County.	Church.	Place.	Missionary.	Stipend.
Essex.........	Good Shepherd.	Bloomingdale.....		
Franklin	St. John's......	St. Regis Lake...	Rev. W. H. Larom .	$100
	St. Luke's	Saranac Lake		
		Santa Clara......		
		St. Regis Falls....	Rev. Phineas Duryea	200
		Paul Smith's Sta.		
	St. Mark's.....	West Bangor. ...	....	
	St. Peter's	Brushton.... ...		60
St. Lawrence..	St. Thomas'....	Lawrenceville....	....	340
Franklin	St. James'.	Hogansburgh.....		
St. Lawrence..	St. John's......	Massena...........	Rev. H. McDougall.	350
	Grace	Louisville Land'g.		
	Grace	Norfolk		
	St. Andrew's...	Norwood	... .	300
	St. Paul's......	Waddington......	Rev. Angus C. Mac-	250
	St. Luke's......	Lisbon.....	donald...... ...	150
	Christ.........	Morristown.....	Rev. J. T. Zorn	300
	Trinity.......	Gouverneur.... ...	Rev. J. A. Dickson .	250
	Trinity Chapel.	Morley..........	Rev. R. G. Hamilton	200
				$2,500

SUMMARY.

	Stations.	Missionaries.	Stipends.
Convocation of Albany....	23	18	$3,800 00
Convocation of Troy...........................	31	16	3,975 00
Convocation of the Susquehanna...................	16	9	2,325 00
Convocation of Ogdensburgh........	19	7	2,500 00
	89	45	$12,600 00

Mr. Selden E. Marvin, Treasurer, read the

REPORT OF THE TREASURER OF THE BOARD OF MISSIONS FROM NO-VEMBER 14, 1889, to NOVEMBER 11, 1890.

RECEIPTS.
Convocation of Albany.

The Cathedral of All Saints.	$1,200 00
St. Peter's, Albany............	1,000 12
St. Paul's, Albany..	364 64
Holy Innocents, Albany...................	50 00
Grace, Albany...	51 00
Trinity, Albany..	20 00
St. Margaret's, Menands...........	
Trinity, Rensselaerville......................................	32 99
St. John's, Cohoes.......	203 00
Trinity, West Troy..... .... ,................................	41 01
St. Andrew's, West Troy	5 00
St. Mark's, Green Island.......................	63 08
Christ, Hudson.....	100 00
All Saints', Hudson	12 00

Evangelist, Stockport.	$8 78
St. Barnabas', Stottville	40 26
St. Paul's, Kinderhook	75 41
Trinity, Claverack	20 00
Our Saviour, Lebanon Springs	20 00
St. Luke's, Clermont.................	10 00
St. Luke's, Chatham....	
St. Mark's, Philmont...	3 89
Christ, Coxsackie...	5 00
St. Luke's, Catskill.............	150 00
Trinity, Athens	13 00
St. Paul's, Oak Hill	5 19
Christ, Greenville............................	7 60
Trinity, Ashland..	
Calvary, Cairo.....	1 48
Gloria Dei, Palenville...	14 10
St. George's, Schenectady...	125 00
Christ, Schenectady	11 26
Christ, Duanesburgh...	56 21
St. Ann's, Amsterdam	34 71
Zion, Fonda......	14 00
Holy Cross, Fort Plain............. ....'	12 67
Good Shepherd, Canajoharie	10 27
St. Columba's, St. Johnsville	5 23
St John's, Johnstown	38 50
Christ, Gloversville.	25 00
Emmanuel, Little Falls........	60 25
Christ, Herkimer.............	51 35
St. Augustine, Ilion	30 00
Grace, Mohawk........................	2 60
St. Alban's, Frankfort.......	8 75
Memorial, Middleville...................	
Trinity, Fairfield........................	
St. James', Rossman's Mills....	6 15
	$4,004 45

Convocation of Troy.

St. Paul's, Troy....	$750 00
St. John's. Troy...	600 00
Christ, Troy	250 00
Holy Cross, Troy.......	195 45
St. Barnabas', Troy.........	61 29
St. Luke's, Troy	4 30
Ascension, Troy	27 00
Trinity, Lansingburgh..	195 00
St. Mark's, Hoosick Falls...	200 00
Trinity, Schaghticoke...	20 00
Messiah, Greenbush	30 00
Epiphany, East Albany.	11 13
St. Giles', Castleton	
Christ, Ballston Spa	150 16
St. Luke's, Mechanicville..	20 00

St. John's, Stillwater...........................	$10 00
Grace, Waterford.............................	59 65
St. Paul's, Charlton..........................	10 00
Calvary, Burnt Hills.........................	25 00
Bethesda, Saratoga Springs....................	200 00
St. Stephen's, Schuylerville..................	
St. John's, East Line........................	
Grace, Jonesville...........................	10 00
St. John's, Conklingville....................	5 50
Zion, Sandy Hill............................	16 81
Trinity, Granville...........................	25 00
Mission, North Granville.....................	10 00
St. James', Fort Edward......................	12 77
St. Paul's, Salem............................	100 88
St. Luke's, Cambridge........................	224 00
St. Paul's, Greenwich........................	3 91
Trinity, Whitehall...........................	87 00
Messiah, Glens Falls.........................	150 00
St. James', Caldwell.........................	
Holy Cross, Warrensburgh.....................	50 00
St. Mary's, Luzerne..........................	22 30
Good Shepherd, Chestertown...................	15 00
St. Sacrament, Bolton........................	8 25
Church of the Cross, Ticonderoga.............	29 90
Christ, Port Henry...........................	21 95
Emmanuel. Mineville.........................	5 00
St. John's, Essex............................	30 00
St. Paul's, Keeseville.......................	15 00
St. James', Ausable Forks....................	16 78
Good Shepherd, Elizabethtown.................	
Keene Valley Mission.........................	20 00
Trinity, Plattsburgh.........................	49 19
Christ, Rouse's Point........................	20 00
St. John's, Champlain........................	20 00
St. Peter's, Ellenburgh......................	10 00
	$3,747 72

Convocation of the Susquehanna.

Christ, Cooperstown..........................	151 00
Grace, Cherry Valley.........................	75 00
Zion, Morris................................	60 00
St. Matthew's, Unadilla......................	50 00
Christ, Gilbertsville........................	20 00
St. James', Oneonta..........................	42 00
Emmanuel, Otego.............................	5 00
St. John's, Richfield Springs................	50 00
Christ, West Burlington......................	
St. Paul's, East Springfield.................	16 50
St. Mary's, Springfield Centre...............	12 00
Holy Spirit, Schenevus.......................	8 00
St. Stephen's, Maple Grove...................	1 00
Mission, Edmeston...........................	3 50

13

St. John's, Delhi...	$100 00
St. Peter's, Hobart.	18 00
Christ, Walton	30 00
St. Paul's, Franklin	22 42
Christ, Deposit.	10 41
Grace, Stamford ...	21 50
St. Paul's, Sidney	12 44
St. Andrew's, Schoharie	31 61
	$740 38

Convocation of Ogdensburgh.

St. John's, Ogdensburgh	500 00
Trinity, Potsdam	663 00
St. Paul's, Waddington	14 00
Christ, Morristown	75 00
Grace, Canton..	4 00
Grace, Norfolk....	3 09
Trinity, Gouverneur.	53 85
St. John's, Massena.	50 00
St. Luke's, Lisbon.	6 00
Zion, Colton	20 65
Trinity Chapel, Morley	11 00
St. Thomas', Lawrenceville	
St. Mark's, Malone.	75 00
St. Peter's, Brushton	6 50
St. Mark's, West Bangor.	
St. James', Hogansburgh.	25 00
St. John's, St. Regis Lake } St. Luke's, Saranac Lake }	85 00
Grace, Louisville Landing ..	
St. Andrew's, Norwood.	2 45
	$1,544 04

Sundry Sources.

Offertories at Convention	110 23
Interest, sundry notes.	38 21
Interest, De Witt Fund.	300 00
Interest, Parochial Fund...	40 00
Interest, Miss Austin Fund.	1,430 00
Interest, Mrs. Green Fund.	210 41
Interest, Tibbits Fund.	120 00
Interest, Vandenburgh bond and mortgage	30 00
Interest, Goss bond.	18 00
Interest, Cornell Steamboat bond	70 00
Interest, Troy and West Troy Bridge bond.	85 00
S. K. T.	40 00
David H. Gay	5 00
Mrs. E. W. N. Wood.	50 00
Friend of Missions.	50 00
Special for Itinerant Missionary	100 00
Balance, Stipend Harrisona returned	42 00
Balance, St. John's Clergy house.	13 03
	$2,701 88

Special.

St. John's, Troy, to St. Luke's, Troy $112 50

Total......... .... $12,850 97

Balance on hand......... .... $914 66

DISBURSEMENTS.

November 14, 1889, balance due Treasurer......... .... $346 48

STIPENDS PAID.

Convocation of Albany.

Rensselaerville.....	Rev. S. C. Thompson	$150 00
Palenville..........	Rev. William Charles Grubbe.....	250 00
Ashland.	Rev. S. T. Brewster	20 83
Coxsackie...... ...	Rev. L. H. Schubert............................	300 00
Hudson & Claverack	Rev. Elmer P. Miller........................ ..	308 33
Clermont..........	Rev. M. E. Wilson.............................	75 00
Philmont...	Rev. Howard McDougall........................	156 25
Chatham	Rev. Isaac Peck...............................	100 00
Lebanon Springs...	Rev. W. C. Stewart.............	116 66
Lebanon Springs...	Rev. A. T. De Learsy........................	75 00
Canajoharie	Rev. John N. Marvin.......................	250 00
Fonda......... ...	Rev. C. C. Edmunds	300 00
Gloversville........	Rev. C. P. A. Burnett	600 00
Mohawk	Rev. M. O. Smith	100 00
Mohawk...... ..	Rev. Alfred Taylor	66 66
Ilion	Rev. William M. Cook..	200 00
Middleville	Rev. W. H. C. Lylburn.....................	400 00
	Rev. Edward Selkirk....	10 00

$3,478 73

Convocation of Troy.

Schaghticoke.......	Rev. William B. Bolmer...................	$291 66
Schaghticoke.......	Rev. T. Dickinson	58 34
Castleton..	Rev. William R. Webb..	187 50
Mechanicville......	Rev. W. G. W. Lewis...........................	225 00
Charlton	Rev. H. R. Timlow.................	100 00
Cambridge	Rev. F. H. T. Horsfield....................	100 00
Granville..........	Rev. William C. Prout.........................	200 00
Salem..............	Rev. John H. Houghton	100 00
Luzerne...........	Rev. C. J. Whipple........................	300 00
Bolton	Rev. C. T. Blanchet	100 00
Chestertown.......	Rev. Alfred Taylor............................	200 00
Chestertown........	Rev. Nassau W. Stephens	100 00
Ticonderoga..... ..	Rev. Henry T. Gregory...	300 00
Port Henry........	Rev. William A. Woodbridge.............. ...	350 00
Keeseville.	Rev. J. William Gill	300 00
Ausable Forks......	Rev. George H. Norton.	152 77
Essex..	Rev. William N. Irish	200 00

Rouse's Point and Champlain .... }	Rev. W. D. U. Shearman....	$250	00
Ellenburgh........	Rev. Silas M. Rogers..........................	200	00
East Albany........	Rev. Thomas White...........................	28	00
		$3,743	27

Convocation of the Susquehanna.

Franklin....	Rev. S. B. Moore..............................	$304	25
Bloomville........	Rev. J. H. Farrar	100	00
Deposit	Rev. S. T. Street.............................	75	00
Deposit...........	C. Onderdonk, Tr...............	75	00
Deposit.......	Rev. F. S. Fisher.......	150	00
Stamford	Rev. A. T. De Learsy.........................	66	67
Oneonta......... ..	Rev. E. A. Hartmann..........................	300	00
Otego.............	Rev. E. A. Hartmann.	45	84
Otego.............	Rev. A. S. Ashley	12	50
Schenevus........	Rev. Robert G. Osborne.....	247	90
Schenevus	Rev. A. S. Ashley......................	58	33
Gilbertsville........	Rev. Horatio Gates............................	50	00
Gilbertsville........	Rev. David McDonald..........	31	25
Maple Grove........	Rev. Horatio Gates	25	00
Maple Grove........	Rev. David McDonald.,.....................	25	00
Sidney.	Rev. Robert N. Parke, D. D....	38	34
West Burlington ...	Rev. Fred. S. Griffin..., ...	100	00
East Springfield...	Rev. John Prout	200	00
		$1,900	08

Convocation of Ogdensburgh.

Waddington.	Rev. A. C. Macdonald.......	$400	00
Massena	Rev. T. Dickinson...	175	00
Massena.	Rev Howard McDougall....	131	25
Morristown........	Rev. Joseph T. Zorn...............	300	00
Gouverneur........	Rev. J. A. Dickson............................	250	00
Morley.............	Rev. R. G. Hamilton....	200	00
Norfolk............	Rev. H. M. P. Pearse	50	00
Saranac Lake......	Rev. W. H. Larom.....	100	00
Brushton	Rev. Nassau William Stephens..................	198	33
Santa Clara........	Rev. Phineas Duryea.	50	00
		$1,854	58

Special.

St. Luke's, Troy................... ....:...........	$112	50

Sundry Purposes.

Ira A. Darling	$60	00
Post-office envelopes..........................	19	62
Printing..........................	12	63
Rev. T. A. Snyder, account Miss Austin Fund........	75	00
Rev. W. R. Woodbridge, Secretary................................	8	42
Rev. C. P. A. Burnett, De Witt Fund.............................	300	00

Mr. Hughes for special services, Lebanon Springs, by order of the
 Board, November 10, 1890 .... $25 00
Balance on hand............... . ... 914 66

Total $12,850 97

RECAPITULATION.

Receipts.

Offertories at Convention... ... $110 32
DeWitt Fund...... .... 300 00
Itinerant Missionary.... .... 100 00
Income securities................. .... 1,991 62
Sundry sources. 200 08
For special purposes... .... 112 50
Convocation of Albany................................. $4,004 45
Convocation of Troy........ .... 3,747 72
Convocation of the Susquehanna 740 38
Convocation of Ogdensburgh............................. 1,544 04
 ———————— 10,086 59

 $12,850 97

Balance on hand, November 11, 1890*............................... $914 66

Disbursements.

Balance due Treasurer..... .... $346 48
 Stipends.
Convocation of Albany................................. $3,478 73
Convocation of Troy......... .... 3,743 27
Convocation of the Susquehanna 1,900 08
Convocation of Ogdensburgh....................... 1,854 58
 ———————— 10,976 66
Sundry purposes..................... .... 175 67
Special purposes.......... .... 112 50
DeWitt Fund.............. .... 300 00
Special appropriation to Mr. Hughes............................ 25 00
Balance on hand.......... .... 914 66

 $12,850 97

In December last, I received from Isaac Pruyn and Walton Van Loan, executors
of the estate of Charlotte Austin, deceased, the sum of $3,060.53, being the balance
of the amount of the property from her estate to the Board of Missions, and making
the total sum so received $29,069.53.

---

* Since received: St. Luke's, Chatham, $5.00; St. Peter's, Hobart, $17.00; making total
balance $936.66.

The Permanent Fund represents the following amounts received from time to time:

Misses Austin	$1,500 00
Elizabeth Sherers	750 00
Mrs. DeWitt	5,000 00
Diocese of New York	2,000 00
Diocese of New York, Parochial Fund	1,000 00
Dr. William Tibbits	2,000 00
L. H. Sears	400 00
Mrs. Hannibal Green	4,750 00
Miss Charlotte Austin	29,069 53
Total	$46,469 53

The Board holds in trust $19,000, received from the executors of Charlotte Austin, deceased, the income from which is to be paid, one-third each, to the Rectors, Wardens and Vestrymen of the following Parishes: Calvary Church, Cairo: Christ Church, Greenville; St. Paul's Church, Oak Hill. ¡

The following amounts from the income of the fund have been paid; to Calvary Church, Cairo, $336.68 ; Christ Church, Greenville, $336.68; St. Paul's Church, Oak Hill, $336.64. Total, $1,010.

I have also paid the Rector of St. Paul's Church, Oak Hill, $75 income from the $1,500 in Permanent Fund, received from the Misses Austin, deceased.

The Board also holds in trust $2,000 in bonds of the Rensselaer and Saratoga Railroad' Company, the income from which is to be paid, one-half each, to St. Luke's Church, Mechanicville, and St. John's Church, Stillwater.

I have received from St. Peter's Church, Albany, for Christ Church, Gloversville, $36.14, Bethesda Church, Saratoga Springs, for Christ Church, Gloversville, $13.10, and remitted the same to the Rector of Christ Church, Gloversville.

SELDEN E. MARVIN,
Treasurer.

The Rev. Charles S. Olmsted presented and read the

REPORT OF THE COMMITTEE ON DIOCESAN MISSIONS.

We are all more or less familiar with the details of our Diocesan Missionary work, and it is not necessary for your Committee, therefore, to dwell upon them here. Rather remembering Cousin's words: "Shew me a beautiful action, and I will imagine one still more beautiful," your Committee rise from their inspection of the reports of the Secretary and the Treasurer of the Board of Missions, not only with gladness and ^dmiration at the amount of work accomplished the past year in this Diocese through the agency of the Board and by the energy and zeal of its Missionaries, but with hearts full of longing for the furtherance of the Gospel still more throughout the vast sphere of our labours.

As the shadows which grave-stones under the sunlight cast upon the grass vanish when the great shadow of the Church falls athwart them, so all these memories of work done, precious as they are, and evermore laid up in God's all-present mind, may well melt into the living and abiding need that in its persuasiveness sheds its meaning upon our souls. Shall not the future be as the past, and more abundant in holy works? Dear brethren, who this day have joined yourselves to the Eucharistic oblation, and through it have tasted of the bitterness of the Cross, ye who have pleaded and applied here to yourselves the passion and death of Jesus, and have known what it is to dwell in Him, and have Him dwell in you, in the virtue and power of that Holy Communion, we ask you, shall we not go forth with renewed earnestness to our fields and vineyards?

We might set before you methods by which you could win happier and richer harvests, but we prefer to lay stress chiefly upon the spirit in which men ought to work. Where there is the true spirit of love and devotion to Jesus, and to the souls for whom He died, this, whether with or without methods, whether with methods in themselves excellent, or with methods defective, and destitute of the highest prudence, will find free course and glory for the Word of God.

While we do not for a moment undervalue organization, nor cast any reflection upon the use of guilds and societies, we do think that there is evermore a danger lurking among us of substituting these things for the real spirit by which only these things can be rightly used, and by which, without any of these things, many victories over the world have been secured to faith.

Our deep desire at this time is to lay stress upon the need we all have of single-hearted and entire devotion to Christ and the Church. To this end, we would say to every member of the Board of Missions, to every Missionary of the Diocese, to every Priest, and to every layman, never undertake any good work simply with reference to some good end at the time to be effected, but always with reference, first of all, to the good in general. This is a deep principle, which must be borne in mind if our labours are to redound to the real honour of religion. If the isolated Missionary is tempted to say within himself, I have nothing to do with other men's work, I must build up my own Mission, and proceeds to attach to himself the affection of the people of his cure, while he leaves them liable to fall away if they remove, or he depart from that particular Mission, then it may be feared that while his motive has not been a selfish or an evil one, it has been a dim and narrow one.

What is a Parish but a thread which with other threads makes up the texture of the Diocese, and what is the Diocese but a part of a system of which other Dioceses are inherent portions. We are to labour for the great end of a general good, to look always for results which only many days can ripen, to do a great many things without any seeming purpose, to sow where others only can reap, to be content to see failure, knowing that out of failure many of the best successes can issue. Pilgrim and Crusader often picked out their path to Jerusalem by the bleached bones of multitudes, who on the way thither had fallen a prey to fatigue, to pestilence, to hunger. to the alien sword; and we ourselves enter into other men's labours, who asked life, but receive the long life of a better world.

And, if in this presence we may, we exhort you to more fervent faith in the promises of God. Remember them, "Who through faith subdued kingdoms, wrought righteousness, obtained promises, stopped the mouths of lions, quenched the violence of fire, escaped the edge of the sword, out of weakness were made strong, waxed valiant in fight, turned to flight the armies of the aliens."

Our hearts go out to the dear and faithful Priests, who in cold and heat, stand fast in the path of their often difficult duties, sometimes without much sympathy, and sometimes in much privation. We know it costs more pains and prudence, more executive ability and insight to build up a Church in a village than to carry on a great town Parish, for in the one case, the Priest has to be his own adviser and his own Curate, at times his own sexton and his own choir, while in the other, scores of rich and strong laymen are at hand to help, and Assistant Ministers and visitors divide the exhausting duties of the house of God. If this Committee can, by any word spoken this evening, wing an arrow of true and loving sympathy, which shall speed into the hearts of our Diocesan Missionaries, and find lodgement there, it will humbly thank God. But with sympathy, it begs leave to repeat, "Have faith in God." He

is with us in all our toils and painful cares. "And this is the promise which He hath promised us," when all is over, "even eternal life."

It is the most difficult as it is the most important lesson in life to learn that each one is born in the best possible time for him, and that he is to work out his salvation under those conditions into which he is thrown. We keep saying: "If we had lived in the days of the fathers," when we live in a day that Divine Wisdom has ordained for us to live in. We forget, therefore, the very precious opportunities now in our power. These difficulties about us are the very mould that is to fashion us after the Image of eternal beauty. Let not the Missionary then say: "O! if I had my brother's Parish, I would do what I can never do here," or "if I had my brother's choir, I would make my services so attractive that crowds would come to them," but let him say, "it is perhaps all work uphillward here, but I must make the most of it. Gregory Thaumaturgus found seventeen Christians in Neo Cæsarea, and left there seventeen heathen. Let me strive with all my special trials like a man, yes, like a man of God, and if I labour and do not faint, in due season, here or there, I shall reap."

It may not be sufficiently realized how many scattered children the Church has in townships where we have no Missions, nor even occasional services. These ought to be visited, registered, supplied with Prayer Books and other Church literature, brought to the Sacrament, and often made nuclei for new Missions and Parishes.

Were the Diocese thoroughly inspected for the purpose of discovering the Church's children in waste places, no doubt several hundreds would be found, and many of them induced to labour for the Church, where, as it is, their money and influence are diverted to the use of the denominations.

It is impossible, with limited time and without money for the purpose, for the settled Clergy to set out on journeys of discovery through large tracts of country. It might be thought a waste of money to employ persons for this purpose. But it seems to this Committee that in the long run, the Diocese would be well repaid, if at once a careful inspection of its waste places could be made by persons in Holy Orders, or even by well-instructed laymen, and a census taken of all baptized and confirmed persons, and of others formerly attached to the Church, and so a basis laid for Mission work in future years. While it would be a mistake to build Churches, or even organize Missions in places where there might be a half dozen Church people, there could be no possible mistake in visiting such places, and from time to time, preaching and administering the Sacrament. We might not see remarkable results, but in other years and under other skies, the Church would enjoy the increase.

The Committee, therefore, recommend the adoption of the following resolution :

Resolved. That the Bishop of the Diocese be requested to appoint a Committee of five persons, which, on conference with the Committee on Archdeaconries, shall consider and report to this Convention on Wednesday, some scheme whereby every child of the Church in this Diocese may be brought under some direct Church influence, and be duly registered in our list of the faithful.

CHARLES S. OLMSTED,
Chairman, Committee.

The resolutions presented in the Report of the Board of Missions, being under discussion, a motion was made by the Rev. Walter C. Stewart, to amend the first resolution by inserting the words $12,000 in place of $10,000, which failed to pass. Missionary addresses were made by the Rev. Messrs. Charles C. Edmunds, Jr., Sheldon M. Griswold and R. J. Adler, of this Diocese, and the Rev. Frederick R. Graves, of the Missionary Jurisdiction of China.

The resolutions were adopted as recommended in the Report of the Board of Missions, and in the Report of the Committee on Diocesan Missions.

The Right Rev. President appointed as the Committee to confer with the Committee on the Duties and Powers of Archdeacons, the Rev. Charles S. Olmsted, the Rev. Walter C. Stewart, the Rev. R. M. Kirby, D. D., Mr. Benjamin F. Hinman and Mr. William L. Du-Bois.

On motion of the Secretary of the Convention, it was

Resolved, That the election of the Board of Missions, and the other business of the Convention in regard to the Missions of the Diocese, be made the order of the day for two o'clock in the afternoon of to-morrow; and that the Convention do now adjourn to meet in the Gymnasium of St. Agnes' School at half-past ten o'clock to-morrow morning.

The Convention adjourned till Wednesday morning.

SECOND DAY.

WEDNESDAY MORNING, NOVEMBER 12, 7:45 O'CLOCK.

The Bishop of the Diocese ordained the Rev. Frederick Stirling Griffin, Deacon, to the Holy Order of Priests, the Rev. R. N. Parke, D. D., the Rev. C. S. Olmsted, the Rev. F. B. Reazor, the Rev. T. B. Fulcher, the Rev. W. C. Stewart and the Rev. C. H. Hatheway joining with the Bishop in the laying on of hands.

The Holy Communion was administered in the Cathedral, the Bishop of the Diocese celebrating, assisted by the Rev. Canon Hatheway.

TEN O'CLOCK.

Morning Prayer was said in the Cathedral by the Dean.

The Right Rev. President took the chair and called the Convention to order in the Gymnasium of St. Agnes' School.

The minutes of the previous day were read and adopted.

The names of the Clergy and Lay Deputies not present on the first day were called by the Secretary, and three Clergymen and Lay Deputies representing six Parishes were found to be present.

The Rev. Dean Robbins presented and read

REPORT NO. 1, OF THE COMMITTEE ON THE CONSTITUTION AND CANONS.

The Committee on Constitution and Canons respectfully report:

(1.) That in their judgment it is expedient that the report of the Special Committee "Upon the Duties and Powers of the Archdeacons and the Archdeaconries and

14

Their Relation to the Board of Missions," which was referred to them, be recommitted to be reported upon at the next Convention.

(2.) That the communication from the Secretary of the General Convention advising the adoption of certain amendments to the Canons relating to the Fund for Aged and Infirm Clergy, be referred to the Trustees of said Fund for their consideration, and that they shall report any action which they may deem expedient in the matter to this Convention.

Your Committee is moved to this action by the wording of Canon XVII, *sec.* 2:

"It shall be the duty of the Trustees to receive applications for relief, and to administer it in accordance with such rules and regulations as they, with the approbation of the Convention, may from time to time adopt."

This would seem to imply that methods of disbursement of moneys should be left in the first instance to the Trustees of the Fund.

(3.) That the motion of the Rev. F. S. Sill, to amend Canon XIV, *sec.* 6, be rejected, pending the action of Convention concerning the whole of Canon XIV, which deals with the subject of Convocation, its duties and officers.

W. L. ROBBINS,	J. W. STEWART,
Secretary.	*Chairman.*

On motion of the Rev. J. D. Morrison, D. D., LL. D., it was

Resolved, That the Committee on the Constitution and Canons be requested to report to this House the proposed Canon on the Clergy Reserve Fund for its consideration.

On motion of the Rev. R. J. Adler, the following amendments to Canon XIV, having been duly presented and referred to the Committee on the Constitution and Canons, and by them reported to the Convention, were adopted.

Resolved, That Canon XIV be amended by striking out, in its title, the word "Convocations," and inserting in place thereof the word "Archdeaconries."

Resolved, That wherever the word "Convocation," or "Convocations," or "Convocational" occurs in Canon XIV it be changed to "Archdeaconry," or "Archdeaconries," or "Archdeaconal," as the case may be, viz.:

Sec. 2, line 3, and sec. 5, line 1, "Archdeaconries:" sec. 2, line 4; sec. 5, lines 2 4, 5 and 7; sec. 6, lines 1, 2, 3, 4, 6, 10, 15 and 17; sec. 7, lines 1, 2, 3, 5, 8 and 11, "Archdeaconry;" and sec. 7, line 14, "Archdeaconal."

The Right Rev. the Bishop of the Diocese announced his concurrence in the amendment.

The Rev. J. Livingston Reese, D. D., presented and read the

REPORT OF THE STANDING COMMITTEE.

The Standing Committee organized December 14, 1889, by electing the Rev. William Payne, D. D., President, and the Rev. J. L. Reese, Secretary.

During the year they have held six meetings.

They have recommended to be admitted candidates for Holy Orders:

W. B. Noble.

William Anderson Stirling.

Marvin Hill Dana.

Edward Tourtellot Carroll.

Frank N. Bouck.
John Montgomery Rich.
Eugene Griggs.
They have recommended for ordination to the Diaconate:
Frederick Stirling Griffin.
Asa Sprague Ashley.
They have recommended for ordination to the Priesthood:
The Rev. Elmer P. Miller.
The Rev. Walter Charles Stewart.
The Rev. Robert Morris Kemp.
The Rev. Frederick Stirling Griffin.
They have given their canonical assent to the consecration of the Rev. William Ford Nicholls, D. D., Assistant Bishop elect of California, and to the consecration of the Rev. Edward R. Atwill, D. D., Bishop elect of West Missouri.

At a meeting held January 4, 1890, at St. Peter's Rectory, Albany, the Bishop announced to the Committee the death of the Hon. Henry R. Pierson, who for ten years had been a member of the Standing Committee. A Minute of his death was entered upon the records of the Committee, and the Hon. John H. Van Antwerp of Albany, was elected to fill the vacancy.

At a meeting held April 14, 1890, the following preamble and resolutions were adopted:

WHEREAS, The Committee of the Diocese of New York have offered the sum of $25,000 in cash as an equivalent for the sum of $28,955 and interest, agreed upon by the Committee of Conference and reported to the Convention of the Diocese of New York, held September 25, 1884; therefore

Resolved, That the Standing Committee acting with the Bishop, advise the Committee of Conference with the Diocese of New York to accept the offer of $25,000 in cash as an equivalent for the claims of this Diocese upon the Diocese of New York for the increase of the Episcopal Fund.

Resolved, That the Standing Committee, acting with the Bishop, take the responsibility of accepting for the Convention of this Diocese the sum of $25,000 as an equivalent for all claims of this Diocese upon the Diocese of New York for the increase of its Episcopal Fund.

ALBANY, *November* 11, 1890.   WILLIAM PAYNE,
J. LIVINGSTON REESE, *Secretary.*   *President.*

Mr. Selden E. Marvin, Treasurer of the Diocese, presented a supplement to the

REPORT OF THE TREASURER OF THE DIOCESE.

I have received from the Treasurer of the Diocese of New York the sum of twenty-five thousand dollars ($25,000), and have given him a receipt, of which the following is a copy:

ALBANY, *November* 13, 1890.

Received from James Pott, Treasurer of the Diocese of New York, the sum of $25,000, this sum being in full of all claims of the Diocese of New York against the Diocese of New York in respect to its Episcopal Fund, it being understood that upon the payment of this money ($25,000) to the Treasurer of the Diocese of Albany, its Convention, now in session, will give a full return to the Diocese of New York of any and all claims touching the Episcopal Fund of the Diocese of Albany.

SELDEN E. MARVIN,
Treasurer.

The Rev. J. Livingston Reese, D. D., presented and read the

REPORT OF THE COMMITTEE TO CONFER WITH A COMMITTEE OF THE DIOCESE OF NEW YORK IN REGARD TO THE EPISCOPAL FUND.

The Committee of Conference with the Diocese of New York in relation to the claims of the Diocese of Albany for an increase of its Episcopal Fund, respectfully report:

The Committee have held one meeting during the year, in the month of April, with a full attendance of its members. There was presented at this meeting the proposition from the Committee of the Diocese of New York, to settle all claims by the immediate payment of $25,000.

In connection with this proposition there were also presented the resolutions of the Standing Committee, acting with the Bishop, advising the acceptance of this offer, and taking the responsibility of acting for the Convention of the Diocese.

Your Committee had no hesitation in accepting at once the advice of the Bishop and the Standing Committee. The offer of the Committee of the Diocese of New York was made in good faith and with the best of feeling for the Diocese of Albany. They had given much time and patient labour to the work assigned them by their Convention. By most faithful and persistent efforts they had succeeded in securing pledges to an amount beyond which they found it impossible to go. Your Committee realized that prompt and decided action was necessary, or the amount already subscribed would be imperilled, and the work of these many years be brought to naught.

The following preamble and resolution were therefore unanimously adopted; a copy was forwarded to the Right Rev. Chairman of the New York Committee:

WHEREAS, The Bishop and the Standing Committee of the Diocese of Albany have advised the Committee of Conference to accept the offer made by the Committee of the Diocese of New York of $25,000 in cash, as an equivalent for the claims of the Diocese of Albany for its Episcopal Fund, and

WHEREAS, The Bishop and the Standing Committee have assumed the responsibility of pledging the Convention of this Diocese to the acceptance of this offer, therefore

Resolved, That this Committee accept the offer of $25,000 in cash, as an equivalent for all claims of the Diocese of Albany upon the Diocese of New York for the increase of the Episcopal Fund.

We further report that the Treasurer of the Diocese of New York has paid to the Treasurer of the Diocese of Albany this sum in full.

The Diocese therefore begins its new Convention year with this large addition to its Episcopal Fund, the income from which will enable the Treasurer to meet promptly the salary of the Bishop, and to cover any indebtedness already incurred.

The Committee also submit with this report the following letter from the Bishop of New York.

DIOCESAN HOUSE, 29 LAFAYETTE PLACE,
NEW YORK, *November* 11, 1890.

MY DEAR DR. REESE.— With this I beg to hand to you as Chairman of the Committee of the Diocese of Albany in the matter of its claims upon the Diocese of New York with reference to the Episcopal Fund of this Diocese, a check for twenty-five thousand dollars ($25,000), being the amount named by your Committee, on behalf of the authorities of the Diocese of Albany, as that which would be accepted as payment in full for all demands.

Personally, I should have been glad if a settlement of this matter could have been reached at an earlier date, and more precisely in accord with the views of those whom you represent. As it is, I am profoundly thankful that the matter has been brought to a conclusion upon terms which do not considerably depart from your original expectations, and with such kindly feeling, as I have reason to hope and believe, on the part of those to whom this payment is now made.

The conclusion of this long-delayed business is largely due to the Rev Clarence Buel, a son of that part of the original Diocese of New York which is now the Diocese of Albany (now, I regret to say, no longer connected with either), and to my valued friend, Mr. James Pott, to whose patient and undiscouraged perseverance, in this business, I am personally greatly indebted. I have designated him to be the bearer of this communication and with it of my affectionate salutations to the Convention of the Diocese of Albany, to its Bishop, my valued brother in the Episcopate, whose personal cares and anxieties it may help, I hope, a little to lighten, and to you, dear friend of many years, whose I am always, with affectionate regard and respect.

HENRY C. POTTER,
Bishop of New York

The Rev. J. LIVINGSTON REESE, D. D., *Chairman, etc.*

The Committee offer the following preambles and resolutions:

WHEREAS, After protracted negotiations between the Convention of the Diocese of Albany and the Convention of the Diocese of New York, through their respective Committees, an arrangement has been made by which the Diocese of Albany has agreed to receive the sum of twenty-five thousand dollars ($25,000), in full of all claim of said Diocese against the Diocese of New York, in respect to its Episcopal Fund; and

WHEREAS, James Pott, Esq., as Treasurer of the Convention of the Diocese of New York, and on behalf of and by authority of said Convention, has now paid to the Treasurer of the Convention of the Diocese of Albany the sum of twenty-five thousand dollars ($25,000);

Resolved, That the Convention of the Diocese of Albany, at present in session, hereby acknowledges the receipt of said sum in full satisfaction for all claims, moral, equitable or otherwise, on the part of the Diocese of Albany, in respect to its Episcopal Fund, against the Diocese of New York, or against any fund or funds of the said Diocese, or against any person who may have under authority of the Diocese of New York collected funds for the said purpose, and of all and every claim of the Diocese of Albany against Trinity Church, New York.

Resolved, That the Secretary of the Convention be authorized to certify these resolutions to the Diocese of New York, and to Trinity Church, New York.

Resolved, That this Convention expresses its grateful obligations to the kind offices and the sincere personal interest of the Bishop of New York in advocating the claims of this Diocese, and in response to his affectionate salutation assures him of the esteem and love of the Clergy and Laity of the Diocese of Albany, whose cause from the first he has so unselfishly and generously maintained.

Resolved, That the thanks of this Convention be returned to the Committee of the Diocese of New York, and especially to the Rev. Clarence Buel and to James Pott, Esq., for their energy and perseverance in completing the work intrusted to them by the Convention of their Diocese.

Resolved, That this Committee be discharged.

J. LIVINGSTON REESE,
J. IRELAND TUCKER,
J. H. VAN ANTWERP,
ERASTUS CORNING,
CHARLES E. PATTERSON.

ALBANY, *November* 12, 1890.

The resolutions presented in the Report of the Committee to Confer with a Committee of the Diocese of New York in regard to the Episcopal Fund were adopted.

On motion of the Rev. J. Livingston Reese, D. D., it was

Resolved, That this Convention welcomes the presence of James Pott, Esq., Treasurer of the Convention of the Diocese of New York, and invites him to a seat in this body.

Mr. James Pott appeared, was presented to the Convention and took a seat on the floor of the house.

On motion of the Rev. J. Livingston Reese, D. D., it was

Resolved, That the Treasurer of the Diocese be instructed by this Convention to hand to the Treasurer of the Episcopal Fund the sum of $25,000, paid him by the Treasurer of the Diocese of New York, for the increase of the Episcopal Fund.

On motion of the Rev. William M. Ogden, it was

Ordered, That the resolution in regard to increasing the salary of the Bishop, which was laid on the table yesterday, be now taken from the table. (See p. 91.)

Pending action in regard to it, the Right Rev. President called the Rev. Joseph Carey, S. T. D., to the chair, and withdrew from the Convention.

During the debate on the resolution of the Rev. Mr. Ogden, the hour for holding the annual elections having arrived, on motion of the Secretary of the Convention, it was

Resolved, That the order of the day be postponed until 12:50 P. M.

The Rev. Thaddeus A. Snively offered the following as a substitute for the resolution under discussion.

Resolved, That a Committee consisting of two Clergymen and three Laymen be appointed to consider the expediency of increasing the Bishop's salary, to report to the next Convention.

A vote being taken in regard to it, it failed of adoption by the Convention.

The following resolution, offered by Mr. George Pomeroy Keese, Lay Deputy from Christ Church, Cooperstown, and accepted by the Rev. Mr. Ogden as a substitute for the original motion, was adopted.

Resolved, That the salary of the Bishop of the Diocese be at the rate of $6,000 per annum, to take effect from the 1st day of November, 1890, and that the Committee on the Salary of the Bishop be requested to readjust the assessment on the Parishes, if in their judgment such change is required.

On motion of the Rev. Charles S. Olmsted, the vote adopting the preceding resolution was made unanimous, in so far as it provides for the increase of the salary of the Bishop.

The hour for the annual elections having arrived, the Right Rev. President, having resumed the chair, appointed the Tellers.

STANDING COMMITTEE.

Clerical Vote.	*Lay Vote.*
The Rev. Charles E. Cragg.	The Rev. Philip W. Mosher.
Mr. P. Remsen Chadwick.	Mr. S. E. Crittenden.

DEPUTIES TO THE GENERAL CONVENTION.

Clerical Vote.	*Lay Vote.*
The Rev. Charles E. Freeman.	The Rev. Frederick N. Skinner.
Mr. William H. Cookson.	Mr. Samuel M. Van Santvoord.

PROVISIONAL DEPUTIES TO GENERAL CONVENTION.

Clerical Vote.	*Lay Vote.*
The Rev. James A. Dickson.	The Rev. John N. Marvin.
Mr. John Keyes Paige.	Mr. John M. Pearson.

The rolls of the Clergy and of the Lay Deputies were called by the Secretaries.

Ballots were received for members of the Standing Committee, for one Deputy to the General Convention, and for one Provisional Deputy to the General Convention.

The Right Rev. President called the Rev. Canon Fulcher to the chair.

The Rev. Chairman announced that the polls were closed, and directed the Tellers to count the votes, for which purpose they had leave to retire.

The Convention took a recess until two o'clock.

TWO O'CLOCK IN THE AFTERNOON.

The Convention re-assembled.

The Right Rev. President took the chair and called the Convention to order.

The reports of the Tellers of ballots for the Standing Committee were received.

REPORT OF THE TELLERS OF THE CLERICAL VOTE FOR THE STANDING COMMITTEE.

Whole number of ballots cast, 57; necessary to a choice, 29; the Rev. William Payne, D. D., received 56 votes; the Rev. J. Livingston Reese, D. D., 57; the Rev. J. Ireland Tucker, S. T. D., 57; the Rev. Fenwick M. Cookson, 57; Mr. Norman B. Squires, 57; Mr. Henry S. Wynkoop, 57, Mr. John I. Thompson, 57; Mr. John H. Van Antwerp, 57; scattering, 1.

CHARLES E. CRAGG,
P. R. CHADWICK.
Tellers.

REPORT OF THE TELLERS OF THE LAY VOTE FOR THE STANDING COMMITTEE.

Whole number of ballots cast, 26; necessary to a choice, 14; the Rev. William Payne, D. D., received 25; the Rev. J. Livingston Reese, D. D., 26; the Rev. J. Ireland Tucker, S. T. D., 26; the Rev. Fenwick M. Cookson, 26; Mr. Norman B. Squires, 26; Mr. Henry S. Wynkoop, 26; Mr. John I. Thompson, 26; Mr. John H. Van Antwerp, 26; scattering, 1.

PHILIP W. MOSHER,
S. E. CRITTENDEN,
Tellers.

The Right Rev. President declared elected as members of

THE STANDING COMMITTEE,

The Rev. William Payne, D. D., the Rev. J. Livingston Reese, D. D., the Rev. J. Ireland Tucker, S. T. D., the Rev. Fenwick M. Cookson, Mr. Norman B. Squires, Mr. Henry S. Wynkoop, Mr. John I. Thompson and Mr. John H. Van Antwerp.

The Tellers of ballots for one Deputy to the General Convention presented their reports.

REPORT OF THE TELLERS OF THE CLERICAL VOTE FOR DEPUTY TO THE GENERAL CONVENTION.

Whole number of ballots cast, 55; necessary to a choice, 28; Mr. John Hobart Warren received 54 votes; scattering, 1.

CHARLES E. FREEMAN,
WILLIAM H. COOKSON,
Tellers.

REPORT OF THE TELLERS OF THE LAY VOTE FOR DEPUTY TO THE GENERAL CONVENTION.

Whole number of ballots cast, 28; necessary to a choice, 15; Mr. John Hobart Warren received 28 votes.

F. N. SKINNER,
S. M. VAN SANTVOORD,
Tellers.

The Right Rev. President announced Mr. John Hobart Warren elected a Deputy to the General Convention.

The Tellers of the votes for one Provisional Lay Deputy to the General Convention presented their reports.

REPORT OF THE TELLERS OF THE CLERICAL VOTE FOR ONE PROVISIONAL LAY DEPUTY TO THE GENERAL CONVENTION.

Whole number of votes cast, 55, necessary to a choice, 28; Mr. Thomas L. Harison received 54 votes, blank 1.

JAMES A. DICKSON,
JOHN KEYES PAIGE,
Tellers.

REPORT OF THE TELLERS OF THE LAY VOTE FOR ONE PROVISIONAL LAY DEPUTY TO THE GENERAL CONVENTION.

Whole number of votes cast, 28; necessary to a choice, 15, Mr. Thomas L. Harison received 28 votes.

J. N. MARVIN,
J. M. PEARSON,
Tellers.

The Right Rev. President announced Mr. Thomas L. Harison elected a Provisional Lay Deputy to the General Convention.

On motion of the Rev. R. G. Hamilton, the ballot was unanimously dispensed with, and Trustees were appointed by the Convention as follows:

OF THE EPISCOPAL FUND.

Mr. J. H. Van Antwerp, Mr. W. Bayard Van Rensselaer, Mr. Theodore Townsend, Mr. Charles W. Tillinghast, 2nd, and Mr. Charles E. Patterson.

OF THE FUND FOR AGED AND INFIRM CLERGYMEN.

Mr. Norman B. Squires, Mr. Robert S. Oliver and Mr. J. J. Tillinghast.

OF THE FUND FOR WIDOWS AND ORPHANS OF DECEASED CLERGYMEN.

Mr. J. W. Tillinghast, Mr. C. W. Tillinghast and Mr. Amasa J. Parker.

TRUSTEES OF THE DIOCESE OF ALBANY UNTIL 1894.

The Rev. J. D. Morrison, D. D., LL. D. and Mr. Levi Hasbrouck.

On motion of the Rev. R. G. Hamilton, the ballot was unanimously dispensed with, and the Rev. Charles C. Edmunds, Jr. and the Rev. Sheldon Munson Griswold were elected Deputies to the Federate Council.

The election of the Board of Missions being in order, nominations were received for the Archdeaconries as presented in the Report of the Secretary of the Convention; and on motion of the Secretary of the Convention, the Rev. W. R. Woodbridge and Mr. William Kemp were nominated for the Diocese at large.

On motion, the ballot was unanimously dispensed with, and the following named persons were elected as the Board of Missions until the next Convention.

BOARD OF MISSIONS.

ARCHDEACONRY OF ALBANY.

The Rev. W. W. Battershall, D. D.   Mr. J. H. Van Antwerp.

ARCHDEACONRY OF TROY.

The Rev. F. M. Cookson.   Mr. George A. Wells.

ARCHDEACONRY OF THE SUSQUEHANNA.

The Rev. Frank B. Reazor.   Mr. Robert M. Townsend.

ARCHDEACONRY OF OGDENSBURGH.

The Rev. R. M. Kirby.   Mr. T. Streatfeild Clarkson.

DIOCESE AT LARGE.

The Rev. W. R. Woodbridge.   Mr. William Kemp.

15

Certain changes having been announced, the apportionment of last year as so modified was adopted, as follows:

PLAN OF APPORTIONMENT TO RAISE MISSIONARY FUND.

ARCHDEACONRY OF ALBANY.

The Cathedral of All Saints	$1,200 00
St. Peter's, Albany	1,000 00
St. Paul's, Albany	400 00
Grace, Albany	50 00
Holy Innocents', Albany	50 00
Trinity, Albany	20 00
Trinity, Rensselaerville	15 00
Trinity, West Troy	45 00
St. Mark's, Green Island	30 00
St. John's, Cohoes	200 00
Trinity, Athens	25 00
Calvary, Cairo	20 00
Gloria Dei, Palenville	10 00
St. Luke's, Catskill	150 00
Christ, Greenville	5 00
St. Paul's, Oak Hill	5 00
Christ, Duanesburgh	50 00
St. George's, Schenectady	125 00
Christ, Schenectady	15 00
St. Ann's, Amsterdam	60 00
Good Shepherd, Canajoharie	10 00
Zion, Fonda	10 00
St. John's, Johnstown	75 00
Trinity, Fairfield	5 00
Christ, Herkimer	60 00
Emmanuel, Little Falls	50 00
St. Augustine's, Ilion	30 00
Trinity, Claverack	12 00
St. Luke's, Clermont	10 00
Our Saviour, Lebanon Springs	20 00
St. John's, Stockport	50 00
St. Mark's, Philmont	20 00
St. Luke's, Chatham	5 00
St. Paul's, Kinderhook	75 00
Christ, Hudson	100 00
Christ, Gloversville	25 00
Grace, Mohawk	15 00
St. Alban's Frankfort	5 00
All Saints', Hudson	.12 00
Holy Cross, Fort Plain	10 00
Of the Memorial, Middleville	20 00
Christ, Coxsackie	5 00
Trinity, Ashland	10 00
St. Margaret's, Menand's Station	5 00
	———— $4,114 00

ARCHDEACONRY OF TROY.

St. Paul's, Troy	$750 00
St. John's, Troy	600 00
Christ, Troy	250 00
Holy Cross, Troy	200 00
Ascension, Troy	150 00
St. Luke's, Troy	20 00
St. Barnabas', Troy	50 00
Epiphany, East Albany	20 00
Messiah, Greenbush	25 00
Trinity, Lansingburgh	150 00
Trinity, Schaghticoke	15 00
St. Mark's, Hoosick Falls	200 00
Grace, Waterford	35 00
Christ, Ballston	150 00
St. John's, East Line	10 00
Grace, Jonesville	10 00
Calvary, Burnt Hills	25 00
St. Paul's, Charlton	10 00
Bethesda, Saratoga	200 00
St. Stephen's, Schuylerville	20 00
St. John's, Conklingville	5 00
St. Paul's, Salem	100 00
St. John's, Stillwater	10 00
St. Luke's, Cambridge	175 00
Trinity, Granville	25 00
North Granville	10 00
St. Paul's, Greenwich	25 00
St. James', Fort Edward	20 00
Zion, Sandy Hill	50 00
Trinity, Whitehall	50 00
St. James', Caldwell	20 00
St. Mary's, Luzerne	20 00
Holy Cross, Warrensburgh	50 00
Messiah, Glens Falls	150 00
Good Shepherd, Chestertown	15 00
Church of the Cross, Ticonderoga	30 00
Christ, Port Henry	31 25
Emmanuel, Mineville	5 00
St. James', Ausable Forks	25 00
St. John's, Essex	30 00
St. Paul's, Keeseville	15 00
Trinity, Plattsburgh	75 00
Christ, Rouse's Point	20 00
St. John's, Champlain	20 00
St. Peter's, Ellenburgh	10 00
Good Shepherd, Elizabethtown	10 00
St. Luke's, Mechanicville	20 00
Keene Valley Mission	25 00
	$3,931 25

ARCHDEACONRY OF THE SUSQUEHANNA.

St. Peter's, Hobart...	$35 00
Christ, Walton...	30 00
St. John's, Delhi...	125 00
Grace, Stamford	20 00
St. Paul's, Franklin	20 00
St. Paul's, Sidney..	5 00
Christ, Butternuts..	25 00
Christ, Cooperstown..	150 00
Grace, Cherry Valley.......................................	75 00
Zion, Morris..	60 00
St. James', Oneonta..	30 00
St. Matthew's, Unadilla....................................	50 00
Christ, West Burlington	5 00
St. Paul's, East Springfield................................	25 00
St. John's, Richfield Springs...............................	50 00
Immanuel, Otego...	5 00
Of the Holy Spirit, Schenevus..............................	15 00
	$725 00

ARCHDEACONRY OF OGDENSBURGH.

St. John's, Ogdensburgh....................................	$500 00
Trinity, Potsdam...	450 00
Trinity, Gouverneur.......................................	50 00
St. John's, Massena..	50 00
Christ, Morristown	75 00
Grace, Norfolk	5 00
St. Paul's, Waddington.....................................	30 00
Grace, Canton	50 00
Trinity, Morley..	25 00
St. Mark's, Malone	75 00
St. Peter's, Brushton.......................................	10 00
St. Thomas', Lawrenceville.................................	5 00
Zion, Colton	20 00
St. Luke's, Saranac Lake...................................	20 00
St. James', Hogansburgh....................................	25 00
St. John's, Chateaugay.....................................	5 00
Grace, Louisville	10 00
St. Mark's, West Bangor....................................	5 00
	$1,410 00

Total...	$10,180 25

RECAPITULATION.

Archdeaconry of Albany....................................	$4,114 00
Archdeaconry of Troy......................................	3,931 25
Archdeaconry of the Susquehanna	725 00
Archdeaconry of Ogdensburgh..............................	1,410 00
	$10,180 25

On motion of the Rev. J. Philip B. Pendleton, the following preamble and resolution were adopted:

WHEREAS, The Memorial of the Convocation of Albany on the subject of a Diocesan Missionary has been referred by this Convention to the Board of Missions, with the request that they consider and act upon it; therefore

Resolved, That in the event of a favorable action being taken upon such Memorial by the said Board, the Sunday Schools of the Diocese be requested to undertake and provide for the salary of such Missionary, as their special contribution toward the Missionary work of the Diocese for the coming year.

The Rev. James Caird presented and read

REPORT NUMBER 2, OF THE COMMITTEE ON CONSTITUTION AND CANONS.

The Committee on the Constitution and Canons, to whom was referred with instructions to report it for the consideration of the Convention, the proposed Canon entitled "The Clergy Reserve Fund," herewith report the same without recommendation.

J. W. STEWART,
Chairman.

On motion of the Rev. J. D. Morrison, D. D., LL. D., the Canon on a Clergy Reserve Fund was adopted by the Convention, and the Bishop of the Diocese announced his concurrence in the change.*

On motion of Mr. James Gibson, Lay Deputy from St. Paul's Church, Salem, it was

Resolved, That the Canon on a Clergy Reserve Fund be numbered XVIII, the numbering of what is now Canon XVIII, and of the subsequent Canons to be changed accordingly.

On motion of the Rev. Fenwick M. Cookson, it was

Resolved, That a Committee consisting of the Rev. Dr. Carey, the Rev. Mr. Ogden, Mr G. Pomeroy Keese and Mr. John I. Thompson, be instructed to inform the Bishop of the Diocese of the action of the Convention in relation to the salary of the Bishop.

On motion of the Rev. James Caird, the following preamble and resolution were adopted:

INASMUCH as the members of this Convention having learned that the Presiding Bishop of the Church has appointed the Bishop of the Diocese of Albany as the Bishop in charge of our foreign Churches in Europe;

Resolved, That we feel that in this selection a great honour has been conferred on him and through him on this Diocese; and while we regret the absence of our Diocesan from among us, we feel it to be a duty for him to accept the appointment; we trust that his labours in administering the affairs of our Church abroad may result in much good, and that in God's time he may, with renewed health, be restored to his Diocese, where he is so highly esteemed and so much beloved.

On motion of the Rev. William C. Pront, it was

Resolved, That the Convention hereby extend its cordial thanks to the Cathedral and Churchmen of Albany for their courteous hospitality to the Twenty-second Convention of the Diocese of Albany.

---

* For the text of this Canon, see p. 91.

On motion of the Secretary, it was

Resolved, That when the Convention adjourn this afternoon, it adjourn to meet in the Cathedral at half-past four o'clock to hear the remainder of the Annual Address of the Bishop of the Diocese; and that at the conclusion of the Address the Convention adjourn *sine die* without further formality.

Resolved, That the Secretary be instructed to print 1,000 copies of the Bishop's Address, apart from the Journal, and to send them to the Clergy of the Diocese as early as possible.

Resolved, That the Secretary be instructed to print 1,250 copies of the Journal of the Convention, and distribute them to the various Parishes.

The Rev. Edgar A. Enos presented the Reports of the Diocesan Branch of the Woman's Auxiliary to the Board of Missions, and of the Girls' Friendly Society.*

The Rev. Frank B. Reazor presented the Reports from the Orphan House of the Holy Saviour, Cooperstown, and of the Committee on the same.

REPORT OF THE SUPERINTENDENT OF THE ORPHAN HOUSE OF THE HOLY SAVIOUR.

November 10, 1890.

There have been 142 children at the Diocesan Orphanage during the past year. The number has seldom been less than 80 at one time, frequently over 90; to-day the number is 98. The remainder have been honourably discharged for self-support, or adoption, or returned to friends. Three excellent girls, brought up at the Orphan-age, have been recently transferred to St. Christina Home for advanced education in teaching, or different branches of work.

There has been steady regularity in the work at the Orphanage, thanks to the fidelity of our excellent staff in the house. It is with most sincere gratitude that we acknowledge the kindness of those friends in the Diocese, who have generously aided us by building the new wing with its improvements, all very much needed.

The health of the children, thanks be to God, has been generally good; many feeble, weak-minded and diseased ones have greatly improved since they came to us. The only death has been that of a badly deformed child, who had the whooping-cough severely.

As usual, among the children are many sad histories. Two victims of the Johns-town flood, a boy and a girl, are among those recently admitted. The most distress-ing cases, however, are those coming from degraded families, where the children have never received sound moral and religious training. All have been to the pub-lic schools. Nevertheless they are, we allude to the unfavourable cases, essentially heathens. During the last few months two half-orphan families, four in each, the eldest girl fourteen, were sent to us; it was said they had never been in a place of worship, they knew nothing of the Holy Scriptures, and had never bent a knee in prayer to their Heavenly Father and Holy Saviour. They had to be taught to kneel.

Earnest, forcible, heartfelt moral teaching of the Ten Great Commandments, in connection with the Holy precepts of our Blessed Lord and Saviour is sorely needed among us Sound home education, the most important form of all education, is too often neglected in American life of all classes, but of course most neglected among the ignorant. The moral tone of our country, with its fanatic devotion to the service of Mammon is becoming painfully low. In the eager pursuit of wealth, the lust of

---

* For which Reports, see end of Appendix B.

the eye, and the pride of life, the Great Commandments of the God we worship are too often forgotten. In this state of things there is necessarily much anxious work to be carried out in every truly Christian Orphanage, that in the humble task and the narrow field allotted to it, there shall be no neglect of plain duty. The moral teaching must be very clear and decided, but never needlessly severe. In this Diocesan Orphanage, from the first days of the work—some twenty years ago—a simple rule has been our guide: "Firmness and kindness in equal measure." The rule has worked well. The children are generally happy and healthy. But their moral and religious teaching is very forcible. Happily, by the gracious mercy of the Heavenly Father and the Holy Saviour, not a few boys and girls, the children of careless private homes, have been rescued from ruin, and trained in this Orphanage for useful Christian lives. Occasionally disappointments have occurred, and we have shortcomings to deplore; nevertheless it is with fervent humble gratitude that we observe that among a number of boys and girls, the industrial, moral and religious improvement has been remarkable. Thanks be to God for all that is good.

Under these circumstances may we not be allowed to ask that the hands of the Diocesan Orphanage may be strengthened? The funds of the Orphan House of the Holy Saviour are not yet fully sufficient for the work intrusted to it. During the past year we have repeatedly been largely in debt for current expenses. On several occasions there has been a deficit of from $500 to $700, and it became necessary to borrow in order to meet the monthly bills for food, fuel, etc. Our funds are also insufficient at present for carrying out a plan, long since formed, for providing the means of teaching the boys some trade by which they may be qualified for self-support. The trades unions refuse to receive apprentices, consequently it will be necessary to teach the boys some useful trade in their Orphanage homes.

Allow me, as Superintendent, under these circumstances, frankly to ask that the present small endowment fund be increased, as soon as may be, by some twenty-five additional free scholarships of $1,000 each. These scholarships might be memorial or parochial in character. Individuals with the means to do an act of truly Christian charity, might thus provide in perpetuity for the sound Christian teaching of a poor child. Strong Parishes could also, by these means, endow in perpetuity a free scholarship under the name of their Church, where one of their needy little ones could be well provided for.

Respectfully submitted,
SUSAN FENIMORE COOPER,
Superintendent Orphan House of the Holy Saviour.

REPORT OF THE TREASURER OF THE ORPHAN HOUSE OF THE HOLY SAVIOUR AT COOPERSTOWN, FOR THE YEAR ENDING SEPTEMBER 30, 1990.

Receipts.

To balance, October 1, 1889	$10 00
From County Treasurer for board of county children	4,120 70
From 58 Churches and Mission Stations	1,442 11
From board of individual children	556 45
From personal subscriptions	199 50
From interest on investments	267 81
From school money	308 26
From miscellaneous	55 01
Borrowed from Endowment Fund	475 67
	$7,435 50

Expenses.

Wages.	$2,069 93
Groceries	968 81
Meat.	484 53
Milk	1,049 66
Clothing	654 95
Fuel	660 88
Lights.	150 00
House stores.	1,096 05
Medicines.	99 51
Repairs.	109 95
Water.	50 00
Miscellaneous.	49 48
By balance.	8 25
	$7,435 50

The following Churches and Mission Stations contributed to the support of the Orphan House during the year ending September 30, 1890:

Cathedral of All Saints	$55 78
St. Peter's, Albany	108 79
St. Paul's, Albany	5 00
Holy Innocents, Albany	21 22
Trinity, Rensselaerville	3 00
Trinity, West Troy	16 00
St. John's, Cohoes	15 00
Trinity, Athens	14 63
St. Luke's, Catskill	39 18
Christ, Duanesburgh	3 00
Christ, Schenectady	4 83
St. George's, Schenectady	17 50
Holy Cross, Fort Plain	2 00
St John's, Johnstown	44 05
Emmanuel, Little Falls	15 21
Our Saviour, Lebanon	3 80
St. John's, Stockport	30 00
St. Mark's, Philmont.	2 82
St. Paul's, Kinderhook	8 50
Christ, Hudson.	10 00
St. Paul's, Troy	158 00
St. John's, Troy	173 08
Christ, Troy	4 93
St. Luke's, Troy	6 05
St. Barnabas', Troy	64 56
Messiah, Greenbush.	5 00
Trinity, Lansingburgh	20 00
Trinity, Schaghticoke	3 03
Messiah, Glens Falls	58 05
St. Mark's, Hoosick Falls	12 00
Christ, Ballston Spa	13 50
St. James', Fort Edward	4 35

Zion, Sandy Hill.....	$11 97
Trinity, Whitehall.....	12 10
Church of the Cross, Ticonderoga...........................	8 45
Christ, Port Henry...........	8 11
Christ, Rouse's Point..... ....---.................. .	10 47
St. John's, Champlain	5 00
St. Peter's, Hobart.......................................	2 75
Christ, Walton...........	32 54
St. John's, Delhi	40 57
Grace, Stamford	7 35
Christ, Cooperstown	45 82
St. Paul's, Franklin	2 50
Grace, Cherry Valley........	10 00
Zion, Morris........	50 00
St James', Oneonta	7 00
St. Matthew's, Unadilla	5 20
St. Paul's, East Springfield	2 00
St. John's, Richfield Springs........................	93 00
Holy Spirit, Schenevus	1 87
St. John's, Ogdensburgh........	44 01
Trinity, Potsdam......................	53 91
Christ, Morristown	2 50
St. Mark's, Malone...........	25 00
St. James', Rossman's Mills...........	5 91
St. James', Lake George.	1 43
Zion, Colton.	1 62
Woman's Auxiliary........	8 17

Respectfully submitted,
LESLIE PELL-CLARKE.
Treasurer.

REPORT OF LESLIE PELL-CLARKE, TREASURER, ORPHAN HOUSE BUILD-
ING FUND, OCTOBER 7, 1890.

Amount due Treasurer, last report.	$2,893 05
Paid on warrant during the year.	182 50
	$3,075 55
Received from subscriptions....	1,345 00
Balance due Treasurer.................	$1,730 55

REPORT OF LESLIE PELL-CLARKE, TREASURER, ORPHAN HOUSE EN-
DOWMENT FUND.

One mortgage, Masonic Lodge	$3,000 00
Two western mortgages	1,000 00
Loaned running expense account, two years	1,255 56
Loaned Building Fund...	333 44
	$5,589 00

Respectfully submitted,
LESLIE PELL-CLARKE,
Treasurer.

REPORT OF THE COMMITTEE ON THE REPORTS FROM THE ORPHAN
HOUSE AT COOPERSTOWN.

The Committee on the Report of the Superintendent and the Treasurer of the Orphan House of the Holy Saviour, Cooperstown, New York, beg leave to recommend the adoption by the Convention of the amendments to the charter of that institution, which were read before the Convention yesterday, believing that by the passage by the State Legislature of the said amendments a greater Diocesan interest in this our Diocesan Orphanage will be aroused.

The following considerations will justify the assumption of your Committee that the Diocese does not yet rise to the full measure of its responsibility to this most worthy and touching work for God's desolate children.

Out of one hundred and seventy-nine Parishes and Mission Stations, all which are canonically required to offer for the Orphanage, only fifty-eight are reported as having made offerings in money.

While your Committee are aware that many Parishes have contributed in kind, they also believe, from the showing of reports, that as a Diocese we are not "caring for our own" in this work as we should.

It is with pleasure that your Committee notes the generally prosperous and improving condition of this institution as shown in the Treasurer's report of an Endowment Fund of $5,589, and in that of the Superintendent.

The Committee would further commend to the thoughtful attention of the Diocese the following suggestion of the Superintendent:

"Allow me," Miss Cooper writes, "frankly to ask that the present small endowment fund be increased as soon as may be by some twenty-five additional free scholarships of $1,000 each. These scholarships might be memorial or parochial in character. Individuals with the means to do an act of Christian charity might thus provide in perpetuity for the sound Christian training of a poor child. Strong Parishes could also by these means, endow, in perpetuity, a free scholarship under the name of their Church, where one of their needy little ones could be provided for."

Miss Cooper also recommends, with practical wisdom, the providing of means to teach the orphan boys trades, which may serve them to great advantage in their riper years, and when the House can no longer mother them. This suggestion is all the more to be thought well of, for the reason, as the Superintendent well says, that the trades unions of the day are in an attitude of opposition to the large use that ought to be made of the apprentice system.

The Committee ventures to express an earnest hope that the enlarging interest in our Orphanage, shown by an increase of some $400 in contributions for the past year, may be yet further augmented until every Parish and Mission Station may be on the list of those who remember the children whom God has given us.

Respectfully submitted,

F. B. REAZOR,
E. R. ARMSTRONG.
S. E. CRITTENDEN,
WILLIAM KEMP.

On motion of the Rev. Charles S. Olmsted, it was

Resolved, That a Committee of three be appointed to present to the Legislature the proposed amendments to the Act of Incorporation of the Orphan House of the Holy Saviour, with the request that they be passed.

The Right Rev. President appointed as such committee, Mr. Melvil Dewey, Mr. Benjamin H. Hall and Mr. Charles E. Patterson.

On motion of Mr. G. Pomeroy Keese, Lay Deputy from Christ Church, Cooperstown, it was

Resolved, That a Committee of five, of which the Bishop shall be Chairman, be appointed to raise the sum of $2,000 to free the Orphan House of the Holy Saviour from debt under the promise that if the amount be raised before January 1, next, the sum of $3,000 is promised as an addition to the Endowment Fund.

The Right Rev. President appointed as members of such Committee, with himself, Mr. A. B. Cox, Mr. T. Streatfeild Clarkson, Mr. John I. Thompson and Mr. J. Russell Parsons, Jr.

The Rev. J. H. Houghton presented and read the following report, the resolution contained in which, was adopted.

REPORT OF THE COMMITTEE ON THE BIBLE AND PRAYER BOOK SOCIETY.

The Committee regard the Bible and Common Prayer Book Society as appearing before us with a spirit so humble and meek after a record of so much good, widely spread, that the Convention should be awakened to a sense of its indebtedness to it and to its privilege and duty to aid it.

Here is an old friend into whose pocket the whole Diocese has had a way of recommending everybody to thrust his hands and he would be sure to draw a gift.

The Rev. and gentlemanly Secretary, proud of the reputation of this, one of the first organizations of the Diocese, has taxed every possible resource to maintain this happy delusion, that the Diocese has a mine of precious books inexhaustible as well as invaluable.

The Report awakens us as with a shock; the Committee has no wish to allay the excitement caused thereby — the pocket has collapsed — the hands so freely thrust in have worn generous holes, and somebody for the future must either refrain from begging or else help to darn the holes.

We are told that some of the best Parishes have done much of the damage and repaired none of the waste. They even complain that the goods furnished are so beautiful that they are mistaken for gift volumes and stolen from the pews, so that the situation is grievous; the Society must not only cease sending out handsome volumes, but it must cease sending out any books at all, save to the most needy Parishes and Missionary Stations.

The Committee thought, at first, that, inasmuch as the kind policy of the Society had ₁made it a sort of Mutual Reserve Institution, no one should draw a benefit unless a contribution had been made within the year. This, however, being considered too severe, we are a unit in the following preambles and resolution:

WHEREAS, The Bible and Common Prayer Book Society cannot pursue its course of usefulness without constant yearly aid;

WHEREAS, Their fund is among the prescribed canonical contributions of the Parishes of this Diocese; therefore be it

Resolved, That the Secretary be recommended to impress this fact on Parishes in the most telling way he can devise, and if necessary to create the conscience, refuse grants to all but Missionary Stations until some contribution to the funds has been made by the applicant.　　(Signed.)

　　　　　　　J. H. HOUGHTON,
　　　　　　　GEORGE B. McCARTEE.
　　　　　　　　　　　For the Committee.

The Rev. David Sprague presented and read the Reports of the Society for Promoting Religion and Learning, of the Treasurer of the

Diocese in regard to moneys sent him for Theological Education, and of the Committee on the same.

REPORT OF THE SOCIETY FOR PROMOTING RELIGION AND LEARNING IN THE STATE OF NEW YORK.

The Superintendent of the Society for Promoting Religion and Learning in the State of New York, as the canonical agent of the Diocese of Albany, for distributing all funds for theological education, would respectfully report:

That of the one hundred and sixteen or more Parishes in the Diocese of Albany, the following six Parishes have contributed and forwarded to the Treasurer of the Society the sum of ninety-nine dollars and seventy-six cents ($99.76) for theological education during the past Conventional year, in accordance with the provisions of the Canon?

1889. Nov. 29. St. Paul's, Troy......	....	$15 00
1890. May 28. Trinity, West Troy.	......	5 00
June 3. Emmanuel, Little Falls		7 00
July 2. Trinity, Potsdam......		31 97
Aug. 7. St. Mark's, Malone......		10 00
Oct. 6. St. Matthew's, Unadilla......		5 79
Oct. 27. St. Paul's, Troy...		25 00
Total...	....	$99 76

This sum of $99.76 forms part of the $1,000 and more which have been expended in aid of students in divinity belonging to the Diocese of Albany during the past year.

It is probably known to the Convention, that the income of the Society is a fixed income, in so far as it seldom goes beyond a certain point, while below that point it is subject to great fluctuations, and it often happens, of course, that students possessing the most legitimate claims to its consideration are refused assistance, and are disheartened and discouraged at the very outset of their career.

We are congratulating ourselves upon the encouraging fact that the number of candidates for the sacred office is increasing at this time. The Seminary was never so full as now, and this report is coming to us from other institutions of the same character. But while this is so, the Society for Promoting Religion and Learning, once so amply endowed for the purposes of its charter, is hindered by lack of means from doing what it would gladly do in furtherance of the great work. Would it be too much to expect that, at least, those of the Clergy of the Diocese of Albany who were educated within the walls of the Seminary, through aid received from the Society for Promoting Religion and Learning, should make an annual contribution to its treasury in accordance with the provisions of their own Canon?

All of which is respectfully submitted,

ANDREW OLIVER,
Superintendent of the Society for Promoting Religion and Learning.

NEW YORK, *November 2, 1890.*

REPORT OF THE TREASURER OF THE DIOCESE OF MONEYS RECEIVED AND DISBURSED FOR THEOLOGICAL EDUCATION.

Receipts.

The Cathedral of All Saints......	$24 71
Through offerings, Cathedral of All Saints	100 00
Christ Church, Hudson	8 70

All Saints' Church of Hoosac	$18 00
Special	3 00
Total	$149 41
Disbursements	$149 41

SELDEN E. MARVIN,
Treasurer.

REPORT OF THE COMMITTEE ON THE REPORT OF THE SOCIETY FOR PROMOTING RELIGION AND LEARNING.

The Committee on the Report of the Society for Promoting Religion and Learning in the State of New York beg leave to report:

That in their opinion the statement of the Superintendent of this Society needs no comment. The question is, "what can most effectually rouse the consciences of the Rectors of the Churches of this Diocese to their duty in this matter?"

Your Committee own that they are unable to say.

DAVID SPRAGUE,
M. ANDRAE,
A. B. COX.

The Rev. Heman R. Timlow, for the Committee on the Society for the Home Study of the Holy Scripture, offered the following resolution, which was adopted.

Resolved, That the Secretary of the Convention be instructed to secure and print in the Journal the Report of the Society for the Home Study of Holy Scripture.

REPORT OF THE SOCIETY FOR THE HOME STUDY OF HOLY SCRIPTURE.

THE PRESIDENT'S PREFACE.

Less than ever this year is there need of any commendation of this report to the intelligent interest, or of this society, to the grateful confidence of the Church. The report carries its own commendation in its spirit, its eloquence and its facts ; and the graduates of our society are *its* letters of commendation known and read by all men, where they are known at all. And yet I cannot forego the honour of this association with those to whom, under God, all is due that has been attained.

I am prompted to emphasize one point in the report, and to call attention to two things which have been deeply borne in upon us, by our experience during this year, in our association with so many young Christian women, in all phases of life and in all parts of the country.

The point for emphasis is this : that with every year of study there comes a larger proportion of honour-certificates ; more in the fourth year than in the third, and more in the second than in the first ; which ought to be an intense encouragement both to teachers and students. Because it means that the mind grows wonted and skilled to use itself ; and that study is easier and more thorough with every year's effort.

For the rest there are words of warning and of help, which I think I ought to speak. The great hindrance to the thorough carrying out of our plan, and indeed of any system of higher and better things, is the acknowledged difficulty of living "in the world and not of it." The *duties* of what is called "Society" must, of course, be attended to ; but the *demands* of society are far more exigent sometimes, than matters of far more importance. It is wiser to be moderate in the discharge of social obligations , and so leave room and time and strength for soberer and more wholesome things ; for the study of God's word, and of things that tend toward the cultivation of the soul and of the mind ; than to leave only the feebleness of the spirit and the weariness of the flesh ; which are unequal to any thing more than the idle unprofitableness of novels and magazines. A fixed purpose, a definite amount of work, a portion of time honestly set apart for the study which this course needs, would make a standard, by which all the proportions of duty, and all the divisions of life could be regulated and arranged,

One last word. Much, of course, of the outlines of this work tends toward exterior questions of Holy Scripture ; the authorship, the authenticity, the age and the external interpretation and application of the passages. But the careful, honest student finds the Bible rather a garden, through which,— as one of the old Targums used to read the third chapter of the Book of Genesis,— "the Word of JEHOVAH walked with the Spirit of the day." And used in this way, great *internal* lessons of higher moral standards and deeper religious convictions will come to those who read.

I have only again to urge upon all Christian women, to whom this opportunity is offered, that they will enter upon what we have found to be a course of study most helpful to their usefulness in home, and Church and school ; that they will help us by larger gifts of money, to increase and extend its advantages: and I am glad to call attention to the great value of the lectures, which, by the kindness of Professors Walpole and Richey, are added to our course ; and to the helpfulness of our enlarged library. Above all, I beg God's continued blessing on our work.

WM. CROSWELL DOANE,
President.

REPORT OF THE ORGANIZING SECRETARY.

I am aware that it is not the usual order of reports to put in the fore-front the work that ought to be done, and to throw into the background that which has been done. And yet, I am disposed so to begin, not only for the wise Apostolic reason— "forgetting those things which are behind, and reaching forth unto those things which are before"— but for the further reason that the chief blessing won from any past effort is clearer insight into the future. As Archbishop Trench has so inimitably phrased it:

> " In doing, is this knowledge won
> To see what yet remains undone."

And in so looking at the requirements of future work, I will venture to repeat a passage from a paper read elsewhere, upon the needs of our religious education.

" In the gracious providence of God, there has sprung up over all our land a quickened interest in our Sunday Schools — a fresh sense of their exceeding importance to the Church of Christ. The depth of this interest finds, perhaps, its truest measure in an equally wide-spread misgiving as to the fitness of its instruments; that is, in plain words, we are facing the fact that our teachers themselves are too ignorant; and the very best of them are bearing this witness against themselves humbly and heroically.

" Nor does the fault lie wholly at their own door. Pressed into the work, often most reluctantly, from a feeling of unfitness, they have simply undertaken to do the best they can; and in proportion, as they have done that best, are they now troubled with a further sense of something strangely false in their position. They, themselves, have been only partially taught, and not at all trained, and yet they have undertaken to teach the highest of all knowledge.

" It must have occurred to them, as to all thoughtful minds, that no such haphazard ways are allowed for any other teachers. Imagine, for one moment, our colleges, or even our common schools, selecting their teachers in like manner. Our very laws protect the children against such incompetency.

" Does then, such a different standard in our Sunday Schools mark our relative estimate of secular and spiritual things? Alas, whether it be so or not, such is the inference too often unconsciously drawn by both teacher and pupil.

" It would be easy to shock our whole Church with well-attested instances of incompetence, but, happily the matter of moment is to provide the remedy rather than to expose the weakness."

Five years of careful observation since these words were penned convince me that this evil is but little abated.

After all, is not this the danger of our Sunday Schools, that we expect from them more than they could give at their best? The Church of England uses them mainly for a class that cannot otherwise be reached; while in her national or voluntary schools, as they are now usually styled, she provides for the religious training of her children in ampler ways, giving them, as instructors, often her clergy, and always her certificated teachers, and that, not once a week, but daily, for forty minutes.

But children of a class in which private education is preferred, are rarely taught thus carefully. In England, as too often here, in proportion as an ampler culture in all other learning is secured, the religious training is slighted. With us the happy exception to this is found in our Church schools for girls, which far outnumber theirs. I have not the slightest doubt that to this fact we owe the blessing that scepticism is so much rarer among Churchwomen here than there. Still outside of these Church schools religious culture lags far behind all other culture, and we allow it to remain so — nay, we are quite content to have it so.

And so it comes to pass that one meets young ladies, brilliant in society, who albeit the daughters of clergymen, have never heard of such a book as Joshua in the Bible, and who, asked to refer to an Epistle, may be seen turning the leaves hard by Chronicles; or searching for King Saul, with just a little bewilderment as to his identity with him of Tarsus, turn anxiously the leaves of the Gospel. "Depend upon it," a Clergyman of wide experience said to me last spring, "the average woman does not know the difference between Elijah and Elisha."

It is a still sadder matter to my mind, that meeting as I so constantly do with young women trained in our colleges to be wise in philosophy and acute in psychology, I rarely meet with one who can at all distinguish a fundamental doctrine of Holy Scripture from the heresies which the Church has condemned in her General Councils. As to all that glorious range of truth that begins with the Incarnation of our Lord and stretches on and on till it reaches the glory of His Everlasting Kingdom — who has ever taught it to them so that it would shape their characters and fix their aims in life? And so it also comes to pass that all our standards grow false, and even the Church comes to be satisfied with women of society instead of women serving the Lord.

While the present Bishop of Durham was in residence as a Canon of Westminster I had the privilege of an hour with him; and I would that I could reproduce by voice or pen the earnestness with which he spoke of this great need. Especially did he feel that the need was sorest among the rich and those of widest social influence. Very notably during the last summer I have found in our mother country among the Church's foremost men, such a keenness of interest and such an all-aliveness of sympathy in every attempt to meet this need, as were full of inspiration. I would that I heard as often like utterances here, from those whose speech is ever full of energizing power.

In sketching thus, as I have tried to do accurately, our present deplorable standards of Christian culture, I have at the same time defined the chief difficulty which confronts our work.

We are constantly receiving requests from our Clergy for supplies of papers giving information of our work, as they hope to get up a large class for us. They are sent; but the result is clearly foreseen. The Rector for his part gains at last a truer knowledge of his people, while the ordinary outcome for us is one student in our simplest section. The rest of his young people he finds are "very busy" and the work "somewhat above them."

Above them indeed! For so superficial has been their previous study, that now, when some simple printed questions on the first four chapters of Acts, call for a definite written answer, and that from memory only, our so-called student is appalled; and so it sometimes comes to pass that she sees no other way out of it than to open her books, and copy something for an answer; a little fact which she sometimes informs us of, but more frequently not. But in either case she take serious offense if we decline to continue such trifling, and ever after she proclaims abroad that we are "fearfully strict," and our questions "awfully hard," and we, ourselves, not qualified for our work, for at least she *was* right, when she had answered that "Paul and Peter and Tertullian and Origen were the Apostolic Fathers." Can any one marvel that we count such students no proper subjects for teaching by correspondence, however sorely they need some other sort of instruction. This is one side and a true side, and alas! only a mere hint of the annoyances and disappointments which it would ill become me to detail. But thus much is due to criticism, which is far from being unfriendly, and which little dreams of this state of things. Moreover, in this slight suggestion of many and varied endurances, I am bearing the strongest possible testimony to the brightness of another side, and the richness of result, which makes us content to bear these inseparable attendants of our work, while growing wisdom enables us to ward off a little more from year to year.

I come now to the record of our work for this term of 1889-90. I need scarcely remind any one of that singular scourge that brought sickness into almost every household, nor of the still stranger depression of mental cheer and vigor that followed in its wake; that with such an extraordinary interruption our record is as high, and in many respects higher than the previous year, means, apart from this drawback, a very marked advance. Our regular students numbered this year two hundred and twenty-one, an increase of twenty above the previous year. Our honorary members numbered thirty, being a gain of eighteen. The number of women holding tickets for the Divinity lectures was one hundred and ten, while about thirty more attended those for Church History at St. John Baptist House.

Inclusive of our correspondents the entire number thus connected with our work was four hundred.

This year, as last, one hundred entered for the June examination in the various classes, but from the cause already mentioned many were obliged to give up all study, and not a few others to defer their examination until another year, so that only sixty-eight actually attempted it. The results were as follows: Students examined in the Acts of the Apostles, twenty, of whom eleven took honours and none failed; in St. John's Gospel, ten, of whom six took honours and none failed; in the Old Testament and Exodus specially, thirteen, of whom eleven took honours and none failed, in St. Paul's Epistles to the Galatians, Ephesians and Philippians, fifteen, of whom thirteen took honours and none failed; in Church History, ten, of whom nine took honours and none failed.

The growing excellence of the papers in those who had reached their third and fourth years is very marked. There are now fifteen who have passed the examinations for four years, thirteen of them with honour. These will now receive from our President the token of honour, which is a silver cross, of the same pattern as the Jerusalem cross. It was at first intended to have them brought from Jerusalem itself. But on further thought it became clear that as these were understood to denote a visit to the Holy Land, we should not use them. A further reason was the large amount of alloy in them. and their rude construction. The work was therefore put into the hands of Hart, Son, Peard & Co., London, with directions to make them of double weight, and of sterling silver, the name of the firm being sufficient security for the excellence of the work itself.

We trust that it will give the same pleasure to those who wear them as badges of life membership that it surely will to those who bestow them as the fitting token of long years of faithful and earnest study of Holy Scripture.

Nearly all of those who have thus completed their regular course are now engaged in post-graduate work of study or reading.

A most interesting class of these has been formed in the Psalms ; the work having this new feature, that there will be no more questions — the papers returned being on certain indicated topics, prepared in any way preferred by the writer. Somewhat singularly, by far the larger portion of books on the Psalter are now out of print, and much time and thought, as well as money, have been expended in the collection of a sufficient number to loan. Our Church History graduates are also reading more fully on various parts of their work. A very rare collection of works is awaiting their use.

It is with an intensity of delight that I can now speak of our library. Up to the close of our third year there was a collection of only two hundred volumes. By October, at the time of our annual meeting last year, there were four hundred volumes. After our removal to this city, and the opening of the office here in November, 1889, the work of adding to the library began in earnest, and by the close of our study-term in June, of this summer, we had seven hundred volumes, and at the present date a few over one thousand volumes. I have given to their selection my utmost care. I have believed fully in the dictum so often repeated by Newman, in his very suggestive lectures on " The Office and Work of Universities," that in such matters " *the supply must precede and create the demand.*" I know all too well, that fiction forms the greater proportion of reading among women ; but I know that woman was made for something better, and I believe firmly that when she really sees that better thing, she will desire it. As it has been, these books do not come in her way as others do. They are costly, and what is more, very many of them are out of print. No such provision as that we are now securing has ever been made, except to a small extent in our Parish libraries ; and no such provision is found in our largest public libraries.

Already there is large and growing use of the books through the mails for the collateral reading of students, and for the Reader's Class, lately inaugurated, both of these extending their use throughout the country. And now we look forward to opening the library on December 1st, for a third use, as a circulating and reference library in this city. It will also be thrown open each Saturday afternoon, as a free reference library to all Sunday-school teachers of all denominations. As already, on our previously limited basis we have had above fifty books out at a time, each of them finding, while out, many readers, I think we may fairly claim that our novel library — i. e., *a library without a novel* — is already a success.

The rule which has governed my selection has been this : In importing new books, which we can do, free of duty, at the rate of twenty-one cents to the shilling, retail price, the most readable have been chosen, the freshest and the brightest or the best in some way. But all along the year as though by a succession of providences, there have come to my eye the books that are out of print, and more or less scarce, some extremely rare. It is somewhat startling to one at first, to find how large a proportion

17

of important works belong to such a list. I have secured at once those which might not be found again for many years ; or, if found, would command a greatly advanced price. Many are the rich treasures of this kind now upon our shelves, some of them enriched with the most interesting autographs of authors.* Next to these, as very limited means has meant limited choice, I have of course preferred the recognized standards upon different subjects, and among these those least easy to find elsewhere. I have had of late to let slip some rare chances of rich treasures, because we have not yet had time to make our wants known to those who we have reason to hope will be benefactors to our work.

Our room, which came to us by a striking Providence, has proved in most respects remarkably adapted to our use ; and small as it is, it has been kept by much contrivance from looking overcrowded. With our revolving book-cases and some interesting pictures, it seems to be as attractive to others as, I may quite simply own, it is beautiful in my own eyes.

I remember as one of the greatest delights of my childhood a simple pastoral pastime. At the swarming of the bees there was always some reluctance on their part to enter a new hive. But a way was found to overcome this, by rubbing the hive with clover blossoms, making it so sweet that they *had* to come. I seem to be doing it now — gathering my little hands full of those luscious pink globes, and then rubbing them into all the recesses of the hive till I am half intoxicated with the sweetness. Even now, I seem to stand watching at a safe distance as the bees also feel the charm, and one after another enters till all are safely housed. Dear friends, whom we are trying to win to wisdom's ways, we have gathered the treasures that are "sweeter than honey and the honey-comb." Will you not also come and make this a home of your thoughts, and a veritable hive of busy, wise and sacred work?

I speak next with profound thankfulness of another onward movement of the past year — the Divinity Lectures for Women, so generously given by Prof. Walpole — a thankfulness in which all who heard them will, I am sure, unite Dealing as they did with the deep things of God, they were yet given so simply and so clearly that the impressions made upon both mind and heart must prove abiding — a store of holy, reverent thought laid up for life-long use. The lectures are not in the least limited to the members of the Society for the Home Study of the Holy Scriptures, having no further connection than being arranged by them. I say this lest our distant members should feel that they have not an equal provision made for them. Would that the benefit could possibly reach all.

At the same time, the Rev. Dr. Richey has continued his course in Church History at St. John Baptist House, the subscription to this being also quite distinct from our membership dues. May the time be hastened by woman's holy importunity, when such helps shall be given all through the Church. I have little doubt that many a Rector would gladly give them, if he knew they were heartily desired.

Another great blessing I may note, coming after long and sore trials. Indeed, if it be true, as has been said, that "difficulties are the stones out of which all God's houses are built," then by that same token we might know our building to be for Him, and might hope from the multitude of those same stones to become a house of goodly size. Our heavy trial has been lack of helpers in the work, and of means to provide for it ; but experience has brought us to a full belief that money will command only a portion of the service which we seek, and that upon such a basis we would run the risk of lowering the whole tone of our work Since the appeal of our

---

*Among them is a copy of Dr Pusey's work on German Rationalism, suppressed soon after its publication in 1829, and, therefore, extremely rare Ours is the copy given by Dr. Pusey to Newman, in 1830, containing both their autographs.

president, the offers of help have come, not all available at once, but cheering in promise. Meantime, till we are fully supplied with such help, we must reluctantly refuse the admission of more members than we can thus care for. I present it earnestly to the consciences of our present members, that a careful observance of directions, so avoiding mistakes, would at once enable us to instruct forty or fifty more. Possibly each thinks only of her own case, and the "only ten minutes" extra, which she asks for at our full hands, whereas she may be quite sure that sixty others will take the same view, and that this means not ten *minutes*, but ten *hours!* With our new office arrangements, the past year has been one of large gain in orderly arrangement, and completed system in all our records ; but all are dependent upon the careful co-operation of our many members ; and, while giving full and rounded measure of glad commendation to the work of our students, at least to the majority of them, it is on this one point that I must still *except* the majority, and say sadly with the Apostle. "In this I praise you not." Numbers always involve regulations, and if each considers herself entitled to exception, there is an end to all order ; for, then, the enforcement of rule in any case becomes a personal matter. I was told last summer, by Mr. Madan, the head-librarian of the Bodleian, of a noble example : When Charles I of England was at Oxford not long before his death, he sent a slip of paper, still carefully preserved, asking for the loan of a book. It was against the rules of the library to allow the books to leave the building, and the librarian had promised to enforce this rule. In a sad strait he took not the book, but the rule, and going himself to the king, fell upon his knees and appealed to him to decide which he should obey, this law or his majesty. The answer of the noble monarch was unhesitating — he himself would obey the law.

Our library rules are very few, but all very necessary ; and we trust that for the common good they will be carefully and cheerfully regarded, and the books themselves so cared-for that they may last for many readers.

Grateful mention is due to our examiners who have so conscientiously, and at the cost of much precious time, rated the papers for the Bishop's examination ; to our correspondents also, whose zeal and devotion have been unflagging and, also, very specially to several of our members who have given days or weeks of invaluable help at our office : while I am sure that all will unite with me in gratitude to our generous benefactors whose names will be found upon the list of donors.

And now, at the close of this report, a few of our students shall be heard telling incidentally, in brief notes, what the work has been to them.

A student of the first year writes: "Indeed it is a matter of thanks that I was led to commence the study when I did. It has been a great help, in many ways, which only God can know." And another in the same class .

"I cannot miss this opportunity of thanking you for the great pleasure and profit I have obtained from these lessons. I have enjoyed them intensely ; no milder word will express it."

It is a Bishop's worthy daughter, full of good works, who writes in her second year "I enjoy Sadler more and more. There is so much depth of meaning, so much that is new, that I have to go very slowly." Another, in the third year, with a teacher's many cares, writes about a work in Exodus : "It is delightful, and, indeed, this year's study has been a revelation to me on many points, and has opened a new world for future study and thought. My interest has never flagged, though it grows harder year by year to *make* the time for study." Another, also in Exodus: "I wish I could tell you how much benefit and pleasure I have received from this winter's study. I feel that I have gained even more spiritual help than I did from the study of St John's Gospel. It has been an entirely new field of thought to me, and such a delightful one."

And still more full are the words from our members of the fourth year: "The study of the Epistle to the Philippians opens delightfully, but certainly it cannot exceed in interest and wonder that to the Ephesians. The whole four years' course has been a delight to me, and I am most grateful for the privilege of this study." An other: "The four years' course has been a great gain to me; a means of growth, both intellectual and spiritual, and it is a great satisfaction to feel so much better fitted to teach and help others." Another faithful helper, as well as student, writes: "The society seems to me more and more one of the greatest practical helps for Churchwomen yet proposed, and the direct influence of the daily study of the Scriptures must of itself promote greater spirituality, as well as intellectual knowledge."

And so cheered by such sure tokens of the blessing of the Lord upon our work, and trusting to Him to guide and strengthen us, and to prosper the work of our hands upon us, we "reach forth unto those things which are before."

The Diocesan distribution of students, is: Alabama 1, California 1, Connecticut 18, Dakota 1, Delaware 5, Georgia 3, Chicago 7, Springfield 3, Indiana 1, Maine 3, Maryland 14, Easton 1, Massachusetts 26, Michigan 7, Western Michigan 1, Minnesota 2, Mississippi 1, Missouri 2, Nebraska 2, New Jersey 7, Newark 5, New York 31, Western New York 3, Albany 15, Central New York 11, Long Island 8, Ohio 2, Southern Ohio 3, Oregon 1, Pennsylvania 8, Central Pennsylvania 5, Pittsburgh 2, Rhode Island 3, South Carolina 1, Tennessee 2, Texas 1, Northern Texas 1, Vermont 1, Virginia 3, Fond du Lac 3, Milwaukee 2, Montreal 1, Nova Scotia 1, Ontario 2, Dioceses 42 — Students 221.

TREASURER'S REPORT.

For the Year Closing July 1, 1890.

Receipts.

Balance from previous year.	$115 82	
Dues of regular members.	391 00	
Subscriptions and donations of honourary members.	170 00	
Donations for general objects.	164 00	
Donations for library.	414 00	
Donations for clerical assistance.	148 00	
		$1,402 82

Expenses.

Printing.	$273 21	
Postage.	67 00	
Stationery.	46 05	
Rent, fire and light.	168 60	
Clerical assistance.	143 94	
Books for library.	393 08	
Furniture for library.	152 06	
Refitting room for library.	27 90	
Library outfit, catalogue, etc.	97 97	
Insurance on library.	11 25	
		1,381 06
Balance on hand.		$21 76
		$1,402 82

The account of this year includes but eleven months, as it has been decided to begin our financial year with the first of July instead of the first of August.

SUSAN B. NELSON,
Treasurer.

The Rev. James A. Dickson presented and read

THE REPORT OF THE COMMITTEE ON NON-REPORTING CLERGY AND PARISHES.

Three letters were received by the Secretary in reply to his letter asking reasons for not reporting to the Convention of 1888, viz.: from the Rev. Messrs. W. H. Cook, G. W. Gates, and Pelham Williams, S. T. D., assigning ill-health, removal from the Diocese and negligence and intense dislike of conventions and routine concerns as reasons for not reporting.

All of which is respectfully submitted.

JAS. A. DICKSON,
T. FLOYD WOODWORTH,
JOHN HORROCKS.

On motion of the Secretary of the Convention, it was

Resolved, That the Secretary of the Convention be and is hereby directed to insert in next year's Journal under a separate head a list of the names of those non-reporting Clergy and Parishes that have failed to return answer to his letter of inquiry ; also, a record of answers received, and the general character of the excuses offered.

Resolved, That the Secretary of the Convention be and is hereby directed to ask of the Parishes from which no report was received at the last Convention, and the Clergy, still canonically resident in the Diocese, who failed to report at the last Convention, their reasons for not complying with the requirements of the Canon; and that a minute of the same be entered in the Journal against the names under the head of non-reporting Clergy and Parishes; and, in any case where the Secretary's request is not complied with, the fact be recorded.

The Rev. Walter C. Stewart, presented and read the following report, the resolution contained in which was adopted.

REPORT OF THE COMMITTEE ON UNFINISHED BUSINESS.

The Committee on Unfinished Business beg to report that there is due,

(1) The report of the Trustees of the Diocese regarding the removal of Chateaugay from the list of parishes. (Journal 1889, p. 116.)

(2) Also, the report from the Committee on the Constitution and Canons with regard to the circumscription of the Diocese, by the exclusion of Deposit. (Journal 1889. p. 131.)

The committee suggest the resolution,

Resolved, That these reports be asked for.

WALTER C. STEWART,
NELSON LA SALLE.

On motion of the Secretary of the Convention, it was

Resolved, That the resolution in regard to the Parish of Christ Church, Deposit, which was referred to the Committee on the Constitution and Canons, be withdrawn from that committee, and laid on the table.

The Rev. William M. Ogden, addressing the Right Rev. President, presented the

REPORT OF THE COMMITTEE APPOINTED TO INFORM THE BISHOP OF THE ACTION OF THIS CONVENTION IN REGARD TO THE SALARY OF THE BISHOP.

That we have great gratification in announcing to the Bishop of the Diocese, the official action of the Convention this morning in passing the following resolution:

Resolved, That the salary of the Bishop be at the rate of $8,000 per annum, to take effect from the first day of November, A. D., 1890.

This resolution, passed by a large majority, was afterward made unanimous. The sentiment of the Convention showed their high appreciation and affectionate regard for their Diocesan.

We recognize the fact that the high position the Diocese holds in the American Church is largely owing to his successful administration during the twenty-two years of his Episcopate.

And each year does but secure him a larger place in the hearts and affections of his people.

WM. M. OGDEN,
G. POMEROY KEESE,
JNO. I. THOMPSON.

The Right Rev. the Bishop of the Diocese made a verbal response.

The Rev. Frederick S. Sill presented and read the following report, the resolutions contained in which were adopted.

REPORT OF THE COMMITTEE ON MORAL INSTRUCTION IN PUBLIC SCHOOLS.

The committee to whom was referred the communication from Rev. George S. Payson, Secretary of the Committee of Arrangements for a conference in New York on November 17th and 18th inst., in regard to the subject of religious instruction in the public schools of the State, and asking that a representation from this Convention be sent to the said conference, beg leave to report:

That they have examined the pamphlet accompanying the request, and find that the principles on which the Conference shapes its proposed action, are as follows:

That our national vigor and permanence are guaranteed only by a religiously grounded morality

That, without claiming it to be the province of the State to teach religion for religion's sake, for the State's own interest there should be in every school maintained by the State the inculcation of such principles of dependence upon God and obligation to Him as are essential to sound learning, safe character and wholesome citizenship.

The object of the Conference is to study this problem in all its details, to attempt its solution, and to secure by friendly co-operation the largest amount of painstaking religious and moral instruction in public schools that is consistent with that liberty of conscience which is guaranteed by the Constitution of the United States.

The specific topics for discussion at this conference are as follows.

(1.) Statistics concerning (a) Moral Instruction, and (b) Religious exercises in the public schools of this State.   Rev. D. G. Wylie, Ph. D., New York.

(2.) What do our Constitution and law hold concerning the teaching of religion in public schools?   William Allen Butler, LL. D.

(3.) What does expediency dictate as to any religious exercises in public schools?

(4.) How far does expediency dictate that State-supported schools should inculcate the principles of morals and religion?

(5.) What should be the ground and character of instruction in morals in our public schools?

(6.) What should this Conference do to carry out its views upon this subject?

With the general principle that the teaching of morals should be based upon the recognition of the existence of God and the responsibility of every human soul to God; that the human soul as made in the image of God is immortal; that a future spiritual state beyond the grave is real, in which every soul shall give account of itself before God, and shall reap that which it has sown, every Christian of every name must be in entire accord. As to the expediency of pressing the claims of religion and morality thus combined upon the hearts and consciences of the young, there can be no question. It is vital to the prosperity of the State. This Convention, by previous action upon the reports of its Committee on Christian Education, notably that of last year, has indorsed this principle.

The simple question remains, whether we are willing to co-operate with other Christian bodies, equally interested with ourselves in the general subject. It is clearly evident that where so many are concerned some sort of concerted action must be taken in order to secure any definite results of general uniformity.

It is felt by your Committee that the Church which this Convention, so far as its local boundaries go, represents, will not in any way compromise itself, or involve itself in any contradiction of its position as a teaching church, if this Convention in union with the Diocese of Long Island, which it seems has appointed a Committee to attend this Conference, should adopt the resolutions which your Committee beg leave to submit:

Resolved, That a Committee of three be appointed by the Bishop to attend the Conference in New York city, of various religious bodies, to consider the subject of Religion in our Public Schools, as outlined by the proposed topics for discussion.

Resolved, That the Communication of the Secretary of the Committee of Arrangements be acknowledged, and the said Secretary informed of the action taken by this Convention.

JOHN H. HOUGHTON,
FREDERICK S. SILL,
T. O. DUROE.

The Right Rev. President appointed as the Committee to attend the Conference on Moral Training in Public Schools, the Rev. Edgar A. Enos, the Rev. John H. Houghton and the Rev. William H. Bown.

The Rev. Charles S. Olmsted presented and read the following report, the resolution contained in which was adopted.

REPORT OF THE COMMITTEE TO CONFER WITH THE COMMITTEE ON ARCHDEACONRIES IN REGARD TO REGISTRATION OF SCATTERED CHILDREN OF THE CHURCH.

The Committee of five to confer with the Committee on Archdeaconries on the subject of an inspection of the waste places of the Diocese in order to bring the scattered children of the Church under its direct influence, beg leave to report that, having had a conference, they recommended to the Convention the adoption of the following resolution:

Resolved, That the Archdeaconries be instructed to consider the subject and to use their utmost endeavours to bring about some feasible scheme for the visitation and registration of such children of the Church, and to report their conclusions upon the subject at the next Annual Convention.

HENRY S. WYNKOOP,
For the Committee on Archdeaconries.

CHARLES S. OLMSTED,
WALTER C. STEWART,
WILLIAM L. DU BOIS.
For the Committee of Five.

Mr. Abram B. Cox presented and read the

REPORT OF THE TRUSTEES OF THE DIOCESE OF ALBANY.

The Trustees of the Diocese of Albany, respectfully report that at a meeting held March 24, 1890, it was resolved to permit the increase of indebtedness upon Christ Church, Gloversville, from $1,500 to $2,000.

At a meeting of the Trustees of the Diocese, held in St. Agnes' School, November 12, 1890, the gift of half an acre of land in the town of Springfield, Otsego county, on which is built the chapel of St. Mary's, was accepted.

A new seal was adopted in place of the old one.

For the Trustees,
A. B. COX,
Secretary.

The following preamble and resolutions presented by the Rev W. W. Battershall, D. D., and seconded by the Rev. Joseph Carey, S. T. D., were adopted

WHEREAS, The Committee to confer with a Committee of the Diocese of New York, in regard to the Episcopal Fund, have for many years been charged with the duty of presenting an equitable claim of this Diocese upon the Episcopal Fund of the Diocese of New York, and the negotiation of this claim has been a matter of deep concern to this Diocese, as well as of great difficulty and complexity; and

WHEREAS, The work of this Committee has at last been concluded by the recognition of the claim, and the payment by the Diocese of New York, of $25,000, which sum has been accepted by this Diocese as a full and satisfactory settlement of the claim; therefore,

Resolved, That this Convention hereby expresses its high appreciation of the zeal, wisdom and ability with which its Committee has conducted the negotiation, and discharged the important trust committed to its hands, and thereby secured a material increase and enrichment of the permanent Episcopal Fund of this Diocese.

Resolved, That this Convention hereby in particular, expresses its gratitude to the Rev. J. Livingston Reese, D. D., for his eminent and effective service in behalf of this Diocese as chairman of the said Committee.

Resolved, That the Convention put on record its sense of satisfaction, not only that the one subject of difference between the older and the younger Diocese is thus removed, but, also, that there has never been any interruption of the kindly and rightful relations between them.

The Rev. E. A. Hartmann presented and read the following reports:

REPORT OF THE WOMAN'S DIOCESAN LEAGUE.

It falls to my lot again as President of the Woman's Diocesan League to report what has been done during the fourth year of our organization, and to state what we ought to accomplish in the fifth year.

From the Treasurer's Report you will see the amounts made from the first year through this year. One can scarcely believe the sum total of $47,622.65 has been the result of our work.

Surely we should be encouraged, and not be staggered at the $7,000 which we must have to complete the $25,000 payment which we women have assumed.

What has been done can be done again.

Let us feel that it is a privilege to be permitted to work to clear off the debt contracted in the building of our beautiful Cathedral. It is an obligation which rests upon us. We cannot get rid of it but in one way — by paying our lawful debts.

Non-parochial branches of the League report good work in their own parishes ; $500 in Lebanon Springs, and about $100 in Franklin.

MARY PARKER CORNING.

TREASURER'S REPORT,

From February, 1889, to February, 1890.

Received.

Offertory St. Paul's Church, Vergennes	$10	76
From the 25th Card Fund	242	20
From Mrs. Corning's Fund	246	05
Gifts from sundry individuals	184	25
Sales of Photographs, Guides, Boxes and small articles	122	14
Sale held 1st week in December, net proceeds	1,547	03
Proceeds of Theatrical Entertainments and Lecture	1,628	50
Collected in several Mite-Boxes	32	54
From Miss Smith's S. S. Class, Christ Church, Troy	25	00
Miss Robbins' S. S. Class, Cathedral	82	60
Cathedral Alms-Box	30	84
From St. Agnes' Guild, in May	58	00
St. Agatha's Guild, at Xmas	35	00
St. Mary's Guild, at All Saints	151	50
Easter Offertory, Cathedral	955	56
All Saints' Day Offertory	366	05
Xmas Day in Offertory	50	00
Subscriptions paid through the Bishop	1,025	00
Interest on deposits in Saving Bank	20	25
Total of Gifts for year	$6,812	77
Balance on hand February, 1889		76
Received from Treasurer of Dues	938	20
Total of Moneys received	$7,751	73

Paid.

For Printing Report, 1889	$13	65
Paid Gavit & Co., for Signs	3	00
For Minute Book for Secretary		85
Whittle, Decorations for Tableaux	12	50
Interest on Mortgage, May 30	350	00
Interest on Mortgage, November 30	350	00
To N. Y. Mutual Life Insurance Co., reduction of Mortgage	4,000	00
Total paid out	$4,780	00
Balance in Savings Bank February 1, 1890	3,021	73
	$7,751	73

18

MONEYS EARNED BY LEAGUE SINCE FEBRUARY 1, 1886.

February, 1886, to 1887...	$13,136 59
February, 1887, to 1888...	15,734 33

Paid to Treasurer of Building Fund..........	$28,870 92
February 1888, to 1889, paid to Mutual Life Insurance Co., to reduce mortgage...............	11,000 00
February, 1889, to 1890, $4,750 paid on mortgage, principal and interest, $3,021.73 in Savings Bank...... ....:.....	7,751 73
	$47,622 65

E. G. D. GARDINER,
Treasurer of Gifts.

REPORT OF THE COMMITTEE ON THE WOMAN'S DIOCESAN LEAGUE.

Your Committee to whom was referred the report of the President of the Woman's Diocesan League, respectfully beg. to say, that the showing of that report is exceedingly gratifying, and is most satisfactory evidence of the wisdom and benefit of its organization. During the four years of its existence it has raised the large amount of $47,622.65. During the past year the result of their work is $7,751.73. This demonstrates one thing, viz.: that while the work has been very quietly done, it has strong life. There is no reason for believing that the $7,000 which still remains due on the pledge of the League, which amounted to $25,000 toward the payment of the indebtedness of the Cathedral of All Saints, will not be forthcoming. The plan and purpose of the League as a Diocesan institution has justified itself, and your Committee are convinced that its continuance, and a more hearty interest among the parishes of the Diocese, will make it a powerful agent for the Church's work in the Diocese, as the Woman's Auxiliary has become a powerful factor in the Church's great missionary work.

Your Committee recommend that the Convention express their appreciation of the work which the women of the Diocese have undertaken and so satisfactorily performed, and the strong desire that they continue and maintain an organization which has shown itself so helpful a factor in Diocesan work.

ERNEST A. HARTMANN,
JNO. KEYES PAIGE

On motion of the Rev. J. Philip B. Pendleton, it was

Resolved, That the Secretary of the Diocese be directed to print in the next Convention Journal copies of the necessary certificates to be used by Churches applying to be admitted into union with this Convention.

On motion of the Rev. Edgar A. Enos, it was

Resolved, That with and as part of the Journal of the Convention there be printed the constitution of the Diocese, and Canons, rules of order, and all written rules governing the calling, holding and procedure of the Conventions of the Diocese.

On motion of the Rev. Richmond Shreve, D. D., the following resolution was referred to the Board of Missions for their consideration:

Resolved, That the Lay people of this Diocese be encouraged to pay the premium of insurance on the lives of the married Missionaries who serve under the Board of Missions — policies to be held in hands of Secretary of Board with blank assignmen *signed by the insured,* to be transferred in case of removal from the Diocese.

The minutes of this day's session were read and adopted.
The Convention took a recess until half-past four o'clock.

HALF-PAST FOUR O'CLOCK IN THE AFTERNOON.

The Convention reassembled in the Cathedral.
The Bishop delivered the remainder of his Annual Address.
Prayers were said by the Rev. W. G. W. Lewis and the Bishop pronounced the Benediction.
The Convention adjourned *sine die.*

WM. CROSWELL DOANE,
Bishop of Albany and President of the Convention.

WM. C. PROUT, *Secretary.*
THOMAS B. FULCHER, *Assistant Secretary.*

APPENDIX.

(A.)

PAROCHIAL REPORTS.

Albany County.

CATHEDRAL OF ALL SAINTS, ALBANY.

THE CATHEDRAL CHAPTER.

Bishop. The Right Rev. William Croswell Doane, S. T. D., LL. D.

Dean. The Rev. Wilford L. Robbins.

Precentor. The Rev. Thomas B. Fulcher.

Treasurer. The Rev. Edgar T. Chapman.

Honorary Canons. The Revs. Edward Selkirk, Richard Temple, F. M. Gray, Edward D. Tibbits, Charles H. Hatheway.

Lay Members. A. Bleecker Banks, Thomas Hun, M. D., Erastus Corning, Selden E. Marvin, Assistant Treasurer, Marcus T. Hun, Vice-Chancellor, Robert S. Oliver.

Parochial.

Baptisms (adults, 17, infants, 85), 102; Confirmed, 79; Marriages, 9; Burials, 31; Communicants, last reported, 548; Present Number, 578; Public Services (Daily Celebration of Holy Communion, Sundays and Holy days, two Celebrations, Daily Matins, and Even Song throughout the year, Private Celebrations of Holy Communion, 14); Sunday School, teachers, 20, pupils, 288; Catechising, number of times, 25; St. Agnes' School, teachers, 30, pupils, 245.

Offerings.

Parochial.—Alms for Poor, $141.20; Current expenses, including salaries, $12,168.23; Increase and Improvement of Church Property, $7,198.89; Other parochial objects: Cathedral building and debt, $452.45; Total, $19,960.77.

Diocesan.—Diocesan Missions, $1,200; Salary of the Bishop, $150; Diocesan Fund, $100; Fund for Aged and Infirm Clergymen, $116.59; Fund for Widows and Orphans of Clergymen, $5; Orphan House of the Holy Saviour, $55.78; The Child's Hospital new building, $2,362.33; Society for Promoting Religion and Learning, $25.71; Other offerings for objects within the Diocese: Woman's Auxiliary, Diocesan Missions, $246.92; St. Margaret's House, $5. Total, $4,267.33.

General.— Domestic and Foreign Missions from Sunday School, $165; Domestic Missions, $164.61; Foreign Missions, $73.53; Jewish Missions, $21.61; Other objects exterior to the Diocese: St. John's Church, Louisville, $75.25; Order Brothers of

Nazareth. $115; Domestic Missions from Woman's Auxiliary, $281.19; Foreign Missions from Woman's Auxiliary, $50.90.   Total, $946.19.
Total amount of Offerings, $25,174.29.

Property.

Church and lot (estimated worth), $300,000.
Other property, $12,000.
Condition of property, good.
Indebtedness, $55,000.
Amount of salary pledged Dean, $3,800.
Amount of salary pledged Precentor, $500.
Number of sittings in the Church 2,375; all free.

ST. PETER'S CHURCH, ALBANY.

Rector. The Rev. Walton W. Battershall, D. D.
Wardens. George S. Weaver, Joseph W. Tillinghast.
Vestrymen. Luther H. Tucker, Henry T. Martin, Theodore Townsend, F. E. Griswold, Robert C. Pruyn, John Macdonald, Thomas S. Wiles, Abraham Lansing.

Parochial.

Baptisms (adults, 15, infants, 17), 32; Confirmed, since last report, 45, present number of confirmed persons, 705; Marriages, 14; Burials, 36; Communicants, last reported, 674, admitted, 45, received, 15, died, 12, removed, 20, present number, 702; Public Services (Sundays, 132, Holy days, 28, other days, 190), 350; Holy Communion (public, 82, private, 23), 105; Sunday School, teachers, 34, pupils, 300; Parish School, teachers, 6, pupils, 23; Sewing School, teachers, 15, pupils, 258.

Offerings.

Parochial.—Repairs to Rectory, $500; Alms at Holy Communion, $847.73; Current expenses, including salaries, $11,791.77; Sunday School, $164.68; St. Peter's Orphanage, $1,385.57; Increase and Improvement of Church Property, $2,489.12; Other parochial objects, Parish Aid Society, $834.52; Chancel Guild, $:07; Christmas Tree, $307; Sewing School, $79.56; Parish Mission Work, $1,158; Endowment Fund, $119.97. Total, $19,834.92.

Diocesan.— Diocesan Missions, $1,000.12; Salary of the Bishop, $150; Diocesan Fund, $120; Mission Church, Gloversville, $36.14; Albany Convocation, $19.03; Convention luncheon, $32; St. Margaret's House (S. S.), $19.80; Orphan House of the Holy Saviour, $58.79; The Child's Hospital (St. Peter's Guild, $128.50, Infant School, $38.60, Sewing School, $10, Dorothy Bissell, $17), $194.10. Total, $1,629.98.

General.— St. Stephen's College, $23.08; Domestic Missions, $300.81; Foreign Missions, $132.97; Indian Missions, $171.95; Home Missions to Coloured Persons, $149.71; Domestic Missions (Sunday School), $24.40; Woman's Auxiliary, $727.94; Bishop of Montana, $169.28; Bishop of Western Texas, $92.48; Church Building Fund, $76.55; Rev. Alex. Crummell, $25; Rev. Thomas W. Cain, Texas, $25. Total, $1,919.17.
Total amount of Offerings, $23,384.07.

Property.

Church and lot (estimated worth), $210,000; Parsonage and lot (freehold lease), $5,000; Parish House, $30,000; Orphanage, $10,000. Total, $255,000.
Amount of salary pledged Rector, $4,000.
Amount of salary pledged Assistant Minister, $1,000.
Number of sittings in the Church (and Chapel), 1,250.

ST. PAUL'S CHURCH, ALBANY.

Rector. The Rev. J. Livingston Reese, D. D.
Wardens. J. H. Van Antwerp, A. P. Palmer.
Vestrymen. John Woodward, George P. Wilson, Robert Geer, Matthew H. Robertson, Eugene Burlingame, Harvey A. Dwight, Wallace N. Horton, James H. Manning.

Parochial.

Baptisms (adults, 7, infants, 64), 71; Confirmed, since last report, 38; Marriages, 18; Burials, 43; Communicants, last reported, 694, admitted, 35, received, 10, died, 18, removed, 40, present number, 685; Sunday School, teachers, 50, pupils, 480.

Offerings.

Parochial.— Alms at Holy Communion, $325: Current expenses, including salaries, $7,960.50; Sunday School, $280.50; Increase and Improvement of Church Property, $452; Other parochial objects, from Sunday School, $404.99; for Poor, $257. Total, $9,679.99.

Diocesan.— Diocesan Missions, $364.64; Salary of the Bishop, $100; Diocesan Fund, $80; Fund for Widows and Orphans of Clergymen, $2,000; The Child's Hospital, $850; Other Offerings for objects within the Diocese, $220.50. Total, $3,615.14.

General.— Deaf Mute Mission, $42; Domestic Missions, $605.53; Foreign Missions, $250; Indian Missions, $60; Home Missions to Coloured Persons, $54.96; Other objects exterior to the Diocese, From Woman's Auxiliary for General Missions, $320; Other objects, $410. Total $1,732.49.

Total amount of Offerings, $15,028.61.

TRINITY CHURCH, ALBANY.

Rector. The Rev. Russell Woodman.
Wardens. William Little, John A. Howe.
Vestrymen. George F. Granger, Richard Story, J. Henry Marlow, Alexander Campbell, Charles Fairchild, Nordin T. Johnston, John Pritchard.

Parochial.

Families, 98; Baptisms (adults, 1, infants, 24), 25; Confirmed, 37, Marriages, 18; Burials, 16; Communicants, died, 8, present number recorded, 237; Public Services, Sundays, morning and evening, Holy days, celebration with sermon, other days, Friday evenings from October 1 to June 1; Holy Communion (public, 50, private, 18), 68. Sunday School, teachers, 20, pupils, 180.

Offerings.

Parochial.— Alms at Holy Communion, $49.20; Current expenses, including salaries. $1,809.19; Increase and Improvement of Church Property, $584.60. Total, $2,442.99.

Diocesan.— Diocesan Missions, $20, Salary of the Bishop, $20, The Child's Hospital (J. A. Howe), $5. Total, $45.

Total amount of Offerings, $2,487.99.

Property.

Church and lot (estimated worth), $40,000.
Parsonage and lot, $2,000.
Number of sittings in the Church, 450; number rented, 194, number free, 248.

GRACE CHURCH, ALBANY.

Rector. The Rev. William Henry Bown.

Wardens. Benjamin F. Hinman, Charles W. White.

Vestrymen. Henry Burn, E. W. Sewell, J. I. Sewell, George B. Longleway, F. H. Gilliland, A. E. Clark, Frank J. Smith, James R. Beauman.

Parochial.

Baptisms, adults and infants, 87; Confirmed, 24; Marriages, 17; Burials, 28; Communicants, last reported, 358, received, 24, present number recorded, 382; Sunday School, teachers, 38, pupils, 380.

Offerings.

Parochial.—Current expenses, including salaries, $3,783.12; Sunday School, $203; Increase and Improvement of Church Property, $377.83; Other parochial objects, $748.39. Total, $5,057.34.

Diocesan.—Diocesan Missions, $71; Salary of the Bishop, $24; Diocesan Fund, $30; Bible and Common Prayer Book Society of Albany, $8.53; Fund for Aged and Infirm Clergymen, $27.42; Fund for Widows and Orphans of Clergymen, $5; The Child's Hospital, $15.00; Other Offerings for objects within the Diocese, $92.46. Total, $273.41.

General.—Domestic and Foreign Missions, $113.48; Jewish Missions, $3.86. Total, $117.34.

Total amount of Offerings, $5,448.09.

Property.

Church and lot (estimated worth), $15,000.

Parsonage and lot, $5,000.

Condition of property, good.

Number of sittings in the Church, 500, all free.

Remarks.

The above report is not complete; the Rev. D. L. Schwartz, the beloved Rector of Grace Church for more than sixteen years, resigned his charge September 1, A. D. 1890; the Parish holds in most affectionate remembrance the long and prosperous ministry of their late Rector. For one month the Parish was without a Rector, during which time the Rev. Charles H. Hatheway conducted the services. The present incumbent became Rector October 1, 1890.

HOLY INNOCENTS' CHURCH, ALBANY.

Rector. The Rev. Richmond Shreve, D. D.

Wardens. S. M. Van Santvoord, W H. Weaver.

Vestrymen. George H. Birchall, G. W Leaning, J. Barrington Lodge, Jr., Dr J. W. Hine, T. J. Tobin, J. P. Reed, H. S McCall, Jr., James Oswald.

Parochial.

Baptisms (adults, 1, infants, 20), 21; Confirmed, since last report, 11; Marriages, 10; Burials, 17; Communicants, last reported, 187, admitted, 10, received, 6, died, 2, removed, 4, present number, 197; Public Services (Sundays, 147, Holy days, 27, other days, 88), 262, Holy Communion (public, 50, private, 13), 63; Sunday School, teachers, 19, scholars, 113, Catechizing, number of children, school, number of times, 20.

Offerings.

Parochial.—Alms at Holy Communion, $72 38, Current expenses, including salaries, $3,218.69; Sunday School, $180 95, Increase and Improvement of Church Property, $355.89. Total, $3,827.91.

Diocesan.—Diocesan Missions, $45.05; Salary of the Bishop, $45; Diocesan Fund, $45; Fund for Aged and Infirm Clergymen, $6; Fund for Widows and Orphans of Clergymen, $6.79; Orphan House of the Holy Saviour, $21.22; The Child's Hospital, $15; Other offerings for objects within the Diocese, St. Peter's Orphanage, Albany, $15. Total, $199.06.

General.—Indian Missions, $60; Home Missions to Coloured Persons, $10; Total, $70.

Total amount of Offerings, $4,086.97.

Property.

Church and lot (estimated worth), $20,000.
Parsonage and lot, $5,000.
Condition of property, good.
Number of sittings in the Church, 340; all free.

TRINITY CHURCH, RENSSELAERVILLE.

Rector. The Rev. Robert Washbon.
Assistant. The Rev. S. C. Thompson.
Wardens. John L. Rice, Nathaniel Teed.
Vestrymen. Charles B. Cross, Dewey Bell, Frank Rice, J. B. Washburn, M. D., James Rider, Luther Fox, Henry Sweet, Frank Frisbee.

Parochial.

Baptisms, infants, 3; Marriages, 2; Burials, 3; Communicants, last reported, 77, died, 3, removed, 3, present number, 71; Public Services, (Sundays, 96, Holy days, 10, other days, 8), 114; Holy Communion, public, 14; Sunday School, teachers, 6, pupils, 20; Catechizing, number of times, 12.

Offerings.

Parochial—Alms at Holy Communion, $19.25; Current expenses, including salaries, $467.71. Total, $486.96.

Diocesan.—Diocesan Missions, $17.88; Salary of the Bishop, $6; Diocesan Fund, $9; Bible and Common Prayer Book Society of Albany, $2.64; Orphan House of the Holy Saviour, $4; The Child's Hospital, $4.32. Total, $43.84.

General.—Domestic Missions, $11; Foreign Missions, $11; Other objects exterior to the Diocese: For Jews, $3. Total, $25.

Total amount of Offerings, $555.80.

Property.

Amount of salary pledged Rector, $105.
Amount of salary pledged Assistant Minister, $300.

ST. JOHN'S CHURCH, COHOES.

Rector. The Rev. Frederick S. Sill.
Wardens. Michael Andrae, John Horrocks.
Vestrymen. George Campbell, Samuel Horrocks, Reuben Lee, William S. Shipley, Luke Kavanaugh, P. Remsen Chadwick, George F. Ford, Harry J P. Green.

Parochial.

Families (besides individuals), 356; Individuals (adults, 1,060, children, 410), 1,470; Baptisms (adults, 8, infants, 43), 51; Confirmed, 19; Marriages, 21; Burials, 37; Churchings, 11; Communicants, last reported, 526, admitted, 20, received, 15, died, 8, removed, 32, present number recorded, 521, actually communicating, 390;

19

Public Services (Sundays, 149, Holy days, 58, other days, 159), 366; Holy Communion (public, 79, private, 10), 89: Sunday School, teachers, 21, pupils, 300; Catechizing, number of times, 27.

Offerings.

Parochial.—Alms at Holy Communion, $244.56; Current expenses, including salaries, $2,855.09; Sunday School, $81.73; Increase and Improvement of Church Property, $1,515.11; Other parochial objects, charitable, $41.31; Bequest for Church Home, $2,527.11. Total, $7,264.91.

Diocesan.—Diocesan Missions, $203; Salary of Bishop, $56; Diocesan Fund, $45; Fund for Aged and Infirm Clergymen, $12; Orphan House of the Holy Saviour, $15; The Child's Hospital, $12; Other offerings for objects within the Diocese: Woman's Diocesan League, $12; Memorial Pillar (part of balance), $200. Total, $555.

General.—Domestic and Foreign Missions, $56.89; Home Missions to Coloured Persons, $17.50; Other objects exterior to the Diocese, Jewish Missions, $7.40; Woman's Auxiliary, $295.11; Other objects, $9. Total, $385.90.

Total amount of Offerings, $8,205.81. *

Property.

Church and lot (estimated worth), $40,000.

Parsonage and lot, $10,000.

Other property, Church Home Fund, $2,527.11.

Home Fund for Poor, $1,500.

Condition of property, very good.

Indebtedness, $5,000.

Amount of salary pledged Rector, $1,500.

Number of sittings in the Church, 800; all free, but 'assigned to families and individuals.

Remarks.

During the year the Church was renovated and much improved by a new carpet, decoration of the walls, and new choir seats placed in the chancel

The bequest of Mrs. Jane Regan for a Church Home, made some years ago, was paid over to the Vestry, and is now invested in the name of the Corporation.

Miss Elizabeth Howe bequeathed to this Parish one-half of the residue of her estate which was found to amount to $1,500, the interest of which is received semi-annually from her executors as trustees, for the benefit of the poor.

Miss Ann Hodgson bequeathed to this Parish the sum of $100 to be used as the Vestry might direct.

The Pledge System has been adopted for the year 1891, with gratifying results at this date. The Envelope System has been in vogue for the past twenty years, and is the only available source of income.

TRINITY CHURCH, WEST TROY.

Rector. The Rev. E. Bayard Smith.

Wardens. William Hollands, John H. Hulsapple.

Vestrymen. William E. Baxter, Charles H. Crabbe, William Doring, Edmund S. Hollands, Thomas Rath, John Scarborough, Bertram F. Stewart, Robert Trimble.

Parochial.

Baptisms (adults 2, infants, 27), 29, Confirmed, since last report, 26; Marriages, 14; Burials, 28; Communicants, last reported, 318, admitted, 24, received, 7, died, 4, removed, 38, present number, 307. Public Services (Sundays, 92, Holy days, 32, other days, 130), 254; Holy Communion (public, 50, private, 3), 53; Sunday School, teachers, 29, pupils, 242; Catechizing, every session.

Offerings.

Parochial.—Alms at Holy Communion, $90.38; Current expenses, including salaries, $2,507.15: Trinity Sunday School, $195.79; St. Gabriel's Sunday School, $104.72; Increase and Improvement of Church Property, $100; Other parochial objects, Ladies' Guild, $15.30; Altrui Guild, $170. Total, $2,733.34.

Diocesan.—Diocesan Missions, $40.82; Salary of the Bishop, $32; Diocesan Fund, $24; Bible and Common Prayer Book Society of Albany, $5; Fund for Aged and Infirm Clergymen, $12; Fund for Widows and Orphans of Clergymen, $20; Orphan House of the Holy Saviour, $16; The Child's Hospital, $12; Society for Promoting Religon and Learning, $5. Total, $166.82.

General.—Domestic Missions, $19; Foreign Missions, $17 61; Other objects exterior to the Diocese, Church Missions to the Jews, $3; Fairview Home, $3; Woman's Auxiliary, $24.30; Box, valued at $25. Total, $91.91.

Total amount of Offerings, $2,992.07.

Property.

Church and lot (estimated worth), $24,000.

Other property, St. Gabriel's, $4,000; Parsonage and lot, $8,000.

Condition of property, good.

Number of sittings in the Church, 377; Chapel, 150; St. Gabriel's, 150.

Number rented, 300.

ST. MARK'S CHURCH, GREEN ISLAND.

Rector. The Rev. R. J. Adler.

Wardens. Richard Leonard, William E. Gilbert.

Vestrymen. Henry Stowell, Edward G. Gilbert, Thomas H. Walker, William H. H. DeMille, Harry Farmer, William W. Butler, James H. Eckler, Louis Harter, Jr.

Parochial.

Families, 171; Individuals, (adults 240, children, 227), 467; Baptisms (adults, 3, infants, 11), 14; Confirmed, since last report, 17; Marriages, 5; Burials, 7; Churchings, 1; Communicants, present number, 190; Public Services (Sundays, 115, other days, 59), 174; Holy Communion (public, 17, private, 3), 20, Sunday School, teachers 15, pupils, 131; Catechizing, all of the School weekly.

Offerings.

Parochial.—Alms at Holy Communion, $16.21; Current expenses, including salaries, $1,455.70; Increase and Improvement of Church Property, $109. Total, $1,580 91.

Diocesan.—Diocesan Missions, $63 08; Salary of the Bishop, $10, Diocesan Fund, $15; From Sunday School for St. Christina Home, $10. Total, $98.08.

General.—Domestic Missions, $15.35, Foreign Missions, $15.40; Jewish Missions, $7.09; Home Missions to Coloured Persons, $2.26; Lenten offerings of Sunday School for General Missions, $13.50, Sunday School offerings for Church Building Fund, $10.47. Total, $64.07.

Total amount of Offerings, $1,743.06.

Property.

Church and lot (estimated worth), $20,000.

Parsonage and lot, $7,000.

Condition of property, good.

Indebtedness, none.

Sittings in the Church and Chapel, all free.

Clinton County.

TRINITY CHURCH, PLATTSBURGH.

Rector. The Rev. Hobart Cook.
Wardens. Peter S. Palmer, George F. Nichols.
Vestrymen. Hon. S. A. Kellogg, Hon. Jno. M. Wever, A. L. Inman, A. M. Warren, Wm. T. Ketchum, Wm. J. McCaffrey, Chas. H. Moore, George S. Weed.

Parochial.

Baptisms, 6; Confirmed, 11; Marriages, 4; Burials, 11; Communicants, present number recorded, 190; Public Services, Sundays, morning and evening, Holy days, morning, Fridays, evening, daily in Lent ; Holy Communion, public, monthly, all great festivals, weekly in Lent; Sunday School, teachers, 6, pupils, 40.

Offerings.

Parochial.— Alms at Holy Communion, $60; Current expenses, including salaries, $1,864.85; Sunday School, $40; Increase and Improvement of Church Property, $340. Total, $2,304.85.

Diocesan.— Diocesan Missions, $44.23; Salary of Bishop, $50; Diocesan Fund, $36 The Child's Hospital, $37.88. Total, $168.11.

General.— Domestic Missions, $11; Jewish Missions, $6; Deaf-mute Missions, $16.05. Total, $33.05.

Total amount of Offerings, $2,506.01.

Property.

Church and lot (estimated worth), $20,000.
Parsonage and lot, $5,000.
Condition of property, good.
Rector's salary, $1,200.
Number of sittings in the Church, 450; all free.

Remarks.

This report for the last Conventional year covers the concluding ministrations of the late Rector, the Rev. Mr. Smyth, and the temporary administration of the Parish under the Rev. Mr. McIlwaine. The retirement of the Rev. Mr. Smyth, owing to greatly prolonged ill health, leaves open record of faithful ministry for the last twelve years, and brings into special notice many substantial tokens of difficult work undertaken and most successfully accomplished. The interests of the Parish during the somewhat protracted interval of vacancy in the rectorship, have been most judiciously and acceptably cared for by the Rev. J. W. McIlwaine, by invitation of the Vestry — the present Rector entering upon his duties in September.

CHRIST CHURCH, ROUSE'S POINT.

Rector. The Rev. W. D. U. Shearman.
Wardens. D White, J. Phillips.
Vestrymen. W. Crook, W. Phillips, C. J. S. Randal, Elmer Bullis, Mr. Wood.

Parochial.

Families, 60; Baptisms, infants, 3; Marriages, 1; Burials, 6; Communicants, last reported, 60, died, 2, removed, 2, present number recorded, 58; Public Services (Sundays, 52, Holy days, 4, other days, 8), 64; Holy Communion (public, 12, private, 3), 15; Sunday School, teachers, 6, pupils, 60.

Offerings.

Parochial.—Current expenses, including salaries, $396.17; Sunday School, $25; Increase and Improvement of Church Property, $120.28. Total, $541.45.

Diocesan.—Salary of the Bishop, $10.

General.—Domestic Missions, $16.

Total amount of Offerings, $567.45.

Property.

Church and lot (estimated worth), $8,000.

Condition of property, good.

Amount of salary pledged Rector, $200.

Number of pews in the Church, 44; number rented, 20, number free, 24.

ST. JOHN'S CHURCH, CHAMPLAIN.

Rector. The Rev. W. D. U. Shearman.

Wardens. James Averill, Jr., Jehiel White.

Vestrymen. Henry Hoyle, Charles R. Ely, Henry Durham, Ransom Graves, James Burroughs.

Parochial.

Families, 15; Baptisms, infant, 1; Confirmed, 3; Marriages, 2; Burials, 3; Churchings, 1; Communicants, admitted, 3, received, 1, died, 2, removed, 1, present number recorded, 32; Public Services (Sundays, 53, Holy days, 14, other days, 29), 96; Holy Communion, public, 39; Sunday School, teachers, 2, pupils, 15.

Offerings.

Parochial.—Current expenses, including salaries, $310.

Diocesan.—Diocesan Missions, $20.

General.—Domestic Missions, $12.

Total amount of Offerings, $542.

Property.

Church and lot (estimated worth), $3,000.

Parsonage and lot, $1,600.

Condition of property, good.

Amount of salary pledged Rector, $400.

Sittings in the Church, all free.

ST. PETER'S CHURCH, ELLENBURGH.

Rector. The Rev. Silas M. Rogers, A. M.

Wardens. William H. Sawyers, Giles H. Corens.

Vestrymen. George Higgins, Hemar Allen. James Higgins, Allen S. Sargent, Byron Emerson, Millard Emerson, and John Hammond.

Parochial.

Baptisms, infants, 12; Confirmed, 2, Marriages, 7; Burials, 5; Communicants, died, 1, present number recorded, 38; Sunday School, teachers, 2, pupils, 20.

Offerings.

Parochial.—Alms at Holy Communion, $5.71; Increase and Improvement of Church Property, $100. Total, $105.71.

Diocesan.—Diocesan Missions, $5, Salary of the Bishop, $2, Diocesan Fund, $1.50; Total, $8.50.

Total amount of Offerings, $114.21.

Property.

Church and lot (estimated worth), $2,000.
Condition of property, good.
Number of sittings in the Church, 150; all free.

ST. PAUL'S CHURCH, ELLENBURGH CENTRE.

Rector. The Rev. Silas M. Rogers, A. M.
Wardens. George W. Carpenter, Orson Hoff.
Vestrymen. Edwin Eldred, C. C. Carpenter, Ryland C. Holt, A. S. Phelps, Stephen Goodspeed, Lyman Carpenter, Alfred Harris, Thomas Harris.

Parochial.

Baptisms (adults, 1. infants, 6). 7; Confirmed, 1; Marriages, 11; Burials, 6; Communicants, admitted, 1, present number recorded, 20.

Offerings.

Parochial.—Alms at Holy Communion, $7.80, Increase and Improvement of Church Property, $86. Total, $93.80.
Diocesan.—Diocesan Missions, $5; Salary of the Bishop, $2; Diocesan Fund, $1.50. Total, $8.50.
Total amount of Offerings, $102.30.

Property.

Church and lot (estimated worth), $2,000.
Condition of property, good.
Number of sittings in the Church, 160; all free.

Columbia County.

CHRIST CHURCH, HUDSON.

Rector. The Rev. John C. Tebbetts, to Sept. 15, 1890.
Wardens. Robert B. Monell, William B. Skinner.
Vestrymen. Henry J. Baringer, John P. Wheeler, M. D., John M. Pearson, Smith Thompson, Arthur C. Stott, Charles W. Bostwick, Clarence Crofts, Frank T. Punderson.

Parochial.

Baptisms (adults, 6. infants, 32), 38; Confirmed, 21; Marriages, 13; Burials, 26; Communicants, present number recorded, 439, Public Services (Sundays, 144, Holy days, 28; other days, 96); Holy Communion (public, 62, private, 10), 72, Sunday School teachers, 27, pupils, 275, Catechizing, number of children, 275.

Offerings.

Parochial —Alms at Holy Communion, $114.29; Current expenses, including salaries, $2,482 80; Sunday School, $111.78, Improvement of Church Property, $568.33; Other parochial objects, $189 35. Total, $3,466 55
Diocesan.—Diocesan Missions, $100; Salary of the Bishop, $60, Diocesan Fund, $36; Fund for Aged and Infirm Clergymen, $6 60, Fund for Widows and Orphans of Clergymen, $8.67, Orphan House of the Holy Saviour, $18 17, The Child's Hospital (building fund, $120, from Sunday School, $25 30), $145 30), Other Offerings objects within the Diocese, $32.79. Total, $407.53.

General.—General Theological Seminary, $8.70; Domestic Missions, $15.43; Foreign Missions, $8.47; Indian Missions, $10; Home Missions to Coloured Persons, $15.78; Other objects exterior to the Diocese, Conversion of Jews, $5.06; General Missions from Children, $42.24; Bishop Leonard, Work in Utah, $15; Woman Worker, $6; Mrs. Buford, box valued at $100. Total, $226.68.

Total amount of Offerings, $4,100.76.

Remarks.

Since September 15 the Parish has been without a Rector, but regular services have been maintained each Sunday, by the Rev. E. S. De G. Tompkins.

CHURCH OF ST. JOHN THE EVANGELIST, STOCKPORT.

Rector. The Rev. Ernest Mariett, from Feb. 9, 1890, to Nov. 10, 1890.

Assistant. The Rev. W. B. Reynolds, Deacon. A. E. Heard, Lay Reader.

Wardens. William H. Van de Carr, Frank C. Kittle.

Vestrymen. F. H. Stott, G. B. Reynolds, Joshua Reynolds, John Wild, Jacob Pultz, F. M. Snyder, F. W. Buss, L. J. Rossman.

Parochial.

Baptisms, infants, 13; Confirmed, 5, Burials, 6; Communicants, last reported, 137, admitted 5, removed, 12, present number recorded, 130; Public Services (Sundays, three every Sunday, Holy days, Holy Communion); Holy Communion (public) weekly; Sunday School, teachers, 12, pupils, 75; Catechizing, number of children, Sunday School and Parish School, number of times, weekly in Sunday School, and daily in Parish School; Parish School, teachers, 3. pupils, 48.

Offerings.

Parochial.—Alms at Holy Communion, $31.14, Current expenses, including salaries, $1,137.78, (of which $31.94 is from St. James' Mission), Sunday School, $183.97 (of which $136.28 is for organ). Parish School, $4.06; Other parochial objects, for new organ, $326.40 (of which $330 is from Ladies' Society); St. James' Mission Sunday School, $8. Total, $1.991.35

Diocesan.—Diocesan Missions, $9.88 (of which $6.15 is from St. James' Mission); Salary of the Bishop, $25, Diocesan Fund, $30; Bible and Common Prayer Book Society of Albany, $14.43; Fund for Aged and Infirm Clergymen, $3.11; Orphan House of the Holy Saviour, $5.91 (from St. James';Mission), Society for Promoting Religion and Learning, $2. Total, $90.33.

General.—Foreign Missions, $1.40, Other objects exterior to the Diocese, American Church Building Fund, $5; Jewish Missions, $2.22. Total, $8.62.

Total amount of Offerings, $2,090.30.

Property.

Church and lot, and Church yard (estimated worth), $15,000.

Parsonage and lot, $4,000.

Other property (school-house), $3,000.

Condition of property, good.

Amount of salary pledged Rector, $1,000.

Number of sittings in the Church, 280, chapel, 150, all free.

Remarks.

This report is complete for only nine months in the items of services.

The Parish is greatly indebted to the Rev. W. B Reynolds, for his faithful services. The weekly Eucharist has been established, and the average attendance has been one-fourth of the actual communicants during the year.

At the Parish Churcht here has been beside the weekly celebration, Morning Prayer and sermon, and Evening Prayer and sermon, every Sunday. Also, Evening Prayer and instruction, Friday evening.

At St. James' Mission the Rector has had a monthly celebration, and every Sunday afternoon, evening prayer and sermon. During Lent, a daily service at the Parish Church, and a service every Thursday evening at the mission.

ST. PAUL'S CHURCH, KINDERHOOK.

Rector. The Rev. Isaac Peck.

Wardens. Henry S. Wynkoop, Edward P. Van Alstyne.

Vestrymen. Francis Silvester, T. F. Woodworth, Wm. H. Fish, Edgar Balls, Frank B. Van Alstyne, James M. Hawley, Andrew Ketterson, Tunis Devoe.

Parochial.

Families, 75; Individuals (adults. 174, children, 112), 286; Baptisms (adults, 3, infants, 20), 23; Confirmed, 8; Marriages, 1; Burials, 8; Communicants, last reported 126, admitted, 10, received, 2, died, 3, removed, 3, present number recorded, 132, actually communicating, 123; Public Services (Sundays, 111, Holy days, 43, other days, 38), 192; Holy Communion (public, 46, private, 7), 53; Sunday School, teachers, 10, pupils, 73; Catechizing, number children, whole school; number of times, weekly.

Offerings.

Parochial.— Alms at Holy Communion, $27.26; Current expenses, including salaries, $1,100; Sunday School, $64.80; Increase and Improvement of Church Property, $175. Total. $1,367.06.

Diocesan.— Diocesan Missions, $15.41 ; Salary of the Bishop, $47 ; Fund for Aged and Infirm Clergymen, $28.38; Fund for Widows and Orphans of Clergymen, $21.44; Orphan House of the Holy Saviour (from Sunday School), $8.50: The Child's Hospital (from Sunday School), $8.50; Other offerings for objects within the Diocese. Bishop's window, $10.93. Total, $140.16.

General.— Lent Reading, $11; Domestic Missions, $30.80; Foreign Missions, $11.16; Home Missions to Coloured Persons, $2; Other objects exterior to the Diocese. Sunday School (Lenten offering) General Missions. $20, Jewish Missions, $3.76, for New York Prayer Book and Bible Society, $1. Total, $79.72.

Total amount of Offerings, $1,586.94.

Property.

Church and lot (estimated worth), $5,000.

Parsonage and lot. $3,000

Condition of property, excellent.

Amount of salary pledged Rector, $700, and Rectory.

Number of sittings in the Church, 150: all free.

Remarks.

In addition to offerings in cash for Missions, the Woman's Auxiliary has sent two barrels of new clothing to the Cooperstown Orphanage, valued at $84; and one barrel to St. Mark's Hospital, Salt Lake City, Utah, valued at $42

The following Memorials have been presented to the Parish during the past year: an oak font cover with brass mountings, a solid silver christening bowel, and a solid silver baptismal shell, a Litany desk of polished brass, an altar rail in antique oak work, polished brass standards; a brass ewer for font; a pair of cut glass cruets, silver mounted, for the Holy Communion; and a Prayer desk in polished brass.

TRINITY CHURCH, CLAVERACK.

Rector. The Rev. Elmer P. Miller.
Wardens. Robert Fulton Ludlow, Richard M. Ludlow.
Vestrymen. Cornelius Shaw, Frank P. Studley, James J. Studley, Arthur A. Rowley.

Parochial.

Families, 25; Baptisms (adults, 2, infants, 4), 6; Confirmed, 7; Burials, 3; Communicants, last reported, 38, admitted, 7, received, 6, died, 1, present number recorded, 45; Public Services (Sundays, 51, Holy days, 8, other days, 35), 94; Holy Communion (public, 21, private, 1), 22; Sunday School, teachers, 5, pupils, 50.

Offerings.

Parochial.— Alms at Holy Communion, $14.09; Current expenses, including salaries, $380.66; Sunday School, $24.27; Increase and Improvement of Church Property, $136. Total, $555.02.
Diocesan.— Diocesan Missions, $12; Salary of the Bishop, $6; Diocesan Fund, $7.50. Total, $25.50.
Total amount of Offerings, $580.52.

CHURCH OF OUR SAVIOUR, LEBANON SPRINGS.

Wardens. Silas G. Owen, William Henry Babcock.
Vestrymen. John G. Field, Francis Myers, J. Harry Cox, Albert B. Parsons, Charles E. Wackerhagen.

Parochial.

Families, 35; Individuals (adults, 69, children, 8), 77; Baptisms (adults, 1, infants, 2), 3; Present number of confirmed persons, 46; Burials, 1; Communicants, last reported, 48, died, 1, removed, 2, present number, 45; Services, Sundays, morning and evening, other days, general festivals; Holy Communion, monthly.

Offerings.

Parochial—Alms at Holy Communion and current expenses, including salary, $432.08; Increase and Improvement of Church Property, $38 06. Total, $470.14.
Diocesan.— Diocesan Missions, $20; Diocesan Fund, $9; Salary of the Bishop, $6; Fund for Aged and Infirm Clergymen, $5; Orphan House of the Holy Saviour, $3.80; The Child's Hospital, $2; Fund for Widows and Orphans of Deceased Clergymen, $2; Bible and Common Prayer Book Society of Albany, $1; Episcopal Fund, $1; Education of Young Men for the Ministry, $1. Total, $50.80.
General.— Domestic Missions, $5; Foreign Missions, $5. Total, $10.
Total amount of Offerings, $530.94.

Property.

Church and lot (estimated worth), $3,000.
Other property, Rectory lot, $273.29.
Condition of property, good
Amount of salary pledged Rector, $300.
Number of sittings in the Church, 150, all free.

Remarks

As reported last year, the ladies of the local branch of the Diocesan League have raised money for a Rectory fund, and have bought and paid for a desirable site adjoining the Church (which is now inclosed in the church-yard), and have quite a sum on hand since that report. They have raised by a Fair and Sale, $500; from an

20

entertainment given by the children staying at Columbia Hall, $35; from unsolicited gifts, $67.50. Making a total of nearly $900 in treasurer's hands, besides several hundred dollars in pledges. If success attends their efforts, the ladies hope by another year to report a Rectory under way, if not completed. Which, in the saving of rent, will assist materially to the small stipend the Church in this place is obliged to offer.

ALL SAINTS' CHURCH, HUDSON.

Rector.   The Rev. Elmer P. Miller.
Wardens.   William H. Cookson, Richard A. Aitkin.
Vestrymen.   Alexander R. Benson, Robert Storms, Franklin Palmer, Benjamin Thompson.

Parochial.

Families, 50; Baptisms (adults, 2, infants, 17), 19; Confirmed, 10; Marriages, 3; Burials, 8, Communicants, last reported, 77, admitted, 10, received, 5, died, 1, present number recorded, 91; Public Services (Sundays, 51, Holy days, 12, other days, 50), 113; Holy Communion (public, 22, private, 2), 24; Sunday School, teachers, 11, pupils, 70.

Offerings.

Parochial.— Alms at Holy Communion, $14.03; Current expenses, including salaries, $521.44; Sunday School, $55; Other parochial objects, old debt, $175. Total, $765.47.

Diocesan.— Diocesan Missions, $12; Salary of the Bishop, $6; Diocesan Fund, $9. Total, $27.

Total amount of Offerings, $792.47.

ST. BARNABAS' CHURCH, STOTTVILLE.

Rector.   The Rev. Frederick Golden Rainey.
Wardens.   Francis Horatio Stott, John J. Plass.
Vestrymen.   C. H. Stott, Jr., Fred. Welch, R. H. Harder, Jr., Fred. Palmer, Levi Plass, Joseph Tanner, Charles Williams, W. H. Tanner.

Parochial.

Families, 112; Individuals (adults, 325, children, 200), 525; Baptisms (adults, 6, infants, 15), 21; Confirmed, 38; Marriages, 5; Burials, 6; Communicants, last reported, 129, admitted, 43, received, 10, died, 2, removed, 2, present number recorded, 172, actually communicating, 121; Public Services (Sundays, 102, Holy days, 10, other days, 60), 172; Holy Communion (public, 23, private, 1), 24; Sunday School, teachers, 27, pupils, 230; Catechizing, number of children, 220; number of times, weekly.

Offerings.

Parochial.— Alms at Holy Communion, $110.16; Current expenses, including salaries, $1,536.63; Sunday School, $364.35; Increase and Improvement of Church Property, $33.87, Other parochial objects, Altar Society, $17; Repairs on Rectory, $135. Total, $2,216.01.

Diocesan.— Diocesan Missions, $21.64, Salary of the Bishop, $25. Diocesan Fund, $18.62; Bible and Common Prayer Book Society of Albany, $10.50; Fund for Aged and Infirm Clergymen, $10. Orphan House of the Holy Saviour, $56. Total, $141.76.

General.— Domestic Missions, $20; Other objects exterior to the Diocese, Jewish Missions, $7.67. Total, $27.67.

Total amount of Offerings, $2,385.44.

Property.

Church and lot (estimated worth), $10,000.
Condition of property, very good.
Amount of salary pledged Rector, $1,200.
Number of sittings in the Church, 350: all free.

Remarks.

The work of enlarging and beautifying the Church is still in progress. When completed it will be a handsome and imposing structure, a credit to a true and loyal people. The improvements will involve an expenditure of $4,500.

ST. LUKE'S MISSION, CHATHAM.

Priest in charge. The Rev. Isaac Peck.

Parochial.

Families, 16; Individuals (adults, 39, children, 18), 57; Confirmed, since last report, 1, present number of confirmed persons, 30; Burials, 1; Communicants, last reported, 24, admitted, 1, received, 5, died, 1, removed, 4, present number, 25; Public Services (Sundays, 50, Holy days, 2, other days, 2), 54; Holy Communion (public, 14, private, 1), 15.

Offerings.

Parochial.— Current expenses, including salaries, $153; Increase and Improvemen of Church Property, $16.52. Total, $169.52.
Diocesan.— Diocesan Missions, $5; Diocesan Fund, $3. Total, $8.
Total amount of Offerings, $177.52.
Amount of salary pledged Rector, $100.

ST. LUKE'S CHURCH, CLERMONT.

Rector. The Rev. M. E. Wilson.
Trustees. Robert Dibblee, Harold Wilson, George Z. Foland, M. E. Wilson, W. C. Doane, H. J. Rivenburg.

Parochial.

Marriages, 1; Burials, 2; Communicants, died, 2, present number recorded, 19; Public Services (Sundays, 44, other days, 4), 48; Holy Communion (public, 10, private, 1), 11.

Offerings.

Parochial — Current expenses, $23.10.
Diocesan.— Diocesan Missions, $10: Salary of the Bishop, $4; Diocesan Fund, $2. Total, $16.
Total amount of Offerings, $39.10

CHURCH OF ST. MARK THE EVANGELIST, PHILMONT.

(No Report.)

Delaware County.

ST. PETER'S CHURCH, HOBART.

Rector. The Rev. John A. Farrar.
Warden. Alexander Haswell Grant.
Vestrymen. George Barlow, Robert McNaught, Alexander McDonald, George Sturges, Charles S. Perkins, James McDonald, Alpheus Rollins, W. J. Calhoun, Orlando B. Foote.

Parochial.

Families, 66; Individuals (adults, 250, children, 130), 380; Baptisms, infants, 2; Present number of confirmed persons, 171; Marriages, 2; Burials, 2; Communicants, last reported, 171, removed, 1, present number, 170; Public Services (Sundays, 200, Holy days, 20, other days, 17), 237; Holy Communion (public, 21, private, 1), 22; Sunday School, teachers, 8; pupils, 80; Catechizing, number of times, 40.

Offerings.

Parochial.— Alms at Holy Communion, $29.86; Current expenses, including salaries, $667; Sunday School, $18.66; Increase and Improvement of Church Property, $124.89; Other parochial objects, $168.45; repairing of organ, $8. Total, $1,016.86.

Diocesan.— Diocesan Missions, $35; Salary of the Bishop, $8; Diocesan Fund, $13; Orphan House of the Holy Saviour, $2.75; Other offerings for objects within the Diocese, for Jews' Conversion Society, $1. Total, $59.75.

Total amount of Offerings, $1,076.61.

Property.

Church and lot (estimated worth), $5,000.
Parsonage and lot, $1,500.
Other property at Hobart, $500.
Condition of property, good.
Amount of salary pledged Rector, $600.
Number of sittings in the Church, 350; number rented, 200; number free, 150.

Remarks.

The number of communicants at Hobart is less this year on account of Grace Mission, Stamford, having been set apart. I hold services at the Mission at Bloomville, every alternate Sunday at 3 P. M.

ST. JOHN'S CHURCH, DELHI.

Rector. The Rev. F. B. Reazor.
Lay Reader. Robert G. Hughston.
Wardens. Charles E. Hitt, Robert G. Hughston.
Vestrymen. John W. Woodruff, Alexander Shaw, George M. Harby, Edwin H. Sheldon, William C. Sheldon, George A. Paine, Herbert Pitcher, John Kemp.

Parochial.

Families, 94, Individuals (adults, 227, children, 110), 337; Baptisms (adults, 4, infants, 19), 23; Confirmed, since last report, 10, present number of confirmed persons, 221; Marriages, 4, Burials, 12; Churching, 1: Communicants, admitted, 12, received, 2, died, 6, removed, 7, present number, 215; Public Services (Sundays, 168, other days, 538), 706; Holy Communion (public, 118, private, 17), 135; Sunday School, teachers, 8, pupils, 65; Catechizing, number of times, every Sunday.

Offerings.

Parochial.— Alms at Holy Communion, $88 15; Current expenses, including salaries, $1,704 59; Sunday School, $63 92, Miscellaneous, $108 88; Other parochial objects, Altar Society, $53 55; Parish League, $90 65. Total, $2,109.74.

Diocesan.— Diocesan Missions, $100, Salary of the Bishop, $30; Diocesan Fund, $20; Bible and Common Prayer Book Society of Albany, $10. Fund for Aged and Infirm Clergymen, $10 54; Fund for Widows and Orphans of Clergymen, $21 02; Orphan House of the Holy Saviour, $40.57; The Child's Hospital, $20.93; Society for Promoting Religion and Learning, $7 44; Other offerings for objects within the Diocese.

Convocation of the Susquehanna, $23.59; box to Child's Hospital, valued at $15; box to Orphanage, Cooperstown, valued at $10. Total, $309.09.

General.— Domestic Missions, $21.75; Indian Missions, $18.01; Home Missions to Coloured Persons, $94; Other objects exterior to the Diocese, Church Mission to Jews, $31.49; Church at Durango, Col. (special), $130; Auxiliary boxes for Dakota and Japan, valued at $110. Total, $390.25.

Total amount of Offerings, $2,809.08.

Property.

Church and lot (estimated worth), $10,000.
Parsonage and lot, $3,500.
Other property, Memorial Chapel and study, $25,000.
Condition of property, good.
Amount of Salary pledged Rector, $1,200.
Number of sittings in the Church, 354, Chapel, 125, total, 479; number free, 141.

Remarks.

On Friday, May 23, 1890, the Memorial Chapel was deeded to the corporation of this Parish by Mr. Edwin H. Sheldon, and the Bishop of the Diocese on the same day dedicated the nave to parochial uses, and consecrated the chancel and altar.

Since the last Parochial Report was made, this exquisite building has been further enriched by an altar of red Lisbon marble and terra cotta, with a *mensa* of white Mexican onyx inlaid with five red jasper crosses.

At the expense of the donor, a Rector's study of great beauty and convenience has been erected in the rear of the Chapel, in immediate communication with both the Church and the Chapel.

In this Chapel the daily offices of the Church are said the year round.

CHRIST CHURCH, WALTON.

Rector. The Rev. Scott B. Rathbun.
Wardens. David H. Gay, George St. John.
Vestrymen. S. H. St. John, John S. Eells, George C. Seeley, S. H. Fancher, Francis Robinson, J. W. St. John, Joseph Harby, Horace E. North.

Parochial.

Families, 108; Baptisms (adults, 1, infants, 4), 5; Confirmed, since last report, 15; Marriages, 2; Burials, 7; Communicants, last reported, 138, admitted, 15, received, 3, died 1, removed, 7, present number, 148; Public Services, Sundays, twice, Holy days, once, other days, Fridays, and daily in Lent; Holy Communion, public, 16; Sunday School, teachers, 11, pupils, 80.

Offerings.

Parochial.—Current expenses, including salaries, $1,565.97; Sunday School, $34.85; Increase and Improvement of Church Property, $112.55; Other parochial objects, Christmas Festival for Sunday School, $30. Total, $1,742.87.

Diocesan.— Diocesan Missions, $39.48; Salary of the Bishop, $30; Diocesan Fund, $24; Orphan House of the Holy Saviour, $5.46; Orphan House of the Holy Saviour, from Sunday School, Lenten offerings, $27.08. Total, $126.02.

General.— Domestic, Foreign and Jewish Missions, $15.80; Other objects exterior to the Diocese, Parish Branch Woman's Auxiliary to Missions, cash, $36; Boxes, value, $43; "Daisy Chain," of King's Daughters, cash, $25; Boxes, $10. Total, $129.80.

Total amount of Offerings, $1,998.69.

Remarks.

The Parish Branch of the Woman's Auxiliary, the Young Ladies Parish Aid, and "The Daisy Chain" of King's Daughters are all in good working order. The first works chiefly for the Orphan House at Cooperstown. The second devote their energies principally to the improvement of the Church, having contributed to that object during the past year, $112.55.

ST. PAUL'S CHURCH, FRANKLIN.

Rector. The Rev. Samuel B. Moore.
Wardens. Henry S. Edwards, Henry A. Mead.
Vestrymen. Eli P. Howe, Alfred Barnes, George Copeland, Jay W. Cook, Edgar Naragon.

Parochial.

Families, 50; Individuals (adults, 130, children, 47), 177; Baptisms (adults, 1, infants, 3), 4; Confirmed, since last report, 5; Present number of confirmed persons, 99; Marriages, 2; Burials, 2; Communicants, last reported, 90, admitted, 5, received, 1, died, 1, removed, 2, present number (corrected list), 84; Public Services (Sundays, 102, Holy days, 32, other days, 45), 179; Holy Communion (public, 27, private, 11), 38; Sunday School, teachers, 4, pupils, 30; Catechizing, number of children, 25; number of times, 45.

Offerings.

Parochial.— Current expenses, including salaries, $908.30; Sunday School, $18.14 Total, $926.44.

Diocesan.— Diocesan Missions, $22.42; Salary of the Bishop, $12; Diocesan Fund, $16.50; Bible and Common Prayer Book Society of Albany, $2; Fund for Aged and Infirm Clergymen, $3; Fund for Widows and Orphans of Clergymen, $2.60; Orphan House of the Holy Saviour, $2.50, The Child's Hospital, $3; Other offerings for objects within the Diocese, Susquehanna Convocation, $2; Lenten Box to Orphan House of the Holy Saviour, value, $9. Total, $75 02.

General.— Domestic and Foreign Missions, $10.62; Other objects exterior to the Diocese, Church Building Fund Commission, $3, Church Mission to the Jews, $2. Total, $15.62.

Total amount of Offerings, $1,017.08.

Property.

Church and lot (estimated worth), $6,500.
Parsonage and lot, $1,500.
Condition of property, good.
Amount of salary pledged Rector, $550.
Number of sittings in the Church, 400; all free.

Remarks.

My resignation of St. Paul's takes effect November 5. During my term of service here much has been accomplished, through the hearty co-operation and mutual sympathy of pastor and people. The Parish is thoroughly united, and the spirit of loyalty and devotion to the Church prevails. Large results, considering the number of communicants and their limited resources, have been attained through the valuable assistance rendered by the Altar Society, the Woman's Diocesan League (which raises the money for Diocesan objects), and the Parish Aid Society. These organizations, during the year, have raised $194 32, included in the above total of offerings.

CHRIST CHURCH, DEPOSIT.

Rector. The Rev. Frederick S. Fisher.

Wardens. William H. Gregory, Titus M. Bixby.

Vestrymen. C. Onderdonk, H. B. Coggshall, Philip Munson, Charles Pinkney, James McDonald, all communicants.

Parochial.

Families, 45; Baptisms (adults, 4, infants, 3), 7; Confirmed, since last report, 15; Marriages, 2; Burials, 3; Communicants, present number, 76; Sunday School, teach. ers, 5, pupils, 40.

Offerings.

Parochial.— Current expenses, including salaries, $700, Sunday School, $43 01; Increase and Improvement of Church Property, $200. Total, $943.01.

Diocesan.— Diocesan Missions, $10.40; Salary of the Bishop, $6. Total, $16.40. Total amount of Offerings, $939.41.

Property.

Church and lot (estimated worth), $1,000.

Condition of property, fair.

Amount of salary pledged Rector, $600.

Number of sittings in the Church, 150; all free.

Remarks.

The present Rector took charge in May.

GRACE MISSION, STAMFORD.

Rector. The Rev. A. T. de Learsy, Missionary in charge since July 1890.

Parochial.

Families, 7; Individuals (adults, 26, children, 9), 35; Baptisms, adults, 1. Burials, 1; Communicants, last reported, 21; Present number recorded, 21, Public Services, Sundays, once from November 1 to June 3, 1890; twice from July 1 to October 31, 1890; Holy Communion, public, once a month, private, once; Sunday School, teachers, 5, pupils, 18.

Offerings.

Parochial.— Alms at Holy Communion, $49.31; Current expenses, including salaries, $337 80; Sunday School, $21.81; Increase and Improvement of Church Property, $30. Total, $458.92.

Diocesan.— Diocesan Missions, $20; Salary of the Bishop, $4; Diocesan Fund, $6; Orphan House of the Holy Saviour, $5.75; also, clothing, etc., value $50. Total, $35.75

General.— Domestic Missions, $7.38.

Total amount of Offerings, $502.05

Property.

Church and lot (estimated worth), $3,000.

Condition of property, good.

Amount of salary pledged Rector, $500.

Number of sittings in the Church, 250, all free.¶

ST. PAUL'S MISSION, SIDNEY.

Missionary. The Rev. Frederick S. Griffin.

Warden. E. Winsor.

Parochial.

Families, 26; Individuals, 72; Confirmed, 6; Communicants, 85; Public Services (Sundays, 84, other days, 11), 45; Holy Communion, 8; Sunday School, teachers, 4, pupils, 14.

Offerings.

Parochial.— Current expenses, $76.22; Special Offering for Communion silver, $30. Total, $96.20.

Diocesan.— Diocesan Missions, $12.44; Diocesan Fund, $1.50. Total, $13.94. Total amount of Offerings, $110.16.

Remarks.

Rev. Dr. Parke, of Unadilla, held services twice a month in Sidney, from November, 1889, to July, 1890, the present Missionary taking charge in July, 1890.

A room has been fitted up at an expense of $150, in which services are held on the second and fourth Sundays in each month, both morning and evening.

EMMANUEL MISSION, GRIFFIN'S CORNERS.

The Rev. F. B. Reazer, in superintendence.

Assistant. Mr. T. W. Challen, Lay Missionary.

Warden. John S. Brown.

Treasurer. Emerson M. Crosby.

Clerk. William A. Ten Broeck.

Parochial.

Families, 10; Individuals (adults, 19, children, 14), 83; Baptisms, infants, 4; Communicants, present number, 7; Public Services (Sundays, 24, Holy days, 2, other days, 7), 33; Holy Communion (public, 3, private, 1), 4; Sunday School, teachers, 3, pupils, 25; Catechizing, number of children, 25; number of times, 17.

Offerings.

Parochial.— Alms at Holy Communion, $4.45; Current expenses, including salaries, $55.43; Increase and Improvement of Church Property, $117. Total, $176.88. Total amount of Offerings, $176.88.

Property.

Lot worth $200. Church now building.

Remarks.

The corner-stone of Emmanuel Church was laid on September 8, and the framework of the Church is now nearly finished. It will seat about 120 persons, and will cost about $2,000.

The Rev. Lewis T. Wattson will hold services about once a month during this winter, very kindly coming up from Kingston, N. Y., for that purpose. Mr. Wright is acting as superintendent of the Sunday School during the winter. About $900 in cash has been paid the Treasurer for the Building Fund and $350 additional is pledged.

Essex County.

CHURCH OF THE CROSS, TICONDEROGA.

Rector. The Rev. Henry T. Gregory.

Wardens. John C. Fenton, Mortimer C. Drake.

Vestrymen. Henry C. Burnet, Lyman Malcolm, Charles H. Baldwin, C. E. Bennett, G. B. Hanford, George B. Bascom, Carlton Cook, Wm. T. Bryan.

Parochial.

Families, 77; Baptisms (adults, 2, infants, 6), 8; Confirmed, since last report, 8; Marriages, 4; Burials, 14; Communicants, last reported, 74, admitted, 4, received, 1, died, 1, removed, 1, present number, 77; Public Services (Sundays, 113, Holy days, 22, other days, 47), 182 ; Holy Communion, public, 28; Sunday School, teachers, 6, pupils, 64; Catechizing, number of children, school; number of times, 20.

Offerings.

Parochial.— Alms at Holy Communion (early service), $5.43; Current expenses, including salaries, $684.93; Sunday School, $19.75; Increase and Improvement of Church Property, $1,341.10; Other parochial objects, entertainment of guests, $10.85. Total, $2,062.06.

Diocesan.— Diocesan Missions, $29.90; Salary of the Bishop, $6; Diocesan Fund, $15; Fund for Aged and Infirm Clergymen, $3.94; Orphan House of the Holy Saviour, $8.45. Total, $63.29.

General.— General Missions (from Sunday School), $29.98; Other objects exterior to the Diocese, Jewish Missions, $1.57; American Church Building Fund Commission, $2.56; Parish Building, St. Mark's, Johnstown, Pa. (Sunday School), $2.46. Total, $36.57.

Total amount of Offerings, $2,161.91.

Property.

Church and lot (estimated worth), $9,000.
Parsonage and lot, $2,500.
Condition of property, good.
Indebtedness on Rectory, $290.
Amount of salary pledged Rector, $500.
Number of sittings in the Church, 270; all free.

Remarks.

Since the last Convention a comfortable and convenient Rectory has been built, with but little assistance from abroad, and is now occupied by the Rector and his family. The small indebtedness, above noted, it is expected will be liquidated during the coming year.

ST. JOHN'S CHURCH, ESSEX.

Rector. The Rev. Wm. Norman Irish.
Wardens. Stephen D. Derby, Andrew J. Tucker.
Vestrymen. Anthony J. B. Ross, Robert Fortune, Moses A. Knowlton, Edward W. Richardson, Lyman R. Thompson, William M. Cowan, Ervin G. Lyon.

Parochial.

Families (Essex, 27, in other towns, 14), 41; Individuals (adults, 109, children, 21), 130; Baptisms, infants, 6; Confirmed, since last report, 3; Marriages, 3; Burials, 3; Communicants, last reported, 80, admitted, 6, received, 4, died, 2, removed, 3, present number, 85;[*] Public Services (Sundays, 100, Holy days, 34, other days, 50), 184; Holy Communion, public, 80.

Offerings.

Parochial.— Alms at Holy Communion, $36.68; Current expenses, including salaries, $365 50; Sunday School, $50; Increase and Improvement of Church Property, $4.17; Other parochial objects, special offering for a family, $55. Total, $511.35.

---

[*]Essex, 56, Lewis, 11, Boquet, 4, Willsborough, 10, Whallonsburgh, 4: 85.

Diocesan.— Diocesan Missions, $30; Salary of the Bishop, $12; Diocesan Fund, $9; Bible and Common Prayer Book Society of Albany, $2.75; Fund for Aged and Infirm Clergymen, $2.25; Fund for Widows and Orphans of Clergymen, $3.78; The Child's Hospital, $10. Total, $69.78.

Total amount of Offerings, $581.13.

Property.

Church and lot (estimated worth), $3,000.
Parsonage and lot, $1,000.
Other property, $550.
Condition of property, good.
Amount of salary pledged Rector, $300.
Number of sittings in the Church, 200; all free.

ST. PAUL'S CHURCH, KEESEVILLE.

Rector. The Rev. J. William Gill.
Wardens. Asa Pierce Hammond, M. D., Francis Cassidy.
Vestrymen. Henry Dundas, James Dundas, Andrew T. Tallmadge, M. D., Frederick W. Cramphorn.

Parochial.

Families, 37; Individuals (adults, 71, children, 23), 94; Baptisms, infants, 8; Confirmed, since last report, 6; Present number of confirmed persons, 52; Marriages, Burials, 3; Communicants, last reported, 44, admitted, 6, received, 2; present number, 52; Public Services (Sundays, 102, Holy days, 50, other days, 50), 202; Holy Communion, public, 12; Sunday School, teachers, 5, pupils, 27; Catechizing, number of times, weekly.

Offerings.

Parochial.— Current expenses, including salaries, $578; Sunday School, $7; Increase and Improvement of Church Property, $187. Total, $772.
Diocesan.— Diocesan Missions, $15; Salary of the Bishop, $10. Total, $25.

Total amount of Offerings, $797.

Property.

Church and lot (estimated worth), $2,000.
Other property, $1,100.
Condition of property, excellent.
Amount of salary pledged Rector, $400.
Number of sittings in the Church, 180; all free.

Remarks.

During the summer months I have held services at Port Kent, in connection with St Paul's. Through the efforts of the Woman's Guild, the Church has been beautifully painted without and within. Too much praise cannot be given for their noble and self-sacrificing labours.

CHRIST CHURCH, PORT HENRY.

Rector. The Rev. William R. Woodbridge.
Assistant. The Rev. Charles E. Cragg.
Wardens. Theodore Tromblee, Jr., William M. J. Botham.
Vestrymen. Frank S. Atwell, George Hoy, T. Reed Woodbridge, Charles W. Woodford, Charles E. Cragg.

Parochial.

Families, 89; Individuals (adults, 95, children, 96), 191; Baptisms, infants, 3; Confirmed, since last report, 1; Present number of confirmed persons, 71; Marriages, 4; Burials, 7; Communicants, last reported, 69, admitted, 1, not known to commune this year, 12, removed, 6, present number, 52; Public Services (Sundays, 92, Holy days, 42, other days, 65), 199; Holy Communion, public, 15; Sunday School, teachers, 5, pupils, 61; Catechizing, number of children, 15; number of times, 5.

Offerings.

Parochial.— Current expenses, including salaries, $662.01; Increase and Improvement of Church Property, $711.57. Total, $1,373.58.

Diocesan.— Diocesan Missions, $21.95; Salary of the Bishop, $6; Diocesan Fund, $12; Orphan House of the Holy Saviour, $8.11; The Child's Hospital, $7.75; Other offerings for objects within the Diocese, Home for the Friendless, $2. Total, $57.81.

General.— Domestic Missions, $2.75; Foreign Missions, $3.81; Other objects exterior to the Diocese, Mission to the Jews, $3.70. Total, $10.26.

Total amount of Offerings, $1,441.65.

Property.

Church and lot (estimated worth), $5,000.
Condition of property, good.
Amount of salary pledged Rector, $416.
Number of sittings in the Church, 180; all free.

Remarks.

Besides the services above reported, there have been held in the Crown Point Mission ten services, including two celebrations of the Holy Communion. And the offerings for current expenses were $24.54.

EMMANUEL MISSION, MINEVILLE.

Missionary. The Rev. William R. Woodbridge.

Parochial.

Families, 26; Individuals (adults, 55, children, 60), 115; Baptisms (adult, 1, infants, 2), 3; Confirmed, since last report, 1; Present number of confirmed persons, 39; Marriages, 1; Burials, 5; Communicants, last reported, 26, admitted, 1, not known to commune this year, 8, present number, 19; Public Services (Sundays, 49, Holy days, other days, 18), 71; Holy Communion, public, 3; Sunday School, teachers, 3, pupils, 3; Catechizing, number of children, 10; number of times, 5.

Offerings.

Parochial.— Current expenses, including salaries, $33.93.
Diocesan.— Diocesan Missions, $5.
Total amount of Offerings, $38.93.

Property.

Church and lot (estimated worth), $1,000.
Condition of property, good.
Number of sittings in the Church, 125; all free.

ST. JAMES' CHURCH, AUSABLE FORKS.

Rector. The Rev. George Herbert Norton.
Warden. James Rogers.
Clerk. A. Bosley.
Treasurer. George Chahorn.

Parochial.

Families, 19; Individuals (adults, 50, children, 17), 67; Baptisms, infants, 4; Confirmed, 8; Marriages, 2; Burials, 2; Communicants, last reported, 45, admitted, 8, died, 1, removed, 14, present number recorded, 88; Public Services (Sundays, 60, Holy days, 3, other days, 5), 68; Holy Communion (public, 5, private, 1), 6; Sunday School, teacher, 1, pupils, 8; Catechizing, number of children, 8; number of times, monthly.

Offerings.

Parochial.— Current expenses, including salaries, $325; Increase and Improvement of Church Property, $10; Other parochial objects, $50. Total, $385.

Diocesan.— Diocesan Missions, $16.78; Salary of the Bishop, $11; Diocesan Fund, $10. Total, $37.78.

Total amount of Offerings, $422.78.

Property.

Church and lot (estimated worth), $12,000.
Condition of property, excellent.
Amount of salary pledged Rector, $500.
Number of sittings in the Church, 225; all free.

Remarks.

During the absence of the Rector in Florida, the Church was closed for nearly five months last winter, during which time no salaries were paid and no stipend drawn. This will largely account for the small number of services, and the reduced total of offerings as compared with last year.

The Parish has met with many discouragements and financial losses, and the outlook is not bright. It has been with great effort that the services have been continued until the close of the Convention year. The Rector will endeavour to keep the Church open until January 1, 1891.

CHURCH OF THE REDEEMER, BLOOMINGDALE.

Missionary. The Rev. Walter H. Larom.
Treasurer. E. G. Ricketson.

Parochial.

Families, 13; Individuals (adults, 27, children, 25), 52; Baptisms (adults, 7, infants, 3), 10; Confirmed, 7; Communicants, last reported, 6, admitted, 7, removed, 1, present number recorded, 12, actually communicating, 9; Public Services (Sundays, 49, other days, 2), 51; Holy Communion, public, 2; Sunday School, teachers, 3, pupils, 36; Catechizing, number of children, whole school; number of times, 2.

Offerings.

Parochial.— Current expenses, including salaries, $65.43; Sunday School, $7; Increase and Improvement of Church Property, $260. Total, $332.43.

Property.

Church and lot (estimated worth), $2,500.
Condition of property, fair.
Number of sittings in the Church, 150; all free.

Remarks.

The offerings for current expenses from this Church have not been sufficient to pay the living expenses of the Missionary, who comes here every Sunday from Saranac Lake, as well as at other times for parochial visitations. (See Report of St. Luke's, Saranac Lake, Franklin county.)

ST. EUSTACE CHURCH, LAKE PLACID.

Missionary. The Rev. Walter H. Larom.
Treasurer of Building Fund. Henry B. Auchincloss.

Parochial.

Families, 5; Individuals (adults, 9, children, 6), 15; Baptisms, infant, 1; Communicants, present number recorded, 6; Public Services, Sundays, 8.

Offerings.

Parochial.—Current expenses, including salaries, $205; Other parochial objects, Church Building Fund, $91. Total, $296.

Remarks.

This Mission has been started this year at the urgent request of a few of the residents and a number of visitors, and services have been held during the summer in the parlor of the Stevens House by the courtesy of the Messrs. Stevens. The Bishop, in a circular asking for subscriptions to the building fund at this place, says: "The time seems to have come for the building of a Church at Lake Placid," and it is hoped that the services held during the summer have been the beginning of a permanent Church establishment. The Mission is called "The Mission of St. Eustace," after St. Eustace the patron Saint of hunters. (See Report of St. Luke's, Saranac Lake, Franklin county.)

ST. ANDREW'S CHURCH, SCHROON LAKE.

(No report.)

Franklin County.

ST. MARK'S CHURCH, MALONE.

Rector. The Rev. Charles Temple.
Wardens. Hon. H. A. Taylor, Dr. R. J. Wilding.
Vestrymen. J. E. Barry, Hon. S. A. Beman, Samuel Greene, A. C. Hadley, Hon. Albert Hobbs, Dr. Calvin Skinner, William Smallman, David Webster.

Parochial.

Families, 129; Individuals (adults, 295, children, 81), 376; Baptisms (adults, 3, infants, 6), 9; Confirmed, since last report, 18; Marriages, 5; Burials, 13; Communicants, last reported, 226, admitted, 18, received, 6, died, 5, removed, 11, present number, 234; Public Services (Sundays, 96, other days, 81), 177; Holy Communion (public, 20, private, 2), 22; Sunday School, teachers, 10, pupils, 75.

Offerings.

Parochial.— Current expenses, including salaries, $2,523.29; Sunday School, $75; Increase and Improvement of Church Property, $271.30. Total, $2,869.59.

Diocesan.— Diocesan Missions, $75; Salary of the Bishop, $30; Diocesan Fund, $66; Bible and Common Prayer Book Society of Albany, $5; Fund for Aged and Infirm Clergymen, $5; Fund for Widows and Orphans of Clergymen, $5; Orphan House of the Holy Saviour, $25; The Child's Hospital, $5; Society for Promoting Religion and Learning, $10; Other offerings for objects within the Diocese, Convocation of Ogdensburgh, $3; Cathedral stall, $100. Total, $329.

General.— Domestic Missions, $15; Foreign Missions, $5; Indian Missions, $5; Home Missions to Coloured Persons, $5; Other objects exterior to the Diocese, Mis-

sions to Jews, $5.50; Missions to Deaf Mutes, $10; Enrollment Fund, $5. T(
$50.50.

Total amount of Offerings, $3,249.09.

Property.

Church and lot (estimated worth), $20,000.
Parsonage and lot, $6,000.
Condition of property, excellent.
Amount of salary pledged Rector, $1.200.
Number of sittings in the Church, 270; all free.

ST. PETER'S CHURCH, BRUSHTON.
(No report.)

ST. JOHN'S CHURCH, CHATEAUGAY.
(No report.)

ST. MARK'S MISSION, WEST BANGOR.
(No report.)

ST. JAMES' MISSION, HOGANSBURGH.

Missionary. The Rev. Howard McDougall.
Warden. Alfred Fulton.

Parochial.

Individuals (adults, 40, children, 17), 57; Baptisms, infants, 3; Present numbe
confirmed persons, 21; Communicants, last reported, 29; Public Services, Sund
22; Sunday School, teachers, 2, pupils, 7; Catechizing, number of children, 7; r
ber of times, 4.

Offerings.

Parochial.— Current expenses, including salaries, $197.92: Increase and Impr
ment of Church Property, $11.13. Total, $209.05.
Diocesan.— Diocesan Missions, $25; Salary of the Bishop, $6; Diocesan Fund.
Total, $36.

Total amount of Offerings, $245.05.

Property.

Church and lot (estimated worth), $3,000.
Parsonage and lot, $800.
Condition of propery, Church in good condition.
Amount of salary pledged Rector, $250.
Number of sittings in the Church, 144; all free.

Remarks.

The Missionary entered upon this work on June 15. By an arrangement with
Parish of St. John, Massena, the services in the place were to be held in the af
noon, during the summer and part of the autumn.

ST. JOHN'S CHURCH IN THE WILDERNESS, PAUL SMITH'S.

Missionary. The Rev. Walter H. Larom.
Warden. Dr. E. L. Trudeau.

Parochial.

Families, 4; Individuals (adults, 8, children, 12), 20; Communicants, last reported, 6; Present number recorded, 6; Public Services, Sundays, 14; Holy Communion, public, 3.

Offerings.

Parochial.— Current expenses, including salaries, $750.27; Increase and Improvement of Church Property, $123.50. Total, $873.77.

Diocesan.— Diocesan Missions, $10; Salary of the Bishop, $2; Diocesan Fund, $19.91. Total, $31.91.

Total amount of Offerings, $905.68.

Property.

Church and lot (estimated worth), $5,000.
Condition of property, excellent.
Number of sittings in the Church, 200; all free.

Remarks.

(See report of St. Luke's, Saranac Lake.)

CHURCH OF ST. LUKE, THE BELOVED PHYSICIAN, SARANAC LAKE.

Missionary. The Rev. Walter H. Larom.
Lay Reader. R. W. Alban Thomson.
Warden. Dr. E. L. Trudeau.

Parochial.

Families, 70; Individuals (adults, 142, children, 61), 203; Baptisms (adults, 4, infants, 12), 16; Confirmed, 12; Burials, 7; Communicants, last re ported, 81; admitted, 12; received, 5; died, 1; removed, 3, present number recorded, 94, actually communicating, 54; Public services (Sundays, 76, Holy days, 18, other days, 53), 147; Holy Communion (public, 34, private, 4), 38; Sunday School, teachers, 9, pupils, 75; Catechizing, whole school; number of times, 40.

Offerings.

Parochial.— Current expenses, including salaries (at Church, $921.70, taken at services at Hotel Ampersand, $400.13), $1,321.83; Sunday School, $35; Increase and Improvement of Church Property, $370; Other parochial objects, Library for village, $200; New organ fund, $109.81; Rectory fund, $545. Total, $2,581.64.

Diocesan.— Diocesan Missions, $10; Salary of the Bishop, $2; Diocesan Fund, $19.90; Bible and Common Prayer Book Society of Albany, $5. Total, $36.90.

Total amount of Offerings, $2,618.54.

Property.

Church and lot (estimated worth) $4,000.
Other property, village library, $2,000.
Condition of property, fair.
Number of sittings in the Church, 200; all free.

Remarks.

The Diocesan assessments here reported as paid, are one-half of the whole amount charged upon this missionary jurisdiction, the other half being charged to the Church at Paul Smith's.

In addition to the number of communicants reported as communicating here, there are always a number of visitors and invalids from other Parishes throughout the country, who avail themselves of the privileges of the Church here.

The Missionary desires to take this opportunity of expressing his appreciation of the help he has received in his summer work at the different posts under his charge, from the following of his brethren, some of whom have come here expressly for that purpose, and others doing so during their own vacations: The Rt. Rev. Benj. H. Paddock, D. D., Bishop of Massachusetts; the Revs. J. D. Morrison, D. D., Thaddeus A. Snively, Jos. W. McIlwaine and Elmer P. Miller, of the Diocese of Albany; the Revs. J. W. Brown, D. D., E. A. Hoffman, D. D., Brady E. Bachus, D. D., and Wm. Everett Johnson, of the Diocese of New York; the Rev. J. W. Lundy, of the Diocese of Pennsylvania; the Rev. Chas. H. Doupé, of the Diocese of Connecticut; the Rev. Chas. J. Mason, of the Diocese of California; the Rev. Richard L. Howell, of the Diocese of Southern Ohio; the Rev. Edwin G. Richardson, of the Diocese of Milwaukee; the Rev. W. B. Tyng Smith, of the Diocese of New Hampshire, and the Rev. D. Harford-Battersby, English Chaplain at Davos Platz, Switzerland. The success of the whole work accomplished is due, in a great measure, to the constant and never tiring energy of my faithful Lay Reader, Mr. R. W. Alban Thomson. The Rev. Milton C. Dotten has taken entire charge of the services at the Church of the Ascension at Saranac Inn, and has also held occasional services at the Wawbeek Lodge.

Public services have been held on Sunday evenings, twenty-six times, in the parlor of the Hotel Ampersand by the courtesy of the managers, Messrs. Eaton & Young, and five times at the Sanitarium by the courtesy of Dr. Trudeau.

MISSION OF THE GOOD SHEPHERD, SANTA CLARA.

Missionary. The Rev. Phineas Duryea, July 26 to Nov. 1, 1890.

Parochial.

Baptisms, infants, 4; *Confirmed, 2; Burials, 4; Communicants last reported, 12 admitted, 2, present number recorded, 14; Public Services, Sundays, 26; Holy Communion, public, 3; Sunday School, teachers, 6, pupils, 50.

Offerings.

Parochial. — Current expenses, including salaries, $150.
Amount of salary pledged Rector, $700.

Remarks.

The foregoing report represents, as nearly as is possible at present, the condition of the Mission. It is, however, very incomplete. It is impossible to give a detailed statement with means of information at hand, the territory being so large and the population changing considerably. I am not yet fully acquainted with the field, or I could be more accurate.

Services are held regularly on Sunday mornings at Santa Clara, and on Sunday afternoons at Tupper Lake station, thirty-eight miles distant by rail. The attendance at this latter service has been large, and the interest in it very manifest. A number of families residing at Brandon, eighteen miles away, attend service at Santa Clara, on Sunday mornings, and are under the pastoral care of the Missionary. It is hoped to have a Church building at Santa Clara within the year.

---

* Confirmed prior to July 26th, but since last report to Convention.

Fulton County.

ST. JOHN'S CHURCH, JOHNSTOWN.

Rector. The Rev. John Brewster Hubbs.
Wardens. Abiram S. Van Voast, Thomas E. Ricketts.
Vestrymen. J. Ricketts, Hon. J. M. Dudley, Hon. J. M. Carroll, Isaiah Yanney, J. I. Younglove, R. J. Evans, Chas. Prindle, C. M. Rowell.

Parochial.

Families, 155; Baptisms (adults, 5, infants, 12), 17; Confirmed, since last report, 18; Marriages, 5; Burials, 12; Communicants, last reported, 247, admitted, 16, received, 4, died, 5, removed, 5, present number, 257; Public Services (Sundays, 135, Holy days, 24, other days, 125), 284; Holy Communion (public, 80, private, 3), 83; Sunday School, teachers, 18, pupils, 150; Catechizing, number of children, 100; number of times, every Sunday.

Offerings.

Parochial.— Alms at Holy Communion, $266.42; Current expenses, including salaries, $2,174.02; Sunday School, $175; Other parochial objects, Guild of All Saints', $477.98; Parochial Mission expenses, $70.80; St. Andrew's Brotherhood, $8.70. Total, $3,172.92.

Diocesan.— Diocesan Missions, $38.50 (Holy Communion alms, in part); Salary of Bishop, $40; Diocesan Fund, $33; Bible and Common Prayer Book Society of Albany, $7.40 (Holy Communion alms); Fund for Aged and Infirm Clergymen, $5; Orphan House of the Holy Saviour, $44.05 (Holy Communion alms, in part); The Child's Hospital, $7.26 (Holy Communion alms); The Child's Hospital Building Fund, $29; Other offerings for objects within the Diocese, Theological education, $100; Cathedral debt, $5; Diocesan library, $25: Albany Convocation, $20.41. Total, $354.62.

General.— Domestic Missions, $10 (Holy Communion alms); Foreign Missions, $12 (Holy Communion alms); Parochial Missions Society, $32.70. Total, $54.70.
Total amount of Offerings. $3,398.97.

Property.

Church and lot (estimated worth) $20,000.
Parsonage and lot, $5,000; Other property, $1,000.
Condition of property, excellent.
Number of sittings in the Church, 350; all free.

CHRIST CHURCH, GLOVERSVILLE.

Rector. The Rev. C. P. A. Burnett.
Warden. William Watson.
Treasurer. James Hull.
Clerk. Emil Alexander.

Parochial.

Families, 55; Individuals (adults, 135, children, 80), 215; Baptisms (adults, 3, infants, 16), 19; Confirmed, 14; Marriages, 2; Burials, 7; Churchings, 9; Communicants, last reported, 90, admitted, 14, received, 4, died, 1, removed, 7, present number recorded, 100, actually communicating, 100; Public Services (Sundays, 151, Holy days, 62, other days, 450), 663; Holy Communion (public, 165, private, 6), 171; Sunday School, teachers, 5, pupils, 60; Catechizing, number of children, all; number of times, 40.

Offerings.

Parochial.— Current expenses, including salaries, $562.50; Sunday School, $22.10; Other parochial objects, on account for furnace, $88. Total, $672.60.

Diocesan.— Diocesan Missions, $25; Salary of the Bishop, $6; Fund for Aged and Infirm Clergymen, $2.56. Total, $33.56.

General.— Jewish Missions, $2.94.

Total amount of Offerings, $709.10.

Property.

Church and lot (estimated worth), $8,000.

Other property, Church furniture, $1,000.

Condition of property, good.

Number of sittings in the Church 380; all free.

Remarks.

With the sum of the offerings of the Sunday School children, given during the last seven years, a stone baptismal font of goodly size, shape and workmanship, was purchased last June and set up in the Church near the doorway.

We have received during the past year, $100 from St. Paul's Church, Troy; $36.14 from St. Peter's Church, Albany; $25 from Christ Church, Troy; and $5 from Trinity Church, Potsdam. This money, given in response to the personal appeal of the Bishop, was used, as the kind donors intended, to decrease our indebtedness on the Church building. A further sum of $500, obtained by adding the same amount to the mortgage on the Church property, was also paid to the builder. The *entire* indebtedness of the Church is now as follows: $2,000 — mortgage at 5 per cent —$150 due the architect; and about $200 still due the builder. A gift of $13.10 from Bethesda Church, Saratoga Springs, received after above settlement with builder, was used to make a payment on account for Church furnace.

Greene County.

ST. LUKE'S CHURCH, CATSKILL.

Rector.   The Rev. Wm. Louis Woodruff.

Lay Reader. H. M. C. Vedder.

Wardens. C. B. Pinckney, William L. Dubois.

Vestrymen. Hon. Jno. H. Bagley, Jr., Chas. E. Willard, Theo. A. Cole, Chas. Trowbridge, Oliver Bourke, Judge M. B. Mattice, Henry T. Jones, W. H. H. Schofield.

Parochial.

Families, 221; Baptisms (adults, 16, infants, 84), 100; Confirmed since last report, 53, present number of confirmed persons, 353; Marriages, 4; Burials, 24; Communicants, last reported, 301, admitted, 53, received, 8, died, 9, removed, 2, present number, 351. Public Services (Sundays, 181, Holy days, 20, other days, 261), 462; Holy Communion (public, 89, private, 9), 98; Sunday School, teachers, 24, pupils, 203;[*] Catechizing, number of children, 175; number of times, 21.

Offerings.

Parochial.— Alms at Holy Communion, $196.76; Current expenses, including salaries, $1,878.30; Sunday School, $84 65; Increase and Improvement of Church Property, $401.25. Total, $2,560.96.

---

[*] September 22, 1889, the attendance at the Sunday School was 47. The attendance Sunday November 9, 1890, was 175, with 24 teachers and 3 officers and the Rector present.

Diocesan.—Diocesan Missions, $150; Salary of the Bishop, $36; Diocesan Fund, $30; Bible and Common Prayer Book Society of Albany, $10; Fund for Aged and Infirm Clergymen, $20; Fund for Widows and Orphans of Clergymen, $20; Orphan House of the Holy Saviour, $39.18; The Child's Hospital, $37. Total, $342.18.

General.— Domestic Missions, $20; Foreign Missions, $20; Other objects exterior to the Diocese, St. Mark's School, Utah, $40; Bishop Leonard, $13; Missions to the Jews, $4; Theological Education, $50. Total, $147.

Total amount of Offerings, $3,050.14.

Amount of salary pledged Rector, $1,200.

Remarks.

The present incumbent took charge of the Parish October 1, 1889. The ladies of the Parish carpeted and partially furnished the Rectory, refitted and repainted the Sunday School room, and have ever during the year abounded in good works for Christ and the Church. Many repairs and improvements have been made by the congregation and vestry in the Rectory and Church property not included in the Treasurer's report. Nearly all the pews are rented and in the face of financial depression in the village the current expenses have been promptly met and a small floating debt nearly paid. The attendance at all services has been good, notably during Lent and week days. Services were also held during the summer at the Prospect Park Hotel. Few country parishes are blessed with a more faithful, earnest band of workers than this. The increase in the Sunday School has been phenomenal, and the influence of the Parish by reason of its labours of love among the poor of the village is steadily increasing. The Rector takes small credit of this gain to himself, for his health has been much impaired during the past ten months.

CHRIST CHURCH, COXSACKIE.

Rector. The Rev. L. H. Schubert, B. D.

Wardens. Dr. N. Clute, N. H. Vosburgh.

Vestrymen. William Farmer, H. J. Hahn, W. R. Reed, J. E. Brown.

Parochial.

Families, 83; Individuals (adults, 68, children, 22), 90; Confirmed, since last report, 2; Marriages, 3; Burials, 10; Communicants, last reported, 48, admitted, 2, received, 3, died, 1, removed, 2, present number, 50; Public Services (Sundays, 96, Holy days, 22, other days, 19), 137; Holy Communion, public, 34; Sunday School, teachers, 3, pupils, 16; Catechizing, every Sunday.

Offerings.

Parochial.— Current expenses, including salaries, $813.75.

Diocesan.— Diocesan Missions, $5; Salary of the Bishop, $12; Diocesan Fund, $36; Fund for Aged and Infirm Clergymen, $6.36. Total, $59.36.

General.— Indian Missions, $5, from Sunday School; Other objects exterior to the Diocese, one box clothes for the Virginia Mission, value, $30. Total, $55.

Total amount of Offerings, $928.11.

Property.

Condition of property, good.

Amount of salary pledged Rector, $600.

Number of sittings in the Church, 200; all free.

Remarks.

During the past three years, the ladies by diligent industry have realized nearly $800 towards a Rectory.

TRINITY CHURCH, ATHENS.

Rector. The Rev. James Wilkins Stewart.
Wardens. S. H. Nichols, N. Clark.
Vestrymen. G. S. Nichols, H. C. Van Loon, F. Beardsley, C. E. Nichols, Wm. Cook, R. Clute, Wm. Decker.

Parochial.

Families, 33; Individuals (adults, 92, children, 50), 142; Baptisms (adults, 1, infants, 10), 11; Confirmed, since last report, 7; Marriages, 2; Burials, 1; Communicants, last reported, 69, admitted, 7, removed, 1, present number, 75; Public Services (Sundays, 100, Holy days, 23, other days, 26), 149; Holy Communion, public, 17; Sunday School, teachers, 9, pupils, 60; Catechizing, number of children, 50; number of times, 48.

Offerings.

Parochial.—Alms at Holy Communion, $23.49; Current expenses, including salaries, $1,000; Sunday School, $33.75. Total, $1,057.24.

Diocesan.—Diocesan Missions, $13; Salary of the Bishop, $20; Diocesan Fund, $21; Bible and Common Prayer Book Society of Albany, $3; Fund for Aged and Infirm Clergymen, $5.66; Orphan House of the Holy Saviour, $8.50; The Child's Hospital, $8.50. Total, $79.66.

General.—Domestic Missions, $6; Foreign Missions, $4.18; Other objects exterior to the Diocese, Jewish Missons, $3.07. Total, $13.25.

Total amount of Offerings, $1,150.15.

Property.

Church and lot (estimated worth), $5,000.
Parsonage and lot, $3,000.
Other property. Endowment Fund, $6,400.
Condition of property, good.
Amount of salary pledged Rector, $700.
Number of sittings in the Church, 250; all free.

ST. PAUL'S CHURCH, OAK HILL.

Rector. The Rev. T. A. Snyder.
Wardens. John H. Cheritree, Charles A. Hall.
Vestrymen. Walter S. Cheritree, Byron Hall, Theodore L. Cheritree, Ambrose H. Flower, Wm. Bell, Charles E. Graham, Hiram Snyder.

Parochial.

Families, 23; Confirmed, since last report, 1; Marriages, 1; Burials, 3; Communicants, last reported, 41, received, 1, died, 2, removed, 1, present number, 39; Public Services (Sundays, 47, Holy days, 13, other days, 12), 72; Holy Communion (public, 34, private, 1), 35.

Offerings.

Parochial.—Current expenses, including salaries, $174.
Diocesan.—Diocesan Missions, $5.19; Diocesan Fund, $3.75; Bible and Common Prayer Book Society of Albany, $1.04. Total, $9.98.
General.—General Missions, $3.62; Jewish Missions, $2. Total, $5.62.
Total amount of Offerings, $189.60.

Property.

Church and lot (estimated worth), $3,000.
Parsonage and lot, $1,500.

Condition of property, in need of repairs.
Amount of salary pledged Rector, $125, and rent of Rectory.
Number of sittings in the Church, 175; all free.

CHRIST CHURCH, GREENVILLE.

Rector. The Rev. T. A. Snyder.
Wardens. T. L. Prevost, E. N. Palmer.
Vestrymen. George W. Robbins, Byron Waldron, James Ponsonby, T. J. Rundle, W. S. Rundle, R. R. Palmer, W. S. Vanderbilt, T. D. Stewart.

Parochial.

Families, 25; Baptisms, adults, 2; Marriages, 1; Burials, 1; Communicants, last reported, 42, died, 1, present number recorded, 41; Public Services (Sundays, 47, Holy days, 12, other days, 13), 72; Holy Communion (public, 32, private, 1), 33.

Offerings.

Parochial.— Current [expenses, including salaries, $181; Other parochial objects, floating debt, $55. Total, $236.
Diocesan.— Diocesan Missions, $7.60; Salary of the Bishop, $12; Diocesan Fund, $3.75; Bible and Common Prayer Book Society of Albany, $1.33; Orphan House of the Holy Saviour, $1.50. Total, $26.18.
General.— General Missions, $8.25; Other objects exterior to the Diocese, Jewish Missions, $2. Total, $10.25.
Total amount of Offerings, $272.43.

Property.

Church and lot (estimated worth), $7,000.
Parsonage and lot, $2,000.
Condition of property, needs repairing.
Amount of salary pledged Rector, $125, and use of Rectory.

TRINITY CHURCH, ASHLAND.

Lay Reader. Eugene Griggs.
Wardens. D. B. Prout, S. W. Chatfield.
Vestrymen. Addison Steele, George S. Smith, Henry P. Smith, F. H. Holcomb, M. D., Merritt McLean.

Parochial.

Families, 32; Individuals (adults, 76, children, 25), 101; Baptisms, infants, 8; Burials, 1; Communicants, last reported, 47, died, 1, present number recorded, 46; Public Services, Sundays, 13; Holy Communion, public, 8; Sunday School, teachers, 2; pupils, no record.

Offerings.

Parochial.— Current expenses, including salaries, $100, paid Rev. W. B. Hall for services during the summer.
Total amount of Offerings, $100.

Property.

Church and lot (estimated worth), $3,000.
Parsonage and lot, $1,000.
Condition of property; Church, good; Rectory, poor.
Number of sittings in the Church, 150; all free.

Remarks.

Trinity Church, Ashland, has been without a Rector for one year. The Rev. W. B. Hall of Racine, Wis., has supplied the people with divine service for eleven successive Sundays. The Bishop has appointed Eugene Griggs, a candidate for Holy Orders, Minister in charge. Services will therefore be maintained during the winter.

CALVARY CHURCH, CAIRO.

Rector. The Rev. Chauncey Vibbard, Jr.
Wardens. Lucius Byington, Levi K. Byington.
Vestrymen. John C. Lennon, George Wickes, George H. Noble, M. D., Edwin E. Darby, John A. Gallatian, Selden H. Hine, Fred. H. Ford, Fred. Goodwin.

Parochial.

Baptisms (adults, 3, infants, 1), 4; Confirmed, since last report, 3; Present number of confirmed persons, 55; Communicants, last reported, 52, admitted, 3, present number, 53; Public Services (Sundays, 40, Holy days, 8, other days, 20), 68; Holy Communion (public, 28, private, 1), 29; Sunday School, teachers, 5, pupils, 35.

Offerings.

Parochial.—Alms at Holy Communion, $10.70; Current expenses, including salaries, $207.33; Sunday School, $5.63; Increase and Improvement of Church Property, $57.80; Other parochial objects, $15; Guild of Calvary Church, $118.60. Total, $415.06
Diocesan.—Diocesan Missions, $1.48; Salary of the Bishop, $4. Total, $5.48.
Total amount of Offerings, $420.54.

Property.

Church and lot (estimated worth), $5,000.
Condition of property, good.
Amount of salary pledged Rector, $250.
Sittings in the Church all free.

GLORIA DEI CHURCH, PALENVILLE.

Rector. The Rev. Wm. Chas. Grubbe.
Reader and Warden. Charles H. Chubb, M. D.

Parochial.

Families, 11; Individuals (adults, 38, children, 7), 45; Baptisms (adults, 1, infants, 2), 3; Confirmed, 7; Burials, 3; Communicants, last reported, 31, admitted, 6, received, 1, died, 1, removed, 7, present number recorded, 30; Public Services (Sundays, 109, Holy days, 10, other days, 114), 233; Holy Communion, (public, 57, private, 6), 63.

Offerings.

Parochial.—Current expenses, including salaries, $372.20; Other parochial objects, on Rectory, $79.95. Total, $452.15.
Diocesan —Diocesan Missions, $14.10; Salary of the Bishop, $5; Diocesan Fund, $9. Total, $28 10.
General.—Domestic and Foreign Missions, $10; Other objects exterior to the Diocese, Church Missions to Jews, $1.35; American Church Building Fund Commission, $4. Total, $15 35.
Total amount of Offerings, $495.6 .

Property.

Church and lot (estimated worth), $6,000.
Parsonage and lot, $1,500.
Condition of property, good.
Amount of salary pledged Rector, $300.
Number of sittings in the Church, 150; all free.

Hamilton County.

MISSION OF THE TRANSFIGURATION, BLUE MOUNTAIN LAKE.

Warden. Thomas A. Gummey.

Services were held in 1890 from the second Sunday in July to the last Sunday in September, inclusive. In all thirty-nine services, of which fifteen were celebrations of the Holy Eucharist. In 1889, the Church was open for services from early in July until the close of December. The village has always been utterly neglected during the winter until the Church attempted to minister to its needs, then the Methodists immediately started a Mission. There were six persons confirmed in 1890. The present number of communicants is four.

During the past summer the property has been improved, by the erection of a rustic fence, and by the addition to the chancel of a handsome credence shelf and altar rail of old oak.

ALFORD A. BUTLER,

Priest in charge.

The undersigned, Warden of the Church of the Transfiguration, Blue Mountain Lake, N. Y., makes the following report of the Mission, for the years 1889 and 1890:

1889.

Receipts through the offertory and other sources.	$557 82
Expenditures for the year 1889	473 44
	$78 88

1890.

Receipts through the offertory and other sources.	$260 16
Expenditures for the year 1890	287 37

The year 1890 shows a deficiency chargeable against the balance in hands of the Warden, from 1889, of $27.21.

The Warden's account at this date is as follows:

Balance from year 1889	$78 88
Deficiency from 1890	27 21
Balance in hands of Warden	**$46 67**

THOMAS A. GUMMEY,

Warden.

November 17, 1890.

Herkimer County.

TRINITY CHURCH, FAIRFIELD.

Rector. The Rev. W. H. C. Lylburn.
Wardens. Reuben Neely, C. W. Nichols.

Vestrymen. William Mather, Jairus Mather, John P. Todd, A. C. Wilson, Frank L. Warne.

Parochial.

Families, 7; Individuals (adults, 16, children, 12), 28; Burials, 1; Communicants, last reported, 16, died, 1, present number recorded, 16, actually communicating, 8; Public Services (Sundays, 52, Holy days, 4), 56 ; Holy Communion, public, 8.

Offerings.

Parochial.— Alms at Holy Communion, $4.80; Current expenses, including salaries, about $120; Increase and Improvement of Church Property, about $25. Total, $149.80.

Property.

Church and lot (estimated worth), $1,000.
Parsonage and lot, $500.
Condition of property, fair.
Amount of salary pledged Rector $2 per Sunday.
Number of sittings in the Church about 200; all free.

Remarks.

There is no reason why this Mission ought not to grow and be a glorious work. There is a large school at Fairfield, and most of the students attend; at present there seems to be a lack of funds to carry on the work, but I feel, if properly managed, time and patience devoted to it, that can be remedied. The Church at Norway is in a bad condition; the building is not fit to use.

GRACE CHURCH, NORWAY.

(See Remarks, Report Trinity Church, Fairfield.)

EMMANUEL CHURCH, LITTLE FALLS.

Rector. The Rev. Sheldon Munson Griswold.
Wardens. R. S. Whitman, W. II. Weeks.
Vestrymen. Charles Bailey, Hon. G. A. Hardin, H. W. Houghton, Hon. A. M. Mills, Hadley Jones, G. W. Searles, Albert Story, E. B. Waite.

Parochial.

Families, about 133; Baptisms (adults, 9, infants, 29), 38; Confirmed, since last report, 11, present number of confirmed persons, about 180; Marriages, 6; Burials, 18; Communicants, last reported, 155, admitted, 12, received, 1, died, 3, removed, 6, present number, 159; Public Services (Sundays, 144, Holy days, 61, other days, 182), 387; Holy Communion (public, 87, private, 3), 90; Catechizing, number of children, school, number of times, weekly.

Offerings.

Parochial.— Alms at Holy Communion, $33.03; Current expenses, including salaries, $2,002.88; Sunday School, $135.66; Increase and Improvement of Church Property, $595.43; Other parochial objects, special for Sexton, $15.13; Easter Offering for floating debt, $171.27. Total, $2,953 40.

Diocesan.— Diocesan Missions, $60.25; Salary of the Bishop, $30: Diocesan Fund, $30, Bible and Common Prayer Book Society of Albany, $7: Fund for Aged and Infirm Clergymen, $8.12; Fund for Widows and Orphans of Clergymen, $10; Orphan House of the Holy Saviour, $15.21; The Child's Hospital, $37; Other offerings for objects within the Diocese, Bishop's window, $31. Total, $228.58.

General.— Domestic Missions, $41.79; Foreign Missions, $40.80; Home Missions to Coloured Persons, $9.61; Other objects exterior to the Diocese, Theological Education, $7; Mission to the Jews, $3.36; American Church Building Fund, $10. Total, $112.56.

Total amount of Offerings, $3,294.54.

Property.

Church and lot (estimated worth), $20,000.

Parsonage and lot, $7,000.

Other property (Chapel, $2,000, house and lots, $4,000), $6,000.

Condition of property, most excellent.

Amount of salary pledged Rector, $1,000.

Number of sittings in the Church and Chapel, 500; nearly all free.

Remarks.

During the year two of the faithful communicants who have passed away have remembered the Parish, in the final distribution of their property. Mrs. Helena T. Warcup made a verbal request that the sum of five hundred dollars should be given from her estate to Emmanuel Church, and it is hoped the amount will soon be paid.

Mrs. Charlotte M. Young devised real estate, valued at about four thousand dollars, and bequeathed a pier-glass to the wardens in trust for Emmanuel Parish. The income from this property will be a permanent addition to the resources of the Parish.

CHRIST CHURCH, HERKIMER.

Rector. The Rev. Chas. C. Edmunds, Jr.

Wardens. Geo. W. Pine, Robt. Earl.

Vestrymen. S. Earl, T. W. Grosvenor, J. D. Henderson, Geo. H. Kelsey, H. G. Munger, C. W. Palmer, W. C. Prescott, H. P. Witherstine.

Parochial.

Baptisms (adults, 6, infants, 21), 27; Confirmed, since last report, 22; Marriages, 10: Burials, 9; Communicants, last reported, 153, admitted, 25, received, 3, died, 3, removed, 14, present number, 166; Public Services (Sundays, 159, Holy days, 34, other days, 125), 318; Holy Communion (public, 95, private, 3), 98; Sunday School, teachers, 9, pupils, 80; Catechizing, Sunday School. weekly; Sewing School, teachers, 10, pupils, 55.

Offerings.

Parochial.— Current expenses, including salaries, $1,408.10; Sunday School, $40; Sewing School, $7.13: Increase and Improvement of Church Property, $325, Other parochial objects, Gift to Choir-master, $50: Gift to Rector, $365; Poor, $17.15; Choir Fund, $40.03. Total, $2,252.41.

Diocesan.— Diocesan Missions, $53.50; Salary of the Bishop, $12; Diocesan Fund, $30; Bible and Common Prayer Book Society of Albany, $8.50; Fund for Aged and Infirm Clergymen, $6.77; Fund for Widows and Orphans of Clergymen, $6.77. Total, $119.54.

General.— Domestic and Foreign Missions, $31.27; Jewish Missions, $3.25. Total, $34.52.

Total amount of Offerings, $2,404.47.

Property.

Church and lot (estimated worth) $25,000,

Parsonage and lot, $4,500.

Other property, Parish building, $4,000.

23

Condition of property, excellent.
Indebtedness, mortgage on Rectory and Parish House, $6,500.
Amount of salary pledged Rector, $1,000 and Rectory.
Number of sittings in the Church, 250; all free.

ST. AUGUSTINE'S CHURCH, ILION.

Rector. The Rev. Wm. Mason Cook.
Wardens. F. C. Shepard, R. L. Winegar.
Vestrymen. George Rix, T. J. Behan, Asa S. Anable, George H. Barlow, Samuel Jess, George H. Dyett, Elmer E. Jenne, Alfred Williamson.

Parochial.

Baptisms (adults, 6, infants, 13), 19; Confirmed, since last report, 12, present number of confirmed persons, 155; Marriages, 5; Burials, 6; Churchings, 2; Communicants, last reported, 149, admitted, 13, received, 5, died, 1 removed, 16, present number of actual communicants, 122; Public Services (Sundays, 137, Holy days, 39, other days, 88), 264; Holy Communion (public, 72, private, 6), 78; Sunday School, teachers, 9, pupils, 85; Catechizing, Sunday School, weekly.

Offerings.

Parochial.— Current expenses, including salaries, $1,331.94; For Sunday School (Library, $30.25, Christmas Fund, $35.80), $66.05; By the Sunday School, $35.74; Other Parochial objects, Payment on mortgage, $150; Altar Guild, $20.80. Total, $1,604.53.

Diocesan.— Diocesan Missions, $30; Salary of the Bishop, $10; Diocesan Fund, $27; Bible and Common Prayer Book Society of Albany, $1.42; Fund for Aged and Infirm Clergymen, $3.78. Total, $72.20.

General.— Domestic Missions, $8.28; Foreign Missions ($10.50 by the Sunday School), $18.77; Other objects exterior to the Diocese, Conversion of the Jews, $1.69. Total, $28.74.

Total amount of Offerings, $1,705.47.

Property.

Church and lot (estimated worth), $6,000.
Parsonage and lot, $3,000.
Condition of property, Church, fair; Rectory, excellent.
Indebtedness.— Mortgage, $2,350; floating debt, $149.10.
Amount of salary pledged Rector, $600.
Number of sittings in the Church, 232; all free.

Remarks.

The Junior Auxiliary sent a box to the Orphan House of the Holy Saviour, Cooperstown, valued at $14.

A flagon and a set of coloured stoles (four) have been presented to the Parish during the year.

The Ladies' Aid Society paid more than half of the $150 on the funded debt, and an equal amount of the interest, which came to more than that sum.

GRACE CHURCH, MOHAWK.

Rector. The Rev. Alfred Taylor.
Wardens. A. W. Haslehurst, E. C Elwood.
Vestrymen. H. D. Alexander, J B. Rafter Charles Spencer, John Brown, E. H. Doolittle, F. L. Van Dusen.

Parochial.

Families, 50; Individuals (adults, 115, children, 45), 160; Baptisms, infants, 2; Confirmed, 1; Burials, 2; Communicants, last reported, 41, admitted, 1, received, 9, present number recorded, 51, actually communicating, 45; Public Services (Sundays, 34, other days, 15), 49; Holy Communion, public, 14; Sunday School, teachers, 4, pupils, 40; Catechizing, number of children, all; number of times, weekly.

Offerings.

Parochial.—Alms at Holy Communion, $7.27; Current expenses, including salaries $420.50. Total, $427.77.

Diocesan.— Salary of the Bishop, $4; Diocesan Fund, $12. Total, $16.

Total amount of Offerings, $443.77.

Property.

Church and lot (estimated worth), $3,500.

Condition of property, good.

Amount of salary pledged Rector, $450.

Number of sittings in the Church, 150; all free.

Remarks.

The above report is for the last four months.

THE CHURCH OF THE MEMORIAL, MIDDLEVILLE.

Rector. The Rev. W. H. C. Lylburn.

Warden. John Molineux.

Treasurer. C. W. Hamlin.

Secretary. George W. Griswold.

Parochial.

Families, 23; Individuals (adults, 68, children, 47), 115; Baptisms (adults, 9, infants, 3), 12; Confirmed, 11; Burials, 1; Communicants, last reported, 42, present number recorded, 53, actually communicating, 53; Public Services (Sundays, 52, Holy days, 14), 66; Holy Communion (public, 59, private, 3), 62; Sunday School, teachers, 6, pupils, 40; Catechizing, number of children, 40; number of times, 47.

Offerings.

Parochial— Alms at Holy Communion, $72.20; Current expenses, including salaries, $416.67; Increase and Improvement of Church Property, $2,500. Total, $2,988.87.

Diocesan.— Salary of the Bishop, $6; Diocesan Fund, $10.50. Total, $16.50.

General.— A box to the Coloured Missions, $60.

Total amount of Offerings, $3,065.37.

Property.

Church and lot (estimated worth), $10,000.

Parsonage and lot, $2,000.

Condition of property, good.

Number of sittings in the Church, 250; all free.

Remarks.

Before the death of Mrs. Ann M. Varney, an active member of the Parish, it was proposed to build a Rectory. After her death and in fulfillment of her wish, she having made no provision for same, her representatives carried out her desire, and contributed the sum of thirteen hundred dollars. Others in the Parish have contributed largely, and by the exertions of parties most interested, the Rectory, costing three thousand dollars has been finished, and there stands to-day a building complete in all its parts, for which the Church may well be proud. Other adornments have been added to beautify the house of God. The Rector presented a prayer-desk and stall as a thank offering for the recovery from a severe illness of his wife.

ST. ALBAN'S CHURCH, FRANKFORT.

Rector. The Rev. Alfred Taylor.

Wardens. Wm. Bennett, Ernest Bennett.

Vestrymen. F. Williams, E. W. Gilligan, R. Rose, S. S. Richards, M. D., C. B. Cleland, Burton Scammell.

Parochial.

Families, 85; Individuals (adults, 80, children, 30), 110; Baptisms, infants, 5. Confirmed, since last report, 4; Present number of confirmed persons, 85; Burials, 2; Communicants, last reported, 23, admitted, 4, received, 6, died, 1, removed, 8, present number, 24; Public Services, Sundays, mornings, Other days, Thursdays; Holy Communion, public, third Sunday in month; Sunday School, teachers, 5, pupils, 30.

Offerings.

Parochial.—Alms at Holy Communion, $5.25; Current expenses, including salaries, $300; Sunday School, $2.17. Total, $307.42.

Diocesan.—Salary of the Bishop, $2.50; Diocesan Fund, $4. Total, $6.50.

Total amount of Offerings, $313.92.

Property.

Church and lot (estimated worth), $2,500.

Condition of property, good.

Amount of salary pledged Rector, $250.

Number of sittings in the Church, 125; all free.

Remarks.

The [above report refers only to the time I have been here, since July of the present year.

Montgomery County.

ST. ANN'S CHURCH, AMSTERDAM.

Rector. The Rev. David Sprague.

Wardens. W. Max Reid, John J. Hand.

Vestrymen. Cyrus B. Chase, Thomas Mansfield, Chas. S. Nisbit, Wm. Ryland, LeGrand S. Strang, Jas. T. Sugden, H. B. Waldron, Jno. K. Warnick.

Parochial.

Families, 380; Individuals, 1,050; Baptisms (adults, 5, infants, 27), 32; Confirmed since last report, 16; Present number of confirmed persons, 400; Marriages, 14 Burials, 22; Communicants, last reported, 256, present number, 270; Public Services, (Sundays, 128, Holy days, 50, other days. 34), 212; Holy Communion (public, 50, private, 3), 53; Sunday School, teachers, 18, pupils, 208; Catechizing, number of children, whole school; number of times, 10.

Offerings.

Parochial.—Alms at Holy Communion, $43.48; Current expenses, including salaries, $2,693.21; Sunday School, $140.13; Increase and Improvement of Church Property, $828.58; Other parochial objects, City Hospital, $47.42. Total, $3,752.82.

Diocesan.—Diocesan Missions, $34.71, Salary of the Bishop, $12; Diocesan Fund, $37.50; Bible and Common Prayer Book Society of Albany, $6.42. Total, $90.63.

General.—Domestic and Foreign Missions, $70; Other objects exterior to the Diocese, Church Temperance Society, $4.60. Total, $74.60.

Total amount of Offerings, $3,913.05.

Property.

Church and lot (estimated worth), $40,000.

Condition of property, excellent.

Indebtedness, about $12,000;

Amount of salary pledged Rector, $1,250.

Number of sittings in the Church, 600; number rented, 450; number free, 150.

ZION CHURCH, FONDA.

Missionary. The Rev. C. C. Edmunds.

Wardens. R. H. Cushney, H. T. E. Brower.

Vestrymen. Henry B. Cushney, Giles H. F. Van Horne, Edward B. Cushney, R. N. Casler, William Fonda, Gershom Banker, Abram Van Horne, Henry Siver.

Parochial.

Families, 21; Individuals (adults, 65, children, 10), 75; Baptisms, infants, 2; Burials, 1; Communicants, last reported, 38, admitted, 1, received, 2, died, 1, removed, 2, present number recorded, 38, actually communicating, 38; Public Services (Sundays, 52, Holy days, 2, Ash Wednesday and each Wednesday in Lent, 6), 60; Holy Communion (public, 14, private, 1), 15.

Offerings.

Parochial.— Alms at Holy Communion, $18.75; Current expenses, including salaries, $470.17. Total, $488.92.

Diocesan.— Diocesan Missions, $14; Salary of the Bishop, $12; Diocesan Fund, $9; Bible and Common Prayer Book Society of Albany, $3. Total, $38.

Total amount of Offerings, $526.92.

Property.

Church and lot (estimated worth), $8,000.

Condition of property, good.

Amount of salary pledged Rector, $300.

Number of sittings in the Church, 150; all free.

R. H. CUSHNEY,

Senior Warden, there being no Rector.

JOHNSTOWN, N. Y., *November* 10, 1890.

During the past year I have continued the services of the Church at Fonda, Montgomery county, every Sunday morning; on Thanksgiving and Christmas days, together with every Wednesday afternoon in Lent. The congregation cannot be said to show much improvement in attending the services, though it does a little better than hold its own, I think. There are a few Church people in Fultonville, whom I visit from time to time, some of whom come to Fonda to attend the services.

Respectfully submitted,

CHARLES C. EDMUNDS.

THE HOLY CROSS CHURCH, FORT PLAIN.

Rector. The Rev. J. N. Marvin.

Lay Reader. T. S. Waters.

Wardens. Douglas Ayres, M. D , Samuel Dennison.
Vestrymen. W. E Diefendorf, A. J. Halliday, T. S. Waters, James Goebel,
Thos. Williams, W. E. Morrison.

Parochial.

Families and parts of families, 69; Individuals (adults, 118, children, 45), 163;
Baptisms (adults, 4, infants, 4), 8; Confirmed, 9; Burials, 2: Communicants, last reported, 48, admitted, 9, received, 13, removed, 1, present number recorded, 69; Public Services (Sundays, 56, Holy days, 13, other days, 42), 111; Holy Communion
(public, 30, private, 3), 33; Sunday School, teachers, 6, pupils, 85; Catechising, number of children, 35.

Offerings.

Parochial.— Alms at Holy Communion, $31.42; Current expenses, including sala-
ries, $707.45; Sunday School, $16.50; Increase and Improvement of Church Property, $50.83; Other parochial objects, Parish paper, $30; Easter offering for Rector,
$50.   Total, $886.20.

Diocesan.— Diocesan Missions, $10.65; Salary of the Bishop, $3; Diocesan Fund, $4;
Fund for Aged and Infirm Clergymen, $1; Fund for Widows and Orphans of Clergy-
men, $1.35; Orphan House of the Holy Saviour, $12 (cash and box); The Child's
Hospital, $3.25.   Total, $35.25.

General.— Domestic Missions, $3; Foreign Missions, $3; Indian Missions, $3;
Home Missions to Coloured Persons, $3; Other objects exterior to the Diocese, Jews,
75 cents.   Total, $12.75.

Total amount of Offerings, $934.20.

Indebtedness, $1,600.

Amount of salary pledged Rector, $500.

Number of sittings in the Church or Chapel, 250; all free.

CHURCH OF THE GOOD SHEPHERD, CANAJOHARIE.

Rector.   The Rev. J. N. Marvin.
Lay Reader.   Theodore S. Waters.
Warden.   Arza Canfield.
Vestrymen.   Randolph Spraker, J. R White, Dr. J. A. Dockstader.

Parochial.

Families and parts of families, 50; Individuals (adults, 91, children, 46), 137;
Baptisms, adults, 1; Confirmed, 4; Marriages, 8; Burials, 4: Communicants, last reported, 63, admitted, 4, received, 2, died, 1, removed, 4, present number recorded,
64; Public Services (Sundays, 122, Holy days, 39, other days, 122), 283; Holy Communion (public, 85, private, 1), 86; Sunday School, teachers, 4, pupils, 33.

Offerings.

Parochial.— Alms at Holy Communion, $17.71; Current expenses, including sala-
ries, $455.35; Sunday School, $19.73; Increase and Improvement of Church Property,
$14.35; Other Parochial objects, $33.   Total, $540 14.

Diocesan.— Diocesan Missions, $10.27; Salary of the Bishop, $6; Diocesan Fund,
$10 50; Orphan House of the Holy Saviour (in cash and garments), $9.69; The
Child's Hospital, $1.61; Other offerings for objects within the Diocese, Lending
Library, $3.   Total, $41.07.

General.— Domestic Missions, $3; Foreign Missions, $3; Indian Missions, $3;
Home Missions to Coloured Persons, $3; Other objects exterior to the Diocese: For
Jews, 75 cents; Bishop Lightfoot Fund, $1.   Total, $13.75.

Total amount of Offerings, $594.96.

Property.

Condition of property, good.
Amount of salary pledged Rector, $350.
Number of sittings in the Church, 200; all free.

ST. COLUMBA'S CHURCH, ST. JOHNSVILLE.

Rector. The Rev. J. N. Marvin.
Warden. Charles Buckingham.
Clerk. Elroy Bartle.

Parochial.

Families and parts of families, 17; Individuals (adults, 27, children, 11), 38; Baptisms (adults, 6, infants, 5), 11 ; Confirmed, 6; Communicants, removed, 1, present number recorded, 10; Public Services (Sundays, 19, other days, 10), 29; Holy Communion, public celebrations in Church of Holy Cross, Fort Plain.

Offerings.

Parochial.— Current expenses, $36.19.
Diocesan.— Diocesan Missions, $5.23.
Total amount of Offerings, $41.42.

Otsego County.

ZION CHURCH, MORRIS.

Rector. The Rev. Walter C. Stewart.
Wardens. N. B. Pearsall, Isaac Mansfield.
Vestrymen. J. R. Morris, G. Clayton Peck, L. S. Pearsall, George A. Yates, 2d, John Smith, C. J. Smith.
Treasurer. T. O. Duroe. Clerk. A. E Yates.

Parochial.

Families, 111; Baptisms (adults, 1. infants, 9), 10: Confirmed, since last report, 8; Present number of confirmed persons, 208; Marriages, 2; Burials, 8; Communicants admitted, 3, died, 5, present number, 208; Public Services (Sundays, 87, Holy days, 13, other days, 120), 220; Holy Communion (public, 19, private, 3), 22; Sunday School, teachers, 14, pupils, 124 ; Catechizing, monthly.

Offerings.

Parochial.— Alms at Holy Communion, $23.43; Current expenses, including salaries, $900; Sunday School, $103.57; Other parochial objects, Christmas tree for Sunday School, $25. Total, $1,052.
Diocesan.— Diocesan Missions, $50; Salary of the Bishop, $45; Diocesan Fund, $54; Fund for Aged and Infirm Clergymen, $2.50; Orphan House of the Holy Saviour, $50; Other offerings for objects within the Diocese, Convocation, $2.60. Total, $204.10.
General.— Objects exterior to the Diocese, St. John's, Louisville, Ky., $24; S. Anne's, Afton, N. Y., $5; Mission to Jews, $15.71. Total, $44.71.
Total amount of Offerings, $1,300.81.

Property.

Church and lot (estimated worth), $20,000
Parsonage and lot, $3,000.

Other property, $10,000.
Condition of property, good.
Amount of salary pledged Rector, $900.
Number of sittings in the Church, 500; all free.

Remarks.

The present Rector assumed charge on the 20th of March, the Parish having been vacant for over seven months. The Rev. William Gardam, who had accepted a call, had fixed the 1st January for his arrival, but at the last moment changed his mind. Much credit is due the Wardens, who acted as Lay Readers, for keeping up the regular services during the vacancy. The report of services and official acts is from the time the Rector entered on his duties. He also had the privilege of administering the Holy Communion twice, and baptising one adult and two children in his former Parish, which was without a Rector.

ST. LUKE'S CHURCH, MONTICELLO (P. O. RICHFIELD).

Wardens. B. L. Woodbury, Clarence Colwell.
Vestrymen. Jonas A. Lidell, Fred. A. Woodbury, John L. Colwell, John Curtiss.

Parochial.

Families, 7; Individuals (adults, 16, children, 2), 18.

Property.

Church and lot (estimated worth), $750.
Other property, $100.

Remarks.

Two years ago we made quite extensive repairs to the Church, which were badly needed. During the last year we have painted the steeple and repaired fences. We sincerely hope to be able in the course of another year to get the Church in condition to hold services in.

ST. MATTHEW'S CHURCH, UNADILLA.

Rector. The Rev. Robert N. Parke, D. D.
Wardens. L. L. Woodruff, B. W. Morse.
Vestrymen. J. F. Sands (clerk), F. B. Arnold, P. G. Clark, M. B. Gregory, S. H. Chapin, W. H. Heslop, A. J. Lewis, C. I. Hayes.

Parochial.

Families, 75; Baptisms, adults, 1; Confirmed, since last report, 9; Marriages, 3; Burials, 9; Communicants, last reported, 155, admitted, 9, received, 1, died, 3, present number, 162; Public Services, (Sundays, 123, Holy days, 35, other days, 41), 199; Holy Communion, public, 32; Sunday School, teachers, 6, pupils, 43; Catechizing, number of times in public, 15.

Offerings.

Parochial.—Alms at Holy Communion, $49.35; Current expenses, including salaries, $1,073.75; Sunday School, $7.79; Increase and Improvement of Church Property, $462.57; Other Parochial objects, $18.04. Total, $1,611.50.

Diocesan.—Diocesan Missions, $50; Salary of the Bishop, $12; Diocesan Fund, $24; Bible and Common Prayer Book Society of Albany, $3.04; Fund for Aged and Infirm Clergyman, $12.79; Orphan House of the Holy Saviour, $5.20; The Child's Hospital, $9.56. Total, $116.59.

General.— Domestic Missions, $5.43; Foreign Missions, $5.51; Other objects exterior to the Diocese, Society for Promoting Christianity Among Jews, $3.02; Education for Holy Ministry, $5.79; St. John's Church, Louisville, Ky., $5.74. Total, $25.49.

Total amount of Offerings, $1,753.58.

Property.

Church and lot (estimated worth), $6,500.
Parsonage and lot, $4,500.
Other property, $600.
Condition of property, good.
Amount of salary pledged Rector, $800.
Number of sittings in the Church, 330.

CHRIST CHURCH, COOPERSTOWN.

Rector. The Rev. Charles S. Olmsted.
Wardens. H. M. Hooker, W. T. Bassett, M. D.
Vestrymen. G. Pomeroy Keese, W. H. Merchant, Henry C. Bowers, Lee B. Crittenden, C. J. Tuttle, S. E. Crittenden, W. D. Boden, R. Heber White.

Parochial.

Baptisms (adults, 3, infants, 54), 57; Confirmed, since last report, 13; Marriages, 1; Burials, 11; Communicants, present number, 281; Public Services, Sundays, all, Holy days, all, other days, Litany days; Holy Communion, Public, every Sunday and Holy day; Sunday School, teachers, 14, pupils, 140; Catechizing, number of children, Sunday School.

Offerings.

Parochial.— Alms at Holy Communion, $201.96; Current expenses, including salaries, $2,451.80; Sunday School, for Salt Lake Mission, $40: By Church for Sunday School, $92; Increase and Improvement of Church Property (addition for Rectory), $822.46; Other Parochial objects, Mite Society, $47.59; Girls' Friendly Society, $120; Woman's Lenten boxes, $400, for surplices, $50. Total, $4,225.81.

Diocesan.—Diocesan Missions, $151; Salary of the Bishop, $60; Diocesan Fund, $36; Bible and Common Prayer Book Society of Albany, $5; Orphan House of the Holy Saviour, $45.80; The Child's Hospital, $5.70; Other offerings for objects within the Diocese, Convocation of the Susquhanna, $18. Total, $321.50.

General.— Domestic Missions, $43.60; Foreign Missions, $26; Indian Missions, $9.25; Home Missions to Coloured Persons, $4.25; Other objects exterior to the Diocese, Mission to Jews, $5.22; Mrs. Buford's Hospital, $5; American Church Building Fund, $8.68; Church in Durango, Colorado, $82; Bishop Johnston's work, $62. Total, $246.

Total amount of Offerings, $4,798.31.

CHRIST CHURCH, GILBERTSVILLE.

Rector. The Rev. David F. MacDonald.
Wardens. Ira L. Ward, C. V. Daniels.
Vestrymen. William F. Ward, E. R. Clinton, C. S. Allaben, B. Murwin, W. R. Kinne, John McCollough, R. M. Stenson, J. Woodlands, C. B. Hull, P. McIntur.

Parochial.

Families, 30; Individuals (adults, 65, children, 55), 130; Communicants, last reported, 46.

24

Offerings.

Parochial.— Increase and Improvement of Church Property, $50.

Diocesan.— Diocesan Missions, $20; Salary of the Bishop, $6.   Total, $26.

General.— Domestic Missions, $3; Other objects exterior to the Diocese, for the Freedmen through Woman's Auxiliary, one barrel clothing, valued at $37; for Mission work in Dakota, $2.   Total, $42.

Total amount of Offerings, $118.

Property.

Church and lot (estimated worth), $3,000.

Parsonage and lot, $1,800.

Other property, $2,500.

Condition of property, good.

Amount of salary pledged Rector, $375.

Number of sittings in the Church, 200; all free.

Remarks.

Our report must necessarily be very incomplete, as we have been without services since March last. The Rev. David MacDonald, who came to us August 17, was un-expectedly called to California on business a month later, and has not as yet returned. We expect, however, services will be continued again before Advent.

IMMANUEL CHURCH, OTEGO.

Deacon in Charge.   The Rev. A. S. Ashley.

Wardens.   Charles Blake, George W. Sherman.

Vestrymen.   James H. Cossart, C. B. Woodruff, George W. Sherman, Jr., William H. Parker, William Birdsall, George H. Goodman, Thaddeus Birdsall.

Parochial.

Families, 22; Individuals (adults, 65, children, 15), 80; Baptisms (adults 4, infants, 1), 5; Confirmed, since last report, 6; Present number of confirmed persons, 30; Mar-riages, 1; Communicants, last reported, 24, admitted, 6, present number, 30; Public Services (Sundays, 36, Holy days, 1, other days, 2), 39; Holy Communion, public, 6; Sunday School, teachers, 2, pupils, 10.

Property.

Church and lot (estimated worth), $5,000.

Condition of property, good.

Number of sittings in the Church, 250; all free.

ST. TIMOTHY'S CHURCH, WESTFORD.

(No Report.)

GRACE CHURCH, CHERRY VALLEY.

Rector.   The Rev. James E. Hall.

Wardens.   A. B. Cox, James M. Phelon.

Vestrymen.   George Neal, W. C. Roseboom, C. D. Walrad, John Walton, J. A. Fonda, A. J. Thompson, F. P. Harriott, Charles Brooks.

Parochial.

Families, 65; Individuals (adults, 132, children. 62), 194; Baptisms, infants, 8; Confirmed, since last report, 2; Present number of confirmed persons, 117; Burials, 4;

Communicants, last reported, 118, admitted, 2, died, 1, removed, 2, present number, 112; Public Services (Sundays, 102, Holy days, 72, other days, 103), 277; Holy Communion (public, 56, private, 3), 59; Sunday School, teachers, 5, pupils, 40; Catechizing, number of children, all; number of times, weekly.

Offerings.

Parochial.— Current expenses, including salaries, $928.07; Sunday School, $17.69. Total, $945.76.

Diocesan.— Diocesan Missions, $75; Salary of the Bishop, $25; Diocesan Fund, $24; Bible and Common Prayer Book Society of Albany, $8.05; Fund for Aged and Infirm Clergymen, $10.90; Fund for Widows and Orphans of Clergymen, $2.50; Orphan House of the Holy Saviour, $10; The Child's Hospital, $11.32; Other offerings for objects within the Diocese, Convocation of the Susquehanna, $23.80. Total, $190.57.

General.— Domestic Missions, $25; Foreign Missions, $25; Home Missions to Coloured Persons, $10; Other objects exterior to the Diocese, Church Mission to Deaf-mutes, $20.97; Church Mission to the Jews, $2.30; Enrollment Fund, $5; Basket makers in this State, $10. Total, $98.27.

Total amount of Offerings, $1,284.60.

Property.

Church and lot, and Parsonage and lot, insured for, $5,000.
Other property, Fund, $6,100.
Condition of property, good.
Amount of salary pledged Rector, $800.
Number of sittings in the Church, 250; all free.

ST. JOHN'S CHURCH, RICHFIELD SPRINGS.

Rector. The Rev. Robert Granger.
Wardens. Niles D. Jewell, James A. Storer.
Vestrymen. J. F. Getman, Wm. A. Ward, James S. Davenport, Myron D. Jewell, Wm. B. Crain, M. D., Henry Greenman, Ira D. Peckham, De Witt W. Harrington.

Parochial.

Families, 123; Individuals (adults 224, children, 71), 295; Baptisms (adults, 11, infants, 30), 41; Confirmed, since last report, 30; Marriages, 3; Burials, 9; Communicants, last reported, 172, admitted, 30, received, 19, died, 1, removed, 2, present number, 218; Public Services (Sundays, 114, Holy days, 14, other days, 67), 195; Holy Communion (public, 34, private, 3), 37; Sunday School, teachers 10, pupils, 83; Catechizing, number of children, all; number of times, twice a month.

Offerings.

Parochial.—Alms for the poor, $67.15; Current expenses, including salaries, $1,821.48; Sunday School, $117.56; Gift to Rector, $200; Increase and Improvement of Church Property, $112; Other parochial objects, Ladies' Guild, $23.88; Parish Herald, $76.38. Total, $2,418.45.

Diocesan.—Diocesan Missions, $50; Salary of the Bishop, $12; Diocesan Fund, $12; Orphan House of the Holy Saviour, $93; Other offerings for objects within the Diocese, Village Bureau of Charities, $20.60. Total, $187.60.

General.—Domestic Missions, $14.50; Other objects exterior to the Diocese, Bishop Johnston, $140. Total, $154.50.

Total amount of Offerings, $2,760.55.

Property.

Church and lot (estimated worth), $13,000.
Parsonage and lot, $6,000.
Other property, Chapel, $2,700.
Condition of property, excellent.
Amount of salary pledged Rector, $900 and Rectory.
Number of sittings in the Church. 400; Chapel, 100; all free.

ST. JOHN'S CHURCH, PORTLANDVILLE.

Missionary. The Rev. Ernest A. Hartmann.
Warden. Hiram Cline.

Parochial.

Families, 4; Individuals, 13; Communicants, last reported, 9, present number recorded, 7; Public Services, Sundays, 11; Holy Communion, public, 4.

Offerings.

Parochial.—Current expenses, including salaries, $12.

Property.

Church and lot (estimated worth), $200.
Condition of property, good.
Number of sittings in the Church, 120; all free.

CHRIST CHURCH, WEST BURLINGTON.

Missionary. The Rev. Frederick Stirling Griffin.
Wardens. Thomas Hickling, Stephen I. Pope.
Vestrymen. B. A. Bailey, Caleb Clark, Lewis Spencer, Elias C. Mather, William Holdredge, John Priest, Stephen Olive, George Thomas.

Parochial.

Families, 30; Individuals (adults, 75, children, 30), 105; Baptisms (adults, 1, infants, 1), 2; Confirmed, since last report, 1; Present number of confirmed persons, 37; Communicants, last reported, 35, admitted, 1, present number, 33; Public Services (Sundays, 12, other days, 4), 16 ; Holy Communion, public, 3; Sunday School, teachers, 5, pupils, 35.

Property.

Church and lot (estimated worth), $4,000.
Parsonage and lot, $750.
Condition of property, excellent.
Amount of salary pledged Rector, $200.
Number of sittings in the Church, 150; all free.

ST. PAUL'S CHURCH, EAST SPRINGFIELD.

Rector. The Rev. John Prout.
Wardens. James H. Cooke, Leslie Pell-Clarke.
Vestrymen. S. A. Young, John Scollard, E. A. Keene, G. Hyde Clarke, Robert L. Walrath, Daniel Gilchrist.

Parochial.

Baptisms (adults, 6, infants, 6), 12; Confirmed, since last report, 3; Marriages, 1; Burials, 3; Communicants, last reported, 57, admitted, 3, died, 2, removed, 3, transferred to register of St. Mary's Church, Springfield Center, 16, present number, 39;

Public Services (Sundays, 86, Holy days, 20, other days, 18), 124; Holy Communion (public, 43, private, 3), 46; Sunday School, teachers, 4, pupils, 85.

Offerings.

Parochial.— Current expenses, including salaries, $575; Sunday School, $9.68; Increase and Improvement of Church Property, $48. Total, $662.68.

Diocesan.— Diocesan Missions, $16.50; Salary of the Bishop, $6; Diocesan Fund, $15; Orphan House of the Holy Saviour, $3; Other offerings for objects within the Diocese, $1. Total, $40.50.

General.— Domestic Missions, $12.35; Foreign Missions, $12.36; Other objects exterior to the Diocese, Bishop Grafton, $5.75. Total, $30.46.

Total amount of Offerings, $733.59.

Property.

Church and lot (estimated worth), $3,750.
Rectory and lot, $3,050.
Condition of property, good.
Amount of salary pledged Rector, $500.
Number of sittings in the Church, 120; all free.

ST. JAMES' CHURCH, ONEONTA.

Rector. The Rev. Ernest A. Hartmann.
Deacon. The Rev. A. Sprague Ashley.
Lay Reader. Robert Perine.
Wardens. John Cope, John D. Rohde.
Vestrymen. Robert M. Townsend, Richard Downes, William H. Hider, A. W. Carr, R. D. Briggs, Robert Perine, S. S. Matteson, James Stewart.

Parochial.

Families, 164; Individuals (adults, 309, children, 142), 451; Baptisms (adults, 4, infants, 24), 28; Confirmed, since last report, 35, present number of confirmed persons, 239; Marriages, 4; Burials, 9; Churchings, 1; Communicants, last reported, 176, admitted, 41, received, 25, removed, 21, present number, 221; Public Services (Sundays, 142, Holy days, 20, other days, 57), 219; Holy Communion (public, 53, private, 1), 54; Sunday School, teachers, 8, pupils, 82; Catechizing, number of times, twice a month.

Offerings.

Parochial.— Alms at Holy Communion, $39.17; Current expenses, including salaries, $998.18; Sunday School, $84.55: Increase and Improvement of Church Property, $29.56; Other Parochial objects, payment of mortgage, $2,000, note, $200. Total, $3,351.46.

Diocesan.— Diocesan Missions, $30; Salary of the Bishop, $6; Diocesan Fund, $12; Orphan House of the Holy Saviour, $7; The Child's Hospital, $5. Total, $60.

General.— Indian Missions, $5.

Total amount of Offerings, $3,416.46.

Property.

Church and lot (estimated worth), $12,000.
Condition of property, good.
Indebtedness, $700.
Amount of salary pledged Rector, $800.
Number of sittings in the Church, 225; all free.

Remarks.

At the time of the last report the Church's indebtedness consisted of bond and mortgage, $2,000, two notes of $200 and $700 respectively, and a floating debt of several hundred dollars. During the past year the mortgage, the note of $200 and the floating debt have been paid. The note of $700 is provided for by cash in hand and pledges. The Church, now free from debt for the first time in nineteen years, was consecrated by the Bishop on the 7th of November, 1890.

In August last, a rearrangement of the Missionary work in the neighborhood of Oneonta was made, by which Schenevus, Portlandville and Otego were associated with this Parish, and placed in charge of the Rector and the Rev. A. Sprague Ashley, Deacon.

ST. MARY'S MISSION, SPRINGFIELD CENTRE.

The Rev. John Prout.
Warden of the Mission. Leslie Pell-Clarke.
Clerk. G. W. Van De Veer.
Treasurer. A. A. Van Horne.

Parochial.

Baptisms (adults, 2, infants, 4), 6; Confirmed, 4; Communicants, admitted, 5, received, 1, transferred from register of St. Paul's, East Springfield, 16, present number recorded, 22, actually communicating, 20; Public Services (Sundays, 38, other days, 3), 41; Holy Communion, public, 12; Sunday School, teachers, 5, pupils, 30.

Offerings.

Parochial.--Current expenses, including salaries, $30.36; Increase and Improvement of Church Property, $63.71. Total, $94.07.
Diocesan.— Diocesan Missions, $12.
General.— Domestic Missions, $3.23; Foreign Missions, $3.23. Total, $6.46.
Total amount of Offerings, $112.53.

Property.

Church and lot (estimated worth), $8,000.
Condition of property, good.
Number of sittings in the Church, 120; all free.

Remarks.

The present is the first report from St. Mary's Mission, and the Parochial items include only such baptisms, etc., as have occurred since June 15. A few baptisms which were earlier are recorded in the register of St. Paul's, East Springfield, and included in the Parish report.

The Church commenced in the autumn of 1889 was completed, and opened for divine service on the second Sunday after Trinity 1890. Consecrated on St. Matthew's day (the 16th Sunday after Trinity), by the Bishop of Albany.

ST. STEPHEN'S CHAPEL, MAPLE GROVE.

Wardens. Clark B. Hull, Henry A. Starr.

Parochial.

Families, 12; Individuals (adults, 27, children, 33), 60; Communicants, last reported, 25, received, 4, removed, 5, present number recorded, 24; Public Services, Sundays, 52. Holy Communion, public, 3; Sunday School, teachers, 3, pupils, 22.

Offerings.

Parochial — Alms at Holy Communion, $3.65; Current expenses, including payment on debt, $65.30; Sunday School, $5.35; Increase and Improvement of Church Property, $40; Belfry, $10; Painting, $11.68. Total, $135.98.

Diocesan.— Diocesan Missions, $3; Salary of the Bishop, $2; Bible and Common Prayer Book Society of Albany, $1; Orphan House of the Holy Saviour, $4. Total, $10.

General.—Domestic Missions, $2; Foreign Missions, $2; Indian Missions, $2; Other objects exterior to the Diocese, old Catholic, $2. Total, $8.

Total amount of Offerings, $155.98.

Property.

Church and lot (estimated worth), $1,000.

Condition of property, good.

Amount of salary pledged Rector, $300.

Number of sittings in the Chapel, 150; all free.

Remarks.

After departure of Rev. H. Gates, our aged benefactor, Rev. Daniel Washburn continued giving us the ministry of the word each Sunday, when with his family, who conducted the music, Sunday School and Parish aid. Rev. S. M. Cook of New York preached once, and Rev. Dr. McDonald having business in California, devolved the services on Mr. Washburn again. With his free provision to us, for years, of chapel room and school, and use of organ even yet, our grateful hearts link the names of priests, from Hughes of Butternuts to Rhames of Morris, and of Bishops Tuttle and Rulison when Rectors of this field, To Mr. Sheldon of Delhi, by the Rev. F. B. Reazor, our thanks are due for an altar, chairs and desk, sightly, antique, rich and heavy.

PERSONAL REPORT.

RT. REV. SIR:

Through December and January last, myself and family helped maintain Church service and Sunday School in St. Stephen's Chapel, Maple Grove, painting within and without, and getting belfry for memorial bell, telling of two in Paradise. During February and March I was again in N. Y. hospitals for treatment of eye and throat; have since supplied place of absent Missionary two months, and attended Convocation specially for promoting diffusion of Church intelligence and for the Spirit's restoration of unity.　　　　Ever faithfully yours,

DANIEL WASHBURN.

THE CHURCH OF THE HOLY SPIRIT, SCHENEVUS.

In charge of the Clergy of the Oneonta Mission.

Parochial.

Families, 18; Individuals (adults, 32, children, 8), 40; Baptisms (adults, 1, infants, 2), 3; Confirmed, 2; Communicants, last reported, 21, admitted, 2, removed, 1, present number recorded, 23; Public Services (Sundays, 50, Holy days, 12, other days, 10), 72; Holy Communion, public, 45.

Offerings.

Parochial.—Alms at Holy Communion, $16.28, Current expenses, including salaries, $199.90; Increase and Improvement of Church Property, $66; Other parochial objects, Special Collection for Tower, $41.48. Total, $323.66.

Diocesan.—Diocesan Missions, 53 cents.

Total amount of Offerings, $324.19.

Property.

Church and lot (estimated worth), $3,000.

Condition of property, good.

Number of sittings in the Church 112; all free.

Rensselaer County.

ST. PAUL'S CHURCH, TROY.

Rector. The Rev. Edgar A. Enos.
Assistant. The Rev. Philip W. Mosher.
Wardens. Joseph M. Warren, Joseph J. Tillinghast.
Vestrymen. Stephen W. Barker, James H. Caldwell, John Clatworthy, Willard Gay, Derick Lane, William W. Morrill, Charles E. Patterson, John I. Thompson.

Parochial.

Families, 388; Individuals (adults and children), 1,589; Baptisms (adults, 9, infants, 38), 47; Confirmed, since last report, 46; Marriages, 13; Burials, 18; Communicants, last reported, 566, admitted, 46, received, 7, died, 3, present number recorded, 616; Public Services (Sundays, 192, Holy days, 138, other days, 560), 890; Holy Communion (public, 172, private, 30), 202; Sunday School, teachers, 21, pupils, 250; Catechizing, every Sunday; Parish School, teachers, 2, pupils, 15; Sisters in residence, 2; Friends of the Sisterhood (an incorporated society), 64; Sewing School, teachers, 24, pupils, 188; Mothers' Meeting, 52; Girls Friendly Society, teachers, 19, girls, 78; Altar Guild, 49; St. Margaret's Guild, 26; Woman's Auxiliary, 85; Young Men's Guild, 83; Ministering Children's League, teachers, 6, pupils, 84.

Offerings.

Parochial.— Alms at Holy Communion (not elsewhere reported), $201.76; Current expenses, including salaries, $9,868.71; Sunday School, $310.10; Parish School, $741.12; Increase and Improvement of Church Property, $528.39; Other parochial objects, Friends of the Sisterhood, $909.86; To Sister Kathryn, $240; Altar Guild, $328 ; St. Margaret's Guild, $100 ; Miscellaneous, $47 ; Special to the Rector, $1,300. Total, $14,574.94.

Diocesan.— Diocesan Missions (allotment, $750, St. Luke's, Troy, $150, Diocesan Itinerant, $100, Gloversville, $100), $1,100; Salary of the Bishop, $250: Diocesan Fund, $120; Bible and Common Prayer Book Society of Albany, $29.21; Fund for Aged and Infirm Clergymen, $20; Fund for Widows and Orphans of Clergymen, $20; Orphan House of the Holy Saviour, $158; The Child's Hospital, $164; Society for PromotingReligion and Learning, $25; Other Offerings for objects within the Diocese, Church Home, Troy, $600, St. Margaret's, Menands, $25; St. Mary s, Luzerne, $23; St. Christina Home, $146.90; Diocesan Missionary Box (estimated), $174.95. Total, $2,826.06.

General.—Domestic Missions ($252: Bp. Garrett, $30, Utah, $10, Louisville, $51, Florida, $10, Johnstown, Pa., $20, Galveston, Tex., $50, Oregon, $30, Missionary Box, Alabama, estimated, $164), $580; Foreign Missions, $50; Indian Missions, $10; Home Missions to Coloured Persons, $80. Total, $720.

Total amount of Offerings, $18,121.

Property.

Church and lot (estimated worth), $75,000.
Parsonage and lot, $15,000.
Chapel and school for boys, $40,000.
Martha Memorial House, $20,000.
Other property, $25.000.
Condition of property, good.
Number of sittings in the Church, 1,200.

Of gifts received during the year mention may be made of a brass processional cross (jeweled) for the Sunday School, the gift of Sister Kathryn.

ST. JOHN'S CHURCH, TROY.

Rector. The Rev. Thaddeus Alexander Snively.

Wardens. Norman B. Squires, Charles W. Tillinghast.

Vestrymen. William A. Thompson, Charles A. McLeod, William M. Sanford, George A. Wells, Francis N. Mann, Edward G. Gilbert, James M. Ide, William P. Mason.

Parochial.

Baptisms (adults, 5, infants, 31), 36; Confirmed, since last report, 25; Marriages, 3; Burials, 26; Communicants, last reported, 465, admitted 28, removed, 7, died, 19, removed, 22, deduct non-communicating, 44, removals without letter, 19, number actually communicating, 396; Sunday School, 225; Catechizing, every Sunday; Parish Sewing School, 88; Woman's Guild, 50; Woman's Auxiliary or Missionary Aid Society, 60; Parish Employment Society, 65; Mothers' Meeting, 28; Flower Society and Altar Guild, 85; Young Men's Free Reading-room, 110; King's Daughters, 66; Reception Brotherhood, 15.

Offerings.

Parochial.— Alms at Holy Communion, etc., $350; Current expenses, including salaries, $7,500; Sunday School, $300; Increase and Improvement of Church Property (Free Reading-room, $200; Parish Visitor, $200; Altar Society, etc., $190; Employment Society, $300; Miscellaneous, $375), $1,265. Total, $9,415.

Diocesan.— Diocesan Missions, including St. Luke's, Troy, $712.50; Salary of the Bishop, $250; Diocesan Fund, $90; Bible and Common Prayer Book Society of Albany, including Mann Bequest for two years, $780; Fund for Aged and Infirm Clergymen and Fund for Widows and Orphans of Clergymen, $59; Orphan House of the Holy Saviour, $189; The Child's Hospital, including Building Fund, $400; Theological Education, $150; Adirondack Sanitarium, $500; Missionary boxes, $250; Church Home of Troy, $600; Other objects, $200. Total, $4,330.50.

General.— Domestic and Foreign Missions, $400; Indian Missions, $15; Home Missions to Coloured Persons, $60; Missionary boxes and other objects exterior to the Diocese, $375; American Church Building Commission, $31.20. Total, $881.20.

Total amount of Offerings, $14,626.70.

Indebtedness, $8,000.

Amount of salary pledged Rector, $3,000.

Number of sittings in the Church, 600; all free.

CHRIST CHURCH, TROY.

Rector. The Rev. Eaton W. Maxcy, S. T. D.

Wardens. Hon. William Kemp, S. C. Tappin.

Vestrymen. Washington Akin, M. D., Peter Black, Charles Cleminshaw, J. W. A. Cluett, John Duke, Thomas H. Magill, Eugene C. Packard.

Parochial.

Families, 125; Individuals (adults, 450, children, 250), 700; Baptisms (adults, 9, infants, 14), 23; Confirmed, since last report, 20; Present number of confirmed persons, 350; Marriages, 2; Burials, 15; Communicants, last reported, 250, admitted, 20, received, 5, died, 3, present number, 272; Public Services (Sundays, 96, Holy days,

10, other days, 60), 176; Holy Communion, public, 15; Sunday School, teachers, 20, pupils, 178; Catechizing, number of times, 40.

Offerings.

Parochial.—Alms at Holy Communion, $75; Current expenses, including salaries, $4,813.28; Sunday School, $250; Increase and Improvement of Church Property, $650; Other parochial objects, $450. Total, $6,238.28.

Diocesan.— Diocesan Missions, $362.50; Salary of the Bishop, $125; Diocesan Fund, $75; Fund for Aged and Infirm Clergymen, $16.75; The Child's Hospital, $17.66; Other offerings for objects within the Diocese, $562. Total, $1,058.91.

Total amount of Offerings, $7,297.19.

Property.

Church and lot (estimated worth), $35,000.
Other property, $4,000.
Amount of salary pledged Rector, $2,500.
Number of sittings in the Church, 600.

CHURCH OF THE HOLY CROSS, TROY.

Rector. The Rev. J. Ireland Tucker.

Parochial.

Baptisms (adults, 13, infants, 23), 36; Confirmed, 23; Marriages, 12; Burials, 25; Communicants, actually communicating, 140; Public Services, Sundays, 2, Holy days, 1, other days, 1; Holy Communion, public, every Sunday and other Holy days; Sunday School, teachers, 12, pupils, 120; Parish School, teachers, 5, pupils, 60.

Offerings.

Diocesan.— Diocesan Missions, $200; Salary of the Bishop, $25; Diocesan Fund, $30; Bible and Common Prayer Book Society of Albany, $10; Fund for Aged and Infirm Clergymen, $25; Fund for Widows and Orphans of Clergymen, $25; Orphan House of the Holy Saviour, $25; The Child's Hospital, $25; Society for Promoting Religion and Learning, $25. Total, $390.

Sittings in the Church, all free.

ST. LUKE'S CHURCH, TROY.

Rector. The Rev. William Brevoort Bolmer.
Wardens. James Wood, John W. Babcock.
Vestrymen. P. Harry Mitchell, Thomas B. Iler, Thomas Marles, Henry E. Darby, Edmund Adams, Daniel Founcks, James Evans, George Haite.

Parochial.

Families, 148; Individuals (adults, 317, children, 233), 550; Baptisms (adults, 1, infants, 20), 21; Marriages, 5; Burials, 6; Churchings, 1: Communicants, last reported, 187, received, 1, removed, 2, present number recorded, 190; Public Services (Sundays, 110, Holy days, 40, other days, 53), 203; Holy Communion (public, 53, private, 6), 59; Sunday School, teachers, 9, pupils, 106; Catechizing, number of children, 50; number of times, 28.

Offerings.

Parochial.— Alms at Holy Communion, $21.73; Current expenses, including salaries, $1,913.29; Sunday School, $27 70: Increase and Improvement of Church Property, $318.75. Total, $2,176.47.

Diocesan.— Diocesan Missions, $4.80; Salary of the Bishop, $10; Diocesan Fund, $30; Orphan House of the Holy Saviour, $6.05. Total, $50.85.
Total amount of Offerings, $2,226.82.

Property.

Church and lot (estimated worth), $23,000.
Parsonage and lot, $4,000.
Other property, $1,700.
Condition of property, in tolerable repair.
Amount of salary pledged Rector, $800 and Rectory.
Number of sittings in the Church, 850; all free.

Remarks.

Rev. J. O. Lincoln resigned May 16. There were eight Sundays that Rev. Mr. Temple officiated. Sunday School was maintained by the Senior Warden and others. On September 1 the present Rector took charge.

FREE CHURCH OF THE ASCENSION, TROY.

Rector. The Rev. James Caird.
Trustees. W. R. Bridges, James Caird, Thomas Cordwell, J. J. Gillespy, David Little, N. B. Squires, F. W. Swett, W. A. Thompson.

Parochial.

Baptisms, infants, 9; Confirmed, 6; Marriages, 4; Burials, 15; Communicants, last reported, 240, present number recorded, 240. Public Services (Sundays, 104, Holy days, 6, other days, 62), 172; Holy Communion, public, 14; Sunday School, teachers, 18, pupils, 180; Catechizing, every Sunday.

Offerings.

Parochial.— Alms at Holy Communion, $10.25; Current expenses, including salaries, $2,110.96; Sunday School, $767.79; Increase and Improvement of Church Property, $75. Total, $2,964.
Diocesan.— Diocesan Missions, $27; Salary of the Bishop, $10; Church Home, Troy, N. Y., $10. Total, $47.
General.— Domestic Missions, $2; Other objects exterior to the Diocese, Women's Auxiliary, $54.07. Total, $56.07.
Total amount of Offerings, $3,067.07.

SAINT BARNABAS' CHURCH, TROY.

Rector. The Rev. William D. Martin.
The Corporation. Rev. Wm. D. Martin, President, Rev. J. Ireland Tucker, S. T. D., Vice-President; A. W. Moffitt, Treasurer, Wm. C. Jamieson, Thomas Entwistle, Wm. M. Morrill, Wm H. Rousseau, Chas. W. Tillinghast, 2d, Horace B. Finley, Secretary.
The Local Committee. Rev. Wm. D. Martin, A. W. Moffitt, Thomas Entwistle, Horace B. Finley.

Parochial.

Families, 50; Individuals (adults, 168, children, 110), 278; Baptisms (adults, 5, infants, 15), 20; Confirmed, since last report, 18; Marriages, 2; Burials, 3; Communicants, last reported, 74, admitted (by confirmation, 28, otherwise, 77), 105, received, 5, died, 4, removed, 11, present number, 169, actually communicating, 161; Public Services (Sundays, 197, Holy days. 91, other days, 602), 890; Holy Communion (public, 233, private, 8), 241; Sunday School, teachers, 7, pupils, 75; Catechizing, number of children (average), 50; number of adults (average), 15; number of times, 52. St. Agatha's Guild, for young women, has 25 members; The Guild of the Holy Childhood, for boys, 20 members; St. Barnabas' Guild (Parochial), for men and women has 40 members; The Brotherhood of St. Barnabas', for men only, has 23 members. Total, 108.

Offerings.

Parochial.—Alms at Holy Communion (early celebrations), $82.90; Current expenses, including salaries, $3,082.45; Sunday School, $32; Increase and Improvement of Church Property, $319.07; Other parochial objects, $258.69; For the purchase of a lot, $677.27; Building Fund, $491.24. Total, $4,943.62.

Diocesan.— Diocesan Missions, $61.29; Salary of the Bishop, $5; Bible and Common Prayer Book Society of Albany, $5.66; Fund for Aged and Infirm Clergymen, $15.06; Orphan House of the Holy Saviour, $4; The Child's Hospital, $9.25; Other offerings for objects within the Diocese: Church Home, Troy, $15.29; Troy Orphan Asylum, $6.18. Total, $121.73.

General.— Domestic Missions, $6.56; Foreign Missions, $4.50; Other objects exterior to the Diocese: For the Jews, $8.93; The Clergymen's Mutual Insurance League, $3.43. Total, $23.42.

Total amount of Offerings, $5,088.77.

Property.

Church and lot (estimated worth), $4,500.

Mission House and lot, $3,500.

Other property (Chancel furniture, etc.), $1,450.

Condition of property. The Church is in good condition; the Mission House is greatly out of repair, and requires constant attention. It should be pulled down.

The Building Fund now amounts to $7,843.36, The Fund for the purchase of a lot to $677.27. Total, $8,520.63.

Indebtedness, a mortgage of $3,600 on the lot.

Amount of salary pledged Rector, $1,200 (no rectory).

Number of sittings in the Chapel, 150, all free.

Remarks.

All amounts for current expenses have come directly through the offertory; for other purposes by pledges and subscriptions. The only assistance that the Parish has received has been $361, from friends in other Parishes, toward the purchase of a lot.

TRINITY CHURCH, LANSINGBURGH.

Rector. The Rev. C. M. Nickerson.

Wardens James McQuide, Peter B. King.

Vestrymen. Eugene Hyatt, E. K. Betts, E. H. Leonard, James M. Snyder, Charles S. Holmes, E. Warren Banker, George F. Nichols, George Daw.

Parochial.

Families, 149; Baptisms (adults, 4, infants, 22), 26; Confirmed, since last report, 18; Marriages, 8; Burials, 17; Communicants, last reported, 227, admitted, 14, received, 13, died, 4, removed, 17, dropped, 2, present number, 231; Public Services (Sundays, 112, Holy days, 30, other days, 42), 184; Holy Communion (public, 42, private, 5), 47; Sunday School, teachers, 20, pupils, 205; Catechizing, number of times, 30.

Offerings.

Parochial.— Alms at Holy Communion, $74; Current expenses, including salaries, $3,297.85; Sunday School, $102.57; Other Parochial objects, Choir vestments, by St. Cecilia Guild, $100; Alms basin, St. Agnes' Guild, $60; Altar hangings, $87. Total, $3,721.42.

Diocesan.— Diocesan Missions, $195; Salary of Bishop, $75; Diocesan Fund, $45; Fund for Aged and Infirm Clergymen, $24.69; Orphan House of the Holy Saviour, $20; The Child's Hospital, $20. Total, $379.69.

General.— Domestic Missions, $82.17; Foreign Missions, $36.68; Other objects exterior to the Diocese, St. Paul's, Durango, Col., $150; Box of clothing for Franklin, N. C., $40. Total, $308.85.

Total amount of Offerings, $4,409.96.

Property.

Church and lot (estimated worth), $50,000.
Parsonage and lot, $5,000.
Other property, Parish House, $4,000.
Condition of property, good.
Amount of salary pledged Rector, $1,500.
Number of sittings in the Church, 374 (number rented, 314, number free, 18), 332.

ST. MARK'S CHURCH, HOOSICK FALLS.

Rector Emeritus. The Rev. George Huntington Nicholls, S. T. D.
Rector. The Rev. George Dent Silliman, S. T. B.
Wardens. Hon. Walter A. Wood, James Russell Parsons.
Vestrymen. John G. Darroch, Wm. S. Nicholls, Marsin D. Greenwood, Isaac A. Allen, Charles M. Coulter, John Hobart Warren, A. Danforth Geer, Nelson Gillespie.

Parochial.

Families, 218; Individuals (adults, 466, children, 272), 738; Baptisms (adults, 5, infants, 25), 30; Confirmed, since last report, 25; Marriages, 10; Burials, 17; Communicants, last reported, 449, admitted, 25, received, 1, died, 10, removed, 33, present number, 432; Public Services (Sundays, 4, Holy days, 2, other days, daily, twice since Advent Sunday, 1889), 875; Holy Communion (public, 182, private, 7), 189; Sunday School, teachers, 15, pupils (including Rector's Bible class), 258; Catechizing, number of children, all; number of times, nearly every Sunday.

Offerings.

Parochial.— For the poor, and a special charity of the Parish, $323.69; Current expenses, including salaries (Treasurer's report since April, 1889), $4,377.23; Sunday School, books, Christmas tree, etc., $219.87; Increase and Improvement of Church Property, $963.31; Other Parochial objects, Parish Hall, etc., $461.13; Theological Education, special, $30. Total, $6,380.23.

Diocesan.— Diocesan Missions, $200; Salary of the Bishop, $26; Diocesan Fund, $45; Bible and Common Prayer Book Society of Albany, $10; Fund for Aged and Infirm Clergymen, $23; Orphan House of the Holy Saviour, $12; The Child's Hospital, $57.   Total, $373.

General.—Domestic Missions, Sunday School, Lenten offering. $28.80; Foreign Missions, $18; Mission to Jews, $7.84; Other objects exterior to the Diocese, "Little Samuel" School, Persia (S. S.), $25; Society for the Increase of the Ministry, $35; Box for St. Cyprian's School, New Berne, N. C., from Woman's Auxiliary, $70; Missions and charities, including two boxes to Cooperstown Ministering Children's League, $53.71. Total, $238.35.

Total amount of Offerings, $6,991.58.

Property.

Church and lot (estimated worth), $25,000.

Parsonage and lot, $7,500.

Condition of property, good.

Amount of salary pledged Rector, $1,500.

All sittings free.

Remarks.

Again, with loving gratitude, the Rector acknowledges the helpful services of the Rector Emeritus, whose aid is still given to the Parish,—a free-will offering.

Little more than a year ago, a branch of the Woman's Auxiliary was formed in the Parish, through the efforts of Mrs. C. E. Patterson, President of the Diocesan Branch. The sum of $317.78 has been raised by its 168 members. Some of its work has been included elsewhere in this report, and the women are now just finishing a box for a Diocesan Missionary, preparatory to beginning work for the Child's Hospital in Albany. The Guild of the Iron Cross, The Ministering Children's League, The Girl's Friendly Society, and The King's Daughters, are all represented in the Parish, and each bears its part in the work done.

TRINITY CHURCH, SCHAGHTICOKE.

Minister. The Rev. T. Dickinson.

Wardens. Edward Searls, J. J. Wetsel.

Vestrymen. Charles E. Corbin, William H. Hawkins, Joseph W. Parker, Ira E. Askins, Frank Signarth.

Parochial.

Families, 37; Individuals (adults, 151, children, 71), 222; Baptisms, 8; Marriages, 1; Burials, 5; Communicants, last reported. 39, admitted, 2, received 1, died, 2, removed, 2, present number recorded, 38, actually communicating, 30; Public Services, Sundays, 2, and on 3d Sunday 3 services, Holy days, 1, other days, Wednesday or Friday, 1; Holy Communion, public, 2, first and third Sundays and great festivals, private, 3; Sunday School, teachers, 4, pupils, 45; Catechizing, number of children, 45; Number of times, weekly.

Offerings.

Parochial —Alms at Holy Communion, $12.89; Current expenses, including salaries, $553 63; Sunday School, $4 82, Increase and Improvement of Church Property, $33 62. Total, $604.96.

Diocesan.—Diocesan Missions, $20; Salary of the Bishop, $6; Diocesan Fund, $9; Bible and Common Prayer Book Society of Albany, $2.36; Fund for Aged and Infirm Clergymen, $3.77; Fund for Widows and Orphans of Clergymen, $3.78. Total, $44.91.

General.—Domestic Missions, $3.49; Foreign Missions, $5.01; Other objects exterior to the Diocese, Promoting Christianity among Jews, $2.33. Total, $10.83.

Total amount of Offerings, $660.70.

Property.

Church and lot (estimated worth), $4,000.
Parsonage and lot, $3,750.
Condition of property, good.
Indebtedness, $2,450.
Amount of salary pledged Rector, $800.
Number of sittings in the Church, 200; all free.

Remarks.

I took charge of this Parish at the request of the Bishop, Sept. 1. This is, therefore, a report more especially of my predecessor.

Since I commenced work, a Junior Ladies Guild has been organized, and a Young Men's Literary Society inaugurated. Both give promise of much good; each organization has about twenty members.

THE CHURCH OF THE MESSIAH, GREENBUSH.

Rector. The Rev. Thomas B. Fulcher.
Wardens. George Low, Alfred S. Curtis.
Vestrymen. David A. Teller, Richard W. Stevens, Fred. A. Akin, Solon L. Slade, William H. Terrell, George Story, William G. Curtis, Harry E. Cole.

Parochial.

Families, 61; Baptisms, infants, 5; Confirmed, since last report, 10; Marriages, 8; Burials, 9; Communicants, last reported, 111, admitted, 10, received, 4, died, 8, removed, 5, present number, 117; Public Services (Sundays, 106, Holy days, 24, other days, 33), 163; Holy Communion (public, 28, private, 10), 38; Sunday School, teachers, 10, pupils, 75; Catechizing, number of children, all, number of times, 12.

Offerings.

Parochial.— Alms at Holy Communion, $34.88; Current expenses, including salaries, $1,104.94; Sunday School, $79.75; Increase and Improvement of Church Property, $293.45; Other parochial objects, rent of Parish rooms, etc., $97.87; Parish House Building Fund, $291.62. Total, $1,902.51.

Diocesan.—Diocesan Missions, $30; Salary of the Bishop, $10; Diocesan Fund, $24; Fund for Aged and Infirm Clergymen, $2.14; Fund for Widows and Orphans of Clergymen, $2; Orphan House of the Holy Saviour, $5; The Child's Hospital, $5. Total, $78.14.

Total amount of Offerings, $1,980.65.

Property.

Church and lot (estimated worth), $6,000.
Other property, $1,000.
Condition of property, fair.
Amount of salary pledged Rector, $800.
Number of sittings in the Church, 150; all free.

Remarks.

It is only just to state that the largely increased offerings of this year are due in great measure to the untiring and faithful work of the two societies of the Parish, together with the Sunday School. " The Ladies' Aid Society " has paid off a long standing coal bill, aided in the improvement and repair of the Church building, and assisted the Treasurer in meeting the current expenses of the Parish. " The Young People's Association " have bent their energies to securing a Fund for the erection of a much-needed Parish House. The fund at the date of this report amounts to $291.62. The Sunday School, with the help of friends, has put in the large nave window at a cost of $225.

FREE CHURCH OF THE EPIPHANY, BATH-ON-THE-HUDSON.

Rector. The Rev. Thomas White.

Parochial.

Families, 43; Baptisms (adults, 4, infants, 22), 26; Confirmed, 10; Marriages, 1; Burials, 14; Communicants, last reported, 157, admitted, 10, received, 1, died, 3, removed, 1, present number recorded, 164; Public Services (Sundays, 123, Holy days, 20, other days, 42), 185; Holy Communion (public, 45, private, 6), 51; Sunday School, teachers, 16, pupils, 200; Catechizing, number of children, 200; number of times, every Sunday.

Offerings.

* Parochial.— Current expenses, including salaries, $803.49; Sunday School, $66.37 ; Increase and Improvement of Church Property, $50 ; Other parochial objects, $57.19. Total, $977.05.

Diocesan.—Diocesan Missions, $6.74; Salary of the Bishop, $4. Total, $10.74.

General.—Domestic Missions, $12.50; Foreign Missions, $12.50. Total, $25.

Total amount of Offerings, $1,012.79.

Property.

Church and lot (estimated worth), $10,000.

Condition of property, good.

Amount of salary pledged Rector, $600.

Number of sittings in the Church, 170, all free.

Remarks.

There have been many gifts for the altar, in memory of friends departed, not taken into account in the above, which deserve recognition; also a beautiful Litany desk from the Young Men's Guild of St. Barnabas', Troy.

ALL SAINTS' CHURCH, HOOSAC.

Rector. The Rev. E. D. Tibbits.

Assistants. The Revs. T. H. R. Luney, W. G. Ivie, J. B. Tibbits.

Wardens. D. P. Griffith, Le G. C. Tibbits.

Vestrymen. Nicholas Brown, Charles Andrews, William Wills, H. C. Babcock.

Parochial.

Families, 80; Baptisms (adults, 5, infants, 5), 10; Confirmed, 4; Marriages, 4; Burials, 2; Communicants, last reported, 105, died, 2, removed, 5, present number recorded, 109, actually communicating, 99, Holy Communion (public, 100, private, 1), 101, Sunday School, teachers, 8; Catechizing, number of times, once a month.

Offerings.

Parochial.— Alms at Holy Communion, $56.57; Current expenses, including salaries, $894.87; Sunday School, $30. Total, $981.44.

Diocesan — Diocesan Missions, $50; Salary of the Bishop, $5; Other offerings for objects within the Diocese, St. Christina's Home, $25. Total, $80.

General.— Home Missions to Coloured Persons, $30.

Total amount of Offerings, $1,091.44

MISSION OF THE HOLY NAME, BOYNTONVILLE.

Priest in charge. The Rev. W. G. Ivie.
Warden. Willis Humiston.
Clerk. P. Slade; Treasurer, F. Snyder.

Parochial.

Baptisms, adults, 5; Confirmed, 8; Burials, 1; Communicants, last reported, 80, died, 3, removed, 2, present number recorded, 28: Holy Communion (public, 29, private, 3), 32.

Remarks.

During the past year at Raymertown, a village five miles south-west of Boyntonville, a new Mission Station (called St. Paul's) has been started. The services have been held at this place every other Sunday in a public hall, and now the use of the district school-house has been secured for the coming year, so that the Priest in charge of Boyntonville will be able to go there every Sunday afternoon. Funds are being raised to erect a suitable church building, and it is hoped that the foundations for it may be laid in the early spring.

ST. GILES' MISSION, CASTLETON.

Missionary. The Rev. William Rollins Webb.

Parochial.

Families, 14; Individuals, 86; Confirmed, since last report, 8; Present number of confirmed persons, 25; Communicants, last reported, 14, present number, 14; Public Services (Sundays, 56, other days, 5), 61; Holy Communion, public, 5: Sunday School, teachers, 2, pupils, 21; Catechizing, number of children, all; number of times, 5.

FINANCIAL REPORT.

Receipts.

Cash on hand, November 1, 1889	$13 82
Through offertory	95 84
Building Fund	36 82
Festivals, etc	84 03
Gifts	40 77
Salary	5 20
Total	$276 48

Disbursements.

Current expenses	$208 84
Balance	67 64
Total	$276 48

Remarks

The following evidences of progress, not included in the above report, should not be omitted, viz.: In December, 1889, the Mission exchanged its inconvenient place of meeting for a large and comfortably fitted up Mission-room. For the furnishing of this the following articles were given: A number of benches formerly used by the Cathedral; a Litany desk and two chancel seats, formerly used by the Cathedral; gifts in Bibles, Prayer Books and Hymnals, from the Bible and Common Prayer Book Society of Albany; silver plated baptismal bowl; marble top support for above; lectern; altar of wood with cross; dorsal curtain. An organ has also been bought and paid for. A "Woman's Auxiliary of St. Giles' Mission" has been organized.

26

At the opening services of the new Mission-room, the first class ever presented was confirmed by the Bishop of the Diocese. There is on deposit as a building fund, $311.13. No report of Sunday School Offerings is made as the treasurer failed to make a report in time for insertion.

St. Lawrence County.

ST. JOHN'S CHURCH, OGDENSBURGH.

Rector. The Rev. J. D. Morrison, D. D., LL. D.
Wardens. Charles Ashley, Louis Hasbrouck.
Vestrymen. James G. Averell, J. C. Sprague, Levi Hasbrouck, Thomas Lawrance, James G. Knap, Egbert Burt, S. Freeman Palmer, Henry F. James.

Parochial.

Baptisms (adults, 7, infants, 41), 48; Confirmed, since last report, 29; Marriages, 9; Burials, 30; Public Services, daily services in Advent, Lent, Ember and Rogation seasons; Holy Communion, public, every Sunday and Holy Day and on Thursdays in Advent and Lent, private, frequent; Sunday School, teachers, 25, pupils, 300; Catechizing, frequent, whole Sunday School and confirmation classes.

Offerings.

Parochial.— Alms at Holy Communion, $146.57; Current expenses, including salaries, $4,033.61: Sunday School, $650; Increase and Improvement of Church Property, $65; Other parochial objects, $600. Total, $5,495.18.

Diocesan.—Diocesan Missions, $500; Specials for Diocesan Missions, $57; Salary of the Bishop, $70; Diocesan Fund, $54; Bible and Common Prayer Book Society of Albany, $21.84; Fund for Aged and Infirm Clergymen, $23.07; Fund for Widows and Orphans of Clergymen, $33.17: Orphan House of the Holy Saviour, $44; The Child's Hospital, $12.50; Other offerings for objects within the Diocese, from Woman's Auxiliary, for Diocesan Missionaries (boxes), $41.30. Total, $356 88.

General.— Domestic and Foreign Missions, $39.50; Other objects exterior to the Diocese, Woman's Auxiliary (money and boxes), Domestic Missions, $126.45; Foreign Missions (money), $42. Total, $207.95.

Total amount of Offerings, $6,560.01.
Amount of salary pledged Rector, $2,000.

Remarks.

The Rector of this Church is under great obligations to the Rev. William H. Harison, D. D., who during the past year has most generously assisted in the services of the Church, and during the Rector's absence has taken the whole duty.

ST. PAUL'S CHURCH, WADDINGTON.

Rector. The Rev A C. Macdonald.
Wardens S. S. Carlisle, S. J. Bower, M. D.
Vestrymen L. J. Proctor, James Cook, Robert Dalzel, Harry Rose, Henry Carlisle.

Parochial.

Families, 37; Individuals (adults, 100, children, 61), 161; Baptisms (adults, 1, infants, 5), 6; Confirmed, since last report, 4: Present number of confirmed persons, 75; Marriages, 3; Burials, 5, Communicants, last reported, 70; received, 1; died, 2; present number, 71: Public Services (Sundays, 156, Holy days, 30, other days, Advent and Lent, 21), 207; Holy Communion (public, 25, private, 5), 30; Sunday School, teachers, 6, pupils, 41; Catechizing, number of children, 40; number of times, several.

Offerings.

Parochial.— Current expenses, including salaries, $425; Sunday School, $14.50; Increase and Improvement of Church Property, $200; Other parochial objects, payment on debt to Mrs. Clemson, $200; Contract for roofing Church, $175. Total, $914.50.

Diocesan.— Diocesan Missions, $24; Diocesan Fund, $9; Bible and Common Prayer Book Society of Albany, $2; Other offerings for objects within the Diocese, contribution to Convocation, $3.45. Total, $38.45.

General.— Domestic Missions, $4.50; Indian Missions, 60 cents. Total, $5.10.

Total amount of Offerings, $958.05.

Property.

Church and lot (estimated worth), $5,000.

Parsonage and lot, $3,000.

Other property, garden and orchard, $50.

Condition of property, good.

Amount of salary pledged Rector, $300.

Number of sittings in the Church, 200; all free.

Remarks.

The attention bestowed upon parochial objects the past year has been eminently satisfactory. The interior of Church, gloomy to a degree, has been changed by the frescoing, so that it is now a thing of beauty, transformed, restored, made more meet for the worship of Almighty God. This work cost $250, a moderate sum, those capable of judging say, for the expenditure of so much labor. In addition to this there is a contract for iron-roofing the Church, a work made necessary by the decayed state of the present shingles. Ways and means are being devised for payment of this. The sum total raised within two years for payment of debt and improvement on property will exceed $750, which may seem small on paper to those who are willing and able to give their thousands, but to us who are a feeble flock, with limited resources, occupying an isolated position, it has meant a great deal. The widow's mite has contributed toward it, and the Master, as of old, is giving His approval Are we satisfied with attainments? No! Our Diocesan contribution is too small and our domestic amount is entirely too low. Efforts, earnest, faithful, must be made to increase them. And the prospects for doing so are brightening.

CHRIST CHURCH, MORRISTOWN.

Rector. The Rev. J. T. Zorn.

Wardens. Joseph Couper, Henry A. Chapman.

Vestrymen. J. A. Phillips, T. W. Pierce, A. L. Palmer, G. E. Pope, Henry Bacon, E. Kingsland, D. C. Church, S. Lamphere.

Parochial.

Baptisms (adults, 2, infants, 3), 5; Confirmed, since last report, 5; Present number of confirmed persons, 4; Marriages, 3; Burials, 9; Communicants, last reported, 117, admitted, 5, received, 1, died, 3, removed, 28, present number, 92; Public Services (Sundays, 102, Holy days, 44, other days, 73), 219; Holy Communion (public, 49, private, 3), 52; Sunday School, teachers, 5, pupils, 40; Catechizing, number of children, 30; number of times, 25.

Offerings.

Parochial.—Alms at Holy Communion, $38.82; Current expenses, including salaries, $758.23. Total, $787.05.

Diocesan.— Diocesan Missions, $75; Salary of the Bishop, $20; Diocesan Fund, $15; Orphan House of the Holy Saviour, $2.50; The Child's Hospital, $11. Total, $123.50.

General.—Domestic and Foreign Missions, $10; Other objects exterior to the Diocese, Christianizing the Jews, $1.45. Total, $11.45.

Total amount of Offerings, $922.

Property.

Church and lot (estimated worth), $3,000.
Parsonage and lot, $2,500.
Other property, two lots in Ogdensburgh, $500.
Condition of property, good.
Amount of salary pledged Rector, $500.
Number of sittings in the Church, 200; all free.

Remarks.

A recent revision of the register has necessitated a large deduction from the number of communicants hitherto reported. The number now reported "removed," embraces the deduction, together with the actual removals taking place during the year. Many names have been borne upon the register, for past years, of persons whose removal was evidently regarded as temporary, but has proved to be permanent. The correction of this over-statement is now made. Some names, hitherto omitted from the register, have been supplied. Yet the "present number" of communicants falls from 117 to 92, and this number still comprises the names of persons removed, but whose removal is not ascertained to be permanent. There is general and culpable neglect of the canonical requirement that persons removing to other Parishes shall bear with them certificates of transfer, and even if this is done, in exceptional cases, it is difficult to ascertain when, or whether at all the actual transfer has taken place. Removals of the younger members of the Church are increasingly frequent, and constitute a serious drain upon our numbers, as they are not counter-balanced by the ordinary accessions.

TRINITY CHURCH, POTSDAM.

Rector. The Rev. R. M. Kirby.
Wardens. Thomas S. Clarkson, Bloomfield Usher.
Vestrymen. E. W. Foster, Milton Heath, C. O. Tappan, T. Streatfeild Clarkson, W. A. Dart, O. G. Howe, H D. Thatcher, L. Usher.

Parochial.

Baptisms (adults, 7, infants, 10), 17; Confirmed, since last report, 12; Present number of confirmed persons, 230; Marriages, 7; Burials, 12; Communicants, last reported, 202, admitted, 13, received, 7, died, 4, removed, 14, present number, 204; Public Services (Sundays, 104, Holy days, 34, other days, 84), 222; Holy Communion, public, 41, private, many times; Sunday School, teachers, 17, pupils, 150; Catechizing, number of children, all; number of times, often.

Offerings.

Parochial — Alms at Holy Communion, $159.46; Current expenses, including salaries, $2,365.11; Sunday School, $129.36; Altar Society, $255.49; Increase and Improvement of Church Property, $4,796.36. Total, $7,705.78.

Diocesan.—Diocesan Missions, $663; Salary of the Bishop, $38; Diocesan Fund, $48; Bible and Common Prayer Book Society of Albany, $15.43; Fund for Aged and Infirm Clergymen (special), $100), $136.76; Fund for Widows and Orphans of Clergymen, $20.75; Orphan House of the Holy Saviour, $53.91; The Child's Hospital, $39.71; Society for Promoting Religion and Learning, $31.97; Other offerings for objects within the Diocese, Convocation of Ogdensburgh, $58.06. Total, $1,100.59.

General.— Home Missions to Jews, $21.11; Domestic Missions, $196; Foreign Missions, $300.03; Indian Missions, $172.91; Church Building Fund, $15; Other objects exterior to the Diocese, Sunday School, for Bishop Brewer, $32.04; Sunday School, for St. Mark's School, Utah, $80. Total, $869.09.

Total amount of Offerings, $9,675.46.

Property.

Church and lot (estimated worth), $60,000.

Parsonage and lot, $4,000.

Condition of property, excellent.

Amount of salary pledged Rector, $1,600.

Number of sittings in the Church, 350; Chapel, 150; all free.

Remarks.

In addition to the amount reported above, the parochial branch of the Woman's Auxiliary has sent boxes into the Mission field having a money value of $225.

During the year I have maintained services at Norwood, giving the people there an afternoon service each Lord's day. The attendance has been fairly good, and as far as they are able, the people of Norfolk availed themselves of these services. At the time of the Bishop's invitation two persons were confirmed at Norwood. The offerings for all purposes amounted to about $300. The Church is completed — is quite an attractive building.

GRACE CHURCH, CANTON.

Rector. The Rev. R. G. Hamilton.

Wardens. Leslie W. Russell, Sheldon Brewer.

Vestrymen. Charles J. Perkins, J. D. Tracey, Cleland Austin, John C. Heeler, Henri H. Lidlaid, H. B. Safford, G. C. Sawyer, one vacancy.

Parochial.

Baptisms (adults, 1, infants, 6),7 ; Confirmed, 4; Marriages, 4; Burials, 6; Communicants, last reported, 104, admitted, 4, died, 1, removed, 10, present number recorded, 97, actually communicating, 75; Public Services (Sundays, 156, Holy days, 27, other days, 100), 283; Holy Communion, public, 75; Sunday School, teachers, 3, pupils, 25; Catechizing, number of times, 12.

Offerings.

Parochial.—Current expenses, including salaries, $872.03; Other parochial objects, interest on Rectory mortgage paid by Ladies' Aid Society, $72. Total, $944.03.

Diocesan.— Diocesan Missions, $4.

Total amount of Offerings, $948.03.

Indebtedness, mortgage on new Rectory, $1,200; deficit on Rector's salary, etc., $361.72.

Remarks.

For the benefit of his successor in this Parish, the present incumbent deems it expedient, in justice to himself and some members of his Parish, to place on record certain facts bearing upon the welfare of the Parish.

The records of the county clerk of St. Lawrence county, N. Y., show the existence of three mortgages on the property of Grace Church, Canton, aggregating $2,283.66. No part of the principal sum or interest has ever been paid.

The records of the Parish show that the Rector will be asked to resign his charge by certain members of the Vestry, on the ground of financial inability to fulfil obligations that are generally considered sacred.

As in all probability this will be the last Parochial Report of this Parish by me as Rector, I beg to place on record my sincere appreciation of the many acts of courtesy extended to the Rector and his family since coming to the Parish.

GRACE CHURCH, NORFOLK.

See Remarks, Report, Trinity Church, Potsdam.

TRINITY CHURCH, GOUVERNEUR.

Rector. The Rev. James Alexander Dickson
Wardens. Aaron B. Cutting, Duncan G. Wood.
Vestrymen J. B. Preston, B. L. Barney, Edward D. Barry, Frank H. Smith, John McCarty.

Parochial.

Families in part or whole, 49; Individuals (adults, 106, children, 49), 155; Baptisms (adults, 4, infants, 11), 15; Confirmed, 6; Marriages, 3; Burials, 10; Communicants last reported, 61, admitted, 6, removed, 2, present number, 66; Public Services, Sundays, 94, Holy days, all, other days, Wednesday evenings; Holy Communion, public, 39; Sunday School, teachers, 7, pupils, 40; Catechizing, every Sunday.

Offerings.

Parochial.— Alms at Holy Communion, $88.57; Current expenses, including salaries, $1,092.82; Sunday School, $19.47; Other parochial objects, Church debt, $475; Repairs on Church, $205.05. Total, $1,880.91.

Diocesan.— Diocesan Missions, $50; Salary of the Bishop, $20; Diocesan Fund, $24; Bible and Common Prayer Book Society of Albany, $3.11. Total, $97.11.

General.— Jewish Missions, $2.

Total amount of Offerings, $1,980.02.

Property

Church and lot (estimated worth), $6,500.
Parsonage and lot, $3,000.
Other property, $350.
Condition of property, fairly good.
Amount of salary pledged Rector, $800.
Number of sittings in the Church, 200; number rented, 185; number free, 15.

ST. JOHN'S CHURCH, MASSENA

Missionary. The Rev. Howard McDougall.
Wardens. H T. Clark, G. A. Smith.
Vestrymen. J. O. Bridges, F. H. Polley, E. R. Foord, F. H. Pitts, L. S. Downing, C. A. Boynton.

Parochial.

Families, 41; Individuals (adults, 102, children, 50), 152; Baptisms, infants, 14; Confirmed since last report, 1, Present number of confirmed persons, 141; Marriages, 2; Burials, 2, Communicants, last reported, 56, admitted, 1, received, 1, present number, 58; Public Services, Sundays, 22; Holy Communion (public, 5, private, 1), 6; Sunday School, teachers, 7, pupils, 50; Catechizing, number of children, 50; number of times, 16.

Offerings.

Parochial.— Current expenses, including salaries, $285.72.

Diocesan.— Diocesan Missions, $50: Salary of the Bishop, $6; Diocesan Fund, $9. Total, $65.

Total amount of Offerings, $350.72.

Property.

Church and lot (estimated worth), $9,000.

Condition of property, good.

Amount of salary pledged Rector, $300.

Number of sittings in the Church, 250; all free.

Remarks.

The Missionary entered upon work in this Church June 15. Among the visitors at Massena Springs are a number of Church people. This increases, for the time, the number of communicants, but is not included in the above statistics. Through the kindness of the Church Periodical Club of New York, some valuable books have been added to the Sunday School library.

ST. LUKE'S CHURCH, LISBON.

Rector. The Rev. A. C. Macdonald.

Parochial.

Families, 12; Individuals (adults, 22, children, 16), 38; Baptisms, infants, 1; Confirmed, 4; Burials, 3; Communicants, last reported, 15, present number recorded, 15, actually communicating, 12; Public Services (Sundays, 36, other days, 4), 40; Holy Communion (public, 4, private, 2), 6; Sunday School, teachers, 4, pupils, 15; Catechizing, number of children, 15; number of times, twice.

Offerings.

Parochial.— Alms at Holy Communion, $6.40; Current expenses, including salaries, $20; Sunday School, 50 cents; Other parochial objects, horse hire, $65; A gift to Mrs. Macdonald, $25. Total, $116.90.

Diocesan.— Diocesan Missions, $6.

Total amount of Offerings, $122.90.

Property.

Church and lot (estimated worth), $2,000.

Condition of property, good.

Remarks.

Interest in the services here is being maintained unabated. The visit to this Church by the Bishop and the Archdeacon on July 6 was greatly enjoyed. A transference of the present vestry-room from end of chancel, to be placed at junction of nave and chancel is a project long contemplated, but we fear, is yet some ways off. The vestry wall forms eastern end of chancel and its removal with other alterations must necessitate a considerable expenditure. Still it is quite desirable and an earnest effort will be made in the spring for accomplishing it. The change commends itself in the heartiest manner to our beloved Diocesan.

ZION CHURCH, COLTON.

Rector. The Rev. G. M. Irish.
Wardens. Thomas S. Clarkson, Myron E. Howard.
Vestrymen. P. Potter, D. J. Culver, M. D., J. W. Lyman, Archie Allen, S. J. Hosley, F. Horton, E. E. Perrine, W. Eacutt.

Parochial. '

Baptisms (adults, 5, infants, 12), 17; Confirmed, since last report, 5; Marriages, 1; Burials, 13; Communicants last reported, 52; admitted, 5, received, 1, died, 1, removed, 12, present number, 45; Public Services (Sundays, 98, Holy days, 12, other days, 54), 164; Holy Communion (public, 33, private, 2), 35; Sunday School, teachers, 9, pupils, 93; Catechizing, number of children, all, number of times, every Sunday.

Offerings.

Parochial.— Alms at Holy Communion, $9.18; Current expenses, including salaries, $1,150.98; Sunday School, $24.09; Increase and Improvement of Church Property, $33.92. Total, $1,218.17.

Diocesan.— Diocesan Missions, $20.65; Salary of the Bishop, $4; Diocesan Fund, $5.14; Fund for Aged and Infirm Clergymen, $2.04; Orphan House of the Holy Saviour, $1.62. Total, $33.45.

General.— Domestic Missions, $81.15; Foreign Missions, $332.43; Other objects exterior to the Diocese, box to Bishop Gobat's School at Jerusalem, $78. Total, $491.58.

Total amount of Offerings, $1,743.20.

Property.

Church and lot and parsonage and lot (estimated worth), $32,000.
Condition of property, excellent.
Amount of salary pledged Rector, $900.
Number of sittings in the Church, 196; all free.

Remarks.

In addition to the above, services have been held every Sunday afternoon at Pierpont Centre.

TRINITY CHAPEL, MORLEY.

Missionary. The Rev. R. G. Hamilton.
Warden. T. L. Harison.
Treasurer. N. P. Whitney.
Clerk. H. N. Fenton.

Parochial.

Baptisms (adults, 2, infants, 2), 4; Confirmed, 2; Marriages, 2; Burials, 3; Communicants, last reported, 60, died, 2, removed, 10, present number recorded, 48, actually communicating, 20; Public Services, Sundays, 51, other days, 25), 76; Holy Communion, public, 18; Sunday School, teachers, 5, pupils, 30; Catechizing, number of times, frequently.

Offerings.

Parochial.—Current expenses, including salaries, $201.11; Sunday School, $50. Total, $251.11.

Diocesan.—Diocesan Missions, $20; Orphan House of the Holy Saviour, 1 box knitted garments.

General.—Domestic Missions, Deer Lodge, Montana, $10.

Total amount of Offerings, $281.11.

Property.

Condition of property, good.

Amount of salary pledged Rector, Missionary Stipend.

ST. ANDREW'S CHURCH, NORWOOD.

See Remarks, Report, Trinity Church, Potsdam.

Saratoga County.

CHRIST CHURCH, BALLSTON SPA.

Rector. The Rev. Charles Pelletreau, B. D.

Wardens. Stephen B. Medbery, John H. Westcot.

Vestrymen. Samuel Haight, Andrew S. Booth, Stephen C. Medbery, Charles M. Brown, James W. Verbeck, William S. Wheeler, Matthew Vassar.

Parochial.

Families and parts of families, 150; Baptisms (adults, 1, infants, 9), 10; Confirmed, 10; Marriages, 4; Burials, 14; Communicants, last reported, 250, admitted, 10, died, 6, removed, 5; Public Services (Sundays, 103, Holy days, all, other days, 100); Holy Communion (public, 27, private, 4), 31; Sunday School, teachers, 11, pupils, 100; Catechizing, frequently.

Offerings.

Parochial.— Alms at Holy Communion, $65; Current expenses, including salaries, $2,370.91; Sunday School, $57; Increase and Improvement of Church Property, $500, Total, $2,992.91.

Diocesan.— Diocesan Missions, $150; Salary of the Bishop, $36; Diocesan Fund, $36; Fund for Widows and Orphans of Clergymen, $9.82; Orphan House of the Holy Saviour, $13.50; The Child's Hospital, $27; Other offerings for objects within the Diocese, East Line House, $45. Total, $317.31.

General.— Domestic Missions, $35; Foreign Missions, $25; Indian Missions, $27; Home Missions to Coloured Persons, $20.43; Other objects exterior to the Diocese, Missions to the Jews, $5.50; Church Building Fund, $5; Missions to $6.50; St. Stephen's College, $22.15; Babcock Scholarship, Dakota, $60. Total, $206.60.

Total amount of Offerings, $3,516.81.

Property.

Church and lot (estimated worth), $18,000.

Parsonage and lot, $10,000.

Other property, $7,000.

Condition of property, excellent.

ST. JOHN'S CHURCH, STILLWATER.

Missionary. The Rev. W. G. W. Lewis.

Wardens. John Stringer, John Bradley.

Vestrymen. E. B. Skinner, Charles Green, George H. Lansing, William Bradley, John Bradley, Jr., John B. Tabor, Joseph Moll, George Hudson, M. D.

Parochial.

Families, 20; Individuals (adults, 47, children, 10), 57; Baptisms, infants, 1; Communicants, last reported, 29, removed, 2, present number recorded, 27; Public Services (Sundays, 46, Holy days, 3, other days, 12), 61; Holy Communion, public, 10.

27

Offerings.

Diocesan.—Diocesan Missions, $10; Fund for Aged and Infirm Clergymen, $1.32; Orphan House of the Holy Saviour, 65 cents. Total, $11.97.

Property.

Church and lot (estimated worth), $4,000.
Amount of salary pledged Rector, $450.
Number of sittings in the Church, 125; all free.

ST. PAUL'S CHURCH, CHARLTON.

Rector. The Rev. Heman R. Timlow.
Wardens. William Taylor, Robert Davis.
Vestrymen. George C. Valentine, Jacob Pink, Robert Wendell, James Thorne, John Marvin, Norman Smith.

Parochial.

Families, 28; Communicants, last reported, 35; Sunday School, teachers, 4, pupils, 20.-

Offerings.

Parochial.— Alms at Holy Communion, $6; Current expenses, including salaries, $226.44; Increase and Improvement of Church Property, $15. Total, $247.44.
Diocesan.— Diocesan Missions, $10; Other offerings for objects within the Diocese, $4. Total, $14.
General.— Domestic Missions, $4.50; Foreign Missions, $4.50; Other objects exterior to the Diocese, $25. Total, $34.
Total amount of Offerings, $291.44.

GRACE CHURCH, WATERFORD.

Rector. The Rev. Charles Elisha Freeman.
Wardens. John Higgins, Roland Henshall Stubbs, M. D.
Vestrymen. John Lawrence, Edward Van Kleeck, Marvin A. Baker, John H. Meeker, William Holroyd, Thomas E. Clayton, Charles H. Kavanaugh, James E. Bootman.

Parochial.

Families, 81; Individuals (adults, 230, children, 98), 328; Baptisms, infants, 9; Confirmed, 18; Marriages, 3; Burials, 8; Communicants, last reported, 166, admitted, 18, received, 7, died, 1, present number recorded, 193, actually communicating, 169; Public Services, (Sundays, 103, Holy days, 51, other days, 42), 196; Holy Communion (public, 66, private, 5), 71; Sunday School, teachers, 8, pupils, 110; Catechizing, number of children, the school; number of times, 25.

Offerings.

Parochial.— Alms at Holy Communion, $89.97; Current expenses, including salaries, $1,519.29; Sunday School, $146.39; Other parochial objects, Sick Fund, $42.50. Total, $1,798.15.
Diocesan.—Diocesan Missions, $59.65; Salary of the Bishop, $35; Diocesan Fund, $30, Bible and Common Prayer Book Society of Albany, $4.72; Fund for Aged and Infirm Clergymen, $5.22; Orphan House of the Holy Saviour, box of clothing. Total, $134.59.
General.—Foreign Missions (by Sunday School), $12.66; Other objects exterior to the Diocese, Church Society for promoting Christianity among the Jews, $2.55. Total, $15.21.
Total amount of Offerings, $1,947. 95.

Property.

Church and lot (estimated worth), $10,000.
Other property, $2,000.
Condition of property, good.
Amount of salary pledged Rector, $1,000.
Number of sittings in the Church, 67; number rented, 42, number free, 25.

Remarks.

Of the total amount of offerings of this Parish, the amount raised by the Parish Guild was $455.47.

ST. LUKE'S CHURCH, MECHANICVILLE.

Missionary. The Rev. W. G. W. Lewis.
Wardens. M. W. Hart, H. O. Bailey.
Vestrymen. S. H. Hall, M. D., J. H. Massey, G. W. Williams, J. H. Thompson, C. H. Keefer, M. D., John Brown, J. H. Cowen.

Parochial.

Families, 60; Individuals (adults, 127, children, 63), 190; Baptisms (adults, 3, infants, 11), 14; Confirmed, 2; Marriages, 2; Burials, 10; Communicants, last reported, 52, admitted, 4, died, 1, present number recorded, 55; Public Services (Sundays, 45, Holy days, 8, other days, 12), 65; Holy Communion public, 15; Sunday School, teachers, 4, pupils, 40.

Offerings.

Parochial.— Alms at Holy Communion, $7; Current expenses, including salaries, $750. Total, $757.
Diocesan.—Diocesan Missions, $20; Fund for Aged and Infirm Clergymen, $1.32; Orphan House of the Holy Saviour, $3.62; The Child's Hospital, $1. Total, $25.94.
General.—General Missions (Sunday School, $7.59), $19.84.
Total amount of Offerings, $802.78.

Property.

Church and lot and Parsonage and lot (estimated worth), $9,000.
Condition of property, good.
Amount of salary pledged Rector, $550.
Number of sittings in the Church, 150; all free.

BETHESDA CHURCH, SARATOGA SPRINGS.

Rector. The Rev. Joseph Carey, S. T. D.
Wardens. James N. Marvin, R. C. McEwen, M. D.
Vestrymen. William A. Sackett, P. Porter Wiggins, Spencer Trask, Daniel Eddy, Walker B. Johnson, George R. P. Shackelford, Winsor B. French, W. B. Gage.

Parochial.

Families, 240; Individuals (adults, 603, children, 530), 1,133; Baptisms (adults, 19, infants, 55), 74; Confirmed, 64; Marriages, 19; Burials, 59; Churchings, 1; Communicants, last reported, 715, admitted, 64, received, 16, died, 19, removed, 24, present number recorded, 752; Public Services (Sundays, 165, Holy days, 31, other days, 329), 525; Holy Communion (public, 98, private, 12), 110; Sunday School, teachers, 63, pupils, including Catharine Street Mission School, 581; Catechizing, number of children, 581: number of times, 52.

Offerings.

Parochial.— Alms at Holy Communion, $365.40; Current expenses, including salaries, $6,339.38; Sunday School, $409.89; Parish House, $1,196 20; Increase and Improvement of Church Property, Rectory, $378.64; Other parochial objects, Altar Society, $43.61; Home of Good Shepherd, $2,054.79; Choir Vestment Society, $54.50; Choir Fund, $377.48. Total, $11,219.89.

Diocesan.— Diocesan Missions, $200; Salary of the Bishop, $40; Diocesan Fund, $63; Bible and Common Prayer Book Society of Albany, $7.20; Fund for Aged and Infirm Clergymen, $20; The Child's Hospital (from Sunday School, including Mission School), $22.52; Other offerings for objects within the Diocese, Balance on Cathedral stalls, $55; Mission at Gloversville, $13.10; Woman's Auxiliary, $54.45. Total, $475.27.

General.— Domestic Missions (Bishop, Western Texas), $140.03; Foreign Missions (Mission to the Jews), $8.90; Indian Missions (Bishop, North Dakota), $24; Other objects exterior to the Diocese, St. Stephen's College, $28.63; For Bishop Perry of Iowa, $14. Total, $235.82.

Total amount of Offerings, $11,930.98.

Property.

Church and lot (estimated worth) $82,000.

Parsonage and lot, $8,500.

Other property, Parish House, $9,500; Home of Good Shepherd, $6,000; Mission Chapel, $1,800.

Condition of property, good.

Indebtedness, on the Church, $9,000; on the Rectory, $3,700; on the Parish House, $4,000.

Amount of salary pledged Rector, $2,100, with Rectory.

Number of sittings in the Church, 1,200; part rented; part free.

Remarks.

On Trinity Sunday a beautiful Processional Cross, the gift of Mr. and Mrs. Samuel A. Sague, in memory of their child Rhobie Frances, was used for the first time.

The Woman's Auxiliary, in addition to other work, sent a box valued at $50, last winter, to the Coloured Missionary at Asheville, N. C.

Through the efforts of Mrs. George S. Adams, wife of the manager of the Grand Union Hotel, some $600 were raised last August for St. Christina Home.

The receipts of the Parish during the past year for current expenses are in excess of previous years, showing a healthy condition financially.

ST. STEPHEN'S CHURCH, SCHUYLERVILLE.

Rector. The Rev. J. Frederick Esch.

Wardens. Peter Davison, J. Hicks-Smith.

Vestrymen. Thos. E. Bullard, Malcom S. Potter, T. B. Aitcheson, John Dix.

Parochial.

Families, 10; Individuals, adults, 40; Baptisms, infants, 3; Confirmed, 5; Marriages, 1; Burials, 1; Communicants, present number recorded, 20; Holy Communion (public, 12, private, 4), 16.

Offerings.

Total amount of Offerings, $225.

Property.

Condition of property, fair.

CALVARY CHURCH, BURNT HILLS.

Rector. The Rev. Heman R. Timlow.

Warden. Edwin Mead.

Vestrymen. Edward K. Wheeler, Robert Keller, Wilson Abbe, Charles H. Upham, Peter Banta, Fred German, John Cotton, M. D., Garret Cavert.

Parochial.

Families, 44; Baptisms, infants, 2; Confirmed since last report, 2; Marriages, 2; Burials, 6; Communicants, present number, 87; Sunday School, teachers, 6, pupils, 33

Offerings.

Parochial.— Alms at Holy Communion, $12; Current expenses, including salaries, $529.20; Other Parochial objects, $54.75. Total, $595.95.

Diocesan.— Diocesan Missions, $25; Salary of the Bishop, $12; Diocesan Fund, $10.13; Other offerings for objects within the Diocese, $25. Total, $72.13.

General.— Domestic Missions, $12.53 ; Foreign Missions, $12.53; Other objects exterior to the Diocese, $15. Total, $40.06.

Total amount of Offerings, $708.14.

Remarks.

During the current year both Wardens of the Church have been removed by death — Calvin S. Wheeler and William H. Wheeler, who have been from the founding of the Church its earnest supporters. Both left legacies to the Church. Through the severe and protracted sickness of the Rector, the Church also suffered by having services interrupted.

Schenectady County.

CHRIST CHURCH, DUANESBURGH.

Rector. The Rev. E. W. Flower.

Lay Reader. Edward Clarence Clark.

Wardens. Alexander McDougall, Ralph W. McDougall.}

Vestrymen. James D. Featherstonhaugh, George Matthews, Alexander Van Pelt, Edward Clark, George A. Snell, Wesley Van Pelt, George L. Matthews, Edward C. Clark.

Parochial.

Families, 80; Baptisms (adults, 3, infants, 7), 10 : Confirmed, since last report, 5; Burials, 7; Communicants, last reported, 94, admitted, 5, received, 2, died, 2, removed, 7, present number, 92; Public Services (Sundays, 101, Holy days, 27, other days, 17), 145. Holy Communion (public, 35, private, 2), 37; Sunday School, teachers, 10, pupils, 80; Catechizing, number of times, every Sunday.

Offerings.

Parochial.— Alms at Holy Communion, not otherwise reported, $13.60; Current expenses, including salaries, $1,346.25; Sunday School, $56.29; Increase and Improvement of Church Property, $311.48. Total, $1,727.62.

Diocesan.— Diocesan Missions, $56.21; Salary of the Bishop, $50; Diocesan Fund, $30; Bible and Common Prayer Book Society of Albany, $2; Fund for Aged and Infirm Clergymen, $3.31; Fund for Widows and Orphans of Clergymen, $1.50; Orphan House of the Holy Saviour, $3; Other offerings within the Diocese, Mission work (special), $6. Total, $152.02.

General.—Domestic Missions, $9.03; Foreign Missions,$6.07; Indian Missions, $2; Home Missions to Coloured Persons, by Woman's Auxiliary, cash value of box clothing $74.04; Other objects exterior to the Diocese, Jewish Missions, $1; American Church Building Fund, $3; Church Building, Johnstown, Pa., $1. Total, $96.14. Total amount of Offerings, $1,975.78.

Property.

Church and lot (estimated worth), $2,000.
Parsonage and lot, $3,000.
Other property, Chapel, $1,500.
Condition of property, good.
Number of sittings in the Church and Chapel, 450; all free.

Remarks.

The Rector has been very efficiently aided in work at the Chapel and in the village of Esperance, by his Lay Reader, Mr. E. C. Clark.

Increased interest and labor are gratefully acknowledged to the "Woman's Auxiliary to the Board of Missions," two branches of which are at work in the Parish. One is composed of women attending the Parish Church, the other of those at the west end of the Parish who attend the Chapel.

ST. GEORGE'S CHURCH, SCHENECTADY.

Rector. The Rev. J. Philip B. Pendleton, S. T. B.
Rector Emeritus. The Rev. William Payne, D. D.
Lay Reader. Gouverneur F. Mosher.
Wardens. Abram A. Van Vorst, Samuel W. Jackson.
Vestrymen. D. Cady Smith, John A. DeRemer, John Keyes Paige, Giles Y. Van de Bogert, Howland S. Barney, T. Low 'Barhydt, Edward D. Palmer, Charles S. Washburn.

Parochial.

Families, 289; Individuals (adults, 600, children, 375), 975; Baptisms (adults, 5, infants, 15), 20; Confirmed, 20; Marriages, 7; Burials, 25; Churchings, 5; Communicants, last reported, 376, admitted, 20, received, 33, died, 9, removed, 15, present number recorded, 405; Public Services (Sundays, 210, Holy days, 101, other days, 131), 442; Holy Communion, (public, 101, private, 11), 112; Sunday School, teachers, 28, pupils, 240, Catechizing, number of children, all, number of times, every Sunday; Industrial School, teachers, 13, pupils, 99; Parish Agencies, St. Mary's Guild, St. Agnes' Guild, St. Paul's Guild, Industrial School, Night School, Parish Paper, Vested Choir.

Offerings.

Parochial.—Alms at Holy Communion, $261.08; Current expenses, including salaries, $3,830.10; Sunday School (not elsewhere included), $145.01; St. Mary's Guild (not elsewhere included), $264.30; Increase and Improvement of Church Property, $325; Other parochial objects, Specials for Sunday School, Parish Kalendar, St. Agnes' Guild, Vested Choir, etc., $550.83. Total, $5,376.32.

Diocesan.—Diocesan Missions (including specials), $219; Salary of the Bishop, $40; Diocesan Fund, $60; Bible and Common Prayer Book Society of Albany, $14.02. Orphan House of the Holy Saviour (including box from Sunday School), $29.50; Other offerings for objects within the Diocese, Schenectady Hospital and Dispensary, $125; Schenectady Children's Home, $20 Total, $513.52.

General.—Domestic Missions, $194; Domestic Missions (Scholarship at Logan, Utah), $40; Foreign Missions, $40, Jewish Missions, $12.88, Home Missions to Coloured Persons, $55; Other objects exterior to the Diocese, Relief of Clergymen, $50.27; Three boxes from children to Springfield Mines, Nova Scotia, $22.50. Total, $414.65.

Total amount of Offerings, $6,304.49.

Property.

Church and lot (estimated worth), $80,000.
Parsonage and lot, $7,000.
Other property, $4,000.
Condition of property, fair.
Indebtedness, $2,300.
Amount of salary pledged Rector, $2,000.
Annuity to Rector Emeritus, $500.
Number of sittings in the Church and Chapel, 850.

Remarks.

The city of Schenectady, owing to the removal here of several large manufacturing industries, has increased its population during the past five years by fully one-fourth. A large number of the employees are single men, and the opportunities for the development of our parochial work are very great. One of our greatest needs is the erection and equipment of a Parish House, by means of which our present work may be concentrated and more efficiently carried on, and new lines of usefulness developed. We have begun a fund (which now amounts to about $600) for this purpose, and we hope that such a structure may be reared in the near future.

CHRIST CHURCH, SCHENECTADY.

Rector. The Rev. Eugene L. Toy.
Lay Reader. Prof. Sidney G. Ashmore, L. H. D.
Wardens. James E. Curtiss, David Guy.
Vestrymen. Samuel T. Benedict, William N. Butler, Henry C. Van Zandt, M. D., David O. Youlen, Prof. Sidney G. Ashmore, L. H. D., Edward E. Kriegsman, John H. Shaffer, Rufus W. Lampman.

Parochial.

Families, and parts of families, 182; Individuals (adults, 270, children, 147), 417; Baptisms, infants, 16; Confirmed, 10, Marriages, 11; Burials, 19; Communicants, last reported, 172, admitted, 10, received, 24, died, 6, removed, 4, present number recorded, 196, number of persons confirmed but not counted as communicants, 28; Public Services (Sundays, 119, Holy days, 51, other days, 25), 195; Holy Communion (public, 43, private, 1), 44; Sunday School, teachers, 14, pupils, 104; Catechizing, number of children, all, number of times, every Sunday.

Offerings.

Parochial.— Alms at Holy Communion, $26.27; Current expenses, including salaries, $1,177.53; Sunday School, $97.41; Guild Room Fund, $51.89; Other Parochial objects, King's Daughters, $23.09; Women's Guild, $250.70. Total, $1,626.89.

Diocesan.—Diocesan Missions, $11.26; Salary of the Bishop, $10; Diocesan Fund, $8.78; Orphan House of the Holy Saviour, $4.83. Total, $34.87.

Total amount of Offerings, $1,661.76.

Property.

Church and lot (estimated worth), $9,000.
Parsonage and lot, $5,000.

Condition of property, very good.
Indebtedness, mortgage, $4,000.
Amount of salary pledged Rector, $800.
Number of sittings in the Church, 180; all free.

Schoharie County.

TRINITY CHURCH, SHARON SPRINGS.

Rector. The Rev. John M. Windsor.
Trustees. A. S. Carhart, Brooklyn, N. Y., President; John H. Gardner, Sr., J. H. Gardner, Jr., Sharon Springs, Mr. Parsons, Mr. Becker, Sharon Springs.

Parochial.

Baptisms (adults, 1, infants, 4), 5; Marriages, 2; Burials, 4; Communicants, present number recorded, 86.

Offerings.

Diocesan.—Salary of the Bishop, $20; Bible and Common Prayer Book Society of Albany, $2.76. Total, $22.76.
General.—Domestic Missions, $6.80.
Total amount of Offerings, $29.56.
Amount of salary pledged Rector, $900.

Warren County.

CHURCH OF THE MESSIAH, GLENS FALLS.

Rector. The Rev. Fenwick M. Cookson.
Wardens. William A. Wait, Leonard G. McDonald.
Vestrymen. A. W. Holden, L. P. Juvet, George Bassinger, Daniel Peck, William H. Robbins, Nelson La Salle, Hugh W. Bowden, Henry W. Coffin.

Parochial.

Baptisms (adults, 16. infants, 43), 59; Confirmed, since last report, 29; Marriages, 7; Burials, 28; Communicants, last reported, 311, admitted, 29, received, 2, died, 5, removed, 8, present number, 329; Public Services (Sundays, 134, Holy days, 35, other days, 73), 242; Holy Communion (public, 38, private, 4), 42; Sunday School, teachers and officers, 26, pupils, 245. Catechizing, number of children, Sunday School, number of times, weekly.

Offerings.

Parochial — Alms at Holy Communion, $54.92; Current expenses, including salaries ($491.40 by Ladies' Society), $2,472.36, Sunday School, $170.43; Increase and Improvement of Church Property ($26.80 by Sunday School), $128.87. Total, $2,826.58.
Diocesan.— Diocesan Missions. $150, Salary of the Bishop, $24; Diocesan Fund, $42, Fund for Aged and Infirm Clergymen, $24.25; Fund for Widows and Orphans of Clergymen, $4.25; Orphan House of the Holy Saviour ($25.57 by Sunday School). $44.57; The Child's Hospital (by Sunday School), $9.84; Other offerings for objects within the Diocese, Bartonville Church ($22.54 by Sunday School), $28.54. Total, $327.45.

General.—Domestic Missions, $29.50; Foreign Missions, $24.15; Other objects exterior to the Diocese, a Mission in Vermont by Sunday School, $12.37. Total, $66.02. Total amount of Offerings, $3,220.05.

Property.

Church and lot (estimated worth), $27,000.
Condition of property, excellent.
Amount of salary pledged Rector, $1,400.
Number of sittings in the Church, 888, assigned; at Harrisena, 150, free.

ST. JAMES' CHURCH, LAKE GEORGE.

Rector. The Rev. Charles H. Lancaster.
Warden. Henry H. Hayden.
Vestrymen. S. R. Archibald, F. G. Tucker, Le Grand C. Cramer, James T. Crandall, Kleber Burlingame, J. B. Phelps, George W. Baker, Jerome N. Hubbel.

Parochial.

Baptisms, adults, 1; Confirmed, since last report, 5; Present number of confirmed persons, 91; Burials, 3; Communicants, died. 2, present number, 92; Public Services, Sundays, 100, Holy days, all, other days, Wednesdays in summer, all Fridays, Lent oftener; Holy Communion (public, 60, private, 3), 63; Sunday School, teachers, 6, pupils, 60; Catechizing, weekly as a rule.

Offerings.

Parochial.— Current expenses, including salaries, $938.48; Sunday School, $60; Increase and Improvement of Church Property, $500. Total, $1,498.48.
Diocesan.— Diocesan Missions, $10; Salary of the Bishop, $10; Orphan House of the Holy Saviour, $1.10. Total, $21.10.
General.-- Domestic and Foreign Missions (from Sunday School), $17.
Total amount of Offerings, $1,536.58.

Property.

Church and lot (estimated worth), $16,000.
Parsonage and lot, $6,000.
Condition of property, good.
Number of sittings in the Church, 200; all free.

Remarks.

A very beautiful Memorial window has been placed in the chancel by Mr. and Mrs. Le Grand Cramer. It is the work of J. C. Spence & Sons, Montreal and England.

HOLY CROSS CHURCH, WARRENSBURGH.

Rector. The Rev. William M. Ogden.
Wardens. Frederick O. Burhans, Henry Griffing.
Vestrymen. Thomas J. Smith, Charles. A. McElroy, John C. Hayes, Jesse Stone, John J. Archer, Albert F. Hayes, Hulyes H. Hill, Seth Reed.

Parochial.

Baptisms (adults, 2, infants, 4), 6; Confirmed, since last report, 3; Present number of confirmed persons, 95; Marriages, 4. Burials, 3; Communicants, last reported, 92, admitted, 1, received, 1, removed, 9, present number, 85; Public Services (Sundays, 156. Holy days, 99, other days, 539), 794; Holy Communion, public, 88; Sunday

28

School, teachers, 3, pupils, 42; Catechizing, number of children, 20; number of times, 12.

Offerings.

Parochial.—Current expenses, including salaries, $2,646.36.

Diocesan.—Diocesan Missions, $50; Salary of the Bishop, $32; Diocesan Fund, $27; Bible and Common Prayer Book Society of Albany, $8.14; Fund for Aged and Infirm Clergymen, $5.30; Fund for Widows and Orphans of Clergymen, $2.86; The Child's Hospital, $4. Total, $129.30.

General.— General Theological Seminary, $2.34; Domestic Missions, $7.68; Other objects exterior to the Diocese, Jewish Missions, 92 cents. Total, $10.94.

Total amount of Offerings, $2,786.60.

Amount of salary pledged Rector, $900.

Number of sittings in the Church, 100; all free.

Remarks.

By the generous gift of Miss Clara and Miss Mary Richards a circulating library of about five hundred volumes has been opened in the Parish House; the benefits of which are offered to all residents of the village, on the payment of a small annual fee. A stereopticon has been purchased for the use of the Sunday School at a cost of $125. The Women's Sewing Society made up and sent a box of clothing to the Child's Hospital at Albany.

ST. MARY'S CHURCH, LUZERNE.

Rector. The Rev. C. J. Whipple.

Wardens. John S. Burneson, Thomas H. Taylor.

Vestrymen. James Clapp, William Beardmore, Joseph J. Wigley, Edward Gell, J. B. Wigley, C. W. Trumbull.

Parochial.

Families, 20; Individuals (adults, 40, children, 31), 71; Baptisms, infants, 8; Confirmed, 3; Burials, 4; Communicants, admitted, 3, removed, 7; Public Services (Sundays, 143, Holy days, 4, other days, 54), 201 ; Holy Communion (public, 31, private, 2), 33; Sunday School, teachers, 3, pupils, 26. Catechizing, number of children, all; number of times, 39.

Offerings.

Parochial.— Alms at Holy Communion, $217.28; Current expenses, including salaries, $661.26; Sunday School, $14.15, Increase and Improvement of Church Property, $215. Total, $1,107.69.

Diocesan.— Diocesan Missions, $22 30; Salary of the Bishop, $6. Diocesan Fund $12, Bible and Common Prayer Book Society of Albany, $2 50. Total, $42.80.

General — Domestic Missions, $10.

Total amount of Offerings, $1,160.49.

Property.

Church and lot (estimated worth) $6,000.

Parsonage and lot, $1,500.

Other property, $500.

Condition of property, good.

Amount of salary pledged Rector, $400.

Number of sittings in the Church, 250; all free.

Remarks.

All official acts at Conklingville are included in the above report.

CHURCH OF THE GOOD SHEPHERD, CHESTERTOWN.

Rector.   The Rev. Nassau William Stephens.

Warden.   Ralph Thurman.

Parochial.

Individuals (adults, 50, children, 33), 83; Baptisms, adults, 6; Confirmed, 6; Marriages, 2; Burials, 1; Communicants, admitted, 6, received, 3, removed, 1, present number recorded, 89, actually communicating, 28; Public Services, Sundays, twice Holy days, evenings, other days, Friday evenings; Holy Communion, public, weekly and Holy days; Sunday School, teachers, 3, pupils, 30; Catechizing, number of children, all; number of times, often.

Offerings.

Parochial.— Alms, $88.75; Current expenses, including salaries, $451.69; Sunday School, $3.64: Other Parochial objects, fair and ice cream, $153.30. Total, $697.38.

Diocesan.— Diocesan Missions, $15; Salary of the Bishop, $6; Diocesan Fund, $12. Total, $33.

General.—Domestic and Foreign Missions, Childrens' Lenten offering and Childrens' Nursery League, $8.40.

Total amount of Offerings, $738.78.

Property.

Church and lot (estimated worth), $3,200.

Condition of property, very good.

Amount of salary pledged Rector, $400.

Number of sittings in the Church, 90; all free.

Remarks.

This report includes the work of my predecessor, the Rev. A. Taylor. On my taking charge in July, I found that the great need of the Mission was a Rectory.

A fair was held, which with minor entertainments netted with a contribution from the Taylor House, Schroon Lake, $137. A guest also gave sufficient paint for the outside of the Rectory.

Services were held at the Taylor House, Schroon Lake, and were well attended, the guests expressing their pleasure, and welcoming the Missionary.

Many of the communicants recorded have removed temporarily and are therefore not shown as actually communicating.

ST. PAUL'S CHURCH, BARTONVILLE.

Rector.   The Rev. Nassau William Stephens.

Warden.   John Barton.

Treasurer.   Scott Barton.

Clerk.   William Hart.

Parochial.

Individuals (adults, 60, children, 40), 100; Baptisms (adults, 9, infants, 4), 13; Confirmed, 8; Marriages, 2; Burials, 1; Communicants, admitted, 8, present number, recorded, 19, actually communicating, 18; Public Services, every Sunday, other days, Wednesdays; Holy Communion, public, monthly; Sunday School, teachers, 3, pupils, 32; Catechizing, number of children, 32; number of times, frequently.

Offerings.

Parochial.— Alms, including Communion alms, $98; Current expenses, including salaries, $150; Other parochial objects, fair, $72. Total, $320.

Total amount of Offerings, $320.

Church and lot (estimated worth), $2,000.
Number of sittings in the Church, 200; all free.

Remarks.

This report includes the work of my predecessor, the Rev. Alfred Taylor.
There is promise of still further growth in this place, notwithstanding strong sec-
tarian opposition.

An organ was presented to this Church by Mr. Thomas Smith of Brooklyn, N. Y.
A brass altar cross and other ornaments are promised.

This Mission is very poor, and quite unable at present to contribute to outside objects, but I hope that with growth of numbers, we shall be able to contribute to Diocesan expenses in the near future.

ST. SACRAMENT CHURCH, BOLTON-ON-LAKE-GEORGE.

Rector. The Rev. Clement T. Blanchet.

Parochial.

Families, 36; Individuals (adults, 57, children, 60), 117; Baptisms (adults, 18, infants, 22), 40; Confirmed, 16; Burials, 5; Communicants, last reported, 50, admitted,
16, removed, 6, present number recorded, 60, actually communicating, 54; Public
Services (Sundays, 110, Holy days, 8, other days, 100), 218; Holy Communion (public, 28, private, 2), 30; Sunday School, teachers, 3, pupils, 30; Catechizing, number
of children, 30; number of times, 12.

Offerings.

Parochial.—Current expenses, including salaries, $665.21; painting Rectory, $100;
debt on Rectory, $500; Interest on debt, $30. Total, $1,295.21.

Diocesan.— Diocesan Missions, $8.25; Salary of the Bishop, $10; Diocesan Fund,
$27. Total, $45.25.

General.— Domestic Missions, $4.90; Foreign Missions, $4.90; Missions among the
Jews, $2; Other objects exterior to the Diocese, Clergy Retiring Fund, $3. Total,
$14.80.

Total amount of Offerings, $1,355.26.

Property.

Church and lot (estimated worth), $8,000.
Parsonage and lot, $3,000.
Condition of property, fair.
Amount of salary pledged Rector, $900.
Number of sittings in the Church, 150; all free.

Remarks.

Ten of the adult baptisms, eight of the infant baptisms, five of the confirmations,
and eight of the communicants reported above are connected with Grace Memorial
Chapel at Sabbath Day Point, some twelve miles north of Bolton, on Lake George,
under the instruction of James F. Chamberlain, an earnest Layman of New York
city, residing at that place the greatest part of the year. The whole number of persons connected with the Church at Sabbath Day Point is now as follows: Baptized
(adults, 13, children, 20), 33, Confirmed there, 8; Communicants, 9.

The Priest in charge at Bolton made two visits, held three services, baptized three
adults and three children at that place during the present year, the other baptisms
were by visiting Clergy from the city of New York. The work there seems to be of

sufficient promise to **be** recognized and encouraged by the Diocesan Board of Missions, and should be put under the pastoral care of the nearest Clergyman of the Church with the understanding that services should be held there once a month when the roads and the weather will permit.

The Church property at Bolton is now happily out of debt, through the special contributions of friends and the proceeds of a fair held for that purpose in the summer.

The painting of the Rectory was done by our own local members, the paint being given by Mr. J. B. Simpson of New York.

Washington County.

ZION CHURCH, SANDY HILL.

Rector. The Rev. Edwin Ruthven Armstrong.

Wardens. Charles Hamilton Beach, John William Wait.

Vestrymen. C. T. Beach, O. R. Howe, G. A. Ingalls, B. G. Knapp, P. F. Langworthy, A. Mott, M. D., John Nichols, S. H. Parks.

Parochial.

Families, 124; Individuals (adults, 308, children, 128), 436; Baptisms (adults, 1889, 3, 1890, 5, infants, 1889, 19, 1890, 15), 42; Confirmed (1889, 16, 1890, 16), 32; Marriages (1889, 1, 1890, 2), 3; Burials (1889, 6, 1890, 10), 16; Churchings, 1; Confirmed persons, 195; Public Services, 268; Holy Communion (public, 66, private, 9), 75; Catechizing, weekly.

Offerings.

Parochial.—Alms at Holy Communion, $48; Current expenses, including salaries, $1,350; Increase and Improvement of Church Property, $500; Other parochial objects, Baptismal ewer, $20; Processional Cross, $35. Total, $1,953.

Diocesan.—Diocesan Missions, $16.81; Salary of the Bishop, $30; Diocesan Fund, $30; Bible and Common Prayer Book Society of Albany, $3.72; Fund for Aged and Infirm Clergymen, $7.19; Orphan House of the Holy Saviour, $11.97. Total, $99.69.

General.— Domestic and Foreign Missions, $23.38; Other objects exterior to the Diocese, Deaf-mutes (Dr. Gallaudet), $6.96. Total, $30.34.

Total amount of Offerings, $2,083.03.

Property.

Church and lot (estimated worth), $12,000.

Parsonage and lot, $3,500.

Condition of property, excellent.

Indebtedness, bank notes outstanding, $500; Mortgage on Rectory, $2,000.

Amount of salary pledged Rector, $900 and Rectory.

Number of sittings in the Church, 300; all free.

Remarks.

For several months prior to February 1, there was no Rector here, wherefore the report submitted at the Convention of 1889 was incomplete. An effort is, therefore, made in the above to make good its defects, and the Baptisms, Confirmations, Marriages and Burials for each year are given definitely.

On Easter Day, 1890, the Baptismal ewer, mentioned above, was provided by the the children of the Sunday School, and during the summer a want felt and expressed in several quarters immediately upon the present incumbent's resumption of work here, was supplied by a number of those interested in the efforts of the late Rector to promote the dignity and reverential character of the services of the sanctuary, the Processional Cross being subscribed for, partly " *in memoriam.*"

The Woman's Auxiliary to the Board of Missions in this Parish has continued to make itself felt and known by its remembrances of the needy within, as well as beyond the Parish and Diocese, and the Guild of St. Mary also has maintained its character among the agencies for good works by its periodical aid sent the Orphan House of the Holy Saviour, and to the Brothers of Nazereth, New York city, as well as by stoles, etc,, furnished Zion Church.

With but two intermissions the Rector has conducted services each Sunday afternoon since May 4, at Adamsville or at Smith's Basin. At the former place the attendance has varied from 86 to 160, and at the latter, from 50 to 95, and at Smith's Basin six of the Baptisms reported above were solemnized.

TRINITY CHURCH, GRANVILLE.

Rector. The Rev. William C. Prout.

Wardens. Jonathan S. Warren, Palmer D. Everts.

Vestrymen. Byron H. Sykes, George W. Henry, Amos W. Wilcox, Orville L. Goodrich, John S. Warren.

Parochial.

Families, 43; Individuals (adults 94, children, 36), 130; Baptisms (adults, 1, infants, 4), 5; Confirmed, since last report, 2; Marriages, 3; Communicants, present number, 57; Public Services (Sundays, 141, Holy days, 34, other days, 25), 200; Holy Communion, public, 76; Sunday School, teachers 5, pupils, 40.

Offerings.

Parochial.—Current expenses, including salaries, $549.50; Other parochial objects, $200. Total, $749.50.

Diocesan.—Diocesan Missions, $25; Diocesan Fund, $15. Total, $40.

General.—General Missions, from Sunday School, $18.

Total amount of Offerings, $807.50.

Property.

Church and lot (estimated worth), $4,000.

Parsonage and lot, $4,500.

Condition of property, Church fair; Rectory good.

Amount of salary pledged Rector, $500.

Number of sittings in the Church, 200; all free.

Remarks.

Of the amount reported above, $261.28 was the result of the labours of the Ladies' Aid Society.

ST. JAMES' CHURCH, FORT EDWARD.

Rector. The Rev. Frederick N. Skinner, S. T. B.

Wardens. James G. Kinne, Francis B. Davis.

Vestrymen. Frederick G. Tilton, Benjamin M. Tasker, George Scott, Jarvis W. Milliman, Albert H. Wicks, John J. Morgan, Robert O. Bascom, William F. Ball.

Parochial.

Families, 110; Individuals (adults, 194, children, 86), 280; Baptisms (adults, 1, infants, 3), 4; Confirmed, 7; Burials, 3; Communicants, last reported, 177, admitted, 18, received, 13, died, 3, removed, 36, present number recorded, 169, actually communicating, about one-half; Public Services (Sundays, 103, other days, 63), 166; Holy Communion, public, 17; Sunday School, teachers, 9, pupils, 82; Catechizing, number of children, all; number of times, frequently.

Offerings.

Parochial.—Alms at Holy Communion, $10.33; Current expenses, including salaries, $1,086.97; Sunday School, $40.94; Other parochial objects, Parish House Fund, $163.39. Total, $1,301.63.

Diocesan.—Diocesan Missions, $12.77; Salary of the Bishop, $15; Diocesan Fund, $12; Orphan House of the Holy Saviour, $4.35. Total, $44.12.

General.— General Missions (Sunday School); $12.04; Other objects exterior to the Diocese, Society for Promoting Christianity among Jews, $2.01; Mission to Deafmutes, $1. Total, $15.05.

Total amount of Offerings, $1,360.80.

Property.

Church and lot (estimated worth), $7,000.

Parsonage and lot, $8,000.

Condition of property, good.

Amount of salary pledged Rector, $800.

Number of sittings in the Church, 250; all free.

Remarks.

This report is full and complete, so far as the Rector's services are concerned. For November and December, 1889, when there was no Rector, the report is as full as it could be made. The Parish has been greatly weakened by losses and removals. It is hoped that a more encouraging report may be made next year. In addition to their work in the Parish, the Ladies' Aid Society last winter sent a box of clothing, etc., to the Orphanage at Cooperstown.

ST. PAUL'S CHURCH, SALEM.

Rector. The Rev. John H. Houghton.

Assistant. The Rev. Harris C. Rush.

Wardens. Hon. James Gibson, Hon. George B. McCartee.

Vestrymen. A. K. Broughton, Frederick Kegler, David Mahaffy, Ephraim Herrick, William Alexander McNish, Frank A. Graham, Geo. B. Martin, Joseph Hofert.

Parochial.

Families, 60; Baptisms, infants, 4; Confirmed, since last report, 17; Marriages, 3; Burials, 8; Churchings, 3; Communicants, last reported, 137, admitted, 8, received, 2, died, 1, removed, 6, present number, 135; Public Services, thrice on all Sundays, four times weekly; Holy Communion, public, each Sunday and Holy day; Sunday School, teachers, 6, pupils, 60.

Offerings.

Parochial.— Alms at Holy Communion, $42.15; Current expenses, including salaries, $1,304.42; Sunday School, $7.91; Increase and Improvement of Church Property, $198.86; Other parochial objects, $64.28. Total, $1,617.62.

Diocesan.— Diocesan Missions, $100.33; Salary of the Bishop, $20; Diocesan Fund, $19.50; Bible and Common Prayer Book Society of Albany, $5; Fund for Aged and Infirm Clergymen, $5; Fund for Widows and Orphans of Clergymen, $4.91; Orphan House of the Holy Saviour, $5; The Child's Hospital, $5. Total, $164.74.

General.— Domestic Missions, $14.83; Foreign Missions, $14.83. Total, $29.66.

Total amount of Offerings, $1,865.02.

Property.

Church and lot (estimated worth), $6,000.

Condition of property, good.

Amount of salary pledged Rector, $700.
Number of sittings in the Church, 260; all free.

Remarks.

At Easter, Rev. H. C. Rush came from Toms River, New Jersey, to assist the Rev. Rector, and after the Convention and Mr. Houghton's resignation, he received the unanimous call to the Rectorship. St. Paul's Hall acquired a large property at Rexleigh during the year, and Rev. J. H. Houghton, will give himself entirely to this branch of the work at Salem.

TRINITY CHURCH, WHITEHALL.

Rectors. The Rev. Alexander McMillan, until February 1, 1890; The Rev. James Otis Lincoln, from May 16, to October 16; The Rev. Reyner E. W. Cosens, from October 26, 1890.

Wardens. Fred. H. McFarran, Edward P. Newcomb.

Vestrymen. R. A. Hall, C. B. Bates, F. S. Cowan, J. C. Hopson, William H. Teft, W. N. Weeks, J. Adams, H. B. Skeels.

Parochial.

Baptisms (adults, 4, infants, 11), 15; Confirmed, 10; Marriages, 2; Burials, 5; Public Services, full daily service as far as possible; Holy Communion, public, 82; Sunday School, teachers, 10, pupils, 100; Catechizing, number of times, 52.

Offerings.

Parochial.— Current expenses, including salaries, $1,479.49; Increase and Improvement of Church Property, $900.95. Total, $2,380.44.

Diocesan.— Diocesan Missions, $25; Salary of the Bishop, $14; Diocesan Fund, $30; Fund for Widows and Orphans of Clergymen, $12.10; Orphan House of the Holy Saviour, $10.06. Total, $91.16.

Total amount of Offerings, $2,471.60.

Amount of salary pledged Rector, $1,120.

Sittings in the Church, all free.

ST. LUKE'S CHURCH, CAMBRIDGE.

Rector. The Rev. Frederick H. T. Horsfield.

Wardens. Henry C. Day, Robert Davis.

Vestrymen. William J. Davis, Thomas Le Grys, Robert Davis, Jr., John Moneypenny, M. D., J. Fennimore Niver, M. D.

Parochial.

Families, 25; Individuals (adults, 75, children, 10), 85; Baptisms (adults, 1, infants, 1), 2; Confirmed, 4; Burials, 2; Communicants, admitted, 4, received, 1, died, 1, removed, 1, present number recorded, 50; Public Services (Sundays, 104, Holy days, 14, other days, 70), 188; Holy Communion, public, 20; Sunday School, teachers, 1, pupils, 10; Catechizing, number of children, 10; number of times, 20.

Offerings.

Parochial.-- Current expenses, [including salaries, $765.77; Sunday School, $25; Increase and Improvement of Church Property, $1,654.27; Other parochial objects, Choir books, $10; Furnace Fund, $8.07; Ladies' Aid, $104. Total, $2,648.11.

Diocesan.— Diocesan Missions, $224; Salary of the Bishop, $6; Diocesan Fund, $15. Total, $245.

General.— General Missions, $41.50; General Clergy Relief Fund, $10.50; A Church in Florida, $2. Total, $54.

Total amount of Offerings, $2,947.11.

Property.

Church and lot (estimated worth), $6,000.
Condition of property, fair.
Amount of salary pledged Rector, $500.
Number of sittings in the Church, 200; all free.

Remarks.

During the year a chancel has been built, containing two memorial windows of beautiful design. A carved baldachin has likewise been put in position. The Rector records his recognition of the kindness of generous friends of the Parish.

ST. PAUL'S CHURCH, GREENWICH.

Lay Reader. David H. Clarkson.
Wardens. Henry L. Mowry, W. R. Hobbie.
Vestrymen. Benjamin T. Kendall, H. B. Bates, S. L. Stillman, W. T. Reynolds George Tucker, Robert Campbell.

Parochial.

Families, 30; Individuals (Adults, 100, children, 50), 150; Baptisms, infants, 1, Confirmed, 8; Communicants, last reported, 56, admitted, 8, received, 20, died, 2, removed, 10, present number recorded, 75, actually communicating, 30; Public Services (Sundays, 40, other days, 2), 42; Holy Communion, public, 2.

Offerings.

Parochial—Current expenses, including salaries, $231.75; Increase and Improvement of Church Property, $170. Total, $401.75.
Diocesan.— Diocesan Missions, $3.91.
Total amount of Offerings, $405.66.

Property.

Church and lot (estimated worth), $7,000.
Condition of property, good.
Number of sittings in the Church, 230; all free.

Remarks.

This Church was closed two years ago last Easter, and no service was held until the 22d of June last, when David H. Clarkson, a student at St. Stephen's College of Annandale, N. Y., came to us as Lay Reader, and remained until the 2d of November.

NORTH GRANVILLE MISSION.

Missionary. The Rev. William C. Prout.

Parochial.

Families, 9; Individuals (adults, 27, children, 6), 33; Baptisms, infants, 2; Burials, 2; Communicants, present number, 14; Public Services (Sundays, 62, Holy days, 2, other days, 25), 89; Holy Communion, public, 11.

Offerings.

Parochial.— Current expenses, including salaries, $131.25.
Diocesan.— Diocesan Missions, $10; Diocesan Fund, $3. Total, $13.
Total amount of Offerings, $144.25.

Property.

Organ and other furniture, $250.
Condition of property, good.
Amount of salary pledged Rector, $100.
Number of sittings in the Chapel, 100; all free.

29

(B.)

PERSONAL REPORTS.

December 20, 1890.

To the Right Rev. W. C. DOANE, D. D., LL. D., *Bishop of Albany:*

MY DEAR BISHOP — During the past year I have been engaged in educational work in St. Paul's Hall, Salem, N. Y.

Very respectfully, your obedient servant,

CHARLES W. BOYD.

EAST LINE, *December* 11, 1890.

The Rev. William H. Cook respectfully reports that his health is too much broken to permit him to look up statistics for parochial report for Jonesville, and he can only send a brief word like this to account for himself to his Bishop.

OSWEGO, N. Y., *November* 14, 1890.

MY DEAR BISHOP DOANE — I beg to report to you that during the past year I have held services twice on nearly every Sunday, and on many Holy days. The principal places of my work have been Sandy Hill, N. Y., Arden, N. C., and Saranac Inn, N. Y. Recently elected to the Rectorship of St. James' Church, Syracuse, N. Y., I have, by my physician's advice, felt reluctantly obliged to decline the interesting work there. The hard lesson had come anew to me that my usefulness depends largely upon a kindly climate. I may therefore turn to southern California this winter, where I trust to undertake regular pastoral duty.

I am, my dear Bishop, very faithfully yours,

MILTON C. DOTTEN.

To the Right Rev. W. C. DOANE, S. T. D., *Bishop of Albany:*

The undersigned respectfully reports as follows.

That having occasion to spend the greater part of the month of August at the Locke House, Indian Lake, he was enabled, through the kindness of the proprietor, Mr. H. G. Locke, to officiate on the first four Sundays of that month. The services on each Sunday consisted of Morning Prayer and a sermon. The attendance at the services was excellent, and much interest was manifested.

HENRY A. DOWS.

FELSENHEIM, KEENE VALLEY, N. Y., *October* 27, 1890.

MY DEAR BISHOP DOANE — For thirty weeks our services have continued uninterruptedly. As many as two hundred have, at times, during the height of the season, been present at the second morning service.

With sincere love, respectfully yours,

GEORGE W. DU BOIS.

SCHAGHTICOKE, N. Y., *November* 10, 1890.

RIGHT REV. DEAR BISHOP — I resigned my Missions of Massena and Hogansburgh, through ill-health, on Easter Day of this year. And from that date until you appointed me this field, September 1, 1890, I officiated from time to time at the request of the proper authorities at Minersville, Pa., and Bethany, Conn. I have baptised the child of a former parishioner at May's Landing, N. J., there being no Church or Mission at that place.

I am, yours obediently,

T. DICKINSON,
Presbyter.

ALBANY, *November* 12, 1890.
To the Right Rev. the Bishop of Albany:

REV. FATHER IN GOD — During the last Conventional year I have been engaged in my duties at St. Agnes' School as Chaplain, Instructor in Latin and Metaphysics, and Treasurer. During the sessions of the school, I have said the daily Morning office of Devotion. From January 1 to November, I was in charge of St. Andrew's Mission, West Troy. I have also officiated in several other Missions and Parishes of the Diocese, and at the Cathedral.

I have celebrated at the Holy Communion 27 times, preached 41 sermons, have said the Morning or Evening Prayer 57 times, and the Burial office twice; besides assisting in the Cathedral 33 times; have baptized 2 adults and 2 infants, and have presented 5 persons for confirmation.

Very faithfully yours,

FREDERICK M. GRAY.

OGDENSBURGH, N. Y., *November* 1, 1890.
To the Right Rev. WILLIAM CROSWELL DOANE, S. T. D., LL. D., *Bishop of Albany:*

RIGHT REV. SIR — During the past year I have taken duty as assigned me by the Rev. Dr. Morrison, Rector of St. John's Church, Ogdensburgh. My clerical acts have been reported to him and are included in his annual report.

Very respectfully,

W. H. HARISON.

TRINITY CLERGY HOUSE, ST. PAUL'S CHURCHYARD,)
NEW YORK, *December* 12, 1890. $

To the Right Rev. the Bishop of Albany:

The Rev. Robert Morris Kemp respectfully reports that during the Conventional year ending November 10, 1890, he has served in St. Paul's Chapel, Trinity Parish, New York city.

1318 BROADWAY, KANSAS CITY, MO., *November* 4, 1890.
The Right Rev. W. C. DOANE, S. T. D., *Albany, N. Y.:*

MY DEAR BISHOP — I have sent to Rev. Mr. Bolmer items for St. Luke's, Troy, during the first half of this past year, and have left in Whitehall items for Trinity Parish during the five months which I spent there. Since leaving Whitehall, I have preached three times, but have not performed any other priestly duties.

Faithfully yours,

JAMES OTIS LINCOLN.

COOPERSTOWN, N. Y.
To the Right Rev. the Bishop of Albany:

I have to report occasional services, mostly outside the Diocese, at sea, and in foreign lands. Respectfully,

W. W. LORD.

SCHENECTADY, *November* 1, 1890.

Dr. Lowell reports that illness has, under the physician's direction, hindered him, peremptorily, from undertaking any official work, or duty, and (much of the time) from being in Church during the year past. This is to his deep regret

PLATTSBURGH, N. Y., *November* 1, 1890.

To the Bishop of Albany :

RIGHT REV. AND DEAR BISHOP — From the time of the last Annual Report until January 1, I was engaged in the duties of the Chaplaincy of Clinton Prison. From January 1 to September 1, I officiated in Trinity Church in this village, during the vacancy of the Rectorship. Yours respectfully,

J. W. McILWAINE.

LAKE WORTH, FLA., *November* 11, 1890.

RIGHT REV. AND DEAR SIR — During the past season, from the middle of June till the first of October, I held services in the Church of the Good Shepherd, St. Hubert's Isle, Racquette Lake. The ministrations of the Missionary there are altogether among summer visitors, and "guides" and their families. The "Rectory" on St. Hubert's Isle has been enlarged and beautified since last year, at a cost of about $3,000, the gift of Mr. and Mrs. William W. Durant. Other improvements have also been made in the way of refurnishing the "Rectory," and adding to the appointments of the Church edifice and Church Island at an expense of about $500. This was met from a fund held by the Mission.

Writing at this distance, without access to the Mission records, I can only give round numbers. In the month of August $400 was added to the Mission fund, the proceeds of a sale of articles by ladies visiting Racquette Lake. The Sunday offerings during the summer ($250) were for the payment of the Missionary's stipend.

During the earlier part of the Convention year (in the winter of 1889 and 1890) I was occupied in Mission work in the Diocese of Florida.

Yours faithfully,

J. N. MULFORD.

To the Right Rev. WILLIAM C. DOANE, D. D.:

MY DEAR BISHOP — I hereby report to you that during the last past conventional year, through the brotherly kindness of our worthy Rector, I have assisted with a good degree of regularity at Morning Prayer on the Lord's Day, at marriages, funerals, the Celebration of the Holy Eucharist, besides fulfilling other ministrations.

GEORGE HUNTINGTON NICHOLLS.

SCHENECTADY, *November* 10, 1890.

The Rev. William Payne, D. D., respectfully reports to the Bishop, that for the past year he has continued to reside in his former Parish, St. George's, bearing the title of Rector Emeritus.

During this year he has assisted the Rector as health and opportunity allowed. He has also rendered such services as asked of him by the Rector of Christ Church from time to time. In addition, he has, in God's good providence, discharged without interruption at any time, the duties that have been incumbent upon him as President of the Standing Committee, and Archdeacon of Albany.

TRINITY CHURCH RECTORY, }
ALBANY, *November* 10, 1890. }

To the Right Rev. WILLIAM CROSWELL DOANE, S. T. D., LL. D., *Bishop of Albany :*

MY DEAR BISHOP — I desire most respectfully to report, that during the past canonical year I have performed the following clerical services. celebrated in the Cathedral of All Saints, once, and assisted in the Celebration fourteen times; December 8, P. M., preached in Church of Messiah, Greenbush, and assisted in the services: December 15, said Morning Prayer, preached and celebrated in Zion Church, Sandy Hill, and P. M., said Evening Prayer and preached: December 22, said Morning

Prayer, and preached at St. Andrew's Church, West Troy: December 20, at St. Andrew's Church, West Troy, said Morning Prayer and preached: 1890, March 28, officiated at Assembly Chamber: April 6, St. Andrew's Church, West Troy, said Morning Prayer, preached and celebrated: April 13, at Grace Church, Waterford, said Morning Prayer, preached and celebrated: April 20, at Trinity Church, West Troy, said Morning Prayer, preached and celebrated: May 4, at St. John's Church, Cohoes, assisted in the service and preached: May 24, Church of Messiah, Greenbush, said Morning Prayer and preached. I have also officiated at 4 burials, and married 27 couples. Respectfully,

EDWARD SELKIRK.

HOFFMAN HALL, NASHVILLE, TENN., *December 9, 1890.*

To the Right Rev. W. C. DOANE, D. D., *Bishop of Albany:*

RIGHT REV. AND DEAR SIR--I beg to report that having resigned the Missions of Mohawk and Frankfort in the beginning of last May, I spent the remainder of the summer at my father's home in Quebec, taking a needed rest, and on September 13, with your consent and approval, entered on my duties as Principal of Hoffman Hall, Nashville, Tenn. I remain, respectfully yours,

M. O. SMITH.

61 EAST SEVENTY-EIGHTH STREET, NEW YORK, *November 10, 1890.*

To the Right Rev. the Bishop of Albany:

MY DEAR BISHOP—Throughout the entire year ill health has compelled me, greatly to my sorrow, to remain at leisure. I am glad, however, to be able to report such improvement as seems to promise a return to active work at no very distant day. Very sincerely yours,

HENRY M. SMYTH.

BELLEVUE, HURON CO., OHIO, *December 9, 1890.*

To the Right Rev. the Bishop of Albany :

Since coming to Ohio I have been engaged in Diocesan Missionary work, officiating at Sunday and week day services, and preaching almost every Sunday.

S. T. STREET.

ALBANY, *November 11, 1890.*

To the Right Rev. WILLIAM CROSWELL DOANE, S. T. D., LL. D., *Bishop of Albany :*

MY DEAR BISHOP — I have to report that during the last conventional year, I have assisted in the services of the Church 31 times; have rendered full services and preached 25 times; celebrated 7 times, and officiated at 4 burials.

Respectfully yours,

RICHARD TEMPLE.

ELIZABETHTOWN, *August 31, 1890.*

DEAR BISHOP DOANE — I have finished my work here for the season and leave to-morrow. Morning Prayer has been said seventeen times; Evening Prayer eight times; Holy Communion ten times; I have officiated at one funeral. The congregations have been good, filling the Church each Sunday, although it has not been packed as it was on the two last Sundays of my stay a year ago. There has not been so large a number of Church people here as last season, but we have had a large percentage of others, both visitors and village people. You will remember that last year we raised money to insure the Church and Rectory for three years. This season we have obtained money enough to give the Church two coats of paint, and the Rectory one, and there is the sum of $50 on hand to pay for the services of next year. I held service at Westport one Sunday evening in the Baptist place of worship. Their minister was sick and it was understood to be a mutual favor.

Very sincerely,
MONTGOMERY H. THROOP, JR.

KINDERHOOK, N. Y., *October* 28, 1890.

To the Bishop of Albany :.

RIGHT REV. AND DEAR BISHOP — I would respectfully report that I have assisted my clerical brethren during the past year whenever they have needed my services.

Very truly yours,
E. S. DE G. TOMPKINS.

ANNUAL REPORT OF THE WOMAN'S AUXILIARY TO THE BOARD OF MISSIONS IN THE DIOCESE OF ALBANY.

Number of Parish Branches, 47 (last year, 35).

Number of Junior Auxiliaries, 21 (last year, none).

Number of boxes sent, 110 (last year, 89).

Valuation of boxes, $5,293.74 (last year, $4,303.34).

Money given, $1,604 19 (last year, $711.93).

Total money and boxes, $6,897.93.

Balance on hand May 8, 1890, $14.85.

F. S. PATTERSON, *President.*

REPORT OF THE GIRLS' FRIENDLY SOCIETY OF AMERICA, DIOCESE OF ALBANY, FOR THE YEAR ENDING NOVEMBER 10, 1890.

Number of branches, 6; St. Paul's, Troy; St. John's, Ogdensburgh: Christ, Cooperstown; St. Mark's, Hoosick Falls; Epiphany, Bath on-the-Hudson; Emmanuel, Little Falls.

Number of Honorary Associates, 13, Working Associates, 41. Total, 54.

Number of Senior members, 119, Junior members, 77. Total, 196.

CONTRIBUTIONS.

St. Paul's Branch.

Orphan House, Cooperstown	$20 00
St. Margaret's Chapel, Menand's	25 00
Galveston, Texas.	50 00
Chanute, Kansas	10 00
St. Christina Home, sheets..................................	11 54
Other Charities..................................	27 00
	$143 54

St. John's, Ogdensburgh.

Child's Hospital, aprons.	
Rev. H. Sawyer, Kansas	$16 25

(Mrs.) A. J. WEISE. *President.*

REPORT OF THE CHILD'S HOSPITAL, ALBANY.

Naturally the leading thought of this year's report is of the new Hospital building, and a retrospect of the history of the work may well find place in these pages.

Sixteen years ago in November, 1874. Bishop Doane suggested to a few ladies that a Child's Nursery and Hospital was much needed. A board of managers was formed and a house on Lafayette street taken; thus the Child's Hospital was started. A year later a larger house was needed and rented; then in 1877, the first Hospital was built; in 1882 a large building was added. In 1884, another house, called St. Margaret's House, was rented for the care of very young babies, and in 1886, a larger house was needed. Thus from the small seed planted in 1874, has the work spread until, with hearts overflowing with joy and gratitude, the Managers on St. Luke's Day, October 18, 1890, attended the laying of the Corner-Stone for a new and larger Hospital. As they listened to the earnest words of the Bishop, and saw around them the suffering little ones for whom he has so faithfully laboured, they felt deeply thankful that under God's mercy the work so nobly begun sixteen years ago has thus grown and prospered.

A year ago an appeal was made to our many friends and the urgent need of a new building stated. Thanks to gifts, both large and small, enough money has been received to build and heat a new building, but there still remains the gas fitting and plumbing, for which about $5,000 more is needed. Then, when complete, it will require furnishing. The Managers feel therefore that they must make still another appeal, knowing full well that a charity that cares for sick and suffering children strikes a tender chord in every heart.

It is indeed necessary that more money should be sent in at an early date in order that contracts can be signed and the work go on without delay. The Managers gratefully acknowledge the generous gifts for the "Building Fund," amounting to very nearly $35,000. As the entire amount needed is not yet complete a list of the contributors will not be printed in this year's report.

The daily work of the Hospital differs little from year to year, doing a great amount of good as can be seen from the "Reports of the Physicians and Surgeons." What better evidence can there be than the fact that during the sixteen years of work 1,981 cases have been treated, of whom a very small proportion have died. The Managers return thanks to the Sisters and Nurses for their faithful, loving service, to the Physicians and Surgeons for their constant, watchful care.

They return also sincere thanks to Mr. Bowditch and his able assistant, Mr. A. M. Blanchard, for the time and care they devote in keeping the accounts of the Hospital.

Each year the Managers appreciate more and more the great benefit the children receive from the summer spent in the open air under the pine trees of St. Christina's Home.

CAROLINE G. HUN, *Secretary.*

SUMMARY OF THE REPORT OF THE MEDICAL STAFF.

	Admitted.		Discharged.			Remaining in Hospital.	Total.
	Male.	Female.	Cured.	Improved.	Died.		
Medical Division	67	50	79	17	12	9	117
Ophthalmic and Aural Division	19	32	31	7	....	13	51
Surgical Division	51	51	28	45	2	27	102
Total	187	133	138	69	14	49	270

ANNUAL REPORT OF ST. MARGARET'S HOUSE FOR THE YEAR ENDING SEPTEMBER
30, 1890.

Charles L. Pruyn in Account with St. Margaret's House.

Receipts.

Annual subscriptions.....	$240 00
Private gifts......	372 00
Board....	3,096 75
Churches, etc..	96 00
Miscellaneous...............	171 86
Due Treasurer October 1, 1890	120 27
Total..............	$4,096 88

Expenditures.

Provisions.............................	$1,369 28
Fuel......	325 27
Clothing...............	57 80
Wages......	1,152 86
Dispensary.........................	135 13
Furniture.............	28 98
Repairs....	67 24
Gas.........................	21 60
Rent, St. Margaret's House........	500 00
Rent, St. Christopher's House..	100 00
Sundries	191 87
Due Treasurer October 1, 1889.......................................	146 85
Total..............	$4,096 88

CHILDREN CARED FOR.

At the Child's Hospital... ...	197
At St. Margaret's House	73
At St. Christina Home, Industrial School..................................	30

ANNUAL REPORT OF THE CHURCH HOME, IN THE CITY OF TROY, FOR THE YEAR 1890.

To the Right Rev. the Bishop of Albany:

The Trustees of the Church Home present the following report for the year 1890:
No report was printed for the year 1889, but it is necessary to state that we closed
that year with a deficiency of $485.14. The payment of this debt prevents our enter-
ing upon the year 1891 with a handsome balance of $559.71. Though even with this
disadvantage, we are enabled to begin the year 1891 with a gratifying balance of
$74.57.

It is to be noted, however, that very little has been spent for repairs. This line
of expense must be greatly increased during the coming year. The property needs
the care of the mason, and the touch of the painter.

The report presents a most satisfactory condition of the Home. This is due to the
watchfulness of the ladies of the Auxiliary committee. During this year the care
and supervision of the expenditures of the household have been intrusted to them,
with the good result that can be noted in the report.

Our Permanent Fund increases slowly. The change of investments, and the constantly lessening rate of interest, keep our income from this source almost unchanged.

We note with extreme sadness the loss of one of our earliest Trustees, Mr. Henry C. Lockwood. His interest in the Home, shown in so many ways, and notably in his long service as Secretary, causes his absence to be deeply felt.

The thanks of the Trustees and Auxiliary Committee are hereby extended to all friends who have remembered the Home, whether in Parish subscriptions, or in special gifts for the support of the Home. We trust that this generous interest will be felt during the coming year.

We give herewith the financial statement for the year 1890:

I. INCOME AND EXPENSE ACCOUNT.

Receipts from Churches, individuals, etc.	$1,484 60
Income from Permanent Fund	1,256 25
Total receipts for the year 1890	$2,740 85
Expended for the year 1890	2,181 14
Balance for the year 1890	$559 71
Deficiency for the year 1889	485 14
Leaving balance December 31, 1890	$74 57

II. PERMANENT FUND.

Amount of Fund, December 31, 1890.		$28,042 70
Invested	$27,900 00	
Cash	142 70	

By order of the Board of Trustees,

January 1, 1891. NORMAN B. SQUIRES, *President.*

(C.)

LIST OF PARISHES IN UNION WITH THE CONVENTION OF THE DIOCESE OF ALBANY, WITH THE DATES OF THEIR ADMISSION.

ALBANY COUNTY.

St. Peter's, Albany, 1787; Trinity, Rensselaerville, 1811; St. Paul's, Albany, 1829; St. John's, Cohoes, 1831; Trinity, West Troy, 1834; Trinity, Albany, 1840; Grace, Albany, 1846; Holy Innocents, Albany, 1850; St. Mark's, Green Island, 1867; Cathedral of All Saints, Albany, 1874.

CLINTON COUNTY.

Trinity, Plattsburgh, 1830; Christ, Rouse's Point, 1853; St. John's, Champlain, 1853.

COLUMBIA COUNTY.

Christ, Hudson, 1794; St. John's, Stockport, 1845; St. Paul's, Kinderhook, 1851; Trinity, Claverack, 1856; Our Saviour, Lebanon Springs, 1882; All Saints', Hudson, 1888; St. Barnabas', Stottville, 1890.

DELAWARE COUNTY.

St. Peter's, Hobart, 1796; St. John's, Delhi, 1822; Christ, Walton, 1831; St. Paul's, Franklin, 1866; Christ, Deposit, 1871.

30

ESSEX COUNTY.

Church of the Cross, Ticonderoga, 1940; St. John's, Essex, 1858; St. Paul's, Keeseville, 1858; Christ, Port Henry, 1878.

FRANKLIN COUNTY.

St. Mark's, Malone, 1831; St. Peter's, Brush's Mills, 1870; St. John's, Chateaugay, 1875.

FULTON COUNTY.

St. John's, Johnstown, 1796.

GREENE COUNTY.

St. Luke's, Catskill, 1801; Christ, Coxsackie, 1806; Trinity, Athens, 1806; St. Paul's, Oak Hill, 1816; Christ, Greenville, 1825; Trinity, Ashland, 1826; Calvary, Cairo, 1832.

HERKIMER COUNTY.

Trinity, Fairfield, 1807; Grace, Norway, 1819; Emmanuel, Little Falls, 1823; Christ, Herkimer, 1854; St. Augustine's, Ilion, 1870; Grace, Mohawk, 1886.

MONTGOMERY COUNTY.

St. Ann's, Amsterdam, 1836; Zion, Fonda, 1867.

OTSEGO COUNTY.

Zion, Morris, 1793; St. Luke's, Richfield, 1803; St. Matthew's, Unadilla, 1810; Christ, Cooperstown, 1812; Christ, Butternuts, 1834; Immanuel, Otego, 1836; St. Timothy's, Westford, 1839; Grace, Cherry Valley, 1846; St. John's, Richfield Springs, 1850; St. John's, Portlandville, 1869; Christ, West Burlington, 1871; St. Paul's, East Springfield, 1871; St. James', Oneonta, 1877.

RENSSELAER COUNTY.

St. Paul's, Troy, 1807; Trinity, Lansingburgh, 1807; St. John's, Troy, 1831; Christ, Troy, 1837; St. Mark's, Hoosick Falls, 1840; Trinity, Schaghticoke, 1846; Messiah, Greenbush, 1853; St. Luke's, Troy, 1867.

ST. LAWRENCE COUNTY.

St. John's, Ogdensburgh, 1820; St. Paul's, Waddington, 1824; Christ, Morristown, 1833; Trinity, Potsdam, 1835; Grace, Canton, 1836; Grace, Norfolk, 1844; Trinity, Gouverneur, 1869; St. John's, Massena, 1870; St. Luke's, Lisbon, 1871; Zion, Colton, 1885.

SARATOGA COUNTY.

Christ, Ballston Spa, 1787; St. John's, Stillwater, 1796; St. Paul's, Charlton, 1805; Grace, Waterford, 1810; St. Luke's, Mechanicville, 1830; Bethesda, Saratoga Springs, 1830; St. Stephen's, Schuylerville, 1846; Calvary, Burnt Hills, 1850.

SCHENECTADY COUNTY.

Christ, Duanesburgh, 1789; St. George's, Schenectady, 1792; Christ, Schenectady, 1869.

WARREN COUNTY.

Messiah, Glen's Falls, 1840, with St. Paul's Chapel, Harrisena; St. James', Caldwell, 1855; Holy Cross, Warrensburgh, 1865, St. Mary's, Luzerne, 1867.

WASHINGTON COUNTY.

Zion, Sandy Hill, 1813; Trinity, Granville, 1815; St. James', Fort Edward, 1845; St. Paul's, Salem, 1860; Trinity, Whitehall, 1866; St. Luke's, Cambridge, 1867; St. Paul's, Greenwich, 1875.

ORGANIZED MISSIONS.

ALBANY COUNTY.

Good Shepherd, Bethlehem; St. Andrew's, West Troy.

CLINTON COUNTY.

St. Paul's, Mooer's Forks; St. Peter's, Ellenburgh; St. Paul's, Ellenburgh Centre; St. Luke's, Chazy; St. John's, Salmon River; all with consecrated buildings.

COLUMBIA COUNTY.

St. Luke's, Chatham; St. Mark's, Philmont.

DELAWARE COUNTY.

Emmanuel, Griffin's Corners; Grace, Stamford.

ESSEX COUNTY.

Emmanuel, Mineville; St. James', Ausable Forks, both with consecrated buildings; Good Shepherd, Bloomingdale.

FRANKLIN COUNTY.

St. Mark's, West Bangor; St. James', Hogansburgh; St. John's in the Wilderness, St. Regis Lake; St. Luke the Beloved Physician, Saranac Lake; all with consecrated buildings.

FULTON COUNTY.

Christ, Gloversville.

GREENE COUNTY.

Gloria Dei, Palenville.

HAMILTON COUNTY.

Good Shepherd, Racquette Lake; Of the Transfiguration, Blue Mountain Lake.

HERKIMER COUNTY.

Of the Memorial, Middleville.

MONTGOMERY COUNTY.

Holy Cross, Fort Plain; Good Shepherd, Canajoharie; St. Columba's, St. Johnsville.

OTSEGO COUNTY.

St. Mary's, Springfield Centre, with consecrated building.

RENSSELAER COUNTY.

St. Giles', Castleton; Holy Name, Boyntonville, with consecrated building.

ST. LAWRENCE COUNTY.

Trinity Chapel, Morley; St. Thomas', Lawrenceville; both with consecrated buildings; Grace, Louisville Landing; St. Joseph's, West Stockholm; All Saints' Barnhart's Island; St. Andrew's, Norwood.

SARATOGA COUNTY.

St. John's, East Line; Grace, Jonesville.

WARREN COUNTY

Good Shepherd, Chester; St. Paul's, Bartonville.

PARISHES NOT IN UNION WITH THE CONVENTION.

ALBANY COUNTY.

Emmanuel, South Westerlo.

COLUMBIA COUNTY.

St. Luke's, Clermont, incorporated July 12, 1859.

ESSEX COUNTY.

St. Andrew's, Schroon Lake.

GREENE COUNTY.

Grace, Prattsville.

HERKIMER COUNTY.

St. Alban's, Frankfort.

RENSSELAER COUNTY.

Holy Cross, Troy; Free Church of the Ascension, Troy; Free Church of the Epiphany, East Albany; All Saints', Hoosac; St. Barnabas', Troy.

SARATOGA COUNTY.

St. John's, Conklingville.

SCHOHARIE COUNTY.

St. Luke's, Middleburgh; St. Andrew's, Schoharie; Trinity Church, Sharon Springs.

WARREN COUNTY.

St. Sacrament, Bolton; Christ, Pottersville.

WASHINGTON COUNTY.

Grace Church, Crandell's Corners.

PLACES OTHER THAN PARISHES OR ORGANIZED MISSIONS, WHERE SERVICES OF THE CHURCH ARE HELD.

CLINTON COUNTY.

Dannemora.

COLUMBIA COUNTY.

Chatham; St. James', Rossman's Mills.

DELAWARE COUNTY.

Esperance; St. Paul's, Sidney; Bloomville; Hamden.

ESSEX COUNTY.

Crown Point; Good Shepherd, Elizabethtown; Lewis; Addison Junction; Keene Valley.

FRANKLIN COUNTY.

Good Shepherd, Santa Clara; Merciful Saviour, St. Regis Falls; Holy Innocents', Brandon.

GREENE COUNTY.

Tannersville.

OTSEGO COUNTY.

Morris Memorial Chapel, Noblesville; Maple Grove; Church of the Holy Spirit, Schenevus; Mt. Vision; Edmeston.

St. Lawrence County.

Cranberry Lake; Pierpont Centre.

Warren County.

St. Paul's, Harrisena; Grace Memorial Chapel, Sabbath-day Point.

Washington County.

North Granville.

•

NON-REPORTING PARISHES.

St. Peter's, Brushton; St. John's, Chateaugay, St. Timothy's, Westford.

NON-REPORTING CLERGY FROM THE JOURNAL OF 1888.

In obedience to the instructions of the Convention of 1889 (see Journal of 1889, p. 57), letters were sent by the Secretary of the Convention to the Clergy from whom no reports were received at the Convention of 1888, viz., the Rev. W. H. Cook, the Rev. G. W. Gates, M. D., the Rev. J. I. Tucker, S. T. D., and the Rev. Pelham Williams, S. T. D.

Replies were received from the Rev. W. H. Cook, the Rev. G. W. Gates, and the Rev. Dr. Williams, assigning ill-health, loss of report in transit, and "chronic" fault, as reasons for failure to report. No reply was received from the Rev. Dr. Tucker.

(D.)

REPORT OF THE SECRETARY OF THE BISHOP'S SALARY COMMITTEE.

1889, Nov. 12, Cash on hand from last report.		$86 12
1890, Nov. 8, Collected during year from various Parishes.		2,355 32
Loaned by the Secretary to help make up the deficiency that has been accumulating owing to the reduction of rate of interest on investments by the Treasurer............		500 00
Contributions, received by the Secretary in response to an appeal to make up this deficiency, above alluded to:		
Mr. H. D. Alexander, Mohawk................	$10 00	
Mrs. J. V. L. Pruyn, Albany...	25 00	
Gen. S. E. Marvin, Albany...	10 00	
	45 00	
		$2,986 44

Contra.

Paid for postal cards, printing circulars, postage, etc......	$22 90	
Remitted to Mr. J. H. Van Antwerp.	2,960 00	
Cash on hand..........	3 54	
		2,986 44

E. & O. E. •

PARISHES IN ARREARS, NOVEMBER 8, 1890.

St. John's, Essex........	$6 00
St Peter's, Brushton.........	16 00
St. James', Hogansburgh................	6 00
Trinity, Athens	10 00

Christ, Greenville...	$6 00
Calvary, Cairo...	
Grace, Prattsville...	
*St. George's, Schenectady.....................................	40 00
St. Luke's, Middleburgh..	2 00
Trinity, Sharon Springs..	10 00
St. John's, Conklingville......................................	9 00
St. James', Caldwell..	20 00
St. James', Fort Edward.......................................	15 00
Trinity, Rensselaerville......................................	8 00
*St. John's, Stockport...	17 50
Trinity, Plattsburgh..	50 00
St. John's, Delhi...	15 00
Christ, Walton..	45 00
Christ, Deposit...	6 00
Epiphany, East Albany...	4 00
St. Barnabas', Troy...	2 50
Christ, Ballston..	36 00
Calvary, Burnt Hills..	6 00
Christ, Herkimer..	8 00
St. Augustine's, Ilion..	10 00
St. Ann's, Amsterdam..	18 00
Zion, Fonda..	6 00
St. Paul's, East Springfield..................................	8 00
Christ, West Burlington.......................................	6 00
*St. John's, Troy...	250 00

In addition to the above there are a number of small Parishes which do not evince any disposition to respond at all.

(E.)

OFFICERS OF THE DIOCESE, TRUSTEES, ETC.

The Right Rev. William Croswell Doane, S. T. D., LL. D., *President.*
The Rev. William C. Prout, *Secretary.*
The Rev. Thomas B. Fulcher, *Assistant Secretary.*
The Rev. Frederick S. Sill, *Registrar.*
Mr. Selden E. Marvin, *Treasurer.*

THE STANDING COMMITTEE.

The Rev. William Payne, D. D.,	Mr. Norman B. Squires,
The Rev. J. Livingston Reese, D. D.,	Mr. Henry S. Wynkoop,
The Rev. J. Ireland Tucker, S. T. D.,	Mr. John I. Thompson,
The Rev. Fenwick M. Cookson,	Mr. J. H. Van Antwerp.

DEPUTIES TO THE GENERAL CONVENTION.

The Rev. William Payne, D. D., the Rev. W. W. Battershall, D. D., the Rev. J. D. Morrison, D. D., LL. D., the Rev Joseph Carey, S. T. D., Mr. G. Pomeroy Keese, Mr. Erastus Corning, Mr. T. Streatfeild Clarkson, Mr. John Hobart Warren.

*Items marked with an asterisk (*) above, were paid after books were closed for the Conventional year, and will appear in next year's accounts

COMMITTEE ON THE CONSTITUTION AND CANONS.

The Rev. J. W. Stewart, the Rev. R. M. Kirby, D. D., the Rev. James Caird, the Rev. Wilford L. Robbins, Mr. James Gibson, Mr. T. Streatfeild Clarkson, Mr. J. D. Henderson.

COMMITTEE ON THE SALARY OF THE BISHOP.

The Rev. Joseph Carey, S. T. D., the Rev. W. W. Battershall, D. D., Mr. J. J. Tillinghast, Mr. Erastus Corning, Mr. W. A. Wood, Mr. J. W. Tillinghast, Mr. John I. Thompson, Mr. Spencer Trask. *Secretary,* Mr. W. W. Rousseau, Troy.

COMMITTEE TO SECURE LEGISLATION FOR THE ORPHAN HOUSE.

Mr. Melvil Dewey, Mr. Benjamin H. Hall, Mr. Charles E. Patterson.

COMMITTEE TO RAISE FUNDS FOR THE ORPHAN HOUSE.

The Bishop of the Diocese, Mr. A. B. Cox, Mr. T. Streatfeild Clarkson, Mr. John I. Thompson, Mr. J. Russell Parsons, Jr.

COMMITTEE TO ATTEND CONFERENCE ON MORAL INSTRUCTION IN PUBLIC SCHOOLS.

The Rev. Edgar A. Enos, the Rev. John H. Houghton, the Rev. William H. Bowen.

THE BOARD OF MISSIONS.

The Right Rev. William Croswell Doane, S. T. D., LL. D., *President.*
The Rev. William R. Woodbridge, *Secretary.*
Mr. Selden E. Marvin, *Treasurer.*

ARCHDEACONRY OF ALBANY.

The Rev. W. W. Battershall, D. D., Mr. J. H. Van Antwerp.

ARCHDEACONRY OF TROY.

The Rev. F. M. Cookson, Mr. George A. Wells.

ARCHDEACONRY OF THE SUSQUEHANNA.

The Rev. Frank B. Reazor, Mr. Robert M. Townsend.

ARCHDEACONRY OF OGDENSBURGH.

The Rev. R. M. Kirby, D. D., Mr. T. Streatfeild Clarkson.

DIOCESE AT LARGE.

The Rev. W. R. Woodbridge, Mr. William Kemp.

ARCHDEACONRIES.

FIRST. ARCHDEACONRY OF ALBANY.

Albany, Greene, Columbia, Schenectady, Montgomery, Fulton, Hamilton and Herkimer counties.
The Rev. William Payne, D. D., *Archdeacon.*
The Rev. F. S. Sill, *Secretary.*
The Rev. E. Bayard Smith, *Treasurer*

SECOND. ARCHDEACONRY OF TROY.

Rensselaer, Saratoga, Washington, Warren, Clinton and Essex counties.
The Rev. Joseph Carey, S. T. D., *Archdeacon.*
The Rev. George D. Silliman, *Secretary.*
Mr. Charles W. Tillinghast, 2d, *Treasurer.*

THIRD. ARCHDEACONRY OF THE SUSQUEHANNA.

Delaware, Otsego and Schoharie counties.
The Rev. Charles S. Olmsted, *Archdeacon.*
The Rev. F. B. Reazor, *Secretary and Treasurer.*

FOURTH. ARCHDEACONRY OF OGDENSBURGH.

St. Lawrence and Franklin counties.
The Rev. J. D. Morrison, D. D., LL. D., *Archdeacon.*
The Rev. Charles Temple. *Secretary.*
Mr. T. Streatfeild Clarkson, *Treasurer.*

EXAMINING CHAPLAINS.

The Rev. J. Ireland Tucker, S. T. D., the Rev. Joseph Carey, S. T. D., the Rev. J. D. Morrison, D. D., LL. D., the Rev. W. N. Irish, the Rev. W. H. Cook, the Rev. Heman R. Timlow, the Rev. Thomas B. Fulcher, the Rev. Edgar A. Enos, the Rev. William G. W. Lewis, the Rev. Wilford L. Robbins, the Rev. G. H. S. Walpole.

THE BIBLE AND COMMON PRAYER BOOK SOCIETY OF ALBANY AND ITS VICINITY.

The Right Rev. William Croswell Doane, S. T. D., LL. D., *President.*
The Rev. J. Ireland Tucker, S. T. D., *First Vice-President.*
The Rev. W. W. Battershall, D. D., *Second Vice-President.*
The Rev. J. W. Stewart, *Third Vice-President.*
The Rev. Thaddeus A Snively, *Corresponding Secretary.*
The Rev. Richmond Shreve, D. D., *Recording Secretary.*
Mr. Henry B. Dauchy, *Treasurer.*

MANAGERS.

Messrs. J. H. Van Antwerp, A. A. Van Vorst, George W. Gibbons, Joseph W. Tillinghast, Francis N. Mann, George A. Wells, John H. Hulsapple, Marcus T. Hun, William C. Buell, John Horrocks, E. G. Dorlan, George B. Warren.

Applications for books may be made to the *Corresponding Secretary*, the Rev. Thaddeus A. Snively, Troy.

All contributions and donations should be sent to the *Treasurer*, Mr. H. B. Dauchy, Troy.

(F.)

DIOCESAN BRANCHES OF GENERAL SOCIETIES.

THE DIOCESAN BRANCH OF THE WOMAN'S AUXILIARY TO THE BOARD OF MISSIONS.

President. Mrs. Melvil Dewey, 315 Madison avenue, Albany.
Vice President. Mrs. Payne, Schenectady.
Treasurer. Mrs. Charles E. Hannaman, 108 First street, Troy.
Corresponding Secretary. Miss Nina E. Browne, 95 Lancaster street, Albany.
Recording Secretary.

Managers.

For the Archdeaconry of Albany: Miss Tweddle, Menand's road, Albany; Mrs. A. Van Nostrand, Schenectady.

For the Archdeaconry of Troy: Mrs. George B. Warren, 19 Second street, Troy; Mrs. R. C. McEwen, Saratoga.

31

For the Archdeaconry of the Susquehanna: Miss E. J. Hughes, Gilbertsville; Miss Laura Gay, Walton.

For the Archdeaconry of Ogdensburgh: Mrs. J. C. Sprague, Ogdensburgh; Mrs. Charles Temple, Malone.

THE DIOCESAN BRANCH OF THE CHURCH TEMPERANCE SOCIETY.

Delegates to the General Council. The Rev. T. A. Snively, Troy; Mr. Henry J. Estcourt, Schenectady.

Honorary Secretary.

Diocesan Committee.

Clerical — The Rev. W. W. Battershall, D. D., Albany; the Rev. Joseph N. Mulford; the Rev. George D. Silliman, Hoosick Falls; the Rev. Hobart Cooke, Plattsburgh; the Rev. John H. Houghton, Salem.

Lay — Messrs. Smith Fine, Albany; William Kemp, Troy; R. C. McEwen, M. D., Saratoga; Henry C. Day, Cambridge; James Rogers, Ausable Forks; Charles Ashley, Ogdensburgh.

THE WOMAN'S DIOCESAN LEAGUE.

Objects.

The objects of the Woman's Diocesan League are, first, to complete the Cathedral building ready for use, and, then, to aid other Church buildings, Missions, schools, and charitable works in the Diocese. Members of the League are free to devote their gifts, now, to any of these purposes.

The Convention by resolution has recommended the formation of Chapters in every Parish in the Diocese.

THE CATHEDRAL CHAPTER.

President. Mrs. Erastus Corning.

Secretaries. Mrs. William B. Van Rensselaer; Mrs. H. E. Bender.

Treasurers. Mrs. Erastus Corning, Jr.; Mrs. J. T. Gardiner.

Chapters in Troy, Stockport, Middleville, Saratoga Springs, Grace Church, Albany, Ogdensburgh, Delhi, Potsdam, Franklin, Philmont, Cohoes, Hoosick Falls, Saranac Lake, Catskill, Brushton, Herkimer, Ilion, West Troy, and in many other places without formal organization.

FUNDS TO WHICH OFFERINGS ARE REQUIRED BY CANON, AND THE NAMES OF THE TREASURERS TO WHOM THE SAME SHOULD BE SENT.

Diocesan Fund. Mr. S. E. Marvin, Albany.

Missions of the Diocese. Mr. S. E. Marvin, Albany.

For Aged and Infirm Clergymen. Mr. S. E. Marvin, Albany.

For Widows and Orphans of Deceased Clergymen. Mr. S. E. Marvin, Albany.

For the Clergy Reserve Fund.

Bible and Common Prayer Book Society of Albany. Mr. H. B. Dauchy, Troy.

Episcopal Fund. Mr. J. H. Van Antwerp, Albany.

Salary of the Bishop. Mr. W. W. Rousseau, Troy.

For the Education of Young Men for the Ministry. The Bishop of the Diocese, or Mr. Richard M. Harison, 31 Nassau street, New York.

Orphan House of the Holy Saviour. Mr. Leslie Pell-Clarke, Springfield Centre, Otsego county.

Domestic and Foreign Missions. Mr. George Bliss, 22 Bible House, New York.

Offerings for the *Child's Hospital* should be sent to Mr. Edward Bowditch, Albany.

For Missionary envelopes and Pledges apply to the *Secretary* of the Board of Missions, the Rev. William R. Woodbridge, Port Henry, Essex county.

(G.)

SUMMARY OF STATISTICS.

From the Bishop's Address, the Parochial, Missionary ana other Reports.

Clergy (Bishop, 1, Priests, 123, Deacons, 8)...................................	132
Ordinations (Deacons, 2, Priests, 3)......................................	5
Candidates for Orders (for the Deacon's Order only, 7, for the Priest's Order, 9)...	16
Postulants...	15
Lay Readers Licensed...................................	21
Parishes in union with Convention..	100
Parishes not in union with Convention..........................	16
Missions (organized, 36, unorganized, 27).....................	63
Churches...	132
Chapels...	21
Sittings in Churches and Chapels	39,097
Free Churches and Chapels	125
Churches otherwise supported	28
Free sittings (including free seats in Churches where there is a pew rental)	29,566
Rectories	73
Corner-stones laid..	2
Churches consecrated	8
Buildings blessed	7
*Families..	6,856
*Individuals (adults, 10,194, children, 5,354, not designated, 2,760)	18,308
Baptisms (adults, 419, infants, 1,559)	1,978
Confirmations	1,401
Communicants (admitted, 1,007, received, 456, died, 270, removed, 632), present number..	18,438
Marriages..	450
Burials	1,060
Sunday School teachers.......................................	1,025
Sunday School pupils	10,658
Parish School teachers	43
Parish School pupils...	343

OFFERINGS.

Parochial.

Alms...	$6,624 46	
Current expenses................................	185,586 22	
Other purposes.................................	80,714 96	
		$272,925 64

Diocesan.

Diocesan Missions	$10,559 34
Salary of the Bishop	2,460 00
Diocesan Fund	2,771 29
Bible and Common Prayer Book Society of Albany	252 18
Aged and Infirm Clergy Fund...................	508 15
Fund for Widows and Orphans of Deceased Clergymen ...	219 14

* Many reports do not give these items.

Orphan Hóuse of the Holy Saviour, including $1,345 for Building Fund........	$3,041 62	
The Child's Hospital (part for Building Fund)	4,668 78	
Theological Education	249 17	
Other purposes........	5,158 79	
		$39,8

General.

General Theological Seminary........	$8 70	
Domestic Missions	3,087 87	
Foreign Missions.	2,170 85	
Indian Missions	512 68	
Home Missions to Coloured Persons.	691 27	
Other purposes...... '.........................	6,505 46	
		12,8
Total amount of Offerings.............		$315,7

TABLE OF CONTENTS.

DIOCESE OF ALBANY.

CONSTITUTION AND CANONS.

CONSTITUTION.

ARTICLE I.

Of the Members of the Convention.

The Diocese of Albany entrusts its legislation to a Convention, to consist as follows: First, of the Bishop, when there is one; of the Assistant Bishop, when there is one. Secondly, of all Clergymen canonically resident in the Diocese for six months previous to the Convention, the restriction of time not to apply to Rectors duly elected or Missionaries duly appointed (provided that no Clergyman suspended from the Ministry shall have a seat); and, Thirdly, of the Lay Delegation from the Cathedral, and of Lay Delegations, consisting of not more than three Deputies from each other Church in union with the Convention, who shall be communicants, and shall have been chosen by the Vestry or Congregation of the same.

ARTICLE II.

Of the Annual Meetings of the Convention.

The Convention shall assemble on the Tuesday after the tenth day of November, in each year, in such place as the Bishop shall appoint, giving fifteen days' notice thereof. In case of his inability to act, the Assistant Bishop, if there be one, shall appoint the place; and, if there be no Bishop, the Standing Committee shall appoint. The place of meeting may be changed for sufficient reason after having been appointed, provided that ten days' notice of such change shall be given.

Every Convention shall be opened with a Sermon and the Holy Communion: and the Preacher shall be appointed by the Bishop, or in case of his inability to act, or if there be no Bishop, by the Standing Committee.

ARTICLE III.

Of Special Conventions.

The Bishop shall have power to call Special Conventions, giving thirty days' notice thereof, and shall do so when requested by a vote of three-fourths of the Standing Committee. When there is no Bishop, the Standing Committee shall have power to call a Special Convention, giving ninety days' notice thereof.

ARTICLE IV.

Of the Cathedral.

"The Cathedral of All Saints in the City and Diocese of Albany" shall be the Cathedral Church of this Diocese. Three Lay Communicants shall be chosen by the Chapter as the Delegation from the Cathedral to the Convention.

ARTICLE V.

Of the Permanent Officers of the Diocese.

The permanent officers of the Diocese shall be: the Bishop of the Diocese (with right to preside, when present in Convention; and when there is an Assistant Bishop, he shall have right to preside in the absence of the Bishop), a Standing Committee, a Secretary, a Treasurer and a Registrar.

ARTICLE VI.

Of the Election of a Bishop.

When a Bishop or an Assistant Bishop is to be elected, the election shall be at the regular Annual Convention, or at a Special Convention duly called for that purpose; and such election shall require a majority of the votes of each order voting separately.

ARTICLE VII.

Of the President of the Convention.

If there be no Bishop of the Diocese, or its *ex-officio* presiding officer be absent, the Convention shall elect a President from among the Clergy, by ballot (unless the ballot be dispensed with by unanimous vote.)

ARTICLE VIII.

Of the Standing Committee.

The Standing Committee shall consist of four Clergymen and four Laymen, to be elected by ballot at each Annual Convention, by a majority of the Clergy and Lay Delegations present, and shall serve until the next Annual Convention and until a new election is made, the functions of which Committee, besides those provided for in the Canons of the General Convention, and in this Constitution, shall be determined by Canon or Resolution of the Convention. But vacancies in the Standing Committee may be filled by a majority of the votes of the remaining members until the next meeting of the Convention.

ARTICLE IX.

Of the Secretary, Treasurer and Registrar.

The Secretary shall be elected at each Annual Convention from the members thereof, by ballot, after nominations (unless the ballot be dispensed with by unanimous vote), and by a majority of the Clergy and Lay Delegations present; and he shall remain in office until his successor shall be elected. His duties shall be those required by the Canons, Resolutions and Rules of Order of the Convention.

The Treasurer and the Registrar shall be elected in a similar manner, and are not required to be members of the Convention. They shall remain in office until the next Annual Convention, and until their successors are elected.

ARTICLE X.

Of the Deliberations of the Convention and of Votes.

The Clergymen and Laymen constituting the Convention shall deliberate in one body, and each Clergyman shall have one vote, and each Lay Delegation one vote, and a majority of the aggregate votes shall be decisive except in the cases provided for in Articles VI, IX and XI.

If five votes require a division, then the voting shall be by orders separately, and the concurrence of a majority of each order shall be necessary to make a decision. But no alteration of the Constitution or Canons shall be valid without the concurrence of the Bishop and of a majority of the Clergy and of a majority of the Lay Delegations; and the Bishop's concurrence shall be presumed unless the contrary be openly expressed by him to the Convention after the vote of the Clergy and Laity and before the adjournment *sine die.*

ARTICLE XI.

Of Altering the Constitution.

The mode of altering the Constitution shall be as follows: A proposition for an amendment shall be introduced in writing and considered in the Convention; and, if approved by a majority, shall lie over till the next Convention, and, if then approved by a two-thirds vote of the Clergy and Lay Delegations present, with the Bishop's concurrence, the Constitution shall be changed accordingly.

CANONS.

CANON I.

Of the List of Clergymen in the Diocese.

SECTION 1. On the first day of each Convention, regular or special, the Ecclesiastical Authority shall present to the Convention a List of the Clergy canonically resident in the Diocese, annexing the names of their respective Parishes, Offices and residences, and the dates of their becoming resident in the Diocese.

SEC. 2. The Secretary shall record this list of names in a book to be kept by him for that purpose.

SEC. 3. From this record shall be made up by the Secretary the list of the Clergymen entitled, according to the Constitution, to seats in the Convention; which list may at any time be revised and corrected by the Convention.

CANON II.

Of the Lay Delegations.

SECTION 1. When the Lay Delegations are chosen by the Vestry, it shall be at a meeting held according to law. In case the Vestry shall not choose Deputies they may be chosen by the congregation in the manner hereinafter prescribed for Churches having no Vestries.

SEC. 2. Deputies from Churches having no Vestries shall be chosen by the Congregation at a meeting of which notice shall have been given during Divine Service on the two Sundays next previous thereto And at such meeting the Rector or Minister shall preside, and the qualifications for voting shall be the same as those required by law for voting at an election for Churchwardens and Vestrymen.

SEC. 3. When Deputies are chosen by a Vestry, the evidence of their appointment shall be a certificate, signed by the Rector of the Church they are chosen to represent and by the Clerk of the Vestry; and if there be no Rector, then the certificate shall state that fact, and shall be signed by the Churchwarden presiding and by the Clerk of the Vestry. The certificate must state the time and place of the election, must show upon its face that the appointment has been made in accordance with all the requirements of the Canons, and shall certify that each Deputy chosen is a Communicant of the Church and entitled to vote for Churchwardens and Vestrymen of the Church he is chosen to represent.

SEC. 4. When Deputies are chosen by the Congregation of any Church, the evidence of their appointment shall be a certificate, signed by the Rector or Minister having charge of the said Church and by the Secretary of the meeting; or if there be no such Rector or Minister, then the certificate shall state that fact, and shall be signed by the officer presiding at the meeting and by the Secretary of the same. The certificate must state the time and place of the election, must show upon its face that the appointment has been made in accordance with all the requirements of the Canons, and shall certify that each Deputy chosen is a Communicant of the Church, and, in the case of the Church having a Vestry, that he is entitled to vote for Churchwardens and Vestrymen of such Church, or, in the case of a Church having no Vestry, that he has belonged for twelve months to the Congregation he is chosen to represent. No other evidence of the appointment of Lay Deputies than such as is specified in this and the preceding section shall be received by the Convention.

SEC. 5. The Secretary of the Convention, when he shall send to any Church or Parish the required notice of the time and place of meeting of any Convention to be held, shall transmit with the same a copy of this Canon and blank printed forms of certificates of appointment of Deputies.

CANON III.

Of the Organization of the Convention.

SECTION 1. If the *ex-officio* presiding officer be not present at the opening of the Convention, the Secretary shall call the members present to order; and the senior Presbyter present, who is a member of the Convention, shall take the chair, and preside until a President is elected, as provided by Article VII of the Constitution.

SEC. 2. The Secretary shall then call the names of the Clergy entitled to seats in the Convention. He shall then call the names of the Churches in union with the Convention, when the Lay Deputies shall present their certificates, which shall be examined by the Secretary, and a committee of two members appointed by the presiding officer. Irregular or defective certificates, and certificates and documents referring to contested seats, shall be temporarily laid aside. The names of the Lay Deputies duly appointed shall then be called, after which the certificates and documents laid aside shall be reported to the Convention, which shall decide upon the admission of the Deputies named therein.

SEC. 3. If twenty Clergymen entitled to vote, and twenty Lay Delegations be present, they shall constitute a quorum; and the presiding officer *ex officio* shall declare the Convention duly organized. The same number of Clergymen and Lay Delegations shall, at any time, be necessary for the transaction of business, except that a smaller number may adjourn from time to time.

SEC. 4. If the presiding officer *ex officio* be not present before the convention is declared to be organized, the temporary Chairman shall direct that the members proceed to elect a President, according to Article VII of the Constitution, who, when elected, shall take the Chair and declare the Convention organized for business.

Sec. 5. The Convention shall then proceed to the election of a Secretary, a Treasurer and a Registrar, according to the Constitution. The Secretary may appoint an Assistant Secretary, also any other assistants he may require, announcing their names to the Convention.

Sec. 6. Any Rules of Order which shall have been previously adopted or sanctioned in the Convention, except such as prescribe the mode of altering the same, shall be in force until changed by the Convention, after having been duly organized.

CANON IV.

Of the Admission of a Church into Union with the Church in this Diocese, and Maintaining such Union.

Section 1. Every Church or Congregation desiring admission into union with the Church in this Diocese, shall present a written application therefor to the Convention, together with a copy of the resolution of the Vestry, or of the Congregation, authorizing such application; in which resolution the said Church, by its Vestry or Congregation, shall agree to abide by, and conform to, and observe, all the Canons of the Church, and all the rules, orders and regulations of the Convention; which copy shall be duly certified by the presiding officer of the Vestry, or of the meeting of the Congregation at which the resolution was adopted, and also by the Clerk of the Vestry or Secretary of the meeting; and shall be authenticated by the seal of the Corporation. The said application shall also be accompanied by the Certificate of Incorporation of the Church, duly recorded, or a copy thereof certified by the officer, whose duty it may be to record or file the same; and also, by a Certificate of the Ecclesiastical Authority, to the effect that he or they approve of the incorporation of such Church, and that such Church, in his or their judgment, is duly and satisfactorily established; and every Church or Congregation applying for admission shall produce satisfactory evidence that not less than twenty-five persons, members of such Church, have habitually, for at least one year preceding such application, attended Divine Service in such Church or Congregation.

Sec. 2. No application for the admission of a Church into union with the Church in this Diocese shall be considered or acted upon, at any meeting of the Convention, unless the same shall have been transmitted to the Secretary of the Convention at least thirty days before the meeting of the Convention. It shall be the duty of the Secretary of the Convention, at least twenty days before the meeting of the Convention, to deliver to a Committee, to be annually appointed (to be called the Committee on the Incorporation and Admission of Churches), all applications for admission into union which shall have been received by him, to be by such Committee examined, considered and reported upon to the Convention.

Sec. 3. Whenever hereafter any Church in union with this Convention shall neglect, for three years in succession, to make a Parochial Report, no Missionary Report being made on its behalf, and shall not, during the same period, have employed a Clergyman as its Parish Minister, nor requested of the Ecclesiastical Authority to have the services of a Missionary, such Church shall be regarded as having forfeited its connection with the Convention, and shall no longer have a right to send a Delegation to the same. The Bishop shall report such Church to the Convention in his Annual Address. Such Church, however, may be re-admitted, upon application to the Convention, accompanied by a report of its condition, and on such terms as shall appear just; such re-admission to take effect from and after the rising of the Convention consenting to such admission.

CANON V.

Of Elections.

All elections by the Convention shall be by ballot, except when the ballot is dispensed with by unanimous consent. And when an election is by ballot, a majority of the votes in each order shall be necessary to a choice.

CANON VI.

Of the Secretary of the Convention.

SECTION 1. It shall be the duty of the Secretary to take and keep the Minutes of the proceedings of the Convention, to attest its public acts, and faithfully to deliver into the hands of his successor all books and papers relating to the business and concerns of the Convention which may be in his possession or under his control). It shall also be his duty to send a printed notice to each Minister, and to each Vestry or Congregation, of the time and place appointed for the meetings of each Convention, and to publish a notice of the meeting in three of the public papers published in the Diocese of Albany, and to perform such other duties as may be required of him by the Convention.

SEC. 2. He shall transmit annually a copy of the Journal of the Convention to each of the Bishops of the Protestant Episcopal Church in the United States, to the Secretary of the House of Deputies of the General Convention, and to the Secretaries of the Diocesan Conventions; and shall ask, on behalf of the Diocese, for copies of the Diocesan Journals in exchange.

SEC. 3. He shall also transmit to every General Convention, in addition to the documents required by the Canons of the General Convention,* a certificate, signed by himself, containing a list of the Clergymen in this Diocese, and the amount of funds paid or secured to be paid (distinguishing them) to the General Theological Seminary, and also a certificate of the appointment of Clerical and Lay Deputies.

SEC. 4. Any expense incurred by a compliance with this Canon shall be paid out of the Diocesan Fund.

SEC. 5. Whenever there shall be a vacancy in the office of Secretary of the Convention, the duties thereof shall devolve upon the Assistant Secretary, if there be one, if not, upon the Secretary of the Standing Committee.

SEC. 6. Whenever, under the provisions of the Constitution, a Special Convention is called for any particular purpose, it shall be the duty of the Secretary, in the notice thereof, to specify such purpose.

CANON VII.

Of the Treasurer of the Diocese.

SECTION 1. It shall be the duty of the Treasurer of the Diocese to receive and disburse all moneys collected under the authority of the Convention, and of which the the collection and distribution shall not be otherwise regulated. He shall report, at each annual meeting of the Convention, the names of the Parishes which have failed to make the required contributions to any of the Diocesan Funds, specifying the funds to which they have failed to contribute and the amount of such deficiency.

SEC. 2. His accounts shall be rendered annually to the Convention, and shall be examined by a Committee acting under its authority.

---

* Title I, Canon 18, Sec IV.

Sec. 3. If the Treasurer of the Convention shall die or resign his office, the Standing Committee shall appoint a Treasurer *ad interim;* to continue in office until an election be made by the Convention.

CANON VIII.

Of the Registrar.

It shall be the duty of the Registrar to collect and preserve, as the property of the Diocese, all documents and papers pertaining to the Diocese, and not in the custody of any other officer; and also the Journals and public documents of other Diocesan Conventions and of the General Convention, and other pamphlets and publications connected with the Church at large.

CANON IX.

Of Deputies to the General Convention.

SECTION 1. The Convention shall, at each regular annual meeting next preceding a stated meeting of the General Convention, elect, by the concurrent ballot of the Clerical and Lay Members, four Clergymen and four Laymen, to act as Deputies from this Diocese to the General Convention. It shall also, in like manner, elect four Clergymen and four Laymen as Provisional Deputies, to act in the case hereinafter mentioned; which Deputies and Provisional Deputies shall hold their respective offices until their successors are elected, and shall be Deputies, or Provisional Deputies, for any General Convention which may be held during their continuance in office.

SEC. 2. Should a vacancy occur by resignation, removal from the Diocese, death, or otherwise, among the Deputies or Provisional Deputies, between the stated times of election, the vacancy shall be supplied by any Convention during or prior to which such vacancy shall occur.

SEC. 3. It shall be the duty of the Deputies elect to signify to the Ecclesiastical Authority, at least ten days before the meeting of the General Convention, their acceptance of the appointment and their intention to perform its duties; in default of which the Ecclesiastical Authority shall designate, from the list of Provisional Deputies, so many as may be necessary to ensure, as far as practicable, a full representation of the Diocese. And the Ecclesiastical Authority shall, in like manner, designate, from the same list of Provisional Deputies, one or more, as the case may be, to supply any deficiency in the representation of this Diocese which may in any way occur. And the person or persons so designated by the Bishop, being furnished with a certificate thereof, shall have all the power and authority of Deputies duly elected by the Convention.

CANON X.

Of the Standing Committee.

The powers and duties of the Standing Committee over and above those given and prescribed by the Canons of the General Convention and by the Constitution of the Diocese of Albany, are further defined as follows:

SECTION 1. If there be no Bishop, or if he be unable to perform his duties, the Standing Committee shall be the Ecclesiastical Authority of the Diocese, *provided* that whenever any duty is specially imposed upon the Clerical Members of the Committee, such duty shall be performed by them only.

SEC. 2. The record of all proceedings upon a presentment of a Clergyman shall be preserved by the Standing Committee.

SEC. 3. The Standing Committee shall make a full report of all their proceedings at every Annual Convention.

CANON XI.

Of Parish Registers and Parochial Reports.

WHEREAS, by the Canons of the General Convention,* it is made the duty of each Clergyman of this Church to "keep a Register of Baptisms, Confirmations, Communicants, Marriages, and Funerals within his Cure, agreeably to such rules as may be provided by the Convention of the Diocese where his Cure lies;" it is hereby ordered that,

SECTION 1. The Record shall specify the name and the time of the birth of the child or adult baptized, with the names of the parents, sponsors or witnesses; the names of the persons confirmed; the names of the persons married, their ages and residences, also the names and residences of at least two witnesses of each marriage; the names of the persons buried, their ages, and the place of burial; and also the time when and the Minister by whom each rite was performed. The list of Communicants shall contain the names of all connected with the Parish or Mission as nearly as can be ascertained. These records shall be made by the Minister in a book provided for that purpose, belonging to each Church; which book shall be the Parish Register, and shall be preserved as a part of the records of the Church.

SEC. 2. AND WHEREAS, by the Canons of the General Convention,† it is " ordered that every Minister of this Church, or, if the Parish be vacant, the Warden shall present, or cause to be delivered, on or before the first day of every Annual Convention, to the Bishop of the Diocese, or, where there is no Bishop, to the President of the Convention, a statement of the number of Baptisms, Confirmations, Marriages and Funerals, and of the number of Communicants in his Parish or Church; also the state and condition of the Sunday Schools in his Parish; and also the amount of the Communion alms, the contributions for 'Missions, Diocesan, Domestic and Foreign, for Parochial Schools, for Church purposes in general, and of all other matters that may throw light on the state of the same," it is hereby further ordered that, in reporting the number of Communicants, he shall distinguish the additions, removals and deaths since the last report, and that, in reporting the contributions for Church purposes in general, he shall include the amount received for sittings in the Church and moneys raised for all Church and Parish purposes, other than those enumerated in this section

SEC. 3. In every case where a Parish is without a Minister, the Parish Register shall be kept by some person appointed by the Vestry or Trustees; and the annual Parochial report shall be presented or forwarded to the Bishop by the Churchwardens or Trustees of the Parish.

CANON XII

Of Vacant Parishes

SECTION 1. Whenever a Parish becomes vacant, it shall be the duty of the Vestry or Trustees to give immediate notice thereof to the Bishop.

SEC. 2. The Bishop shall appoint those of the Clergy in the Diocese who can with most convenience discharge the duty, to supply such vacant Parishes as have been reported to him, at such times as may be deemed convenient and proper. And the Clergy so appointed, shall make a full report to the Bishop concerning the state of the Parishes which they have visited. It shall be the duty of the Parishes thus supplied to defray all the expenses incident to such occasional services.

---

* Title I, Canon 15, Sec 5   † Title I, Canon 18, Sec. 1.

CANON XIII.

Of Offerings.

SECTION 1. Whereas it is the duty of all Christians, as faithful stewards of God, to set apart regularly a portion of their income as God's portion, "every one as God hath prospered him," to be used for the maintenance and extension of His kingdom, and the relief of His poor; this Church enjoins this duty upon all her members.

SEC. 2 It shall be the duty of every Congregation of this Diocese to contribute, at least once in each year, by weekly or monthly offerings, or in some other systematic way, to the Missions of the Diocese; the Domestic and Foreign Missions and other departments of Missionary work under the control of the General Convention; the support of the Episcopate; the expenses of the Convention; the education of young men for the Holy Ministry; the distribution of the Bible and Book of Common Prayer; the support of aged and infirm Clergymen: the relief of the widows and orphans of deceased Clergymen; and the support and education of orphan children; the offerings to be sent to the Treasurers of the funds for which they are made, and the amounts of all such contributions to form distinct items in the Annual Parochial Report.

SEC. 3. "The Protestant Episcopal Society for Promoting Religion and Learning in the State of New York," in which we have an interest in common with our mother Diocese, shall be the agent of this Diocese for the education of young men for Holy Orders. A copy of its Annual report, if obtained from its Superintendent, shall be laid by the Secretary of the Convention before each Annual Convention.

SEC. 4. "The Bible and Common Prayer Book Society of Albany and its Vicinity" shall be the agent of this Diocese for the Distribution of the Bible and the Book of Common Prayer, and shall present a full report of its proceedings to each Annual Convention.

SEC. 5. The Orphan House of the Holy Saviour, at or near Cooperstown, shall be the Diocesan Orphanage, and shall make a report of its proceedings and condition to each Annual Convention.

CANON XIV.

Of the Missions of the Diocese and of Archdeaconries.

The Church in this Diocese, acknowledging her responsibility, in common with the whole Church, for the fulfilment of the charge of our Lord to preach the Gospel to every creature, and especially for the extension of the Church throughout the Diocese, declares that it is the duty of the Convention, as her representative body, to care for the Missionary work, and that every baptized Member of the Church is bound, according to his ability, to assist in carrying it on. To this end it is hereby enacted as follows:

SECTION 1. "The Board of Missions of the Protestant Episcopal Church in the Diocese of Albany," incorporated by an Act of the Legislature of the State of New York, passed February 16, 1870, shall be entrusted with the general charge and direction of the work of Missions within the Diocese, and particularly with the custody and management of all money or property given or acquired for that object, subject to the provisions of this Canon and to such written instructions as may from time to time be given to them by the Convention and entered upon the Journal thereof.

SEC. 2. The said Board of Missions shall consist of the Bishop, who shall be *ex officio* the President thereof; and of ten other members, one Clergyman and one Layman resident within the limits of each of the Archdeaconries hereinafter provided for, and nominated by said Archdeaconry, and one Clergyman and one Layman who

may be resident anywhere within the Diocese, and shall be nominated in open Conver
tion, all of whom shall be annually chosen by the Convention, and by ballot unles
the same be unanimously dispensed with. All vacancies occurring in the Boar
during the recess of the Convention, may be filled by the Board.

SEC. 3. The evening session of the Convention on the first day of each Annu
Meeting shall be devoted to the reception and consideration of the Report of the Boar
of Missions and of its Treasurer, the election of the Board, and other business co
nected with the subject.

SEC. 4. The Board of Missions shall meet on the day after the adjournment of th
Convention in each year, and elect a Secretary and a Treasurer. The Board ma
hold other meetings during the year, according to its own rules, and shall meet o
the day preceding the Annual Convention, to audit the accounts of the Treasure
and to adopt a report to the Convention.

SEC. 5. The Diocese shall be divided into districts called Archdeaconries, the titl
and limits of which shall be as follows: The Archdeaconry of Albany shall compri
the counties of Albany, Greene, Columbia, Schenectady, Montgomery, Fulto
Hamilton and Herkimer. The Archdeaconry of Troy shall comprise the counties
Rensselaer, Saratoga, Washington, Warren, Clinton and Essex. The Archdeacon
of the Susquehanna shall comprise the counties of Delaware, Otsego and Schohari
The Archdeaconry of Ogdensburgh shall comprise the counties of St. Lawrence a
Franklin.

SEC. 6. The Bishop shall be *ex officio* the head of each Archdeaconry. He sha
however, annually appoint an Archdeacon on the nomination of each Archdeaconr
from among the Clergy thereof, who shall be the Executive Officer of the Archde
conry. Each Archdeaconry, moreover, shall annually elect a Secretary and Treasure
who shall make annual reports to the Convention. The Archdeacon in the absen
of the Bishop shall preside at all the meetings of the Archdeaconry, and may also l
present without a vote at the meetings of the Board of Missions. He shall be charge
with the duty of visiting the Mission Stations and vacant Parishes, and, with th
consent of the Clergy in charge, the other Parishes receiving Missionary aid with
the limits of his Archdeaconry, to ascertain their condition, to give such advi
as may be required, reporting the result of his inquiries and observations to the Bisho
It shall also be his duty to stir up an increased Missionary interest and zeal, and
urge more liberal offerings for the work of Church extension. And furthermore th
Archdeacon and the Clerical and Lay Members of the Board of Missions from ea
Archdeaconry shall be an Advisory Committee of the Board, whose duty it shall be
counsel the Board as to the amount which should be expended in, and the amou
which should be raised by the Archdeaconry which they represent, and to use the
best efforts to secure the required amount of Missionary offerings from their Arc
deaconry.

SEC. 7. Each Archdeaconry shall hold two meetings a year at such places within i
boundaries as it may designate. Other meetings may be held as the Archdeacon
may order. At all meetings of the Archdeaconry every Clergyman canonically re
dent within its boundaries shall be entitled to a seat; also three Laymen from ea
Parish or Mission Station within the limits of the Archdeaconry. Each Clergym
and each Lay Delegation shall have one vote. Any number of members present a
meeting duly called shall be competent to transact business. The meetings of Arc
deaconry shall have for their main purpose the presentation of the claims of the M
sion work of the Diocese and the Church. Such Missionaries as may be membe
shall report concerning their work, and provision may be made for especial need
the Missionary work within the boundaries of the Archdeaconry. Contributions

local work shall not interfere with the claims of the Diocesan Board of Missions, and shall be reported to the Treasurer thereof, and included in his Annual Report to the Convention. It shall also be the object of these Archdeaconal meetings to bring the Clergy together in fraternal intercourse and to promote their spiritual and intellectual life. Each Archdeaconry shall make its own rules as to the arrangement of services.

Sec. 8. All Missionaries shall be appointed by the Board of Missions on the nomination of the Bishop, and may be removed with his approval. But in case of a vacancy in the Episcopate, or of the absence of the Bishop from the Diocese, or of his being otherwise unable to perform his duties, the Board of Missions shall have the power of appointing and removing Missionaries.

Sec. 9. It shall be the duty of every member of the Church in the Diocese to contribute as God hath prospered him, to the funds of the Board of Missions; and every Clergyman having Parochial or Missionary charge shall impress this duty upon his people, and cause one or more Offertories to be made annually for that object.

Sec. 10. The Treasurer of the Board of Missions shall include in his Annual Report all sums certified to him as expended in local Missionary work. He shall also receive, report and pay over any special contributions from Parishes or individuals in accordance with the instructions of the contributors.

Sec. 11. The travelling expenses of the members of the Board of Missions and of the Archdeacons, attending the meetings of the Board, shall be paid out of its treasury.

Sec. 12. Any Mission Station designated by the Board of Missions may be organized by the Bishop on the application of any residents in its neighbourhood. But such station shall not be established within the Parochial Cure of any other Minister or Ministers, without either the consent of such Minister or of a majority of such Ministers, or with the advice of the Standing Committee of the Diocese. The Bishop may appoint, upon the organization of the Mission, a Churchwarden, a Clerk, and a Treasurer, which officers shall thereafter be elected by the Congregation annually in Easter week, in the same manner as provided for the choice of Deputies to Convention by section 2, of Canon II of this Diocese. They shall, as far as possible, discharge the duties which belong to their respective offices in incorporated Parishes.

Sec. 13. The title of all property, real or personal, given or purchased for the use of any Mission Station, shall be vested in "The Board of Missions of the Protestant Episcopal Church, in the Diocese of Albany."

Canon XV.

Of the Episcopal Fund.

Section 1. The fund for the support of the Episcopate in this Diocese, now provided, together with that which may be hereafter contributed or acquired, and any accumulation accruing from the investment thereof, shall be entrusted to the Corporation, entitled "The Trustees of the Episcopal Fund of the Diocese of Albany," incorporated by an Act of the Legislature of the State of New York, passed April 28, 1869. The Trustees composing said Corporation shall be five in number, who shall be appointed by the Convention, and shall hold their offices during the pleasure thereof.

Sec. 2. All moneys belonging to the said fund shall be loaned by the said Trustees upon security of real estate, or invested in stock of the United States, or of this State, or of the city of New York, at their discretion; and all securities and investments shall be taken or made in their corporate name above mentioned, and they shall have power, from time to time, to change such investments. A statement signed by the Trustees or a majority of them, exhibiting the condition of said fund

and securities, together with the receipts and disbursements during the year, shall be reported to the Convention at every annual meeting thereof.

CANON XVI.

Of the Diocesan Fund.

SECTION 1. WHEREAS it is indispensable to provide a fund for defraying the necessary expenses of the Convention, including the expenses of those of the Clergy who may have to travel from a distance to the Convention, and also the cost of maintaining a suitable residence for the Bishop; it is hereby required of every Congregation in this Diocese to pay to the Treasurer of the Convention on or before the day of its annual meeting, a contribution at such a rate per cent upon the salary of its Clergyman as shall have been determined by the previous Convention to be required for the purposes above-mentioned.

SEC. 2. AND WHEREAS, by the Canons of the General Convention,* it is made "the duty of the several Diocesan Conventions to forward to the Treasurer of the General Convention, at or before any meeting of the General Convention, three dollars for each Clergyman within such Diocese;" therefore, it shall be the duty of the Treasurer to retain annually out of the Diocesan Fund, one dollar for each Clergyman in this Diocese, as a special fund, to be paid over to the Treasurer of the General Convention at each meeting of the same.

CANON XVII.

Of the Aged and Infirm Clergy Fund.

SECTION 1. The fund now existing, together with all contributions hereafter received for the support of Aged and Infirm Clergymen, shall be entrusted to the Corporation entitled "The Trustees of the Fund for the support of the Aged and Infirm Clergy of the Protestant Episcopal Church in the Diocese of Albany," incorporated by an Act of the Legislature of the State of New York, passed February 16, 1870. The said Trustees shall consist of the Bishop and the Treasurer of the Diocese, together with three Lay Trustees, who shall be appointed annually by the Convention. Vacancies occurring in the number of the Lay Trustees during the recess of the Convention may be filled by the remaining Trustees.

SEC. 2 It shall be the duty of the Trustees to receive applications for relief, and to administer it in accordance with such rules and regulations as they, with the approbation of the Convention, may from time to time adopt.

SEC. 3. The Trustees shall present a detailed report of their proceedings and of the condition of the fund to every Annual Convention.

CANON XVIII.

Of the Clergy Reserve Fund.

SECTION 1. A fund shall be established to be known as the Clergy Reserve Fun of the Diocese of Albany.

SEC. 2. It shall be the duty of each Parish and Mission station in the Diocese contribute one offering annually in behalf of this fund.

SEC. 3 The fund thus formed shall be permitted to accumulate until it shall amoun to $20,000, and the income shall then be divided into annuities of $300, which shall be paid to the beneficiaries of the fund.

SEC. 4. The beneficiaries of the fund shall be the Clergy of the Diocese according to the seniority of their canonical residence.

---

* Title III, Canon 1, Sec. 5.

SEC. 5. No Clergyman shall be a beneficiary of the fund whose salary or stipend exceeds $1,000 per annum. Nor shall any Clergyman receive the annuity who has allowed the Parish or Mission under his charge to neglect its annual contribution to the fund.

SEC. 6. The principal of the fund shall not be impaired.

SEC. 7. The trustees of the fund shall be the Bishop of the Diocese, the Rector of St. Peter's Church, Albany, the Rector of St. Paul's Church, Troy, the Treasurer of the Diocese, and the Lay members of the Board of Missions designated by the Archdeaconries of the Diocese. And they are hereby authorized to form a corporation under the Laws of the State of New York, whose object shall be to carry into effect the provisions of this Canon, and to provide for the receipt by the corporation so to be formed, of real and personal estate by gifts, purchase, devise, bequest or otherwise, for the purposes of said corporation.

CANON XIX.

Of the Fund for the Widows and Orphans of Deceased Clergymen.

SECTION 1. The fund now existing, together with all contributions hereafter received for the relief of widows and orphans of Deceased Clergymen shall be entrusted to the Corporation entitled "The Trustees of the Fund for the Widows and Orphans of Deceased Clergymen of the Protestant Episcopal Church in the Diocese of Albany," incorporated by an Act of the Legislature of the State of New York, passed February 16, 1870. The said Trustees shall consist of the Bishop and the Treasurer of the Diocese, together with three Lay Trustees, who shall be appointed annually by the Convention. Vacancies occurring in the number of the Lay Trustees during the recess of the Convention may be filled by the remaining Trustees.

SEC. 2. It shall be the duty of the Trustees to receive applications for relief, and to administer it in accordance with such rules and regulations as they, with the approbation of the Convention, may from time to time adopt.

SEC. 3. The Trustees shall present a detailed report of their proceedings and of the condition of the fund to every Annual Convention.

CANON XX.

Of the Trial of a Clergyman not being a Bishop.

Whenever any Minister of this Diocese, not being a Bishop thereof, shall become "liable to presentment and trial" under the provisions of any Canon of the General or Diocesan Convention, the mode of proceeding in this Diocese shall be as follows:

SECTION 1. The trial shall be on a presentment in writing, addressed to the Bishop of the Diocese, specifying the offences of which the accused is alleged to be guilty, with reasonable certainty as to time, place and circumstances. Such presentment may be made by the major part in number of the members of the Vestry of any Church of which the accused is Minister, or by any three Presbyters of this Diocese entitled to seats in the Convention, or as hereinafter mentioned. Whenever, from public rumor or otherwise, the Bishop shall have reason to believe that any Clergyman is under the imputation of having been guilty of any offence or misconduct for which he is liable to be tried, and that the interest of the Church requires an investigation, it shall be his duty to appoint five persons, of whom three at least shall be Presbyters, to examine the case; a majority of whom may make such examination; and if there is, in their opinion, sufficient ground for presentment, they shall present the Clergyman accordingly.

SEC. 2. A presentment being made in any one of the modes above prescribed, the Bishop, if the facts charged shall not appear to him to be such as constitute an of-

fence, may dismiss it; or if it allege facts, some of which do and some of which do not constitute an offence, he may allow it in part and dismiss the residue, or he may permit it to be amended. When it shall be allowed in whole or in part, the Bishop shall cause a copy of it to be served on the accused; and shall also nominate twelve Presbyters of this Diocese entitled to seats in the Convention, and not being parties to the presentment, and cause a list of their names to be served on the accused, who shall, within thirty days after such service, select five of them, and notify their names in writing to the Bishop; and if he shall not give such notification to the Bishop within the said thirty days, the Bishop shall select five: and the Presbyters so selected shall form a Board for the trial of the accused, and shall meet at such time and place as the Bishop shall direct, and shall have power to adjourn from time to time, and from place to place (but always within the Diocese), as they shall think proper.

SEC. 3. A written notice of the time and place of their first meeting shall be served, at least thirty days before such meeting, on the accused, and also on one of the persons making the presentment.

SEC. 4. If, at the time appointed for the first meeting of the Board of Presbyters, the whole number of five shall not attend, then those who do attend may adjourn from time to time; and if, after one adjournment or more, it shall appear to them improbable that the whole number will attend within a reasonable time, then those who do attend, not being less than three, shall constitute the board, and proceed to the trial, and a majority of them shall decide all questions.

SEC. 5. If a Clergyman presented shall confess the truth of the facts alleged in the presentment, and shall not demur thereto, it shall be the duty of the Bishop to proceed to pass sentence; and if he shall not confess them before the appointment of a Board for his trial, as before mentioned, he shall be considered as denying them.

SEC. 6. If a Clergyman presented, after having had due notice, shall not appear before the Board of Presbyters appointed for his trial, the Board may, nevertheless, proceed as if he were present, unless for good cause they shall see fit to adjourn to another day.

SEC. 7. When the Board proceed to the trial, they shall hear such evidence as shall be produced, which evidence shall be reduced to writing and signed by the witnesses, respectively; and some officer authorized by law to administer oaths may, at the desire of either party, be requested to administer an oath or affirmation to the witnesses, that they will testify the truth, the whole truth, and nothing but the truth, concerning the facts charged in the presentment. If, on or during the trial, the accused shall confess the truth of the charges, as stated in the presentment, the Board may dispense with hearing further evidence, and may proceed at once to state their opinion to the Bishop as to the sentence that ought to be pronounced.

SEC. 8. Upon the application of either party to the Bishop, and it being made satisfactorily to appear to him that any material witness cannot be procured upon the trial, the Bishop may appoint a Commissary to take the testimony of such witness. Such Commissary may be either a Clergyman or a Layman, and the party so applying shall give to the other at least six days' notice of the time and place of taking the testimony. If the person on whom the notice shall be served shall reside more than forty miles from the place of examination, notice of an additional day shall be given for every additional twenty miles of the said distance. Both parties may attend and examine the witness: and the questions and answers shall be reduced to writing and signed by the witness, and shall be certified by the Commissary, and enclosed under his seal, and transmitted to the Board, and shall be received by them as evidence. A witness examined before such Commissary may be sworn or affirmed in manner aforesaid.

SEC. 9. The Board, having deliberately considered the evidence, shall declare in a writing signed by them, or a majority of them, their decision on the charges contained in the presentment, distinctly stating whether the accused be guilty or not guilty of such charges, respectively, and also stating the sentence (if any) which, in their opinion, should be pronounced; and a copy of such decision shall be, without delay, communicated to the accused; and the original decision, together with the evidence, shall be delivered to the Bishop, who shall pronounce such canonical sentence as shall appear to him to be proper, provided the same shall not exceed in severity the sentence recommended by the Board; and such sentence shall be final. Before pronouncing any sentence, the Bishop shall summon the accused, and any three or more of the Clergy, to meet him at such time as may, in his opinion, be most convenient, in some Church to be designated by him, which shall, for that purpose, be open at the time to all persons who may choose to attend; and the sentence shall then and there be publicly pronounced by the Bishop. But the Bishop, if he shall be satisfied that justice requires it, may grant a new trial to the accused, in which case a new Board of Presbyters shall be appointed, the proceedings before whom shall be conducted as above mentioned.

SEC. 10. All notices and papers contemplated in this Canon may be served by a summoner or summoners, to be appointed for the purpose by the Bishop, and whose certificate of such service shall be evidence thereof. In case of service by any other person, the facts shall be proved by the affidavit of such person. A written notice or paper delivered to a party, or left at his last place of residence, shall be deemed a sufficient service of such notice or paper.

SEC. 11. The defendant may have the privilege of appearing by counsel; in case of the exercise of which privilege, and not otherwise, those who present shall also have the like privilege.

SEC. 12. If the Ecclesiastical Authority of any other Diocese shall, under the provisions of the Canons of the General Convention, or otherwise, make known to the Ecclesiastical Authority of this Diocese, charges against a Presbyter or Deacon thereof, such communication shall be a sufficient presentation of him for trial; and the trial shall take place as above provided. The Bishop shall appoint some competent person as Prosecutor, who shall be considered as the party making the presentment.

CANON XXI.

Of Differences between Ministers and their Congregations.

SECTION 1. Whenever there shall be any serious difference between the Rector of any Church in this Diocese and the Congregation thereof, it shall be lawful for a majority of the Vestry or Trustees to make a representation to the Bishop, stating the facts in the case and agreeing, for themselves and for the Congregation which they represent, to submit to his decision in the matter, and to perform whatever he may require of them by any order which he may make under the provisions of this Canon, and shall at the same time serve a copy of the representation on the Rector.

SEC. 2. It shall be the duty of the Bishop, at all stages of the proceeding, to seek to bring them to an amicable conclusion, and in such case the agreement between the parties, signed by them and attested by the Bishop, shall have the same force as an order made under section 4 of this Canon.

SEC. 3. If the matter shall not be amicably settled within a reasonable time, the Bishop shall convene the Clerical Members of the Standing Committee and shall give notice to the parties to appear before him and present their proofs and arguments at such time and place as he may appoint, and he may adjourn and continue the hearing in the matter in his discretion.

SEC. 4. When the hearing is concluded, the Bishop shall make such an order in regard to the matter as he may think to be just and for the true interests of the Church; and such order may require the Rector to resign his Rectorship, and may require the Church to pay a sum of money to the Rector; and it shall be the duty of the Rector and of the Church and every member thereof to submit to and abide by such order as the final and conclusive determination of all matters of dif. ference between them. *Provided,* that no order shall be made under this or the next succeeding section of this Canon, unless with the advice and concurrence of at least two Clerical Members of the Standing Committee, who shall have been present at the hearing.

SEC. 5. If it shall be made to appear to the Bishop that any agreement made under section 2 of this Canon, or any order made under section 4 of this Canon, or of this section, shall have been disregarded by any of the parties concerned, or if an application be made to him to modify such order, he may convene the Clerical Members of the Standing Committee, and after hearing such further proofs and arguments as may be presented to him, make such further order in the matter as he may think proper with the same effect as an order made under section 4 of this Canon.

SEC. 6. If any Church or Congregation shall persistently neglect or refuse to obey any order made under this Canon, it shall be the duty of the Bishop to exhort the members of such Congregation to submit to the authority and discipline of the Church; and if they will not do so, the Convention may proceed to dissolve the union between the Church so offending and the Convention of this Diocese, and may take such other action in the matter as it may think expedient. *Provided,* that no such action shall be held or taken to be a surrender of any right which either the Church in this Diocese, or such members of such Congregation as submit to the authority and discipline of the Church may have in the corporation of such Church, or in any property belonging thereto.

SEC. 7. Whenever the Standing Committee shall be acting as the Ecclesiastical Authority of the Diocese, the Clerical Members thereof shall perform the duties herein required of the Bishop; and they shall request the Bishop of some other Diocese to attend the hearing of the case, and shall make no order therein but with his advice and assistance.

CANON XXII.

Of Amendments of the Canons.

No new Canon or amendment of a Canon shall hereafter be adopted by the Convention, unless at least one day's previous notice thereof shall have been given in open Convention, nor, unless by unanimous consent, until the same shall have been referred to, and reported upon by a Committee of at least two Presbyters and two Laymen. All propositions to amend the Canons shall be in the form of a Canon, and such sections as shall be amended shall be re-enacted in full in their amended form.

ADMISSION OF CHURCHES.

ADVICE AND INSTRUCTIONS TO CHURCHES APPLYING FOR ADMISSION INTO UNION WITH
THE PROTESTANT EPISCOPAL CHURCH IN THE DIOCESE OF ALBANY.

Under Canon IV, in order to be admitted into union with the Church in this Diocese, the Church or congregation must (in sufficient time to allow the papers to be transmitted to, *and he received by* the Secretary of the Convention at least thirty days before the meeting of the Convention) adopt a resolution, at a legally convened and held meeting of the Vestry, or (*in the case of Churches incorporated without Vestries*), of the congregation, authorizing the application for such admission to be made, and agreeing to abide by, and conform to, and observe all the Canons of the Church, and all the rules, orders and regulations of the Convention. A copy of this resolution must be duly certified by the presiding officer of the Vestry, or of the meeting of the congregation at which the resolution was adopted, and also by the Clerk of the Vestry, or Secretary of the meeting of the congregation, and must also be authenticated by the seal of the corporation.

In Churches having Vestries, this resolution should be adopted by the Vestry. In Churches incorporated without Vestries, it should be adopted by the congregation.

The following form of resolution is recommended:

Resolved, That [*here set forth the corporate name or title by which the Church is known in law as the same is described in the Certificate of Incorporation*] desire admission into union with the Church in the Diocese of Albany, and do make application therefor to the Convention of the Church in this Diocese; and do hereby agree to abide by, and conform to, and observe all the Canons of the Church, and all the rules, orders and regulations of the Convention.

The resolution must be entered accurately and at length on the minutes of the Vestry, or of the meeting of the congregation, as the case may be.

The Canon requires an application *in writing,* to the Convention, asking admission, which must then be made out. This may be signed by the Rector (if there be one), and by one or both of the Wardens, *and* by the Clerk of the Vestry; or, in the case of Churches without Vestries, by the Minister, or by the presiding officer of the meeting at which the resolution was adopted, *and also* by the Clerk of such meeting.

The following form of application is recommended:

To the Convention of the Protestant Episcopal Church in the Diocese of Albany:

The Church or congregation duly incorporated and known in law by the name of [*here set forth the corporate name or title of the Church, as the same is described in the Certificate of Incorporation*], in pursuance, and by authority of a resolution of the [*Vestry or congregation as the case may be*] of the said Church, hereby applies for admission into union with the Church in this Diocese; and presents herewith a duly certified and authenticated copy of the resolution of the said [*Vestry or congregation, as the case may be*] adopted on the   day of   189 , authorizing such application, and agreeing to abide by, and conform to, and observe all the Canons of the Church, and all the rules, orders and regulations of the Convention. *Also,* the Certificate of Incorporation of the Church (*or in case the original certificate is not presented, then say, " a duly certified copy of the Certificate of the Incorporation of the Church*), which was duly recorded in the office of the (Clerk or Register, *as the case may be*), of the   county of   on the   day of 189 , in Book   of Certificates of Religious Incorporations, (*or whatever may be the official designation of the book in which such Certificates are recorded in the county in which such Church is located*), page . *Also*, a certificate of the Bishop that he approves of the incorporation of such Church, and that such Church, in his judgment, is duly and satisfactorily established. *And also*, evidence that not less than twenty-five persons, members of such Church, have habitually, for at least one year preceding the date of this application, attended Divine Services in such Church or congregation.

Dated at in the county of and State of New York, this day of 189 .

By order of the [*Vestry or congregation as the case may be*].

> A. B., *Rector.*
> C. D., *Warden.*
> E. F., *do.*
> G. H., *Clerk.*

Or, in case of Churches having no Vestries:

> A. B., *Minister.*
> C. D., *Presiding officer of the Meeting of the Congregation.*
> E. F., *Secretary of the Meeting of the Congregation.*

The Canon also requires that the application be accompanied by the following papers:

I. A duly certified and authenticated copy of the resolution of the Vestry or congregation authorizing the application, etc.

II. The original, or a certified copy of the Certificate of Incorporation.

III. The certificate of the Bishop's approval of the incorporation, and that, in his judgment, the Church is duly and satisfactorily established.

IV. The evidence that not less than twenty-five persons, members of such Church, have habitually, for at least one year preceding the date of the application, attended Divine Service in the Church or congregation.

The following is recommended as a form for certifying the resolution of the Vestry or of the congregation:

At a meeting of the [*Vestry or congregation, as the case may be*] of the Church or congregation known as [*here set forth the corporate name or title of the Church, as the same is described in the Certificate of Incorporation*], duly convened, and held according to law, at on the day of 18 , the following resolution was adopted.

"*Resolved*, That [*here copy, in the precise words, and at length, and accurately, resolution as adopted and entered on the Minutes.*"]

Which is hereby certified by A B., the Rector of the said Church [*or, if there no Rector, then* C. D., the Warden, who presided at the meeting of the Vestry which the resolution was adopted, there being no Rector of the said Church], also by E. F., the Clerk of the Vestry, and is also authenticated by the seal of corporation.

Dated at in the county of the day of 189 .

> A. B , *Rector*
> [*or*] C D *Warden presiding*
> E. F. *Clerk of the Vestry*

In the case of Churches having no Vestries, the certificate may be as follows:

Which is hereby certified by A. B., Minister of the Church, *or* C. D., the Presiding officer of the meeting of the congregation at which the resolution was adopted, and also by E. F., the secretary of the said meeting, and is also authenticated by the seal of the corporation.

Dated, etc. (as above).

A. B., *Minister.*
[*or*] C. D., *Presiding officer of the Meeting of the Congregation.*
E. F., *Secretary of the Meeting.*

[SEAL.]

The following is submitted (with the approval and authority of the Bishop) as the form for his certificate:

I do hereby certify, that I approve of the incorporation of a Church known as [*here set forth the corporate name or title of the Church as the same is described in the Certificate of Incorporation*], and that such Church, in my judgment, is duly and satisfactorily established.

Dated at   the   day of   in the year of our Lord one thousand eight hundred and

Bishop.

The following is recommended as a form for the presentation of the evidence of the number of persons habitually attending the Church:

We, the undersigned, do hereby certify and declare, that we are, and for one year last past have been connected with, or been members of, and well acquainted with the affairs and condition of, the Church or congregation known as [*here set forth the corporate name or title of the Church as the same is described in the Certificate of Incorporation*], and that we have had means of knowing, and do know, the number of persons habitually attending the said Church during one year past; and that not less than twenty-five persons, members of such Church, have habitually, for at least one year preceding this date, attended Divine Service in such Church or congregation.

Dated at   in the county of   the   day of 189 .

This certificate should be signed by the Rector, or officiating Minister, if there be one, and by one or both of the Wardens, or by two or more of the Trustees (in the case of a Church incorporated without a Vestry), or by other known and reputable parties who can certify to the fact set forth.

The application, together with the requisite papers (as before set forth), must be transmitted to the Secretary of the Convention, at least thirty days before the meeting of the Convention.

The Canon (Section 2, Canon IV.) expressly declares that " no application for the admission of a Church into union with the Church in this Diocese, shall be considered or acted upon at any meeting of the Convention, unless the same shall have been transmitted to the Secretary of the Convention at least thirty days before the meeting of the Convention."

DIOCESAN INSTITUTIONS.

THE SISTERHOOD OF THE HOLY CHILD JESUS.

ST. AGNES' SCHOOL, ALBANY.

THE CHILD'S HOSPITAL, ALBANY.

THE ST. MARGARET'S HOUSE, ALBANY.

THE CHURCH HOME, TROY.

THE ST. CHRISTINA HOME, SARATOGA.

THE ST. CHRISTOPHER HOME, EAST LINE.

THE ORPHAN HOUSE OF THE HOLY SAVIOUR, COOPERSTOWN.

THE BIBLE AND COMMON PRAYER BOOK SOCIETY OF ALBANY AND VICINITY.

ST. PAUL'S HALL, SALEM.

PAROCHIAL INSTITUTIONS.

ST. PETER'S ORPHANAGE, ALBANY.

THE MARTHA MEMORIAL HOUSE, TROY.

THE MARY WARREN FREE INSTITUTE, TROY.

DIOCESE OF ALBANY.

Convention Journal,
A. D., 1891.

JOURNAL OF THE PROCEEDINGS

OF THE

TWENTY-THIRD ANNUAL CONVENTION

OF THE

Protestant Episcopal Church

IN THE

DIOCESE OF ALBANY,

WHICH ASSEMBLED IN

ALL SAINTS CATHEDRAL, ALBANY, N Y.

TUESDAY, NOVEMBER 17,

A. D., 1891

ALBANY, N. Y.:

WEED, PARSONS & COMPANY, PRINTERS.

1891.

LIST OF THE CLERGY

IN THE

DIOCESE OF ALBANY

IN THE ORDER OF CANONICAL RESIDENCE

NOVEMBER 17, 1891.

Showing the dates of becoming resident, and in case of those not gaining residence by Ordination, the name of the Diocese from which each was received.

Date of Reception.	Diocese from which received.	Name.
1868. Nov. 15.	At Primary Convention.	The Rt. Rev. WILLIAM CROSWELL DOANE, D. D., *Oxon.*, LL. D., *Cantab.*, Bishop.
" "	" "	The Rev. JOSEPH CAREY, S. T. D.
" "	"	The Rev. EDGAR T. CHAPMAN.
" "	"	The Rev. JOSEPH N. MULFORD.
" "	"	The Rev. GEORGE H. NICHOLLS, S. T. D.
" "	"	The Rev. J. LIVINGSTON REESE, D. D.
" "	"	The Rev. WILLIAM S. ROWE.
" "	"	The Rev. DAVID L. SCHWARTZ.
" "	"	The Rev. JOHN B. TIBBITS, Deacon.
" "	"	The Rev. J. IRELAND TUCKER, S. T. D.
" "	" "	The Rev. ROBERT WASHBON.
" Dec. 1.	New York - - -	The Rev. JAMES WILKINS STEWART.
1869. Sept. 22.	Montreal - - -	The Rev. CHARLES H. LANCASTER.
1870. Mar. 7.	Massachusetts - -	The Rev. FENWICK M. COOKSON.
" June 12.	- - - - -	The Rev. WILLIAM CURTIS PROUT.
" Dec. 6.	Pennsylvania - - -	The Rev. JAMES CAIRD.
1871. April 12.	Montreal - - -	The Rev. J. D. MORRISON, D. D., LL. D.
" July 12.	Vermont - - -	The Rev. J. W. McILWAINE.
" Sept. 27.	New York - -	The Rev. ERASTUS WEBSTER.
" Nov. 21.	Massachusetts - -	The Rev. WILLIAM R. WOODBRIDGE.
1872. July 14.	- - - - -	The Rev. JOHN H. HOUGHTON.
1874. May 18.	New York - - -	The Rev. WILLIAM CHARLES GRUBBE.
" Aug. 3.	Western New York -	The Rev. WALTON W. BATTERSHALL, D. D.
" Sept. 17.	- - - - -	The Rev. THEODORE A. SNYDER.
" Sept. 29.	Central New York -	The Rev. MOSES E. WILSON.
" Oct. 7.	Pennsylvania - - -	The Rev. R. J. ADLER.
" Nov. 1.	- - - - -	The Rev. HENRY M. SMYTH.

Date of Reception.	Diocese from which received.	Name.
1875. Nov. 5.	New York - - -	The Rev. CHARLES C. EDMUNDS.
1876. Mar. 12.	- - - - -	The Rev. WILLIAM B. REYNOLDS, Deacon.
" Mar. 18.	New York - - -	The Rev. RICHARD TEMPLE.
" Aug. 22.	Central New York -	The Rev. WILLIAM N. IRISH.
" Sept. 26.	North Carolina - -	The Rev. WILLIAM W. LORD, D. D.
" Dec. 11.	New York - - -	The Rev. CHARLES S. OLMSTED.
1877. Jan. 24.	- - - -	The Rev. CHAS. EDWARD CRAGG, Deacon.
" Mar. 1.	Newark - - -	The Rev. ERNEST A. HARTMANN.
" May 31.	- - - -	The Rev. SCOTT B. RATHBUN.
1878. Feb. 27.	Montana - - -	The Rev. EUGENE L. TOY.
1879. Jan. 1.	Long Island - -	The Rev. THOMAS B. FULCHER, B. D.
" July 18.	- - - -	The Rev. JOHN N. MARVIN.
" July 15.	Massachusetts - -	The Rev. SILAS M. ROGERS.
1880. Mar. 29.	Connecticut - - -	The Rev. HEMAN R. TIMLOW.
" May 23.	- - - -	The Rev. JOHN PROUT.
" June 1.	- - - - -	The Rev. CHARLES C. EDMUNDS, Jr.
" Oct. 18.	Massachusetts - -	The Rev. FREDERICK H. T. HORSFIELD.
1881. Jan. 8.	Western New York -	The Rev. CHARLES M NICKERSON, D. D.
" Mar. 1.	Massachusetts - -	The Rev. THADDEUS A. SNIVELY
" Mar. 14.	Central New York -	The Rev. ROBERT GRANGER.
" Dec. 19.	New York - - -	The Rev. GEORGE DENT SILLIMAN.
1882. Jan. 9.	Newark - - -	The Rev. WILLIAM HENRY HARISON, D.D.
" Feb. 23.	Utah - - -	The Rev. R. M KIRBY
" Nov. 7.	Connecticut - -	The Rev. HOBART COOKE.
" Dec. 28.	Rhode Island - - -	The Rev. CLEMENT J WHIPPLE.
1883. Feb. 12.	Central New York -	The Rev. E. BAYARD SMITH.
" May 5.	Delaware - - -	The Rev. W G. W LEWIS.
" Oct. 31.	New York - - -	The Rev. C. P A BURNETT.
1884. Jan. 8.	Western New York -	The Rev. W. D. U. SHEARMAN.
" Jan. 20.	- - - -	The Rev. JAMES A. DICKSON.
" Feb. 13.	Fredericton - - -	The Rev. FREDERICK B. SILL.
" Mar. 4.	Ohio - - -	The Rev. SAMUEL T STREET.
" May 27.	Newark - - -	The Rev. CHARLES PELLETREAU.
" June 3.	- - - -	The Rev. EDWARD S. DeG. TOMPKINS.
" June 9.	- - - - -	The Rev. DAVID SPRAGUE.
" July 12.	- - - -	The Rev. RUSSELL WOODMAN.
1885. Jan. 10.	Springfield - - -	The Rev. JAMES E. HALL.
" Mar. 16.	Exeter, England - -	The Rev. THOMAS H. R. LUNEY.
" May 1.	Central Pennsylvania -	The Rev. J. PHILIP B. PENDLETON, S.T.B.
" May 30.	- - - -	The Rev. CHARLES TEMPLE.
" May 31.	- - - -	The Rev. SHELDON M. GRISWOLD.
" Aug. 6.	Maine - - -	The Rev. RICHMOND SHREVE, D. D.
" Oct. 10.	- - - -	The Rev. EDWARD DUDLEY TIBBITS.
" Nov. 5.	Wisconsin - - -	The Rev. LOUIS HECTOR SCHUBERT.
" Dec. 18.	Connecticut - - -	The Rev. EATON W. MAXCY, D. D.
1886. Mar. 8.	Western New York -	The Rev. WILLIAM B. BOLMER.
" June 7.	Massachusetts - - -	The Rev. JAMES O. LINCOLN.
" Aug. 2.	Iowa - - -	The Rev. NASSAU W. STEPHENS.
" Sept. 24.	Yedo - - -	The Rev. CLEMENT THEOPHILUS BLANCHET.
" Nov. 13.	Central Pennsylvania -	The Rev. DANIEL WASHBURN.
1887. Jan. 15.	Connecticut - -	The Rev. FRANK B. REAZOR.
" Feb. 12.	- - - -	The Rev. JOSEPH T. ZORN.
" May 19.	Connecticut - -	The Rev. EDGAR A. ENOS.
" Aug. 1.	New York - - -	The Rev. CHARLES E. FREEMAN
" Aug. 1.	New York - - -	The Rev. WILLIAM ROLLINS WEBB.
" Sept. 24.	New York - - -	The Rev. J. FREDERICK ESCH.
" Nov. 5.	Massachusetts - -	The Rev. WILFORD LASH ROBBINS, D. D.
1888. Jan. 20.	Southern Ohio - -	The Rev. HENRY T. GREGORY.
" Jan. 28.	New Hampshire - -	The Rev. FREDERICK MORLAND GRAY.
" May 18.	Pittsburgh - - -	The Rev. WILLIAM MASON COOK, S. T. B.
" May 20.	- - - -	The Rev. GEORGE MERIWETHER IRISH.
" May 22.	Springfield - - -	The Rev. THOMAS WHITE.

Date of Reception.	Diocese from which received.	Name.
1888. Sept. 3.	Tennessee - - -	The Rev. ALFRED TAYLOR.
" Oct. 7.	- - - -	The Rev. WALTER CHARLES STEWART.
" Nov. 20.	Nova Scotia - -	The Rev. ANGUS C. MACDONALD.
" Nov. 20.	Pennsylvania - - -	The Rev. CHARLES W. BOYD, Deacon.
" Dec. 21.	- - - -	The Rev. FREDERICK G. RAINEY.
1889. Jan. 14.	New Hampshire - -	The Rev. ISAAC PECK.
" Jan. 21.	New Jersey - -	The Rev. THOMAS DICKINSON.
" Mar. 8.	Maine - - -	The Rev. WILLIAM DICKINSON MARTIN.
" April 15.	Maine - - - -	The Rev. ROBERT N. PARKE, D. D.
" June 16.	- - - -	The Rev. ELMER PLINY MILLER.
" June 16.	- - - -	The Rev. MEREDITH OGDEN SMITH, Deacon.
" Sept. 23.	New York - -	The Rev. JOHN McCARTHY WINDSOR.
" Sept. 23.	Springfield - - -	The Rev. HOWARD McDOUGALL.
" Oct. 31.	Missouri - - -	The Rev. E. W. FLOWER.
" Nov. 1.	New York - -	The Rev. WALTER HASKINS LAROM.
" Dec. 27.	Easton - - -	The Rev. A. T. DeLEARSY.
1890. Jan. 10.	East Carolina - -	The Rev. FREDERICK NASH SKINNER.
" Feb. 5.	Western New York -	The Rev. E. RUTHVEN ARMSTRONG.
" Mar. 14.	Massachusetts - -	The Rev. ERNEST MARIETT.
" April 25.	New Jersey - -	The Rev. HARRIS COX RUSH.
" May 8.	Rochester, England -	The Rev. S. C. THOMPSON.
" June 4.	- - - -	The Rev. ASA SPRAGUE ASHLEY.
" June 7.	- - - -	The Rev. FREDERICK STIRLING GRIFFIN.
" June 7.	Central New York -	The Rev. CHAUNCEY VIBBARD, Jr.
" July 20.	Frederickton - -	The Rev. CHARLES H. HATHEWAY.
" Sept. 24.	Vermont - - - -	The Rev. FREDERICK SHUBALL FISHER.
" Oct. 13.	New York - - -	The Rev. WILLIAM HENRY BOWN.
" Nov. 1.	Durham, England .	The Rev. REYNER EDWARD WILLIAM COSENS.
" Nov. 8.	Colorado - - -	The Rev. PHINEAS DURYEA.
1891. Jan. 8.	Montreal - - -	The Rev. HERBERT LUTHER WOOD.
" Jan. 22.	Quebec - - -	The Rev. ROBERT WYNDHAM BROWN.
" April 26.	- - - -	The Rev. EUGENE GRIGGS.
" May 5.	New Jersey - -	The Rev. ARTHUR LOWNDES.
" May 8.	Minnesota - -	The Rev. RICHMOND H. GESNER.
" May 19.	Southern Ohio - -	The Rev. WILLIAM H. GOODISSON.
" June 3.	- - - -	The Rev. FREEBORN GARRETTSON JEWETT, Jr., Deacon.
" June 14.	- - - -	The Rev. JAMES FREDERIC OLMSTED, Deacon.
" July 9.	Vermont - - -	The Rev. CLARENCE MORTIMER CONANT, M. D.
" Aug. 13.	Connecticut - -	The Rev. CLARENCE ERNEST BALL.
" Sept. 10.	- - - -	The Rev. GEORGE LYNDE RICHARDSON, Deacon.
" Oct. 15.	Milwaukee - - -	Th Rev. GEORGE G. CARTER, S. T. D.
" Oct. 19.	Connecticut - -	The Rev. GEORGE BRINCKERHOFF RICHARDS, Deacon.
" Oct. 28.	- - - -	The Rev. HARRY ELMER GILCHRIST, Deacon.
" Nov. 8.	- - - -	The Rev. JOHN G. URLING, L. Th., Deacon.
" Nov. 15.	New York - - -	The Rev. GEORGE B. JOHNSON.

AN ALPHABETICAL LIST OF THE CLERGY.

The Right Rev. WILLIAM CROSWELL DOANE, D. D., *Oxon.*, LL. D., *Cantab.*, Bishop, Albany.

The Rev. R. J. ADLER, Rector, St. Mark's Church, Green Island, Albany county.

The Rev. E. RUTHVEN ARMSTRONG, Rector, Zion Church, Sandy Hill, Washington county.

The Rev. ASA SPRAGUE ASHLEY, Providence, R. I.

The Rev. CLARENCE ERNEST BALL, Missionary, Church of the Good Shepherd, Canajoharie, and Church of the Holy Cross, Fort Plain, Montgomery county.

* The Rev. WALTON W. BATTERSHALL, D. D., Rector, St. Peter's Church, Albany, Albany county.

The Rev. CLEMENT T. BLANCHET, Missionary, St. Sacrament Church, Bolton, Warren county.

The Rev. W. B. BOLMER, Rector, St. Luke's Church, Troy, Rensselaer county.

The Rev. WILLIAM HENRY BOWN, Rector, Grace Church, Albany, Albany county.

The Rev. CHARLES W. BOYD, Missionary, St. Paul's Church, Greenwich, Washington county.

The Rev. ROBERT WYNDHAM BROWN, Rector, St. Peter's Church, Brushton, and Missionary, St. Mark's Church, West Bangor, Franklin county, and St. Thomas' Church, Lawrenceville, St. Lawrence county.

* The Rev. C. P. A. BURNETT, Missionary, Christ Church, Gloversville, Fulton county.

The Rev. JAMES CAIRD, Rector, Free Church of the Ascension, Troy, Rensselaer county.

* The Rev. JOSEPH CAREY, S. T. D., Rector, Bethesda Church, Saratoga Springs, Saratoga county.

The Rev. GEORGE G. CARTER, S. T. D., Rector, All Saints' Church, Hudson, and Trinity Church, Claverack, and Missionary, Columbia county.

* The Rev. EDGAR T. CHAPMAN, Canon and Treasurer, Cathedral of All Saints, Albany; Priest in charge, St. Margaret's Mission, Menands Station. P. O., Troy road, Albany.

The Rev. CLARENCE MORTIMER CONANT, M. D., Missionary, Church of the Holy Name, Boyntonville, Rensselaer county.

* The Rev. WILLIAM MASON COOK, S. T. B., Rector, St. Augustine's Church, Ilion, Herkimer county.

The Rev. HOBART COOKE, Rector, Trinity Church, Plattsburgh, Clinton county.

* The Rev. FENWICK M. COOKSON, Rector, Church of the Messiah, Glen's Falls, Warren county.

The Rev. *Reyner Edward William Cosens*, Rector, Trinity Church, Whitehall, Washington county.

The Rev. CHARLES EDWARD CRAGG, Assistant Minister, Christ Church, Port Henry, Essex county.

* The Rev. *A. T. DeLearsy*, Bellevue, Ohio.

The Rev. *Thomas Dickinson*.

The Rev. JAMES A. DICKSON, Rector, Trinity Church, Gouverneur, and Missionary, St. Lawrence county.

* The Rev. *Phineas Duryea*.

* The Rev. CHARLES C. EDMUNDS, Missionary, Zion Church, Fonda, Montgomery county. P. O., Johnstown, Fulton county.

* The Rev. CHARLES C. EDMUNDS, Jr., Rector, Christ Church, Herkimer, Herkimer county.

The Rev. EDGAR A. ENOS, Rector, St. Paul's Church, Troy, Rensselaer county.

The Rev. *John Frederick Esch*, Rector, St. Stephen's Church, Schuylerville, Saratoga county.

* The Rev. FREDERICK S. FISHER, Rector, Christ Church, Deposit, and Missionary, Delaware county.

The Rev. E. W. FLOWER, Rector, Christ Church, Duanesburgh, Schenectady county.

* The Rev. CHARLES E. FREEMAN, Rector, Grace Church, Waterford, Saratoga county.

* The Rev. THOMAS B. FULCHER, B. D., Canon and Precentor, Cathedral of All Saints, Albany, Albany county.

The Rev. HARRY ELMER GILCHRIST, Missionary, Church of the Holy Spirit, Schenevus, Otsego county.

* The Rev. RICHMOND H. GESNER, Rector, Zion Church, Morris, Otsego county.

The Rev. WILLIAM H. GOODISSON, Rector, St. Paul's Church, Franklin, and Missionary, Delaware county.

The Rev. ROBERT GRANGER, Rector, St. John's Church, Richfield Springs, Otsego county.

The Rev. FREDERICK MORLAND GRAY, Honorary Canon, Cathedral of All Saints, and Chaplain, St. Agnes' School, Albany, Albany county.

The Rev. HENRY T. GREGORY, Rector, Church of the Cross, Ticonderoga, and Missionary, Essex county.

* The Rev. FREDERICK STIRLING GRIFFIN, Missionary, St. Paul's Church, Sidney, Delaware county, Christ Church, West Burlington, and at Edmeston, Otsego county.

The Rev. EUGENE GRIGGS, Rector, St. Peter's Church, Hobart, Delaware county.

* The Rev. SHELDON M. GRISWOLD, Rector, Christ Church, Hudson, Columbia county.

The Rev. WILLIAM CHARLES GRUBBE, Rector, Gloria Dei Church, Palenville, and Missionary, Greene county.

* The Rev. JAMES E. HALL, Rector, Grace Church, Cherry Valley, Otsego county.

* The Rev. *William Henry Harison*, D. D., Ogdensburgh, N. Y.

* The Rev. ERNEST A. HARTMANN, Rector, St. James' Church, Oneonta, Otsego county.

The Rev. CHARLES H. HATHEWAY, Honorary Canon, Cathedral of All Saints, Albany, also Missionary, St. Andrew's Church, West Troy, Albany county, and St. Giles', Castleton, Rensselaer county.

* The Rev. FREDERICK H. T. HORSFIELD, Rector, St. Luke's Church, Cambridge, Washington county.

* The Rev. JOHN H. HOUGHTON, Rector, Rexleigh School, Salem, Washington county.

* The Rev. GEORGE M. IRISH, Rector, Zion Church, Colton, St. Lawrence county.

The Rev. WILLIAM N. IRISH, Rector, St. John's Church, Essex, and Missionary, Essex county.

The Rev. FREEBORN GARRETTSON JEWETT, Jr., Assistant Minister, St. Paul's Church, Albany, Albany county.

The Rev. GEORGE B. JOHNSON, Rector, Church of Our Saviour, Lebanon Springs, and Missionary, Columbia county.

* The Rev. R. M. KIRBY, D. D., Rector, Trinity Church, Potsdam, St. Lawrence county.

The Rev. *Charles H. Lancaster*, Priest in charge, Trinity Church, Granville, and at North Granville, Washington county.

The Rev. WALTER HASKINS LAROM, Missionary, Church of St. Luke the Beloved Physician, Saranac Lake, and St. John's in the Wilderness, St. Regis Lake, Franklin county, and Good Shepherd, Bloomingdale, Essex county.

The Rev. WILLIAM G. W. LEWIS, Rector, Immanuel Church, Otego, and Missionary, Otsego county.

The Rev. *James O. Lincoln*, Topeka, Kansas.

The Rev. *William W. Lord*, D. D., Cooperstown, Otsego county.

The Rev. ARTHUR LOWNDES, Rector, St. Mark's Church, Philmont, and Missionary, Columbia county.

The Rev. THOMAS H. R. LUNEY, Officiating, All Saints' Church, Hoosac, Rensselaer county.

The Rev. ANGUS C. MACDONALD, Rector, St. Paul's Church, Waddington, and Missionary, St. Luke's Church, Lisbon, St. Lawrence county.

* The Rev. HOWARD McDOUGALL, Missionary, St. John's Church, Massena, and Grace Church, Louisville Landing, St. Lawrence county, and St. James', Hogansburgh, Franklin county.

The Rev. J. W. McILWAINE, Rector, St. James' Church, Fort Edward, Washington county.

The Rev. ERNEST MARIETT, Rector, Emmanuel Church, Little Falls, Herkimer county.

The Rev. *William Dickinson Martin*, Anniston, Ala.

The Rev. JOHN N. MARVIN, Rector, St. John's Church, Johnstown, Fulton county.

The Rev. EATON W. MAXCY, D. D., Rector, Christ Church, Troy, Rensselaer county.

* The Rev. ELMER P. MILLER, Rector, St. Luke's Church, Catskill, Columbia county.

The Rev. J. D. MORRISON, D. D., LL. D., Rector, St. John's Church, Ogdensburgh, St. Lawrence county.

The Rev. *Joseph N. Mulford*, Lake Worth, Florida.

The Rev. *George H. Nicholls*, S. T. D., Rector Emeritus, St. Mark's Church, Hoosick Falls, Rensselaer county.

* The Rev. CHARLES M. NICKERSON, D. D., Rector, Trinity Church, Lansingburgh, Rensselaer county.

* The Rev. CHARLES S. OLMSTED, Rector, Christ Church, Cooperstown, Otsego county.

* The Rev. JAMES FREDERIC OLMSTED, Newburgh, N. Y.

* The Rev. ROBERT N. PARKE, D. D., Rector, St. Matthew's Church, Unadilla, Otsego county,

The Rev. ISAAC PECK, Rector, St. Paul's Church, Kinderhook, and Missionary, St. Luke's Mission, Chatham, Columbia county.

* The Rev. CHARLES PELLETREAU, Rector, Christ Church, Ballston Spa, Saratoga county.

* The Rev. J. PHILIP B. PENDLETON, S. T. B., Rector, St. George's Church, Schenectady, Schenectady county.

* The Rev. JOHN PROUT, Rector, St. Paul's Church, East Springfield, and Missionary, Otsego county.

* The Rev. WILLIAM C. PROUT, Rector, Christ Church, Schenectady, Schenectady county.

The Rev. FREDERICK G. RAINEY, Rector, St. Barnabas' Church, Stottville, Columbia county.

* The Rev. *Scott B. Rathbun*, Flat Rock, N. C.

* The Rev. *Frank B. Reazor*, Orange, N. J.

The Rev. *J. Livingston Reese*, D. D., Rector, St. Paul's Church, Albany, Albany county.

The Rev. WILLIAM B. REYNOLDS, Assistant Minister, Church of St. John the Evangelist, Stockport, Columbia county.

The Rev. GEORGE BRINCKERHOFF RICHARDS, Assistant Minister, St. Peter's Church, Albany, Albany county.

The Rev. *George Lynde Richardson*, Faribault, Minnesota.

The Rev. WILFORD LASH ROBBINS, D. D., Dean, Cathedral of All Saints, Albany, Albany county.

The Rev. SILAS M. ROGERS, Rector, St. Peter's Church, Ellenburgh, and St. Paul's Church, Ellenburgh Centre, and Missionary, Clinton county.

The Rev. *William S. Rowe.*

* The Rev. HARRIS COX RUSH, Rector, St. Paul's Church, Salem, Washington county.

The Rev. *Louis H. Schubert*, Coxsackie, N. Y.

* The Rev. *David L. Schwartz.*

* The Rev. W. D. U. SHEARMAN, Rector, St. John's Church, Champlain, and Missionary, Clinton county.

The Rev. RICHMOND SHREVE, D. D., Rector, Church of the Holy Innocents, Albany, Albany county.

* The Rev. FREDERICK S. SILL, Rector, St. John's Church, Cohoes, Albany county.

* The Rev. GEORGE D. SILLIMAN, Rector, St. Mark's Church, Hoosick Falls, Rensselaer county.

* The Rev. *Frederick Nash Skinner*, Wilmington, N. C.

* The Rev. E. BAYARD SMITH, Rector, Trinity Church, West Troy, Albany county.

* The Rev. *Meredith Ogden Smith*, Nashville, Tennessee.

The Rev. HENRY M. SMYTH, New York city.

The Rev. THADDEUS A. SNIVELY, Rector, St. John's Church, Troy, Rensselaer county.

The Rev. THEODORE A. SNYDER, Rector, Christ Church, Greenville, and St. Paul's. Church, Oak Hill, Greene county.

* The Rev. DAVID SPRAGUE, Rector, St. Ann's Church, Amsterdam, Montgomery county.

The Rev. *Nassau W. Stephens*, Boonton, N. J.

* The Rev. JAMES WILKINS STEWART, Rector, Trinity Church, Athens, and Missionary, Greene county,

The Rev. WALTER CHARLES STEWART, Honorary Canon, Cathedral of All Saints, Diocesan Missionary. P. O. Albany.

The Rev. SAMUEL T. STREET, Missionary, Trinity Church, Schaghticoke, Rensselaer county.

The Rev. ALFRED TAYLOR, Missionary, Church of the Good Shepherd, Chestertown, Warren county.

*The Rev. CHARLES TEMPLE, S. T. B., Rector, St. Mark's Church, Malone, Franklin county.

The Rev. RICHARD TEMPLE, Honorary Canon, Cathedral of All Saints, Albany, Albany county.

The Rev. S. C. THOMPSON, Assistant Minister, Trinity Church, Rensselaerville, Albany county.

* The Rev. EDWARD DUDLEY TIBBITS, Rector, All Saints' Church, Hoosac, Priest in charge, Church of the Holy Name, Boyntonville, Rensselaer county, Honorary Canon, Cathedral of All Saints.

The Rev. John B. *Tibbits*, Officiating, All Saints' Church, Hoosac, Rensselaer county.

The Rev. HEMAN R. TIMLOW, Rector, Calvary Church, Burnt Hills, and St. Paul's Church, Charlton, and Missionary, Saratoga county.

The Rev EDWARD S. DeG. TOMPKINS, Kinderhook, Columbia county.

* The Rev. EUGENE L. TOY, Rector, Church of St. John the Evangelist, Stockport, Columbia county.

* The Rev. JOHN IRELAND TUCKER, S. T. D., Pastor, Church of the Holy Cross, and Principal of the Warren Free Institute, Troy, Rensselaer county.

The Rev. *John G. Urling*, L. Th., Lexington, Ky.

The Rev. CHAUNCEY VIBBARD, Jr., Rector, Calvary Church, Cairo, Greene county.

* The Rev. ROBERT WASHBON, Rector, Trinity Church, Rensselaerville, and Missionary, Berne and Westerlo, Albany county.

The Rev. DANIEL WASHBURN, Maple Grove, Otsego county.

* The Rev. *William Rollins Webb*, Baltimore, Md.

The Rev. *Erastus Webster*, Acra, Greene county.

* The Rev. CLEMENT J. WHIPPLE, Rector, St. Mary's Church, Luzerne, Warren county, and Missionary, St. John's Church, Conklingville, Saratoga county.

* The Rev. THOMAS WHITE, Missionary, Church of the Epiphany, Bath, Rensselaer county.

The Rev. *Moses E. Wilson*, Rector, St. Luke's Church, Clermont, and Missionary, Columbia county.

The Rev. *John M. Windsor*, Tuxedo, N. Y.

The Rev. HERBERT LUTHER WOOD, Rector, Christ Church, Rouse's Point, and Missionary, Clinton county.

The Rev. WILLIAM R. WOODBRIDGE, Rector, Christ Church, Port Henry, and Missionary, Emmanuel Mission, Mineville, Essex county.

The Rev. RUSSELL WOODMAN, Rector, Trinity Church, Albany, Albany county.

The Rev. JOSEPH T. ZORN, Missionary, Christ Church, Morristown, St. Lawrence county.

I certify the above to be a correct list of the clergy canonically resident in the Diocese of Albany.

WM. CROSWELL DOANE,
Bishop.

ALBANY, *November* 17, 1891.

LIST OF LAY DEPUTIES.

The names of those who were not known to be present are printed in *italics*.

County.	Church.	Deputies.
Albany	Cathedral of All Saints	Gen. Selden E. Marvin.
		Oscar L. Hascy.
		Charles J. Oaks.
	St. Peter's, Albany	F. E. Griswold.
		John T. Perry.
		Charles L. Pruyn.
	Trinity, Rensselaerville	John L. Rice.
		Nathaniel Teed.
		Charles B. Cross.
	St. Paul's, Albany	Andrew B. Jones.
		Harvey J. Cady.
		Ira Porter, Jr.
	St. John's, Cohoes	Michael Andrae.
		John Horrocks.
		George F. Ford.
	Trinity, West Troy	William Hollands.
		John H. Hulsapple.
		Robert Trimble.
	Trinity, Albany	*George F. Granger.*
		Nordine T. Johnson.
		J. Henry Marlow.
	Grace, Albany	Benjamin F. Hinman.
		Charles W. White.
		Frank J. Smith.
	Holy Innocents, Albany	S. M. Van Santvoord.
		James Oswald.
		Henry S. McCall, Jr.
	St. Mark's, Green Island	Richard Leonard.
		William W. Butler.
		Robert W. Porter.
Clinton	Trinity, Plattsburgh	*E. T. Gilliland.*
		John C. Smith.
		W. A. Drowne.
Columbia	Christ, Hudson	John M. Pearson.
		Charles W. Bostwick.
		Clarence L. Crofts.
	St. John's, Stockport	*Leonard J. Rossman.*
		William H. Van de Carr.
		Joshua Reynolds.
	St. Paul's, Kinderhook	H. S. Wynkoop.
		E. P. Van Alstyne.
		W. H. Fisk.
	Trinity, Claverack	*Cornelius Shaw.*
		Frank P. Studley.
		J. J. Studley.
	All Saints', Hudson	William H. Cookson.
		Richard A. Aitkin.
		Alexander R. Benson.
	Our Saviour, Lebanon Spg's.	Charles E. Wackerhagen
		J. Harry Cox.

County.	Church.	Deputies.
Columbia	St. Barnabas', Stottville	Richard H. Harder, Jr.
		Frederick H. Welch.
		John J. Plass.
Delaware	Christ, Walton	David H. Gay.
		Horace E. North.
		Joseph Harby.
	St. Paul's, Franklin	*George Copeland.*
		Jay W. Cook.
		E. P. Howe.
	Christ, Deposit	*William H. Gregory, M. D.*
		Titus M. Bixby.
		James McDonald.
Essex	Of the Cross, Ticonderoga	M. C. Drake.
		S. S. Paige.
	St. Paul's, Keeseville	*Asa Pierce Hammond, M. D.*
		Henry Dundas.
		Francis Cassidy.
	Christ, Port Henry	*Frank S. Atwell.*
		William M. J. Botham.
		Charles W. Woodford.
Fulton	St. John's, Johnstown	Thomas E. Ricketts.
		James I. Younglove.
		Fred Linus Carroll.
Greene	St. Luke's, Catskill	John H. Bagley.
		Walton Van Loan.
		Henry T. Jones.
	Trinity, Athens	*Samuel H. Nichols.*
		Robert Cleet.
		Frank Van Schaaick.
	St. Paul's, Oak Hill	*Walter S. Cheritree.*
		Charles A. Hall.
		Ambrose H. Flower.
	Christ, Greenville	*E. N. Palmer.*
		W. S. Rundle.
		Byron Waldron.
	Calvary, Cairo	*Levi K. Byington.*
		John C. Lennon.
		Edwin E. Darby.
Herkimer	Trinity, Fairfield	*Reuben Neely.*
		C. W. Nichols, M. D.
	Christ, Herkimer	Robert Earl.
		J. D. Henderson.
		W. C. Prescott.
	St. Augustine's, Ilion	Geo. P. Rix.
		Walter C. Rix.
		J. L. Osgood.
	Grace, Mohawk	A. W. Haslehurst.
		D. J. Fitch, M. D.
		Frank L. Van Dusen.
Montgomery	St. Ann's, Amsterdam	H. B. Waldron.
		W. Max Reid.
		Geo. De Hart.
	Zion, Fonda	Richard H. Cushney.
		Giles H. F. Van Horne.
		Henry T. E. Brower.
Otsego	Zion, Morris	T. O. Duroe.
		Isaac Mansfield.
		J. Rutherford Morris.
	St. Matthew's, Unadilla	George B. Fellows.
		William J. Thompson.
		Andrew J. Lewis.
	Christ, Cooperstown	G. Pomeroy Keese.
		Horace M. Hooker.
		Simeon E. Crittenden.

2

County.	Church.	Deputies.
Otsego	Christ, Butternuts	*Thomas Swinyard.*
		Ira L. Ward.
		Charles V. Daniels.
	Immanuel, Otego	*Charles Blake.*
		James S. Cossaart, M. D.
		C. Bennett Woodruff.
	Grace, Cherry Valley	A. B. Cox.
		Wm. C. Roseboom.
		Fred. P. Harriott.
	St. Paul's, E. Springfield	G. Hyde Clarke.
		H. L. Wardwell.
		James H. Cooke.
	St. James', Oneonta	*James Stewart.*
		R. M. Townsend.
		Richard Downes.
Rensselaer.	St. Paul's, Troy	Joseph J. Tillinghast.
		John I. Thompson.
		Henry B. Dauchy.
	Trinity, Lansingburgh	James McQuide.
		Peter B. King.
		George F. Nichols.
	St. John's, Troy	Norman B. Squires.
		Benjamin H. Hall.
		Francis N. Mann.
	Christ, Troy	Hon. William Kemp.
		Dr. Washington Akin
		J. W. A. Cluett.
	St. Mark's, Hoosick Falls	John G. Darroch.
		Geo. B. Pattison.
		James Russell Parsons, Jr
	Trinity, Schaghticoke	*Thomas L. Doremus.*
		William H. Hawkins.
		Edward Searls.
	Messiah, Greenbush	*William H. Terrell*
		Alfred L. Curtis.
		Harry E. Cole.
	St. Luke's, Troy	*James Wood.*
		Thomas B. Iler.
		Henry E. Darby.
St. Lawrence.	St. John's, Ogdensburgh	*Charles Ashley.*
		Louis Hasbrouck.
		Levi Hasbrouck.
	Christ, Morristown	*Joseph Couper.*
		Asa L. Palmer.
		E. H. Miller.
	Trinity, Potsdam	*T. Streatfeild Clarkson.*
		E. W. Foster.
		C. O. Tappan.
	Trinity, Gouverneur	Aaron B. Cutting.
		Edward D. Barry.
	Zion, Colton	*Thomas S. Clarkson.*
		Myron E. Howard.
		Frederick Horton.
Saratoga	Christ, Ballston Spa	John H. Westcot.
		Andrew S. Booth.
		Charles M. Brown.
	St. Paul's, Charlton	John Marvin.
		George O. Valentine.
		William Taylor.
	Grace, Waterford	*Roland H. Stubbs.*
		John H. Meeker.
		Henry S. Tracy.
	Bethesda, Saratoga Springs	William A. Sackett.
		Spencer Trask.
		William B. Husetis.

County.	Church.	Deputies.
Saratoga..............	Calvary, Burnt Hills........	John Colton, M. D.
		Garret Uavert.
		Peter N. Banta.
Schenectady..........	Christ, Duanesburgh........	James D. Featherstonhaugh.
		Ralph W. McDougall.
		George Matthews.
	St. George's, Schenectady...	Abram A. Van Vorst.
		John Keyes Paige.
		Charles S. Washburn.
	Christ, Schenectady	Prof. Sidney G. Ashmore.
		Edward E. Kriegsman.
		Robert J. English.
Warren	Messiah, Glen's Falls.......	William A. Wait.
		Nelson La Salle.
		James A. Holden.
	Holy Cross, Warrensburgh..	Henry Griffing.
		Thomas J. Smith.
		Emerson S. Crandall.
	St. Mary's, Luzerne........	John S. Burneson.
		H. J. Martine.
		W. J. Kinnear.
Washington	Zion, Sandy Hill...........	Charles Hamilton Beach.
		John William Wait.
		Albert Mott, M. D.
	Trinity, Granville.........	Palmer D. Everts.
		Orville L. Goodrich.
		John S. Warren.
	St. James', Fort Edward....	Francis B. Davis.
		Benjamin M. Tasker.
		John J. Morgan.
	St. Paul's, Salem.	James Gibson.
		George B. McCartee.
		George B. Martin.
	St. Luke's, Cambridge......	Henry C. Day.
		J. Fennimore Niver, M. D.
		Robert Davis, Jr.

DIOCESE OF ALBANY.

RULES OF ORDER.

1. After the administration of the Holy Communion, the President shall take the chair, and call the Convention to order.

2. If the President *ex officio* is not present at the opening of the Convention, the Secretary of the last Convention shall call the Convention to order, when the Presbyter, senior by ordination, present, shall take the chair; and in such case, immediately after the organization of the Convention, a President shall be elected from among the clergy.

3. When the President takes the chair, no member shall continue standing, or shall afterward stand, unless to address the Chair.

ORDER OF BUSINESS.
FIRST DAY.

4. After the Convention is called to order, the roll of the clergy and of the parishes entitled to representation shall be called by the Secretary of the last Convention; the certificates of the lay deputies, as presented, being referred to a committee consisting of the Secretary and two members appointed by the President. If a quorum of twenty clergy and a representation of twenty parishes be present, the President shall declare the Convention duly organized.

5. The first business shall be the election of a Secretary, a Treasurer, and a Registrar. The Secretary may appoint one or more Assistant Secretaries, announcing their names to the Convention.

6. Notices, resolutions, motions and other miscellaneous business shall then be in order.

7. The following committees shall be appointed by the President:

    A. On the Admission of Parishes into Union with the Convention.

    B. On the Constitution and Canons.

    C. On the Treasurer's Accounts.

    D. On the Diocesan Fund and Mileage of the Clergy.

    E. On Diocesan Missions.

    F. On the Bishop's Salary and the Episcopal Fund.

    G. On the Fund for the Widows and Orphans of Deceased Clergymen.

    H. On the Aged and Infirm Clergy Fund.

    I. On the General Theological Seminary.

    J. On the Society for Promoting Religion and Learning.

    K. On unfinished business.

    L. On non-reporting Clergy and Parishes.

8. Business for these committees shall be received in the following order:

    A. Report of the Treasurer.

    B. Report of the Board of Diocesan Missions.

    C. Report of the Trustees of the Episcopal Fund and of the Bishop's Salary.

DIOCESE OF ALBANY.

RULES OF ORDER.

1. After the administration of the Holy Communion, the President shall take the chair, and call the Convention to order.

2. If the President *ex officio* is not present at the opening of the Convention, the Secretary of the last Convention shall call the Convention to order, when the Presbyter, senior by ordination, present, shall take the chair; and in such case, immediately after the organization of the Convention, a President shall be elected from among the clergy.

3. When the President takes the chair, no member shall continue standing, or shall afterward stand, unless to address the Chair.

ORDER OF BUSINESS.
FIRST DAY.

4. After the Convention is called to order, the roll of the clergy and of the parishes entitled to representation shall be called by the Secretary of the last Convention; the certificates of the lay deputies, as presented, being referred to a committee consisting of the Secretary and two members appointed by the President. If a quorum of twenty clergy and a representation of twenty parishes be present, the President shall declare the Convention duly organized.

5. The first business shall be the election of a Secretary, a Treasurer, and a Registrar. The Secretary may appoint one or more Assistant Secretaries, announcing their names to the Convention.

6. Notices, resolutions, motions and other miscellaneous business shall then be in order.

7. The following committees shall be appointed by the President:
    A. On the Admission of Parishes into Union with the Convention.
    B. On the Constitution and Canons.
    C. On the Treasurer's Accounts.
    D. On the Diocesan Fund and Mileage of the Clergy.
    E. On Diocesan Missions.
    F. On the Bishop's Salary and the Episcopal Fund.
    G. On the Fund for the Widows and Orphans of Deceased Clergymen.
    H. On the Aged and Infirm Clergy Fund.
    I. On the General Theological Seminary.
    J. On the Society for Promoting Religion and Learning.
    K. On unfinished business.
    L. On non-reporting Clergy and Parishes.

8. Business for these committees shall be received in the following order:
    A. Report of the Treasurer.
    B. Report of the Board of Diocesan Missions.
    C. Report of the Trustees of the Episcopal Fund and of the Bishop's Salary.

D. Report of the Trustees of the Fund for the Widows and Orphans of Deceased Clergymen, and the Treasurer of the same.

E. Report of the Trustees of the Aged and Infirm Clergy Fund, and the Treasurer of the same.

F. Report of the Society for Promoting Religion and Learning.

These reports, and those mentioned in the next rule, shall be referred to the appropriate committees, and shall not be read until such committees be ready to report upon them.

9. A. Report of the Committee on Applications of Parishes for Admission.

B. Report of the Secretary of the Convention.

C. Report of the Standing Committee of the Diocese.

D. Report of the Registrar of the Diocese.

E. Report of the Secretary and Treasurer of the Bible and Prayer Book Society of Albany and its Vicinity.

F. Reports from the Orphan House of the Holy Saviour, Cooperstown.

G. Reports of Special Committees appointed at the last Convention.

H. Miscellaneous business.

SECOND DAY.

10. On the second and each succeeding day of the session, after Daily Morning Prayer, the order of business, which shall not be departed from without the consent of two-thirds of the members present, or a special order of the day previously voted, shall be as follows:

A. Reading, correcting and approving the minutes of the previous day.

B. Calling the roll of members absent on the previous day.

C. Reports from the Regular Committees of the House, in the order of their appointment.

D. Reports from Special Committees, in the order of their appointment.

E. Unfinished business.

F. Miscellaneous business.

11. The Bishop's Address is in order at any time.

12. The annual election shall be held at noon on the second day, and continued at the order of the House until completed.

13. All reports embodying long statements of accounts shall be accompanied with a brief abstract of them, and such abstracts only shall be printed in the Journal.

GENERAL.

14. When any member is about to speak, he shall rise from his seat, and shall, with due respect, address himself in an audible tone of voice to the President, confining himself strictly to the point in debate.

15. No member shall speak more than twice in the same debate without leave of the House; nor more than once, until every other member wishing to speak shall have spoken.

16. No motion shall be considered as before the House unless it be seconded, and reduced to writing when required, and announced by the Chair.

17. The mover may withdraw a motion or resolution at any time before amendment or decision, with the consent of the Convention; in which case it shall not be entered upon the minutes.

18. When a question is under consideration, it shall be in order to move to lay it upon the table, to postpone it indefinitely, to postpone it to a time certain, to commit it, to amend it, or to divide it; and motions for any of these purposes shall have precedence in the order here named.

19. If the question under debate contains several distinct propositions, the same

shall be divided at the request of any member, and a vote taken separately; except that a motion to strike out and insert shall be indivisible.

20. All amendments shall be considered in the order in which they are moved. When a proposed amendment is under consideration, a motion to amend the same may be made. No after amendment to such second amendment, shall be in order; but a substitute for such second amendment, or a substitute for the whole matter, may be received. No proposition on a subject different from that under consideration shall be received under colour of a substitute.

21. A motion to lay upon the table shall be decided without debate.

22. A motion to adjourn shall always be in order when no member is speaking; and, if unqualified, shall be decided without debate. If negatived, it shall not be renewed until some other business has intervened.

23. When a question is put by the President, it shall be determined by the sound of voices, for or against it; but any three members may require a count of the votes, and tellers for that purpose shall then be appointed by the Chair; or any five votes may require that the decision be by yeas and nays and by orders, which shall be done by calling the roll of the clerical members and parishes represented, and the votes shall be entered on the Journal.

24. When the President is putting any question, the members shall continue in their seats, and shall not hold any private discourse.

25. Every member present shall vote when a question is put, unless excused by a vote of the House.

26. A motion once determined, whether in the affirmative or the negative, shall stand as the judgment of the Convention, and shall not again be considered during the same session, unless the motion to reconsider be made by one of the majority on the first decision, and be carried by a vote of two-thirds of the members present.

27. All questions of order shall be decided by the President, subject to an appeal to the House; and on such appeal no member shall speak more than once, without leave of the Convention.

28. All committees shall be appointed by the President, unless otherwise ordered by the Convention.

29. The reports of all committees shall be in writing; and unless recommitted, shall be received of course, without motion for acceptance. They shall be entered on the minutes, unless otherwise ordered. If recommending or requiring any action or expression of opinion by the Convention, they shall be accompanied by a resolu-tion or resolutions for its consideration.

30. No rule of order shall be suspended, unless by a vote of two-thirds of the members present; nor shall any be changed or rescinded without one day's previous notice.

31. No member shall absent himself from the session of the Convention without leave of the President.

32. Before the final adjournment of the Convention, the minutes of the last day's proceedings shall be read, corrected and approved.

33. When the Convention is about to rise, every member shall keep his seat until the President leaves the chair.

STANDING ORDER.

OF THE CONDUCT OF ELECTIONS.

WHEREAS, it is expedient to provide by a standing order, for the manner of conducting all elections by ballot in the Convention of the Diocese of Albany, it is hereby ordered as follows :

1. The President of the Convention shall appoint one clergyman and one layman to be tellers of the clerical vote, and one clergyman and one layman to be tellers of the lay vote, for each office that is to be filled except that all the members of any committee, board or delegation shall be voted for upon one ticket, and only one set of tellers shall be appointed therefor. Vacancies, arising from temporary absence or otherwise, shall be supplied by the President.

2. When the election is to be held, the tellers for the clerical vote shall take their places, together, on one side of the house or place of meeting, and the tellers for the lay vote, together, upon the other side; and the Secretary shall supply them with the necessary boxes, and also with lists of the clergy entitled to seats in the Convention, and of the parishes entitled to representation, on which lists, as each vote is deposited, they shall make a mark against the name of the clergyman or parish voting; and these lists, signed by the tellers, shall be returned with their reports to the Convention. The names of the clergy and of the parishes shall be called by the Secretaries, and the votes shall be received by the tellers.

3. So soon as voting shall appear to have ceased, the President shall announce that the polls are about to be closed, and not less than ten minutes after such announcement, he may direct the tellers to count the votes, for which purpose they shall have leave to retire. The tellers shall then proceed to count the votes, and shall make written reports, stating the whole number of votes cast, and the number cast for each person, except that when less than five votes are cast for any one person, it shall suffice to include all such votes under the head of scattering. These reports shall be signed by the tellers respectively, and shall be entered upon the Journal, and the President shall announce the result.

4. In case of any contest arising as to the right of any person to cast a vote, the tellers shall submit the question to the Convention before the closing of the polls.

5. If in regard to any office there shall not be a majority of votes, either in the clerical or in the lay order, for any one person, or if there shall not be a concurrence of the two orders, the Convention shall forthwith proceed to another ballot, for such and so many offices as have not been filled at the first ballot; and such second and all other ballots shall be conducted in the same manner as above provided. In case there shall still remain any vacancy to be supplied after such second ballot, further ballots may be held at the order of the Convention.

6. Immediately before any ballot, it shall be in order for the nomination of any person to be made and seconded. But nominations for members of the Standing Committee and for Deputies and Provisional Deputies to the General Convention shall be made on the first day of the Convention, at the call of the President, under the order of "Miscellaneous Business;" and it shall be the duty of the Secretary of the Convention to prepare, for the use of the Convention on the second day, ballots for these several offices, containing the names of all persons nominated for each office, respectively, with a note indicating the whole number to be chosen. No speech or debate shall be allowed upon such nomination, or while the Convention is holding an election.

JOURNAL.

All Saints' Cathedral Church, Albany, N. Y.
Tuesday, November 17, A. D., 1891.

This being the place designated by the Bishop of the Diocese and the day appointed by the Constitution, for the meeting of the Twenty-third Annual Convention of the Diocese of Albany, the Bishop, and a number of the Clergy and Lay Deputies assembled in All Saints' Cathedral Church at half-past ten o'clock in the morning.

The Bishop of the Diocese administered the Holy Communion, being assisted in the service by the Rev. Archdeacons Carey, Morrison, Olmstead and Sill.

In place of the sermon, the Bishop delivered a portion of his Annual Address.

THE BISHOP'S ADDRESS.

There are circumstances, my well beloved Brethren of the Clergy and Laity, which bring us to this meeting of the Convention with more sober and more serious sense of both privilege and responsibility, of the solemnities of parting and the sweetness of meeting again, than ever before.

The year, so far as you and I are concerned in our relations to each other, has been unusual from the fact that I have been absent from the Diocese for four months, not in pursuit of rest or pleasure, but in the discharge of duties imposed upon me by the Presiding Bishop; and consequently we have been less together than ever before, because I have been obliged to delegate to others my welcome duty of visiting you in your Parishes, and because I have been withdrawn both from the accustomed and the unusual gatherings which ordinarily bring us together from time to time.

I have a sense of infinite thankfulness that God has enabled me to accomplish my first visitation of the Continental Churches, not only in

3

safety but with very great satisfaction, and I hope with some service besides to our work on the Continent of Europe; and that in my absence work went on with its accustomed thoroughness and faithfulness in the Institutions and Parishes over which God has set those who are indeed such "workers with me unto the Kingdom of God," as are "a comfort unto me."

Over and above this, as marking with intense significance and emphasis this Convention and this year, we have been called upon as we have never been before to face the fact (which must come home especially to those of us who have been associated from the beginning with this Diocese) of the changes which time will make, of the emptiness which death brings about, in the ranks of those who have been side by side with us in counsel and labours in our immediate portion of the Kingdom.

You will, I am sure, realize that I have keenly felt my inability to join with the other Clergy in their tribute of reverent love, the last service we can render, and the last gift we can offer, to those with whom we have been associated in our life work.

The Rev. Mr. Selkirk and the Rev. Dr. Payne died during my absence in Europe, Mr. Ogden's death and Dr. Hopkins', (who always seemed one of us,) and Mr. Norton's and Dr. Lowell's occurred when I was too far away to be able to be present at their burials. And I was arrested, on my way to the burial of Mr. Cook, by a telegram announcing my brother's desperate illness. It is only left to me, in this record of the experiences of the past year, to make a very loving minute of my reverent affection for these men; five of whom were in the Diocese at the time of my election to the Episcopate; and whose departure leaves in the Diocese only eleven of us, (we *were* sixty Clergymen) who were in the primary Convention of Albany.

Reading the lesson at Evensong on the Sunday of Ogden's translation I was intensely struck with the differences and varieties among the Saints whom St. Paul catalogues in that wonderful record in the 11th chapter of the Epistle to the Hebrews; and as I remembered the crown of venerable years which Payne and Selkirk wore, and the comparative freshness of Ogden's youth, I recognized in the first two the death of those who like Jacob "worshipped leaning on the top of his staff;" and in the other of the man who "was not, because God took him," and who certainly had this testimony before his death, that "he pleased God." Then I thought of that picture of the Heavenly City, which our Old Testament Seer paints, how the streets shall be full of old men leaning on their staves for very age, and of the young rejoicing in their youth.

Canon Selkirk's death was absolutely unexpected to me. He had laid out for himself a work, a good deal of which was completed, and to whose finishing he looked forward as the labour of his last years. When I parted from him at the gathering of the Clergy on the day before

I left Albany, he was full of interest in it, and apparently full of vigourous ability to accomplish what few men could have done as well as he, namely, to write out the story of the Church's life and work in this old town. He has left behind him, in the Church property belonging to Trinity Parish, a memorial of patient, steady, constant work. It was impossible of course, or at least, improbable, that any man could have been, for more than fifty years, living in one place, and occupied in one work, without encountering opposition and accumulating certain prejudices of unfriendliness; but I am thankful to feel that long before his death, there came to him the recognition, on all hands, of what he had been able to do; and that he has left behind him abundant evidence of the fact that, remaining poor himself, he has made many rich in the property which he accumulated for the Church. His connection with the Cathedral was a great pleasure to me, and to all of us who were associated with him. He had a real enjoyment in the services, and in the welcome which always awaited him in his accustomed place there; and to me, I confess, few things have given more satisfaction in connection with the establishment of the Cathedral than the ability to give to him title and place of honour, and such work as he was able to do; so that he did not feel himself, when the necessity of resigning his more active labours came, as entirely laid aside. I have already had occasion to express my own personal obligation to the Rector of St. Peter's Church, for the sermon which he preached here on the occasion of Mr. Selkirk's funeral. Far beyond the mere question of eloquence and affection, it was marked by such discrimination and delicacy of feeling and taste, that I am only too glad to adopt as my own its admirable expression of what is left behind, as the heritage to this city and Diocese, of a long life spent in the service of the Church.

I venture to suggest to the Convention that it would be wise to obtain, if possible, the partially completed History of the Church in Albany, and to put it into the hands of our admirable Registrar (who has a gift in that direction), to use the materials which would thus come into his hands; and if possible to secure the publication of the book, as a memorial of Canon Selkirk's long and laborious life.

Personally, there could hardly have been a greater loss in the ranks of the Clergy of this Diocese, than came in the death of Dr. Payne. He was really the Senior Priest of the Diocese in years of life and service, and in the positions with which from the beginning, and I am glad to say, with unbroken continuance, the Diocese delighted to honour him. To me, from my very first meeting with him, he has been loyal and loving in every possible way, and intensely helpful in every word and act of sympathy and service, as my counsellor and friend. He was abundantly qualified in all his gifts of mind and heart, for the positions which he was called to fill; and I had the sense always, when I went to him, or when he came to me, of a very deep and true love between us which, spite of the difference in our years (for I look back now and feel that when I began my work among you I was almost a boy), drew us most closely and intimately together. The memorial which the Standing Committee have put upon their Minutes, and which will be read and published in this Journal, is not one whit too strong in its description of his rare character. He was a Priest after the manner of George Herbert's description. And it was given to him, as to few men that I know, to enrich the accumulated experiences of his pastoral life and theological reading, with the perpetual acquisitions of new lines of thought and life which kept him abreast with all the fresher theology and work of the century in which we live. Even when the feebleness and infirmity of age crept upon him, he remained young inside, and not only was constant to the last in his discharge of the various duties, both Parochial and Diocesan, which gathered about him, but kept his full and vigorous interest in every thing that concerned the Church's life.

He asked me on the day when I parted from him, the 2d of February, if I would do two things: go to his son's grave in the beautiful cemetery in Rome, and see his son's widow in Paris. I gathered, from the abundant growth of ivy and violets about the grave under the old Roman Pyramid, a few flowers which I sent him, and which only reached him in time to be laid, with other tributes of living love, in his coffin; and I was only able to see his grandchild and her mother after they and I had received the news that he had gone to join those whom he had "loved and lost awhile." A letter from Schenectady told me another thing which touched me very deeply; that among the very last thoughts which he expressed about things and people of this earth, was his interest in seeing published, in the paper in Schenectady, the statement of the various attentions which had been shown me abroad. To have been honoured by intimate association for two and twenty years with such a man, and to have won, not only his sympathy but his warm affection, while of course it deepens the sorrow of his loss, makes a memory which I shall carry with me to the end of my life, with infinite thankfulness to God.

While I am speaking of "the Elders" which are among us, who ought to be counted "worthy of double honour," let me remind the Convention that there are two priests in the Diocese who have come this year to the golden anniversary of their ordination. The Rev. George H. Nicholls, S. T. D., was ordained Deacon on the 8th of June, and the Rev. Robert Washbon, on the 27th of June, A. D., 1841. They have laboured in the Word and doctrine in the Diocese; and are still where they were when the Diocese was organized, giving to the Church such service as they are able to render, and blessing us with the daily example of their holy lives. I am sure the Diocese will need no suggestion of mine to take such action as may express our reverent recollection of their labours, and our realization of the blessing and benefit of what they have been, and of what they are to us, in the constant and continual power of their influence and their prayers.

The news of the sudden summons of William Meredith Ogden came to me on a lovely summer Sunday afternoon, just at the close of my own service in the Chapel at North-East Harbour. That it was an intense shock from its suddenness and surprise I need hardly say; but as the sense of it grew in upon me more and more, I could not help feeling, that for one who had lived the life that he had lived, it was a glorious ending of earthly labour, to be taken instantly from the delivery of his Master's message to hear from Him the assurance of its acceptance at His hands. What could be more beautiful, as a pathway into Paradise than the story of that Sunday morning, with the Early Celebration at half-past seven, with the sweet and pleasant home life in the Rectory, with the care of the children committed to him in the Sunday School, with the full service of the Morning Prayer in which he took his part, in the music as well as in the reading of the Office, and then — in the middle of a sentence, "The Lord is in His Holy Temple, let all the earth keep silence before Him," to pass from the earth into that Holy Temple in which the Lord reveals Himself in clearer and fuller vision.

It seems to me that being dead he yet speaks to us in the fact and the manner of his last sermon; for the text was taken from the First General Epistle of St. Peter, in which he quotes the Thirty-fourth Psalm, and his very last words were, "I read a scientific article —," so that he was combining, in rich and real ways, the Old and the New Testament Scriptures and the revelation of God in nature, to bring out the absolute harmony which always is among the three. And one can not but feel that God fulfilled to him the text that "His Eyes were over him and His Ears open to his prayers," for when he asked "of Him a long life He gave it unto him even for ever and ever."

The Archdeacon said of him, "It was a glorious death, delivering his Master's message, and in the House of God he loved so well," and I am sure we shall all accept with most entire cordialty the admirable Minute, drawn up by Mr. Cookson and adopted by the Clergy who were present at his burial, as the words we ourselves would use to tell our common sorrow:

"For thirty-one years, save a few days, he had exercised the office of his ministry at St. John the Evangelist's in Montreal, at Plattsburgh, Franklin, Ticonderoga, Gouverneur and Warrensburgh, everywhere with great devotion and faithfulness and with a solemn consciousness of the responsibility laid upon him.

"His blameless life, his manly frankness, his steadfastness of purpose and principle, his gentleness of spirit, his affectionate interest in his people were known of all men, and he won and held confidence and esteem in every place where he ministered.

"For the last sixteen years he had gone in and out among the people of this village as priest and friend, and his memory will be ever fragrant among his own flock and among those who were not his.

"With hand pointing heavenward, while the words of teaching and persuasion were falling from his lips, God suddenly took him away from the service of the earthly sanctuary to the nobler worship of the temple 'not made with hands, eternal in the heavens.'

"We cannot mourn for him, nor do other than thank God for taking him in a way so full of honour, but we mourn for his dear children and friends and for his devoted parish, while we pray God that they and we may follow his 'good example,' and so may be ready when our summons comes.

I have before me as I write, a note which came to me from him on the 13th of March, to tell of another great sorrow which had befallen the Warrensburgh Church in the death of Miss Sarah Burhans, one of the old Church family to whom both the Parish and the Diocese owe so much of generous help in every way; and to whom I owe so much, as having been my kind and faithful friends for all these years. Speaking in the letter to me of the possibility of changing his place of work, which would involve leaving what he felt was a fairly comfortable provision for life, he says, "I am quite quiescent, content and willing to leave the matter wholly in the hands of Divine Providence. Death and removals the last two years have greatly thinned out our numbers, and I sometimes think that with so large a Church property and the wealth which can be reached, the experiment of a new man here might be a gain;" and in this contentment and quiescence we must accept the Providential ordering which has removed him, and made, what would have been to you and to me a most unwilling experiment, a necessity which we are compelled to accept.

I cannot speak too strongly of Ogden's work in Warrensburgh. Quiet and withdrawn from public notice, he built up there, largely as I know by his wise and patient perseverance, a very noble "plant," as business men would call it; and quite in keeping with the material advances has been the spiritual upbuilding. He was infinitely painstaking in all the details of his pastoral work, having a true sense of his responsibility; and he filled out the ideal of a country parson and a parish priest with unusual completeness; while to me, he was, since ever I came into the Diocese, a most loyal and loving brother and friend.

It is impossible for me not to put in my Diocesan Address some record of my feeling about a man who for thirty years has filled a foremost place in the history of our American Church.

Knowing Dr. Hopkins as intimately as I did, I am abundantly aware of the very marked faults of his character, of that curious subtleness of mind which tempted him to indulge in dialectics and speculations, and to prefer often rather tortuous ways of reaching the ends at which he aimed. It was a matter of temperament and mental constitution, and I think was the chief snare and difficulty of his life. Making this frank avowal, which I have often made to him, I honestly believe that no man in the American Church has ever served her interests with purer devotion, with more unselfish love, or with finer intellectual appreciation of the responsibilities and possibilities of her position in the world.

In all the varied departments of Art, musical, architectural, ecclesiological; as a poet and a preacher, as a literary man and a theologian, he was one of the rare examples of a man who could be master of many trades. His instinctive taste was accurate to a minute degree; the courage of his convictions never failed him; he was prophetic almost in many of his theories in regard to the life and work of the Church.

Looked at through this long distance, his editorial career in the *Church Journal*, brilliant as it was beyond any other in American Church newspapers, must be qualified by two facts: one which makes it greater, and the other, which is of course to be deplored. He and Dr. Mahan were ahead of their time in many of the plans and proposals which they advocated. Familiar to us now, partly by adoption in fact and partly by general acceptance in theory, they were then novel and strange and unpopular; but many a gain in doctrinal recognition and in practical advantage is due to the advocacy in the *Church Journal*, with persistent and earnest ability, of such measures as were under warm discussion then.

I remember Dr. Hopkins telling me some years ago, that in reading the old editorials he was sometimes at a loss to know which were his and which were Mahan's, so one-minded were they in the work they had in hand.

The other qualifying fact is the severity, sometimes almost coarse in its strength, with which the editorials were now and then marred. Judging from our own times, the tendency to this sort of appeal is an editorial temptation deeply to be regretted, especially when it descends into the modern political arena of personal abuse. But in Dr. Hopkins' case, however caustic and cruel the writing was, there was never in the writer the bitterness of personal enmity or individual dislike. They were hot times that made hot tempers, and then, as now, they hindered instead of helping on the cause.

My pleasantest associations with my brother date back to the days, when he was working as a Missionary in this Diocese, in the beautiful region of Lake Champlain and the Adirondacks. Day after day we spent together driving through the exquisite country, every inch of which he knew and loved; and I can never forget how he beguiled the weariness of the way, with his keen artistic enjoyment of all that was beautiful, with his unfailing brightness and humour, with his freshness about all matters of Theology, old or new, and with the kindness of his personal courtesy.

It was my privilege to gather in the good harvest of his faithful spiritual sowing over the large and difficult missionary district where he served; and then to ordain him to the Priesthood and appoint him to the Rectorship of Plattsburgh which he filled with a new life and spirit. And the recollection of the gentleness and peace of his last years is like the sunset glow at the end of a long day. Clearheaded to the very latest moment of his life, calmly facing what was before him, with the sweetest patience he talked "about the exodus which he should accomplish," with the courage and composure of, not resignation merely, but acceptance of God's Will. And when the story comes to be written of the sacrifices and self denials of his life, when it comes to be realized that this man of highest intellectual power and most admirable intellectual furnishing, lived and died with the very smallest and most meagre provision for his personal support, I am sure that this Church will count him and his work among the most important factors in her great advance in clear conceptions of the Catholic Faith and Order, and in the practical application of primitive principles to present needs.

Speaking from an almost interior intimacy with the man, and recog—nizing, as I frankly do, mistakes and faults which are common to us all, I desire to lay my tribute upon his grave, and to record my conviction of the unselfishness, the devotion, the self-denial, the consecration of most unusual gifts, with no personal ambitions to gratify and no personal ends to serve, to the glory of the Master whom he loved and the upbuilding and extension of His Kingdom on earth.

The news came to me by telegram on the 18th of August of the very sudden death of the Rev. George H. Norton, who had been for many years our Missionary at Au-Sable Forks, and only this year had gone be the Missionary at Greenwich. We must add him to the long list, that year, of those whom we remember at our commemorative celebration. Mr. Norton was ill on Saturday, but struggled through the reading the service in the Church on Sunday the 16th, immediately after which he went to St. Luke's Hospital in New York, where, very unexpectedly, in spite of the faithful care of those who nursed him, he died. Just before he died he rose from his bed and knelt by the side of it in prayer.

His service in this Diocese has been an unusual service. In the face of extreme difficulties he has been able to maintain work where only Divine guidance could have kept him free from hindering complications; and those who came to know him last will join, with his old parishioners in Au-Sable Forks and with me, in recognizing that by his death we are the poorer for the loss of a man of real ability as a preacher, of bright and cheerful and entire sympathies with all that is best in human nature, and of earnest and successful service to that highest human nature, the Incarnate Master, in Whose Merits and Mediation we minister for Him.

The death of the Rev. Dr. R. T. S. Lowell, following so soon upon the

death of his distinguished brother, adds one more name to the too long
list of losses from our Clergy, and takes one more away from the number
of the older men who were in the Diocese in its early days. My memory of Dr. Lowell dates back to my boyhood, when I remember his coming to my father's house, the original and realization of "The New
Priest of Conception Bay," with the fervour of his youth still upon him,
and the flavour of his most romantic and devoted life in the middle of
the scenes, which he painted with so much power and beauty in that book.

He served with great faithfulness and acceptance in the Parish of Duanesburgh, which was his wife's ancestral home; discharged his duties with
the accurate ability of his admirable scholarship in Union College; and,
although not in any definite charge for many years, he was ready always
for any kindly help that he could render in a vacant Parish or to a
brother unable to do his work.

In 1889 he reported several services and Celebrations of the Holy Communion, with the little note added, "Has helped his brother priest, the
Rector of the Parish in which he lives, as occasion offered." His last
report to me on the 1st of November, 1890, was that "illness had, under
the physician's direction, hindered him peremptorily from undertaking
any official work or duty, and much of the time from being in Church
during the year past. This is to his deep regret."

And now that he has gone to that higher and untiring activity of those
who "cease not day nor night," we recall with loving admiration and
honour the dignity of his bearing, his devotion to duty, his thorough
priestly and pastoral instinct, and the distinction which he won in the
field of letters, both of poetry and of fiction; with the clear and comforting recollection that in whatever sphere or place he wrought, his talents
were consecrated to the high and holy service of his Master.

The death of the Rev. William Henry Cook occurred on the 8th of
October at his temporary home in Ballston. He too, was one of the few
remaining Clergy of our Primary Convention, and his passing away, while
it leaves of course its edge of sorrow in the sense of loss, was a merciful
gift of God to him and to those who had so long and so tenderly watched
his increasing feebleness and suffering. He was one of the few of the
Clergy of Northern New York whom I recognized as a friend when I
first came into it in 1867. His brother was my parishioner in St. John's,
Hartford, and it was by his death-bed that I first met him. So that my
association with him is the longest of any clerical association with this
Diocese, and I may truly say it is one of the most loving and pleasant of
all my memories. In his old home at Keeseville, in the brighter days
no welcome was more cordial, and no hospitality more lavish, more loving or more refined than met me there. He has always "endured hardness as a good soldier of Jesus Christ;" but the witness which his house-

4

hold at all times bore, and which the education of his children still bears, to the possibilities of maintaining all the amenities of cultivated life on the smallest conceivable stipend, made him the very realization of Goldsmith's parson who was "passing rich on forty pounds a year." He has done splendid missionary work in this Diocese wherever he has been; and up to and even beyond the strength of his declining years he worked, not only till the twilight but till the dark came on. He knows how dear he was to me, and I know how true and loving a friend and brother he has always been to me. Nothing but the summons to go to my brother, who was suddenly and desperately ill, prevented my presence at his burial, to which I was going, when the telegram turned my steps the other way. If service and suffering ever made perfect any Priest, I am well assured that he will stand "perfect and complete before the Son of Man."

This thinning of the ranks, of the men who have stood by me from the first, tells me, at any rate, more than any inward feeling of advancing years, how the time goes on toward the point when the change must come, not only in the faithful following, but in the leadership, which such followers make easy and happy to a Bishop in his work.

Prominent among the losses which come to us this year among our staunch and faithful lay people is the death of Mr. Edwin Sheldon, to whom in many ways this Diocese owes much. His own intense love for those who went before him, and for the place of his ancestral home gave him a strong interest, not only in the Parish in Delhi, but in the Diocese in which it was situated; and his large-minded Churchmanship made him from the start a kind and cordial friend in the work which I was trying to do in Albany. I am very glad to know that the family interest still continues; that a generous memorial of him is to be made by his children in the building of a new Rectory, and in the care for the maintenance of the services of the Parish.

I record here permanently what I said when the intelligence of his death first reached me. "In the large and widespread activities of his business relations, in his association with one of the great and successful banking concerns in the country, he was widely recognized as a man of wisdom, energy, ability and of integrity incorruptible.

There is far more than this in him that one loves to recall; in his cultivated taste, the reach and range of his information and his interests, and the variety and extent of his generous giving. Almost his last words to me last summer were of his delight in foreign travel, and his warm sympathy with the work of our Chapels abroad : with the pleasant expression of his wish that he could have been in Italy with me that winter. As I call up the impression of my intercourse with him, the leading traits of his character seem to me to have been gentleness, graciousness and genuineness; rare refinement and simplicity of taste and manner; quick perceptions, and instant instincts of generosity. His home love was very strong. His heart turned to the homestead in Delhi; and he was content and delighted to be there; loving the hills, and the river and the valley ; and, above all, the associations and memories which clustered about them; and he adorned the place with exquisite gifts. The Memorial Chapel, which he only completed last year, is, in its every detail, as finished and perfect as reverence and liberality and taste and affection could make it.

This was one of the points in Mr. Sheldon's character which always touched me very deeply; what one may call his natural affections ; not merely for, what many men lavish their love on, wife and children; but his filial and fraternal love, the honour in which he held the memory of his father and mother, the great love of his brotherliness, and his strong feeling about his birthplace were rare and beautiful. And all the while his affections were set on things above. He died as he had lived, in the faith and favour of God, in the peace of Christ, in charity with all the world."

The death of Mr. John H. Cheritree takes from me another of the life-long friends of my Episcopate. He was my host always in his pleasant home at Oak Hill. He had been for many years Senior Warden of the Parish. He officiated in any vacancy of the Rectorship as Lay Reader; and the family in all its connections has been the chief support of the Church in that little village, from which, in every one of all his varied services, he will be very greatly missed and very truly mourned.

I have to record also, the death of a very venerable lady from the Parish of St. Paul's Church, Troy; Mrs. Joseph M. Warren. Intimately associated for a very long period of years, with all the best life and work of that old Parish, there is hardly a family name in our Diocese of Albany that must for all time be held in higher honour than hers; and although withdrawn from the activities of duty, she never lost her living and loving interest in every thing that could promote the welfare of the Parish; and after many years of waiting, that would have been weary but for the grace of patience that was given to her, she has been permitted at last to depart in peace.

Our sympathy must go out abundantly to her husband who so long has filled with such honorable generosity and faithfulness, the position of Warden of the old Parish, and to her children, in whom her influence and example will still go on to benefit and bless the Church.

During my absence the news reached me of the death of Mr. P. Remsen Chadwick, who had been for many years, by the inheritance of his good name, closely connected with all the best things in this Diocese of Albany. He was a man of great power of work and endurance, who had done noble service in the war, and had come, as "a good soldier of Jesus Christ," in time of peace to serve his Heavenly Master with the same loyalty, fearlessness and faithfulness.

More could not be said of him than that he carried out and carried on the beautiful example of his father and mother; and the testimony of his Rector and fellow vestrymen is not too strongly worded when it says of him: "In his personal character he endeared himself to us all. His genial manner and his upright consistency attracted and won the esteem of his associates. He was a faithful communicant and supporter of the Church, and in every way advanced its spiritual and material prosperity. For several years he represented this Parish in the Diocesan Convention. We rejoice over the evidence of faith and love in this servant of God, and cherish his memory as one who was faithful unto death."

The record of this year's deaths must be still further enlarged, by the fact of the death of Mr. Charles Stott, who, though never in anywise connected with the public affairs of the Diocese, has been a most valuable and important factor in its work. He was a man whose splendid physical nature indicated the strength of purpose and the power of will which were within. Of invincible integrity and remarkable business ability, with great powers of administration, generous and earnest in his support of the Church in Stockport, almost the founder and builder both of the village and the Church of Stottville, he lent all the influence of his life to the maintenance of things that were "honest and of good report."

No man has ever shared the pleasure of his patriarchal home without realizing the unusual power and attractiveness of the man, and in that home, which it is difficult to think of without his presence, the bereavement is bitter, indeed.

Two dear old friends have been taken away, whose loss will be most seriously felt in their own Parish of Glens Falls, and whose kindly greeting, which grew kindlier with every year, I shall be most sorry to miss. Dr. Austin Wells Holden and his wife, after forty years of married life together, died within six months of each other — she going first — this year.

The Doctor himself was a man of very marked character, prominent in various departments of life. As a physician, both at home, and in the army during the war; as a citizen interested in all educational matters in his own town, as a student and author, he filled an important place in Glens Falls: and he and his wife together were perfectly devoted to every good and gracious work, not only "giving alms of their goods," but going about and doing good whenever and wherever there was need. They have been most faithful and devoted members of the Church. He held my License as a Lay Reader; and was for nearly fifty years a member of the Vestry of the Church of the Messiah; and she was as devout and devoted as he.

Their old age was ripe with something more than years, and green with something more than physical health; for it was the old age of matured Christian character, and it was fragrant and fresh with the beauty of earnest and keen interest in all good things.

I have spoken in connection with the great loss at Warrensburgh of the death of Miss Sarah Burhans. I must add a word of very loving testimony to the graciousness of her hospitality, to her intelligent interest in Church matters, and to her uniform kindness and courtesy, both when she administered her father's house in his life-time, and when she continued, after his death, the pleasant welcome which always awaited me there.

I may not fail to mention the death of a true friend and very earnest Churchman, for many years Vestryman of St. Paul's Church, Troy, Mr. Willard Gay, associated in various directions with Church work and Churchmen; a man of highest integrity and business capacity, with most loving and reverent devotion not only to his Parish but to the interests of the Diocese.

I must add my testimony to that which the Rector of the Parish has already paid to the faithfulness of a very old parishioner of Ballston, Miss Mary Rebecca Smith, who had been for fifty years actively identified with Christ Church and had taught two generations of children in the Parish School, and of whom I am sure the Rector has not said too much in writing, "There was no person in the whole community so generally known or more sincerely respected for the consistency of a Christian life."

This record, which would be so painful but for the stimulus of its memory and the joyfulness of its hope, cannot end yet. In the north, Mr. Duncan J. Wood has died, and the Parish of Gouverneur will wait long before it finds his equal in generous, intelligent devotion to the Parish: while I must miss one of the laymen, who was a Churchman by conviction and on principle, with intense and entire recognition of all in the Church that is Catholic and primitive. Dr. Darling was really the founder of the Church in Bangor, my host always, and my companion in many of the drives through the Missions that were connected with it. A prominent and beloved physician, a kind and cordial friend, coming late in life to the knowledge of the Church, he devoted himself to its interests with loyal zeal, and will be greatly missed from its services — in which he always led the singing — and from its support. And the Church lost a most successful Missionary worker, and the work, which Mr. Larom is doing so wonderfully in the Northern Adirondack region one of its chief supporters, in the death of Mr. R. W. Alban Thompson, one of my lay readers, and a most devoted and faithful servant of his Master. Almost on the same day that Mr. Cook died, one of the leading laymen of Christ Church, Ballston, Mr. Samuel Haight, was taken very suddenly away. His death is not only a loss of the most real kind to his Rector and to me, but it deprives the Parish there of his generous and intelligent support, and takes away from the community a man who stood for everything that means integrity and energy in business, and wise and wide-awake interest in the affairs of the village.

One of the old names in this Diocese known through three generations for all things that were " pure and lovely and of good report " is the name of Leonard, and while, thank God, it still remains in the Parish of Lansingburgh, one of the most valuable members of the family has passed away this year.

Miss Leonard bore in her outward appearance the evidence of character which it expressed. She was a woman of rare and gracious dignity, living up to the traditions of the old name, whose main object in life was to advance the interest of the village and of the Parish in the village. Most devoutly religious and thoroughly in earnest, she was the Rector's fast and faithful friend and a very lovely illustration of the kind of woman which the system of the Church trains.

Dr. Nickerson says of her what I can thoroughly endorse, that " she was really the Lady Bountiful of the village, the first resort of every person in want or trouble, the common adviser and friend of all. Her death will be deeply felt here not only because we have lost one of our most liberal and devout Church members, but because a sweet and lovely and noble woman has been taken away."

The Parish at Herkimer, already sorely bereaved by the death of Miss Bartow, who had been always among its most faithful worshippers and generous supporters, mourns very deeply the unexpected death of Mr. Samuel Earl, one of the strong men, intellectually and in public spirit, of the place, and a warm supporter of the Church, and the friend of all of us who are interested in it.

The minute of the Vestry is the reverent expression of the common sense of sorrow: " Active and interested from almost the very beginnings of parochial life, he has ever since been closely associated with all its developments, to which he has contributed not a little. Regular and prompt in attendance, alike at Divine Worship and at meetings of the Vestry, outspoken in counsel and vigorous in action, naturally conservative and a lover of old things and old ways, generous in giving, warm hearted and kindly in address, proud of the growth and prosperity of the parish of which he was a most efficient support, he was one whose voice and figure will be greatly missed."

Other than merely personal reasons constrain me to speak of the death of Dr. J. Francis Williams, which, as we think suddenly, has ended an earthly career not merely of rare promise but of rich fulfilment. It seems incredible to those who knew him that he could have done so much and died so young; and the record I think is worth making as a lesson to us all, young men and old, of the duty of redeeming the time, be it long or short, of every life.

The story of this short life is consistent and continuous from the beginning, and its characteristic is manliness. He quitted himself like a man in our great Church School at Concord, winning high honour and the warm commendation and confidence of Dr. Coit; at our own Polytechnic School in Troy, where he stood for everything that was best in character and scholarship; in the places of his foreign studying; in his professorships; in his scientific investigations; thorough, careful, faithful, honourable, always and everywhere.

What underlies it all is the entire consistency of his Christian life as a faithful communicant of the Church; and what touches me most closely is that a light has gone out from the dear old Salem homestead which has been a true *deversorium viatoris* to me for twenty years and more.

What Coleridge said of Matthew Arnold we may take and say here: "We may revive with the dews of love the fading flowers of memory and wind them into a wreath for Hope to wear."

And all our Cathedral people will realize with what affectionate reverence for his memory, I add, to the long list of this year's dead, the name of Mr. Leonard G. Hun, dead in his prime. No man in Albany stood higher in the respect and confidence of his profession, and of all who knew him. His mind was more than brilliant at its best, mastering the most abstruse studies in a way that gave him high honour at West Point, and then enabled him to win a foremost position as a lawyer. His religious convictions were of the sort that come, when a quiet man, accepting the great principles of the Faith, makes them the rule of his life. I have never been much disposed to think that Christianity needed for its defense a list of the great names of its adherents. But it is strong evidence, against the charge that religion rests upon the sandy basis of superstition or the swampy bottom of mere emotion, to find a thoughtful well-balanced, thoroughly trained, judicial mind accept and act out the Church's system of life and faith and worship, as the calm conclusion of his ripest thought.

Outside of the Diocese I must recall with you grave and serious losses, as we count them here on earth, which have come in the deaths of the Bishops of Massachusetts, Georgia and Milwaukee; and of Bishop Boone.

Bishop Paddock had certainly shown, in the administration of one of the most difficult and important of the Dioceses in America, that he was fully endowed by God, not only with the authority, but with the grace of his Office.

It was my pleasure two years ago to find the strong hold that he had upon the affections of his own people, when I ministered for him in some of his country Parishes. And the testimony which was borne to him by the Clergy of the great central city of his See shows, how he had won their confidence and affection as their leader.

Full of the aggressive missionary spirit for the Church, painstaking and accurate to an unusual degree in all the cumbersome details of our

Office, consecrated with the most entire devotion to his Master's service, and a man with whom one could not be without realizing at once the beauty and holiness of his life, he has left behind him such a memory and such memorials, as any one of us will be thankful to hope may "follow and enter in with us," at the end.

My clearest recollections of him are connected with the work in which he was deeply interested, and to which he gave both love and labour to the the last, as a most active member of the Hymnal Committee; and I am thankful to bear my tribute to the worth and value of one of the most faithful Bishops I have ever known.

Bishop Beckwith's death removes from the House of Bishops one of its greatest preachers, and takes from the intimate communion of our fellowship, a truly genial and delightful friend.

It is part of the pain of our wide severance from one another, that we can know, personally, little of the Diocesan work and duty of those of our brothers, who are removed from us by as many miles as separate Georgia from Albany; but the tokens of the sorrow in his Diocese are so many and so real, that one feels sure that the strong cords with which Bishop Beckwith drew his brethren to him in their association in the House, must have made him very closely dear to his own Clergy and people.

The death of the Bishop of Milwaukee has the element in it of a very true personal sorrow. We had been together in College as young men, and had kept always, even though we seldom met in later years, the old and close confidence of early and intimate friendship; and I welcomed with great pleasure his coming into the House of Bishops, although I was at the last prevented from doing what I was glad to have him want me to do, preaching the sermon and taking part in his Consecration.

He was a man of rare strength of character and soundness of judgment, with the full courage of his own convictions, and with great practical ability. His bearing and influence in our House were marked and evident from the first; and he bade fair to be, both in the counsels of the House of Bishops and in the work of his own Diocese, most valuable. Even in his short Episcopate he has left his mark in the work that he was able to accomplish, and the influence that he had already secured, to a degree that will make it very difficult for any one to fill his place.

Bishop Boone's life ended where it began, in the far East. Born, as it were, to the Episcopate and to the Episcopate *in China*, he had given all the love and the life of his ministry to Foreign Missions. And through many difficulties and constant dangers he bore himself manfully, till, just in the moment when the harvest was whitening, the faithful labourer passed to his reward.

May I not ask you also, while we are thinking and speaking of the bereavements in our American Episcopate, to remember the great sorrow to me, and the great loss to our Mother Church of England, which has overwhelmed us in the death of Archbishop Magee. I may say truly that he had been for thirteen years my very kind personal friend; and no one can have come in contact with him in such ways as I was privileged to do, in the Lambeth Conferences and in his own delightful home at Peterborough, without realizing how closely he attached himself, in his loving and generous nature, to those who knew him.

The public record of his life is too well known to need more than most passing reference here. To a nature of intense and entire devotion to duty, he added the rare gift of great eloquence, and the almost rarer gift of a courage that seemed sometimes almost presumptuous. The mystery of his death, just as he had reached the point of highest influence and honour, is one of those things which bring us face to face with a truth which is easier to write than to accept, that only God (if I may say so reverently) would dare to order, in the way He sometimes does, the issues and events of life.

His immediate predecessor in the See of York was a man whom none could know and not honour. With the clearest and most crystal intellect, with an innate power of ruling, with marked ability as writer, preacher and administrator, he joined, what men who never saw him in his home would fail to recognize, great tenderness and sweetness in all his human relations; and I am glad, with the memory of many years of almost intimate acquaintance with the one and of courteous and kindly relations with the other, to bear my tribute of reverent sympathy with the Church of England, and with the households of the two departed Bishops, in their loss.

To these and to all the faithful departed, the Lord grant everlasting rest, and the Light of the Life Eternal.

The stir of excitement which moved upon the face of our own ecclesiastical waters during my absence in Europe reached me, there. I think I may be permitted to say in reference to the two subjects which created such momentary commotion in America, that so far as I had any share in one of them, namely, in the question of the confirmation of the election of the Bishop of Massachusetts, I was infinitely thankful to find that, as usual, the action of our Standing Committee, taken of course (as it would have been even if I had been at home) in entire independence of me, was just what I ventured to be sure of and just what I desired.

Looking at the different methods of filling vacancies in our Episcopal Sees here and in England, one is, I am sure, abundantly satisfied that ours is the more primitive and the better way.

That a Bishop should be chosen by the people whom he is to serve, that both laymen and Clergymen should have a voice in the selection, is not only wise from natural considerations, but far more in accordance with the practice of the primitive Church.

5

I say this, realizing that nominally the people have a voice in an English election, first, because the appointment comes from the Crown as the chief representative of the nation, and secondly, that the so-called "Congé d'élire" gives the Cathedral Chapter a participation in the choice. But of course both these lay and Clerical sharings are nominal rather than real. And I say it also with a full realization of the fact that God has wonderfully overruled the English method, in the selection of a very remarkable body of men, and in the avoidance of the excitement and anxiety which sometimes attend our Episcopal elections. But in reference to our own American plan, primitive and admirable as it is, it seems to me that there are some safeguards which ought to be observed.

I cannot but think that so far as the action of the Standing Committee is concerned, its chief duty is to assure the Church at large that in the technical detail of an election, and in the technical testimonials to the fact, all things have been done "decently and in order;" and unless some knowledge, not possessed by the electing body, has come to them before or after the election, their consent is comparatively simple and easy. And while I believe that Bishops have a higher function and a higher responsibility in the action that they are called upon to take, in admitting, to their own Order, one who is to take part with them in the general government of the Church, I am very sure, with our present arrangement, when the testimonial has to be given by Bishops residing over the wide extent of our great country, that it is very dangerous for any individual sitting really as "Judex in camera," to judge, by his own standards, the question of the orthodoxy of a man permitted to hold the teaching office of the Priesthood, and certified by those who are supposed to know him best, as sound in the faith.

There are conceivable cases where it will be the duty even of a single individual to refuse, and every man of course, as things are now, must act according to his conscience. Nor, I think, should any Bishop be questioned or condemned if in his deliberate judgment he is compelled to the painful necessity of refusing his consent. For myself I am free to say, that knowing a man to be honourable and responsible, I should hesitate to refuse my consent to his Consecration if he were willing to take upon himself the solemn Consecration Vows. But in saying this, I beg to be understood as neither judging nor condemning those who take a different view of their responsibility. On the contrary, I thoroughly respect any man who, having strong convictions, has the courage to act upon them. But I do believe that two things must come about before long; one, the limitation of time within which either consent or refusal should be sent in, no Bishop being allowed to withhold one or the other expression; and the other thing, which I suppose can only be secured when this huge Continent is broken into Provinces, namely, that instead of asking the consent of the whole bench, only the neighboring Bishops, who can know of their own knowledge about the man, and who if difficulties and doubts arise can meet and take counsel together, should be expected to act.

It goes without saying, or ought to, that a Bishop consenting to the Consecration of a Bishop-elect, does not thereby commit himself to an acceptance of his individual opinions. And it seems to me the wildest folly to imagine that the standards of doctrine or order are altered or lowered in the Church at large, when a majority admits to the Episcopate a man, supposed by the minority to fall below those standards in his teaching or in his practice.

Meanwhile I hope that we shall not fail to learn some lessons from what has now become really the philosophy of history; many of which Dean Church, in his most admirable book on the Oxford Movement, has drawn to the life.

And if any of you have read the life of the late Archbishop of Canterbury, especially that portion of it which deals with the events connected with the election of Bishop Hampden to Hereford, and of Bishop Temple to Exeter, you will, I am sure, feel with me that all the Cassandra prophecies of misfortune made sometimes by a few and sometimes by many, sometimes even by the greatest and wisest men and sometimes by men less great and wise, fail somehow of their fulfilment in their application, not to a human institution, but to the Church of God, which He guides by His overruling Providence and by His indwelling Spirit. In those two cases in England, one may say, without unkindness, that the one was innocuous to the last degree, and by the confession of his opponents completely purged himself from all taint of unsound doctrine; while the other appointment placed upon the Episcopal bench of the Church of England, a man evidently much misunderstood by those who judged him, who won all hearts in the Diocese of Exeter; who rules the enormous Diocese of London to-day, with a hand strong and even, as his heart is brave and true and his head wise and clear; and of whom it is not too much to say that he is the foremost Bishop in England, in the combination of courage and comprehensiveness, with moral, spiritual and intellectual power.

Whatever else we may learn, my dear friends, we have reason I am sure to realize that it is unwise to measure men too much by a standard of our own opinions, and most unwise to fancy that we are any of us set to take into our own hands God's administration and government of His Church.

Above all, I wish that we might come to feel the danger of pushing our arguments toward the attainment of an end by prophesying results which are beyond our ken or our control. Unfulfilled prophecies react like the Australian boomerang. To have threatened the Church with disruption; to have denounced the House of Bishops as being favourers and fosterers of heresy ; to have insisted that if they appointed over this "business of overseeing," a man chosen, by those who were called upon to choose, as of honest report, they would alter the Faith and change the Order of the Church; all this either alarms people who are ignorant of the facts of the case when the deprecated result is obtained, or brings confusion (I wish it might also bring confession) upon the heads of those, who, in their eagerness to attain an end, have ventured into the unsafe region of foretelling future events, and prophesying consequences.

The spirit of quietness and confidence especially in Divine Institutions and a Divine Order, seems to me a safer and more Christian spirit, than the anxious unrest which is self-confident and unquiet; and which, particularly when it addresses itself in general public utterances to the outside world, creates mistaken opinions and produces mischievous results.

I turn to another matter, which filled the minds and eyes and mouths of men, namely, the invitation to certain ministers of the denominations to give public teaching in consecrated buildings at hours not set apart for the worship of the congregation, and at services announced to be special and peculiar. I am free to say that on all accounts, in my judgment, such action is eminently unwise.

It cannot be done without two things. In the first place, it conveys a wrong impression to the people at large, that those who are asked to speak in our Churches are recognized by us as qualified according to our Canons to minister in holy things; and in the next place, it carries with it either an acknowledgment on the part of the person inviting that the man whom he asks, is asked, as though he were a clergyman in good standing in this Church, which of course is not true; or else it implies a circumlocution, which hardly fulfils a high idea of honesty; or a discourtesy, because it covers a slur upon the orders of the minister, inasmuch as he is asked, not as a Clergymen, but as an expert layman in some field of Christian science and teaching.

I sincerely hope that no Clergyman of this Diocese will invite into his pulpit any clergyman not, "according to the Canons of this Church," qualified to teach. Of course there is a deeper point in this, namely, that we are not only controlled and governed by our Canons, as to the authority to minister in holy things, but that we are controlled and governed by certain standards of doctrine, up to which every teacher, with whom we share the responsibility of training our people, ought fully to come.

And while the prophetic and the priestly functions are separate in character, they are united in the office of those who are set apart to minister in holy things; and the authorized clergyman is recognized by the congregation naturally as combining both. So that we cannot, without inevitable misunderstanding, admit any one to the exercise of the prophetic office, who is not qualified to minister as Priest.

But, having said this, I feel bound also to say that I recognize in the different opinion and different action of the men who have followed this course, of which I disapprove, the possibility, and, indeed, the certainty of honest convictions in their own minds, that they are furthering in this way the great cause, which lies, and ought to lie, deep in the heart of every Christian man, namely, the breaking down of the wretched divisions which weaken Christendom throughout the world, in its onslaught against error and sin.

I can not help thinking, therefore, that whatever our individual action may be, we should be slow in denunciation of those who differ from us. And, as one reads the story of the Jew Apollos, whom Aquila and Priscilla found teaching at Ephesus, and neither silenced nor condemned nor separated themselves from him, but "took him unto them and expounded unto him the way of God more perfectly," so we should, as the opportunity comes to us, deal with these men who are often "mighty in the Scriptures," and who are certainly "instructed in the way of the Lord, and fervent in the Spirit," that we may help them to "speak and teach diligently the things of the Lord, with more perfect knowledge" of the Catholic Order and Faith.

My own strong conviction is that the only true method to promote the Unity of the Church is to insist upon, in loving strength and thoroughness, the whole scheme and order of teaching, government and worship which we have received and hold in trust for all the world. And, that, if, in addition to this insistence, we illustrate by our lives, and by our pastoral and priestly character, the working of the Grace of God in us, as sealed through His appointed means, we shall do better to "stand in our lot to the end of the days," concerned rather with praying than with planning; and realizing that we may not lightly speak against any, even though they be not with us, by whom it pleases Jesus Christ to cast out the evil spirits from the lives of men. I am very sure beside that there are innumerable works and ways of common interest in the great public movements for the improvement of society, in which we can more and more be associated with others who are not of our household of faith. But the longer I live the more I feel that we must guard ourselves carefully against making our own mental operations the measure of God's revelations of truth, or of God's condescensions of work; and the more, also, I feel, how far wiser each one of us is, in his own place and way, to strive and pray for the coming and consummation of the Kingdom, than to waste our time and strength in the idleness and bitterness of controversy.

I believe that we ought to realize that we are living in an age of very peculiar stir and movement in religious matters. There is one problem that fills the hearts of all intelligent and thoughtful Christians to-day as it has not for many years, and there is one puzzle that is taxing the minds of Christian men as much as the problem stirs their hearts. The problem is the best method of reaching a real unity; and the puzzle is the ad-

justment, of what we believe to be God's own chosen and appointed
methods of work, with the very evident blessing which rests upon work
that is done in methods different from those which we hold; and hold to
be of absolute institution and requirement.   Of course, there are those
who prefer the ease and comfort of living in times that are free from
what have come to be called "burning questions;" who would rather
live before they are raised, or after they are solved; but, inasmuch as the
questions always existed, and the solution must be in God's time and in
God's way, I think that we ought rather to rejoice that we are permitted
to have a part in any prayers or any plans that may work out His definite purpose and will.   But the danger of such times is always the double
danger of impatience and self-will: of mistaking strong convictions of
one's own conscience for the plain revelations of God's will; of measur-
ing every thing human and divine, by just what seems to us to be the
wise and right way; and out of that come, what certainly more than
any thing else hinders unity, mutual recrimination and reproach, and
the forcing apart of those, who in the providence of God are now one, at
any rate, in the holding of the Faith and Order of the Catholic Church.
The appearance of our own branch of the Church, for instance, divided
against itself, with the accusations of disloyalty and unfaithfulness freely
hurled on the one side, and of exclusiveness and narrowness on the other,
makes a spectacle which certainly has little in it to attract those who are
separated from us by their own organizations.

I am well aware that there is danger of a loose holding of things which
in themselves are fundamental and essential, and of melting truth to an
evaporated residuum in the heat of an unwise and unlawful love.   But it
seems to me that much that has gone on among us during the last year,
ought to recall us to a sense of the great need of humbler estimates of
ourselves and kindlier judgments of each other.

I can not, for instance, for a moment believe that any thing ever did
justify, or ever could justify, the setting up of a ministry, out of the direct and divine line of authority which comes to us from Christ, through
the Apostles and their successors.

I should be very clear in my own mind that the old puzzle which for
many years has amused the minds of some people, as to what men ought
to do, cast away on a desert island without a ministry, solved itself by
the simple solution that *if* God withdrew that which He had once given,
it would mean that men were to do without it; and that the doing without it was far safer than any wilful attempt to substitute a human provision, in the stead of that which God once gave and then withdrew.
And the other puzzle, as to what should be done, if the ministry of divine Institution failed from the earth, has the added solution, in my
mind, that it is *impossible*, and idle therefore, to imagine it; and most
unwise to make so shadowy a thing the premiss of an argument for the

validity of ministries constituted otherwise than we believe God's word to allow. He has promised to be with His Church "alway, even unto the end of the world" in the *same promise* which carried with it the commission and authority of the Apostolic Ministry; and the two things must stand together.

But, at the same time, if anybody can find in this kind of theorizing, an explanation of the acknowledged fact, that the abundant blessing of God rests on the ministry of men lacking the link which binds us to the Apostolic Church, I do not see why we should be irritated into violent denunciations. For myself, I utterly disagree with the premisses and the conclusion. I readily recognize that true spiritual results are attendant upon the ministries of the great denominations. I find myself relieved from any contradiction, or any weakening, of my own positive belief in the absolute importance of a duly authorized Ministry, by feeling, that God does not tie Himself to the institutions to which He ties us; that one cannot speak lightly of anyone who casts out devils in His name; that there is some middle line of evident truth and divine reconciliation between our Lord's two statements, "He that is not with Me is against Me," and, "He that is not against us is for us;" that men who have inherited the systems of separation are not responsible, but are, according to their inheritance, earnest and real; and in their earnestness and reality are accepted and blessed of God; and above all, that it behooves us, as inheritors of the ancient Faith and Order of the Church to humble ourselves in the dust; first, because no great schism has ever risen in the Church that was not due to her own unfaithfulness at the time; and secondly, because if men's responsibility is to be measured by their opportunity, we are shamed constantly by the holier lives, the larger liberality and the intenser zeal of the Christian bodies about us.

Believing as I do that the grace of Baptism is independent of the authority of the baptizer, and accepting, so far at any rate, the decree of Trent because it agrees with Catholic decisions far earlier than Trent, that Baptism with the proper matter and the correct form is valid even when administered by a heretic; and believing that there is no forced construction when one applies the rubric in the Office for the Communion of the Sick to those who "are hindered by an impediment," which I believe God counts "just," of inherited ignorance and impossibility; I have no question but that those who are not of us are truly baptized into the Kingdom of God on earth, and do really "eat and drink the Body and Blood of our Saviour Christ profitably to their soul's health, although they do not receive the Sacrament with their mouth."

I may be absolutely wrong in my method of satisfying my own mind upon this troublesome question. There may be many solutions beside these two which I have suggested. I only beg you to realize that whatever one's own views may be, we have no right to lay them down as exclusively and certainly correct; no right to condemn others who explain the difficulty in other ways; and that we are really hindering the enlarged unity of the whole Christian Church by presenting the broken front of brother Churchmen, not only differing, but quarreling among themselves, about questions which are not plainly revealed, and can not be positively settled, until we shall see in the clear light of God's unveiling.

The time, it seems to me, has gone by when anybody attaches much importance to a state of things, which, within even our memory, loomed once into very great significance on the ecclesiastical horizon; whether we should or should not take part in meetings and actions of the American Bible Society; whether the rope of sand, feebler than the old confederation of the thirteen states, miscalled the Evangelical Alliance, should have our countenance and support. Questions like these, I think, have passed out of sight, in the clear conviction, that this momentary union, which covered a deep-seated and permanent separation, broke to the heart the promise which it made to some ears. And that, in itself, seems to me a matter of very real thankfulness. For the first step toward the attainment of a real thing, is dissatisfaction with unreality. A man's pursuit of the great things of life does not begin, until the days are over when a child felt itself busy, playing with a bubble or pursuing a butterfly. In reaching for the more substantial satisfaction of actual unity, some people are disposed to give a *quasi* recognition to non-episcopal clergymen not only by inviting them to preach in their Churches; but by taking part with them in union meetings for various purposes of one kind and another; and I am bound, however I may differ from the methods pursued, to respect the underlying purpose which, however mistaken in the means, has undoubtedly a holy motive which may not be despised. That is to say, I thoroughly respect and sympathize with the end that is proposed; while I differ entirely from the means that are applied; but again I say, it seems to me unjust, unwise, ungenerous, unsafe, to attack bitterly the loyalty of these men to the Church.

I believe there are instances and occasions when it may be very wise for us to join with the ministers and the members of the religious denominations, in condemnation of some great public evil or in pursuit of some great public good. I felt myself, if I may say so without egotism, honoured to co-operate with the Ministerial Association of Albany, of which I am not a member, and with which I never met before, in the onslaugh which we made together and successfully against the evasion, under th pretence of religion or philanthropy, of the laws of the state of New Yor against gambling, which goes on continually in fairs and bazaars, hel sometimes by religious bodies and sometimes by benevolent association "doing evil that good may come." And I have not hesitated to ask one instance a Clergyman to speak, not in his clerical character but the Secretary of the Prison Reform Association, in the Cathedral, abo the work of that Association. It seems to me that intelligent men can see and draw the line. And I can not see how any advance is made toward even a kindlier and closer relation among Christians of various names, by giving them access to the pulpit, when it is perfectly understood that by the very fundamental charter of the Church in her Prayer Book and Constitution, none of us can or would dare to ask those men to minister at the Altar.

The subject is a very large one and reaches out into very many directions, and has varied and interesting applications. I am free to say to you, as your Bishop, that when the opportunity offers for joint action, with those who are not actually of us, in public matters and moral issues, I believe we ought to take advantage of it. And in dealing with an institution which is growing more and more into prominence in this country, The Young Men's Christian Association, I believe that if instead of denouncing it, or falling in with its new plans of separate services of worship and preaching, we can keep such hold upon the men who are controlling it as to influence them to confine it to its own legitimate lines of Christian beneficence, and to prevent it from its evident tendency to intrude into the teaching functions of the Church, we shall do wisely and well. Meanwhile, the value of this Church as a factor in the great problem of the restored unity of Christendom, with most respectful recognition of the work of other bodies, and with the entire abstinence from the bitterness of controversy against them or among ourselves; is, I believe, to stand fast in our old ways, to sit still and see the salvation of God; to illustrate by our lives, our earnestness, our intelligent reasons, the principles we hold ; and to attract the restless and uncertain movements of religious life toward that which, because it is ancient and of divine authority, can afford to possess itself in patience.

It is quite true that this Church which we call the Episcopal Church is relatively small, compared with what we might call Roman Episcopalianism; or with Non-Episcopal Protestantism. But it is also true, as against the numerical* claim of Protestantism, even in our century, that the enormous proportion of Christians in the world to-day are under Episcopal government; and as against all claims, it is true that a larger number of persons come to *us* from the various religious bodies, than to any other body of Christians in America.

And I believe it is a matter worth our while to realize, that the question of the importance of the Institution called the Church does not turn upon a single text in the Bible, but on the drift of our Lord's teachings;

---

* Taking only the English speaking Christians throughout the world to-day, thirty-eight millions out of one hundred millions are under Episcopal government, and the proportion would be much greater still, if the estimate included universal christendom, and added to the " Episcopalians," the members of ·the Roman and Eastern Communions.

that it does not depend upon theoretical interpretations of the Bible, but upon the practical working of Christianity in the world as begun by those whom the Master made its founders after Him; and that for Churchmen the witness of the Prayer Book is binding upon us, in the Preface to the Ordinal, in the Ordination office, in the Litany, in the Ember Prayers in the Collect for St. Peter's Day, in the Institution Office; above all, in the Nicene definition of the Church as One in its unchangingness, Catholic in its lineal connection with the Church of the upper room and the mountain of the Ascension, with the Church to which men were added by Holy Baptism, in which St. Peter and St. John and St. Paul laid on hands for the giving of the Holy Ghost, in which men continued steadfastly in the doctrine as well as the "fellowship of the Apostles, and in the breaking of the bread and in the prayers." Over against all theories of baptism as a sort of continued Jewish rite, stands the fact of the commission to the disciples, which is the charter of Christ's continued presence and work in the world. Christian Baptism with water, "In the name of the Father and of the Son and of the Holy Ghost," is the divinely appointed method of making disciples. And over against all imaginings that the Church is not made prominent in the New Testament Scriptures, is the fact that our Lord preached as did St. Philip after Him and all the rest, the Kingdom of God as inseparable from the Name of Jesus Christ; that His whole life was spent, not in winning multitudes, but in founding a Ministry; and that the theory of a head without a body or of a body without a head, that is of Christ without the Church or of the Church without Christ, is alike monstrous and impossible.

I pass on now to the record of my work this year, which involves, of course, two things — variety in the field of its discharge and smaller results at home; but as I have said to you, both in the letter announcing my acceptance of the charge of our foreign Churches and in the letter which I addressed to the Clergy in July, I have felt that wherever I was acting under authority, I was doing the Church's work and discharging the duties of my Office, whose grave responsibility I constantly feel, is that it makes a man not merely the Overseer of a Diocese, but a Bishop in the Church of God.

On Tuesday, November 11, the 22d annual Convention of the Diocese met in the Cathedral. I delivered a charge to the Clergy and lay people upon the subject of what is called to-day the "Higher Criticism" in the place of the sermon, and celebrated the Holy Communion assisted by the Rev. Archdeacons Carey, Morrison and Olmsted, the Rev. J. Ireland Tucker, S. T. D., and the Dean of the Cathedral. Rather more than the usual number of Clergy and lay delegates were present, and a good many matters of importance were fairly and carefully considered. The business of the Convention was completed in the early afternoon, and delivered my Address in the Cathedral and pronounced the Benediction, after which the Convention adjourned without day.

The acts of most importance were connected with the Report of the Standing Committee that the Diocese of New York had paid "the sum of $25,000, in cash, as an equivalent for all claims of this Diocese from the Diocese of New York for the increase of its Episcopal fund." The letter of the Bishop of New York, and the presence of Mr. James Pott, the Treasurer, to whose interest in this matter its success is not a little due, and the adoption of the resolutions offered by the Committee, with special recognition of Bishop Potter's interest and of the service rendered by the Rev. Clarence Buel and Mr. Pott, mark, of course, an important era in the history of this Diocese.

Not the least pleasure of this transaction came to me in the acknowledgment on the part of the Convention of Dr. Reese's eminent and effective service as Chairman of our Committee, and in the unanimous adoption by the Convention of the last of the three resolutions containing the record of our sense of satisfaction, not only that the one subject of difference between the older and the younger Diocese had been removed, but that there never had been any interruption of the kindly and rightful relations between them.

I desire here to put on record permanently what in the surprise of the moment I could only say imperfectly at the time, my recognition of the most warm, and as I think, extravagant expression of personal affection and kindness to me which marked the final passage of the resolution on this subject. And I trust that the Parishes will recognize practically and promptly, that in a business transaction of this sort there ought to be neither fear nor suspicion of personal feeling, that it is a transaction which belongs to the clerk's office and the counting room, and that if and when the Committee having the matter in charge shall feel it wise to readjust, as I think ought to be done, the assessment upon the different Parishes, "those who are strong will be willing" and able "to bear the infirmities of the weak," and a distribution, of what ought not it seems to me, to be a burden, be made that will secure three things. First, the removal of any undue pressure upon the smaller Parishes; secondly, the removal, from the list, of Missions that are virtually extinct; and thirdly, the prompt payment to the Treasurer of the quota assigned to each Parish, so that both he and the Bishop may be relieved from the perpetual inconvenience and embarrassment of payments postponed. I speak this frankly for your own sakes, and in no way personally for mine; and because it enables me to beg the Vestries and members of the different corporations in the Diocese to realize, that instead of counting the obligation of the payment for religious service as rather sentimental and of secondary consequence, there ought to be more promptness, more punctuality more punctiliousness in pecuniary relations that in any wise concern Religion and the Church, than in any other commercial transactions in the world. The payment of Missionaries by the Board, the payment of Rectors by the Parishes, the payment of pledges made to our different Treasurers, fulfilment of canonical obligations for offerings to different objects, these and all kindred matters, it seems to me, lie along the line of that very highest virtue, honesty, which will "owe no man any thing."

The next matter of chief consequence in the Convention was the final determination instructing the Board of Missions to create and fill the office of Diocesan Missionary. I confess I was very glad of it then, and as I have said elsewhere in this Address, I am the more glad of it since the Board acted under the instructions of the Convention. I very readily gave my consent to the change of the Canons by which the name of Convocation was changed to the name Archdeaconry.

The meeting of the Board of Missions in the evening was spirited and earnest, with good addresses from our own Missionaries,.and an earnest ·appeal from the Rev. Frederick R. Graves, of our Chinese Mission. I was glad of the opportunity of saying then what I repeat now, that situated as we are, with such pressing demands for our own immediate Missionary necessities, we are peculiarly tempted to depreciate our duty to the general Missions of the Church; and I am the more bound therefore to press upon the Clergy and people of this Diocese the fact that in our position and according to our proportion of ability we are bound, I think first of all to give both to the foreign and domestic Missions of the Church regularly and generously, in order that no tinge of selfishness may diminish the sweet savour of our offering as it goes up to God.

I think I ought not to fail to mention my warm approval of the new Canon numbered 18, of the Clergy Reserve Fund. I only hope that it will not be allowed to remain a dead letter on our book of Canons, but that every Clergyman shall see to it that the second section of the Canon is complied with; and I take leave to say *here* and now, that I think it would be eminently wise for this Convention, to order printed on a card a list of the offerings which are canonically required from every Parish in the Church, either by the General or by the Diocesan Convention, with a blank left to be filled in by each Rector, of a stated day in every year when those offerings shall be taken; the card to be hung not only in the Vestry but in the porch of every Church in the Diocese, so that the matter may be before the minds and eyes of both Clergy and people.

On the evening of November 26th, in Grace Church, Albany, preached and confirmed two persons.

December 31st, in the afternoon, at St. Paul's Church, Albany, preached and confirmed thirteen persons.

On Monday, January 19, at a meeting of the Archdeaconry of Albany in St. John's Church, Cohoes, I preached and confirmed seventeen persons.

Our Diocesan Missionary, the Rev. W. C. Stewart, made an address that same evening and began the impression which his service to the Diocese, as his report will show, has gone on to deepen and increase, of the importance of the position and of his admirable adaptation to fill it. It is, of course, in its first year largely tentative, and I am free to say that he has accomplished far more than I hoped in my most sanguine moments. With its lines of work more clearly defined, its usefulness more fully recognized, and his own experience ripening him for its discharge, I am abundantly assured that still larger results will continue to appear In a way, of course, it lightens my work by gathering and giving to me information about certain details which I should otherwise have had to get myself; in another way, like every improvement in machinery, it increases my work by opening new opportunities for its exercise, and I am very glad to welcome it on both these grounds.

On Tuesday, January 22, acting under the authority of the Bishop of Vermont, I blessed the new Chancel of Trinity Church, Rutland, preaching the sermon and celebrating the Holy Communion.

It was a noble service, and the cordial welcome and generous hospitality were very grateful to me. I felt a special interest, from the fact that the Rector under whom such admirable results have been wrought out was a candidate for Holy Orders in this Diocese, and began his preparation for the Sacred Ministry under my direction.

On Friday, January 23d, in the evening, in St. John's Church, Troy, I preached and confirmed fourteen persons.

On Sunday, the 25th, the Feast of the Conversion of St. Paul, I admitted Miss Emma Janes, a postulant in the Sisterhood of the Holy Child Jesus, and celebrated the Holy Communion.

On Tuesday, the 27th, at a meeting of the Archdeaconry of Troy, in the Church of the Holy Cross, I preached and celebrated the Holy Communion, and was present afterward at a meeting of the Archdeaconry, and took part in two most pleasant events; first, the address of cordial God speed to me, and then the passing of a resolution of sympathy with the venerable Priest, the Rev. John Henry Hopkins, D. D., my friend, intimate and beloved for many years, much of whose active ministry was passed in this Diocese.

On Wednesday, January 28th I blessed the new Altar in Christ Church, Hudson, preaching and celebrating the Holy Communion. The re-arrangement of the Chancel is an admirable addition to the beauty of a beautiful Church in the part of it which ought to be *most* beautiful. It preserves a sweet and sacred memory which never can die out, I know, before God or in the hearts of the people in that Parish, and which I certainly never can forget; and it preserves it in the *most* fitting way; not only that the Altar is the place of constant commemoration, and closest communion with the saints at rest; but that in this case artistic skill has been joined with sisterly love, in accomplishing the result.

On January the 30th, in the evening, in the Church of the Holy Innocents, Albany, I confirmed eight persons and preached.

On Saturday, January 31, I confirmed in private in the Cathedral one person from the Cathedral congregation, and, also, on that same day organized St. Sacrament Mission, Bolton, appointing Mr. J. B. Simpson, Warden, Mr. A. W. Dickinson, Treasurer, and Mr. Randall H. Wilson, Clerk. The Church had hitherto been without ecclesiastical organization, being held simply by a Board of Trustees, who have faithfully discharged their duty, and have handed the property over to the Diocese, free from debt and largely increased in its value.

On Monday, February 2, in the Cathedral, being the Feast of the Purification and the twenty-second anniversary of my consecration to the Episcopate, I preached, confirmed twenty persons and celebrated the Holy Communion. Fourteen of the candidates were from the School and therefore from the Cathedral, and the others were presented, two by the Rector of Green Island, one from the Church of the Ascension, Troy, one by the Missionary at St. Andrew's, West Troy, and two by the Rector of Trinity Church, Albany. A large congregation gathered; twenty-four of the Clergy came to keep the Feast with me and bid me God-speed on my journeying; and the Bishop of Indiana made us glad by his presence, a Bishop whom Albany is glad to claim her share in, both by family relations, and from the fact that the earliest prophecy of his great work was in our Diocese. At the gathering at my daughter's house afterward, I had the pleasure of seeing the Clergy personally, and little thought that I should never again see two who were there, Dr. Payne and Mr. Selkirk, their thoughts filled with prayers for my protection against the dangers of the sea, little dreaming that *I* should come back safely, not to find them.

On Tuesday, February 3, I was present at a meeting of the House of Bishops called to nominate a Bishop for Japan, and on the 4th, Wednesday, at one o'clock, we sailed on the Trave, sped on our way by kindliest farewells from hosts of friends, and followed, as I know I was, through all my journeyings, with faithful and constant prayers.

On Sunday, February 8, I said the Morning Prayer and preached on *shipboard*, and on Wednesday, being Ash Wednesday, I said the service with a few Church people who were *on board*.

On Friday, the 13th, late at night, we landed at Bremen, after a smooth and *most* comfortable passage, to find good news awaiting me of all at home. I went immediately to Berlin, where I was anxious to look into the question which had been proposed to me, about the necessity of establishing an American Chapel in that great Capital. It is quite true that there are large numbers of Americans from time to time residing in Berlin, as students of the Arts and Modern Languages; but the Rector of the English Church, St. George's, makes all Americans most welcome who will come, and there is room enough and to spare in the Church, so that I was entirely satisfied that there was no need of separate organization for Americans in Berlin. My very clear conviction in regard to the founding of American Chapels abroad is that in accordance with the agreement among the Bishops at Lambeth, they ought not to be established, where the English Church already exists and makes sufficient provision for our people to attend its services; and I am equally satisfied that where there are enough resident Americans to support the services, the right and duty of establishing them is plain.

I was more than ever impressed during my Visitation of the Continental Churches this year with the three-fold use to which their erection and maintenance lends itself. First, as providing for our own people, who, for various reasons, by no means always merely pleasure seeking, are abroad for longer or shorter times; and who ought, of course, where they are in sufficient numbers, to look after the building and its support themselves; secondly, upon national grounds, to offer to *all* Americans, a service that shall keep them in touch and contact with home. I found, even in my brief experience this year, that familiarity with the Prayer Book and the inevitable attraction of our Church service, does away with many misconceptions of the Church, and attracts to her, many persons, who, coming to know the Church in the beauty of her Worship, look for it, when they come home, and attach themselves permanently to us. And thirdly, by no means least, although I mention it last, the witness of our American Church in its pure and unbroken relations to all that is primitive and Catholic, absolutely unembarrassed by any relations to the State, is a constant presentation to thoughtful men in Roman Catholic countries, of the noble ideal of "a free Church in a free State," toward which, as the possible outcome in the establishment of National Churches abroad, many hearts and heads in Europe are coming more and more to look.

I am bound, I think, in the consideration of serious dangers, to call the attention of those to whom my words may come, to what seems to me a serious risk, thoughtlessly incurred, by American parents in sending their children abroad, unguarded and uncared for, to the various temptations of these great European Capitals; where the whole standard of life is very different from ours; where the relations which at home, *because* of our different standards, are perfectly safe, between young men and young women, become unsafe, if not improper; and where, often, by the testimony of those who are on the ground, the gravest results follow.

I cannot but feel, from what I heard and saw in Berlin, Dresden and Paris, that too many American men and women are either ignorant of, or indifferent to, the dangers to which their children are exposed; and I do not hesitate to say, that in my judgment, no young man or young woman ought to be sent to any of these cities, for any purpose whatever, without sufficient means to guard against emergencies of illness and expense, and without being definitely under the charge of some older person, to whom they would naturally turn for guidance, and who would have some oversight of them in their daily lives. I was very glad to find in Berlin a most admirable Presbyterian minister and his wife, who, without attempting any definite religious organization, give themselves to the establishment of a friendly, personal relation with the students whom they can reach. And in Paris I found that the Rev. W. W. Newell and his wife were interested and engaged in a similar work. I am thankful to say, that, so far as Paris is concerned, under the direction and at the suggestion of the Rev. Dr. Morgan, we have determined to begin services in the Latin quarter, in the midst of the students who live and work there; which, I am still more thankful to say, are to be carried on under the direction of Mr. Newell, whom I had the great pleasure of confirming in Paris, and who has since been admitted as a candidate for Orders in the Church, and will be ordered Deacon in the early winter, I trust.

I had the pleasure of preaching morning and evening in St. George's Church, Berlin, through the courtesy of the Rector, and celebrated the Holy Communion at the morning service; and I must put on record here what I should repeat in every instance but for the monotony of the repetition, that we were overwhelmed with cordial courtesies and social and personal attentions of every sort, not only from the very admirable men who represent the United States Government as our Ministers and Consuls in these European cities, but from all, both American and English Church people, whom we met everywhere.

I felt, of course, that they were rendered to the Office and to my representative position, but to whatever the honour was done, the pleasure and enjoyment were ours.

On Friday, February 20, in St. John's Church, Dresden, I preached and ordained Priest the Rev. Thomas Wilson Bevan, presented by Mr. Caskey who, together with Mr. Gilderdale, united with me in the Laying on of Hands. I celebrated the Holy Communion. In the afternoon, I made an Address at the Lenten service; and Saturday evening I received such of the people as came, in the Rector's house, where he made us cordially welcome.

On Sunday morning, the 22d, I preached and celebrated in St. John's Church, and in the afternoon I preached and confirmed eight persons in St. John's Church; and in the evening I preached in the English Church of All Saints, at Mr. Gilderdale's courteous invitation. The death of this wise and faithful Priest, which occurred not long after, is a great loss to the work of the English Church abroad, and is a personal sorrow to me and to all who ever came to know him.

Our Church in Dresden is a very beautiful building. Mr. Caskey has certainly accomplished a remarkable work, and is ready, with earnest pastoral instinct to serve and care for the American people resident or transient there.

On the 23d I was present at a Parish meeting at which some changes were made in the Constitution of the Parish to conform it more to American precedent, and by which my old friend, Mr. John Bard was elected Warden, and the vacancies in the Vestry were filled.

On Sunday, March 1, in St. James' Church, Florence, I preached and celebrated the Holy Communion. It was a great comfort and pleasure to me to make my pilgrimage to the shrine in the beautiful English cemetery in Florence, where my mother is buried. The little Church, in spite of its, to say the least, uncentral and inconspicuous position, holds its own, numbers earnest and admirable people among its officers and congregation, and is a comfort to the Americans who live here, or pass through this most intense and interesting city of the world.

On Sunday, the 8th of March, I celebrated the Holy Communion in St. Paul's Church in Rome, the Bishop of Minnesota preaching the sermon. It was a great pleasure to find the daily Lenten service in the Church, with an added celebration of the Holy Communion on Thursdays, which the Bishop of Minnesota took on Thursday, the 12th of March; and to find the real rooting of this work which has been so long in the hands of Dr. Nevin. The Church itself, which is very beautiful, is a standing and valuable witness, in the face of the Latin additions to our common Christianity, to primitive truth, both in its outward form and in the spirit of its teaching and work; and like the other Chapels on the Continent, it furnishes the opportunity, often desired, for people to whom the step is difficult at home to come for confirmation; as three Americans did when I administered confirmation this year.

The St. Paul's House, where sick people are cared for, and from which trained nurses are often supplied, is a practical and valuable benefaction, and I was glad to help on (I hope towards its completion), the Rectory, which, when it is finished, will not only furnish suitable rooms for the Priest in charge, but will give important additions to the working power of the Parish.

On Sunday, the 15th, in the morning, I preached and celebrated the Holy Communion and confirmed seven persons in St. Paul's Church, Rome; and on Monday morning I confirmed one more person in the Church.

I went to Nice the next day, where I found a very complete establishment of the Church: a beautiful Building, with a convenient and delightful Rectory, and a satisfactory condition of the whole work. I preached in the Church on the 18th, in the morning, and on the 19th, I preached, confirmed ten persons and celebrated the Holy Communion.

One of the persons confirmed was the son of the Rev. Mr. Schwartz, who was present, with Mr. Boardman, the old Rector of the Church of the Holy Innocents, Albany, and made me feel all the more at home, as surrounded by Clergy associated always in my mind with Albany.

On Saturday, the 21st, in Geneva, I met the Rt. Rev. Dr. Herzog, the Bishop of the Catholic Christian Church of Switzerland, and Dr. Weibel, President of the Council, and signed a formal contract by which we are to have joint occupation of a very admirable Church building which the Christian Catholics are erecting in Lucerne. I confess this was one of the great pleasures of my European Visitation, because I believe we can do nothing that will so much tend to help on the only true reform that can come in the Roman Communion, namely, that which is from within; and because I believe that the witness, which our common occupation of the consecrated building will bear, will be a powerful and perpetual evidence, of a practical sort, of our great longing for the restored unity of Christendom. I had hoped to have part in the ceremony of the laying of the Corner-stone. But an unexpected difficulty about the land deferred it until the 18th of August, when Dr. Weibel telegraphed me it was laid with due and fitting solemnity.

On Sunday, the 22d, in Emmanuel Church, Geneva, I preached and celebrated the Holy Communion, and confirmed thirteen persons. Here too, I found not strength, because the congregation is small, but unity and an admirable administration of affairs.

Not being able to make my Visitation to the Church in Paris on Easter Day, I went immediately to London; where I had the constant privilege and enjoyment of such services and teachings as one can find in that great centre of English Christianity. It was my intense pleasure to hear the Bach Passion music on Tuesday night in Holy Week, in the Cathedral, and the sight of the vast congregation, and the great array of surpliced singers and musicians reaching out into the dome, the splendid music, and the noble effect of the congregation rising and joining in the familiar hymns, are never to be forgotten.

I had the comfort of celebrating at eight o'clock in the North Chapel, on Good Friday, and of being present at the Three Hours Service in the Cathedral afterward. The impressiveness of the service, and specially of the silence in the Cathedral, was very marked. And the whole keeping of Good Friday made one feel how strong a hold religion has in London, when such great bodies of men gather and take their part in the solemnities of our worship. Noble as the great musical services are in St. Paul's, I think I was almost more struck on Good Friday, by the sound of the great multitude of people singing the hymns without any instrument, and led by the single voice of the officiating Priest, than by any thing I had ever heard, even there.

On Easter Day I preached and celebrated the Holy Communion in the

Savoy Chapel, and enjoyed the Evensong service in the Cathedral in the afternoon; and then listened with great edification to the sermon which the Bishop of London preached at night to a congregation, many of whom *stood,* silent and packed in the Cathedral, through the whole service and sermon.

I returned on the 8th of April to Paris, and in the beautiful Church of the Holy Trinity, on the morning of Sunday, April 12, I preached, celebrated the Holy Communion and confirmed twenty-seven persons. In the evening, in the rooms occupied by the Rev. Mr. and Mrs. Newell, in " the Latin quarter," I made an Address to a very goodly company of the young students in Paris, having previously dined by invitation of the President in the Club rooms of the Artists' Association. My object was to look a little more thoroughly and on the spot, into the possibility and importance of making some spiritual provision for the large number of young Americans who are both living and studying in the old quarter of the Sorbonne. Mr. and Mrs. Newell have been for some time doing a most gracious work among them, combining religious instruction with personal and social interest and influence which are so attractive and precious to people far away from home; and as I had determined, at the suggestion of the Rector of the Holy Trinity in Paris, to make the attempt to provide services especially for them, I was anxious to see for myself just what the position of things was. I am very thankful to say that after we had decided to make the move and to open religious services regularly in the Latin quarter in the autumn, Mr. Newell, who, by his devotion and character and ability, by his thorough knowledge of the people and by his already large influence over them, is the man of all men to make the movement a success, concluded, after due consideration, to apply to be admitted to Orders in the Church, and was confirmed with two others, when I came back to Paris on the morning of the 12th of May. I gave him at once a License as a Lay Reader under Dr. Morgan's direction, and he has since been recommended to me by the Standing Committee of this Diocese as a candidate for Holy Orders, and will, I hope, be able to be ordained at the expiration of the required time. I am free to say that this *most* welcome surprise made, I think, sufficient reason and return for my European tour.

Our stay in Paris was largely occupied with very constant and gracious hospitalities from the Rector, from our American minister, Mr. Reid, and from the great number of kindly friends whom we either found or made there. The Parish is strong, united and full of life. And the service is unusually reverent and beautiful.

On Sunday, the 19th, I celebrated early in the Church of the Holy Trinity, preached at the morning service at which the Bishop of Minnesota celebrated, and preached again in the Church at Evensong. This ended my official duty, which, in spite of a month's half-illness and half-health, making duty sometimes difficult, was really one long pleasure from the great kindness and cordiality of our own Clergy and people and of others whom we were privileged to meet.

I spent the next three weeks at Aix les Bains, the guest of my *most* dear and kind friend, Mr. J. Pierpont Morgan; and on my way back to England held a special confirmation for three persons in the Church at Paris.

On Sunday, the 17th of May, I preached and celebrated the Holy Communion in St. Gabriel's Church, Warwick Square, London, where the Rector is my old friend the son of Canon Ellison, and a son-in-law of the late Archbishop Tait; and in the afternoon I had the pleasure of speaking to a body of about fifty boys, gathered into what the Curate calls his "Perseverance Class." It was a meeting of very deep interest to me. Just how far such a work could be done among our own people I am not sure, but I am very sure that something of the sort would be of the greatest use in our parochial organization. Its object is to hold together young people after their confirmation, and to keep them in continual contact with the Priest, and in constant thoughtfulness and regularity about their reception of the Holy Communion. I certainly commend the idea to the Clergy as likely to help them in what we all know to be one of the most difficult of our duties, namely, the guarding of young people after Confirmation, from straying away.

On the 20th of May I went to Cambridge as the guest of the Vice Chancellor, the Rev. Dr. Butler, Master of Trinity, and the next day, surrounded by kind friends, I had the great honour and pleasure of receiving the degree of Doctor of Laws from that venerable University, *conferred* upon me, to my great surprise. I found added satisfaction in the fact that I owed its conferring in very large degree, to the wishes expressed three years ago by Bishop Lightfoot, and recently by the Archbishop of Canterbury, and the present Bishop of Durham, and the Rev. Canon Browne.

On Sunday, May 24, I preached for the Archbishop's Assyrian Mission in St. Peter's, Eaton Square, by the appointment of his Grace.

On Tuesday, the 26th, accompaned by some gracious friends, I went to Oxford, and after a delightful day with my dear old friend, Dr. Sewell, Warden of New College, I was presented by Archdeacon Palmer, to the Vice Chancellor and received from him the degree of Doctor in Divinity. By the kindness of the Warden, I was permitted to wear the gown of his brother, Dr. William Sewell, Founder and Master of Radley; and the day will be always really "a scarlet day" in my memory, as bringing to me what all men I am sure account, the *other* very highest possible Academic honour in the world.

On Sunday, the 31st of May, in old St. Mary's, Cambridge, I preached of the University Sermons, the Ramsdell Sermon as it is called, taking the place of my friend the Bishop of Rochester, who was unable owing to illness, to fulfil his appointment.

I was glad to render some return, small as it was, to the University, in consideration of the honour it had done me, glad to lift my voice again in that historic Church, and glad to feel that in some small way I could render a service to Bishop Davidson.

We sailed from Liverpool on the 2d day of June, in the good ship Majestic, which well deserves her name, and had one of those passages which rob the sea of its terrors, and turn an ocean voyage into a yachting cruise. Due partly to the ship, partly to the delightful company in which we journeyed, I felt that it was due still more to the constant prayers that followed me and brought me safely to my own country again, in the early morning of June 10.

I preached on board, on the morning of Sunday, the 7th, the Bishop of Minnesota giving the Benediction, and the Captain reading the Lessons at my request, with an intelligent reverence and earnestness which I wish all our Clergy could imitate in that most important and valuable part, it seems to me, of our public ministrations except the Celebration of the Sacraments, the rendering of the Holy Word of God; and at eight o'clock, on the evening of the 10th of June, I was in the house which is another home to me, by the kindness of my gracious friend, Mrs. J. V. L. Pruyn; and later, among the dear children of St. Agnes School, who, with the many friends that were gathered for the musical evening which closes the term there, gave me the heartiest of welcomes, and filled my heart anew with thankfulness and affection, and a desire to give myself with more devotion than before, to the work which God has been good enough to enable me to do.

The next day was very fully occupied. I celebrated the Holy Communion early in the Cathedral, and made the Address to the Post-graduates, who gathered in goodly number to keep the twenty-first anniversary of the graduating at the School. At eleven, in the great school-room, I presided at the graduating exercises; and afterward in the Cathedral, delivered my Address, with the diplomas and Benediction, to the unusually large class of twenty-two girls who graduated this year. The occasion was full of deep feeling and great satisfaction to me. I have felt the loss, to me, of the months of constant intercourse with the children, and especially with the graduates; but I was reassured, in the firm conviction with which I left home, that the wise and faithful hands to whom the work has been so long entrusted would carry it on and out without me as well as though I were there; and as it turned out, the loss was only mine, and the condition of the School was admirable throughout the whole term.

I am minded here to lift my voice in protest against the recklessness with which statements in regard to disease and its causes are made in the interests of all sorts of people. This year, for reasons which I do not think it would be hard to find, it seemed to be the interest of some people to make strong assertions about an epidemic disease in Albany, and to attribute it to the water supply. There were only two cases of serious illness in the School, but owing to the wild assertions of the newspapers, great alarm was felt by parents as to the possible risks of their children. Some were withdrawn and anxiety was spread abroad in many households throughout the country. The fact is, that owing to the extreme care which is exercised in boiling and filtering all the water, and to the wholesomeness of the life in every way, I venture to say that there is no community of one hundred and fifty people anywhere in the world living in one house, or in a row of houses, where there is such absolute freedom from illness, as in St. Agnes School.

While I thoroughly believe in tracing the causes of disease and in removing them, I am sure that nothing is gained by the publication of statements of an alarming character, especially when they have small foundation in fact. The testimony of twenty-one years of our school life, during which time, out of the hundreds of children only two have died, is witness to the fact, both of the healthfulness of the city and of the carefulness of the administration of the School.

At two o'clock I laid the Cornerstone of the Graduates' Hall, which the Society of Graduates have undertaken to build, to furnish better accommodations for the public exercises of the School, and as a memorial of their gratitude to their intellectual Mother.

It is begun, as so much else has been begun in connection with our work, in faith, without funds as yet in hand to do more than lay the foundations; but I believe that in this case, as in so many other cases, the foundations will grow, because work that is done in faith is apt to be after the manner of seed, which "has life within itself."

At a meeting of the Trustees of the Corning Foundation the next morning, I signed the contract for the additional building which the Trustees have erected at the east end of the School, intended not to furnish accomodation for more pupils, but better accommodation for the number of pupils we have always received. The building is to contain recitation rooms, a large kindergarten room, and a row of dormitories, in order that we may be able to use for only special cases what is commonly known as the Third Dormitory, avoiding in this way almost entirely the necessity of climbing stairs. All this is quite in keeping with the purpose which I expressed in my Address to the graduates, "to make the School more and more live up to and work out its ideals; recognising that this means material improvements in the buildings, more apparatus, a larger library, and teaching that keeps up *pari passu* with all the advances and changes of the times."

In the evening, in the Cathedral, I preached and confirmed fifty-six persons, which, with fourteen previously confirmed and four later on, make seventy-four for the year.

Sunday, June 14, in the Cathedral, I preached and ordered Deacon Mr. James F. Olmsted and Mr. J. Montgomery Rich. The former was presented by his brother, the Archdeacon of the Susquehanna, and the latter by the Rev. Canon Gray. I am sorry to say that the Diocese gains nothing by the addition of these two young men, as I immediately transferred them, much against my wishes, to other jurisdictions.

In the evening, in Trinity Church, Albany, I preached and confirmed eight persons.

Monday, June 15, in the afternoon, in Christ Church, Gloversville, I preached and confirmed five persons; and in the evening, in St. John's Church, Johnstown, where I am thankful to find Mr. Marvin successfully and satisfactorily established in the Rectorship, I preached and confirmed nineteen persons.

On Tuesday, the 16th, in the morning, in Christ Church, Herkimer, I preached and confirmed twenty-six persons. Owing to the lateness of the train, I was compelled greatly to hasten my Visitation, and to my great regret obliged to leave the Celebration of the Holy Communion to the Rector, in order that I might reach my next appointment in time. In the afternoon I was present at the closing of the training school in the St. Christina Home, and was very glad to give the prizes which had been earned during the year. It was a very interesting occasion, and indeed its whole work, I think, is full of interest and promise. I am glad to express, for one of very many gracious services to me and to my work, my very cordial thanks to Canon Fulcher, who cares for the spiritual training of these children, is most helpful about their musical training, and brings to the Sisters while they are here, with the full consent of the Rector of the Parish, the weekly Celebration of the Holy Communion in the little Chapel of the Home.

In the evening, in Bethesda Church, Saratoga, I preached and confirmed fifty-nine persons. The service was very impressive, and I am abundantly satisfied that here, as in other places, the Clergy feel with me not merely the relief of the shortened service by the omission of the Evening Prayer, but the advantage of bringing into more prominence the Office of Confirmation, by letting it stand alone.

I desire to call the attention of the Clergy to a method of administering Confirmation, which I have been led for various reasons lately to adopt. I need hardly say that it is with no desire of any personal convenience; but the more or less confusion which pertains when candidates are obliged to kneel by the railing and then rise to make room for others, has been always an annoyance to me; and the serious objection of keeping people too long upon their knees by having the Bishop go from one to another as they are kneeling, is very evident. I have, therefore,

where it was agreeable to the Rector, had a chair placed at the opening
of the Chancel gate, and had all the candidates come up into the choir
and stand, and then come, one by one, and kneel in front of me to receive
the Laying on of Hands; and after that retire to the Choir and remain
standing until they kneel for the closing Collect and Benediction.   The
special beauty of the arrangement to me is that it brings out what is so
marked about the Confirmation office, the separateness and individuality;
and the giving to each person his own gift.   I am in nowise disposed
to insist upon it in any instance; but I am inclined to suggest it to the
Clergy, as in my judgment, the most impressive method of administering
the Holy Ordinance.

On the evening of June 17, in Grace Church, Albany, I preached and
confirmed twenty-five persons, an earnest of good things for the future
of this Parish under its new administration.

On Thursday, June 18, I was present at a meeting of the Trustees of
St. Stephen's College, Annandale, and made the Address in the Chapel
in connection with the laying of the Cornerstone of Hoffman Hall.   I
did not take part in the actual laying of the Cornerstone, as Bishop Potter's thoughtful urgency enabled me to escape the downpour to which he
was compelled to expose himself; but the rain was the only drawback to
the great pleasure of the day.   The College was never in more admirable
condition; and the report of the Warden, with its clear outlines of distinction between a College and a University, and its strong arguments in
favour of the former, was full of that strong sense and intellectual grasp
which go to make up Dr. Fairbairn's enviable reputation as a Master of
Philosophy and a Master of Education as well.   It was a great satisfaction to me that the College on this occasion honored the Dean of the
Cathedral with the title of Doctor in Divinity, rarely well bestowed, I
think, in this case; and also recognized the fitness and faithfulness of
Canon Fulcher by giving him the degree of Bachelor in Divinity; which
if not *in* course, might, I think, be well said to be *of* course, when a
graduate of the College has so won his way to its honours.

In the evening, in St. Barnabas' Church, Troy, I preached and confirmed nineteen persons.

On Friday, the 19th, in the evening, in All Saints' Chapel, Hoosac, I
preached and confirmed thirteen persons.   The Chapel is more beautiful
than ever, since the addition of the new tapestry hangings and the wrought-
iron brackets, which bear witness to the generous and loving taste of the
Rector.   The reaching out of the Church to care for the region that lies
in the range of Hoosac is a noble evidence of the true missionary spirit ;
and Mr. Tibbits' devoted energy is laying strong foundation for the future.

Saturday, the 20th, in the morning, I preached and consecrated
abas' Church, Stottville; celebrated the Holy Communion

and confirmed twelve persons, of whom one was confirmed in private. The Church is very greatly improved by its enlargement and is the centre of a good and earnest work.

In the afternoon, in Christ Church, Hudson, with the Church crowded and with every best token of energy and life, I preached and confirmed thirty-two persons; and in the evening, in St. Luke's Church, Catskill, where to the infinite advantage of the Parish Mr. Miller has become Rector, I preached and confirmed twenty-eight persons.

On Sunday morning, June 21, in St. Paul's Church, Troy, I preached and confirmed thirty-three persons and celebrated the Holy Communion; and in the afternoon, in Trinity Church, Lansingburgh, I preached and confirmed seventeen persons; and in the evening, in the Free Church of the Ascension, Troy, I preached and confirmed eighteen persons.

On Monday morning I confirmed three persons for the Cathedral, one in private. In the afternoon, in the Church of the Epiphany, Bath, I preached and confirmed fourteen persons; and in the evening, in St. Mark's, Green Island, I preached and confirmed fourteen persons.

Up to this point the number of confirmations is 890, of whom the Bishop of Delaware confirmed in St. Augustine's, Ilion, 13; in Emmanuel Church, Little Falls, 10; in St. George's, Schenectady, 24; in St. Ann's Church, Amsterdam, 48; in St. Paul's Church, Bartonville, 10; in the Church of the Good Shepherd, Chestertown, 18; and in St. Paul's Church, Salem, 10; and the Bishop of Wyoming and Idaho confirmed 29 in St. Peter's Church, Albany, and 21 in St. Paul's Church, Albany; and of whom I myself, confirmed, as I have already reported, in Europe, 68.

On the 23d of June, I officiated at the marriage of one of my St. Agnes' children, acting with the courteous consent of the Rector, in the beautiful Church at Mamaroneck; and on the 25th of June, I found myself in my dear place of summer rest and refreshing, where I have been able to keep the usual round of our services, on Sunday morning and afternoon, and on Wednesday morning and Friday evening, with two sermons a week and the Celebration on all Holy Days and Sundays.

I must again call the attention of the Diocese with more emphasis, or at least with, I hope, more effect than ever to what I really consider to be a disgraceful and discreditable record. The Orphan House at Cooperstown, which cares for a hundred children, exists, I may so say, upon two things — the faith, devotion and practical wisdom of Miss Cooper in its administration, and the fact that the poormasters of Otsego county find it the best and most economical place for the children who but for this house would be sent to the degrading surroundings of the poor-house.

The Diocese itself virtually does nothing, except that in a few instances children are supported, coming from different Parishes in the Diocese by small payments from their relatives. Meanwhile, in the first place, money is seriously needed for repairs that are absolutely essential to the

8

house itself; and the income is entirely insufficient for the support of the Institution; so that it has come to be the question on the part of the Trustees whether they can go on any longer to do more than receive children who are absolutely paid for. I am very glad to say that so far they have determined to continue their act of faith and mercy, but the Diocese really must rise to a recognition of its duty towards this most admirable institution.

I am disposed to suggest, to every Clergyman of the Diocese that he should organize, perhaps in his Sunday School, a perfectly informal guild of young people under his own direction, with the double promise, first, to remember the Orphan House in their prayers from time to time, and secondly, to give themselves to gathering subscriptions toward its support. And I ask the Convention distinctly in the appointment of the Committee upon the Report of the Superintendent this year, to instruct that Committee to make some practical suggestion by which every Parish in the Diocese may be moved to contribute something annually toward the decent support of the Orphan House.

On Sunday, the 30th of August, in the Chapel of St. Mary's by the Sea, North-east Harbor, I confirmed one person.

On Thursday, September 10th, in St. John's, Troy, I ordained deacon Mr. George Lynde Richardson, presented by the Rev. Mr. Snively. There was a very goodly gathering of the clergy present, who enjoyed with me both the dignity of the service and the delightful hospitality of the ladies of the Parish.

On the 11th of September, in the Chapel at Tannersville, I preached and confirmed four persons, having the great pleasure of finding there the Bishop of Tennessee, who gave the benediction at the close of the service.

On the 12th, in the morning, I consecrated Emmanuel Church at Griffin's Corners. The building up of this work is due to the devotion and energy of the lay reader, Mr. Challen, who is also a candidate for Holy Orders; and whose missionary spirit and capacity give promise of the best things in his ministry. The request to consecrate was read by the Rev. Mr. Reazor, who has fostered and fathered this work, and the sentence of consecration by the Diocesan Missionary. The coming of the choir from Kingston with the rector, Rev. Mr. Wattson, added very much to the beauty of the service.

On Sunday, September the 13th, in Zion Church, Sandy Hill, I preached, confirmed nine persons, two of whom were from Fort Edward, and celebrated the Holy Communion; and in the evening in the Church of the Messiah, Glens Falls, I preached and confirmed eleven persons, more than ever impressed by the beauty of the new Chancel and the excellence of the choir.

On the 14th, in the morning, in the Church of St. Sacrament, Bolton,

I preached and confirmed five persons and celebrated the Holy Communion. In the afternoon, in the Union Church at Sabbath Day Point, I preached and confirmed four persons. Every thing here is due to the long loving service of Mr. Chamberlain the lay reader, who in the ripeness of his age, with the freshness of youth, devotes himself to real missionary work in this region. It is a rare sight to see a gentleman of education and literary taste and habit, devoting the leisure of his life to work among those plain simple people. The sight of his library and his manuscript translations from the Fathers really had about it a flavour of Oxford which was most refreshing. I have been rarely more touched than I was during the service when one of the candidates for confirmation laid her little baby close to the chancel steps upon the floor so that it might not miss its mother, and, with the child almost touching the skirts of her dress, knelt for the grace of confirmation. The kindly hospitality of old Albany friends added much to the pleasures of my visit, and General Banks added to the comforts of the visitation also, as did Mr. Simpson by carrying me from point to point on their steam launches.

On Thursday, the 17th, I officiated at the marriage of a dear friend in Bar Harbour.

On Sunday, the 27th, I celebrated and preached for the last time this summer at the dear chapel at North-east.

On Tuesday, the 29th, the Feast of St. Michael, after the celebration in the Cathedral, I blessed the new building of the Child's Hospital, which is finished and paid for by the generous gifts of those who have always cared for this gracious charity, both with the open hands of their giving and the outstretched hands of their prayers. It is a perfect building, nobly planned in all its details and thoroughly adapted to its work, but thankful as I am that we have been permitted to accomplish this, it is to me only a stimulus to the carrying on of the very necessary additions of new buildings for St. Margaret's House and for the Sisters' House; which ought to come soon.

On the 1st of October, in the Church of the Memorial, Middleville, I preached and confirmed fourteen persons, six of whom came from Fairfield, and celebrated the Holy Communion. In the afternoon, at the Church in Mohawk, I preached and confirmed six persons.

On the 5th, Monday, in the evening, in Trinity Church, Whitehall, I preached and confirmed eight persons, and afterward used a service of benediction for the new building which has been completed for the Sunday-school and parochial gatherings. A beautiful and admirable building it is too, and sure to be very helpful in the practical workings of the parish.

On the 6th of October, in Christ Church, Port Henry, in the afternoon, I preached and confirmed three persons; and in the evening in Trinity Church, Plattsburgh, I preached and confirmed twenty-seven persons, of whom fourteen came from our new mission just organized at Lyon Mountain. They were presented by the Diocesan Missionary, Mr. Stewart, whose energetic interest, I think, has fixed, for permanent establishment and growth, the work which was begun by the Archdeacon in the summer. There seems to me a real opening here for the establishment of an important mission, which in the summer can be associated with the work of Loon Lake, and so mark one step further forward in the region of our northern mountains.

October 7th, in the morning, in Christ Church, Rouses Point, I preached and confirmed six persons and celebrated the Holy Communion. In the evening at St. John's Church, Champlain, I preached and confirmed seven persons.

On the 8th, I preached a sermon at the meeting of the Archdeaconry of Ogdensburgh, in St. Mark's Church, Malone, and was present afterward at the business meeting of the Convocation at which the Archdeacon presided: at which I was more than ever impressed with the vigour, energy and working power of this northern Archdeaconry. In the evening in the same Church I confirmed three persons who had driven with Mr. Stewart twenty-four miles from Lyon Mountain, to be confirmed, having been prevented from coming with the others to Plattsburgh.

On the 9th, in the afternoon, in the Church at Colton, I preached and confirmed nine persons, and in the evening in Trinity Church, Potsdam, I preached and confirmed nineteen, two coming from Hogansburgh for the confirmation. The Church is more beautiful than ever. The vested choir with the platform carried out into the nave adds greatly, both to the beauty of the service and the impressiveness of the building. I missed here the greeting of my kind old friend Mr. Dart, one of the prominent laymen of the Parish, who had *filled* not only important stations of public trust, but honourably *filled* the position of a christian man, of a loyal citizen and of a gracious and kindly friend.

On the 10th of October, in Christ Church, Morristown, I preached and confirmed nine persons; and on the 11th of October, in St. John's Church, Ogdensburgh, I preached and confirmed thirty persons. The service here is finished and beautiful; the whole life and work of the Parish vigorous and fine; and the vested choir is a great addition to the worship.

On the 14th of October, I took part in the consecration of the Rev. Phillips Brooks as Bishop of the Diocese of Massachusetts. The impressive service, the noble sermon ringing to the echo, with primitive truth and apostolic order, and the dignity and earnestness of the man upon whom hands were laid that day, made an augury for his episcopate, which I believe will be fulfilled and be filled full of great results for the Church.

On the 16th, in St. Paul's Church, Salem, I preached and advanced to priesthood the Rev. Clarence Mortimer Conant, presented by the Rev Houghton, who with the Rev. Mr. Rush joined in the laying on of hands, confirmed two persons and celebrated the Holy Communion. In the afternoon I had great pleasure in witnessing the athletic sports of the boys on the ball ground of St. Paul's Hall. The spirit of the School was really catching, and I believe great things are in store for the future of this place; which even now is doing good service for the Church, and which, when its feet can be set in the larger room of "the King's Meadow," will bring forth richer results in the important work of a thorough christian training for boys.

On Sunday, St. Luke's day, the 18th of October, I organized St. Matthew's Mission at Lyon Mountain, appointing as officers: O. W. Arthur, warden; Joseph A. Forkey, treasurer, and L. G. Moir, clerk.

In the evening, at St. Mark's, Philmont, I preached and confirmed twelve persons, delighted to find the parish earnest and united under the new administration.

On Thursday, October the 22d, in New York, I formally opened and blessed the house for the Society for the Home Study of the Holy Scripture. Letters were read by the Dean of the General Theological Seminary, from the presiding Bishop, and from the Bishop of New York, of cordial approval and appreciation. The Reverend Professor Walpole, who has lent most valuable aid to us in our work, made an address after mine. The building is charmingly situated, commodious and convenient, and is a great step forward in this very important work. More and more as it goes on is the value of it proved, both in its spiritual effect upon the students, and in its developing power to make careful and competent teachers in the Church. The main want is still the want of workers and of means. I earnestly appeal for generous support; and if the hearts of any women in the Diocese are touched, not only to take advantage of its opportunity to study, but to put themselves in some definite connection as helpers in the work, I shall be very thankful if they will send their names to Miss Smiley or to me.

Sunday, October the 25th, I preached in the morning in the Church at Highland Falls, in the Diocese of New York, and in the afternoon baptized a child in private.

Monday, the 26th, in the evening, in St. James', Oneonta, I preached and confirmed five persons.

On Tuesday, the 27th, at Cooperstown, I presided at a meeting of the Trustees of the Orphan House of the Holy Saviour, and was met again by the painful and I think shameful statement of the inability of the managers, with the strictest economy, to pay the running expenses of the home, due mainly to the fact that our own Churches are absolutely careless about their collections, and indifferent even to the duty of supporting the children whom they send there. It is impossible for the Trustees to go on, with any honesty, caring for so many children, unless larger means are given them for their support. In the evening I preached and confirmed twelve persons in Christ Church, and was present at this part of the meeting of the Archdeaconry of the Susquehanna. The next morning I had the great satisfaction of blessing the new Sanctuary, which has been added with singular skill and taste to the old building, making it really now one of the most beautiful and effective Churches in the Diocese. The Bishop of Delaware, to my great pleasure, was with me and preached the sermon. There was a goodly gathering of clergy. The surpliced choir were in their places for the first time and sang extremely well. The new Sanctuary is built in memory of Mrs. Jane Averell Carter by her children, and is complete and exquisite. My heart was stirred to add a few words after the admirable sermon of the Bishop of Delaware, because I could not let the memory of my dear friend be so beautifully embalmed, for perpetual remembrance and perpetual commemoration, without a word telling of my own estimate of the great value of her example and her influence; and of my warm appreciation of the beautiful gift of her children to the Church. During the service I ordered Deacon the Reverend Harry Elmer Gilchrist, who has been doing such work as a lay reader, as gives good promise for his usefulness in the ministry. The whole service was *most* interesting and beautiful.

On Thursday, the 2Jth, in the morning, at Christ Church, Walton, I preached, confirmed six persons and celebrated the Holy Communion. It was pleasant to be once again with my dear old friend Mr. St. John, and while I was sorry to find the parish still unoccupied, and missed the presence of the last Rector and his family, I was glad to find some fruits waiting to be gathered in from the old sowing, and to meet again the Reverend Mr. Creveling, who assisted me at the service and presented the candidates.

In the evening, in St. John's Church, Delhi, I preached and confirmed nine persons, renewing, in the presence of Mr. Roazor at the service, my very deep sense of the loss which has come to us all by his removing from the Diocese.

The next morning, at St. Peter's Church, Hobart, I preached, celebrated the Holy Communion and confirmed twelve persons, the first fruits of the new Rector's ministry there.

On Saturday evening, October 31st, I lighted the fire on the hearth of the school-room at St. Agnes for the nineteenth time, rejoicing in the unusual prosperity of the school and in the renewal of the memories of all those years; and after this we took formal possession of the new building which adds very greatly to the material furnishing of the school, equipped, as I believe it is now, in every way, for better service than even it has been before. to train girls in all that is best, spiritually, intellectually, morally, and physically.

On Sunday, November 1st, we kept our Dedication Festival in the ▉▉▉dral with many added elements of thankfulness for the blessings of the past year. Foremost among them was the universal sense of glad-ness that the Dean had decided to remain in the position which he has filled with such marked advantage to all the best Cathedral interests, and with such great comfort to all of us who are associated with him in the work.

In material gifts we had good reason to rejoice, in what I cannot help feeling are the evidences of life and a power of growth in the building it-self. Ever since the Dedication day, something has grown in the build-ing, or come to it, in the way of added ornament. This year have come more carvings of columns, and of the arches over the Doors; the painted Tapestries at the east end have been given by the Guild of St. Mary; two beautiful brass Candelabra by Dr. T. M. Trego; a very noble Processional Cross (a bit of old work of the fifteenth century) by Dr. Jeffery; and a new set of the fairest linen, most beautifully embroidered by one of our faithful women. The stone mullions of the window, given by women all over the Diocese, as a token of personal love to me, are waiting the glass, through which, please God, the Christmas sun will shine; and the mosaics, which are to fill the four tympana in the Choir and Sanctuary, are on their way across the water. The legend of these mosaics, given by the four living children of Mr. and Mrs. Amasa J. Parker, is the family legend "*fideli certa merces*," and speaks of them, in the strong and simple language of our marriage service, with unusual truth, as having " lived faithfully together " for fifty-five years. Meanwhile, both in increased congregations, in extending service to the city, and I trust in deepened spiritual life, the whole work keeps pace with these material tokens of God's blessing.

I must say here, before the window comes, with what grateful surprise I received on the very eve of my departure for Europe last February the gift gathered from many places by faithful friends here and faithful women everywhere throughout the Diocese, for the east window. I have always greatly desired to avoid making the Cathedral itself a memorial in any wise to myself, but I am only too glad to associate their names and the recollection of the continual and cordial help which has come to me from the women of the Diocese in all my work; and it will be no little part of the pleasure which the window will bring to me to feel that it tells the story, familiar to the Church everywhere since holy women ministered to our dear Lord, of the devo-tion which has always consecrated them and their substance and their service to Him.

The correspondence which is printed in the Cathedral Guide which passed between us at the time, I am glad to insert as an appendix to this Address, in order that it may reach those who have contributed toward this beautiful gift.

Wednesday, November 4, in the Cathedral at the early celebration, I admitted two Probationers to the Sisterhood of the Holy Child Jesus.

On Sunday morning, the 8th of November, I preached in the Chapel of Vassar College to a congregation which greatly interested me, four hundred young girls, whom I found not only intelligent and earnest in the use of our service for Morning Prayer, but very deeply interested in sacred studies, and I was more than glad to find that their instruction in the Holy Scriptures was very thorough, with a perfectly fearless recognition of all that modern criticism is feeling after in the study of the text and with a reverent interpretation and acceptance of the Holy Scriptures as the Word of God.

The following week I spent in New York presiding at the meetings of the Board of Managers; of the Committee on the Standard Prayer Book, and of the Committee on the Hymnal.

And on the 10th of November in St. Ann's Church, Brooklyn, I married the Rev. Ralph Wood Kenyon, once connected with the Diocese of Albany.

On Saturday, the 14th, in the Cathedral, I confirmed one person in the morning; and in the afternoon, in St. Paul's Church, Albany, I confirmed twenty-one persons and made an address. It was a service full of deep feeling, as the circumstances naturally would compel. We were all as one in the earnest hope, that the compulsory withdrawal of the Rector from the work, which for twenty-seven years he has done with such devotion and ability and every token of God's blessing, will restore him not only to his health, but, please God, to his work again here.

On Sunday afternoon, November 15th, I preached and confirmed twenty persons in the Church of the Holy Cross, Troy. The service was never so beautiful in this most beautiful Church; almost the *fons et origo* of not only choral service, but of reverent ritual in the use of the Book of Common Prayer in this country.

And there is no Church in the Diocese, to which I go back from year to year and from time to time, with a stronger sense of the power and influence of pastoral work and personal example and perpetual worship; nor is there any place fuller to me of sacred associations with all that I can remember of the past.

I beg to call the attention of the Clergy of the Diocese again to the Diocesan Lending Library. The Report of this year's work is that 164 new books have been added by gift and purchase and 215 books have been drawn out during the year by 33 of the Clergy. Of course this abundantly indicates the necessity and the value of the establishment of the Library; and while I am thankful for what it has accomplished, I must confess to some feeling of disappointment that it has not done more.

Its establishment grew out of the intense conviction which impresses me at every turn of the compulsory poverty of so many of our clerical libraries; and while as I go about from place to place I am overborne with the sense of the *res angusta domi* (which I think must have been written to describe a parsonage), and with the strain of constant economy which wears so much upon a clergyman's life; I have felt more deeply the *hunger of the mind* which must beset men who are thinkers and teachers ; who come in contact everywhere not only with the old but with the new religious questions which are in the minds of all men. It was out of this strong impression, that I proposed the founding of this Library.

I beg that the Clergy will utilize it more than they do. The machinery is very simple and the cost almost nothing; and I can conceive of nothing that will so absolutely repay the effort and the expense, in the return that it will make of increased ability to "fulfil the Ministry which they have received of the Lord Jesus."

I have had the great pleasure of organizing All Saints' Mission at Round Lake, appointing Dr. P. C. Curtis as Warden, Mr. H. Hoyt, as Treasurer and Mr. George L. Thorn as Clerk, and also the Mission of St. Simon and St. Jude at Worcester, appointing Mr. Charles Fredenburgh as Warden, Mr. Richard Colbeck as Treasurer, and Mr. William J. Cavanaugh as Clerk, and also the Mission of St. John in the Wilderness, Copake, appointing Mr. J. C. Chesborough as Warden. In connection with this last statement I beg to congratulate the Diocese upon the fact that the Church building and Rectory connected with this old Parish which is now extinct, have been through the wisdom and perseverance of our Diocesan Missionary rescued for the Church. Owing to a difficulty and defect in the title we had really lost our hold upon the building which had lapsed into use for a Methodist congregation, but the property now has been deeded to the Trustees of the Diocese of Albany, and I hope very soon to be able to make arrangements for combining Copake with Chatham for regular services of the Church.

The summary of my acts is as follows:

Confirmations, 1166; * Celebrations of Holy Communion, 32; * Sermons, 71; Addresses, 11; Clergy dismissed, 9; Died, 6; Received, 9; Added by Ordination, 7. Present number of Clergy: Bishop, 1; Priests, 121; Deacons, 12; Total, 134. Priests ordained, 3; Deacons ordained, 7; Total, 10. Postulants admitted, 2; Total Postulants, 8. Candidates for Deacon's order admitted, 8; Total candidates for Deacon's order, 19; Candidates for Priest's order admitted, 11; Total Candidates for Priest's order, 19; Total Candidates for Holy Orders, 26. Lay-Readers Licensed, 18; Total Lay-Readers, 18. Probationers admitted, 3. Missions organized, 5; Churches Consecrated, 2; Corner-Stones laid, 1; Buildings, etc., blessed, 5. * Baptisms: Infants, 1; Total, 1. * Marriages, 3. Notices of deposition, 18.

---

*Not included in the Cathedral report.

I have attended the regular meetings of the Board of Missions; the Cathedral Chapter; the Trustees of the Corning Foundation; the Managers of the Child's Hospital; and of St. Margaret's House; the Trustees of the Orphan House of the Holy Saviour; the Diocesan Branch of the Woman's Auxiliary; the Woman's Diocesan League; the Trustees of the various Diocesan Funds; the Bible and Prayer Book Society, and three of the four Archdeaconries. I have also attended meetings of the House of Bishops, the Trustees of the General Theological Seminary, and of St. Stephen's College; the Board of Managers of the Missionary Society; the Committees on the Prayer Book and Hymnal, and the Society for the Home Study of Holy Scripture.

ORDINATIONS.

November 12, 1890. The Rev. Frederick Stirling Griffin, to the Priesthood, in the Cathedral.

December 18, 1890. The Rev. Asa Sprague Ashley, to the Priesthood, in the Cathedral.

April 26, 1891. Eugene Griggs, to the Diaconate, by Bishop Coleman, in St. George's Church, Schenectady.

June 3, 1891. Freeborn Garrettson Jewett, to the Diaconate, by Bishop Williams, in the Church of the Holy Trinity, Middletown, Connecticut.

June 14, 1891. James F. Olmsted, to the Diaconate, in the Cathedral.

June 14, 1891. John Montgomery Rich, to the Diaconate, in the Cathedral.

September 10, 1891. George Lynde Richardson, to the Diaconate, in St. John's Church, Troy.

October 16, 1891. The Rev. Clarence Mortimer Conant, to the Priesthood, in St. Paul's Church, Salem.

October 28, 1891. Harry Elmer Gilchrist, to the Diaconate, in Christ Church, Cooperstown.

November 8, 1891. John G. Urling, to the Diaconate, by Bishop Dudley, in the Church of the Merciful Saviour, Louisville, Kentucky.

CLERGYMEN RECEIVED FROM OTHER DIOCESES.

1891.

January 8. The Rev. Herbert Luther Wood, from the Diocese of Montreal.

January 22. The Rev. Robert Wyndham Brown, from the Diocese of Quebec.

May 5. The Rev. Arthur Lowndes, from the Diocese of New Jersey.

May 8. The Rev. Richmond H. Gesner, from the Diocese of Minnesota.

May 19. The Rev. W. H. Goodisson, from the Diocese of Southern Ohio.

July 9. The Rev. Clarence Mortimer Conant, from the Diocese of Vermont.

August 13. The Rev. Clarence Ernest Ball, from the Diocese of Connecticut.

October 15. The Rev. George G. Carter, S. T. D., from the Diocese of Milwaukee.

October 19. The Rev. George Brinckerhoff Richards, from the Diocese of Connecticut.

November 15. The Rev. George B. Johnson, from the Diocese of New York.

CLERGYMEN DISMISSED TO OTHER DIOCESES.

1890.

November 12. The Rev. Robert M. Kemp, to the Diocese of New York.

1891.

January 4. The Rev. S. B. Moore, to the Diocese of Massachusetts.

January 29. The Rev. John B. Hubbs, to the Diocese of Western Michigan.

January 31. The Rev. Philip W. Mosher, to the Diocese of Western Michigan.

February 5. The Rev. Wm. G. Ivie, to the Diocese of Long Island.

February 12. The Rev. R. G. Hamilton, to the Diocese of Springfield.

April 9. The Rev. J. A. Farrar, to the Diocese of Easton.

July 14. The Rev. John M. Rich, to the Diocese of Colorado.

September 14. The Rev. Milton C. Dotten, to the Diocese of California.

CANDIDATES FOR PRIEST'S ORDER.

September 29, 1886. Mr. Alvin J. Vandebogart.

December 23, 1886. The Rev. Meredith O. Smith.

May 19, 1888. Mr. John C. Woodworth.

October 18, 1888. The Rev. James F. Olmsted.

April 29, 1889. The Rev. George Lynde Richardson.

June 10, 1889. Mr. George Kilpatrick McNaught.

December 2, 1889. The Rev. Freeborn Garrettson Jewett, Jr.

January 6, 1890. Mr. Anton Augustine Müller.

October 10, 1890. Mr. Marvin Hill Dana.

October 27, 1890. Mr. Thurston Walker Challen.

November 17, 1890. The Rev. Eugene Griggs.

November 17, 1890. Mr. Edward T. Carroll.

December 25, 1890. Mr. George Arthur Ingalls.

January 6, 1891. The Rev. Harry Elmer Gilchrist.
January 12, 1891. Mr. Frank N. Bouck.
October 1, 1891. Mr. Harry Sherman Longley.
October 18, 1891. Mr. Keble Dean.
November 6, 1891. Mr. George William Farrar.
November 6, 1891. Mr. Frederic Henry Farrar.

CANDIDATES FOR DEACON'S ORDER.

April 26, 1883. Mr. Gulian V. P. Lansing.
December 17, 1885. Mr. Alvin J. Vandebogart.
June 4, 1887. Mr. George K. McNaught.
October 3, 1887. Mr. George H. Rhames.
October 3, 1887. Mr. Charles H. Moore.·
December 1, 1887. Mr. John C. Woodworth.
November 19, 1888. Mr. Keble Dean.
September 15, 1890. Mr. William Anderson Stirling.
September 15, 1890. Mr. Marvin Hill Dana.
November 8, 1890. Mr. Frank N. Bouck.
November 8, 1890. Mr. Edward T. Carroll.
December 15, 1890. Mr. George Arthur Ingalls.
January 6, 1891. Mr. Anton Augustine Müller.
March 9, 1891. Mr. Harry Sherman Longley.
April 13, 1891. Mr. Gouverneur Frank Mosher.
May 18, 1891. Mr. William Whitney Newell.
October 5, 1891. Mr. George William Farrar.
October 5, 1891. Mr. Frederic Henry Farrar.
October 17, 1891. Mr. William Francis Parsons.

POSTULANTS.

February 16, 1885. Robert Perine.
May 12, 1885. Isaac Borts, M. D.
March 22, 1887. Charles Hegamin, Jr.
March 3, 1888. E. Townsend Jones, M. D.
May 1, 1889. George Henry Chase.
May 27, 1889. William Croswell Doane Willson.
July 1, 1891. William Robert Golden.
September 29, 1891. Hamilton Douglass Bentley MacNeil.

CORNER-STONES LAID.

June 11, 1891. "Graduates' Hall," St. Agnes' School, Albany.

CHURCHES CONSECRATED.

June 20, 1891. St. Barnabas' Church, Stottville.
September 12, 1891. Emmanuel Church, Griffin's Corners.

BENEDICTIONS.

January 28, 1891. Altar, Christ Church, Hudson.

September 29, 1891. The new building for the Child's Hospital, Albany.

October 5, 1891. Parish building, Trinity Church, Whitehall.

October 22, 1891. House for the Society for the Home Study of Holy Scripture, New York, N. Y.

October 28, 1891. Sanctuary of Christ Church, Cooperstown.

MISSIONS ORGANIZED.

January 31, 1891. St. Sacrament Mission, Bolton.

October 18, 1891. St. Matthew's Mission, Lyon Mountain.

October 29, 1891. St. Simon and Jude Mission, Worcester.

November 1. All Saints' Mission, Round Lake.

November 15. St. John in the Wilderness, Copake.

LAY-READERS LICENSED.

1890.

December 10. W. J. Thompson, for the Diocese.

December 10. Frederick W. Cornell, for the Diocese.

December 22. Wm. J. Bower, Grace Church, Canton.

1891.

January 12. Frank N. Bouck, for the Diocese.

January 23. David C. Wright, Church of Our Saviour, Lebanon Springs.

January 29. Wm. C. Noyes, Church of the Cross, Ticonderoga.

January 29. Albert E. Heard, Christ Church, Hudson.

February 3. George W. Searles, Emmanuel Church, Little Falls.

February 3. Merrick Freeman, Emmanuel Church, Little Falls.

February 9. Alex. R. Benson, All Saints' Church, Hudson.

February 17. J. C. Chesbrough, St. John's Church, Copake Iron Works.

July 1. Edward Carroll, St. John's Church, Johnstown.

July 15. Charles Judd, St. Paul's Church, Kinderhook.

September 15. H. D. B. McNeil, Christ Church, Hudson.

October 10. Maurice G. B. Randall, Trinity Church, Lansingburgh.

October 31. Webster W. Jennings, Calvary Church, Cairo.

November 2. G. Charles Bowles, Church of the Holy Spirit, Schenevus.

November 6. Anton A. Müller, for the Diocese.

NOTICES OF CLERGY DEPOSED.

1890.

October 31. Henry L. Teller, Priest, by the Bishop of Central New York.

November 8. John Lester Morton, Priest, by the Bishop of New York.

November 27. Edmund Smith Middleton, Priest, by the Bishop of Massachusetts.

December 16. Frederick Olney Barstow, Priest, by the Assistant Bishop of California.

1891.

January 13. J. Buchanan Drysdale, Priest, by the Bishop of Long Island.

January 19. Philip P. Ruse, Deacon, by the Bishop of Central Pennsylvania.

February 6. James Harvey Gray, Deacon, by the Bishop of Pittsburgh.

February 26. John Bingley Garland, Priest, by the Bishop of South Dakota.

February 27. Henry Keely Boyer, Deacon, by the Bishop of Central Pennsylvania.

February 27. William Louis Woodruff, Priest, by the Assistant Bishop of Central Pennsylvania.

March 1. James J. Hamilton Reedy, Deacon, by the Bishop of Iowa.

March 4. John Coleman, Deacon, by the Assistant Bishop of Minnesota.

March 13. Charles S. Daniel, Priest, by the Bishop of Pennsylvania.

May 5. George H. Rice, Priest, by the Bishop of Colorado.

June 17. Lyman H. Merrill, Minister, by the Bishop of Delaware.

August 19. Samuel F. Myers, Priest, by the Bishop of The Platte.

September 25. Howard MacQueary, Priest, by the Bishop of Ohio.

October 23. H. Digby Johnston, Priest, by the Bishop of Colorado.

APPENDIX TO THE BISHOP'S ADDRESS.

CORRESPONDENCE.

The earnest wish of the friends of Bishop Doane to put in the East window of the Cathedral of All Saints of Albany, as a tribute of their love for him, and their appreciation of his work, has been accomplished. Unknown to the Bishop, the necessary money was contributed by willing hands and loving hearts, and on Saturday, the thirty-first of January, the good news was communicated to him by means of the following letter:

DEAR BELOVED BISHOP:

We have collected a sum of money toward the erection of the East window at All Saints' Cathedral, and offer it to you as a token of our affection, and as a slight recognition of the great work you have done, not only at Albany, but everywhere you go. Already we have had sent in more than Mr. Gibson thought necessary for the glass, and are now accumulating towards the stone mullions of the window. Long before you will need to draw on the fund, the amount will be made up, but we wanted you to know of the undertaking before going abroad, so as to be able to give the orders, and see the designs in London before returning home. With very best wishes for a prosperous journey, and speedy return to us,

Very truly yours,

ALICE C. MOIR, *President.*
ESTELLE DEP. VAN VECHTEN, *Treasurer.*
ANNA M. TALCOTT, *Secretary.*

A book containing a list of the names of subscribers was given the Bishop at the same time, and the great pleasure and gratification experienced by him will be seen in his reply:

DEAR FRIENDS:

I ought by this time to be beyond surprise as to any gracious and generous act to me, from the dear friends, whose list of names upon the book of the givers, your names lead, and represent; names two of which — dear Mrs. Varney's and dear Edwin Sheldon's — we can only remember now at the altar of our Eucharistic commemoration; names, all of which in this old home city, in the Parishes of the Diocese, in the cities of my earlier and later friendships — Boston, Philadelphia and New York, and in my beloved North East Harbour — stand for long, true and loyal love. I thought such people could not surprise me with any kindness, for I am so used to it at their hands. But I confess myself overcome and overwhelmed.

The loving words, the wide-spread embrace, the generous gift, the gracious thought; the hope of all it means of added glory and beauty to the dear Cathedral; the cheer with which it sends me off; the over-estimate of my own service, which would have come so far short in its attainment but for the upholding of my hands by your love, and gifts and prayers; and the wonderful quietness with which you have accomplished this, and kept it even from my suspicions; all these stir me to intense gratitude to God; to hearty thanks to you all; to a deeper love for my beloved friends and people, and to a higher hope and purpose of what we still may do for God's glory together.

I beg you to make known to all who have taken part in this last token of affection, how I am helped, and humbled, and held up. Tell them and be sure yourselves, that my prayer is, that God will abundantly bless and keep you all; and that I am, with renewed assurance of my love,

Your most grateful and faithful Bishop and friend,

ALBANY, *January 31st,* 1891.   WM. CROSWELL DOANE.

AN OLD-TIME PROPHECY.

I am indebted to the Rev. Mr. Hooper for the following extracts which are of interest from their antiquity, and as showing the long ago expectation of what has now been in part fulfilled.

Mr. John Wells, a merchant from Albany who went to Montreal with the army of occupation, writes to Sir William Johnson, on the 30th of March, 1764, "When the Bishop arrives at Albany that part of the country will flourish," and Mr. James Rivington, Royal Printer of New York, and proprietor of Rivington's *Gazette,* writes also to Sir William from New York, on the 11th of June, 1764, "A Bishop of Albany will soon be established with an appointment of £1500 per annum and a handsome palace."

It is certainly a recommendation of the chosen name of the See and I am very glad for myself that the "handsome palace" is after the manner of Solomon's purpose, "builded for the Lord and not for man."

WM. CROSWELL DOANE.

After the service, the Convention was called to order by the Bishop of the Diocese, in the gymnasium of St. Agnes' School.

In accordance with Section 1, Canon I, of the Diocese, the Bishop presented a List of Clergy canonically resident in the Diocese.

The Secretary called the roll of the Clergy, and one hundred were found to be present.[*]

The roll of Parishes entitled to representation was called, and the Bishop appointed the Rev. Walter H. Larom and Mr. John Horrocks with the Secretary, as a committee, to examine the credentials of the Lay Deputies.

The Committee presented the credentials of seventy-three Parishes as correct.

The Secretary then called the names of the Deputies, and forty-five Parishes were found to be represented.[†]

A constitutional quorum being present, the Right Rev. President declared the Convention organized and ready for business.

The election of officers being in order, on motion of the Hon. R. H. Cushney, the ballot was unanimously dispensed with.

The Rev. William C. Prout was elected Secretary, Mr. Selden E. Marvin, Treasurer, and the Rev. Frederick S. Sill, Registrar.

The Secretary appointed the Rev. Thomas B. Fulcher as the Assistant Secretary.

On motion of the Secretary of the Convention, it was

Resolved, That the Rules of Order of the last Convention be adopted for this Convention.

Resolved, That section 6 of the Standing Order for the Conduct of Elections be amended so as to read as follows:

6. Immediately before any ballot, it shall be in order for the nomination of any person to be made and seconded. But nominations for members of the Standing Committee and for Deputies and Provisional Deputies to the General Convention shall be made on the first day of the Convention, at the call of the President, under the Order of "Miscellaneous Business," and it shall be the duty of the Secretary of the Convention to prepare, for the use of the Convention on the second day, ballots for these several offices, containing the names of all persons nominated for each office respectively, with a note indicating the whole number to be chosen. No speech or debate shall be allowed on such nomination or while the Convention is holding an election.

Resolved, That all standing resolutions in regard to the nomination of persons for office be rescinded.

On motion of the Rev. W. C. Prout, it was

Resolved, That Clergymen of other Dioceses, Professors and Students of Theology in this Church, and all persons holding any office or trust under the Convention, if not members thereof, being present, be invited to seats in the Convention.

---

[*] See List of Clergy, page 6.　　　[†] See List of Lay Deputies, page 10.

On motion of the Secretary of the Convention, it was

Resolved, That the order of services and sessions for this Convention be as follows : That a recess be taken from five to eight o'clock this evening; that at eight o'clock the Convention assemble in the Cathedral for the annual Missionary service and meeting; that to-morrow the Holy Communion be celebrated at eight o'clock in the morning, and the Morning Prayer and Litany said at ten o'clock, in the Cathedral; the business session shall be resumed in this place at half-past ten with the usual recesses from one to two and from five to eight o'clock.

On motion of the Rev. Joseph Carey, S. T. D., it was

Resolved, That the portion of the Bishop's Address relating to the Clergymen of the Diocese, including Rev. Dr. John Henry Hopkins, who have died during the year, be referred to a Committee to prepare a suitable memorial minute in relation to their lives and character, to be entered upon the Journal of the Convention.

The Right Rev. President appointed as such Committee, the Rev. Joseph Carey, S. T. D., the Rev. Richard Temple, and the Rev. Charles M. Nickerson, D. D.

The Rev. W. C. Prout gave notice of the following amendment to Canon XIV, which, on his motion, was referred to the Committee on the Constitution and Canons.

Resolved, That Canon XIV, section 13, be amended by the addition of the words " or in the Trustees of the Diocese of Albany."

The Right Rev. President appointed the regular Committees.

ON THE INCORPORATION AND ADMISSION OF CHURCHES.

The Rev. J. Philip B. Pendleton.   Mr. Richard H. Cushney,
    Mr. Benjamin H. Hall.

ON THE CONSTITUTION AND CANONS.

The Rev. J. W. Stewart,   Mr. James Gibson,
The Rev. R. M. Kirby, D. D.,   Mr. T. S. Clarkson,
The Rev. James Caird,   Mr. J. D. Henderson.
The Rev. Wilford L. Robbins, D. D.

ON THE ACCOUNTS OF THE TREASURER.

Mr. William Kemp.   Mr. F. E. Griswold.

ON THE DIOCESAN FUND AND MILEAGE OF THE CLERGY.

The Rev. Charles Temple,   Mr. G. Hyde Clark,
The Rev. Edward Dudley Tibbits.   Mr. Eli P. Howe,
    Mr. William Hollands.

ON DIOCESAN MISSIONS.

The Rev. Eaton W. Maxcy, D. D.,   Mr. Abram A. Van Vorst,
The Rev. Wm. Henry Brown.   Mr. John Keyes Paige,
    Mr. John T. Perry.

ON THE BISHOP'S SALARY AND THE EPISCOPAL FUND.

The Rev. C. M. Nickerson, D. D.,   Mr. John H. Bagley,
The Rev. J. N. Marvin.   Mr. Sidney G. Ashmore,
    Mr. Henry Griffing.

10

On the Fund for Widows and Orphans of Deceased Clergymen.

The Rev. Ernest Mariett.   Mr. T. O. Duroe,
           Mr. Ralph W. McDougall.

On the Aged and Infirm Clergy Fund.

The Rev. Russell Woodman.   Mr. James McQuide,
           Mr. Edward Searls.

On the General Theological Seminary.

The Rev. E. Bayard Smith,   Mr. William A. Sackett,
The Rev. William M. Cook,   Mr. Robert Earl.
The Rev. Frederick S. Fisher.

On the Society for Promoting Religion and Learning.

The Rev. Charles C. Edmunds, Jr. Mr. Francis B. Davis,
           Mr. Charles E. Wackerhagen.

On Unfinished Business.

The Rev. Hobart Cooke.   Mr. Benjamin F. Hinman,
           Mr. James Russell Parsons, Jr.

On Non-Reporting Clergy and Parishes.

The Rev. George M. Irish.   Mr. Michael Andrae,
           Mr. Henry C. Day.

On the Registrar's Report.

The Rev. William B. Bolmer.   Mr. Geo. B. Pattison,
           Mr. Walton Van Loan.

On the Orphan House at Cooperstown.

The Rev. Ernest A. Hartmann, Mr. J. Rutherford Morris,
The Rev. James E. Hall.   Mr. Fred. L. Carroll.

On the Salary of the Bishop.

The Rev. Joseph Carey, S. T. D., Mr. J. J. Tillinghast,
The Rev. W. W. Battershall, D. D. Mr. Erastus Corning,
           Mr. Walter A. Wood,
           Mr. J. W. Tillinghast,
           Mr. W. W. Rousseau,
           Mr John I. Thompson,
           Mr. Spencer Trask.

On the Society for the Home Study of Holy Scripture.

The Rev. George G. Carter, S. T. D., Mr. Andrew S. Booth,
The Rev. Joseph T. Zorn.   Mr. Levi Hasbrouck,
The Rev. George B. Johnson   Mr. Ralph W. McDougall.

On the Woman's Diocesan League.

The Rev. Richmond Shreve, D. D., Mr. S. M. Van Santvoord,
The Rev. Walter C. Stewart.   Mr. Richard Leonard,
           Mr. Sidney G. Ashmore.

The reports of the Treasurer of the Diocese; of the Board of Diocesan Missions; of the Trustees of the Episcopal Fund and of the Committee on the Salary of the Bishop; of the Trustees of the Fund for the Widows and Orphans of Deceased Clergymen, and of the Treasurer of the same; of the Trustees of the Aged and Infirm Clergy Fund, and of the Treasurer of the same; of the Registrar of the Diocese; of the Superintendent and of the Treasurer of the Orphan House of the Holy Saviour, Cooperstown; of the Society for Promoting Religion and Learning; of the Bible and Common Prayer Book Society, were received and referred to the appropriate Committees.

The Rev. J. Philip B. Pendleton presented and read

THE REPORT OF THE COMMITTEE ON THE INCORPORATION AND ADMISSION OF CHURCHES.

The Committee on the Incorporation and Admission of Churches report that they have received, through the Secretary of the Convention, an application to be admitted into union with the Convention of the Diocese of Albany, from St. Mark's Church, Philmont, Columbia county.

They have examined the Articles of Incorporation and other papers accompanying the said application, and find them to be in accordance with the requirements of Canon IV, and, therefore, recommend the adoption of the following resolution:

Resolved, That the Church of St. Mark, Philmont, Columbia county, be admitted into union with the Convention.

ALBANY, N. Y., *November* 17, 1891.

Respectfully submitted,
J. PHILIP B. PENDLETON,
Chairman.

On motion of the Secretary of the Convention, the resolution recommended in the Report of the Committee on the Incorporation and Admission of Churches was adopted; and St. Mark's Church, Philmont, Columbia county, was admitted into union with the Convention.

The Secretary of the last Convention presented and read the following :

REPORT OF THE SECRETARY OF THE CONVENTION.

ALBANY, *November* 17, 1891.

To the Convention of the Diocese of Albany:

The Secretary of the Diocese respectfully presents the following report.

Twelve hundred copies of the Bishop's Address and twelve hundred copies of the Journal of the Convention were printed and distributed.

Letters were sent to the Clergy who failed to report to the Convention of 1889. Four replies were received.

Application for admission into union with the Convention was duly received from St. Mark's Church, Philmont, Columbia county, and forwarded to the chairman of the Committee on the Incorporation and Admission of Churches.

The Convention will need to elect this year the Standing Committee and Trustees of the several funds as usual, also four clerical and four lay Deputies to the General Convention, and four clerical and four lay Provisional Deputies. In consequence of the amendment to the act for the Incorporation of the Orphan House of the Holy Saviour, Cooperstown, there are to be nine Trustees of the Orphan House elected by the Convention.

Nominations for members of the Board of Missions have been received: For the Archdeaconry of Albany, the Rev. Walton W. Battershall, D. D., and Mr. John H. Van Antwerp; for the Archdeaconry of Troy, the Rev. Fenwick M. Cookson and Mr. George A. Wells; for the Archdeaconry of the Susquehanna, the Rev. Robert N. Parke, D. D., and Mr. Robert M. Townsend; for the Archdeaconry of Ogdensburgh, the Rev. R. M. Kirby, D. D., and Mr. T. Streatfeild Clarkson.

A large number of Journals of other Dioceses and other documents have been received and forwarded to the Registrar.

Respectfully submitted,

WM. C. PROUT,
Secretary of the Convention.

The Rev. Richmond Shreve, D. D., read

THE REPORT OF THE BIBLE AND COMMON PRAYER BOOK SOCIETY OF ALBANY AND ITS VICINITY.

The Bible and Common Prayer Book Society of Albany and Its Vicinity respectfully report that, during the year since the last Convention, there have been granted 5,007 volumes. Of this total number, 3,715 came from the Society itself, and consisted of 522 Bibles, 2 of which were for use in the Chancel; 2,239 Prayer Books, 41 of these being of the larger size; and 954 Hymnals, of which 14 were 12mo, and 45 musical editions. The remaining 1,292 volumes were provided by the "Mann Bequest," as auxiliary to the Society, through the Rector and Vestry of St. John's Church, Troy. This additional list included 1 large Lectern Bible, 1,101 Hymnals (40 with the music), and 190 books for Parish and Sunday School libraries.

If it be noticed that the number granted during this Conventional year is smaller than that reported twelve months ago, the explanation is to be found in the double fact: the former unusually large total had supplied the immediate demand; and the income of the Society is limited.

An abstract of the Report of the Treasurer, Mr. H. B. Dauchy, of Troy, will make this latter statement more emphatic.

The Permanent Fund remains as it was last year, without increase .. $13,385
Special Prayer Book Fund.................. 300

SUMMARY OF RECEIPTS AND EXPENDITURES FOR THE YEAR.

Receipts.

Received from fifty-one Parishes..................................	$427
Received from the "Mann Bequest"........	320
Received from the income of Permanent Fund........................	908
Balance on hand, last Report.............................	195
Total Receipts....	$1,851 2

Expenditures.

Paid for books "Mann Bequest"........	$14 00
Paid for Bibles, Prayer Books and Hymnals	1,629 94
Cash Balance on hand..................................	7 28
Total Expenditures......................	$1,851 22

While the Society may regret that the Balance in hand is $120.00 less than that of the last Report, it notes, with gratitude and pleasure, that, in response to the appeal made at the last Convention, the number of contributing Parishes has increased from thirty-seven (37) to fifty-one (51), and the amount received has also nearly doubled. Five Parishes may be mentioned in a special " Roll of Honour," as having contributed *twice* during the year: St. John's, Johnstown; St. John's, Delhi; St. Matthew's, Unadilla; Bethesda, Saratoga Springs; St. John the Evangelist, Stockport.

There is urgent need for yet fuller interest and still larger offerings during the coming year, because of the probable largely increased expenditure necessary for the issuance of the completed Prayer Book, after the next General Convention of the Church.

Of all the agencies which justly claim a proportion of the offerings of the members of the Church in this Diocese, the Society yields the position of priority and importance to but one: the direct call of the Missionary cause, the living voice and presence of the commissioned Priest.

Closely following, and often bringing spiritual strength and comfort in places where the Clergyman has not come, and cannot come, is the generous distribution of copies of the inspired Word, and of the loftiest of human compositions, the Book of Common Prayer. To send these is the grateful work of this Society,

All of which is respectfully submitted,
RICHMOND SHREVE,
Recording Secretary.

Mr. A. B. Cox, Lay Deputy from Grace Church, Cherry Valley, presented the following report, which was accepted and the committee discharged :

REPORT OF THE COMMITTEE TO RAISE FUNDS FOR THE ORPHAN HOUSE OF THE HOLY SAVIOUR.

To the Convention of the Diocese of Albany :

Your Committee to raise the sum of $2,000 for the Orphan House of the Holy Saviour respectfully report as follows :

Receipts.

1890. Dec. 9.	From Wm. E. Thorn	$100 00
16.	From Rev. R. Washbon, for Trinity Church, Rensselaerville.	10 00
12.	From Rev. Charles E. Freeman	5 00
17	From Rev. T. A. Snyder	10 00
18.	From Rev. E. W. Flower, Christ Church, Duanesburgh	5 77
18.	From Rev. W. C. Stewart, Zion Church, Morris	76 50
20.	From Mrs. Sarah A. Gage	25 00
23.	From John I. Thompson	100 00
23.	From E. Ray Thompson	50 00
23.	From James L. Thompson	25 00
23.	From Mrs. W. Howard Hart	50 00
23.	From Robert H. Thompson	25 00
23.	From William Kemp	25 00
23.	From George B. Cluett	25 00
23.	From J. W. A. Cluett	25 00
23.	From T. Streatfeild Clarkson, collections from Ogdensburgh.	45 00
23.	From T. Streatfeild Clarkson, collections from Potsdam	260 00
24.	From Mrs. A. B. Cox	150 00

24.	From A. B. Cox...........................	$150 00
24.	From Rev. J. E. Hall, for Grace Church, Cherry Valley	20 66
27.	From Jonas H. Brooks.............................	5 00
27.	From Mrs. Harriet Langdon Pruyn........	25 00
27.	From L. H. Tucker....................................	25 00
27.	From Rev. W. W. Battershall, D. D..	33 00
27.	From Rt. Rev. Wm. Croswell Doane, D. D..................	35 00
27.	From James B. Jermain...............................	25 00
30.	From J. H. Van Antwerp...	25 00
30.	From George H. Birchall, Treasurer Holy Innocents, Albany,	22 70
30.	From Rev. S. M. Griswold, Christ Church, Hudson..........	25 16
30.	From Rev. F. S. Griffin, from his Missions................	5 00
30.	From W. H. Weaver....................................	25 00
1891. Jan. 1.	From Rev. A. T. de Learsy, Grace Church S. S., Stamford...	10 00
7.	From Rev. F. B. Reazor, St. John's Church, Delhi..........	118 55
13.	From Miss A. E. Tweddle.............	50 00
13.	From Mrs. C. E. Benedict..............................	10 00
13.	From J. G. Damroch	5 00
13.	From Danforth Geer	5 00
13.	From Frank H. White..................................	3 00
13.	From Rev. G. H. Nicholls, S. T. D.	5 00
13.	From Le Grand C. Tibbits.............	5 00
13.	From J. R. Parsons........................	10 00
13.	From Ellen C. Parsons	5 00
13.	From J. R. Parsons, Jr........	15 00
13.	From Mrs. W. W. Campbell	100 00
15.	From Rev. Wm. R. Woodbridge, for Christ Church, Port Henry.	19 51
15.	From Rev. Wm. R. Woodbridge, for Emmanuel Church, Mineville.	8 29
24.	From Miss C. E. Tunnicliff, for Ladies of St. John's Church, Richfield Springs.....	150 00
Feb. 3.	From Mrs. Elizabeth V. Price.......	25 00
10.	From John I. Thompson	25 00
		$2,003 14

Disbursements.

Paid Second National Bank of Cooperstown to be applied on note of Treasurer of Orphan House, as follows:

1890. Dec. 24	....	$1,162 27
30	....	276 52
1891. Jan. 13.	....	241 55
15	....	122 80
24	....	150 00
Feb. 9.	....	25 00
10.	....	25 00
		$2,003 14

A. B. Cox,
Treasurer of Committee.

The Secretary of the Convention, at the request of Mr. Melvil Dewey, presented, as the Report of the Committee to secure legislation for the Orphanage, the amendments to the Act of Incorporation as passed by the last Legislature. The Report was accepted and the Committee discharged.

REPORT OF THE COMMITTEE ON LEGISLATION FOR THE ORPHAN HOUSE OF THE HOLY SAVIOUR.

LAWS OF NEW YORK. — By Authority.

[Every law, unless a different time shall be prescribed therein, shall commence and take effect throughout the State, on and not before the twentieth day after the day of its final passage, as certified by the Secretary of State. Sec. 12, title 4, chap. 7, part 1, Revised Statutes.]

CHAP. 340.

AN ACT to amend chapter one hundred and five of the Laws of eighteen hundred and seventy, entitled "An act to incorporate the Trustees of the Orphan House and Industrial School of the Holy Saviour, near Cooperstown, New York."

APPROVED by the Governor May 6, 1891. Passed, three-fifths being present.

The People of the State of New York, represented in Senate and Assembly, do enact as follows :

SECTION 1. Section three of chapter one hundred and five of the Laws of eighteen hundred and seventy, entitled "An act to incorporate the Trustees of the Orphan House and Industrial School of the Holy Saviour, near Cooperstown, New York," is hereby amended so as to read as follows :

§ 3. The Corporation shall be managed by a Board of Trustees, which shall consist of the Bishop of the Protestant Episcopal Church in the Diocese of Albany, who shall be ex-officio President of the same, the Rector of Christ Church, Cooperstown, Susan Fenimore Cooper, during her life-time, and nine other persons. Said nine Trustees shall be elected by the Annual Diocesan Convention of said Diocese. At the first annual election held after the passage of this act, nine Trustees shall be elected, who shall divide themselves by lot into three classes, three of whom shall hold office for one year, three for two years and three for three years. At each annual election thereafter, three Trustees only shall be elected to hold office for three years. The Board of Trustees may fill any vacancy in the office of Trustee, by appointment, to serve until the next annual election, at which time a Trustee shall be elected to fill such vacancy for the unexpired term. By their corporate name said Trustees shall be persons in law capable of suing and being sued, and they and their successors may have and use a common seal, and the same may alter and change at pleasure; may make By-Laws for the management of the affairs of said Corporation not inconsistent with the Constitution and Laws of this State or the United States; may appoint servants and teachers for the Institution under their charge, and allow them a suitable compensation for their services; may appoint a Secretary and Treasurer, and cause a Record to be kept of the proceedings of the Board of Trustees in a book or books which shall be open to the inspection of the said Convention, or any Committee of the same; shall make an Annual Report to the said Convention, showing in detail their proceedings, the condition of the property and funds intrusted to their charge, and their receipts and expenditures; shall conform to any instructions or directions of the said Convention touching the management and care of said Orphanage, and the property and funds of the same, provided the same shall be in writing and entered on the

Journals of the said Convention. The Trustees of said Corporation who shall be in office at the date of the passage of this act shall hold the same until the annual election herein provided for and until their successors are elected.

§ 2. This act shall take effect immediately.

STATE OF NEW YORK, } *ss.:*
Office of the Secretary of State, }

I have compared the preceding with the original law on file in this office, and do hereby certify that the same is a correct transcript therefrom and of the whole of said original law.

FRANK RICE,
Secretary of State.

The Rev. Edgar A. Enos presented the Report of the Committee on Moral Instruction in Public Schools; which was accepted and the Committee discharged.

REPORT OF THE COMMITTEE TO ATTEND A CONFERENCE ON MORAL INSTRUCTION IN PUBLIC SCHOOLS.

The Committee appointed to attend a Conference on Moral Instruction in Public Schools, held in the City of New York in November last, under the call of the Presbyterian Synod of New York, respectfully report that on account of Parish engagements they were unable to attend said Conference.

EDGAR A. ENOS,
JOHN H. HOUGHTON,
WM. H. BOWN.

The Rev. William C. Prout gave notice of a proposed amendment to Canon XIV, which on his motion was referred to the Committee on the Constitution and Canons.

Resolved, That Canon XIV, Section 3, be amended by the addition of the following words: "provided that said election and other business may be deferred to the second day."

On motion of the Rev. Frederick S. Sill, it was

Resolved, That the resolution* of the Rev. Mr. Pendleton, to be found on page 117 of last year's Journal, be referred to the several Archdeaconries in order that the matter may be acted on by them.

The Right Rev. President announced the order of nominations for the Standing Committee and for Deputies and Provisional Deputies to the General Convention; and read the following

LETTER OF THE REV. DR. REESE.

My dear Bishop:

I do not expect to be able to attend any meeting of the Standing Committee the coming year. You know how difficult it sometimes is to get a two-thirds attendance,

---

* The resolution was as follows:

WHEREAS, The Memorial of the Convocation of Albany on the subject of a Diocesan Missionary, has been referred by this Convention to the Board of Missions, with the request that they consider and act upon it, therefore

Resolved, That in the event of favorable action being taken upon such Memorial by the said Board, the Sunday Schools of the Diocese be requested to undertake and provide for the salary of such Missionary, as their special contribution toward the Missionary work of the Diocese for the coming year.

which in some cases is required by the Canon. Will you therefore see that my name does not go before the Convention as a proposed member of that Committee, and assure the Convention of the gratitude I feel for the honor they have conferred from the date of the Primary Convention ?

. ALBANY, *November* 16, 1891.

Respectfully and sincerely,
J. LIVINGSTON REESE.

On motion of the Rev. W. W. Battershall, D. D., the following preamble and resolution were adopted :

IN VIEW of the letter of the Rev. Dr. Reese, member and Secretary of the Standing Committee of this Diocese since its organization, declining a renomination to this position ;

Resolved, That a Committee be appointed by the Chair, who shall present to this Convention a minute expressive of its grateful appreciation of the long and eminent service rendered by Dr. Reese to the Church in this Diocese.

The Right Rev. President appointed as such Committee, the Rev. W. W. Battershall, D. D., the Rev. Thaddeus A. Snively and Mr. Giles H. F. Van Horne.

Nominations for the Standing Committee were presented as follows: the Rev. J. Ireland Tucker, S. T. D., the Rev. Fenwick M. Cookson, the Rev. Wilford L. Robbins, D. D., the Rev. James Caird, Mr. Norman B. Squires, Mr. Henry S. Wynkoop, Mr. John I. Thompson and Mr. John H. Van Antwerp, nominated by Gen. Selden E. Marvin.

Nominations for Deputies to the General Convention were presented as follows: the Rev. W. W. Battershall, D. D., the Rev. J. D. Morrison, D. D., LL. D., the Rev. Joseph Carey, S. T. D., nominated by the Rev. W. C. Prout ; the Rev. James Caird, by the Rev. David Sprague ; the Rev. Charles C. Edmunds, Jr., by Mr. J. D. Henderson ; the Rev. J. Philip B. Pendleton, by the Rev. W. C. Prout ; the Rev. John H. Houghton, by Mr. John Horrocks ; the Rev. William C. Prout, by Prof. Sidney G. Ashmore ; the Rev. Edgar A. Enos, by the Rev. John H. Houghton ; the Rev. Robert N. Parke, D. D., by the Rev. R. H. Gesner ; Mr. G. Pomeroy Keese, Mr. Erastus Corning, Mr. T. Streatfeild Clarkson, Mr. John Hobart Warren, by the Rev. W. C. Prout ; and Mr. Charles E. Patterson, by the Rev. Edgar A. Enos.

Nominations for Provisional Deputies to the General Convention were presented as follows: the Rev. Edgar A. Enos, the Rev. R. M. Kirby, D. D., the Rev. Charles S. Olmsted, the Rev. George D. Silliman, nominated by the Rev. W. C. Prout ; the Rev. Charles M. Nickerson, D. D., by the Rev. Richmond Shreve, D. D.; Mr. Leslie Pell-Clarke, Mr. Spencer Trask, Mr. Edward Sheldon and Mr. Thomas L. Harison, nominated by the Rev. W. C. Prout.

11

On motion of the Rev. George D. Silliman, it was

Resolved, That a Committee be appointed to take into consideration that part of the Bishop's Address relating to the Rev. Dr. Nicholls and the Rev. Robert Washbon, this being the fiftieth year of their ordination, therefore their "golden wedding."

The Right Rev. President appointed as such committee, the Rev. George D. Silliman, the Rev. J. Ireland Tucker, S. T. D., and Mr. Nathaniel Teed.

Mr. James Gibson, Lay Deputy from St. Paul's Church, Salem, presented and read

REPORT NUMBER I, OF THE COMMITTEE ON THE CONSTITUTION AND CANONS.

The Committee on Canons to whom was referred the following amendment to Canon XIV, recommend that it be adopted.

A CANON TO AMEND CANON XIV.

Section 3 of Canon XIV, is hereby amended so as to read as follows:

SEC. 3. The evening session of the Convention on the first day of each Annual Meeting shall be devoted to the reception and consideration of the Report of the Board of Missions and of its Treasurer, the election of the Board, and other business connected with the subject; provided that said election and other business connected with the subject may be deferred to the second day.

J. W. STEWART,
Chairman.

On motion of the Rev. J. Philip B. Pendleton, it was

Resolved, That a committee be appointed to consider and report to this Convention upon the changes that have been proposed in the Book of Common Prayer by the last General Convention, notice of which changes has been communicated to this Convention by the Secretary of the General Convention.

The Right Rev. President appointed as such committee, the Rev. J. Philip B. Pendleton, the Rev. John H. Houghton, the Rev. Richmond Shreve, D. D., Mr. Selden E. Marvin and Mr. Henry B. Dauchy.

On motion of the Rev. W. W. Battershall, D. D., it was

Resolved, That the Diocesan Missionary of this Diocese be accorded a seat without vote at the meetings of the Board of Missions.

The reports of the Treasurer of the Diocese, and of the Committee on same, and of the Committee on the Diocesan Fund were presented and read.

REPORT OF THE TREASURER OF THE DIOCESE.

ALBANY, *November* 17, 1891.

Herewith find statement of receipts and disbursements on account of the Diocesan Fund for the year, showing as follows.

Receipts.

Balance on hand as reported to last Convention	$341 79
From individuals	10 00
From Parishes	2,242 55
From Diocese of New York	25,000 00
Total	$27,594 34

Disbursements.

For mileage...	$240 06
For Secretary's expenses...	71 00
For Secretary's salary...	250 00
For taxes, insurance and repairs Bishop's house......................	455 69
For assessment General Convention....................................	130 00
For Bishop's traveling expenses..	300 00
For printing	692 69
For Registrar...	10 00
Paid J. H. Van Antwerp, Treasurer Episcopal Fund	25,000 00
Total.	$27,149 44
Balance...	$444 90

It will be necessary for the Convention at this meeting to provide for the following objects. mileage to clergymen in attendance upon Convention; printing the Journal of the Convention; taxes and repairs Bishop's house; sundry current expenses; one-third dues to General Convention; salary of the Secretary; traveling expenses of the Bishop.

For the above purposes I suggest the following estimate of the sums that will be required :

For mileage...	$250 00
For printing	700 00
For taxes and repairs Bishop's house.................................	600 00
For sundry current expenses...	150 00
For one-third dues, General Convention...............................	130 00
For salary of the Secretary..	250 00
For Bishop's traveling expenses	300 00

To provide the above amount I recommend the Convention order an assessment of three (3) per centum upon the salaries paid or pledged the Clergymen by the Parishes and Mission Stations; one-half payable April 1st, and one-half payable October 1st, 1892.

I further recommend that the Treasurer be directed to pay to each Clergyman in attendance upon the Convention and belonging to this Diocese, residing a distance of twenty miles from Albany, his actual traveling expenses, provided that in no case shall he pay to exceed seven cents a mile.

SELDEN E. MARVIN,
Treasurer, Diocese of Albany.

REPORT OF THE COMMITTEE ON THE ACCOUNTS OF THE TREASURER.

The Committee to whom was referred the Report of the Treasurer of the Diocese, have examined the same, together with the vouchers for expenditures, and find the same correct.

WILLIAM KEMP,

ALBANY, N. Y., *November* 17, 1891.   F. E. GRISWOLD.

REPORT OF THE COMMITTEE ON THE DIOCESAN FUND AND MILEAGE OF THE CLERGY.

The Committee on the Diocesan Fund and Mileage of the Clergy recommend the adoption of the following resolution:

Resolved, That the recommendations of the Treasurer of the Diocese be adopted by this Convention as follows: 1st, that an assessment be levied on the Parishes and Mission Stations of this Diocese equal to three *per centum* of the salaries paid or pledged to be paid to the clergy by such Parishes or Mission Stations, one-half payable April 1st, 1892, the other half on October 1st, 1892; and 2nd, that the Treasurer be directed to pay to each Clergyman in attendance at this Convention and belonging thereto, residing a distance of twenty miles from Albany, his actual traveling expenses, provided that in no case shall he pay more than seven cents per mile.

CHARLES TEMPLE,
Chairman.

The resolution recommended by the Committee on the Diocesan Fund was adopted.

The Rev. C. M. Nickerson, D. D., presented the following reports:

REPORT OF THE TRUSTEES OF THE EPISCOPAL FUND.

ALBANY, *November* 16, 1891.

To the Convention:

The undersigned, Trustees of the Episcopal Fund, respectfully report, that they hold the following securities for the Fund.

Bond of Grace Church, Waterford	$500 00
Bond of St. John's Church, Cohoes	800 00
Bond and mortgage of J. Judge, 6 per cent	1,500 00
Bond and mortgage of D. McElveney, 5 per cent.	5,000 00
Bond and mortgage of L. Sautter, 6 per cent	6,000 00
Bond and mortgage of J. Kennah, 6 per cent	6,000 00
Bond and mortgage of J. A. Clark, 5 per cent	8,000 00
Bond and mortgage of Smead & Northcott, 4½ per cent.	8,500 00
Bond and mortgage of L. Hasbrouck, 5 per cent	5,000 00
Bond and mortgage of J. E. Birdsall, 5 per cent	20,000 00
Deposit in Savings Bank, 4 per cent.	2,543 02
Total	$63,843 02

Two dollars have been received from the "Church of Our Saviour, Lebanon Springs," for the capital of the Fund, in addition to the $25,000 received during last Convention from the Diocese of New York on the compromise of our claim of $40,000 on it, as sanctioned by our Convention.

This addition to Albany's Episcopal Fund was immediately deposited in bank on interest, and as soon as possible thereafter invested, in five per cent bonds and mortgages.

The rate on the Smead and Northcott mortgage of $8,500, hitherto at 4½ per cent, is raised, by agreement, to 5 per cent, after November 1. The interest* on all the securities in the Fund has been promptly paid, when due.

As soon as a satisfactory small mortgage is obtainable, the money on deposit in savings bank will be invested in it.

Respectfully submitted,
J. H. VAN ANTWERP,
WM. BAYARD VAN RENSSELAER,
C. WHITNEY TILLINGHAST, 2ND.,
THEODORE TOWNSEND.

---

* **The rate** of interest on the principal of the fund now averages five and one quarter per cent per annum.

REPORT OF THE TREASURER OF THE EPISCOPAL INCOME FUND.

J. H. Van Antwerp, Treasurer, in account with the Episcopal Income Fund:

1891.   *Dr.*

Feb. 1. To interest received from bank on deposit of $25,000, received
                 from Diocese of New York........................... .... $256 18
May 1. To 9¼ months' interest, Sautter mortgage, 6 per cent........   290 00
             To 10 months' interest, Kennah mortgage, 6 per cent. 300 00
             To 10 months' interest, Clark mortgage, 5 per cent 333 33
Nov. 1. To 12 months' interest, Judge mortgage, 6 per cent 90 00
             To interest, Hasbrouck mortgage, to November 1, 5 per cent..   173 08
             To interest, Birdsall mortgage, to November 1, 5 per cent.....   697 22
             To interest, Savings Bank deposit, to November 1, 4 per cent...   101 72
             To interest, Northcott mortgage, to November 1, 4½ per cent..   382 50
             To interest, McElveney mortgage, to November 1, 5 per cent..   250 00
             To interest, Sautter mortgage, 6 months, to November 1, 6 per
                 cent..   180 00
             To interest, Kennah mortgage, 6 months, to November 1, 6 per
                 cent. 180 00
             To interest, Clark mortgage, 6 months, to November 1, 5 per
                 cent 200 00
             To interest, Grace Church, Waterford, to November 1 ....   64 17
             To interest, St. John's Church, Cohoes, to November 1 ......   70 00
             To dividends, January, April and July (October dividend passed),
                 on Missouri Pacific Railroad stock in name of Bishop, in trust,
                 $10 each............. ....   30 00
   16. To remittances received from W. W. Rousseau, Secretary of
                 , Bishop's Salary Committee........ ... .   3,145 00
                                                                                                       ————
                 Total $6,743 20
                                                                                                       ════

Cr.

1890.
Nov. 12. By payment of balance due.... .... $3 28
             By payment of balance due Bishop on his salary, October 1, 1890,   250 00
1891.
Jan. 9. By payment of the Bishop's salary one month, from October 1
                 to November 1, 1890, at $5,000 per annum.................   416 67
Nov. 11. By payment of salary to Bishop, one year, from November 1,
                 1890, to November 1, 1891 ....:................... ...   6,000 00
             By balance.... ... .   73 25
                                                                                                       ————
                                                                                                       $6,743 20
                                                                                                       ════

As will be observed, the interest payments on the bonds and mortgages, etc., in
the Episcopal Fund, have been made up and collected in full to the 1st instant ; so
that they will come in hereafter, semi-annually, May 1 and November 1, and correspond with payments due at those periods to the Bishop for his salary, the other two
quarterly dates, being February and August.

E. & O. E., *November* 16, 1891.

Respectfully submitted,

J. H. Van Antwerp,
Treasurer of the Episcopal Fund, Diocese of Albany.

REPORT OF THE COMMITTEE ON THE SALARY OF THE BISHOP.

OFFICE OF BISHOP'S SALARY COMMITTEE, }
TROY, N. Y., *November 17, 1891.* }

To the Convention of the Diocese of Albany :

The Bishop's Salary Committee begs to report that agreeably to the action of the Convention last year, the Committee, after several meetings and careful deliberation, adopted a * new schedule of assessments to meet the requirements of the Diocese—a schedule which it was the aim and desire of the Committee to make as fair and equitable as possible to all the Parishes.

The almost unanimous acceptance of the new schedule by the various Parishes, and the promptitude with which the calls of the Secretary have been responded to, have been a source of great gratification to the Committee as they must also be to your Bishop and the entire Diocese.   Respectfully,

WM. W. ROUSSEAU,
Secretary.

STATEMENT OF WM. W. ROUSSEAU, SECRETARY OF BISHOP'S SALARY
COMMITTEE.

1890.
Nov. 18. Cash on hand last report............. .... $3 54
1891.
Nov. 13. Received since last report from various Parishes.............. 3,185 18

                                                                 $3,188 72

1891.   *Contra.*
Nov. 18. † Remitted since last report to J. H. Van Antwerp,
                Treasurer, by checks...................... .... $3,020 00
      9. Paid on account, note...... .... 100 00
            Paid 1 year interest to March on note of $500....... 25 00
            Postage, blanks, postal cards, notices, etc........... 39 05
     13. Cash on hand.................................. . 4 67
                                                        ———— $3,188 72

REPORT OF THE COMMITTEE ON THE BISHOP'S SALARY AND THE EPISCOPAL FUND.

The Committee to whom was referred the Report of the Treasurer of the Episcopal Fund and Bishop's Salary respectfully report, that they have examined the Reports of the Trustees of the Episcopal Fund and of the Treasurer of the same, and find them to be correct.

The Committee would suggest that the assessments levied by the Committee on the Bishop's Salary be published in the Journal.

The Committee offer the following resolution:

Resolved, That the thanks of the Convention are due to Mr. W. W. Rousseau for his painstaking and judicious readjustment of the assessments on the Parishes of this Diocese.

C. M. NICKERSON,
J. N. MARVIN,
S. G. ASHMORE.

---

* For schedule of Assessments, see Appendix D
† Nov. 17. Received check $125 additional from Mr Rousseau, Secretary; $3,145 in all. —
Treasurer Episcopal Fund

The resolution recommended in the Report of the Committee on the Bishop's Salary and the Episcopal Fund was adopted.

The Rev. Ernest Mariett presented and read the following reports:

REPORT OF THE TRUSTEES OF THE FUND FOR THE SUPPORT OF WIDOWS AND ORPHANS OF DECEASED CLERGYMEN.

DIOCESE OF ALBANY. }
ALBANY, *November* 17, 1891. }

The Trustees of the Fund for the Support of the Widows and Orphans of Deceased Clergymen present herewith the report of the Treasurer showing the receipts and disbursements for the year.

Receipts.

Balance on hand as reported to last Convention	$2,155 06
From Parishes	202 69
From investments	255 00
Total	$2,612 57

Disbursements.

For Investment	$1,500 00
For Special	100 00
Balance	1,012 75
	$2,612 75

The Trustees hold the following securities contributed by St. Paul's Church, Albany·

One United States Registered 4 per cent bond	$1,000 00
Two Chicago, Burlington and Quincy Railroad, Nebraska Extension, 4 per cent bonds	2,000 00
One Chicago, Burlington and Quincy Railroad 4 per cent bond	1,000 00
One Wabash Railway 5 per cent bond	1,000 00
Total	$5,000 00
And three bonds $500 each	1,500 00
Making Permanent Investment	$6,500 00

WM. CROSWELL DOANE, *President,*
SELDEN E. MARVIN, *Treasurer,*

The Committee on the Report of the Trustees of the Fund for the Support of the Widows and Orphans of Deceased Clergymen respectfully report that they have examined the same and found it correct.

The Committee notes that only twenty-seven Parishes have contributed to the Fund during the year, and that the total of the offerings is less than that of the previous year. In view of this fact, the Committee commend that worthy object to the consideration of those Parishes that have not been accustomed to contribute to the Fund.

ERNEST MARIETT,
T. O. DUROE,
R. W. McDOUGALL.

The Rev. Russell Woodman read the report of the Trustees of the Fund for Aged and Infirm Clergymen, and of the Committee on the same.

REPORT OF THE TRUSTEES OF THE FUND FOR AGED AND INFIRM CLERGYMEN.

DIOCESE OF ALBANY, }
ALBANY, *November* 17, A. D., 1891. }

The undersigned, Trustees of the Fund for the Support of Aged and Infirm Clergymen respectfully report that the receipts and disbursements for the year have been as reported in detail by the Treasurer, and are as follows:

Receipts.

Balance on hand as reported to last Convention.....	$308 39
From Parishes......	522 75
From interest on investments........	841 62
From individuals...........	2 00
Total.................................	$1,674 76

Disbursements.

For Stipends	1,000 00
Balance on hand	$674 46

The Trustees have the following securities which constitute the Permanent Fund:

Bond and mortgage, Bishop's house.............................	$3,600 00
Perry judgment, Bishop's house.............................	6,565 86
Learned bond and mortgage	4,000 00
Burnett bond and mortgage	1,700 00
Troy and Lansingburgh Railroad bond..............	1,000 00
United States Registered 4 per cent bond.....................	1,000 00
New York, Lake Erie and Western Railroad bond	1,000 00
Loan on demand note..	700 00
Total..	$19,565 86

Which represents the following receipts:

Diocese of New York	$10,000 00
St. Paul's Church, Albany	2,000 00
Miss Burr Legacy, Diocese of New York...	2,000 00
Total.......	$14,000 00

The Trustees do not think the Fund is in a condition at present to warrant a diversion of any portion of the income to the Clergymen's Retiring Fund. In their judgment any balance remaining over could more properly be used with our own beneficiaries, and in increasing the principal of the Fund.

The Trustees do not deem it expedient to take any action upon the communication of the Secretary of the General Convention under date May 13, 1890, reported to the last Convention and referred to them, believing the present operation of the disposition of the fund is satisfactory, and together with the Canon on the Clergy Reserve Fund is in accordance with the Canon of the Diocese of Newark.

WM CROSWELL DOANE, *President.*
SELDEN E. MARVIN, *Treasurer.*

REPORT OF THE COMMITTEE ON THE AGED AND INFIRM CLERGY FUND.

The Committee on the Report of the Trustees of the Aged and Infirm Clergy Fund find there stands to the credit of the Fund a cash balance of $674.76. Forty-seven Parishes have contributed to this fund in the past year the sum of $522.75. The gain in amount contributed is not proportionate to the increase in number of Parishes contributing.

To the suggestion and resolution sent to the Trustees as to the advisability of purchasing an interest for some of the more aged of the Clergy in the Clergymen's Retiring Fund, they report as follows: The Trustees do not think the Fund in a condition at present to warrant a diversion of any portion of the income to the Clergymen's Retiring Fund. In their judgment any balance remaining over could more properly be used with our own beneficiaries and in increasing the principal of the Fund.

The Committee have examined the Report of the Treasurer of the Fund and find it correct.

RUSSELL WOODMAN.

The Secretary of the Convention read the Reports of the Society for Promoting Religion and Learning, of the Treasurer of the Diocese in regard to moneys sent him for Theological Education, and of the Committee on the same.

REPORT OF THE SOCIETY FOR PROMOTING RELIGION AND LEARNING IN THE STATE OF NEW YORK.

The Superintendent of the Society for Promoting Religion and Learning in the State of New York, as the Canonical agent of the Diocese of Albany for distributing all funds for theological education, would respectfully report, that during the past Conventional year the following sums have been contributed for the purposes of the Society within the Diocese of Albany:

1890.

Nov. 6.	St. John's Church, Delhi	$7 44
12.	St. Paul's Church, Salem........................	5 00
18.	Church of Our Saviour, Lebanon Springs	1 00
1891.		
May 14.	St. Luke's Church, Troy	4 01
June 20.	Christ Church, Hudson.............................	13 44
Sept. 18.	St. Paul's Mission, Sidney........................	10 00
28.	St. Paul's Church, Troy..........	14 25
Nov. 1.	Church of Our Saviour, Lebanon Springs.....	1 00
	Total.........	$56 14

This sum of $56.14 has been included in the sum of $1,200 and upwards, which has been appropriated by the Society in aid of students in Divinity pursuing their studies in St. Stephen's College, Annandale, and in the General Theological Seminary.

All which is respectfully submitted,

ANDREW OLIVER,
Superintendent.

12

REPORT OF THE TREASURER OF THE DIOCESE OF SUMS RECEIVED FOR THEOLOGICAL EDUCATION.

DIOCESE OF ALBANY, }
ALBANY, *November* 17, A. D., 1891. }

Receipts.

Holy Cross, Troy...	$25 00
Christ, Duanesburgh..	3 09
Trinity, Potsdam...	22 19
	$50 28

Disbursements.

Rev. Joseph T. Zorn...	$25 00
Bishop Doane...	25 28
	$50 28

REPORT OF THE COMMITTEE ON THE REPORT OF THE SOCIETY FOR PROMOTING RELIGION AND LEARNING.

The Committee on the Report of the Society for Promoting Religion and Learning beg leave to report that they have examined the Report of the Superintendent of the Society for Promoting Religion and Learning, and the Report of the Treasurer for the Diocese of sums received for theological education, and find the same correct. In this connection they would call the attention of the Clergy to the desirability of sending sums intended to aid theological education to the Treasurer of the Diocese, to be used at the discretion of the Bishop, rather than to the Superintendent of the Society in New York. Only eight Parishes seem to have made an offering this year, and it would seem as if the Diocese might more generally contribute to this important object.

CHARLES C. EDMUNDS, JR.,
FRANCIS B. DAVIS,
CHARLES E. WACKERHAGEN.

The Rev. George M. Irish presented the

REPORT OF THE COMMITTEE ON NON-REPORTING CLERGY AND PARISHES.

The Committee on Non-Reporting Clergy and Parishes would respectfully report that at the Convention of 1889, there were lacking reports from seven Parishes, Trinity, Plattsburgh, St. John's, Chateaugay; Trinity, Fairfield; Grace, Norway; Grace, Norfolk; St. Stephen's, Schuylerville, and St James', Caldwell. To the Secretary's inquiries, answers were received as follows The reason for no report from St. John's, Chateaugay, was that there had been no services held there for three years; at St. Stephen's, Schuylerville, no Clergyman was in charge at the time; the Rev. C. H. Lancaster reported that sickness and affliction in his Parish at Caldwell prevented his reporting. From the remaining places no answer was received. The Rev. H. M Smyth was prevented from reporting by ill-health

GEORGE M. IRISH,
M ANDRAE.

On motion the resolutions of the last Convention in regard to Non-Reporting Clergy and Parishes were adopted:

Resolved, That the Secretary of the Convention be and is hereby directed to insert in next year's Journal under a separate head a list of the names of those non-reporting Clergy and Parishes that have failed to return answer to his letter of inquiry; also, a record of answers received, and the general character of the excuses offered.

Resolved, That the Secretary of the Convention be and is hereby directed to ask of the Parishes from which no report was received at the last Convention, and the Clergy, still canonically resident in the Diocese, who failed to report at the last Convention, their reasons for not complying with the requirements of the Canon; and that a minute of the same be entered in the Journal against the names under the head of non-reporting Clergy and Parishes; and in any case where the Secretary's request is not complied with, the fact be recorded.

The Rev. Frederick S Sill read the Registrar's Report, and Mr. Walton Van Loan, Lay Deputy from St. Luke's Church, Catskill, that of the Committee on the Report of the Registrar.

REPORT OF THE REGISTRAR, 1891.

The Registrar would respectfully report that the file of Journals for the year 1890 is complete.

Journals of 1891 have been received from all the Dioceses except Albany, Kansas, New Hampshire, New York, Springfield, and Western New York, whose Conventions are held late in the year, and Long Island, Maryland, Massachusetts and Minnesota, where Journals have been delayed. Several Journals of the Missionary Convocations have come to hand and been filed.

A few miscellaneous pamphlets have been received and catalogued.

The Registrar acknowledges the receipt of $10 from the Treasurer of the Diocesan Fund. Expenses, amount overdrawn as per last report, $3.11; binding, $1.50; sundry, 43 cents; total, $5.04; balance on hand, $4.96. For the coming year he would ask for an appropriation from the Diocesan Fund of $5 to add to this balance, for the special purpose of binding.

During several years a large number of duplicate Journals of all the Dioceses has been accumulating until a large trunk is now full of them. What shall be done with them? None of them are of any value to us, and as none antedate the year 1877, and they are for the most part for the years 1880 to 1890, they are not apparently valuable to any other Diocese. Several lists of Journals wanted have come to the Registrar, but all were for years other than those included in his duplicates. The Registrar would suggest that they be sold for waste paper, and the proceeds applied to the appropriation asked for above.

The following Journals are still wanted to complete the sets: Tennessee, 1882. Ohio, 1879, 1884; also, Reports of the Child's Hospital previous to 1884.

We are indebted to the Diocesan Library for four volumes of early Journals of New York, four years of which we did not have. They belonged to the library of the late Canon Selkirk.

FREDERICK S. SILL,
Registrar.

REPORT OF THE COMMITTEE ON THE REGISTRAR'S REPORT.

The Committee on the Registrar's Report, considering the thoroughness with which he has accomplished so much, and at so little cost, and the present and prospective value of the results of his labours, hope the Convention will cheerfully adopt the following resolution:

Resolved, That the Registrar be authorized to draw on the Treasurer of the Diocesan Fund for the sum of $5, according to the request in his report; and that he be authorized to dispose of the duplicate Journals in his possession as he may think best.

W. B. BOLMER,
WALTON VAN LOAN.

On motion of Mr. Van Loan the resolution recommended in the Report of the Committee on the Registrar's Report was adopted.

The following resolution was offered by the Rev. W. W. Battershall, D. D.:

Resolved, That Mr. Selden E. Marvin be designated Treasurer of the Clergy' Reserve Fund.

Pending its discussion the following resolution offered by the Rev. Thaddeus A. Snively was adopted as a substitute for it :

Resolved, That the Trustees of the Clergy Reserve Fund be requested to present a report to the Convention to-morrow.

On motion of Hon. William A. Sackett, Lay Deputy from Bethesda Church, Saratoga, it was

Resolved, That the Order of Miscellaneous Business be laid on the table.

The Rev. W. W. Battershall, D. D., gave notice of a proposed amendment to Canon XVIII, which on his motion was referred to the Committee on the Constitution and Canons.

Resolved, That Canon XVIII, section 7, be amended as follows: Insert " who shall be Treasurer of the Fund," after the words "Treasurer of the Diocese;" and insert the words " and the Archdeacons of the Diocese," in place of the words "and the Lay Members of the Board of Missions designated by the Archdeaconries of the Diocese."

On motion of Mr. J. D. Henderson, Lay Deputy from Christ Church, Herkimer, the Convention took a recess.

HALF-PAST FIVE O'CLOCK IN THE AFTERNOON.

The Evening Prayer was said in the Cathedral, the Dean and the Precentor officiating.

EIGHT O'CLOCK IN THE EVENING.

The Convention reassembled in the Cathedral.

A special Missionary Service, set forth by the Bishop, was said, the Rev. the Precentor of the Cathedral, and the Rev. W. H. Bown officiating.

After the service the Right Rev. President took the chair and called the Convention to order.

The Rev. W. R. Woodbridge, Secretary of the Board of Missions, read the

REPORT OF THE BOARD OF MISSIONS.

The Board of Missions respectfully report that there are 97 Mission Stations in the Diocese, of which 8 are newly adopted, viz.: Dolgeville and Cullen in Herkimer county, Boyntonville in Rensselaer county, Round Lake in Saratoga county, Lyon

Mountain in Clinton county, Monticello and Worcester in Otsego county, Cobleskill in Schoharie county. Twenty stations are just now without Missionaries, several having been recently vacated, and no appointments having been made to some of the new stations.

During the past year one of our Missionaries has died. The Rev. George H. Norton, after three years of faithful service at Au Sable Forks, laboured abundantly and with much success at Greenwich for a few months during the past year, from which work he was suddenly called to the rest of Paradise, on the 16th day of August last.

The Board would also here record the death of the Rev. William H. Cook at the age of eighty-two years, which took place at Ballston on the 8th day of October last. He had served as Missionary in the Diocese ever since its organization, and only resigned his work at East Line at the last Convention.

There are now at work 50 Missionaries in 75 stations. And of these 37 were at work a year ago, and 13 have been appointed since that time.

The Board is happy to report that all the stipends of the Missionaries (including the Diocesan Missionary) have been paid, and no debt rests upon the Board.

But it must be noted that this is in a large measure owing to the fact that the Convention year was begun with a balance of about $900 in the treasury.

In view of this, and of the opening of five new stations, and of the need of larger stipends for some stations, we should not let any self-congratulation lead us into carelessness or neglect of regular and systematic giving. The offerings of the Parishes ought to be forwarded quarterly to the Treasurer in order to provide for the punctual payment of stipends. To do this requires system and perseverance.

It would be interesting to know in how many congregations there is any regular plan or system in the collection of offerings for this special purpose, whether weekly, monthly, or quarterly, by pledges or by subscription books, and what plan seems the most practical and effective.

If we are to look for any notable increase of the offerings in the future, we must interest the children, who are growing up to be the men and women of our Parishes, and educate them to recognize their duty and privilege of helping this most important work of the Diocese.

At the last Convention it was proposed that the Clergy be requested to interest the Sunday School children in making special offerings toward providing the salary of the Diocesan Missionary; and the Board is glad to report that special offerings for this purpose have been made by thirteen Sunday Schools, amounting in all to $358.33.

Such a good beginning gives promise of greater results in the coming year if the Clergy and people unite in faithfully training up the children in the habit of giving according to their ability to build up God's Church.

According to the reports sent in last year, there were 10,658 Sunday School pupils in this Diocese. If from each of these an average of only 14 cents a year (or 1¼ cents a month) were received, there would be almost enough to pay the $1,500 salary of the Diocesan Missionary, and even an average of 10 cents a year would provide for more than two-thirds of that salary.

It is evident that the payment of that salary should not be from the offerings now pledged by the Parishes, as all of these are needed for the stipends of other Missionaries in their several stations. Cannot something more definite be done to bring the offerings of the Sunday Schools to the support of this new work of the Diocesan Missionary?

There is much to encourage us for the future if each will in his place faithfully do his part for the work of Diocesan Missions.

Our freedom from the burden of debt, the good done and promised by the children's special offerings, and the effective work of the Diocesan Missionary, whose report will, we think, fully vindicate the wisdom of such an appointment; all these things cheer us to go right onward in our Mission work, until we may rejoice in occupying every field that is white for the harvest, and until we may be justified in appropriating more than the almost stereotyped sum of $10,000 for the work of a year.

There has been brought to the notice of the Board the proposal made by the Rev. Dr. Shreve at the last Convention, that the Lay people be encouraged to pay the premium of insurance on the lives of the married Missionaries. And the Board thereupon resolved to commend the Rev. Dr. Shreve's proposal, and recommend its carrying out whenever it may be feasible.

In conclusion the Board recommend the adoption of the following resolutions:

Resolved, That it be made the duty of the Diocesan Missionary to present a report of his work at the Missionary meeting on the first evening of the Convention.

Resolved, That the sum of $10,000 be appropriated from the offerings of the Parishes and Mission stations for the work of Missions in this Diocese for the coming year.

Appended to this Report is a list of the stations, missionaries and their stipends.

All of which is respectfully submitted in behalf of the Board of Missions.

WILLIAM R. WOODBRIDGE,
Secretary.

MISSIONS IN THE DIOCESE OF ALBANY.

ARCHDEACONRY OF ALBANY.

County.	Church.	Place.	Missionary.	Stipend
Albany..	Trinity	Rensselaerville...	Rev. R. Washbon and Rev. S. C. Thompson.	$150
	St. Andrew's...	West Troy.	Rev. C. H. Hatheway.	50
Greene.	Gloria Dei	Palenville	Rev. W. C. Grubbe .	250
	Grace..........	Prattsville.	....	250
	Trinity	Ashland.		
	Trinity	Athens., ...	Rev J. W. Stewart ..	
	Christ.	Coxsackie	... ...	300
Herkimer.....	Trinity	Fairfield		
	Grace...... ..	Norway.	Rev E C Hoskins	400
	Memorial.	Middleville		
	St. Albans.	Frankfort.		
	Grace...... ..	Mohawk	....	200
	St. Augustine's.	Ilion..	Rev. W. M. Cook ...	200
		Dolgeville.... ...	Rev. Ernest Mariett.	200
		Cullen	....	
Fulton..	Christ.	Gloversville..	Rev. C. P. A. Burnett.	500
Montgomery...	Zion............	Fonda	Rev. C. C. Edmunds..	300
	Good Shepherd.	Canajoharie	Rev. C. E. Ball	250
	Holy Cross.....	Fort Plain.......		
Columbia. ...	St. Luke's.	Clermont	Rev. M. E. Wilson...	100
	All Saints'.....	Hudson	Rev. G. G. Carter, S. T. D.	300
	Trinity	Claverack		
	St. John in the Wilderness ..	Copake.... .	....	
	St. Luke's.	Chatham	Rev. Isaac Peck..	100
	St. Mark's	Philmont.	Rev. Arthur Lowndes.	500
	Our Saviour....	New Lebanon ...	Rev. Geo. B Johnson	300
		Lebanon Springs..		
				$4,350

ARCHDEACONRY OF TROY.

County.	Church.	Place.	Missionary.	Stipend
Rensselaer...	St. Giles'.......	Castleton..........	Rev. C. H. Hatheway.	$200
	Trinity.... ...	Schaghticoke.....	Rev. S. T. Street.. .	350
	Holy Name...	Boyntonville.....	Rev. C. M. Conant...	
Saratoga......	St. Stephen's. ..	Schuylerville.....	....	100
	St. John's.....	Stillwater. ....}		225
	St. Luke's.....	Mechanicville ...}	....	
	St. Paul's.....	Charlton...... .}	Rev. H. R. Timlow,	
		West Charlton...}	D. D.........	100
	St. John's.....	East Line........}		
	Grace	Jonesville......}		
	All Saints'......	Round Lake......	....	
	St. John's ...	Conklingville...}	Rev. C. J. Whipple .	300
Warren.......	St. Mary's... ..	Luzerne. ....}		
	Good Shepherd.	Chestertown ....}	Rev. Alfred Taylor..	200
	St. Paul's ...	Bartonville. ...}		100
	St. Sacrament..	Bolton	Rev. C. T. Blanchet..	100
Washington..	St. Luke's.....	Cambridge.... ...	Rev. F.H.T. Horsfield.	100
	St. Paul's ...	Greenwich.... ...	Rev. Chas. W. Boyd..	300
	Trinity....	Granville.......}	Rev. C. H. Lancaster.	200
		North Granville..}		
	St. Paul's.....	Salem.............	Rev. H. C. Rush.....	100
Essex.........	Of the Cross...	Ticonderoga......	Rev. H. T. Gregory ..	300
	Christ	Port Henry.....}	Rev. W. R. Wood-	
	Emmanuel.. ..	Mineville.......}	bridge...	350
	St. John's......	Essex.	Rev. W. N. Irish. ...	200
	Good Shepherd.	Bloomingdale	Rev. W. H. Larom ...	
	St. James'.....	Ausable Forks. ...	....	250
	St. Paul's.....	Keesevil e	Rev. J. W. Gill.... .	300
Clinton.	Christ.........	Rouse's Point	Rev. H. L. Wood....	100
	St. John's	Champlain.	Rev.W.D.U.Shearman	250
	St. Peter's,...	Ellenburgh.......}	Rev. S. M. Rogers....	200
	St. Paul's... ..	Ellenburgh Cen..}		
	St. Matthew's ..	Lyon Mountain	....	
	St. John's	Salmon River......	Rev. Hobart Cooke. ..	100
				$4,425

ARCHDEACONRY OF THE SUSQUEHANNA.

County.	Church.	Place.	Missionary.	Stipend
Delaware......	Christ..........	Deposit...........	Rev. F. S. Fisher....	$300
		Bloomville...... ..	Rev. E. Griggs	200
	St. Paul's.....	Franklin	Rev. W. H. Goodisson.	300
	Grace	Stamford..	....	200
	St. Paul's......	Sidney .... }		
Otsego	Christ....... ...	West Burlington.}	Rev. F. S. Griffin	300
		Edmeston ....}		
		Monticello........		
	Immanuel.. ..	Otego...... ...	Rev. W. G. W. Lewis	175
	St. John's.....	Portlandville.....}	Rev. E. A. Hartmann	300
	St. James'.....	Oneonta ......}		
	Christ	Gilbertsville.....}	Rev. D. F. MacDonald	125
	St. Stephen's ...	Maple Grove.....		
	St. Paul's.......	E. Springfield....}	Rev. John Prout.....	200
	St. Mary's.....	Springfield Centr. }		
	Holy Spirit.....	Schenevus.		
	St. Simon and St.		Rev. Harry E. Gil-	
	Jude.........	Worcester ....}	christ.............	125
Schoharie....	....	Cobleskill. .....}		
				$2,050

ARCHDEACONRY OF OGDENSBURGH.

County.	Church.	Place.	Missionary.	Stipend
Franklin.. . .	St. John's......	St. Regis Lake...	Rev. W. H. Larom :	$100
	St. Luke's......	Saranac Lake ...		
		Santa Clara......		
		St. Regis Falls...	....	200
		Paul Smith's Sta.		
	St. Mark's......	West Bangor	Rev. R Wyndham	60
	St. Peter's	Brushton	Brown.........	340
St. Lawrence..	St. Thomas'	Lawrenceville....		
Franklin......	St. James'.. ..	Hogansburgh	Rev. Howard McDou-	
St. Lawrence..	St. John's	Massena........	gall.......... ...	350
	Grace.. .. .	Louisville Land'g		
	Grace.........	Norfolk.	Rev. R. M. Kirby,	
	St. Andrew's....	Norwood	D. D............	300
	St. Paul's	Waddington.	Rev. A. C. Macdon-	
	St. Luke's.	Lisbon	ald............ ..	400
	Christ	Morristown........	Rev. J. T. Zorn	300
	Trinity........	Gouverneur........	Rev. J. A. Dickson...	250
	Trinity Chapel..	Morley..	....	200
				$2,500

SUMMARY.

	Stations.	Missionaries.	Stipends.
Archdeaconry of Albany....	27	16	$4,350 00
Archdeaconry of Troy	34	20	4,425 00
Archdeaconry of the Susquehanna	18	9	2,050 00
Archdeaconry of Ogdensburgh.....	18	7	2,500 00
	97	*52	$13,325 00

Mr. Selden E. Marvin, Treasurer, read the

REPORT OF THE TREASURER OF THE BOARD OF MISSIONS FROM NOVEMBER, 1890, TO NOVEMBER, 1891.

RECEIPTS.

Balance as reported to last Convention... .... $914 66

Archdeaconry of Albany.

The Cathedral of All Saints.	1,200 00
St. Peter's, Albany	762 60
St. Paul's, Albany	300 00
Grace, Albany...........................	50 00
Holy Innocents, Albany. .. .. ·	50 00
Trinity, Albany......	20 00
Trinity, Rensselaerville.	15 01
Trinity, West Troy	27 31
St. Mark's, Green Island.	40 61

* This total does not agree with that given in the Report, for the reason that in this summary, which was made by the Secretary of the Convention, the Rev C. H Hatheway is counted in the Archdeaconries of Albany and Troy, and the Rev Walter H. Larom in the Archdeaconries of Troy and Ogdensburgh.—W. C. P L

St. John's, Cohoes..	$253 74
Trinity, Athens	8 00
Calvary, Cairo..	
Gloria Dei, Palenville..	12 82
St. Luke's, Catskill..	150 00
Christ, Greenville...	4 00
St. Paul's, Oak Hill..	4 00
Christ, Coxsackie..	5 00
Trinity, Ashland...	
Christ, Duanesburgh...	50 00
St. George's, Schenectady....................................	125 00
Christ, Schenectady..	15 00
St. Ann's, Amsterdam	28 33
Good Shepherd, Canajoharie..................................	10 00
Holy Cross, Fort Plain.......................................	
Zion, Fonda...	10 00
St. John's, Johnstown..	75 01
Christ, Gloversville..	25 00
Trinity, Fairfield..	
Christ, Herkimer..	60 00
Emmanuel, Little Falls.......................................	47 26
St. Augustine's, Ilion..	30 00
Grace, Mohawk..	15 00
St. Alban's, Frankfort..	
Memorial, Middleville..	20 00
Trinity, Claverack...	12 00
St. Luke's, Clermont...	10 00
Our Saviour, Lebanon Springs................................	20 00
St. John the Evangelist, Stockport............................	9 39
St. Barnabas', Stottville	25 00
St. Mark's, Philmont...	23 00
St. Luke's, Chatham, (1890, $5; 1891, $5).....................	10 00
St. Paul's, Kinderhook.......................................	125 80
Christ, Hudson..	111 87
All Saints', Hudson..	12 00
St. Margaret's, Menands......................................	5 00
	$3,777 25

Archdeaconry of Troy.

St. Paul's, Troy	$750 00
St. John's, Troy..	500 00
Christ, Troy...	250 00
Holy Cross, Troy..	250 00
Ascension, Troy..	35 25
St. Luke's, Troy...	28 09
St. Barnabas', Troy	50 00
Epiphany, East Albany..	
Messiah, Greenbush..	80 00
St. Giles', Castleton...	1 00
Trinity, Lansingburgh..	214 00
Trinity, Schaghticoke	15 00
St. Mark's, Hoosick Falls.....................................	110 40

13

All Saints', Hoosac	$26 82
Grace, Waterford	85 00
Christ, Ballston Spa	80 25
St. John's, East Line	
Grace, Jonesville	10 00
Calvary, Burnt Hills	22 00
St. Paul's, Charlton	5 00
Bethesda, Saratoga Springs	200 00
St. Stephen's, Schuylerville	
St. John's, Conklingville	5 00
St. Luke's, Mechanicville	20 00
St. John's, Stillwater	10 00
St. Paul's, Salem	78 67
St. Luke's, Cambridge	180 00
Trinity, Granville	12 50
Mission, North Granville	10 00
St. Paul's, Greenwich	25 00
St. James', Fort Edward	18 00
Zion, Sandy Hill	18 87
Trinity, Whitehall	25 00
St. James', Caldwell	
St. Mary's, Luzerne	20 00
Holy Cross, Warrensburgh	50 00
Messiah, Glens Falls	75 00
Good Shepherd, Chestertown	15 00
St. Paul's, Bartonville	4 78
St. Sacrament, Bolton	22 00
Church of the Cross, Ticonderoga	30 44
Christ, Port Henry	34 87
Emmanuel, Mineville	5 00
St. James', Ausable Forks	
St. John's, Essex	30 00
St. Paul's, Keeseville	15 00
Mission, Racquette Lake	50 00
Trinity, Plattsburgh	75 00
Christ, Rouse's Point	6 80
St. John's, Champlain	20 00
St. Peter's, Ellenburgh	10 00
	$3,468 74

Archdeaconry of the Susquehanna.

St. Peter's, Hobart	$35 00
Christ, Walton	52 43
St. John's, Delhi	125 00
Grace, Stamford	20 00
St. Paul's, Franklin	20 00
St. Paul's, Sidney	6 00
Christ, Deposit	12 32
Christ, Gilbertsville	25 00
Christ, Cooperstown	170 88
Grace, Cherry Valley	75 00
Zion, Morris	38 00

St. James', Oneonta ...	$40 00
St. Matthew's, Unadilla	50 00
Christ, West Burlington	5 50
St. Paul's, East Springfield	25 00
St. John's, Richfield Springs	50 00
Immanuel, Otego	5 00
Holy Spirit, Schenevus	
St. Andrew's, Schohorie	6 71
	$761 84

Archdeaconry of Ogdensburgh.

St. John's, Ogdensburgh	$500 00
Trinity, Potsdam	685 00
Trinity, Gouverneur	50 00
St. John's, Massena	26 25
Christ, Morristown	50 00
Grace, Norfolk	5 00
St. Paul's, Waddington	19 00
Grace, Canton	
Trinity Chapel, Morley	
St. Thomas', Lawrenceville	50
Zion, Colton	15 05
Grace, Louisville Landing	
St. Mark's, Malone	75 00
St. Peter's, Brushton	10 00
St. Luke's, Saranac Lake	20 00
St. James', Hogansburgh	25 00
St. Mark's, West Bangor	5 00
	$1,485 80

For Missionary at Large.

Christ, Duanesburgh	$25 00
Christ, Herkimer	10 00
Christ, Hudson	51 10
Christ Sunday School, Port Henry	2 74
Christ, Cooperstown	30 00
St. John's, Ogdensburgh	110 00
Trinity, Potsdam	55 00
St. Luke's, Saranac Lake	15 00
St. Mark's, Malone	15 00
Trinity, Gouverneur	5 00
St. Mark's Sunday School, Green Island	3 91
St. George's Sunday School, Schenectady	20 00
St. Peter's Sunday School, Albany	15 58
	$358 33

Miss Austin Fund for Cairo, Greenville and Oak Hill.

Income from securities received from executors	$1,010 00

Sundry Sources.

Offertories at Convention.............................	$90 85
M. M., Plattsburgh........	20 00
Income, Miss Austin Fund....	1,555 00
Income, Mrs. Hannibal Green Fund............................	250 00
Income, Mrs. De Witt Fund........	300 00
Income, Parochial Fund	40 00
Iuterest, Vandenburgh bond	30 00
Interest, Goss bond...	12 00
Interest, Houghton bond..	30 00
Interest, Troy and West Troy Bridge bond.............	35 00
Interest, Cornell Steamboat bond......	70 00
Interest, Tibbits Fund....	120 00
Interest, Sundry notes	32 00
Mrs. E. W. N. Wood....	50 00
	$2,634 35

Specials.

St. John's, Troy, to St. Luke's, Troy...........................	100 00
St. John's, Troy, to St. Luke's, Saranac Lake....................	100 00
	$200 00
Total...	$14,560 97
By balance....... .....`....	$268 06

DISBURSEMENTS.

FOR STIPENDS.

Archdeaconry of Albany.

Rensselaerville	Rev. Samuel C. Thompson................ ..	$161 29
West Troy..............	Rev. C. H. Hathaway.............	200 00
Palenville........	Rev. William Charles Grubbe	250 00
Ashland...............	Rev. Eugene Griggs.	156 25
Coxsackie	Rev. L. H. Schubert	300 00
Mohawk................	Rev. Alfred Taylor....	183 34
Ilion....	Rev. W. M. Cook	200 00
Middleville...	Rev. Edward C. Hoskins.	300 00
Dolgeville.............	Rev. Ernest Mariett...	100 00
Gloversville......... ..	Rev. C. P. A. Burnett.	500 00
Fonda..................	Rev. C. C. Edmunds.... ....;	300 00
Canajoharie............	Rev. John N. Marvin.........	62 50
Canajoharie........	Rev. Clarence E. Ball.	62 50
Hudson	Rev. Elmer P. Miller...	87 50
Hudson	Rev. George G. Carter.............	50 00
Chatham...............	Rev. Isaac Peck....................... ...	100 00
Clermont.........	Rev. M. E. Wilson	75 00
Philmont...	Rev. Arthur Lowndes	264 00
Lebanon Springs	Rev. E. J. Johnston Smith...	12 00
Lebanon Springs	Rev. D. C. Wright	40 00
Lebanon Springs........	Rev. Montgomery H. Throop, Jr.	75 00
		$3,479 38

Archdeaconry of Troy.

Castleton	Rev. C. H. Hatheway	$200 00
Schaghticoke	Rev. T. Dickinson	233 34
Schaghticoke	Rev. Irving Towsly	29 16
Schaghticoke	Rev. S. T. Street	58 34
East Albany	Rev. Thomas White	100 00
Mechanicville	Rev. W. G. W. Lewis	37 50
Charlton	Rev. H. R. Timlow	100 00
Schuylerville	Rev. J. F. Esch	100 00
Luzerne	Rev. C. J. Whipple	300 00
Chestertown	Rev. Nassau William Stephens	191 66
Chestertown	Rev. Alfred Taylor	25 00
Bolton	Rev. C. T. Blanchet	100 00
Ausable Forks	Rev. George H. Norton	41 67
Cambridge	Rev. F. H. T. Horsfield	100 00
Greenwich	Rev. George H. Norton	175 00
Greenwich	Rev. F. M. Gray	25 00
Granville	Rev. W. C. Prout	200 00
Salem	Rev. H. C. Rush	100 00
Ticonderoga	Rev. Henry T. Gregory	300 00
Port Henry	Rev. William R. Woodbridge	350 00
Essex	Rev. William N. Irish	200 00
Keeseville	Rev. J. William Gill	300 00
Champlain	Rev. W. D. U. Shearman	250 00
Ellenburgh	Rev. Silas M. Rogers	200 00
Rouse's Point	Rev. Herbert Luther Wood	83 33
		$3,800 00

Archdeaconry of the Susquehanna.

Deposit	Rev. F. S. Fisher	300 00
Sidney	Rev. F. S. Griffin	300 00
Stamford	Rev. A. T. DeLearsy	66 67
Stamford	Rev. Phineas Duryea	49 99
Bloomville	Rev. Eugene Griggs	75 00
Franklin	Rev. William Henry Goodisson	137 50
Oneonta	Rev. E. A. Hartmann	300 00
Schenevus	Rev. A. S. Ashley	87 50
Schenevus	Rev. Harry Elmer Gilchrist	62 50
Gilbertsville	Rev. David F. McDonald, D. D.	225 00
East Springfield	Rev. John Prout	200 00
Otego	Rev. W. G. W. Lewis	65 63
Otsego County	Rev. F. N. Bouck	50 00
		$1,919 79

Archdeaconry of Ogdensburgh.

Morristown	Rev. Joseph T. Zorn	300 00
Morristown	Rev. Joseph T. Zorn (special)	50 00
Morley	Rev. R. G. Hamilton	33 33
Massena	Rev. Howard McDougall	350 00
Norfolk	Rev. R. M. Kirby, D. D	265 00
Waddington	Rev. Angus C. Macdonald	400 00
Waddington	Rev. Angus C. Macdonald (special)	100 00

Gouverneur	Rev. James A. Dickson......................	$250 00
Santa Clara...........	John Hurd for Rev. Mr. Green	50 00
Santa Clara	Rev. Phineas Duryea......	33 33
Santa Clara.............	Rev. Nassau William Stephens	47 20
Saranac Lake...........	Rev. W. H. Larom....	100 00
Brushton	Rev. R. Wyndham Brown.........	340 00
		$2,318 86

General Missionary.

Rev. Walter C. Stewart, 9 months.....	1,125 00

Sundry Purposes.

Post office envelopes	$19 62	
Rev. Wm. R. Woodbridge, expenses	12 00	
Amount returned St. Andrew's, Schoharie....................	31 61	
Henry Stowell, printing	1 65	
Rev. T. A. Synder, Misses Austin Fund for St. Paul's, Oak Hill	75 00	
		139 88

De Witt Fund.

Rev. C. P. A. Burnett	300 00

Miss Austin Fund for Cairo, Oak Hill and Greenville.

Rector, Wardens and Vestrymen, Calvary, Cairo..............	$336 68	
Rev. T. A. Snyder, St. Paul's, Oak Hill......	336 64	
Rev. T. A. Snyder, Christ, Greenville........	336 68	
		1,010 00

Specials.

St. Luke's, Troy....	100 00
St. Luke's, Saranac Lake.........	100 00
Balance.	268 06
	$14,560 97

DIOCESE OF ALBANY,
ALBANY, *November* 17, A. D., 1891.

Herewith find statement of receipts and disbursements rendered in detail, for the year, showing as follows :

RECEIPTS.

Balance on hand as reported to last Convention...........		$914 66
Offertories at Convention......		90 35
Salary General Missionary........		358 33
Income securities ... .-.........		2,474 00
Sundry sources.......		70 00
Income Miss Austin Fund for Cairo, Oak Hill and Greenville.....		1,010 00
Archdeaconry of Albany........ .. .. ·	$3,777 25	
Archdeaconry of Troy	3,468 74	
Archdeaconry of the Susquehanna	761 84	
Archdeaconry of Ogdensburgh	1,435 80	
		9,443 63
Total...		$14,360 97

DISBURSEMENTS.

Stipends.

Archdeaconry of Albany	$3,479 38
Archdeaconry of Troy	3,800 00
Archdeaconry of the Susquehanna........	1,919 79
Archdeaconry of Ogdensburgh............................	2,318 86
	$11,518 03
General Missionary................	1,125 00
Sundry purposes .... '.	139 88
De Witt Fund........	300 00
Miss Austin Fund for Cairo, Oak Hill and Greenville..................	1,010 00
	$14,092 91
Balance on hand..........	268 06
	$14,360 97
Balance on hand...	$268 06

The Permanent Fund represents the following amounts:

Misses Austin	$1,500 00
Elizabeth Sherers.......	750 00
Mrs. De Witt	5,000 00
Diocese of New York........	2,000 00
Diocese of New York Parochial Fund.....	1,000 00
Dr. William Tibbits.............................	2,000 00
L. H. Sears...	400 00
Mrs. Hannibal Green	4,750 00
Miss Charlotte Austin,...	29,069 53
Total........	$46,469 53

The Board holds in trust $19,000 received from the executors of Charlotte Austin, deceased, the income from which is to be paid, one-third each to the Rector, Wardens and Vestrymen of the following Parishes : Calvary Church, Cairo; Christ Church, Greenville; St. Paul's Church, Oak Hill.

The Board holds in trust $2,000 of the bonds of the Rensselaer and Saratoga Railroad Company, the income from which is to be paid one-half each to St. Luke's Church, Mechanicville, and St. John's Church, Stillwater.

SELDEN E. MARVIN,
Treasurer Board of Missions.

RECEIPTS FOR CLERGY RESERVE FUND.

St. Peter's, Albany.......................	$21 31
St. John's, Ogdensburgh.........	32 67
Christ, Herkimer...	7 00
St. Luke's, Saranac Lake	2 50
	$63 48

REPORT OF RECEIPTS AND } DISBURSEMENTS OF THE GENERAL MISSIONARY FROM FEBRUARY 20, 1891, TO NOVEMBER 10, 1891.

RECEIPTS.

Church of our Saviour, Lebanon Springs......................	$12 00
St. John in the Wilderness, Copake.........................	21 00

St. Luke's, Milton Centre..............................	$6 87
All Saints' Mission, Round Lake........................	10 91
Grace Mission, Jonesville..............................	10 20
Trinity, Schaghticoke..................................	12 90
St. Mark's, Hoosick Falls..............................	2 00
St. Luke's, Mechanicville..............................	3 03
St. Mark's, Philmont...................................	5 00
St. Andrew's, Schoharie................................	2 35
Zion, Morris..	27 25
St. James', Oneonta...................................	11 05
Christ, Gilbertsville..................................	3 60
St. Mark's, Malone....................................	7 82
Christ, Port Henry....................................	3 34
Archdeaconry of the Susquehanna.......................	7 00
Archdeaconry of Albany................................	1 08
Cathedral of All Saints, Albany.......................	117 93
	$264 83

DISBURSEMENTS.

For personal expenses................................	$141 58	
For Communion set....................................	116 30	
		257 88

Balance on hand.. $6 95

The Committee appointed to examine the Treasurer's Report of the Board of Missions find the disbursements correct, vouchers having been furnished therefor.

FENWICK M. COOKSON,
GEORGE A. WELLS.

The Rev. Walter Charles Stewart, Diocesan Missionary, presented the

REPORT OF THE DIOCESAN MISSIONARY.

On the 15th November last, the Bishop did me the honour of offering me the position of Diocesan Missionary: a position which I finally concluded, not without considerable anxiety and misgiving, to accept, regarding it as a call to important work from one whom it was a pleasure as well as a duty to obey. It was arranged that the duties of the office should commence on the 1st February; and, in order to carry out the idea that the Cathedral should be the centre of the general missionary work of the Diocese, a place was assigned me on the staff of the Cathedral clergy. On the 3d February, circular letters were sent to the four Archdeacons announcing the appointment and inviting suggestions. The general lines on which it was proposed to prosecute the work were indicated in these letters by requests for information regarding places: (1) Where the Church has no foothold but where Church families are to be found, (2) where Parishes or Missions had once been established, but had lapsed; and (3) where weak and irregularly supplied Missions still exist. Cards were also subsequently sent to most of the reverend clergy asking for information regarding points in their neighbourhood suitable for missionary operations, and for any general information which might prove useful. It is unnecessary to go into details of the various and varied answers received; suffice it that I avail myself of this opportunity to return thanks to the large number of my brethren who so kindly complied with my request. It will, of course, be readily understood that it would be impossible for any one to cover the large area of this Diocese, investigating all the possibilities held out, and at the same time to accomplish any thing that would prove of permanent value. Consequently, the chief aim kept in view was to establish, to restore, or to strengthen where prospects seemed hopeful; though inquiries regarding other places, where work in the future might tell, were not neglected.

In laying before you a brief review of some of the work accomplished, it may be as well, for the sake of classification, to follow the order above given.

I. Of places where the Church has no foothold, but where Church families are to be found, there may be mentioned:

(1) Round Lake. Though this place is best known as a Methodist camp-meeting ground it has also some claims as a summer resort. There are a few Church people resident all the year round, and quite a number who own summer cottages and spend the season. Others have said they would like to go there if only they could obtain the services of the Church. My first visit was paid on the 26th March, for the purpose of investigating, and on the 6th April I returned and baptized two children. Since then occasional services have been held in a hall loaned to us; the Holy Communion administered; an adult and another child baptized, and a Sunday School established. During summer the number of pupils enrolled was seventy, but the average for winter is forty. Prospects seeming to be favourable, a meeting was held to discuss the situation, which resulted in a petition being sent to the Bishop asking him to organize a Mission, while a pledge of $300 was made toward the support of a missionary. The executive committee of the Round Lake Association generously granted a ninety-nine years' lease, renewable at expiry and forever, of a piece of ground ninety feet square in an excellent location on which to erect a Church building. A local architect has contributed the plans, estimates, etc., and the supervision of the work, while a number of artisans and labourers have promised to give their services in lieu of cash subscriptions. Nine hundred dollars have already been subscribed toward the building fund, and operations will be commenced as soon as the lease has been signed on behalf of the Board of Missions. Toward the furnishing of the Church the following gifts have been promised, some of which have been already made : The windows, by the Rev. Canon Chapman; an Altar through Rev. Edgar A. Enos; altar-cross and altar-rail by the Rev. Robert Granger, Richfield Springs; sanctuary chair, stall, prayer-desk, and two stools, through Archdeacon Olmsted; a communion set, through the Rev. James E. Hall, Cherry Valley; altar-linen by the Sunday School of St. Mark's, Philmont, through the Rev. Arthur Lowndes; Bible for the lectern and Prayer Books for the chancel, by the local Sunday School; and an embroidered dossal by a Philadelphia lady. There are at present here three candidates for confirmation.

(2) Lyon Mountain, in Clinton county, is a mining camp with a population of about 3,000. The Archdeacon of Ogdensburgh, being in that neighbourhood last summer, and having held one or two services there, was so impressed with the possibilities for mission work, that he reported the matter to the Bishop, who lost no time in asking me to go and investigate. There were a faithful few of our people, who greatly longed for the advent of Mother Church, and quite a number ready to learn about her. I spent three weeks here, holding services, and visiting, and canvassing some of the neighbouring districts. Later, I returned to carry on the movement which had been inaugurated; and, on the 2d October, baptized two children in Standish, six miles distant. On the 4th October, I baptized eight adults and twelve children. On the evening of the 6th, a special train was chartered to take us to Plattsburgh — an hour and a half's ride — where, in Trinity Church, I had the privilege of presenting to the Bishop fourteen candidates for the apostolic rite of the laying on of hands. Through the courtesy of the Rev. Hobart Cooke, I was permitted to baptize

14

a young lady before the confirmation services began. On the 8th October, I baptized two more adults, and that afternoon started with three more candidates, in a cold and drizzly rain, for a twenty-four miles drive to Malone, where I had the satisfaction of presenting three for confirmation. The average age of these seventeen candidates was a little over thirty-six; nine were males, and eight females. Subsequently a petition was sent to the Bishop praying for the organization of a Mission and pledging at least $300 toward the support of a Missionary. Here, also, a Sunday School was established with every prospect of growth and development. I have reason for believing that if this point is faithfully worked it will be a self-supporting Parish in two years.

(3) Cullen, in Herkimer county, is a small village, about two miles and a half from Richfield Springs, which has hitherto possessed neither Church nor meeting-house. For some years the wife and daughters of Mr. D. Jones Crain, who has a country house there, have maintained a Sunday School. This year Mr. Crain has been building a Chapel, which we had hoped would be ready for occupation this winter, but circumstances have occurred to prevent its being completed before next spring, when it will be turned over to the Board of Missions. Those who have graduated from the Sunday School will form the nucleus of what promises to be a lively mission.

(4) At Worcester, in Otsego county, a Mission has been organized by the Bishop in response to a petition addressed him. The people are very enthusiastic. Services are held regularly in the Baptist meeting-house, the use of which has been kindly tendered. There are at least three candidates for confirmation here. The Mission has been placed in charge of the Rev. H. E. Gilchrist under the supervision of the Diocesan Missionary.

II. Of places where Parishes or Missions had been once established but had lapsed, mention may be made of:

(1) Copake Iron Works. While the situation here *seemed* hopeless, I was determined that one more effort should be made to undo the wrong which had been done in the past. The history of affairs here is, perhaps, an old story to many, but I may be allowed to touch briefly on a few of its salient points. The Church of St. John-in-the-Wilderness was consecrated by Bishop Chase in 1852, and services were regularly maintained till 1878 From this time on till 1883, the services were very irregular, owing in a large degree to the eccentricity of the vestry. In that year they finally decided not to call a rector, and since that time until very recently there have been no services of the Church there. (For a comprehensive view of the case see Convention Journals for 1886, p. 126, and 1887, p. 122) On the 16th November, 1886, the parish was declared extinct by the Convention, and the Trustees of the Diocese were directed to take possession of the temporalities. But neither the Trustees, as a body, nor the Bishop, as their representative, could obtain actual possession, though repeated efforts were made. The chief obstacle lay in the fact that the deed of gift of the property was not to be found, and no record of it had been entered in the County Clerk's office. In the meantime the Methodists, who at sundry times previously had held their exercises in the Church, were invited by the *soi-disant* vestry to occupy the Church and make such use of it as seemed good in their eyes. This they did, and when I paid my first visit there I found them " holding the fort " with characteristic enthusiasm. To do them justice it may be said that, when I announced my determination to take possession on behalf of the Diocese, they offered to let me have the use of the Church when they were not themselves using it; and seemed grieved when I declined their kindly offer. It would take too long to go into the details of the various arguments, moral and physical, which were employed to

convince them of our right to the property; suffice it to say that, in the end, they moved away their belongings and sought "fresh fields and pastures new." But, while we thus obtained *de facto* possession, there was still a possibility of its being questioned *de jure*. While things were in this uncertain condition, it was learned that the trustees of the estate on which the property was situated had sold a large tract of land, including the Church lot, to a person who subsequently gave a quit-claim deed of the Church lot to a gentleman whose parents were buried there. On application being made to him he consented to give the Trustees of the Diocese a quit-claim deed of the property exclusive of the little burying-ground which he desired to reserve for his family. So now the Church is once more the property of the Diocese. It has been thoroughly overhauled and renovated, decorated under the personal supervision of Mr. J. Neville Stent, of New York, who contributed the designs, and presents a very handsome appearance. On the 18th October it was my privilege to conduct services and celebrate the Holy Communion in this, in a double sense, restored edifice. It is an act of the barest justice to acknowledge here the self-sacrificing assistance rendered by Mr. I. C. Chesbrough and his daughter, Mrs. F. P. C. Peck. A Mission has been organized here in place of the extinct Parish. Services has been kept up with tolerable regularity since the end of February, Mrs. Peck having fitted up a temporary Chapel in her house. For some weeks the Rev. B. F. Cooley, of Westfield, Mass., took charge of the Mission, and the Rev. Canon Temple has also officiated on various occasions. I have here baptized three adults and three children, and buried one child. There are four candidates for confirmation.

(2) At Richfield, in Otsego county, locally known as Monticello, stands St. Luke's Church, one of the oldest in the Diocese, dating from 1803. For nearly fifteen years there have been no services held here. The growth of the more popular Richfield Springs, and the removal of many Church families have contributed to the decline of the Parish. But a remnant of the old stock has been left; and year by year the Parish organization has been kept up and perpetuated in the hope that a brighter time would come. At the time of my first visit all things seemed to point out our opportunity. The Baptists had closed their meeting-house and given up the field, and the Universalist body was moribund. Occasionally a student was found to come and preach, but usually their edifice remained closed. I was fortunate at this time in being able to secure the services, as Lay-reader, of a student from the General Theological Seminary. Mr. T. N. Bouck entered on his duties on the 11th June, remaining till the 15th September, and doing most faithful and efficient work. He reported an attendance at the services of "from 80 to 100, rain or shine, every Sunday." A Sunday School was started here also with a fair attendance. It was my privilege in this old Church to administer the Holy Communion and to baptize an adult and two children. There is an excellent field here for active, earnest, missionary work. It is a pleasure to be able to report that, until a Missionary can be sent here, the Rev. Robert Granger, of Richfield Springs, has kindly consented to give services on Sunday afternoons.

(3) At Milton Centre, two and a half miles from Ballston, is the little Church of St. Luke, built ten years ago through the exertions of that indefatigable Missionary the Rev. Walter Delafield. At that time a tannery was located here, round which a large settlement had grown. But the tannery was subsequently burned down, the plant removed to Ballston, and with it went the operatives. There remains, however, a small community, and farm-houses are scattered all over the district. The services I held here on the 3d May were the first since 9th January, 1887. There are at least nine communicants living here. No services of any kind are to be had

nearer than Ballston, and an average of fifty people have attended on the occasions when I was there. On the 7th June I baptized six children; and I also celebrated. · A Sunday School has been organized, with an average attendance of nineteen pupils and four teachers. Whatever the report of others may be, I can only say that the few people here seem to be actually what they profess to be — desirous of having at least occasionally the benefits and the comforts of the Church. The difficulty in the way of supplying regular services at stated intervals lies in the isolation of its position from any Missionary jurisdiction to which it might otherwise be attached.

(4) Under this heading may appropriately be mentioned Schoharie. That some organization once existed here is plain from a minute of the Trustees of the Diocese at a meeting held 11th June, 1885 (see Journal 1886, p. 126) when the Rev. E. A. Hartmann was directed to take steps toward the recovery of the Church property or of the proceeds of its sale. By an arrangement suggested by the Rev. E. W. Flower, of Duanesburgh, he has undertaken to give services here once a month during summer and fall while I continue them during winter and spring. Mr. Flower reports as follows — commencing in April — " evening prayer and sermon, 7; Holy Communion, 7; average attendance in evening, 20, average attendance at Holy Communion in morning, 7; baptized one child. Eight communicants desire and appreciate services, six or seven more confirmed, but indifferent." To this record I add one service, with sermon, in the evening, and one celebration of the Holy Communion. At each celebration a collection was taken for Diocesan Missions.

III. Under the caption of weak or irregularly supplied Missions may be included:

(1) Schenevus. This has had a very precarious and vacillating existence. At times it has almost seemed as if it would have to be given up. It is mentioned more because it is believed that at last it has entered on a season of prosperity, and because this is due indirectly to the work of the Diocesan Missionary. It had no organization of any kind, beyond what was known as " The Parish Guild," and was very unreliable in the matter of financial support. The Rev. H. E. Gilchrist, who was placed here as Lay-reader during his period of candidateship, had begun to make his influence felt. At this time the Diocesan Missionary proposed forming a Missionary circuit, comprising Schenevus, Worcester, Cobleskill, Schoharie and Middleburgh. It was this which stirred up the people of Schenevus to see what they really could do, the result being that they pledged themselves to pay $450 a year provided that they had service once every Sunday, and that the Missionary resided there. The Church was incorporated by consent of the Bishop, and steps will be taken next year looking to union with the Convention.

(2) Lebanon Springs has been, in some respects, exceedingly unfortunate. So situated that it cannot join forces with another Parish or Mission, it has struggled under the burden of its poverty bravely. I know no congregation in the Diocese showing, comparatively speaking, such good work under great discouragements. It was my happiness to go there twice and administer the Holy Communion. For one year and eight months they have had no Rector, but it is a matter of great thankfulness that such a man as the Rev. George B. Johnson has consented to become their Rector.

(3) Grace Mission, Jonesville, was committed to me, so to speak, in loving and tender words by the venerable William H. Cook, whose declining years had been given to the work here and at East Line It is more than a year since he was obliged to give up his ministrations, and but recently he has entered on the rest of Paradise. He wrote "They (of Jonesville) are the best congregation I have ever known, and richly deserve the ministrations of a Priest." Numerically weak, they are strong in loyalty and faith. I have held occasional services here, administered

the Holy Communion, and baptized one child. There are four candidates for confirmation here.

(4) Schuylerville. I went there at the Bishop's request to make some inquiries. All that need be said is that, with a pretty Church, well-furnished, Rectory and Parish School buildings on the one hand, and large mills on the other, there seems to be every indication of hopeful possibilities under the right man. Unfortunately, owing to various causes, the Parish at present is run to the ground.

IV. Of places other than those classed as above brief mention may be made of:

(1) Tannersville. An unorganized Mission with hopeful prospects. It was started by Mrs. Alexander Hemsley in 1879, when services were held by a Deacon in the Union meeting-house in the village. In 1880 clerical friends were asked to officiate and they proposed that the offertories be devoted to a Church building fund. The corner-stone of the Church of St. John-the-Evangelist was laid by Father Field, in July, 1884, and the first service held in August, 1886. The first sermon was preached and Holy Communion celebrated by Father Maturin. Since then there have been services every summer by various Priests, and the following statistics may be noted; Baptisms, 78; confirmations, 33; marriages, 1; burials, 5. The property is being improved this year. I held services here and celebrated this summer, and consulted with these interested regarding future plans. It is hoped that arrangements can be made for all the year round ministrations.

(2) Four miles distant is the larger village of Hunter. Hitherto, for the past four years, summer services have been held. This year, owing to my not being informed in time, there were none. Mr. S. D. Van Loan, who has been so energetic in the work here, reports that they have $254.63 invested and bearing six per cent interest; a promise of $50 and a lot on which to build; another promise of $50; a promise of $200 and a very desirable lot on which to build, and all the stone for the building, provided that the Church be built of stone, or, if a frame structure, that it cost not less than $4,000. It is hoped that an arrangement can be made by which Hunter and Tannersville may be joined together as one Mission.

(3) In Prattsville, also in Greene county, a Parish was incorporated forty-seven years ago, but "the using up of bark, used in tanning, and the opening up of the country by railroads (none of which came near this place) resulted in the closing up of all the fifteen or sixteen manufactories, the best part of the population left — with the result that the Church, which had been strong and useful, was with the village, stranded." There are five communicants here — well-stricken in years — and there is no material for the up-building of the Church.

(4) Lewis, in Essex county, was sugggested by the Rev. W. N. Irish, as a good field for work. In his company I visited the place and found a few Church people who said they would be glad to have services. They offered to raise $200 toward a Missionary's salary. It was proposed that it should be joined with Elizabethtown, five miles distant; but the Rev. H. M. Smyth, who took duty there last summer, and who was asked to look into the matter, reported that he did not think any thing could be done in winter at Elizabethtown, though he thought both points ought to be worked in summer. There are eleven known communicants at Lewis, and there may be more in the neighbourhood. The only services are semi-monthly meetings conducted by the Congregational minister at Westport.

(5) I visited Poland, in Herkimer county, in company with the Rev. C. C. Edmunds, Jr., and the Rev. W. M. Cook. While the outlook here is not very bright, arrangements were made for week-day services to be given by some of the neighbouring clergy with a view to feeling the way for more definite work if that be deemed advisable.

(6) Portlandville, in Otsego county, is in a state of rapid decline. Hitherto it has been worked in connection with Schenevus; but, under the scheme which I have suggested for the Missionary at that place, this could be no longer done; but the Archdeacon of the Susquehanna, the Rev. E. A. Hartmann, and myself will see to their having such ministrations as are possible.

(7) At Middleburgh, Schoharie county, we have a Church (St. Luke's) and Rectory, but only three individuals belonging to the Church. The Rectory is rented for $100 a year and the proceeds used in keeping the Church in repair — at least, so I was informed — in anticipation of some brighter times to come. As there seems to be no reasonable hope of any such thing, I call the attention of the Board of Missions to the advisability of securing this income for its own use.

(8) Cobleskill, with a population of over 2,000, ought to prove a fruitful field. The Lutherans hold sway here and are extremely jealous of any other body. Arrangements have been made, however, for the Missionary at Schenevus to work this point also. It is too early yet too be able to report any thing.

(9) At my suggestion, the late Rector of Trinity Church, Schaghticoke, undertook services occasionally at Crandall's Corners — a place which very much needs the light of the gospel. His removal, however, has caused a temporary cessation of the work, which I trust may be continued by the present incumbent.

Other places have been investigated but nothing of any practical value has been accomplished, beyond keeping them in view.

The brief experience of the past few months has but confirmed the opinion I already held, viz.: that there was work enough for an itinerant Missionary in each Archdeaconry; and it is to be hoped the time is not far distant when such appointments can be made. In the meantime it is worth while considering the question of grouping together two or more Missionary stations and forming circuits. The idea is not new; it was referred to in the Bishop's address last year (Journal 1890, p. 35), and more fully set forth the year previous by the Rev. Edgar A. Enos in the practical report read by him on the report of the Board of Missions (Journal 1889, p. 103). One of the suggestions contained in that report has become a fact, namely, the appointment of the General Missionary, attached to the Cathedral staff, and under the personal supervision of the Bishop; and I believe that the other suggestion will prove to be the solution of the difficulties now experienced. I have had this in view in some of the suggestions I have made to the Bishop. For example, at Jonesville and East Line, the salary pledged is in each case $100. It will be easily understood, first that $200 is not sufficient to keep even the most self-sacrificing man, and, secondly, that to make this up to a living salary would be too great a demand on the Board of Missions. By adding the Mission at Round Lake there is added $300 salary. And I may say here, in passing, that Jonesville has pledged $150 for the coming year. This gives three stations in a circuit of nine miles offering a total of $550 toward the support of a Missionary. For this work the Board can afford to give $250 additional, so that $800 and a Rectory can now be offered. Again, West Burlington, with a pledge of $200, has hitherto stood in an inconveniently isolated position and has been worked with Sidney. Edmeston, four miles distant, is a practically new station and contributes nothing Monticello, where the pledge is $250, is thirteen miles from West Burlington. Five miles beyond is Cullen, with a pledge of $150. By grouping these four stations we have a circuit of twenty-two miles with a total pledge of $600, to which the Board could add $250, and offer $850 and Rectory Otherwise the Board would have to face the question of making up two separate, salaries or cutting off two stations from its list.

Not the least pleasant part of my work has been the nearer intercourse with so many of both the clergy and laity of the Diocese, and I desire to put on record my appreciation of the unvarying kindness and hospitality shown me on all sides.

I have handed to the Treasurer of the Board a financial statement showing receipts and expenditures, with a small balance to the credit of the Board. And I append the following statistics covering a period of seven and a half months:

Services, 60; sermons, 65; addresses, 9 ; celebrations of Holy Communion, 22; Baptisms, adults, 15, children, 30, total, 45; confirmations, 17; Missions organized, 3; Parish, 1; Sunday Schools established, 5; funerals, 4; marriages, 1. I also took part in the services at the Cathedral five times and celebrated twice.

All of which is respectfully submitted.

WALTER C. STEWART.

ALBANY, N. Y., 17th *November*, 1891.

The Rev. Eaton W. Maxcy, D. D., presented and read

THE REPORT OF THE COMMITTEE ON DIOCESAN MISSIONS.

The Report of the Committee on the Report of the Board of Missions has its principal value as introducing the subject to the Convention at its Missionary Session and opening the way for discussion and action. It has the disadvantage of reporting upon a theme in which its members, however profound their interest, cannot be presumed to be in knowledge the peers of a Board, who, from the nature of the case, are familiar above others with the mission field as a whole. We believe that never yet has the Board presented a resolution nor proposed any measure which it would not have been safe to adopt and act upon without discussion. Such is the confidence we believe the Convention of this Diocese has in those to whom it has entrusted this important work. If the suggestions which your Committee may present, after carefully pondering the report referred to them, shall lead not simply to a hearty endorsement of the measures recommended, but to an aroused interest in the Convention of the Diocese, they will only find a result like that which the study of the report has produced on themselves.

They would call your attention to the fact that these brethren in the Missionary field are labouring in localities which require a greater vigour and enthusiasm than many, not to say most, of the settled Parishes in our Diocese. With an established Parish — with its cherished associations reaching into a distant past — with many of the people long familiar with churchly ways — with some devoted spirits who are ready to cooperate freely and generously in the Church's work—it is far more easy to toil faithfully and perseveringly than in the regions where are many of our most devoted labourers. There is no place for the idle and despondent in any Parish, but to press on through the year where the attendants are few, where the community is quiet, where the resources of every character are most limited, where emphatically the work is one of faith, sometimes laying the foundation from the very lowest course, sometimes gathering the scattered and discouraged, pressing on amidst misconceptions of the Church most difficult to overcome, these are the things that " try men's souls."

We have considered the report which has to do with this kind of toil with deepening appreciation of the character of those engaged in it. We hope that the brethren will find in this Convention such interest in their services that they will return with renewed zeal and confidence.

We also would call attention to the fact that there is a great amount of undeveloped efficiency which might be available could the anxiety of many of the Missionaries in regard to temporalities be diminished.

It was a conviction of this character which led a Committee like ours to venture to suggest some time since the possibility of a scheme of fewer Missionaries with larger salaries, as a more effective agency. We are inclined to the belief that the suggestion is by no means groundless, and it is consonant with the proposition which has been made in another Diocese, to consolidate in our large cities some of the struggling Parishes. But we think that the difficulty in our own Mission field could easily be met by increased contributions for those already engaged in the arduous work.

We do not believe that the Board would favour nor the Convention approve a suggestion to remove a single faithful toiler nor the omission of any fairly established services. The fields have been selected which have seemed to be indicated by Divine Providence and we would not dare to take a single step backward. We are convinced that a more generous provision for those already engaged would soon result in an increased efficiency that would be evident in blessed results.

If we live in an age in which doubt and unbelief are for the time increasing, when even our remote villages feel the influence of a press which disseminates sentiments antagonistic to "the faith once (for all) delivered to the saints," it is also true that we are members of a Church which clings with increasing fervour to the *revealed* truth, and steadily bears on the standard which Divine hands entrusted to it. These Missionary Parishes present fields like those in which the fathers toiled when the Church was young. They are fields like those which parishes, now strong and active, were once in days which are so near to us that we can almost think of them as belonging to our own time. And we can say too that the men whom our Board has placed in their various stations will compare not unfavourably in earnestness of spirit and godly fidelity, in labour and sturdiness of faith, with their brethren of the former days. They are loyal and true and we believe the call for their sustentation will be met as the urgency of the call is understood.

We would have impressed upon the various Parishes the necessity of promptness in remittances to the Treasurer, and would urge that quarterly the contributions should be forwarded.

The Committee, in conference with the General Missionary, have been deeply interested in the story of his work during the past year. It is perhaps too much to expect that a single year's experience should be deemed decisive of the wisdom of a policy in connection with a large mission field like that of this Diocese. But at least it is certain that the success of his efforts fully warrants the continuance of his services for the coming year, and we most heartily approve the resolution of the Board embodied in their report, providing that a summary of his work should be presented at the missionary meeting of the first evening of the session.

On a former occasion a suggestion was made in our Convention which aimed at bringing forward the agency of the Sunday Schools of the Diocese in this important work. From all that has come to the knowledge of the Committee they believe that the plan has not been fairly tried. But even the limited extent to which the suggestion has been followed has been fruitful of very substantial returns. We most strongly recommend the general use of this agency which has already approved itself. A greater definiteness in regard to it is evidently desirable, and we would submit the *proposal* that a Sunday to be known as the Children's Missionary Sunday be indicated as a time for Missionary contributions from the Sunday Schools of the Diocese. If in this way the salary of the General Missionary were provided for (and we think it could be), there would be not only a very substantial assistance to the Board in their financial work, but a deepened interest among the children of the Parishes and in consequence among their elders. The General Missionary would become the Children's Missionary and as such find a most cordial welcome ever his duties might call him.

The amount proposed for expenditure for the coming year, is called for in a manner most evident to those who give all their thought to our field with its fifty missionaries and its seventy-five stations. Eight new stations now send out the Macedonian cry in chorus with those previously struggling in the work for Christ and His Church.

We most heartily recommend the appropriation called for.

All which is respectfully submitted.

EATON W. MAXCY,
WM. HENRY BOWN,
A. A. VAN VORST,
JOHN KEYES PAIGE,
JOHN T. PERRY,
Committee.

On motion of the Secretary of the Convention, it was

Resolved, That the election of the Board of Missions, and the other business of the Convention in regard to the Missions of the Diocese, be made the order of the day for eleven o'clock in the forenoon of to-morrow ; and that the Convention do now adjourn to meet in the Gymnasium of St. Agnes' School at half-past ten o'clock to-morrow morning.

The Convention adjourned till Wednesday morning.

SECOND DAY.

WEDNESDAY MORNING, NOVEMBER 18, 7:45 O'CLOCK.

The Bishop of the Diocese ordained the Rev. Eugene Griggs, Deacon, to the Holy Order of Priests, the Rev. C. S. Olmsted, the Rev. T. B. Fulcher, and the Rev. C. H. Hatheway joining with the Bishop in the laying on of hands.

The Holy Communion was administered in the Cathedral, the Bishop of the Diocese celebrating, assisted by the Rev. Canons Fulcher and Hatheway.

TEN O'CLOCK.

Morning Prayer was said in the Cathedral by the Dean.

The Right Rev. President took the chair and called the Convention to order in the Gymnasium of St. Agnes' School.

The minutes of the previous day were read and adopted.

The names of the Clergy and Lay Deputies not present on the first day were called by the Secretary, and three Clergymen and Lay Deputies representing five Parishes were found to be present.

The Rev. Hobart Cooke presented and read the

REPORT OF THE COMMITTEE ON UNFINISHED BUSINESS.

The Committee on Unfinished Business beg leave to report the following * business standing over from the last Convention.

----

* These matters of business were all reported to the Convention by the Committees having them in charge, and finally disposed of.

15

1. A Report from the Trustees of the Aged and Infirm Clergy Fund regarding the support of the aged and infirm clergy.

2. The amendments of the Rev. R. J. Adler to Canon XIV, "Upon the Duties and Powers of the Archdeacons and Archdeaconries, and their Relation to the Board of Missions."

3. A Report from the Trustees of the Diocese in regard to Chateaugay.

HOBART COOKE,

B. F. HINMAN.

The Rev. George D. Silliman presented and read the

REPORT OF THE COMMITTEE ON THE * REPORT OF THE BIBLE AND
COMMON PRAYER BOOK SOCIETY OF ALBANY AND VICINITY.

The Committee appointed recommend the adoption of the report of the Recording Secretary. Furthermore, they acknowledge the potent influence of the Prayer Book in Missionary work, as being the proper interpreter of Holy Scripture. The Prayer Book is the silent teacher of the Church. At the meeting of the Missionary Council in Detroit, the Secretary of the Board of Missions declared: "I would sow this land with the Prayer Book, as the greatest spiritual benefit that can be bestowed upon our generation. I would take it into every house, and offer it at a price, or leave it as a gift, so that no family should be without it." It has fallen under the observation of this Committee within a week that the Prayer Book was the Missionary that brought an adult person to baptism. It is the great expositor of Church doctrine and Bible truth. The Bible and Common Prayer Book Society always deals with a generous hand. It should be sustained.

The Committee observe, with pleasure, the increased number of Parishes, which during the year have contributed to the fund, and pray that every Parish may make an offering for this object, on Whitsun-Day.

Signed for the Committee,

GEORGE D. SILLIMAN,

Chairman.

The Rev. Fenwick M. Cookson presented and read the

REPORT OF THE STANDING COMMITTEE.

The Standing Committee organized December 15, 1890, by electing the Rev. Wm. Payne, D. D., President, and the Rev. Dr. Reese, Secretary.

During the year they have held nine meetings.

They have recommended to be admitted candidates for Holy Orders: George Arthur Ingalls; Harry Elmer Gilchrist; Harry S. Longley; John G. Urling; Gouverneur Frank Mosher; William Whiting Newell. George William Farrar; Frederic Henry Farrar.

They have recommended for ordination to the Diaconate. Eugene Griggs; George L. Richardson; James Frederic Olmsted; Freeborn Garrettson Jewett, Jr; John Montgomery Rich; John George Urling; Harry Elmer Gilchrist; William Francis Parsons.

They have recommended for ordination to the Priesthood. The Rev. Asa Sprague Ashley, the Rev Eugene Griggs; the Rev. Clarence Mortimer Conant; the Rev. Freeborn Garrettson Jewett, Jr., the Rev. George Brinckerhoff Richards.

They have given their canonical assent to the consecration of· The Rev. Henry Melville Jackson, as Assistant Bishop of Alabama; the Rev. Davis Sessums, A. M., as

---

* For the Report of the Bible and Common Prayer Book Society, see page 78.

Assistant Bishop of Louisiana; the Rev. Phillips Brooks, D. D., as Bishop of Massachusetts; the Rev. Isaac L. Nicholson, S. T. D., as Bishop of Milwaukee.

The Committee refused to give its assent to the consecration of the Rev. John Wright Chapman, to the Missionary Episcopate of Alaska, as in its judgment no such vacancy exists as is required by section 16, canon 16, title 1, of the Digest.

From the 2d of February until the return of the Bishop from Europe, the Standing Committee was, under the hand and seal of the Bishop, the ecclesiastical authority of the Diocese. Acting as such, letters of transfer were given to the Rev. J. A. Farrar to the Diocese of Easton; to the Rev. Frederick N. Skinner to the Diocese of East Carolina, and to the Rev. A. T. DeLearsy to the Diocese of Ohio.

Letters dimissory were received from the Diocese of New Jersey for the Rev. Arthur Lowndes, and from the Diocese of Minnesota for the Rev. Richmond H. Gesner.

The Committee present to the Convention, along with this report, their Minute adopted and entered upon their records, in relation to the death of their loved and honoured President, the late Rev. William Payne, D. D. The Rev. Dr. Tucker was elected President *pro tem.* of the Committee.

ALBANY, *November* 17, 1891.　　　　　Respectfully submitted,

J. LIVINGSTON REESE,　　　　　　　　　J. IRELAND TUCKER,
　　Secretary.　　　　　　　　　　　　　*Chairman, pro tem.*

MINUTE OF THE STANDING COMMITTEE IN RELATION TO THE DEATH OF THE REV. DR. PAYNE.

The Standing Committee of the Diocese of Albany, having heard of the death of the Rev. William Payne, D. D.. with deep sorrow for their own loss, but with devout thankfulness to Almighty God for the beautiful life and Christian example of their late honoured and beloved President, order the following Minute to be placed upon their records:

For forty-one years the Rev. William Payne, D. D., was identified with the work of the Church in what is now the Diocese of Albany. For thirty-seven years the Rector of St. George's, Schenectady, his high scholarship, his persuasive eloquence, and his gentle, courteous manners gathered about him a congregation of devoted Churchmen, whose influence was felt through this part of the State. Always a welcomed guest at the old Northern Convocation, a prominent figure among as noble a band of earnest, cheerful, faithful workers as the Church has ever had, his faith and his influence helped to lay the foundations of the new Diocese of Albany. When the infirmities of age and the need of rest from exhausting parochial cares compelled him to resign active parish life, he never lost his sympathy with the Church's work, nor failed to give it his time and his heart.

From the date of the Primary Convention of the Diocese in 1868, he has been honoured by the Diocese in representing it in the General Convention. The love and confidence of his brethren made him for the last sixteen years the Archdeacon of the Convocation of Albany. For eighteen years he has been a member of the Standing Committee; and from the time of his election its loved and honoured President. Devoted and conscientious in the performance of the duties of his most responsible office, never absent from its meetings, gentle yet firm when his convictions called him to act, he won the devoted love and confidence of his associates.

The Blessed Master whom he served has now called our loved brother and father to his rest. Dearly as we loved him, so ripened were his Christian graces and so ready he was for his crown of rejoicing. we would not wish to call him back from his exceeding great reward.

We thank God for all he did and was; for his work, so well done; for his beautiful example of purity and patience; and for the benediction he leaves behind in the memory of a life that was lived as in the presence of the Loving Master, and that now beyond the reach of suffering and death, and gifted with new powers to fulfil the will of God, he beholds with unclouded vision the Saviour's glory.

SCHENECTADY, *March* 23, 1891.

The Order of the Day was taken up, being the election of the Board of Missions and other business connected with the Missions of the Diocese.

The election of the Board of Missions being in order, nominations were received for the Archdeaconries as presented in the Report of the Secretary of the Convention; and on motion of Gen. Selden E. Marvin, the Rev. W. R. Woodbridge and Mr. William Kemp were nominated for the Diocese at large.

On motion of the Secretary of the Convention, the ballot was unanimously dispensed with, and the following named persons were elected as the Board of Missions until the next Convention.

BOARD OF MISSIONS,

ARCHDEACONRY OF ALBANY.

The Rev. W. W. Battershall, D. D.   Mr. J. H. Van Antwerp.

ARCHDEACONRY OF TROY.

The Rev. F. M. Cookson.   Mr. George A. Wells.

ARCHDEACONRY OF THE SUSQUEHANNA.

The Rev. Robert N. Parke, D. D.   Mr. Robert M. Townsend.

ARCHDEACONRY OF OGDENSBURGH.

The Rev. R. M. Kirby.   Mr. T. Streatfeild Clarkson.

DIOCESE AT LARGE.

The Rev. W. R. Woodbridge.   Mr. William Kemp.

The * resolutions recommended in the Report of the Board of Missions were adopted.

On motion of the Rev. Richmond Shreve, D. D., it was

Resolved, That the subject of Clerical Insurance be referred to a committee, who shall draw up a plan of action as definitely as may be and report to the next Convention.

The Right Rev. President appointed as such committee, the Rev. Richmond Shreve, D. D., the Rev. Walter C. Stewart, Mr. John Keyes Paige, Mr. F. E. Griswold, and Mr. S. M. Van Santvoord.

Certain changes having been announced, the apportionment of last year as so modified was adopted, as follows:

---

* See page 96.

PLAN OF APPORTIONMENT TO RAISE MISSIONARY FUND.

ARCHDEACONRY OF ALBANY.

The Cathedral of all Saints	$1,200 00
St. Peter's, Albany	1,000 00
St. Paul's, Albany	400 00
Grace, Albany	50 00
Holy Innocents', Albany	50 00
Trinity, Albany	20 00
Trinity, Rensselaerville	15 00
Trinity, West Troy	45 00
St. Andrew's, West Troy	5 00
St. Mark's, Green Island	30 00
St. John's, Cohoes	250 00
Trinity, Athens	25 00
Calvary, Cairo	10 00
Gloria Dei, Palenville	10 00
St. Luke's, Catskill	150 00
Christ, Greenville	5 00
St. Paul's, Oak Hill	5 00
Christ, Duanesburgh	80 00
St. George's, Schenectady	125 00
Christ, Schenectady	20 00
St. Ann's, Amsterdam	60 00
Good Shepherd, Canajoharie	10 00
Zion, Fonda	10 00
St. John's, Johnstown	75 00
Trinity, Fairfield	5 00
Christ, Herkimer	60 00
Emmanuel, Little Falls	50 00
St. Augustine's, Ilion	30 00
Trinity, Claverack	12 00
St. Luke's, Clermont	10 00
Our Saviour, Lebanon Springs	20 00
St. John's, Stockport	25 00
St. Barnabas', Stottville	25 00
St. James', Rossman's Mills	5 00
St. Mark's, Philmont	20 00
St. Luke's, Chatham	5 00
St. John's, Copake	5 00
St. Paul's, Kinderhook	75 00
Christ, Hudson	100 00
All Saints', Hudson	12 00
Christ, Gloversville	25 00
Grace, Mohawk	15 00
St. Alban's, Frankfort	5 00
Holy Cross, Fort Plain	10 00
Of the Memorial, Middleville	20 00
Christ, Coxsackie	5 00
Trinity, Ashland	5 00
St. Margaret's, Menand's Station	5 00
	——————
	$4,199 00

ARCHDEACONRY OF TROY.

St. Paul's, Troy..	$750 00
St. John's, Troy	600 00
Christ, Troy	250 00
Holy Cross, Troy...	200 00
Ascension, Troy..	150 00
St. Luke's, Troy	20 00
St. Barnabas', Troy..	50 00
Epiphany, East Albany.....................................	5 00
Messiah, Greenbush..	25 00
Trinity, Lansingburgh	150 00
Trinity, Schaghticoke	15 00
St. Mark's, Hoosick Falls	200 00
All Saints', Hoosac...	30 00
Holy Name, Boyntonville...................................	5 00
Grace, Waterford	35 00
Christ, Ballston..	125 00
St. John's, East Line	5 00
Grace, Jonesville...	10 00
All Saints, Round Lake	5 00
Calvary, Burnt Hills..	25 00
St. Paul's, Charlton..	10 00
Bethesda, Saratoga...	200 00
St. Stephen's, Schuylerville................................	5 00
St. John's, Conklingville...................................	5 00
St. Paul's, Salem...	100 00
St. John's, Stillwater.......................................	10 00
St. Luke's, Cambridge	175 00
Trinity, Granville..	25 00
North Granville..	10 00
St. Paul's, Greenwich......................................	25 00
St. James', Fort Edward....................................	20 00
Zion, Sandy Hill...	50 00
Trinity, Whitehall	50 00
St. James', Caldwell..	20 00
St. Mary's, Luzerne	20 00
Holy Cross, Warrensburgh..................................	50 00
Messiah, Glens Falls	150 00
Good Shepherd, Chestertown	15 00
St. Paul's, Bartonville	8 00
Church of the Cross, Ticonderoga	30 00
Christ, Port Henry	31 25
Emmanuel, Mineville.......................................	5 00
St. James', Ausable Forks..................................	25 00
St. John's, Essex	35 00
St. Paul's, Keeseville	15 00
Trinity, Plattsburgh	75 00
Christ, Rouse's Point	15 00
St. John's, Champlain......................................	20 00
St. Peter's, Ellenburgh	10 00
Good Shepherd, Elizabethtown..............................	10 00

ARCHDEACONRY OF TROY — *Continued.*

St. Matthew's, Lyon Mountain............................	$5 00	
St. Luke's, Mechanicville..	20 00	
Keene Valley Mission	25 00	
		$3,924 25

ARCHDEACONRY OF THE SUSQUEHANNA.

St. Peter's, Hobart........	$35 00	
Christ, Walton	30 00	
St. John's, Delhi..	125 00	
Grace, Stamford	20 00	
St. Paul's, Franklin	20 00	
St. Paul's, Sidney....	5 00	
Christ, Butternuts	25 00	
Christ, Cooperstown.	150 00	
Grace, Cherry Valley.................................	75 00	
Zion, Morris........	50 00	
St. James', Oneonta	30 00	
St. Matthew's, Unadilla	50 00	
Christ, West Burlington............	5 00	
St. Paul's, East Springfield........................	50 00	
St. John's, Richfield Springs..	50 00	
Immanuel, Otego.....	5 00	
Of the Holy Spirit, Schenevus	10 00	
St. Simon and St. Jude's, Worcester............	5 00	
		740 00

ARCHDEACONRY OF OGDENSBURGH.

St. John's, Ogdensburgh.......	$500 00	
Trinity, Potsdam............	450 00	
Trinity, Gouverneur	50 00	
St. John's, Massena	50 00	
Christ, Morristown...	50 00	
Grace, Norfolk...........	5 00	
St. Paul's, Waddington............................	30 00	
Grace, Canton.......................................	50 00	
Trinity, Morley.......................................	25 00	
St. Mark's, Malone....	100 00	
St. Peter's, Brushton	10 00	
St. Thomas', Lawrenceville	5 00	
Zion, Colton....................	20 00	
St. Luke's, Saranac Lake	20 00	
St. James', Hogansburgh........	25 00	
St. Mark's, West Bangor....................	5 00	
		1,395 00

Total		$10,258 25

RECAPITULATION.

Archdeaconry of Albany	$4,199 00
Archdeaconry of Troy	3,924 25
Archdeaconry of the Susquehanna	740 00
Archdeaconry of Ogdensburgh............	1,395 00
	$10,258 25

On motion of the Rev. W. C. Stewart, it was

Resolved, That all Parishes or Missions receiving aid from the Board of Missions shall report annually to said Board whether they have paid the amount pledged by them as salary; or, if not, what amount has been paid.

The Rev. William M. Cook presented and read the

REPORT OF THE COMMITTEE ON THE GENERAL THEOLOGICAL SEMINARY.

Your Committee respectfully report : That there are five students from this Diocese now pursuing their studies at the General Theological Seminary. It appears from the Journal of the last Convention that only $8.70 were contributed by our Parishes for a twelve month toward the support of the Seminary, or $1.74 per student; and whilst there is reason to believe that the reports this year will make a better showing, we desire to call the attention of the Convention to this matter, and to urge that larger offerings, gifts and bequests be made to this institution, which is now, more than ever, in fact as well as name, the *general* school of theology of the Church.

In this report the Committee cannot omit to put on record its profound sense of gratification at the high standard of excellence which the Seminary has attained in scholarship and spirituality of life. Of this inward grace, the increase of material wealth and prosperity is the outward and visible expression. The number of students for the last two years is unprecedented in the history of the Seminary, one hundred and twenty having been enrolled at the end of the Christmas term in 1890. The accommodations for the students are still inadequate, although two new dormitories were completed within the last year. We note with especial pleasure and thankfulness, the completion of the Chapel of the Good Shepherd. It stands not only as the fitting memorial of her by whom it was built and endowed, but as the real centre of all the daily life and work of the Seminary.

E. BAYARD SMITH,
WM. M. COOK,
FREDERICK S. FISHER,
W. A. SACKETT,
ROBERT EARL.

On motion of the Secretary of the Convention, it was

Resolved, That the twelfth rule of order be suspended so far as it relates to the election of Trustees.

On motion of the Secretary of the Convention, the ballot was unanimously dispensed with, and Trustees were appointed by the Convention as follows :

OF THE EPISCOPAL FUND.

Mr. J. H. Van Antwerp, Mr. W. Bayard Van Rensselaer, Mr. Theodore Townsend, Mr. Charles W. Tillinghast, 2nd, Mr. Dean Sage.

OF THE FUND FOR AGED AND INFIRM CLERGYMEN.

Mr. Norman B. Squires, Mr. Robert S. Oliver, and Mr. J. J. Tilling-

hast.

Of the Fund for Widows and Orphans of Deceased Clergymen.

Mr. J. W. Tillinghast, Mr. C. W. Tillinghast, and Mr. Amasa J. Parker.

Of the Orphan House of the Holy Saviour at Cooperstown.

The Rev. Walton W. Battershall, D. D., the Rev. J. Philip B. Pendleton, the Rev. Thaddeus A. Snively, Mr. Leslie Pell-Clarke, Mr. G. Pomeroy Keese, Mr. A. B. Cox, W. T. Bassett, M. D., Mr. T. Streatfeild Clarkson, and Mr. G. Hyde Clarke.

Trustees of the Diocese of Albany until 1895.

The Rev. Frederick S. Sill and Mr. John H. Bagley.

Deputies to the Federate Council.

The Rev. William H. Harison, S. T. D., the Rev. Ernest Mariett, and Mr. J. D. Henderson.

The Rev. Dean Robbins presented

REPORT NUMBER 2, OF THE COMMITTEE ON THE CONSTITUTION AND CANONS.

The Committee on the Constitution and Canons to whom were referred certain proposed amendments to Canon XVIII, recommend their adoption, and offer the following Canon to the Convention:

A CANON TO AMEND CANON XVIII.

Canon XVIII, sec. 7, is hereby amended so as to read as follows :

SEC. 7. The trustees of the fund shall be the Bishop of the Diocese, the Rector of St. Peter's Church, Albany, the Rector of St. Paul's Church, Troy, the Archdeacons of the Diocese, and the Treasurer of the Diocese, who shall be the Treasurer of the fund. And they are hereby authorized to form a corporation under the Laws of the State of New York, whose object shall be to carry into effect the provisions of this Canon, and to provide for the receipt by the corporation so to be formed, of real and personal estate by gifts, purchase, devise, bequest or otherwise, for the purposes of said corporation.

The Committee further report adversely on the amendments to Canon XIV, proposed by the Committee on the Duties and Powers of the Archdeacons and the Archdeaconries.   For the Committee,

J. W. STEWART.

Chairman.

The recommendations of the Committee were adopted, and Canon XVIII, sec. 7, was amended as proposed; and the Right Rev. the Bishop of the Diocese, announced his concurrence in the amendment.

The Rev. Joseph Carey, S. T. D., presented and read the Report of the Committee on Memorials of Deceased Clergy, which was adopted by a rising vote.

16

REPORT OF THE COMMITTEE ON MEMORIALS OF DECEASED CLERGYMEN.

The Committee to whom was intrusted the duty of preparing a Memorial Minute respecting the lives and character of the deceased Clergymen of whom the Bishop has spoken so tenderly and lovingly in his Address, beg leave to report the following

MINUTE.

Seven consecrated servants of the Lord who were with us one year ago, to-day are not, for God has taken them. It is with no ordinary emotion that we miss from our ranks the familiar forms of our brethren beloved in the Lord, fellow-workers and fellow-helpers unto the Kingdom of God, with whom we have often taken sweet counsel together in our Diocesan assemblies.

These brethren in all the years that they were associated with us proved a tower of strength, and stimulated us by their words and works unto noble effort in the up-building of our dear Church. Because they were so true and loving and faithful, our loss seems all the greater, but the Church in Paradise has added to her precious jewels by their going from us, when the King in His beauty called them. As we realize that they are in everlasting peace, and that light perpetual shines on them, we solace ourselves in the knowledge of their felicity.

Canon Edward Selkirk, the first whose feet touched the eternal shore, was a life-long example of the faithful Priest, who, amidst storm and sunshine, was found in his place of duty ministering to Christ's flock, and illustrating in his daily walk and conversation the teachings of his Divine Master. His memory will evermore be em-balmed in the history of Trinity Church, Albany, where he served so long, and in All Saints' Cathedral, where, in his ministries of love, he passed his closing days.

The saintly life of William Payne, Doctor in Divinity, was a benediction during a long course of years of unremitting toil to St. George's Church, Schenectady. One felt instinctively in his presence that his was a noble Christian manhood, rich in its fruitage. Walking in and out among his people he taught them by precept and ex-ample the beauty of our holy religion. He breathed only pure thoughts, and was "an Israelite indeed in whom was no guile." His noble service to the Church, in his Parish, in our Diocesan Council, in his office as Archdeacon of Albany, and in the General Convention, can never be forgotten. His judgment was clear, his heart tender and strong, and his friendship ever true. His name, like precious ointment poured out, fills our hearts with its fragrance.

No truer Priest of God ever served at His Altar than William Meredith Ogden, Rector of the Holy Cross, Warrensburgh. For long years he ministered in his ap-pointed place; and in the Diocese he was known and loved for his steadfastness and sterling qualities of head and heart. He was loyalty itself to his Bishop and his brethren, and every interest of the Church found a place in his affections. In the full vigour of his manhood, on the Lord's Day, while proclaiming the message of life, in God's house, the sudden summons came which called him up higher to blessed ministries of Paradise.

George Herbert Norton, youngest of all the seven gone from us, "used the office of a Deacon well and purchased to himself a good degree, and great boldness in the faith which is in Christ Jesus." Full of zeal and with his heart thoroughly in his work he won the respect and love of those to whom he ministered. With aptitude as a teacher, and possessed of strong convictions, he never failed to edify his hearers. His earthly life, all too short, ended in the midsummer, has nevertheless in it a com-pleteness, and his memory is that of the just which is blessed.

The death of John Henry Hopkins, Doctor of Laws and of Theology, after a long sickness borne with patient waiting for the coming of the Lord, removes from the

American Church a man who largely influenced the thought and action of his day. Whether in Church journalism, in which he had a peculiar fitness, or in the pulpit, or in our Church Councils, he was always fresh and edifying. In some respects he was ahead of his time, but he lived to see many of the measures advocated by him adopted by the Church for her extension. As one of the worthy champions of the faith and order of the Church during the greater part of the nineteenth century he will live in our ecclesiastical history for all time.

We recall the memory of Robert T. S. Lowell, Doctor of Divinity, with reverence and affection. No one could look into his refined face without seeing the light of heaven reflected there. To all his mental accomplishments there was added a Christian courtesy which lent a charm to his presence and his conversation. Quietly and unostentatiously he served his Lord with all his best thought and action. The influence of such a life for good cannot be measured by human words.

As we make mention of the name of Rev. William Henry Cook, there rises before our vision the saintly face of the venerable Missionary, who for long years laboured in loving service done for his beloved Master. There was a sweetness in his disposition which drew men towards him and a dignity in his mien which commanded respect and reverence. In the midst of all his arduous labours he still found time for study, remembering that "the Priest's lips should keep knowledge;" and so he ever edified his flock. Such faithfulness as his has its reward, and such a death is right dear in the sight of the Lord.

These all having died in faith, are now numbered with God's saints in glory everlasting. While their names are in our hearts and on our sacred dyptichs, they are also written in the Lamb's Book of Life.

All of which is respectfully submitted.

For the Committee,

JOSEPH CAREY.

Chairman.

The Rev. J. Philip B. Pendleton, S. T. B., presented and read the

REPORT OF THE COMMITTEE ON PROPOSED CHANGES IN THE PRAYER BOOK.

The Committee to whom was referred the notification of Proposed Changes in the Prayer Book, beg leave to report that with the majority of the alterations proposed, we think that the Diocese of Albany would be in sympathy, while as to particulars we have such confidence in the judgment of our Deputies to the General Convention that we should advise leaving the final determination of the advisability of all changes to them.

Respectfully submitted.

J. PHILIP B. PENDLETON,
JOHN H. HOUGHTON,
RICHMOND SHREVE,
SELDEN E. MARVIN,
H. B. DAUCHY.

The Rev. Dean Robbins presented and read

REPORT NUMBER 8, OF THE COMMITTEE ON THE CONSTITUTION AND CANONS.

The Committee on the Constitution and Canons to whom was referred a proposed amendment to Canon XIV, sec. 18, recommend its adoption, as follows:

A CANON TO AMEND CANON XIV.

Canon XIV, section 13, is hereby amended so as to read as follows:

SEC. 13. The title of all property, real or personal, given or purchased for the use of any Mission Station, shall be vested in "The Board of Missions of the Protestant Episcopal Church, in the Diocese of Albany," or in "The Trustees of the Diocese of Albany."

For the Committee,

J. W. STEWART,
Chairman.

On motion, the proposed amendment to Canon XIV, section 13, was adopted; and also the amendment to Canon XIV, section 3,* recommended in Report Number 1, of the Committee on the Constitution and Canons; and the Right Rev. the Bishop of the Diocese, announced his concurrence in both amendments.

The hour for the annual elections having arrived, the Right Rev. President appointed the Tellers.

STANDING COMMITTEE.

Clerical Vote.	*Lay Vote.*
The Rev. Eugene L. Toy.	The Rev. Elmer P. Miller.
Mr. A. W. Haslehurst.	Mr. Sidney G. Ashmore.

DEPUTIES TO THE GENERAL CONVENTION.

Clerical Vote.	*Lay Vote.*
The Rev. F. G. Jewett, Jr.	The Rev. George B. Richards.
Mr. Walton Van Loan.	Mr. T. O. Duroe.

PROVISIONAL DEPUTIES TO THE GENERAL CONVENTION.

Clerical Vote.	*Lay Vote.*
The Rev. A. S. Ashley.	The Rev. F. H. T. Horsfield.
Mr. H. S. Wynkoop.	Mr. John Keyes Paige.

The rolls of the Clergy and of the Parishes were called by the Secretaries.

Ballots were received for members of the Standing Committee, and for Deputies and Provisional Deputies to the General Convention.

The Right Rev. President announced that the polls were closed, and directed the Tellers to count the votes, for which purpose they had leave to retire.

The Rev. Ernest A. Hartmann read the Reports from the Orphan House of the Holy Saviour, at Cooperstown, and of the Committee on the same; during the reading of which reports, the Right Rev. L. R. Brewer, S. T. D., Bishop of Montana, entered the Hall, and was received by the Convention standing, and given a seat by the side of the Right Rev. President.

* See page 81.

REPORT OF THE SUPERINTENDENT OF THE ORPHAN HOUSE OF THE
HOLY SAVIOUR, OCTOBER 29, 1891.

The number of children at the Diocesan Orphanage during the past year has generally varied between 90 and 102. For the greater part of the year the number was one hundred. The entire number during the year was one hundred and thirty. Of these thirty-five were dismissed to their friends, or for self-support. The work, thanks to God, has gone on with the usual regularity. The religious, moral and industrial training of the children has been carried on with the utmost patient fidelity, by our excellent working staff. The improvement in many of the children has been very great. The school has been declared by the Commissioner to be one of the best in this district, the children answering with more than usual intelligence. It has also been remarked by experienced observers that there is much less of evil in this school than among the children of the public schools of the State. With humble thankfulness we record the fact that we have been mercifully guarded from all serious illness. The children have generally been very healthy.

The great trial of the year has been the sadly heavy indebtedness for current expenses, amounting, October 1, to $2,011. There have been several causes for this indebtedness. During the past year prices for all staple articles of food, needed at the Orphanage, have been much higher than usual. In some cases the prices were more than doubled. At the same time the size of the family was largely increased, numbering generally one hundred and sixteen to provide for. Unhappily during this year of need the offerings from the Church Parishes were reduced to less than one-half of their previous amount. An additional cause of the present indebtedness is also clearly to be traced to the fact that there has been a sad failure in payments for Church children on the part of friends in different Parishes throughout the Diocese. In many cases, where children were paid for at first, payment ceased entirely after a time, owing to sickness, lack of work, or death of the friends who placed the orphans with us, while the Parishes from which the children were received made no effort to meet fully the expenses of those desolate ones. Last year there were twenty children in the house entirely unpaid for, supported solely at the expense of the Orphanage. In a number of these cases the failure in payment had been going on for years. Another class of Church children have been very inadequately paid for, fifty cents or one dollar a week being all that poor widows earning their living could afford to pay. Some fifteen half orphans were last year included in this class. With only the small beginning of an endowment to cover such a large number of deficient payments on the part of the Church, indebtedness was unavoidable. To dismiss some thirty-five helpless orphans with cold-hearted indifference was not to be thought of. In this distressing condition of the Orphanage it only remains for us to appeal prayerfully and solemnly to our fellow Churchmen for aid in this hour of great need. We ask for relief from them as earnestly as we should for ourselves if we were in need of food, shelter and Christian care. We ask for relief with anxious sorrow. We ask for relief in the name of the Most Holy, Most Merciful Saviour.

Do not compel us by careless indifference to close the doors of the Diocesan Orphanage!

It is clear that a much larger endowment is needed to cover occasional deficiencies. Free scholarships of $1,000, either Memorial or simply Parochial in character, bearing interest, would be of great assistance.

Regular annual subscriptions from individuals would also afford great relief.

We have received children from sixteen out of the nineteen counties of the Diocese, at least such is our belief, though in several instances it was not easy to state with accuracy the particular county to which a child belonged. Children have been brought to us from the most southern and the most northern counties; from Catskill to the shores of the St. Lawrence. They have come to us in large numbers from th counties beyond the Hudson, and from those bordering on Central New York.

At the recent meeting of the Board of Trustees, held at the Orphanage, October 2〜 1891, the following resolution was passed :

"*Resolved*, That, until the income of the Orphan House shall warrant a large extension of its charity, the Superintendent be requested to receive no child exce〜 with the consent of the majority of the Executive Committee, unless the Parish fro〜 which the child comes shall agree through its Rector to contribute to the Orphanage an amount not less than $100 a year for the support of the child, except in cases where the superintendent of the poor in any county in the State becomes responsible."　　　　Respectfully submitted,

SUSAN FENIMORE COOPER,
Superintendent Orphan House of the Holy Saviour.

REPORT OF THE TREASURER OF THE ORPHAN HOUSE OF THE HOLY SAVIOUR AT COOPERSTOWN, FOR THE YEAR ENDING SEPTEMBER 30, 1891.

Receipts.

To balance October 1, 1890	$8 25
County treasurer for county children	4,876 87
Forty Churches and Missions	701 13
Board of children	840 01
Personal subscriptions	387 00
Interest on investments	275 00
School money	246 75
Miscellaneous	88 00
Borrowed from Endowment Fund	500 00
Borrowed from other funds	217 84
Due Treasurer	1,293 81
To balance	21 68
	$8,906 08

Expenses.

Wages	$2,378 54
Groceries	1,119 18
Meat	603 44
Milk	1,179 07
Clothing	987 66
Fuel	762 67
Lights	240 50
Furniture	198 27
House stores	986 25
Medicines	83 47
Repairs	41 17
Water	50 00
Miscellaneous	381 81
	$8,906 08

The following Churches contributed to the support of the Orphan House during the past year, in money, as follows:

All Saints' Cathedral	$46 82
Grace, Albany	5 00
St. Mark's, Green Island	8 55
Trinity, West Troy	13 50
Trinity, Plattsburgh	15 00
Trinity, Athens	8 50
St. Luke's, Catskill	27 00
St. George's, Schenectady	28 85
St. Paul's, Kinderhook	16 42
Christ Church, Hudson	7 01
St. Margeret's, Menand's	5 00
St. Paul's, Troy	140 00
St. John's, Troy	32 65
Holy Cross, Troy	25 00
St. Luke's, Troy	11 76
Christ Church, Troy	10 58
St. Barnabas', Troy	4 84
Trinity, Lansingburgh	22 00
Trinity, Schaghticoke	1 50
All Saints, Hoosac	10 00
Christ Church, Ballston Spa	13 26
St. Luke's, Mechanicville	4 75
St. James', Fort Edward	5 17
Zion, Sandy Hill	38 02
Church of the Cross, Ticonderoga	12 53
Christ Church, Walton	22 00
Christ Church, Cooperstown	59 60
Grace, Cherry Valley	23 19
St. James', Oneonta	5 00
St. Matthew's, Unadilla	3 00
Christ Church, West Burlington	2 25
Christ Church, Herkimer	5 00
Christ Church, Gilbertsville	2 00
St. John's, Ogdensburgh	18 75
Trinity, Potsdam	44 61
Christ Church, Morristown	1 39
St. Paul's, Salem	5 00
St. Paul's, Greenwich	3 00
Zion, Colton	1 12
Christ Church, Greenville	2 50
	$701 12

BUILDING FUND.

Balance due Treasurer last report	$1,730 55
Paid Steam Heating Company	345 00
	$2,075 55

Received from A. B. Cox, Treasurer. $3,003 14
Balance charged running account.......... .... 72 4

$3,075 5

ENDOWMENT FUND.

One mortgage, Masonic Lodge........ .... $3,000
One western mortgage... 500
Loaned running expenses three years... .... 1,755 5
Loaned Building Fund... 333 4

$5,589 00

Respectfully submitted,
LESLIE PELL-CLARKE,
Treasurer.

REPORT OF THE COMMITTEE ON THE REPORTS FROM THE ORPHAN HOUSE OF THE HOLY SAVIOUR.

Your Committee on the Reports of the Superintendent and the Treasurer of the Orphan House of the Holy Saviour beg leave to say that the Act of Incorporation as amended by the Convention of 1890, was passed by the Legislature, and received the approval of the Governor, May 6, 1891.

The Committee have read with great pleasure the opening paragraph of the admirably presented report of the Superintendent, which has reference to the care for and the instruction of the children committed to its keeping. The health of the large household has been good, which is evidence that the sanitary arrangements of the institution are all that can be desired. The School Commissioner has declared its school to be one of the best in the district, which goes to show the excellent educational privileges provided for the children committed to its keeping.

The remainder of the report, however, which has to do with the matter of indebtedness for the ordinary current expenses, is written with a sad pen. While it exacts sympathy for the large hearted Superintendent, who, after so many years of noble self-devotion, finds that the institution, which in its material aspect has grown so satisfactorily, must still needs go begging for the support of its work, at the same time it must fill us with shame because it is owing to our failure to do what under the canons the orphanage has the right to expect us to do, that it is not only in debt, but that its doors have been closed absolutely to the knock of destitute orphans.

The Orphan House of the Holy Saviour is a Diocesan Institution in Otsego Co.; it is not a county institution attached to and fathered by the Diocese. It seems such a statement ought to be made, because the money contributed towards its support by the Diocese is so small, that were it the only source of income, the number of inmates would be necessarily so few as scarcely to justify its existence. The Treasurer reports $8,906.03 as the amount paid for current expenses during the past year. It will be interesting to note how this was provided. Offerings from 41 Parishes, $701.12, Interest on investments, $275, School money, $246.75, Personal subscriptions, $387. Paid for the care of county children, $4,376.57 ; Borrowed from its endowment and and other funds, $717.84; Advanced by the Treasurer, $1,293.81.

This means that the money contributed by the Diocese, added to the income of the Orphanage derived from vested funds and board of children, made only $1,816.13, or about one-fifth of the whole amount ; that the sum obtained from other sources left a balance required to meet the current expenses ; that to make up this deficiency, the Treasurer was compelled to advance $1,293.91, in addition to the amount secured by borrowing $717.84 from its own life.

These figures speak in many ways, but they do suggest and at the same time furnish an answer to the question : To what extent does the Diocese estimate the Orphan House of the Holy Saviour as a Diocesan Institution?

It appears that if the 138 Parishes and Mission Stations who did not contribute any money had made canonical offerings in proportion to the amount paid by the 41 Parishes who did contribute, the sum would have reached $3,050. This would have provided amply for the current expenses, and kept the door of the House open to the orphans of the Diocese who are destitute, and for whose maintenance no means cans be provided. It would have relieved the Trustees of the sad necessity for passing the resolution which appears in the Superintendent's report, which practically makes it impossible for any orphan to gain admittance, unless security is forthcoming that $100 a year will be paid for its support — an action which to a very large degree limits its usefulness and its blessing.

Your Committee does not ask why 188 out of 179 Parishes and Mission St

A Prayer for the Orphan House of the Holy Saviour, in Cooperstown. Commended for Use in the Diocese of Albany, by the Bishop.

O God, without whom nothing is strong, nothing is holy, vouchsafe to look down in mercy upon the work undertaken at this Orphan House of the Holy Saviour for Thy service, and the good of children in need of Christian care. Be pleased, O Lord, to grant all good blessings of guidance, protection, support and sanctification to this work undertaken in the Name of the Holy Saviour, our blessed Lord Jesus Christ. Amen.

The resolution recommended in the Report of the Committee on the Reports from the Orphan House was adopted.

On motion of Mr. G. Hyde Clarke, Lay Deputy from St. Paul' Church, East Springfield, it was

Resolved, That every Clergyman be requested to organize in his Sunday School a Guild of young persons under his own direction, with the double purpose, first, to remember the Orphan House of the Holy Saviour in their prayers from time to time; and secondly, to give themselves to gathering subscriptions toward it support.

Pending the discussion of the Reports from the Orphan House, the hour for recess having arrived, on motion of the Rev. Thaddeus A. Snively, the recess was postponed fifteen minutes.

The reports of the Tellers of votes for the Standing Committee were received.

REPORT OF THE TELLERS OF THE CLERICAL VOTE FOR THE STANDING COMMITTEE. ·

Whole number of ballots cast, 85; necessary to a choice, 43 votes; the Rev. J. Ireland Tucker, S. T. D., received 83 votes; the Rev. Fenwick M. Cookson, 80; the

17

Rev. Wilford L. Robbins, D. D., 79; the Rev. James Caird, 72; the Rev. George
Silliman, 5: Mr. Norman B. Squires, 85; Mr. Henry S. Wynkoop, 85; Mr. John
Thompson, 85; Mr. John H. Van Antwerp, 85; scattering, 18.

EUGENE L. TOY,
ALEX. W. HASLEHURST.
Tellers.

REPORT OF THE TELLERS OF THE LAY VOTE FOR THE STANDING COMMITTEE.

Whole number of ballots cast, 40; necessary to a choice, 21 votes; the Rev. J. Ireland Tucker, S. T. D., received 40 votes; the Rev. Fenwick M. Cookson, 40; the Rev. Wilford L. Robbins, D. D., 40; the Rev James Caird, 38; Mr. Norman B. Squires, 40; Mr. Henry S. Wynkoop, 40; Mr. John I. Thompson, 40; Mr. John H. Van Antwerp, 40; scattering, 2.

ELMER P. MILLER,
SIDNEY G. ASHMORE.
Tellers.

The Right Rev. President declared elected as members of the Standing Committee, the Rev. J. Ireland Tucker, S. T. D., the Rev. Fenwick M. Cookson, the Rev. Wilford L. Robbins, D. D., the Rev. James Caird, Mr. Norman B. Squires, Mr. Henry S. Wynkoop, Mr. John I. Thompson, and Mr. John H. Van Antwerp.

The Tellers of votes for Deputies to the General Convention presented their reports.

REPORT OF THE TELLERS OF THE CLERICAL VOTE FOR DEPUTIES TO THE GENERAL CONVENTION.

Whole number of ballots cast 83; necessary to a choice, 42 votes: the Rev. Walton W. Battershall, D. D., received 74 votes; the Rev. J. D. Morrison, D. D., LL D., 7C the Rev. Joseph Carey, S. T. D., 52; the Rev. C. C. Edmunds, Jr., 40; the Rev Edgar A. Enos, 17; the Rev. R. M. Kirby, D. D., 17; the Rev. William C. Prout, 1.5; the Rev. James Caird, 13; the Rev. John H. Houghton, 12, the Rev. Robert N. Parke, D. D., 11; the Rev. J. Philip B. Pendleton, 7, Mr G. Pomeroy Keese, 70; Mr. Erastus Corning, 69; Mr. T. Streatfeild Clarkson, 77; Mr. John Hobart Warren, 71; Mr. Charles E. Patterson, 34; scattering, 3.

F. G. JEWETT, JR.,
WALTON VAN LOAN,
Tellers.

REPORT OF THE TELLERS OF THE LAY VOTE FOR DEPUTIES TO THE GENERAL CONVENTION.

Whole number of ballots cast, 37; necessary to a choice, 19 votes; the Rev. Walton W. Battershall, D. D., received 32 votes; the Rev. J. D. Morrison, D. D., LL. D., 33; the Rev. Joseph Carey, S. T. D., 26; the Rev. Charles C. Edmunds, Jr., 18; the Rev. John H. Houghton, 8; the Rev. William C. Prout, 8, the Rev. R. M. Kirby, D. D., 7; Mr. G. Pomeroy Keese, 33; Mr. Erastus Corning, 32; Mr. T. Streatfeild Clarkson, 30; Mr. John Hobart Warren, 31; Mr. Charles E. Patterson, 17; scattering, 16.

One ballot voted for five Lay Deputies, and was cast out as regards the Lay Deputies. The four clerical votes on this ballot being correct, the clerical portion of the ballot was counted.

GEORGE B. RICHARDS,
T. O. DUROE,
Tellers.

The Right Rev. President declared elected as Deputies to the General Convention, the Rev. Walton W. Battershall, D. D., the Rev. J. D. Morrison, D. D., LL. D., the Rev. Joseph Carey, S. T. D., Mr. G. Pomeroy Keese, Mr. Erastus Corning, Mr. T. Streatfeild Clarkson, and Mr. John Hobart Warren.

There being one vacancy on the list of Clerical Deputies to General Convention so elected, on motion of the Rev. Thaddeus A. Snively, it was

Resolved, That the Secretary of the Convention be directed to cast the ballot of the Convention for the Rev. Charles C. Edmunds, Jr., for Deputy to the General Convention.

The Secretary cast the ballot of the Convention as directed; the Tellers reported the result, and the Right Rev. President declared the Rev. Charles C. Edmunds, Jr., elected a Deputy to the General Convention.

The Tellers of votes for Provisional Deputies to the General Convention presented their reports.

REPORT OF THE TELLERS OF THE CLERICAL VOTE FOR PROVISIONAL. DEPUTIES TO THE GENERAL CONVENTION.

Whole number of ballots cast, 82; necessary to a choice, 42 votes; the Rev. Edgar A. Enos received 76 votes; the Rev. R. M. Kirby, D. D., 62; the Rev. Charles S. Olmsted, 76; the Rev. George D. Silliman, 80; Mr. Leslie Pell-Clarke, 76; Mr. Spencer Trask, 81; Mr. Edward Sheldon, 82; Mr. Thomas L. Harison, 82; scattering, 13.

A. S. ASHLEY,
H. S. WYNKOOP,
Tellers.

REPORT OF THE TELLERS OF THE LAY VOTE FOR PROVISIONAL DEPUTIES TO THE GENERAL CONVENTION.

Whole number of ballots cast, 37; necessary to a choice, 19 votes; the Rev. Edgar A. Enos received 35 votes; the Rev. R. M. Kirby, D. D., 37; the Rev. Charles S. Olmsted, 37; the Rev. George D. Silliman, 37; Mr. Leslie Pell-Clarke, 37; Mr. Spencer Trask, 37; Mr. Edward Sheldon, 37; Mr. Thomas L. Harison, 37; scattering, 2.

F. H. T. HORSFIELD,
JNO. KEYES PAIGE,
Tellers.

The Right Rev. President declared elected as Provisional Deputies to the General Convention, the Rev. Edgar A. Enos, the Rev. R. M. Kirby, D. D., the Rev. Charles S. Olmsted, the Rev. George D. Silliman, Mr. Leslie Pell-Clarke, Mr. Spencer Trask, Mr. Edward Sheldon, and Mr. Thomas L. Harison.

The Rev. Walton W. Battershall, D. D., for the committee appointed to prepare a minute in relation to the Rev. Dr. Reese, reported the following minute, which was adopted by the Convention:

MINUTE IN RELATION TO THE REV. DR. REESE.

INASMUCH as the Rev. J. Livingston Reese, D. D., has informed this Convention that ill-health and protracted absence make it impossible for him to accept a re-nomination to the Standing Committee of which he has been a member since the formation of the Diocese, and for many years its Secretary, this Convention hereby expresses, and enters upon its records, its grateful appreciation of the long and eminent service rendered by Dr. Reese to the Church in this Diocese.

Prominent in the organization of the Diocese, he has given conspicuous proof of his concern for and devotion to its interests. He brought to his position in the Standing Committee an administrative skill, a habit of order and promptitude, a clearness of judgment and a fidelity to trust, which have made him an invaluable member of the committee, and have enabled him to discharge the laborious and responsible duties of its secretaryship with singular efficiency. To his unwearied labor and unfailing tact, as Chairman of the Committee on the claim of this Diocese on the mother Diocese of New York with reference to the Episcopal Fund, may be attributed in large measure the friendly spirit which characterized the long negotiation, and the amicable adjustment of the claim.

In this grateful recognition of his service to the Diocese, this Convention would also express its deep respect and warm affection for one who has given an able and fruitful ministry to one of the largest Parishes of the Diocese, and whose personal qualities have endeared him to his people and his brethren in the priesthood. May the adorable Head of the Church add to his ministry many honoured and useful years.

WALTON W. BATTERSHALL,
THADDEUS A. SNIVELY,
G. H. F. VAN HORNE.

The Convention took a recess until two o'clock.

TWO O'CLOCK IN THE AFTERNOON.

The Convention re-assembled.

The Right Rev. President took the chair and called the Convention to order.

The Rev. George D. Silliman presented and read the Report of the Committee to prepare a suitable Minute upon the fiftieth anniversary of the Ordinations of the Rev. Dr. Nicholls and the Rev. Mr. Washbon, the resolution contained in which was unanimously adopted.

REPORT OF THE COMMITTEE TO PREPARE A MINUTE UPON THE FIF-
TIETH ANNIVERSARY OF THE ORDINATIONS OF THE REV. GEORGE
HUNTINGTON NICHOLLS, S. T. D., AND THE REV. ROBERT WASHBON.

In accordance with the recommendation of the Bishop in his annual address to the
Convention, the Committee, appointed to prepare a proper Minute upon the fiftieth
anniversary of the Ordinations of the Rev. George Huntington Nichols, S.T. D., Rector
Emeritus of St. Mark's Church, Hoosick Falls, and of the Rev. Robert Washbon,
Rector of Trinity Church, Rensselaerville, place on record the feeling of profound
gratitude of the Convention to Almighty God, that these two faithful servants of the
Church have been spared to carry on the work of CHRIST'S Kingdom for so many
years.

Let it be noted, that counting backward thirty-eight times the period since their
ordinations would bring us back to the times of the Apostles. The fiftieth anniversary of a wedding is called a golden wedding and the fiftieth anniversary of an ordination is a golden day, such as falls to the lot of very few men to enjoy.

The Rev. Dr. Nicholls was ordered Deacon by Bishop Brownell of Connecticut, on
June 8th, 1841 ; Priest, on St. Andrew's Day, 1842. After doing Missionary work
for a time, he was called to the Parish of St. Luke's, Glastonbury, Conn. He was
elected Rector of St. John's Church, Salisbury, Conn., in the Spring of 1846. In
1854, he was called to Cherry Valley, N. Y., whence he came in the Spring of 1865
to Hoosick Falls. It will be seen that the greater part of his priesthood has been
spent in this Diocese. He still continues to celebrate the Sacred Mysteries at the
Altar, where he has served so long, and is held in loving estimation by the numbers
to whom he has ministered for such a length of years.

The Rev. Robert Washbon has served at Rensselaerville since the time of his Ordination, June 27, 1841. Ordered Priest, 1842. His Rectorship indicates most faithful service in the one field, connected with a large Missionary work outside his Parish.
The Church in Oneonta owes its existence to his efforts.

These aged servants have reared for them "monuments more enduring than brass,
and more sublime than the regal elevation of pyramids," for they live in the hearts
and lives of many who have gone hence, and of others who still live to bless them in
their lives. These Teachers of the Truth are blessed indeed, for they are of those
of whom it is said that "They that turn many to righteousness shall shine as the
stars for ever and ever." Therefore be it

Resolved, That the Convention of the Diocese of Albany sends its most cordial
greetings to these aged servants of the Most High God, who have served so many
years in the kingdom of our LORD JESUS CHRIST on earth, and extends to them the
assurance of its love and prayers for their continued good health.

GEORGE D. SILLIMAN,
J. IRELAND TUCKER.
NATHANIEL TEED,

The Rev. George G. Carter, S. T. D., presented and read the

REPORT OF THE COMMITTEE ON THE REPORT OF THE SOCIETY FOR THE
HOME STUDY OF HOLY SCRIPTURE AND CHURCH HISTORY.

Your Committee on the Report of the Society for the Home Study of Holy Scripture
and Church History, desire to congratulate the Society upon the happy opening of
its new house in New York city, and upon the evidence, which has been laid before
them, that, while the number of the students is increasing, and the range of their
studies is widening, the quality of the work, as shown by the results of the examina-

tions is steadily improving. The formal report from the society itself has been
ferred until its plans for new work, and especially for lectures during the winter i
spring, can be perfected; but enough is known of these to justify the hope and c
fidence of your Committee that the usefulness of the society will become far grea
in the future than ever in its happy and fruitful past. They are glad to find that
students already represent so many Dioceses of the American Church, and they le
forward to a gradual uplifting, through such studies as theirs, of the aims and sta
ards of those also who are engaged in training the children of the Church. T
society needs help in establishing itself firmly in its new home in New York, anc
heartily commended to the interest and care of the Church in the Diocese.

Communications should be addressed to the Secretary of the S. H. S. H. S., 1
428 West 20th street, New York city.

All of which is respectfully submitted.

GEORGE G. CARTER,
GEORGE B. JOHNSON,
J. T. ZORN,
LEVI HASBROUCK.

On motion of the Rev. George G. Carter, S. T. D., it was

Resolved, That the Secretary of the Convention be instructed to procure, and ho
printed in the Journal, the report of the Society for the Home Study of H
Scripture and Church History.

REPORT OF THE SOCIETY FOR THE HOME STUDY OF HOLY SCRIPTU
AND CHURCH HISTORY.

The issuing of our annual report has been delayed in part by the unusual pi
sure incident to the removal of our office and library, but in part, also, by the
creased demands of the work — the *doing* leaving but little time for the *telling*.

For the same reason we have been compelled to almost studiously avoid publicity-
adding too much to an already overwhelming labor. True, our well-wishers of
urge it as the most hopeful way of providing help and helpers. But somehow
result of every notice in our Church papers has invariably been an increase of *be
ficiaries* but not of *benefactors*. Often as it has been repeated it does not seem
be understood, except within the society itself, that no one connected with it recei
any salary. The small annual dues of two dollars a year cover little more than pe
age, stationery and the printing of study papers. The added donations of our me
bers barely suffice for the rent, and occasionally a little clerical assistance. Uf
such a basis as this, the moment that our numbers exceed our own powers of wo
each added student must mean actual loss. The salary of a really competent sec
tary would require far more than the doubling of our present dues. The ladies w
sometimes assist in the work are always amazed at the multiplicity of details wh
it involves and the amount of almost mechanical labor required, which yet can o
be intrusted to a clear-headed and most accurate helper. But even a chance vis'
who should attempt to lift the letter-file of a single year, with hands failing bene
its weight, might dimly apprehend the heavier strain which the brain must b
that reads, and considers, and answers the thousands within it. And all this, be
noted, is in addition to the proper work of organizing and guiding, and the perso
instruction of a large proportion of the students which ought to have the unhampe
energies of at least one mind. Such are the immense difficulties of this wo

Our success cannot be measured by mere numbers. These have dropped from
reported last year to 210 for this year. Yet the amount of actual study has far

ceeded that of any previous year, and this, too, in the face of that strange distemper which made the majority of students sufferers or the nurses of the suffering. In our higher section this was almost the sole cause of interrupted work, and it compelled many to at least postpone their June examination for a year. But even with this most serious hindrance there were sixty-three who returned papers, only five less than the previous year. The standard of scholarship was higher than ever before. This year, as the last, not one failed to pass. But while last year there were fifty out of sixty-eight who took honors there were this year fifty-eight out of the sixty-three—a record surely of rare excellence. There were many others who studied as thoroughly, and who could, no doubt, have passed, and some of them with high honors, but who shrank from an ordeal of which they had no experience. Also, among those who pass — missing honor — there are sometimes one or two of our best students who fail because they encounter something untoward at this final crisis. Probably no human wisdom could devise a system of examinations perfectly fair and free from all objections and dangers. Still with all this necessary imperfection they accomplish a good to be attained in no other way.

This year there were nineteen of our members who completed their four years' course, fourteen of them in Holy Scriptures and five in Church History. The blessing and the bestowal of the Jerusalem Cross upon these, by our President, the Bishop of Albany, was one of the most interesting features of our annual meeting. There have now been thirty-two of those well-won medals thus awarded.

One lady who graduated last year in Holy Scriptures, also graduated this year in Church History—the only instance thus far of the two completed courses. This raises the number of our actual graduates to twenty this year.

It is proposed in future to give to those who have finished the *two* courses another medal. The design for it, only, has thus far been prepared. It is the beautiful Triquetra Knot, in the form of a Greek cross, which is found on some ancient monuments in Cornwall. No less than twelve of the graduates of these two years in Holy Scriptures have begun this year the Church History course. Entering upon their work with well-trained minds they form a class of specially high promise. No words can express the delight of giving guidance and supplying help to such a class — undertaking their work as they do, with the noblest of motives, to know what they may of the Church they so love, that they may render a fuller service to their Lord. Last year nearly all our graduates entered at once upon post-graduate work in the Psalms, and this year there is another class of ten, several of them being those who went through the course without taking the June examination. I cannot speak too warmly in praise of some of the papers sent in upon the Psalms. This class does not receive questions or examinations, but only a list of headings upon which they prepare their papers. Very few of the books required for their study can be purchased at all by the students, being out of print, and those which can be purchased are in several volumes and very expensive. Here, if at any stage, should the students be met with generous aid. A very large and choice collection of works upon the Psalms has been made in our library for this purpose, and they are all freely loaned. In like manner has large preparation been made for collateral reading in Church History.

But the most cheering outcome of our work is found in the fact that of those who have been so long under training nearly all are now giving religious instruction in some way to others. Many of them are on our own staff of correspondents. Others have Bible classes, and others classes in Sunday Schools. They will help, indeed, to raise the standard of all such study. They also bring other students to us with a very different preparation from that with which some have come. They still depend upon us largely for books to aid in their preparation or with which to help their perplexed friends. In this quite natural way we more and more approach the true ideal of a society rather than of a school—becoming, in fact, a sort of bureau for Bible teachers.

I trust to be pardoned for any personality which it involves in defending briefly the strict standards of the society. No doubt criticism wounds a little. It seems usually agreed, also, that women, far more than men and children, are acutely sensitive to it. But then, it costs the giver somewhat also—enough, at least, to make it quite unselfish. But without it there surely can be no true training. It does not mean *blame* even when mistakes are very great. Blame should fall upon them when neglect has caused the ignorance, and rests only on the student when earnest endeavor fails. No doubt we are strict. But we should have been a horde of mere stragglers but for this. No doubt the question often touches the very points where one is least prepared. But their object is not *testing* but *training*. They lead the student to be observant. They free her from that greatest foe to real thought — vagueness. Such questions as are often given would be very unjust in a *bona fide* examination. But in that they do not occur. Beginners unaccustomed to thorough work no doubt are a little vexed, and probably some have dropped off by reason of it. But it is more and more understood and valued. One of our students, after graduating, took a special course in the Boston Society for Home Study. She had endured a fair share of criticism, but she reported to me with great glee that her new instructor pronounced her notes the best ever received.

It is with special thankfulness that I speak of the growth of our library, mainly as the result of definite donations. Last year we reported 1,000 books. This number has now reached 1,400, but the accession of 600 of these was made between Oct. 1, 1890, and Oct. 1, 1891. There were also added to these the past summer 200 more— mostly large and valuable works — from the director's private library. The book-plates upon these is marked " loaned until recalled," but with the expectation that they will pass into the permanent possession of the library.

We have had the past year an extraordinary success in securing long sought for treasures. The recent addition of Dr. Neale's Liturgiology—a work extremely rare —completes a collection by that author alone of 76 volumes, inclusive of a few du-plicates. It only lacks a few of his works for children, and a pamphlet or two, to make it absolutely complete. The same may very nearly be said, also, of such authors as Keble, Liddon, Moberly, Mozley, Pusey, Newman, Manning, Canon Carter, Bennett, the Wilberforces, Isaac Williams, Trench, Bright and Church. Nor have the earlier standards been slighted, but, alas, Bull, and Beveridge, and even Izaak Walton, are almost unknown, even as names, to thousands of otherwise intelligent Christian women It cannot be so for long if the Church awakens to her duty.

In Church History we have now above 300 volumes, embracing the standard works, from the Fathers down, including many very rare works. A good beginning has been made in Church Art, and a very full collection upon the Catechism. But above all we aim to supply the books which shall further the study of the Bible itself.

"But do women really read these books?" has been asked more than once in our library. A sufficient answer lies open in our register where are the titles of more than 500 volumes, that travelled up and down the land last year as mighty teachers. Of these, every one appears to have returned safely to its lodging, very few of them, indeed, showing signs of their long journey. Few can realize what care has been required to reach such a result. But our working system is now settled, and the extension of the work will be comparatively easy. There is no charge to any member of our society for these books unless retained over time — and when once the simple fact is comprehended that as a rule it costs less for the books to travel to the borrower through the mails than it would for the borrower in our cities to pay her car fare to the library and back, we trust that very many more will hail the idea of a library that comes to their own doors.

But let no one dream that a benefit costing so little to the reader can be sustained with little cost. To give our library full efficiency it needs greatly the gift of at least a few thousand dollars, and a well trained librarian in constant charge. Who will give herself to such a work, so full of blessing to others ? And will not all who read this remember that a very small gift from each would place one more book upon our shelves, to remain a blessing for long years to come?

To build up such a library calls for a perseverance that is even persistency. Many years ago, when one of a party among the lakes of Killarney, our jaunting car was followed for a mile or more by a plucky little girl, who bare-headed and barefooted pursued us with the incessant cry: "The price of a book ; the price of a book." We could never quite divine her object, but somehow that persevering pursuit, that untiring call of the little maiden, comes to mind as somewhat apropos to our own begging. So that we also are ready to cry out to the passers-by: "The price of a book! the price of a book." Only we will trust that their generosity will reverse the order of things so far as that the givers will also do the running.

It remains to report the crowning blessing of our fifth year of work — the new Home of the Society.

The visitors who found their way aloft to the small room occupied for the last two years in University Place, could all bear witness to its overcrowded state even as a library, while those who shared in its office work can alone know its serious straits and inconveniences — involving the constant loss of time. The purpose for which it had been taken—as a cradle in which to nurse the infant library—had been fairly answered—but the time had come when the need to step out of it was imperative. It was not, however, until after much searching, and many disappointments, that the house was found. In its location, fronting as it does the Chapel of the Good Shepherd, and the campus of the General Theological Seminary, we recognize a most kindly Providence. It is also adapted as very few houses would be to our needs. The large undivided parlors required no change to become the lecture and reading-rooms, while the extension on the same floor, with its large south windows, provided a quite ideal library. A range of spacious closets in the rear hall exactly met the requirements of our office work.

The one disadvantage was that while the house was thoroughly well built, it was not in good surface repair. Very sore was the struggle of expelling the demons of dust and disorder. A thorough renovation of nearly every room was requisite and by the terms of our lease was assumed by us — a reduction being allowed. Sufficient progress was made to allow of the final opening and blessing of the library and reading-room on October 22nd. The day proved extremely inclement; but this did not hinder a goodly company from assembling. The beautiful and impressive office was performed by the Bishop of Albany, our beloved President, in whose honour the reading-room is to be named the Albany room, the furnishing having been provided for by himself and his personal friends. The Bishop of New York was unavoidably absent but kindly sent his blessing and good wishes in a letter, as did also our Presiding Bishop and the Bishops of Central New York and Minnesota, Dr. Dix and Dr. Mortimer. Among those present were Bishop Coleman of Delaware, the Rev. Dean Hoffman, the Rev. Dr. Houghton, the Rev. Dr. Walpole, Dr. Davenport and Dr. Gallaudet, Senator Edmunds and wife, with many others whose coming was felt

18

to be an honour. The address of Bishop Doane, who was fully robed for the occasion, was one of his happiest, and was uplifting and stimulating to all. Huldah, the prophetess, dwelling in Jerusalem in the college was set before us as an example worthy to be followed in these latter days. Dr. Walpole followed showing the need of a great ENTHUSIASM in all such work and its blessed power. The crosses given to the graduates were arranged upon a table in the form of a crown. Three only of the members were present to receive them at the Bishop's hands, but as the list was read each name was brought into most pleasant remembrance.

Our members will be interested to know the destination of the other portions of the house. It is to be devoted to the same object for which the lot at Saratoga was given, a Home for Bible Study. No means have yet been provided to carry out the work there which would naturally belong to the summer. Meantime, the portion of this house not required by the society was comparatively easy to prepare for a corresponding use at other seasons.

The very success of the work effected by correspondence points on to the need of a further and fuller provision for those who aim to take a true part in the great work of a higher religious education. The library itself is a great educator, and placed as the Home is so close to the General Theological Seminary, whose Dean and whose professors have shown us such kindness, we are in the very atmosphere of the Church's highest Christian culture, with counsel and aid very ready at hand. Our full plan embraces in the future, and we earnestly hope a not distant one, a professor whose special duty will be the training of our women in all that will best prepare them for Christian work. Even the residence at such a centre for a week or two may be of inestimable benefit. Instructions which are given elsewhere are easily included among the privileges, and some of the most successful of our city clergy will gladly welcome our guests to inspect their methods of parish work. It will be the happy office devolving on myself to guide our guests in their quest of books and to answer as far as possible the many questions which all earnest students are sure to bring. Now, also, those who come to assist us with generous gifts of time and talents can find a home where while helping others they may themselves be helped. We desire that our graduates should all feel that this is *their home* to which they will ever be welcomed and the very thought of which may bring them rest and refreshment. Already they have hailed the prospect of it with delight, and their generous gifts are helping in the preparation of the rooms, so that we trust soon to have a lodging prepared for them in " Bethlehem " and " Bethesda," and " Elim " and " Philadelphia." " The High Hall " awaits some further gifts to make it a charming retreat for study.

In giving a name to this portion of the house as a whole — a much neglected saint has been chosen — the woman whose high privilege it was to see in the Babe of forty days, brought into the temple courts as any other babe, her Lord and Saviour — the fulfilment of that life-long prayer with which she had been serving God — so now at the end to give thanks likewise and to speak of Him Incarnate to all them that looked for redemption. Such silent service, such patient prayer, such true teaching of Him be ours, who shall dwell, whether for days or for years, in ST. ANNA's HOUSE. And may God graciously turn hither hearts whether from stricken homes or lonely paths, or so it be His call even out of the full flush of a joyous life, to join in loving and cheering companionship while they seek to raise higher and yet higher for their sisters far and near the standard of sacred study and to build themselves and others up upon their most holy faith, becoming indeed in fact if not in name a SOCIETAS FIDEI SANCTISSIMAE.

The Rev. Walton W. Battershall, D. D., presented and read the

REPORT OF THE TRUSTEES OF THE CLERGY RESERVE FUND.

The Trustees of the Clergy Reserve Fund beg leave to report that during the past year only four Parishes of the Diocese have contributed to the fund, namely:

St. Peter's, Albany..	$21 31
St. John's, Ogdensburgh.	32 67
Christ Church, Herkimer	7 00
St. Luke's, Saranac Lake.......................	2 50
Aggregating................................	**$63 48**

They also report that Canon XVIII, regarding the Clergy Reserve Fund, section 7, has been altered by the Convention, so as to make the Treasurer of the Diocese the Treasurer of the Fund, and the Archdeacons of the Diocese Trustees of the Fund in the place of the Lay Members of the Board of Missions.

· The Trustees call the attention of the Clergy of the Diocese to the provisions of section 5 of the above Canon, and strongly urge every Rector and Clergyman in charge of Mission Stations to order an offering for the Fund during the coming year and send the same to the Treasurer of the Diocese.

On behalf of the Trustees,

WALTON W. BATTERSHALL.

Mr. A. B. Cox, Lay Deputy from Grace Church, Cherry Valley, presented and read the

REPORT OF THE TRUSTEES OF THE DIOCESE OF ALBANY.

The Trustees of the Diocese of Albany report, that a meeting was held in St. Agnes' School on the 17th day of November, 1891, pursuant to a call by the Bishop. At which were present, the Bishop presiding, Rev. Drs. J. D. Morrison and Joseph Carey, Rev. Mr. Charles S. Olmsted, Messrs. Benjamin H. Hall, Levi W. Hasbrouck and A. B. Cox, Secretary.

The Bishop presented a deed of two adjoining pieces of land, containing together one acre and three-quarters of an acre, in the town of Bolton, Warren county, N. Y., on which is situated the "Church of St. Sacrament, Bolton, Lake George." This deed was made by Rev. Fenwick M. Cookson, Referee, appointed by the Warren county court to transfer the property to the Trustees, and was recorded in the Warren county clerk's office.

It was voted that the Trustees take and accept the property described in the above-mentioned deed.

The Secretary presented the quit-claim deed of William Lyman Pomeroy and Jane E. Pomeroy, his wife, to the Trustees, of a piece of land known as the "Church lot," in the town of Copake, Columbia county, N. Y., on which is situated "The Church of St. John in the Wilderness," and the Rectory, reserving a burial lot inclosed by an iron fence "fifty feet east and west by twenty-six feet north and south," with a right of ingress to it and egress from it.

It was voted that the Trustees take and accept the property described in the above-mentioned deed with the reservation therein specified.

The Secretary was directed to procure the necessary certificate and have the deed recorded in the Columbia county clerk's office.

The Rev. W. C. Prout presented the deed of Hiram Every and Hannah E. Every, his wife, of a piece of land in the town of Kortright, Delaware county, N. Y., to the Trustees, containing one-quarter of an acre of land, and recorded in the Delaware county clerk's office.

It was voted that the Trustees take and accept the property described in the above-mentioned deed.

On motion of the Rev. Dr. Morrison, it was resolved that the following preamble and resolutions be presented to the Diocesan Convention and their adoption recommended:

WHEREAS, St. John's Church of Chateaugay, in Franklin county, N. Y., has abandoned its organization and no religious services have been held therein for more than two years past ; therefore

Resolved, That, in pursuance of chapter 110 of the Laws of 1876, and section 3 of chapter 23 of the Laws of 1882, the Parish and Church of St. John's of Chateaugay, in Franklin county, N. Y., aforesaid, have become and are extinct.

Resolved, That the Trustees of the Diocese of Albany be directed to take possession of the real and personal property and temporalities of said extinct Church and manage the same in such manner as warranted by law.

The Secretary presented an informal lease by Mrs. Anna Pell of Newport, R. I., to the Trustees, at a nominal rent, of a stone building with adjoining grounds, situated in the hamlet of Springfield Centre, Otsego county, N. Y., for use as a Parish House, attached to St. Mary's Mission, Springfield Centre, and holding the Trustees blameless of all charges which may be levied against said Parish House.

On motion, it was resolved that the Trustees are not empowered to hold property on the terms expressed in the instrument, and that they express their regret to Mrs. Pell at their inability to accept the offer so generously extended.

On motion the meeting adjourned.

A meeting was held in St. Agnes' School on the 18th day of November, 1891, pursuant to a call by the Bishop, at which were present, the Bishop presiding, Rev. Drs. J. D. Morrison and Joseph Carey, Rev. Mr. Frederick S. Sill, and Messrs. Benjamin H. Hall, Levi W. Hasbrouck, John H. Bagley, and A. B. Cox, Secretary.

Mr. Hall presented a warranty deed of Margaret L. Fale of Pittstown, Rensselaer county, N. Y., to the Trustees, of a parcel of land containing 12,500 square feet in said town of Pittstown, on which land it is proposed to erect a church edifice, the foundation and basement story of which have been already laid, at an expense of about $800. This organization to be known as St. Paul's Mission, Raymerstown. The deed was recorded in the Rensselaer county clerk's office

It was voted that the Trustees take and accept the property described in the above-mentioned deed.

The Secretary stated to the Trustees that Mr. Chesborough suggests that the Trustees put a mortgage of $500 upon the Rectory, and one acre of land adjoining it, in the town of Copake, Columbia county, N. Y., and that the money thus borrowed be expended in putting the building in thorough repair, so that it can be rented for a sufficient sum to pay the interest and gradually the principal.

On motion of Mr. Hall the Trustees declared their unwillingness at this time to take the action suggested by Mr. Chesborough, and expressed their earnest wish that those who have the immediate charge and enjoy the services of the Church at Copake, will endeavor to put the Rectory connected therewith in proper condition.

Mr. Benjamin H. Hall was elected Treasurer in place of Hon. Jas. M. Dudley who ceased to be a member of the Trustees at the last election.

On motion the meeting adjourned.

All of which is respectfully submitted.

A. B. COX, *Secretary.*

On motion the resolutions recommended in the Report of the Trustees of the Diocese were adopted as follows:

WHEREAS, St. John's Church of Chateaugay, in Franklin county, N. Y., has abandoned its organization, and no religious services have been held therein for more than two years past; therefore

Resolved, That in pursuance of chapter 110 of the Laws of 1876, and section 8 of chapter 23 of the Laws of 1882, the Parish and Church of St. John's of Chateaugay, in Franklin county, N. Y., aforesaid, have become and are extinct.

Resolved, That the Trustees of the Diocese of Albany be directed to take possession of the real and personal estate and temporalities of said extinct Church, and manage the same in such manner as warranted by law.

On motion of the Rev. Canon Stewart, it was

Resolved, That the case of the Church of St. Luke's, Middleburgh, be referred to the Trustees of the Diocese.

The Rev. Richmond Shreve, D. D., presented the Report of the Woman's Diocesan League, and of the Committee on the same.

REPORT OF THE WOMAN'S DIOCESAN LEAGUE.

The President of the Woman's Diocesan League reports that the League is actively engaged in raising the interest on the Cathedral debt.

The debt which the Bishop has assumed has been reduced from $75,000 to $44,000, and by the first of January will be further reduced to $40,000.

The amount of money raised by the League since the last Convention is $4,245.66

The President wishes to mention particularly two Churches which have never failed to send contributions as Parishes — Grace Church, Albany, and St. Mary's Church, Luzerne. She feels most gratefully the interest and energy shown by the members of the League.

REPORT OF THE COMMITTEE ON THE REPORT OF THE WOMAN'S DIOCESAN LEAGUE.

The Christian world can never fully repay the debt it owes to the help received from woman's work. It is sometimes possible to do little more than gratefully acknowledge her enthusiastic devotion, her lofty purity of motive, her unswerving perseverance; and gladly to congratulate her upon well-merited success.

Your Committee deem it a privilege to be allowed to do thus much in recognition of the labours of the Woman's Diocesan League.

Not yet six (6) years old, this organization has laid upon the Cathedral Altar some $54,000, and it looks upon the coming days of further work with womanly hopefulness and courage.

The Committee express the hope that the League may, in the not distant years, see the spires of "All Saints" — finished and paid for — stand pointing to the Heavens, and, that first object of their existence being accomplished, its members may make other places glad with the fruitage of their continued work.

Signed for the Committee,

RICHMOND SHREVE,
Chairman.

On motion of the Rev. Archdeacon Olmsted it was

Resolved, That the thanks of the Convention be heartily given to the Dean and Chapter of All Saints' Cathedral, the Trustees of St. Agnes' School and the Church people of Albany for their hospitality during its present delightful session.

On motion of the Rev. Charles S. Olmsted it was

Resolved, That the Rev. J. Ireland Tucker, S. T. D., the Rev. Walton W. Battershall, D. D., the Rev. Wilford L. Robbins, D. D., the Rev. J. D. Morrison, D. D., L.L. D., the Rev. Joseph Carey, S. T.(D., the Rev. James Caird, the Rev. R. M. Kirby, D. D., the Rev. Fenwick M. Cookson, the Rev. Richard Temple, Mr. John I. Thompson, Mr. A. B. Cox, Mr. Erastus Corning, Mr. Joseph M. Warren, Gen. S. E. Marvin, Mr. T. Streatfeild Clarkson, Mr. L. Averill Carter, Prof. Sidney G. Ashmore, Mr. John Keyes Paige, Mr. G. Pomeroy Keyes and the Hon. William A. Sackett be a Committee to take into consideration the due celebration of the twenty-fifth anniversary of the consecration of the first Bishop of Albany, and the raising of money for a suitable memorial of his successful episcopate.

On motion of the Rev. C. M. Nickerson, D. D., it was

Resolved, That the name of the Rev. C. S. Olmsted be added to those mentioned in the resolution appointing a Committee on the celebration of the twenty-fifth anniversary of the consecration of the first Bishop of Albany.

On motion of the Rev. W. W. Battershall, D. D., it was

Resolved, That the Committee on the celebration of the twenty-fifth anniversary of the consecration of the first Bishop of Albany be empowered to increase their number by the addition of five names, and to fill vacancies.

The following resolution offered by the Rev. J. D. Morrison, D. D., L.L. D., was, on motion of the Rev. Richmond Shreve, D. D., laid on the table :

Resolved, That an assessment of one per cent on the salaries paid to clergymen in this Diocese, be laid on the Parishes and Missions, to defray the expense of the entertainment of the clergy of the Diocese in attendance at next Convention.

On motion of the Rev. J. D. Morrison, D. D., LL. D., it was

Resolved, That the Secretary of the Diocese be instructed to print in the Journal of Convention the Speeches made by the Public Orator of the University of Cambridge, and by Archdeacon Palmer at Oxford, in presenting the Bishop of this Diocese for the Degrees of Doctor of Laws and Doctor in Divinity, conferred upon him by those Universities, respectively, in May of this year.

Resolved, That the Secretary be instructed to print a translation* of the addresses.

SPEECH DELIVERED ON MAY 21 BY THE PUBLIC ORATOR, DR. SANDYS, FELLOW AND TUTOR OF ST. JOHN'S, IN PRESENTING THE BISHOP FOR THE DEGREE OF LL. D.

"DIGNISSIME DOMINE, DOMINE PROCANCELLARIE, ET TOTA ACADEMIA : — Quem tres abhinc annos in episcopis nonnullis titulo nostro decorandis imprudentes praetermisimus, eum hodie ad nos feliciter advectum non sine gaudio singulari salutamus. Salutamus episcopum episcopi filium, filiorum suorum in Christo re

---

* The following translations of the speeches given in the text have been prepared with much care and pains, the effort being to render the spirit and significance of them rather than to give an exact literal translation.--W. C. P.

SPEECH OF THE PUBLIC ORATOR AT CAMBRIDGE.

MOST HONOURABLE CHANCELLOR, VICE-CHANCELLOR AND MEMBERS OF THE UNIVERSITY : — One, whom we inadvertently passed by when honouring certain Bishops with our degree three years ago, has now happily returned to us. Most heartily and sincerely we bid him welcome. To him as a Bishop and son of a Bishop, and in very deed the father of his own sons in Christ, we offer our cordial greeting. We are here to welcome him who, beyond the Atlantic, was

vera patrem, qui trans aequor Atlanticum tres et viginti abhinc annos episcopus Albanensis consecratus, Angliam nostram idcirco identidem invisit, ut ecclesiarum nostrarum cathedralium non modo aedificia sed etiam instituta penitus perdisceret, atque e tot exemplis optimum quicque suos in usus converteret. Olim verbis quam exquisitis ecclesiarum illarum dignitatem descripsit,—aedem pulchritudine venerabili urbem subiacentem coronantem et consecrantem, horas praetereuntes sono suavi nuntiantem, saeculorum praeteritorum memoriam cotidie renovantem, mentesque a terrestribus ad coelestia revocantem. Idem nuper animo quam grato in sede sua episcopali templum ex ipsis fundamentis sensim surgens aspexit, ubi provinciae totius velut ara focusque constitutus est ; ubi tot columnae, manuum piarum liberalitate exstructae, nominum insignium, nominum sacrorum, nominum dilectorum memoriam conservant ; ubi tot fenestrae lucidae, aut Gregorii Magni, aut Bedae Venerabilis, aut Sancti Albani, primi martyris Anglici, aut Sanctae Margaretae, reginae Caledonicae, historiis illustrantur ; ubi tot donorum splendor novus sanctitatis priscae velut imagine illuminatur ; ubi crucis denique signum, lapidibus pretiosis decoratum et episcopi ipsius in sinu suspensum, corda sursum ad civitatem coelestem vocat, cuius fundamenta sunt omni lapide pretioso ornata, portaeque singulae ex singulis margaritis conditae. Dei domum tam augustam procul contemplati, recordamur arcae divinae tabernaculum Iudaeorum a rege his fere verbis olim dedicatum:—*Afferte Domino gloriam et honorem ; afferte dona et introite in atria eius ; adorate Dominum in decore sancto.* Duco ad vos virum admodum reverendum Willelmum Croswell Doane, Episcopum Albanensem."

SPEECH DELIVERED AT OXFORD ON MAY 28 BY ARCHDEACON PALMER IN PRESENTING BISHOP DOANE FOR THE DEGREE OF S. T. D.

" INSIGNISSIME VICE CANCELLARIE VOSQUE EGREGII PROCURATORES : Praesento vobis virum spectatissimum, tam doctrina quam virtute praestantem, Willelmum Croswell Doane, Albaniae in America Septentrionali episcopum. Nescit ecclesia Christi regnorum et civitatium fines, nescit respublica ut aiunt litterarum. Nobis semper mos fuit ut neminem qui bonis artibus inclaruerit a nobis alienum putemus. Quod si Gallos, Germanos, Italos, libenter amplectimur, quali adfectu animi eos de-

consecrated Bishop of Albany three and twenty years ago, and has since made repeated visits to England in order to thoroughly study not only the external beauties of our Cathedra Churches, but also the Cathedral institution itself that he might adapt the best to his own special purposes.

In what choice language has he described the majestic beauty of our churches — the temple of the Lord, fair and venerable, "crowning and consecrating the town which nestles at its feet; which takes its time from the Cathedral chimes and is tuneful with the Cathedral choir;" renewing day by day the memory of by-gone ages, and calling away men's minds from things of earth to things of heaven.

He also, within recent years, has looked with pride and thankfulness upon the slow but steady growth of a Cathedral Church, of which the foundations were laid by himself at his own Episcopal seat, and where have been placed the sacred hearth and altar, as it were, of the whole Diocese. There, many pillars, reared through the generosity of pious and loving hands, preserve the memory of distinguished, sacred and beloved names. There the bright hues of many windows tell the stories of Gregory the Great and the venerable Bede, of Saint Alban, the first martyr of England, and Margaret, Scotland's sainted Queen. There the new splendour of many costly gifts is made still brighter by the very representation, as it were, of the sanctity of the past. There, in fine, the image of the Cross, adorned with precious stones, hangs upon the breast of the Bishop himself, and summons the hearts of men to that city of the Heavens whose foundations " were garnished with all manner of precious stones, and whose every several gate was of one pearl." While viewing from afar so noble a house of God, we are re-

bemus excipere quos stirpe nostra ortos ac paene nostrates maioris cujusdam Brit-
anniae cives licet appellare? Huius quem vobis hodie praesento, nomen tam apud
nostros quam apud suos notum est. Patris illustris, illustris filius, episcopus episcopi, tum paternis virtutibus tum suis commendatur. Ipse adhuc iuvenis, id quod
hac in Academia usitatum est, ecclesiae ministeria cum professoris munere coniunxit.
Idem annos abhinc viginti duo factus episcopus ita dioecesim rexit, immo regit hodie,
ut neque litterarum, neque Dei cultus unquam visus sit oblivisci. Illud testantur
ludi quos instituit, imprimis vero is qui Sanctae Agnes nomine celebratur puellarum
doctrinae magnum addidit momentum; hoc missi quaquaversus pastores, collectae
Christi oves quae fuerant dispersae. Νοσοκομεία quid dicam instituta? Is scilicet
qui Pastoris Boni exemplum sibi proposuit tam corporibus hominum quam animabus
voluit consulere. His proximis annis ecclesiam cathedralem, rem apud suos paene
inusitatam, opus mirabile mirabiliore studio molitus est. Episcopum verum agnos-
cimus, re non verbo reverendum. Hunc igitur talem virum vobis praesento, ut ad-
mittatur ad gradum Doctoris in Sacra Theologia honoris causa.

On motion of the Rev. Eaton W. Maxcy, D. D., it was

Resolved, That the proposition of the Committee on the Report of the Board of
Missions that a special Sunday be set apart for contributions by the Sunday Schools
for the support of the General Missionary, be recommended to the Archdeacons of the
Diocese, for favorable consideration.

minded of the tabernacle of the Ark of God once dedicated by the King of the Jews in almost
these very words: *Ascribe unto the Lord glory and honour ; bring presents and come into His
courts ; worship the Lord in the beauty of holiness.*

I present to you the Right Rev. William Croswell Doane, Bishop of Albany.

SPEECH OF ARCHDEACON PALMER AT OXFORD.

Most Distinguished Vice-Chancellor and you Eminent Proctors, I present to you a man most
worthy of regard, excelling both in learning and in virtue, William Croswell Doane, Bishop of
Albany in North America.

The Church of Christ knows not, the republic (so named) of letters knows not the boundaries of kingdoms, or of States. Our custom always has been to hold no one as estranged from
us, who has gained renown in good arts. If then we cheerfully take to our embrace French-
men, Germans, Italians, with what emotion of soul ought we to receive men, whom, as sprung
from our own stock, and almost of our own country, we may rightly call the citizens of
some greater Britain. Well known, both amongst our countrymen and his own, is the name of
him whom I present to you to-day. The illustrious son of an illustrious father, the Episcopal
son of an Episcopal father, he is commended to us by the virtues of his father, as by his own.
As is the custom also in this University, he in early manhood united the ministry of the
Church with the office of a teacher. Twenty-two years ago, he too, was made a Bishop, and
through these years he has so ruled his Diocese (yea, so rules it to-day), as to seem never for-
getful either of letters or of the worship of God. To this on the one hand bear witness the
schools, which he has founded, especially that one, which, widely known by the name of
Saint Agnes, has greatly influenced the onward movement in the education of girls; on the
other, testify the shepherds, sent in every direction, by whose labours have been gathered
into one fold the sheep of Christ, which had been scattered abroad. Why need I mention the hospital which he has founded? He in truth, setting before himself the example
of the Good Shepherd, has been mindful to care for the bodies as well as for the souls of
men. In these later years, with zeal truly wonderful, he has undertaken a wonderful work,
the building a Cathedral Church, an achievement almost without precedent among his countrymen. In him we acknowledge a true Bishop, worthy of reverence in deed not in name.
This man, therefore, so worthy, I present to you, that he may be admitted to the honourary
degree of Doctor in Sacred Theology.

On motion of the Secretary of the Convention it was

Resolved, That when the Convention adjourn this afternoon, it adjourn to meet in the Cathedral at half-past four o'clock to hear the remainder of the Annual Address of the Bishop of the Diocese; and that at the conclusion of the Address the Convention adjourn *sine die* without further formality.

Resolved, That the Secretary be instructed to print 1,000 copies of the Bishop's Address, apart from the Journal, and to send them to the Clergy of the Diocese as early as possible.

Resolved, That the Secretary be instructed to print 1,250 copies of the Journal of the Convention, and distribute them to the various Parishes.

The minutes of this day's session were read and adopted.

The Convention took a recess until half-past four o'clock.

HALF-PAST FOUR O'CLOCK IN THE AFTERNOON.

The Convention reassembled in the Cathedral.

The Bishop delivered the remainder of his Annual Address.

Prayers were said by the Rev. Dean Robbins, and the Bishop pronounced the Benediction.

The Convention adjourned *sine die.*

WM. CROSWELL DOANE,
Bishop of Albany and President of the Convention.

WILLIAM C. PROUT, *Secretary.*

THOMAS B. FULCHER, *Assistant Secretary.*

19

APPENDIX.

(A.)

PAROCHIAL REPORTS.

Albany County.

CATHEDRAL OF ALL SAINTS, ALBANY.

THE CATHEDRAL CHAPTER.

Bishop. The Right Rev. William Croswell Doane, D. D., *Oxon*, LL. D., *Cantab.*
Dean. The Rev. Wilford L. Robbins, D. D.
Precentor. The Rev. Thomas B. Fulcher, B. D.
Treasurer. The Rev. Edgar T. Chapman.
Honorary Canons. The Revs. Richard Temple, F. M. Gray, Edward D. Tibbits, Charles H. Hatheway, Walter C. Stewart.
Lay Members. A. Bleecker Banks, Thomas Hun, M. D., Erastus Corning, Selden E. Marvin, Assistant Treasurer, Marcus T. Hun, Vice-Chancellor, Robert S. Oliver.

Parochial.

Families, 197; Individuals, 1035; Baptisms (adults, 23, infants, 81), 104; Confirmed, since last report, 72; Present number of confirmed persons, 622; Marriages,13; Burials, 41; Communicants, last reported, 578, present number, 587; Public Services, Daily Celebration of Holy Communion, Sundays and Holy Days, 2 celebrations; Daily Matins and Even Song throughout the year; Holy Communion, private celebrations, 18, Sunday School, teachers, 18, pupils, 245; Catechizing, number of times, 30; St. Agnes' School, teachers, 30, pupils, 250.

Offerings.

Parochial.— Current expenses, including salaries, $13,866.60; Sunday School, $150; Increase and Improvement of Church Property, $5,000; Other parochial objects: Specials, $366.78; Woman's Auxiliary to Board of Missions, $54.14. Total, $19,437.52.

Diocesan.— Diocesan Missions, $1,200; Salary of the Bishop, $150; Diocesan Fund, $114; Fund for Aged and Infirm Clergymen, $12; Fund for Widows and Orphans of Clergymen, $5; Orphan House of the Holy Saviour, $46.32; The Child's Hospital, $657.32; Society for Promoting Religion and Learning, $100; St. Peter's Church, Ellenburgh, $100; Diocesan Library, $25; Diocesan Missionary (Sunday School), $20; Church Vestments (Sunday School), $30. Total, $2,459.64.

General.— Domestic and Foreign Missions (Sunday School, $90.10), $305.98; Missions to Jews, $27.90. Total, $333.88.

Total amount of Offerings, $22,231.04.

Property.

Church and lot (estimated worth), $300,000.
Other property, $12,000.

Condition of property, good.
Indebtedness, $52,200.
Amount of salary pledged Dean, $3,800.
Amount of salary pledged Precentor, $500.
Number of sittings in the Church, 2,375; all free.

ST. PETER'S CHURCH, ALBANY.

Rector. The Rev. Walton W. Battershall, D. D.
Assistant. The Rev. George B. Richards.
Wardens. George S. Weaver, Joseph W. Tillinghast.
Vestrymen. Luther H. Tucker, Henry T. Martin, Theodore Townsend, F. E.
Griswold, Robert C. Pruyn, John MacDonald, Thomas S. Wiles, Abraham Lansing.

Parochial.

Families, 384; Individuals, 1,200; Baptisms (adults, 9, infants, 12), 21; Confirmed,
since last report, 29; Present number of confirmed persons, 712; Marriages, 19;
Burials, 35; Communicants, last reported, 702, admitted, 29, received, 18, died, 22,
removed, 15; present number, 712; Public Services (Sundays, 134, Holy days, 30,
other days, 190), 354; Holy Communion (public, 86, private, 24), 110; Sunday School,
teachers, 39, pupils, 300; Parish School, teachers, 5, pupils, 22; Sewing School,
teachers, 15, pupils, 289.

Offerings.

Parochial.— Alms at Holy Communion, $926.20; Current expenses, including sal-
aries, $12,695.87; Sunday School, $88.70; St. Peter's Orphanage, $1,163.10; Increase
and Improvement of Church Property, $6,571.83; Other parochial objects: Chancel
Guild, $185; Parish Aid Society, $801.55; Parish Mission Work, $1,164.51; Christmas
Tree, $267; Sewing School, $101.24; Endowment Fund, $118.94. Total, $24,083.94.

Diocesan.— Diocesan Missions, $762.55; Salary of the Bishop, $150; Diocesan
Fund, $120; Bible and Common Prayer Book Society of Albany, $28.40; Debt on Orphan House Holy Saviour, $38; Orphan House of the Holy Saviour, $36.08; The
Child's Hospital (from Sunday School), $15.10; The Child's Hospital (from Sewing
School), $14.44; St. Christina Home (from Sunday School), $14; Other offerings for
objects within the Diocese Diocesan Missionary (Sunday School), $15.58; Clergy Re-
serve Fund, $21.31. Total, $1,215.46.

General.— Domestic Missions, $306.69, Foreign Missions, $114.18; Indian Missions,
$130; Home Missions to Coloured Persons, $105.69; Bishop of Wyoming and Idaho,
$88.92; Woman's Auxiliary, $780.54; Domestic Missions (Sunday School), $23.16;
Church Building Fund, $135.73; Bishop of Western Texas, special, $500; Bishop of
Wyoming and Idaho, special, $200; Mission in Mexico, special, $100. Total,
$2,484.91.

Total amount of Offerings, $27,784.31.

Property.

Church and lot (estimated worth), $210,000 ; Parsonage and lot (estimated worth,
freehold lease), $5,000; other property, Parish house, $30,000; Orphanage, $10,000.
Total, $255,000.

Condition of property, good.
Amount of salary pledged Rector, $4,000.
Amount of salary pledged Assistant Minister, $1,000.
Number of sittings in the Church and Chapel, 1,250.

Remarks.

Since the last report, three memorial windows have been placed in the chancel, which make the series of the chancel windows complete. The pictorial 'treatment of these windows gives in the upper portion the angelic choir, and in the lower portion scenes in the life of St. Peter. The windows recently put in are as follows : The window to the memory of Mrs. John De Witt Pelts (the fifth in the series), gives the healing of the cripple at the Beautiful Gate of the Temple, and bears the following text and inscription : " In the name of Jesus Christ of Nazareth, rise up and walk." " In loving memory of Mary Marvin Learned, wife of John De Witt Pelts, who died November 23d, A. D., 1888, in the 83d year of her age." The window in memory of Mrs. Amasa J. Parker (the first of the series), gives the scene of the call of St. Peter, with the following text and inscription, " Follow me, and I will make you fishers of men." " To the Glory of God, and in loving memory of Harriet Langdon Parker, daughter of Edmund and Katherine Langdon Roberts of Portsmouth, N. H., and beloved wife of Amasa J. Parker of Albany. At Rest June 27th, 1889. ' Her children arise up and call her blessed. Her husband also, and he praiseth her.' " The window to memory of Judge Parker (the last of the series), displays the scene of the deliverance of St. Peter from prison, with the following text and inscription : " The Angel of the Lord came upon him, and a light shined in the prison." " Amasa J. Parker, at Rest, 13th of May, 1890, æt. 83. Faithful unto death."

ST. PAUL'S CHURCH, ALBANY.

Rector. The Rev. J. Livingston Reese, D. D.

Assistant. The Rev. Freeborn G. Jewett, Jr.

Wardens. J. H. Van Antwerp, John Woodward.

Vestrymen. George P. Wilson, Robert Geer, Matthew H. Robertson, Eugene Burlingame, Harvey A. Dwight, Wallace N. Horton, James H. Manning, E. B. Holden.

Parochial.

Families, 304; Individuals (adults, 834, children, 404), 1,238; Baptisms (adults, 12, infants, 40), 52 ; Confirmed, since last report, 54; Marriages, 13; Burials, 46; Communicants, last reported, 685, admitted, 54, received, 20, died, 17, removed, 35, present number, 707; Sunday School, teachers, 50, pupils, 450.

Offerings.

Parochial.— Alms at Holy Communion, $336; Current expenses, including salaries, $7,085.90; Sunday School, $312; From Sunday School, $350; Increase and Improvement of Church Property, $997; Parochial Missions, $562.35; For Poor, $270; Other parochial objects, $670.25. Total, $10,583.50.

Diocesan.— Diocesan Missions, $302.44; Salary of the Bishop, $100; Diocesan Fund, $80; Other offerings for objects within the Diocese, $152. Total, $634.44.

General.— General Missions, $177.78; Domestic Missions, $691.55; Foreign Missions, $305; Indian Missions, $60 ; Other objects exterior to the Diocese, $570. Total, $1,804.33.

Total amount of Offerings, $13,022.27.

TRINITY CHURCH, ALBANY.

Rector. The Rev. Russell Woodman.

Wardens. William Little, John A. Howe.

Vestrymen. John Pritchard, Richard Norris, George F. Granger, Charles Fairchild, J. Henry Marlow, Alexander Campbell, Nordin T. Johnson, Richard Story.

Parochial

Families, 111; Baptisms (adults, 2, infants, 26), 28: Confirmed, since last report, 11; Marriages, 14; Burials, 24; Communicants, last reported, 237, received, 10, died, 1, removed, 28, present number, 225; Public Services, Sundays, morning and evening with sermon, Holy days, Holy Communion, other days, Friday evenings, October to June; Holy Communion, public, 28; Sunday School, teachers, 20, pupils, 170; Catechizing, monthly. Sewing School, teachers, 7, pupils, 40.

Offerings.

Parochial.— Alms at Holy Communion, $50.46; Current expenses, including salaries, $2,000 ; Improvement and repair of Church Property, $800. Total, $2,850.46.

Diocesan.— Diocesan Missions, $20; Salary of the Bishop, $20; Diocesan Fund, $10; The Child's Hospital (from John A. Howe), $5· Total, $55.

General.— Domestic Missions, $5.36; Indian Missions, $5. Total, $10.36.

Total amount of Offerings, $2,915.82.

Property.

Church and lot (estimated worth), $40,000.

Remarks.

The Rectory is in good repair; the Church is in fair condition. Each year improvements are made, and its condition bettered.

GRACE CHURCH, ALBANY.

Rector. The Rev. William Henry Bown.

Wardens. B. F. Hinman, Charles W. White.

Vestrymen. Frank J. Smith, James C. Sewell, Henry Burn, Frederick Gilliland, George B. Longleway, Edward Sewell, James Beauman, William Rankin.

Parochial.

Baptisms (adults, 7, infants, 38), 45; Confirmed, since last report, 25; Marriages, 15; Burials, 36; Communicants, last reported, 358, admitted, 25, received, 5, died 2, removed, 2, present number, 384. Public Services (Sundays, 116, Holy days, 23, other days, 90), 229 Holy Communion (public 59, private, 15), 74, Sunday School, teachers. 38, pupils, 380; Catechizing, weekly

Offerings.

Parochial —Current expenses, including salaries, $1,864 30; Sunday School, $255.16; Increase and Improvement of Church Property, $76 06, Other parochial objects, $1,117 57 Total, $3,313 69

Diocesan. — Diocesan Missions, $50. Salary of the Bishop, $32; Bible and Common Prayer Book Society of Albany, $5 78. Orphan House of the Holy Saviour, $5 Total, $92.78.

General — Domestic and Foreign Missions, $24 78; Jewish Missions, $9.85. Total, $31 63.

Total amount of Offerings, $3,440 50

Property.

Church and lot (estimated worth), $15,000

Parsonage and lot (estimated worth), $5,000.

Condition of property, good

Indebtedness, mortgage, $2,000

Number of sittings in the Church, 500, all free

THE CHURCH OF THE HOLY INNOCENTS, ALBANY.

Rector. The Rev. Richmond Shreve, D. D.
Wardens. S. M. Van Santvoord, W. H. Weaver.
Vestrymen. J. Barrington Lodge, Jr., G. H. Birchall, E. W. Leaning, James Oswald, J. W. Hine, H. S. McCall, Jr., Robert Parker, William Riley.

Parochial.

Baptisms, infants, 23; Confirmed, since last report, 8; Marriages, 7; Burials, 19; Communicants, last reported, 197, admitted, 8, received, 7, died, 6, removed, 17, present number, 189; Public Services (Sundays, 149, Holy days, 25, other days, 82), 256; Holy Communion (public, 48, private, 23), 71; Sunday School, teachers, 18, pupils, 138; Catechizing, school, number of times, 17.

Offerings.

Parochial. — Alms at Holy Communion, $53.21; Current expenses, including salaries, $3,091.22; Sunday School, $188.40; Increase and Improvement of Church Property, $301.34. Total, $3,634.17.

Diocesan. — Diocesan Missions, $50; Salary of the Bishop, $30; Diocesan Fund, $45; Bible and Common Prayer Book Society of Albany, $5; Fund for Aged and Infirm Clergymen, $7.14; Fund for Widows and Orphans of Clergymen, $8.15; Orphan House of the Holy Saviour, $47.70; The Child's Hospital, $8.59. Total, $201.58.

General. — Foreign Missions, $10; Indian Missions, $60; American Church Building Fund, $5. Total, $75.

Total amount of Offerings, $3,910.75.

Property.

Church and lot, estimated worth, $20,000.
Parsonage and lot, estimated worth, $5,000.
Condition of property, good.
Indebtedness on Rectory, $2,000.
Number of sittings in the Church, 340; all free.

TRINITY CHURCH, RENSSELAERVILLE.

Rector. The Rev. Robt. Washbon.
Assistant. The Rev. S. C. Thompson.
Wardens. John L. Rice, Nathaniel Teed.
Vestrymen. C. B. Cross, Frank Rice, Dewey Bell, J. B. Washburn, M. D., Jas. Rider, Luther Fox, Henry Sweet, Frank Frisbee.

Parochial.

Families, 22; Baptisms (adults, 2, infants, 1), 3; Present number of confirmed persons, 57; Marriages, 2; Burials, 3, Communicants, last reported, 71, died, 2, removed 2; Public Services (Sundays, 94, other days, 29), 123; Holy Communion (public, 15, private, 4), 19; Sunday School, teachers, 6, pupils, 20; Catechizing, number of times, 12.

Offerings.

Parochial. — Alms at Holy Communion, $20.80, Current expenses, including salaries, $342.27. Total, $363.07.

Diocesan. — Diocesan Missions, $15, Salary of the Bishop, $8, Diocesan Fund, $9; Fund for Aged and Infirm Clergymen, $3.24, Orphan House of the Holy Saviour, $10. Total, $45.24.

General.— Domestic Missions, $9.25; Foreign Missions, $9.25.   Total, $18.50.
Total amount of Offerings, $426.81.
Amount of salary pledged Rector, $105.
Amount of salary pledged Assistant Minister, $300.

ST. JOHN'S CHURCH, COHOES.

Rector.   The Rev. Frederick S. Sill, B. D.
Wardens.   Michael Andrae, John Horrocks.
Vestrymen.   George Campbell, Samuel Horrocks, Reuben Lee, William S. Shipley, Luke Kavanaugh, George F. Ford, Harry J. P. Green, Robert R. Chadwick.

Parochial.

Families, 340; Individuals (adults, 1,040, children, 430), 1,470; Baptisms (adults, 2, infants, 33), 35; Confirmed, since last report, 17; Marriages, 19; Burials, 41; Churchings, 2; Communicants, last reported, 521; admitted, 12, received, 13, died, 15, removed, 11, present number, 520, actual number during year, 324; Public Services (Sundays, 156, Holy days, 63, other days, 173), 392; Holy Communion (public, 81, private, 11), 92; Sunday School, teachers, 18, officers, 5, pupils, 300.

Offerings.

Parochial. — Alms at Holy Communion, $55.19; Current expenses, including salaries, $2,881.44; Sunday School, $123.08 ($37.70 more included elsewhere); Increase and Improvement of Church Property, $195.68; Howe Poor Fund, $71.06; King's Daughters, for sick, $27.45; Jane Ryan Fund, increase, $140.90; Chancel Committee, $129.12; Sunday School Improvements, $215; Reduction of Debt, $1,350. Total, $5,188.92.
Diocesan.— Diocesan Missions, $253.75; Salary of the Bishop, $90; Diocesan Fund, $45; Bible and Common Prayer Book Society of Albany, $25; Fund for Aged and Infirm Clergymen, $10; Orphan House of the Holy Saviour, $25; Cathedral, $133.34; Archdeaconry of Albany, $20.50. Total, $602.59.
General.— Domestic Missions (from the Sunday School), $36.22 ; Foreign Missions (from the Sunday School), $36.22; Home Missions to Coloured Persons (Woman's Auxiliary), $10; Jewish Missions, $7; Woman's Auxiliary, $221.66, Lambertville. N. J., Church, $40; Annandale Professorship Fund, $10   Total, $361.10.
Total amount of Offerings, $6,152.61.

Property.

Church and lot (estimated worth), $40,000.
Parsonage and lot (estimated worth) $10,000.
Other property, Howe Fund, $1,500; Church Home Fund, $2,668.01.
Condition of property, very good.
Indebtedness, $3,650.
Amount of salary pledged Rector, $1,500.
Number of sittings in the Church, 800.
Number rented, none; number free, all, but assigned to families.

Remarks.

The debt has been reduced $1,350. The offerings each Sunday have largely increased. A new boiler is being placed in the Church at a cost of over $500, and the organ has been greatly improved at a cost of $125, neither of which items has been included in the above statistics, as the work is not finished. An effort will be made to clear the property entirely from debt during the next year. The number of burials has been larger than in any other twelve months in the history of the Parish.

TRINITY CHURCH, WEST TROY.

Rector. The Rev. E. Bayard Smith.

Wardens. William Hollands, John H. Hulsapple.

Vestrymen. William E. Baxter, Charles H. Crabbe, William Doring, Edmund S. Hollands, Thomas Rath, John Scarborough, Bertram F. Stewart, Robert Trimble.

Parochial.

Families, 200; Individuals (adults, 400, children, 300), 700; Baptisms (adults, 2, infants, 40), 42; Marriages, 6; Burials, 28; Communicants, last reported, 307, received, 1, died, 7, removed, 29, present number, 272; Public Services (Sundays, 95, Holy days, 18, other days, 114), 227; Holy Communion (public, 50, private, 3), 53; Trinity Sunday School, teachers, 18, pupils, 133; St. Gabriel's Sunday School, teachers, 11, pupils, 88; Total teachers, 29, pupils, 221; Catechizing, every session.

Offerings.

Parochial.— Alms at Holy Communion, $65.27; Current expenses, including salaries, $2,451.53; Trinity Sunday School, $43.03; St. Gabriel's Sunday School, $51.20; Chapel, $18.87; Shingling the Church, $161.31; Daughters of the Cross (earnings), $194.81; Carpeting the Church, $295.88; Stenciling the Church, $30; Draining the cellar, $50.18; Painting Guild Rooms, $20; St. Agatha's Guild, $16.66. Total, $3,398.24.

Diocesan.— Diocesan Missions, $27.31; Salary of the Bishop, $40; Diocesan Fund, $34; Fund for Aged and Infirm Clergymen, $11; Fund for Widows and Orphans of Clergymen, $13; Orphan House of the Holy Saviour, $13.50; The Child's Hospital, $15; Education of Young Men for the Holy Ministry, $7; Other offerings for objects within the Diocese, Woman's Auxiliary, $45.07. Total, $195.88.

General.— Domestic Missions, $7.50; Foreign Missions, $6; Humane Society, $4; Mission to the Jews, $6. Total, $23.50.

Total amount of Offerings, $3,617.62.

Property.

Church and lot (estimated worth), $24,000.

Parsonage and lot (estimated worth), $8,000.

Other property, St. Gabriel's Chapel, $4,000.

Condition of property, good.

Number of sittings in the Church, 377, apportioned; Trinity Chapel, 150, free; St. Gabriel's Chapel, 150, free.

Remarks.

The Church has been kalsomined and renovated throughout by the "Daughters of the Cross." A new carpet, the gift of Misses Altane and Libbie N. Fraser has been laid, door mats have been presented by Miss A. Fraser, and the Church beautifully stenciled, the gift of Miss L. N. Fraser. The Guild rooms have been newly painted, and the vestry room carpeted. The cellar has been drained at considerable expense, the gift of Miss A. Fraser. A new sidewalk has been laid in front of the Church, and the roof shingled, the latter by the gift of the children of the Sunday School.

ST. MARK'S CHURCH, GREEN ISLAND.

Rector. The Rev. R. J. Adler.

Wardens, Richard Leonard, Wm. E. Gilbert.

Vestrymen. Henry Stowell, Harry Farmer, Wm. W. Butler, James H. Eckler, Louis Harter, Jr., Fred. S. Uhle, Robert W. Porter, James Madden.

20

Parochial.

Families, 173; Individuals (adults, 239, children, 232), 471; Baptisms (adults, 4, infants, 9), 13; Confirmed, since last report, 16; Present number of confirmed persons, 228; Marriages, 4; Burials, 8; Churchings, 1; Communicants, present number, 187; Public Services (Sundays, 115, other days, 63), 178; Holy Communion (public, 17, private, 4), 21; Sunday School, teachers, 13, pupils, 142; Catechizing, the whole school, weekly.

Offerings.

Parochial.—Alms at Holy Communion, $14.54; Current expenses, including salaries, $1,880.78. Total, $1,895.32.

Diocesan.— Diocesan Missions ($3.90 of which from S. S. for Diocesan Missionary), $49.42; Salary of the Bishop, $12; Diocesan Fund, $15; Bible and Common Prayer Book Society of Albany, $6.05; Increase of the Episcopate Fund, $3.05; Fund for Aged and Infirm Clergymen, $4.80; Orphan House of the Holy Saviour (from S. S.), $3.55; The Child's Hospital (from S. S.), $2; St. Christina Home (from S. S.), $10. Total, $105.87.

General.— General Missions ($14.78 of which from S. S.), $24.88; Domestic Missions, $14.55; Foreign Missions, $13.25; Missions to Jews, $2.37; Home Missions to Coloured Persons, $5.87; American Church Building Fund ($19.05 of which from S. S.), $28.05; Church Building, Lu Verne, Minn. (from Daughters of the King), $28.22. Total, $117.14.

Total amount of Offerings, $2,118.33.

Property.

Church and lot (estimated worth), $20,000.
Parsonage and lot (estimated worth), $7,000.
Condition of property, good.
Sittings in the Church and Chapel, all free.

Remarks.

There is a fund accumulating for the improvement of the Church property, the amount and expenditure of which will be reported upon completion; the contracts are let and the work now in progress.

ST. ANDREW'S CHURCH, WEST TROY.

Missionary. The Rev. Canon Hatheway.

Parochial.

Families, 30; Individuals (adults, 55, children, 60), 115; Baptisms (adults, 1, infants, 4), 5; Confirmed, since last report, 1; Present number of confirmed persons, 42; Burials, 1; Communicants, admitted, 2, removed, 6, present number, 39; Public Services (Sundays, 54, other days, 10), 64; Holy Communion (public, 12, private, 3), 15; Sunday School, teachers, 9, pupils, 45, Catechising, number of children, 45, number of times, 15.

Offerings.

Parochial.— Current expenses, including salaries, $432 13; Sunday School, $41.02; Other parochial objects, about $475. Total, $948 15.

Diocesan.— St. Christina Home, $2.52.

Total amount of Offerings, $950.67.

Property.

Church and lot (estimated worth), about $1,300
Condition of property, not very good.

Clinton County.

TRINITY CHURCH, PLATTSBURGH.

Rector. The Rev. Hobart Cooke.
Lay Reader. John Henry Booth.
Wardens. George F. Nichols, Wm. T. Ketchum.
Vestrymen. Hon. S. A. Kellogg, Hon. Jno. M. Wever, A. L. Inman, A. M. Warren, Hon. Geo. S. Weed, John Ross, Millard F. Parkhurst, Edward T. Gilliland.

Parochial.

Baptisms (adults and infants), 12; Confirmed, since last report, 13; Marriages, 10; Burials, 10; Communicants, present number, 208; Public Services (Sundays, Holy days, other days), 273; Holy Communion (public and private), 60; Sunday School, teachers, 14, pupils, 109.

Offerings.

Parochial.— Alms at Holy Communion, $87.24; Current expenses, including salaries, $2,095; Sunday School, $195; Increase and Improvement of Church Property, $1,500; Home of the Friendless, $16; Special charities, $400. Total, $4,293.24.

Diocesan.— Diocesan Missions, $75; Salary of the Bishop, $60; Diocesan Fund, $45; Orphan House of the Holy Saviour (Sunday School), $15; The Child's Hospital (Sunday School, $15), $30. Total, $225.

General.— Domestic and Foreign Missions, $23.25.

Total amount of Offerings, $4,541.49.

Property.

Church and lot (estimated worth), $20,000.
Parsonage and lot (estimated worth), $6,000.
Condition of property, excellent.
Amount of salary pledged Rector, $1,500.
Number of sittings in the Church, 450; all rented.

Remarks.

During the past year the Rectory has been thoroughly renovated and greatly improved by the additions of steam heat, electric light, and the modern conveniences of water supply throughout the house. The members of the Altar Society have provided a beautiful Communion Set of Sterling Silver, large size, for use in private communions; also a handsome Credence Table of quartered oak. The members of St. Mary's Guild, as memorial of the Rev. John Henry Hopkins, S. T. D., who organized the Guild during his Rectorship here, have made an offering of an oak Litany Desk of unusually fine material and workmanship, which, with the Credence Table, was given place in the Church with appropriate benediction on All Saints Day. The Ladies Aid Society have sent boxes of clothing and useful articles to The Child's Hospital at Albany, and to the Orphan House of the Holy Saviour at Cooperstown; and mainly through members of this Society, some largely generous home charities have been most happily devised and successfully accomplished.

CHRIST CHURCH, ROUSE'S POINT.

Rector. The Rev. Herbert Luther Wood.
Wardens. William Crook, Chas. Randall.
Vestrymen. I. H. Vanbuskirk, J. R. Sperry, W. S. Phillips, J. R. Myers, Alexander Wood.

Parochial.

Families, 76; Baptisms, infants, 3; Confirmed, since last report, 6; Present number of confirmed persons, about 100; Burials, 8; Communicants, last reported, 58, received, 2, died, 3, removed, 2, present number, 54; Public Services (Sundays, 103, Holy days, 4, other days, 8), 115; Holy Communion (public, 12, private, 1), 13; Sunday School, teachers, 6, pupils, 46; Catechizing, weekly in Sunday School.

Offerings.

Parochial.— Current expenses, including salaries, $130; Weekly offertory, $264. Total, $394.

Diocesan.— Diocesan Missions, $6.82; Salary of the Bishop, $12; Bible and Common Prayer Book Society of Albany, $3. Total, $21.82.

General.— Domestic and Foreign Missions (S. S. Mite boxes, Lenten offering), $17.61. Total amount of Offerings, $432.93.

Property.

Church and lot, (estimated worth), $3,000.
Condition of property, not in good condition.
Amount of salary pledged Rector, $900.
Number of sittings in the Church, 275; number rented, 216; Number free, 65.

Remarks.

It is impossible to make out all the returns asked for. Another year I hope to supply all the needful information.

ST. JOHN'S CHURCH, CHAMPLAIN.

Rector. The Rev. W. D. U. Shearman.
Wardens. James Averill, J. White.
Vestrymen. Henry Hoyle, C. R. Ely, James DeF. Burroughs, Ransom Graves, James Hackett, M. D.

Parochial.

Families, 15; Individuals (adults, 45, children, 22), 67; Baptisms, infants, 2; Confirmed, since last report, 7; Present number of confirmed persons, 42; Marriages, 9; Communicants, last reported, 32, admitted, 7, received, 3, removed, 2, present number, 40. Public Services (Sundays, 94 Holy days, 12, other days, 12), 128: Holy Communion, public. 38. Sunday School, teachers, 3, pupils, 18.

Offerings.

Parochial.— Current expenses, including salaries, $577.37; Sunday School, $10; Increase and Improvement of Church Property, $100. Total, $687.37.

Diocesan.— Diocesan Missions, $20, Salary of the Bishop, $6; Diocesan Fund, $7; Offering for Archdeaconry of Troy, $3. Total, $36.

General.— Domestic Missions, $11.50.
Total amount of Offerings, $734.87.

Property.

Church and lot (estimated worth), $3,000.
Parsonage and lot (estimated worth), $1,600.
Condition of property, good.
Amount of salary pledged Rector, $450.
Number of sittings in the Church, 200; all free.

ST PETER'S CHURCH, ELLENBURGH.

Rector. The Rev. Silas M. Rogers, A. M.
Wardens. William L. Sawyer, Giles H. Carew.

Vestrymen. George Higgins, Bryan Emerson, James Higgins, Heman Allen, Millard Emerson, Allen L. Sargent, John Hammond.

Parochial.

Baptisms (adults, 1, infants, 8), 9, Marriages, 9; Burials, 12; Communicants, died, 2, present number, 36; Sunday School, teachers, 4, pupils, 20.

Offerings.

Parochial.— Alms at Holy Communion, $7.41; Increase and Improvement of Church Property, $145. Total, $152.41.

Diocesan.—Diocesan Missions, $5; Salary of the Bishop, $2; Diocesan Fund, $1.50. Total, $8.50.

Total amount of Offerings, $160.91.

Property.

Church and lot (estimated worth), $2,000.
Condition of property, good.

ST. PAUL'S CHURCH, ELLENBURGH CENTRE.

Rector. The Rev. Silas M. Rogers, A. M.

Wardens. George W. Carpenter, Orson Haff.

Vestrymen. Lyman Carpenter, Alfred Harris, C. C. Carpenter, Thomas Harris, Ryland Holt, Stephen Goodspeed, A. S. Phelps.

Parochial.

Baptisms (adults, 2, infants, 4), 6; Marriages, 6; Burials, 4; Communicants, present number, 20.

Offerings.

Parochial. — Alms at Holy Communion, $4.91; Increase and Improvement of Church Property, $24.50. Total, $29.41.

Diocesan.— Diocesan Missions, $5; Salary of the Bishop, $2; Diocesan Fund, $1.50. Total, $8.50.

Total amount of Offerings, $37.91.

Property.

Church and lot (estimated worth), $2,000.
Condition of property, good.

ST. MATTHEW'S MISSION, LYON MOUNTAIN.

(See Report of the Diocesan Missionary, page 107.)

Columbia County.

CHRIST CHURCH, HUDSON.

Rector. The Rev. Sheldon Munson Griswold.

Wardens. R. B. Monell, W. B. Skinner.

Vestrymen. H. J. Baringer, J. P. Wheeler, M. D., J. M. Pearson, A. C. Stott, C. W. Bostwick, C. L. Crofts, F. T. Punderson, James Eisemann.

Parochial.

Families and parts of families, about, 250; Baptisms (adults, 8, infants, 31), 39; Confirmed, since last report, 33; Present number of confirmed persons, 470; Marriages, 14; Burials, 19; Communicants, last reported, 439, admitted, 30, received, 8, died, 5, removed, 6, present number recorded, 466, actual present number, between 253 and 300; Public Services (Sundays, 141, Holy days, 55, other days, 313), 509; Holy Communion (public, 101, private, 9), 110; Sunday School, teachers, 27, pupils, 300, Catechizing, number of children, whole school, number of times, every week.

Offerings.

Parochial.— Alms at Holy Communion, $113.20; Current expenses, including sala - ries, $3,808.37; Sunday School, $97.49; Increase and Improvement of Church Prop- erty, $1,518.23; Other parochial objects, Expenses lenten preachers, Parish paper and sundry items, $221.72. Total, $4,759.01.

Diocesan.— Diocesan Missions, $111.37; Salary of the Bishop, $66; Bible and Com- mon Prayer Book Society of Albany, $18; Fund for Aged and Infirm Clergymen. $17.25; Fund for Widows and Orphans of Clergymen, $10.49; Orphan House of the Holy Saviour, $31.92; The Child's Hospital (from Sunday School), $22.19; Society for Promoting Religion and Learning, $13.44; Child's Hospital Building Fund (from Sunday School), $5.40; Diocesan Missionary (from Sunday School), $51.10. Total. $347.16.

General. — Domestic Missions, $6.77; Foreign Missions, $15; Home Missions to Coloured Persons, $10.19; Missions to the Jews, $7; St. Mark's School, Salt Lake city (from Sunday School), $40. Total, $78.96.

Total amount of Offerings, $5,185.13.

Property.

Church and lot (estimated worth), $40,000.

Parsonage and lot (estimated worth), $7,000.

Other property, $3,000.

Condition of property, first class.

Indebtedness, bond and mortgage on Rectory, $1,500; note, $1,100; Floating, $500.

Amount of salary pledged Rector, $1,500.

Number of sittings in the Church, 500; number rented, 363.

Remarks.

In addition to the above, about $430 was sent in money and clothing to various places within and without the Diocese by different Guilds.

The Rector also conducted seven services at the House of Refuge for Women. During the year the Altar Society placed in the Choir and Sanctuary a mosaic pave- ment, with steps of Tennessee marble, and gave a very beautiful white festival super- frontal for the Altar, and new choir stalls — all of which are included in the item of increase of Parish property. Not included in the above report, however, are the fol- lowing gifts from different persons· An Altar rail of brass, a Litany desk, a marble Credence, and Altar hangings of the various colours.

There has also been erected a memorial Altar, which deserves especial notice and permanent record in this place, and of which the following is a description.

The Altar itself is of a warm tint of white marble from the Sacarezza quarries, and is composed of a few massive pieces. The mensa is a solid block, eight inches thick, and is supported along the face of the Altar by interlaced romanesque arches which are in turn borne by nine columns of variously coloured brcia marbles. The capi- tals of white marble are wrought diversely. The interlaced arches are decorated with vine-like foliations on their faces, each arch having its own vine form alter- nating a zig-zag or saw-tooth pattern with a circular one. The crowning feature of the work is to be seen above the re-table, with its *Ter Sanctus* marked in gold, in the two angels kneeling on either side with their wings raised to meet and touch above the Altar cross, forming thereby a reredos. The entire work was the gift to

Christ Church of Dr.'J. P. Wheeler, one of its Vestry, in loving memory of a sainted wife and a little son long since at rest in Paradise, viz., Alice Freeborne Wheeler, 1875, and George F. Wheeler, 1869.

ALL SAINTS' CHURCH, HUDSON.

Rector. The Rev. Elmer P. Miller, to March 1, 1891. The Rev. George G. Carter, from Oct. 1, 1891.

Wardens. William H. Cookson, Richard A. Aitkin.

Vestrymen. Alexander R. Benson, Robert Storms, Benjamin Thompson, George Palmer.

Parochial.

Families, 52; Baptisms (adults, 1, infants, 2), 3; Communicants, last reported, 91: Public Services (Sundays, 56, Holy days, 6, other days, 36), 98; Holy Communion, public, 13; Sunday School, teachers, 11, pupils, 65; Catechizing, number of children, all.

Offerings.

Parochial.— Current expenses, including salaries, $325; Sunday School, $61.57; Increase and Improvement of Church Property, $25. Total, $411.57.

Diocesan.— Diocesan Missions, $12; Salary of the Bishop, $6; Diocesan Fund, $9; Orphan House of the Holy Saviour, $5. Total, $32.

Total amount of Offerings, $443.57.

Property.

Church and lot (estimated worth), $6,000.

Condition of property, good.

Sittings in Church, all free.

Remarks.

As the present Rector took charge of the Parish only in October, after it had been vacant for seven months, this report is defective and incomplete. The statistics of last year are followed in certain points, where changes, if made at this time, would be misleading.

CHURCH OF ST. JOHN THE EVANGELIST, STOCKPORT.

Rector. The Rev. Eugene L. Toy.

Assistant. The Rev. William Benjamin Reynolds, Deacon.

Wardens. William H. Van de Carr, Frank C. Kittle.

Vestrymen. F. H. Stott, G. B. Reynolds, Joshua Reynolds, John Wild, Jacob Pultz, F. M. Snyder, F. W. Buss, L. J. Rossman.

Parochial.

Families, 116; Individuals (adults, 271, children, 126), 397; Baptisms, infants, 9; Present number of confirmed persons, about 130, Marriages, 2; Burials, 6: Communicants, last reported, 130, received, 1, died, 2, removed, 8, present number, 121, Public Services, four every Sunday except second Sunday in the month, then three; Holy days, all (celebration); other days, in Lent, five times a week; Holy Communion, public, every Sunday and Saint's day, Sunday School, teachers and officers, 21, pupils, 139; Catechizing, number of children, the two Sunday Schools, number of times, frequently; Parish School, teachers, 2, pupils, 34.

Offerings.

Parochial.— Alms at Holy Communion, $18.71; Current expenses, including salaries, $1,574.65; Sunday School, $51.84. Parish School, $4.64; Increase and Improvement of Church Property, $286.07. Total, $1,935.91.

Diocesan.— Diocesan Missions, $9.39; Salary of the Bishop, $26; Diocesan Fund, $27; Bible and Common Prayer Book Society of Albany, $2.70; Fund for Widows and Orphans of Clergymen, $2.46. Total, $67.55.

General.--Theological Education, $3.78; Domestic Missions, $24.22; Foreign Missions, $1.27; Home Missions to Coloured Persons, $1.23; The Church Society for Promoting Christianity among the Jews, $3.59; The Brothers of Nazareth, $2.38. Total, $36.47.

Total amount of Offerings, $2,089.93.

Property.

Church and lot and Churchyard (estimated worth), $15,000.
Parsonage and lot (estimated worth), $4,000.
Other property, School-house, $3,000; Organ, $1,500.
Condition of property, very good.
Amount of salary pledged Rector, $900.
Number of sittings in the Church, 280; Chapel, 150; all free.

Remarks.

The present Rector entered upon his duties May 15, 1891.

ST. PAUL'S CHURCH, KINDERHOOK.

Rector. The Rev. Isaac Peck.
Wardens. Henry S. Wynkoop, Edward P. Van Alstyne.
Vestrymen. Francis Silvester, T. F. Woodworth, W. H. Fish, Edgar Balis, Frank B. Van Alstyne, James M. Hawley, Andrew Ketterson, Tunis Devoe.

Parochial.

Families, 75; Individuals (adults, 176, children, 115), 291; Baptisms, infants, 12; Present number of confirmed persons, 143; Marriages, 2; Burials, 2; Communicants, last reported, 132, admitted, 1, received, 2, died, 2, removed, 3, present number, 130; Public Services (Sundays, 120, Holy days, 45, other days, 47), 212; Holy Communion (public, 46, private, 2), 48; Sunday School, teachers, 10, pupils, 76; Catechizing, number of children, whole school, number of times, weekly.

Offerings.

Parochial.— Alms at Holy Communion, $47.85; Current expenses, including salaries, $1,250; Sunday School, $68; Increase and Improvement of Church Property, $175. Total, $1,540.85.

Diocesan.— Diocesan Missions, $35.80; Salary of the Bishop, $36; Diocesan Fund, $21 ; Fund for Widows and Orphans of Clergymen, $17.08; Orphan House of the Holy Saviour (from Sunday School), $10.65; The Child's Hospital (from Sunday School), $10.65, Orphan House (from Woman's Auxiliary), $5.77; Express barrel to Orphanage, $1.65. Total, $138.60.

General.— Domestic Missions, $12.55; Foreign Missions, $24.70; Indian Missions, $2.85 ; General Missions (Sunday School Lenten Offerings), $17.32; Jewish Missions, $4.80. Total, $62.22.

Total amount of Offerings, $1,741.67.

Property.

Church and lot (estimated worth), $5,000.
Parsonage and lot (estimated worth), $3,000.
Condition of property, excellent.
Amount of salary pledged Rector, $700 and Rectory.
Number of sittings in the Church, 150; all free.

Remarks.

In addition to offerings in cash for Missions, the Woman's Auxiliary has sent a barrel of new clothing to the Cooperstown Orphanage, valued at $67.

To the memorials have been added a Bishop's chair of carved oak, and a desk for service book at font, also of carved oak.

TRINITY CHURCH, CLAVERACK.

Rector. The Rev. Elmer P. Miller, to March 1, 1891; the Rev. George G. Carter, from October 1, 1891.

Wardens. Robert Fulton Ludlow, Richard M. Ludlow.

Vestrymen. Cornelius Shaw, Frank P. Studley, James J. Studley, Arthur A. Rowley.

Parochial.

Families, 23; Present number of confirmed persons, 47; Marriages, 3; Communicants, last reported, 45, received, 2, removed, 4, present number, 43; Public Services (Sundays, 50, Holy days, 6, other days, 12), 68; Holy Communion (public 10, private, 1), 11; Sunday School, teachers, 4, pupils, 30; Catechizing, number of children, all.

Offerings.

Parochial.— Alms at Holy Communion, $14.72; Current expenses, including salaries, $385.31; Sunday School, $40. Total, $440.03.

Diocesan.— Diocesan Missions, $12; Salary of the Bishop, $6; Diocesan Fund, $6. Total, $24.

General.— Domestic Missions, $3.50; Foreign Missions, $3.50. Total, $7.

Total amount of Offerings, $471.03.

Number of sittings in the Church, 150; all free.

CHURCH OF OUR SAVIOUR, LEBANON SPRINGS.

Rector. The Rev. George B. Johnson.

Wardens. William Henry Babcock, Silas G. Owen.

Vestrymen. John G. Field, Francis Myers, J. Harry Cox, Albert B. Parsons, Charles E. Wackerhagen.

Parochial.

Families, 35; Individuals (adults, 69, children, 8), 77; Present number of confirmed persons, 46; Communicants, last reported, 45; Present number, 45; Public Services, Sundays, morning and evening, other days, general festivals; Holy Communion, weekly during the summer —as could procure a celebrant the rest of the year; Sunday School, teacher, 1, pupils, 8.

Offerings.

Parochial.— Alms at Holy Communion and current expenses, including salaries, $297.84.

Diocesan.— Diocesan Missions, $20; Salary of the Bishop, $6; Diocesan Fund, $9; Bible and Common Prayer Book Society of Albany, $1; Increase of the Episcopate Fund, $1; Fund for Aged and Infirm Clergymen, $5; Fund for Widows and Orphans of Clergymen, $2, Orphan House of the Holy Saviour, $3.75; The Child's Hospital. $2; Education of Young Men for the Ministry, $1. Total, $50.75.

General.— Domestic Missions, $5; Foreign Missions, $5. Total, $10.

Total amount of Offerings, $358.59.

Property.

Church and lot (estimated worth), $3,000.

Parsonage lot (estimated worth), $275.

21

Condition of property, good.

Amount of salary pledged Rector, $300.

Number of sittings in the Church, 150; all free.

Remarks.

Although this Parish has had no regularly appointed Rector or Missionary the past year, yet services have been maintained nearly the entire year, and the Holy Communion was celebrated weekly through July and August and frequently during the rest of the year: the Parish has also been enabled to maintain its usual offerings for Diocesan and general funds. As reported last year, nearly $900 was in the hands of the treasurer for a rectory building, and a lot purchased and paid for, adjoining the Church (and now inclosed in the Church grounds). Since that time the ladies have added over $200 to above amount within the Parish. There are also pledges in hand for several hundred dollars additional. The building committee are now considering plans, and we hope next year to report a rectory, and thereby add to the small stipend this little Parish can offer, the amount usually paid for the rental of a house.

ST. BARNABAS' CHURCH, STOTTVILLE.

Rector.   The Rev. Frederick Golden Rainey.

Wardens.   Francis Horatio Stott, John J. Plass.

Vestrymen.   C. H. Stott, Jr., Fred. A. Welch, R. H. Harder, Jr., W. H. Tanner, Fred. H. Palmer, James Shortell, David Cooper, Levi Plass.

Parochial.

Families, 106; Individuals (adults, 300, children, 200), 500; Baptisms, infants, 15; Confirmed, since last report, 12; Present number of confirmed persons, 186; Marriages, 11; Burials, 9; Communicants, last reported, 129, admitted, 12, received, 1, present number, 186, actually communicating, 120; Public Services (Sundays, 105, Holy days, 10, other days, 70), 185; Holy Communion (public, 28, private, 1), 29; Sunday School, teachers, 29, pupils, 210; Catechizing, number of children, 210, number of times, weekly.

Offerings.

Parochial. — Alms at Holy Communion, $108.20; Current expenses, including salaries, $1,471.81; Sunday School, $241 83; Increase and Improvement of Church Property, $4,813.50; Altar Society, $78.   Total, $6,713.34.

Diocesan.— Diocesan Missions, $25; Salary of the Bishop, $26; Diocesan Fund, $25; Bible and Common Prayer Book Society of Albany, $17; Fund for Aged and Infirm Clergymen, $10; The Child's Hospital, $40.56. Total, $143.56.

General.— Domestic Missions, $9.44; Foreign Missions, $20; Jewish Missions, $10. Total, $39.44.

Total amount of Offerings, $6,896.34.

Property.

Church and lot (estimated worth), $10,000.

Condition of property, very good.

Amount of salary pledged Rector, $1,200.

Number of sittings in the Church, 400; all free.

Remarks.

The Ladies' Parish Aid have devoted their energies principally to the repairing and furnishing the Church, having contributed during the past year the large sum of $1,829.39. A nobler and more zealous band of Christian women would be difficult to find.

ST. MARK'S CHURCH, PHILMONT.

Rector. The Rev. Arthur Lowndes.

Wardens. George Baker, Frank S. Harder.

Vestrymen. G. E. Clum, S. W. Richardson, G. W. Palmer, J. L. Gale, H. J. Krooss, R. L. Hermance.

Parochial.

Families, 49; Individuals (adults, 73, children, 24), 97; Baptisms (adults, 3, infants, 5), 8; Confirmed, since last report, 12; Present number of confirmed persons, 58; Marriages, 1; Communicants, present number, 47; Public Services (Sundays, 150, Holy days, 15, other days, 15), 180; Holy Communion, public, 38 ; Sunday School, teachers, 6, pupils, 39; Catechizing, number of children, the Sunday School, number of times, every Sunday.

Offerings.

Parochial.— Alms at Holy Communion, $21.98; Current expenses, including salaries, $606.34; Sunday School, $9.45; Increase and Improvement of Church Property, $76.59; Interest on debt, $180; Payment on debt, $251; The Altar Guild for Altar vessels, $150; St. Mark's Guild (exclusive of $85 applied to reduction of debt and $45 to current expenses), $68.96; Choir Guild, $43.59; Balances in hand in Guilds, $130. Total, $1,537.86.

Diocesan.— Diocesan Missions, $23; Salary of the Bishop, $6. Total, $29.

General.— Domestic Missions, $2.72; Foreign Missions, $2.71. Total, $5.43.

Total amount of Offerings, $1,572.29.

Property.

Church and lot (estimated worth), $10,000.

Condition of property, excellent.

Indebtedness, on Church (by bond and mortgage), $2,750.

Amount of salary pledged Rector, $650.

Number of sittings in the Church, 300; all free.

Remarks.

The present Rector entered upon his incumbency on St. Mark's Day, 1891. The number of celebrations refers only to those held during the present incumbency, as the Rector has no means of knowing the number held from November, 1890, to April 25, 1891. The other statistics are for the whole Diocesan year, November 1, 1890. to October 31, 1891.

ST. LUKE'S CHURCH, CLERMONT.

Rector. The Rev. M. E. Wilson.

Trustees. Robert Dibblee, Harold Wilson, G. Z. Foland, M. E. Wilson, W. C. Doane, H. G. Rivenburg.

Parochial.

Marriages, 1; Burials, 1; Communicants, removed, 1, present number, 18; Public Services (Sundays, 33, Holy days, 4), 37; Holy Communion, public, 10.

Offerings.

Parochial.— Current expenses, $20.25.

Diocesan.— Diocesan Missions, $10; Salary of the Bishop, $4; Diocesan Fund, $2. Total, $16.

Total amount of Offerings, $36.25.

ST. LUKE'S MISSION, CHATHAM.

Priest in charge. The Rev. Isaac Peck.

Parochial.

Families, 18; Individuals (adults, 40, children, 18), 58; Baptisms (adults, 1, infants, 4), 5; Present number of confirmed persons, 43; Marriages, 1; Burials, 1; Communicants, last reported, 25, present number, 25; Public Services (Sundays, 46, Holy days, 1), 47; Holy Communion, public, 12.

Offerings.

Parochial.— Current expenses, including salaries, $109.80.
Diocesan.— Diocesan Missions, $5; Salary of the Bishop, $2. Total, $7.
Total amount of Offerings, $116.80.
Amount of salary pledged Rector, his expenses.

ST. JOHN'S MISSION, COPAKE IRON WORKS.

See Report of the Diocesan Missionary, page 108.

Delaware County.

ST. PETER'S CHURCH, HOBART.

Rector. The Rev. Eugene Griggs.
Wardens. A. H. Grant, George Barlow.
Vestrymen. Robert McNaught, George Sturges, Charles S. Perkins, Alpheus Rollins, W. J. Calhoun, Orlando B. Foot.

Parochial.

Families, 55; Individuals (adults, 120, children, 35), 155; Baptisms (adults, 1, infants, 4), 5; Confirmed, since last report, 12; Present number of confirmed persons, 106; Burials, 2; Communicants, last reported, 170, admitted, 12, received, 3, died, 1, removed, 4, error of last report in excess, 74, present number, 65; Public Services (Sundays, 50, Holy days, 4, other days, 12), 66; Holy Communion, public, 2; Sunday School, teachers, 7, pupils, 44, Catechizing, number of times, 6.

Offerings.

Parochial.—Current expenses, including salaries, $575; Sunday School, $25; Increase and Improvement of Church Property, $150. Total, $750.
Diocesan.— Diocesan Missions, $18; Salary of the Bishop, $15; Diocesan Fund, $4.52; Bible and Common Prayer Book Society of Albany, $2.50; Fund for Widows and Orphans of Clergymen, $3; Orphan House of the Holy Saviour, $3.10; Expense of Convocation, $3.02; Clergy Reserve Fund, $3.86. Total, $53.
Total amount of Offerings, $803.

Property.

Church and lot (estimated worth), $5,000.
Parsonage and lot (estimated worth), $1,500.
Other property, $500.
Condition of property, good.
Amount of salary pledged Rector, $500.
Number of sittings in the Church, 350; all free.

These statistics date from June 21, last, when I took charge of St. Peter's Parish. I hold services once a month at Bloomville, but the outlook there is far from encouraging, two of the four communicants there having removed from the place. They have a building lot, however, and a few hundred dollars with which to begin a chapel.

ST. JOHN'S CHURCH, DELHI.

Rector. The Rev. F. B. Reazor.

Wardens. C. E. Hitt, R. G. Hughston.

Vestrymen. Alexander Shaw, G. M. Harby, G. A. Paine, J. W. Woodruff, Wm. C. Sheldon, Herbert Pitcher, John Kemp, S. E. Smith.

Parochial.

Families, 88; Individuals, 320; Baptisms (adults, 5, infants, 9), 14; Present number of confirmed persons, 214; Marriages, 3; Burials, 16; Churchings, 1; Communicants, last reported, 215, admitted, 3, received, 5, died, 7, removed, 9, present number, 207, actually communicating, 181; Public Services (Sundays, 179, other days, 562), 741; Holy Communion (public, 114, private, 18), 132; Sunday School, teachers, 7, pupils, 82; Catechizing, number of children, all, number of times, every Sunday.

Offerings.

Parochial.— Alms at Holy Communion, $72.88; Current expenses, including salaries, $1,777.08; Sunday School, $47.20; Altar Society, $41.48; St. Andrew's Brotherhood, $14.85; Parish Endowment Fund, $1,684.10. Total, $3,637.59.

Diocesan.— Diocesan Missions, $125; Bible and Common Prayer Book Society of Albany, $17.70; Fund for Aged and Infirm Clergymen, $15.50; Orphan House of the Holy Saviour, $118.55; The Child's Hospital, $20.12; Archdeaconry of the Susquehanna, $20.12; St. Margaret's Chapter, boxes Child's Hospital and Orphanage, $20.01. Total, $337.

General.— General Theological Seminary, $5.47; Domestic Missions, $12; Foreign Missions, $44.46; Home Missions to Coloured Persons, $46.48; Church Missions to Jews, $17.10; Boxes, Domestic Missions by Auxiliary, $78.15. Total, $203.66.

Total amount of Offerings, $4,178.25.

Property.

Church and lot (estimated worth), $10,000.

Parsonage and lot (estimated worth), $3,500.

Other property, Memorial Chapel, $25,000.

Condition of property, good.

Amount of salary pledged Rector, $1,200.

Number of sittings in the Church, 354; in Chapel, 125; total, 479; number free, 141.

Remarks.

Owing to the resignation of the present Rector this report does not extend beyond October 1, 1891.

During the past year Mr. Edwin B. Sheldon and Mrs. Fitzhugh Whitehouse have purchased a fine building site in connection with the Church lot upon which is building, at their expense, a handsome Rectory.

CHRIST CHURCH, WALTON.

Rector. The Rev. Scott B. Rathbun, until July 2, 1891.

Wardens. David H. Gay, George St. John.

Vestrymen. S. H. St. John, Francis Robinson, John S. Eells, George C. Seeley, Samuel H. Fancher, Julius W. St. John, Joseph Harby, Horace E. North.

Parochial.

Families, 106; Individuals (adults, 269, children, 81), 350; Baptisms, infants, 11; Confirmed, since last report, 6; Present number of confirmed persons, 164; Marriages, 3; Burials, 7; Communicants, last reported, 148, admitted, 1, received, 6, died, 3, removed, 7, present number, 145; Public Services, Sundays, twice, Holy days, once, Fridays, once, other days, once, during Lent, once; Holy Communion, public, say 20; Sundays School, teachers, 12, pupils, 70.

Offerings.

Parochial.— Current expenses, including salaries, $1,385.85; Sunday School, $69.81; Increase and Improvement of Church Property, $20.45; Individuals, Woman's Auxiliary, clothing for poor children in the Parish, $8; Knights of Temperance, $46.22; Archdeaconry of the Susquehanna, mileage of Clergy, October, 1891, $6; Hymnals for Choir, $8.25; Cassock for the Clergyman, $11.35. Total, $1,555.93.

Diocesan.— Diocesan Missions, $52.10; Salary of the Bishop, $20; Woman's Auxiliary for Orphan House of the Holy Saviour, box of clothing, $25; Woman's Auxiliary, membership fees, $1; Diocesan Missionary, $5; Lending Library, $5. Total, $108.10.

General.— Domestic Missions, $5; Foreign Missions (Japan, $10, Shanghai, $5), $15; Indian Missions, Pine Ridge Agency (Mr. Cook), $13; Home Missions to Coloured Persons in the South, $5; Woman Worker, Utah, $7; Brownville, Tenn., $12; other objects, $9. Total, $66.

Total amount of Offerings, $1,730.03.

Remarks.

The Parish Branch of Woman's Auxiliary, the Young Ladies' Parish Aid Society, and the Daisy Chain of King's Daughters are doing good work. The first named work for the Orphan House, Cooperstown, Foreign, Domestic and Indian Missions, and other objects in which they are aided by the Daisy Chain of King's Daughters. And the Young Ladies' Parish Aid Society reports the purchase of Hymnals for the choir, and a Cassock for the Clergyman, together $19.60.

ST. PAUL'S CHURCH, FRANKLIN.

Rector. The Rev. William H. Goodisson.

Wardens. Henry S. Edwards, Henry A. Mead.

Vestrymen. Eli P. Howe, Alfred Barnes, George Copeland, Jay W. Cook, Edgar Naragon.

Parochial.

Families, 50; Baptisms, infants, 2; Present number of confirmed persons, 93; Marriages, 1; Burials, 1; Communicants, last reported, 84, died, 3, removed, 3, present number, 78; Public Services (Sundays, 52, Holy days, 4, other days, 23), 79; Holy Communion (public, 6, private, 1), 7; Sunday School, teachers, 4, pupils, 38; Catechizing, number of times, 15.

Offerings.

Parochial.— Alms at Holy Communion, $15.

Diocesan.— Diocesan Missions, $20; Salary of the Bishop, $16; Diocesan Fund, $7.50, for the six months to date of Convention. Total, $43.50.

General.— Jewish Missions, 90 cents.

Total amount of Offerings, $59.40.

Property.

Church and lot (estimated worth), $6,500.
Parsonage and lot (estimated worth), $1,500.
Condition of property, good.
Amount of salary pledged Rector, $500.
Number of sittings in the Church, 400; all free.

Remarks.

I assumed the rectorship of St. Paul's, May 17. During these six months of service no small progress and encouragement have been manifested. By means of the Altar Society, the Woman's Diocesan League and the Parish Aid Society, money has been raised for Diocesan objects and the Church kept out of debt.

As there has been but six months of work, some of our best opportunities for raising money and contributing to other objects were lost, and what we desired to do we could not. But we hope to send up a more full and satisfactory report to the next annual Convention.

CHRIST CHURCH, DEPOSIT.

Rector. The Rev. Frederick S. Fisher.
Wardens. William H. Gregory, M. D., Titus M. Bixby.
Vestrymen. C. Onderdonk, H. B. Coggshall, Philip Munson, Charles Pinckney, James McDonald.

Parochial.

Families, 45; Individuals (adults, 103, children, 46), 149; Baptisms (adults, 5, infants, 14), 19; Present number of Confirmed persons, 86; Burials, 1; Communicants, last reported, 76, received, 3, removed, 4, present number, 75; Public Services, Sundays, all, Holy days, all, other days, Fridays; Sunday School, teachers, 5, pupils, 40; Catechizing, number of times, Sundays.

Offerings.

Parochial.— Alms at Holy Communion, $17.54; Current expenses, including salaries, $700; Sunday School, $36.29; for Sunday School, $13.78. Total, $767.61. Brass Altar Cross by the Sunday School; brass Vases and Altar Desk by Charles Pinney, Esq.; brass Receiving Basin by the Rector; also a Hymn Marker, set of green Hangings, white Dossal and Curtains.

Diocesan.— Diocesan Missions, $12.32; Salary of the Bishop, $6; Bible and Common Prayer Book Society of Albany, $3.10; Archdeaconry of the Susquehanna, $1.20. Total, $22.62.

General.— Domestic Missions, $8.06, by the Sunday School.
Total amount of Offerings, $798.29.

Property.

Church and lot (estimated worth), $1,000.
Condition of property, fair.
Amount of salary pledged Rector, $600.
Number of sittings in the Church, 150; all free.

Remarks.

A lot of land has been secured and is finely located for the much desired and much needed new Church Building.

GRACE CHAPEL, STAMFORD.

Rector. The Rev. Mr. De Learsy, four months, Rev. Mr. Duryea, four months, vacant four months, and vacant at present.

Warden. Albert Clist.

Clerk, Dr. E. W. Landon.

Treasurer, John Elliott.

Parochial.

Families, 12; Individuals (adults, 30, children 20), 50; Baptisms (adults, 2, infants, 5), 7; Confirmed, since last report, 2; Present number of confirmed persons, 25; Communicants, died, 1, removed, 5, present number, 21; Public Services (Sundays, 56, Holy days, 7, other days, 15), 78; Holy Communion (Public, 17, private, 2), 19; Sunday School, teachers, 4, pupils, 28.

Offerings.

Parochial.— Alms at Holy Communion, $42.38; Current expenses, including salaries, $309.89; Sunday School, $11.02; Increase and Improvement of Church Property, $14. Total, $377.29.

Diocesan.— Diocesan Missions, $20; Salary of the Bishop, $6; Diocesan Fund, $9; Fund for Aged and Infirm Clergymen, $6; Orphan House of the Holy Saviour, clothing, etc., valued at $35; The Child's Hospital, $10; Other Offerings for objects within the Diocese, $12. Total, $98.

General.— Domestic Missions, $6.50.

Total amount of Offerings, $481.79.

Property.

Church and lot (estimated worth), $2,500.

Condition of property, good.

Amount of salary pledged Rector, $450.

Number of sittings in the Church, 250; all free.

Remarks.

The Ladies' Guild raised $450 at their annual fair in August, which they placed in the Stamford National Bank, to be used for the benefit of the Chapel.

ST. PAUL'S MISSION, SIDNEY.

Rector. The Rev. Fred. Stirling Griffin.

Warden. E. Winsor.

Treasurer, D. K. Bowers.

Parochial.

Families, 34; Individuals (adults, 74, children, 29), 103; Baptisms, infants, 8; Present number of confirmed persons, 38; Marriages, 3; Communicants, last reported, 35, received, 6, removed, 3, present number, 30, Public Services (Sundays, 68, Holy days, 39, other days, 49), 156; Holy Communion (public, 50, private, 1), 51; Sunday School, teachers, 5, pupils, 26.

Offerings.

Parochial.— Alms at Holy Communion, $9.83; Current expenses, including salaries, $160; Sunday School, $5.31; Increase and Improvement of Church Property, $335. Total, $510.14.

Diocesan.— Diocesan Missions, $6; Salary of the Bishop, $3; Diocesan Fund, $3; Bible and Common Prayer Book Society of Albany, $2.25; Fund for Aged and Infirm Clergymen, $2; Orphan House of the Holy Saviour, $1.50; Society for Promoting

Religion and Learning, $10; Other Offerings for objects within the Diocese, $5.25. Total, $33.

Total amount of Offerings, $543.14.

Amount of salary pledged Rector, $100.

EMMANUEL MISSION, GRIFFIN'S CORNERS.

The Rev. Eugene Griggs, in charge.

Lay-reader. Thurston W. Challen.

Warden. Nathaniel Wright.

Clerk. William A. Ten Broeck.

Treasurer. Emerson W. Crosby.

Parochial.

Families, 7; Individuals (adults, 13, children, 11), 24; Confirmed, since last report, 1; Present number of confirmed persons, 5; Communicants, last reported, 5, admitted, 1, died, 1, present number, 5; Public Services (Sundays, 29, Holy days, 2, other days, 4), 35; Holy Communion, public, 3; Sunday School, teachers, 2, pupils, 20; Catechizing, number of children, 20, number of times, 15.

Offerings.

Parochial.— Alms at Holy Communion, $31.62; Current expenses, including salaries, $39.82; Increase and Improvement of Church Property, $109.86. Total, $181.30.

Diocesan.— Mission at Sidney, $7.25.

General.— Church Mission to Deaf Mutes, $7.89.

Total amount of Offerings, $196.44.

Property.

Church and lot (estimated worth), $2,500.

Condition of property, excellent.

Indebtedness, due to workmen, $150.

Number of sittings in the Church, 120; number free, 120.

Remarks.

During the history of the Mission to the end of this summer, it has been in charge of the Rev. F. B. Reazor, of Delhi, with Thurston W. Challen, as lay-reader. Mr. Challen has been there during the summer only. During the winter of 1890–91 the Rev. Lewis F. Wattson, of Kingston, held monthly services. The Church was finished during the past summer and consecrated on September 12, 1891.

Essex County.

CHURCH OF THE CROSS, TICONDEROGA.

Rector. The Rev. Henry T. Gregory.

Wardens. John C. Fenton, M. C. Drake.

Vestrymen. George B. Bascom, John H. Bryan, Carlton Cook, George B. Hanford, Robert Hanna, Lyman Malcolm, William C. Noyes.

Parochial.

Families, 72; Baptisms (adults, 1, infants, 5), 6; Present number of confirmed persons, 97; Marriages, 2; Burials, 8; Communicants, last reported, 77, admitted 2, received, 6, died, 3, present number, 82; Public Services (Sundays, 100, Holy days, 10, other days, 60), 170; Holy Communion, public, 30; Sunday School, teachers, 6, pupils, 75; Catechizing, number of children the school, number of times, frequently.

22

Offerings.

Parochial.— Alms at Holy Communion (early service), $3.56; Current expenses, including salaries, $616.57; Sunday School, $27.18; Increase and Improvement of Church Property, $709.81; Insurance, $86.25. Total, $1,443.37.

Diocesan.— Diocesan Missions, $30.44; Salary of the Bishop, $10; Diocesan Fund, $15; Fund for Aged and Infirm Clergymen, $4.50; Orphan House of the Holy Saviour, $12.53. Total, $72 47.

General.— General Missions, $24.70; Jewish Missions, $3.48. Total, $28.18.

Total amount of Offerings, $1,544.02.

Property.

Church and lot (estimated worth), $9,000.
Parsonage and lot (estimated worth), $2,500.
Condition of property, good.
Amount of salary pledged Rector, $500.
Number of sittings in the Church, 270; all free.

Remarks.

Included in the Offerings this year, though actually given last year and not recorded, is a beautiful Altar rail erected as a memorial.

The debt on the Rectory has been paid and a water motor has been attached to the organ.

ST. JOHN'S CHURCH, ESSEX.

Rector. The Rev. Wm. Norman Irish.

Wardens. Stephen D. Derby, Andrew J. Tucker.

Vestrymen. Anthony J. B. Ross, Robert Fortune, Moses A. Knowlton, Edward W. Richardson, Lyman R. Thomson, William M. Cowan, Ervin G. Lyon.

Parochial.

Families, 50; Individuals (adults, 74, children, 19), 93; Baptisms (adults, 1, infants, 5), 6; Present number of confirmed persons, 72; Marriages, 1, Burials, 4; Communicants, last reported, 85, received, 6, died, 3, removed, 16, present number, 72; Public Services (Sunday, 104, Holy days, 30, other days, 40), 174; Holy Communion, public, 30; Sunday School, teachers, 4, pupils, 18; Catechizing, every Sunday.

Offerings.

Parochial.— Alms at Holy Communion, $42.37, Current expenses, including salaries, $335; Sunday School, $45.40, Increase and Improvement of Church Property, $6.95. Total, $429.72.

Diocesan.— Diocesan Missions, $30; Salary of the Bishop, $16 ; Diocesan Fund, $9; Fund for Aged and Infirm Clergymen, $3 25; Fund for Widows and Orphans of Clergymen, $2.50; The Child's Hospital, $49.40. Total, $116 15.

General.— Domestic Missions, $5; Foreign Missions, $5; For the Jews, $1.54. Total, $11.54.

Total amount of Offerings, $551.41.

Property.

Church and lot (estimated worth), $3,000.
Parsonage and lot (estimated worth), $1,000.
Other property, $575.
Condition of property, good.
Amount of salary pledged Rector, $300.
Number of sittings in the Church, 200; all free

ST. PAUL'S CHURCH, KEESEVILLE.

Rector. The Rev. Jno. W. Gill.

Wardens. Asa Pierce Hammond, M. D., Francis Cassidy.

Vestrymen. Henry Dundas, Andrew T. Tallmadge, M. D., Frederick W. Cramphorn, Philip Harrison.

Parochial.

Families, 39; Individuals (adults, 74, children, 27), 101; Baptisms, infants, 14; Present number of confirmed persons, 52: Marriages, 10; Burials, 9; Communicants, last reported, 52, removed, 2, present number, 50; Public Services (Sundays, 98, Holy days, 25, other days, 50), 173; Holy Communion (public, 7, private, 3), 10; Sunday School, teachers, 5, pupils, 27; Catechizing, number of children, 27; number of times, weekly.

Offerings.

Parochial.— Current expenses, including salaries, $578; Sunday School, $15; Increase and Improvement of Church Property, $150. Total, $743.

Diocesan.— Diocesan Missions, $15; Salary of the Bishop, $10. Total, $25.

General.— Missions to the Jews, $2.10.

Total amount of Offerings. $770.10.

Property.

Church and lot. (estimated worth), $2,000.

Parsonage and lot (estimated worth), $1,250.

Condition of property, good.

Amount of salary pledged Rector, $400.

Number of sittings in the Church, 180; number free, 180.

Remarks.

During the summer months I have held services at Port Kent, in connection with St. Paul's. I now have taken charge of the services at St. James' Church, Ausable Forks, N. Y.

CHRIST CHURCH, PORT HENRY.

Rector. The Rev. Wm. R. Woodbridge.

Assistant. The Rev. Charles E. Cragg.

Wardens. Theodore Tromblee, Jr., Wm. M. J. Botham.

Vestrymen. Frank S. Atwell, George Hoy, Charles W. Woodford, Wallace T. Foote, Jr., Charles P. Parker.

Parochial.

Families, 41; Individuals (adults, 91, children, 105), 196; Baptisms, infants, 7; Confirmed, since last report, 3; Present number of confirmed persons, 72; Marriages, 4; Burials, 5; Communicants, last reported, 52, died, 1, removed, 2, present number, 44; Public Services (Sundays, 102, Holy days, 26, other days, 61), 189; Holy Communion, public, 16; Sunday School, teachers, 5, pupils, 59; Catechizing, number of children, 20, number of times, 5.

Offerings.

Parochial.— Current expenses, including salaries, $894.52; Sunday School, $14.20; Increase and Improvement of Church Property, $24.68. Total, $933.40.

Diocesan.— Diocesan Missions, $37.81; Salary of the Bishop, $10; Diocesan Fund, $12.48; Bible and Common Prayer Book Society of Albany, $8; Orphan House of the Holy Saviour, $19.51; The Child's Hospital, $7.18; Home for the Friendless, Plattsburgh, $4.32. Total, $99.30.

General.— Domestic Missions (of which from Sunday School, $2.35), $5.55; Foreign Missions (of which from Sunday School, $3.30), $6.40; Jewish Missions, $7.94. Total, $19.89.

Total amount of Offerings, $1,052.59.

Property.

Church and lot (estimated worth), $5,000.
Condition of property, good.
Amount of salary pledged Rector, $416.
Number of sittings in the Church, 180; all free.

Remarks.

There have also been held 11 services in Crown Point Mission, including 1 celebration of the Holy Communion.

EMMANUEL MISSION, MINEVILLE.

Missionary. The Rev. Wm. R. Woodbridge.

Parochial.

Families, 26; Individuals (adults, 51, children, 59), 110; Baptisms (adults 1, infants, 12), 13; Present number of confirmed persons, 35; Marriages, 1; Burials, 5; Communicants, last reported, 19, received, 1, died, 1, removed, 1, present number, 12; Public Services (Sundays, 48, Holy days, 4, other days, 20), 72; Holy Communion, public, 3; Sunday School, teachers, 3, pupils, 21; Catechizing, number of children, 10, number of times, 4.

Offerings.

Parochial.— Current expenses, $29.25.
Diocesan.— Diocesan Missions, $5; Orphan House of the Holy Saviour, $3.29. Total, $8.29.

Total amount of Offerings, $37.54.

Property.

Church and lot (estimated worth), $1,000.
Condition of property, good.
No salary pledged Rector.
Number of sittings in the Church, 125; all free.

ST. JAMES' CHURCH, AU SABLE FORKS.

The Rev. Jno. W. Gill, Priest in charge.
Warden. James Rogers.

Parochial.

Families, 21; Individuals (adults, 91, children, 35), 126; Baptisms, infants, 4; Present number of confirmed persons, 46; Burials, 4, Communicants, last reported, 76, died, 4, removed, 20; Public Services (Sundays, 19, other days, 1), 20; Holy Communion, public, 3; Sunday School, teachers, 5, pupils, 30; Catechizing, number of times, 8.

Offerings.

Parochial.— Alms at Holy Communion, $4; Current expenses, including salaries, $207. Total, $211.

Property.

Church and lot (estimated worth), $12,000.
Other property, $2,000.
Condition of property, good.
Amount of salary pledged Rector, $200.
Number of sittings in the Church, 200; number free, 200.

CHURCH OF THE REDEEMER, BLOOMINGDALE.

Rector. The Rev. Walter H. Larom.
Warden. E. G. Ricketson.

Parochial.

Families, 13; Individuals (adults, 28, children, 26), 54; Present number of confirmed persons, 14; Communicants, last reported, 12, removed. 1, present number, 11; Public Services (Sundays, 40, other days, 1), 41; Holy Communion, public, 6; Sunday School, teachers, 3, pupils, 36.

Offerings.

Parochial.—Current expenses, including salaries, $38.81; Sunday School, $6. Total, $44.81.

Property.

Church and lot (estimated worth), $2,500.
Condition of property, good.
Number of sittings in the Church, 150; number free, all.

ST. EUSTACE CHURCH, LAKE PLACID.

Rector. The Rev. Walter H. Larom.
Treasurer of Building Fund. Henry B. Auchincloss.

Parochial.

Families, 5; Individuals (adults, 9, children, 6), 15: Communicants, 6; Public Services, Sundays, 10.

Offerings.

Parochial.—Current expenses, including salaries, $240.54; Building Fund, $40. Total, $280.54.

Remarks.

This Mission was started one year ago at the earnest request of a few of the residents and a number of visitors, and services have been held for two summers in the parlor of the Stevens House by the courtesy of the Messrs. Stevens, and in the parlor of the Union Lake House by the courtesy of the proprietor, Mr. William Martin. The Bishop, in a circular asking for subscriptions to the building fund at this place, says: "The time seems to have come for the building of a Church at Lake Placid, and it is hoped that the services held during the summer have been the beginning of a permanent Church establishment." The Mission is called St. Eustace after St. Eustace, the patron Saint of hunters.

CHURCH OF THE GOOD SHEPHERD, ELIZABETHTOWN.

Rector. The Rev. Henry Mason Smyth.

Parochial.

Present number of confirmed persons, 4; Communicants, present number 4; Public Services, Sunday morning and evening through July, August and September; Holy Communion, public, weekly in July and August.

Offerings.

Parochial.— Current expenses, including salaries, $265.85; Increase and Improvement of Church Property, $7.50; Other parochial objects, repairing and furnishing the Rectory, $237.20. Total, $510.55.

Property.

Church and lot (estimated worth), $4,000.
Parsonage and lot (estimated worth), $2,000.
Condition of property, the very best.
Sittings in the Church all free.

Remarks.

The Church was opened for the summer on the first Sunday in July, and Services were continued until October. The attendance was excellent, and the interest manifested in the Services and general welfare of the Mission most gratifying, although confined largely to visitors at the hotels.

An appeal for the furnishing of the Rectory met with a cheerful response, and the project was carried to completion in a satisfactory manner, although not begun until the latter part of the season. A portion of a fund accumulated during the previous summer was utilized for the purpose. It would seem that the offerings might be depended upon hereafter to afford suitable support for a Missionary with a family during the summer months.

ST. ANDREW'S CHURCH, SCHROON LAKE.

(No report.)

Franklin County.

ST. MARK'S CHURCH, MALONE.

Rector. The Rev. Charles Temple.
Wardens. Hon. H. A. Taylor, Dr. R. J. Wilding.
Vestrymen. J. O. Ballard, Jas. E. Barry, Samuel Greene, A. C. Hadley, Hon. Albert Hobbs, M. S. Mallon, W. E. Smallman, David Webster.

Parochial.

Families, 122, Individuals (adults, 290, children, 75), 365; Baptisms, infants, 1; Marriages, 5; Burials, 8; Communicants, last reported, 234, died, 2, present number, 232; Public Services (Sundays, 95, other days, 80), 175; Holy Communion, public, 35, Sunday School, teachers, 10, pupils, 80; Catechizing, number of children, all, number of times, every Sunday.

Offerings.

Parochial. — Alms at Holy Communion, $19.93; Current expenses, including salaries, $1,615 50; Sunday School, $82.86; Increase and Improvement of Church Property, $250, Balance to close Church debt, $338; Sundries, $63.45. Total, $2,369.74.

Diocesan — Diocesan Missions, $97.82; Salary of the Bishop, $36; Diocesan Fund, $66; Fund for Aged and Infirm Clergymen, $5; Orphan House of the Holy Saviour, $25; Mission at Maple Grove, Box, $25. Total, $254.82.

General — Domestic Missions, $15, Foreign Missions, $15; Indian Missions, $5, Home Missions to Coloured Persons, $5; Mission to Jews, $7. Total, $47.

Total amount of Offerings, $2,671.56.

Property.

Church and lot (estimated worth), $20,000.

Parsonage and lot (estimated worth), $6,000.
Condition of property, excellent.
Amount of salary pledged Rector, $1,200.
Number of sittings in the Church, 270; all free.

ST. PETER'S CHURCH, BRUSHTON.

Rector. The Rev. R. Wyndham Brown.
Warden. W. S. Lawrence.
Vestrymen. W. Corbin Brush, J. C. Farnsworth, W. H. Smith, Robert Dunlap, G. W. Harris, James E. Brady, James Pickering.

Parochial.

Families, 18; Individuals (adults, 40, children, 16). 56; Baptisms, infants, 4; Present number of confirmed persons, 22; Marriages, 1; Burials, 1; Churchings, 1; Communicants, admitted, 1, removed, 1, present number, 13; Public Services (Sundays, 43; Holy days, 8, other days, 10), 61; Holy Communion, public, 14; Sunday School, teachers, 4, pupils, 20; Catechizing, number of children, 15, number of times, 12.

Offerings.

Parochial. — Alms at Holy Communion, $10; Current expenses, including salaries, $290.50; Sunday School, $7; Sunday offertories, $90; Ladies' Aid Society, on account of mortgage on the Rectory, $140.75. Total, $538.25.
Diocesan — Diocesan Missions, $10; Salary of the Bishop, $8; Diocesan Fund, $7.95. Total, $25.95.
Total amount of Offerings, $564.20.

Property.

Church and lot (estimated worth), $3,000.
Parsonage and lot (estimated worth), $1,500.
Condition of property, good.
Indebtedness, balance of mortgage due on Rectory, $90.
Amount of salary pledged Rector, $800.
Number of sittings in the Church, 150; all free.

ST. MARK'S CHURCH, WEST BANGOR.

Rector. The Rev. R. Wyndham Brown.
Warden. C. A. Crooks.

Parochial.

Families, 15; Individuals (adults, 28, children, 20), 48; Present number of confirmed persons, 20; Burials, 1; Communicants, last reported, 19, died, 1, present number, 18; Public Services (Sundays, 43, Holy days, 1), 44; Holy Communion, public, 2; Sunday School, teachers, 3, pupils, 20.

Offerings.

Parochial.—Alms at Holy Communion, $2; Current expenses, including salaries, $100; Sunday School, $6. Total, $108.
Diocesan.—Diocesan Missions, $5; Salary of the Bishop, $4; Diocesan Fund, $2.25. Total, $11.25.
Total amount of Offerings, $119.25.

Property

Church and lot (estimated worth), $1,500.
Condition of property, very good.

Amount of salary pledged Rector, $75.
Number of sittings in the Church, 200; all free.

ST. JAMES CHURCH, HOGANSBURGH.

Missionary. The Rev. Howard McDougall.
Warden. Alfred Fulton.
Treasurer. Gurdon Stoves Mills.

Parochial.

Families, 15; Individuals (adults, 40, children, 15), 55; Baptisms, infants, 1; Confirmed, since last report, 2; Present number of confirmed persons, 22; Communicants, last reported, 29, admitted, 2, removed, 1, present number, 20; Public Services, Sundays, 36; Sunday School, teachers, 2, pupils, 8; Catechizing, number of children 8, number of times, 10.

Offerings.

Parochial.—Current expenses, including salaries, $203.64; Sunday School, $1.50; Increase and Improvement of Church Property, $5.63.   Total, $210.77.
Diocesan.—Diocesan Missions, $25; Salary of the Bishop, $8; Diocesan Fund, $5. Total, $38.
Total amount of Offerings, $248.77.

Property.

Church and lot (estimated worth), $3,000.
Parsonage and lot (estimated worth), $800.
Condition of property : Parsonage out of repair, Church in good condition.
Amount of salary pledged Rector, $250.
Number of sittings in the Church, 144; all free.

ST. JOHN'S CHURCH IN THE WILDERNESS, PAUL SMITH'S.

Rector. The Rev. Walter H. Larom.
Warden. Dr. E. L. Trudeau.

Parochial.

Families, 4, Individuals (adults, 8, children, 12), 20, Communicants, last reported, 6, present number, 6, Public Services, Sundays, 12, Holy Communion, public, 3.

Offerings.

Parochial.—Current expenses, including salaries, $758 55; Other parochial objects, $20.   Total, $778.55.
Diocesan.—Included in offering of St. Luke, Saranac Lake.

Property.

Church and lot, estimated worth, $5,000.
Condition of property, excellent.
Number of sittings in the Church, 200, all free.

ST. LUKE THE BELOVED PHYSICIAN CHURCH, SARANAC LAKE

Rector. The Rev. Walter H. Larom
Lay Reader. William S. Hance.
Warden. E. L. Trudeau, M. D.

Parochial.

⅄milies, 68; Individuals (adults, 152, children, 50), 202; Baptisms (adults, 4, in-
s, 16), 20; Confirmed, since last report, 1; Present number of confirmed persons,
Marriages, 4; Burials, 10; Communicants,* last reported, 94, admitted, 2, reed. 3, died, 3, removed, 16, present number, 75; Public Services (Sundays, 76,
y days, 17, other days, 42), 135; Holy Communion (public, 40, private, 4), 44;
day School, teachers, 11, pupils, 80; Catechizing, number of times, 40.

Offerings.

ꞁrochial.—Current expenses, including salaries, at Church, $874.30; Sunday
ꞁol, $60; Increase and Improvement of Church Property, $125; At Hotel Amper-
l, $461.89; At Algonquin Hotel, $8.58; At Rustic Lodge, $8.50; Village Library,
); Organ Fund, $50; Rectory Fund, $980. Total, $3,138.27.
ꞁocesan.—Diocesan Missions, $20; Salary of the Bishop, $6; Clergy Relief Fund,
₀. Total, $28.50.
eneral.—Foreign Missions, $50.
ɔtal amount of Offerings, $3,216.77.

Property.

ꞁurch and lot (estimated worth), $4,000.
ꞁrsonage and lot (estimated worth), $3,300.
ondition of property, fair.
ꞁmber of sittings in the Church, 200; all free.

Remarks.

ꞁublic services have been held in the Drawing Room of the Hotel Ampersand
ꞁnty-six times during the year, by the courtesy of the managers, Messrs. Eaton
ꞁoung.

Fulton County.

ST. JOHN'S CHURCH, JOHNSTOWN.

ꞁector. The Rev. J. N. Marvin.
ꞁy Reader. Edward T. Carroll.
Vardens   Abiram S. Van Voast, Thomas E. Ricketts.
ꞁestrymen. Hon. J. M. Dudley, Hon. J. M. Carroll, J. Ricketts, Isaiah Yanney,
. Younglove, R. J. Evans, Charles Prindle, John Uhlinger.

Parochial.

ꞁamilies, 188, parts of families, 36. Baptisms (adults, 8, infants, 16), 24; Confirmed,
ꞁe last report, 19, Marriages, 7, Burials, 11. Communicants, last reported, 257,
ꞁitted, 19, received, 33, died, 5, removed, 1, present number, 303; Public Services
ꞁndays, 138, Holy days. 26, other days, 125), 289; Holy Communion (public, 64,
ꞁate, 7), 71; Sunday School, teachers, 23, pupils, 150; Catechizing, weekly.

Offerings.

ꞁrochial.--Alms at Holy Communion, $44.17; Current expenses, including salaries,
ꞁ78.74, Sunday School, $233 39. St. Andrew's Brotherhood, $83.80; Parish Room,

---

ꞁarge number of communicants reside in Saranac and communicate regularly, but they
ꞁot be counted as regular communicants of St. Luke's Church. They are invalids who re-
ꞁ sometimes for a few months, sometimes for several years, and number about 40.

$89; Guild of All Saints ($511.84, less $336.34, accounted for elsewhere), $175.50; Communion Set, $76.50 ; St. John's Register, $79.25.   Total, $3,060.35.

Diocesan.—Diocesan Missions, $75; Salary of the Bishop, $45; Diocesan Fund, $33; Bible and Common Prayer Book Society of Albany, $6.33; Orphan House of the Holy Saviour (special), $5; Archdeaconry of Albany, $2.54. Total, $166.87.

General.—Domestic Missions (special), $8; Foreign Missions, $16.70; Home Missions to Coloured Persons (special), $10; Mission to the Jews, $3.88; Church Building Fund, $3. Total, $41.58.

Total amount of Offerings, $3,268.80.

Property.

Church and lot (estimated worth), $20,000.

Parsonage and lot (estimated worth), $5,000.

Other property, $1,000.

Condition of property, good.

Number of sittings in the Church, 350.

CHRIST CHURCH, GLOVERSVILLE.

Rector. The Rev. C. P. A. Burnett.

Warden. James Eysaman.

Treasurer. James Hull.

Clerk. Emil Alexander.

Parochial.

Families, 63; Individuals (adults, 175, children, 83), 258; Baptisms (adults, 7, infants, 20), 27; Confirmed, since last report, 5; Present number of confirmed persons, 138; Marriages, 6; Burials, 9; Churchings, 9; Communicants, last reported, 100, admitted, 5, died, 1, removed, 3, present number, 101; Public Services (Sundays, 156, Holy days, 66, other days, 430), 652; Holy Communion (public, 176, private, 5), 181; Sunday School, teachers, 5, pupils, 58; Catechizing, number of children, all, number of times, 40.

Offerings.

Parochial.— Current expenses, including salaries, $698.76; Sunday School, $16.64; Increase and Improvement of Church Property, $22.50; Sunday School, Christmas Festival, $25.01. Total, $762.91.

Diocesan — Diocesan Missions, $25; Salary of the Bishop, $10; Diocesan Fund, $7.50, Fund for Aged and Infirm Clergymen, $1.81. Total, $44.31.

General — Mission to the Jews, $6.43.

Total amount of Offerings, $813.65.

Property.

Church and lot (estimated worth), $8,000.

Other property, church furniture, $1,000.

Condition of property, good.

Indebtedness, mortgage at five per cent, $2,000.

Number of sittings, in the Church, 330; all free.

Greene County.

ST. LUKE'S CHURCH, CATSKILL.

Rector. The Rev. Elmer P. Miller.

Wardens. Wm. L. Du Bois, Henry T. Jones.

Vestrymen. M. B. Mattice, Robert Selden, Theo. A. Cole, W. H. H. Schofield, C. E. Willard, C. H. Trowbridge, Oliver Bourke, W. S. C. Wiley.

Parochial.

Families, 245; Baptisms (adults, 3, infants, 27), 30; Confirmed since last report, 27; Present number of confirmed persons, 347; Marriages, 8; Burials, 28; Communicants, last reported, 322, admitted, 27, received, 15, died, 7, removed, 10, present number, 347; Actually communicating, 270; Public Services (Sundays, 135, Holy days, 16, other days, 137), 288; Holy Communion (public, 58, private, 14), 72; Sunday School, teachers, 21, pupils, 160; Catechizing, number of times, nearly every week.

Offerings.

Parochial. — Alms at Holy Communion, $130.37; Current expenses, including salaries, $1,837.75; Sunday School, $98.80 ; Increase and Improvement of Church Property, $230; Sunday School Library, $51.43; Sunday School Excursion, $162.80; Parish Reading Room, $60; Paid on Church debt, $86.03. Total, $2,657.18.

Diocesan. — Diocesan Missions, $150; Salary of the Bishop, $30; Diocesan Fund, $36; Bible 'and Common Prayer Book Society of Albany (from Holy Communion Alms), $10; Fund for Aged and Infirm Clergymen, $10; Fund for Widows and Orphans of Clergymen, $10; Orphan House of the Holy Saviour, $20.34; The Child's Hospital (by Sunday School), $45. Total, $311.34.

General.— Domestic Missions, $20; Foreign Missions, $20; Missions to the Jews $3.35; St. Mark's School, Utah (by Sunday School), $40. Total, $83.35.

Total amount of Offerings, $3,051.87.

Amount of salary pledged Rector, $1,200.

CHRIST CHURCH, COXSACKIE.

Rector. The Rev. L. H. Schubert, B. D.

Wardens. Dr. N. Clute, N. H. Vosburgh.

Vestrymen. Wm. K. Reed, J. E. Brown, H. J. Hahn, Wm. Farmer.

Parochial.

Families, 23; Individuals (adults, 39, children, 20), 59; Baptisms, infants, 4; Burials, 5, Communicants, last reported, 50, removed, 3, excommunicated, 18, present number, 29; Public Services (Sundays, 88, Holy days, 14, other days, 17), 119; Holy Communion, public, 30; Sunday School, teachers, 3, pupils, 15.

Offerings.

Parochial.—Current expenses, including salaries, $657.60.

Diocesan. — Diocesan Missions, $10; Salary of the Bishop, $12. Total, $22.

Total amount of Offerings, $679.60.

Property.

Amount of salary pledged Rector, $600.

Number of sittings in the Church, 200, all free.

Remarks.

The Rector resigned Nov. 1, 1891.

TRINITY CHURCH, ATHENS.

Rector. The Rev. James Wilkins Stewart.

Wardens. S. H. Nichols, H. C. Van Loon.

Vestrymen. G. S. Nichols, R. Clute, Wm. Cook, F. Beardsley, Frank Van Schaick, Frank Nichols, George Nedtwick, M. Davenport.

Parochial.

Families, 36; Individuals (adults, 107, children, 45), 152; Baptisms (adults, 2, infants, 1), 3; Marriages, 3; Burials, 7; Communicants, last reported, 75, died, 2, removed, 1, present number, 72; Public Services (Sundays, 96, Holy days, 15, other days, 34), 145; Holy Communion (public, 15, private, 1), 16; Sunday School, teachers, 7, pupils, 60; Catechizing, number of children, 50, number of times, 46.

Offerings.

Parochial. — Alms at Holy Communion, $18.02; Current expenses, including salaries, $900; Sunday School, $24.55. Total, $942.57.

Diocesan. — Diocesan Missions, $8; Salary of the Bishop, $20; Diocesan Fund, $21; Bible and Common Prayer Book Society of Albany, $3; Fund for Aged and Infirm Clergymen, $5; Orphan House of the Holy Saviour, $8.50; The Child's Hospital, $8.50. Total, $74.

General.— Domestic Missions, $6; Foreign Missions, $10.18; Jewish Missions, $3.06. Total, $19.24.

Total amount of Offerings, $1,035.81.

Property.

Church and lot (estimated worth), $5,000.
Parsonage and lot (estimated worth), $3,000.
Other property, Endowment Fund, $8,000.
Amount of salary pledged Rector, $700.
Number of sittings in the Church, 250; all free.

ST. PAUL'S CHURCH, OAK HILL.

Rector. The Rev. T A. Snyder.
Wardens. W. S. Cheritree, C. A. Hall.
Vestrymen. Byron Hall, Wm. Bell, Theodore L. Cheritree, Ambrose H. Flower, Charles E. Graham, Hyram Snyder. H. Irving Graham, Rome Adams.

Parochial.

Burials, 3; Communicants, last reported, 39, died, 3, present number, 36; Public Services (Sundays, 46, Holy days, 7, other days, 10), 63; Holy Communion (public, 32, private, 1), 33.

Offerings.

Parochial. — Alms at Holy Communion, $8.20; Current expenses, including salaries, $263.45 Total, $271.65.

Diocesan — Diocesan Missions, $4; Diocesan Fund, $3.75 Total, $7.75.

General. — Domestic and Foreign Missions, $3, Jewish Missions, $1.43. Total, $4.43.

Total amount of Offerings, $283.83.

Amount of salary pledged Rector, $125 and rent of Rectory.

CHRIST CHURCH, GREENVILLE.

Rector. The Rev. T. A. Snyder.
Wardens. E. N. Palmer, W. S. Rundle.
Vestrymen. Byron Waldron, W. S. Vanderbilt, L. D. Stewart, R. R. Palmer, James Ponsonby, E. A Galation, E. L Wood, T. J. Rundle.

Parochial.

Baptisms, infants, 1; Marriages, 1; Burials, 3; Communicants, last reported, 41, died, 2, present number, 39: Public Services (Sundays, 50, Holy days, 14, other days, 10), 74; Holy Communion, public, 38.

Offerings.

Parochial.— Alms at Holy Communion, $20.04; Current expenses, including salaries, $143.78; Increase and Improvement of Church Property, about $900. Total, $1,063.82.

Diocesan.— Diocesan Missions, $4; Diocesan Fund, $3.75; Orphan House of the Holy Saviour, $2.50. Total, $10.25.

General.—Domestic and Foreign Missions, $4.50; Jewish Missions, $1.80. Total, $6.30.

Total amount of Offerings, $1,080.37.

Property.

Indebtedness, on repairing Rectory, $400. On Rector's salary, $38.10.
Amount of salary pledged Rector, $125, and use of Rectory.

TRINITY CHURCH, ASHLAND.

Wardens. Darius B. Prout, Willis Chatfield.

Vestrymen. Addison Steele, George S. Smith, Henry P. Smith, Merritt McLean, Homer Holcomb, M. D.

Parochial.

Families, 16; Burials, 1; Communicants, removed, 5, present number, 35; Public Services, Sundays, 40; Holy Communion, public, 5.

Offerings.

Parochial.—Current expenses, including salaries, $175.
Diocesan.—Salary of the Bishop, $4.
Total amount of Offerings, $179.

Property.

Church and lot (estimated worth), $3,000.
Parsonage and lot (estimated worth), $1,000.
Number of sittings in the Church, 150; all free.

Remarks.

The Parish was served by Mr. Eugene Griggs as Lay Reader, from Nov. 1 until his ordination, April 26, and after that date he remained in charge until the 1st of June. Services were held on eleven Sundays in the Summer by the Rev. Watson B. Hall of Racine, Wis.

CALVARY CHURCH, CAIRO.

Rector. The Rev. Chauncey Vibbard.
Lay Reader. Webster W. Jennings.
Wardens. Lucius Byington, Levi K. Byington.
Vestrymen. Edwin E. Darby, John C. Lennon, George H. Noble, M. D., Selden H. Hine, John L. Van Hoesen, Alfred Bennett, John K. Palen, Nelson Carman.

Parochial.

Families, 39; Individuals (adults, 75, children, 35), 110; Present number of confirmed persons, 59; Marriages, 1; Burials, 4; Communicants, last reported, 52, removed, 1, present number, 51; Public Services (Sundays, 104, Holy days, 16, other days, 52), 172; Holy Communion, public, 55; Sunday School, teachers, 5, pupils, 33.

Offerings.

Parochial.—Alms at Holy Communion, $23.84; Current expenses, including salaries, $378.31; Sunday School, $15.80; Increase and Improvement of Church Property, $157.77. Total, $575.72.

Diocesan.—Salary of the Bishop, $6; Diocesan Fund, $7.50; Fund for Aged and Infirm Clergymen, $6. Total, $19.50

General.—Domestic Missions, $1.

Total amount of Offerings, $596.22.

Property.

Church and lot (estimated worth), $4,000.

Parsonage and lot (estimated worth), $1,000.

Condition of property, good.

Amount of salary pledged Rector, $250.

Number of sittings in the Church, 200; number free, all.

GLORIA DEI CHURCH, PALENVILLE.

Rector   The Rev. Wm. Chas. Grubbe.

Warden and Treasurer.   Charles H. Chubb, M. D.

Parochial.

Families, 10; Individuals (adults, 38, children, 10), 48; Baptisms (adults, 1, infants, 2), 3; Present number of confirmed persons, 28; Burials, 4; Communicants, last reported, 30, removed, 2, present number, 28; Public Services (Sundays, 100, Holy days, 17, other days, 83), 200; Holy Communion (public, 66, private, 2), 68.

Offerings.

Parochial — Current expenses, including salaries, $412.63; Increase and Improvement of Church Property, $63.89. Total, $476.52.

Diocesan.— Diocesan Missions, $12 82; Salary of the Bishop, $8; Diocesan Fund, $9. Total, $29.82.

General.—Domestic Missions, $5; Foreign Missions, $7.75; General Missions (by Sunday School), $2, Jewish Missions, $2.16. Total, $16.91.

Total amount of Offerings, $523 25

Property

Church and lot (estimated worth), $6,000.

Parsonage and lot (estimated worth), $1,500.

Condition of property, good

Amount of salary pledged Rector, $300.

Number of sittings in the Church, 150; all free.

Hamilton County.

CHURCH OF THE TRANSFIGURATION, BLUE MOUNTAIN LAKE.

Rector   The Rev Alford A Butler

Warden.   Thomas A Gummey

Parochial

Families, 3; Individuals (adults, 5, children, 19), 24; Baptisms, infants, 2; Present number of confirmed persons, 3. Communicants, removed, 1, present number, 3;

Public Services (Sundays, 20, Holy days, 2), 22; Holy Communion, public, 14; Sunday School, teachers 1, pupils, 11.

Offerings.

Parochial.— Alms at Holy Communion, $11.40; Current expenses, including salaries, $230.84. Total, $242.24.

Property.

Church and lot (estimated worth), $5,000.
Condition of property, good.
Number of sittings in the Church, 150; all free.

Remarks.

This Church is a Mission, and used so far during summer seasons of about thirteen weeks only, and the services on Sundays and Holy days are well attended by the native population and summer residents. The Rector has been in Europe this summer owing to ill-health, and his place has been supplied by three Clergymen, viz.: Rev. George C. Foley, Rector of Trinity Church, Williamsport, Penn., for July; Rev. Sheldon M. Griswold of Christ Church, Hudson, N. Y., for August, and Rev. Horatio O. Ladd, Deacon from New York city, for September. A very successful Mother's meeting has been started with much encouragement from the native population. Two hundred and seventy dollars or thereabouts are in the hands of a lady, a friend of the Mission, toward the building of a Rectory, which it is hoped will be erected next year, and when completed we look forward to permanent services.

THOMAS A. GUMMEY,
Warden.

Herkimer County.

TRINITY CHURCH, FAIRFIELD.

Rector. The Rev. Edward C. Hoskins.
Wardens. Reuben Neeley, C. W. Nichols, M. D.
Vestrymen. Jairus Mather, John P. Todd, A. C. Wilson, Frank L. Warne, D. D. Warne.

Parochial.

Families, 10; Individuals (adults, 39, children, 7), 46; Baptisms (adults, 8, infants, 5), 13; Confirmed, since last report, 6; Present number of confirmed persons, 17; Burials, 1; Communicants, last reported, 8, admitted, 7, died, 1, present number, 18; Public Services, Sundays, 37; Holy Communion, public, 9.

Offerings.

Parochial. Alms at Holy Communion, $14.60; Current expenses, including salaries, $77.59. Total, $92.19.

Property.

Church and lot (estimated worth), $1,000.
Parsonage and lot (estimated worth), $500.
Condition of property, fair.
Amount of salary pledged Rector, $2 per Sunday.
Number of sittings in the Church, 200; all free.

Remarks.

The Principal of the Fairfield Seminary, Prof. D. D. Warne, is in sympathy with the Church, and has been elected and serves as a Vestryman. The students attend the services quite frequently, and some regularly. Quite a number of the students assist in the singing.

EMMANUEL CHURCH, LITTLE FALLS.

Rector. The Rev. Ernest Mariett.
Assistant. The Rev. C. M. Conant, from December 1, 1891.
Wardens. R. S. Whitman, E. B. Waite.
Vestrymen. Geo. W. Searles, Albert Storey, Hadley Jones, Hon A. M. Mills, Judge Geo. A. Hardin, Harry Houghton, Chas. Bailey.

Parochial.

Families, about 140; Individuals, 125; Baptisms (adults, 2, infants, 15), 17; Confirmed, since last report, 10; present number of confirmed persons, about 165; Marriages, 5; Burials, 9; Communicants, last reported, 159, admitted, 10, received, 8, died, 1, removed, 15, present number, 156; Public Services (Sundays, 144, Holy days, 20. other days, 300), 464; daily morning prayers; Holy Communion (public, 87, private, 2), 89; Sunday School, teachers, 12, pupils, 100; Catechizing, number of children, whole school, number of times, weekly.

Offerings.

Parochial.— Alms at Holy Communion, $37.96; Current expenses, including salaries, $1,690; Sunday School, $131.43; Increase and Improvement of Church Property, $346.15; Other parochial objects, $116; For mission work in parish and Dolgeville, $800. Total, $3,121.54.

Diocesan.— Diocesan Missions, $47.26; Salary of the Bishop, $40; Diocesan Fund, $30; Bible and Common Prayer Book Society of Albany, $5.07; Fund for Aged and Infirm Clergymen, $2.25; Fund for Widows and Orphans of Clergymen, $4; Orphan House of the Holy Saviour, $7.50; The Child's Hospital, $8; Society for Promoting Religion and Learning, $2.02; Other offerings for objects within the Diocese, $65 Total, $211.10.

. General. — Domestic Missions, $4; Foreign Missions, $3.22; Home Missions to Coloured Persons, $6.20; Other objects exterior to the Diocese, $87.25; Jewish Missions, $5.06. Total, $105.73.

Total amount of Offerings, $3,438.27.

Property.

Church and lot (estimated worth), $20,000.
Parsonage and lot (estimated worth), $7,000.
Other property (Chapel, $2,000, house and lot, $4,000), $6,000.
Condition of property, good.
Amount of salary pledged Rector, $1,000.
Number of sittings in the Church, 500; number rented, all.

Remarks.

A Mission was begun by the Rector at Dolgeville, a town of fifteen hundred inhabitants, eight miles distant from Little Falls, in May last. Service and Sunday School have been maintained without interruption. There are many signs of growth and interest. A congregation of about one hundred has been gathered and in the spring it is the intention to build a Church.

CHRIST CHURCH, HERKIMER.

Rector. The Rev. Charles Carroll Edmunds, Jr.
Wardens. Geo. W. Pine, Robert Earl.
Vestrymen. T. W. Grosvenor, G. H. Kelsey, J. D Henderson, H. G. Munger, C. W. Palmer, W. C. Prescott, H. P. Witherstine.

Parochial.

Baptisms (adults, 10, infants, 24), 34; Confirmed, since last report, 24; present number of confirmed persons, about 190; Marriages, 12, Burials, 17; Communicants, last reported, 166, admitted, 29, received, 3, died, 8, removed, 12, present number 178; Public Services (Sundays, 170, Holy days, 48, other days, 135), 353; Holy Communion (public, 89, private, 7), 96; Sunday School, teachers, 11, pupils, 90; Catechizing, number of children, all, number of times, every week; Sewing School, teachers, 8, pupils, 60.

Offerings.

Parochial.—Current expenses, including salaries, $1,807.99; Sunday School, $106.29; Sewing School, $9.51; Increase and Improvement of Church Property, $2,748.55; Poor, $39.86; Altar Fund, $23.84; Piano, $125. Total, $4,860.04.

Diocesan. — Diocesan Missions, $60; Salary of the Bishop, $31; Diocesan Fund, $30; Bible and Common Prayer Book Society of Albany, $7; Fund for Aged and Infirm Clergymen, $7.65; Fund for Widows and Orphans of Clergymen, $7.65; Salary Diocesan Missionary, $10; Clergy Reserve Fund, $7. Total, $160.80.

General.— Domestic Missions, $16.81, Foreign Missions, $16.81; American Church Building Fund, $6; China Mission, $37.32; Jewish Mission, $5. Total, $81.94.

Total amount of Offerings, $5,102.28.

Property.

Church and lot (estimated worth), $25,000.
Parsonage and lot (estimated worth), $4,500.
Other property, Parish building, $4,000.
Indebtedness; mortgage on rectory and parish building, $5,000.
Amount of salary pledged Rector, $1,000.
Number of sittings in the Church, 250; all free.

Remarks.

There is every prospect of the debt on the Rectory and Parish Building being paid off during the next few months.

ST. AUGUSTINE'S CHURCH, ILION.

Rector. The Rev. Wm. Mason Cook.
Wardens. F. C. Shepard, R. L. Winegar.
Vestrymen. Geo. P. Rix, T. J. Behan, Geo. H. Barlow, Samuel Jess, Geo. H Dyett, Elmer E. Jenne, Alfred Williamson, N. A. Hanchett.

Parochial.

Families, 106; Individuals not thus included, 30; Baptisms (adults, 6, infants, 12), 18; Confirmed, since last report, 13; Present number of confirmed persons, 172; Marriages, 7; Burials, 14; Churchings, 1; Communicants, last reported, 122, admitted, 12, received, 3, died, 2, removed, 1, present number, 134; Public Services (Sundays, 129, Holy days, 29, other days, 91), 249; Holy Communion (public, 70, private, 5), 75; Sunday School, teachers, 9, pupils, 84; Catechizing, number of children, school, number of times, nearly every Sunday; Industrial School, teachers, 5, pupils, 73.

Offerings.

Parochial.— Current expenses, including salaries, $1,072.63; Sunday School (Christmas Fund), $40; Increase and Improvement of Church Property, $154.29; Other parochial objects, Payment on mortgage, $100; Sunday School, for various objects, $44.06; Offerings by Altar Guild, $41.87; Gift for the funded debt, $10. Total, $1,462.76.

Diocesan.— Diocesan Missions, $30; Salary of the Bishop, $12; Diocesan Fund, $18; Fund for Widows and Orphans of Clergymen, $15.62; Orphan House of the Holy Saviour, $10; The Child's Hospital, $6.15. Total, $91.77.

General.—Domestic Missions, $9.13; Foreign Missions ($11.94 by the Sunday School), $21.07; Church Society for Conversion of the Jews, $2.49. Total, $32.69.

Total amount of Offerings, $1,587.22.

24

Property.

Church and lot (estimated worth), $6,000.
Parsonage and lot (estimated worth), $3,000.
Condition of property, good.
Indebtedness, mortgage, $2,250.
Amount of salary pledged Rector, $600.
Number of sittings in the Church, 232; all free.

Remarks.

At Easter the Parish received the gift of a handsome Altar and Credence from Christ Church, Hudson, together with a set of red hangings.

The parochial branch of the Junior Auxiliary sent a box to the Orphanage at Cooperstown, valued at about $15, besides contributing the items given above of $10 to the same institution, and $6.15 to the Child's Hospital.

GRACE CHURCH, MOHAWK.

Rector. The Rev. Alfred Taylor until Oct. 1, 1891: since that date the Parish has been vacant.

Wardens. Alex. W. Haslehurst, Edgar C. Elwood.

Vestrymen. H. D. Alexander, J. D. Fitch, M. D., F. L. Van Dusen, Chas. Spencer, E. H. Doolittle, James B. Rafter, John Brown.

Parochial.

Families, about 50; Individuals (adults, 115, children, 45),160; Baptisms (adults, 1, infants, 6), 7; Confirmed, since last report, 7; Present number of confirmed persons recorded, 61; Marriages, 1; Burials, 5; Communicants, last reported, 51.

Offerings.

Parochial.— Alms at Holy Communion, $24.31; Current expenses, including salaries, $579.45; Increase and Improvement of Church Property, $51; Other parochial objects, $255.27. Total, $910.03.

Diocesan.— Diocesan Missions, $15; Salary of the Bishop, $6. Total, $21.

General.— Domestic Missions, $3.59; Mission for the Jews, $1. Total, $4.59.

Total amount of Offerings, $935.62.

Property.

Church and lot (estimated worth), $3,500.
Condition of property, good.
Amount of salary pledged Rector, $450.
Number of sittings in Church, 150; all free.

CHURCH OF THE MEMORIAL, MIDDLEVILLE.

Rector. The Rev. Edward C. Hoskins.

Warden. John Molineux.

Treasurer. C. W. Hamlin, M. D.

Secretary. George W. Griswold.

Parochial.

Families, 34; Individuals (adults, 95, children, 32), 127; Baptisms (adults, 11, infants, 8), 19, Confirmed, since last report, 8; Present number of confirmed persons, 65; Burials, 6; Communicants, last reported, 53, admitted, 9, removed, 2, present number, 59; Public Services (Sundays, 100, Holy days, 17, other days, 24), 141; Holy Communion (public, 47, private, 2), 49; Sunday School, teachers 6, pupils, 23.

Offerings.

Parochial.—Alms at Holy Communion, $55.12; Current expenses, including salaries, $276.44; Sunday School, $14.81; Increase and Improvement of Church Property, $350; Incidentals, $43.80. Total, $740.17.

Diocesan.— Diocesan Missions, $20; Salary of the Bishop, $6. Total, $26.

Total amount of Offerings, $766.17.

Property.

Church and lot (estimated worth), $10,000.

Parsonage and lot (estimated worth), $2,000.

Condition of property, good.

Number of sittings in the Church, 200; all free.

CULLEN.

See Report of the Diocesan Missionary, page 108.

POLAND.

See Report of the Diocesan Missionary, page 111.

Montgomery County.

ST. ANN'S CHURCH, AMSTERDAM.

Rector. The Rev. David Sprague.

Wardens. W. Max Reid, Jno. J. Hand.

Vestrymen. Cyrus B. Chase, Thos. Mansfield, Chas. S. Nisbet, William Ryland, LeGrand S. Strang, Jas. T. Sugden, Hicks B. Waldron, Jno. K. Warwick.

Parochial.

Families, nearly 400; Individuals, nearly 1,100; Baptisms (adults, 9, infants, 22), 31; Confirmed, since last report, 48; Present number of confirmed persons, over 400; Marriages, 6; Burials, 21; Communicants, last reported, 270, admitted, 40, received, 28, died, 4, removed, 6, present number, 328; Public Services, exclusive of Holy Communion (Sundays, 100, Holy days, 55, other days, 40), 195; Holy Communion (public, 50, private, 3), 53; Sunday School, teachers, 18, pupils, 230; Catechizing, number of children, whole school, number of times, 10.

Offerings.

Parochial.— Alms at Holy Communion, $44.62; Current expenses, including salaries, $3,488.33; Sunday School, $130; Increase and Improvement of Church Property, $876.75; Children's Home, $6.08; City Hospital, $22.50; Library for S. S., $140. Total, $4,708.28.

Diocesan.— Diocesan Missions, $28.33; Salary of the Bishop, $16; Diocesan Fund, $15; Bible and Common Prayer Book Society of Albany, $5.90; Orphan House of the Holy Saviour, $5.34. Total, $70.57.

General.—General Missions, $70.

Total amount of Offerings, $4,848.85.

Property.

Church and lot (estimated worth), $50,000.

Other property, three building lots, $1,500.

Condition of property, admirable.

Indebtedness, about $12,500.
Amount of salary pledged Rector, $1,350.
Number of sittings in the Church, 600; number rented, 500; number free, 100.

ZION CHURCH, FONDA.

Missionary. The Rev. C. C. Edmunds.
Wardens. Richard H. Cushney, Henry T. E. Brower.
Vestrymen. Henry B. Cushney, Giles H. F. Van Horne, Edward B. Cushney, Richard N. Casler, William Fonda, John S. Van Horne, Robert Agune, Henry Siver.

Parochial.

Families, 27; Individuals (adults, 79, children, 13), 92; Baptisms, infants, 1; Present number of confirmed persons, 51; Burials, 1; Communicants, last reported, 38, omitted, 3, admitted, 3, received, 5, present number, 46; Public Services (Sundays, 52, Holy days, 3, other days, 6), 61; Holy Communion, public, 12.

Offerings.

Parochial.—Alms at Holy Communion, $26.14; Current expenses, including salaries; $415.70. Total, $441.84.

Diocesan.— Diocesan Missions, $10; Salary of the Bishop, $12; Diocesan Fund, $9, Bible and Common Prayer Book Society of Albany, $3. Total, $34.

Total amount of Offerings, $475.84.

Property.

Church and lot (estimated worth), $8,000.
Condition of property, good.
Amount of salary pledged Missionary, $300.
Number of sittings in the Church, 150; all free.

CHURCH OF THE HOLY CROSS, FORT PLAIN.

The Rev. Clarence Ernest Ball, Priest in charge.
Lay Reader. Theo. S. Waters.
Warden. Douglas Ayres, M. D.
Clerk. Theo. S. Waters.

Parochial.

Families and parts of families, 60; Individuals (adults, 118, children, 45), 163; Baptisms, infants, 5; Marriages, 1; Burials, 1; Communicants, last reported, 69, received, 1.

Offerings.

Parochial.— Current expenses, including salaries, estimated, $220.
Indebtedness, $1,600.
Amount of salary pledged Rector, $500
Number of sittings in the Church, 250, all free

Remarks.

The Rev. J. N. Marvin, former Missionary, left the work after the first Sunday in February, 1891, and the present Missionary took up the work the second Sunday in August. In the interval only lay service was held, and that only for a small portion of the time. Since taking up his work the present Missionary has been unable to revise accurately the figures so as to represent the true state of the Church at the present date, and so has taken in part the figures as given in the report a year ago.

CHURCH OF THE GOOD SHEPHERD, CANAJOHARIE.

The Rev. Clarence Ernest Ball, Priest in charge.
Lay Reader. Theo. S. Waters.
Warden. Arza Canfield.
Clerk. Randolph Spraker.

Parochial.

Families and parts of families, 50; Individuals (adults, 91, children, 46), 137; Baptisms, infants, 1; Marriages, 1; Communicants, 64.

Offerings.

Parochial.— Current expenses, including salaries, $266; Sunday School, $6.80; Parish School, $5. Total, $277.80.

Diocesan.— Diocesan Missions, $10; Salary of the Bishop, $2; Diocesan Fund, $5.25; Ophan House of the Holy Saviour (boxes), estimated, $15. Total, $32.25.

Total amount of Offerings, $309.55.*

Amount of salary pledged Rector, $350.
Number of sittings in the Church, 200; all free.

Remarks.

See note under report of the Church of the Holy Cross, Fort Plain.

Otsego County.

ZION CHURCH, MORRIS.

Rector. The Rev. R. H. Gesner, B. D.
Wardens. Isaac Mansfield, Nelson B. Pearsall.
Vestrymen. J. Rutherford Morris, G. Clayton Peck, George A. Yates, 2nd, John Smith, C. J. Smith, George A. Sanderson.
Treasurer. T. O. Duroe.
Clerk. A. E. Yates.

Parochial.

Families, 135; Individuals (adults, 425, children, 125), 550; Baptisms (adults, 4, infants, 7), 11; Present number of confirmed persons, 207; Marriages, 5; Burials, 7; Communicants, last reported, 208, received, 11, died, 4, removed, 8, present number, 207; Public Services (Sundays, 140, Holy days, 30, other days, 47), 217; Holy Communion (public, 17, private, 2), 19; Sunday School, teachers, 14, pupils, 124; Catechizing, number of times, bi-monthly.

Offerings.

Parochial.— Alms at Holy Communion, $36.52; Current expenses, including salaries, $1,112.17; Sunday School, $16.53; New Rectory fund, $129. Total, $1,294.22.

Diocesan.— Diocesan Missions, $60; Salary of the Bishop, $24; Diocesan Fund, $24; Orphan House of the Holy Saviour, $76.50; Archdeaconry of the Susquehanna, $4; Rectory Fund, Lebanon Springs, $13.60. Total, $202.10.

General.— Domestic Missions, $8.39; Foreign Missions, $16.10. Total, $24.49.

Total amount of Offerings, $1,520.81.

Property.

Church and lot (estimated worth), $20,000.
Parsonage and lot (estimated worth), $3,000.

---

* The amount reported, $266 for current expenses, does not include the Offerings while the services were held by Lay Reader. The Offerings were taken by him in lieu of compensation—amount not reported to the Treasurer, nor can it be estimated.

Condition of property, Church in fine condition; Rectory needs rebuilding.

Amount of salary pledged Rector, $1,000.

Number of sittings in Zion Church, 500; New Lisbon Chapel, 150; Morris Memorial Chapel, 75; all sittings free.

Remarks.

The present Rector entered upon his duties on March 8, 1891. He has started the fund for a new Rectory, of which the Parish stands greatly in need. The St. Agnes' Guild for young girls, organized in July, has enlisted the services of many willing hands and is doing efficient work.

The Ladies' Aid Society and the Young Ladies' Guild sent valuable boxes to the Child's Hospital at Albany, and the Orphanage at Cooperstown.

The Rector's thanks are due the Rev. D. F. MacDonald, D. D., for kindly giving one service during the month at the Morris Memorial Chapel.

The Chapel at New Lisbon is doing good work, owing to the faithful laymen who show personal interest in its welfare.

ST. LUKE'S CHURCH, RICHFIELD.

See Report of the Diocesan Missionary, page 109.

ST. MATTHEW'S CHURCH, UNADILLA.

Rector. The Rev. Robert N. Parke, D. D.

Wardens. Lloyd L. Woodruff, Bennitt W. Morse.

Vestrymen. Andrew J. Lewis, Milo B. Gregory, Clark I. Hayes, Paris G. Clark, M. D., William H. Heslop, J. Fred. Sands, S. Horace Chapin, Samuel S. North.

Parochial.

Families, 98; Individuals (adults, 218, children, 64), 282; Baptisms (adults, 1, infants, 3), 4; Present number of confirmed persons, 144; Marriages, 3; Burials, 9; Communicants, received, 2, died, 1, removed, 5, present number, 139; Public Services (Sundays, 124, Holy days, 18, other days, 55), 197; Holy Communion (public, 33, private, 2), 35; Sunday School, teachers, 6, pupils, 38; Catechizing, number of times, 14.

Offerings.

Parochial.— Alms at Holy Communion, $45, Current expenses, including salaries, $1,215.79; Increase and Improvement of Church Property, $12.07. Total, $1,272.86.

Diocesan.— Diocesan Missions, $50; Salary of the Bishop, $16; Diocesan Fund, $24; Bible and Common Prayer Book Society of Albany, $3 96; Fund for Aged and Infirm Clergymen, $9 45; Fund for Widows and Orphans of Clergymen, $2; Orphan House of the Holy Saviour, $3; The Child's Hospital, $2. Total, $110.41.

General.— Domestic Missions, $11.22, Foreign Missions, $3.16; Society for Promoting Christianity among Jews, $7.20. Total, $21.58.

Total amount of Offerings, $1,404.85

Property.

Church and lot (estimated worth), $6,500.

Parsonage and lot (estimated worth), $4,500.

Other property, $600.

Condition of property, good.

Amount of salary pledged Rector, $800.

Number of sittings in the Church, 330.

Remarks.

The children of the Sunday School are instructed and catechized by the Rector every Sunday, as a leading part of the exercises of the school.

The falling off from 162 to 139 communicants finds its explanation in the fact that a thorough revision of the recorded list had to be made before the real number of living and resident communicants could be reported. The result is that a number of names were dropped of persons who had been some time dead or removed.

CHRIST CHURCH, COOPERSTOWN.

Rector. The Rev. Charles S. Olmsted.

Wardens. Wilson T. Bassett, M. D., Horace M. Hooker.

Vestrymen. G. Pomeroy Keese, W. H. Merchant, Lee B. Cruttenden, R. Heber White, S. E. Crittenden, Henry C. Bowers, Charles J. Tuttle, Wm. D. Boden.

Parochial.

Families, 145; Individuals, 545; Baptisms (adults, 4, infants, 23), 27; Confirmed, since last report, 12; Present number of confirmed persons, 297; Marriages, 4; Burials, 9; Communicants actually communicating, 231; Public Services (Sundays, 147, Holy days, 33, other days, 136), 316; Holy Communion (public, 72, private, 5), 77; Sunday School, teachers, 14, pupils, 140; Catechizing, number of children, school, number of times, about 35.

Offerings.

Parochial.— Alms at Holy Communion, $208.60; Current expenses, including salaries, $1,979.87; Sunday School, $126.57; Increase and Improvement of Church Property, $15,000; Woman's Lenten Work, $374; Mite Society, $44.50; Choir, $185. Total, $17,918.48.

Diocesan.— Diocesan Missions, $170.88; Salary of the Bishop, $80; Diocesan Fund, $45; Bible and Common Prayer Book Society of Albany, $5; Fund for Aged and Infirm Clergymen, $6.28; Fund for Widows and Orphans of Clergymen, $6.28; Orphan House of the Holy Saviour, $59.60; Archdeaconry of the Susquehanna, $27: Diocesan Missionary, $30; Missionary at Otego, $21.76; Church at Sidney, $42.15; Theological Education, $60.62. Total, $554.57.

General.— Domestic Missions, $32.26; Foreign Missions, $6.54; Indian Missions, $12.50; Home Missions to Coloured Persons, $12.50; American Church Building Fund, $10; Sunday School, for Scholarship Salt Lake City, $40. Total, $113.80.

Total amount of Offerings, $18,586.85.

Remarks.

The Carter Memorial Chancel, consecrated on the Festival of St. Simon and Jude, is a marvel of beauty. It was built by the four children of the late Mrs. Jane Russell Carter in her memory, and contains the altar given by her to the parish seven years ago.

CHRIST CHURCH, GILBERTSVILLE.

Rector. The Rev. David F. MacDonald.

Wardens. Ira L. Ward, Chas. V. Daniels.

Vestrymen. Wm. F. Ward, Thomas Swingard, E. R. Clinton, J. R. Woodlands, J. G. McCulloch, R. M. Stenson, B. F. Marvin, Wm. R. Kinne.

Parochial.

Families, 41; Individuals (adults, 89, children, 28), 117; Present number of confirmed persons, 58; Marriages, 3; Burials, 6, Communicants, received, 5, died, 3, removed, 11, present number, 67; Public Services (Sundays, 104, Holy days, 15, other days [Lenten] 20), 139; Holy Communion, public, 22; Sunday School, teachers, 6, pupils, 25; Catechizing, number of times, 4.

Offerings.

Parochial.— Alms at Holy Communion, $30; Current expenses, including salaries $445; Sunday School, $7; Increase and Improvement of Church Property, $48; Other parochial objects, $5.50; Guild Charities, $15. Total, $550.50.

Diocesan.— Diocesan Missions, $25; Salary of the Bishop, $6; Orphan House of the Holy Saviour, $2; The Child's Hospital (Box), $27; Orphanage of Holy Saviour (Box), $20; Special Collection for Missions, given to Dr. Stewart, Diocesan Missionary, $3.60; Expenses of Convention, $3. Total, $86.60.

General.— Domestic Missions, $5; Foreign Missions, $5; Indian Missions, $2.16; Missions for Jews, $1. Total, $13.16.

Total amount of Offerings, $650.26.

Property.

Church and lot (estimated worth), $3,000.
Parsonage and lot (estimated worth), $1,800.
Other property, $2,500.
Condition of property, good.
Amount of salary pledged Rector, $475.
Number of sittings in the Church 200; all free.

Remarks.

The number of services at the three points, Gilbertsville, Maple Grove and Morris Chapel comes to two hundred. It is but a little over a year since I have had charge of Gilbertsville and Maple Grove. My predecessor, the Rev. Mr. Gates, had almost all the infants baptized and the youth of the two places confirmed. This must account for our lack of baptisms and confirmations. This locality is remarkable for its scarcity of children. We have a Branch of Woman's Auxiliary, consisting of twelve most active members; also a "Ladies Guild" operating for benefit of the Parish and its poor; also a "Junior Branch of Woman's Auxiliary," working for a "Lady Missionary," in China. This branch of children has pledged $15 for the above purpose, and expects to do even more. Our "Branch of Woman's Auxiliary," besides a number of charities and two boxes, has pledged $36 for "Enrolment Fund" to be presented at next General Convention. Besides these, we have a small society called "King's Daughters," consisting of ten little girls.

Morris Chapel is one of the Missionary points in charge of the Rector in Morris parish. The Rev. Mr. Gesner has so many points to serve as Missionary that he cannot give as many services to the chapel as he would like. Therefore, with his express permission, I give the people there services every fourth Sunday of the month.

EMMANUEL CHURCH, OTEGO.

Rector. The Rev. William G. W. Lewis.

Wardens. Charles Blake, George Sherman, Jr.

Vestrymen. Wm. Birdsall, James H. Cossart, M. D., F. D. Shumway, C. B. Woodruff, Wm. Parker, John H. Martin, M. D., Geo. H. Goodman, E. Wyman.

Parochial.

Families, 26; Individuals (adults, 61, children, 15), 76, Baptisms (adults, 2, infants, 2), 4; Present number of confirmed persons, 39, Marriages, 2; Burials, 1; Communicants, last reported, 30, received, 8, died, 1, present number, 37; Public Services (Sundays, 56, Holy days, 4, other days, 16), 76; Holy Communion (public, 16, private, 1), 17; Sunday School teachers 3, pupils, 15, Catechizing, number of times, 4.

Offerings.

Parochial.— Current expenses, including salaries, $475; Sunday School, $5; Increase and Improvement of Church Property, $200. Total, $680.

Diocesan.— Diocesan Missions, $5; Salary of the Bishop, $6; Bible and Common Prayer Book Society of Albany, $1; Fund for Aged and Infirm Clergymen, $1; Fund for Widows and Orphans of Clergymen, $3.78; Orphan House of the Holy Saviour, Box valued at $10; Archdeaconry, $2.25. Total, $29.03.

General.— Domestic Missions, $3.47; Foreign Missions, $1.35. Total, $4.82.

Total amount of Offerings, $713.85.

Property.

Church and lot (estimated worth), $5,000.

Condition of property, good.

Amount of salary pledged Rector, $400.

Number of sittings in the Church 250; all free.

ST. TIMOTHY'S CHURCH, WESTFORD.

See Remarks, Report, Grace Church, Cherry Valley.

GRACE CHURCH, CHERRY VALLEY.

Rector. The Rev. James E. Hall.

Wardens. A. B. Cox, J. M. Phelon.

Vestrymen. Geo. Neal, J. A. Fonda, F. P. Harriott, C. Brooks, C. D. Wolrad, Alvin Brown, A. J. Thompson, W. C. Roseboom.

Parochial.

Families, 60; Individuals (adults, 136, children, 65), 201; Baptisms, infants, 4; Present number of confirmed persons, 113; Marriages, 4; Burials, 5; Communicants, last reported, 112, died, 3, present number, 109; Public Services (Sundays, 100, Holy days, 60, other days, 100), 260; Holy Communion (public, 52, private, 6), 58; Sunday School, teachers, 5, pupils, 40; Catechizing, number of children, all, number of times, weekly.

Offerings.

Parochial.— Current expenses, including salaries, $1,047.02; Sunday School, $9.48. Total, $1,056.50.

Diocesan.— Diocesan Missions, $75; Salary of the Bishop, $25; Diocesan Fund, $24; Bible and Common Prayer Book Society of Albany, $11.43; Fund for Aged and Infirm Clergymen, $4; Fund for Widows and Orphans of Clergymen, $5; Orphan House of the Holy Saviour, $13.19; The Child's Hospital, $9.71; Orphan House debt, $20.66; Orphan House, special "in memory of Little Mary," $10; Archdeaconry of the Susquehanna, $6.63. Total, $204.62.

General.— Foreign Missions, $25; Indian Missions, $25; Nashotah, $10; Mrs. Buford's Hospital, $5.20; Basket makers, $10; Enrolment Fund, $20. Total, $95.20.

Total amount of Offerings, $1,356.82.

Property.

Church and lot, and parsonage and lot, insured for $5,000.

Other property, Fund, $6,600.

Condition of property, good.

Amount of salary pledged Rector, $800.

Number of sittings in the Church, 250; all free

Remarks.

At St. Timothy's, Westford, I officiated six times; and celebrated the Holy Communion twice.

ST. JOHN'S CHURCH, RICHFIELD SPRINGS.

Rector. The Rev. Robert Granger.

Wardens. N. D. Jewell, James A. Storer.

Vestrymen. Henry Greenman, W. B. Ward, M. D. Jewell, W. B. Crain, M. D., De Witt W. Harrington, I. D. Peckham, Frank Getman.

Parochial.

Families, 126; Individuals (adults, 268, children, 92), 360; Baptisms (adults, 4, infants, 11), 15; Present number of confirmed persons, 228; Marriages, 2; Burials, 10; Communicants, admitted, 4, died, 2, removed, 10, present number, 213; Public Services (Sundays, 100, Holy days, 16, other days, 58), 174; Holy Communion (public, 20, private, 2), 22; Sunday School, teachers, 9, pupils, 85; Catechizing, number of children, all, number of times, 13.

Offerings.

Parochial. — Current expenses, including salaries, $1,872.92; Sunday School, $105.14; Increase and Improvement of Church Property, $494.87; The Poor, $56.51; Village Bureau of Charities, $20.60; Ladies' Sewing Society, $454.80; Ladies' Guild, $32.06; Gift to Rector, $200. Total, $3,236.90.

Diocesan.— Diocesan Missions, $50; Salary of the Bishop, $16; Diocesan Fund, $12; Orphan House of the Holy Saviour, $150. Total, $228.

General.— Domestic Missions, $36.78; Foreign Missions, $9.69; Two barrels of goods to Church Home for Coloured People, Lawrenceville, Va., $35; One box of goods to Ontonagon, North Michigan, $23. Total, $104.47.

Total amount of Offerings, $3,569.37.

Property.

Church and lot (estimated worth), $13,000.

Parsonage and lot (estimated worth), $6,000.

Other property, Chapel, $2,700.

Condition of property, perfect.

Amount of salary pledged Rector, $900 and Rectory.

Number of sittings in the Church, 400; all free.

ST. JOHN'S CHURCH, PORTLANDVILLE.

See Report of the Diocesan Missionary, page 112.

CHRIST CHURCH, WEST BURLINGTON.

Rector. The Rev. Frederick Stirling Griffin.

Warden. Stephen I. Pope.

Vestrymen. B. A. Bailey, Caleb Clark, Lewis Spencer, Elias C. Mather, William Holdredge, John Priest, Stephen Olive, S. W. Gardner.

Parochial.

Families, 30; Individuals (adults, 75, children, 25), 100; Baptisms (adults, 3, infants, 2), 5; Present number of confirmed persons, 37; Burials, 3; Communicants, died, 1, present number, 34; Public Services (Sundays, 36, Holy days, 2, other days, 7), 45; Holy Communion (public, 18, private, 2), 20; Sunday School, teachers, 4, pupils, 30.

Offerings.

Diocesan.— Diocesan Missions, $5.50; Salary of the Bishop, $6; Bible and Common Prayer Book Society of Albany, $1.50; Orphan House of the Holy Saviour, $4.40; The Child's Hospital, sewing; Other offerings for objects within the Diocese, $1. Total, $18.40.

Property.

Church and lot (estimated worth), $4,000.
Parsonage and lot (estimated worth), $750.
Condition of property, excellent.
Amount of salary pledged Rector, $200.
Number of sittings in the Church, 150; all free.

Remarks.

At Edmeston services have been held on Sunday evenings every two weeks for the past year.

ST. PAUL'S CHURCH, EAST SPRINGFIELD.

Rector. The Rev. John Prout.
Wardens. James H. Cooke, Leslie Pell-Clarke.
Vestrymen. S. A. Young, John Scollard, G. Hyde Clarke, Daniel Gilchrist, R. L. Walrath, E. A. Keene.

Parochial.

Baptisms, infants, 1; Marriages, 1; Burials, 2; Communicants, last reported, 39, died, 1, present number, 38; Public Services (Sundays, 83, Holy days, 32), 115; Holy Communion, public, 43; Sunday School, teachers, 5, pupils, 30.

Offerings.

Total amount of Offerings, $1,152.19.

Property.

Church and lot (estimated worth), $4,350.
Parsonage and lot (estimated worth), $3,050.
Condition of property, good.
Amount of salary pledged Rector, $500.
Number of sittings in the Church, 120; all free.

Remarks.

The Parish has received from Mr. G. Hyde Clarke the gift of an excellent organ, which is placed as a memorial of the late Mr. George Clarke, and the Vestry has erected for an organ chamber a Transept to the Chancel, the total addition to the value of the Church property being $650.

During the summer Services were held by the Rector at Hyde Hall — four miles from this village — on alternate Sunday afternoons.

ST. JAMES' CHURCH, ONEONTA.

Rector. The Rev. Ernest A. Hartmann.
Lay Reader. Robert Perine.
Wardens. John Cope, John D. Rohde.
Vestrymen. Robert M. Townsend, Richard Downes, A. W. Carr, R. D. Briggs, S. S. Matteson, James Stewart, Hobert B. Somers, James O. Beach.

Parochial.

Families, 151; Individuals (adults, 290, children, 140), 430; Baptisms (adults, 4, infants, 20), 24; Confirmed, since last report, 6; Present number of confirmed persons, 235; Marriages, 4; Burials, 6; Communicants, last reported, 221, admitted. 6, received, 14, removed, 15, present number, 226; Public Services (Sundays, 129, Holy days, 20, other days, 59), 208; Holy Communion (public, 50, private, 1), 51; Sunday School, teachers, 11, pupils, 98; Catechizing, number of times, frequently.

Offerings.

Parochial,— Alms at Holy Communion, $12.51; Current expenses, including salaries, $1,054.88; Sunday School, $76.60; Increase and Improvement of Church Property, $51.44; Other parochial objects, Paid on note, $500; Village Benevolent Society, $8.33. Total, $1,703.76.

Diocesan.— Diocesan Missions, $40; Salary of the Bishop, $10; Diocesan Fund, $24; Orphan House of the Holy Saviour, $5; A Church Building, $23; Diocesan Missionary, $11. Total, $113.

General.— Domestic Missions, $14; Foreign Missions, $5; Mission to the Jews, $3.50. Total, $22.50.

Total amount of Offerings, $1,839.26.

Property.

Church and lot (estimated worth), $12,000.
Condition of property, good, insured.
Number of sittings in the Church, 225; all free.

ST. MARY'S (MISSION) CHURCH, SPRINGFIELD CENTRE.

Priest. The Rev. John Prout.
Warden of the Mission. Leslie Pell-Clarke
Clerk. S. W. Vandeveer.
Treasurer. A. A. Van Horne.

Parochial.

Baptisms (adults, 3, infants, 1), 4; Burials, 1; Communicants, 22, present number, 22; Public Services (Sundays, 34, Holy days, 4), 38; Holy Communion, 11; Sunday School, teachers, 5, pupils, 30.

Offerings.

Total amount of Offerings, $146.43.

Property.

Church and lot (estimated worth), $8,000.
Condition of property, good.
Number of sittings in the Church, 120; all free.

Remarks.

There has been given to the "Trustees of the Diocese of Albany" a lease of a house in Springfield Centre, for the term of ten years, to be used by St. Mary's Mission as a Parish House. It is the gift of Mrs. Anna Pell, and is proving a valuable help in the work of the Mission.

ST. STEPHEN'S CHURCH, MAPLE GROVE.

The Rev. David F. MacDonald in charge.
Wardens. Henry A. Starr, C. B. Hull.
Vestrymen. W. J. Aylsworth, L. W. Davis, Frank C. Hull.

Parochial.

Families, 9; Individuals (adults, 15, children, 6), 21; Present number of confirmed persons, 22; Communicants, last reported, 24, removed, 2, present number, 22; Public Services (Sundays, 53, Holy days, 3), 56; Holy Communion (public, 10, private, 1), 11; Sunday School, teachers, 3, pupils, 20.

Offerings.

Parochial.—Alms at Holy Communion, $5.80; Sunday School, $7.62; Increase and Improvement of Church Property, $81.35. Total, $94.78.

Diocesan.—Salary of the Bishop, $2; Diocesan Fund, $2. Total, $4.

Total amount of Offerings, $98.78.

Property.

Church and lot (estimated worth), $1,000.

Condition of property, good.

Indebtedness, $250.

Number of sittings in the Church, 150; all free.

Remarks.

Maple Grove has a very beautiful Chapel built of wood, and furnished in Churchly style. Lately Mr. Washburn of Washington, D. C., has presented it with a very handsome Marble Font; and the Rev. Mr. Cook of New York city gave it a very nice Communion Service. All last winter I went to Maple Grove, a distance of five miles from Gilbertsville, to hold the services ; but being unable to have a conveyance of my own, I go there now twice a month, the *first* and *third* Sundays. The Sundays on which I am absent the Rev. Daniel Washburn gives the people one service. Thus, really, Maple Grove is not without a service throughout the year. As may be seen from the financial report above the Chapel is in debt to the Building Association, to the amount of $250. This small debt this weak but worthy band of Church people is slowly and with great difficulty struggling to wipe out. It would be a most excellent charity should some noble, Christian heart lift this oppressive burden from off this little community, either entirely or partially. The partial payments made towards this debt are made by monthly subscriptions from five to fifty cents. I pray God, that by another year, some kind heart will favorably listen to this weak appeal.

CHURCH OF THE HOLY SPIRIT, SCHENEVUS.

Harry Elmer Gilchrist, Catechist and Missionary in charge.

Warden. John H. Fowler.

This Mission is organized at present under a Guild with John H. Fowler, Warden

Parochial.

Families, 28; Individuals (adults, 57, children, 20), 77; Present number of confirmed persons, 28; Communicants, last reported, 21, admitted, 5, removed, 1, present number, 25; Public Services, Sundays, 33; Holy Communion, public, 3.

Offerings.

Parochial.—Alms at Holy Communion, $4.38 ; Current expenses, including salaries, $151.91; Increase and Improvement of Church Property, $11.46. Total, $167.75.

Diocesan.— Bible and Common Prayer Book Society of Albany, $1.71.

Total amount of Offerings, $169.46.

Property.

Church and lot (estimated worth), $3,000.
Condition of property, good.
Amount of salary pledged Missionary, $350, or $30 per month.
Number of sittings in the Church, 100; all free.

Remarks.

This record dates from Whitsunday, May 17, 1891, the time I assumed charge, to October 1, 1891.

MISSION OF ST. SIMON AND ST. JUDE, WORCESTER.

See Report of the Diocesan Missionary, page 108.

Rensselaer County.

ST. PAUL'S CHURCH, TROY.

Rector. The Rev. Edgar A. Enos.
Wardens. Joseph M. Warren, Joseph J. Tillinghast.
Vestrymen. Stephen W. Barker, James H. Caldwell, John Clatworthy, Derick Lane, William W. Morrill, Charles E. Patterson, John I. Thompson.

Parochial.

Baptisms (adults, 10, infants, 38), 48; Confirmed, since last report, 31; **Marriages, 7**; Burials, 15; Communicants, last reported, 613, admitted, 31, received, 26, died, 7, removed, 9, present number, 654; Public Services (Sundays, 192, Holy days, 138, other days, 560), 890; Holy Communion (public, 173, private, 18), 191; Sunday School, teachers, 18, pupils, 250; Catechizing, every Sunday; Parish School, teachers, 1, pupils, 12.

Offerings.

Parochial.— Alms at Holy Communion, not elsewhere reported, $484.60 ; Current expenses, including salaries, $11,477.04; Sunday School, $155.50; Parish School, $734.60; Friends of the Sisterhood, $2,647.48; Altar Guild, $547; Memorial Window, $2,000, Vestments and ornaments, $500. Total, $18,546.22.

Diocesan.— Diocesan Missions (Allotment, $750, St. Luke's, Troy, $100, Salary of Diocesan Missionary, $128), $978; Salary of the Bishop, $200, Diocesan Fund, $90; Bible and Common Prayer Book Society of Albany, $30; Fund for Aged and Infirm Clergymen, $25.84; Fund for Widows and Orphans of Clergymen, $25.84; Orphan House of the Holy Saviour, $160; The Child's Hospital, $23.20; Society for Promoting Religion and Learning, $14 25; Clergy Reserve Fund, $27; Church Home, Troy, $500; Orphan Asylum, Troy, $100; Young Woman's Association, Troy, $25, St. Christina Home, Saratoga, $294; Window, St. Margaret's Church, Menands, $225. Total, $2,718.13.

General.— Domestic Missions (Bishop Knickerbocker, $125, other fields, $175 Missionary boxes [estimated], $425.56), $725.56, Foreign Missions, $63.51; Indian Missions, $10. Home Missions to Coloured Persons, $25. Total, $824.07.

Total amount of Offerings, $22,088.42.

Property.

Church and lot (estimated worth), $75,000.
Parsonage and lot (estimated worth), $15,000.

Chapel and School for Boys, $40,000.
Martha Memorial House, $20,000.
Other property, $25,000.
Condition of property, good.

Remarks.

Of gifts received during the year, mention may be made of a processional cross (set with fifty-two jewels), designed and made by Tiffany & Co., New York, the gift of Mrs. William Howard Hart.

ST. JOHN'S CHURCH, TROY.

Rector. The Rev. Thaddeus Alexander Snively.
Wardens. Norman B. Squires, Charles W. Tillinghast.
Vestrymen. Edward G. Gilbert, James M. Ide, C. A. McLeod, Francis N. Mann, William P. Mason, William M. Sanford, William A. Thompson, George A. Wells.

Parochial.

Baptisms (adults, 11, infants, 20), 31; Confirmed, since last report, 14; Marriages, 4; Burials, 24; Communicants, last reported, 896, admitted, 14, received, 7, died, 11, removed, 6, present number, 400; Sunday School, 225; Catechizing, every Sunday; Sewing School, 140; Woman's Guild, 60; Employment Society, 65; Mother's Meeting, 31.

Offerings.

Parochial.—Alms at Holy Communion, $310; Current expenses, including salaries (estimated), $7,500; Sunday School, $300; Increase and Improvement of Church Property, $150; Other parochial objects: Parish Visitor's Work, $200; Altar Society, $170; Employment Society, $310; Sewing School, $75; Miscellaneous, $200. Total, $9,215.

Diocesan.— Diocesan Missions, including special, $700; Salary of the Bishop, $250; Diocesan Fund, $90; Bible and Common Prayer Book Society of Albany, $300; Fund for Aged and Infirm Clergymen, $25; Fund for Widows and Orphans of Clergymen, $25; Orphan House of the Holy Saviour, $40; The Child's Hospital, $150; Other offerings for objects within the Diocese: Missionary Board, $200; Church Home of Troy, $500; Miscellaneous, $150. Total, $2,430.

General.— Domestic and Foreign Missions, $230; Indian Missions, $30; Home Missions to Coloured Persons, $40; Missionary boxes and other objects exterior to the Diocese, $400; American Church Building Commission, $30; Theological Education, $200. Total $930.

Total amount of Offerings, $12,575.

Property.

Indebtedness, $8,000.

CHRIST CHURCH, TROY.

Rector. The Rev. Eaton W. Maxcy, S. T. D.
Wardens. Hon. William Kemp, S. C. Tappin.
Vestrymen. Washington Akin, M. D., Peter Black, Charles Cleminshaw, J. W. A. Cluett, George Churchill, Thomas H. Magill, Charles A. Nimmo, Eugene C. Packard.

Parochial.

Families, 125; Individuals (adults, 450, children, 250), 700; Baptisms (adults, 4, infants, 9), 13; Present number of confirmed persons, 350; Marriages, 8; Burials, 20; Communicants, received, 10, died, 7, removed, 3, present number, 250; Public Services (Sundays, 96, Holy days, 10, other days, 60), 166; Holy Communion (public 15, private, 2), 17; Sunday School, teachers 16, pupils, 160; Catechizing, number of times, 40.

Offerings.

Parochial.— Alms at Holy Communion, $100; Current expenses, including salaries, $4,768.70; Sunday School, $241.86; Other parochial objects, $758.49. Total, $5,869.05.

Diocesan.— Diocesan Missions, $250; Salary of the Bishop, $124; Diocesan Fund, $75; Fund for Aged and Infirm Clergymen, $25.65; Fund for Widows and Orphans of Clergymen, $32.94; Orphan House of the Holy Saviour, $10.58. Total, $518.17.

General.— Foreign Missions, $2.

Total amount of Offerings, $6,389.22.

Property.

Church and lot (estimated worth), $35,000.

Other property, $4,000.

Amount of salary pledged Rector, $2,500.

Number of sittings in the Church, 600.

THE CHURCH OF THE HOLY CROSS, TROY.

Rector. The Rev. J. Ireland Tucker.

Parochial.

Baptisms (adults, 15, infants, 10), 25; Confirmed since last report, 20; Marriages, 14; Burials, 20; Communicants, present number, 145; Public Services, Sundays, 2, Holy days, 1, other days, 1; Holy Communion, public, Sundays and Saints' days; Sunday School, teachers, 14, pupils, 130; Parish School, teachers, 4, pupils, 60.

ST. LUKE'S CHURCH, TROY.

Rector. The Rev. William Brevoort Bolmer.

Wardens. James Wood, John W. Babcock.

Vestrymen. Henry E. Darby, Thomas Marles, P. Harry Mitchell, Daniel Francks, George Haite, Edmund Adams, Thomas B. Iler, James Evans.

Parochial.

Families, 150; Individuals (adults, 320, children, 240), 560; Baptisms (adults, 2, infants, 38) 40; Confirmed, since last report, 1; Present number of confirmed persons, 250, Marriages, 5; Burials, 22; Churchings, 4; Communicants, last reported, 190, admitted, 1, received, 1, died, 4, removed, 1, present number, 192; Public Services (Sundays, 156, Holy days, 72, other days, 42), 270; Holy Communion (public, 74, private, 7), 81; Sunday School, teachers, 10, pupils, 109; Catechizing, number of children, 100, number of times, 48.

Offerings.

Parochial.— Alms at Holy Communion, $49.75; Current expenses, including salaries, $1,509.72; Sunday School, $56.94; Poor women in child-bed, $1.75. Total, $1,618.16.

Diocesan.— Diocesan Missions, $28.39; Salary of the Bishop, $10; Diocesan Fund, $15; Bible and Common Prayer Book Society of Albany, $5.63; Fund for Aged and Infirm Clergymen, $6.29; Fund for Widows and Orphans of Clergymen, $6.29; Orphan House of the Holy Saviour, $11.76, Society for Promoting Religion and Learning, $4.01. Total, $87.37.

General.— Domestic Missions, $5.29; Foreign Missions, $4.10; Indian Missions, $3.63; American Church Building Fund, $4.60; Conversion of the Jews, $4.48. Total, $22.10.

Total amount of Offerings, $1,727.63.

Property.

Church and lot (estimated worth), $23,000.

Parsonage and lot (estimated worth), $4,000.

Other property, $1,700.

Condition of property, tolerable.

Amount of salary pledged Rector, $1,000, and Rectory.

Number of sittings in the Church, 850; all free.

FREE CHURCH OF THE ASCENSION, TROY.

Rector. The Rev. James Caird.

Trustees. William R. Bridges, James Caird, Thomas Cordwell, J. J. Gillespie, N. B. Squires, William A. Thompson.

Parochial.

Baptisms (adults, 11, infants, 17), 28; Confirmed, since last report, 18; Marriages, 3; Burials, 17; Communicants, present number, 240; Public Services (Sundays, 104, Holy days, 8, other days, 62), '174; Holy Communion, public, 14; Sunday School, teachers, 20, pupils, 180; Catechizing, every Sunday.

Offerings.

Parochial.—Current expenses, including salaries, $2,069.28; Sunday School, $475; Increase and Improvement of Church Property, $239.28. Total, $2,783.56.

Diocesan.— Diocesan Missions, $35.25; Salary of the Bishop, $10; Church Home, $10; Helping Hand Mission, $10. Total, $65.25.

Total amount of Offerings, $2,848.81.

ST. BARNABAS' CHURCH, TROY.

Rector. The Rev. Geo. A. Holbrook.

The Corporation. Rev. Geo. A. Holbrook, President. Rev. J. Ireland Tucker, S. T. D., Vice-President; A. W. M. Moffitt, Treasurer; William C. Jamieson, Thomas Entwistle, Wm. W. Morrill, Wm. W. Rousseau, Chas. W. Tillinghast, 2d, Horace B. Finley, Secretary.

The Local Committee. Rev. Geo. A. Holbrook, A. W. M. Moffitt, Thos. Entwistle, Wm. C. Jamieson, H. B. Finley.

Parochial.

Baptisms (adults, 6, infants, 19), 25; Confirmed, since last report, 19; Marriages, 8; Burials, 15; Communicants, last reported, 161, admitted, 31, received, 3, died, 8, removed, 22, present number, 170; Public Services (Sundays, 152, Holy days, 76, other days, 468), 696; Holy Communion (public, 163, private, 9), 172; Sunday School, teachers, 8, pupils, 94, Catechizing, number of children, 94, number of times, 52.

Offerings.

Parochial.— Alms at Holy Communion, $73.03; Current expenses, including salaries, $3,719.49; Sunday School, $42.90; Increase and Improvement of Church Property, $277.80; St. Barnabas Building Fund, $742.22; St. Barnabas Mortgage Fund, $95.76; For the Poor, $4.15. Total, $4,955.35.

Diocesan.—Diocesan Missions, $50; Salary of the Bishop, $7; Bible and Common Prayer Book Society of Albany, $2.57; Fund for Aged and Infirm Clergymen, $11.11; Orphan House of the Holy Saviour, $4.34, The Child's Hospital, $3.33; The Church Home, Troy, $6.33; Troy Orphan Asylum, $3.27. Total, $86.95.

General.— Domestic Missions, $7.32; Foreign Missions, $3.88; The Clergymen's Mutual Insurance League, $1.79; Church Mission to the Jews, $5.82; Society St. John Evangelist, for new Church at Oxford, Eng., $5. Total, $123.51.

Total amount of Offerings, $5,065.81.

26

Property.

Church and lot (estimated worth), $4,500.
Mission House and lot (estimated worth), $3,500.
Other property (chancel furniture, etc.), $1,450.
Condition of property, good.
Indebtedness, a mortgage of $3,600 on Mission House and lot.
The Building Fund now amounts to $8,780.69.
The Mortgage Fund now amounts to $767.03.
Amount of salary pledged Rector, $1,200. (No Rectory.)
Number of sittings in the Church, 200; all free.

Remarks.

It is to be noted that the report of services and celebrations is only for the period since Quinquagesima, when the present Rector took charge. All other reports are for the Convention year. During the last summer, the entire property of St. Barnabas was put in complete repair. The front wall of the Mission House was rebuilt, the roof shingled, the Guild rooms papered and painted. The interior of the Church was redecorated, and the roof put in repair.

TRINITY CHURCH, LANSINGBURGH.

Rector. The Rev. Charles Metcalf Nickerson.
Wardens. James McQuide, Peter B. King.
Vestrymen. Eugene Hyatt, E. K. Betts, E. H. Leonard, J. M. Snyder, Charles S. Holmes, E. Warren Banker, Geo. F. Nichols, Geo. W. Daw.

Parochial.

Baptisms (adults, 2, infants, 12), 14; Confirmed, since last report, 16; Present number of confirmed persons, 267; Marriages, 4; Burials, 17; Communicants, last reported, 231, admitted, 10, received, 7, died, 3, removed, 1, present number, 244; Public Services (Sundays, 133, Holy days, 18, other days, 76), 227; Holy Communion (public, 30, private, 6), 36; Sunday School, teachers, 23, pupils, 205; Catechizing, number of times, 30.

Offerings.

Parochial.— Alms at Holy Communion, $105; Current expenses, including salaries, $3,952.69; Sunday School, $75; Increase and Improvement of Church Property, $640; St. Stephen's Mission, $355.58; Special subscriptions for pay of singers not included in "salaries," $500; Altar cloth, $75; Hymnals and vestments, $75. Total, $5,778.27.

Diocesan.— Diocesan Missions, $214; Salary of the Bishop, $60; Diocesan Fund, $45; Bible and Common Prayer Book Society of Albany, $12.72; Fund for Aged and Infirm Clergymen, $39.78; Orphan House of the Holy Saviour, $20, The Child's Hospital, $25; Box, Orphanage (Cooperstown), $82, Box, Fairview Home, [$12; Archdeaconry of Troy, $5. Total, $516.50.

General.— Domestic Missions, $55.11; Foreign Missions, $27.56; Bishop of Indiana, $39. Total, $121.67.

Total amount of Offerings, $6,416.44.

Property.

Church and lot (estimated worth), $50,000.
Parsonage and lot (estimated worth), $5,000.
Other property (Parish House) $4,000.
Condition of property, good.

Amount of salary pledged Rector, $1,500.

Number of sittings in the Church, 876. Number rented, 314; number free, 60.

Remarks.

Of the Barton fund for the poor $850 has been spent this year.

On the first Sunday in July I started St. Stephen's Mission in the fourth ward. The building where service is held is a mile from the Parish Church, and a little farther from the nearest Church in Troy (St. Barnabas). There is a Sunday School of 55 pupils. There has been a large attendance at the evening service. One service and Sunday School is held every Sunday. If the fourth ward grows at the rate it has for the past five years this Mission will become self-sustaining within a few years.

ST. MARK'S CHURCH, HOOSICK FALLS.

Rector Emeritus. The Rev. Geo. Huntington Nicholls, S. T. B.

Rector. The Rev. Geo. Dent Silliman, S. T. B.

Wardens. Hon. Walter A. Wood, J. Russell Parsons.

Vestrymen. John G. Darroch, Wm. S. Nicholls, Marvin D. Greenwood, Isaac A Allen, Charles A. Coulter, A. Danforth Geer, Nelson Gillespie, James A. Beckett.

Parochial.

Families, 219; Individuals (adults, 464, children, 242), 706; Baptisms (adults, 6, infants, 31), 37; Marriages, 1; Burials, 12; Communicants, last reported, 431, admitted, 4, received, 5, died, 6, removed, 36, present number, 398; Public Services 3 every Sunday, 2 every Holy day, other days, 2 each; total, 771; Holy Communion (public, 185, private, 12), 197; Sunday School, teachers, 17, pupils, 250; Catechizing, number of children, all, number of times, nearly every week.

Offerings.

Parochial.— For the Poor, $75.28; Current expenses, including salaries, per Treasurer's report, $3,007.75; Sunday School, $270.62; Increase and Improvement of Church Property, $545; General Parish Expenses, $427.90. Total, $4,326.55.

Diocesan.— Diocesan Missions, $110.40; Salary of the Bishop, $40; Diocesan Fund, $45; Bible and Common Prayer Book Society of Albany, $13.22; Fund for Aged and Infirm Clergymen, $14.94; Orphan House of the Holy Saviour, $15.56; The Child's Hospital, $31.61; Society for Promoting Religion and Learning, $15.94; Society for the Increase of the Ministry, $18.46. Total, $305.13.

General.— Domestic Missions, $12.78; Foreign Missions, $16.75; Mission to the Jews, $7; Sunday School, for Little Samuel School, Persia, $25; Sunday School, Easter, Domestic and Foreign Missions, $30.07; Sunday School, Chinese League, $10. Total, $101.60.

Total amount of Offerings, $4,733.28.

Property.

Church and lot (estimated worth), $25,000.

Parsonage and lot (estimated worth), $7,500.

Condition of property, good.

Amount of salary pledged Rector, $1,500.

Number of sittings in the Church, 200; all free.

Remarks.

From year to year the Rector has gratefully to acknowledge the kindly aid of the venerable Rector Emeritus.

Included in the report of the offerings for Diocesan Missions, is the sum of $10 given by the Sunday School, from its Easter Offering, and also $5 from the Jr. Auxiliary and Ministering Children's League.

The Parish Branch of the Woman's Auxiliary has received the sum of $211.54 from gifts and subscriptions, during the year ending Oct., 1891. It has sent out five boxes, one valued at $350 to a Diocesan Missionary, and three to the Child's Hospital.

The King's Daughters have given $10, included in the offerings for the poor; also, $10 to the Fresh Air Fund, $2 to St. Christina Home.

The Ministering Children's League and Junior Auxiliary present the following report of their work during the year ending Nov. 1, 1891:

Box to St. Lawrence Co. (Missionary)	$53 76
" Child's Hospital, Albany	24 00
St. Christina Home	2 00
Diocesan Missions	5 00
Box to Shoshone Agency	102 81
Material for work and printing	13 27
	$200 84

TRINITY CHURCH, SCHAGHTICOKE.

Rector. The Rev. S. T. Street.

Wardens. Edward Searles, W. H. Hawkins.

Vestrymen. C. E. Corbin, Robert Barth, Frank Sigworth, J. W. Parker, Ira E. Askins.

Parochial.

Families, about 48; Individuals, 118; Baptisms (adults, 1, infants, 6), 7; Present number of confirmed persons, 76; Marriages, 2; Burials, 1; Communicants, last reported, 38, removed, 4, present number, 34; Sunday School, teachers, 4, pupils, 29.

Offerings.

Parochial.—Current expenses, including salaries, $532.96; Increase and Improvement of Church Property, $59.74. Total, $592.70.

Diocesan.—Diocesan Missions, $15; Salary of the Bishop, $6; Diocesan Fund, $9; Bible and Common Prayer Book Society of Albany, $2; Fund for Aged and Infirm Clergymen, $1.50; Fund for Widows and Orphans of Clergymen, $1.50; Orphan House of the Holy Saviour, $1.50. Total, $36.50.

Total amount of Offerings, $629.20.

Property.

Church and lot (estimated worth), $4,000.

Parsonage and lot (estimated worth), $3,750.

Indebtedness, $2,450.

Amount of salary pledged Rector, $300.

Number of sittings in the Church, 200; all free.

Remarks.

No record being left by my predecessor I am unable to make a full report of his work.

THE CHURCH OF THE MESSIAH, GREENBUSH.

Rector. The Rev. Thomas B. Fulcher.

Wardens. George Low, William H. Terrell.

Vestrymen. Jacob V. B. Teller, Richard W. Stevens, George Story, Harry E. Cole, Alfred L. Curtis, Charles H. Smith, Theo. A. McKean, Benjamin F. Allen.

Parochial.

Families, 60; Baptisms, infants, 4; Marriages, 1; Burials, 10; Communicants, last reported, 117, received, 6, died, 5, removed, 7, present number, 111; Public Services (Sundays, 106, Holy days, 25, other days, 29), 160; Holy Communion (public, 34, private, 10), 44; Sunday School, teachers, 10, pupils, 75; Catechizing, number of children, all, number of times, 12.

Offerings.

Parochial.— Alms at Holy Communion, $67.11; Current expenses, including salaries, $1,212.65; Sunday School, $60.56; Other parochial objects, $58.88. Total, $1,399.20.

Diocesan.— Diocesan Missions, $30; Salary of the Bishop, $10; Diocesan Fund, $24; Fund for Aged and Infirm Clergymen, $1.75; Fund for Widows and Orphans of Clergymen, $1.75; Orphan House of the Holy Saviour, $7; The Child's Hospital, $6. Total, $80.50.

General.—General Missions, $5.

Total amount of Offerings, $1,484.70.

Property.

Church and lot (estimated worth), $6,000.
Other property, $1,000.
Condition of property, fair.
Indebtedness, none.
Amount of salary pledged Rector, $800.
Number of sittings in the Church, 150; all free.

Remarks.

The Rector, having been recalled to the full duties of his office as Precentor in the Cathedral, resigned Nov. 1, 1891.

CHURCH OF THE EPIPHANY, EAST ALBANY.

Rector. The Rev. Thomas White.

Parochial.

Families, 42; Baptisms (adults, 2, infants, 11), 13; Confirmed, since last report, 14; Marriages, 9; Burials, 7; Communicants, last reported, 164, admitted, 14, received, 2, removed, 3, present number, 177; Public Services (Sundays, 103, Holy days, 26, other days, 34), 163; Holy Communion (public, 44, private, 2), 46; Sunday School teachers, 13, pupils, 150; Catechizing, every Sunday.

Offerings.

Parochial.— Current expenses, including salaries, $979.31; Sunday School, $64.88. Total, $1,044.19.

Diocesan.— Diocesan Missions, $4.

General.— Domestic Missions, $17.50; Foreign Missions, $17.50. Total, $35.

Total amount of Offerings, $1,083.19.

Property.

Church and lot (estimated worth), $10,000.
Condition of property, good.
Indebtedness $611.
Amount of salary pledged Rector, $600.

Remarks.

In the report of work for the year I have not enumerated the services which were so kindly rendered by my brethren in the Ministry, the Rev. Canon Fulcher, Mr. Stewart and Mr. Hatheway. My thanks are also due to Mr. Palmer, of Holy Innocents', for lay-service during my absence during the summer.

The indebtedness included under the last clause, is for improvements made by the village in grading and paving the streets — not from any expense incurred by the Parish. During the last year there has been collected nearly $200 for a Rectory.

ALL SAINTS' CHURCH, HOOSAC.

Rector. The Rev. E. D. Tibbits.

Assistants. The Rev. H. R. Luney, Rev. J. B. Tibbits.

Wardens. LeG. C. Tibbits, H. C. Babcock.

Vestrymen. L. C. Boyle, G. M. Bovie, G. M. Andrews, E. J. Brown, H. E. Hallenbeck, H. Myers, C. E. Pierce.

Parochial.

Baptisms (adults, 19, infants, 23), 42; Confirmed, since last report, 13; Present number of confirmed persons, 112; Marriages, 8; Burials, 6; Communicants, last reported, 109, died, 1, removed, 7, present number, 112, actual communicants during past year, 95; Holy Communion (public, 115, private, 2), 117; Sunday School, teachers, 8, pupils, 92; Catechizing, number of times, 7; Parish School, teachers, 3, pupils, 18.

Offerings.

Parochial.— Current expenses, including salaries, $1,369.01; Sunday School, $16.75. Total, $1,385.76.

Diocesan.— Diocesan Missions, $26.82; Salary of the Bishop, $6; Orphanage, Cooperstown, $9.09. Total, $41.91.

General.— Home Missions to Coloured Persons (Sunday School, at Christmas), $30; Jewish Missions, $6.58. Total, $36.58.

Total amount of Offerings, $1,464.25.

THE MISSION CHURCH OF THE HOLY NAME, BOYNTONVILLE.

Rector. The Rev. E. D. Tibbits.

Priest in charge. The Rev. Clarence M. Conant, M. D.

Warden. Willis Porter Humiston.

Parochial.

Families, 20; Individuals (adults, 37, children, 16), 53; Baptisms (adults, 1, infants, 3), 4; Confirmed, since last report, 3; Present number of confirmed persons, 25; Marriages, 1; Communicants, last reported, 30, admitted, 3, removed, 10, present number, 25; Public Services, Sundays, 10:30 A. M., 7 P. M., Holy days, 4 P. M., other days, Thursdays; Holy Communion (public, 12, private, 3), 15; Sunday School, teachers, 3, pupils, 26; Catechizing, number of children, about 20, number of times, 4.

Offerings.

Parochial.— Alms at Holy Communion, about $30; Increase and Improvement of Church Property, $100 (for a bell). Total, $130.

Property.

Church and lot (estimated worth), including a Parish Hall, $2,200.

Condition of property, excellent; Hall needs painting.

Number of sittings in the Church, about 200; all free.

Remarks.

The Rev. E. D. Tibbits has presented this Mission with a very sweet-tone bell, cast by Meneely of Troy. Sunday, July 19th, 1891, he visited the Mission, blessed the bell and celebrated Holy Communión.

ST. GILES' MISSION, CASTLETON.

Missionary. The Rev. Charles H. Hatheway.

Parochial.

Families, 7; Individuals, 10; Baptisms (adults, 1, infants, 3), 4; Communicants, removed, 2, present number, 15; Public Services (Sundays, 52, other days, 11), 63; Holy Communion, public, 7.

Offerings.

Parochial.—Current expenses, including salaries, $358.72.
General.—Domestic Missions, $1.
Total amount of Offerings, $359.72.

Property.

Amount of salary pledged Rector, $200.

ST. PAUL'S MISSION, RAYMERSTOWN.

A Mission in this village, to be known as St. Paul's, has been maintained by the Rev. E. D. Tibbits and his assistants during the past year. Evening Prayer with Sermon is given every Sunday, a Sunday School preceding, which is well attended Seven children have been brought to Holy Baptism. Mr. Tibbits has presented the Mission with a fine building site, upon which a foundation for a frame Church (for which the plans have been drawn) to cost about $2,000 has been laid, but whose erection is deferred for want of funds. There is one communicant resident in the village and a number of persons are seeking confirmation. Much interest was evinced in the work by a large attendance upon the occasion of the laying of the Corner Stone, Sunday afternoon, Sept. 13th, 1891, by the Rev. E. D. Tibbits, assisted by the Rev. George D. Silliman of Hoosick Falls and the Rev. Clarence M. Conant (then deacon) in charge. A stirring Missionary address was made by the Rev. Mr. Silliman. The Corner Stone was the gift of St. Margaret's Guild of St. Paul's Church, Troy, and contained the usual enclosures.

St. Lawrence County.

ST. JOHN'S CHURCH, OGDENSBURGH.

Rector. The Rev. J. D. Morrison, D. D., LL.D.
Wardens. Charles Ashley, Louis Hasbrouck.
Vestrymen. Levi Hasbrouck, J. C. Sprague, James G. Knap, Egbert N. Burt, J. G. Averill, S. F. Palmer, Thomas Lawrence.

Parochial.

Families, 280; Individuals (adults, 720, children, 350), 1070; Baptisms (adults, 7, infants, 35), 42; Confirmed, since last report, 29; Present number of confirmed persons, 550; Marriages, 12; Burials, 30; Communicants, removed, 48, present number, 480; Holy Communion (public, Sundays and Holy days, and Thursdays in Lent, and daily in Holy week, private, frequent); Sunday School, teachers, 32, pupils, 249; Catechizing, number of children, whole school, number of times, monthly.

Offerings.

Parochial.—Alms at Holy Communion, $169; Current expenses, including salaries, $4,091.92; Sunday School, $400; Mortgage on Rectory due Nov. 1, 1891, $5,800; Choir Stalls in Chancel and Re-carpeting of Church, $600; Altar Society and Vestment Committee, $250. Total, $10,810.92.

Diocesan.—Diocesan Missions, $610; Salary of the Bishop, $110; Diocesan Fund, $57; Bible and Common Prayer Book Society of Albany, $35.11; Fund for Aged and Infirm Clergymen, $35.53; Orphan House of the Holy Saviour, $18.75; Clergy Reserve Fund, $32.67; Woman's Auxiliary Boxes, $139.95. Total, $1,039.01.

General.—Domestic and Foreign Missions, $170.08; Indian Missions, $5.75; Home Missions to Coloured Persons, $4.36; Jewish Missions, $30.18; Woman's Auxiliary Money, $67.00. Total, $267.87.

Total amount of Offerings, $12,107.80.

Property.

Church, Chapel and lot (estimated worth), $100,000.
Parsonage and lot (estimated worth), $12,000.
Condition of property, good.
Amount of salary pledged Rector, $2,000.
Number of sittings in the Church, 1,000; in Chapel, 250.

Remarks.

In the amount given to Diocesan Missions is included the sum of $110, given for salary of the Diocesan Missionary. Of that amount the Woman's Auxiliary gave $35, and the Sunday School, $35. In November a mortgage on the Rectory came due and was promptly paid. During the last twenty years the parish has built Church and Chapel, and has purchased a Rectory. The heavy obligations incurred have all been met, and the Parish to-day does not owe a penny.

ST. PAUL'S CHURCH, WADDINGTON.

Rector. The Rev. Angus C. Macdonald.
Wardens. Joseph Graves, S. J. Bower, M. D.
Vestrymen. James I. Cook, Robert Dalzel, Clarence Montgomery, John Rule, William Forsyth.

Parochial.

Families, 37; Individuals (adults, 102, children, 62), 164; Baptisms (adults, 4, infants, 5), 9; Present number of confirmed persons, 75; Marriages, 2; Burials, 8; Communicants, last reported, 71, died, 1, present number, 70; Public Services (Sundays, 150, Holy days, 10, other days, 32, Advent and Lent), 192; Holy Communion (public, 24, private, 1), 25; Sunday School, teachers, 6, pupils, 40; Catechising, number of children, 40, number of times, several.

Offerings.

Parochial.— Current expenses, including salaries, $270; Sunday School, $10; Increase and Improvement of Church property $100; Amount paid on decoration, $1.50; Paid Organist, $50; Interest and sinking fund, $15; Woman's Aid Society in hands of Treasurer, $62; Donation by Church and citizens to Rector, $75. Total, $782.

Diocesan.— Diocesan Missions, $30; Salary of the Bishop, $9; Diocesan Fund, $9; Archdeaconry Offertory, $2.50. Total, $50.50.

General.— Domestic Missions, $5; Children's Lenten Offerings, $5. Total, $10.

Total amount of Offerings, $792.50.

Property.

Church and lot (estimated worth), $5,000.
Parsonage and lot (estimated worth), $3,000.
Other property, $3,900.
Condition of property, good.
Indebtedness, amount borrowed for roofing Church, $195.
Amount of salary pledged Rector, $300.
Number of sittings in the Church, 200; all free.

Remarks.

On Whitsunday, in addition to the due commemoration of the Festival, an effort which proved satisfactory was made, as the initiative, in commemorating the establishment of St. Paul's Church in this village. Among other things an historical sermon was preached. This Church possesses the proud distinction of being the Mother Church in the county of St. Lawrence. Its seventy-fifth anniversary will occur in October, 1893. As to Church progress in the past year, one matter alone is noted. Parochial contributions have exceeded our anticipations, while extra parochial have not diminished. Indeed, with the depressed financial condition of our town the Church, in holding its own, is doing something remarkable.

CHRIST CHURCH, MORRISTOWN.

Rector in charge and Missionary. The Rev. J. T. Zorn.
Wardens. Joseph Couper, Henry A. Chapman.
Vestrymen. J. A. Phillips, T. W. Pierce, A. L. Palmer, G. E. Pope, Henry Bacon, E. Kingsland, O. P. Phillips, E. H. Miller.

Parochial.

Families, 45; Individuals (adults, 86, children, 44), 130; Baptisms (adults, 7, infants, 5), 12; Confirmed, since last report, 10; Present number of confirmed persons, 96; Marriages, 1; Burials, 4; Communicants, last reported, 92, admitted, 10, received, 2, removed, 8, present number, 96; Public Services (Sundays, 104, Holy days, 47, other days, 85), 236; Holy Communion (public, 59, private, 2), 61; Sunday School, teachers, 5, pupils, 40; Catechizing, number of children, 40, number of times, 20.

Offerings.

Parochial.— Alms at Holy Communion, $16.30; Current expenses, including salaries, $541.34. Total, $557.64.

Diocesan.— Diocesan Missions, $50; Salary of the Bishop, $19.50; Diocesan Fund, $12; Bible and Common Prayer Book Society of Albany, $2; Fund for Aged and Infirm Clergymen, $1.82; Orphan House of the Holy Saviour, $1.89; The Child's Hospital, $11.52; Salary of Diocesan Missionary, $3. Total, $100.73.

General.— Domestic and Foreign Missions, $15.48; Other objects exterior to the Diocese, $1.61; Jewish Missions, $1.33. Total, $18.42.

Total amount of Offerings, $676.79.

Property.

Church and lot (estimated worth), $3,000.
Parsonage and lot (estimated worth), $1,800.
Condition of property, fair.
Amount of salary pledged Rector, $400.
Number of sittings in the Church, 200; all free.

27

TRINITY CHURCH, POTSDAM.

Rector. The Rev. R. M. Kirby, D. D.
Wardens. Thomas S. Clarkson, Bloomfield Usher.
Vestrymen. E. W. Foster, M. Heath, T. Streatfeild Clarkson, C. O. Tappan, L. Usher, H. D. Thatcher, O. G. Howe, J. G. McIntyre.

Parochial.

Baptisms (adults, 9, infants, 7), 16; Confirmed, since last report, 16; Present number of confirmed persons, 246; Marriages, 11; Burials, 11; Communicants, last reported, 204, admitted, 16, received, 9, died, 4, removed, 7, present number, 218; Public Services (Sundays, 104, Holy days, 33, other days, 70), 207; Holy Communion (public, 44, private, frequent); Sunday School, teachers, 16, pupils, 145; Catechising, number of children, all, number of times, often.

Offerings.

Parochial.—Alms at Holy Communion, $190.43; Current expenses, including salaries, $3,099.83; Sunday School, $231.62; Increase and Improvement of Church Property, $80; Altar Society, $131.58. Total, $3,733.41.

Diocesan.—Diocesan Missions, $635; Salary of the Bishop, $50; Diocesan Fund, $48; Bible and Common Prayer Book Society of Albany, $11.76; Fund for Aged and Infirm Clergymen, $38.06; Fund for Widows and Orphans of Clergymen, $29.32; Orphan House of the Holy Saviour, $44.61; The Child's Hospital, $61.62; Society for Promoting Religion and Learning, $22.19; For Debt on Orphan House of the Holy Saviour, $260; Convocation of Ogdensburgh, $24.42; For General Missionary, $50. Total, $1,274.98.

General.—Domestic Missions, $228.65; Foreign Missions, $314.13; Indian Missions, $163.45; Bishop Leonard, Utah and Nevada, $150; St. Mark's School, Salt Lake City, Utah, $80; Bishop Knickerbocker, $32.82; Mrs. Buford by Woman's Auxiliary, $20; National City, California, $60. Total, $1,044.05.

Total amount of Offerings, $6,052.44.

Property.

Church and lot (estimated worth), $60,000.
Parsonage and lot (estimated worth), $4,000.
Condition of property, excellent.
Amount of salary pledged Rector, $1,600.
Number of sittings in the Church, 350, Chapel, 150; all free.

Remarks.

Services have been maintained at Norfolk and Norwood during several months of the year, the Rev. R. L. Mathison, of the Diocese of Connecticut, officiating. The offerings at these services for all purposes amounted to $130.

GRACE CHURCH, CANTON.

(No Report.)

GRACE CHURCH, NORFOLK.

See Remarks, Report, Trinity Church, Potsdam.

TRINITY CHURCH, GOUVERNEUR.

Rector. The Rev. James Alexander Dickson.
Warden. Aaron B. Cutting.

Vestrymen. J. B. Preston, Edward D. Barry, Frank H. Smith, John McCarty, James D. Easton.

Parochial.

Families, 45 in part or whole; Individuals (adults, 100, children, 40), 140; Baptisms (adults, 1, infants, 4), 5; Present number of confirmed persons, 68; Marriages, 4; Burials, 7; Communicants. last reported, 66, received, 2, died, 8, removed, 1, present number, 64; Public Services (Sundays, 94, Holy days, 28, other days, Wednesday evenings); Holy Communion (public, 37, private, 1), 38; Sunday School, teachers, 7; Catechizing, number of children, 40, number of times, several.

Offerings.

Parochial.—Alms at Holy Communion, $88.57; Current expenses, including salaries, $1,035; Sunday School, $18.42; Increase and Improvement of Church Property, $304.28. Total, $1,446.27.

Diocesan.—Diocesan Missions, $50; Salary of the Bishop, $26; Diocesan Fund, $24; Diocesan Missionary, $5. Total, $105.

Total amount of Offerings, $1,551.27.

Property.

Church and lot (estimated worth), $6,500.
Parsonage and lot (estimated worth), $3,000.
Other property, $350.
Condition of property, first-class.
Amount of salary pledged Rector, $800.
Number of sittings in the Church, 200; number rented, 175; number free, 25.

ST. JOHN'S CHURCH, MASSENA.

Rector. The Rev. Howard McDougall.
Wardens. H. T. Clark, G. A. Snaith.
Vestrymen. E. H. Pitts, E. R. Foord, J. O. Bridges, Henry Warren, L. S. Dominy, R. H. Wilson.

Parochial.

Families, 40; Individuals (adults, 108, children. 50), 158; Baptisms, infants, 1; Confirmed, since last report, 1; Present number of confirmed persons, 80; Burials, 3; Communicants, last reported, 58, admitted, 1, received, 2, died, 1, present number, 60; Public Services (Sundays, 52, Holy days, 5, other days, 7), 64; Holy Communion, public, 14; Sunday School, teachers, 7, pupils, 55; Catechizing, number of times, 30.

Offerings.

Parochial.—Current expenses, including salaries, $400; Sunday School, $9.14; Bond and Mortgage on Church, $265. Total, $674.14.

Diocesan.—Diocesan Missions, $26.25; Salary of the Bishop, $8; Diocesan Fund, $9. Total, $43.25.

General.—Domestic and Foreign Missions (Sunday School Lenten Offerings), $10.05.
Total amount of Offerings, $727.44.

Property.

Church and lot (estimated worth), $4,000.
Condition of property, good.
Amount of salary pledged Rector, $300.
Number of sittings in the Church, 250; all free

Remarks.

The congregations of St. John's Church are increased by the visitors at Massena Springs during the summer. Two hundred dollars were raised through entertainments given for the benefit of the Church at the Hatfield House and the Massena Springs Park. Sixty-five dollars were added to this amount by the Ladies' Aid Society of the Parish.

ST. LUKE'S CHURCH, LISBON.

Rector. The Rev. Angus C. Macdonald.

Parochial.

Families, 13; Individuals (adults, 25, children. 16), 41; Baptisms (adults, 1, infants, 1), 2; Present number of confirmed persons, 17; Burials, 1; Communicants, last reported, 15, admitted, 2. present number, 14; Public Services (Sundays, 80, other days, 4), 84; Holy Communion (public, 4, private, 1), 5; Sunday School, teachers, 3, pupils. 15; Catechizing, number of children, 15, a number of times.

Offerings.

Parochial.— Alms at Holy Communion, $5.40; Current expenses, including salaries, $50; Horse hire for Missionary, $68; Amount for roofing Church, $62. Total, $185.40. Diocesan.— Diocesan Missions, $1.50.
Total amount of Offerings, $186.90.

Property.

Church and lot (estimated worth), $2,000.
Condition of property, good.

Remarks.

All idea of the contemplated alteration of the vestry-room of St. Luke's had to be abandoned when it was discovered that the roof of the whole building required reshingling. And to this object all efforts have been directed for the past six months. The result is that $65 is now in our hands for that purpose.

ZION CHURCH, COLTON.

Rector. The Rev. George M. Irish.
Wardens. Thomas S. Clarkson, Myron E. Howard.
Vestrymen. P. Potter, J. W. Lyman, Archie Allen, S. J. Hosley, W. Eacutt, A. H. Gustin, Eugene Moore, F. Horton.

Parochial.

Families, 76; Individuals, adults and children, 291; Baptisms (adults, 13, infants, 11), 24; Confirmed, since last report, 9; Present number of confirmed persons, 63; Marriages, 3: Burials, 7; Communicants, last reported, 45; admitted, 9: present number, 54; Public Services (Sundays, 96, Holy days, 17, other days, 54), 167; Holy Communion, public, 27; Sunday School. teachers, 9, pupils, 80; Catechizing, number of children, all, number of times, frequently.

Offerings.

Parochial.— Alms at Holy Communion (not elsewhere reported), $6.70; Current expenses, including salaries, $1,182.45; Sunday School. $6.76; Increase and Improvement of Church Property, $416.65. Total, $1,612.56.

Diocesan.— Diocesan Missions, $15.05; Salary of the Bishop, $4; Diocesan Fund, $4.50; Bible and Common Prayer Book Society of Albany, $1.28; Fund for Aged and Infirm Clergymen, $1.06; Orphan House of the Holy Saviour, $1.17. Total, $27.06.

General.—Domestic Missions, $81.26; Foreign Missions, $343.59; Mary Baldwin Scholarship at Jaffa, $15.29; Box to Bishop Gobat's School, Jerusalem, $60. Total, $500.14.

Total amount of Offerings, $2,139.76.

Property.

Church and lot and Parsonage and lot (estimated worth), $33,400.
Condition of property, excellent.
Amount of salary pledged Rector, $900.
Number of sittings in the Church, 200; all free.

Remarks.

In addition to those included in the above report, services have been held each Sunday afternoon (with the exception of four Sundays), at Pierpont Centre.

ST. THOMAS' CHURCH, LAWRENCEVILLE.

Rector. The Rev. R. Wyndham Brown.
Warden. William Kingston.

Parochial.

Families, 8; Individuals (adults, 20, children, 6), 26; Baptisms, infants, 2; Present number of confirmed persons, 14; Communicants, last reported, 14, present number, 14; Public Services (Sundays, 43, Holy days, 1), 44; Holy Communion, public, 4.

Offerings.

Parochial.— Alms at Holy Communion, $1.50; Current expenses, including salaries, $50. Total, $51.50.

Diocesan.— Diocesan Missions, 50 cents; Salary of the Bishop, $3.60. Total, $4.10.
Total amount of Offerings, $55.60.

Property.

Church and lot (estimated worth), $3,000.
Parsonage and lot (estimated worth), $1,000.
Condition of property, fair.
Amount of salary pledged Rector, $120.
Number of sittings in the Church, 200; all free.

TRINITY CHAPEL, MORLEY.

(No Report.)

ST. ANDREW'S CHURCH, NORWOOD.

See Remarks, Report, Trinity Church, Potsdam.

Saratoga County.

CHRIST CHURCH, BALLSTON SPA.

Rector. The Rev. Charles Pelletreau.
Wardens. Stephen B. Medbery, John H. Westcot.
Vestrymen. George L. Thompson, Matthew Vassar, James W. Verbeck, Andrew S. Booth, Charles M. Brown, William S. Wheeler, Stephen C. Medbery.

Parochial.

Families and parts of families, 150; Baptisms (adults, 2, infants, 16), 12; Marriages, 2; Burials, 26; Communicants, last reported, 250, died, 7, removed, 4; Public Services, Sundays, 108, Holy days, all, other days, 100; Holy Communion (public, 27, private, 5), 32; Sunday School, teachers, 11, pupils, 120; Catechising, number of times, often.

Offerings.

Parochial.— Alms at Holy Communion, $60; Current expenses, including salaries, $1,990.59; Sunday School, $70.17; Other parochial objects, $920.07; Christmas tree, $40; Contributions to poor families (special), $50. Total, $3,130.68.

Diocesan.— Diocesan Missions, $111.95; Salary of the Bishop, $42; Diocesan Fund, $36; Orphan House of the Holy Saviour, $13.26; The Child's Hospital, $76; East Line Home (money, $45, box of clothing, etc., $39, fruit, vegetables and groceries, $40), $134. Total, $413.01.

General.— Domestic Missions, $32; Foreign Missions, $25; Indian Missions, $25; Home Missions to Coloured Persons, $35; Mission to Jews, $10; Hospital for Coloured People, $48; Babcock Scholarship, Dakota, $50. Total, $225.

Total amount of Offerings, $3,768.84.

Property.

Church and lot (estimated worth), $18,000.
Parsonage and lot (estimated worth), $10,000.
Other property, $7,000.
Condition of property, excellent.
Amount of salary pledged Rector, $1,500.
Number of sittings in the Church, 350.

Remarks.

Since the last report the Church has put in handsome new pews, a new carpet, new pew cushions, the vestibule floor has been laid in tiles, and steam heat has taken the place of hot air.

ST. JOHN'S CHURCH, STILLWATER.

(No Report.)

ST. PAUL'S CHURCH, CHARLTON.

Rector. The Rev. Heman R. Timlow.
Wardens. William Taylor, Robert C. Davis.
Vestrymen. George C. Valentine, John Marvin, Robert Wendell, Jacob Pink.

Parochial.

Families, 25; Burials, 1; Communicants, present number, 26; Sunday School, teachers, 3, pupils, 15.

Offerings.

Parochial.—Alms at Holy Communion, $6; Current expenses, including salaries, $220. Total, $226.

Diocesan.—Diocesan Missions, $7; Other offerings for objects within the Diocese, $10. Total, $17.

General.— Domestic Missions, $4; Foreign Missions, $4; Other objects external to the Diocese, $22.43. Total, $30.43.

Total amount of Offerings, $273.43.

GRACE CHURCH, WATERFORD.

Rector. The Rev. Charles E. Freeman, S. T. B.

Wardens. John Higgins, Roland Henshall Stubbs, M. D.

Vestrymen. Charles B. Laithe, Edward Van Kleeck, Marvin A. Baker, John H. Meeker, William Holroyd, Thomas E. Clayton, Charles H. Kavanaugh, James E. Bootman.

Parochial.

Families, 85; Individuals (adults, 211, children, 92), 303; Baptisms (adults, 2, infants, 6), 8; Present number of confirmed persons, 189; Marriages, 6; Burials, 10; Communicants, last reported, 169, received, 3, died, 2, removed, 1, present number, 169; Public Services (Sundays, 100, Holy days, 50, other days, 45), 195; Holy Communion (public, 68, private, 6), 74; Sunday School, teachers, 6, pupils, 78; Catechising, number of children, school, number of times, every Sunday.

Offerings.

Parochial. — Alms at Holy Communion, $66.07; Current expenses, including salaries, $1,594.46; Sunday School, $90.33. Total, $1,750.86.

Diocesan.—Diocesan Missions, $35; Salary of the Bishop, $64.17; Diocesan Fund, $30; Bible and Common Prayer Book Society of Albany, $6.29; Fund for Aged and Infirm Clergymen, $3; Fund for Widows and Orphans of Clergymen, $2; Archdeaconry of Troy, $19.60. Total, $160.06.

General.—General Theological Seminary, $3.93; Foreign Missions (by Sunday School), $7.70; Church Society for Promoting Christianity among the Jews, $1.43. Total, $13.06.

Total amount of Offerings, $1,923.98.

Property.

Church and lot (estimated worth), $10,000.

Other property, $2,000.

Condition of property, good.

Amount of salary pledged Rector, $1,000.

Number of sittings in the Church, 335; number rented, 210, number free, 100.

Remarks.

Of the total amount of offerings of this Parish, the amount raised by the Parish Guild was $536.60.

ST. LUKE'S CHURCH, MECHANICVILLE.
(No report.)

BETHESDA CHURCH, SARATOGA SPRINGS,

Rector. The Rev. Joseph Carey, S. T. D.

Wardens. James M. Marvin, R. C. McEwen, M. D.

Vestrymen. William A. Sackett, Spencer Trask, Daniel Eddy, Walker R. Johnson, George R. P. Shackelford, Winsor B. French, W. B. Gage, William B. Huestis.

Parochial.

Families, 242; Individuals (adults, 605, children, 533), 1,138; Baptisms (adults, 23, infants, 50), 73; Confirmed, since last report, 61; Present number of confirmed persons, 768; Marriages, 21; Burials, 60; Churchings, 2; Communicants, last reported, 752, admitted, 61, received, 8, died, 22, removed, 46, present number, 753; Public Services (Sundays, 168, Holy days, 32, other days, 331), 531; Holy Communion (public, 99, private, 14), 113; Sunday School, teachers, 65, pupils, including Catharine St. Mission School, 587; Catechizing, number of children, 587; number of times, 52.

Offerings.

Parochial.— Alms at Holy Communion, $340.17; Current expenses, including
ries, $5,455.57; Sunday School, $278.12; Parish House, $1,391.30; Choir Vest
Society, $40; Choir Fund, $96.84; Altar Society, $11.68; Church Indebted
$2,500; Home of Good Shepherd, $1,400.55. Total, $11,514.23.

Diocesan — Diocesan Missions, $200; Salary of the Bishop, $70; Diocesan I
$63; Bible and Common Prayer Book Society of Albany, $12.30; Fund for
and Infirm Clergymen, $26.25; The Child's Hospital, $20; Archdeaconry of '
$14.98; Woman's Auxiliary Society, $57.05. Total, $463.53.

General.—To President Potter for Hobart College from Mrs. Stickney, $1
Domestic Missions, to Church in Ashville from Woman's Auxiliary, $35; I
Missions to Coloured Persons, $10.75; Church Mission to the Jews, $16.22; For
T. W. Cain, Galveston, Texas, $5; Clergy Retiring Fund, $24.64; Home Stu
Scriptures, $18.11; Increase of the Ministry, $21.60. Total, $1,131.32.

Total amount of Offerings, $13,109.08.

Property.

Church and lot (estimated worth), $82,000.

Parsonage and lot (estimated worth), $9,000.

Other property, Parish house, including new house, $16,000, Home of Good ;
herd, $6,000, Mission Chapel, $1,800.

Condition of property, good.

Indebtedness (On Church, $6,800, on Rectory, $3,700, on the old Parish h
$3,000), $13,500.

Amount of salary pledged Rector, $2,100 with Rectory.

Number of sittings in the Church, 1,200; part rented, part free.

Remarks.

The year is marked by the securing of a subscription of $8,500 for the Cl
debt, with $1,000 additional conditionally. Part of the money subscribed has all
been paid. The great event of the year is Mr. and Mrs. James A. Moore's m
cent gift of the building adjoining the Parish house to the Church for the enl
ment of our Parish work. God's blessing on the Parish is manifest, and the Cl
is stronger in Saratoga to-day than ever before.

ST. STEPHEN'S CHURCH, SCHUYLERVILLE.

Rector. The Rev. J. F. Esch (resigned October 19, 1891).

Wardens. P. Davison, J. H. Smith.

Vestrymen. T. E. Bullard, J. Dix.

Parochial.

Present number of confirmed persons (in the Parish and vicinity, upon the b
19; Burials, 1.

Property.

Church and lot (estimated worth), $8,000.

Parsonage and lot (estimated worth), $1,500.

Other property, School-house, $200.

Condition of property, good.

Sittings in the Church all free.

CALVARY CHURCH, BURNT HILLS.

Rector. The Rev. Heman R. Timlow.

Wardens. Edward Mead, Peter Banta.

Vestrymen. Charles H. Upham, John Wheeler, Robert Keller, Garret Cavert, John Cotton, M. D., Fred. German, Willie Larkins.

Parochial.

Families and parts of families, 50; Baptisms, infants, 4; Burials, 4; Sunday School, teachers, 6, pupils, 30.

Offerings.

Parochial.— Alms at Holy Communion, $9.78, Current expenses, including salaries, $481; General Parish purposes, $74.22. Total, $565.

Diocesan.— Diocesan Missions, $22; Salary of the Bishop, $12; Bible and Common Prayer Book Society of Albany, $6.56. Total, $40.56.

General.— Domestic Missions, $11.59; Foreign Missions, $12 ; Other objects exterior to the Diocese, $15. Total, $38.59.

Total amount of Offerings, $644.15.

GRACE MISSION, JONESVILLE.

See Report of the Diocesan Missionary, page 110.

ALL SAINTS' MISSION, ROUND LAKE.

See Report of the Diocesan Missionary, page 107.

ST. LUKE'S CHURCH, MILTON CENTRE.

See Report of the Diocesan Missionary, page 109.

Schenectady County.

CHRIST CHURCH, DUANESBURGH.

Rector. The Rev. E. W. Flower.

Lay Reader. Edward Clarence Clark.

Wardens. Alexander McDougall, Ralph W. McDougall.

Vestrymen. James D. Featherstonhaugh, Alexander Van Pelt, Wesley Van Pelt, George Matthews, George D. Matthews, Edward Clark, Edward C. Clark, George Snell.

Parochial.

Families, 76; Individuals (adults, 127, children, 47), 174; Baptisms (adults, 1, infants, 3), 4; Present number of confirmed persons, about 110; Marriages, 2; Burials, 6; Communicants, last reported, 92, received, 1, died, 2, removed, 1, present number, 90; Public Services (Sundays, 112, Holy days, 25, other days, 22), 159; Holy Communion (public, 41, private, 3), 44; Sunday School, teachers, 7, pupils, 43; Catechizing, number of times, 50.

Offerings.

Parochial.— Alms at Holy Communion, $23.03; Current expenses, including salaries, $1,593.98; Sunday School, including Christmas tree, $53.33; Increase and Improvement of Church Property, $220.75; Local charities, $33. Total, $1,924.09.

Diocesan. — Diocesan Missions, $75: Salary of the Bishop, $50; Diocesan Fund, $30; Bible and Common Prayer Book Society of Albany, $1.56; Fund for Aged and Infirm Clergymen, $6; Fund for Widows and Orphans of Clergymen, $2.51; Orphan House of the Holy Saviour, $5.77; The Child's Hospital, $5.56; Theological Education, $3.09; Orphan House of the Holy Saviour, box from Woman's Auxiliary, $30. Total, $209.49.

28

General.— Domestic Missions, $14.66; Foreign Missions, $13.11; Indian Missions, $1.32; Home Missions to Coloured Persons, $1.95; Jewish Missions, $1; American Church Building Fund, $4.60; Clergymen's Retiring Fund, $4.06; Coloured Missions, box from Woman's Auxiliary, $43; Enrolment Fund, $5. Total, $87.70.

Total amount of Offerings, $2,231.28.

Property.

Church and lot (estimated worth), $2,000.
Parsonage and lot (estimated worth), $3,000.
Other property, Chapel, $1,500.
Condition of property, good.
Number of sittings in the Church and Chapel, 450; all free.

Remarks.

In addition to parochial work the Rector has visited the village of Schoharie and held a number of services which are separately reported.

ST. GEORGE'S CHURCH, SCHENECTADY.

Rector. The Rev. J. Philip B. Pendleton, S. T. B.
Lay Reader. Gouverneur F. Mosher.
Wardens. Abram A. Van Vorst, Samuel W. Jackson.
Vestrymen. D. Cady Smith, John A. DeRemer, John Keyes Paige, Giles Y. Van de Bogert, Howland S. Barney, T. Low Barhydt, Edward D. Palmer, Charles S. Washburn.

Parochial.

Families, 319; Individuals (adults, 670, children, 400), 1,070; Baptisms (adults, 5, infants, 29), 34; Confirmed, since last report, 24; Present number of confirmed persons, 500; Marriages, 8; Burials, 39; Churchings, 3; Communicants, last reported 405, admitted, 28, received, 44, died, 10, removed, 10, present number, 457; Public Services (Sundays, 228, Holy days, 78, other days, 195), 501; Holy Communion (public, 100, private, 7), 107; Sunday School, teachers, 29, pupils, 250; Catechising, number of children, all, number of times, every Sunday; Industrial School, teachers, 14, pupils, 110; Parish Agencies, St. Mary's Guild, 110 members; St. Agnes' Guild, 37 members; St. Andrew's Guild, 46 members; Industrial School, Night School, Vested Choir, Parish Paper.

Offerings.

Parochial.— Alms at Holy Communion, $328.74; Current expenses, including salaries, $3,867.13; Sunday School (not reported elsewhere), $173.49; Floating Indebtedness, $465; Increase and Improvement of Church Property, $200; St. Mary's Guild (not reported elsewhere), $376.04; St. Agnes' Guild, $123.86; St. Andrew's Guild, $4.29. Specials for Sunday School, Vested Choir, Parish Kalendar, Vestments, etc., $552.11. Total, $6,090.26.

Diocesan.— Diocesan Missions (allotment, $125, General Missionary, $45, Mission at Sidney, $10, Specials for Missionaries, $40), $220; Salary of the Bishop, $50; Diocesan Fund, $60; Bible and Common Prayer Book Society of Albany, $23.03; Orphan House of the Holy Saviour, $23.85; The Child's Hospital (value of box), $50; Diocesan Lending Library, $10; Women's Diocesan League, $6; Schenectady Hospital and Free Dispensary, $56.10. Total, $507.97.

General.— Domestic Missions (including boxes to Missionaries), $245; Jewish Missions, $23.69; Foreign Missions, $20; Indian Missions, $15; Home Missions to Coloured Persons, $20; Other objects exterior to the Diocese: Scholarship in St. John's School, Logau, Utah, $40; Woman Workers in Utah, $10; Theological Education,

$25; Relief of Clergymen, $40.63; Toward erection of Churches in various places, $40. Total, $479.32.

Total amount of Offerings, $7,077.55.

Property.

Church and lot (estimated worth), $35,000.

Parsonage and lot (estimated worth), $8,000.

Other property, $4,000.

Condition of property, good.

Indebtedness, $2,500.

Amount of salary pledged Rector, $2,000.

Number of sittings in the Church and Chapel, 850.

Remarks.

During the past year the Parish and the Rector have experienced a two-fold affliction in the deaths of the venerable and esteemed resident priests, the Rev. William Payne, D. D., and the Rev. Robert T. S. Lowell, D. D. The former had been connected with the Parish for forty-two years, thirty-six of which were spent as Rector and six as Rector Emeritus, while the latter had been residing here for nearly twenty years. Both of these servants of God passed to their reward after many years of faithful service, and their works do follow them. Their lives have been a source of benediction to us, and they leave behind many tender and helpful memories.

CHRIST CHURCH, SCHENECTADY.

Rector. The Rev. William Curtis Prout, November 1, 1891.

Wardens. James E. Curtiss, David Guy.

Vestrymen. Wm. N. Butler, Henry C. Van Zandt, M. D., David O. Youlen, Prof. Sidney G. Ashmore, Edward E. Kriegsman, John H. Shaffer, Rufus W. Lampman, Robert J. English.

Parochial.

Families, and parts of families, 182; Individuals (adults, 270, children, 150), 420; Baptisms, infants, 10; Marriages, 6; Burials, 13; Communicants, present number, about 195; Public Services (Sundays, 119, Holy days, 26, other days, 51), 196; Holy Communion, public, 48; Sunday School, teachers and officers, 15, pupils, 85; Catechizing, number of children, the Sunday School, number of times, every Sunday.

Offerings.

Parochial.— Alms at Holy Communion, $35.91; Current expenses, including salaries (from the Woman's Guild $103.97), $1,396.24; Sunday School, $81.45; Other parochial objects: Legacy of Mrs. Hough applied on mortgage, $500; for interest on mortgage (from the Woman's Guild), $206.25; Guild Room Fund (legacy of Mrs. Rogers, $500; legacy of Mrs. Watkins $100; cash subscriptions $15.77), $615.77; carpeting and furnishing vestry-room (from the King's Daughters), $21. Total, $2,856.62.

Diocesan.— Diocesan Missions, $15; Salary of the Bishop, $10; Diocesan Fund, $24. Total, $49.

General.— General Missions, $3; Other objects exterior to the Diocese: Missionary box sent by Woman's Guild valued at $35; Christmas box sent by the King's Daughters valued at $35. Total, $73.

Total amount of Offerings, $2,978.62.

Property.

Church and lot (estimated worth), $10,000.

Parsonage and lot (estimated worth), $5,000.

Condition of property, good.
Indebtedness, mortgage $3,500.
Amount of salary pledged Rector, $800 and Rectory.
Number of sittings in the Church, 180; all free.

Remarks.

Three bequests of generous friends of the Parish have been received within the year; one of $500 from the estate of Mrs. Elizabeth W. Rogers, whose husband was at one time Rector of the Parish; one of $500 from that of Mrs. Ann S. Hough; and the third of $100 from that of Mrs. J. De Lancey Watkins. The first and third of these bequests have been added to the fund for a Parish building; the second was applied to the reduction of the bonded debt.

The Parish was without a Rector from the middle of May until the first of November; during which period the services were maintained with but one Sunday's intermission, by the Lay Reader, Prof. Sidney G. Ashmore, and the junior warden, Mr. David Guy.

Schoharie County.

TRINITY CHURCH, SHARON SPRINGS.

Rector. The Rev. Percy St. Michael Podmore.
Trustees. Amory T. Carhart, President; John W. Gardner, Jr., Secretary; John H. Gardner, Seth Parsons, Alfred W. Gardner.

Parochial.

Baptisms, infants, 2; Marriages, 1; Burials, 5; Public Services, Sundays, 100; Holy Communion, public, 12.

Offerings

Parochial.—Current expenses, including salaries, $1,200
Diocesan.—Salary of the Bishop, $20.
* Collections in Church for the year ending July 21, 1891, $506.

Property.

Church and lot (estimated worth) $6,000.
Parsonage and lot (estimated worth), $5,000.
Condition of property, good.
Amount of salary pledged Rector, $900
Number of sittings in the Church, 300, all free.

Remarks

There has been no resident Rector here since Mr. Windsor left; the supply has come from visiting clergy Already there has been a marked improvement in all respects. The celebrations have been well attended, the Sunday School scholars are increasing. I have been in charge since Sept. 7, 1891, and feel very hopeful for the future.

ST ANDREW'S MISSION, SCHOHARIE

The Rev. E. W. Flower, officiating.

---

* This is taken from the balance sheet of the Treasurer of the Board of Trustees.

Parochial.

Families, 7; Individuals (adults, 13, children, 5), 18; Baptisms, infants, 1; Present number of confirmed persons, 11; Communicants, present number, 8; Public Services, 8; Holy Communion, public, 8.

Offerings.

Parochial. — Alms at Holy Communion, reported below for Diocesan Missions; Current expenses, including salaries, $2.35.

Diocesan.—Diocesan Missions, $6.71.

Total amount of Offerings, $9.06.

Remarks.

There is no property except a supply of Prayer and Hymn Books, and a Silver Communion Service, and a full set of Altar Linen.

It is reported that a lot which was owned by the former parish, was sold a number of years since by order of the court for $200, and the money never accounted for by the person appointed to receive it.

There are a few earnest communicants who value the services, but there is not much promise of growth. The services are held in a private parlor. One evening service, and a celebration of the Holy Communion, were held during the summer by the Rev. Canon Stewart.

COBLESKILL.

See Report of the Diocesan Missionary, page 112.

MIDDLEBURGH.

See Report of the Diocesan Missionary, page 112.

Warren County.

CHURCH OF THE MESSIAH, GLENS FALLS.

Rector. The Rev. Fenwick Mitford Cookson.

Wardens. William A. Wait, Leonard G. McDonald.

Vestrymen. Louis P. Juvet, George H. Bassinger, Daniel Peck, William H. Robbins, Nelson LaSalle, Henry W. Coffin, M. D., Hugh A. Bowden, James A. Holden.

Parochial.

Families, 183; Baptisms (adults, 4, infants, 16), 20; Confirmed, since last report, 12; Marriages, 10; Burials, 15; Communicants, last reported, 329, admitted, 12, received, 8, died, 4, removed, 5, present number, 340; Public Services (Sundays, 135, Holy days, 29, other days, 75), 239; Holy Communion (public, 56, private, 3), 59; Sunday School, teachers, 23, pupils, 230. Catechizing, number of children, Sunday School, number of times, weekly.

Offerings.

Parochial.— Alms at Holy Communion, $50.29; Current expenses, including salaries, $3,093.82; Sunday School, $117.54; Increase and Improvement of Church Property, $92. Total, $3,353.65.

Diocesan.— Diocesan Missions, $75; Salary of the Bishop, $40; Diocesan Fund,

\$42; Bible and Common Prayer Book Society of Albany, \$6.03; Orphan House o the Holy Saviour, \$20.76; The Child's Hospital, \$7.14. Total, \$190.93.

General.—Domestic Missions, \$20; Jewish Missions, \$1.35; A Western Mission \$12.70. Total, \$34.05.

Total amount of Offerings, \$3,578.63.

Property.

Church and lot (estimated worth), \$27,000.

Condition of property, excellent.

Amount of salary pledged Rector, \$1,400.

Number of sittings in the Church, 388, assigned; at Harrisena, 150, free.

Remarks.

The Ladies' Society render most generous and valuable service, and it is the chie source of support of the vested choir.

The Altar Society provide in all things for the sanctuary. A beautiful brass eagl lectern in memory of Mrs. Elizabeth Buell Holden, a devout and most faithfu woman, who died Jan. 20, 1891, was placed in the Church on Easter day by her hu band, Dr. Austin W. Holden, and her son, James A. Holden.

On July 19, 1891, Dr. Austin W. Holden died. He was a vestryman or warden o the parish almost continuously since its organization in 1840, and was many time its delegate to the Convention of the Diocese of New York, and later of the Dioces of Albany, and was ever an intelligent and earnest advocate of the interests of th Church. He was for a long time a licensed lay-reader, and to the last, within fe months, a faithful and constant teacher in the Sunday School.

A handsome brass alms-basin was given to the Church on Easter day by Mrs. J W. Finch.

THE PARISH OF THE HOLY CROSS, WARRENSBURGH.

Wardens. Frederick Burhans, Henry Griffing.

Vestrymen. James Herrick, Emerson S. Crandall, Halsey Herrick, Thomas J Smith, Chas. F. Burhans, Charles White, Halsey B. Hayes.

Parochial.

Baptisms (adults, 4, infants, 8), 12; Burials, 8; Communicants, last reported, 85 died, 4.

Offerings.

Parochial.—Current expenses, including salaries, \$2,234.94.

Diocesan — Diocesan Missions, \$50; Salary of the Bishop, \$38; Diocesan Fund \$27, Bible and Common Prayer Book Society of Albany, \$6; Fund for Aged and In firm Clergymen, \$9.19; Fund for Widows and Orphans of Clergymen, \$3.33. Total \$133.52.

General.— General Theological Seminary, \$3 67, Domestic Missions, \$17.35; Pro moting Christianity among the Jews, \$2.39. Total, \$23.41.

Total amount of Offerings, \$2,391.87.

Remarks

The report from this Parish would not be complete unless we placed on record be fore the Diocese at large our sense of the great loss that we have sustained in the sud den death of our beloved Rector who ministered to us wisely and faithfully for six teen years. It is a loss that is deeply felt by every member of the Parish, bot young and old, for all had learned to love him, because of his impartial kindness t every person in our community and his readiness in season and out of season to serv one in sickness and in death. The Rev. William Meredith Ogden was a pattern Priest who never forgot his priesthood, while at the same time his high regard for his office placed no barrier around him to prevent the humblest from approaching him with the utmost confidence. He was always at his post offering daily morning and evening prayer, whether with the many or the few, and as his life had been one of ministrations, so he died robed in his Priestly vestments with wise and comforting words on his lips teaching the flock that God had committed to his care.

" May he rest in peace and may perpetual light shine upon him."

We regret that we are not able to give a more complete Parochial Report (not having the private register of the late Rector).

ST. MARY'S CHURCH, LUZERNE.

Rector. The Rev. C. J. Whipple.

Wardens. Thomas H. Taylor, H. J. Martine.

Vestrymen. James Clapp, John S. Burneson, J. J. Wigley, Edward Gell, W. J. Kinnear, J. B. Wigley, George Gell, G. W. Beardmore.

Parochial.

Families, 24; Individuals (adults, 54, children, 25), 79; Baptisms, infants, 7; Present number of confirmed persons, 42; Burials, 1; Communicants, received, 3, removed, 1, Communicants in Conklingville, 12; Public Services (Sundays, 125, Holy days, 12, other days, 69), 206; Holy Communion (public, 37, private, 1), 38; Sunday School, teachers, 2, pupils, 24; Catechizing, number of children all, number of times, 30.

Offerings.

Parochial.— Alms at Holy Communion, $223.84; Current expenses, including salaries, $612.21; Sunday School, $45; Increase and Improvement of Church Property, $502; Other parochial objects, $90. Total, $1,473.05.

Diocesan.— Diocesan Missions, $20; Salary of the Bishop, $8; Diocesan Fund, $12. Total, $40.

General.— Domestic Missions, $4.16.

Total amount of Offerings, $1,517.21.

Property.

Church and lot (estimated worth), $6,000.

Parsonage and lot (estimated worth), $1,500.

Other property, $500.

Condition of property, good.

Amount of salary pledged Rector, $400.

Number of sittings in the Church, 250; all free.

Remarks.

All the Diocesan assessments against St. John's Church, Conklingville, have been fully paid during the past year, which, however, are not included in the above report.

' CHURCH OF THE GOOD SHEPHERD, CHESTERTOWN.

Priest in charge, The Rev. Alfred Taylor.

Warden. Ralph Thurman.

Treasurer. S. H. Bevans.

Clerk. James F. Holley.

Parochial.

Families, 27; Individuals (adults, 67, children, 35), 102; Baptisms (adults, 18, infants, 3), 21; Confirmed since last report, 18; Communicants, last reported, 39, admitted, 17, received, 5, removed, 3, present number, 58; Public Services, twice every Sunday, holy days, nearly all, other days, Fridays; Holy Communion, public, weekly private, once; Sunday School, teachers, 3, pupils, 25.

Offerings.

Parochial.— Alms at Holy Communion, $3.36; Current expenses, including salaries, $332; Sunday School, $3.54; Increase and Improvement of Church Property, $50; Purchase and decoration of Rectory, $2,300. Total, $2,688.90.

Diocesan.— Diocesan Missions, $15; Salary of the Bishop, $6; Diocesan Fund, $12. Total, $33.

Total amount of Offerings, $2,721.90.

Property.

Church and lot (estimated worth), $3,200.
Parsonage and lot (estimated worth), $2,300.
Condition of property, excellent.
Amount of salary pledged Rector, $400.
Number of sittings in the Church 100; all free.

Remarks.

This report is as full as I can make it, some things being omitted for the lack of proper entry in the register. I have only been in charge since October 1st, and for four months preceding there had been no regular service.

R. Thurman, Esq., has during the year refurnished the church with lamps more useful and more beautiful than any we have had since it was built. The Rectory is also the gift of Mr. and Miss Thurman, to whose generous benefactions the Church on many occasions has been indebted.

ST. PAUL'S CHURCH, BARTONVILLE.

Priest in charge. The Rev. Alfred Taylor.
Warden. John Barton.
Treasurer. Scott Barton.
Clerk. Alfred A. Hart.

Parochial.

Families, 18; Individuals (adults, 44, children, 20), 64; Baptisms (adults, 13, infants, 10), 23. Confirmed, since last report, 10; Present number of confirmed persons 35; Burials, 1: Communicants, last reported, 19, admitted, 10, received, 6, present number, 35; Public Services, every Sunday, Holy days, occasionally, other days Wednesdays; Holy Communion, public, monthly; Sunday School, teachers, 3, pupils, 32.

Offerings.

Parochial — Current expenses, including salaries, $152.95.

Property.

Church and lot (estimated worth), $3,000.
Condition of property, very good
Amount of salary pledged Rector, $100
Sittings in the Church all free.

ST. SACRAMENT CHURCH, BOLTON-ON-LAKE-GEORGE.

Rector. The Rev Clement T. Blanchet, B. D.
Lay Reader. James F. Chamberlain, Esq , Sabbath-Day Point.

Warden. John B. Simpson.
Treasurer. Asa W. Dickinson.
Clerk. Randall W. Wilson.

Parochial.

BOLTON.

Families, 38; Individuals (adults, 60, children, 66), 126; Baptisms (adults, 5, infants, 10), 15; Confirmed, since last report, 5; Present number of confirmed persons, 55; Marriages, 4; Burials, 3; Communicants, last reported, 52, admitted, 5, received, 1, died, 1, removed, 4, present number, 55; Public Services (Sundays, 164, Holy days, 4, other days, 100), 268; Holy Communion (public, 25, private, 1), 26; Sunday School, teachers, 5, pupils, 60; Catechizing, number of children, all, number of times, 12.

SABBATH-DAY-POINT.

Families, 12; Individuals (adults, 18, children, 34), 52; Baptisms (adults, 4, infants, 12), 16; Confirmed, since last report, 4; Present number of confirmed persons, 12; Communicants, last reported, 8, admitted, 4, removed, 2, present number, 10; Public Services, Sundays, 4; Holy Communion, public, 2; Sunday School, teachers, 1, pupils, 15.

Offerings.

Parochial. — Alms at Holy Communion, and Current expenses, including salaries, $434.99; Sunday School, $15. Total, $449.99.

Diocesan.—Diocesan Missions, $10; Salary of the Bishop, $10; Diocesan Fund, $27. Total, $47.

General.—Domestic Missions, $2.32; Foreign Missions, $2.32; Indian Missions, $2.32; Home Missions to Coloured Persons, $2.32; Work among the Jews, $2.32; Clergy Retiring Fund, $4. Total, $15.60.

Total amount of Offerings, $512.59.

Property.

Church and lot (estimated worth), $8,000.
Parsonage and lot (estimated worth), $3,000.
Condition of property, good.
Amount of salary pledged Rector, $900.
Number of sittings in the Church, 150; all free.

Remarks.

The above statistics include those for Sabbath-Day Point some twelve miles further down the lake, under our earnest and efficient Lay Reader, James F. Chamberlain, Esq.

The figures for Sabbath-Day Point have reference only to the work done there since I was requested to take the general oversight of it by the Bishop some three years ago. It appears, however, that much excellent work had previously been done there which cannot easily be put down in figures, but which may be inferred from the following facts: When Mr. Chamberlain first made his summer residence at Sabbath-Day Point some eighteen or twenty years ago, there were no members of our Church in the whole town of Hague in which Sabbath-Day Point is situated. There are now twelve families, including thirty-three adults and thirty-four children; twenty-three of these adults have been baptized and eighteen confirmed, and thirty-three of the children have also been baptized, and about half of them are now under catechetical instruction. Besides those twelve families, there are eight more which have been visited and instructed, and from among whom we may look for excellent fruit in the near future. Our efficient Lay Reader has not reported his frequent

29

visits, services, cottage lectures and catechetical instructions, which would average three or four each week for eight or nine months of the year. The children reported as Sunday School pupils are gathered into three small groups at different places and instructed at different hours almost every Sunday in the year, and although their parents are not included in the classes, they often hear the instruction given, and some are thus won to the Saviour, and to His Church. The summary of the work would therefore be as follows: Families, 12; adults, 33; children, 34; baptized, adults, 23, children, 33; whole number confirmed, 18; owing to deaths and removals the present number of communicants is 10 besides the Lay Reader.

It seems only right to note the pleasant fact that the Church of St. Sacrament at Bolton is now entirely out of debt, its property in excellent condition, and for the first time in its existence of twenty-two years, in union with the Diocese. Our present corporation is composed of local members, and works very satisfactorily. For this happy state of affairs we are largely indebted (under God) to the sympathetic and patient efforts of the Rev. F. M. Cookson of Glens Falls.

. We are also indebted to Mr. John B. Simpson, our present Warden, for a new and handsome Estey Chapel organ, and for earnest effort in raising about half of the incumbent's salary during the past summer. Also to many friends for helping make up arrears on salary last spring, and for donation of clothing for our poor people.

Washington County.

ZION CHURCH, SANDY HILL.

Rector. The Rev. Edwin Ruthven Armstrong.
Lay Reader. George Arthur Ingalls.
Wardens. Charles Hamilton Beach, John William Wait.
Vestrymen. C. T. Beach, D. Harrington, G A. Ingalls, P. F. Langworthy, Albert Mott, M. D., John Nichols, S. H. Parks, Charles Young.

Parochial.

Families, 129; Individuals (adults, 319, children, 184), 503; Baptisms (adults, 1, infants, 13), 14; Received (clinically baptized), 1; Confirmed, since last report, 7; Present number of confirmed persons, 193; Marriages, 2, Burials, 10; Communicants, died, 2, removed, 7; Public Services, 492, Holy Communion (public, 95, private, 8), 103; Catechizing, weekly.

Offerings.

Parochial.— Alms at Holy Communion, $81 31; current expenses, including salaries, $1,350; Sunday School, $25; Increase and Improvement of Church Property (retable), $13; Sunday School Christmas tree, $15; Smith's Basin Christmas tree, $19. Total, $1,503.31.

Diocesan.— Diocesan Missions, $13.37; Salary of the Bishop, $30; Diocesan Fund, $30; Bible and Common Prayer Book Society of Albany, $8.75; Fund for Aged and Infirm Clergymen, $14 67, Orphan House of the Holy Saviour, $28.02; The Child's Hospital, $12.58; Archdeaconry expenses, $2.74. Total, $140.13.

General.— Domestic and Foreign Missions, $2 88 from the Sunday School; Mission to the Jews, $8.72; American Church Building Fund, $1.55. Total, $13.15.

. Total amount of Offerings, $1,656.59.

Property

Church and lot (estimated worth), $12,000.
Parsonage and lot (estimated worth), $3,500.

Miller Fund, invested for literature, $300.

Condition of property, excellent.

Indebtedness, (1) bank notes outstanding, $750; (2) mortgage on Rectory, $2,000.

Amount of salary pledged Rector, $900 and Rectory.

Number of sittings in the Church, 300; all free.

Remarks.

During the past year services have been maintained with such marked appreciation at Adamsville in the township of Hartford and at Smith's Basin in the town of Kingsbury, that five of those confirmed were from the outskirts of the Parish. The people of those districts too have given the Rector a valuable horse, by the help of which the work has been greatly facilitated.

Zion Church has been enriched also in the past year by a gift from the Sunday School of a neat cover for the font in oak and bronze, and by a pair of Eucharistic Candlesticks, a thank offering for improved health vouchsafed to a communicant.

TRINITY CHURCH, GRANVILLE.

Rector. The Rev. C. H. Lancaster, November 1, 1891.

Wardens. Jonathan S. Warren, Palmer D. Everts.

Vestrymen. Byron H. Sykes, Amos W. Wilcox, George W. Henry, Orville L. Goodrich, John S. Warren.

Parochial.

Families, 49; Individuals (adults, 100, children, 40), 140; Baptisms, infants, 4; Marriages, 5; Burials, 2; Communicants, present number, about 60; Public Services (Sundays, 142, Holy days, 30, other days, 25), 197; Holy Communion, public, 70; Sunday School, teachers, 6, pupils, 40.

Offerings.

Parochial.— Current expenses, including salaries, $880.87; Sunday School, $72.11; Increase and Improvement of Church Property, $160. Total, $1,112.98.

Diocesan.— Diocesan Missions, $12.50; Salary of the Bishop, $6; Diocesan Fund, $7.50. Total, $26.

General.— General Missions (from Sunday School), $16.06.

Total amount of Offerings, $1,155.04.

Property.

Church and lot (estimated worth), $4,000.

Parsonage and lot (estimated worth), $4,000.

Condition of property, good.

Indebtedness, mortgage on Rectory, $1,800; floating debt about $100.

Amount of salary pledged Rector, $400, and use of Rectory.

Number of sittings in the Church, 200; all free.

Remarks.

Of the money reported above, $214 14 were secured by the efforts of the Ladies' Aid Society.

ST. JAMES' CHURCH, FORT EDWARD.

Rector. The Rev. Joseph W. McIlwaine.

Wardens. James G. Kinne, Francis B. Davis.

Vestrymen. Frederick G. Tilton, Benjamin M. Tasker, George Scott, Jarvis W. Milliman, Albert H. Wicks, John J. Morgan, Robert O. Bascom, Robert A. Linendoll, M. D.

Parochial.

Families and parts of families, 102; Individuals (adults, 200, children, 108), 303⇌ Baptisms (adults, 7, infants, 12), 19; Confirmed, since last report, 2; Present number of confirmed persons, 157; Marriages, 1; Burials, 5; Communicants, admitted, 3, died, 2, removed, 15, present number, 60; Public Services, Sundays, morning and evening, Holy days, Lent, daily, other days, Wednesday evening; Holy Communion, public, monthly and chief festivals; Sunday School, teachers, 8, pupils, 60; Catechizing, number of children, all, number of times, frequently.

Offerings.

Parochial.— Alms at Holy Communion, $14; Current expenses, including salaries, $1,050; Sunday School, $25.90. Total, $1,089.90.

Diocesan.— Diocesan Missions, $18; Salary of the Bishop, $30: Diocesan Fund, $18 ; Orphan House of the Holy Saviour, $5.19. Total, $71.19.

General.— General Missions, $30.14; Mission to Deaf-Mutes, $2.50; Mission to Jews, $1.96. Total, $34.60.

Total amount of Offerings, $1,195.69.

Property.

Church and lot (estimated worth), $7,000.

Parsonage and lot (estimated worth), $3,000.

Condition of property, good.

Amount of salary pledged Rector, $600.

Number of sittings in the Church, 250; all free.

Remarks.

The above report covers the last six months of the Rectorship of the Rev. Frederick N. Skinner.

ST. PAUL'S CHURCH, SALEM.

Rector. The Rev. Harris C. Rush.

Wardens. Hon. James Gibson, Hon. George B. McCartee.

Vestrymen. A. K. Broughton, Frederick Kegler, David Mahaffy, Ephraim Herrick, William Alexander McNish, Frank A. Graham, George B. Martin, Joseph Hofert.

Parochial.

Families, 60; Baptisms (adults, 4, infants, 8), 12; Confirmed, since last report, 12; Present number of confirmed persons, 166; Marriages, 2; Burials, 10; Communicants, last reported, 135, admitted, 13, received, 2, died, 3, removed, 1, added, 9,, present number, 155; Public Services, thrice on all Sundays, other days, four times weekly; Holy Communion, public, each Sunday and Holy day, private, four times; Sunday School, teachers, 8, pupils, 50 ; Catechizing, number of times, frequently.

Offerings.

Parochial. Alms at Holy Communion, $57.96; Current expenses, including salaries, $1,341.32 , Parish debt, $500. Total, $1,899.28.

Diocesan.— Diocesan Missions, $73.67. Salary of the Bishop, $30; Diocesan Fund, $21; Bible and Common Prayer Book Society of Albany, $5; Fund for Aged and Infirm Clergymen, $5, Fund for Widows and Orphans of Clergymen, $5; Orphan House of the Holy Saviour, $5. Total, $144.67.

General.—Domestic Missions, $7.48. Foreign Missions, $7.48; Society for Promoting Christianity among the Jews, $5.08. Total, $20.04.

Total amount of Offerings, $2,063.99.

Property.

Church and lot (estimated worth), $6,000.
Amount of salary pledged Rector, $700.
Number of sittings in the Church, 260; all free.

TRINITY CHURCH, WHITEHALL.

Rector. The Rev. Reyner E. W. Cosens.
Wardens. Edward P. Newcomb, Fred. H. McFarran.
Vestrymen. Robert A. Hall, C. B. Bates, F. S. Cowan, William H. Tefft, W. N. Week's, I. Adams, Hiram B. Skeels.

Parochial.

Families, 118; Individuals (adults, 258, children, 78), 336; Baptisms (adults, 2, infants, 9), 11; Confirmed, since last report, 8; Present numper of confirmed persons, 200; Marriages, 6 ; Burials, 6 ; Communicants, last reported, 174, admitted, 8, received, 3, died, 2, removed, 5, present number, 178; Public Services, daily, *during the year,* total number of public services, 551, sermons, instructions and Bible classes, 153; Holy Communion (public, 81, private, 4), 85; Sunday School, teachers, 7, pupils, average attendance, 50; Catechizing, frequent.

Offerings.

Parochial.— Current expenses, including salaries, $1,276.25 ; Parish School, $543.98. Total, $1,820.23.
Diocesan.— Diocesan Missions, $25 ; Salary of the Bishop, $20. Total, $45.
Total amount of Offerings, $1,865.23.

Property.

Condition of property, good.
Indebtedness, $250.
Amount of salary pledged Rector, $1,000.
Sittings in the Church all free.

ST. LUKE'S CHURCH, CAMBRIDGE.

Rector. The Rev. Frederick H. T. Horsfield.
Wardens. Henry C. Day, Robert Davis.
Vestrymen. William J. Davis, Thomas Le Grys, Robert Davis, Jr., John Money-penny, M. D., J. Fenimore Niver, M. D.

Parochial.

Families, 25; Individuals (adults, 75, children, 10), 85; Present number of confirmed persons, 50; Marriages, 1; Burials, 3; Communicants, received, 1, died, 1, removed, 2, present number, 50; Public Services (Sundays, 104, Holy days, 15, other days, 75), 194; Holy Communion (public, 30, private, 2), 32; Sunday School, teachers, 1, pupils, 10.

Offerings.

Parochial.— Alms at Holy Communion, $15; Current expenses, including salaries, $716.12; Sunday School, $20; Increase and Improvement of Church property, $800; Final payment of Furnace, $89.41; Ladies' Aid, $104. Total, $1,744.53.
Diocesan.— Diocesan Missions, $180; Salary of the Bishop, $10; Diocesan Fund, $15; Orphan House of the Holy Saviour, $25. Total, $230.
Total amount of Offerings, $1,974.53.

Property.

Church and lot (estimated worth), $6,000.
Condition of property, fair.
Amount of salary pledged Rector, $500.
Number of sittings in the Church, 200; all free.

Remarks.

A handsome Pulpit of carved oak, the work of Geissler, New York, has been erected in the Church in loving memory of the late Rev. Sydney Kent, M. A., a former Rector of the Parish.

A beautiful Chancel Chair — and a valuable "Fair linen cloth" have been presented to the Parish.

ST. PAUL'S CHURCH, GREENWICH.

Rector. The Rev. Chas. W. Boyd (Deacon), appointed November 7, 1891.
Wardens. H. L. Mowry, W. R. Hobbie.
Vestrymen. B. F. Kendall, George Tucker, H. B. Bates, Robt. Campbell, S. L. Stillman, W. E. Reynolds.

Parochial.

Families, 30; Individuals (adults, 100, children, 45), 145; Baptisms, infants, 1; Marriages, 1; Burials, 3; Communicants, last reported, 56, received, 4, died, 3, removed, 12, present number, 45; Public Services, two each Sunday for 11 months, one each Sunday for 1 month; Holy days, one, other days, Friday during Lent; Holy Communion, public, 4; Sunday School, teachers 5, pupils, 35.

Offerings.

Parochial.— Current expenses, including salaries, $491.33; Sunday School, $18.11; Increase and Improvement of Church Property, $215; Contribution for the Jews, $3.87; General expenses, $216.18. Total, $944.49.

Diocesan.— Diocesan Missions, $25; Salary of the Bishop, $4; Diocesan Fund, $15. Total, $44.

Total amount of Offerings, $988.49.

Property.

Church and lot (estimated worth), $7,000.
Condition of property, good.
Indebtedness, mortgage with interest due, about $400.
Amount of salary pledged Rector, $500.
Number of sittings in the Church, 230.

Remarks.

David H. Clarkson, Lay Reader was our supply during November, 1890, and Canon Gray of Albany, in December.

The Rev. Geo. Herbert Norton was appointed resident Rector in January, and filled the position most acceptably until his very sudden death, August 18. Since then we have had a number of different clergymen, but have had services at least once every Sunday, and most of the time twice.

NORTH GRANVILLE MISSION.

Missionary. The Rev. C. H. Lancaster.

Parochial.

Families, 9. Individuals (adults, 27, children, 6), 33, Marriages, 1; Communicants, present number, 14; Public Services (Sundays, 57, Holy days, 2, other days, 25), 84; Holy Communion, public, 6.

Offerings.

.hial.— Current expenses, including salaries, $154.35; Sunday School, $10.40.
;164.75.

san.— Diocesan Missions, $10; Salary of the Bishop, $4; Diocesan Fund, $3.
;17.

amount of Offerings, $181.75.

Property.

1 and furniture, $250.

.tion of property, good.

.nt of salary pledged Missionary, $100.

CRANDALL'S CORNERS.

See Report of the Diocesan Missionary, page 112.

ADAMSVILLE.

See Remarks, Report, Zion Church, Sandy Hill.

SMITH'S BASIN.

See Remarks, Report, Zion Church, Sandy Hill.

(B.)

PERSONAL REPORTS.

101 WESTMINSTER ST., PROVIDENCE, R. I., *October* 31, 1891.

ι BISHOP — I have just returned from Europe, and as I desire not to be put
n the delinquent list of non-reporting Clergy, I write to say that my last ser-
Otego was on Easter evening, and before leaving I made out a full report of
·k during the six months I was there. I left the report in the Parish Regis-
)tego, thinking it would be of service to my successor, and I suppose that the
·ill send it with his own to you at the Convention in November.

Respectfully yours,

A. S. ASHLEY.

TROY ROAD, ALBANY, *November* 17, 1891.

Right Rev. WM. C. DOANE, D. D., LL. D.:

)EAR BISHOP — I beg leave to report that during the last conventional year I
ntinued the work of establishing the Church at Menands.
services of the Church have been regularly maintained. I have celebrated
y Communion on every Lord's Day, and on all festivals. I have Baptized 4
ind 9 children, have performed 3 Marriages, and buried 5 persons.

Faithfully yours,

EDGAR T. CHAPMAN.

Right Rev. W. C. DOANE, D. D., LL. D., *Bishop of Albany :*

.ndersigned respectfully reports as follows:
:iated at the Locke House, Indian Lake, on the five Sundays in August of the
year. On each occasion the Holy Communion was celebrated, the total num-
·ersons communicating being 9. I also read Morning Prayer on each Sunday,
ached.

In this work I enjoyed the hearty co-operation of the proprietor of the hotel, M⸍ '
H. G. Locke, and of a number of other persons, not of our own Communion.

　　　　　　　　　　　　　　　　　　HENRY A. DOWS.

　　　　　　　JOHNSTOWN, N. Y., *November* 16, 1891.

To the Right Rev. WM. C. DOANE, D. D., LL. D.:

DEAR BISHOP — Enclosed with this, my personal report, is the parochial report of
the Parish at Fonda.

I have held the Sunday Morning Services, as arranged for, throughout the past
year, without an omission, and in addition a Service on Christmas day, Ash Wednesday, Good Friday and every Wednesday in Lent. Have visited the Church people
there and in Fultonville, at their homes, quite often, and more especially in some
calls upon the sick. There is no marked change in Church matters in Fonda.
Though a " feeble folk " as far as numbers are concerned, there is nothing to discourage, but, on the other hand, I trust it is a good thing to have kept the work going.
Several persons come regularly to the Services from Fultonville, and several other
irregularly.

　　　　　　　　　　　　Yours sincerely,

　　　　　　　　　　　　　　CHARLES C. EDMUNDS.

　　　HOOPERS VALLEY, TIOGA CO., N. Y., *December* 10, 1891.

To the Right Rev., the Bishop of Albany:

RIGHT REV. AND DEAR SIR — Immediately after my resignation of St. Stephen's
Church, Schuylerville, I returned to the Diocese of Central New York and took charge
of a former Parish of mine. 　　　　　　Truly yours,

　　　　　　　　　　　　　　　　J. F. ESCH.

　　　　　　　OGDENSBURG, N. Y., *November* 1, 1891

The Right Rev. WILLIAM CROSWELL DOANE, D. D., LL. D.:

RIGHT REV. SIR — During the past year I have, when desired, assisted the Rev.
Dr. Morrison, Rector of St. John's Church, Ogdensburg, and also taken the full duty
in Grace Church, Canton, for the three months ending August 1, 1891.

　　　　　　　　　　　　Very respectfully,

　　　　　　　　　　　　　　W. H. HARISON.

　　　　　REXLEIGH SCHOOL, SALEM, N. Y., *November* 17, 1891.

RIGHT REV. AND DEAR BISHOP—You touch Salem often enough to know that your
Priest has not retired from the Parish of St. Paul for lack of work.

One of the most active and stirring centers of Church life is Rexleigh School, over
which for the year past I have presided.

I beg to report " progress " in all parts of its manifold life, and trust that ere I
write again some generous heart may provide our new building and set us in Rexleigh's broad meadows among the great schools of the land.

　　　　　　　　　　　　Always dutifully yours,

　　　　　　　　　　　　　　JOHN H. HOUGHTON.

　　　　　　　COOPERSTOWN, *November* 7, 1891.

I have to report to the Bishop an occasional service and such religious work as circumstances and the state of my health would permit.

　　　　　　　　　　　　Respectfully,

　　　　　　　　　　　　　　W. W. LORD.

　　　　　　　LAKE WORTH, FLA., *November* 20, 1891.

MY DEAR BISHOP — During the past summer I have held services at the Church
of the Good Shepherd, on Racquette Lake, from the middle of June till October

This Mission receives no aid from the Board of Missions, but during the season just closed has sent our offering of $50 to Diocesan Missions. The Church and Rectory on St. Hubert's Isle are both in complete condition, and elaborately furnished. Every thing pertaining to the work on Racquette Lake is lovingly cared for by interested friends. The Missionary seeks to extend his ministrations both to summer visitors and to the guides and their families on the lake. Yours sincerely,

J. N. MULFORD.

In charge of the Church of the Good Shepherd, Racquette lake, Hamilton county.

HOOSICK FALLS, *November* 10, 1891.

Right Rev. WILLIAM C. DOANE, D. D., LL. D.:

MY DEAR BISHOP — In complying with the canonical requirement to report to you for the year last past, I have only to repeat what I have formerly reiterated.

By God's blessing and through the brotherly kindness of our worthy Rector and other brethren I have had the privilege of frequently celebrating the Holy Eucharist and assisting in the services of the Church on the Lord's Day with a good degree of regularity. Faithfully yours,

G. H. NICHOLLS.

NEWBURGH, N. Y., *December* 7, 1891.

To the Right Rev. the Bishop of Albany :

The Rev. James F. Olmsted respectfully reports that since his ordination to the Diaconate, June 14, 1891, he has served as Assistant Minister in St. George's Church, Newburgh, N. Y.

SEABURY HALL, FARIBAULT, MINN., 21st *November*, 1891.

Right Rev. W. C. DOANE, D. D., LL. D., *Bishop of Albany :*

MY DEAR BISHOP — Since my ordination in September; I have been engaged as tutor in Greek and Metaphysics in the preparatory department of Seabury Divinity School, and have also pursued special studies in the Divinity course. On Sundays I have regularly assisted the Rector of St. James' Parish, St. Paul.

Faithfully yours,

GEORGE LYNDE RICHARDSON.

GRAND HOTEL DU LAC,
VEVEY, SUISSE, *October* 2, 1891.

MY DEAR BISHOP — Since the last meeting of the Diocesan Convention of Albany, I have taken part in the Confirmation services at Nice; assisted the Rev. Dr. Nevin of St. Paul's Church, Rome, two Sundays, and preached and celebrated one Sunday in the American Church at Geneva. Yours in Christ,

D. L. SCHWARTZ.

BOONTON, N. J., *November* 10, 1891.

MY DEAR BISHOP DOANE — I beg to report that since resigning the Mission at Santa Clara, I have preached every Sunday and celebrated, baptized two adults for the Rector of this Parish. In case no reports are received from Chestertown or Santa Clara, I would like to state that thirty-eight were baptized, mostly adults, and twenty-nine confirmed at Chester and Bartonville, and eighteen baptized at Santa Clara since last report. Yours most respectfully,

NASSAU WILLIAM STEPHENS.

ALBANY, N. Y., *Nov.* 17, 1891.

To the Right Rev. WILLIAM C. DOANE, D. D., LL. D., *Bishop of Albany :*

MY DEAR BISHOP — I hereby report to you that during the past conventional year I have assisted in services of the Church thirty-four times, have rendered full ser-

30

vices and preached twenty-seven times, celebrated nine times, and officiated at three funerals. Respectfully yours,

RICHARD TEMPLE.

757 NORTH CLARK ST., CHICAGO, *Sept.* 9, 1891.

DEAR BISHOP DOANE—With reference to my work this Summer at Lebanon Springs, I report as follows: In the Church of Our Saviour, Lebanon Springs, I conducted morning and evening prayer, and preached on each of the nine Sundays of July and August. The Church was fairly well filled at the morning service. There were three public celebrations of the Holy Eucharist, with an average of about thirteen communions made A fair was held for the Rectory Fund, netting about two hundred dollars. Very sincerely,

MONTGOMERY H. THROOP, JR.

KINDERHOOK, *Sept.* 28, 1891.

To the Right Rev. the Bishop of Albany:

The Rev. E. S. DeG. Tompkins respectfully reports that he has resided at Kinderhook during the past year, and assisted his reverend brethren as they had need.

20 LEXINGTON AVE., LEXINGTON, KY., *Nov.* 9, 1891.

The Right Rev. W. C. DOANE, D. D., LL. D. :

RIGHT REV. FATHER—I beg very respectfully to inform you that Bishop Dudley yesterday, 24th Sunday after Trinity, ordained me Deacon at Louisville, Ky., at the 11 A. M. service. The congregation was good and very much interested. The Bishop told me he would write you at once and inform you of his ordaining me, at the same time he said I too should-write you. Praying the Lord of the Harvest to give me wisdom and discretion to labour in His Vineyard in the Holy office to which I have been ordered, and requesting your Episcopal prayers and blessing.

I am, Right Rev. Father, very respectfully yours,

JOHN G. URLING.

To the Right Rev. the Bishop of Albany:

RIGHT REV. AND DEAR SIR—Personally, it seems to me unnecessary to add to what Dr. McDonald may have said of my services at St. Stephen's Chapel, Maple Grove, where what I could do, the past year, has been freely rendered — three or four public services each month and on Holy days, some catechizing, and three funerals — a memorial font and communion silver contributed ; but chiefly giving Church intelligence, by tracts, and such works as Littledale's, Odenheimer's and Lane's Notes of English Church History. Being in my 70th year, my eyesight does not improve, and it is with great difficulty I can officiate at all — yet I do, so that the Church may keep her ground, and win souls, and glorify God.

D. WASHBURN.

WINDSOR AVE., BALTIMORE, MD., *Nov.* 24, 1891.

Right Rev. WM. CROSWELL DOANE, D. D., LL. D. :

MY DEAR BISHOP—During the past Conventional year I have been engaged in ministerial work, with his permission, in the Diocese of the Bishop of Maryland. The records of all such services and other ministerial acts, held and performed by me, are entered in the registers of the various parishes in which they were rendered, to be included in their reports to the Diocesan at the annual convention.

Very respectfully,

WM. ROLLINS WEBB.

TUXEDO PARK, *Dec.* 28, 1891.

The Right Rev. WM. C. DOANE, D. D., LL. D.:

The Rev. John M. Windsor respectfully reports : That having resigned the rectorship of Trinity Church, Sharon Springs, to take effect May 1, 1891, he removed with his family to New York city, where he preached and celebrated the Holy Communion at St. Matthew's Church, in that city, on Sunday, the third day of the same month, and on the afternoon of that day was seized with an illness that confined him to his bed for nearly three weeks, and disabled him for work until the middle of July, when he accepted an invitation to preach at "St. Mary's Church in Tuxedo, N. Y.," on the nineteenth of that month, and on the same day was engaged by the Rector, and also by the Warden of the Church, to remove his family to Tuxedo, and take charge of the parish for ten weeks, or during the Rector's absence in England. The time of the Rector's vacation having been extended, the vestry afterward engaged him to continue in charge for the winter of 1891–92 or, for an indefinite period.

REPORT OF THE TRUSTEES OF THE CORNING FOUNDATION FOR CHRISTIAN WORK IN THE DIOCESE OF ALBANY.

The work of the Foundation has been carried on with gratifying success during the past year. The trustees have held their usual meetings. They have granted permission to the Society of Graduates to put up a building on the school grounds to be called "Graduates Hall" (the foundation of this building has been laid); they have erected an additional building, at the east end of the school, containing recitation rooms, kindergarten room, and a row of dormitories ; they have also erected a new building for the Child's Hospital, and the old hospital building has been given over to the uses of St. Margaret's House. Number of teachers and lecturers in the school 43; pupils, 252.

THOMAS B. FULCHER,
Nov. 1, 1891. *Secretary of the Board.*

ANNUAL REPORT OF THE CHILD'S HOSPITAL, ALBANY.

In publishing this sixteenth annual report of the Child's Hospital, the principal event to record is the completion and opening of the new building. Thanks to the gifts so freely given, the work progressed rapidly, and on the 29th of September, the Feast of St. Michael and All Angels, the completed building was opened. An impressive service was held, and a number of persons were present and enjoyed going through the wards and rooms. So generous had been the gifts that after furnishing, a small balance was left, to be used as may be needed.

Those who have inspected the building cannot fail to appreciate its beauty and the way in which it meets every requirement. The Managers feel that the thoroughness with which the work is done is due to the painstaking care given by Mr. Kilbourne, the superintendent, and Mr. Dodge, the contractor, and they extend to them their sincere thanks.

As the Hospital is now enlarged a much larger number of children can be cared for, but to do this requires a greater expenditure of money, and it is earnestly hoped that the good work done may induce many, not yet givers, to aid in the work done for Him "who went about doing good." The daily routine goes on in about the same manner, year by year. Many new children appear, but a few of the old ones remain to welcome the visitor. Their happy faces testify to the loving care of the Hospital. A visit to the play-room is one not soon forgotten. The sunny room, with its plants and toys, is an ideal place to play in.

The managers have a deep sense of the faithful, loving service which is rendered o the children, and of the constant and watchful care of the physicians and surgeons.

To Mr. Bowditch and Mr. Blanchard, sincere thanks are again due, and never so much as this year, for the additional time spent in keeping the accounts of the Building Fund, as well as the yearly accounts.

As in past years the children spent the summer months at the St. Christina Home, returning stronger and happier for the change from the city to the country, and very grateful to the many kind friends in Saratoga and Troy who add so much to their pleasure and comfort during the summer months. May more friends be raised up to aid us in carrying on the work, and may the Good Father bless all future efforts as the past has been blest.

CAROLINE G. HUN, Secretary.

SUMMARY OF THE REPORT OF THE MEDICAL STAFF.

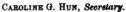

	Admitted.		Discharged.			Remaining in Hospital.	Total.
	Male.	Female.	Cured.	Improved.	Died.		
Medical Division..........................	41	36	49	5	8	15	77
Ophthalmic and Aural Division.	15	31	39	6	.....	1	46
Surgical Division.......	57	57	29	36	2	47	11
Total.............................	113	124	117	47	10	63	237

ANNUAL REPORT OF ST MARGARET'S HOUSE FOR THE YEAR ENDING SEPTEMBER 30, 1891.

Charles L. Pruyn, Treasurer, in Account with St. Margaret's House.

Receipts.

Annual subscriptions.	$225 00
Private gifts....	280 50
Board	2,277 19
Churches, etc	79 82
Alms box....	55
Moneys borrowed to meet current expenses	300 00
Amount due Treasurer	96 30
	$3,259 36

Repairs........	$25	47
Rent St. Margaret's House...................................	350	00
Rent St. Christopher's House................................	75	00
Sundries..............................	346	09

$3,259 36

CHILDREN CARED FOR.

At the Child's Hospital.........	178
At St. Margaret's House....	79
At St. Christiana Home, Industrial School................	36

ANNUAL REPORT OF THE GIRLS' FRIENDLY SOCIETY OF AMERICA, DIOCESE OF ALBANY.

Number of branches, 7; St. Paul's, Troy; St. John's, Ogdensburg; Christ, Coopers-town; St. Mark's, Hoosick Falls; Epiphany, Bath-on-the-Hudson; Emmanuel, Little Falls; Christ, Herkimer.

Number of Working Associates, 43; Honorary Associates, 20; Members, 139; Candidates, 87.

CONTRIBUTIONS.

St. Paul's Branch, Troy.

Parochial work, $205; sick members, $26.50; Orphanage, Cooperstown, $10; St. Christina Home, $8.. .... $249 50

St. Mark's Branch, Hoosick Falls.

St. Christina Home....... .... 2 00

St. John's Branch, Ogdensburg.

Mission work 10 00

Epiphany Branch, Bath-on-the-Hudson.

Rectory Fund, $75; Choir, $15; Child's Hospital, Albany, 1 doz. pillow cases 90 00

$351 50

TROY, N. Y., *Nov.* 16, 1891. A. L. WEISE, *President.*

ANNUAL REPORT OF THE WOMAN'S AUXILIARY TO THE BOARD OF MISSIONS IN THE DIOCESE OF ALBANY.

Number of Parish Branches, 53.
Number of Junior Auxiliaries, 31.
Number of boxes sent, 110.
Valuation of boxes, $5,202.99.
Money given, $2,175.27.
Total money and boxes, $7,378.26.
Balance on hand May 8, 1891, $372.79.

THE DIOCESAN LENDING LIBRARY.

Number of volumes in Library, 990.
Books loaned, 126.

Number of readers, 69.
Total amount of moneys received, $359.
Total amount of moneys expended, $344.86.
Balance on hand, $14.14.
The Library needs both funds and books.

THE CHURCH PERIODICAL CLUB.

This club receives magazines and books and distributes them for circulation among Clergymen and Mission stations. There are branches in 37 Dioceses.
Number of regular contributors, about 1,600.
Number of periodicals in regular circulation, 4,008.
Books given, 9,337.
Odd papers and magazines, 63,000.

MRS. MELVIL DEWEY, *President.*

ANNUAL REPORT OF THE CHURCH HOME IN THE CITY OF TROY FOR THE YEAR 1891.

To the Right Rev. the Bishop of Albany:

The Trustees of the Church Home present the following report for the year 1891:

FINANCIAL STATEMENT.

I. *Income and Expense Account.*

Received from churches, individuals, etc.	$1,409 58
Received from Income Permanent Fund	1,454 50
Balance on hand from 1890	74 57
	$2,938 65
Expended for the year 1891	2,810 70
Showing balance on hand December 31, 1891	$127 95

II. *Permanent Fund.*

Amount of Fund December 31, 1890, last report	$28,042 70
Received from entrance fees	100 00
Received from Mr. J. W. Fuller, legacy	1,250 00
Total Fund, December 31, 1891	$29,392 70

By order of the Board of Trustees,

NORMAN B. SQUIRES,

January 1, 1892.   *President.*

(C.)

LIST OF PARISHES IN UNION WITH THE CONVENTION OF THE DIOCESE OF ALBANY, WITH THE DATES OF THEIR ADMISSION.*

ALBANY COUNTY.

St. Peter's, Albany, 1787; Trinity, Rensselaerville, 1811; St. Paul's, Albany, 1829; St. John's, Cohoes, 1831; Trinity, West Troy, 1834; Trinity, Albany, 1840; Grace, Albany, 1846; Holy Innocents, Albany, 1850; St. Mark's, Green Island, 1867; Cathedral of All Saints, Albany, 1874

* Dates earlier than 1868 are those of admission to union with the Convention of the Diocese of New York before the organization of the Diocese of Albany.

CLINTON COUNTY.

Trinity, Plattsburgh, 1830; Christ, Rouse's Point, 1853; St. John's, Champlain, 1853.

COLUMBIA COUNTY.

Christ, Hudson, 1794; St. John's, Stockport, 1845; St. Paul's, Kinderhook, 1851; Trinity, Claverack, 1856: Our Saviour, Lebanon Springs, 1882; All Saints', Hudson, 1888; St. Barnabas', Stottville, 1890; St. Mark's, Philmont, 1891.

DELAWARE COUNTY.

St. Peter's, Hobart, 1796; St. John's, Delhi, 1822; Christ, Walton, 1831; St. Paul's, Franklin, 1866; Christ, Deposit, 1871.

ESSEX COUNTY.

Church of the Cross, Ticonderoga, 1840; St. John's, Essex, 1853; St. Paul's, Keeseville, 1853; Christ, Port Henry, 1873.

FRANKLIN COUNTY.

St. Mark's, Malone, 1831; St. Peter's, Brush's Mills, 1870.

FULTON COUNTY.

St. John's, Johnstown, 1796.

GREENE COUNTY.

St. Luke's, Catskill, 1801; Christ, Coxsackie, 1806; Trinity, Athens, 1806; St. Paul's, Oak Hill, 1816; Christ, Greenville, 1825; Trinity, Ashland, 1826; Calvary, Cairo, 1832.

HERKIMER COUNTY.

Trinity, Fairfield, 1807; Grace, Norway, 1819; Emmanuel, Little Falls, 1823; Christ, Herkimer, 1854; St. Augustine's, Ilion, 1870; Grace, Mohawk, 1886.

MONTGOMERY COUNTY.

St. Ann's, Amsterdam, 1836; Zion, Fonda, 1867.

OTSEGO COUNTY.

Zion, Morris, 1793; St. Luke's, Richfield, 1803; St. Matthew's, Unadilla, 1810; Christ, Cooperstown, 1812; Christ, Butternuts, 1834; Immanuel, Otego, 1836; St. Timothy's, Westford, 1839; Grace, Cherry Valley, 1846; St. John's, Richfield Springs, 1850; St. John's, Portlandville, 1869; Christ, West Burlington, 1871; St. Paul's, East Springfield, 1871; St. James', Oneonta, 1877.

RENSSELAER COUNTY.

St. Paul's, Troy, 1807; Trinity, Lansingburgh, 1807; St. John's, Troy, 1831; Christ, Troy, 1837; St. Mark's, Hoosick Falls, 1840; Trinity, Schaghticoke, 1846; Messiah, Greenbush, 1853; St. Luke's, Troy, 1867.

ST. LAWRENCE COUNTY.

St. John's, Ogdensburgh, 1820; St. Paul's, Waddington, 1824; Christ, Morristown, 1833; Trinity, Potsdam, 1835; Grace, Canton, 1836; Grace, Norfolk, 1844; Trinity, Gouverneur, 1869; St. John's, Massena, 1870; St. Luke's, Lisbon, 1871; Zion, Colton, 1885.

SARATOGA COUNTY.

Christ, Ballston Spa, 1787; St. John's, Stillwater, 1796; St. Paul's, Charlton, 1805; Grace, Waterford, 1810; St. Luke's, Mechanicville, 1830; Bethesda, Saratoga Springs, 1830; St. Stephen's, Schuylerville, 1846; Calvary, Burnt Hills, 1850.

SCHENECTADY COUNTY.

Christ, Duanesburgh, 1789; St. George's, Schenectady, 1792; Christ, Schenectady, 1869.

WARREN COUNTY.

Messiah, Glens Falls, 1840, with St. Paul's Chapel, Harrisena ; St. James', Caldwell, 1855; Holy Cross, Warrensburgh, 1865 ; St. Mary's, Luzerne, 1867.

WASHINGTON COUNTY.

Zion, Sandy Hill, 1813; Trinity, Granville, 1815; St. James', Fort Edward, 1845; St. Paul's, Salem, 1860; Trinity, Whitehall, 1866; St. Luke's, Cambridge, 1867; St. Paul's, Greenwich, 1875.

ORGANIZED MISSIONS.

ALBANY COUNTY.

Good Shepherd, Bethlehem; St. Andrew's, West Troy.

CLINTON COUNTY.

St. Paul's, Mooer's Forks; St. Peter's, Ellenburgh ; St. Paul's, Ellenburgh Centre St. Luke's, Chazy; St. John's, Salmon River; all with consecrated buildings; S Matthew's, Lyon Mountain.

COLUMBIA COUNTY.

St. Luke's, Chatham; St. John's in the Wilderness, Copake.

DELAWARE COUNTY.

Emmanuel, Griffin's Corners; Grace, Stamford.

ESSEX COUNTY.

Emmanuel, Mineville; St. James', Ausable Forks, both with consecrated buildings; Good Shepherd, Bloomingdale.

FRANKLIN COUNTY.

St. Mark's, West Bangor; St. James', Hogansburgh; St. John's in the Wilderness, St. Regis Lake; St. Luke the Beloved Physician, Saranac Lake, all with consecrated buildings.

FULTON COUNTY.

Christ, Gloversville.

GREENE COUNTY.

Gloria Dei, Palenville.

HAMILTON COUNTY.

Good Shepherd, Racquette Lake; Of the Transfiguration, Blue Mountain Lake.

HERKIMER COUNTY.

Of the Memorial, Middleville.

MONTGOMERY COUNTY.

Holy Cross, Fort Plain; Good Shepherd, Canajoharie; St. Columba's, St. Johnsville.

OTSEGO COUNTY.

St. Mary's, Springfield Centre, with consecrated building; St. Simon and St. Jude's, Worcester.

RENSSELAER COUNTY.

St. Giles', Castleton; Holy Name, Boyntonville, with consecrated buildings.

St. Lawrence County.

Trinity Chapel, Morley; St. Thomas', Lawrenceville, both with consecrated buildings; Grace, Louisville Landing; St. Joseph's, West Stockholm; All Saints', Barnhart's Island; St. Andrew's, Norwood.

Saratoga County.

St. John's, East Line; Grace, Jonesville; All Saints', Round Lake.

Warren County.

Good Shepherd, Chester; St. Paul's, Bartonville; St. Sacrament, Bolton, all with consecrated buildings.

PARISHES NOT IN UNION WITH THE CONVENTION.

Albany County.

Emmanuel, South Westerlo.

Columbia County.

St. Luke's, Clermont, incorporated July 12, 1859.

Essex County.

St. Andrew's, Schroon Lake.

Greene County.

Grace, Prattsville.

Herkimer County.

St. Alban's, Frankfort.

Otsego County.

Church of the Holy Spirit, Schenevus.

Rensselaer County.

Holy Cross, Troy; Free Church of the Ascension, Troy; Free Church of the Epiphany, East Albany; All Saints', Hoosac; St. Barnabas', Troy.

Saratoga County.

St. John's, Conklingville.

Schoharie County.

St. Luke's, Middleburgh; St. Andrew's, Schoharie; Trinity, Sharon Springs.

Warren County.

Christ, Pottersville.

Washington County.

Grace, Crandell's Corners.

PLACES OTHER THAN PARISHES OR ORGANIZED MISSIONS, WHERE SERVICES OF THE CHURCH ARE HELD.

Albany County.

St. Margaret's, Menand's Station.

Clinton County.

Dannemora; Standish.

Columbia County.

Chatham; St. James', Rossman's Mills.

Delaware County.

Esperance; St. Paul's, Sidney; Bloomville; Hamden.

Essex County.

Crown Point; Good Shepherd, Elizabethtown; Lewis; Addison Junction; Keene Valley.

31

FRANKLIN COUNTY.

Good Shepherd, Santa Clara; Merciful Saviour, St. Regis Falls; Holy Innocents, Brandon.

GREENE COUNTY.

Tannersville; Hunter.

HAMILTON COUNTY.

Locke House, Indian Lake.

HERKIMER COUNTY.

Cullen; Poland; Dolgeville.

OTSEGO COUNTY.

Morris Memorial Chapel, Noblesville; Maple Grove; Mt. Vision; Edmeston.

RENSSELAER COUNTY.

St. Stephen's, Lansingburgh; Raymertown.

ST. LAWRENCE COUNTY.

Cranberry Lake; Pierpont Centre.

SARATOGA COUNTY.

St. Luke's, Milton Centre.

SCHOHARIE COUNTY.

Cobleskill.

WARREN COUNTY.

St. Paul's, Harrisena; Grace Memorial Chapel, Sabbath-day Point.

WASHINGTON COUNTY.

North Granville; Adamsville; Smith's Basin.

NON-REPORTING PARISHES.

Grace, Norway; Grace, Canton; St. John's, Stillwater; St. Luke's, Mechanicville St. James, Caldwell.

NON-REPORTING CLERGY AND PARISHES FROM THE JOURNAL OF 1889

In obedience to the instructions of the Convention (see Journal 1890, p. 133), letter were sent to the Clergy, and to the officers of those Parishes from whom no report were received at the Convention of 1889. Replies were received from the Rev Messrs. Lancaster and Smyth, assigning ill-health as the reason for failure to repor from St. John's, Chateaugay, that there had been no services for three years; an from St. Stephen's, Schuylerville, that there had been no clergymen at the tim of the Convention in 1889. From Fairfield, Norway, Norfolk and Plattsburgh, r replies were received.

(D.)

ASSESSMENTS FOR THE BISHOP'S SALARY.

Albany County.		Assessed.	Paid
Cathedral of All Saints, Albany		$150 00	$150
St. Peter's	"	150 00	150
St. Paul's,	"	100 00	100
Trinity,		20 00	20
Grace,		32 00	32
Holy Innocents,		30 00	30
St. John's, Cohoes		20 00	20
Trinity, West Troy		40 00	40
Trinity, Rensselaerville		8 00	8
St. Mark's, Green Island		12 00	12

	Assessed.	Paid.
Clinton County.		
Trinity, Plattsburgh	$60 00	$60 00
Christ Church, Rouse's Point ....:.............	12 00	12 00
St. John's, Champlain......	6 00	6 00
Centreville and Chateaugay.....		
St. Peter's, Ellenburgh...	4 00	4 00
St. John's, Salmon River..................................		
Columbia County.		
Christ Church, Hudson.	66 00	66 00
St. John's, Stockport...............	26 00	26 00
St. Paul's, Kinderhook...........................	36 00	36 00
St. John's, Copake.....		
Trinity, Claverack.....................	6 00	6 00
Church of Our Saviour, Lebanon Springs	6 00	6 00
St. Luke's, Clermont...........	4 00	4 00
St. Barnabas', Stottville	26 00	26 00
All Saints', Hudson	6 00	6 00
St. Mark's, Philmont...........	6 00	6 00
St. Luke's, Chatham .....:.......................	2 00	2 00
Delaware County.		
St. Peter's, Hobart	20 00	20 00
St. John's, Delhi......	40 00	40 00
Christ, Walton..	20 00	20 00
St. Paul's, Franklin..	16 00	16 00
Christ Church, Deposit	6 00	6 00
Grace, Stamford	6 00	6 00
St. Paul's, Sidney......	3 00	3 00
Essex County.		
Of the Cross, Ticonderoga.......	10 00	10 00
St. John's, Essex. ... .•:...............	16 00	16 00
Christ Church. Port Henry...............	10 00	10 00
Emmanuel, Mineville.............................		
St. James, Ausable Forks.....	16 00	
St. Andrews, Schroon Lake...........	4 00	4 00
St. Paul's, Keeseville.	10 00	10 00
Franklin County.		
St. Mark's, Malone...............................	36 00	36 00
St. Peter's, Brushton...........	8 00	8 00
St. Mark's, W. Bangor	4 00	4 00
St. James, Hogansburgh....	8 00	8 00
St. John's, St. Regis.............		
St. Luke's, Saranac.	6 00	6 00
Good Shepherd, Santa Clara....	4 00	
Fulton County.		
St. John's, Johnstown.. ... ...;	50 00	50 00
Redeemer, Northampton....		
Christ Church, Gloversville....	10 00	10 00
Greene County.		
St. Luke's, Catskill.....	30 00	30 00
Christ Church, Coxsackie.........	12 00	12 00

	Assessed.	Paid.
Greene County—Continued.		
Trinity, Athens.....................................	$20 00	$20 00
St. Paul's, Oak Hill................................	6 00	
Christ Church, Greenville...........................	12 00	
Trinity, Ashland...................................	4 00	4 00
Calvary, Cairo.....................................	6 00	6 00
Gloria Dei, Palenville..............................	8 00	8 00
Grace, Prattsville.................................		
Herkimer County.		
Emmanuel, Little Falls..............................	40 00	40 00
Christ Church, Herkimer.............................	16 00	16 00
Grace, Mohawk.....................................	6 00	6 00
St. Augustine's, Ilion..............................	12 00	12 00
Trinity, Fairfield.................................	4 00	4 00
Memorial, Middleville..............................	6 00	6 00
Grace, Norway.....................................		
Montgomery County.		
St. Ann's, Amsterdam...............................	20 00	10 00
Zion, Fonda.......................................	12 00	12 00
Good Shepherd, Canajoharie..........................	8 00	8 00
Holy Cross, Fort Plain..............................	4 00	
Otsego County.		
Zion, Morris......................................	24 00	24 00
St. Matthew's, Unadilla............................	16 00	16 00
Christ Church, Cooperstown..........................	80 00	80 00
Christ Church, Gilbertsville........................	6 00	6 00
Immanuel, Otego....................................	6 00	6 00
St. Timothy's, Westford............................		
St. John's, Portlandville...........................	4 00	
Grace, Cherry Valley...............................	25 00	25 00
St. Paul's, E. Springfield...........................	10 00	10 00
St. John's, Richfield Springs........................	16 00	16 00
Christ Church, W. Burlington........................	6 00	6 00
St. James, Oneonta.................................	10 00	10 00
St. Stephen's Chapel................................	2 00	2 00
Holy Spirit, Schenevus..............................	4 00	3 00
Rensselaer County.		
St. Paul's, Troy...................................	200 00	200 00
St. John's, "	176 00	176 00
Christ Ch., "	124 00	124 00
Holy Cross, "	50 00	50 00
Ascension. "	10 00	10 00
St. Luke's, "	10 00	10 00
St Barnabas', "	6 00	4 50
Trinity, Lansingburgh..............................	60 00	60 00
Trinity, Schaghticoke..............................	6 00	6 00
Messiah, Greenbush.................................	10 00	10 00
Epiphany, E. Albany................................	4 00	4 00
St. Mark's, Hoosick Falls...........................	40 00	40 00
All Saints', Hoosac................................	6 00	6 00

	Assessed.	Paid.
St. Lawrence County.		
St. John's, Ogdensburgh	$100 00	$100 00
St. Paul's, Waddington.	12 00	12 00
Christ Church, Morristown	26 00	19 50
Trinity, Potsdam	50 00	50 00
Grace, Canton	14 00	
Grace, Norfolk	6 00	
St. Andrew's, Norwood	4 00	4 00
Trinity, Gouverneur	26 00	26 00
St. John's, Massena	8 00	8 00
Trinity, Morley	6 00	
Grace, Louisville Landing		
St. Thomas, Lawrenceville		
St. Luke's, Lisbon		
Zion, Colton	4 00	4 00
St. Phillip's, Madrid		
All Saints, Barnhart Island		
Saratoga County.		
Christ Church, Ballston Spa	42 00	42 00
St John's, East Line		
St. Paul's, Charlton	4 00	
Grace, Waterford	10 00	
Bethesda, Saratoga Springs	70 00	*85 00
St. Stephen's, Schuylerville	6 00	
Calvary, Burnt Hills	12 00	12 00
St. John's, Conklingville	4 00	4 00
St. John's, Stillwater	4 00	4 00
St. Luke's, Mechanicville	4 00	4 00
Grace, Jonesville	4 00	4 00
Schenectady County.		
St. George's, Schenectady	60 00	60 00
Christ Church, Schenectady	10 00	10 00
Christ Church, Duanesburgh	50 00	50 00
Schoharie County.		
St. Luke's, Middleburgh	4 00	4 00
Trinity, Sharon Springs	20 00	20 00
Warren County.		
Messiah, Glens Falls	40 00	40 00
Harrisena		
Holy Cross, Warrensburgh	38 00	38 00
St. Mary's, Luzerne	8 00	8 00
Good Shepherd, Chestertown	6 00	6 00
St. John's, Conklingville		4 00
St. Sacrament, Bolton	10 00	10 00
St. James', Caldwell	10 00	
Washington County.		
Zion, Sandy Hill	30 00	30 00
Trinity, Granville	6 00	6 00

* Fifteen dollars overpaid, making entire amount overpaid 1890–91, $35.00.

Washington County—Continued.	Assessed.	Paid.
Mission, North Granville...	$4 00	$4 00
St. James', Fort Edward...	30 00	15 00
St. Paul's, Salem...	30 00	30 00
Trinity, Whitehall	20 00	20 00
St. Luke's, Cambridge...	10 00	10 00
St. Paul's, Greenwich	4 00	4 00

(E.)

OFFICERS OF THE DIOCESE, TRUSTEES, ETC.

The Right Rev. William Croswell Doane, D. D., LL. D., *President.*
The Rev. William C. Prout, Schenectady, *Secretary.*
The Rev. Thomas B. Fulcher, Albany, *Assistant Secretary.*
The Rev. Frederick S. Sill, Cohoes, *Registrar.*
Mr. Selden E. Marvin, Albany, *Treasurer.*

THE STANDING COMMITTEE.

The Rev. J. Ireland Tucker, S. T. D., Troy, *President;* the Rev. Fenwick M. Cookson, Glens Falls, *Secretary;* the Rev. Wilford L. Robbins, D. D., the Rev. James Caird, Mr. Norman B. Squires, Mr. Henry S. Wynkoop, Mr. John I. Thompson, Mr. J. H. Van Antwerp.

DEPUTIES TO THE GENERAL CONVENTION.

The Rev. W. W. Battershall, D. D., the Rev. J. D. Morrison, D. D., LL. D., the Rev. Joseph Carey, S. T. D., the Rev. Charles C. Edmunds, Jr., Mr. G. Pomeroy Keese, Mr. Erastus Corning, Mr. T. Streatfeild Clarkson, Mr. John Hobart Warren.

PROVISIONAL DEPUTIES TO THE GENERAL CONVENTION.

The Rev. Edgar A. Enos, the Rev. R. M. Kirby, D. D., the Rev. C. S. Olmsted, the Rev. George D. Silliman, Mr. Leslie Pell-Clarke, Mr. Spencer Trask, Mr. Edward Sheldon, Mr. Thomas L. Harison.

DEPUTIES TO THE FEDERATE COUNCIL.

The Rev. J. Ireland Tucker, S. T. D., the Rev. Fenwick M. Cookson, the Rev. George D. Silliman, the Rev. Wilford L. Robbins, D. D., the Rev. C. C. Edmunds, Jr., the Rev. S. M. Griswold, the Rev. Wm. H. Harison, D. D., the Rev. Ernest Mariett, Mr. N. B. Warren, Mr. G. Pomeroy Keese, Mr. R. H. Cushney, Mr. Robert Earl, Mr. J. I. Thompson, Mr. F. J. Fitch, Mr. Charles E. Patterson, Mr. J. D. Henderson.

TRUSTEE OF THE GENERAL THEOLOGICAL SEMINARY UNTIL NOVEMBER 15, 1893.

The Rev. Joseph Carey, S. T. D.

TRUSTEES OF THE EPISCOPAL FUND.

Mr. J. H. Van Antwerp, Albany, *Treasurer;* Mr. W. Bayard Van Rensselaer, Mr. Theodore Townsend, Mr. Charles W. Tillinghast, 2d, Mr. Dean Sage.

TRUSTEES OF THE FUND FOR AGED AND INFIRM CLERGYMEN.

The Right Rev. William Croswell Doane, D. D., LL. D., Mr. Selden E. Marvin, *Treasurer;* Mr. Norman B. Squires, Mr. Robert S. Oliver, Mr. J. J. Tillinghast.

TRUSTEES OF THE FUND FOR WIDOWS AND ORPHANS OF DECEASED CLERGYMEN.

The Right Rev. William Croswell Doane, D. D., LL. D., Mr. Selden E. Marvin, *Treasurer;* Mr. J. W. Tillinghast, Mr. C. W. Tillinghast, Mr. Amasa J. Parker.

TRUSTEES OF THE ORPHAN HOUSE OF THE HOLY SAVIOUR, COOPERS-TOWN.

The Right Rev. William Croswell Doane, D. D., LL. D., *President.*
The Rev. Charles S. Olmsted, Cooperstown, *Secretary.*
Mr. Leslie Pell-Clarke, Springfield Centre, *Treasurer.*
Miss Susan Fenimore Cooper, Cooperstown, *Superintendent.*

TRUSTEES.

Mr. A. B. Cox, Mr. Leslie Pell-Clarke, Mr. G. Hyde Clarke, until Convention, 1892.
The Rev. Thaddeus A. Snively, Mr. T. Streatfeild Clarkson, W. T. Bassett, M. D., until Convention, 1893.
The Rev. Walton W. Battershall, D. D., the Rev. J. Philip B. Pendleton, S. T. B., Mr. G. Pomeroy Keese, until Convention, 1894.

TRUSTEES OF THE DIOCESE OF ALBANY.

The Right Rev. William Croswell Doane, D. D., LL. D., *President.*
Mr. A. B. Cox, Cherry Valley, *Secretary.*
Mr. Benjamin H. Hall, Troy, *Treasurer.*

TRUSTEES.

The Rev. Joseph Carey, S. T. D., until 1892.
Mr. Benjamin H. Hall, until 1892.
The Rev. Charles S. Olmsted, until 1893.
Mr. Abram B. Cox, until 1893.
The Rev. J. D. Morrison, D. D., LL. D., until 1894.
Mr. Levi Hasbrouck, until 1894.
The Rev. Frederick S. Sill, until 1895.
Mr. John H. Bagley, until 1895.

COMMITTEE ON THE INCORPORATION AND ADMISSION OF CHURCHES.

The Rev. J. Philip B. Pendleton, S. T. B., Mr. Richard H. Cushney, Mr. Benjamin H. Hall.

COMMITTEE ON THE CONSTITUTION AND CANONS.

The Rev. J. W. Stewart, the Rev. R. M. Kirby, D. D., the Rev. James Caird, the Rev. Wilford L. Robbins, D. D., Mr. James Gibson, Mr. T. Streatfeild Clarkson, Mr. J. D. Henderson.

COMMITTEE ON THE SALARY OF THE BISHOP.

The Rev. Joseph Carey, S. T. D., the Rev. W. W. Battershall, D. D., Mr. J. J. Tillinghast, Mr. Erastus Corning, Mr. J. W. Tillinghast, Mr. W. W. Rousseau, Mr. John I. Thompson, Mr. Spencer Trask. *Secretary,* Mr. W. W. Rousseau, Troy.

COMMITTEE ON CLERICAL INSURANCE.

The Rev. Richmond Shreve, D. D., the Rev. Walter C. Stewart, Mr. John Keyes Paige, Mr. F. E. Griswold, Mr. S. M. Van Santvoord.

COMMITTEE ON THE OBSERVANCE OF THE TWENTY-FIFTH ANNIVER-
SARY OF THE CONSECRATION OF THE FIRST BISHOP OF ALBANY.

The Rev. J. Ireland Tucker, S. T. D., the Rev. Walton W. Battershall, D. D., the
Rev. Wilford L. Robbins, D. D., the Rev. J. D. Morrison, D. D., LL. D., the Rev.
Joseph Carey, S. T. D., the Rev. James Caird, the Rev. R. M. Kirby, D. D., the Rev.
Fenwick M. Cookson, the Rev. Richard Temple, the Rev. Charles S. Olmsted, Mr.
John I. Thompson, Mr. A. B. Cox, Mr. Erastus Corning, Mr. Joseph M. Warren, Gen.
Selden E. Marvin, Mr. T. Streatfeild Clarkson, Mr. L. Averill Carter, Prof. Sidney G.
Ashmore, Mr. John Keyes Paige, Mr. G. Pomeroy Keese, the Hon. William A.
Sackett.

THE BOARD OF MISSIONS.

The Right Rev. William Croswell Doane, D. D., LL. D., *President.*
The Rev. William R. Woodbridge, *Secretary.*
Mr. Selden E. Marvin, *Treasurer.*

ARCHDEACONRY OF ALBANY.
The Rev. W. W. Battershall, D. D., Mr. J. H. Van Antwerp.

ARCHDEACONRY OF TROY.
The Rev. F. M. Cookson, Mr. George A. Wells.

ARCHDEACONRY OF THE SUSQUEHANNA.
The Rev. Robert N. Parke, D. D., Mr. Robert M. Townsend.

ARCHDEACONRY OF OGDENSBURG.
The Rev. R. M. Kirby, D. D., Mr. T. Streatfeild Clarkson.

DIOCESE AT LARGE.
The Rev. W. R. Woodbridge, Mr. William Kemp.

ARCHDEACONRIES.

FIRST. ARCHDEACONRY OF ALBANY.
Albany, Greene, Columbia, Schenectady, Montgomery, Fulton, Hamilton and
Herkimer counties.
The Rev. Frederick S. Sill, *Archdeacon.*
The Rev. Richmond Shreve, D. D., *Secretary.*
The Rev. E. Bayard Smith, *Treasurer.*

SECOND. ARCHDEACONRY OF TROY.
Rensselaer, Saratoga, Washington, Warren, Clinton and Essex counties.
The Rev. Joseph Carey, S. T. D., *Archdeacon.*
The Rev. George D. Silliman, *Secretary.*
Mr. Charles W. Tillinghast, 2d, *Treasurer.*

THIRD. ARCHDEACONRY OF THE SUSQUEHANNA.
Delaware, Otsego and Schoharie counties.
The Rev. Charles S. Olmsted, *Archdeacon.*
The Rev. Ernest A. Hartmann, *Secretary and Treasurer.*

FOURTH. ARCHDEACONRY OF OGDENSBURG.
St Lawrence and Franklin counties.
The Rev. J. D. Morrison, D. D., LL. D, *Archdeacon.*
The Rev. Charles Temple, *Secretary.*
Mr. T. Streatfeild Clarkson, *Treasurer.*

EXAMINING CHAPLAINS.

The Rev. J. Ireland Tucker, S. T. D., the Rev. Joseph Carey, S. T. D., the Rev. J. D. Morrison, D. D., LL. D., the Rev. W. N. Irish, the Rev. Thomas B. Fulcher, B. D., the Rev. Edgar A. Enos, the Rev. William G. W. Lewis, the Rev. Wilford L. Robbins. D. D., the Rev. G. H. S. Walpole, the Rev. George B. Johnson, the Rev. George G. Carter, S. T. D.

THE BIBLE AND COMMON PRAYER BOOK SOCIETY OF ALBANY AND ITS VICINITY.

The Right Rev. William Croswell Doane, D. D., LL. D., *President.*
The Rev. J. Ireland Tucker, S. T. D., *First Vice President.*
The Rev. W. W. Battershall, D. D., *Second Vice-President.*
The Rev. J. W. Stewart, *Third Vice-President.*
The Rev. Thaddeus A. Snively, *Corresponding Secretary.*
The Rev. Richmond Shreve, D. D., *Recording Secretary.*
Mr. Henry B. Dauchy, *Treasurer.*

MANAGERS.

Messrs. J. H. Van Antwerp, A. A. Van Vorst, George W. Gibbons, Joseph W. Tillinghast, Francis N. Mann, George A. Wells, John H. Hulsapple, Marcus T. Hun, William C. Buell, John Horrocks, E. G. Dorlan, George B. Warren.

Applications for books may be made to the *Corresponding Secretary*, the Rev. Thaddeus A. Snively, Troy.

All contributions and donations should be sent to the *Treasurer*, Mr. H. B. Dauchy, Troy.

(F.)

DIOCESAN BRANCHES OF GENERAL SOCIETIES.

THE DIOCESAN BRANCH OF THE WOMAN'S AUXILIARY TO THE BOARD OF MISSIONS.
President. Mrs. Melvil Dewey, 315 Madison avenue, Albany.
Vice-Presidents. Mrs. Payne, Schenectady; Mrs. McEwen, Saratoga Springs.
Treasurer. Mrs. Charles E. Hanaman, 103 First street, Troy.
Corresponding Secretary. Miss E. M. Sands, 201 Elm street, Albany.
Recording Secretary.

Managers.

For the Archdeaconry of Albany: Miss Tweddle, Menand's road, Albany, for Albany, Montgomery and Fulton counties; Mrs. A. Van Nostrand, Schenectady, for Greene, Columbia, Schenectady, Hamilton and Herkimer counties.

For the Archdeaconry of Troy: Miss Mary E. Gilbert, 189 Second street, Troy, for Rensselaer, Washington and Saratoga counties; Mrs. Wm. S. Wheeler, Ballston Spa, for Warren, Essex and Clinton counties.

For the Archdeaconry of the Susquehanna: Miss E. J. Hughes, Gilbertsville, for Otsego and Schoharie counties: Miss Laura Gay, Walton, for Delaware county.

For the Archdeaconry of Ogdensburg: Mrs. Chas. Temple, Malone, for Franklin county; Mrs. Thomas L. Knap, Ogdensburg, for St. Lawrence county.

DIOCESAN LENDING LIBRARY COMMITTEE.

Mrs. Melvil Dewey, *Chairman*, 315 Madison avenue, Albany; Miss E. W. Boyd, *Treasurer*, St. Agnes' School, Albany.

CHURCH PERIODICAL CLUB.

Miss Mary F. Burt, Rensselaerville. *Diocesan Correspondent.*

THE DIOCESAN BRANCH OF THE CHURCH TEMPERANCE SOCIETY.

Delegates to the General Council. The Rev. T. A. Snively, Troy; Mr. Henry J. Estcourt, Schenectady.

Honorary Secretary.

Diocesan Committee.

Clerical—The Rev. W. W. Battershall, D. D., Albany; the Rev. Joseph N. Mulford; the Rev. George D. Silliman, Hoosick Falls; the Rev. Hobart Cooke, Plattsburgh; the Rev. John H. Houghton, Salem.

Lay—Messrs. Smith Fine, Albany; William Kemp, Troy; R. C. McEwen, M. D., Saratoga; Henry C. Day, Cambridge; James Rogers, Ausable Forks; Charles Ashley, Ogdensburg.

THE WOMAN'S DIOCESAN LEAGUE.

Objects.

The objects of the Woman's Diocesan League are, first, to complete the Cathedral building ready for use, and, then, to aid other Church buildings, Missions, schools, and charitable works in the Diocese. Members of the League are free to devote their gifts, now, to any of these purposes.

The Convention by resolution has recommended the formation of Chapters in every Parish in the Diocese.

THE CATHEDRAL CHAPTER.

President. Mrs. Erastus Corning.

Secretaries. Mrs. William B. Van Rensselaer; Mrs. H. E. Bender.

Treasurers. Mrs. Erastus Corning, Jr.; Mrs. J. T. Gardiner.

Chapters in Troy, Stockport, Middleville, Saratoga Springs, Grace Church, Albany, Ogdensburg, Delhi, Potsdam, Franklin, Philmont, Cohoes, Hoosick Falls, Saranac Lake, Catskill, Brushton, Herkimer, Ilion, West Troy, and in many other places without formal organization.

FUNDS TO WHICH OFFERINGS ARE REQUIRED BY CANON, AND THE NAMES OF THE TREASURERS TO WHOM THE SAME SHOULD BE SENT.

Diocesan Fund. Mr. S. E Marvin, Albany.

Missions of the Diocese. Mr. S E. Marvin, Albany.

For Aged and Infirm Clergymen. Mr. S. E. Marvin, Albany.

For Widows and Orphans of Deceased Clergymen. Mr. S. E Marvin, Albany.

For the Clergy Reserve Fund Mr. S. E. Marvin, Albany.

Bible and Common Prayer Book Society of Albany. Mr. H. B. Dauchy, Troy.

Episcopal Fund. Mr J H. Van Antwerp, Albany.

Salary of the Bishop Mr. W. W. Rousseau, Troy.

For the Education of Young Men for the Ministry. The Bishop of the Diocese, or Mr. Richard M. Harison, 31 Nassau street, New York.

Orphan House of the Holy Saviour. Mr. Leslie Pell Clarke, Springfield Centre, Otsego county.

Domestic and Foreign Missions. Mr. George Bliss, 22 Bible House, New York.

Offerings for the *Child's Hospital* should be sent to Mr. Edward Bowditch, Albany.

For Missionary envelopes and pledges apply to the *Secretary* of the Board of Missions, the Rev. William R. Woodbridge, Port Henry, Essex county.

(G.)

SUMMARY OF STATISTICS.

From the Bishop's Address, the Parochial, Missionary and other Reports.

Clergy (Bishop, 1, Priests, 121, Deacons, 12)	134
Ordinations (Deacons, 7, Priests, 3)	10
Candidates for Orders (for the Deacon's Order only, 7, for the Priest's Order, 19)	26
Postulants	8
Lay-Readers Licensed	18
Parishes in union with Convention	100
Parishes not in union with Convention	17
Missions (organized, 43, unorganized, 38)	81
Churches	134
Chapels	19
Sittings in Churches and Chapels	42,509
Free Churches and Chapels	127
Churches otherwise supported	26
Free sittings (including free seats in Churches where there is a pew rental)	30,925
Rectories	75
Corner-stone laid	1
Churches consecrated	2
Buildings blessed	5
*Families	8,865
*Individuals (adults, 13,887, children, 6,855, not designated, 4,619)	24,861
Baptisms (adults, 428, infants, 1,358)	1,786
Confirmations	1,166
Communicants (admitted, 683, received, 442, died, 280, removed, 661), present number	17,662
Marriages	494
Burials	1,138
Sunday School teachers	1,077
Sunday School pupils	12,455
Parish School teachers	32
Parish School pupils	318

OFFERINGS.

Parochial.

Alms	$6,426 69	
Current expenses	185,978 50	
Other purposes	110,881 98	
		$303,287 17

Diocesan.

Diocesan Missions	$9,962 31
Salary of the Bishop	3,185 18
Diocesan Fund	2,252 55
Bible and Common Prayer Book Society of Albany	427 11
Aged and Infirm Clergy Fund	524 75

* Many reports do not give these items.

Clergy Reserve Fund........................	$97 34	
Fund for Widows and Orphans of Deceased Clergymen....	202 69	
Orphan House of the Holy Saviour (including $2,003.14 raised by special committee)..........................	3,129 26	
The Child's Hospital	1,498 47	
Theological Education...	189 85	
Other purposes	3,784 95	
		$25,204 ◄

General.

General Theological Seminary...........................	$18 43	
Domestic Missions...	3,546 60	
Foreign Missions.......................................	2,250 58	
Indian Missions....	700 85	
Home Missions to Coloured Persons	502 70	
Other purposes	6,054 08	
		13,073 ≡

Total amount of Offerings..........................	$341,564 ≡

TABLE OF CONTENTS.

DIOCESE OF ALBANY.

CONSTITUTION AND CANONS.

CONSTITUTION.

ARTICLE I.

Of the Members of the Convention.

The Diocese of Albany entrusts its legislation to a Convention, to consist as follows: First, of the Bishop, when there is one; of the Assistant Bishop, when there is one. Secondly, of all Clergymen canonically resident in the Diocese for six months previ. to the Convention, the restriction of time not to apply to Rectors duly elected or sionaries duly appointed (provided that no Clergyman suspended from the Ministry all have a seat); and, Thirdly, of the Lay Delegation from the Cathedral, and of Delegations, consisting of not more than three Deputies from each other Church inion with the Convention, who shall be communicants, and shall have been sen by the Vestry or Congregation of the same.

ARTICLE II.

Of the Annual Meetings of the Convention.

The Convention shall assemble on the Tuesday after the tenth day of November, in h year, in such place as the Bishop shall appoint, giving fifteen days' notice reof. In case of his inability to act, the Assistant Bishop, if there be one, shall ap- nt the place; and, if there be no Bishop, the Standing Committee shall appoint. a place of meeting may be changed for sufficient reason after having been appointed, vided that ten days' notice of such change shall be given.

Every Convention shall be opened with a Sermon and the Holy Communion; and Preacher shall be appointed by the Bishop, or in case of his inability to act, or if re be no Bishop, by the Standing Committee.

ARTICLE III.

Of Special Conventions.

The Bishop shall have power to call Special Conventions, giving thirty days' notice reof, and shall do so when requested by a vote of three-fourths of the Standing mmittee. When there is no Bishop, the Standing Committee shall have power to ll a Special Convention, giving ninety days' notice thereof.

ARTICLE IV.

Of the Cathedral.

"The Cathedral of All Saints in the City and Diocese of Albany" shall be the Cathedral Church of this Diocese. Three Lay Communicants shall be chosen by the Chapter as the Delegation from the Cathedral to the Convention.

ARTICLE V.

Of the Permanent Officers of the Diocese.

The permanent officers of the Diocese shall be: the Bishop of the Diocese (with right to preside, when present in Convention; and when there is an Assistant Bishop, he shall have right to preside in the absence of the Bishop), a Standing Committee, a Secretary, a Treasurer and a Registrar.

ARTICLE VI.

Of the Election of a Bishop.

When a Bishop or an Assistant Bishop is to be elected, the election shall be at the regular Annual Convention, or at a Special Convention duly called for that purpose; and such election shall require a majority of the votes of each order voting separately.

ARTICLE VII.

Of the President of the Convention.

If there be no Bishop of the Diocese, or its *ex-officio* presiding officer be absent, the Convention shall elect a President from among the Clergy, by ballot (unless the ballot be dispensed with by unanimous vote.)

ARTICLE VIII.

Of the Standing Committee.

The Standing Committee shall consist of four Clergymen and four Laymen, to be elected by ballot at each Annual Convention, by a majority of the Clergy and Lay Delegations present, and shall serve until the next Annual Convention and until a new election is made, the functions of which Committee, besides those provided for in the Canons of the General Convention, and in this Constitution, shall be determined by Canon or Resolution of the Convention. But vacancies in the Standing Committee may be filled by a majority of the votes of the remaining members until the next meeting of the Convention.

ARTICLE IX.

Of the Secretary, Treasurer and Registrar.

The Secretary shall be elected at each Annual Convention from the members thereof, by ballot, after nominations (unless the ballot be dispensed with by unanimous vote), and by a majority of the Clergy and Lay Delegations present; and he shall remain in office until his successor shall be elected. His duties shall be those required by the Canons, Resolutions and Rules of Order of the Convention.

The Treasurer and the Registrar shall be elected in a similar manner, and are not required to be members of the Convention. They shall remain in office until the next Annual Convention, and until their successors are elected.

ARTICLE X.

Of the Deliberations of the Convention and of Votes.

The Clergymen and Laymen constituting the Convention shall deliberate in one body, and each Clergyman shall have one vote, and each Lay Delegation one vote, and a majority of the aggregate votes shall be decisive except in the cases provided for in Articles VI, IX and XI.

If five votes require a division, then the voting shall be by orders separately, and the concurrence of a majority of each order shall be necessary to make a decision. But no alteration of the Constitution or Canons shall be valid without the concurrence of the Bishop and of a majority of the Clergy and of a majority of the Lay Delegations; and the Bishop's concurrence shall be presumed unless the contrary be openly expressed by him to the Convention after the vote of the Clergy and Laity and before the adjournment *sine die.*

ARTICLE XI.

Of Altering the Constitution.

The mode of altering the Constitution shall be as follows: A proposition for an amendment shall be introduced in writing and considered in the Convention; and, if approved by a majority, shall lie over till the next Convention, and, if then approved by a two-thirds vote of the Clergy and Lay Delegations present, with the Bishop's concurrence, the Constitution shall be changed accordingly.

CANONS.

CANON I.

Of the List of Clergymen in the Diocese.

SECTION 1. On the first day of each Convention, regular or special, the Ecclesiastical Authority shall present to the Convention a List of the Clergy canonically resident in the Diocese, annexing the names of their respective Parishes, Offices and residences, and the dates of their becoming resident in the Diocese.

SEC. 2. The Secretary shall record this list of names in a book to be kept by him for that purpose.

SEC. 3. From this record shall be made up by the Secretary the list of the Clergymen entitled, according to the Constitution, to seats in the Convention; which list may at any time be revised and corrected by the Convention.

CANON II.

Of the Lay Delegations.

SECTION 1. When the Lay Delegations are chosen by the Vestry, it shall be at a meeting held according to law. In case the Vestry shall not choose Deputies they may be chosen by the congregation in the manner hereinafter prescribed for Churches having no Vestries.

SEC. 2. Deputies from Churches having no Vestries shall be chosen by the Congregation at a meeting of which notice shall have been given during Divine Service on the two Sundays next previous thereto. And at such meeting the Rector or Minister shall preside, and the qualifications for voting shall be the same as those required by law for voting at an election for Churchwardens and Vestrymen.

Sec. 3. When Deputies are chosen by a Vestry, the evidence of their appointment shall be a certificate, signed by the Rector of the Church they are chosen to represent and by the Clerk of the Vestry; and if there be no Rector, then the certificate shall state that fact, and shall be signed by the Churchwarden presiding and by the Clerk of the Vestry. The certificate must state the time and place of the election, must show upon its face that the appointment has been made in accordance with all the requirements of the Canons, and shall certify that each Deputy chosen is a Communicant of the Church and entitled to vote for Churchwardens and Vestrymen of the Church he is chosen to represent.

Sec. 4. When Deputies are chosen by the Congregation of any Church, the evidence of their appointment shall be a certificate, signed by the Rector or Minister having charge of the said Church and by the Secretary of the meeting; or if there be no such Rector or Minister, then the certificate shall state that fact, and shall be signed by the officer presiding at the meeting and by the Secretary of the same. The certificate must state the time and place of the election, must show upon its face that the appointment has been made in accordance with all the requirements of the Canons, and shall certify that each Deputy chosen is a Communicant of the Church, and, in the case of the Church having a Vestry, that he is entitled to vote for Churchwardens and Vestrymen of such Church, or, in the case of a Church having no Vestry, that he has belonged for twelve months to the Congregation he is chosen to represent. No other evidence of the appointment of Lay Deputies than such as is specified in this and the preceding section shall be received by the Convention.

Sec. 5. The Secretary of the Convention, when he shall send to any Church or Parish the required notice of the time and place of meeting of any Convention to be held, shall transmit with the same a copy of this Canon and blank printed forms of certificates of appointment of Deputies.

CANON III.

Of the Organization of the Convention.

Section 1. If the *ex-officio* presiding officer be not present at the opening of the Convention, the Secretary shall call the members present to order; and the senior Presbyter present, who is a member of the Convention, shall take the chair, and preside until a President is elected, as provided by Article VII of the Constitution.

Sec. 2. The Secretary shall then call the names of the Clergy entitled to seats in the Convention. He shall then call the names of the Churches in union with the Convention, when the Lay Deputies shall present their certificates, which shall be examined by the Secretary, and a committee of two members appointed by the presiding officer. Irregular or defective certificates, and certificates and documents referring to contested seats, shall be temporarily laid aside. The names of the Lay Deputies duly appointed shall then be called, after which the certificates and documents laid aside shall be reported to the Convention, which shall decide upon the admission of the Deputies named therein.

Sec. 3. If twenty Clergymen entitled to vote, and twenty Lay Delegations be present, they shall constitute a quorum; and the presiding officer *ex officio* shall declare the Convention duly organized. The same number of Clergymen and Lay Delegations shall, at any time, be necessary for the transaction of business, except that a smaller number may adjourn from time to time.

Sec. 4. If the presiding officer *ex officio* be not present before the convention is declared to be organized, the temporary Chairman shall direct that the members proceed to elect a President, according to Article VII of the Constitution, who, when elected, shall take the Chair and declare the Convention organized for business.

SEC. 5. The Convention shall then proceed to the election of a Secretary, a Treasurer and a Registrar, according to the Constitution. The Secretary may appoint an Assistant Secretary, also any other assistants he may require, announcing their names to the Convention.

SEC. 6. Any Rules of Order which shall have been previously adopted or sanctioned in the Convention, except such as prescribe the mode of altering the same, shall be in force until changed by the Convention, after having been duly organized.

CANON IV.

Of the Admission of a Church into Union with the Church in this Diocese, and Maintaining such Union.

SECTION 1. Every Church or Congregation desiring admission into union with the Church in this Diocese, shall present a written application therefor to the Convention, together with a copy of the resolution of the Vestry, or of the Congregation, authorizing such application; in which resolution the said Church, by its Vestry or Congregation, shall agree to abide by, and conform to, and observe, all the Canons of the Church, and all the rules, orders and regulations of the Convention; which copy shall be duly certified by the presiding officer of the Vestry, or of the meeting of the Congregation at which the resolution was adopted, and also by the Clerk of the Vestry or Secretary of the meeting; and shall be authenticated by the seal of the Corporation. The said application shall also be accompanied by the Certificate of Incorporation of the Church, duly recorded, or a copy thereof certified by the officer, whose duty it may be to record or file the same; and also, by a Certificate of the Ecclesiastical Authority, to the effect that he or they approve of the incorporation of such Church, and that such Church, in his or their judgment, is duly and satisfactorily established; and every Church or Congregation applying for admission shall produce satisfactory evidence that not less than twenty-five persons, members of such Church, have habitually, for at least one year preceding such application, attended Divine Service in such Church or Congregation.

SEC. 2. No application for the admission of a Church into union with the Church in this Diocese shall be considered or acted upon, at any meeting of the Convention, unless the same shall have been transmitted to the Secretary of the Convention at least thirty days before the meeting of the Convention. It shall be the duty of the Secretary of the Convention, at least twenty days before the meeting of the Convention, to deliver to a Committee, to be annually appointed (to be called the Committee on the Incorporation and Admission of Churches), all applications for admission into union which shall have been received by him, to be by such Committee examined, considered and reported upon to the Convention.

SEC. 3. Whenever hereafter any Church in union with this Convention shall neglect, for three years in succession, to make a Parochial Report, no Missionary Report being made on its behalf, and shall not, during the same period, have employed a Clergyman as its Parish Minister, nor requested of the Ecclesiastical Authority to have the services of a Missionary, such Church shall be regarded as having forfeited its connection with the Convention, and shall no longer have a right to send a Delegation to the same. The Bishop shall report such Church to the Convention in his Annual Address. Such Church, however, may be re-admitted, upon application to the Convention, accompanied by a report of its condition, and on such terms as shall appear just; such re-admission to take effect from and after the rising of the Convention consenting to such admission.

Canon V.

Of Elections.

All elections by the Convention shall be by ballot, except when the ballot is dispensed with by unanimous consent. And when an election is by ballot, a majority of the votes in each order shall be necessary to a choice.

Canon VI.

Of the Secretary of the Convention.

Section 1. It shall be the duty of the Secretary to take and keep the Minutes of the proceedings of the Convention, to attest its public acts, and faithfully to deliver into the hands of his successor all books and papers relating to the business and concerns of the Convention which may be in his possession or under his control. It shall also be his duty to send a printed notice to each Minister, and to each Vestry or Congregation, of the time and place appointed for the meetings of each Convention, and to publish a notice of the meeting in three of the public papers published in the Diocese of Albany, and to perform such other duties as may be required of him by the Convention.

Sec. 2. He shall transmit annually a copy of the Journal of the Convention to each of the Bishops of the Protestant Episcopal Church in the United States, to the Secretary of the House of Deputies of the General Convention, and to the Secretaries of the Diocesan Conventions; and shall ask, on behalf of the Diocese, for copies of the Diocesan Journals in exchange.

Sec. 3. He shall also transmit to every General Convention, in addition to the documents required by the Canons of the General Convention,* a certificate, signed by himself, containing a list of the Clergymen in this Diocese, and the amount of funds paid or secured to be paid (distinguishing them) to the General Theological Seminary, and also a certificate of the appointment of Clerical and Lay Deputies.

Sec. 4. Any expense incurred by a compliance with this Canon shall be paid out of the Diocesan Fund.

Sec. 5. Whenever there shall be a vacancy in the office of Secretary of the Convention, the duties thereof shall devolve upon the Assistant Secretary, if there be one; if not, upon the Secretary of the Standing Committee.

Sec. 6. Whenever, under the provisions of the Constitution, a Special Convention is called for any particular purpose, it shall be the duty of the Secretary, in the notice thereof, to specify such purpose.

Canon VII.

Of the Treasurer of the Diocese.

Section 1. It shall be the duty of the Treasurer of the Diocese to receive and disburse all moneys collected under the authority of the Convention, and of which the the collection and distribution shall not be otherwise regulated. He shall report, at each annual meeting of the Convention, the names of the Parishes which have failed to make the required contributions to any of the Diocesan Funds, specifying the funds to which they have failed to contribute and the amount of such deficiency.

Sec. 2. His accounts shall be rendered annually to the Convention, and shall be examined by a Committee acting under its authority.

---

* Title I, Canon 18, Sec. IV.

SEC. 5. The Convention shall then proceed to the election of a Secretary, a Treasurer and a Registrar, according to the Constitution. The Secretary may appoint an Assistant Secretary, also any other assistants he may require, announcing their names to the Convention.

SEC. 6. Any Rules of Order which shall have been previously adopted or sanctioned in the Convention, except such as prescribe the mode of altering the same, shall be in force until changed by the Convention, after having been duly organized.

CANON IV.

Of the Admission of a Church into Union with the Church in this Diocese, and Maintaining such Union.

SECTION 1. Every Church or Congregation desiring admission into union with the Church in this Diocese, shall present a written application therefor to the Convention, together with a copy of the resolution of the Vestry, or of the Congregation, authorizing such application; in which resolution the said Church, by its Vestry or Congregation, shall agree to abide by, and conform to, and observe, all the Canons of the Church, and all the rules, orders and regulations of the Convention; which copy shall be duly certified by the presiding officer of the Vestry, or of the meeting of the Congregation at which the resolution was adopted, and also by the Clerk of the Vestry or Secretary of the meeting; and shall be authenticated by the seal of the Corporation. The said application shall also be accompanied by the Certificate of Incorporation of the Church, duly recorded, or a copy thereof certified by the officer, whose duty it may be to record or file the same; and also, by a Certificate of the Ecclesiastical Authority, to the effect that he or they approve of the incorporation of such Church, and that such Church, in his or their judgment, is duly and satisfactorily established; and every Church or Congregation applying for admission shall produce satisfactory evidence that not less than twenty-five persons, members of such Church, have habitually, for at least one year preceding such application, attended Divine Service in such Church or Congregation.

SEC. 2. No application for the admission of a Church into union with the Church in this Diocese shall be considered or acted upon, at any meeting of the Convention, unless the same shall have been transmitted to the Secretary of the Convention at least thirty days before the meeting of the Convention. It shall be the duty of the Secretary of the Convention, at least twenty days before the meeting of the Convention, to deliver to a Committee, to be annually appointed (to be called the Committee on the Incorporation and Admission of Churches), all applications for admission into union which shall have been received by him, to be by such Committee examined, considered and reported upon to the Convention.

SEC. 3. Whenever hereafter any Church in union with this Convention shall neglect, for three years in succession, to make a Parochial Report, no Missionary Report being made on its behalf, and shall not, during the same period, have employed a Clergyman as its Parish Minister, nor requested of the Ecclesiastical Authority to have the services of a Missionary, such Church shall be regarded as having forfeited its connection with the Convention, and shall no longer have a right to send a Delegation to the same. The Bishop shall report such Church to the Convention in his Annual Address. Such Church, however, may be re-admitted, upon application to the Convention, accompanied by a report of its condition, and on such terms as shall appear just; such re-admission to take effect from and after the rising of the Convention consenting to such admission.

Sec. 3. The Standing Committee shall make a full report of all their proceedings at every Annual Convention.

CANON XI.

Of Parish Registers and Parochial Reports.

WHEREAS, by the Canons of the General Convention,* it is made the duty of each Clergyman of this Church to "keep a Register of Baptisms, Confirmations, Communicants, Marriages, and Funerals within his Cure, agreeably to such rules as may be provided by the Convention of the Diocese where his Cure lies;" it is hereby ordered that,

SECTION 1. The Record shall specify the name and the time of the birth of the child or adult baptized, with the names of the parents, sponsors or witnesses; the names of the persons confirmed; the names of the persons married, their ages and residences, also the names and residences of at least two witnesses of each marriage; the names of the persons buried, their ages, and the place of burial; and also the time when and the Minister by whom each rite was performed. The list of Communicants shall contain the names of. all connected with the Parish or Mission as nearly as can be ascertained. These records shall be made by the Minister in a book provided for that purpose, belonging to each Church; which book shall be the Parish Register, and shall be preserved as a part of the records of the Church.

SEC. 2. AND WHEREAS, by the Canons of the General Convention,† it is " ordered that every Minister of this Church, or, if the Parish be vacant, the Warden shall present, or cause to be delivered, on or before the first day of every Annual Convention, to the Bishop of the Diocese, or, where there is no Bishop, to the President of the Convention, a statement of the number of Baptisms, Confirmations, Marriages and Funerals, and of the number of Communicants in his Parish or Church; also the state and condition of the Sunday Schools in his Parish; and also the amount of the Communion alms, the contributions for 'Missions, Diocesan, Domestic and Foreign, for Parochial Schools, for Church purposes in general, and of all other matters that may throw light on the state of the same," it is hereby further ordered that, in reporting the number of Communicants, he shall distinguish the additions, removals and deaths since the last report, and that, in reporting the contributions for Church purposes in general, he shall include the amount received for sittings in the Church and moneys raised for all Church and Parish purposes, other than those enumerated in this section.

SEC. 3. In every case where a Parish is without a Minister, the Parish Register shall be kept by some person appointed by the Vestry or Trustees; and the annual Parochial report shall be presented or forwarded to the Bishop by the Churchwardens or Trustees of the Parish.

CANON XII.

Of Vacant Parishes.

SECTION 1. Whenever a Parish becomes vacant, it shall be the duty of the Vestry or Trustees to give immediate notice thereof to the Bishop.

SEC. 2. The Bishop shall appoint those of the Clergy in the Diocese who can with most convenience discharge the duty, to supply such vacant Parishes as have been reported to him, at such times as may be deemed convenient and proper. And the Clergy so appointed, shall make a full report to the Bishop concerning the state of the Parishes which they have visited. It shall be the duty of the Parishes thus supplied to defray all the expenses incident to such occasional services.

* Title I, Canon 15, Sec 5.   † Title I, Canon 18, Sec. 1.

Canon XIII.

Of Offerings.

Section 1. Whereas it is the duty of all Christians, as faithful stewards of God, to set apart regularly a portion of their income as God's portion, "every one as God hath prospered him," to be used for the maintenance and extension of His kingdom, and the relief of His poor; this Church enjoins this duty upon all her members.

Sec. 2. It shall be the duty of every Congregation of this Diocese to contribute, at least once in each year, by weekly or monthly offerings, or in some other systematic way, to the Missions of the Diocese; the Domestic and Foreign Missions and other departments of Missionary work under the control of the General Convention; the support of the Episcopate; the expenses of the Convention; the education of young men for the Holy Ministry; the distribution of the Bible and Book of Common Prayer; the support of aged and infirm Clergymen; the relief of the widows and orphans of deceased Clergymen; and the support and education of orphan children; the offerings to be sent to the Treasurers of the funds for which they are made, and the amounts of all such contributions to form distinct items in the Annual Parochial Report.

Sec. 3. "The Protestant Episcopal Society for Promoting Religion and Learning in the State of New York," in which we have an interest in common with our mother Diocese, shall be the agent of this Diocese for the education of young men for Holy Orders. A copy of its Annual report, if obtained from its Superintendent, shall be laid by the Secretary of the Convention before each Annual Convention.

Sec. 4. "The Bible and Common Prayer Book Society of Albany and its Vicinity" shall be the agent of this Diocese for the Distribution of the Bible and the Book of Common Prayer, and shall present a full report of its proceedings to each Annual Convention.

Sec. 5. The Orphan House of the Holy Saviour, at or near Cooperstown, shall be the Diocesan Orphanage, and shall make a report of its proceedings and condition to each Annual Convention.

Canon XIV.

Of the Missions of the Diocese and of Archdeaconries.

The Church in this Diocese, acknowledging her responsibility, in common with the whole Church, for the fulfilment of the charge of our Lord to preach the Gospel to every creature, and especially for the extension of the Church throughout the Diocese, declares that it is the duty of the Convention, as her representative body, to care for the Missionary work, and that every baptized Member of the Church is bound, according to his ability, to assist in carrying it on. To this end it is hereby enacted as follows:

Section 1. "The Board of Missions of the Protestant Episcopal Church in the Diocese of Albany," incorporated by an Act of the Legislature of the State of New York, passed February 16, 1870, shall be entrusted with the general charge and direction of the work of Missions within the Diocese, and particularly with the custody and management of all money or property given or acquired for that object, subject to the provisions of this Canon and to such written instructions as may from time to time be given to them by the Convention and entered upon the Journal thereof.

Sec. 2. The said Board of Missions shall consist of the Bishop, who shall be *ex officio* the President thereof; and of ten other members, one Clergyman and one Layman resident within the limits of each of the Archdeaconries hereinafter provided for, and nominated by said Archdeaconry, and one Clergyman and one Layman who

may be resident anywhere within the Diocese, and shall be nominated in open Convention, all of whom shall be annually chosen by the Convention, and by ballot unless the same be unanimously dispensed with. All vacancies occurring in the Board during the recess of the Convention, may be filled by the Board.

SEC. 3. The evening session of the Convention on the first day of each Annual Meeting shall be devoted to the reception and consideration of the Report of the Board of Missions and of its Treasurer, the election of the Board, and other business connected with the subject; provided that said election and other business connected with the subject may be deferred to the second day.

SEC. 4. The Board of Missions shall meet on the day after the adjournment of the Convention in each year, and elect a Secretary and a Treasurer. The Board may hold other meetings during the year, according to its own rules, and shall meet on the day preceding the Annual Convention, to audit the accounts of the Treasurer, and to adopt a report to the Convention.

SEC. 5. The Diocese shall be divided into districts called Archdeaconries, the titles and limits of which shall be as follows: The Archdeaconry of Albany shall comprise the counties of Albany, Greene, Columbia, Schenectady, Montgomery, Fulton, Hamilton and Herkimer. The Archdeaconry of Troy shall comprise the counties of Rensselaer, Saratoga, Washington, Warren, Clinton and Essex. The Archdeaconry of the Susquehanna shall comprise the counties of Delaware, Otsego and Schoharie. The Archdeaconry of Ogdensburgh shall comprise the counties of St. Lawrence and Franklin.

SEC. 6. The Bishop shall be *ex officio* the head of each Archdeaconry. He shall, however, annually appoint an Archdeacon on the nomination of each Archdeaconry, from among the Clergy thereof, who shall be the Executive Officer of the Archdeaconry. Each Archdeaconry, moreover, shall annually elect a Secretary and Treasurer, who shall make annual reports to the Convention. The Archdeacon in the absence of the Bishop shall preside at all the meetings of the Archdeaconry, and may also be present without a vote at the meetings of the Board of Missions. He shall be charged with the duty of visiting the Mission Stations and vacant Parishes, and, with the consent of the Clergy in charge, the other Parishes receiving Missionary aid within the limits of his Archdeaconry, to ascertain their condition, and to give such advice as may be required, reporting the result of his inquiries and observations to the Bishop. It shall also be his duty to stir up an increased Missionary interest and zeal, and to urge more liberal offerings for the work of Church extension. And furthermore the Archdeacon and the Clerical and Lay Members of the Board of Missions from each Archdeaconry shall be an Advisory Committee of the Board, whose duty it shall be to counsel the Board as to the amount which should be expended in, and the amount which should be raised by the Archdeaconry which they represent, and to use their best efforts to secure the required amount of Missionary offerings from their Archdeaconry.

SEC. 7. Each Archdeaconry shall hold two meetings a year at such places within its boundaries as it may designate. Other meetings may be held as the Archdeaconry may order. At all meetings of the Archdeaconry every Clergyman canonically resident within its boundaries shall be entitled to a seat; also three Laymen from each Parish or Mission Station within the limits of the Archdeaconry. Each Clergyman and each Lay Delegation shall have one vote. Any number of members present at a meeting duly called shall be competent to transact business. The meetings of Archdeaconry shall have for their main purpose the presentation of the claims of the Mission work of the Diocese and the Church. Such Missionaries as may be members shall report concerning their work, and provision may be made for especial needs of the Missionary work within the boundaries of the Archdeaconry. Contributions to

local work shall not interfere with the claims of the Diocesan Board of Missions, and shall be reported to the Treasurer thereof, and included in his Annual Report to the Convention. It shall also be the object of these Archidiaconal meetings to bring the Clergy together in fraternal intercourse and to promote their spiritual and intellectual life. Each Archdeaconry shall make its own rules as to the arrangement of services.

SEC. 8. All Missionaries shall be appointed by the Board of Missions on the nomination of the Bishop, and may be removed with his approval. But in case of a vacancy in the Episcopate, or of the absence of the Bishop from the Diocese, or of his being otherwise unable to perform his duties, the Board of Missions shall have the power of appointing and removing Missionaries.

SEC. 9. It shall be the duty of every member of the Church in the Diocese to contribute as God hath prospered him, to the funds of the Board of Missions; and every Clergyman having Parochial or Missionary charge shall impress this duty upon his people, and cause one or more Offertories to be made annually for that object.

SEC. 10. The Treasurer of the Board of Missions shall include in his Annual Report all sums certified to him as expended in local Missionary work. He shall also receive, report and pay over any special contributions from Parishes or individuals in accordance with the instructions of the contributors.

SEC. 11. The travelling expenses of the members of the Board of Missions and of the Archdeacons, attending the meetings of the Board, shall be paid out of its treasury.

SEC. 12. Any Mission Station designated by the Board of Missions may be organized by the Bishop on the application of any residents in its neighbourhood. But such station shall not be established within the Parochial Cure of any other Minister or Ministers, without either the consent of such Minister or of a majority of such Ministers, or with the advice of the Standing Committee of the Diocese. The Bishop may appoint, upon the organization of the Mission, a Churchwarden, a Clerk, and a Treasurer, which officers shall thereafter be elected by the Congregation annually in Easter week, in the same manner as provided for the choice of Deputies to Convention by section 2, of Canon II of this Diocese. They shall, as far as possible, discharge the duties which belong to their respective offices in incorporated Parishes.

SEC. 13. The title of all property, real or personal, given or purchased for the use of any Mission Station, shall be vested in "The Board of Missions of the Protestant Episcopal Church, in the Diocese of Albany," or in "The Trustees of the Diocese of Albany."

CANON XV.

Of the Episcopal Fund.

SECTION 1. The fund for the support of the Episcopate in this Diocese, now provided, together with that which may be hereafter contributed or acquired, and any accumulation accruing from the investment thereof, shall be entrusted to the Corporation, entitled "The Trustees of the Episcopal Fund of the Diocese of Albany," incorporated by an Act of the Legislature of the State of New York, passed April 28, 1869. The Trustees composing said Corporation shall be five in number, who shall be appointed by the Convention, and shall hold their offices during the pleasure thereof.

SEC. 2. All moneys belonging to the said fund shall be loaned by the said Trustees upon security of real estate, or invested in stock of the United States, or of this State, or of the city of New York, at their discretion; and all securities and investments shall be taken or made in their corporate name above mentioned; and they shall have power, from time to time, to change such investments. A statement, signed by the Trustees or a majority of them, exhibiting the condition of said fund

may be resident anywhere within the Diocese, and shall be nominated in open Convention, all of whom shall be annually chosen by the Convention, and by ballot unless the same be unanimously dispensed with. All vacancies occurring in the Board during the recess of the Convention, may be filled by the Board.

SEC. 3. The evening session of the Convention on the first day of each Annual Meeting shall be devoted to the reception and consideration of the Report of the Board of Missions and of its Treasurer, the election of the Board, and other business connected with the subject; provided that said election and other business connected with the subject may be deferred to the second day.

SEC. 4. The Board of Missions shall meet on the day after the adjournment of the Convention in each year, and elect a Secretary and a Treasurer. The Board may hold other meetings during the year, according to its own rules, and shall meet on the day preceding the Annual Convention, to audit the accounts of the Treasurer, and to adopt a report to the Convention.

SEC. 5. The Diocese shall be divided into districts called Archdeaconries, the titles and limits of which shall be as follows: The Archdeaconry of Albany shall comprise the counties of Albany, Greene, Columbia, Schenectady, Montgomery, Fulton, Hamilton and Herkimer. The Archdeaconry of Troy shall comprise the counties of Rensselaer, Saratoga, Washington, Warren, Clinton and Essex. The Archdeaconry of the Susquehanna shall comprise the counties of Delaware, Otsego and Schoharie. The Archdeaconry of Ogdensburgh shall comprise the counties of St. Lawrence and Franklin.

SEC. 6. The Bishop shall be *ex officio* the head of each Archdeaconry. He shall, however, annually appoint an Archdeacon on the nomination of each Archdeaconry, from among the Clergy thereof, who shall be the Executive Officer of the Archdeaconry. Each Archdeaconry, moreover, shall annually elect a Secretary and Treasurer, who shall make annual reports to the Convention. The Archdeacon in the absence of the Bishop shall preside at all the meetings of the Archdeaconry, and may also be present without a vote at the meetings of the Board of Missions. He shall be charged with the duty of visiting the Mission Stations and vacant Parishes, and, with the consent of the Clergy in charge, the other Parishes receiving Missionary aid within the limits of his Archdeaconry, to ascertain their condition, and to give such advice as may be required, reporting the result of his inquiries and observations to the Bishop. It shall also be his duty to stir up an increased Missionary interest and zeal, and to urge more liberal offerings for the work of Church extension. And furthermore the Archdeacon and the Clerical and Lay Members of the Board of Missions from each Archdeaconry shall be an Advisory Committee of the Board, whose duty it shall be to counsel the Board as to the amount which should be expended in, and the amount which should be raised by the Archdeaconry which they represent, and to use their best efforts to secure the required amount of Missionary offerings from their Archdeaconry.

SEC. 7. Each Archdeaconry shall hold two meetings a year at such places within its boundaries as it may designate. Other meetings may be held as the Archdeaconry may order. At all meetings of the Archdeaconry every Clergyman canonically resident within its boundaries shall be entitled to a seat; also three Laymen from each Parish or Mission Station within the limits of the Archdeaconry. Each Clergyman and each Lay Delegation shall have one vote. Any number of members present at a meeting duly called shall be competent to transact business. The meetings of Archdeaconry shall have for their main purpose the presentation of the claims of the Mission work of the Diocese and the Church. Such Missionaries as may be members shall report concerning their work, and provision may be made for especial needs of the Missionary work within the boundaries of the Archdeaconry. Contributions to

Sec. 5. No Clergyman shall be a beneficiary of the fund whose salary or stipend exceeds $1,000 per annum. Nor shall any Clergyman receive the annuity who has allowed the Parish or Mission under his charge to neglect its annual contribution to the fund.

Sec. 6. The principal of the fund shall not be impaired.

Sec. 7. The trustees of the fund shall be the Bishop of the Diocese, the Rector of St. Peter's Church, Albany, the Rector of St. Paul's Church, Troy, the Archdeacons of the Diocese, and the Treasurer of the Diocese, who shall be the treasurer of the fund. And they are hereby authorized to form a corporation under the Laws of the State of New York, whose object shall be to carry into effect the provisions of this Canon, and to provide for the receipt by the corporation so to be formed, of real and personal estate by gifts, purchase, devise, bequest or otherwise, for the purposes of said corporation.

CANON XIX.

Of the Fund for the Widows and Orphans of Deceased Clergymen.

Section 1. The fund now existing, together with all contributions hereafter received for the relief of widows and orphans of Deceased Clergymen shall be entrusted to the Corporation entitled "The Trustees of the Fund for the Widows and Orphans of Deceased Clergymen of the Protestant Episcopal Church in the Diocese of Albany," incorporated by an Act of the Legislature of the State of New York, passed February 16, 1870. The said Trustees shall consist of the Bishop and the Treasurer of the Diocese, together with three Lay Trustees, who shall be appointed annually by the Convention. Vacancies occurring in the number of the Lay Trustees during the recess of the Convention may be filled by the remaining Trustees.

Sec. 2. It shall be the duty of the Trustees to receive applications for relief, and to administer it in accordance with such rules and regulations as they, with the approbation of the Convention, may from time to time adopt.

Sec. 3. The Trustees shall present a detailed report of their proceedings and of the condition of the fund to every Annual Convention.

CANON XX.

Of the Trial of a Clergyman not being a Bishop.

Whenever any Minister of this Diocese, not being a Bishop thereof, shall become "liable to presentment and trial" under the provisions of any Canon of the General or Diocesan Convention, the mode of proceeding in this Diocese shall be as follows:

Section 1. The trial shall be on a presentment in writing, addressed to the Bishop of the Diocese, specifying the offences of which the accused is alleged to be guilty, with reasonable certainty as to time, place and circumstances. Such presentment may be made by the major part in number of the members of the Vestry of any Church of which the accused is Minister, or by any three Presbyters of this Diocese entitled to seats in the Convention, or as hereinafter mentioned. Whenever, from public rumor or otherwise, the Bishop shall have reason to believe that any Clergyman is under the imputation of having been guilty of any offence or misconduct for which he is liable to be tried, and that the interest of the Church requires an investigation, it shall be his duty to appoint five persons, of whom three at least shall be Presbyters, to examine the case; a majority of whom may make such examination; and if there is, in their opinion, sufficient ground for presentment, they shall present the Clergyman accordingly.

Sec. 2. A presentment being made in any one of the modes above prescribed, the Bishop, if the facts charged shall not appear to him to be such as constitute an of-

fence, may dismiss it; or if it allege facts, some of which do and some of which do not constitute an offence, he may allow it in part and dismiss the residue, or he may permit it to be amended. When it shall be allowed in whole or in part, the Bishop shall cause a copy of it to be served on the accused; and shall also nominate twelve Presbyters of this Diocese entitled to seats in the Convention, and not being parties to the presentment, and cause a list of their names to be served on the accused, who shall, within thirty days after such service, select five of them, and notify their names in writing to the Bishop; and if he shall not give such notification to the Bishop within the said thirty days, the Bishop shall select five: and the Presbyters so selected shall form a Board for the trial of the accused, and shall meet at such time and place as the Bishop shall direct, and shall have power to adjourn from time to time, and from place to place (but always within the Diocese), as they shall think proper.

SEC. 3. A written notice of the time and place of their first meeting shall be served, at least thirty days before such meeting, on the accused, and also on one of the persons making the presentment.

SEC. 4. If, at the time appointed for the first meeting of the Board of Presbyters, the whole number of five shall not attend, then those who do attend may adjourn from time to time; and if, after one adjournment or more, it shall appear to them improbable that the whole number will attend within a reasonable time, then those who do attend, not being less than three, shall constitute the board, and proceed to the trial, and a majority of them shall decide all questions.

SEC. 5. If a Clergyman presented shall confess the truth of the facts alleged in the presentment, and shall not demur thereto, it shall be the duty of the Bishop to proceed to pass sentence; and if he shall not confess them before the appointment of a Board for his trial, as before mentioned, he shall be considered as denying them.

SEC. 6. If a Clergyman presented, after having had due notice, shall not appear before the Board of Presbyters appointed for his trial, the Board may, nevertheless, proceed as if he were present, unless for good cause they shall see fit to adjourn to another day.

SEC. 7. When the Board proceed to the trial, they shall hear such evidence as shall be produced, which evidence shall be reduced to writing and signed by the witnesses, respectively; and some officer authorized by law to administer oaths may, at the desire of either party, be requested to administer an oath or affirmation to the witnesses, that they will testify the truth, the whole truth, and nothing but the truth, concerning the facts charged in the presentment. If, on or during the trial, the accused shall confess the truth of the charges, as stated in the presentment, the Board may dispense with hearing further evidence, and may proceed at once to state their opinion to the Bishop as to the sentence that ought to be pronounced.

SEC. 8. Upon the application of either party to the Bishop, and it being made satisfactorily to appear to him that any material witness cannot be procured upon the trial, the Bishop may appoint a Commissary to take the testimony of such witness. Such Commissary may be either a Clergyman or a Layman, and the party so applying shall give to the other at least six days' notice of the time and place of taking the testimony. If the person on whom the notice shall be served shall reside more than forty miles from the place of examination, notice of an additional day shall be given for every additional twenty miles of the said distance. Both parties may attend and examine the witness; and the questions and answers shall be reduced to writing and signed by the witness, and shall be certified by the Commissary, and enclosed under his seal, and transmitted to the Board, and shall be received by them as evidence. A witness examined before such Commissary may be sworn or affirmed in manner aforesaid.

SEC. 9. The Board, having deliberately considered the evidence, shall declare in a writing signed by them, or a majority of them, their decision on the charges contained in the presentment, distinctly stating whether the accused be guilty or not guilty of such charges, respectively, and also stating the sentence (if any) which, in their opinion, should be pronounced; and a copy of such decision shall be, without delay, communicated to the accused; and the original decision, together with the evidence, shall be delivered to the Bishop, who shall pronounce such canonical sentence as shall appear to him to be proper, provided the same shall not exceed in severity the sentence recommended by the Board; and such sentence shall be final. Before pronouncing any sentence, the Bishop shall summon the accused, and any three or more of the Clergy, to meet him at such time as may, in his opinion, be most convenient, in some Church to be designated by him, which shall, for that purpose, be open at the time to all persons who may choose to attend; and the sentence shall then and there be publicly pronounced by the Bishop. But the Bishop, if he shall be satisfied that justice requires it, may grant a new trial to the accused, in which case a new Board of Presbyters shall be appointed, the proceedings before whom shall be conducted as above mentioned.

SEC. 10. All notices and papers contemplated in this Canon may be served by a summoner or summoners, to be appointed for the purpose by the Bishop, and whose certificate of such service shall be evidence thereof. In case of service by any other person, the facts shall be proved by the affidavit of such person. A written notice or paper delivered to a party, or left at his last place of residence, shall be deemed a sufficient service of such notice or paper.

SEC. 11. The defendant may have the privilege of appearing by counsel; in case of the exercise of which privilege, and not otherwise, those who present shall also have the like privilege.

SEC. 12. If the Ecclesiastical Authority of any other Diocese shall, under the provisions of the Canons of the General Convention, or otherwise, make known to the Ecclesiastical Authority of this Diocese, charges against a Presbyter or Deacon thereof, such communication shall be a sufficient presentation of him for trial; and the trial shall take place as above provided. The Bishop shall appoint some competent person as Prosecutor, who shall be considered as the party making the presentment.

CANON XXI.

Of Differences between Ministers and their Congregations.

SECTION 1. Whenever there shall be any serious difference between the Rector of any Church in this Diocese and the Congregation thereof, it shall be lawful for a majority of the Vestry or Trustees to make a representation to the Bishop, stating the facts in the case and agreeing, for themselves and for the Congregation which they represent, to submit to his decision in the matter, and to perform whatever he may require of them by any order which he may make under the provisions of this Canon, and shall at the same time serve a copy of the representation on the Rector.

SEC. 2. It shall be the duty of the Bishop, at all stages of the proceeding, to seek to bring them to an amicable conclusion; and in such case the agreement between the parties, signed by them and attested by the Bishop, shall have the same force as an order made under section 4 of this Canon.

SEC. 3. If the matter shall not be amicably settled within a reasonable time, the Bishop shall convene the Clerical Members of the Standing Committee and shall give notice to the parties to appear before him and present their proofs and arguments at such time and place as he may appoint; and he may adjourn and continue the hearing in the matter in his discretion.

SEC. 4. When the hearing is concluded, the Bishop shall make such an order in regard to the matter as he may think to be just and for the true interests of the Church; and such order may require the Rector to resign his Rectorship, and may require the Church to pay a sum of money to the Rector; and it shall be the duty of the Rector and of the Church and every member thereof to submit to and abide by such order as the final and conclusive determination of all matters of difference between them. *Provided*, that no order shall be made under this or the next succeeding section of this Canon, unless with the advice and concurrence of at least two Clerical Members of the Standing Committee, who shall have been present at the hearing.

SEC. 5. If it shall be made to appear to the Bishop that any agreement made under section 2 of this Canon, or any order made under section 4 of this Canon, or of this section, shall have been disregarded by any of the parties concerned, or if an application be made to him to modify such order, he may convene the Clerical Members of the Standing Committee, and after hearing such further proofs and arguments as may be presented to him, make such further order in the matter as he may think proper with the same effect as an order made under section 4 of this Canon.

SEC. 6. If any Church or Congregation shall persistently neglect or refuse to obey any order made under this Canon, it shall be the duty of the Bishop to exhort the members of such Congregation to submit to the authority and discipline of the Church; and if they will not do so, the Convention may proceed to dissolve the union between the Church so offending and the Convention of this Diocese, and may take such other action in the matter as it may think expedient. *Provided*, that no such action shall be held or taken to be a surrender of any right which either the Church in this Diocese, or such members of such Congregation as submit to the authority and discipline of the Church may have in the corporation of such Church, or in any property belonging thereto.

SEC. 7. Whenever the Standing Committee shall be acting as the Ecclesiastical Authority of the Diocese, the Clerical Members thereof shall perform the duties herein required of the Bishop; and they shall request the Bishop of some other Diocese to attend the hearing of the case, and shall make no order therein but with his advice and assistance.

CANON XXII.

Of Amendments of the Canons.

No new Canon or amendment of a Canon shall hereafter be adopted by the Convention, unless at least one day's previous notice thereof shall have been given in open Convention; nor, unless by unanimous consent, until the same shall have been referred to, and reported upon by a Committee of at least two Presbyters and two Laymen. All propositions to amend the Canons shall be in the form of a Canon, and such sections as shall be amended shall be re-enacted in full in their amended form.

ADMISSION OF CHURCHES.

Under Canon IV, in order to be admitted into union with the Church in this Diocese, the Church or congregation must (in sufficient time to allow the papers to be transmitted to, *and be received by* the Secretary of the Convention at least thirty days before the meeting of the Convention) adopt a resolution, at a legally convened and held meeting of the Vestry, or (*in the case of Churches incorporated without Vestries*), of the congregation, authorizing the application for such admission to be made, and agreeing to abide by, and conform to, and observe all the Canons of the Church, and all the rules, orders and regulations of the Convention. A copy of this resolution must be duly certified by the presiding officer of the Vestry, or of the meeting of the congregation at which the resolution was adopted, and also by the Clerk of the Vestry, or Secretary of the meeting of the congregation, and must also be authenticated by the seal of the corporation.

In Churches having Vestries, this resolution should be adopted by the Vestry. In Churches incorporated without Vestries, it should be adopted by the congregation.

The following form of resolution is recommended:

Resolved, That [*here set forth the corporate name or title by which the Church is known in law as the same is described in the Certificate of Incorporation*] desire admission into union with the Church in the Diocese of Albany, and do make application therefor to the Convention of the Church in this Diocese; and do hereby agree to abide by, and conform to, and observe all the Canons of the Church, and all the rules, orders and regulations of the Convention.

The resolution must be entered accurately and at length on the minutes of the Vestry, or of the meeting of the congregation, as the case may be.

The Canon requires an application *in writing*, to the Convention, asking admission, which must then be made out. This may be signed by the Rector (if there be one), and by one or both of the Wardens, *and* by the Clerk of the Vestry; or, in the case of Churches without Vestries, by the Minister, or by the presiding officer of the meeting at which the resolution was adopted, *and also* by the Clerk of such meeting.

The following form of application is recommended:

To the Convention of the Protestant Episcopal Church in the Diocese of Albany:

The Church or congregation duly incorporated and known in law by the name of [*here set forth the corporate name or title of the Church, as the same is described in the Certificate of Incorporation*], in pursuance, and by authority of a resolution of the [*Vestry or congregation as the case may be*] of the said Church, hereby applies for admission into union with the Church in this Diocese; and presents herewith a duly certified and authenticated copy of the resolution of the said [*Vestry or congregation, as the case may be*] adopted on the   day of   189 , authorizing such application, and agreeing to abide by, and conform to, and observe all the Canons of the Church, and all the rules, orders and regulations of the Convention. *Also,* the Certificate of Incorporation of the Church (*or in case the original certificate is not presented, then say, "a duly certified copy of the Certificate of the Incorporation of the Church*), which was duly recorded in the office of the (Clerk or Register, *as the case may be*), of the   county of   on the   day of   189 , in Book   of Certificates of Religious Incorporations, (*or whatever may be*

Sec. 4. When the hearing is concluded, the Bishop shall make such an order in regard to the matter as he may think to be just and for the true interests of the Church; and such order may require the Rector to resign his Rectorship, and may require the Church to pay a sum of money to the Rector; and it shall be the duty of the Rector and of the Church and every member thereof to submit to and abide by such order as the final and conclusive determination of all matters of difference between them. *Provided,* that no order shall be made under this or the next succeeding section of this Canon, unless with the advice and concurrence of at least two Clerical Members of the Standing Committee, who shall have been present at the hearing.

Sec. 5. If it shall be made to appear to the Bishop that any agreement made under section 2 of this Canon, or any order made under section 4 of this Canon, or of this section, shall have been disregarded by any of the parties concerned, or if an application be made to him to modify such order, he may convene the Clerical Members of the Standing Committee, and after hearing such further proofs and arguments as may be presented to him, make such further order in the matter as he may think proper with the same effect as an order made under section 4 of this Canon.

Sec. 6. If any Church or Congregation shall persistently neglect or refuse to obey any order made under this Canon, it shall be the duty of the Bishop to exhort the members of such Congregation to submit to the authority and discipline of the Church; and if they will not do so, the Convention may proceed to dissolve the union between the Church so offending and the Convention of this Diocese, and may take such other action in the matter as it may think expedient. *Provided,* that no such action shall be held or taken to be a surrender of any right which either the Church in this Diocese, or such members of such Congregation as submit to the authority and discipline of the Church may have in the corporation of such Church, or in any property belonging thereto.

Sec. 7. Whenever the Standing Committee shall be acting as the Ecclesiastical Authority of the Diocese, the Clerical Members thereof shall perform the duties herein required of the Bishop; and they shall request the Bishop of some other Diocese to attend the hearing of the case, and shall make no order therein but with his advice and assistance.

CANON XXII.

Of Amendments of the Canons.

No new Canon or amendment of a Canon shall hereafter be adopted by the Convention, unless at least one day's previous notice thereof shall have been given in open Convention; nor, unless by unanimous consent, until the same shall have been referred to, and reported upon by a Committee of at least two Presbyters and two Laymen. All propositions to amend the Canons shall be in the form of a Canon, and such sections as shall be amended shall be re-enacted in full in their amended form.

In the case of Churches having no Vestries, the certificate may be as follows:

Which is hereby certified by A. B., Minister of the Church, *or* C. D., the Presiding officer of the meeting of the congregation at which the resolution was adopted, and also by E. F., the secretary of the said meeting, and is also authenticated by the seal of the corporation.

Dated, etc. (as above).

[SEAL.]

> A. B., *Minister.*
> [*or*] C. D., *Presiding officer of the Meeting of the Congregation.*
> E. F., *Secretary of the Meeting.*

The following is submitted (with the approval and authority of the Bishop) as the form for his certificate:

I do hereby certify, that I approve of the incorporation of a Church known as [*here set forth the corporate name or title of the Church as the same is described in the Certificate of Incorporation*], and that such Church, in my judgment, is duly and satisfactorily established.

Dated at   the   day of   in the year of our Lord one thousand eight hundred and

> *Bishop.*

The following is recommended as a form for the presentation of the evidence of the number of persons habitually attending the Church:

We, the undersigned, do hereby certify and declare, that we are, and for one year last past have been connected with, or been members of, and well acquainted with the affairs and condition of, the Church or congregation known as [*here set forth the corporate name or title of the Church as the same is described in the Certificate of Incorporation*], and that we have had means of knowing, and do know, the number of persons habitually attending the said Church during one year past; and that not less than twenty-five persons, members of such Church, have habitually, for at least one year preceding this date, attended Divine Service in such Church or congregation.

Dated at   in the county of   the   day of 189 .

This certificate should be signed by the Rector, or officiating Minister, if there be one, and by one or both of the Wardens, or by two or more of the Trustees (in the case of a Church incorporated without a Vestry), or by other known and reputable parties who can certify to the fact set forth.

The application, together with the requisite papers (as before set forth), must be transmitted to the Secretary of the Convention, at least thirty days before the meeting of the Convention.

The Canon (Section 2, Canon IV.) expressly declares that " no application for the admission of a Church into union with the Church in this Diocese, shall be considered or acted upon at any meeting of the Convention, unless the same shall have been transmitted to the Secretary of the Convention at least thirty days before the meeting of the Convention."

the official designation of the book in which such Certificates are recorded in the county in which such Church is located), page . *Also*, a certificate of the Bishop that he approves of the incorporation of such Church, and that such Church, in his judgment, is duly and satisfactorily established. *And also*, evidence that not less than twenty-five persons, members of such Church, have habitually, for at least one year preceding the date of this application, attended Divine Services in such Church or congregation.

Dated at   in the county of   and State of New York, this   day of   189 .

By order of the [*Vestry or congregation as the case may be*].

> A. B., *Rector*.
> C. D., *Warden*.
> E. F., *do*.
> G. H., *Clerk*.

Or, in case of Churches having no Vestries:

> A. B., *Minister*.
> C. D., *Presiding officer of the Meeting of the Congregation*.
> E. F., *Secretary of the Meeting of the Congregation*.

The Canon also requires that the application be accompanied by the following papers:

I. A duly certified and authenticated copy of the resolution of the Vestry or congregation authorizing the application, etc.

II. The original, or a certified copy of the Certificate of Incorporation.

III. The certificate of the Bishop's approval of the incorporation, and that, in his judgment, the Church is duly and satisfactorily established.

IV. The evidence that not less than twenty-five persons, members of such Church, have habitually, for at least one year preceding the date of the application, attended Divine Service in the Church or congregation.

The following is recommended as a form for certifying the resolution of the Vestry or of the congregation:

At a meeting of the [*Vestry or congregation, as the case may be*] of the Church or congregation known as [*here set forth the corporate name or title of the Church, as the same is described in the Certificate of Incorporation*], duly convened, and held according to law, at   on the   day of   18 , the following resolution was adopted:

"*Resolved*, That [*here copy, in the precise words, and at length, and accurately, the resolution as adopted and entered on the Minutes.*"]

Which is hereby certified by A. B., the Rector of the said Church [*or, if there be no Rector, then* C. D., the Warden, who presided at the meeting of the Vestry at which the resolution was adopted, there being no Rector of the said Church]. and also by E. F., the Clerk of the Vestry, and is also authenticated by the seal of the corporation.

Dated at   in the county of   the   day of 189.

[SEAL.]

> A. B., *Rector*.
> [*or*] C. D. *Warden presiding*
> E. F., *Clerk of the Vestry*.

In the case of Churches having no Vestries, the certificate may be as follows:

Which is hereby certified by A. B., Minister of the Church, *or* C. D., the Presiding officer of the meeting of the congregation at which the resolution was adopted, and also by E. F., the secretary of the said meeting, and is also authenticated by the seal of the corporation.

Dated, etc. (as above).

A. B., *Minister.*
[*or*] C. D., *Presiding officer of the Meeting*
of the Congregation.
E. F., *Secretary of the Meeting.*

[SEAL.]

The following is submitted (with the approval and authority of the Bishop) as the form for his certificate:

I do hereby certify, that I approve of the incorporation of a Church known as [*here set forth the corporate name or title of the Church as the same is described in the Certificate of Incorporation*], and that such Church, in my judgment, is duly and satisfactorily established.

Dated at   the   day of   in the year of our Lord one thousand eight hundred and

Bishop.

The following is recommended as a form for the presentation of the evidence of the number of persons habitually attending the Church:

We, the undersigned, do hereby certify and declare, that we are, and for one year last past have been connected with, or been members of, and well acquainted with the affairs and condition of, the Church or congregation known as [*here set forth the corporate name or title of the Church as the same is described in the Certificate of Incorporation*], and that we have had means of knowing, and do know, the number of persons habitually attending the said Church during one year past; and that not less than twenty-five persons, members of such Church, have habitually, for at least one year preceding this date, attended Divine Service in such Church or congregation.

Dated at   in the county of   the   day of 189 .

This certificate should be signed by the Rector, or officiating Minister, if there be one, and by one or both of the Wardens, or by two or more of the Trustees (in the case of a Church incorporated without a Vestry), or by other known and reputable parties who can certify to the fact set forth.

The application, together with the requisite papers (as before set forth), must be transmitted to the Secretary of the Convention, at least thirty days before the meeting of the Convention.

The Canon (Section 2, Canon IV.) expressly declares that "no application for the admission of a Church into union with the Church in this Diocese, shall be considered or acted upon at any meeting of the Convention, unless the same shall have been transmitted to the Secretary of the Convention at least thirty days before the meeting of the Convention."

DIOCESAN INSTITUTIONS.

THE SISTERHOOD OF THE HOLY CHILD JESUS.

ST AGNES' SCHOOL, ALBANY.

THE CHILD'S HOSPITAL, ALBANY.

THE ST. MARGARET'S HOUSE, ALBANY.

THE CHURCH HOME, TROY.

THE ST. CHRISTINA HOME, SARATOGA.

THE ST. CHRISTOPHER HOME, EAST LINE.

THE ORPHAN HOUSE OF THE HOLY SAVIOUR, COOPERSTOWN.

THE BIBLE AND COMMON PRAYER BOOK SOCIETY OF ALBANY AND VICINITY.

REXLEIGH SCHOOL, SALEM.

PAROCHIAL INSTITUTIONS.

ST. PETER'S ORPHANAGE, ALBANY.

THE MARTHA MEMORIAL HOUSE, TROY.

THE MARY WARREN FREE INSTITUTE, TROY.

Diocese of Albany.

Convention Journal,

A. D., 1892.

---

together with the

MINUTES OF THE MEETING

of the

FEDERATE COUNCIL,

which assembled in

NEW YORK CITY

DECEMBER 28, 1892.

JOURNAL OF THE PROCEEDINGS

OF THE

Twenty-Fourth Annual Convention

OF THE

Protestant Episcopal Church

IN THE

DIOCESE OF ALBANY,

WHICH ASSEMBLED IN

ALL SAINTS' CATHEDRAL, ALBANY, N. Y.,

TUESDAY, NOVEMBER 15,

A. D., 1892.

ALBANY, N. Y.:
AMASA J. PARKER, RECEIVER FOR WEED, PARSONS & CO., PRINTER.
1892.

LIST OF THE CLERGY

IN THE

DIOCESE OF ALBANY

IN THE ORDER OF CANONICAL RESIDENCE

NOVEMBER 15, 1892.

Showing the dates of becoming resident, and in case of those not gaining residence by Ordination, the name of the Diocese from which each was received.

Date of Reception.	Diocese from which received.	Name.
1868. Nov. 15.	At Primary Convention.	The Rt. Rev. WILLIAM CROSWELL DOANE, D. D. *Oxon.*, LL. D. *Cantab.*, Bishop.
" " " "	" " " "	The Rev. JOSEPH CAREY, S. T. D.
" " " "	" " " "	The Rev. EDGAR T. CHAPMAN.
" " " "	" " " "	The Rev. JOSEPH N. MULFORD.
" " " "	" " " "	The Rev. GEORGE H. NICHOLLS, S. T. D.
" " " "	" " " "	The Rev. J. LIVINGSTON REESE, D. D.
" " " "	" " " "	The Rev. WILLIAM S. ROWE.
" " " "	" " " "	The Rev. DAVID L. SCHWARTZ.
" " " "	" " " "	The Rev. JOHN B. TIBBITS, Deacon.
" " " "	" " " "	The Rev. J. IRELAND TUCKER, S. T. D.
" Dec. 1.	New York - - -	The Rev. JAMES WILKINS STEWART.
1869. Sept. 23.	Montreal - - -	The Rev. CHARLES H. LANCASTER.
1870. Mar. 7.	Massachusetts - - -	The Rev. FENWICK M. COOKSON.
" June 12.	- - - - -	The Rev. WILLIAM CURTIS PROUT.
" Dec. 6.	Pennsylvania - -	The Rev. JAMES CAIRD.
1871. April 12.	Montreal - - -	The Rev. J. D. MORRISON, D. D., LL. D.
" July 12.	Vermont - - -	The Rev. J. W. MCILWAINE.
" Nov. 21.	Massachusetts - - -	The Rev. WILLIAM R. WOODBRIDGE.
1872. July 14.	- - - - -	The Rev. JOHN H. HOUGHTON.
1874. May 12.	New York - - -	The Rev. WILLIAM CHARLES GRUBBE.
1874. Aug. 3.	Western New York -	The Rev. WALTON W. BATTERSHALL, D. D.
" Sept. 17.	- - - - -	The Rev. THEODORE A. SNYDER.
" Sept. 29.	Central New York -	The Rev. MOSES E. WILSON.
" Oct. 7.	Pennsylvania - -	The Rev. R. J. ADLER.
" Nov. 1.	- - - - -	The Rev. HENRY M. SMYTH.

List of Clergy.

Date of Reception.	Diocese from which received.	Name.
1875. Nov. 5.	New York - - -	The Rev. CHARLES C. EDMUNDS.
1876. Mar. 12.	- - - -	The Rev. WILLIAM B. REYNOLDS, Deacon.
" Aug. 22.	Central New York -	The Rev. WILLIAM N. IRISH.
" Sept. 26.	North Carolina -	The Rev. WILLIAM W. LORD, D. D.
" Dec. 11.	New York - -	The Rev. CHARLES S. OLMSTED.
1877. Jan. 24.	- - -	The Rev. CHAS. EDWARD CRAGG, Deacon.
" Mar. 1.	Newark - - -	The Rev. ERNEST A. HARTMANN.
1878. Feb. 27.	Montana - - -	The Rev. EUGENE L. TOY.
1879. Jan. 1.	Long Island - -	The Rev. THOMAS B. FULCHER, B. D.
" July 13.	- - - -	The Rev. JOHN N. MARVIN.
" July 15.	Massachusetts -	The Rev. SILAS M. ROGERS.
1880. May 28.	- - - -	The Rev. JOHN PROUT.
" June 1.	- - - -	The Rev. CHARLES C. EDMUNDS, Jr.
" Oct. 18.	Massachusetts -	The Rev. FREDERICK H. T. HORSFIELD.
1881. Jan. 8.	Western New York	The Rev. CHARLES M. NICKERSON, D. D.
" Mar. 1.	Massachusetts -	The Rev. THADDEUS A. SNIVELY.
" Mar. 14.	Central New York -	The Rev. ROBERT GRANGER.
" Dec. 19.	New York - -	The Rev. GEORGE DENT SILLIMAN.
1882. Jan. 9.	Newark - - -	The Rev. WILLIAM HENRY HARISON, D. D.
" Feb. 28.	Utah - - -	The Rev. R. M. KIRBY.
" Nov. 7.	Connecticut - -	The Rev. HOBART COOKE.
" Dec. 26.	Rhode Island -	The Rev. CLEMENT J. WHIPPLE.
1883. Feb. 12.	Central New York -	The Rev. E. BAYARD SMITH.
" May 5.	Delaware - -	The Rev. W. G. W. LEWIS.
" Oct. 31.	New York - -	The Rev. C. P. A. BURNETT.
1884. Jan. 20.	- - - -	The Rev. JAMES A. DICKSON.
" Feb. 13.	Fredericton - -	The Rev. FREDERICK S. SILL, S. T. B.
" Mar. 4.	Ohio - - -	The Rev. SAMUEL T. STREET.
" May 27.	Newark - - -	The Rev. CHARLES PELLETREAU.
" June 8.	- - - -	The Rev. EDWARD S. DEG. TOMPKINS.
" June 9.	- - - -	The Rev. DAVID SPRAGUE.
" July 12.	- - - -	The Rev. RUSSELL WOODMAN.
1885. Jan. 10.	Springfield - -	The Rev. JAMES E. HALL.
" Mar. 16.	Exeter, England -	The Rev. THOMAS H. R. LUNEY.
" May 1.	Central Pennsylvania	The Rev. J. PHILIP B. PENDLETON S.T.B.
" May 30.	- - - -	The Rev. CHARLES TEMPLE.
" May 31.	- - - -	The Rev. SHELDON M. GRISWOLD.
" Aug. 6.	Maine - - -	The Rev. RICHMOND SHREVE, D. D.
" Oct. 10.	- - - -	The Rev. EDWARD DUDLEY TIBBITS.
" Nov. 5.	Wisconsin - -	The Rev. LOUIS HECTOR SCHUBERT.
" Dec. 18.	Connecticut - -	The Rev. EATON W MAXCY, D. D.
1886. Mar. 8.	Western New York -	The Rev. WILLIAM B. BOLMER.
" Sept. 24.	Yedo - - -	The Rev. CLEMENT THEOPHILUS BLANCHET.
" Nov. 13.	Central Pennsylvania -	The Rev. DANIEL WASHBURN.
1887. Feb. 12.	- - -	The Rev. JOSEPH T. ZORN.
" May 19.	Connecticut - -	The Rev. EDGAR A. ENOS, D. D.
1887. Aug. 1.	New York - -	The Rev. CHARLES E. FREEMAN.
" Nov. 5.	Massachusetts -	The Rev. WILFORD LASH ROBBINS, D. D.
1888. Jan. 20.	Southern Ohio -	The Rev. HENRY T GREGORY.
" Jan. 23.	New Hampshire -	The Rev. FREDERICK MORLAND GRAY.
" May 18.	Pittsburgh - -	The Rev. WILLIAM MASON COOK, S. T. B.
" May 20.	- - -	The Rev. GEORGE MERIWETHER IRISH.
" May 22.	Springfield - -	The Rev. THOMAS WHITE.
" Sept. 3.	Tennessee - -	The Rev. ALFRED TAYLOR.
" Oct. 7.	- - -	The Rev. WALTER CHARLES STEWART.
" Nov. 20.	Nova Scotia - -	The Rev. ANGUS C. MACDONALD.
" Dec. 21.	- - -	The Rev. FREDERICK G. RAINEY.
1889. April 15.	Maine - - -	The Rev. ROBERT N. PARKE, D. D.
" June 16.	- - -	The Rev. ELMER PLINY MILLER.
" Sept. 23.	New York - -	The Rev. JOHN McCARTHY WINDSOR.
" Sept. 23.	Springfield - -	The Rev. HOWARD McDOUGALL.
" Oct. 31.	Missouri - -	The Rev. E. W. FLOWER.

Date of Reception.	Diocese from which received.	Name.
1889. Nov. 1.	New York - - -	The Rev. WALTER HASKINS LAROM.
1890. Feb. 8.	Western New York -	The Rev. E. RUTHVEN ARMSTRONG.
" Mar. 14.	Massachusetts - -	The Rev. ERNEST MARIETT.
" April 25.	New Jersey - -	The Rev. HARRIS COX RUSH.
" May 8.	Rochester, England -	The Rev. S. C. THOMPSON.
" June 7.	Central New York -	The Rev. CHAUNCEY VIBBARD, Jr.
" July 20.	Fredericton - - -	The Rev. CHARLES H. HATHEWAY.
" Sept. 24.	Vermont - - -	The Rev. FREDERICK SHUBALL FISHER.
" Oct. 18.	New York - - -	The Rev. WILLIAM HENRY BOWN.
1891. Jan. 8.	Montreal - - -	The Rev. HERBERT LUTHER WOOD.
" Jan. 22.	Quebec - - - -	The Rev. ROBERT WYNDHAM BROWN.
" Feb. 12.	Ohio - - - -	The Rev. GEORGE A. HOLBROOK.
" April 26.	- - - - -	The Rev. EUGENE GRIGGS.
" May 5.	New Jersey - -	The Rev. ARTHUR LOWNDES.
" May 8.	Minnesota - - -	The Rev. RICHMOND H. GESNER.
" June 8.	- - - - -	The Rev. FREEBORN GARRETTSON JEWETT, Jr.
" June 14.	- - - - -	The Rev. JAMES FREDERIC OLMSTED.
" July 9.	Vermont - - -	The Rev. CLARENCE MORTIMER CONANT.
" Aug. 13.	Connecticut - - -	The Rev. CLARENCE ERNEST BALL.
" Sept. 10.	- - - - -	The Rev. GEORGE LYNDE RICHARDSON.
" Oct. 15.	Milwaukee - - -	The Rev. GEORGE GALEN CARTER, S. T. D.
" Oct. 19.	Connecticut - -	The Rev. GEORGE BRINCKERHOFF RICHARDS.
" Oct. 28.	- - - - -	The Rev. HARRY ELMER GILCHRIST.
" Nov. 15.	New York - - -	The Rev. GEORGE B. JOHNSON.
1891. Dec. 8.	Long Island - -	The Rev. JOHN WILLIAM GILL.
" Dec. 17.	- - - - -	The Rev. WILLIAM FRANCIS PARSONS.
1892. Jan. 4.	Georgia - - -	The Rev. THOMAS BOONE.
" Jan. 26.	Long Island - -	The Rev. JAMES R. L. NISBETT.
" Jan. 26.	Massachusetts - -	The Rev. CREIGHTON SPENCER.
" Mar. 5.	New York - - -	The Rev. HAMILTON CADY.
" Mar. 24.	Central New York -	The Rev. HARRY A. R. CRESSER.
" Mar. 26.	Ontario - - -	The Rev. FRANK SLADEN GREENHALGH.
" April 11.	Springfield - - -	The Rev. JOHN H. MOLINEUX.
" April 11.	Springfield - -	The Rev. PERCY ST. MICHAEL PODMORE.
" May 8.	- - - - -	The Rev. WILLIAM WHITNEY NEWELL, Deacon.
" May 23.	Central New York -	The Rev. ELMER R. EARLE.
" June 29.	Rupert's Land - -	The Rev. ALFRED L. FORTIN.
" July 12.	Ontario - - -	The Rev. DAVID JENKINS.
" Aug. 3.	New York - - -	The Rev. EDWARD CARLTON HOSKINS.
" Sept. 24.	New York - - -	The Rev. EARNEST WEBSTER DUSTAN, Deacon.
" Oct. 11.	Long Island - -	The Rev. HENRY R. FREEMAN.
" Nov. 14.	Pittsburgh - - -	The Rev. JOHN E. BOLD.
" Nov. 16.	- - - - -	*The Rev. JOHN MILLS GILBERT, Deacon.
" Nov. 16.	- - - - -	*The Rev. CHARLES ALBERT HOWELLS, Deacon.

* Ordered Deacon on the second day of the Convention after the list was prepared for the Convention, and added by permission of the Bishop.

W. C. P.

AN ALPHABETICAL LIST OF THE CLERGY.

This mark * designates the Alumni of the General Theological Seminary.

The Right Rev. WILLIAM CROSWELL DOANE, D. D. *Oxon.*, LL. D. *Cantab.*, Bishop, Albany.

The Rev. R. J. ADLER, Rector, St. Mark's Church, Green Island, Albany county.

The Rev. E. RUTHVEN ARMSTRONG, Rector, St. James' Church, Caldwell, Warren county. P. O., Lake George.

The Rev. CLARENCE ERNEST BALL, Missionary, Church of the Good Shepherd, Canajoharie, and Church of the Holy Cross, Fort Plain, Montgomery county.

* The Rev. WALTON W. BATTERSHALL, D. D., Rector, St. Peter's Church, Albany, Albany county.

The Rev. CLEMENT T. BLANCHET, Missionary, St. Sacrament Church, Bolton, Warren county.

*The Rev. JOHN E. BOLD, Missionary, St. James' Church, Oneonta, Otsego county.

The Rev. W. B. BOLMER, Rector, St. Luke's Church, Troy, Rensselaer county.

The Rev. THOMAS BOONE, Missionary, All Saints' Church, Round Lake, Grace Mission, Jonesville, and St. John's Church, East Line, Saratoga county.

The Rev. WILLIAM HENRY BOWN, Rector, Grace Church, Albany, Albany county.

The Rev. ROBERT WYNDHAM BROWN, Rector, Grace Church, Canton, and Missionary, Trinity Chapel, Morley, St. Lawrence county.

* The Rev. C. P. A. BURNETT.

* The Rev. HAMILTON CADY, Rector, Church of the Holy Cross, Warrensburgh, Warren county.

The Rev. JAMES CAIRD, Rector, Free Church of the Ascension, Troy, Rensselaer county.

* The Rev. JOSEPH CAREY, S. T. D., Rector, Bethesda Church, Saratoga Springs, Saratoga county.

The Rev. GEORGE GALEN CARTER, S. T. D., Rector, All Saints' Church, Hudson, and Trinity Church, Claverack, and Missionary, Columbia county.

* The Rev. EDGAR T. CHAPMAN, Canon and Treasurer, Cathedral of All Saints, Priest in charge, St. Margaret's Mission, Menands Station. P. O., Troy road, Albany.

The Rev. CLARENCE MORTIMER CONANT, Missionary, Church of the Memorial, Middleville, and Trinity Church, Frankfort, Herkimer county.

* The Rev. WILLIAM MASON COOK, S. T. B., Rector, St. Augustine's Church, Ilion, and Missionary, St Alban's Church, Frankfort, Herkimer county.

The Rev. HOBART COOKE, Rector, Trinity Church, Plattsburgh, Clinton county.

* The Rev. FENWICK M. COOKSON, Rector, Church of the Messiah, Glen's Falls, Warren county.

The Rev. CHARLES EDWARD CRAGG, Assistant Minister, Christ Church, Port Henry, Essex county.

The Rev. HARRY A. R. CRESSER, Rector, Church of the Messiah, Greenbush, Rensselaer county.

The Rev. JAMES A. DICKSON, Rector, Trinity Church, Gouverneur, and Missionary, St. Lawrence county.

* The Rev. EARNEST WEBSTER DUSTAN, Rector, Trinity Church, Sharon Springs, Schoharie county.

The Rev. ELMER R. EARLE, Missionary, Grace Church, Norfolk, and St. Andrew's, Norwood, St. Lawrence county.

* The Rev. CHARLES C. EDMUNDS, Missionary, Zion Church, Fonda, Montgomery county. P. O., Johnstown, Fulton county.

* The Rev. CHARLES C. EDMUNDS, Jr., Rector, Christ Church, Herkimer, Herkimer county.

The Rev. EDGAR A. ENOS, D. D., Rector, St. Paul's Church, Troy, Rensselaer county.

* The Rev. FREDERICK S. FISHER, Rector, Christ Church, Deposit, and Missionary, Delaware county.

The Rev. E. W. FLOWER, Rector, Christ Church, Duanesburgh, Schenectady county.

The Rev. ALFRED L. FORTIN, Rector, St. Peter's Church, Brushton, and St. Mark's, West Bangor, Franklin county, and Missionary, St. Thomas' Church, Lawrenceville, St. Lawrence county.

* The Rev. CHARLES E. FREEMAN, New York city.

The Rev. HENRY R. FREEMAN, Rector, St. John's Church, Troy, Rensselaer county.

* The Rev. THOMAS B. FULCHER, B. D., Canon and Precentor, Cathedral of All Saints, Albany, Albany county.

* The Rev. RICHMOND H. GESNER, Rector, Zion Church, Morris, Otsego county.

The Rev. JOHN MILLS GILBERT, Missionary, Calvary Church, Burnt Hills, and St. Paul's, Charlton, Saratoga county.

The Rev. HARRY ELMER GILCHRIST, Rector, Zion Church, Sandy Hill, Washington county.

The Rev. JOHN WILLIAM GILL, Rector, St. Paul's Church, Keeseville, and Missionary, St. James', Ausable Forks, Essex county.

The Rev. ROBERT GRANGER, Rector, St. John's Church, Richfield Springs, Otsego county.

The Rev. FREDERICK MORLAND GRAY, Honorary Canon, Cathedral of All Saints, and Chaplain, St. Agnes' School, Albany, Albany county.

The Rev. FRANK SLADEN GREENHALGH, Missionary, St. John's Church, Massena, St. Lawrence county.

The Rev. HENRY T. GREGORY, Rector, Church of the Cross, Ticonderoga, and Missionary, Essex county.

The Rev. EUGENE GRIGGS, Missionary, Church of the Holy Spirit, Schenevus, and St. Simon and St. Jude's, Worcester, Otsego county.

* The Rev. SHELDON M. GRISWOLD, Rector, Christ Church, Hudson, Columbia county.

The Rev. WILLIAM CHARLES GRUBBE, Rector, Gloria Dei Church, Palenville, and Missionary, Greene county.

* The Rev. JAMES E. HALL, Rector, Grace Church, Cherry Valley, Otsego county.

* The Rev. WILLIAM HENRY HARISON, D. D., Ogdensburgh, N. Y.

* The Rev. ERNEST A. HARTMANN.

The Rev. CHARLES H. HATHEWAY, Honorary Canon, Cathedral of All Saints, Albany, also Missionary, St. Andrew's Church, West Troy, Albany county, and St. Giles', Castleton, Rensselaer county.

The Rev. GEORGE A. HOLBROOK, Rector, St. Barnabas' Church, Troy, Rensselaer county.

* The Rev. FREDERICK H. T. HORSFIELD, Rector, St. Luke's Church, Cambridge, Washington county.

* The Rev. EDWARD CARLTON HOSKINS, Missionary, St. Luke's Church, Mechanicville, and St. John's, Stillwater, Saratoga county.

* The Rev. JOHN H. HOUGHTON, Rector, Rexleigh School, Salem, Washington county.

The Rev. CHARLES ALBERT HOWELLS, Missionary, Christ Church, West Burlington, Good Shepherd, Cullen, St. Luke's, Monticello, and at Edmeston, Otsego county.

* The Rev. GEORGE M. IRISH, Rector, Zion Church, Colton, St. Lawrence county.

The Rev. WILLIAM N. IRISH, Rector, St. John's Church, Essex, and Missionary, Essex county.

The Rev. DAVID JENKINS, Missionary, St. James' Church, Hogansburgh, and at Fort Covington, St. Lawrence county.

The Rev. FREEBORN GARRETTSON JEWETT, Jr., Rector, St. Paul's Church, Albany, Albany county.

The Rev. GEORGE B. JOHNSON, Rector, Church of Our Saviour, Lebanon Springs, and Missionary, Columbia county.

* The Rev. R. M. KIRBY, D. D., Rector, Trinity Church, Potsdam, St. Lawrence county.

The Rev. CHARLES H. LANCASTER, Rector, Trinity Church, Granville, and Missionary at North Granville, Washington county.

The Rev. WALTER HASKINS LAROM, Missionary, Church of St. Luke the Beloved Physician, Saranac Lake, and St. John's in the Wilderness, St. Regis Lake, Franklin county, and Good Shepherd, Bloomingdale, Essex county.

The Rev. WILLIAM G. W. LEWIS, Rector, Immanuel Church, Otego, and Missionary, Otsego county.

The Rev. WILLIAM W. LORD, D. D., Cooperstown, Otsego county.

The Rev. ARTHUR LOWNDES, Rector, St. Mark's Church, Philmont, and Missionary, Columbia county.

The Rev. THOMAS H. R. LUNEY, Officiating, All Saints' Church, Hoosac, Rensselaer county.

The Rev. ANGUS C. MACDONALD, Rector, St. Paul's Church, Waddington, and Missionary, St. Luke's Church, Lisbon, St. Lawrence county.

* The Rev. HOWARD McDOUGALL, Missionary, Grace Mission, Stamford, Delaware county.

The Rev. J. W. McILWAINE, Rector, St. James' Church, Fort Edward, Washington county.

The Rev. ERNEST MARIETT, Rector, Emmanuel Church, Little Falls, and Missionary, Dolgeville, Herkimer county.

The Rev. JOHN N. MARVIN, Rector, St. John's Church, Johnstown, Fulton county.

The Rev. EATON W. MAXCY, D. D., Rector, Christ Church, Troy, Rensselaer county.

* The Rev. ELMER P. MILLER, Rector, St. Luke's Church, Catskill, Greene county.

The Rev. JOHN H. MOLINEUX, Rector, Trinity Church, Whitehall, Washington county.

The Rev. J. D. MORRISON, D. D., LL. D., Rector, St. John's Church, Ogdensburgh, St. Lawrence county.

The Rev. JOSEPH N. MULFORD, Missionary, Church of the Good Shepherd, Raquette Lake, Hamilton county.

The Rev. WILLIAM WHITNEY NEWELL, Paris, France.

The Rev. GEORGE H. NICHOLLS, S. T. D., Rector Emeritus, St. Mark's Church, Hoosick Falls, Rensselaer county.

* The Rev. CHARLES M. NICKERSON, D. D., Rector, Trinity Church, Lansingburgh, Rensselaer county.

The Rev. JAMES R. L. NISBETT, Rector, Christ Church, Walton, Delaware county.

* The Rev. CHARLES S. OLMSTED, Rector, Christ Church, Cooperstown, Otsego county.

* The Rev. JAMES FREDERIC OLMSTED, Rector, St. John's Church, Champlain, and Missionary, Christ Church, Rouse's Point, Clinton county.

* The Rev. ROBERT N. PARKE, D. D., Rector, St. Matthew's Church, Unadilla, Otsego county.

The Rev. WILLIAM FRANCIS PARSONS, Rector, St. Paul's Church, Greenwich, Washington county, and St. Stephen's, Schuylerville, Saratoga county.

* The Rev. CHARLES PELLETREAU, Rector, Christ Church, Ballston Spa, Saratoga county.

* The Rev. J. PHILIP B. PENDLETON, S. T. B., Rector, St. George's Church, Schenectady, Schenectady county.

The Rev. PERCY ST. MICHAEL PODMORE.

* The Rev. JOHN PROUT, Rector, St. Paul's Church, East Springfield, and Missionary, St. Mary's, Springfield Centre, Otsego county.

* The Rev. WILLIAM C. PROUT, Rector, Christ Church, Schenectady, Schenectady county.

The Rev. FREDERICK G. RAINEY, Rector, St. Barnabas' Church, Stottville, Columbia county.

The Rev. J. LIVINGSTON REESE, D. D., Albany, Albany county.

The Rev. WILLIAM B. REYNOLDS, Assistant Minister, Church of St. John the Evangelist, Stockport, Columbia county.

The Rev. GEORGE BRINCKERHOFF RICHARDS, Assistant Minister, St. Peter's Church, Albany, Albany county.

The Rev. GEORGE LYNDE RICHARDSON, Assistant Minister, St. Paul's Church, Albany, Albany county.

The Rev. WILFORD LASH ROBBINS, D. D., Dean, Cathedral of All Saints, Albany, Albany county.

The Rev. SILAS M. ROGERS, Rector, St. Peter's Church, Ellenburgh, and St. Paul's Church, Ellenburgh Centre, and Missionary, Clinton county.

The Rev. WILLIAM S. ROWE.

*The Rev ¿HARRIS COX RUSH, Rector, St. Paul's Church, Salem, Washington county.

The Rev. LOUIS H. SCHUBERT, Glenham, N. Y.

* The Rev. DAVID L. SCHWARTZ, Cherry Valley, N. Y.

The Rev. RICHMOND SHREVE, D. D., Rector, Church of the Holy Innocents, Albany, Albany county.

* The Rev. FREDERICK S. SILL, Rector, St. John's Church, Cohoes, Albany county.

* The Rev. GEORGE D. SILLIMAN, Rector, St. Mark's Church, Hoosick Falls, Rensselaer county.

* The Rev. E. BAYARD SMITH, Rector, Trinity Church, West Troy, Albany county.

The Rev. HENRY M. SMITH, Missionary, Christ Church, Gloversville, Fulton county.

The Rev. THADDEUS A. SNIVELY, Troy, N. Y.

The Rev. THEODORE A. SNYDER, Rector, Christ Church, Greenville, and St. Paul's Church, Oak Hill, Greene county.

* The Rev. CREIGHTON SPENCER, Rector, St. John's Church, Delhi, Delaware county.

* The Rev. DAVID SPRAGUE, Rector, St. Ann's Church, Amsterdam, Montgomery county.

* The Rev. JAMES WILKINS STEWART, Rector, Trinity Church, Athens, and Missionary, Greene county.

The Rev. WALTER CHARLES STEWART, Honorary Canon, Cathedral of All Saints, Diocesan Missionary. P. O. Albany.

The Rev. SAMUEL T. STREET, Rector, Grace Church, Waterford, Saratoga county.

The Rev. ALFRED TAYLOR, Missionary, Church of the Good Shepherd, Chestertown, and St. Paul's, Bartonville, Warren county.

* The Rev. CHARLES TEMPLE, S. T. B., Rector, St. Mark's Church, Malone, Franklin county.

The Rev. S. C. THOMPSON, Missionary, Trinity Church, Rensselaerville, Albany county.

* The Rev. EDWARD DUDLEY TIBBITS, Rector, All Saints' Church, Hoosac, Priest in charge, Church of the Holy Name, Boyntonville, Rensselaer county, Honorary Canon, Cathedral of All Saints.

The Rev. JOHN B. TIBBITS, Officiating, All Saints' Church, Hoosac, Rensselaer county.

The Rev. EDWARD S. DEG. TOMPKINS, Missionary, Christ Church, Coxsackie, Greene county. P. O. Kinderhook, N. Y.

* The Rev. EUGENE L. TOY, Rector, Church of St. John the Evangelist, Stockport, Columbia county.

* The Rev. JOHN IRELAND TUCKER, S. T. D., Pastor, Church of the Holy Cross, and Principal of the Warren Free Institute, Troy, Rensselaer county.

The Rev. CHAUNCEY VIBBARD, Jr., Dansville, N. Y.

The Rev. DANIEL WASHBURN, Maple Grove, Otsego county.

The Rev. CLEMENT J. WHIPPLE, Rector, St. Mary's Church, Luzerne, Warren county, and Missionary, St. John's Church, Conklingville, Saratoga county.

* The Rev. THOMAS WHITE, Missionary, Church of the Epiphany, Bath, Rensselaer county.

The Rev. MOSES E. WILSON, Rector, St. Luke's Church, Clermont, and Missionary, Columbia county.

The Rev. JOHN M. WINDSOR, Tuxedo, N. Y.

The Rev. HERBERT LUTHER WOOD.

The Rev. WILLIAM R. WOODBRIDGE, Missionary, Christ Church, Morristown, St. Lawrence county.

The Rev. RUSSELL WOODMAN, Rector, Trinity Church, Albany, Albany county.

The Rev. JOSEPH T. ZORN, Missionary, Calvary Church, Cairo, Greene county.

I certify the above to be a correct list of the clergy canonically resident in the Diocese of Albany.

WM. CROSWELL DOANE,
Bishop.

ALBANY, *November* 15, 1892.

2

LIST OF LAY DEPUTIES.

County.	Church.	Deputies.
Albany	Cathedral of All Saints	Gen. Selden E. Marvin.
		Dr. Howard Van Rensselaer.
		Thomas R. Wade.
	St. Peter's, Albany	Thomas S. Wiles.
		William G. Rice.
		George Gibbons.
	Trinity, Rensselaerville	Nathaniel Teed.
		John L. Rice.
		David D. L. McCullough.
	St. Paul's, Albany	Thomas W. Larwood.
		Frederick C. Manning.
		Frederick W. Ridgway.
	St. John's, Cohoes	Michael Andrae.
		John Horrocks.
		Robert R. Chadwick.
	Trinity, West Troy	William Hollands.
		John H. Hulsapple.
		John Scarborough.
	Trinity, Albany	George F. Granger.
		Nordine T. Johnston.
		J. Henry Marlow.
	Grace, Albany	Benjamin F. Hinman.
		Frank J. Smith.
		Charles W. White.
	Holy Innocents, Albany	S. M. Van Santvoord.
		H. S. McCall, Jr.
		James Oswald.
	St. Mark's, Green Island	Richard Leonard.
		William W. Butler.
		Louis Harter, Jr.
Clinton	Trinity, Plattsburgh	John Henry Booth.
		Charles Halsey Moore.
		Edward T. Gilliland.
Columbia	Christ, Hudson	Arthur C. Stott.
		Clarence L. Crofts.
		Samuel B. Coffin.
	St. John's, Stockport	William H. Van de Carr.
		Joshua Reynolds.
		John H. Wild.
	St. Paul's, Kinderhook	Henry S. Wynkoop.
		Edward P. Van Alstyne.
		Franklin B. Van Alstyne.
	Trinity, Claverack	James J. Studley.
		Robert Fulton Ludlow.
		John A. Nichols.
	Our Saviour, Lebanon Springs.	John G. Field.
		Charles E. Wackerhagen.

County.	Church.	Deputies.
Columbia	All Saints, Hudson	William H. Cookson.
		Alexander R. Benson.
		Robert V. Noble.
	St. Barnabas', Stottville	John J. Plass.
		Frederick H. Palmer.
		William H. Tanner.
	St. Mark's, Philmont	George Baker.
		Richard A. Woodruff.
		Frank S. Harder.
Delaware	St. John's Delhi	Herbert A. Pitcher.
		Sherill E. Smith.
		George A. Paine.
	Christ, Walton	David H. Gay.
		Edwin W. Pond.
		John H. Townsend.
	Christ, Deposit	William H. Gregory.
		Charles Pinkney.
		Titus M. Bixby.
Essex	Of the Cross, Ticonderoga	S. S. Paige.
	St. Paul's, Keeseville	Francis Cassidy.
		Philip Harrison.
		James Dundas.
	Christ, Port Henry	Charles W. Woodford.
		W. M. J. Botham.
		Charles A. Neide.
Fulton	St. John's, Johnstown	Abiram S. Van Voast.
		Isaiah Yanney.
		James I. Younglove.
Greene	St. Luke's, Catskill	John H. Bagley.
		Walton Van Loan.
		Robert Selden.
	Christ, Coxsackie	Henry J. Hahn.
		Robert J. Washbol.
		N. A. Calkins.
	Trinity, Athens	Henry C. Van Loan.
		Samuel H. Nichols.
		Robert Cleat.
	St. Paul's, Oak Hill	Walter S. Cheritree.
		Byron Hall.
		Ambrose Flower.
	Christ, Greenville.	William S. Vanderbilt.
		Byron Waldron.
		Winfield S. Rundle.
Herkimer	Trinity, Fairfield	Reuben Neely.
		Charles W. Nichols.
		George Barnes.
	Christ, Herkimer	Robert Earl.
		John D. Henderson.
		George W. Pine.
	St. Augustine's, Ilion	J. L. Osgood.
		Walter S. Baker.
		Frank N. Quaife.
	Grace, Mohawk	A. W. Haselhurst.
		E. C. Elwood.
		Dr. J. D. Fitch.
Montgomery	St. Ann's, Amsterdam	Hicks B. Waldron.
		William Ryland.
		William Perry.
	Zion, Fonda	Richard H. Cushney.
		Giles H. F. Van Horne
		Edward B. Cushney.

County	Church.	Deputies.
Otsego	Zion, Morris	T. Octavius Duroe. J. Rutherford Morris. George G. Sanderson.
	St. Matthew's, Unadilla........	George B. Fellows. William H. Heslop. Lloyd L. Woodruff.
	Christ, Cooperstown.......,....	G. Pomeroy Keese. S. E. Crittenden. S. Averill Carter.
	Christ, Butternuts.............	Thomas Swinyard. Charles Daniels. Ira L. Ward.
	Immanuel, Otego..	Charles Blake. George H. Sherman, Jr. James H. Cossaart.
	Grace, Cherry Valley...... ...	A. B. Cox. W. C. Roseboom. F. P. Harriott.
	St. John's, Richfield Springs ...	D. W. Harrington. J. D. Cary. M. D. Jewell.
	Chirst, West Burlington	Albert Austin. William Holdridge. John Priest.
	St. Paul's, E. Springfield . ..	Leslie Pell-Clarke. James H. Cooke. G. Hyde Clarke.
	St. James', Oneonta	Robert M. Townsend. Richard Downs. Silas S. Matterson.
Rensselaer........ ,.....	St. Paul's, Troy..............	Joseph J. Tillingbast. John I. Thompson. Thomas Buckley.
	Trinity, Lansingburgh........	James McQuide. Peter B. King. George W. Daw.
	St. John's, Troy......	Norman B. Squires. Francis N. Mann. Benjamin H. Hall.
	Christ, Troy	J. W. A. Cluett. Dr. Washington Akin. Hon. William Kemp.
	St. Mark's, Hoosick Falls	John G. Darroch. James R. Parsons, Jr. George B. Pattison.
	Trinity, Schaghticoke	Almadus Wilkinson. Thomas L. Doremus. Edward Searles.
	Messiah, Greenbush..........	George Low. Richard W. Stevens. Harry E. Cole.
	St. Luke's, Troy.....	James Wood. Thomas B. Iler. Henry E. Darby.
St. Lawrence	St. John's, Ogdensburgh......	Charles Ashley. Levi Hasbrouck. Frank Chapman.
	Christ, Morristown	Frank B. Kingsland. Henry A. Chapman.
	Trinity, Potsdam.............	T. Streatfeild Clarkson. Edward W. Foster. Charles O. Tappan.

County.	Church	Deputies.
St. Lawrence	Grace, Canton....	Cleland Austin.
		Hammond Safford.
	Trinity, Gouverneur	Aaron B. Cutting.
		Frank H. Smith.
	Zion, Colton	Thomas S. Clarkson.
		Myron E. Howard.
Saratoga	Christ, Ballston Spa..........	Irving W. Wiswall.
		David L. Wood.
		Andrew S. Booth.
	St. John's, Stillwater	Joseph Moll.
		Charles Green.
		John Stringer.
	Grace, Waterford	Dr. Roland H. Stubbs
		John H. Meeker.
		Henry S. Tracy.
	St. Luke's, Mechanicville.....	Madison W. Hart.
		Herbert O. Bailey.
		Samuel H. Hall.
	Bethesda, Saratoga Springs ...	William A. Sackett.
		G. R. P. Shackleford
		R. C. McEwen.
	St. Stephen's, Schuylerville...	Peter Davison.
		J. Hicks Smith.
		John A. Dix.
	Calvary, Burnt Hills	Charles H. Upham.
		William H. Larkin.
Schenectady	Christ, Duanesburgh	Alexander McDougall
		Ralph W. McDougall
		Edward C. Clark.
	St. George's, Schenectady	Abram A. Van Vorst.
		John Keyes Paige.
		Charles S. Washburn
	Christ, Schenectady..........	David Guy.
		Sidney G. Ashmore.
		John H. Shaffer.
Warren	Messiah, Glen's Falls.........	William A. Wait.
		Nelson La Salle.
		James A. Holden.
	St. James', Caldwell	George W. Bates.
		Samuel R. Archibald.
		George H. Cramer.
	Holy Cross, Warrensburgh....	Frederick O. Burhans
		Thomas J. Smith.
		Henry Griffing.
	St. Mary's, Luzerne	John S. Burneson.
		Homer J. Martin.
		Thomas H. Taylor.
Washington	Zion, Sandy Hill	John William Wait.
		Charles Titus Beach.
		Albert Mott, M. D.
	Trinity, Granville..	Orville L. Goodrich
		John S. Warren.
		Silas E. Everts.
	St. James', Fort Edward.......	Francis B. Davis.
		George Scott.
		Benjamin M. Tasker.
	St. Paul's, Salem.............	James Gibson.
		George B. Martin.
		Solomon W. Russell.

County.	Church.	Deputies.
Washington	Trinity, Whitehall	F. H. McFarran.
		H. B. Skeels.
		C. B. Bates.
	St. Luke's, Cambridge	Henry C. Day.
		John Moneypenny.
		William J. David.
	St. Paul's, Greenwich	Henry L. Mowry.
		Benjamin F. Kendall.
		Thomas Reid.

DIOCESE OF ALBANY.

RULES OF ORDER.

1. After the administration of the Holy Communion, the President shall take the chair, and call the Convention to order.

2. If the President *ex officio* is not present at the opening of the Convention, the Secretary of the last Convention shall call the Convention to order, when the Presbyter, senior by ordination, present, shall take the chair; and in such case, immediately after the organization of the Convention, a President shall be elected from among the clergy.

3. When the President takes the chair, no member shall continue standing, or shall afterward stand, unless to address the Chair.

ORDER OF BUSINESS.
FIRST DAY.

4. After the Convention is called to order, the roll of the clergy and of the parishes entitled to representation shall be called by the Secretary of the last Convention; the certificates of the lay deputies, as presented, being referred to a committee consisting of the Secretary and two members appointed by the President. If a quorum of twenty clergy and a representation of twenty parishes be present, the President shall declare the Convention duly organized.

5. The first business shall be the election of a Secretary, a Treasurer, and a Registrar. The Secretary may appoint one or more Assistant Secretaries, announcing their names to the Convention.

6. Notices, resolutions, motions and other miscellaneous business shall then be in order.

7. The following committees shall be appointed by the President:
   A. On the Admission of Parishes into Union with the Convention.
   B. On the Constitution and Canons.
   C. On the Treasurer's Accounts.
   D. On the Diocesan Fund and Mileage of the Clergy.
   E. On Diocesan Missions.
   F. On the Bishop's Salary and the Episcopal Fund.
   G. On the Fund for the Widows and Orphans of Deceased Clergymen.
   H. On the Aged and Infirm Clergy Fund.
   I. On the General Theological Seminary.
   J. On the Society for Promoting Religion and Learning.
   K. On unfinished business.
   L. On non-reporting Clergy and Parishes.

8. Business for these committees shall be received in the following order:
   A. Report of the Treasurer.
   B. Report of the Board of Diocesan Missions.
   C. Report of the Trustees of the Episcopal Fund and of the Bishop's Salary.

D. Report of the Trustees of the Fund for the Widows and Orphans of Deceased Clergymen, and the Treasurer of the same.

E. Report of the Trustees of the Aged and Infirm Clergy Fund, and the Treasurer of the same.

F. Report of the Society for Promoting Religion and Learning.

These reports, and those mentioned in the next rule, shall be referred to the appropriate committees, and shall not be read until such committees be ready to report upon them.

9. A. Report of the Committee on Applications of Parishes for Admission.

B. Report of the Secretary of the Convention.

C. Report of the Standing Committee of the Diocese.

D. Report of the Registrar of the Diocese.

E. Report of the Secretary and Treasurer of the Bible and Prayer Book Society of Albany and its Vicinity.

F. Reports from the Orphan House of the Holy Saviour, Cooperstown.

G. Reports of Special Committees appointed at the last Convention.

H. Miscellaneous business.

SECOND DAY.

10. On the second and each succeeding day of the session, after Daily Morning Prayer, the order of business, which shall not be departed from without the consent of two-thirds of the members present, or a special order of the day previously voted, shall be as follows:

A. Reading, correcting and approving the minutes of the previous day.

B. Calling the roll of members absent on the previous day.

C. Reports from the Regular Committees of the House, in the order of their appointment.

D. Reports from Special Committees, in the order of their appointment.

E. Unfinished business.

F. Miscellaneous business.

11. The Bishop's Address is in order at any time.

12. The annual election shall be held at noon on the second day, and continued at the order of the House until completed.

13. All reports embodying long statements of accounts shall be accompanied with a brief abstract of them, and such abstracts only shall be printed in the Journal.

GENERAL.

14. When any member is about to speak, he shall rise from his seat, and shall, with due respect, address himself in an audible tone of voice to the President, confining himself strictly to the point in debate.

15. No member shall speak more than twice in the same debate without leave of the House; nor more than once, until every other member wishing to speak shall have spoken.

16. No motion shall be considered as before the House unless it be seconded, and reduced to writing when required, and announced by the Chair.

17. The mover may withdraw a motion or resolution at any time before amendment or decision, with the consent of the Convention; in which case it shall not be entered upon the minutes.

18. When a question is under consideration, it shall be in order to move to lay it upon the table, to postpone it indefinitely, to postpone it to a time certain, to commit it, to amend it, or to divide it; and motions for any of these purposes shall have precedence in the order here named.

19. If the question under debate contains several distinct propositions, the same

shall be divided at the request of any member, and a vote taken separately; except that a motion to strike out and insert shall be indivisible.

20. All amendments shall be considered in the order in which they are moved. When a proposed amendment is under consideration, a motion to amend the same may be made. No after amendment to such second amendment, shall be in order; but a substitute for such second amendment, or a substitute for the whole matter, may be received. No proposition on a subject different from that under consideration shall be received under colour of a substitute.

21. A motion to lay upon the table shall be decided without debate.

22. A motion to adjourn shall always be in order when no member is speaking; and, if unqualified, shall be decided without debate. If negatived, it shall not be renewed until some other business has intervened.

23. When a question is put by the President, it shall be determined by the sound of voices, for or against it; but any three members may require a count of the votes, and tellers for that purpose shall then be appointed by the Chair; or any five votes may require that the decision be by yeas and nays and by orders, which shall be done by calling the roll of the clerical members and parishes represented, and the votes shall be entered on the Journal.

24. When the President is putting any question, the members shall continue in their seats, and shall not hold any private discourse.

25. Every member present shall vote when a question is put, unless excused by a vote of the House.

26. A motion once determined, whether in the affirmative or the negative, shall stand as the judgment of the Convention, and shall not again be considered during the same session, unless the motion to reconsider be made by one of the majority on the first decision, and be carried by a vote of two-thirds of the members present.

27. All questions of order shall be decided by the President, subject to an appeal to the House; and on such appeal no member shall speak more than once, without leave of the Convention.

28. All committees shall be appointed by the President, unless otherwise ordered by the Convention.

29. The reports of all committees shall be in writing; and unless recommitted, shall be received of course, without motion for acceptance. They shall be entered on the minutes, unless otherwise ordered. If recommending or requiring any action or expression of opinion by the Convention, they shall be accompanied by a resolution or resolutions for its consideration.

30. No rule of order shall be suspended, unless by a vote of two-thirds of the members present; nor shall any be changed or rescinded without one day's previous notice.

31. No member shall absent himself from the session of the Convention without leave of the President.

32. Before the final adjournment of the Convention, the minutes of the last day's proceedings shall be read, corrected and approved.

33. When the Convention is about to rise, every member shall keep his seat until the President leaves the chair.

STANDING ORDER.

OF THE CONDUCT OF ELECTIONS.

WHEREAS, it is expedient to provide by a standing order, for the manner of conducting all elections by ballot in the Convention of the Diocese of Albany, it is hereby ordered as follows:

1. The President of the Convention shall appoint one clergyman and one layman to be tellers of the clerical vote, and one clergyman and one layman to be tellers of the lay vote, for each office that is to be filled except that all the members of any committee, board or delegation shall be voted for upon one ticket, and only one set of tellers shall be appointed therefor. Vacancies, arising from temporary absence or otherwise, shall be supplied by the President.

2. When the election is to be held, the tellers for the clerical vote shall take their places, together, on one side of the house or place of meeting, and the tellers for the lay vote, together, upon the other side; and the Secretary shall supply them with the necessary boxes, and also with lists of the clergy entitled to seats in the Convention, and of the parishes entitled to representation, on which lists, as each vote is deposited, they shall make a mark against the name of the clergyman or parish voting; and these lists, signed by the tellers, shall be returned with their reports to the Convention. The names of the clergy and of the parishes shall be called by the Secretaries, and the votes shall be received by the tellers.

3. So soon as voting shall appear to have ceased, the President shall announce that the polls are about to be closed, and not less than ten minutes after such announcement, he may direct the tellers to count the votes, for which purpose they shall have leave to retire. The tellers shall then proceed to count the votes, and shall make written reports, stating the whole number of votes cast, and the number cast for each person, except that when less than five votes are cast for any one person, it shall suffice to include all such votes under the head of scattering. These reports shall be signed by the tellers respectively, and shall be entered upon the Journal, and the President shall announce the result.

4. In case of any contest arising as to the right of any person to cast a vote, the tellers shall submit the question to the Convention before the closing of the polls.

5. If in regard to any office there shall not be a majority of votes, either in the clerical or in the lay order, for any one person, or if there shall not be a concurrence of the two orders, the Convention shall proceed forthwith to another ballot, for such and so many offices as have not been filled at the first ballot; and such second and all other ballots shall be conducted in the same manner as above provided. In case there shall still remain any vacancy to be supplied after such second ballot, further ballots may be held at the order of the Convention.

6. Immediately before any ballot, it shall be in order for the nomination of any person to be made and seconded. But nominations for members of the Standing Committee and for Deputies and Provisional Deputies to the General Convention shall be made on the first day of the Convention, at the call of the President, under the order of "Miscellaneous Business;" and it shall be the duty of the Secretary of the Convention to prepare, for the use of the Convention on the second day, ballots for these several offices, containing the names of all persons nominated for each office, respectively, with a note indicating the whole number to be chosen. No speech or debate shall be allowed upon such nomination, or while the Convention is holding an election.

JOURNAL.

All Saints' Cathedral Church, Albany, N. Y.
Tuesday, November 15, A. D., 1892.

This being the place designated by the Bishop of the Diocese and the day appointed by the Constitution, for the meeting of the Twenty-fourth Annual Convention of the Diocese of Albany, the Bishop, and a number of the Clergy and Lay Deputies assembled in All Saints' Cathedral Church at half-past ten o'clock in the morning.

The Bishop of the Diocese administered the Holy Communion, being assisted in the service by the Rev. Archdeacons Carey, Morrison, Olmsted and Sill.

In place of the sermon, the Bishop delivered a portion of his Annual Address.

THE BISHOP'S ADDRESS.

My Dear Brethren of the Clergy and Laity, I make you welcome once more, at this feast of our ingathering, into the Cathedral Church, and ask you to make with me, before we come to our Holy Communion, first of all, that which is always prominent at such a service as this, our commemoration of the faithful whom God has taken from us in the past year; and then to consider the summary of the acts of the great Triennial Council of our national Church.

The store in Paradise, of those who have lived and wrought with us in the Master's service here, has grown very largely this year, and there is consequently a very deep sense of emptiness and loss left behind.

Five of the Clergy have passed away, the Rev. Mr. Washbon, of Rensselaerville, one of the most marked and conspicuous figures of this Diocese, in its Conventions years ago and in its missionary work; the Rev. Mr. Timlow, than whom I do not know a priest more richly furnished, not only in theology, but in all departments of godly and good learning; the Rev. Mr. Webster, who had been laid aside from active work for so many years, that I fancy he had almost passed out of the memory of those who are in the Diocese to-day; but who, when I first came here, was full of wise and practical zeal in his work in the Catskill mountain region ; (Mr. Vibbard administered the Holy Communion to him two days before his death and laid him at rest in the little churchyard at Acra on the last day of last year;) the Rev. Mr. Rowden, a stranger in a strange land, who had been but a very little while with us, working amid discouragements and difficulties that would have disheartened most men, and permitted soon to lay his life down, in order that he might find it again; and the Rev. Canon Temple, lovely in his daily walk and conversation; a trained and thorough scholar; a large-hearted and devoted pastor; a courteous Christian gentleman; a true and loyal friend.

I have spoken somewhat at length already of three of these priests; and I simply repeat here the tribute which I paid to them at the time of their taking away, with a very earnest hope, not only that men will be found to take up the spirit in which they did their work, but that you and I may learn more and more the lesson, which is taught us by their good examples, and pressed home upon us as the ranks are thinned from year to year, of our duty of more earnest work while it is day.

The Rev. Dr. Timlow, who has been for many years a faithful missionary at Burnt Hills and Charlton, died after a lingering illness, leaving behind him in his Parish the memories of a most faithful and wise pastor, a preacher of real spiritual and intellectual power, and a gentleman with all the charm of cordial courtesy which that name implies. He was a scholar by every instinct and habit of his nature, a constant student, and a man, whose conversation, as I had reason to know in my drives with him over his mission and when I was the guest in his delightful home, was full of freshness, of the fragrance of books old and new, and of the keenest zest in all theological questions.

His book upon the Ministry is one of the most admirable and valuable books that have been written in our day, and ought to be more widely known and read than it is; and the whole memory of the man is full of sweetness and attraction, and of the comforting assurance of the blessed Christian hope.

The death of Mr. Rowden, at Lyon Mountain, was pathetic to an unusual degree. He had been only a short time in the Diocese, to which he came from the Diocese of Pennsylvania; he had thrown himself into an almost hopeless task with intense energy, and had made himself respected and beloved in the community in which he was at work.

He seemed to have been absolutely solitary, without relatives or friends in this country. He was ministered to most tenderly by the faithful physician and the kindly people of the place, and by the Rector of Plattsburgh, the Rev. Hobart Cooke, who gave the Holy Communion to him shortly before he died, and buried him afterward, by my directions, in Plattsburgh.

I am glad to commemorate him as a faithful priest, and I remember with infinite pity the loneliness of his life and death ; and with great thankfulness the fact that he has passed from all that is desolate and painful in this world, to the companionship and communion of the saints in Paradise.

The death of the Rev. Mr. Washbon takes out of the Diocese almost its oldest priest. He had been steadfast, for nearly all the years of his long ministry, to one place of work. He was a missionary after the manner of old "Father Nash," who felt himself responsible for any circle that he could possibly reach in driving or in walking. He was known from house to house, in the whole large and lonely neighborhood of the rough country in which he lived, and was always an ideal missionary.

The circumstances of his death were touching, with a very real pathos, and I think I am not violating the sacred confidence of sorrow, in making known to those who knew him the expression of the note, which communicated to me the fact of the almost simultaneous death of this good man and his admirable wife : "I write with a sad heart to tell you that this morning at half-past six o'clock the kind, good woman who has been such a comfort and care-taker of my father entered into rest. We thought her getting better, but her heart gave way like the broken string of a sweet instrument of music, which she truly was ; her life always so full of gentle harmonies of duty and charity; and this morning my own dear father, ripe in years and rich in the love of all who knew him, passed quietly away, and we have laid the two side by side in peaceful sleep. His death was as gentle as the falling of the dew. When he received the Holy Communion, with his wife, shortly before the end came, he said, 'I do this to show my faith in Christ as the Son of God.'"

The Rev. Richard Temple, always since its organization an honoured and beloved priest of the Diocese, passed away in peace and into peace on the 5th day of October, A. D., 1892. I had only left him three days before, he and I both knowing that we should not meet again on earth. It was a great trial that my positive duty, as a member of the House of Bishops, hindered my personal presence at his burial. My last memory of him lingers with infinite comfort in my mind, as I turned from his bedside the day after I gave him his last Communion, and he said softly the single word "happy."

Canon Temple was intensely and essentially a holy man. It was the first and last impression that he made, I think, on every one. Scholar, student, pastor, accurate in affairs, genial in home-life, lovely in every human, as he was loyal in every ecclesiastical, relation, clear and strong in his theological convictions, and devout as he was devoted in his priestly life; his soul was that of a little child, simple and sweet and pure. He was, here, one of those on whom the Master's sentence was impressed, on whom, in far fuller sense, I believe it has now been passed, "of such is the Kingdom of God." I am glad to adopt and put on record the admirable minutes adopted by the Cathedral Chapter.

Among our own Bishops one has passed away, the Rt. Rev. Dr. Galleher, Bishop of Louisiana, whose character was a rare combination of brave manhood and gentle courtesy, which makes up the name and marks the nature of a gentleman. Few have held higher rank in our House of Bishops in personal charm, in intellectual force, in spiritual fervour; and his Diocese as well as his brethren loved him dearly.

Almost one of our own Bishops, the beloved Metropolitan of Canad has been so identified with the growth and life of the Church on this Continent, that we mourn his death as though one of our own number had been taken away. He was a power in the Catholic revival. He came to America exchanging the sacred shades of Oxford, the companionship of its great scholars and schools, and the serene sweetness of English pastoral life for the bleak and barren loneliness of what New Brunswick was fifty years ago. He was a scholar of rare ripeness, a born leader of men; strong as a lion in his maintenance of the faith; full of elegant accomplishments, architect as well as musician. And he was a man of most holy self-denying life, to whom "to live was Christ," to whom we humbly hope, "to die" has been "gain," grave and grievous as the loss to us. I am glad to add this very vigorous description of him from the *Canadian Gazette:*

"Of an essentially modest and retiring nature, yet as a scholar, a preacher, a musician, a master of terse and nervous English, and a Hebraist, the late Bishop had few equals. His translation of Job has to many students thrown entirely new light on that little understood book, while his anthems and other musical compositions ought to be known to others besides the choir of his Cathedral, whom for many years he exclusively trained. Music, in fact, was his great study and solace, and no more enthusiastic Handelian than the octogenarian Bishop attended the last Handel festival. Possessed of these qualities and of a keen sense of humour — humour that as regards others was perfectly stingless, but which led him to recount stories about and against himself — is there any wonder that those who might call themselves his intimate friends regarded such a man with ever increasing respect and love? With all his quiet demeanour he was ready with a quick rejoinder. The head of a deputation that wished to bring something to his knowledge was so poor a speaker that he could only get as far as — 'My lord, your lordship is ignorant —' After a pause, the same words again; and for a third time the same words once more, when the Bishop remarked: — 'Well, Mr. Archdeacon, we are all agreed on that point, let us take the next.' It was Bishop Medley who, when a somewhat violent partisan began his speech by ostentatiously exclaiming 'My lord, I am a very Low Churchman,' quietly interposed the remark ' I hope you mean a very humble Churchman.' In his later years, especially, the Bishop had to bear — and bore uncomplainingly — many severe trials. A year or two ago a slip on ice incapacitated for some time his right arm, and caused him great suffering. The brave old man instantly set to work to write — and for some time did write — with his left hand. No sketch of Bishop Medley's life can conclude without a reference to her who for so many years cheered him on and so efficiently shared and assisted him in all his work. But even to her in her bereavement there can be but the one -thought, that for him the change is ' far better.' Yet to her and to his friends there cannot but rise the feeling that the Church and the world are distinctly the poorer for that the grave which he had so long set aside for himself under the east window of his Cathedral has to-day closed upon ' John Fredericton, Metropolitan of Canada.' "

There have been large losses too among the laymen of this Diocese. From Zion Church, Sandy Hill, Mr. Charles H. Beach has been taken away, one of my first and firmest friends. He had been for years and years in the active lay administration of Parish matters, the staunch friend and supporter of the Rector, and always devoted to the best interests of the Church, and I believe he was a Deputy to our Diocesan Convention from its organization until his death. When I last saw him he was hoping to be present, at our meeting in November, but the feebleness of the disease so increased that he was unable to come, and on the 21st of December, 1891, he entered, in the ripeness of his years into the richness of his reward.

The death of the Hon. Walter A. Wood, of Hoosick Falls, is not only the taking away from me of one of my earliest and dearest friends in the Diocese, but means the removal from the village which he really created, and the Parish of which he was the chief stay, a man whose place can never be made good in this world. I have never been more impressed at any burial than I was by his. Of the twenty-five hundred men who were in line it seemed to me that there was not one to whom his death was not a personal sorrow; and the tributes of affection and admiration which came really from every quarter of the world told the story as nothing else could tell it, of how a man of great ability, of entire unselfishness, of strict integrity and of most generous interest in all which promotes the best interests of mankind, is really set among the princes of the earth. I can add nothing to what I have said of him under the first pressure of my great sorrow, and so I put it here on permanent record, and add in the Appendix the resolutions of the Trustees of the Corning Foundation, of which Mr. Wood had been a member since its organization.

One of the old and staunch standbys of St. John's Church, Cohoes, has passed away this year, Mr. Samuel Horrocks, who came from England where he had been a choir boy in his Parish Church, and took his place in the choir of St. John's, from which I believe he was never absent, and where I always remember his reverent presence.

Mr. George F. Ford, who was a very faithful Vestryman of the Church and one of our Delegates to the Convention last year, and Treasurer of the Sunday School, has also died; one of the men, his Rector writes me, who could always be depended on and who had become thoroughly devoted to and identified with the work of the Church.

From the old Parish at Walton the taking away of Mr. George St. John is really the removal of a man who not only seemed to be, but was, a pillar. His life has been one of singular purity and beauty, and his character, one of those tender and attractive characters savouring not a little of the rare beauty of the holy saint whose name he bore. He was a man whom people loved because his heart was full of all most sweet and kindly things, and I confess that few of the laymen of the Diocese have come so near to me in all personal ways as he did, and few men whom I knew have lived a life more lovely and of good report. He was devoted to the Church in Walton, which he remembered very generously in his will, and he illustrated, not only in his giving but in his living, all that one wants to see illustrated in the public life of an intelligent and earnest Churchman.

I add what I wrote at the time that the news of his death came to me, so that it may find its place upon the diptychs of our Diocese.

You will all miss, not for the first time, because he was away last year, the Hon. James M. Dudley, who was a Vestryman of St. John's Church, Johnstown, and for very many years had been prominent in the councils of the Diocese. He was our most active man perhaps in the Board of Trustees in the Diocese of Albany, and one of the men to whom I looked for counsel and advice, and who lent his ripe legal judgment to the settlement of the question about the division of the funds of the Diocese of New York with ours. Faithful in all responsibilities, civil and religious, a wise and earnest man, he was one of the old landmarks of the Diocese of Albany, who will be sorely missed.

The death of Dr. Clute has taken away one of the very oldest laymen of the Diocese, both in years and in service.

He had been interested in and identified with the parish at Coxsackie since ever I knew it, and although withdrawn by infirmity of late years from attendance at its services he was in his place when he could be, and had always at heart the advancement of the parish.

He was a truly venerable man in that his years entitled him to that adjective and his character deserved the veneration which it implies.

I must add to this already long list the name of Mr. Nelson B. Pearsall, a very marked man, whose devotion to the Church was, I really think, the strongest and intensest characteristic of his life. There was nothing that he did not do with heart and hands for the welfare of the

Church in Morris, as Warden, Vestryman, Lay Reader; and he never was so happy, I am quite sure, as when he was either engaged in the worship, or occupied in the service, of the Church. I cordially adopt the strong expression of the Rector, Wardens and Vestrymen, as my own.

"Mr. Pearsall was a man of child-like faith and unfeigned love. Like Zacharias of old, he walked in all the statutes of the Lord blameless. His hand was ever outstretched to the need of the Church and his neighbors. He was as modest as self-sacrificing, as gentle and generous as he was pure-souled and high-minded. His loyalty to Christ was equalled by his stainless honour. Exquisitely tender-hearted, his charity was as wide as his knowledge. He 'sought not his own,' but always the good of others.

"Ripe in years and full of gracious qualities, he has gone to his rest and reward. He has left us the precious memorial of a life consecrated to the Saviour, and of a Christ-like benevolence to his fellow-men.

"In this great loss to the Church we do not forget the deep bereavement of his family. That God will graciously comfort and keep them in this time of adversity is our sincere and affectionate prayer."

Among the laymen whose loss will be chiefly felt in Albany I have to record the death of Mr. Montgomery H. Throop. He had been largely withdrawn from public life and public notice by his deafness, but he had done valuable service to his own profession both as counsellor and as codifier of the laws; he was a most earnest and devout Christian man, he was a scholar of large and liberal reading, and he was very generous and faithful in his love for the Cathedral, and in his gifts to its building and its support. It was a great pleasure to see him sitting, as I have seen him out of service hours, taking in the beauty of the building which he dearly loved, and which he has exchanged now for the greater glories of the "temple made without hands."

I have put in the Appendix what I wrote of him the day he died, and add his name to those whom we remember at our Celebration to-day with very real affection and reverence.

The Rev. Mr. Goodisson of Franklin had been so short a time in the Diocese that I confess I am unable to speak of him from any personal knowledge, but he left the record of a priest of earnest life and good report, and his death has taken from us an earnest labourer in this portion of the vineyard of the Lord. It was most sudden, but to a man who lived as he had lived it was not unprepared. And I am glad to note the prompt and generous course which the Vestry of the Church adopted towards his bereaved family.

I have spoken elsewhere of the death of Mr. Stephen Warren whose name is identified with the Church of the Holy Cross in Troy.

Colonel Milton Heath, a man of strength and force, with great Christian kindliness and gentleness, has died in Potsdam.

4

Although not long a resident in that parish he was a very faithful attendant upon its services, and his venerable and kindly presence will be greatly missed from the Church, where I always saw him, and which he served and loved very truly.

There is a certain amount of naturalness about the long record of the deaths of "honourable women not a few," who have passed into the rest and refreshment of Paradise since our last gathering. The most venerable of them all, a true "mother in Israel," was Mrs. Augustus Chapman, who died in the beautiful old homestead in Morristown, in her ninety-fourth year, in June. The family have been always staunch upholders of the Church there, and it was my great refreshment in my visits to Morristown always to have a little while at any rate with her, recalling her vivid memories of the past, and refreshed by the charm and brightness of her conversation. She was a woman of real dignity and beauty of presence and graceful with the old-time courtesies of life, and has been a close and kind friend to me for five and twenty years.

Mrs. Stillwell, who has been taken away from the Mohawk Church, was a courtly woman, in whom the type of her ancestry repeated itself in dignity, in ability, and in the hospitality which she dispensed with liberal hand. The village as well as the Church will miss her always, and I am thankful that the home at least is not to be broken up, nor the influence lost, since she leaves those behind her who will perpetuate her interest and her presence.

At the ripe age of eighty-two Mrs. Roebuck died last March, in Morley. Connected with the Harison family, to whom the Church in this Diocese owes so much, she made one of those homes for me which is associated with the very brightest memories of my Episcopal life. She was a woman of infinite brightness of mind, and most genial courtesy and cordiality of manner, thoroughly devoted to the Church and a most loyal, faithful friend. She lies in the shadow of the beautiful Chapel there, which owes its existence to the family of which she was a member, and her death closes, I am afraid, a chapter of delightful recollections to me. "After a long life of usefulness and love, and in the blessed hope of a blessed immortality," as Mr. Harison wrote me, "she has passed into peace."

Mrs. Daniel Yost has died in Fort Plain, and will be greatly missed by the Church people there and by me, as representing one of the old names of the Mohawk valley, and as warmly and generously interested in all Church work there.

The record of my services contains an allusion to the burial of Mrs. John L. Thompson of Troy. To speak of her life is to speak of the history of St. Paul's Church, of which she has been a most constant and devout member for more than half this century. I can truly say that I never remember a service in St. Paul's since I was Bishop at which she was not present. Her "due feet" never failed to seek the refreshment of its worship, and she was like Anna, both before and after her widowhood, "departing not from the temple, but serving God with fastings and prayers." It was a holy, quiet, peaceful life, with most blessed influences about it, which have told in the training of her large family of children, all of whom "rise up and call her blessed."

Only a year ago we had occasion to send our message of greeting to dear Dr. Nicholls of Hoosick Falls, on the fiftieth anniversary of his ordination. We must not fail to send him a thought of sympathy this year, now that his life has been broken in two. It is too sacred and beautiful a story to speak of in any public way, but never was priest's wife more faithful and helpful in her husband's life than she, never more beautiful relation between man and wife than theirs, and certainly never more gentle and gracious nature, developed alike by great home happiness and blessings and by great personal trials and sorrows.

I am glad to add to this address a minute of my affectionate admiration of her, and to ask you to remember, when we come to our Blessed Eucharist, these and the other of the faithful who have departed this life in God's faith and fear, asking for them light and peace and rest eternal, and for us the long and blessed influence of their example under which to live, and the learning of the lesson of the deaths, so that our last end may be like theirs.

Mrs. Charles Temple died in what seemed the very prime of life, in strange and striking contrast to the ripe years which these other holy women had attained. But God does not put in His sickle until the individual harvest is ripe in every soul, and I am quite sure from a long knowledge of Mrs. Temple, for she was a graduate of St. Agnes School, that her character was rich and ready with every sort of ripening that can come in mind and heart and soul. She was a sweet and gracious woman, a true helpmeet to her husband, most valuable and highly valued in the parish at Malone, and I add her name with very loving remembrance to the long list of those, with whom we can only be in communion now in the Great Offering, and in loving thoughts and prayers.

One of the holiest and most earnest women I ever knew, Miss Maria Brooks of Little Falls, died there on the very day of my Visitation, the 3rd of May.

She had been active in all parochial work, in the organization of the Girls' Friendly Society, and in the Woman's Auxiliary, a teacher in the Sunday School and a member of the choir for twenty-five years, a true and intelligent Churchwoman, constantly at the weekly Celebration and the early Morning Prayer, and a kind and true friend to me, one of those who from the beginning were interested in the building of the Cathedral and always made me welcome in the most cordial way.

A memorial of her love and interest is already in St. Agnes School in a valuable collection of shells, which by her wish her sister sent there after her death; and she will long be remembered by all who knew her as a beautiful example of the Christian life trained and lived in the Church's way.

The death of Miss Hasbrouck, following closely upon that of my venerable friend Miss Harison, removes another who may be truly called a shining light in the parish of St. John's, Ogdensburg. She had passed into and beyond the ripeness of old age, but still retained her fresh interest in all good things, and she leaves behind a memorable and beautiful example.

Miss Louisa Partridge, always associated in my mind with my dear old friend Dr. Kedney, passed away from Potsdam, after a life, as her Rector truly says, "of much practical goodness and bright Christian service. She was a wise helper and a diligent worker in the parish, with clear insight and resolute will;" and the Rector truly says that they all feel that with her a strong stay has gone.

THE GENERAL CONVENTION.

And so I come to speak to you of the General Convention.

We are apt to speak "great swelling words" about these meetings, and to count each gathering of more importance than the last. But I think one is safe in saying, that, in the blessed temper of brotherly kindness; in the unusual accord between the two Houses; in the splendid glow of missionary ventures; in the happy conclusion of the long and anxious work of Prayer Book revision, and in the important results secured by the adoption of the Standard Prayer Book, the authorized Hymnal, and the Canons of ordination, no more marked and useful General Convention ever assembled.

There is striking and pleasant coincidence in the fact that three of the authorized collections of hymns have been set forth in the city of Baltimore. In 1808, "at eight o'clock, A. M.," the hymns set forth by the Convention were ordered to be inserted in all future editions of the Book of Common Prayer, and the edition of the hymns thus set forth by the authority of the Convention was made the standard copy. And on the 24th day of October, 1871, in Baltimore, which was the year of my first attendance in the House of Bishops, the Joint Committee on the Hymnal was directed to arrange for and supervise the printing of the first edition of the last Hymnal. And now in Baltimore the new Hymnal has been authorized this year.

The meetings of the Board of Missions were conducted with great spirit and the consideration of every matter connected with its work attracted large attendance. The reports which were presented upon every subject and from every quarter of the missionary work were full of interest and encouragement. The thronging crowds of people who came to all the meetings of the Board, and at the various missionary services, were most impressive. And no nobler scene and fact stirred the Church gathered in Baltimore than the first meeting of the Woman's Auxiliary, when twelve hundred women were together at the Holy Communion, and when an offering of nearly twenty thousand dollars was made. The Convention created five new missionary districts, in Oklahoma, in Western Colorado, in Northern Michigan, in Southern Florida, and in a portion of the State of Washington (in the last instance I am glad to say, departing from geographical terminology, by calling the two districts, from the names of the see cities, Olympia and Spokane). And five Bishops were elected to fill the jurisdictions. A Bishop was elected also for Japan, and the nomination of the Bishop of China failed in the House of Deputies, only because a constitutional quorum was not present in the lay delegations.

A much more satisfactory relation too was established about the work in Mexico. It seems almost impossible to impress upon the minds of many people just what the true condition of things there had come to be. The unfortunate complications of years ago seemed surely to have taken possession of the intelligence of the Church, as inherent and essential parts of it. It is useless to recapitulate the mistakes and misfortunes of the past, but it is discreditable to deal with them as though they still existed. They have really passed away. " The Mexican muddle " has become the Mexican Mission. The late Bishop has ceased to claim or exercise jurisdiction. The huge Church building which was both ban and burthen to the work is sold. The few adherents of Bishop Riley have come in under the care of the Priest to whom the oversight of the congregations in Mexico is committed, and they are absolutely at one. The society in New York which upheld the old division is dissolved. Its work has grown till it cares for thirty-six congregations, with thirty clergymen and lay-readers. And it had never fairer promise than to-day.

The attempt to discredit it ecclesiastically, by questioning our right to be there, on the grounds that we recognize the orders of the Roman Church was most emphatically discredited after a vigorous debate, in which the Presiding Bishop took the effective part. And it stands to-day recognized, established and commended by the great Missionary Body of the Church, and asks your generous gifts, with a powerful appeal such as it never had before.

I am free to say that the confusion of thought in some clear minds about this matter is an amazement to me. In a sense it is true that it is neither a Foreign Mission because it is not to heathen, nor a Domestic Mission because it lies outside the territorial jurisdiction of the United States of America. But it is neither Foreign nor Domestic, because it is *both ;* Foreign because it is to people in another country, and Domestic because it is to those who are of the "household of faith;" in communion with us upon the old primitive Creeds, Sacraments and Orders of the Church. The theory of intrusion into Mexico is based upon the fallacy that the Bishop of Rome has jurisdiction, there, which is utterly untenable. There is not and never was a national Church in Mexico. And the very principles not only of the Anglican Reformation but of the Catholic Church require our maintainance of this "primitive principle of jurisdiction." Ultramontane assertions are bad enough, but ultramarine assumptions are simply intolerable. The lieutenants of the Bishop of the City of Rome, who represent him, are intruders everywhere. Before Trent the Roman episcopate outside the seven-hilled city was, as the Archbishop of Canterbury called it, "an Italian Mission"; since Trent it is a Tridentine intrusion. And the men in Mexico who ask our help come clearly within the accurate definitions which the Bishops at Lambeth laid down in 1878, and reiterated in 1888: "excommunicated on account of their refusal for conscience sake to accept the novel doctrines promulgated by the authority of the Church of Rome, and who yet desire to maintain in its integrity the Catholic faith and to remain in full communion with the Catholic Church."

The action of the Lambeth Conference in 1878 was quoted in the report of the committee on the relation of the Anglican communion to the old Catholics and other reforming bodies in 1888. "We declare that all sympathy is due from the Anglican Church to churches and individuals protesting against these errors of the Church of Rome, and to those who are drawn to us in the endeavour to free themselves from the yoke of error and superstition we are ready to offer all help and such privileges as may be acceptable to them and are consistent with the maintenance of our own principles as enunciated in our formularies." And the resolution which was passed, *nemine contradicente*, was this, "Without desiring to interfere with the rights of Bishops of the Catholic Church to interpose in cases of extreme necessity, we deprecate any action that does not regard the primitive and established principles of jurisdiction and the interests of the whole Anglican communion." While the primitive and established principles of jurisdiction in ordinary cases are that no man shall play the αλλοτριο επισκοπος which our version translates "a busybody in other men's matters," it is abundantly plain from the instances cited that such an appeal as this comes within that primitive principle of jurisdiction which is described in the well-known phrase "episcopatus unus, cujus a singulis pars in solidum tenetur": and that we are bound *on* the primitive principles of jurisdiction to refuse to recognize the right of the Bishop of Rome to claim jurisdiction in Mexico.

These men are cut off from the Sacraments of Salvation because they cannot accept the recent and wrong terms of Communion which Rome began at Trent when she changed the Creed of Chalcedon to read "I believe in one Holy *Roman*, Catholic and Apostolic Church;" thereby making herself the first of the sects of the sixteenth century; and to which changes she has gone adding from time to time. And so far as their claim is concerned and our duty, they are as plain and clear as the calls which have been heard and heeded in the cases of the old Catholics in Switzerland and Germany. Yes, and behind that they are as plain and clear, as the Presiding Bishop so strongly put it, as the appeal which was heard and the duty which was done in the case of Paul of Samosata, or when the Bishops of Italy stood by Athanasius and the Western Bishops upheld St. Basil. In the beginning, the action of this Church was closely parallel to these latter cases; for it was to the Bishops that the appeal was made and by the Bishops that the action was taken, in accordance with the tenth article of the Constitution of this Church. And I take leave to say that the drawing of this question into discussion before the House of Deputies was done, not by the advocates but by the opponents of the Mexican mission.

The action of the General Convention upon the proposition to give a certain sort of alternate authentication to the Revised Version of the New Testament is worthy, in my judgment, of most profound gratitude to God. It goes without the saying that no more important subject can occupy the mind of the Church. It seems to me playing *with* words, if not playing *on* them, to say that the standard Bible is "hypothetical" and "mythical," and that "no *copy* of the standard Bible exists." This last statement was certainly true of the standard Prayer Book until last month, for the old standard was an *edition* and not a *book*. But it cannot be forgotten that after three years' discussion and reference to a joint committee, of which Bishop White was chairman, the General Convention in 1826 adopted the *edition* of the authorized version of the English Bible published by Eyre and Strahan in 1806 and 1812 as the standard Bible of this Church; and further specified an American publisher or bookseller, S. Potter, as having it for sale with the imprint of 1813. We are certainly not prepared to substitute for it, the inferior English translation of the questionable Greek version of the Revised New Testament. And nothing much more distressing and disastrous could be imagined, than to present, to the people gathered to hear the word of God, one reading in one place and another in another. It would certainly be *wrongly* "dividing the word." It would certainly be "the author of confusion in the Churches." And it is matter of true pride and satisfaction to me that the clear, strong, masterly presentation of the case which prevailed, was made by a Committee of which the Rector of St. Peter's, Albany, was Chairman. Those of us to whom the peculiar force of his English is familiar will not doubt much as to the authorship of the Report; which I print in the appendix to this Address.

A new departure was introduced this year, into the sessions of the General Convention which has much positive and still more prospective value. The Houses, which have been always in the habit of sitting together as a Board of Missions, agreed this year to sit together, if I may say so, as a Board of Christian Education, to receive the report of the Church University Board of Regents, which is a creation of the General Convention, and to deal with such questions concerning education as might be presented. After the reading of the report stirring speeches were made by the Bishops of Minnesota and Georgia, by Dr. Gailor, the Vice-Chancellor of the University of the South, and by Mr. Silas McBee.

The Board presents itself as organized and ready to work. It has definite propositions as to increasing the endowments of Schools and Colleges allied to the Church, founding post-graduate scholarships and fellowships to be awarded upon competitive examination, holding themselves ready to receive, by gift or bequest, funds for these purposes, and establishing themselves as a permanent educational bureau, to whom educational questions and suggestions may be addressed and by whom they may be dealt with.

The three years' work has been simply preliminary and sketchy, but it is greatly hoped that the Board will take up some definite matters of interest and importance now, and will prove itself of value to the Church. Meanwhile the joint committees on Christian Education have had leave to sit together, and have presented certain practical resolutions which the Convention adopted.

The adoption of the Hymnal was matter of great gratification to me. Naturally enough, during the three months' discussion after the final report of the Commission was published, only the critics who had faults to find had much to say; and for a while it looked as though the Hymnal was to be positively and universally condemned.

As chairman of both committees that have dealt with this question of hymns I am able to say that the subject was studied after full access to all the leading hymnals in the English language, with the greatest possible care, by sub-committees, and by every member of the Commission; and we all most cordially endorse the admirable introduction of the Hymnal into the House of Deputies made by the Rev. Dr. Nelson with such quiet clearness and such persuasive force, as the expression of our deliberate judgment and the result of our thorough examination.

I am still myself clearly of the opinion that the Hymn Book, as the Commission presented it, is a better book than that which has been adopted, after omissions and restorations, which the Convention agreed to. But the strong sense of association, partly with words and partly with tunes, carried the day and many of the popular hymns have been restored; in order to accomplish which, some omissions largely recommended by the Commission itself, had to be made.

It is a curious fact that only two of the omitted hymns found universal commendation by the votes of forty delegates in the House of Deputies; and

still more curious to me that those two hymns were " Brightest and Best of
the Sons of the Morning," and the hymn "Come, Holy Spirit, Heavenly
Dove;" the first of which, pretty as it is as a carol, certainly has no mark
of conformity to the best Canons of hymnology; and the second of which
represents the congregations who are pleased to sing it in an attitude of
"grovelling," which I confess hardly seems to me consistent with an
uplifted sense of the privilege of adoration, or with a true description of
the attitude of worshippers. Its last two lines have always seemed to me
most descriptive of the effect, which such a thought would necessarily produce upon the act of worship "Hosannas languish on our
tongues, and our devotion dies."

I confess it was an infinite satisfaction to me that after many
fluctuations of discussion and decision, although the royalty was allowed
upon the Hymnal, in deference to the past custom of the Church, the
Prayer Book is to be published without copyright and without royalty.
The necessary certificates from the Custodian abundantly protect the
Prayer Book from coarse and careless editions; and indeed the whole
question of copyright in books like the Prayer Book and the Hymnal
depends upon that which may be always relied on, the honour of the
publishing houses; but to put a royalty upon the Book of Common
Prayer seemed to me a contradiction in terms. It ought to be considered as the universal heritage of people who worship in the English
tongue.

At this very Convention, steps were taken to organize a Board of
Trustees for the larger distribution of the Prayer Book. And in the
face of such a fact I am free to say, that the putting of a royalty upon
the book would have been eminently unwise and inconsistent. Indeed
it was the judgment of learned and liberal laymen, that instead of helping,
it would really hinder, the pressing and important cause of providing for
the aged and infirm Clergy and for the widows and orphans of Clergymen.
And I have great hope too that out of all this discussion, will come fuller
and wiser arrangements for this neglected and most necessary duty,
which ought to be lifted entirely out of the rank of eleemosynary institutions. Plans are on foot to provide for it, upon the principle of a
pension fund, to the benefits of which, every clergyman shall be entitled,
when he arrives at a certain age, having remained in good standing in
the Ministry. I am glad to feel that this is the same idea which
was suggested some years ago by Archdeacon Morrison, and failed then
to command the attention of the Diocese, which I hope it will secure
now. Officers in the Church should certainly be treated with the same
consideration and with the same deference to their self-respect as the
Nation treats the Officers of its Army.

As not unconnected with this thought, I beg to notice one decision of
the House of Deputies at the last Convention.

It has been, I believe, from its early organization, a custom in the House of Bishops at the first session of its triennial meeting, to have read to the assembled Bishops, standing in reverent silence, the names of any Bishops who have died since the last meeting, with the dates of their respective deaths, and then to unite immediately in the saying of the All Saints Collect and other suitable prayers.

I notice with great satisfaction that the House of Deputies of the General Convention has this last year decided to make a change in its formal method of calling to mind the names of the members who have passed away, and in place of the memorial which heretofore was prepared by a committee, to adopt the simple and solemn custom which has been the invariable rule in the House of Bishops.

I am minded to follow, in our own Diocesan Convention, these examples, and I propose hereafter, at the opening of my Convention Address, to read to you the names of the Clergy and faithful lay people who have been our fellow-workers, and have passed away since our last assembling, and then to use some suitable commemorative prayers. Nothing, I think, can be so reverent a tribute of our love for those who have gone. In the appendix to the Address there can still be printed such personal notices of my own, or of the Vestries of the different Parishes, as may pay fuller and more detailed tributes to the faithful departed.

Naturally and inevitably the interest of the General Convention this year centres in, and gathers about, the fact that it closed the work of revision of the Book of Common Prayer, which since 1880 has not only occupied the time and thought of committees and commissions, but which has drawn the minds and hearts of Churchmen in England and America very much to this delicate and difficult work.

Before entering upon the general discussion of this subject, I desire to pay my tributes of respect to three men, — one of whom has concealed himself behind an *incognito*, — I mean the layman who has made possible the superb printing both of the Report and of the Book, and the distribution of it to every member of both houses of the Convention. The other two, the Rev. Dr. Huntington and the Rev. Dr. Hart, have been a very large part of the success of this whole undertaking. We lost, in the last three years of the work of the Commission and regained for the Committee on the Standard Book, the invaluable services of Dr. Huntington; but he had given us, during the critical time, the unstinted help of his clear judgment, his thorough knowledge, his cultivated taste, and his broad-minded consideration of the whole subject of liturgics, with reference to what was in conformity to Catholic and Anglican use, and in demand by the necessities of our own country and age. To Dr. Hart's unerring accuracy, sound learning and unwearied labour we owe the searching thoroughness of the Report and the actual perfectness of the Standard Prayer Book.

It will not certainly be out of place to review the salient points of this important story, beginning with the resolution which was virtually a resolution of inquiry passed in the General Convention of 1880, "Resolved, that a joint committee to consist of seven Bishops, seven presbyters and seven laymen be appointed to consider and to report to the next General Convention whether in view of the fact that this Church is soon to enter upon the second century of its organized existence in this country, the changed conditions of the national life do not demand certain alterations in the Book of Common Prayer in the direction of liturgical enrichment and increased flexibility of use."

There are three very distinct points involved in this proposed inquiry The first, adaptation to the new conditions of the national life; the next, liturgical enrichment; and the third, increased flexibility of use. I may speak with a certain amount of authority in regard to this whole matter because I had the honour of being appointed one of the seven Bishops who composed the joint committee in the General Convention of 1880. I have been continuously on the committee, was appointed chairman of it in Chicago in 1886, and at the last General Convention when we brought in our final report, became the chairman of the committee on the Standard Book and have been, I may say literally, in contact and in sympathy with the whole movement.

The first proposition in 1880, as I remember, struck almost everybody with a sense of suspicion and alarm. There are great numbers of people in this world, to whom any large and strong proposition of this sort suggests at first sight one or the other of these two things. And it has been rather curious to notice how they have lingered on in minds of very different constitution and for reasons very widely apart, for twelve years; have hindered and hampered more or less the progress of the work by a combination of entirely opposite opinions, against certain phases of it; and have succeeded, not in preventing the general purpose, but in seriously marring its perfectness.

The suspicion was that, because this proposition originated from what was supposed to be one of the Broad Church leaders some secret gall of vagueness and vapidity was concealed under the language of the resolution. And in spite of all the evidences of results, in spite of an acknowledgment all round that the work has been done in no narrow and partisan interest, curiously enough, even in cases where the proposition coincided absolutely with the peculiar partisanship involved, a certain number of individuals have held aloof from, and hindered, what I am quite sure they would all acknowledge in the main to have been, a sound progress in the direction of liturgical improvement. On the other hand, and combining with the men who held these views, was that most respectable and venerable body of men, to whom the mere fact of long attachment and association had so endeared the precise shape of the American Book of Common Prayer, that they could not brook the thought of the dotting of an i or the crossing of a t.

The third company of opposers, considerably the smallest of the three, consisted of persons, who, desiring much larger and more sweeping changes, opposed the more moderate proposals of the various committees in the hope that, this movement being made a failure, room would be found for them to carry out their views.

In spite of all this, and more and more as the work went on, an agreement with very unusual unanimity was reached in regard to all the most important changes which the committee proposed.

Just what the changed condition in the national life was in the minds of the movers of the resolution I am not prepared to say, but I am very sure of one thing, and that is that in the minds of the revisers two things largely answered to this condition; in the first place, the feeling that the Prayer Book should be made more the great manual of public worship for all who professed and called themselves Christians; partly by making its title-page broader in the omission of the language which apparently confines its use to members of the Protestant Episcopal Church in the United States of America; partly by accepting the fact, that in our day and generation the multiplication of shorter services is better adapted to the habits of the people, and more likely to attract them, than the prolongation of a few services in the day. They felt also the necessity and importance of providing Prayers and Offices for circumstances and occasions like Rogation Days, the Fourth of July, our Harvest Homes, and for some separate and individual demands.

As to the other two points of the language of the resolution, the first is certainly plain enough, and was constantly in the minds of the committee and has evidently commended itself to the Church. What has been accomplished may readily be seen, by any one who will run over the additions which have been already adopted. To have restored the Feast of the Transfiguration and made it a red letter day; to have replaced the full form of the Benedictus, and to have put into Evensong the Magnificat and the Nunc Dimittis; to have insisted upon the use of the Nicene Creed in the Communion Office, on the chief Feasts commemorating the life of our Lord: these and other matters which will readily suggest themselves to anybody's mind who is familiar with the work of the last twelve years, are certainly very *rich* enrichments of the Liturgy. And as to the question of flexibility of use, while not so much has been done perhaps as might have been, the shortened form of Morning Prayer and Evensong; the right to omit sometimes the Ten Commandments in the Office for the Holy Communion; the larger freedom about the use of the Litany; these will sufficiently indicate the action of the committee and its acceptance by the Church in this direction. I am free to say that the only very grave omissions, for neither of which the House of Bishops is responsible, which the General Convention has made in the direction of liturgical enrichment, have been the failure to accept the Collect, Epistle and Gospel proposed for use when the Holy Communion is celebrated at the time of a burial ; the refusal to allow the use of the words " Thanks be to Thee, O Christ, for this Thy Holy Gospel," after the Gospel; and the failure to accept the proposal, which passed the House of Bishops, to put the Prayer of Humble Access immediately before the reception of the Holy Communion and after the Consecration Prayer.

The two last points would have conformed our Communion Office more literally to that of the Scottish Church, whose form we have, thank God, been always permitted to retain; and would, I think, farther than that, have set before the people, in the first place, the attitude in which they approach the Blessed Sacrament just at the time of the approach; and would have enabled them to realize the infinite and ineffable gift, which has come to us in the Holy Gospel.

And now has come about in the good providence of God the final conclusion of this long and anxious labour. As I contrast the feeling of the first committee and of the Church but twelve years ago, with the feeling which was so intense and strong this last October, it seems to me like the difference between the setting out upon a trackless sea in a new ship and with an untried and unaccustomed crew, and the sailing in, with all on board safe and secure, to a peaceful haven of rest and calm. With very rare exceptions the changes adopted in 1889, were finally passed in 1892 (forty-four out of fifty-two). Of the proposals that were lost, two were in my judgment most undesirable. The resolution substituting Psalm sixty-four for Psalm sixty-nine was mercifully lost. This proposition had not come at all from the Revision Committee. The theory that the sixty-ninth Psalm, because a portion of it declares the wrath of God against impenitent sin, is unsuitable for use on the Day when the Saviour laid His Life down to save us from our sins, is one of those bits of soft and specious sentimentalism which need correction and rebuke. The Psalm, as everybody knows, is an almost historical prophecy of our Lord's suffering. It must have been in His own mind and heart when, " that the Scripture might be fulfilled, He said I thirst; " and the foresight of the Psalmist saw the awful scene on Calvary. But is the story of the Cross only the story of the Saviour slain for sinners? Is there not behind it as the background, the awful lesson of His hatred and horror at sin. The very same lips which spoke the blessed words in the act of the completed Sacrifice, " Father, forgive them, for they know not what they do; " said in that awful hour of His first Oblation of Himself on the night in which He was betrayed: " None of them is lost but the Son of Perdition that the Scripture might be fulfilled." And this, and the one hundred and ninth Psalm *are* the Scripture so fulfilled. Moreover, in the first chapter of the book of the Acts, St. Peter gives an interpretation of the Psalm, in his description of the traitor's awful fate. And in the interest of the grand principles of moral theology, men must be taught that the Holiness of God is so absolutely holy, that while the sinner is loved and forgiven, the sin is intolerably hateful to God.

Of the good gains in the last General Convention we shall count the added and adopted versicles at Evensong, the prayers for Unity, for the Rogation Days and Missions, the Penitential office, the Thanksgiving for a Child's Recovery, the Vigil Collects, the added Collects, Epistles and Gospels for Christmas Day and Easter Day, the greater freedom in the use of "the Summary of the Law," and the insertion of the Kyrie after it, the new Offertory sentence, "Remember the words of the Lord Jesus," the introduction into the Exhortation in the Marriage Service, of the words "is an honourable estate instituted of God in the time of man's innocency, signifying unto us the mystical union that is betwixt Christ and His Church, which holy estate Christ adorned and beautified with His presence and first miracle that He wrought in Cana of Galilee," and the additional prayers inserted in the Office for the Burial of the Dead, the last of which has the sanction of the 1st Book of Edward VI, and brings us into touch with the Scottish Church, to whom we are already in such deep debt.

I am glad to say that the Triennial Report from this Diocese to the General Convention shows an increase over the Report of 1889, in the number of Clergy, Baptisms, Confirmations, Communicants, Mission Stations, Sunday School scholars, contributions, endowments, gifts to objects outside the Diocese, and in Candidates for Holy Orders and Lay-readers.

Of matters still pending, the most important are the appointment of a Commission, in consultation with the Convocation of Canterbury to suggest such of the more important and better translations from the Revised Version, as may wisely be put into our authorized Bible in the form of marginal readings; the presentation of a Canon for the restoration of Suffragan Bishops to the Church; the change of the name of Assistant Bishop to Bishop-Coadjutor, which was unanimously adopted, in its first instance, in the House of Deputies after having passed the House of Bishops, and goes down to the Dioceses for final action at the next Convention because it involves a change in an article of the Constitution; and most perhaps of all, the appointment of a Constitutional Commission, to whom is to be referred a general survey of the Constitution and Canons of the Church, with a view of bringing them into fuller harmony with the enlarged life of the Church, into more consistency among themselves, and into more carefully considered language in legal points.

The Convention found its fitting close in the impressive service in *Emmanuel* Church, at which I had the privilege of reading for the first time by authority, out of the sheets of the Standard Book itself, the shortened form of Evensong with the new versicles; the Rev. Dr. Hart, secretary of the Prayer Book committee, reading the Lessons. The Hymns rang out with the full power of voice of the choir and the great congregation which thronged the Church. And no one who heard there or since the Pastoral Letter can fail to feel, not only that it represented in clearest and most dignified words, the mind and manner of its distinguished writer, the Bishop of Mississippi, but that it represents as I think few Letters of the sort have done before, the mind of the whole Church in most practical and valuable ways.

I am bound to say that the apparent ignoring of the work of Sisters in that portion of the Pastoral which dwells upon the duty of women consecrating themselves to God's service, is due to the fact that there is, and I am very glad there is, no canonical regulation of Sisterhoods attempted in this Church. But I must bear my witness here, after many years of trial, to the invaluable help and comfort which have come to me from the Sisterhood of the Holy Child Jesus: and I must also say that it is a perpetual pain and astonishment to me that they are left, so few in number, to undertake the almost superhuman task of the great amount of work which already presses upon them; while we are hindered from meeting the demands that come to us from all quarters of putting Sisters at work, in other parishes besides those of Albany and Troy.

THE CATHEDRAL.

On the 22d day of last February, there came to me, in reply to a request which I had no thought could bring such a response, the generous and gracious offer from a very dear friend which, as you know, has since enabled us to remove all remainder of debt from our Cathedral property in Albany. It was a touch of flame lighted by very faithful love, which kindled instantly the waiting and generous interest of my many friends. Five thousand dollars came to me the next day in Troy, and so the good work went on, until, long before the appointed time, the whole amount and more was secured. I am glad to put on record the fact that on the 2d day of March, my sixtieth birthday, the $27,000 needed to make good the original offer of $13,000 had been subscribed.

It is idle for me to speak again of the enormous relief and intense satisfaction of this result. You have in hand the sermon which I preached on the day of the commemoration of benefactors, and I only say again, what is true, that a very, very large part of the comfort and pleasure of all this has come first, from the fulness and readiness of the giving, and next, from the universal cordialness of sympathy, with which the Diocese from one end to the other received it.

You will, I am sure, notice with great pleasure the added decorations in the Cathedral since we met here last ; the beautiful East window, the wall mosaics, not only exquisite in themselves but lovely in the remembrance which they perpetuate, and to me intensely satisfactory because there is no particle of artificial colour, but every separate piece of stone is just as God made it; and the two carved doors, the Benefactors' door and the Baptistery door; the first the gift of the children of St. Agnes School —most appropriately because it is the door through which the graduating classes go in and out each year—carved in memory "of the benefactors and of the mercies vouchsafed to us" through them in the relief of the Cathedral from debt; and the second a nameless gift, which on the whole is to me the most beautiful bit of modern carving that I know anywhere. It is all done by the same faithful artist under whose hand the stones in the Cathedral have leaped into life, except for the Head of Christ, which is carved by Mr. Hinton's son.   The motive of the carving of the Baptistery door, as you will see, is in the first place that the foliage is of the grape vine and the true olive tree into which we are engrafted by our incorporation into Christ; while under the overshadowing of the Holy Spirit, on one side are the fruits of the Spirit, a pair of turtle doves representing love, a soaring lark for joy, a brooding dove over the water for peace, a pelican for long suffering, and a bird on its nest for gentleness; and on the other side, with the two crossed fishes, the old representation of those who are born in the water, are the five points of the whole armour of God, the breastplate, the shield, the helmet, the sword and the sandals.

I must add in this connection a word as to the future of the work. The Cathedral paid for, as you see it, by no means ceases to claim from you to whom it belongs, namely, every Clergyman and every member of the Church in the Diocese, your constant and generous interest.   It is yours as you are all proud to recognize now; but because it is yours you are in part responsible for all that still remains to be done.   I have pledged myself never to ask any thing more for the carrying on of the building to its completion, but in other directions I should feel myself derelict to one of my first duties if I did not keep constantly and urgently before the people its needs, in connection both with the building, and the work that it is set to do.   So far as the enrichment of the building in its interior is concerned, that will be cared for undoubtedly by individual gifts, but for the extension of its work and influence, and for the comfort and convenience of the Diocese we absolutely need that the Chapter House should be built without delay.   You certainly must realize how greatly every interest would be advanced, if this Convention and all other Church gatherings could be suitably housed, as they would be by a proper Chapter House.   The Diocesan library and the Cathedral library, the Woman's Auxiliary, and Diocesan meetings for any purpose would all find their natural home in it; and it would be the centre of all the Cathedral works of charity and mercy.

It can be built as the Cathedral has been, by laying the entire foundation and ground plan, carrying it up to a certain height in stone, and then finishing it with a temporary roof until the time comes when it can be fully carried out. It ought to be begun without delay, and it ought to enlist the sympathy and interest and generous help of every one in the Diocese.

Beside this there ought to be at least a partial endowment for the work that the Cathedral has to do. This lies very near my heart. I venture to say without fear of contradiction that there are no Institutions in the whole Church such as we have in this Cathedral city, in St. Agnes School, the Child's Hospital and its kindred houses, the Sisterhood and the Cathedral itself that have been carried on for so many years without any endowment. Of course it has been a very great strain and anxiety for me and for those who labour with me to do this. It still is. And I think it ought to be lifted, or at least somewhat lightened. There is nothing I feel more strongly about than that there should be an effort to procure an endowment for parts of the Cathedral work; and that from no desire to relieve the stated worshippers of their regular and generous giving, but rather to enable them to direct their gifts more largely to more general interests, and to make permanent and not dependent upon any temporary congregation the support of the services and of the charities, and also of some of the missionary work connected with the Cathedral. An endowment for the music and for the support of one Canon would accomplish this.

I propose to begin the fund without delay, and I hope to live long enough to see it rise to a sufficient amount.

I frankly acknowledge with emphasis that it is my very earnest hope and purpose before I lay my work down to see this accomplished, to see much larger provision of scholarships in St. Agnes School, more beds endowed in the Child's Hospital, and two buildings built besides the Chapter House, viz., the Sisters' House, and a permanent and more convenient house in which the babies of St. Margaret's may be properly cared for.

It seems wise for me to call the attention of the Clergy to two things, both of which have become matters of practical interest and importance in the Diocese during this year.

In one of the parishes a clergyman just before leaving, without any notification whatever to me or to the persons immediately concerned, marked upon his parish register, and left to astonish and torment his successor, a statement that he had excommunicated eighteen of the communicants of his parish. I immediately ordered the record to be altered, and gave notice to the clergyman that the action was entirely illegal and invalid. It must be noticed that a solemn and serious act of this sort could

6

only be done with the most careful observance of the canon law. A separation from the Holy Communion is one of the most serious and awful sentences that can possibly be passed. It can only be put into operation according to the canon, with notice given to the individual accompanied by a notice to the Bishop, to whom the persons involved have the right of appeal. Title 2, Canon 12, section 2 of the Digest contains the clear statement of the way in which persons are to be repelled from the Holy Communion agreeably to the rubric, and any action taken without due regard to all the prescriptions of that canon is *ipso facto* null and void. I do not think it necessary from any other experience; but this possibility makes me think it wise to beg the Clergy to remember, that this awful exercise of the power of the keys should be never used, except under the most pressing necessity; and under no circumstances should be used for the adjustment of personal differences or in vindication of personal wrongs. If the discipline of the Church is brought into disrespect, as it too often is, by laxity, it will lose all its force and value if it is made contemptible by the introduction of personal feeling, and by carelessness in its administration.

I beg you also to remember in the matter of parochial organization that there is provision made in the civil law of this State for making a change in the number of the vestrymen of a parish. Here, too, I must say, because it involves important civil and legal interests, the prescriptions of the law must be most accurately and carefully observed; and I beg to call the attention of the Clergy to the law as it stands to-day, which I have reprinted in the appendix to the Address

As we turn to our Blessed Communion with each other and with our Lord, I am thankful to feel that we come to it under the solemn sanction of the teaching of to-day's Epistle, into whose earnest words of prayer and thankfulness I can enter with all my heart; "thanking my God upon every remembrance of you all, and always in every prayer of mine making request with joy for your fellowship," with Christ, with me, with one another, "in the Gospel." Only let us remember the force of that which follows, "from the first day until now," which has in it the solemn warning of the danger lest any of us should fall away. "Until now," which does not merely mean this present day of speaking, but which leads us on and up to think of that other "*Now*," that present moment of appearing each one of us before the Judge, and so sets us earnestly to ask that "He who hath begun the good work in us will perform it until the day of Jesus Christ."

What fitter thoughts or fitter words can fill our hearts and mouths before the Altar to-day, as we think of the whole household which the Church is, or of the portion of it in this great American continent of which we have been speaking, or of our own small portion of "the great family in Heaven and earth" which is named after Him "whose Name is above every name," than to beseech God that He will keep, as we thank Him that He has kept, "His household the Church in continual godliness," and to pray that "free from all adversities by His protection, we may be devoutly given to serve Him in good works, to the glory of His Name."

RECORD OF VISITATIONS.

It is my pleasant duty to record the story of the year's work in the diocese.

Our last Convention gathered, as you will remember, in the Cathedral, on the 17th of November, with one hundred and three Clergy present, and ninety-four laymen representing forty-nine Parishes. I delivered the portion of my Address which stands instead of a Charge, at the opening service, and celebrated the Holy Communion assisted by the Archdeacons, the Dean and the Secretary of the Convention.

I think our missionary meeting at night was in many ways the best we ever had, and I am quite sure that the impression made by our Diocesan Missionary not only convinced any who needed convincing of the value of his work, but has brought forth the fruit of securing from the Sunday Schools in the different Archdeaconries, the necessary money to support the work without intrenching upon the other income of the Board.

At the early Celebration on Wednesday I ordered the Rev. Eugene Griggs Priest, presented by the Archdeacon of the Susquehanna, who, with Canons Fulcher and Hatheway, united in the imposition of hands.

The session continued, pleasantly and constantly occupied through the day, and its labours were brought to a close early enough, to enable some of us to take short part in the meeting of the Diocesan branch of the Woman's Auxiliary, and enabled me to deliver my Address before the Evensong, at the close of which the Convention adjourned without day.

The Board of Missions held its first meeting in my library that night, with perhaps less than the usual effort at cutting down expenses, because the ability was given to us in various ways to assign the stipends and somewhat enlarge the work.

On Monday, the 30th of November, in the morning I said the Litany in the Cathedral, in connection with the Office of Intercession for Missions on St. Andrew's Day, and in the evening, in St. Luke's Church, Troy, I preached and confirmed twenty persons.

On Sunday, the 13th of December, I celebrated in Mt. Calvary Church Baltimore, early; and preached at the eleven o'clock service in Grace Church; and at night in St. Paul's Church, Baltimore, I preached before the St. Paul's Guild. It was a very noble service and a splendid gathering of men, and it was a great pleasure to me to be once more associated with my dear old friend Dr. Hodges, and to see how thoroughly grounded and rooted the work is under him, in that old mother Church of Baltimore.

On my return home we were arrested, by the first accident that has ever befallen me during my many journeyings in the twenty-three years of my Episcopate. It was a merciful escape, involving only alarm and delay, except for the shock and sorrow of the death of two of the employes of the road. I was greatly impressed with the comfort of the daily Celebration in the Cathedral, which enabled me almost instantly upon my arrival at home in the early morning, to go and give thanks to God for His merciful deliverance of my own life, and of the lives of those who are very dear to me.

On Thursday, the 17th of December, in the Cathedral, I ordered Priest the Rev. James Frederic Olmsted, presented by Mr. Cookson, the Rev. George Brinckerhoff Richards and the Rev. Freeborn Garrettson Jewett, presented by the Rev. Dr. Battershall; and I also ordered Deacon William Francis Parsons, presented by the Rev. Dr. Chambré of the Diocese of Massachusetts. I preached and celebrated the Holy Communion.

On Tuesday, the 22nd, I preached and celebrated the Holy Communion and consecrated the Church of the Holy Spirit in Schenevus, and confirmed four persons, one of whom came from the Worcester Mission.

On the 23rd, in the evening, in St. Andrew's Mission Chapel, West Troy, I preached and confirmed five persons.

On the 24th of December, in the afternoon, in the Cathedral, I held a service of benediction of the east window and of the wall mosaics, in the sanctuary and choir of the Cathedral.

On Friday, January 1st, I said the prayer and gave the benediction at the inauguration of the Governor of New York.

Tuesday, January 12th, I presided at the meeting of the Board of Managers in New York; and on Monday, January 18th, I was present and made an address in the Cathedral, at the meeting of the Archdeaconry of Albany.

Tuesday, January 19th, in Hoosick Falls, I officiated at the burial of my dear friend, Mr. Walter A. Wood. The service had in it every evidence of the consciousness of what a friend had been taken away from the village which he founded, and whose every best interest he furthered and fostered with constant and most generous care.

It is said that there were two thousand five hundred men in the lines between which the funeral procession passed, and who followed it through a bleak and cold wind to the Maple Grove Cemetery. Every shop was closed in the village, and all business gave way to the common desire to do great honour to his good memory.

On Wednesday evening I made an address on the subject of what I saw of religious work and life in Europe, before the Young Men's Christian Association in Albany.

Tuesday, the 26th, in St. Paul's Church, Troy, I preached and blessed the new Altar and celebrated the Holy Communion, and was present afterward at the meeting of the Archdeaconry of Troy.

Wednesday, the 27th, at the early Celebration in the Cathedral I admitted Miss Julia Janes a full Sister, in the Sisterhood of the Holy Child Jesus.

February 2nd I kept the twenty-third anniversary of my Consecration in the Cathedral,—not only by the early Celebration in the morning, but by baptizing at Evensong four of the St. Agnes girls,— with many intense memories and infinite gratitude, for the goodness of God during all these years of such imperfect service.

On the 6th of February I made an address to the children of the Sunday Schools in Albany gathered in the Cathedral. I hope this will be a yearly custom in the city as establishing the cordial and sisterly relations among the City Parishes, with the Cathedral which is the natural centre of ecclesiastical life.

On Monday, the 8th, I made a speech before a meeting in the interests of a decent Excise law at the Cooper Institute in New York; and on Tuesday, I presided at the meeting of the commission on the Standard Prayer Book and of the Board of Managers.

On Wednesday, the 10th, I officiated in St. Peter's Church, Albany, at the wedding of a dear child, dear by every inherited and personal relation, the daughter of close friends; whom I had baptized, confirmed and graduated from St. Agnes School.

The honour came to me that day of a unanimous election as Regent of the University of New York, which I accepted, and in which I have done such service as I could render, because it came to me with no political element in it and is in no sense a political office; and because I felt that it was an opportunity for me to serve in larger ways the interests of higher education, in which both by instinct and inheritance I have the deepest concern.

On the 11th I officiated at the burial of my old friend and my father's, Mr. Stephen Warren, in the lovely Church of the Holy Cross in Troy. It was a service of great beauty and fitness, flooded with recollections of many years and many friends. Mr. Warren's life was one of quiet occupation in private affairs, but it was distinguished by three gracious distinctions, in an unusual degree, personal unselfishness, filial devotion and fraternal love.

On Saturday, the 13th, I went to Burnt Hills and officiated at the burial of the Rev. Dr. Timlow. There were four clergy with me, Canon Fulcher, Mr. Prout, Mr. Pendleton and Mr. Snively, and there would have been more, but for the difficulty of reaching the place over the drifted roads. There were innumerable indications of the deep reverence and affection in which his congregation held this most admirable man.

On Tuesday, the 8th of March, in the evening, and on Wednesday and Thursday following, I conducted the Retreat for the students in the Chapel of the General Theological Seminary, to my own great interest and, as I have reason to hope from the kindly words of several of the students, not without profit and help to them.

I celebrated early in the Chapel on Wednesday morning; and on Thursday morning at the second Celebration I ordained the Rev. Hamilton Cady to the Priesthood, who was presented by his father. It was a fitting close of the Retreat, an object lesson of the solemnity and dignity of the priestly office; and it was a great pleasure to me personally, because it recalled very close relations which go back through many years, with my old friend, Dr. Cady; whose son I am more than glad to welcome as one of the Clergy of this Diocese.

On Saturday, the 12th, I was present at the meeting of the Cathedral Chapter of the Woman's Diocesan League, at which the whole amount of the debt was reported raised, and at both which meetings action was taken in the form of resolutions which I print in the Appendix to this Address. I am quite sure it is one of the events in our Diocesan life which is most worthy of commemoration.

On Sunday, 20th of March, I preached in St. George's Church, New York, and in the evening I had the great pleasure of listening to one of the noble sermons of the Lord Bishop of Derry in the course on Christian Evidences.

On Thursday, the 24th, I made my annual Visitation of the Church Home in Troy, preached and celebrated the Holy Communion.

On Friday, the 25th, in the evening, in the Cathedral, I preached and confirmed sixty-nine persons, and on the next morning I confirmed one person who was unable to be present the evening before, making seventy in the Cathedral this year.

On Sunday morning, the 27th, in the Cathedral, I preached the sermon at the service appointed for "the commemoration of benefactors and of thanksgiving for mercies vouchsafed to us," offered upon the Altar the complete sum of $40,009, and celebrated the Holy Communion.

March 28th, in the Cathedral, I confirmed Mr. Charles A. Howells, a Methodist minister now a candidate for Holy Orders, and working most acceptably as a Lay Reader in one of the Missions of the Diocese.

On the 30th of March, in the evening, in St. John's Church, Cohoes, I preached and confirmed thirty-one persons.

Sunday, April the 3rd, in St. John's Church, Troy, I preached and confirmed eighteen persons. I had no thought at the time that it was to be my last service there in connection with the Rev. Mr. Snively's rectorship of the Parish, which he has resigned to the great regret of his people. I am myself truly sorry to lose one who has been with me during his whole ministry, with the short interval of absence in the Diocese of Massachusetts, and who has left behind him, in the greatly-improved condition of his Church in Troy, a marked evidence of his success.

Sunday, April 10th, in St. Peter's Church, in the morning, I preached and confirmed fifty persons, and in the evening, in St. Paul's Church, Albany, I preached and confirmed nineteen persons.

On Monday, the 11th, I took part in the burial of Mr. George Henry Warren in the Church of the Holy Cross, Troy. The service was made more impressive, if it could be, by the fact that the body of his son was brought, and lay by his in the Chapel, and was interred afterward in the family vault in the cemetery. The service was most touching; musically speaking, I think perfect in its fitness, and it gathered up in my heart memories of all my earlier life, when we were young together in the dear old Mount Ida home.

On Tuesday evening, April 12th, in the Church of the Holy Innocents in Albany, I preached and confirmed seven persons.

April 13th, in the evening, in Trinity Church, Albany, I preached and confirmed thirty-five persons. The service in every way gave manifest evidence of faithful and successful work.

April 14th, in the evening, in Grace Church, I preached and confirmed twenty-eight persons, thankful to find here too the old life and stir in the service and in the pastoral care.

Friday, the 15th, being Good Friday, I preached the three hours' service in the Cathedral, with a congregation larger and more impressed, it seemed to me, than ever before.

Our Easter feast in the Cathedral this year was gladder than ever in the five hundred communions that were made, in the great congregations which filled the building, and in the glorious outburst of most thankful praise.

Tuesday, the 19th, in Trinity Church, West Troy, I preached and confirmed twenty-one persons.

Wednesday, the 20th, I was present at a meeting of the Church University Board of Regents in St. Bartholomew's House, and in the evening, in All Souls' Church, I had the great pleasure of marrying my old friend, Mr. von Eltz.

April 22nd, in the evening, in Trinity Church, Lansingburgh, I preached and confirmed forty-nine persons. It was a noble service in every way, and while the number of the class confirmed was accounted for in part by the presence of candidates from the mission which Dr. Nickerson has opened between Lansingburgh and Troy, it of course all pointed to the fact of the loving labour of the Rector of the Parish.

Sunday, the 24th of April, the Lord Bishop of Derry preached in the Cathedral, winning all our hearts by the charm of his presence and the power of his preaching.

April 25th, in the evening, in St. Mark's Church, Green Island, I preached and confirmed ten persons.

April 26th, in the evening, in Christ Church, Ballston, I preached and confirmed seven persons.

April 27th, in the morning, at Fort Edward, I preached and confirmed three persons and celebrated the Holy Communion.

In the afternoon, in Zion Church, Sandy Hill, I preached and confirmed twelve persons, and in the evening, in the Church of the Messiah, Glens Falls, I preached and confirmed twenty persons. This Church is one of the most beautiful of our country Churches, and the service is very admirably rendered. I am always surprised when I find such results as are secured here from a boy choir in a country village. Where it can be well done it certainly is the most attractive kind of choir for religious music, but I am somewhat inclined to advise against their introduction for the mere sake of surpliced men and boys. They are the most difficult of all choirs to maintain, and I think, when they are not well trained, they are the most discordant and undesirable.

I greatly wish that the attention of the Clergy and choristers could be more given to the singing of hymns. The rich and ringing Services and Anthems have their own place in the public worship of God, and when and where they are well rendered, they promote devotion and do honour to God. But ambitious attempts at a Cathedral service are far from edifying. And even the finest choral service is inadequate and injurious, at the expense of real congregational singing especially in familiar hymns.

April 28th, in the morning, in St. Mary's Church, Luzerne, I preached, celebrated and confirmed six persons, and in the evening, in Bethesda Church, Saratoga, I preached and confirmed fifty-three persons. The music here, also, is of the very best.

Friday, the 29th, in the morning, I preached, confirmed seven persons and celebrated the Holy Communion and consecrated All Saints' Church, Round Lake. There was a very goodly gathering of Clergy, the Request to consecrate was read by the Missionary, Mr. Boone, who is most successfully caring for this place and the two adjoining Missions of Jonesville and East Line, and the Sentence of Consecration by the Archdeacon. It is the best result in the way of a Church building, for the money spent upon it, that I know anywhere.

In the afternoon, in Grace Chapel, Jonesville, I preached and confirmed six persons. Small in numbers, there is no Mission in the Diocese that is so full of earnest devotion on the part of the lay people as this Mission.

In the evening, in St. John's Church, East Line, I preached. The day was very full of memories of dear Mr. Cook, with whom I had been so often in these Churches and into whose labours, now that he has passed to his rest and reward, the present Missionary has entered with great efficiency.

Sunday morning, May 1st, in St. Paul's Church, Troy, I preached and celebrated and confirmed thirty-eight persons.

In the afternoon, in Christ Church, Schenectady, I preached and confirmed twelve persons, and in the evening, in St. George's Church, I preached and confirmed thirty persons. The growth of the Church in this old town is very marked. It is the outcome of the years of faithful work and holy living of the dear old Rector, Dr. Payne, and of much faithful service done here by Mr. Toy; and the fruits which Mr. Pendleton's energy and Mr. Prout's devotion are gathering now are very sure to increase. Of course the new life of the place, owing to the introduction of new manufactories, has something to do with it, but the Church there is really vigorous and strong.

May 2nd, in the morning, in Zion Church, Fonda, I preached and celebrated the Holy Communion.

In the afternoon, in St. John's Church, Johnstown, I preached and confirmed twenty-four persons; and in the evening, in Christ Church, Gloversville, I preached and confirmed seven persons. The outlook in these two places was never so good as now, under the wise and energetic administration of the two faithful Priests in charge, and I have great hopes that the Church in Gloversville will grow up to its possibilities in this thriving town.

May 3rd, in the morning, in the Church of the Good Shepherd, Canajoharie, I preached, celebrated the Holy Communion and confirmed one person

In the afternoon, in the Church of the Holy Cross, Fort Plain, I preached; and in the evening in Emmanuel Church, Little Falls, I preached and confirmed fourteen persons.

May 4th, in the morning, in the Chapel used for St. John's Mission in Dolgeville, I preached, confirmed seven persons and celebrated the Holy Communion. I have had a good many hard drives in the course of my Episcopate, but I think this was the worst of all, and it gave me a new sense of the exposures of our Missionaries who make these drives continually, and of the devotion of the Rector of Little Falls to whom the successful planting of this Mission is due. I was thankful to know that a railway was in process of building and likely to be completed before I made another visitation, and I look with great hope toward the establishment of a strong Mission here in a place which is full of energy and life.

This announcement from the newspaper tells to my great pleasure of the next step in the progress of the work:

"The twentieth Sunday after Trinity — Oct. 20, 1892 — will always be remembered as a Golden Number in the calendar of Dolgeville. After eighteen months of hard work, self-sacrifice, patience, persistent conflict against odds of all sorts, the intrepid rector of Emmanuel Church, Little

7

Falls — Rev. Mr. Mariett — who founded the mission here, laid the foundation stone of the new church at 3 o'clock in the afternoon."

In the afternoon, in St. Augustine Church, Ilion, I preached and confirmed fifteen persons; and in the evening, in St. Alban's Church, Frankfort, I preached and confirmed six persons. Mr. Cook has added this Mission to his own abundant and admirable work in Ilion and is encouraged about its prospects.

May 5th, in the morning, in Christ Church, Herkimer, I preached, celebrated the Holy Communion and confirmed thirteen persons.

In the afternoon, in the old Church at Fairfield, I preached and confirmed three persons, with really a large congregation, due to the revival of the old Fairfield Seminary which bids fair to be one of our strong country Academies. The place becomes of increased importance in view of this, and I greatly hope there will be a building up of the old Parish.

In the evening, in the Church of "The Memorial," Middleville, I preached and confirmed four persons.

May 6th, in the evening, in St. Anne's Church, Amsterdam, I preached and confirmed twenty-three persons.

Sunday, May 8th, in the afternoon, in St. Barnabas' Church, Troy, I preached and confirmed eighteen persons.

May 10th, in the evening, in Christ Church, Hudson, I preached and confirmed seventeen persons.

May 11th, in the morning, in Trinity Church, Athens, I preached and confirmed eight persons and celebrated the Holy Communion, enjoying the welcome and accustomed hospitality of the Rector and his wife. I am glad to call your attention this year to the fact that Mr. Stewart's name is to be added to the list of those faithful Priests who have passed the golden anniversary of their Ordination. Still fresh in heart and mind and with much vigour of body, he is carrying on his good work, and I am sure that his brethren in the Diocese will desire to make some minute on our Journal of congratulation to him, and of thankfulness to God for the long and beautiful memory of his ministerial service, so much of which has been given to the Church in this Diocese.

In the afternoon, in Trinity Church, Claverack, I preached and confirmed two persons, and in the evening, in All Saints' Church, Hudson, I preached and confirmed four persons.

May 12th, in the morning, in St. John's Church, Stockport, I preached, celebrated the Holy Communion and confirmed twenty-two persons. It was an ideal service in a country Church. The organ has been brought down stairs to the great improvement of the music in every way, and Mr. Toy's work here and in Rossman's Mills is evidently beginning to tell. I was glad to hear from him that the organization of the King's Daughters had been successfully and satisfactorily at work.

In the afternoon, in the Chapel at Rossman's Mills I preached and confirmed six persons; and in the evening, in St. Barnabas' Church, Stottville, I preached and confirmed seven persons.

Sunday evening, the 15th, I preached and confirmed sixteen persons in St. Mark's Church, Philmont. I am glad to find the Church strengthening, and I am thankful that Mr. Lowndes has been able to take advantage of the very generous offer of Mr. Aken to build a Parish House, which is of unusual importance in a place like this; where so many young people are gathered in the mills, who can be reached through such opportunities of social gathering and attractive amusements, as a guild house will afford.

May 16th, in the morning, in St. Paul's Church, Kinderhook, I preached, confirmed eight persons and celebrated the Holy Communion.

May 18th, in the evening, in the Church of the Holy Cross, Warrensburgh, I preached and confirmed five persons. I was greatly divided here between the missing of dear Ogden who always used to welcome me so cordially to his beautiful Rectory, and rejoicing to welcome Mr. Cady to his new work here. Staying for the first time for many years, in the old house that used to be my home brought back many memories of dear old Colonel Burhans.

May the 19th, in the morning, in St. Paul's Church, Bartonville, I preached, celebrated the Holy Communion and confirmed six persons; and in the afternoon, in the Church of the Good Shepherd, Chestertown, I preached and confirmed three persons. Mr. Thurman has added, to his many gracious and generous gifts to this Parish, almost its most important, in the giving of a delightful Rectory, in which I found Mr. Taylor and his wife comfortably established.

May 20th, in the morning, in the Church of St. Sacrament, Bolton, I preached, confirmed eight persons and celebrated the Holy Communion. Two of the candidates came from Sabbath-day Point, since it was more convenient, in the difficulties of transportation, for them to be brought to Bolton, than for me to go to the little Chapel at Sabbath-day Point as I had originally proposed.

May 22nd, in the afternoon, in Grace Church, Waterford, I preached and confirmed seventeen persons, one of whom came from Lansingburgh. I regret to report to the Convention that Mr. Freeman, after a very successful ministry here, has resigned and left the Diocese; and I am glad to restore the name to our clergy list in the person of an old friend— young as he is in years — the Rev. Henry R. Freeman who is now Rector of St. John's Church, Troy.

In the evening, in Christ Church, Troy, I preached and confirmed eighteen persons.

May 23rd, in the afternoon, in the Church of the Cross, Ticonderoga, I preached and confirmed ten persons; and in the evening, in Christ Church, Port Henry, I preached and confirmed two persons.

May 24th, in the morning, I preached, celebrated the Holy Communion and confirmed three persons in Emmanuel Church, Mineville.

In the afternoon, in St. John's Church, Essex, I preached and confirmed three persons; and in the evening, in St. Paul's Church, Keeseville, I preached and confirmed seven persons.

May 25th, in the morning, in St. James' Church, Au Sable Forks, I preached, celebrated the Holy Communion and confirmed fourteen persons. This is one of the few instances I have ever met, where in two towns that are decaying and diminishing, the Church is increasing and strengthening. It must mean hard and faithful work on the part of the Missionary, Mr. Gill.

In the evening, in Trinity Church, Plattsburgh, I preached and confirmed sixteen persons.

May 26th, in the morning, in Christ Church, Rouse's Point, I preached, confirmed five persons and celebrated the Holy Communion; and in the evening, in St. John's Church, Champlain, I preached and confirmed two persons.

May 27th, in the morning, in St. Peter's Church, Ellenburgh, I preached, celebrated the Holy Communion and confirmed three persons. I was very sorry to miss my visitation to Ellenburgh Centre, owing to the impossibility of meeting the train in time.

In the evening, in St. Mark's, Malone, I preached and confirmed sixteen persons, entering with intense sympathy into the shadow of bereavement which has fallen upon the Rector, and glad to find the spontaneous tribute of well-deserved love which the people had paid to Mrs. Temple, in the Eagle Lectern which they had placed in the Church in her dear memory, and which I blessed during that service.

May 28th, in the morning, I preached, confirmed one person and celebrated the Holy Communion in Grace Church, Norfolk; and in the afternoon, in St. Andrew's Church, Norwood, I preached and confirmed six persons. Mr. Earle is just entering upon his work here with every promise of success.

Sunday, the 29th, in Trinity Church, Potsdam, I preached, confirmed twelve persons and celebrated the Holy Communion; and in the afternoon, in Zion Church, Colton, I preached and confirmed nine persons. How much the whole of this northern work is indebted to the old Church family in Potsdam no one can fully know.

Monday, May 30th, in the afternoon, in St. Peter's Church, Brushton, I preached and confirmed two persons; and in the evening, in St. John's Church, Massena, I preached and confirmed six persons.

Tuesday, the 31st, I celebrated at Massena early; and in the afternoon, in Fort Covington, in a hall which is used for their worship, I preached and confirmed two persons. This is my first visitation to this Mission, and I found not much strength but very real spirit and earnestness, so that I greatly hope good may come of the planting of the Church here.

In the evening, in Hogansburgh, I preached; Canon Stewart, who was with me, baptizing a child.

Wednesday, June 1st, in the afternoon, in Trinity Church, Gouverneur, I preached and confirmed ten persons; and in the evening, after a noble service in St. John's Church, Ogdensburgh, I preached and confirmed forty-one persons.

I was sorry to be obliged to turn back and give up the visitation at Waddington and Lisbon, owing to a cold which came upon me from officiating in a Church, cold and damp after long closing, and which, although I fought it off for a good while, was really the beginning of the breaking up of my later June Visitations.

From the 4th of June until the 7th I was occupied with the examinations in St. Agnes School; and on Sunday the 5th, in the afternoon, in St. Margaret's Chapel, Menands, I preached and confirmed eleven persons.

Tuesday the 7th I presided at a meeting of the Trustees of the General Theological Seminary in New York, and was present for a little while at the reception for the Society for the Home Study of Holy Scripture and Church History in the delightful house which Miss Smiley has opened. It seems like the college in which Hulda the prophetess lived, full of the atmosphere of literary religion, and where I am very sure, by this new step which houses the Society, much has been accomplished toward making it more permanent. It has never done better work than the last year and its prospects seem to me full of hope.

In the evening, in the Carnegie Music Hall, acting for the Chancellor of the University, I conferred the degree of Bachelor of Law upon one hundred and nine graduates of the New York Law School.

On the 9th of June the twenty-first class graduated from St. Agnes School. The gathering in the schoolroom had all its usual brightness and beauty, and the service in the Cathedral at which I delivered my Address and gave the Benediction to the graduates was attractive as ever.

In the evening, in St. John's Church, Troy, I married one of the old graduates of the School.

On the 11th of June, St. Barnabas' Day, four girls, who had completed the course of training in the St. Christina Home, were sent out with the certificates and medals showing their faithfulness in the training work. It was one of the most interesting and delightful acts of my Episcopate. The Home itself is not known as it ought to be, but it is a ch place and the whole atmosphere and influence are of the ver

one of the children received a Savings' bank book containing certificates
of the money which she had deposited out of her earnings, so that each
one had a little capital with which to start life, in money as well as in all
garnered influences and teachings of their four years there; and they each
received a gold medal, a Chi Rho in a circle, on which was engraved on
one side "St. Christina Home," and on the other, the rare legend of that
rare life which in its few years accomplished so much, "If your life is
short make it long by good works and deeds." Besides this each one
had a little book given them of practical suggestions about household
economy. The medals were hung around the neck of each child by Mrs.
Trask, and I am sure that the memory of that day will linger long in
the minds, not of the children only, but all who were present.

I must renew my thanks to Canon Fulcher for his faithfulness in both
the spiritual and musical training of the children, my expression of the
infinite benefaction of this gracious gift of Mr. and Mrs. Trask, and my
hope that the future of the work may tell in every way for the making
both of good servants and of good masters and mistresses; the latter of
which, by the bye, seems to me to be quite as essential as the former, and
rather more difficult.

In the afternoon I confirmed one person in the Cathedral; and on
Sunday the 12th I ordered Priest Mr. George Lynde Richardson and Mr.
W. Francis Parsons, and also, acting for the Bishop of Maryland, Mr.
Lawson Carter Rich. Mr. Rich was presented by the Rev. Mr. Clapp
of the Diocese of Maryland, Mr. Richardson by the Dean, and Mr. Parsons by Canon Fulcher. I preached and celebrated the Holy Communion; and in the afternoon, in the Church of the Holy Cross, I preached
and confirmed ten persons; and in the evening, in the Free Church of the
Ascension, Troy, I preached and confirmed ten persons.

June 13th, in the morning, in the Cathedral, I ordered Priest Mr.
Harry Elmer Gilchrist, presented by the Dean, he having been prevented
unexpectedly from being ordained on Sunday; and I have also to report
that acting for me the Bishop of Ontario ordered Priest on Trinity Sunday, in his Cathedral in Ottawa, the Rev. Mr. Greenhalgh.

June 13th, in the afternoon, I confirmed two persons in private for
St. Peter's Church, Albany.

June 14th, in New York, I was present at a meeting of the Committee
on Missionary Services in connection with the meeting of the General
Convention, and presided afterward at a meeting of the Board of Managers.

June 15th, in the afternoon, in Trinity Chapel, Sharon Springs, I
preached and confirmed twenty-two persons; and in the evening, in Grace
Church, Cherry Valley, I preached and confirmed eleven persons.

June 16th, in the morning, in St. Paul's Church, East Springfield, I
preached, confirmed seven persons and celebrated the Holy Communion;
but here, owing I think to the effect of the intense heat, affecting me the

more, of course, because I had not thoroughly regained my health, I was taken ill, and to my infinite regret and disappointment was obliged to give up all further Visitations. By the very good providence fo God and the great kindness of my dear friend and brother, the Bishop of Delaware, the rest of the Visitations which I had appointed were all accomplished, so that the disappointment was only mine; and it is a disappointment which no one but a Bishop can realize, not to be with his own Clergy and his own people and to do his own work; but I am sure the Clergy and people share with me the sense of very deep gratitude to the Bishop for his most acceptable Visitations.

He reports to me that on the 17th of June, in Zion Church, Morris, he confirmed forty-five persons.

On the 20th of June, in St. John's, Delhi, he confirmed thirteen persons.

On the 21st, in St. Paul's, Franklin, he confirmed two persons.

On the 22nd, in the Church at Sidney he confirmed four in the morning; and in the evening, in St. Matthew's, Unadilla, eight persons.

On the 23rd of June he laid the corner-stone of the new Church in Deposit and confirmed fifteen persons, one of whom was confirmed in private; and in the evening, in St. James' Church, Oneonta, he confirmed fifteen persons.

On Friday, the 24th, in Christ Church, Cooperstown, he confirmed eighteen persons, one being from East Springfield.

On the 25th, in Calvary Church, Cairo, he confirmed five persons who had been prepared by Mr. Vibbard and were presented by Mr. Podmore, Mr. Vibbard unfortunately having been obliged to give up his work for the time.

On Sunday, the 26th, in St. Peter's Church, Hobart, he confirmed five persons; and in Grace Church, Stamford, in the evening, he confirmed six persons.

On the 28th, in Trinity Church, Granville, he confirmed ten persons in the morning; and in the afternoon, in Cambridge, two persons. The candidates in Granville were presented by the Rev. Mr. Cookson, dear Mr. Lancaster, though better, being unable to do more than be present at the service.

On the 29th of June, Bishop Coleman gave the benediction to the various additions to the old St. Luke's Church in Cambridge, and was with the Clergy of the Archdeaconry of Troy who met at that time and place. Both the service and the alterations to the Church are reported to me by he Bishop, and by those who were present, as having been most attractive; and the tokens of both spiritual and material improvement in the place are cause of great thankfulness, to the Rector, under whose faithful ministrations they have been accomplished, and to me. We must not forget to-day to remember him in earnest sympathy in the great sorrow which has come to him in the death of his only son.

In the evening, in St. Mark's Church, Hoosick Falls, the Bishop con-firmed fifty-two persons; and on the 30th, in the morning, in Trinity Church, Schaghticoke, he confirmed fourteen; and in the evening, in All Saints' Chapel, Hoosac, he confirmed twenty-seven persons, making a total of two hundred and forty-one persons confirmed by him, giving the impression, both to him and to me, as I am sure it will to you to whom this report comes, of very vigorous and admirable work in the Parishes which he visited.

I was so much better for a short stay ·in North East Harbour, that I was able to obey the summons of the Presiding Bishop and go to Middletown·to a meeting of a committee of the House of Bishops on the Lectionary, on the 1st of July; and after that I was occupied in Albany on the 4th, 5th and 6th of July with the meetings of the University Con-vocation, presiding part of the time, and intensely interested in the able and admirable discussion of various educational subjects, which was carried on by many of the leading College and Academy Professors and Teachers in the State of New York.

I gave the degrees of Bachelor of Library Science to nine persons who had graduated from the Library School on the 5th of July, acting for the Chancellor; and was glad indeed to be able, as one of the Regents of the University, to have any, even small, part in the things that pertain to the advancement of the highest education in our Empire State.

During my holiday in dear North East Harbour I celebrated twelve times, preached fifteen sermons, baptized a child, and buried the son of my dear friend Stephen Smallidge. He was a Christian boy of excellent promise, and the great sorrow of his early death was not a little com-forted, I am sure, by the universal sympathy of the people there.

On Thursday, September 9th, in the morning, in Christ Church, Duanesburg, I preached and confirmed six persons and celebrated the Holy Communion; and in the evening in Trinity Church, Rensselaer-ville, I preached and confirmed four persons.

September 10th, in the morning, in Christ Church, Greenville, I preached, celebrated the Holy Communion and confirmed three persons; and in the afternoon in St. Paul's Church, Oak Hill, I preached and con-firmed three persons.

Sunday, September 11th, in the morning, in St. Luke's Church, Cats-kill, I preached, confirmed nineteen persons and celebrated the Holy Communion.

On Thursday, September 15th, in the morning, in St. Luke's Church, Mechanicville, I preached, celebrated the Holy Communion, and con-firmed ten persons and one in private, making eleven persons; and in the afternoon, in St. John's Church, Stillwater, I preached and confirmed two persons.

On Friday the 16th, in the morning, in St. Stephen's Church, Schuylerville, I preached, celebrated the Holy Communion and confirmed two persons; and in the afternoon, in St. Paul's Church, Greenwich, I preached and confirmed thirteen persons.

Sunday the 18th, in the morning, I preached and celebrated the Holy Communion in the old Church at Monticello or Richfield.` It was an interesting service, gathering a goodly number of people from the neighbourhood, and showing a certain amount at any rate of promise of work, if sufficient effort can be put forth to make it energetic and real. The building has been admirably restored, its old lines and characteristics being kept, but the whole thing put in beautiful order, clean and fresh, by the generous interest of Mr. Tailer of New York.

In the afternoon, in the Chapel at Cullen, an extremely pretty and Churchly building erected by Mr. D. J. Crain as a memorial to his father and mother, I preached and baptized a little child. Here, too, the congregation was large, and if, as I greatly hope, we may be able to make these two points a mission station by themselves, I think that good results will come from it. At any rate it was a comfort, both to "dig again the wells which our fathers" had made, and to open a new well, which I hope will be of water springing forth to everlasting life.

In the afternoon, in St. John's Church, Richfield Springs, I preached and confirmed forty-two persons, with two in private, making forty-four.

On Monday the 19th, in the morning, in Christ Church, West Burlington, I preached, celebrated the Holy Communion and confirmed two persons.

On the 20th, in the evening, I preached and confirmed eleven persons in the little chapel at Schroon. I am thankful to hope that the mission work here may be resumed, under circumstances of considerable promise, and after long discontinuance, much against my will.

On the 21st, and for the two following days, I was in Retreat under the direction of the Right Reverend the Lord Bishop of Nassau, for whose wise and holy teachings, the seventy Clergy who were there with me are very grateful to God, as we are for the peace and refreshment of the quiet days.

On the 25th I organized the Mission of the Good Shepherd at Cullen, appointing as Warden, Mr. Dunham Jones Crain; as Treasurer, Mr. Arthur Northrup, and as Clerk, Mr. Jefferson Lyman.

On Wednesday the 27th, in the evening, in St. Paul's Church, Salem, I preached and confirmed five persons; and on the morning of the 28th, in Hoosick Falls, I confirmed one person in private.

The Bishop of Springfield was kind enough to confirm, at Sabbath-day Point, five persons prepared and presented by his old friend and mine, Mr. Chamberlain, the Lay Reader, whose holy life and earnest work are perennial in their fruitage as they must be perpetual in

8

Of the fourteen hundred and seventy confirmed this year, two hundred and forty-one were confirmed by the Bishop of Delaware; five by the Bishop of Springfield; and nine by the Bishop of Missouri. All the Parishes but four have been visited, two of which were vacant and in the others the appointment was postponed at the clergyman's request; and all the Missions except six, one of which was also given up at the request of the Missionary. And as I shall be compelled to make my visitation this year of the Foreign Chapels I give notice to the clergy that I shall not attempt any regular or full visitation of the Diocese next year; which is the less necessary because of the unusual fulness of the visits during the year past. I shall of course expect to make and keep some appointments, especially in the places where no confirmations have been reported.

On Friday, September 30, I gave the Holy Communion to my dear brother, Canon Temple, which was truly his viaticum.

October 3d, acting for the Presiding Bishop, as Vice-President of the Board of Managers, I laid the corner stone of the new Missions House in New York; a grand step forward for the convenient dispatch of the necessary business of the Board; a noble evidence to the growth and strength of the Missionary spirit; and a perpetual and permanent witness, in the great commercial and the great Church centre of this country, to the fact that this Church is set for the advancement and establishment of the Kingdom of God in the world.

October 4th, in the morning, I presided at an adjourned meeting of the Trustees of the General Theological Seminary in New York. In the afternoon I went to Baltimore, where three full weeks of hard and incessant work were lightened by the pleasure of most congenial companionship, most loving hospitality and a home life of greatest comfort and refreshment; by constant intercourse with dear and honoured brethren in the Episcopate, and by the successful accomplishment of important measures which have occupied my mind and heart and time for many years. There are certain "class" sentiments which can scarcely be realized outside of those whom they affect. And I can truly say that the coming together of our nearly seventy Bishops has in it an element of strength and refreshing, and our breaking up after weeks of close and constant and most affectionate communion, a sense of loss and loneliness which nothing else in life contains. Besides the constant work of the House of Bishops, I spoke in Baltimore four times, on Parochial Missions, on Church Unity, for the increase of the restoration fund of the Lord Bishop of Newfoundland, and for our General Missions; preached once in St. Luke's Church, where I also celebrated the Holy Communion, and addressed a meeting of women held under Miss Smiley's direction, to press the work of the Society for the Home Study of Holy Scripture and Church History, with especial reference to the training of mothers to teach their children.

And on the last Sunday in the Session, I preached in the morning in the venerable old Christ Church in Philadelphia, the last of a course of four sermons, on Prayer Book Revision; and addressed the Trustees, Faculty and students of the Philadelphia Divinity School at a most stirring service in St. James' Church, in the evening.

I ask the Clergy very specially to notice another matter of importance. The Woman's Diocesan League, as they will remember, was organized as its name implies, with the intention of including, in its membership, its work and its gifts, all the Parishes of the Diocese. While it never realized its aim in this particular, although it more than realized it in other results, there were for some years many branch leagues in various Parishes, and always individual members connected with it from many Parishes where there was no formal organization of a chapter. As the years have gone on these parochial branches have fallen gradually off, until I believe there is no one left except in Grace Church, Albany. With the payment of the debt on the Cathedral, it might be supposed by many that the need for the League had passed away, but the central Cathedral chapter of the League takes no such view and has no intention of disbanding. The only question that it considers and asks me to put before the Diocese is, whether it shall change its name from the Woman's Diocesan to the Woman's Cathedral League. It must not belie its name. It can only be Diocesan if the Parishes of the Diocese desire to make it a part of the Diocesan machinery.

I have no wish to push the matter upon the Clergy or the people, though I am bound to say that in my judgment it has in it great possibilities of doing for the Diocese what the Woman's Auxiliary is doing for the Church at large. It was founded distinctly and in terms to aid the Bishop in Diocesan works and interests. It recognized the fact that every Bishop must know better than any one else where there is need for help in the Institutions, Parishes or Missions of the Diocese. Its fundamental principle is that it should be an agency extending through the Diocese, before which the Bishop could put, from time to time, efforts and interests to be aided in due proportion, according to its constitution and by-laws.

I leave this matter with the Clergy and with the women of their Parishes to say whether it shall go on as it was originally proposed or not. I must ask them to act upon it promptly and as soon as the Convention adjourns, for our annual meeting is in February, and we must be governed in the course which will be taken then by the replies which I shall receive.

On the 31st of October I lighted the Hallowe'en fire on the hearth at St. Agnes' School, with the kindling at the same time of twenty-five years of memory, bringing out into clear light the old traditions of the house.

I am a little surprised, full as the School is and strongly as it has grown in its hold on the public confidence, to find that this year there are comparatively few of the children from our own Diocese, and I think the Clergy ought to feel, and the people too, that this is the true place in which our own children of the Diocese should be trained. I can answer for it that there is no better place, and for the best future interests of the Church in this Diocese, nothing is more important than the training up of a body of Christian women with the best intellectual advantages, and in the atmosphere and tone of the Church.

On the 6th of November, acting for me most kindly and most acceptably to the congregation, the Bishop of Missouri confirmed nine persons in Christ Church, Gilbertsville.

On the 10th of November I presided at a meeting of the Board of Managers in New York, and on the 11th I was present at the quarterly meeting of our branch of the Woman's Auxiliary in Christ Church, Cooperstown. We had the great pleasure and stimulus of addresses from the Bishops of Montana, Utah and Nevada, and Wyoming and Idaho, and a goodly gathering of women; but I am sorry to find that there are still less than one-third of our Parishes which have in them branches of the Auxiliary. It is a great mistake; this organisation is in the American Church to stay and grow, and the Parish that is without it is behind the age. It is quite as important for the Parishes themselves to have the stir of this interest in their own life as it is for the Board of Missions to have a general representation of its work in this way.

I beg that the Parishes will not be deterred from making the organization because they are small. The arrangement wisely made by the central board of a purchasing committee, and the division of labour, so that many Parishes together can make up a single box, make it possible for every smallest place do a valuable part of the work. I trust that this coming year will show a large increase of parochial branches.

I think I ought to inform the Clergy that the number of Churches and Sunday-Schools contributing to the Child's Hospital this year is smaller than it has been for a good while. I am sure that this is not intentional, and I beg to assure them that it is very important to us, with our enlarged building and the increased number of children, that offerings should come to us from every Parish in the Diocese. The benefits of the Hospital, as it is well understood, are free to all, come from where they may, and without any money if there is no money to be paid; and as it is unlimited in its benefactions. I think there should be no limitation about its support.

The summary of my acts is as follows:

Confirmations, 1470; * Celebrations of Holy Communion, 40; * Sermons, 104; Addresses, 7; Clergy dismissed, 10; Died, 5; Received, 10; Added by Ordination, 2; Present number of Clergy: Bishop, 1; Priests, 123; Deacons, 5; Total, 129. Priests ordained, 9; Deacons ordained, 1; Total, 10. Postulants admitted, 4; Total Postulants, 11. Candidates for Deacon's order admitted, 7; Total Candidates for Deacon's order, 21; Candidates for Priest's order admitted, 5; Total Candidates for Priest's order, 14; Total Candidates for Holy Orders, 22. Lay-Readers licensed, 19; Total Lay-Readers, 19. Sisters admitted, 1. Missions organized, 1; Churches consecrated, 2; Corner-Stones laid, 1; Benedictions, 4. * Baptisms: Infants, 1; * Marriages, 3; * Burials, 5. Notices of deposition, 12.

I have attended the regular meetings of the Board of Missions; the Cathedral Chapter; the Trustees of the Corning Foundation; the Managers of the Child's Hospital; and of St. Margaret's House; the Trustees of the Orphan House of the Holy Saviour; the Diocesan Branch of the Woman's Auxiliary; the Woman's Diocesan League; the Trustees of the various Diocesan Funds; the Bible and Prayer Book Society; and two of the four Archdeaconries. I have also attended the Sessions of the General Convention at Baltimore; meetings of the Board of Managers of the Missionary Society; of the Board of Regents of the Church University; of the Trustees of the General Theological Seminary; of the Commission on the Standard Prayer Book; of the Committee on the Hymnal; of the Committee (of the House of Bishops) on the Lectionary; of the Committee on Missionary Services in Connection with the Meeting of the General Convention; and the Society for the Home Study of Holy Scripture.

ORDINATIONS.

November 18, 1891. The Rev. Eugene Griggs, to the Priesthood, in the Cathedral.

December 17, 1891. William Francis Parsons, to the Diaconate, in the Cathedral.

December 17, 1891. The Rev. James Frederic Olmsted, to the Priesthood, in the Cathedral.

December 17, 1891. The Rev. George Brinckerhoff Richards, to the Priesthood, in the Cathedral.

December 17, 1891. The Rev. Freeborn Garrettson Jewett, to the Priesthood, in the Cathedral.

March 10, 1892. The Rev. Hamilton Cady, to the Priesthood, in the Chapel of the General Theological Seminary.

---

* Not included in the Cathedral report.

May 8, 1892. William Whitney Newell, to the Diaconate, in St. Luke's Church, Paris, France, by the Bishop of New York (acting for me).

June 12, 1892. The Rev. George Lynde Richardson, to the Priesthood, in the Cathedral.

June 12, 1892. The Rev. William Francis Parsons, to the Priesthood, in the Cathedral.

June 12, 1892. The Rev. Frank Sladen Greenhalgh, to the Priesthood, in the Cathedral at Ottawa by the Bishop of Ontario (acting for me).

June 13, 1892. The Rev. Harry Elmer Gilchrist, to the Priesthood, in the Cathedral.

Clergymen Received from Other Dioceses.

1891.

December 8. The Rev. John W. Gill, from the Diocese of Long Island.

1892.

January 4. The Rev. Thomas Boone, from the Diocese of Georgia.

January 26. The Rev. James R. L. Nisbett, from the Diocese of Long Island.

January 26. The Rev. Creighton Spencer, from the Diocese of New York.

March 6. The Rev. Hamilton Cady, from the Diocese of New York.

March 24. The Rev. Harry Cresser, from the Diocese of Central New York.

March 25. The Rev. W. H. Dean, from the Diocese of Central New York.

March 26. The Rev. Frank Sladen Greenhalgh, from the Diocese of Ontario.

April 11. The Rev. John H. Molineux, from the Diocese of Springfield.

April 11. The Rev. Percy St. Michael Podmore, from the Diocese of Springfield.

May 23. The Rev. Elmer R. Earle, from the Diocese of Central New York.

June 29. The Rev. Alfred L. Fortin, from the Diocese of Rupert's Land.

July 12. The Rev. David Jenkins, from the Diocese of Ontario.

August 3. The Rev. Edward C. Hoskins, from the Diocese of New York.

September 24. The Rev. Earnest W. Dustan, from the Diocese of New York.

October 11. The Rev. Henry R. Freeman, from the Diocese of Long Island.

November 14. The Rev. John E. Bold, from the Diocese of Pittsburgh.

CLERGYMEN DISMISSED TO OTHER DIOCESES.

1891.

November 18. The Rev. James Otis Lincoln, to the Diocese of West Missouri.

November 18. The Rev. Wm. D. Martin, to the Diocese of Alabama.

November 18. The Rev. M. O. Smith, to the Diocese of Tennessee.

November 18. The Rev. F. N. Skinner, to the Diocese of East Carolina.

November 18. The Rev. A. T. De Learsy, to the Diocese of Ohio.

November 18. The Rev. F. B. Reazor, to the Diocese of Newark.

November 24. The Rev. Phineas Duryea, to the Diocese of South Carolina.

December 12. The Rev. William R. Webb, to the Diocese of Maryland.

December 18. The Rev. Scott B. Rathbun, to the Diocese of North Carolina.

December 31. The Rev. R. E. W. Cosens, to the Diocese of Southern Ohio.

1892.

January 19. The Rev. J. F. Esch, to the Diocese of Central New York.

April 27. The Rev. John G. Urling, to the Diocese of Kentucky.

May 17. The Rev. W. H. Dean, to the Diocese of Southern Ohio.

June 17. The Rev. Asa Sprague Ashley, to the Diocese of Connecticut.

July 7. The Rev. C. W. Boyd, to the Diocese of Pennsylvania.

July 11. The Rev. Nassau W. Stephens, to the Diocese of Pittsburgh.

July 15. The Rev. Thomas Dickinson, to the Diocese of Western Michigan.

July 22. The Rev. W. D. U. Shearman, to the Diocese of California.

September 21. The Rev. Fred. S. Griffin, to the Diocese of Long Island.

October 31. The Rev. Isaac Peck, to the Diocese of Long Island.

CANDIDATES FOR PRIEST'S ORDER.

May 19, 1888. Mr. John C. Woodworth.

October 10, 1890. Mr. Marvin Hill Dana.

October 27, 1890. Mr. Thurston Walker Challen.

November 17, 1890. Mr. Edward T. Carroll.

January 12, 1891. Mr. Frank N. Bouck.

October 1, 1891. Mr. Harry Sherman Longley.

October 18, 1891. Mr. Keble Dean.
November 6, 1891. Mr. George William Farrar.
November 6, 1891. Mr. Frederic Henry Farrar.
January 28, 1892. Mr. Frederick St. George McLean.
February 11, 1892. Mr. William Anderson Stirling.
September 29, 1892. Mr. Alexander Haswell Grant, Jr.
September 29, 1892. Mr. Lewis Gouverneur Morris.
September 29, 1892. Mr. Robert Perine.

CANDIDATES FOR DEACON'S ORDER.

April 26, 1883. Mr. Gulian V. P. Lansing.
October 3, 1887. Mr. George K. Rhames.
October 3, 1887. Mr. Charles H. Moore.
December 1, 1887. Mr. John C. Woodworth.
November 19, 1888. Mr. Keble Dean.
September 15, 1890. Mr. William Anderson Stirling.
September 15, 1890. Mr. Marvin Hill Dana.
September 16, 1890. Mr. John Mills Gilbert.
November 8, 1890. Mr. Frank N. Bouck.
November 8, 1890. Mr. Edward T. Carroll.
March 9, 1891. Mr. Harry Sherman Longley.
April 13, 1891. Mr. Gouverneur Frank Mosher.
October 5, 1891. Mr. George William Farrar.
October 5, 1891. Mr. Frederic Henry Farrar.
November 18, 1891. Mr. Robert Perine.
November 18, 1891. Mr. Frederick St. George McLean.
March 5, 1892. Mr. Lewis Gouverneur Morris.
March 5, 1892. Mr. Charles A. Howells.
June 6, 1892. Mr. John S. Warren.
September 19, 1892. Mr. Alexander Haswell Grant, Jr.
November 14, 1892. Mr. Homer B. Williams.

POSTULANTS.

May 12, 1885. Isaac Borts, M. D.
March 22, 1887. Charles Hegamin, Jr.
March 3, 1888. E. Townsend Jones, M. D.
May 1, 1889. George Henry Chase.
May 27, 1889. William Croswell Doane Willson.
July 1, 1891. William Robert Golden.
September 29, 1891. Hamilton Douglass Bentley MacNeil.
July 1, 1892. Albert L. Longley.
September 29, 1892. Edmund Norman Curry.
October 1, 1892. James Lewis Lasher.
November 8, 1892. Homer B. Williams.

CORNER-STONES LAID.

June 23,1892. Christ Church,Deposit. (By the Bishop of Delaware.)

CHURCHES CONSECRATED.

December 31, 1891. The Church of the Holy Spirit, Schenevus.
April 29, 1892. All Saints' Church, Round Lake.

BENEDICTIONS.

December 24, 1891. The East Window and Mosaics in the Sanctuary and Choir of the Cathedral.
January 26, 1892. The new Altar in St. Paul's Church, Troy.
May 27, 1892. The new Lectern in St. Mark's Church, Malone.
June 29, 1892. Various additions to St. Luke's Church, Cambridge. (By the Bishop of Delaware.)

MISSIONS ORGANIZED.

November 19, 1891. The Mission of.

LAY-READERS LICENSED.

1891.

December 8. Jay Zorn, for the Diocese.
December 23. George Maxwell, St. Ann's Church, Amsterdam.

1892.

January 6. Herbert Keble Betts, All Saints' Church, Hoosac.
March 8. Harry S. Longley, All Saints' Church, Hoosac.
April 11. Charles A. Howells, for West Burlington and Edmeston.
April 12. Edmund Norman Curry, St. Barnabas' Church,Troy.
April 23. William H. Philips, for Loon Lake, Franklin county.
May 21. Gouverneur F. Mosher, for the Diocese.
May 21. Daniel G. Thomas, for Norfolk and Norwood.
July 15. Lewis G. Morris, St. James' Church, Oneonta.
July 28. John S. Warren, Trinity Church, Granville.
July 28. Arthur Clapton, St. Paul's Church, Albany.
July 28. Herbert I. Hamilton, St. Paul's Church, Albany.
August 3. Willard D. Johnson, Zion Church, Morris.
August 15. Alexander H. Grant, Jr., St. Peter's Church, Hobart.
August 26. David Guy, Christ Church, Schenectady.
August 26. Sidney G. Ashmore, Christ Church, Schenectady.
October 5. Frederick Craige, St. Luke's Church, Catskill.
November 8. Robert Perine, for the Diocese.

9

NOTICES OF CLERGY DEPOSED.

1891.

December 23.   Francis E. Shober, Priest, by the Bishop of New York.

1892.

January 17. James Field Spalding, D. D., Priest, by the Bishop of Massachusetts.

January 25.   Edward Rainsford, by the Bishop of New Jersey.

March 2.   Edward John Peeke Bell Williams, Priest, by the Bishop of Missouri.

March 7.   D. Wilson Taylor, Deacon, by the Bishop of Virginia.

March 21.   Rene Vilatte, Priest, by the Bishop of Fond du Lac.

April 8.   James Hattrick Lee, Priest, by the Bishop of Western New York.

May 10.   Samuel Earp, Ph. D., Priest, by the Bishop of Michigan.

June 1.   F. S. DeMattos, Priest, by the Bishop of Colorado.

June 1.   John Harrington, Deacon, by the Bishop of Colorado.

July 5.   W. Leggett Kolb, Priest, by the Bishop of Pennsylvania.

October 2.   George Clement King, Deacon, by the Bishop of New York.

APPENDIX TO THE BISHOP'S ADDRESS.

THE PAYMENT OF THE CATHEDRAL DEBT.

ACTION OF THE CATHEDRAL CHAPTER.

The following resolutions, moved by the Dean of the Cathedral, were unanimously adopted by the Cathedral Chapter, at a special meeting held on March 12, 1892 :

The Chapter of All Saints Cathedral, having heard the statement made by the Bishop of the fact that he had been enabled to secure the necessary amount of money to pay off the entire indebtedness which rests upon the Cathedral, now desire to put on record, first of all, their devout thankfulness to God for this great gift.

They ask the Bishop, further, to express to the generous friend who has made possible this result, their appreciation of the noble offer which contained in it even a larger outcome than he intended.

They desire to express to the women of the Diocesan League their cordial recognition of the patience and faithfulness with which they have worked on toward the diminution of the debt and the payment of the interest ; and they ask the Bishop, also, in communicating this good news to the Congregation of the Cathedral, to press upon them their responsibility, out of a sense of their gratitude, for the generous maintenance of the services in the Cathedral ; whose enjoyment comes, of course, first of all to them, and for which they are so largely indebted to the generous gifts of Churchmen outside of the immediate Congregation; and the Chapter pledge themselves meanwhile, as a token of their own gratitude, to every earnest endeavour to advance the best interests of the Cathedral in all spiritual and material ways.

For the Bishop's personal share in this glad consummation of so many hopes and prayers, the members of the Chapter feel that no words that they can utter are adequate. Unwavering faith and tireless labour have borne rich fruit. The example of how work may be done for God is among the most inspiring of the lessons which the Cathedral shall ever teach to those who have watched its growth year by year, under the guidance of him to whom, under God, it owes its signal success, and its abundant promise for the future.

They also resolve to carve the central doorway of the north transept, as a thank-offering for mercies vouchsafed and a memorial of benefactors, on the day when the Cathedral is freed from debt, March 15, A. D., 1892.

And they resolve that the Dean be requested to arrange for a service of Offering and Commemoration on such Sunday near the 15th of March as he and the Bishop may appoint.

Attest: T. B. FULCHER,
Secretary.

THE PASTORAL LETTER TO THE CLERGY.

ALBANY, *March* 15, 1892.

MY DEAR AND REVEREND BRETHREN:

You have been for so many years sharers in my anxieties and efforts in regard to the building of the Cathedral Church, and it is so essentially part and parcel of our Diocesan work, that I must put you in possession of the great joy and relief that have come to me, in the fact that on this day, March 15th, I am able to thank God that the whole debt which had been resting upon the property is provided for, and before the 1st of July will be paid.

Under God, this is due to the kindness and generosity of a dear friend, who proposed to me that if before this date two-thirds of the debt could be secured he would himself pay the one-third; and this liberal offer of more than $13,000, God has used as the seed and stimulus from which has resulted the entire payment of the debt.

The gracious and generous response which has come to me, not only in the way of lavish giving, but still more in the way of loving, personal expression and of interest in the Cathedral, has made the task of this last asking, pleasure instead of pain. From various quarters, quite as much outside as inside the Diocese, in sums ranging from $5,000 to $1, the whole amount has been secured within less than the three weeks; and as I look back upon the years of anxiety and toil, in which the women of the Diocesan League have been such patient and noble helpers, and try to realize that all our care and worry have been relieved in so short a time; I am more than ready to assent to what the Dean of the Cathedral said in answer to the question, "Where did the money come from?" "It came from Heaven."

I am sending this to you, asking that on the fourth Sunday in Lent, which is Refreshment Sunday, when I shall offer on the Cathedral Altar the moneys that shall have been paid in, you will make this gracious fact known to your people; and that just before the final Benediction in the Morning Service you will say "the Memorial of Benefactors;" and will remember, at the Celebration of the Holy Communion on that day, the Cathedral and its benefactors, not forgetting the Bishop and the Diocese and all its Clergy and People.

Believe me always
Most faithfully your brother and friend,
WM. CROSWELL DOANE.

THE SERVICE.

The Morning Prayer on Sunday was said as usual, followed by the hymn "O God, our help in ages past."

After the Bishop's Address the choir sang the Te Deum, using Martin's Service in D.

The Introit was the Hymn "Ancient of Days," the words of which were written by the Bishop for the bicentennial service in Albany, and the music by Dr. Jeffery, the organist of the Cathedral. The third verse of the Hymn was changed for better application to this occasion to read :

> " O Holy Jesus, Giver of salvation,
>   Who didst within the Temple's porch appear
> Upon its holy feast of dedication,
>   Own this Thy Temple, grant Thy Presence here."

The Office of the Holy Communion.

For the Introit, the Hymn " Ancient of Days."

At the Offering of the Alms :

O God, Who didst fill with the glory of Thy Presence the Temple which Thy servants built of old unto Thee, and Whose blessed Son did approve and honour, by His bodily presence at the Feast of Dedication, the religious services which hallow the houses in which Thy Name is set up as a Memorial forever ; we pray Thee to accept the offering, which all unworthily, we bring to Thee this day, by which this Holy House is freed from all encumbrance, and wholly made Thine own. And because holiness becometh Thine house forever, consecrate us, we pray Thee, as holy temples to Thyself. Grant that Thy dear Son may be with those that are gathered together here in His Name, and may dwell in their hearts by faith ; and so possess our souls by the grace of Thy Holy Spirit, that nothing which defileth may enter into us ; but that being cleansed from all worldly and carnal affections, we may ever be devoutly given to serve Thee in good works, through Jesus Christ our Lord and Saviour. Amen.

Instead of Gloria in Excelsis :

> " Visit, Lord, the earthly temple
>   Where Thy Presence we implore ;
> Here receive the rising incense
>   From the hearts that Thee adore ;
> Sprinkle here Thy Benedictions,
>   Dews of healing evermore.
> Mete Thou here the promised measure,
>   Running o'er and closely prest
> Foretaste of the eternal pleasure
>   By the saints in light possest ;
> There our heart is, there our treasure,
>   Paradise and Home and Rest. *Amen.*"

Before the final Benediction :

The Memorial of Benefactors.

Blessed be Thy Name, O Lord our God, that it hath pleased Thee to put it into the hearts of Thy servants to free our Cathedral Church from all indebtedness, and to make it only and altogether Thine own.

Bless, we humbly beseech Thee, all those by whose pains, care and cost this work is happily completed. Bless their families and their substance ; remember them concerning this kindness that they have showed for the House of their God : bless Thy servant the Bishop, and all the Priests and Deacons who minister for Thee in this Diocese, and the Congregations committed to their charge ; and grant that all who shall enjoy the blessing of this Cathedral Church may use it right faithfully, to the Glory of Thy Name ; through Jesus Christ our Lord. Amen.

AND THESE TWO COLLECTS.

Cleanse Thou us, O Good Lord, and so shall we be cleansed : and grant that as Thy Blessed Son was presented in the Temple in Substance of our Flesh, so with pure and clean hearts we may ever present ourselves before Thee, to offer up spiritual Sacrifices to the honour of Thy great Name, through the same Jesus Christ our Lord. Amen.

O God, Whom heaven and earth cannot contain, who yet humblest Thyself to make a habitation here among men, where we may continually call upon Thy Name; visit, we beseech Thee, this place with Thy loving kindness, and cleanse it by Thy grace, that all who shall call upon Thee herein may feel Thy mercy and find Thy protection, through Jesus Christ our Lord. Amen.

THE REV. ROBERT WASHBON.

At the annual business meeting of the wardens and vestrymen of Trinity Church, Rensselaerville, Nathaniel Teed was elected treasurer; Frank Rice, collector; Charles B. Cross, clerk; John L. Rice, superintendent of Church grounds and cemetery; Dewey Bell, superintendent of rectory and grounds. The following resolutions were also adopted:

Inasmuch as it hath pleased Almighty God in His wise providence to remove from this world the soul of our deceased rector. Therefore, be it

Resolved, That while we bow in humble submission to the divine will, we do express our deep sense of the loss sustained by the Church and this whole community in the death of Rev. Robert Washbon.

Resolved, That we do recognize in the late Rev. Mr. Washbon, in every best quality, a man of mark in the Church of God.

For half a century he has served as priest at the altar of the Church here, of unusual ability and learning he has adorned it as a preacher and brought strength and confidence to its officers and communicants. He has lived in the most important historic period of the American Church, has mingled with its great men now fast disappearing, and was on familiar terms with many of its leading minds now living. Not inconsistently with his great breadth of view, he was a man of singular devotion to duty and marked spirituality of life. In parochial life — as a pastor and priest over the people of God, as a witness for Christ and a dispenser of the means of grace vouchsafed by the divine spirit — he was always equal to the Church's best standard of service.

In domestic and social life, as a husband and father and friend and as a man among men, he was beloved and respected by all classes, he "adorned the doctrine of Christ in all things," and was ever on the side of truth, integrity and purity, bringing knowledge to the ignorant, rebuke to the erring and dishonest, wise counsel to the perplexed and doubtful, help to the destitute, and conviction and strength to the strong.

His last few years had been encumbered with failing health and a gradual weakening of his natural powers, and unwillingly he gave up active

retirement. During this time he suffered much, but all was borne with dignity and patient gentleness.

"In the communion of the Catholic Church; in the confidence of a certain faith; in the comfort of a reasonable, religious and holy faith; in favor with God and in perfect charity with men," he has been gathered unto the fathers. May he rest in the assurance of a joyful resurrection.

Resolved, That a copy of these memorial resolutions be entered upon the minutes of the society and a copy with the sympathy of the Church be sent to his son.

THE REV. CANON TEMPLE.

God in His wise providence having called to his rest the Rev. Richard Temple, honorary canon of the Cathedral of All Saints, we, the Dean and chapter of the Cathedral, desire to put on record our sense of sorrow in the loss which we have suffered and of sympathy with the wife and kindred of the deceased.

As a priest Canon Temple has done long and faithful service for the Church. To a fine scholarship and enthusiasm were added a lofty purity of life and a courtesy of manner which assured success in the highest sense to all his work for God. During the later years of his life, when increasing infirmity made more active service impossible, Canon Temple still filled a place of usefulness in the Cathedral Church, which will sorely miss his presence in the years to come. New meanings were revealed in Holy Scriptures, when he read the lessons in the public worship of the Cathedral, by the deep sincerity of utterance which spake whereof it knew, and many are the testimonies which have come to us of blessing received through this simplest yet most powerful preaching of the Word.

We extend most hearty sympathy to the family now sorely afflicted. Comfort can alone be found in the assurance that for such a one, ripe in all graces of character and strong in faith, "to depart and be with Christ is far better."

WILFORD L. ROBBINS,
Dean.

THOMAS B. FULCHER,
Secretary.

THE HON. WALTER A. WOOD.

It is not too much to say that the great circle of the world to-day lies under the shadow of sorrow which more or less touches all hearts with a sense of sympathy. The deaths of a Royal duke and a Roman cardinal in England and of a distinguished Judge in our own State have fallen simultaneously, and at the same time comes the news, which affects smaller numbers, but which, nevertheless, will be felt far and wide and mourned very truly and deeply, of the death of Walter A. Wood.

He was a natural nobleman in all that makes nobility and manhood; he was a prince in the Church if not of it, by the possession of the gifts and graces which princes ought to have; he was a man imbued with the essential elements of justice, according to that summing up of the divine requirements, "to do justly, to love mercy, to walk humbly with God."

It is hard to hold the pen back when it is writing of so dear a friend; a gentleman so high bred in his courtesy; a benefactor of his kind; a public servant faithful to every trust; a private citizen who made, adorned and blessed the village in which he lived, crowning its busy streets with the hum of honorable and successful industry, as his beautiful home crowned it with the grace of cordial hospitality, with the dignity of honours won the wide world over in competitions of skill, with the charm of domestic happiness, with the blessed beauty of a consistent Christian life.

Mr. Wood's life, as the world knows it, has been full of courage and enterprise. The labour of constant devotion to business was brightened to him not with the mere motive of money-making, which, nevertheless, it attained, but with the perpetual interest of an inventiveness that was never restless or unpractical, and an ambition for improvement which made each success attained the step toward something better. In the accumulation of his fortune, men were not only bettered by his generous use of money, but the men who helped him make it were advancing their own prosperity as well. The honours that were showered upon him in medals and decorations. the constant material improvement in the houses and families of his workmen, and the increased opportunities for doing good, were the real satisfactions of his success. No labour troubles ever distracted the kindly relations which were close and personal between workman and employer, in the great works of which he was head and heart and often labouring hand.

An intense American, he was to me the type of the only nobility that we know in America, which wins and wears the crown of labour; and the grace of his presence, his courtly carriage, his courtesy and dignity, made him the peer of princes everywhere; while the good heart that was in him held him so erect and strong in courage and in character that, at three score years and sixteen, he bore no trace or token of old age.

There are deep places in which this grief gathers itself, as water in the pools of a stream, into whose profound sorrow one may look, but of which one may not speak; but outside of his own home there is a shadow in many a house in his own village and in Washington, in Albany and in Troy, wherever he was known, under which as we walk, we know that life will be lonelier and poorer for the taking out of it of a noble, generous, gracious friend.

For twenty-three years he has been to me the truest, the closest and the kindest of friends. I count it among the privileges of my episcopate to have known him and to have loved him, and his name goes now with the dear names of other men who were his friends as they were mine, upon the tablets of quick and constant remembrance, for whom I thank God, and for whom I pray God, that "He will show them mercy in that day." WILLIAM CROSWELL DOANE.

MR. GEORGE ST. JOHN.

The death of Mr. George St. John takes out of the diocese of Albany one of its noblest and truest laymen, and from me, one of my dearest and best friends. Our relations to each other were a sort of "love at first sight," and for almost a quarter of a century it has strengthened and deepened, mutually, I think ; on my part I know ; so that I mourn for him as among those closest to him.

He was in many respects an ideal man. Endowed by nature with very gracious gifts of mind and heart and body, they had been developed by a discipline of years, a very tribulation, in the real meaning of the word, which had separated the chaff and left the pure golden grain of a fine and beautiful character, and over all was the consecration of the grace of God. Patient, brave, gentle, courteous, "given to hospitality," simple as "the pure in heart" are, lavish in affection, in service, in his gifts ; tender, with the very freshest sympathies ; true, with a rare devotion to the Church, to his home duties, and to his friends ; his heart, that lay long under darkest shadow, never lost its sunniness to men, nor its trust in God. He was the kind of Christian gentleman who recalls and revives the ideal of true chivalry ; and I am sure that no purer soul ever passed from its earthly tabernacle into the blessed rest of the faithful in Paradise, more justly and truly mourned by all who ever came within the circle of his influence, which charmed all alike, men and women and children, servants and dependents, and even beasts with their quick instinct to detect true from false.

May God rest him and refresh him with light and peace, and reward him when He cometh in "His kingdom," with the joy of his Lord.

WILLIAM CROSWELL DOANE.

The following resolutions were passed by the wardens and vestrymen of Christ Church, Walton, at a meeting held April 13, 1892 :

WHEREAS, It has pleased Almighty God in His wise Providence to take from us our esteemed brother and junior warden, George St. John, who during so many years past has identified himself with, and been a strong support to our Church and parish, now therefore, be it

Resolved, That we desire to place upon record our deep feeling of respect and love for his life, character and works, both as vestryman, junior warden and communicant of the Church. That we tender to his family our most sincere sympathy for them in their bereavement, and

· WHEREAS, By his last will and testament he has emphasized most strongly his earnest affection for our parish, in his endowment gift of twenty thousand ($20,000) dollars, be it further

Resolved, That while accepting the gift, with sincere gratitude to Almighty God, and to the generous giver of the same, we desire to place upon record our earnest hope that his noble example may prove an incentive to every member of the parish to contribute faithfully to the support of this Church, to the honour and glory of our Heavenly Father. That the Clerk of the Vestry is directed to send a copy of these resolutions to the family of the deceased, and for publication.

MR. CHARLES HAMILTON BEACH.

At a meeting of the rector, warden and vestrymen of Zion Church, Sandy Hill, N. Y., held December 21, 1891, the following preamble and resolutions were adopted :

WHEREAS, Mr. Charles Hamilton Beach, late senior warden of this Parish, departed this life on the 18th inst, the rector, warden and vestrymen of Zion Church desire to place on record their high estimate of his character and untiring labours in behalf of the Church.

His name appears on the second page of the Parish Record, dated March 29, 1842, as that of a newly elected vestryman. This office he held until 1848, and again from 1856 to 1859, inclusive. He was junior warden from 1860 to 1883, and senior warden from 1883 until his death.

As delegate to the Diocesan Convention of 1868, he took part in the separation of the Diocese of Albany from that of New York, and went as delegate to many succeeding conventions of this Diocese.

One of those to whose zeal and perseverance the building and consecration of our Parish Church are due. He supervised the erection of the belfry, placing the cross thereon with his own hands, and set the stone corbels, which are largely his own work, on the interior of the walls.

A mere statement, however, of offices held by one who has been prominent in the history of this Parish from its earliest days, leaves untold his many self-sacrifices made in the service of Christ and His Church. He shrank from no work in their behalf, however rough and arduous.

As a courteous Christian gentleman, he won the respect of the entire community in which he lived.

Therefore be it

Resolved, I. That we, the rector, warden and vestrymen of Zion Church, express to the family of the late senior warden our sympathy with them in their sorrow.

II. That copies of this preamble and resolutions be sent to the local newspapers, the bereaved family and the Bishop of Albany.

CHAS. A. YOUNG,
Clerk pro tem.

MR. MONTGOMERY H. THROOP.

It was something more than its suddenness, which startled and shocked Albanians yesterday, when the news of Montgomery H. Throop's death was passed from mouth to mouth. It was a sense of loss; the recognition of the fact that a man was gone out of our common city life, whose personality had made itself felt in positive and prominent ways. Identified, by residence, with Albany for nearly a score of years, it was an identification with all its best interests. And few men withdrawn by physical infirmity from the concerns and contests of public life, have mingled as much as Mr. Throop did, with the men and the movements of the city and the time.

His professional labours were confined necessarily to matters of counsel and of the codifying of laws. But he was a lover of his profession, true to its best traditions, learned in the law, and a just-minded man like the counsellor of Arimathea.

Neither his studies nor his learning were limited by legal lines. His mind was beautifully trained and beautifully furnished. A great lover of books and an incessant reader, he had the pure literary tastes and instincts of the true scholar. And with that quickening of the inner senses, by which God compensates men for the dulling of the outer senses, his perceptions were clear and fine.

Most of all I love to think of him in those higher aspects of character, which go to make up the remembrance that a good man leaves behind him, and the record which goes in with him to the other life. The extreme sweetness of his nature, his gentleness, his patience, his dignity, his purity impressed themselves from within upon the expression of his face, and made him a very lovable man to all who knew him. There was in his soul that sort of peace of which Augustine spoke to Monica, as of a man who heard, "without the din of words." "Kept in the tabernacle of God from the strife of tongues," he seemed to live in an atmosphere of holy sounds. And in my constant intercourse of many years I found him, with every healthy interest in earthly duties and enjoyments, an uplifted man. Reverent, simple-hearted, sincere, guileless like Nathanael, earnest and devout in his religious life, he has left behind him the legacy of a fragrant memory and the example of a holy life. There is something very striking in the manner of his death, whose suddenness was not unexpected by him. It was of God's great mercy that he was permitted to come home only on Friday, to be in his place in the Cathedral, which he most dearly loved, on Sunday morning; to reach his own home in time to die quietly, where he was wont to "take his rest in sleep." Passing from the worship of God in the church on earth, in which he had so partial a share, to the full enjoyment of the perfect worship of paradise he has realized the mercy of the Master's miracle on the coasts of Decapolis. For God has taken him "aside from the multitude" and spoken the word "Epphatha, be opened," and even those who love him best will learn the unselfish patience to say, "He hath done all things well."

W. C. D.

MRS. GEORGE H. NICHOLLS.

In the death of Mrs. George Huntington Nicholls, there has passed away from the earth one of the purest and sweetest women who ever graced it with a holy and beautiful life. Descended directly through eight generations from the very best of the old Connecticut stock, the Phelps and Beaches, whose name she bore, she inherited from them the characteristics of staunch and strong convictions, of high standards, and of unfaltering devotion to principle.

10

The thought which seemed to fill the holy atmosphere of her sick room during a long and suffering illness was the benediction of the Master to the pure in heart and to the peacemakers.

Faithful and helpful to her husband in a married life that covered almost fifty years, and lovely and loving in all the relations that grew out of it to two generations of descendants, and to the people who were committed to his care, she filled out with rare completeness all that is best and most blessed in the influences of a priest's wife.

Somehow she seemed to live apart in many ways from the outside world; in which, nevertheless, she took a keen interest and discharged every duty; but as one who is "kept secretly in God's tabernacle from the strife of tongues," the very infirmity of her deafness always seemed to me to hold her soul, as Monica's was at Ostia, away from the ruder noises of earth, and within clear and close hearing of those things which the Holy Spirit speaketh to the soul, without what one of the old Fathers called "the din of words."

To be in her presence during the time of her health and strength was always a pleasure and a help; but there came, in the last months of her life, to those who had the privilege of seeing her in her sick room, an influence of teaching and of blessing which never can be lost. Looking and watching, with intervals of hope, for the time of her departure, which she had thought near at hand for several months, the calm composure of her trust in God kept her from any impatience; and so she waited on, until at last, with the quietness of sleep, the end came to her, and she passed into the closer vision of the "King in His beauty" as one who had long lived in "a land that was not very far off."

Patience and purity and peacefulness were the leading features of her life; and as she both shared and gave on earth the blessing of those qualities, we thank God that she has passed on now to receive the fulness of the blessing which the Master promised to those in whose lives these fair fruits are manifested as the gifts of His grace.

REPORT OF COMMITTEE ON REVISED VERSION OF THE HOLY SCRIPTURES.

The Special Committee, to whom was referred the Memorial of the Convention of the Diocese of Massachusetts, requesting this "Convention to consider what action, if any, is necessary on its part, to make the discretionary use of the Revised Version of the Holy Scriptures in Public Worship lawful, at least so far as the reading of the Lessons is concerned; and to take such action:" respectfully report that they consider the authorization of the General Convention necessary to make the reading of the Revised Version in the public worship of the Church lawful; and that they deem it inexpedient for this Convention to give such authorization. All the members of the Committee, with one important exception, concur in this judgment; and, in view of this dissent, as well as the gravity and interest of the subject, the majority beg leave to briefly indicate the reasons which have determined their judgment.

The necessity of Conventional legislation for the lawful use of the Revised Version in the Lections of service arises from the fact, that, from the very beginnings and through all the history of the Church in this country, there has been in constant and unchallenged use one exclusive version of the Holy Scriptures, which has won for itself the title of "Authorized Version," which bears upon its title-page the claim "Appointed to be read in Churches," and which, with hardly a shadow of question, is referred to, in the title of Canon 19, Title I, as "The Standard Bible of this Church." Like other things which stand among the great prescriptions of the Church and the world, the sanction under which we use King James' Version must be found in the actual fact, rather than any formal document. Granted that no man can lay his finger on the time or place of ;its authorization either in the Church of England or the Church in America. Granted that it won its way simply by its intrinsic excellence, the fact remains. For well nigh three hundred years it has been in universal and exclusive use in the Lectionary of the Church. Surely an unbroken use of three centuries, whatever the defect of documentary sanction, justifies its claim to the title of "Authorised Version," by which title it is repeatedly referred to in the Preface to the Revised Version.

If this be so, it is evident that it ought not, and, properly speaking, can not be displaced by any other version in the worship of any congregation of this Church, until competent authority shall so pronounce.

The Memorial of the Diocese of Massachusetts brings before us the question : Is it expedient that this Convention, here and now, authorize the Revised Version of 1884 side by side with the King James Version of 1611. Reasons strong and pertinent, and demanding careful consideration, may be urged for granting the prayer of the Memorial. In the minds of the majority of your Committee, however, every thing that would seem to favour the authorization of the Revised Version is overwhelmingly counter-balanced by the considerations which have influenced their action. They are as follows :

(1) The authorized version of 1611 is so embedded in and interwoven with the common thought, the literature and the spiritual history of English speaking people of the last three centuries, that the use of any other version in the Lections of the Church would be attended with a distinct loss of that voice of authority, and the power of appeal and richness of association, with which the words of the King James Version speak to the heart and the conscience.

(2) The permission to read the Revised Version in the Services of the Church would produce confusion, needless diversity, annoyance and debate, and, moreover, would seriously vitiate the devotional use of the Holy Scriptures, by flinging the word of God into the arena of criticism in the very act of its use in the public offices of worship. The plea that translations other than those of King James Version are used in the Psalter, the Canticles, the offertory sentences and Comfortable words of the Communion Office, while certainly indicating a large freedom in the composition of the Prayer Book, can hardly be urged to justify the optional use of two rival versions of the Holy Scripture in the Lectionary of the Church.

(3) Whatever be the merits of the Revised Version its general superiority to the Authorized Version is still in dispute. Unquestionably the Revisionists of 1884 had knowledge of Critical Canons which were unrecognized, and the command of a critical apparatus which was inaccessible in 1611 : and we concede that they brought to their task a profound learning and a high purpose. Without doubt the results of their work are of great value to the student and the theologian and the preacher. But it must be remembered that even in regard to its critical features, the new version has not yet emerged from the region of controversy. Eminent scholars strenuously question the textual theories upon which the Greek text of the Revision was determined, and in many cases, the accuracy of the translation even that of the text. Certainly, in the minds of the Revisers, a preponderating value has been ascribed to the four great uncials, which has obscured the value of the other critical material, and which must be counted a passing fashion in the domain of biblical scholarship.

But if the critical claims of the revision are not unchallenged, concerning its literary merits unfortunately there is no controversy. It is generally conceded that the Revisionists in their recasting of the language of the King James Version, have not only carried the work beyond their instructions, but have hopelessly mutilated and defaced the chief of English classics. Despite their professions and their ef████ they have failed to retain the tone and rhythm of the old version. Not ██

revision marred by capricious and unnecessary changes of language; in many cases it evinces a striking disregard of English idiom, and perplexes the reader with cumbersome and pedantic phrases. The few instances where the original has been put in a more exact English equivalent are outweighed by innumerable passages, which obscure the sense, and offend the ear by verbal inaptitudes. Truth is forevermore sacred and priceless, but it does not appear that its gains overbalance its losses in the Revised Version.

(4) As regards the Church of England, and, by implication, the Church in America, the Revision of 1884 stands in the position of an unaccredited report indefinitely laid on the table. The Convocation of Canterbury, which appointed the Revision Committee, has refrained from putting its imprimatur upon their work.

The Revised Version is obviously an essay, an experiment, a contribution to a revision, which shall be the result of the larger knowledge of the future, and be undertaken with the more unquestioned sanction of the Church.

In comparison with the curiosity and enthusiasm which greeted its publication, its history of the last ten years is full of significance. It is not too much to say, that in despite of its merits, it has failed to satisfy the scholarship, or commend itself to the literary sense and religious consciousness of the age. It is a valuable document, a monument of careful and learned workmanship, but it is a tentative effort, a structure still echoing with the sounds of the hammer, and in no sense does it justify the claim that it be placed alongside of the great version, which has moulded the language, and is enshrined in the affection and reverence of all English speaking peoples.

In view of these considerations, your Committee deem that any action of this Convention touching the Revised Version would be premature and harmful; and we therefore recommend the adoption of the following resolution:

Resolved, That it is inexpedient for this Convention to authorize the reading of the Revised Version of the Holy Scripture in the Public Worship of the Church. The resolution was adopted by the House of Deputies.

* FROM A SERMON ON THE GENERAL CONVENTION OF 1892, PREACHED IN GRACE CHURCH, NEW YORK, BY THE REV. WILLIAM R. HUNTINGTON, D. D.

I can not leave this subject without paying a personal tribute to a prelate but for whose aid in the House of which he is a distinguished ornament, liturgical revision would, humanly speaking, have long ago come to nought. To the fearlessness, the patience, the kindly temper, and the resolute purpose of Wm. Croswell Doane, Bishop of Albany, this Church for these results stands deeply and lastingly indebted. When others' courage failed them, he stood firm; when friends and colleagues were counselling retreat, and under their breath were whispering "Fiasco!" and "Collapse!" his spirit never faltered.

He has been true to a great purpose, at the cost of obloquy sometimes, and to the detriment even of old friendships. Separated from him by a dozen shades of theological opinion, and by as many degrees of ecclesiastical bias, I render him here and now that homage of grateful appreciation which every Churchman owes him.

---

* This extract from the sermon of the Rev. Dr. Huntington was added to the other part of the appendix to the Bishop's Address by vote of the Convention.— W. C. P.

After the service, the Convention was called to order by the Bishop of the Diocese, in the Gymnasium of St. Agnes' School.

In accordance with Section 1, Canon I, of the Diocese, the Bishop presented a List of Clergy canonically resident in the Diocese.*

The Secretary called the roll of the Clergy, and ninety-eight were found to be present, as follows:

The Right Rev. William Croswell Doane, D. D., LL. D., Bishop of the Diocese.

The Reverend.

R. J. Adler,
E. R. Armstrong,
C. E. Ball,
W. W. Battershall, D. D.,
C. T. Blanchet,
J. E. Bold,
W. B. Bolmer,
Thomas Boone,
W. H. Bown,
R. W. Brown,
Hamilton Cady,
James Caird,
Joseph Carey, S. T. D.,
G. G. Carter, S. T. D.
E. T. Chapman,
C. M. Conant,
W. M. Cook, S. T. B.,
Hobart Cooke,
F. M. Cookson,
C. E. Cragg,
Harry Cresser,
J. A. Dickson,
E. R. Earle,
C. C. Edmunds, Jr,
E. A. Enos, D. D.,
F. S. Fisher,
E. W. Flower,
A. L. Fortin,
H. R. Freeman,
T. B. Fulcher, B. D.,
R. H. Gesner,
H. E. Gilchrist,
J. W. Gill,
Robert Granger,
F. M. Gray,
H. T. Gregory,
Eugene Griggs,
S. M. Griswold,
W. C. Grubbe,

The Reverend.

J. E. Hall,
C. H. Hatheway,
G. A. Holbrook,
E. C. Hoskins,
J. H. Houghton,
G. M. Irish,
W. N. Irish,
David Jenkins,
F. G. Jewett, Jr.,
G. B. Johnson,
R. M. Kirby, D. D.,
C. H. Lancaster,
W. H. Larom,
W. G. W. Lewis,
Arthur Lowndes,
T. H. R. Luney,
A. C. Macdonald,
J. W. McIlwaine,
Ernest Mariett,
J. N. Marvin,
E. P. Miller,
J. H. Molineux,
J. D. Morrison, D. D., LL. D.,
C. M. Nickerson, D. D.,
J. R. L. Nisbett,
C. S. Olmsted,
R. N. Parke, D. D.,
Charles Pelletreau,
J. P. B. Pendleton, S. T. B.,
John Prout,
W. C. Prout,
F. G. Rainey,
W. B. Reynolds,
G. B. Richards,
W. L. Robbins, D. D.,
S. M. Rogers,
H. C. Rush,
Richmond Shreve, D. D.,
F. S. Sill,

* See List of Clergy, pp. 8-9.

The Reverend.
  G. D. Silliman,
  E. B. Smith,
  H. M. Smyth,
  T. A. Snyder,
  Creighton Spencer,
  David Sprague,
  J. W. Stewart,
  W. C. Stewart,
  S. T. Street,
  Alfred Taylor.

The Reverend.
  Charles Temple,
  S. C. Thompson,
  E. D. Tibbits,
  E. S. DeG. Tompkins,
  E. L. Toy,
  J. I. Tucker, S. T. D.,
  Daniel Washburn,
  W. R. Woodbridge,
  Russell Woodman.

The roll of Parishes entitled to representation was called, and the Bishop appointed the Rev. George B. Richards and Mr. S. M. Van Santvoord as a committee, with the Secretary, to examine the credentials of the Lay Deputies.

The Committee presented the credentials of eighty-two Parishes as correct.*

The Secretary then called the names of the Deputies, and sixty Parishes were found to be represented, as follows:

County.	Church.	Deputies.
Albany	Cathedral of All Saints	Selden E. Marvin.
		Thomas R. Wade.
	St. Peter's, Albany,	Thomas S. Wiles.
		William G. Rice.
	Trinity, Rensselaerville	Nathaniel Teed.
		John L. Rice.
		David D. L. McCulloch.
	St. Paul's, Albany	Thomas W. Larwood.
		Frederick C. Manning.
	St. John's, Cohoes	Michael Andrae.
		John Horrocks.
		Robert P. Chadwick.
	Trinity, West Troy	William Hollands.
	Trinity, Albany	George F. Granger.
		Nordine T. Johnston.
	Grace, Albany	Benjamin F. Hinman.
		Charles W. White.
	Holy Innocents', Albany	S. M. Van Santvoord.
		H. S. McCall, Jr.
		James Oswald.
	St. Mark's, Green Island	Richard Leonard.
		William W. Butler.
Clinton	Trinity, Plattsburgh	Edward T. Gilliland.
Columbia	Christ, Hudson	Samuel B. Coffin.
	St. John the Evangelist, Stockport.	William H. Van de Carr.
	St. Paul's, Kinderhook	Henry S. Wynkoop.

* See List of Lay Deputies, pp. 10-14.

County.	Church	Deputies.
Columbia	Trinity, Claverack...	John A. Nichols.
	Our Saviour, Lebanon Springs,	Charles E. Wackerhagen.
	All Saints', Hudson..... ...	Robert V. Noble.
	St. Barnabas', Stottville.. ...	William H. Tanner.
	St. Mark's, Philmont	George Baker.
		Richard A. Woodruff.
		Frank S. Harder.
Delaware....	Christ, Walton..	David H. Gay.
		Edwin W. Pond.
Essex	Of the Cross, Ticonderoga ...	S. S. Paige.
	Christ, Port Henry	Charles W. Woodford.
Fulton............. ...	St. John's, Johnstown	Abiram S. Van Voast.
		Isaiah Yanney.
		James I. Younglove.
Greene	St. Luke's, Catskill..	John H. Bagley.
		Walton Van Loan.
	Christ, Coxsackie...........	Henry J. Hahn.
	Trinity, Athens	Henry C. Van Loan.
	St. Paul's, Oak Hill	Walter S. Cheritree.
Herkimer.............	Christ, Herkimer........ ..	John D. Henderson.
		George W. Pine.
	Grace, Mohawk	E. C. Elwood.
Montgomery	St. Ann's, Amsterdam	William Ryland.
		William Perry.
	Zion, Fonda	Richard H. Cushney.
		Giles H. F. Van Horne.
		Edward B. Cushney.
Otsego	Zion, Morris	T. Octavius Duroe.
		J. Rutherford Morris.
		George A. Sanderson.
	St. Matthew's, Unadilla	George B. Fellows.
	Christ, Cooperstown.	G. Pomeroy Keese.
		L. Averill Carter.
	Grace, Cherry Valley	A. B. Cox.
	St. John's, Richfield Springs..	M. D. Jewell.
	St. John's, East Springfield..	Leslie Pell-Clarke.
		James H. Cooke.
	St. James', Oneonta	Robert M. Townsend.
		Richard Downs.
Rensselaer....	St. Paul's, Troy........	Joseph J. Tillinghast.
		John I. Thompson.
		Thomas Buckley.
	Trinity, Lansingburgh... ...	James McQuide.
		Peter B. King.
		George W. Daw.
	St. John's, Troy............	Norman B. Squires.
		Francis N. Mann.
	Christ, Troy	William Kemp.
	St. Mark's, Hoosick Falls....	John G. Darroch.
		James R. Parsons, Jr.
		George B. Pattison.

County.	Church.	Deputies.
Rensselaer............	Trinity, Schaghticoke	Almadus Wilkinson.
		Edward Searles.
	Messiah, Greenbush....	George Low.
		Richard W. Stevens.
		Harry E. Cole.
St. Lawrence..........	St. John's, Ogdensburg	Levi Hasbrouck.
	Trinity, Potsdam............	T. Streatfeild Clarkson.
Saratoga.....	Christ, Ballston Spa	Andrew S. Booth.
	St. John's, Stillwater........	John Stringer.
	Bethesda, Saratoga Springs ..	William A. Sackett.
	St. Stephen's, Schuylerville..	John A. Dix.
	Calvary, Burnt Hills	Charles H. Upham.
		William H. Larkin.
Schenectady	Christ, Duanesburgh	Edward C. Clark.
	St. George's, Schenectady....	Abram A. Van Vorst.
		John Keyes Paige.
	Christ, Schenectady	David Guy.
		Sidney G. Ashmore.
		John H. Shaffer.
Warren	Messiah, Glens Falls	William A. Wait.
		James A. Holden.
	Holy Cross, Warrensburgh .	Henry Griffing.
Washington	St. James', Fort Edward.....	George Scott.
		Benjamin M. Tasker.
	St. Paul's, Salem....	James Gibson.
	St. Luke's, Cambridge	Henry C. Day.

A constitutional quorum being present, the Rt. Rev. President declared the Convention organized and ready for business.

The election of officers being in order, on motion of Mr. William A. Sackett, the ballot was unanimously dispensed with.

The Rev. William C. Prout was elected Secretary, Mr. Selden E. Marvin, Treasurer, and the Rev. Frederick S. Sill, Registrar.

The Secretary appointed the Rev. Thomas B. Fulcher as the Assistant Secretary.

On motion of the Rev. W. C. Prout, it was

Resolved, That Clergymen of other Dioceses, Professors and Students of Theology in this Church, and all persons holding any office or trust under the Convention, if not members thereof, being present, be invited to seats in the Convention.

The Rt. Rev. President having announced the invitation, the Rev. John Anketell, of the Diocese of Vermont, the Rev. George F. Breed, of the Diocese of Long Island, the Rev. Geo. H. Fenwick (canonically resident in the Diocese of Tennessee, but) missionary at Chatham and Copake in this Diocese, the Rev. William M. Grosvenor, of the Diocese of Massachusetts, the Rev. Richard C. Searing, of the Diocese of Vermont, the Rev. W. Ball Wright (canonically resident in the Diocese of

Michigan, but) missionary at Port Henry and Mineville, in this Diocese, Mr. John Mills Gilbert, lay-reader at Burnt Hills and Charlton, Mr. D. W. Godard, lay-reader at Saranac Lake, and Mr. Charles Albert Howells, lay-reader at West Burlington, took seats in the Convention.

On motion of the Secretary, it was

Ordered, That the order of services and sessions for this Convention be as follows: That a recess be taken from five to eight o'clock this evening; that at eight o'clock the Convention assemble in the Cathedral for the annual Missionary service and meeting; that to-morrow the Holy Communion be celebrated at half-past seven o'clock in the morning, and the Morning Prayer said at ten o'clock, in the Cathedral; the business session shall be resumed in this place at half-past ten with the usual recesses from one to two and from five to eight o'clock.

On motion of the Rev. Arthur Lowndes, it was

Resolved, That in future the parochial returns to the Diocesan Convention contain a column showing the amount of insurance held on the buildings belonging to the Parish or Mission.

Resolved, That the Secretary be instructed to print as an addition to the Journal such parts of the laws of the State of New York as relate to the election and qualifications of Wardens and Vestrymen, and the provisions for holding Vestry meetings.

The following resolution, offered by the Rev. William Mason Cook, S. T. B., was on his motion referred to the Committee on the Diocesan Fund :

Resolved, That the Treasurer of the Diocese be empowered to pay to each delegate to the General Convention from this Diocese the sum of fifty dollars ($50) on account of expenses in attending future meetings of the General Convention.

On motion of the Rev. Joseph Carey, S. T. D., it was

Resolved, That so much of the Bishop's Address as deals with the Woman's Diocesan League be referred to the Committee on the League, for the purpose of bringing this important agency in our Church work in a formal way before this Convention.

Resolved, That the portion of the Bishop's Address relating to the Woman's Auxiliary be referred to a committee to take the matter into consideration and to report to this Convention.

The Right Rev. President appointed as the Committee on the Woman's Auxiliary, the Rev. Freeborn Garrettson Jewett, Jr., the Rev. Harris Cox Rush, Mr. Edgar C. Elwood, Mr. Samuel B. Coffin and Mr. George W. Pine.

On motion of the Secretary of the Convention, it was

Resolved, That the Trustees of the Diocese be requested to inquire into the condition of affairs in the parish of Grace Church, Norway, Herkimer county.

On motion of the Rev. Frederick S. Sill, it was

Resolved, That the Secretary be instructed to insert at the end of the Appendix to the Bishop's Address the public utterance of the Rev. Dr. Huntington, in a late sermon on the General Convention, in regard to the part taken by the Bishop of Albany in the matter of the Revision of the Prayer Book.   •

On motion of the Rev. Henry T. Gregory, it was

Resolved, That so much of the Bishop's Address as relates to the Funds for Aged and Infirm Clergymen and for Widows and Orphans of Deceased Clergymen be referred to the Committee on the Aged and Infirm Clergy Fund.

11

The Right Rev. John Franklin Spalding, D. D., Bishop of Colorado, entered the hall and was received by the Convention standing, and given a seat by the side of the Right Rev. President of the Convention.

The Right Rev. President appointed the regular committees.

On the Incorporation and Admission of Churches.

The Rev. J. Philip B. Pendleton.	Mr. Richard H. Cushney.
	Mr. John H. Bagley.

On the Constitution and Canons.

The Rev. J. W. Stewart,	Mr. James Gibson,
The Rev. R. M. Kirby, D. D.,	Mr. J. D. Henderson,
The Rev. Edgar A. Enos, D. D.,	Mr. R. M. Townsend.
The Rev. Charles M. Nickerson, D. D.	

On the Accounts of the Treasurer.

Mr. Leslie Pell-Clarke.	Mr. Henry Griffing.

On the Diocesan Fund and Mileage of the Clergy.

The Rev. Sheldon M. Griswold.	Mr. George Low,
	Mr. Charles H. Upham,
	Mr. James I. Younglove.

On Diocesan Missions.

The Rev. Charles M. Nickerson, D. D.,	Mr. Levi Hasbrouck,
The Rev. Elmer P. Miller.	Mr. J. Russell Parsons, Jr.

On the Bishop's Salary and the Episcopal Fund.

The Rev. Ernest Mariett,	Mr. James H. Holden,
The Rev. Richmond H. Gesner.	Mr. Benjamin F. Hinman,
	Mr. Michael Andrae.

On the Fund for the Widows and Orphans of Deceased Clergymen.

The Rev. George D. Silliman.	Mr. James H. Holden,
	Mr. Myron D. Jewell.

On the Aged and Infirm Clergy Fund.

The Rev. George G. Carter, S. T. D.	Mr. Thomas R. Wade,
	Mr. George W. Daw.

On the General Theological Seminary.

The Rev. Charles Temple,	Mr. Edward C. Clark,
The Rev. Richmond H. Gesner,	Mr. George B. Pattison.
The Rev. George M. Irish.	

On the Society for Promoting Religion and Learning.

The Rev. David Sprague.	Mr. Frank S. Harder,
	Mr. James H. Cooke.

On Unfinished Business.

The Rev. R. J. Adler.

Mr. Samuel B. Coffin,
Mr. Henry J. Hahn.

On Non-Reporting Clergy and Parishes.

The Rev. John N. Marvin.

Mr. James McQuide,
Mr. William H. Van de Carr.

On the Registrar's Report.

The Rev. Hobart Cooke.

Mr. William Hollands,
Mr. David Guy.

On the Orphan House at Cooperstown.

The Rev. E. W. Flower,
The Rev. D. F. McDonald, D. D.

Mr. Walton Van Loan,
Mr. T. Octavius Duroe.

On the Salary of the Bishop.

The Rev. Joseph Carey, S. T. D.,
The Rev. W. W. Battershall, D. D.

Mr. J. J. Tillinghast,
Mr. Erastus Corning,
Mr. J. W. Tillinghast,
Mr. W. W. Rousseau,
Mr. John I. Thompson,
Mr. Spencer Trask,
Mr. William G. Rice.

On the Society for the Home Study of Holy Scripture.

The Rev. George B. Johnson,
The Rev. William C. Grubbe,

Mr. John Keyes Paige,
Mr. George B. Fellows,
Mr. Edward T. Gilliland.

On the Woman's Diocesan League.

The Rev. Edward Dudley Tibbits,
The Rev. James A. Dickson.

Mr. Charles E. Wackerhagen,
Mr. Charles W. White,
Mr. Thomas Buckley.

On the Bible and Prayer Book Society.

The Rev. Edgar A. Enos, D. D.,
The Rev. Eugene L. Toy,
The Rev. George A. Holbrook.

Mr. William A. Sackett,
Mr. Henry C. Day,
Mr. Sidney G. Ashmore.

The reports of the Treasurer of the Diocese: of the Board of Diocesan Missions; of the Trustees of the Episcopal Fund and of the Committee on the Salary of the Bishop; of the Trustees of the Fund for the Widows and Orphans of Deceased Clergymen, and of the Treasurer of the same; of the Trustees of the Aged and Infirm Clergy Fund, and of the Treasurer of the same; of the Registrar of the Diocese; of the Superintendent and of the Treasurer of the Orphan House of the Holy Saviour, Cooperstown; of the Society for Promoting Religion and Learning, and of the Treasurer of the Diocese, of Moneys re___ for Theological Education ; of the Bible and Common Prayer Book Society, were received and referred to the appropriate Committees. The Report of the Trustees of the Clergy Reserve Fund was received and referred to the Committee on the Aged and Infirm Clergy Fund.

The Secretary of the last Convention presented and read the follow-ing

REPORT OF THE SECRETARY OF THE CONVENTION.

ALBANY, *November* 15, 1892.

To the Convention of the Diocese of Albany :

The Secretary of the Diocese respectfully presents the following report :

One thousand copies of the Bishop's Address and 1,250 copies of the Journal of the Convention were printed and distributed.

Letters were sent to the Parishes that failed to report to the Convention of 1890. Only one reply was received; from St. Peter's Church, Brushton.

The Convention will need to elect this year the Standing Committee and the Trus_ tees of the several funds, and two Trustees of the Diocese to supply the places of two whose terms of office now expire, and three Trustees of the Orphan House of the Holy Saviour, at Cooperstown, in place of three, whose terms of office now expire. And by a change in the Canon of General Convention, we are to elect one Presbyter and one layman, as members of the Missionary Council.

Two Special Committees appointed at the last Convention are to report; that on Clerical Insurance, and that on the Observance of the Twenty-fifth Anniversary of the Consecration of the first Bishop of Albany. Appended to this report and forming part of it is a Communication from the General Assembly of Congregational Ministers and Churches, in regard to the law of the State relating to wills.

Nominations for members of the Board of Missions have been received : For the Convocation of Albany, the Rev. Walton W. Battershall, D. D., and Mr. John H. Van Antwerp; for the Convocation of Troy, the Rev. Fenwick M. Cookson and Mr. George A. Wells; for the Convocation of the Susquehanna, the Rev. Robert N. Parke, D. D., and Mr. R. M. Townsend; for the Convocation of Ogdensburg, the Rev. R. M. Kirby, D. D., and Mr. T. Streatfeild Clarkson.

A large number of Journals of other Dioceses and other documents have been re-ceived and forwarded to the Registrar.

Respectfully submitted,

WM. C. PROUT,

Secretary of the Convention.

COMMUNICATION FROM THE GENERAL ASSOCIATION OF CONGREGA-TIONAL MINISTERS AND CHURCHES.

SYRACUSE, *May* 9, 1892.

To REV. W. C. PROUT, *Sec'y of the Convention of the Albany Diocese, etc.:*

DEAR SIR — At a meeting of the General Association of Congregational Ministers and Churches, held at Brooklyn, May 19, 1891, the undersigned were appointed a Committee to present to other religious bodies within the State, for their considera-tion, the following resolutions, offered by the Central Association:

WHEREAS, The Laws of 1860, chap. 360, an act relating to wills, section 1, pro-vides that " no person having a husband, wife, child or parent, shall by his or her last will and testament, devise or bequeath to any benevolent, charitable, literary, scientific, religious or missionary society, association or corporation, in trust or otherwise, more than one-half of his or her estate after the payment of his or her debts, and such devise or bequeath shall be void to the extent of one-half and no more;" and,

WHEREAS, The Laws of 1848, chap. 319, an act for the incorporation of benevolent, charitable, scientific and missionary societies, section 6, of said act provides, "That no devise or bequest to any corporation founded under said act shall be valid in any will which shall not have been made and executed at least two months before the death of the testator;" and,

WHEREAS, We believe the foregoing restrictions and limitations are arbitrary and abridge the rights of individuals and often defeat and hinder the work of the benevolent and missionary societies; and,

WHEREAS, We believe the objects sought by such restrictions and limitations are already fully secured by ample provision in our statutes, and the obstacles hereby complained of are exceptional in their character, not applying to forms of bequest other than educational and benevolent; therefore it is

Resolved, By the Central Association of Congregational Ministers and Churches of New York, that said restrictions and limitations ought to be repealed by the Legislature of this State.

Resolved, That the State Association of our Ministers and Churches which meets at Brooklyn the 19th instant, be requested to take action for conferring with religious bodies representing other denominations in order to secure a united effort to procure the repeal of these obnoxious laws.

We beg leave to present these resolutions to you, which were adopted by our State Association, and to ask you to present them to the Convention of the Diocese of Albany, of which you are clerk, at their next annual meeting, with a view to their appointing one or more brethren to act upon a Committee of Conference in regard to presenting some law to the Legislature of New York in due time, should the object thus sought seem desirable upon careful consideration.

Whenever any action shall be taken by your body and any person appointed to act on a Conference Committee, will you please notify us so that we may call a meeting?

With fraternal sentiments we remain, yours faithfully,

EDWARD N. PACKARD,
AUGUSTUS F. BEARD,
WM. A. ROBINSON,
Committee.

By E. N. PACKARD, *Syracuse, Chairman.*

Mr. J. D. Henderson, Lay Deputy from Christ Church, Herkimer, offered a motion that the communication from the General Assembly of Congregational Ministers and Churches be laid on the table; which motion failed to pass.

On motion of the Rev. J. D. Morrison, D. D., LL. D., of the Convention, it was

Resolved, That the communication from the General Assembly of Congregational Ministers and Churches be referred to a Special Committee.

The Right Rev. President appointed as such Committee the Rev. J. D. Morrison, D. D., LL. D., the Rev. J. Philip B. Pendleton, S. T. B., Mr. William A. Sackett, Mr. J. D. Henderson, and Mr. James Gibson.

The Rev. Fenwick M. Cookson, Secretary of the Standing Committee, presented and read the

REPORT OF THE STANDING COMMITTEE.

The Standing Committee of the Diocese met on November 18, 1891, and organized by the election of the Rev. J. Ireland Tucker, S. T. D., President, and the Rev. Fenwick M. Cookson, Secretary.

At its first meeting after organization the following resolution was adopted:

Resolved, That we would record our sincere regret that the Rev. J. Livingston Reese, D. D., for almost sixteen years the efficient Secretary of the Standing Committee of the Diocese, should feel obliged by ill health to decline re-election as a member of the Committee and to withdraw from the duties he has so ably fulfilled, and that we express to him our great respect, and our hope that his health may soon be restored.

The Committee has held six meetings during the year.

It has recommended the following postulants for candidateship for Holy Orders: Messrs. Robert Perine, Frederick St. George McLean, Charles Albert Howells, Lewis Gouverneur Morris, John S. Warren, Alexander Haswell Grant, Jr., and Homer B. Williams. It has recommended the following candidates, for ordination to the Diaconate: Messrs. William W. Newell, Charles Albert Howells and John Mills Gilbert.

It has recommended the following Deacons for ordination to the Priesthood: the Rev. James Frederic Olmsted, the Rev. Harry Elmer Gilchrist, the Rev. Hamilton Cady, the Rev. George Lynde Richardson and the Rev. W. F. Parsons.

The Committee has given its canonical consent to the election of an Assistant Bishop in the Diocese of Springfield, and to the consecration of the Bishop-elect, the Rev. Charles R. Hale, S. T. D., LL. D.

It has also given canonical consent to the consecration of the Bishop-elect of the Diocese of Texas, the Rev. George H. Kinsolving.

An application from the Standing Committee of the Diocese of Oregon, asking for consent to the election of an Assistant Bishop for that Diocese, was laid on the table, because of the nearness of the session of the General Convention.

Respectfully submitted,

J. IRELAND TUCKER,
President.

FENWICK M. COOKSON, *Secretary.*
ALBANY, *November* 14, 1892.

The Rev. Richmond Shreve, D. D., presented and read the

REPORT OF THE COMMITTEE ON CLERICAL INSURANCE.

To the Right Rev. the Bishop, and the Convention of the Diocese of Albany:

Your Committee to whom was intrusted the consideration of the subject of Clerical Insurance, with instructions to draw up, if practicable, a plan of operation by which the objects sought might be obtained, beg leave to report:

1. Recognizing that the Church's work in this Diocese, outside the few cities and larger towns, is almost altogether of a missionary character, they believe that any strengthening aid given to this department of Diocesan work will advance the true interests of the Church.

2. Believing, also, that any relief from temporal anxiety which may be gained for the missionary worker will tend, in its measure, to increase his efficiency and usefulness:

They therefore recommend that a system of Clerical Insurance, the principle of which has already been indorsed by two successive Conventions and by the Board of Missions, be carried into effect as soon as possible upon the following plan, which is in its nature official as well as personal.

(a) When a policy of insurance is placed upon any life, each person so insured shall give to the Treasurer of the Diocese an assignment of all the right, title and interest accruing, in consequence of such insurance, to his surviving heirs.

(b) If at the time of his death the insured shall be canonically resident and at work within the Diocese, the interest of the principal amount insured, at the best percentage obtainable consistent with security, shall be paid by the Treasurer to the surviving widow or minor children of the deceased. Such payment of interest shall cease and determine at the time of such widow's death or re-marriage; and in case of minor children, when they attain legal age. The principal amount shall thenceforward be subject to the control of the Board of Missions

(c) If the insured shall have removed from the Diocese, or shall have accepted a rectorship within it, which yields a stipend of $1,000 or over, per annum, the amount insured shall at once upon maturity become the property of the Board of Missions.

(d) The amount of each policy taken under this plan shall be $1,000.

The Committee offer the following resolution : '' That the Convention authorize the addition of one-half of one per cent per annum to the ordinary assessment for Diocesan Fund, which additional sum shall be devoted to the payment of Clergy Insurance premiums.''

RICHMOND SHREVE,
WALTER C. STEWART,
JNO. KEYES PAIGE.

On motion of the Rev. W. G. W. Lewis, it was

Resolved, That the Report of the Committee on Clerical Insurance be referred to the Committee on the Diocesan Fund.

The Right Rev. President having called for nominations for offices in the gift of the Convention, the Rev. William H. Bown nominated for members of the Missionary Council, the Rev. J. Philip B. Pendleton, S. T. B., and Mr. Benjamin H. Hall. The Rev. William C. Pront nominated for the Standing Committee, the Rev. J. Ireland Tucker, S. T. D., the Rev. Fenwick M. Cookson, the Rev. Wilford L. Robbins, D. D., the Rev. James Caird, Mr. Norman B. Squires, Mr. Henry S. Wynkoop, Mr. John I. Thompson and Mr. John H. Van Antwerp.

The Secretary read the Report of the Registrar, and that of the Committee on the same, and on motion the recommendation of the Committee was adopted.

REPORT OF THE REGISTRAR, 1892.

The Registrar would respectfully report that the file of Diocesan Journals for the year 1891 is complete. He has had thirty-eight volumes of these Journals bound. Journals for the year 1892 have been received from forty-four Dioceses, leaving eight to be heard from. Also the Journals of Foreign Jurisdictions, and of the Missionary Jurisdictions of Montana and W. Texas.

The Registrar is indebted to Mr. S. N. Sanford, the Registrar of Ohio, for the Journals of Ohio of the years 1879 and 1864, which complete our set. Tennessee, 1882, is still missing. The duplicate Journals referred to last year have not been disposed of, a suggestion having been made that they might be useful to some public or State Library. Pamphlets, including sermons, addresses, charges, etc., have been received from the Bishop. the Secretary of the Convention, and the Rev. Drs. Carey and Shreve.

The Registrar has been in correspondence with several other Diocesan Registrars, among them the Registrar of the Diocese of Melbourne, Australia, to whom he sent our Journal and a copy of our Constitution and Canons, with other information, in reply to a request sent to the Bishop. The Registrar acknowledges the receipt of $5.00 from the Treasurer of the Diocesan Fund. Balance on hand, as per last report, $4.96 ; total cash received, $9.96 ; expenses binding thirty-eight volumes of Journals at 35 cents, $13.30 ; postage, $1.50 ; sundry fares, $1.80 ; mucilage, 10 cents. Total, $16.70. Account overdrawn, $6.74. An appropriation of $10, for the coming year, is needed to offset this deficiency, and to provide for binding and other purposes.

FREDERICK S. SILL,
Registrar.

REPORT OF THE COMMITTEE ON THE REGISTRAR'S REPORT.

Your Committee on the Report of the Registrar respectfully beg leave to say : that they find the Report faithfully presented regarding all details with Statement of Receipts and Expenses, leaving the amount of $6.74 due the Registrar.

Your Committee recommend the appropriation of $10 for the coming year to meet necessary expenses of binding, postage, stationery, etc.

HOBART COOKE,
November 15, 1892.   WM. HOLLANDS.

On motion of the Secretary of the Convention, it was

Resolved, That a Committee be appointed to prepare and present to the Convention a suitable minute in regard to the fiftieth anniversary of the ordination of the Rev. James Wilkins Stewart.

The Right Rev. President appointed as such Committee, the Rev. Walton W. Battershall, D. D., the Rev. Elmer P. Miller, Mr. John H. Bagley and Mr. Henry J. Hahn.

The Secretary read the Reports of the Society for Promoting Religion and Learning, and of the Treasurer of the Diocese of Receipts and Disbursements for Theological Education.

REPORT OF THE SOCIETY FOR PROMOTING RELIGION AND LEARN-ING IN THE STATE OF NEW YORK.

The Superintendent of the Society for Promoting Religion and Learning in the State of New York, as the Canonical Agent of the Diocese of Albany for distributing all funds for Theological Education, respectfully reports :

That during the past Conventional year, the Society has received and distributed the following sums from Parishes in the Diocese.

1891.
Sept. 28. St. Paul's Church, Troy.................................... $14 25
Nov. 12. Church of Our Saviour, Lebanon Springs.. .... 1 00
    24. St. Mark's Church, Hoosick Falls. 15 94
    1892.
Mar. 18. Christ Church, Hudson........ .... 4 49
May 17. St. Augustine's Church, Ilion..... .... 3 00
June 7. St. Paul's Church, Salem............. .... 2 88
    13. St. Matthew's Church, Unadilla.......... .. .. 4 41
Aug. 7. St. Paul's Mission, Sidney 5 00

    Total..... .... **$50 97**

During the same period the sum of thirteen hundred dollars and upwards has been contributed by the Society in aid of Candidates for Holy Orders in the Diocese of Albany.

All which is respectfully submitted,

ANDREW OLIVER,
Superintendent.

. NEW YORK, *November,* 1892.

REPORT OF THE TREASURER OF THE DIOCESE OF RECEIPTS AND DISBURSEMENTS FOR THEOLOGICAL EDUCATION.

ALBANY, *November* 15, A. D. 1892.

RECEIPTS.

St. John's, Cohoes.............................. ... . $4 00
Christ, Duanesburgh.... .... 7 85
Christ, Herkimer.......................... .... 7 00
Memorial, Middleville.............................. .... 3 21
Trinity, Fairfield 1 71
Christ, Hudson.......... .... 10 00
Trinity, Claverack.... .... 14 00
St. John's, Troy... .... 50 00
Trinity, Lansingburgh. 17 19
Grace, Waterford....... .... 13 00
Bethesda, Saratoga Springs.... . ... 25 00
Messiah, Glens Falls.................................... . 9 02
Good Shepherd, Chestertown........ .. .. 4 15
Church of the Cross, Ticonderoga 5 91
Christ, Port Henry............. .... 8 86
Emmanuel, Mineville 5 60
St. James', Ausable Forks........ .... 10 48
St. Paul's, Keeseville.............. .... 4 40
St. Paul's, East Springfield 11 08
Trinity, Potsdam......... .... 58 76
St. Mark's, Malone....... .... 10 00
    ——— **$280 72**

DISBURSEMENTS.

For stipends........... .... **$280 72**

SELDEN E. MARVIN,

The Rev. David Sprague presented and read the

REPORT OF THE COMMITTEE ON THE SOCIETY FOR PROMOTING RELIGION AND LEARNING.

Your Committee to whom was referred the Report of the Society for the Promotion of Religion and Learning respectfully report:

It is a very easy matter, ordinarily, to hear a report and to go back again to our Parishes as if we had not heard. Yet it would seem as if there was something in this report of the Society for the Promotion of Religion and Learning that would leave a ringing sound in our ears.

Your Committee find that only eight Parishes of this Diocese have contributed during the past year to the Society which is the "Canonical Agent of the Diocese of Albany for distributing all funds for Theological Education." They find that the sum of $50.97 has been contributed, where the sum of $1,300 has been received in aid of Candidates for Holy Orders in this Diocese.

Your Committee find in these facts reason for great regret and sense of shame. They recognize in the appeal which is made to the Parishes of this Diocese an appeal to our sense of honor and to our conscience. While noting with pleasure the increased number of Parishes contributing to the cause of Theological Education in this Diocese, yet they feel bound to put on record their opinion that every Parish in the Diocese should make at least one annual offering specifically to the Society for the Promotion of Religion and Learning.

DAVID SPRAGUE,
F. S. HARDER,
J. H. COOKE.

On motion of the Secretary, it was

Resolved, That the Committee on the Constitution and Canons be requested to consider and report whether any change is necessary or desirable in Sec. 3 of Canon XIII.

The Secretary read the Reports of the Trustees of the Aged and Infirm Clergy Fund, and of the Trustees of the Clergy Reserve Fund.

REPORT OF THE TRUSTEES OF THE FUND FOR AGED AND INFIRM CLERGYMEN.

DIOCESE OF ALBANY, }
ALBANY, *November* 15, A. D. 1892. }

The undersigned Trustees of the Fund for the Support of Aged and Infirm Clergymen respectfully report that the receipts and disbursements for the year have been as reported in detail by the Treasurer, and are as follows:

RECEIPTS.

Balance on hand as reported to last Convention..............	$674 76
From Parishes.....	499 80
From Interest on Investments...	864 12
Total..	$2,038 68

DISBURSEMENTS.

For Stipends............................	1,500 00
Balance	$538 68

The Trustees have the following securities which constitute the Permanent Fund :

Bond and Mortgage Bishop's House.....	$3,600 00
Perry Judgment Bishop's House.	6,815 86
Learned Bond and Mortgage............	4,000 00
Burnett Bond and Mortgage...	1,700 00
Troy and Lansingburgh R. R. Bond....	1,000 00
United States Registered 4 per cent Bond.	1,000 00
New York, Lake Erie and Western R. R. Bond......................	1,000 00
Loans on demand...	950 00
Wabash Railway Bonds.	2,000 00
Total..	$21,565 86

which represents the following receipts :

Diocese of New York...	$10,000 00
St. Paul's Church, Albany.............	4,000 00
Miss Burr Legacy, Diocese of New York..........	2,000 00
Leonard G. Hun Bequest...........	250 00
	$16,250 00

During the year the Treasurer received on account of the Perry Judgment Bishop's House the sum of $250, reducing this security from $6,565.86 to $6,315.86.. The Treasurer also received as a contribution to the Fund from St. Paul's Church, Albany, two (2) $1,000 5 per cent Bonds of the Wabash Railway Company ; also, in cash, $250 from the estate of Leonard G. Hun, deceased.

WM. CROSWELL DOANE, *President,*

SELDEN E. MARVIN, *Treasurer.*

REPORT OF THE TREASURER OF THE CLERGY RESERVE FUND FROM NOVEMBER 19, 1891, TO NOVEMBER 15, 1892.

RECEIPTS.

Balance on hand as reported to last Convention..........................	$63 48
St. Peter's, Albany	26 10
St. John's, Cohoes...	4 68
Christ, Schenectady	1 50
Trinity, Claverack..	2 00
Our Saviour, Lebanon Springs	1 00
St. Paul's, Troy...	97 00
Grace, Waterford	2 86
St. Sacrament, Bolton	1 88
Trinity, Granville	1 30
Church of the Cross, Ticonderoga..............................	2 75
Immanuel, Otego...	1 00
St. Peter's, Hobart.......................................	8 86
St. John's, Ogdensburg	141 86
Trinity, Potsdam...........	27 00
Christ, Herkimer....	4 50
Total..	$381 77

SELDEN E. MARVIN,

The Rev. George G. Carter, S. T. D., presented and read Report Number 1 of the Committee on the Aged and Infirm Clergy Fund, and the resolution recommended in it was adopted.

REPORT NUMBER 1 OF THE COMMITTEE ON THE AGED AND INFIRM CLERGY FUND.

Your Committee on the Report of the Trustees of the Aged and Infirm Clergy Fund find that the disbursements are more than three times as great as the receipts from Parishes. Forty-three Parishes have contributed, being about one-third of the entire number. The Fund has lost on balance, during the year, $136.06. The receipts are less, and the number of contributing Parishes is less than last year, while the calls upon the income were just fifty per cent greater. In view of the fact that the proper and necessary claims upon every such Beneficiary Fund inevitably increase as they grow older, your Committee venture to submit that this Fund is even now in a dangerous condition, and they offer the following resolution: *Resolved*, That it is the sense of this Convention that an offering should be taken up each year in every Parish and Organized Mission for this purpose, and that something of. the income should be added to the Invested Funds, whenever immediate claims will admit.

Respectfully submitted.

GEORGE G. CARTER,
GEORGE W. DAW.

The Secretary read the Reports of the Treasurer of the Diocese, of the Committee on the Treasurer's Accounts, and Report No. 1 of the Committee on the Diocesan Fund and Mileage of the Clergy, and on his motion the resolutions of the Committee on the Diocesan Fund were adopted.

REPORT OF THE TREASURER OF THE DIOCESE.

ALBANY, *November* 15, 1892.

Herewith find statement of Receipts and Disbursements for the year showing as follows :

RECEIPTS.

Balance on hand as reported to last Convention....	$444 90
From Parishes......	2,501 76
Total...............	$2,946 66

DISBURSEMENTS.

For mileage..	$258 79
For Secretary's expenses.......	100 00
For Secretary's salary.	250 00
For Bishop's traveling expenses...	300 00
For sundries......	25 75
For taxes, Bishop's house.....	354 24
For Registrar	5 00
For one-third dues, General Convention...............................	147 00
For printing..	682 56
Total	$2,123 34
Balance	823 32
	$2,946 66

It will be necessary for the Convention at this meeting to provide for the following objects: Mileage to Clergymen in attendance upon Convention; printing the Journal of the Convention; taxes and repairs Bishop's house; sundry current expenses; one-third dues to General Convention; salary of the Secretary; traveling expenses of the Bishop.

For the above purposes I suggest the following estimate of the sums that will be required.

For mileage..	$300 00
For printing.	700 00
For taxes and repairs Bishop's house.	600 00
For sundry current expenses	150 00
For one-third dues General Convention	180 00
For salary of the Secretary.	250 00
For Bishop's traveling expenses.	300 00

To provide the above amount I recommend the Convention order an assessment of three (3) per centum upon the salaries paid or pledged the Clergymen by the Parishes and Mission Stations; one-half payable April 1, and one-half payable October 1, 1893.

I further recommend that the Treasurer be directed to pay to each Clergyman in attendance upon the Convention and belonging to this Diocese, residing a distance of twenty miles from Albany, his actual traveling expenses, provided that in no case shall he pay to exceed seven cents a mile.

SELDEN E. MARVIN,
Treasurer.

REPORT OF THE COMMITTEE ON THE ACCOUNTS OF THE TREASURER.

The Committee to whom was referred the Report of the Treasurer of the Diocese, have examined the same, together with the vouchers for expenditures, and find the same correct.

ALBANY, *November* 15, 1892.

LESLIE PELL–CLARKE,
HENRY GRIFFING.

REPORT NUMBER 1, OF THE COMMITTEE ON THE DIOCESAN FUND AND MILEAGE OF THE CLERGY.

The Committee on the Diocesan Fund and Mileage of the Clergy respectfully report that they have considered the estimates of the Treasurer of the Diocese and recommend their adoption.

The Committee have also considered the resolution of the Rev. William M. Cook, which was referred to them, in regard to payment of the expenses of Deputies from this Diocese to the General Convention, and recommend its adoption. They present the following resolutions for the action of the Convention:

Resolved, That the Treasurer of the Diocese be empowered to pay to each delegate to the General Convention from this Diocese the sum of fifty dollars ($50) on account of expenses in attending future meetings of the General Convention.

Resolved, That one-third of the stipulated amount be provided each year from the Diocesan Fund.

Resolved, That the recommendations of the Treasurer of the Diocese be adopted by this Convention as follows: First, that an assessment be levied upon the Parishes and Mission Stations of this Diocese equal to three per centum of the salaries paid or pledged to be paid to the Clergy by such Pa —half payable April 1, 1893, and the other half October 1, 1893 ; and second, that the Treasurer be directed to pay to each Clergyman in attendance at this Convention and belonging thereto, residing a distance of twenty miles or more from Albany, his actual traveling expenses, provided that in no case shall he pay more than seven cents per mile.

> SHELDON M. GRISWOLD,
> CHARLES PELLETREAU,
> JAMES I. YOUNGLOVE,
> CHARLES H. UPHAM,
> GEO. LOW.

The Rev. J. D. Morrison, D. D., LL. D., presented and read the Report of the Committee on the Communication from the General Association of Congregational Ministers and Churches, the recommendation of which report was adopted.

REPORT OF THE COMMITTEE ON THE COMMUNICATION FROM THE GENERAL ASSOCIATION OF CONGREGATIONAL MINISTERS AND CHURCHES IN THE STATE OF NEW YORK.

The Committee, to whom was referred the Communication from the General Association of Congregational Ministers and Churches in the State of New York, asking for the appointment by this Convention of a Committee of Conference, with a view to obtaining from the Legislature the repeal of several sections of the present statutes relating to the non-validity of certain bequests made to religious, benevolent and educational corporations, respectfully report that they have given the above communication their thoughtful consideration.

After a careful examination, however, of the restrictions complained of in the existing statutes, notwithstanding in some instances their apparent harshness and seemingly unnecessary severity, your Committee think that it would be unwise to take any measures toward their repeal, and they are, furthermore, of the opinion that the opening up of this subject for revision in these particulars might jeopardize the retention of other and more important provisions, which ought, by all means, to be retained.

They, therefore, recommend the adoption of the following resolution.

Resolved, That the Secretary of the Convention be instructed to send a copy of this report to the Committee of the General Association of Congregational Ministers and Churches in the State of New York, and to inform them that for the reasons mentioned above, this Convention deems it inexpedient to appoint a Committee to confer on the subject.

> J. D. MORRISON,
> J. PHILIP B. PENDLETON,
> WILLIAM A. SACKETT,
> JAMES GIBSON,
> J. D. HENDERSON.

The Rev. Edward Dudley Tibbits presented and read the Report of the Committee on the Woman's Diocesan League, the resolution of which report was adopted. (Ayes, 57; noes, 20.)

REPORT OF THE COMMITTEE ON THE WOMAN'S DIOCESAN LEAGUE.

The Committee appointed to consider that portion of the Bishop's Address relative to the Woman's Diocesan League having given the matter careful attention, respectfully report that they fully coincide with the Bishop's suggestion and move the following resolution:

Resolved, That the organization known as the Woman's Diocesan League be continued, and that each Parish be urged to organize under such a plan and for such purposes as the Bishop may approve.

E. D. TIBBITS, *Chairman.*

J. A. DICKSON,

C. E. WACKERHAGEN,

C. W. WHITE,

J. H. BAGLEY.

The following resolution, offered by the Rev. J. D. Morrison, D. D., LL. D., was, with his consent, referred to the Committee on the Observance of the Twenty-fifth Anniversary of the Consecration of the First Bishop of Albany:

Resolved, That so much of the Bishop's Address as refers to a Chapter House, in which this Convention may hold its sessions, be referred to a Committee which shall report thereon to this Convention.

The Rev. Freeborn G. Jewett, Jr., presented and read the following

REPORT OF THE COMMITTEE ON THE WOMAN'S AUXILIARY TO THE BOARD OF MISSIONS.

Your Committee feel it a privilege to be able to review the report presented by the Diocesan Branch of the Woman's Auxiliary to the Board of Missions, especially at this time when such a wonderful impetus has been given to their work by the enthusiasm and consecration displayed at the triennial meeting held during the sitting of the General Convention at Baltimore. While our Diocesan Branch has grown during the past year it has not grown in the proportion that it ought. There are within the confines of the Diocese, 153 Churches and Chapels and 81 Missions, but in this number only 45 have Parish Branches of the Auxiliary. This is largely, we are sure, due to the indifference of the Clergy toward this important branch of Church work. There are women enough to work and women enough willing to work if the Clergy would only urge them to it. It may be hard to interest men in some forms of Church activity, but, thank God, women respond heartily and willingly. Your Committee earnestly urge the Rectors of Parishes to first learn something about the Woman's Auxiliary themselves, and then to form Branches under their care. Let not the smaller Parishes be afraid to form Branches because of their inability to do great things. It is with regret that we speak, in this connection, of the lapsed Branches of which there are 19. It is bad enough not to put one's hand to the plow at all, it is infinitely worse to turn back at the first sign of fatigue. Financially the Diocesan Branch has done well. The number of boxes sent during the year was 110, representing in money value $5,647.42. The total financial statement included in money and boxes reaches the sum of $7,538.44. At first hearing that sounds well, but it is only an increase over the previous year of $160.18 That surely is argument enough for more Branches and for more activity in the now existing Branches.

All of which is respectfully submitted.

FREEBORN G. JEWETT, Jr.,

HARRIS C. RUSH,

SAMUEL B. COFFIN.

The Secretary of the Convention read the reports from the Orphan House of the Holy Saviour:

REPORT OF THE SUPERINTENDENT OF THE ORPHAN HOUSE OF THE HOLY SAVIOUR, NOVEMBER 12, 1892.

During the past year there have been 104 children at the Orphan House of the Holy Saviour. Of this number three girls have been sent to St. Christina Home; one girl has been adopted in a very respectable family; one boy has been sent to an idiot asylum; one boy and two girls have been taken to the State Industrial School at Rochester; and twenty-one other children have been dismissed for self-support, or been returned to friends who can now care for them. The number in the House to-day is seventy-six.

The general health of the children, thanks be to God, has been very good. There has been no death, and no case of serious illness. But scarlet fever prevailed in the house for about four months. There were 26 cases, all very mild. The Orphanage was placed in strict quarantine by the Board of Health from March until June. The sick children were closely confined to the Infirmary, where they were made very comfortable under the care of an experienced nurse, and most faithfully watched over by our excellent physician, Dr. Bassett. On the full recovery of the last little patient, the quarantine being raised, a service of thanksgiving was held in the school-room.

The building is now in very good condition, having been thoroughly repaired throughout during the summer. The exterior has been painted for the first time, six ladies of the neighborhood having united to bear the necessary expense. Two fire-escapes of the best kind have also been provided. Let us pray that they may never be needed. The expense was heavy, but it was a duty to provide them in case of danger to the children.

The women of the Diocese have been very kind in sending clothing and bedding to the Orphanage. Their different contributions in this way have been of great assistance, and much diminished our outlay in the clothing department. There are, however, certain articles not included in the boxes which we are still obliged to pay for, such as some boys' clothing, hats for boys and girls, stockings and shoes. The shoe bills have generally amounted to about $500 annually.

Free Scholarships of $1,000, endowed either by individuals or by Parishes, continue to be a great need of the Orphan House of the Holy Saviour. Children, entirely destitute, with strong claims upon the charity of our Church, apply for shelter and fostering care at the Diocesan Orphanage. But the Superintendent is told that they must be rejected, unless fully paid for. Our doors are closed against them for the want of Free Scholarships.

Respectfully submitted.

SUSAN FENIMORE COOPER,
Superintendent, Orphan House of the Holy Saviour.

REPORT OF THE TREASURER OF THE ORPHAN HOUSE OF THE HOLY SAVIOUR AT COOPERSTOWN FOR THE YEAR ENDING SEPTEMBER 30, 1892.

RECEIPTS.

County Treasurer for board of Children....	$3,915 16
Seventy Churches and Missions	1,818 59
Individuals for Children's board..........................	783 11

Personal Subscriptions.	$281 08
Interest on Investments...	240 00
School Money	372 82
Two Bequests.................................	4,250 59
	$11,611 35

EXPENSES.

Wages..	$2,548 60
Groceries..	989 76
Meat	612 86
Milk..	1,084 08
Clothing...........................	784 83
Fuel..	770 84
Light..	206 47
Furniture...	16 63
House Stores	529 81
Medicines..	117 04
Repairs...	6 00
Water	50 00
Flour..	415 58
Miscellaneous..................................	184 36
Treasurer's Note paid.......	1,334 22
Extra Repairs on Orphau House.	936 82
Carried to Endowment Fund	1,000 00
Balance on Hand........	23 45
	$11,611 35

Respectfully submitted.

LESLIE PELL–CLARKE,
Treasurer.

STATEMENT OF CONDITION OF ORPHAN HOUSE ENDOWMENT FUND, SEPTEMBER 30, 1892.

On Hand per last report...	$3,500 00
Invested in Cooperstown Savings Bank.....	1,000 00
	$4,500 00

Respectfully submitted.

LESLIE PELL–CLARKE,
Treasurer.

LIST OF CHURCHES, MISSIONS AND SUNDAY-SCHOOLS CONTRIBUTING TO THE SUPPORT OF THE ORPHAN HOUSE, FROM OCTOBER 1, 1891.

ARCHDEACONRY OF ALBANY.

The Cathedral of All Saints............................	$57 60
St. Peter's, Albany...............................	144 24
St. Paul's, Albany.................................	67 48
Grace, Albany....	15 00

13

Holy Innocents', Albany	$11 8
Trinity, Rensselaerville.	13 0
Trinity, West Troy	14 0
St. Mark's, Green Island	13 4
St. John's, Cohoes	25 0
Trinity, Athens	5 8
Calvary, Cairo	4 0
St. Luke's, Catskill	50 0
Christ Church, Duanesburgh	11 1
St. George's, Schenectady	30 7
Christ Church, Schenectady	20 0
Good Shepherd, Canajoharie	14 7
St. John's, Johnstown	37 5
Christ Church, Herkimer	13 6
Our Saviour, Lebanon Springs	4 0
St. John's, Stockport	7 6
St. Barnabas', Stottville	27 0
All Saints', Hudson	18 3
Christ Church, Gloversville	13 0
St. Alban's, Frankfort	1 0
Holy Cross, Fort Plain	5 0
St. Margaret's, Menands	4 0
	$628 8

ARCHDEACONRY OF TROY.

St. Paul's, Troy	$142 0
St. John's, Troy	48 1
Christ Church, Troy	75 2
Holy Cross, Troy	20 0
St. Barnabas', Troy	3 6
Messiah, Greenbush	7 0
Trinity, Lansingburgh	20 0
St. Mark's, Hoosick Falls	51 0
All Saints', Hoosac	52 0
Grace, Waterford	13 2
Christ Church, Ballston Spa	20 0
St. Paul's, Salem	5 0
St. Luke's, Cambridge	25 0
Zion, Sandy Hill	35 0
Holy Cross, Warrensburg	6 1
Messiah, Glens Falls	33 3
Church of the Cross, Ticonderoga	7 4
Christ Church, Port Henry	20 0
Trinity, Plattsburgh	25 0
Christ Church, Rouse's Point	5 3
St. Luke's, Mechanicville	6 2
	$620 8

ARCHDEACONRY OF THE SUSQUEHANNA.

Christ Church, Gilbertsville.............	$5 00
St. Peter's, Hobart.................	8 10
St. John's, Delhi....	20 18
Grace, Stamford.......	7 50
St. Paul's, Franklin	8 93
Christ Church, Cooperstown......	89 58
Grace, Cherry Valley.....	54 64
Zion, Morris............. ... .'.......	20 00
St. James', Oneonta..	26 00
St. Matthew's, Unadilla..	28 16
St. Paul's, East Springfield..	2 00
St. Mary's, Springfield Centre.......	7 01
St. John's, Richfield Springs..	108 25
Emmanuel, Otego...	2 00
Christ Church, Deposit	2 50
St. Stephen's, Maple Grove	1 11
	$375 91

ARCHDEACONRY OF OGDENSBURG.

St. John's, Ogdensburg..	$37 40
Trinity, Potsdam...	117 36
Trinity, Gouverneur..	5 00
Christ Church, Morristown	2 04
St. Mark's, Malone...	30 00
Zion, Colton....	1 13
	$192 93

RECAPITULATION.

Archdeaconry of Albany, contributed	$628 87
Archdeaconry of Troy, contributed.......................	620 88
Archdeaconry of the Susquehanna, contributed...................	375 91
Archdeaconry of Ogdensburg, contributed...........	192 93
	$1,818 59

Respectfully submitted.
LESLIE PELL-CLARKE,
Treasurer.

The Rev. E. W. Flower presented and read the

REPORT OF THE COMMITTEE ON THE REPORTS FROM THE ORPHAN HOUSE OF THE HOLY SAVIOUR.

Your Committee on the Reports of the Superintendent and the Treasurer of the Orphan House of the Holy Saviour beg leave to express their gratification with the Reports of both the Superintendent and Treasurer in that they make such an excellent showing of the prosperity of this Diocesan Charity.

Last year we were shamed by the report of great negligence on the part of many Parishes and Missions of the Diocese to contribute to the work of the Orphanage, and the consequent inability of the Treasurer to meet the necessary current expenses without incurring a debt of nearly $2,000.

This year the deficiency of the last year has not only been paid, but all expenses have been met, leaving a balance on hand of $23.45. This good report has been made possible by two bequests, aggregating $4,250.59, and also by reason of a marked increase in the number of contributing Parishes and Missions.

Seventy Parishes and Missions have sent offerings this year amounting to $1,818.59, as against forty-one Parishes and $701.02 last year.

And yet there are still many delinquents, and your Committee would respectfully urge the importance of an annual collection at least from every Parish and Mission in the Diocese, in order that the usefulness of the Institution may be augmented.

We also commend most heartily the request of the Superintendent for endowments of $1,000 Scholarships.

All of which is respectfully submitted,

DAVID F. McDONALD,
E. W. FLOWER,
WALTON VAN LOAN,
T. O. DUROE.

The Rev. Richmond Shreve, D. D., presented and read the Report of the Bible and Common Prayer Book Society of Albany and its vicinity ; and the Rev. Edgar A. Enos, D. D., that of the Committee on the same.

REPORT OF THE BIBLE AND COMMON PRAYER BOOK SOCIETY OF ALBANY AND ITS VICINITY.

The Bible and Common Prayer Book Society of Albany and its Vicinity, has pleasure in reporting that, during the past conventional year, there have been distributed through its regular channels no fewer than 4374 volumes, as follows :

217 Bibles (two of which were for Lectern use); 1962 Prayer Books : 2195 Hymnals ; total, 4374.

Beside these, through the " Mann Bequest " which, under the kind co-operation of the authorities of St. John's Church, Troy, lends its valued aid to this Society, there were distributed 390 additional volumes, consisting of Bibles, Prayer Books, Hymnals, with and without music, Sunday-School Library Books, and twelve " Helps to the Study of the Bible."

The grand total of books sent out during the year was, therefore, 4764. Sixty (60) separate grants have been made . To Parishes, 56 ; to Albany Academy, 1 : to House of Refuge, Hudson, 1 ; to Sanitarium, Saranac Lake, 1 ; to St. Paul's School, Salem, 1 ; total, 60.

The Society gladly records its obligations to the Rev. James Caird, who has, during the latter portion of this year, faithfully and well fulfilled the duties of the Corresponding Secretary.

The Report of the Treasurer, Mr. H. B. Dauchy, of Troy, shows some facts which give pleasure ; but, also, in other statements cannot but cause regret.

The Permanent Fund has, by the authority of the Society, been increased to $18,400

The Special Prayer Book Fund is as before, $300.

Following is a summary of Receipts and Expenditures for the year.

RECEIPTS.

Cash on hand at last Report..	$76 28
Received from Income Permanent Fund..	902 50
Received from " Mann Bequest " (St. John's Church, Troy)..............	400 00
Received from 45 Parishes	283 18
Received for Books sold.	20 50
Total...	$1,682 46

EXPENDITURES.

Paid Rev. Rev. T. A. Snively "Mann Bequest"....................... ...	$175 00
Paid Bibles, Prayer Books and Hymnals.	836 37
Paid for recording assignment, Mortgage.........	85
Total...	$1,012 22
Leaving cash balance on hand............	$670 24

In view of the fact that there was a larger number of Books sent out this year than last, the large Cash Balance on hand is a gratifying feature ; but the Receipts of $283.18 from 45 Parishes do not compare favorably with the $427.11 from 51 Parishes of last Report.

The Society feels that its work this coming year is of special importance.

The completion of the revision of the Prayer Book marks a momentous epoch in the history of the American Church. When twelve years ago, in obedience to a general desire which, for many reasons, found only a partial expression, liturgical scholars and devout men in the Church were appointed to this task, and they set out upon their great work, their earlier movements were tentative, and perhaps not altogether without hesitation on their own part. Themselves conservative and humble in their greatness, they recognized the magnitude of their undertaking. Working at times in the face of misunderstandings, seldom encouraged by the plaudits of their fellow Churchmen, not unfrequently hampered by criticism from supposed superior culture and technical knowledge, they yet labored on through years of silent industry, enduring toil, and patient courage, until a grateful Church to-day accepts and rejoices in the outcome of their work, and gives them, in the name of God, her warmest thanks.

Thus in one of the loftiest exercises of her independent existence as a National Church, this American Branch of the great Body Catholic has set forth her own " *Use* " and order for Divine Worship, in which she has not only restored some comparatively modern devotional utterances from her English mother's speech, which she had lost for a little while; but, also, proved that she "thought it not robbery" to reach back with reverent and untrembling hands into the Centuries of the ancient days, and take *as her own* the treasures of devotion which enriched the Apostolic Worship. Linking thus together the earlier and the later years of Christian story, she greatly strengthens her position as pleading for the re-union of Christendom.

In this revised and enriched Prayer Book as her heritage and possession, the ecclesiastical daughter in America appears even fairer and more beautiful than her Anglican mother, and with loving salutation, bids her take courage when she shall undertake for herself the great work now so happily completed here.

Nor is it only with the larger name of *American* Churchmen that it is ours to look with gratitude upon these facts to-day.

This Society has for its members the Clergy and all the baptized lay people of the Diocese of *Albany*. And among the honored men who have rendered each signal service to the whole Church was one whose Catholic spirit lent its devoutness, and whose cultured mind gave of its treasures to largely aid in this labor; whose gentle firmness, resolute spirit, unwearied patience and unfaltering courage—his colleagues themselves tell us—turned possible failure into blessed success. Of him we speak with grateful pride and respectful affection as our own Right Rev. William Croswell Doane, President of this Society, and Bishop of Albany.

We would fail of a pleasing duty while recording those things which are of deepest interest to "The *Bible* and Common Prayer Book Society," were we to forget that when the General Convention was asked to authorize for public use the Revised Version of the Scriptures, it was the Rev. Dr. Battershall, of Albany, who, as Chairman of the Committee, saved the Church from that (even permissive) disaster.

Recognizing that we are now face to face with "a condition, not a theory," the Society has authorized the purchase of not less than five thousand copies of the new Prayer Book, as soon as they can be obtained, with the Society's imprint upon the title page, for free distribution throughout the Churches of the Diocese. Very earnestly do we beg the Clergy to remember that much money will be needed, this coming year, under these new circumstances. The Laity will come to the assistance of the work if prompted and led by their Pastors.

The thanks of this Society are cordially rendered to the Rev. G. H. S. Walpole, D. D., Professor in the General Theological Seminary, for his kindness in coming to preach the Sermon before them last evening, and for the marked ability and gracious power with which he fulfilled his mission. A copy of the Sermon has been requested by the Society for publication

The Corresponding Secretary of the Society for the ensuing year is the Rev Henry R. Freeman, Rector of St. John's Church, Troy.

All which is respectfully submitted,
RICHMOND SHREVE,
Recording Secretary.

REPORT OF THE COMMITTEE ON THE REPORT OF THE BIBLE AND COMMON PRAYER BOOK SOCIETY OF ALBANY AND ITS VICINITY.

Your Committee, having examined the Report of the Bible and Prayer Book Society of Albany and its vicinity, have nothing but commendation for the admirable presentation of the work accomplished by that Society during the Convention Year just closing. We note that both the number of Parishes contributing, and the total amount of contributions, are less this year than last; but, on the other hand, the balance in the Treasury at the present date is some six hundred dollars more than that of last year. There has been, also, a substantial increase in the Permanent Fund of the Society.

In view of the excellent results of the "Mann Bequest" of St. John's Parish, Troy, your Committee are of the opinion that similar bequests would be of great advantage to the work of the Society in the future; especially in view of the increased demands which are now to be made upon it, for the circulation of the Revised Prayer Book, and its substitution for the old one.

Finally, your Committee desire to express their cordial agreement with the Report submitted to them, in respect of its expression of loyalty to the authorized version of the Holy Scriptures, as against the Westminster Revision of 1881.

EDGAR A. ENOS,
Chairman.
EUGENE L. TOY,
GEO. A. HOLBROOK,
SIDNEY G. ASHMORE,
WM. A. SACKETT.

The Rev. R. J. Adler presented the

REPORT OF THE COMMITTEE ON UNFINISHED BUSINESS.

The Committee on Unfinished Business respectfully report that there was no business left unfinished at the last Convention, except such as is in the charge of Committees or has been already reported to this Convention.

Respectfully submitted.

R. J. ADLER,
For the Committee.

The following resolution offered by the Rev. Walton W. Battershall, D. D., having been put by the Secretary, was adopted.

Resolved, That a Committee be appointed to present a resolution which shall express the grateful appreciation of this Convention of the work of the Bishop of this Diocese on the revision of the Prayer Book.

The Right Rev. President declining to act under it, the Secretary of the Convention appointed as such Committee, the Rev. Walton W. Battershall, D. D , the Rev. Edgar A. Enos, D. D., and Mr. James Gibson.

On motion of the Rev. Walton W. Battershall, D. D., it was

Resolved, That, in view of the special need which exists this year for the large gratuitous distribution of Prayer Books, and in view of the recognition of this need by the Albany Bible and Prayer Book Society, this Convention urges upon the Clergy of the Diocese the claim of this Society for an annual offering from each Parish.

On motion of the Rev. Joseph Carey, S. T. D., it was

Resolved, That the members of this Convention desire to make record of their deep sense of obligation to the generous friend of the Diocese, who, in connection with other liberal givers, by his princely offering, in February last, enabled the Bishop to free the Cathedral from indebtedness.

On motion of the Secretary of the Convention, it was

Ordered, That the last clause of the Order of Services and Sessions of this Convention be amended to read as follows: "The business session shall be resumed in this place after the hearing of the Bishop's Address, which is appointed for half-past ten o'clock."

Resolved, That the election of the Board of Missions and the other business of the Convention in regard to the Missions of the Diocese be made the order of the day for 11:55 o'clock in the forenoon of to-morrow; and that the Convention now take a recess and reassemble in the Cathedral at eight o'clock to hear the Reports of the Board of Missions and of the Treasurer of the Board, and other Reports connected with them.

The Convention took a recess.

HALF-PAST FIVE O'CLOCK IN THE AFTERNOON.

The Evening Prayer was said in the Cathedral, the Dean and the Precentor officiating.

EIGHT O'CLOCK IN THE EVENING.

The Convention reassembled in the Cathedral.

A special Missionary Service, set forth by the Bishop, was said, the Dean and the Precentor of the Cathedral and the Rev. W. Ball Wright officiating.

After the service the Right Rev. President took the chair and called the Convention to order.

The Rev. W. R. Woodbridge, Secretary of the Board of Missions, read the

REPORT OF THE BOARD OF MISSIONS.

The Board of Missions respectfully present the following report.

During the past year four Missionaries in active service in this Diocese have been called away from their earthly labors by death and have gone to receive their reward from the Lord of the Harvest. The following memorial notices of them on the records of the Board are by their direction herewith presented:

1. The Rev. Heman R. Timlow, D. D., Missionary for twelve years past at Charlton, in Saratoga county, and Rector of Calvary Church, Burnt Hills, after a painful and lingering illness, departed this life on Wednesday, February 10, A. D. 1892, at the age of fifty-eight years. He has left behind him in his Parishes the memory of a faithful Pastorate, a true Christian courtesy and a rare scholarship, combined with most spiritual preaching. In his death the Church has lost a most loyal son, and the Diocese a devoted Missionary. But the world is always better for the living of such a life as his, and for the faithful but unostentatious work that he did his Master shall surely reward him openly.

2. In the death of the Rev. Edward C. M. Rowden, Missionary at Lyon Mountain, in Clinton county, which occurred February 15, A. D. 1892, there was a peculiar sadness rarely met with. He seemed absolutely alone, in the sense that he had not a single relative on this Continent, nor could the address of any of his family be found. But he was ministered to most kindly by the friends he had made during his few weeks of service in that difficult field, and his grave was kindly provided in the family lot of one of his devoted admirers. He endured hardness as a good soldier of Jesus Christ in the severe work of the new Mission, and in the face of open opposition he showed a manly and yet courteous perseverance, which extorted the respect and admiration even of those who opposed his work. Though dying a stranger without an earthly home, we rejoice to think of him as now "with Christ, which is far better." And for such faithful servants we may feel sure there is waiting a crown of righteousness in the day of Christ's appearing.

3. The Rev. Robert Washbon, Missionary at Rensselaerville and vicinity in Albany county, was not only the oldest Missionary in the Diocese, but was at work there before the Diocese was organized. After a long and devoted ministry, most of it in the same neighborhood, and in what many would think a rough country, this faithful servant of Christ gently fell asleep, and entered into the rest of Paradise on March 5, A. D. 1892.

No human calculation can fully estimate the far-reaching influence of such a life as his, always steadfast in the work of the Lord, full of love and good works toward every soul for whom Christ died, so far as he could reach them with his ministrations. But *something* shall be made known of his work in the day when the Lord shall make up his jewels; and to many a rejoicing soul shall be said the "Well done, good and faithful servant, enter thou into the joy of thy Lord."

4. The Rev. William Henry Goodisson died on the 22d day of October, A. D. 1892, at the age of 53. For about eighteen months he was Missionary at St. Paul's Church, Franklin. His death came as a sudden and grievous shock to his family and personal friends. But to the faithful servant who is about his Master's business, it matters little when the call comes to join the multitude of the redeemed in the blessed rest of Paradise.

The Board of Missions hereby puts on record its thankfulness for the good examples of these servants of God, who, having finished their course in faith, do now rest from their labors; together with the earnest hope that many more Missionaries may be raised up in this Diocese to follow them in all virtuous and godly living.

The Board further reports that there have been under its care during the past year 95 Mission Parishes and Stations, calling for the service of 61 Missionaries, as follows :

	Stations.	Missionaries.
In the Archdeaconry of Albany	24	18
In the Archdeaconry of Troy	35	22
In the Archdeaconry of the Susquehanna.	18	11
In the Archdeaconry of Ogdensburg	18	10
	95	61

Just at present 7 Stations are vacant, which are usually served by 4 Missionaries. So that to-day we have 87 Stations occupied by 56 Missionaries. For the needs of these Stations, many of them poor and weak, and of their Missionaries, all faithful and laborious, the Board has apportioned such stipends as seemed possible from the funds provided for this most important work in the Diocese. Its importance may be seen in the fact that of the 160 Parishes and organized Missions in this Diocese, 94 are Mission Stations, or nearly three-fifths of the whole number, dependent on stipends, and in many cases there is need of increased stipends which cannot be granted until the people's offerings are sent in more abundantly. In this connection it is encouraging to learn that in one small Parish there has been a notable advance this year. The Church of Our Saviour, Lebanon Springs, which a few years ago did not give any thing to Diocesan Missions, has for some years given $20, and this year their offerings advanced to $33.57, an increase of 68 per cent. If any such average increase could be made throughout the Diocese, the total offerings for our Mission work would amount to the goodly sum of $16,875, instead of the $10,000 which has been voted in Convention so many years.

It is to be hoped that other Parishes may have done as well, and that others will be stimulated to follow their good examples.

The echo of Missionary zeal and practical Missionary work comes to us from the General Convention which established five new Missionary jurisdictions and provided Bishops for them.

The idea of Mission, *i. e.*, of the sending forth and the uplifting the light of the Gospel, is more and more recognized as the supreme duty, the weightiest responsibility, and the most blessed privilege of the Church and her individual members. We have 12 Missionary jurisdictions within the United States, and yet it is a noticeable fact that we have more than one-half as many Missionaries at work in this Diocese as are reported in all these jurisdictions, so that ours is most distinctly an extensive and important Missionary field; and because it is such, it calls the more loudly for the prayers and the offerings of the people to strengthen the weaker Parishes, and to plant Missions in new and promising fields.

14

It is not any special cause for pride that the Treasurer is able to report no considerable debt at the close of this year, for the year began with a balance of $268.06, while the year before began with a balance of $914.66. It is certainly to be hoped that we are not going to allow ourselves to drop into the old habit of closing the year in debt. Let us rather aim at putting an increasing balance at the beginning of the year to provide for special and advanced Mission work.

The Board cannot close this Report without alluding with thankfulness to the account rendered by one of its oldest Missionaries, the Rev. Silas M. Rogers, who for nearly fourteen years has been laboring most faithfully in the villages of Ellenburgh and Ellenburgh Centre, in Clinton county. In that time he has brought about the rebuilding of one Church, and the building of a new one at the latter station. He has Baptised 153 persons and presented 48 for Confirmation. His patient and devoted labors, quietly but perseveringly continued, while not obtruding themselves upon the eyes of men, are doubtless noted in the book of God's remembrance and shall be greatly rewarded in God's own good time — while their influence is felt in many lives of those who have come under his ministrations. May the Lord of the Harvest send forth many more laborers with his consecrated devotion, and give to this His servant many more seals for his ministry.

With this is presented the list of Stations, Missionaries and Stipends, as they stand to-day.

All of which is respectfully submitted, by order of the Board.

WILLIAM R. WOODBRIDGE,
Secretary.

MISSIONS IN THE DIOCESE OF ALBANY.

ARCHDEACONRY OF ALBANY.

County.	Church.	Place.	Missionary.	Stipend.
Albany	Trinity...... ...	Rensselaerville.....	Rev. S.C.Thompson.	$150
	St. Andrew's...	West Troy.........	Rev. C.H.Hatheway.	200
Greene... ...	Gloria Dei	Palenville........	Rev. W. C. Grubbe.	250
	Grace.....	Prattsville.......	....	250
	Trinity.........	Ashland.........		
	Trinity..	Athens...........	Rev. J. W. Stewart.	
	Christ.........	Coxsackie..... ...	Rev. E. S. De G. Tompkins..... ..	300
Herkimer.....	Trinity.........	Fairfield.........	Rev. C. M. Conant..	400
	Memorial......	Middleville... ..		
	Grace....... ...	Mohawk	....	200
	St. Augustine's.	Ilion...........	Rev. W. M. Cook.	200
	St. Alban's.....	Frankfort.		100
		Dolgeville.........	Rev. Ernest Mariett.	200
Fulton	Christ.........	Gloversville........	Rev. H. M. Smyth ..	400
Montgomery ..	Zion.........	Fonda.............	Rev. C.C. Edmunds.	200
	Good Shepherd.	Canajoharie.....	Rev. C. E. Ball...	250
	Holy Cross....	Fort Plain		
Columbia.....	St. Luke's. ...	Clermont	Rev. M. E. Wilson..	100
	All Saints'.....	Hudson..........	Rev. G. G. Carter, S. T. D.	300
	Trinity.........	Claverack........		
	St. Luke's......	Chatham........		
	St. John-in-the-Wilderness...	Copake	Rev. G. H. Fenwick.	300
	St. Mark's......	Philmont.........	Rev. A. Lowndes...	500
	Our Saviour....	Lebanon Springs...	Rev. Geo.B.Johnson.	300

ARCHDEACONRY OF TROY.

County.	Church.	Place.	Missionary.	Stipend.
Rensselaer....	St. Giles'.......	Castleton.........	Rev. C.H.Hatheway.	$200
	Trinity........	Schaghticoke.... ⎫	Rev. M. O. Smith..	350
	St. Paul's....	Raymerstown.... ⎭		
	Holy Name....	Boyntonville.......	Rev. E. D. Tibbits.	200
Saratoga......	St. Stephen's...	Schuylerville.......	Rev. W. F. Parsons.	100
	St. John's.....	Stillwater........ ⎫	Rev. E. C. Hoskins.	150
	St. Luke's. ..	Mechanicville.... ⎭		
	St. Paul's.....	Charlton......... ⎫	Rev. J. M. Gilbert..	100
		West Charlton... ⎭		
	St. John's.....	East Line........ ⎫		
	Grace..........	Jonesville........ ⎬	Rev. Thos. Boone..	250
	All Saints'....	Round Lake..... ⎭		
	St. John's.. ...	Conklingville ... ⎫	Rev. C. J. Whipple.	300
	St. Mary's.....	Luzerne......... ⎭		
	St. Andrew's...	Schroon Lake......	Rev. C. B. Perry....	
Warren.......	Good Shepherd.	Chestertown...... ⎫	Rev. A. Taylor... ⎰	200
	St. Paul's.....	Bartonville ..... ⎭		100
	St. Sacrament..	Bolton..........	Rev. C. T. Blanchet.	100
Washington ..	St. Luke's......	Cambridge........	Rev.F.H.T.Horsfield	100
	St. Paul's......	Greenwich........	Rev. W. F. Parsons.	300
	Trinity.........	Granville........ ⎫	Rev.C.H. Lancaster.	300
		North Granville.. ⎭		
	St. Paul's.....	Salem............	Rev. H. C. Rush...	100
Essex	Of the Cross...	Ticonderoga......	Rev. H. T. Gregory.	300
	Christ	Port Henry ..... ⎫	Rev.W. Ball Wright	350
	Emmanuel.....	Mineville..... .. ⎭		
	St. John's......	Essex	Rev. W. N. Irish...	
	Good Shepherd.	Bloomingdale......	Rev. W. H. Larom..	
	St. Paul's......	Keeseville........ ⎰	Rev. J. W. Gill. ⎰	300
	St. James'.....	Ausable Forks... ⎱		200
Clinton.......	Christ......	Rouse's Point.... ⎫	Rev. J.F. Olmsted ⎰	100
	St. John's......	Champlain....... ⎭		250
	St. Peter's.....	Ellenburgh....... ⎫	Rev. S. M.Rogers. ⎰	
	St. Paul's....	Ellenburgh Centre ⎭		⎰100
	St. John's......	Salmon River......	Rev. Hobart Cooke..	

ARCHDEACONRY OF THE SUSQUEHANNA.

County.	Church.	Place.	Missionary.	Stipend.
Delaware.....	Christ..........	Deposit	Rev. F. S. Fisher...	$300
	St. Peter's.....	Hobart	....	300
	St. Paul's......	Franklin	Rev.Grenville Rath-	
			bun........	300
	Grace...	Stamford..........	Rev. H. McDougall.	200
	St. Paul's......	Sidney	....	300
Otsego........	Christ...... ...	West Burlington . ⎫		
		Edmeston........ ⎪		
	Good Shepherd.	Cullen........... ⎬	Rev. C. A. Howells.	250
	St. Luke's.....	Monticello.. .. ... ⎭		
	Immanuel.. ...	Otego............	Rev.W.G.W.Lewis.	200
	Holy Spirit....	Schenevus .... ⎫		
	Sts. Simon &		⎬	Rev. E. Griggs.....	250
	Jude........	Worcester........ ⎭		
	St. James'.....	Oneonta......... ⎫	Rev. J. F. Bold....	300
	St. John's.....	Portlandville...... ⎭		
	Christ..........	Gilbertsville .... ⎫	Rev.D.F.MacDon- ⎰	⎰125
	St. Stephen's...	Maple Grove.... ⎬	ald, D. D...... ⎱	100
	St. Paul's......	East Springfield.. ⎪		
	St. Mary's. ...	Springfield Centre ⎭	Rev. John Prout....	200

ARCHDEACONRY OF OGDENSBURG.

County.	Church.	Place.	Missionary.	Stipend.
Franklin......	St. John's...... St. Luke's	St. Regis Lake... Saranac Lake ... Santa Clara ..... S. Regis Falls... Paul Smith's Sta.	Rev. W. H. Larom.	$100 200
	St. Mark's..... St. Peter's. ...	West Bangor . Brushton	Rev. A. L. Fortin..	340
St. Lawrence..	St. Thomas'...	Lawrenceville. ...		
Franklin.. ..	St. James'.....	Hogansburgh .... Fort Covington...	Rev. David Jenkins.	325
St. Lawrence..	St. John's......	Massena............	Rev. F.S.Greenhalgh	325
	Grace .... St. Andrew's...	Norfolk..... .... Norwood...........	Rev. E. R. Earle....	700
	St. Paul's ... St. Luke's.....	Waddington..... Lisbon	Rev. A.C. Macdonald	400
	Christ..........	Morristown........	Rev. W. R. Wood- bridge...........	300
	Trinity........	Gouverneur........	Rev. J. A. Dickson.	250
	Trinity Chapel.	Morley............	Rev. R. Wyndham Brown...........	200

Mr. Selden E. Marvin, Treasurer, read the

REPORT OF THE TREASURER OF THE BOARD OF MISSIONS, NOVEMBER 19, 1891, TO NOVEMBER 15, 1892.

RECEIPTS.	For Salary of the Diocesan Missionary, from Sunday Schools.	Missions.
By balance reported last Convention.........	......	$268 06
Archdeaconry of Albany.		
The Cathedral of All Saints............................	$40 00	$1,200 00
St. Peter's, Albany................................	117 05	902 56
St. Paul's, Albany......................	20 00	400 00
Grace, Albany................................... ...	5 00	50 00
Holy Innocents, Albany	15 00	50 00
Trinity, Albany...............	5 00	20 00
Trinity, Rensselaerville	......	21 29
Trinity, West Troy..................................	4 00	45 00
St. Gabriel's, West Troy.......	3 14	
St. Andrew's, West Troy.......	......	5 00
St. Mark's, Green Island	7 22	38 37
St. John's, Cohoes..............................	15 00	269 90
Trinity, Athens.................................	......	6 30
Calvary, Cairo..................................	1 00	10 60
Gloria Dei, Palenville....	......	15 00
St. Luke's, Catskill...............................	15 00	150 00
Christ, Coxsackie....................	......	
Trinity, Ashland................	......	

Christ, Greenville.....	......	$10 05
St. Paul's, Oak Hill........	......	7 57
Christ, Duanesburgh............	$20 00	60 00
St. George's, Schenectady............	25 00	125 00
Christ, Schenectady.................	5 00	20 37
St. Ann's, Amsterdam........	25 00	56 05
Good Shepherd, Canajoharie.........	......	10 00
Holy Cross, Fort Plain	......	('91) 10 00
	......	18 65
Zion, Fonda........	......	18 00
St. John's, Johnstown........	20 00	75 94
Christ, Gloversville............	......	25 00
Memorial, Middleville........	......	20 00
Trinity, Fairfield........	......	('91) 5 00
	. ....	('92) 5 00
Christ, Herkimer	10 00	70 60
Emmanuel, Little Falls........	24 87	23 68
St. Augustine's, Ilion........	5 51	30 00
St. Alban's, Frankfort........	......	5 00
Grace, Mohawk........	......	15 00
Trinity, Claverack........	10 00	17 11
St. Luke's, Clermont........	......	10 00
Mission, Canaan........	......	6 89
Our Saviour, Lebanon Springs........	......	27 18
St. John's, Stockport........	10 00	25 00
St. Barnabas', Stottville........	... ..	25 00
St. James', Rossman's Mills	5 00	5 00
St. Mark's, Philmont........	10 00	21 00
St. Luke's, Chatham........	......	5 00
St. John's, Copake	......	5 00
St. Paul's, Kinderhook.....	4 26	126 85
Christ, Hudson........	24 08	125 78
All Saints', Hudson........	10 00	12 39
St. Margaret's, Menands	......	5 00

Archdeaconry of Troy.

St. Paul's, Troy........	110 00	1,282 00
St. John's, Troy	......	600 00
Christ, Troy........	......	250 00
Holy Cross Sunday-school, Troy....	......	50 00
Holy Cross, Troy........	8 36	307 62
Ascension, Troy.... ..	......	44 25
St. Luke's, Troy........	......	30 98
St. Barnabas', Troy........	7 84	51 05
St. Giles', Castleton........	......	6 00
Epiphany, East Albany........	5 00	
Messiah, Greenbush........	... ..	25 00
Trinity, Lansingburgh........	... ..	200 00
Trinity, Schaghticoke........	......	15 00
St. Mark's, Hoosick Falls........	25 00	100 00
All Saints', Hoosac........		30 00
Holy Name, Boyntonville........		

St. Luke's, Mechanicville............................	......	$15 00
St. John's, Stillwater................................ ...	......	10 00
Grace, Waterford..,..............	......	374 00
Christ, Ballston Spa.................................	$15 00	102 64
St. John's, East Line	3 00	5 00
Grace, Jonesville....................................	3 00	10 00
All Saints', Round Lake..........	4 00	5 00
Calvary, Burnt Hills..................................	......	25 00
St. Paul's, Charlton.................................	......	
Bethesda, Saratoga Springs..........	60 00	300 00
St. Stephen's, Schuylerville..........................	......	5 00
St. John's, Conklingville............................	......	5 00
St. Paul's, Salem.........	......	59 40
St. Luke's, Cambridge.............................. .	......	366 00
Trinity, Granville...................................	......	9 22
Mission, North Granville.............................	......	10 00
St. Paul's, Greenwich...........	......	
St. James', Fort Edward..	10 00	20 00
Zion, Sandy Hill...................................	... ..	16 76
Trinity, Whitehall	.. ..ī	50 00
St. James', Caldwell......	......	
St. Mary's, Luzerne.	......	20 00
Holy Cross, Warrensburgh.....	5 00	50 00
Messiah, Glens Falls................................	10 00	150 00
St. Sacrament, Bolton......................	......	10 00
Good Shepherd, Chestertown.........................	......	15 00
St. Paul's, Bartonville.........	......	
Cross, Ticonderoga.................................	5 00	30 00
Christ, Port Henry................................ ...	5 00	81 25
Emmanuel, Mineville................................	......	1 98
St. Andrew's, Schroon..........................	... ..	4 16
Mission, Westport..................................	......	10 85
St. James', Ausable Forks...........................	... ..	25 00
St. John's, Essex.................	5 00	33 36
St. Paul's, Keeseville..............................	......	15 00
Trinity, Plattsburgh.................................	......	100 00
Christ, Rouse's Point.. ....··	5 00	16 63
St. John's, Champlain	......	20 00
St. Peter's, Ellenburgh..........	......	10 00
Good Shepherd, Elizabethtown	......	
Keene Valley Mission.............	......	

Archdeaconry of the Susquehanna.

Christ, Cooperstown................................	45 58	150 00
Grace, Cherry Valley............................	......	75 00
Zion, Morris.	......	60 00
Christ, Gilbertsville.............	11 25	25 00
St. James', Oneonta.................................	16 50	30 00
St. Matthew's, Unadilla..............................	10 00	50 00
Christ, West Burlington..............................	......	5 00
St. Paul's, East Springfield..........	......	50 00
St. John's, Richfield Springs............................	8 00	50 44

tego....	......	$5 00
Schenevus ...	......	
l St. Jude, Worcester... ...	... ..	
Iobart.... ...	......	6 00
m...	$5 00	30 00
elhi...	20 00	125 00
iit...	......	15 89
ord...	... ..	23 71
ranklin...	. ....	11 60
idney	5 00	10 50

Archdeaconry of Ogdensburg.

gdensburg... ...	......	500 00
dam... '...	.... .	1,000 00
rerneur... ...	......	50 00
lassena ...	......	25 58
stown...	......	50 00
l, Norwood... ...	......	5 00
lk... ...	......	5 00
/addington... ...	......	30 00
n...	......	50 00
el, Morley ..,... ...	......	25 00
Lawrenceville	......	5 00
... ...	4 00	20 00
Malone...	... ..	100 00
Brushton...	......	10 00
laranac Lake... ...	......	20 00
Iogansburgh...	5 00	25 00
West Bangor... ...		
ort Covington...	......	4 12
ch Woman's Auxiliary...	430 00	
of Ogdensburg...	220 00	
Ioughton... ...	10 00	
		1,535 30

Sundry Sources.

t Convention...	$87 63	
100l...	10 00	
N. Wood...	50 00	
Austin Fund...	1,555 00	
Hannibal Green Fund... ...	250 00	
DeWitt Fund	100 00	
chial Fund...	40 00	
denburgh Bond...	30 00	
s Bond	6 00	
ighton Bond...	25 00	
y and West Troy Bridge Bond...	35 00	
aell Steamboat Bond ...	70 00	
bits Fund.....	120 00	
thern Pacific Bond	50 00	
dry Notes	42 57	
lissions... ...	100 00	
		2,571 20

Fund for Cairo, Greenville and Oak Hill Income from received from Executors 1,010 00

Special.

St. John's Church, Troy, to Epiphany, Bath........................

$16,

Balance..

$

Amounts received since making out above report and for 1892:

St. Paul's, Greenwich............................	$25 00
St. John's, Dolgeville............................	5 00
St. Paul's, Salem............................	8 41
Christ, West Burlington..........................	8 00
Good Shepherd, Elizabethtown....................	10 00

$

DISBURSEMENTS.

STIPENDS.

Archdeaconry of Albany.

Rev. Samuel C. Thompson, Rensselaerville...............	$150 00
Rev. C. H. Hatheway, West Troy......................	200 00
Rev. Wm. Chas. Grubbe, Palenville..................	250 00
Rev. E. S. DeG. Tompkins, Coxsackie................	300 00
Rev. E. C. Hoskins, Middleville....................	100 00
Rev. C. M. Conant, Middleville....................	300 00
Rev. Wm. M. Cook, Ilion and Frankfort..............	300 00
Rev. Ernest Mariett, Dolgeville.	200 00
Rev. C. P. A. Burnett, Gloversville................	41 67
Rev. Henry M. Smyth, Gloversville..................	437 50
Rev. C. C. Edmunds, Fonda.	200 00
Rev. C. E. Ball, Canajoharie and Fort Plain........	250 00
Rev. G. G. Carter, Hudson and Claverack...........	300 00
Rev. Arthur Lowndes, Philmont.	500 00
Rev. George B. Johnson, Lebanon Springs...........	300 00
Rev. Isaac Peck, Chatham........................	25 00
Right Rev. Bishop Doane for amount paid a Clergyman, Chatham and Copake..........................	37 50
Rev. G. H. Fenwick, Chatham and Copake............	112 50
Rev. M. E. Wilson, Clermont......................	75 00

$4,

Archdeaconry of Troy.

Rev. Charles Pelletreau, spl., East Line............	$25 00
Rev. Thomas White, spl., East Albany.	50 00
Rev. C. H. Hatheway, Castleton....................	200 00
Rev. S. T. Street, Schaghticoke....................	336 37
Rev. Edw. D. Tibbits, Boyntonville................	200 00
Rev. E. C. Hoskins, Mechanicville................	112 50
Rev. H. R. Timlow, Charlton	50 00
Rev. D. M. Elwood and others, Charlton...........	27 00
Rev. Thomas Boone, Round Lake and Conklingville......	250 00
Rev. C. J. Whipple, Luzerne	300 00
Rev. Alfred Taylor, Chestertown and Bartonville......	300 00

Rev. C. T. Blanchet, Bolton....................	$100 00
Rev. C. H. Lancaster, Granville	300 00
Rev. F. H. T. Horsfield Cambridge.....	100 00
Rev. Geo. H. Norton, Greenwich and Schuylerville.......	15 00
Rev. Charles W. Boyd, Greenwich and Schuylerville.....	200 00
Rev. W. F. Parsons, Greenwich and Schuylerville	133 34
Rev. H. C. Rush, Salem.................................	100 00
Rev. Henry T. Gregory, Ticonderoga...................	300 00
Rev. Wm. R. Woodbridge, Port Henry...................	262 50
Rev. J. Wm. Gill, Keeseville and Ausable Forks	500 00
Rev. H. L. Wood, Rouse's Point....................... ..	66 67
Rev. W. D. U. Shearman, Champlain........	31 25
Rev. James F. Olmsted, Rouse's Point and Champlain.....	100 00
Rev. Silas M. Rogers, Ellenburgh	160 00

$4,159 68

Archdeaconry of the Susquehanna.

Rev. F. S. Fisher, Deposit...............................	$300 00
Rev. Eugene Griggs, Bloomville........................	275 00
Rev. W. H. Goodisson, Franklin...............	300 00
Rev. Howard McDougall, Stamford.................	200 00
Rev. F. S. Griffin, Sidney....	250 00
Rev. W. G. W. Lewis, Otego.	200 00
Rev. H. E. Gilchrist, Schenevus and Worcester..........	187 50
Rev. E. A. Hartmann, Oneonta......................	275 00
Rev. David McDonald, D. D., Gilbertsville and Maple Grove.	225 00
Rev. John Prout, East Springfield.................... ..	200 00
Mr. C. A. Howells, West Burlington....................	187 50
Mr. Thurston Challen, spl., Griffin's Corners.............	50 00

2,650 00

Archdeaconry of Ogdensburg.

Rev. E. C. M. Rowden, Lyon Mountain............... ...	$66 67
Rev. W. H. Larom, Saranac Lake...	100 00
Rev. R. Wyndham Brown, Brushton and West Bangor...	170 00
Rev. Alfred Louis Fortin, Brushton and West Bangor.....	132 23
Rev. Wilfred H. Dean, Hogansburgh and Fort Covington.	121 87
Rev. David Jenkins, Hogansburgh and Fort Covington....	108 33
Rev. Angus C. Macdonald, Waddington and Lisbon.......	400 00
Rev. Joseph T. Zorn, Morristown.....	175 01
Rev. F. B. Cossitt, Morristown	37 50
Rev. Wm. R. Woodbridge, Morristown	75 00
Rev. James A. Dickson, Gouverneur....................	250 00
Rev. R. M. Kirby, D. D., Norwood and Norfolk..........	58 33
Rev. E. R. Earle, Norwood and Norfolk.............	349 99
Rev. R. M. Kirby, D. D., special, Norwood and Norfolk...	175 00
Rev. F. S. Greenhalgh, Massena.......................	216 66
Rev. Joseph T. Zorn, Santa Clara	75 00
Rev. R. Wyndham Brown, Morley	100 00

2,611 59

Sundries.

Rev. C. P. A. Burnett, De Witt Fund	$150 00
Henry Stowell, printing........	9 15

15

Postage, Envelopes..............	$19 62	
Rev. W. G. W. Lewis, expenses	20 00	
Charles Van Benthuysen & Son, printing.................	11 00	
Rev. F. M. Gray, expense...........	6 90	
Rev. W. R. Woodbridge, expense......................	17 27	$233 94
Rev. T. A. Snyder, for 1 year's interest Austin Fund of $1,500........		75 00

Diocesan Missionary.

One year's salary..................		1,500 00

Miss Austin Fund for Cairo, Greenville and Oak Hill.

Calvary Church, Cairo...... ....,....	$336 68	
Christ Church, Greenville...............	336 66	
St. Paul's Church, Oak Hill.....	336 66	1,010 00

Special.

St. John's Church, Troy, to Epiphany, Bath.........		25 00
		$16,344 33
Balance..		228 85
		$16,573 18

We, the undersigned, a Committee appointed to examine the accounts of the Treasurer, respectfully report they find the same to be correct, vouchers having been furnished for the disbursements made.

JOSEPH CAREY,
WILLIAM KEMP,
Committee.

November 14, 1892.

DIOCESE OF ALBANY,
ALBANY, *November* 15, A. D., 1892.

Herewith find statement of receipts and disbursements for the year, showing as follows:

RECEIPTS.

Balance on hand as reported to last Convention....................		$268 06
Offertories at Convention		87 63
Income from securities		2,323 57
Sundry sources.		160 00
Income Miss Austin Fund for Cairo, Greenville and Oak Hill....... ..		1,010 00
Special		25 00
Salary of the General Missionary		1,535 30
Archdeaconry of Albany.................................	$4,206 63	
Archdeaconry of Troy........	4,309 15	
Archdeaconry of the Susquehanna	723 14	
Archdeaconry of Ogdensburg.............	1,924 70	11,163 62
Total.		$16,573 18

DISBURSEMENTS.

Stipends.

Archdeaconry of Albany	$4,079 17	
Archdeaconry of Troy	4,159 63	
Archdeaconry of the Susquehanna	2,650 00	
Archdeaconry of Ogdensburg	2,611 59	
		$13,500 39
Salary of the General Missionary		1,500 00
Sundry purposes		808 94
Special		25 00
Miss Austin Fund for Cairo, Greenville and Oak Hill		1,010 00
Total		$16,844 33
Balance of account		$228 85
Received during the Convention		51 41
Balance in hand Nov. 17, 1892		$280 26

The permanent Fund represents the following amounts:

Misses Austin	$1,500 00
Elizabeth Sherers	750 00
Mrs. De Witt	5,000 00
Diocese of New York	2,000 00
Diocese of New York Parochial Fund	1,000 00
Dr. William Tibbits	2,000 00
L. H. Sears	400 00
Mrs. Hannibal Green	4,750 00
Miss Charlotte Austin	29,069 53
	$46,469 53

The Board holds in trust $19,000, received from the executors of Charlotte Austin, deceased, the income from which is to be paid, one-third each to the Rector, Wardens and Vestrymen of the following Parishes: Calvary Church, Cairo; Christ Church, Greenville; St. Paul's Church, Oak Hill.

The Board also holds in trust $2,000 of the bonds of the Rensselaer and Saratoga Railroad Company, the income from which is to be paid one-half each to St. Luke's Church, Mechanicville, and St. John's Church, Stillwater.

SELDEN E. MARVIN,
Treasurer.

REPORT OF RECEIPTS AND DISBURSEMENTS OF THE DIOCESAN MIS-SIONARY.

RECEIPTS.

Balance on hand	$6 95
Cobleskill	2 00
Christ Church, Gloversville	10 00
St. John in the Wilderness, Copake	4 00
Holy Spirit, Schenevus	3 76
St. Luke's, Milton Centre	2 61
Fort Covington	3 50
St. James', Hogansburgh	5 60

St. Luke's, Richfield.	$3 15
Good Shepherd, Cullen..	12 27
St. Andrew's, Schroon Lake..................................	28 86
St. Luke's, Chatham.	11 14
Zion, Morris.......	9 00
St. Stephen's, Maple Grove.................................	1 50
Christ Church, Gilbertsville...................	5 11
St. Paul's, Sidney.......	7 00
Archdeaconry of the Susquehanna...........	2 98
Archdeaconry of Troy...	2 36

$121 79

DISBURSEMENTS.

For personal expenses........... .... $133 74

Received from Christ Church, Cooperstown, for salary of Diocesan Missionary, and
paid to Mr. Selden E. Marvin, $15.53.

The Rev. Walter Charles Stewart, Diocesan Missionary, presented the

REPORT OF THE DIOCESAN MISSIONARY.

In making the report for the year just ending, it may be as well to begin with a
reference to some of the places mentioned in last year's report. With one exception
all the new Missions organized have thrived and done well. That exception is the
Mission of St. Matthew, in Lyon Mountain. It may be remembered that I spoke
somewhat enthusiastically of the prospects here, and, to all appearances, the
enthusiasm was justified. The attendances at the services were uniformly large
and interested: there were 21 baptisms and 16 confirmations; the sum of $300
had been pledged and guaranteed toward the support of a Missionary; and all
signs seemed to point to a bright future. Then came misfortune. Numerous dis-
charges took place among the employes of the company, and, by some peculiar process of natural selection, the unfortunate ones who lost their places were those who
were identified with our Mission. The company said that was a mere coincidence —
and probably to the same cause may be attributed the fact that the boasts of the
Methodists that they would sweep us away came true, for which curious condition
they have thanked God and taken courage. The saddest part of the affair was the
death of the Missionary, the Rev. E. C. Rowden, who had entered heartily into the
work and was doing good service in spite of great difficulties when he was stricken
down.

To turn to brighter things. Last year I reported the organization of a Mission
(All Saints') at Round Lake and stated that an effort was being made to build a
Church, and I am glad now to be able to say that thirteen months after my first visit
the Church was not only built but consecrated, when I had the pleasure of reading the
first service in it. It is a very pretty and well-appointed structure. During the
summer season so large was the attendance that, though extra seats were placed in
every available space, people were turned away. It is unnecessary for me to say
more, as the report of the Missionary, the Rev. Thomas Boone, will give the details
of the work done.

Another Church which has been finished since last report is that of the Good
Shepherd at Cullen, in Herkimer county. This is a little gem, one of the daintiest
buildings in the Diocese, and withal thoroughly churchly and complete in every detail. The altar, lectern and windows are memorials, and memorial tablets adorn
the walls. This is the gift of the Hon. D. Jones Crain to the Diocese, and I have

had the pleasure of turning over to the Trustees of the Diocese the title deeds to the property. On the 12th of June I read the service here for the first time, when the Rev. Robert Granger, of Richfield Springs, and Mr. C. A. Howells, the Lay-reader of the Mission, were present and assisted. Since that time services have been held regularly every two weeks.

On St. Barnabas' Day, acting for the Bishop, I laid the corner-stone of St. Luke's Church, Chatham. The usual service was read by the Missionary in charge, the Rev. George H. Fenwick ; the lessons were read by the Rev. Geo. B. Johnson, of Lebanon Springs ; and addresses were made by the venerable Archdeacon Sill, and the Rev. Professor Johnson, of Berkeley Divinity School. For fourteen years this Mission has been existing in a more or less precarious condition, for the last two or three years having been served by the Rector of Kinderhook, and the services were held in an upstairs room in a business block. Last year I suggested to the Bishop the advisability of setting it off as a separate Mission, or of connecting it with Copake, in order that it might be developed, believing it would eventually become a self-sustaining Parish. This was done, but not until the 14th of June was a Missionary appointed. In the meantime, however, a piece of land in a very desirable situation opposite the new school was purchased for a church lot; and as I have said, the corner-stone was laid on the 24th of August. I am assured that the guild-room will be ready for occupation by Christmas, and that by February the Church will be completed. But this is not all. Hitherto the Mission only pledged and paid $100 a year ; but with the prospect of autonomous life, and having a resident Priest, the people have received such a stimulus that they have pledged $500 a year, and have regularly paid each installment as it became due. The Missionary says he believes that if he is allowed to concentrate all his energies here the Mission will become an independent Parish in three, if not two, years. In my last Report I gave a sketch of the history of the unorganized Mission of St. John the Evangelist, at Tannersville. I am happy to say now that it has been handed over to the Diocese and organized by the Bishop, thus adding one more to the list of regular stations. I made arrangement for the supply of services there during the summer, the work being carried on by the Rev. Arthur Lowndes, of Philmont, and the Rev. Canon Hatheway. I trust I shall be able to make arrangements with the Rector at Palenville, to carry on the services every two weeks during the winter. Services were, this summer, also maintained at Hunter, four miles from Tannersville. The Rev. S. D. Van Loan, who started the work here and who has collected a good deal of money toward building a Church, writes me that he expects to be there next summer to try to accomplish the erection of a Church. At no distant date, I trust these two points will be united under the charge of a Missionary. During the winter and spring, I had been inquiring into the possibilities at Westport, on Lake Champlain. While it does not seem probable that any thing of a permanent character can be accomplished, for some time at least, it was found possible by attaching it to Elizabethtown, to create another summer station. Father Sargent, O. H. C., who held services there, reports that not only summer visitors but many of the residents attended, and he expresses the hope that the services may be continued. The Rev. W. R. Woodbridge, who also officiated here, concurs in the report. Occasional visits will be made during the coming winter and spring and the needs of the few Church people attended to.

Ashland, in Greene county, has been without regular ministrations for about a year and a half, but during the summer the Rev. W. B. Hall, of Racine, Wisconsin, who has a residence there, officiated for several weeks. It is hoped that arrangements may yet be made whereby work in this region may be revived ; in the meantime it is under the supervision of the Diocesan Missionary.

In the spring I visited the Mission at Fort Covington on the Canadian border, holding services and celebrating the Holy Communion. I also had the pleasure of presenting to the Bishop for confirmation two persons, the first fruits of this Mission, one of whom came in from the Presbyterian body. I also held service in the neighboring Mission of St. James at Hogansburgh. While staying here I availed myself of the opportunities afforded me of making several visits in that region. Not the least interesting experience here were my visits to the reservation of the St. Regis Indians, many of whom I was glad to notice among the reverent worshippers at the Church. As a result of a long drive into the country I was enabled to baptize a child whose parents gladly brought her to the Church for that purpose.

Mooers' Forks was visited in order to inquire into the possibility of reviving work here. But it did not seem feasible. I had the pleasure, however, of baptizing two children in the Church, this being the first time the doors of the edifice had been opened in years. Since that time a request has come to the Board of Missions from the Presbyterians for leave to use our Church; and there may be here a hint worthy of consideration by that Board.

The situation at Sidney is worth a passing glance. The Mission of St. Paul, which had been so wisely and self-sacrificingly served by the Rev. F. S. Griffin, shows every prospect of growth and success. But it needs fostering care for a time. The growth of the town is so great that the demand for houses far exceeds the supply. When a factory now in process of erection is completed it is estimated that five hundred new people will come into town; and another factory, which will give employment to many more people, is soon to be built. Two lots—one for Church and the other for Rectory—have been secured. About $1,000 is in hand toward the building fund, and I trust next spring the erection of a Church will be commenced. It is believed by the local Churchmen, and I am inclined to concur in their belief, that if this point be faithfully worked for the next three years it will be a self-supporting Parish.

Last summer I went up to Schroon Lake. In some old copies of the Convention Journal I had seen parochial reports from St. Andrew's Chapel there, but none had appeared for four years. I wrote to the Junior Warden, who invited me to go up and visit the place. On doing so I found that summer services had been held during these last four years, but the expenses had been so great that no money was left in the Treasury for winter services. I remained here for some time, officiating on Sundays, and trying to revive the work. It seemed too bad that, with about fifty communicants among the residents of the place, and with a nice Chapel, these poor people should be without the comforts of the Church. The natives are almost entirely dependent upon what they can make during the short summer season when the city folks come here. It is a matter of great thankfulness that I am able to report having secured the sum of $600, so that, for a year at least, there will be a Missionary at work in this field. Another cause for gratitude is the fact that the place is filled. While here I baptized seven adults and six children. One of those baptized was over eighty-two years of age. I also presented eleven to the Bishop for confirmation. Had there not been, unfortunately, some uncertainty as to the exact date of the Bishop's visitation, eight more would have been added to the list, as they were all prepared, but at too great a distance to notify in time.

It is unnecessary to specify in detail all the other places I have visited and served. It must be enough to remark that there are places where there is no hope for growth, where one can but go occasionally to minister and to give such comfort as one may till they die a natural death. During the period of my active service—for I was absent three months on leave, and one month by reason of sickness—I held 61 services and took part in 20 more; preached 61 sermons and made 9 addresses; celebrated the Holy Communion 22 times; baptized 9 adults and 14 children, making a total of 23;

and presented 13 candidates for confirmation. There have been three Missions organized; one revived; one new one started; summer services have been supplied in three places; two new Churches built; and one corner-stone laid during the past year.

WALTER C. STEWART.

The Rev. Charles M. Nickerson, D. D., presented and read the

REPORT OF THE COMMITTEE ON DIOCESAN MISSIONS.

The Report of the Board of Missions, submitted to your Committee, is a document fitted to give rise to reflections congratulatory or the reverse according to the point of view of the person taking it into consideration.

As an exhibit of the Missionary activity and interest in Missions of the Diocese of Albany compared with the Missionary activity and interest in Missions of other Dioceses, it makes a fairly creditable showing. As Diocesan Missionary appropriations go, the $13,734 expended by the Board during the last year is a tidy bit of money; only two or three Dioceses, and they the wealthiest in the land, have done better.

Nowhere else does the Missionary machinery appear to have run more smoothly, and with fewer stoppages and interruptions traceable to the unskillful adjustment of its several parts.

Nowhere else is the Diocesan Council, acting in its capacity of Missionary Committee of the Whole, so seldom called upon to listen to desponding appeals to make good a deficit which is the only too apparent outcome of pledges unfulfilled and of the apathy of Rectors and their congregations. But as an indication of the disposition of the Churchmen of this Diocese to make a liberal use of the means God has given them for the upbuilding of His kingdom, the report of the Board, it must be confessed, comes something short of what one would like to see, for it shows that the work intrusted to the Board is the one thing in the Diocese of Albany that is standing still. There has been activity everywhere along the line except just here. To go no further back than ten years, the number of Clergy has increased from 119 to 129, or 9 per cent; the number of Parishes and Missions stations from 147 to 179, or 32 per cent; the number of persons annually confirmed, from 1,086, to 1,588, or nearly 50 per cent; the number of communicants from 13,226 to 16,507, or 25 per cent. The sum total of contributions from $240,118 to $338,207, or 41 per cent.

The offerings for Diocesan Missions have increased not one dollar. The sum voted ten years ago, yes twenty years ago, was $10,000, and that was precisely the sum voted last year, and it is the sum likely to be voted this year, unless the members of the Council here assembled resolve in earnest to look their responsibilities and their opportunity in the face.

In thus venturing to call attention to the fact that the offerings for Missions have remained unchanged, while those for all other purposes have increased from 25 to 50 per cent, your Committee are aware that they are laying themselves open to the charge of only repeating what has been said here every year, in the memory of the oldest member of this Council.

It is an old story, but is it not on that account all the more a reproach to us? Ought we not seriously to try to do something to get out of this twenty-year-old rut of a ten thousand dollar appropriation? Might we not at least venture to make it $11,000, if for no other reason than for the sake of a change? The result might be a report by our Treasurer to the next Convention of an overdraft unprecedented in the history of the Diocese. But would that be an altogether unmixed calamity? It might stimulate us to exertions we are slow to make because things seem ⟶   ⟶ are.

On the eve of the assembling of the Council of a ⟩

bearing a smile of satisfaction on his face, said to a prominent lay delegate: " We shall make a grand report to-morrow — all Missionary stipends paid and $50 in the treasury." " I am very sorry to hear it," was the reply. " The best thing you can do is at once to call all your Missionary board together and appropriate $100 extra salary to your most deserving Missionary, so that you may report a fifty dollar deficit. If you do not do that every parson in the Council will go home convinced that he is at liberty to let the next year's contribution of his Parish drop off $50, and then where will you be?" While not venturing to predict that any such result will follow the announcement of a surplus made to us to-night, your Committee are nevertheless of the opinion, drawing their conclusions from this report and the almost identical reports of the last twenty years, that the very ease with which the endeavored has been achieved, the absence of effort and the rarity of urgent appeals to each and every member of the Council to bestir himself to relieve the Diocese from the charge of leaving its pledges to its Missionaries unredeemed, the conviction we all share that our Bishop will bring whatever he lays his hands to to a successful issue, whether we give him a very active support or not, have engendered in the minds of Clergy and laymen a comforting assurance that the Missionary board has all the money it really requires for the effective prosecution of its work, and that in the hurry and press of meeting the new parochial needs which continually arise, a harassed Rector, and a prudent Senior Warden may safely defer the assumption of an increased apportionment to the happy millennium all Rectors hope for but few are permitted to see, the millennium of a surplus in the parochial treasury. Therefore we present the following resolution:

Resolved, That $11,000 be the amount to be raised for Missionary purposes in the Diocese for the coming year.

All of which is respectfully submitted.

C. M. NICKERSON,
ELMER P. MILLER,
LEVI HASBROUCK,
JAMES RUSSELL PARSONS, Jr.

The Convention adjourned to the following day.

SECOND DAY.

WEDNESDAY MORNING, NOVEMBER 16, 7:30 O'CLOCK.

The Bishop of the Diocese ordered Deacons Mr. John Mills Gilbert, presented by the Rev. Clarence M. Conant, and Mr. Charles Albert Howells, presented by the Rev. Canon Fulcher, and the Holy Communion was administered, in the Cathedral, the Bishop of the Diocese celebrating, assisted by the Rev. Canon Hatheway.

10 O'CLOCK.

Morning prayer was said in the Cathedral by the Dean.

The Bishop of the Diocese read the portion of his Annual Address containing the record of visitations.

11:15 O'CLOCK.

The Right Rev. President took the chair and called the Convention to order in the Gymnasium of St. Agnes' School.

The minutes of the previous day were read and adopted.

The names of the Clergy and Lay Deputies not present on the first day were called by the Secretary.

The Rev. John M. Gilbert, the Rev. Charles A. Howells, the Rev. Eaton W. Maxcy, D. D., the Rev. Clement J. Whipple, and Messrs. George Gibbons, of St. Peter's Church, Albany, Edward P. Van Alstyne, of St. Paul's Church, Kinderhook, Clarence L. Crofts, of Christ Church, Hudson, Robert J. Washbon, of Christ Church, Coxsackie, Benjamin H. Hall, of St. John's Church, Troy, Henry S. Tracy, of Grace Church, Waterford, G. R. P. Shackelford, of Bethesda Church, Saratoga Springs, and Ralph W. McDougall, of Christ Church, Duanesburgh, answered to their names and took their seats in the Convention.

The Right Rev. President presented a communication which he had received from the Commissioners of Statutory Revision, which, on motion of the Rev. Canon Stewart, was referred to the Committee on the Constitution and Canons.

COMMUNICATION FROM THE COMMISSIONERS OF STATUTORY REVISION.

STATE OF NEW YORK,
OFFICE OF THE COMMISSIONERS OF STATUTORY REVISION,
ALBANY, *Nov.* 15, 1892.

Rt. Rev. WILLIAM C. DOANE, D. D., LL. D., 29 Elk street, Albany, N. Y. :

Dear Sir — The Commissioners of Statutory Revision are about to undertake a revision of the draft of the Religious Corporations Law presented by them to the Legislature of last winter with a view to its enactment by the Legislature this year. The former draft was unsatisfactory to some of the authorities of the Episcopal Church. The only desire of the Commission is to present a bill which meets the views of the various Churches which are brought under its provisions, especially so far as regards matters of internal government. As there is a Convention of the Diocese now being held at Albany, if such a course is proper, I would respectfully suggest that you bring the matter to the attention of the Convention. I understand there are only a few points as to which there is a conflict of opinion, and if we can determine the sense of your Diocese as to these, it will be of great assistance to us in framing a satisfactory bill.

At a later day, when your duties are less exacting, I should like to call upon you, and go over with you the bill section by section.

I send you two copies of the bill as proposed at the last session of the Legislature.

Very respectfully yours,
R. C. CUMMING,
With Revision Commission.

16

The Rev. George Dent Silliman presented and read the Reports of the Trustees of the Fund for Widows and Orphans of Deceased Clergy—men, and of the Committee on the same.

REPORT OF THE TRUSTEES OF THE FUND FOR THE SUPPORT OF WIDOWS AND ORPHANS OF DECEASED CLERGYMEN.

DIOCESE OF ALBANY,
ALBANY, *November* 15, 1892.

The Trustees of the Fund for the Support of the Widows and Orphans of Deceased Clergymen present herewith the Report of the Treasurer, showing the Receipts and Disbursements for the year:

RECEIPTS.

Balance on hand as reported to last Convention........	$1,012 75
From Parishes...	271 15
From Investments.......	210 00
Total	$1,493 90

DISBURSEMENTS.

For special stipends........	$250 00
Balance..............................	1,243 90
Total.. ..	$1,493 90

The Trustees hold the following securities, presented by St. Paul's Church, Albany:

One United States Registered 4 per cent. Bond	$1,000 00
Two Chicago, Burlington & Quincy Railroad, Nebraska Extension, 4 per cent. Bonds.....	2,000 00
One Chicago, Burlington & Quincy Railroad 4 per cent. Bond...........	1,000 00
One Wabash Railway 5 per cent. Bond..........................	1,000 00
Total	$5,000 00
Also three Bonds of $500 each·...........	1,500 00
Making permanent Investment.................	$6,500 00

WILLIAM CROSWELL DOANE,
President.
SELDEN E. MARVIN,
Treasurer.

REPORT OF THE COMMITTEE ON THE FUND FOR WIDOWS AND OR-PHANS OF DECEASED CLERGYMEN.

The Committee on the Report of the Trustees of the Fund for the Support of the Widows and Orphans of Deceased Clergymen, having examined the accounts and vouchers, find them correct.

The Fund has not increased rapidly. Many Parishes do not contribute. It seems to be a fair question suggested by the Bishop's Address whether the multiplication of agencies for the collection of funds does not weaken the cause instead of strength-ening it. There are three Canons for the Relief of Aged and Infirm Clergy, their Widows and Orphans. It is the opinion of the Committee that in the consolidation of all the funds raised for the purpose there would be wisdom and strength.

All of which is respectfully submitted.

GEORGE D. SILLIMAN,
JAMES A. HOLDEN,
MYRON D. JEWELL.

The Rev. Sheldon Munson Griswold presented and read Report, Number 2, of the Committee on the Diocesan Fund ; the recommendations of which were adopted.

REPORT, NUMBER 2, OF THE COMMITTEE ON THE DIOCESAN FUND.

Your Committee, to whom was referred the Report of the Committee appointed to prepare a plan for the insurance of the Missionaries of the Diocese, respectfully report, that after careful consideration of the plan suggested and the appended resolution, they recommend its adoption with the following amendments, viz.: that the words in clause (B) "and at work" be stricken out ; and that in clause (B) and also, clause (C) for the words "Board of Missions," there be substituted in each case the words " Treasurer of the Diocese, for the increase of the Insurance Fund."

Signed for the Committee,

SHELDON MUNSON GRISWOLD,

Chairman.

The resolution and plan of Clerical Insurance, reported by the Committee on Clerical Insurance, were then adopted with the amendments recommended by the Committee on the Diocesan Fund, as follows :

PLAN OF CLERICAL INSURANCE.

(*a*) When a Policy of Insurance is placed upon any life, each person so insured shall give to the Treasurer of the Diocese an assignment of all the right, title and interest, accruing in consequence of such insurance to his surviving heirs.

(*b*) If at the time of his death the insured shall be canonically resident within the Diocese, the interest of the principal amount insured,at the best per cent. obtainable, consistent with security, shall be paid by the Treasurer to the surviving widow or minor children of the deceased. Such payment of interest shall cease and determine at the time of such widow's death or remarriage, and, in the case of minor children, when they attain legal age. The principal amount shall thenceforward be subject to the control of the Treasurer of the Diocese for the increase of the Insurance Fund.

(*c*) If the insured shall have removed from the Diocese, or shall have accepted a Rectorship within it, which yields a stipend of $1,000 or over, per annum, the amount insured shall at once upon maturity become the property of the Treasurer of the Diocese for the increase of the Insurance Fund.

(*d*) The amount of each policy taken out under this plan shall be $1,000.

Resolved, That the Convention authorizes the addition of one-half of one per cent. per annum to the ordinary assessment for Diocesan Fund, which additional sum shall be devoted to the payment of Clergy Insurance Premiums.

The order of the day was taken up, being the election of the Board of Missions and other business connected with the Mission work of the Diocese.

It having been announced that the Rev. William R. Woodbridge desired to be relieved from service as Secretary of the Board of Missions. on motion of the Secretary of the Convention, it was

Resolved, That a Committee be appointed to prepare a minute expressing the sense of the Convention of the high value of the services of the Rev. William R. Woodbridge as Secretary of the Board of Missions

The Right Rev. President appointed as such Committee, Rev. William O. Prout, the Rev. Walter C. Stewart and Mr. George B. Pattison.

The election of the Board of Missions being in order, nominations were received for the Archdeaconries as presented in the Report of the Secretary of the Convention; and, on motion of the Rev. Canon Fulcher, the Rev. Charles Temple and Mr. William Kemp were nominated for the Diocese at large.

On motion of the Secretary of the Convention, the ballot was unanimously dispensed with, and the following named persons were elected as the Board of Missions until the next Convention.

BOARD OF MISSIONS.

ARCHDEACONRY OF ALBANY.
The Rev. W. W. Battershall, D. D.   Mr. J. H. Van Antwerp.

ARCHDEACONRY OF TROY.
The Rev. F. M. Cookson.   Mr. George A. Wells.

ARCHDEACONRY OF THE SUSQUEHANNA.
The Rev. Robert N. Parke, D. D.   Mr. Robert M. Townsend.

ARCHDEACONRY OF OGDENSBURG.
The Rev. R. M. Kirby, D. D.   Mr. T. Streatfeild Clarkson.

DIOCESE AT LARGE.
The Rev. Charles Temple.   Mr. William Kemp.

The resolution recommended in the Report of the Board of Missions was adopted, as follows:

Resolved, That $11,000 be the amount to be raised for Missionary purposes in this Diocese the coming year.

Certain changes having been announced, the apportionment of last year as so modified was adopted, as follows:

DIOCESE OF ALBANY.

PLAN OF APPORTIONMENT TO RAISE MISSIONARY FUND.

Archdeaconry of Albany.

The Cathedral of all Saints	$1,200 00
St. Peter's, Albany...	1,000 00
St. Paul's, Albany	300 00
Grace, Albany	50 00
Holy Innocents', Albany...............	50 00
Trinity, Albany..........	20 00
Trinity, Rensselaerville	15 00
Trinity, West Troy.	45 00
St. Andrew's, West Troy	5 00
St. Mark's, Green Island...............	30 00
St. John's, Cohoes...	250 00

, Athens.............	$25 00
', Cairo	10 00
Dei, Palenville	10 00
.e's, Catskill...................................	150 00
Greenville	5 00
l's, Oak Hill	5 00
Duanesburgh.........	60 00
rge's, Schenectady.....................	200 00
Schenectady	20 00
's, Amsterdam	60 00
hepherd, Canajoharie...	15 00
imba's, St. Johnsville	2 50
onda	10 00
n's, Johnstown	75 00
. Fairfield.........	5 00
Herkimer.....	60 00
uel, Little Falls................................	50 00
ustine's, Ilion.....	35 00
n's, Dolgeville.....	10 00
Claverack	12 00
e's, Clermont	10 00
lour, Lebanon Springs	20 00
n's, Stockport	25 00
abas' Stottville	25 00
es', Rossman's Mills.................................	5 00
k's, Philmont	20 00
e's, Chatham	5 00
n's, Copake	5 00
l's, Kinderhook	75 00
Hudson	100 00
its', Hudson	12 00
Gloversville	25 00
Mohawk...................	15 00
n's, Frankfort...	5 00
oss, Fort Plain	5 00
Memorial, Middleville	20 00
Coxsackie	5 00
Ashland.	5 00
garet's, Menand's Station	5 00
	$4,171 50

Archdeaconry of Troy.

l's, Troy...	$750 00
l's, Troy..........	600 00
Troy...................................	250 00
oss, Troy..........	200 00
n, Troy.....................................	50 00
s's, Troy.....	20 00
abas', Troy	50 00
y, East Albany...................................	5 00
, Greenbush......	25 00
Lansingburgh..........	150 00

Trinity, Schaghticoke	$15 00
St. Mark's, Hoosick Falls..................................	150 00
All Saints', Hoosac	30 00
Holy Name, Boyntonville..............	5 00
St. Giles', Castleton....................	10 00
Grace, Waterford....	85 00
Christ, Ballston......................	100 00
St. John's, East Line.......................................	5 00
Grace, Jonesville	10 00
All Saints', Round Lake..................................	5 00
Calvary, Burnt Hills	25 00
St. Paul's, Charlton .. ..,..........	10 00
Bethesda, Saratoga...... ....,..............	200 00
St. Stephen's, Schuylerville...............	5 00
St. John's, Conklingville.....	5 00
St. Paul's, Salem............................	60 00
St. John's, Stillwater....	10 00
St. Luke's, Cambridge.......................................	175 00
Trinity, Granville...........	25 00
North Granville.................................	10 00
St. Paul's, Greenwich	25 00
St. James', Fort Edward.............................	20 00
Zion, Sandy Hill.	50 00
Trinity, Whitehall...	50 00
St. James', Caldwell	20 00
St. Mary's, Luzerne	20 00
Holy Cross, Warrensburgh........	50 00
Messiah, Glens Falls......................................	150 00
Good Shepherd, Chestertown	15 00
St. Paul's, Bartonville	8 00
Church of the Cross, Ticonderoga.........................	30 00
Christ, Port Henry...	31 25
Emmanuel, Mineville	5 00
St. James', Ausable Forks	15 00
St. John's, Essex...	80 00
St, Paul's, Keeseville...................	15 00
Trinity, Plattsburgh	75 00
Christ, Rouse's Point.........	15 00
St. John's, Champlain	20 00
St. Peter's, Ellenburgh....................................	10 00
Good Shepherd, Elizabethtown........	10 00
St. Luke's, Mechanicville....	20 00

3,674 25

Archdeaconry of the Susquehanna.

St. Peter's, Hobart	$35 00
Christ, Walton.	30 00
St. John's, Delhi...	125 00
Grace, Stamford	20 00
St. Paul's, Franklin	20 00
St. Paul's, Sidney	5 00
Christ, Butternuts....	25 00

Christ, Cooperstown.....	$150 00	
Grace, Cherry Valley...........................	75 00	
Zion, Morris..............................	55 00	
St. James', Oneonta...........	30 00	
St. Matthew's, Unadilla	50 00	
Christ, West Burlington...........................	5 00	
St. Paul's, East Springfield	50 00	
St. John's, Richfield Springs..........	50 00	
Immanuel, Otego	5 00	
Of the Holy Spirit, Schenevus	10 00	
St. Simon and St. Jude's, Worcester.........	5 00	
		$745 00

Archdeaconry of Ogdensburg.

St. John's, Ogdensburg.........	$500 00	
Trinity, Potsdam.........................	450 00	
Trinity, Gouverneur.....................................	50 00	
St. John's, Massena	50 00	
Christ, Morristown	40 00	
Grace, Norfolk.......	5 00	
St. Paul's, Waddington...............	30 00	
Grace, Canton..	50 00	
Trinity, Morley	25 00	
St. Luke's, Lisbon...	5 00	
St. Andrew's, Norwood.........................	10 00	
St. Mark's, Malone	100 00	
St. Peter's, Brushton......................................	10 00	
St. Thomas', Lawrenceville	5 00	
Zion, Colton	20 00	
St. Luke's, Saranac Lake	20 00	
St. James', Hogansburgh	25 00	
St. Mark's, West Bangor........................	5 00	
		1,400 00
Total.........................		$9,990 75

RECAPITULATION.

Archdeaconry of Albany	$4,171 50
Archdeaconry of Troy	3,674 25
Archdeaconry of the Susquehanna...	745 00
Archdeaconry of Ogdensburg...........	1,400 00
	$9,990 75

The Rev. James W. Stewart presented and read Report No. 1,
of the Committee on the Constitution and Canons; the resolution contained in which was adopted.

REPORT, NUMBER 1, OF THE COMMITTEE ON THE CONSTITUTION AND CANONS.

The Committee on the Constitution and Canons, having considered the communication in regard to the Revision of the Religious Corporations Law, referred to them
by the Convention, respectfully recommend the adoption of the following preambles
and resolution :

WHEREAS, The attention of the Convention has been called to the proposed action of the Commissioners of Statutory Revision in regard to the revision of the draft of the Religious Corporations Law, presented by them to the Legislature of last winter, with a view to its enactment by the Legislature of this winter; and

WHEREAS, The Commission express the desire "to present a bill which meets the views of the various Churches that are brought under its provisions, especially so far as regards matters of internal government":

Resolved, That this Convention respectfully requests the Bishop of New York to call, at an early date, a meeting of the Federate Council to consider the proposed draft and to secure joint action in the interest of the Church in the State of New York.

For the Committee,
J. W. STEWART,
Chairman.

The hour for the annual elections having arrived, the Right Rev. President appointed the Tellers;

STANDING COMMITTEE.

Clerical Vote.	*Lay Vote.*
The Rev. George B. Richards.	The Rev. George L. Richardson.
Mr. G. R. P. Shackelford.	Mr. John A. Dix.

On motion, it was

Resolved, That the Secretary of the Convention be instructed to cast the ballot of the Clergy, and Mr. John A. Dix, that of the laity, for the members of the Standing Committee as nominated by the Secretary of the Convention on yesterday.

The ballots were cast accordingly, and the Right Rev. President declared elected as members of

THE STANDING COMMITTEE,

The Rev. J. Ireland Tucker, S. T. D., the Rev. Fenwick Mitford Cookson, the Rev. Wilford Lash Robbins, D. D., the Rev. James Caird, Mr. Norman B. Squires, Mr. Henry S. Wynkoop, Mr. John I. Thompson and Mr. John H. Van Antwerp.

On motion of the Secretary of the Convention the ballot was dispensed with, and the following elections were made:

MEMBERS OF THE MISSIONARY COUNCIL.

The Rev. J. Philip B. Pendleton, S. T. B., and Mr. Benjamin H. Hall.

TRUSTEES OF THE EPISCOPAL FUND.

Mr. J. H. Van Antwerp, Mr. W. Bayard Van Rensselaer, Mr. Charles W. Tillinghast, 2nd, Mr. Dean Sage, Mr. Robert C. Pruyn.

TRUSTEES OF THE FUND FOR AGED AND INFIRM CLERGYMEN.

Mr. Norman B. Squires, Mr. Robert S. Oliver, and Mr. J. J. Tillinghast.

The Rev. George B. Johnson read the reports of the Society for the
Home Study of the Holy Scripture, and of the Committee on the same;
and the resolutions of the Report of the Committee were adopted.

REPORT OF THE SOCIETY FOR THE HOME STUDY OF HOLY SCRIPTURE AND CHURCH HISTORY.

BY THE ORGANIZING SECRETARY.

In the review of our sixth year's work and the forecast of the seventh, there is
great cause for thankfulness and joy. It is my privilege to emphasize that which
statistics feebly tell — an increase of earnestness and perseverance — higher aims apparent and richer results in the instruction of others.

In the seventy-five new members admitted this autumn we see fresh tokens of a
serious purpose. The ranks of the do-littles are dwindling, soon we trust to disap-
pear. The entrance examination now used sets before the student at once her needs,
and guarantees her steadiness. We ought not to reckon among the failures the large
numbers disabled by illness, so reducing the figures of the past year, but swelling
those of this. The most cheering feature of our opening has been in fact the very
large number of former students who after intervals of from one to four years have
returned to us with renewed ardor.

Our membership roll for the year 1891-92 numbered 215; of these, 100 entered for
the June examination. Only 58 really took it. Of these, 18 were in the Acts, 5
in St. John, 15 in Exodus and 2 in the Epistles. In Church History, 18. Out of the
total of 58, there were 51 who passed with honor; 6 others, all in their first year's
work, satisfactorily, and only 1 failed, with extenuating causes. Our graduates
were 8, the low number being due to the prevalent sickness. It will be compen-
sated in the unusually large class of 1893. It should not be overlooked that outside
of these figures is found a very much larger number, not attempting a final examination, but returning papers throughout the year showing both mental and spiritual
profit of a high order.

Our class record for the future year stands thus: 84 in the first year's course, 48 in
the second, 15 in the third, and 27 in the fourth; 3 in the post-graduate course, and
31 in Church History; also 19 regular readers, and 15, mostly graduates, doing
special reading. Readers and honorary members who often re-enter later, will no
doubt make our total 250, and adding those who attend lectures and our correspondents, who are of necessity deeper and more constant students, we may estimate our
entire membership as 300.

17

Could all these students of Holy Scripture and of the History of the Church be gathered together from their widely scattered homes, and could our Bishops and Clergy survey them from some gallery — somewhat as they of late have been themselves surveyed — no other appeal would be needed and my pen might pause here, and trust to the inspiring spectacle. Even a glance would reveal the fact that they were no common company. Wives and mothers as well as daughters, leaders in all works for the Church and charity; women whose influence is powerful in the social circle — such are many, if not the most. Surely the right training of these can be second only to that of our theological students, whose numbers they at least equal.

As a matter of fact no other work in the Church is so scantily sustained. Not a single salary of any sort is provided for, and the director bears almost alone the burden of soliciting the funds required by its general needs. Upon her fall alone the multitudinous details of a work heavy enough for a trained staff of four or five. It is inevitable that its highest interests suffer.

There are but two possible ways of meeting this need — the best I believe would be by gifted women giving their lives to the work unremunerated save by the Great Rewarder — the second by a salary such as would secure a really competent and well-trained and permanent helper.

The work has so grown that it cannot possibly be properly done by helpers coming in for a few hours or days. The uncertainty and inaccuracy which without the slightest blame attach to such work, rebound heavily upon the one who must fill every gap and set right every mistake? This year five months of work, beginning with July and outlasting November, with rare intermissions of a few days, have been required to wind up the clerical duties of last year and to reach the point where actual instruction begins. And this with the most careful system. Sometimes even in a so-called vacation, the labor that begins at 9 o'clock one morning goes on till 1 o'clock of the next morning. Should this burden be unlifted by another summer, the director will feel herself compelled to refuse any further admissions and confine herself to the care of those already in. Six years of such sore struggle may well make one pause, and ask if such martyrdom be really called for, and whether it be not a higher duty to so state the case, that others may realize their responsibility in the matter.

And here may I go on a little further to point out as the real root of the difficulty, the amazing slumber of our Church over the whole question of religious education; and especially such education for women? We look with pity upon the Dark Ages. But what if some women then could have foreseen *us* with our thousands of fair ladies cultured in all other knowledge — with hands skilled in music, painting and embroidery — and yet profoundly ignorant of the one book we profess to honor above all others — knowing far less of it than Christian women did in those same Dark Ages before it was printed and criticised and neglected; and withal laying its counsels so little to heart that for a hundred lives given up then so gladly to serve God, there is now barely one? True indeed that the many do each *a little* for Him as they can spare time from other foremost concerns. But is it true that Christian devotedness has increased? Was not the pithy French writer correct when he said of our age, " We whirl more but we advance less?" Do our Bishops and our Clergy at all understand that the great majority of the women who are communicants in our churches have far less knowledge of the Bible than they have of scores of novels — that they are utterly unable to give the most meagre outline of the history of the Church or to define to their children and friends the fundamental doctrines of the Gospel, or to distinguish them from the heresies which they hear and read on every hand? Is that a safe condition for either men or women?

I saw lately on two successive days two sights which put the Church to shame for this indifference. One was Bryn Mawr College, the other the Drexel Institute. At the former the President drew my special attention to a newly-erected building, a noble structure for laboratory work only; one floor was given up to chemistry, all the rest to biology; the apparatus was abundant, the libraries most learned, the professors picked men and women from all countries.

I had loved as a child and given my warmest sympathies to the ardent girl who had developed into the Dean whose rare learning and still more exceptional administrative power had planned and guided this highest work for women in our land. There, too, I saw hundreds of young women — doing what? — learning to turn the keys of earthly knowledge and to trace the secrets of life in plants and animals. For this they could forego the sweets of home. For this they gave up the charms of society, at least as to its chief fascinations. And it was even intimated to me that celibacy, so long condemned as unnatural and dangerous in the religious life, was in this cause a splendid sacrifice! All day and half that night the question rang its changes through my soul, "What is the Church of God doing to train her children, her daughters, to trace out the laws of *spiritual* life and give them the wisdom that alone completes all knowledge?" And when the next day at the Drexel Institute I saw the munificent gifts which were devoted to the development of skill in the higher handicrafts so to secure a better living for this brief life, another question pursued me day and night, "Was there no one in this Church of God in our great country wise and far-sighted enough to bestow his or her wealth to provide for at least the training of a few who should teach others also how to make the fullest preparation for the long, endless life that lies *beyond* this? Was there really no child of light as wise as the children of this world?"

A paper read at the recent Church Congress at Folkstone gave some startling evidence that the Church of England was not training her clergy as thoroughly as did the Roman, and that Baptists and Wesleyans far outstripped her in the generous encouragement given to young men of promise without means, and especially to train such as missionaries and lay helpers.

Equally startling to the Church in our own land should be the simple fact of an activity all around us in fitting women for nobler work. And alas! now that we begin to awaken we find that the very idea of such a devotion has almost perished from among us, or that the few who feel it are pressed into work for which they are not prepared.

As carefully as one re-lights the expiring fire upon the hearth-stone, should the feeble sparks of such devotedness be fanned till haply by God's great grace they may leap into a flame.

It remains for me to touch upon four other branches of this work more or less dependent upon it.

1. The Library.— The work connected with this has greatly extended. Five hundred volumes went last year to all parts of the land, and again without the loss of one. When one notes the percentage of even solid reading in other libraries those figures will not seem small. So far as my inquiries reach each loan represents from five to ten readers. Very slowly the busy ladies of New York are discovering that there *is* such a library, and the almost bewilderment of joy over its treasures would if witnessed richly reward our benefactors.

Said a college president to me with a sigh: "We have only $3,000 a year to spend on our library." And I could not repress a smile, when replying that we had so much as $300.

And besides our $300 has somehow been made to do so much, and so wonderfully have treasures seemed to drop at our feet that the books seem to be really of ten-fold value. The history of the collection is almost a romance. Sooner or later whatever has been needed and desired comes to us, till hundreds of books, always marked in catalogues as scarce or very rare, stand upon our shelves. The most recent treasure is a very perfect copy of St. Bernard, printed only three years later than the discovery of America.

2. The Lectures.— There were three courses of these last winter arranged under difficulties which we trust are but temporary. The Advent Course upon the Second Coming of our Lord and the Lenten Course upon the Psalms were very well attended. A small class in the Catechism — for training — and a class in New Testament Greek were also conducted in the same room.

3. St. Anna's Hall.— The establishment of this has suffered sorely from the want of more help and helpers. That the rooms have been renovated and were partially furnished is cause for gratitude, and still more so that at different times so many as eight ladies availed themselves of its opportunities for study and reading and lectures. So long as the director is obliged in her solitary person to meet the duties of organization, instruction, lectures, head librarian, accountant, solicitor of funds and housekeeper, with other sundries, she cannot hope to develope largely what is waiting to be done in this new direction. She trusts also to be sustained in the judgment unanimous among the trustees, that it must not be allowed to become a mere boarding-house under any pressure of false economy. Two ladies are expecting to devote themselves to the work in about two years, and meantime we trust that some not unworthy results may be quietly achieved. It is greatly to be desired that as many of our members as possible will avail themselves of the privileges of such a house though it may be only for a short time.

4. The League of St. Lois.— Some association of mothers has long been contemplated — as a branch of our work — of mothers who should take up the sacred duty of instructing their own children in the Holy Scripture, and most of whom would probably need some special preparation and aid. At a drawing room meeting held during the General Convention at Baltimore, the subject was first presented, and the organization of it under the above name was committed to Mrs. Albert Sioussat, the President of the Maryland Branch of the Woman's Auxiliary. It is most earnestly commended to the prayers and cooperation of all mothers. The olden chain of St. Lois, St. Eunice and St. Timothy may yet be repeated among us, and give us, as then, in the third generation at least, many a godly Bishop.

Thus on every side the possibilities of our work grow upon us. Score upon score of grateful letters from our students tell what it is more and more meaning to them. One after another offers whatever lies in her power of gifts of time or money. And from those who cannot join our ranks come a growing sympathy and more generous support. So that with all the difficulties and delays of cherished hopes we can indeed thank God and take courage.

SARAH F. SMILEY.

REPORT OF THE COMMITTEE ON THE REPORT OF THE SOCIETY FOR THE HOME STUDY OF HOLY SCRIPTURE AND CHURCH HISTORY.

Your Committee on the Report of the Society for the Home Study of Holy Scripture and Church History commend to the Convention the careful study of the Report itself. We cannot express too high an opinion of the value of the work that is undertaken, and the zeal and energy with which it is carried on.

We call special attention to what is said as to the widespread ignorance of Holy Scripture on the part of women in other respects highly educated. This ignorance is by no means confined to women. It is well known that candidates for Holy Orders are often found to be most imperfectly acquainted with even the bare facts of Bible History.

This ignorance is due primarily to the neglect of the duty of reading the Bible, a duty imperative upon all who believe that the Bible contains the one record of God's Revelations to mankind.

This neglect arises from many causes. To two we venture to call special attention. One is the widespread disuse of the daily service, especially in country places. Though attended by few, the daily service sets before the people a standard of what the Church expects of her children in respect of devotion and the reading of Holy Scripture. In old times many made a practice of reading the daily psalms and lessons. Though unable to be present at the service, children were taught that it was a duty to read a chapter of the Bible every day, just as much as to say their prayers. We fear that the Clergy often take it for granted that these simple religious duties are performed by their people, and fail to press their importance.

Again, while there has been the greatest possible improvement in the printing of other books, Bibles are still commonly printed in fine type, and in a generally unattractive fashion. It is impossible to procure a copy of the four Gospels, printed in attractive form, for distribution to children. We submit that this is a great practical hindrance to the reading of the Bible of the present day.

Your Committee present the following resolutions:

Resolved, That, subject to the discretion of the Bishop, the Secretary of the Convention be instructed to have printed in the Journal the Report of the Society for the Home Study of Holy Scripture and Church History.

Resolved, That the Bishop be requested to consider under what conditions the daily service may wisely be restored, especially in country Parishes, and, in his discretion, to give his counsel to the Clergy on this subject.

Resolved, That it be referred to the Bible and Common Prayer Book Society of Albany and its vicinity, to consider the expediency of providing for the publication of the four Gospels and the Acts of the Apostles in an attractive volume, in large type, and arranged in paragraphs, with a view to encouraging the reading of Holy Scripture by children; and that they be requested to report to the next Convention.

Resolved, That it be commended to such as have the means to provide for the support of the work of this Society.

GEORGE B. JOHNSON,
WM. CHARLES GRUBBE,
JOHN KEYES PAIGE.

The Rev. George G. Carter, S. T. D., presented and read

REPORT, NUMBER 2, OF THE COMMITTEE ON THE AGED AND INFIRM CLERGY FUND.

Your Committee, to which was referred the Report of the Treasurer of the Clergy Reserve Fund, together with that portion of the Bishop's Address treating of the subject, beg leave to report that they find that this Fund is now less than two years old; that last year four Parishes contributed to it the sum of $63.48; and that this year fifteen Parishes have contributed $318.59. The Fund, therefore, is now $381.77. Nearly one-half of it has been contributed by the Parish of St. John's, Ogdensburg.

The Canon creating the Fund, provides that there shall be no disbursements until the principal shall amount to at least $20,000. At that time the income is to be distributed among the Clergy longest in residence in the Diocese, under carefully-arranged provisions.

The Diocese appears to have here the seed-corn of a most important provision for the Clergy. It is, as yet, only the seed; but if the Parishes generally will begin to work for the cause with the energy which has been already displayed by one, there may soon be a consecration of the first-fruits. Then a true

ing the needs of the elder Clergy, will come into immediate operation. The propriety of meeting these needs, in some such way as this, is, we believe, unquestioned. A provision to which each year of work in the Diocese will bring the faithful Priest distinctly nearer, and which will seek him out at his post by a considerate and almost impersonal rule, as one who has proceeded *in course* to a good Diocesan Degree ; surely this will be doing a most gracious work. And the value of this Fund may lie, not merely in its service to those honored Priests who may be its beneficiaries, but in its vindication of a principle. If the principle now finds the practical recognition which it rightly demands, it is too vital not to find fresh applications and grow fruitful in new ways.

Your Committee recommend the passage of the following resolutions :

Resolved, That the Clergy Reserve Fund is commended, with increased confidence and urgency, to the Christian liberality of all the Parishes.

Resolved, That a Commission consisting of two Presbyters and three laymen, with the Bishop as Chairman, be appointed by the Chair, to examine into the working of the Clerical Pension system, where it may be now in operation, and to report to the next Convention what additional legislation upon the subject, if any, may in their judgment be called for at this time,

All which is respectfully submitted.

GEORGE G. CARTER,
GEORGE W. DAW,
Committee.

The resolutions recommended in the above Report were adopted ; and the Right Rev. President appointed as members of the Commission on the Clerical Pension system, the Rev. J. D. Morrison, D. D., LL. D., the Rev. George G. Carter, S. T. D., Mr. Selden E. Marvin, Mr. Levi Hasbrouck and Mr. Leslie Pell-Clarke.

On motion of the Rev. James Caird, the following preamble and resolution were adopted :

Whereas, Since our last Convention, the Rev. T. A. Snively has resigned the office of Corresponding Secretary of the Albany Bible and Prayer Book Society which he filled during a period of nearly six years, distributing in that time about 29,086 volumes, to the Parishes, Mission Stations, Schools and Charitable Institutions of the Diocese ; be it

Resolved, That we, the members of this Convention, place on record our appreciation of the interest he manifested in this work, the time and thought he devoted to it, the generous manner he treated every call made upon him, as well as the kindly spirit with which he discharged the trust committed unto him by his brethren.

The Rev. J. W. Stewart presented and read

REPORT, NUMBER 2, OF THE COMMITTEE ON THE CONSTITUTION AND CANONS.

The Committee on Constitution and Canons to whom it was referred to inquire whether any change is necessary in section 3 of Canon XIII, respectfully recommend that it be amended by striking out the word "the," and inserting in its place the word "an," before the word "agent" in the third line of said section.

The following Canon is offered for the adoption of the Convention :

A Canon to amend Canon XIII, Section 3 :

Section 3 of Canon XIII is hereby amended so as to read as follows :

SEC. 3. "The Protestant Episcopal Society for Promoting Religion and Learning in the State of New York," in which we have an interest in common with our mother Diocese, shall be an agent of this Diocese for the education of young men for Holy Orders. A copy of its Annual Report, if obtained from its Superintendent, shall be laid by the Secretary of the Convention before each Annual Convention.

Respectfully submitted for the Committee.

J. W. STEWART,
Chairman.

On motion of the Secretary of the Convention the amendment to Canon XIII, section 3, was adopted by the Convention; and the Right Rev. the Bishop of the Diocese announced his concurrence in the change.

The Secretary of the Convention read the Reports of the Trustees of the Episcopal Fund, of the Treasurer of the Episcopal Fund, of the Committee on the Salary of the Bishop, and of the committee on the same; and the resolution recommended by the Committee was adopted.

REPORT OF THE TRUSTEES OF THE EPISCOPAL FUND.

To the Convention :

The undersigned Trustees of the Episcopal Fund respectfully report that they hold the following securities for the Fund:

Bond and mortgage of J. Judge, 6 per cent....	$1,500 00
Bond and mortgage of D. McElveney, 5 per cent	5,000 00
Bond and mortgage of L. Sautter, 6 per cent.......	6,000 00
Bond and mortgage of J. Kennah, 6 per cent....	6,000 00
Bond and mortgage of J. E. Birdsall, 5 per cent	20,000 00
Bond and mortgage of Smead & Northcott, 5 per cent	8,500 00
Bond and mortgage of L. Hasbrouck, 5 per cent.....	5,000 00
Bond and mortgage of Harriet Martin, 5 per cent	2,500 00
Bond of Grace Church, Waterford...	500 00
Bond of St. John's Church, Cohoes..........................	800 00
Certificate of deposit in New York State National Bank.................	8,000 00
Balance of deposit in National Savings Bank......................	47 07
Total..	**$63,847 07**

A combination of circumstances made it judicious to assign and receive payment for Mrs. J. E. Clark's bond and mortgage, she being deceased, $8,000. Another mortgage for that amount has been arranged for, and the $8,000 deposited in bank invested in it shortly. It will be observed that $2,500 of the balance in savings bank reported last year, has been invested in a bond and mortgage of that amount (May 5). Only $4.05 have been added to the principal of the fund;

Contributed by St. Mark's Church, Green Island...........................	$3 05
Contributed by Church of Our Saviour, Lebanon Springs	1 00
	$4 05

Respectfully submitted.

J. H. VAN ANTWERP,
WM. BAYARD VAN RENSSELAER,
C. WHITNEY TILLINGHAST, 2ND,
THEODORE ~~~~~~

ALBANY, *Nov.* 15, 1892.

t.:. REPORT OF THE TREASURER OF THE EPISCOPAL INCOME FUND.

J. H. Van Antwerp Treasurer, in account with the Episcopal Income Fund :

1892.   Dr.

Nov. 1. To balance Nov. 16, 1891......	$73 25
To 1 year's interest, Sautter mortgage.........................	360 00
To 1 year's interest, Kennah mortgage....	360 00
To 1 year's interest, Hasbrouck mortgage......................	250 00
To 1 year's interest, Birdsall mortgage...................	1,000 00
To 1 year's interest, Northcott mortgage.	425 00
To 1 year's interest, McElveney mortgage......................	250 00
To 1 year's interest, Judge mortgage..........................	90 00
To 6 months' interest, Clark mortgage..............	200 00
To 5½ months' interest, Clark mortgage	185 60
To 6 months' interest, Martin mortgage.....................	62 50
To 1 year's interest, bond Grace Church, Waterford.............	35 00
To 1 year's interest, bond St. John's Church, Cohoes	56 00
To interest from National Savings Bank.......................	51 84
14. To remittances received from Mr. Rousseau, Secretary Bishop's Salary Committee..	2,700 00
Total.	$6,099 19

Cr.

Nov. 14. By salary paid the Bishop, one year, ending Nov. 1, 1892......	6,000 00
Balance...	$99 19

My credit of $2,700 as the amount received by me from the Secretary of the Bishop's Salary Committee, is $125 less than his report of the amount sent me by him, *this* year; because of a remittance of $125 he made Nov. 16, 1891, which I included in my report to the Convention *last* year, and which *he* did *not* include in his report to the Convention *last* year, but in his report for *this* year; which prevents our figures from agreeing in *both* years; but accounts for the money in full.

See Convention Journal for 1891, pages 87 and 88.

Respectfully submitted.

J. H. VAN ANTWERP,
Treasurer of the Episcopal Fund, Diocese of Albany.

ALBANY, E. & O. E., *November* 16, 1892.

REPORT OF THE COMMITTEE ON THE SALARY OF THE BISHOP.

W. W. Rousseau, Secretary, in account with J. H. Van Antwerp, Treasurer:

1892.

Nov. 12. Received from various Parishes since last account for Bishop's Salary*......... ....$3,022 17	

1891.	Contra.	
Nov. 16. Check to J. H. Van Antwerp..............	$125 00	
1892.		
Jan. 14. Paid on account of W. W. Rousseau, *note*....	150 00	
15. Check to J. H. Van Antwerp......................	250 00	
Feb. 18. '' '' ''	125 00	

* For Assessment for the Bishop's Salary see Appendix D.

Mar.	8.	Check to J. H. Van Antwerp...			$50 00
Apr.	5.	" " "			250 00
	23.	" " " ....'.....			175 00
	29.	" " "			100 00
June	4.	" " "			125 00
July	6.	" " "			150 00
	8.	" " "			25 00
Aug.	1.	" " "			300 00
	10.	" " "			90 00
Sept.	24.	" " "			100 00
Oct.	6.	" " "			175 00
	23.	" " "			225 00
Nov.	5.	" " "			200 00
	11.	" " "			275 00
	12.	" "			85 00
		Paid H. Stowell, printing postals..			8 76
		Clerk hire, postage stamps, etc....................			27 00
		Cash on hand......................			11 41
					$3,022 17

1892.

Nov. 12. Cash on hand for new account.......................... .. ... $11 41

SUMMARY.

Total amount sent J. H. Van Antwerp since last account.... .... $2,825 00
Paid on account note... ... ... 150 00
Sundries 35 76

REPORT OF THE COMMITTEE ON THE BISHOP'S SALARY AND THE EPISCOPAL FUND.

The Committee to whom was referred the Report of the Treasurer of the Episcopal Fund and Bishop's Salary, respectfully report that they have examined the Reports of the Trustees of the Episcopal Fund and of the Treasurer of the same, and find them to be apparently correct, although no vouchers accompany the Report.

The Committee offer the following resolution:

Resolved, That the question of the increase of the Episcopal Fund be referred to the Committee on the Observance of the twenty-fifth anniversary of the Consecration of the first Bishop of Albany.

ERNEST MARIETT,
F. S. FISHER,
R. H. GESNER,
B. F. HINMAN,
M. ANDRAE,
JAMES. A. HOLDEN.

The Rev. Canon Stewart presented and read the Report of the Committee to draft a suitable minute with regard to the services of the Rev. W. R. Woodbridge as Secretary of the Board of Missions, which minute was adopted by the Convention:

18

MINUTE ON THE WITHDRAWAL OF THE REV. WILLIAM R. WOOD-
BRIDGE FROM THE BOARD OF MISSIONS.

The Committee to whom was referred the preparation of a minute in regard to the
withdrawal of the Rev. W. R. Woodbridge from the Secretaryship of the Board of
Missions presents the following :

Whereas, The Rev. W. R. Woodbridge has declined a renomination to the Board of
Missions, and in view of the faithful and efficient services he has rendered to the
Board as its Secretary for the last thirteen years, the Convention desires to put on
record its appreciation of his long and persevering labors and its sense of the loss
sustained by his withdrawal from the Councils of the Board.

WILLIAM C. PROUT,
WALTER C. STEWART,
GEORGE B. PATTISON.

The Rev. Charles S. Olmsted presented and read the

REPORT OF THE COMMITTEE ON THE PROPER OBSERVANCE OF THE
TWENTY-FIFTH ANNIVERSARY OF THE CONSECRATION OF THE FIRST
BISHOP OF ALBANY.

The Committee on the Proper Observance of the twenty-fifth anniversary of the
Consecration of the First Bishop of Albany begs leave to report that it has just held
an important meeting, at which it has added to its number the Rev. Dr. Enos, the
Rev. Dr. Nickerson, the Rev. S. M. Griswold, the Rev. H. R. Freeman, Mr. Leslie
Pell-Clarke, and Mr. Nathan B. Warren.   The Rev. Dr. Tucker was made permanent
Chairman and the Rev. Charles S. Olmsted, Recording and Corresponding Secretary.

The Rev. Dr. Tucker, Dean Robbins and Gen. Marvin were appointed a Committee
to order the services in honor of the Consecration, and the second day of February,
1894, was fixed as the time.

It was decided that the Memorial of the Consecration Anniversary take the form
of a Chapter House to the Cathedral, and that steps should be taken shortly to set
forth to the Diocese the object, plan, and funds required.

CHAS. S. OLMSTED,
For the Committee.

The Rev. Walton W. Battershall, D. D., presented and read the
following Report, which was unanimously adopted by a rising vote.

REPORT OF THE COMMITTEE ON THE FIFTIETH ANNIVERSARY OF THE
ORDINATION OF THE REV. JAMES WILKINS STEWART.

Resolved, That this Convention extends to the Reverend James Wilkins Stewart
its cordial congratulations on the fiftieth anniversary of his ordination to the sacred
ministry, and the long and devoted service to the Church, which is registered by this
anniversary.   Ordained Deacon by Bishop Onderdonk in St. Mark's Church, New
York, on July 3, 1843, he has spent most of his ministry in the Diocese of Albany,
having been Rector at the Churches in Malone, Johnstown and Athens.   During his
Rectorship in the latter place, the Parish Church was built.   For twelve years he
has been a member, and for several years the Chairman of the Committee on Constitution and Canons.   This Convention hereby expresses its appreciation of the personal character and Priestly work of our Reverend Brother, and prays the adorable
head of the Church that many years may yet be added to his unblemished and fruitful Priesthood in the Church of God.

WALTON W. BATTERSHALL,
For the Committee.

The Rev. J. W. Stewart addressed the Convention.

The following resolution, offered by the Rev. J. D. Morrison, D. D., LL. D., was, on his motion, referred to the Committee on the Diocesan Fund, with instructions to report to the next Convention:

Resolved, That the expense of entertaining the Clerical members of the Diocese in attendance on the sessions of the Convention is properly a charge on the whole Diocese of Albany, and the Committee on the Diocesan Fund is requested to take the subject under consideration, and report thereon to the next Convention.

The Rev. Walton W. Battershall, D. D., presented and read the Report of the Committee to prepare a minute in regard to the work done by the Bishop of the Diocese in the Revision of the Prayer Book; which report was unanimously adopted by the Convention by a rising vote.

REPORT OF THE COMMITTEE ON THE SERVICES OF THE BISHOP OF ALBANY IN THE WORK OF PRAYER BOOK REVISION.

Resolved, That this Convention hereby records its appreciation of the eminent services which the Bishop of this Diocese, as a member of the Committee on the Revision of the Book of Common Prayer, has rendered to the American Church, and indirectly to Anglican Christendom. Evincing from the first a large interest and a deep faith in an enterprise which was beset with prejudice and apprehension, he brought to bear refinements of taste and resources of learning, which were invaluable contributions in the progress of the work, and determining factors in the final result. In presenting and championing the reports of the Committee in the Upper House, he has had an honorable and conspicuous share in an historic labor, to which this Church is indebted for an Order of Worship, which has at once been enriched with restorations on the lines of Catholic faith and devotion, and has been more perfectly adjusted to the needs of modern life.

WALTON W. BATTERSHALL,
EDGAR A. ENOS.

The Right Rev. the Bishop of the Diocese addressed the Convention.

On motion of the Rev. Richmond H. Gesner it was

Resolved, That this Convention tenders its hearty thanks to the Dean and Chapter of All Saints' Cathedral, the Trustees of the St. Agnes' School and the Church people of Albany for their cordial and generous hospitality, during its present session.

The Rev. Richmond H. Gesner presented and read the

REPORT OF THE COMMITTEE ON THE GENERAL THEOLOGICAL SEMINARY.

It is the pleasant duty of the Committee on the General Theological Seminary to report the gratifying and encouraging condition of that venerable institution. Never before in its history have so many students been enrolled as are now pursuing their studies under the efficient corps of instructors. A chair of Christian Ethics and Philosophy has recently been established, to which the Rev. Philander K. Cady, D. D., has been nominated. Dr. Cady's rare talents so acceptably displayed in the chair of Christian Evidences are ample guarantee of his success in this new department of theological learning. Materially and financially the Seminary has been greatly advanced by noble benefactions, amounting to

Dean and his family. The picturesque and ancient East Building has been torn down and on its site the new Professors' houses, whose corner-stone was laid at the last Commencement, are already approaching completion. In another year the Dean hopes to build a new gymnasium and refectory, of which the Seminary has long stood in urgent need. The Dean and Trustees are earnestly striving to complete the quadrangle with an imposing array of suitable buildings. The Board of Trustees have held two meetings in the past year, at which the Right Rev. the Bishop of this Diocese presided, one at the last Annual Commencement, the other on the 31st of October last. They are now aiming to raise sufficient funds for scholarships, so that young men seeking Holy Orders may not be compelled, during their attendance at the Seminary, to seek work which proves interruptive of complete devotion to their sacred studies. They are thus seeking in every way to increase the efficiency of the Seminary curriculum. The Dean has arranged for a course of lectures on the Missionary and Charitable work of the Church, as well as upon the more specifically Theological subjects. The daily services rendered chorally in the beautiful memorial Chapel are well attended. The dignified and reverent worship has become a wholesome and influential factor in shaping the spiritual life of the students, and in setting a standard for the doing of " all things decently and in order."

Respectfully submitted.

CHARLES TEMPLE,
Chairman.

R. H. GESNER,
GEORGE M. IRISH,
EDWARD CLARENCE CLARK,
GEORGE B. PATTISON.

On motion of the Secretary of the Convention, it was

Resolved, That the time for taking the recess be postponed twenty minutes.

The Secretary of the Convention read the

REPORT OF THE COMMITTEE ON NON-REPORTING CLERGY AND PARISHES.

The Committee on Non-Reporting Clergy and Parishes respectfully report:

That in answer to the Secretary's letter, but one reply was received — from St. Peter's, Brushton: excuse, absence of Missionary.

J. N. MARVIN,
W. H. VANDE CARR.

On motion the following resolutions from the Journal of last year were continued in force for this year:

Resolved, That the Secretary of the Convention be and is hereby directed to insert in next year's Journal under a separate head a list of the names of those non-reporting Clergy and Parishes that have failed to return answer to his letter of inquiry; also, a record of answers received, and the general character of the excuses offered.

Resolved, That the Secretary of the Convention be and is hereby directed to ask of the Parishes from which no report was received at the last Convention, and the Clergy, still canonically resident in the Diocese, who failed to report at the last Convention, their reasons for not complying with the requirements of the Canon; and that a minute of the same be entered in the Journal against the names under the head of Non-reporting Clergy and Parishes; and in any case where the Secretary's request is not complied with, the fact be recorded.

On motion of the Rev. Joseph Carey, S. T. D., it was

Resolved, That the Secretary be instructed to print 1,000 copies of the Bishop's Address, apart from the Journal, and to send them to the Clergy of the Diocese as early as possible.

Resolved, That the Secretary be instructed to print 1,250 copies of the Journal of the Convention, and distribute them to the various Parishes.

On motion of Mr. A. B. Cox, Secretary of the Trustees of the Diocese of Albany, leave was given to have his report printed in its place in the Journal.

REPORT OF THE TRUSTEES OF THE DIOCESE.

The Trustees of the Diocese of Albany report that a meeting was held in the gymnasium of St. Agnes' School, Albany, after the adjournment of the Diocesan Convention on the 16th day of November, 1892, pursuant to a call by the Bishop, at which were present, the Bishop presiding, Rev. Drs. J. D. Morrison and Joseph Carey, Rev. Mr. Frederick S. Sill, Messrs. Benjamin H. Hall, Levi W. Hasbrouck and A. B. Cox, Secretary.

The Secretary presented the deed of William Lyman Pomeroy and wife, mentioned in last year's report, and reported that he had procured the necessary certificate and had the deed recorded in the Columbia County Clerk's office.

The Secretary presented the deed of Chas. J. Knapp, guardian of Florence and Morris Knapp, infants, to the Trustees, for the consideration of $500, of a piece of land on the corner of Cottage and Monument streets, in the village of Deposit, N. Y., to be held in trust for Christ Church, Deposit; also a release of dower from Mrs. Alice S. Knapp to the Trustees, for the consideration of $96.22 of the same piece of land and on the same conditions of trust.

It was voted that the Trustees take and accept the property described in the above-mentioned deed and release.

The Secretary presented the deed of Dunham Jones Crain and Hannah Ann Crain to the Trustees, of a piece of land about fifty by seventy feet situated at Cullen, on the westerly side of the highway leading from Richfield Springs to Jordanville, between the residences of Joseph R. Petrie and Jacob Crossway, with the building erected thereon for a Church and known as the Good Shepherd, subject to the conditions that if the Trustees or their successors shall allow the burial of a person on the property, or shall omit to hold a service of the Protestant Episcopal Church upon the premises for the space of twelve months, the property shall revert to the original holders. Two policies of insurance accompanied the deed.

On motion it was resolved that the Trustees take and accept the property described in the above-mentioned deed.

After hearing a statement from Mr. J. D. Henderson, Lay Delegate from Christ Church, Herkimer, in relation to the condition of Grace Church, Norway, it was resolved that the following preamble and resolutions be presented to the next Diocesan Convention and their adoption recommended.

Whereas, Grace Church at Norway, in Herkimer county, N. Y., has abandoned its organization, and no religious services have been held therein for more than two years past, therefore

Resolved, That, in pursuance of chapter 110 of the Laws of 1876, and section 3 of chapter 28 of the Laws of 1882, the Parish and Church of Grace Church of Norway, in Herkimer county, N. Y., aforesaid, have become and are extinct.

Resolved, That the Trustees of the Diocese of Albany be directed to take possession of the real and personal property and temporalities of said extinct Church and manage the same in such manner as warranted by law.

The Rev. E. D. Tibbets stated to the Trustees that the corporation of St. Paul's Church at Raymertown desired to place a mortgage of $700 on their property.

On motion the matter was referred to Rev. Dr. Carey and Mr. Hall, with power to act.

All of which is respectfully submitted.

A. B. Cox,
Secretary.

On motion of the Rev. Charles C. Edmunds, Jr., it was

Resolved, That after the reading of the minutes and the customary devotions, the Convention adjourn *sine die.*

The minutes of this day's session were read and adopted.

The Bishop of the Diocese briefly addressed the Convention; and after saying some collects, pronounced the Benediction.

The Convention adjourned *sine die.*

WM. CROSWELL DOANE,
Bishop of Albany and President of the Convention.

WILLIAM O. PROUT, *Secretary.*

THOMAS B. FULCHER, *Assistant Secretary.*

APPENDIX.

(A.)

PAROCHIAL REPORTS.

Albany County.

CATHEDRAL OF ALL SAINTS, ALBANY.

THE CATHEDRAL CHAPTER.

Bishop. The Rt. Rev. Wm. Croswell Doane, D. D., LL. D.
Dean. The Rev. Wilford L. Robbins, D. D.
Precentor. The Rev. Thomas B. Fulcher, B. D.
Treasurer. The Rev. Edgar T. Chapman.
Honorary Canons. The Revs. F. M. Gray, Edward D. Tibbits, Charles H. Hatheway, Walter C. Stewart.
Lay Members. A. Bleecker Banks, Thomas Hun, M. D., Erastus Corning, Selden E. Marvin, Assistant Treasurer, Marcus T. Hun, Vice-Chancellor, Robert S. Oliver.

Parochial.

Families, 196 ; Individuals, 1,085 ; Baptisms (adults, 20, infants, 87), 107 ; Confirmed, since last report, 72 ; Present number of confirmed persons, 674 ; Marriages, 10 ; Burials, 62 ; Communicants, last reported, 587, present number, 632 ; Public Services, Daily Celebration of Holy Communion, Sundays and Holy days, 2 celebrations ; Daily Matins and Even Song throughout the year ; Holy Communion, private, 34 ; Sunday School, teachers, 20, pupils, 246 , Catechising, number of times, 25 ; St. Agnes' School, teachers, 30, pupils, 250.

Offerings.

Parochial.— Alms at Holy Communion, $428.52 ; Current expenses, including salaries, $13,539.17 ; Sunday School, $230 75 ; Payment of Debt, $50,823.30 ; Cathedral Branch Woman's Auxiliary, $613.65 ; St. Mary's Guild, $18 ; St. Agatha's Guild, $15 ; Guild Room, $115 ; Benefactors' door Cathedral, $317.37 ; Choir Endowment Fund, $57.13. Total, $66,157.89.

Diocesan.— Diocesan Missions, $1,200 , Salary of the Bishop, $150 ; Diocesan Fund, $150 ; Fund for Aged and Infirm Clergymen (Debt, $250), $271 ; Fund for Widows and Orphans of Clergymen, $5 ; Orphan House of the Holy Saviour, $57.60 ; The Child's Hospital, $265 ; Society for Promoting Religion and Learning, $24.11 ; St. Margaret's House Building Fund, $450 ; St. John's Church, East Line, $17.68 ; Woman's Diocesan League, $145. Total, $2,735.39.

General.— Domestic Missions, $261.89 ; Foreign Missions, through Sunday School $72.02 ; Russian Sufferers, $70.41. Total, $404.32.

Total amount of Offerings, $69,297.60.

Property.

Church and lot (estimated worth), $350,000.
Other property, $12,000.
Amount of salary pledged Dean, $5,000.
Amount of salary pledged Precentor, $1,300.
Number of sittings in the Church, 2,375; all free.

ST. PETER'S CHURCH, ALBANY.

Rector. The Rev. Walton W. Battershall, D. D.
Assistant. The Rev. George B. Richards.
Wardens. George S. Weaver, Joseph W. Tillinghast,
Vestrymen. Henry T. Martin, Luther H. Tucker, Theodore Towns
Griswold, Robert C. Pruyn, Thomas S. Wiles, Abraham Lansing, Willia

Parochial.

Individuals, 1,250; Baptisms (adults, 9, infants, 30), 39; Confirmed,
report, 53; Present number of confirmed persons, 730; Marriages, 11
33; Communicants, last reported, 712, admitted, 53, received, 10, di(
moved, 34, present number, 730; Public services (Sundays, 140, Holy
other days, 190), 360; Holy Communion (public, 90, private, 22), 112; Sund
teachers, 39, pupils, 300; Parish School, teachers, 5, pupils, 20; Sewi
teachers, 15, pupils, 200.

Offerings.

Parochial.—Alms at Holy Communion, $1,184.94; Current expenses,
salaries, $12,681.67; Sunday School, $147.64; St. Peter's Orphanage,
Increase and Improvement of Church Property, $5,074.51; Chancel G(
Parish Aid Society, $504.77; Christmas Tree, $268; Endowment Fund, $14
ing School, $57.35. Total, $21,465.33.

Diocesan.—Diocesan Missions, $902.56; Salary of the Bishop, $150; Dioc(
$120; Diocesan Missionary, $100; Diocesan Missionary from Sunday Scho
St. Christina's Home, from Sunday School, $10; Orphan House of the Hol
$108.16; The Child's Hospital, from Sewing School, $14; Society for
Religion and Learning, $19.65; Clergy Reserve Fund, $26.10; Conventi(
eon, $50. Total, $1,517.52.

General.—Domestic Missions, from Sunday School, $100; Domestic
$301.87; Foreign Missions, $165.66; Indian Missions, $127.79; Home M
Coloured Persons, $103.88; Woman's Auxiliary, $707.05; Russian Famin(
Church Building Fund, $29.57. Total, $1,788.61.

Total amount of Offerings, $24,771.46.

Property.

Church and lot (estimated worth), $210,000; Parsonage and lot
worth), $5,000; other property, Parish House, $30,000; Orphanage, $10,0(
$255,000.

Condition of property, good.
Amount of salary pledged Rector, $4,000.
Amount of salary pledged Assistant Minister, $1,000.
Number of sittings in the Church and Chapel, 1,250.

ST. PAUL'S CHURCH, ALBANY.

Rector. The Rev. Freeborn G. Jewett, Jr.
Assistant. The Rev. George L. Richardson.

Wardens.   John H. Van Antwerp, John Woodward.

Vestrymen.   Geo. P. Wilson, Robert Geer, Matthew H. Robertson, Eugene Burlingame, Henry A. Dwight, Wallace N. Horton, James H. Manning, Edgar B. Holden.

Parochial.

Families, 325; Individuals (adults, 842, children, 387), 1,229; Baptisms (adults, 8, infants, 39), 47; Confirmed, since last report, 40; Marriages, 13; Burials, 32; Communicants, last reported, 707, admitted, 41, received, 30, died, 12, removed, 14, present number, 752; Public Services (Sundays, 174, other days. 105), 279; Holy Communion (public, 20, private, 15), 35; Sunday School, teachers, 47, pupils, 475.

Offerings.

Parochial.— Alms at Holy Communion, $604.39; Current expenses, including salaries, $6,821.92, Sunday School, $796.81; Increase and Improvement of Church Property, $2,821.80; Other parochial objects, $774.13; Parochial Missions, $378.66. Total, $12,197.71.

Diocesan.— Diocesan Missions, $400; Salary of the Bishop, $100; Diocesan Fund, $80; Bible and Common Prayer Book Society of Albany, $10; Fund for Aged and Infirm Clergymen, $1,000; Fund for Widows and Orphans of Clergymen, $1,000; Orphan House of the Holy Saviour, $17.48; Other offerings for objects within the Diocese, $95. Total, $2,702.48

General.— Domestic Missions, $286.16; Foreign Missions, $202.44; Other objects exterior to the Diocese, $621.83. Total, $1,110.43.

Total amount of Offerings, $16,010.62.

TRINITY CHURCH, ALBANY.

Rector.   The Rev. Russell Woodman.

Wardens.   William Little, John A. Howe.

Vestrymen.   John Pritchard, Richard Norris, George F. Granger, Charles E. Fairchild, Norden T. Johnston, Alexander Campbell, J. Henry Marlow, Edward Johnston.

Parochial.

Baptisms (adults, 1, infants, 34), 35 ; Confirmed, since last report, 36 ; Marriages, 27 ; Burials, 31; Churchings, 1 ; Communicants, last reported, 225, received, 6, died, 2, removed, 23, received Easter Day, 197; Public Services, Sundays, morning and evening, with sermon, throughout year; Holy days, Holy Communion; other days, Friday nights, from November to June ; Holy Communion, public, every Sunday, private, 15 ; Sunday School, teachers, 21, pupils, 183 ; Catechizing, monthly ; Parish Sewing School, teachers, 6, pupils, 50.

Offerings.

Parochial.— Alms at Holy Communion, $51.64 : Current expenses, including salaries, $1,909.50 ; Sunday School, $36; Increase and Improvement of Church Property, $400. Total, $2,397.14.

Diocesan.— Diocesan Missions, $20 ; Salary of the Bishop, $20 ; Diocesan Fund, $5 ; The Child's Hospital (J. A. Howe), $5. Total, $50.

General.— Domestic Missions, $6.48 ; Foreign Missions, $7.82 ; Indian Missions, $5 ; Other objects exterior to the Diocese, $5 ; Enrolment (Mr. and Mrs. Howe's S. S. class), $7.42. Total, $31.72.

Total amount of Offerings, $2,478.86.

Property.

Church and lot (estimated worth) $40,000

19

Parsonage and lot (estimated worth), $8,000.
Condition of property, good.

GRACE CHURCH, ALBANY, N. Y.

Rector.　The Rev. William Henry Bown.
Wardens.　Benjamin F. Hinman, Charles W. White.
Vestrymen.　Frank J. Smith, James C. Sewell, Henry Burn, Frederick Gilliland,
George B. Longleway, Edward Sewell, James Beauman, William Rankin.

Parochial.

Baptisms (adults, 5, infants, 31), 36; Confirmed, since last report, 27; Marriages, 14;
burials, 29; Communicants, last reported, 384, admitted, 27, received, 10, died, 3,
removed, 6, present number, 412; Public Services (Sundays, 120, Holy days, 25, other
days, 90), 235; Holy Communion (public, 60, private, 18), 78; Sunday School,
teachers, 38, pupils, 380; Catechizing, weekly.

Offerings.

Parochial.—Current expenses, including salaries, $2,495.13; Sunday School,
$318.70; Increase and Improvement of Church Property, $730.83; Other parochial
objects, $378.91.　Total, $3,923.57.

Diocesan.—Diocesan Missions, $50; Salary of the Bishop, $32; Diocesan Fund,
$15; Bible and Common Prayer Book Society of Albany, $10; Fund for Aged and Infirm Clergymen, $6; Orphan House of the Holy Saviour, $10; The Child's Hospital,
$17.　Total, $140.

General.—Domestic and Foreign Missions, $101.98; Home Missions to Coloured
Persons, $50.　Total, $151.98.

Total amount of Offerings, $4,215.55.

Property.

Church and lot (estimated worth), $15,000.]
Parsonage and lot (estimated worth), $5,000.
Condition of property, good.
Indebtedness, mortgage, $2,000.
Number of sittings in the church, 500; all free.

Remarks.

During the year the Church has been thoroughly renovated and a new tin roof put
upon it at an expense of about $800.　This amount was raised and paid by the
Ladies' Aid Society.

HOLY INNOCENTS' CHURCH, ALBANY.

Rector.　The Rev. Richmond Shreve, D. D.
Wardens.　S. M. Van Santvoord, W. H. Weaver.
Vestrymen.　J. Barrington Lodge, Jr., E. W. Leaning, H. S. McCall, Jr., James
Oswald, Robert Parker, William Riley, Thomas Kyle, Thomas J. Tobin.

Parochial.

Baptisms (adults, 1, infants, 23), 24 ; Confirmed, since last report, 7 ; Marriages,
12 ; Burials, 15 ; Communicants, last reported, 189, admitted, 7, received, 4, died, 4,
removed, 5, present number, 191; Public Services (Sundays, 147, Holy days, 26,
other days, 79), 253 ; Holy Communion (public, 57, private, 15), 72 ; Sunday School,
teachers, 17, pupils, 130 ; Catechizing, number of children, whole school, number of
times, 20.

Offerings.

Parochial. — Current expenses, including salaries, $2,663.72 ; Sunday School, $134.92 ; Increase and Improvement of Church Property, $36.56. Total, $2,835.20.

Diocesan — Diocesan Missions, $50 ; Salary of the Bishop, $30 ; Diocesan Fund, $45 ; Bible and Common Prayer Book Society of Albany, $4.68 ; Fund for Aged and Infirm Clergymen, $6.23 ; Fund for Widows and Orphans of Clergymen, $5.28 ; Orphan House of the Holy Saviour, $11.35 ; Clergy Reserve Fund, $4.68 ; Diocesan Missionary salary, $15 ; Convention, $10. Total, $182.22.

General. — Foreign Missions, $52.55 ; Indian Missions, $60 ; Home Missions to Coloured Persons, $4.50 ; American Church Building Fund Commission, $4.68. Total, $121.73.

Total amount of Offerings, $3,139.15.

Property.

Church and lot (estimated worth), $20,000.
Parsonage and lot (estimated worth), $5,000.
Condition of property, good.
Indebtedness on Rectory, $2,000.
Number of sittir gs in Church, 840; all free.

TRINITY CHURCH, RENSSELAERVILLE.

Missionary. The Rev. S. C. Thompson.
Wardens. John L. Rice, Nathaniel Teed.
Vestrymen. C. B. Cross, Frank Rice, Dewey Bell, J. B. Washburn, M. D., James Rider, Luther Fox, Henry Sweet, Frank Frisbee.

Parochial.

Families, 25 ; Individuals (adults, 87, children, 21), 108 ; Baptism (adult), 1 ; Confirmed, since last report, 4 ; Present number of confirmed persons, 54 ; Burials, 9 ; Communicants, admitted, 4, received, 2, died, 4, removed 2, present number, 50 ; Public Services (Sundays, 82, other days, 22), 104 ; Holy Communion (public, 14, private 1), 15 ; Sunday School, teachers, 6, pupils, 20 ; Catechizing, number of times, 11.

Offerings.

Parochial. — Alms at Holy Communion, $18.73 ; Current expenses, including salaries, $352.57 ; Increase and Improvement of Church Property, $100. Total, $471.30.

Diocesan. — Diocesan Missions, $21.29 ; Salary of the Bishop, $8 ; Diocesan Fund, $9 ; Fund for Aged and Infirm Clergymen, $9.03 ; Orphan House of the Holy Saviour, $13. Total, $60.32.

General. — Mrs. Buford's Hospital, $11.
Total amount of Offerings, $542.02.
Amount of salary pledged Missionary, $300.

ST. JOHN'S CHURCH, COHOES.

Rector. The Rev. Frederick S. Sill, B. D.
Wardens. Michael Andrae, John Horrocks.
Vestrymen. George Campbell, Reuben Lee, William S. Shipley, Luke Kavanaugh, Harry J. P. Green, Robert R. Chadwick, Charles H. Disbrow, William T. Ford.

Parochial.

Families, 360 ; Individuals (adults, 1,015, children, 450), 1,465 ; Baptisms (adults, 4, infants, 49), 53 ; Confirmed, since last report, 81; Marriages, 14; Burials, 29 ; Churchings, 5; Communicants, last reported, 520, admitted, 36, received, 20, died 10, removed, 22, present number, 544; Public Services (Sundays, 160, Holy days, 66, other days, 148), 374; Holy Communion (public, 78, private, 11), 89; Sunday School, teachers and officers, 24, pupils, 300; Catechizing, number of times, 15.

Offerings.

Parochial.—Alms at Holy Communion, $77.81; Current expenses, including salaries, $3,019.13; Sunday School, $100.81; Increase and Improvement of Church Property, $855.89; Reduction of Debt, $950; Howe Poor Fund, $57.20; King's Daughters for Sick, $17.32; Jane Ryan Fund, increase, $169.61. Total, $5,247.77.

Diocesan.—Diocesan Missions, $269.90; Salary of the Bishop, $56; Diocesan Fund, $45; Bible and Common Prayer Book Society of Albany, $5.94; Fund for Aged and Infirm Clergymen, $18.55; Orphan House of the Holy Saviour, $11; Theological Education, $14; Diocesan Missionary (S. S.), $15. Total, $480.39.

General.—Domestic Missions, $48.39; Foreign Missions, $48.38 (S. S. $78.27; Indian Missions, $10 (Wom. Aux.); Home Missions to Colored Persons, $10 (Wom. Aux.); Other objects exterior to the Diocese: Jewish Mission in Palestine, $15; Annandale Professorship Fund, $13; Woman's Auxiliary, $294.25 (Total, $329.25); Japan Mission, $5 (Wom. Aux.); Alaska Mission, $5 (Wom. Aux.); China Mission, $5 (Wom. Aux.). Total, $454.02.

Total amount of Offerings, $6,182.18.

Property.

Church and lot (estimated worth), $40,000.
Parsonage and lot (estimated worth), $10,000.
Other property, Howe Fund, $1,500; Church Home Fund, $2,837.62.
Condition of property, very good.
Indebtedness, mortgage, $2,700.
Amount of salary pledged Rector, $1,500.
Number of sittings in the Church and Chapel, 800; all free, but assigned.

Remarks.

A plan has been set on foot by the Vestry for the entire removal of the mortgage debt by Easter, 1893.

A vested choir will be introduced at Christmas, consisting of the present number of girls, women and men, with a number of boys added.

A new boiler for heating the Church was put in last December, and the organ has been put in thorough repair during the year.

TRINITY CHURCH, WEST TROY.

Rector. The Rev. E. Bayard Smith.
Wardens. William Hollands, John H. Hulsapple.
Vestrymen. William E. Baxter, Charles H Crabbe, William Doring, Edmund S. Hollands, Thomas Rath, John Scarborough, Bertram F. Stewart, Robert Trimble.

Parochial.

Families, 200; Individuals (adults, 400, children, 300), 700; Baptisms (adult, 1, infants, 23), 24; Confirmed, since last report, 21; Marriages, 11; Burials, 21; Communicants, last reported, 272, admitted, 22, received, 7, died, 4, removed, 16, present number, 281; Public Services (Sundays, 96, Holy days, 18, other days, 123), 237; Holy Communion (public, 50, private, 2), 52; Trinity Sunday School, teachers, 18, pupils 133; St. Gabriel's Sunday School, teachers, 9, pupils, 87; Catechizing, every session.

Offerings.

Parochial.— Alms at Holy Communion, $64.17; Current expenses, including salaries, $2,456.76; Sunday School, Trinity, $80.09; St. Gabriel's, $93.88; Daughters of the Cross, $152.91; Carpet at St. Gabriel's, $22. Total, $2,869.81.

Diocesan.— Diocesan Missions, $45; Salary of the Bishop, $60; Diocesan Fund, $24; Fund for Aged and Infirm Clergymen, $8; Fund for Widows and Orphans of Clergymen, $5; Orphan House of the Holy Saviour, $14, The Child's Hospital, $18; Diocesan Missionary (Trinity S. S., $4, St. Gabriel's S. S., $3.14), $7.14. Total, $181.14.

General.— Domestic Missions, $10; Foreign Missions, $8; Church Mission to the Jews, $3; St. Mark's, Fort Dodge, Iowa, $9; Woman's Auxiliary, $16.90. Total, $46.90.

Total amount of Offerings, $3,097.85.

Property.

Church and lot (estimated worth), $24,000.
Parsonage and lot (estimated worth), $8,000.
Other property, $4,000.
Condition of property, excellent.
Number of sittings in the Church, 377, apportioned; Trinity Chapel, 150, free; St. Gabriel's Chapel, 150, free.

Remarks.

The exterior of the Church and Parish Building has been painted through the efforts of the Daughters of the Cross. The Chancel of St. Gabriel's Chapel has been carpeted.

ST. MARK'S CHURCH, GREEN ISLAND.

Rector. The Rev. R. J. Adler.

Wardens. Richard Leonard, Wm. E. Gilbert.

Vestrymen. Henry Stowell, Harry Farmer, Wm. W. Butler, James H. Eckler, Louis Harter, Jr., Robert W. Porter, J. Andrew Best, John Watson.

Parochial.

Families, 152; Individuals (adults, 215, children, 261), 476; Baptisms (adults, 7, infants, 11), 18; Confirmed, since last report, 17; Present number of confirmed persons, 210; Marriages, 7; Burials, 11; Churchings, 2; Communicants, present number, 176; Public Services (Sundays, 117, other days, 65), 182; Holy Communion (public, 16, private, 3), 19; Sunday School, teachers, 13, pupils, 135; Catechizing, the whole school, weekly.

Offerings.

Parochial.—Alms at Holy Communion, $19.16; Current expenses, including salaries, $1,522.02; Improvement of Church Property, $1,175.85. Total, $2,717.03.

Diocesan.— Diocesan Missions ($7.22 of which from S. S.), $45.59; Salary of the Bishop, $12; Diocesan Fund, $15; Bible and Common Prayer Book Society of Albany, $4.98; Increase of the Episcopate Fund, $4.15; Fund for Aged and Infirm Clergymen, $4.30; Orphan House of the Holy Saviour ($6.80 of which from S. S.), $13.45; The Child's Hospital, for St. Christina Home, from S. S., $10.00. Total, $109.47.

General.— Domestic Missions, $12.25; Foreign Missions, $11.05; General Missions (S. S. Lenten offering), $34.38; Home Missions to Jews, $6.08; American Church Building Fund, $8.08. Total, $71.84.

Total amount of Offerings, $2,898.34.

Property.

Church and lot (estimated worth), $20,000.

Parsonage and lot (estimated worth), $7,000,
Condition of property, good.
Sittings in the Church and Chapel, all free.

Remarks.

Of the above $1,175,85 contributed for Improvement of Church Property, $975.85 have been expended on a steam-heating plant and repairs; and $200 contributed, one-half each, by the Daughters of the King and the Sunday School, have placed in the west end of the Church three beautiful windows, representing "Faith, Hope and Charity." A "Permanent Fund" has been started, on account of which $100 (not included above) is now on deposit.

ST. ANDREW'S, WEST TROY.

Missionary.   The Rev. Canon Hatheway.

Parochial.

Families, 18; Individuals (adults, 44, children, 50), 94: Baptisms (adults), 2; Confirmed, since last report, 5; Present number of confirmed persons, 43; Marriage, 1; Communicants, last reported, 46, admitted, 2, removed, 5, present number, 43; Public Services (Sundays, 50, Holy days, 2, other days, 11), 63; Holy Communion, public, 12; Sunday School, teachers, 8, pupils, 45; Catechizing, number of children, 45, number of times, 12.

Offerings.

Parochial.— Current expenses, including salaries, $504.76.
General.— Domestic Missions, $5; Foreign Missions, $2 38; Total, $7,38.
Total amount of Offerings, $512.14.

Property.

Condition of property, good.
Amount of salary pledged Rector, $450.
Sittings in the Church, all free.

Remarks.

The Church has just been painted thoroughly inside and out. Three new windows have been put in and six stained glass windows replace the old ones. New gutters and repairs on the tower and roof have been made, so that the Church is now in excellent condition. The congregation is well kept up and interest shown in the welfare of the Church. The Ladies' Guild is the main stay of the Mission, and its members are noted for their energy and success.

ST. MARGARET'S CHURCH, MENANDS.

Priest in charge.   The Rev. Edgar T. Chapman.

Parochial.

Families, 20 ; Individuals (adults, 75, children, 35), 110 ; Baptisms (adults, 8, infants, 17), 25 ; Confirmed, since last report, 23 ; Present number of confirmed persons, 62 : Marriages, 9 ; Burials, 19 ; Communicants, last reported, 62, present number, 62 ; Public Services (2 each Sunday, 1 each Holy day, other days, from Advent to Trinity, daily) ; Holy Communion (public), Sundays and Holy days; Sunday School, teachers, 5, pupils, 25 ; Catechizing, number of children, 25, number of times, monthly.

Offerings.

Diocesan.— Diocesan Missions, $5; Orphan House of the Holy Saviour, $5 ; The Child's Hospital, $5.   Total, $15.

Clinton County.

TRINITY CHURCH, PLATTSBURGH.

Rector. The Rev. Hobart Cooke.
Lay Reader. John Henry Booth.
Wardens. George F. Nichols, William T. Ketchum.
Vestrymen. Hon. S. A. Kellogg, Hon. John M. Wever, A. L. Inman, A. M. Warren, Hon. George S. Weed, John Ross, Millard F. Parkhurst, Edward T. Gilliland.

Parochial.

Baptisms (adults, 7, infants, 8), 15; Confirmed, since last report, 16; Marriages, 5; Burials, 16; Communicants, present number, 230; Public Services, 286; Holy Communion, 82; Sunday School, teachers, 12, pupils, 114.

Offerings.

Parochial.— Alms at Holy Communion, $70; Current expenses, including salaries, $2,492.74; Sunday School, $236; Home of the Friendless, $35. Total, $2,833.74.

Diocesan.— Diocesan Missions, $100; Salary of the Bishop, $60; Diocesan Fund, $45; Orphan House of the Holy Saviour, $25; The Child's Hospital, $25. Total, $255.

General.— Domestic and Foreign Missions, $50; Jewish Missions, $7. Total, $57.

Total amount of Offerings, $3,145.74.

Property.

Church and lot (estimated worth), $20,000.
Parsonage and lot (estimated worth). $6,000.
Condition of property, excellent.
Amount of salary pledged Rector, $1,500.
Number of sittings in the Church, 450; all rented.

Remarks.

Among the Parochial activities of the year, the Ladies' Society has sent boxes of clothing and useful articles to The Child's Hospital, Albany. The St. Mary's Guild has accomplished much efficient work. Boxes of clothing, etc., have been sent to The Orphan House of the Holy Saviour, at Cooperstown; large supplies of magazines, papers and books, also knitted woolen helmets and gauntlets, forwarded for the men at the Life-Saving stations on Long Island and Coney Island; valuable assistance rendered with generous contributions of money to the Sunday School work; and a marble cross provided for the grave of the Rev. E. C. M. Rowden, late Missionary at Lyon Mountain, buried in Riverside cemetery in this Parish.

CHRIST CHURCH, ROUSE'S POINT.

Missionary. The Rev. James F. Olmsted.
Wardens. John Phillips, William Crook.
Vestrymen, J. R. Sperry, J. R. Myers, Alexander Wood, H. L. Clark, Frank E. Vail.

Parochial.

Families, 70; Individuals (adults, 140, children, 50), 190; Baptisms, infants, 14; Confirmed, since last report, 5; Present number of confirmed persons, about 100; Marriages, 3; Burials, 7; Communicants, last reported, 54, admitted, 5, present number, 59; Public Services (Sundays), 87; Holy Communion (public, 19

1), 18 ; Sunday School, teachers, 6, pupils, 46 ; Catechizing, number of children school, number of times, weekly.

Offerings.

Parochial.—Alms at Holy Communion, $25.84 ; Current expenses, including salaries, $777.95 ; Sunday School, $12. Total, $815.79.

Diocesan.—Diocesan Missions, $16.63 ; Salary of the Bishop, $12 ; Diocesan Fund, $12 ; Sunday School pledge for Diocesan Missionary, $5. Total, $45.63.

General.—Indian Missions, $1.25 ; Home Missions to Coloured Persons, $4.28 ; Church Temperance Society, $8 ; Russian Relief Fund, $12.30 ; Society for Promoting Christianity among the Jews, $2.30. Total, $23.13.

Total amount of Offerings, $884.55.

Property.

Church and lot (estimated worth), $8,000.

Condition of property, fair.

Amount of salary pledged Rector, $400.

Number of sittings in the Church (rented, 105, free, 110), 215.

ST. JOHN'S CHURCH, CHAMPLAIN.

Rector. The Rev. James F. Olmsted.

Wardens. James Averill, Jr., Jehiel C. White.

Vestrymen. Henry Hoyle, James De F. Burroughs, James M. Hackett, M. D., John H. Crook.

Parochial.

Families, 28; Individuals (adults, 48, children, 32), 80; Baptisms (adult, 1, infants, 5), 6; Confirmed, since last report, 2; Present number of confirmed persons, 47; Marriages, 1; Burials, 1; Communicants, last reported, 40, admitted, 2, received, 3, died, 1, removed, 2, present number, 45; Public Services (Sundays, 61, Holy days, 7, other days, 15), 83, Holy Communion public, 31; Sunday School, teachers, 4, pupils, 19; Catechizing, number of children, 19, number of times, Sundays.

Offerings.

Parochial.—Alms at Holy Communion, $28.43; Current expenses, including salaries, $500; Sunday School, $20.22; Increase and Improvement of Church Property, $390. Total, $838.65.

Diocesan.—Diocesan Missions, $20, Salary of the Bishop, $6; Diocesan Fund, $12. Total, $38.

General — Domestic and Foreign Missions (Sunday School offering), $16.22.

Total amount of Offerings, $992.87.

Property.

Church and lot (estimated worth), $3,000.

Parsonage and lot (estimated worth), $1,600.

Condition of property, good.'

Indebtedness, note, $250.

Amount of salary pledged Rector, $400.

Number of sittings in the Church, 200; all free.

ST. PETER'S CHURCH, ELLENBURGH.

Rector. The Rev. Silas M. Rogers, A. M.

Wardens. William H. Sawyer and Giles H. Carew.

Vestrymen. James Higgins, Allen Sargent, Heman Allen, Bryan Emerson, John Hammond, Millard Emerson, William Shutts, Charles Livingston.

Parochial.

Baptisms (infants), 7; Confirmed, since last report, 8, Marriages, 6; Burials 5; Communicants, admitted, 3, present number, 40; Holy Communion, public, first Sunday of each month ; Sunday School, teachers, 2, pupils, 20; Catechizing, number of times, 12.

Offerings.

Parochial.—Alms at Holy Communion, $5.51; Sunday School, $8; Increase and Improvement of Church Property, $393.44. Total, $406.95.

Diocesan.— Diocesan Missions, $5; Salary of the Bishop, $4; Diocesan Fund, $3; Fund for Aged and Infirm Clergymen, $2. Total, $14.

General.-- Foreign Missions, $4.

Total amount of Offerings, $424.95.

Property.

Church and lot (estimated worth), $2,000.

Condition of property, good.

Number of sittings in the Church, 150.

ST. PAUL'S CHURCH, ELLENBURGH CENTRE.

Rector. The Rev. Silas M. Rogers, A. M.

Wardens. Orson Haff and George W. Carpenter.

Vestrymen. Oliver Sancomb, Alfred Harris, Thomas Harris, C. C. Carpenter, Lyman G. Carpenter, Judson H. Cole, Aden Hazletine and Stephen Goodspeed.

Parochial.

Baptisms (adults, 2, infants, 2), 4 ; Marriages, 1 ; Burials, 8 ; Communicants' present number, 28.

Offerings.

Parochial. — Alms at Holy Communion, $3.53 ; Increase and Improvement of Church Property, $50. Total, $53.53.

Diocesan.— Diocesan Missions, $5.

Total amount of Offerings, $58.53.

Property.

Church and lot (estimated worth), $2,000.

Condition of property, good.

Number of sittings in the Church, 160.

Columbia County.

CHRIST CHURCH, HUDSON.

Rector. The Rev. Sheldon Munson Griswold.

Lay Readers. Mr. A. E. Heard and Mr. H. D. Mac Neil.

Wardens. W. B. Skinner, H. J. Baringer.

Vestrymen. J. P. Wheeler, M. D., John M. Pearson, A. C. Stott, C. W. Bostwick, Clarence L. Crofts, F. T. Punderson, James Eisemann, Samuel B. Coffin.

Parochial.

Families (about), 250; Baptisms (adults, 10, infants, 28), 38; Confirmed, since last report, 17; Present number of confirmed persons, 487; Marriages, 17; Burials, 27; Communicants, last reported, 466, admitted, 18, died, 4, removed, 2, present number, 488; Public Services (Sundays, 150, Holy days, &c. Holy Com-

20

munion (public, 103, private, 17), 120; Sunday School, teachers, 28, pupils, 260; Catechizing, number of children, whole school, number of times, weekly.

Offerings.

Parochial.— Alms at Holy Communion, $103.36; Current expenses, including salaries, $3,238.93; Sunday School, $220.36; Increase and Improvement of Church Property, $189.95; Other Parochial objects, $2,431.65. Total, $6,179.95.

Diocesan.— Diocesan Missions, $124.68; Salary of the Bishop, $66; Diocesan Fund, $128.77; Bible and Common Prayer Book Society of Albany, $13.86; Fund for Aged and Infirm Clergymen, $17; Fund for Widows and Orphans of Clergymen, $4.83; Orphan House of the Holy Saviour, $14.98; The Child's Hospital (from S. S.), $20; Society for Promoting Religion and Learning, $21.91; Diocesan Missionary (from S. S., $12), $19.57. Total, $416.62.

General.— Domestic Missions, $51.15; Foreign Missions, $14.16; Mr. Partridge's work in China, $15; Bishop Leonard, Scholarship St. Mark's School (from S. S.), $80; American Church Building Fund, $21.13; Missions to the Jews, $7.35; Enrolment Fund, $10. Total, $198.79.

Total amount of Offerings, $6,794.66.

Property.

Church and lot (estimated worth), $40,000.
Parsonage and lot (estimated worth), $7,000.
Other property, $3,000.
Condition of property, first class.
Indebtedness, floating (about), $1,200.
Amount of salary pledged Rector, $1,500.
Number of sittings in the Church, 500; rented, 367.

Remarks.

The Junior Auxiliary presented the Parish with a piano. The above report does not include money and boxes sent away by various guilds. The Rector also held seven services and preached seven times at the House of Refuge for Women.

ALL SAINTS' CHURCH, HUDSON.

Rector. The Rev. George G. Carter.
Wardens. William H. Cookson, Richard A. Aitken.
Vestrymen. Alexander R. Benson, George H. Palmer, Robert Storm, Benjamin Thompson.

Parochial.

Families, 38; Confirmed, since last report, 4; Present number of confirmed persons, about 100; Burials, 11; Communicants, last reported, 91, admitted, 4, received, 8, died, 2, removed, 12; present number, 89; Public Services (Sundays, 106, Holy days, 36, other days, 92), 234; Holy Communion (public), 85; Sunday School, teachers, 15, pupils, 140; Catechizing, number of children, all, number of times, 52.

Offerings.

Parochial.—Alms at Holy Communion, $66.36; Current expenses, including salaries, $539.38; Sunday School, $53.38; Increase and Improvement of Church Property, $213.65; Proposed new Sunday School building, $52.50. Total, $925.27.

Diocesan.—Diocesan Missions, $40.39; Salary of the Bishop, $9; Diocesan Fund, $6; Orphan House of the Holy Saviour (from S. S.), $13.35; The Child's Hospital, $7.61. Total, $76.35.

General.—Missions to the Jews, $1.54; Russian Relief Fund, $6. Total, $7.54.
Total amount of Offerings, $1,009.16.

Property.

Condition of property, good.
Indebtedness, none.
Amount of salary pledged Rector. $300.
Number of sittings in the Church, 200; all free.

Remarks.

A very beautiful Chalice and Paten, in silver parcel-gilt, and a silver Baptismal
shell, have been given by a devoted family in the congregation; three generations
uniting in these memorial offerings. They were used for the first time on the Feast
of St. Michael and All Angels.

THE CHURCH OF ST. JOHN THE EVANGELIST, STOCKPORT.

Rector. The Rev. Eugene L. Toy.
Assistant. The Rev. William B. Reynolds, Deacon.
Wardens. William H. Van de Carr, Jacob H. Pultz.
Vestrymen. F. H. Stott, G. B. Reynolds, John H. Wild, F. M. Snyder, F. W.
Buss, R. B. Reynolds, Frank Stenerwald, O. Hanson.

Parochial.

Baptisms (adults, 1, infants, 6), 7 ; Confirmed, since last report, 28 ; Present number of confirmed persons, about 150 ; Marriages; 1 ; Burials, 4 ; Communicants, last
reported, 121, admitted, 27, received, 3, removed, 2, present number, 149 ; Public
Services (Sundays, 192, Holy days, 46, other days, 35), 273 ; Holy Communion (public, 88, private, 4), 92 : Sunday School, teachers, 28, pupils, 170 ; Catechising, number of children, the two schools, number of times, every Sunday ; Parish School,
teachers, 2, pupils, 36.

Offerings.

Parochial.— Alms at Holy Communion, $15.36 ; Current expenses, including sal-
aries, $1,759.26 ; Sunday School, $68.46 ; Parish School, $194.90 ; The Woman's
Guild, $33 ; The King's Daughters, $139. Total, $2,209.98.

Diocesan.— Diocesan Missions, $30 ; Salary of the Bishop, $26 ; Diocesan Fund,
$27 ; Orphan House of the Holy Saviour, $17.67 ; Salary of the Diocesan Missionary,
$15. Total, $115.67.

General.— For General Missions, $34.82 ; Church Society for Promoting Christian-
ity Among Jews, $1.79 ; Russian Famine Relief Fund, $7. Total, $43.61.
Total amount of Offerings, $2,369.26.

Property.

Church and lot (estimated worth), $15,000.
Parsonage and lot (estimated worth), $4,000.
Other property, Parish school-house, $3,000.
Organ, $1,500.
Condition of property, very good.
Amount of salary pledged Rector, $900.
Number of sittings in the Church and Chapel, 330 ; all free.

Remarks.

The balance on hand of the Communion Alms and Sunday School offerings is
reported. The larger part is reported as used for other purposes, viz.: Missions,
Cooperstown, etc. The Altar in the Parish Church has been placed upon a solid oak

base. A new re-table, two brass vases and a cross were given during the year. Two of Frink's patent ten-lamp reflectors have been placed in the Church and one will soon be hung in the Chancel. Service and Sunday School are held at the Chapel at Rossman's Mills every Sunday.

ST. PAUL'S CHURCH, KINDERHOOK.

Wardens. Henry S. Wynkoop, Edward P. Van Alstyne.

Vestrymen. Francis Silvester, T. F. Woodworth, F. B. Van Alstyne, Tunis Devoe, Edgar Balls, Andrew Ketterson, James M. Hawley, William Heeney.

Parochial.

Families, 75; Individuals (adults, 180, children, 105), 285; Baptisms (adults, 2, infants, 12), 14; Confirmed, since last report, 8; Present number of confirmed persons, 188; Burials, 2; Communicants, last reported, 130, admitted, 8, died, 1, removed, 4, present number, 133; Public Services (Sundays, 127, Holy days, 37, other days, 51), 215; Holy Communion (public, 42, private, 2), 44; Sunday School, teachers, 7, pupils, 70; Catechizing, number of children, whole school, number of times, 30.

Offerings.

Parochial.—Alms at Holy Communion, $13.28; Current expenses, including salaries, $1,200; Increase and Improvement of Church Property, $150. Total, $1,363.28.

Diocesan.— Diocesan Missions, $60.90; Salary of the Bishop, $36; Bible and Common Prayer Book Society of Albany, $1.59; Fund for Aged and Infirm Clergymen, $16; Orphan House of the Holy Saviour (from S. S.), $10.97; The Child's Hospital (from S. S.), $10.97. Total, $136.43.

General. — Foreign Missions (to complete and furnish Church of Nativity, Wuchang), $6.13; Mission to Jews, $5.97; General Missions from S School, $27 23. Total, $39.38.

Total amount of Offerings, $1,539.09

Property.

Church and lot (estimated worth), $5,000.
Parsonage and lot, $3,000.
Condition of property, excellent.
Amount of salary pledged Rector, $700.
Number of sittings in the Church, 150; all free.

Remarks.

The Rev Isaac Peck resigned the Rectorship, June 25, 1892, and since then the Parish has had no Rector.

TRINITY CHURCH, CLAVERACK.

Rector. The Rev. George G Carter

Wardens. R. Fulton Ludlow, Richard M Ludlow

Vestrymen. Cornelius Shaw, Arthur Rowley, James J. Studley, Franklin P. Studley

Parochial.

Families, 24 ; Present number of confirmed persons, about 55 ; Communicants, last reported, 43, admitted, 4, received, 6, removed, 3, present number, 50 ; Public Services (Sundays, 52, Holy days, 6, other days, 30), 88, Holy Communion, public, 28; Sunday School, teachers, 5, pupils, 30; Catechizing, number of children, all, number of times, 28.

Offerings.

Parochial.—Current expenses, including salaries, $317.82 ; Sunday School, $40 ; Increase and Improvement of Church Property. $22.42 ; Altar Vases, and Hymn Board, $19.50.   Total, $399.74.

Diocesan.—Diocesan Missions, $27.11 ; Salary of the Bishop, $6 ; Diocesan Fund, $6 ; Fund for Aged and Infirm Clergymen, $3.50 ; Fund for Widows and Orphans of Clergymen, $1.50 ; Orphan House of the Holy Saviour, $6.25 ; The Child's Hospital, $5 ; Society for Promoting Religion and Learning, $14.   Total, $69.36.

General.—General Missions, $5.84 ; Russian Relief Fund, $6.34 ; Missions to the Jews, $2.54.   Total, $14.22.

Total amount of Offerings, $483.32.

Property.

Condition of property, good.

Amount of salary pledged Rector, $200.

THE CHURCH OF OUR SAVIOUR, LEBANON SPRINGS.

Rector.   The Rev. George B. Johnson.

Wardens.   Silas G. Owen, Wm. Henry Babcock.

Vestrymen.   John G. Field, Francis Myers, J. Harry Cox, Albert B. Parsons, Charles E. Wackerhagen.

Parochial.

Families, 18; Individuals (adults, 46, children, 16), 62; Baptisms, infants, 1; Present number of confirmed persons, 35; Marriages, 1; Burials, 5; Communicants, last reported, 45, admitted, 1, died, 2, removed, 1, present number, 31; Public Services (Sundays, 101, Holy days, 62, other days, 444), 607; Holy Communion (public, 66, private, 3), 69; Sunday School, teachers, 3, pupils, 12.

Offerings.

Parochial.—Current expenses, including salaries, $405.98.

Diocesan.—Diocesan Missions, $33.57; Salary of the Bishop, $6.00; Diocesan Fund, $9; Bible and Common Prayer Book Society of Albany, $1; Increase of the Episcopate Fund, $1; Fund for Aged and Infirm Clergymen, $2.25; Fund for Widows and Orphans of Clergymen, $2; Orphan House of the Holy Saviour, $4;* The Child's Hospital, $2; Society for Promoting Religion and Learning, $1; Clergy Reserve Fund, $1.   Total, $62.82.

General.—Domestic and Foreign Missions, $13.26;* Home Missions to Coloured Persons, $1.35.   Total, $14.61.

Total amount of Offerings, $483.41.

Property.

Church and lot (estimated worth), $3,000.

Parsonage lot (estimated worth), $275.

Other property (funds in hand for Rectory), $1,200.

Condition of property, good.

Amount of salary pledged Rector, $300.

Number of sittings in the Church, 150; all free.

Remarks.

Mrs. Morrison, of New York city, has presented to the Church a very handsome Communion Service of solid silver, as a memorial of her parents, Mr. and Mrs. E. C.

* The offerings for the Orphan House of the Holy Saviour and $3.55 of the offerings for Missions me from the children of the Sunday School.

King, the latter of whom, for many years a communicant of this Parish, died during the last winter. By the will of the late Mr. Merriman M. Field, a communicant, who died last April, there has been left to the Church a bequest of $500.

During the summer, four services were held on Sunday afternoons at Canaan, at the house of Mr. Sidney C. Beale. There was a fair attendance, for the most part of Churchmen that were boarding in Canaan. The offerings, which amounted to $6.89, were devoted to Diocesan Missions.

ST. BARNABAS' CHURCH, STOTTVILLE.

Rector. The Rev. Frederick Golden Rainey.
Wardens. Francis Horatio Stott, John J. Place.
Vestrymen. C. H. Stott, Jr., Fred. A. Welch, R. H. Harder, Jr., Wm. H. Tanner, Fred. H. Palmer, James Shortell, David Cooper, Levi Place.

Parochial.

Families, 100; Individuals (adults, 280, children, 200), 480; Baptisms (adults, 4, infants, 20), 24; Confirmed, since last report, 7; Present number of confirmed persons, 189; Marriages, 5; Burials, 10; Communicants, last reported, 185, admitted, 7, died, 3, present number, 189; Public Services (Sundays, 95, Holy days, 13, other days, 73), 181; Holy Communion (public, 35, private, 5), 40; Sunday School, teachers, 28, pupils, 202; Catechising, number of children, 202, number of times, weekly.

Offerings.

Parochial.—Alms at Holy Communion, $137.86; Current expenses, including salaries, $1,447.58; Sunday School, $54.89; Increase and Improvement of Church Property, $181.96; Altar Society, $135; the Ladies' Aid Society, $135. Total, $2,061.79.

Diocesan.— Diocesan Missions, $25; Salary of the Bishop, $26; Diocesan Fund, $30; Fund for Aged and Infirm Clergymen, $13; Orphan House of the Holy Saviour, $27; The Child's Hospital, $27; All Saints' Mission, Round Lake, $50. Total, $198.

General. — Domestic Missions, $13; Foreign Missions, $10; General Missions (S. S), $50; the Jews, $8. Total, $81.

Total amount of Offerings, $2,360.79.

Property.

Church and lot (estimated worth), $10,000.
Amount of salary pledged Rector, $1,200.
Number of sittings in the Church, 400; all free.

Remarks.

The Parish Aid Society have nearly $700 in the bank toward the building of a Rectory.

ST. MARK'S CHURCH, PHILMONT.

Rector. The Rev. Arthur Lowndes.
Wardens. George Baker, Frank Sutterland Harder.
Vestrymen. George Edward Clum, Henry Kroosz, S. W. Richardson, Richard Allen Woodruff, M. D.
Vestry Clerk. F. W. Herington.

Parochial.

Families, 50; Individuals (adults, 92, children, 31), 123; Baptisms (adults, 9, infants, 5), 14; Confirmed, since last report, 16; Present number of confirmed persons, 91; Marriages, 1; Burials, 1, Communicants, last reported, 47, admitted, 29, received, 4, restored, 3, removed, 3, present number, 80; Public Services (Sundays, 216, Holy days, 56, other days, 20), 292; Holy Communion (public), 87; Sunday School, teachers, 5, pupils, 38; Catechizing, The Sunday School, monthly.

Offerings.

Parochial.—Current Expenses, including salaries, $895.90; Sunday School, $16.41; Increase and Improvement of Church Property (payment of Church mortgage), $3,066; Other Parochial objects; Reduction of an old floating debt, $50; piano for choir room, $50; Altar vases from class confirmed, St. Luke's Day, 1891, $20; Silver Credence Paten from class confirmed May, 1892, $25; from St. Mark's Guild (for choir stalls, $43.81; surplices and cassocks, $55.07, to Altar Fund, $25, exclusive of $6.50 paid on mortgage included above), $123.88; Offering for staff for Processional Cross, $15; Altar Guild, $25.76. Total, $4,287.95.

Diocesan.—Diocesan Missions, $21; Salary of the Bishop, $6; Fund for Widows and Orphans of Clergymen, $5; Orphan House of the Holy Saviour (box), $15; The Child's Hospital (box), $15; Diocesan Missionary, $10. Total, $72.

General.—Domestic and Foreign Missions ($6 from Sunday School as Lenten offering), $16; The Clergyman's Retiring Fund Society, $12. Total, $28.

Total amount of Offerings, $4,387.95.

Property.

Church and lot (estimated worth), $10,000.

Condition of property, excellent.

Indebtedness, one note given to free Church from mortgage, $400; one note, given to consolidate several outstanding debts before present Rector's incumbency, for $200, on which $50 has been paid, $150.

Amount of salary pledged Rector, $650.

Number of sittings in the Church, 300; all free.

Remarks.

A box of Altar linen was sent by the Sunday School to All Saints' Church, Round Lake, on All Saints' Day, 1891.

A surpliced choir was introduced Christmas day, 1891.

The certificate of incorporation not having been legally drawn up in 1885, a special bill had to be obtained from the State Legislature to validate the attempted incorporation. This bill was approved by the Governor, April 15, 1892.

In the amount of $3,066, under the head of payment of mortgage, is included the sum of $1,500 given to the Rector from friends outside of the Parish in answer to his appeal indorsed by the Bishop.

The Church is also indebted to the Cathedral Chapter for the very stately Altar Cross formerly on the Cathedral Altar.

A guild hall, choir room, study and rectory are in the course of erection. The corner-stone of the guild hall, which is the gift of Mr. James Aken, was laid by James Ten Eyck, the Grand Master of the Masons in the State of New York, on October 22.

ST. LUKE'S CHURCH, CLERMONT.

Rector. The Rev. M. E. Wilson.

Trustees. Robert Dibblee, Harold Wilson, George Z. Foland, M. E. Wilson, W. C. Doane, H. J. Rivenburg.

Parochial.

Communicants, present number, 18; Public Services, Holy days, 5, 46; Holy Communion, public, 9.

Offerings.

Parochial.— Parochial objects, $19.62.

Diocesan.— Diocesan Missions, $10 ; Salary of the Bishop, $4 ; Diocesan Fund, $2. Total, $16.

Total amount of Offerings, $35.62.

THE CHURCH OF ST. JOHN IN THE WILDERNESS, COPAKE IRON WORKS.

Missionary. The Rev. George H. Fenwick.

Warden. J. C. Chesbrough.

Parochial.

Baptisms, infants, 3 ; Communicants, died, 1, removed, 2, present number, 8 ; Public Services (Sundays, 28, other days, 2), 30 ; Holy Communion (public, 15, private, 3), 18.

Offerings.

Parochial.— Alms at Holy Communion, $51.04 ; Current expenses, including salaries, $138.05. Total, $189.09.

Property.

Church and lot (estimated worth), $2,500.

Parsonage and lot (estimated worth), $3,000.

Condition of property, fairly good.

Indebtedness (Rectory debt, repairs, etc., $200, Church decoration, $240, floating debt, $13.44), $453.44.

Amount of salary pledged Missionary, $150.

Number of sittings in the Church, 150 ; all free.

ST. LUKE'S CHURCH, CHATHAM.

Missionary. The Rev. George H. Fenwick.

Trustees. W. Tetherly, Samuel Moffet, James Cook, Frederick Greenough.

Parochial.

Families, 20 ; Baptisms (adults, 2, infants, 1), 3 ; Communicants, present number, 10.

Offerings.

Parochial.— Current expenses, including salaries, $500.

Property.

Church and lot (estimated worth), $700.

Amount of salary pledged Missionary, $500.

Remarks.

I began to labor here last June, and we already have in course of construction what we hope will be a beautiful and perfectly appointed Church, which will cost about $5,000. We hope to have the Church opened for Divine Worship in about three months. Money to the amount of $2,000 has been already subscribed. This amount it is hoped will be increased during the winter, while the work is under way.

Delaware County.

ST. PETER'S CHURCH, HOBART.

Rector. The Rev. Eugene Griggs.

Wardens. A. H. Grant, George Barlow.

Vestrymen. W. J. Calhoun, George Moore, Robt. McNaught, Roswell Barlow, Frank McCourt, Geo. Sturges, James Porteus, O. B. Foot.

Parochial.

Families and parts of families, 38; Individuals (adults, 65, children, 35), 110; Baptisms (adults, 2, infants, 8), 10; Confirmed, since last report, 5; Present number of confirmed persons, 74; Marriages, 1; Burials, 11; Communicants, last reported, 65, admitted, 5, died 6, removed, 12, present number, 52; Public Services (Sundays, 91, Holy days, 3, other days, 1), 95; Holy Communion (public, 18, private, 1), 19; Sunday School, teachers, 6, pupils, 35; Catechizing, number of times, frequently.

Offerings.

Parochial.— Alms at Holy Communion, $28; Current expenses, including salaries, $550; Sunday School, $15; Increase and Improvement of Church Property, $100. Total, $693.

Diocesan.— Diocesan Missions, $6; Salary of the Bishop, $15; Bible and Common Prayer Book Society of Albany, $1.85; Fund for Widows and Orphans of Clergymen, $3.27; Orphan House of the Holy Saviour, $6, in work; The Child's Hospital, work, value not estimated; Expenses of Archdeaconry, $1.32. Total, $33.44.

General.— Domestic and Foreign Missions (Lenten Offering of S. S.), $5. Total amount of Offerings, $731.44.

Property.

Church and lot (estimated worth), $5,000.
Parsonage and lot (estimated worth), $1,500.
Condition of property, Church, very good; Rectory, poor.
Amount of salary pledged Rector, $500.
Number of sittings in the Church, 350; rented, 100; free, 250.

Remarks.

A Chalice and Cruet were purchased with the Easter Offering, at a cost of $14. The Church has been newly painted, so that it is now in good condition.

ST. JOHN'S CHURCH, DELHI.

Rector. The Rev. Creighton Spencer.
Wardens. Charles E. Hitt, R. G. Hughston.
Vestrymen. Alexander Shaw, G. M. Harby, G. A. Paine, J. W. Woodruff, Wm. C. Sheldon, H. A. Pitcher, John A. Kemp, S. E. Smith.

Parochial.

Families, 98; Individuals, 301; Baptisms (adults, 4, infants, 13), 17; Confirmed, since last report, 22; Present number of confirmed persons, 218; Burials, 15; Communicants, last reported, 207, admitted, 21, received, 1, died, 3, removed, 15, present number, 211; Public Services (Sundays, 168, Holy days, 47, other days, 76), 291; Holy Communion (public, 86, private 5), 91; Sunday School, teachers, 8, pupils, 72; Catechizing, number of children, all, number of times, every Sunday.

Offerings.

Parochial.—Alms at Holy Communion, $63.84; Current expenses, including salaries, $1,982.78; Sunday School, $24.91; Other parochial objects: Added to Endowment Fund, $405.74; Parish League, $126 ($100 given to Endowment Fund); Altar Society, $31.25. Total, $2,534.52.

Diocesan.—Diocesan Missions, $125; Salary of the ▓▓▓▓▓▓▓▓▓▓▓▓▓▓ $30;

21

Diocesan Fund, for 1891 and 1892, $72; Fund for Aged and Infirm Clergymen, $20; Orphan House of the Holy Saviour, $20.13; The Child's Hospital, $20.10; Other offerings for objects within the Diocese: Archdeaconry of the Susquehanna, for salary of Diocesan Missionary, $20; Woman's Auxiliary's boxes to Child's Hospital and Orphan House of the Holy Saviour, valued at $55.20. Total, $412.43.

General.—Domestic Missions (from the Sunday School), $35; Indian Missions, $21.19; Other objects exterior to the Diocese: Woman's Auxiliary's box for Domestic Missions, valued at $41.50; Jewish Missions, $5.10. Total, $102.79.

Total amount of Offerings, $3,049.74.

Property.

Church and lot (estimated worth), $10,000.
Parsonage and lot (estimated worth), $3,500.
Other property, Memorial Chapel, $25,000.
Condition of property, good.
Amount of salary pledged Rector, $1,200.
Number of sittings in the Church, 388; free, 36.
The 125 sittings in the Chapel are all free.

Remarks.

This report is for the thirteen months from October 1, 1891, to November 1, 1892. Of the 22 persons confirmed during this period, 9 were prepared by the Rev. F. B. Reazor, and were presented by him after his resignation of the Rectorship. The present Rector took charge January 2, 1892, Edwin B. Sheldon, Esq., and Mrs. Fitzhugh Whitehouse are building a handsome Rectory for the Parish.

CHRIST CHURCH, WALTON.

Rector. The Rev. James R. L. Nisbett.

Wardens. David H. Gay, Samuel H. St. John.

Vestrymen. John S. Eells, George C. Seeley, Samuel H. Fancher, Julius W. St. John, Joseph Harby, Horace E. North, Edwin W. Pond, John H. Townsend.

Parochial.

Families, 116; Individuals, 354; Baptisms (adult, 1, infants, 3), 4; Present number of confirmed persons, 159; Marriages, 3; Burials, 9; Communicants, last reported, 145, received, 4, died, 6, removed, 11, present number, 131; Public Services (Sundays, 140, Holy days, 38, other days, 104), 283; Holy Communion (public, 72, private, 7), 79; Sunday School, teachers and officers, 16, pupils, 110; Catechizing, number of children, all, number of times, 5.

Money raised and expended.

Parochial.—Alms at Holy Communion, $39.54; Current expenses, including salaries, $2,406.84; Sunday School, $85.17; Increase and Improvement of Church Property, about $800; Roofing Church, etc., $200; Piano for Lecture Room, $275; Sanctuary Guild, about $20. Total, $3,326.55.

Diocesan.— Diocesan Missions, $30; Salary of the Bishop, $20; Diocesan Fund, $36; to Christ Church, Deposit, $8.44; from Woman's Auxiliary to Diocesan Missions, $20; From Woman's Auxiliary to Orphan House, Cooperstown, value of boxes $35. Total, $149.44.

General.— Domestic Missions (from Woman's Auxiliary), $20; Foreign Missions (from Woman's Auxiliary), $20; Society for Promoting Christianity among the Jews, $7.51; Russian Famine Relief Fund, $11.70; Church Temperance Society, $2.25. Total, $61.46.

Total amount of Offerings, $3,537.45.

Property.

Church and lot (estimated worth), $12,000.
Parsonage and lot (estimated worth), $4,000.
Other property, $2,400.
Condition of property, very good.
Indebtedness, none.
Amount of salary pledged Rector, $1,200.
Number of sittings in the Church, 300; rented, 240; free, 60.

Remarks.

During the past year the Parish has sustained an irreparable loss in the death of its Junior Warden, Mr. George St. John, the full value of whose faithfulness and generosity to the Parish will only be realized as time passes and discloses what a bulwark he has been to the Church in faithfulness of life and work. He closed his long list of generous gifts by leaving in his will an endowment fund of $20,000.

The death of Mr. Francis Robinson left another vacant seat in the Church and Vestry, and caused us to mourn another earnest and devout soul.

The Church has been lighted with electricity during the past year.

The Parish branch of the Woman's Auxiliary has raised — In addition to its Missionary Offerings recorded in their proper places — about $110.

The Sanctuary Guild numbers about forty active members, and the St. Andrew's Association (a parochial society for men) about thirty members. I assumed the Rectorship of the Parish on December 19, 1891.

ST. PAUL'S CHURCH, FRANKLIN.

Wardens. Henry S. Edwards, E. P. Howe.
Vestrymen. George Copeland, Alfred Barnes, Edgar Naragon, H. E. Baldwin.

Parochial.

Families, 50; Baptisms (adults, 2, infant, 1), 3; Confirmed, since last report, 2; Present number of confirmed persons, 74; Burials, 4; Communicants, admitted, 2, died, 1, removed, 5, present number, 64.

Offerings.

Parochial.—Current expenses, including salaries, $1,254; Sunday School, $8.49; Parish School, $374.93; Altar Society, $22.26; Dorcas Guild, $5; for young Churchman, $4.90; Unspecified, $12.27. Total, $1,676.85.

Diocesan.—Diocesan Missions, $11.60; Salary of the Bishop, $16; Bible and Common Prayer Book Society of Albany, $3.93; Fund for Aged and Infirm Clergymen, $3.93; Orphan House of the Holy Saviour, $3.93; Other Offerings for Objects within the Diocese, Archdeaconry, $4. Total, $43.39.

General.—General Missions, $8.34; Russian sufferers, $3.12; Jewish Missions, $1. Total, $12.46.

Total amount of Offerings, $1,732.70.

Property.

Church and lot (estimated worth), $6,500.
Parsonage and lot (estimated worth), $1,500.
Condition of property, good.
Amount of salary pledged Rector, $500.
Number of sittings in the Church, 400; all free.

This report is of necessity incomplete. The Rector died very suddenly, and some of the data necessary to the making of a correct report have been lost.

CHRIST CHURCH, DEPOSIT.

Rector. The Rev. Frederick S. Fisher.
Wardens. W. H. Gregory, T. M. Bixby.
Vestrymen. C. Onderdonk, H. B. Coggshall, Philip Munson, Charles Pinkney, James McDonald.

Parochial.

Families, 46 ; Individuals (adults, 105, children, 46), 151 ; Baptisms (adults, 5, infants, 11), 16 ; Confirmed, since last report, 15 ; Present number of confirmed persons, 94 ; Marriages, 2 ; Burials, 5 ; Communicants, last reported, 75, admitted, 14, received, 1, died, 1, removed, 6, present number, 83 ; Public Services, Sundays, all, Holy days, all, other days, Fridays ; Holy Communion, public, monthly and Holy days ; Sunday School, teachers, 5, pupils, 41 ; Catechizing, number of times, all Sundays.

Offerings.

Parochial.— Current expenses, including salaries, $700 ; Increase and Improvement of Church Property, $6,000 ; Easter Special, $10 ; Parish Purposes, $50 ; For the Sunday School, $14.17 ; Archdeaconry, $1.50. Total, $6,775.67.

Diocesan.— Diocesan Missions, $15.89 ; Salary of the Bishop, $6 ; Bible and Common Prayer Book Society of Albany, $2 ; Orphan House of the Holy Saviour, $2.50. Total, $26.39.

General.— Domestic and Foreign Missions, $6.82.

Total amount of Offerings, $6,818.88.

Property.

Church and lot (estimated worth), $7,500.
Other property, old Church, $1,000.
Condition of property, good.
Indebtedness, on new Church, $1,500.
Amount of salary pledged Rector, $600.
Number of sittings in new Church, 248 ; all free.

Remarks.

In the year past a stone Church has been built on a new lot. The new location is far better and more accessible than the old site. The Church at the time of the Convention is not yet quite finished. Already we feel the good effects of a proper Church Building in a better part of the village. Those effects are as yet, to be sure, promises only, but promises that we think will increase the Parish. And the Parishioners, for this fulfillment of a long delayed and much-desired Church, are full of thanks to those that have helped the enterprise and with praise to God.

GRACE CHURCH, STAMFORD.

Missionary. The Rev. Howard McDougall.
Warden. Albert Clist.

Parochial.

Families, 20 . Individuals (adults, 37, children, 18), 55 ; Baptisms (adults, 5, infants, 8), 13 ; Confirmed, since last report, 6 . Present number of confirmed persons. 33 ; Marriages, 1 ; Communicants, last reported, 21, admitted, 6, received, 2, removed 1, present number, 30 ; Public Services (Sundays, 101, Holy days, 15, other days, 9), 125 ; Holy Communion public, 27 ; Sunday School, teachers, 5, pupils, 31; Catechizing, number of times, 30.

Offerings.

Parochial.— Alms at Holy Communion (at early Service, $4.21, at late service, $66.90), $71.11 ; Current expenses, including salaries, $604.86 ; Sunday School, $47.45 ; Increase and Improvement of Church Property, $43.79 ; Other Parochial objects, $32. Total, $799.21.

Diocesan.— Diocesan Missions, $23.71 ; Salary of the Bishop, $6 ; Diocesan Fund, $9 ; Orphan House of the Holy Saviour, $7 50 ; two packages of clothing (valued at), $15. Total, $61 21.

General.— Domestic and Foreign Missions (S. S. Lenten offering), $14.

Total amount of Offerings, $874.42.

Property.

Church and lot (estimated worth), $2,500.
Condition of property, good.
Amount of salary pledged Missionary, $450.
Number of sittings in the Church, 200 ; all free.

Remarks.

A fair was held in August, by the Church Guild and summer visitors, at which over $500 were realized. Also, a Thank Offering of $25 was made by a Church-woman from New York city.

ST. PAUL'S MISSION, SIDNEY.

Missionary. The Rev. Fred. S. Griffin.
Warden. E. Winsor.
Treasurer. D. M. Bowers.

Parochial.

Families, 37; Individuals (adults, 83, children, 30), 113; Baptisms (adult, 1, infants, 6), 7; Confirmed, since last report, 4; Present number of confirmed persons, 41; Marriages, 1 ; Burials, 5; Communicants, last reported, 30, admitted, 4, received, 1, died, 2, removed, 1, present number, 32; Public Services (Sundays, 99, Holy days, 31, other days, 80), 210; Holy Communion, public, 62; Sunday School, teachers, 4, pupils, 28.

Offerings.

Parochial.—Alms at Holy Communion, $8.31; Current expenses, including salaries, $200; Sunday School, $16.49; Increase and Improvement of Church Property, $695; New organ for the Mission, $65; Christmas tree festival, $12; Flowers for Altar, $8. Total, $1,004.80.

Diocesan.—Diocesan Missions, $15.50; Salary of the Bishop, $3; Diocesan Fund, $3; Bible and Common Prayer Book Society of Albany, $3.85; Fund for Widows and Orphans of Clergymen, $2.75; Orphan House of the Holy Saviour, $1.75; Society for Promoting Religion and Learning, $5; Archdeaconry Fund, $2. Total, $36.85.

Total amount of Offerings, $1,041.65.

Property.

Lot upon which to build a Chapel has been purchased for $1,000.
Amount of salary pledged Missionary, $100.

Essex County.

CHURCH OF THE CROSS, TICONDEROGA.

Rector. The Rev. Henry T. Gregory.

Wardens. John C. Fenton, Carlton Cook.

Vestrymen. L. Malcolm, G. B. Bascom, G. B. Hanford, W. T. Bryan, J. H. ___ Bryan, W. C. Noyes, Frederick Higgins, R. M. Wilbur.

Parochial.

Families, 70; Baptisms (adults, 2, infants, 7), 9; Confirmed, since last report, 10== ; Marri ges, 3; Burials, 4; Communicants, last reported, 83, admitted, 9, received, 2___ , removed 3, present number, 90; Public Services (Sundays, 78, Holy days, 6, othe=== days, 44), 128; Holy Communion, public, 27; Sunday School, teachers. 3, pupils, 85== ; Catechizing, number of children, Sunday School, number of times, nearly every=== Sunday.

Offerings.

Parochial.—Current expenses, including salaries, $677.33; Sunday School, $42.28== ; Increase and Improvement of Church Property, $90. Total, $809.61.

Diocesan.—Diocesan Missions, $30; Salary of the Bishop, $10; Diocesan Fund___ $15; Bible and Common Prayer Book Society of Albany, $4.98; Fund for Aged and=== Infirm Clergymen, $4.44; Fund for Widows and Orphans of Clergymen, $3.22== ; Orphan House of the Holy Saviour, $7.44; Education for the Ministry, $5.91== ; Clergy Reserve Fund, $2.75; Archdeaconry of Troy, $3.12; Toward salary of Dioce——· san Missionary, $5. Total, $90.86.

General.—General Missions (Sunday School, $25.45), $33.56; Jewish Missions___ , $2.72. Total, $36.28.

Total amount of Offerings, $936.75.

Property.

Church and lot (estimated worth), $9,000.

Parsonage and lot (estimated worth), $2,500.

Condition of property, good.

Amount of salary pledged Rector, $500.

Number of sittings in the Church, 270; all free.

Remarks.

The Church has been painted and the order given for a furnace to be put into the= Rectory. For this the Parish is indebted to the Ladies' Aid Society, which, by legiti— mate work, without entertainments, has obtained the money for these purposes.

ST. JOHN'S CHURCH, ESSEX.

Rector. The Rev. Wm. Norman Irish.

Wardens. Stephen D. Derby, Andrew J. Tucker.

Vestrymen. Anthony J. B. Ross, Robert Fortune, Moses Knowlton, Edward W. Richardson, Lyman R. Thompson, William M. Cowan.

Parochial.

Families, 50; Individuals (adults, 70, children, 15), 85; Baptisms (adults, 2, infant, 1), 3; Confirmed, since last report, 3; Burials, 8; Communicants, last reported (72, which ought to have been), 80, admitted, 3, received 5, present number, 88;* Public Services (Sundays, 104, Holy days, 12, other days, 64), 180; Holy Communion, public, 16; Sunday School, teachers, 4, pupils, 12, Catechizing, every Sunday.

---

* Including Lewis, Willsborough and vicinity.

Offerings.

Parochial.—Alms at Holy Communion, $38.33; Current expenses, including salaries, $404.83; Sunday School, $42.24; Increase and Improvement of Church Property, $10. Total, $495.40.

Diocesan.—Diocesan Missions, $38.36; Salary of the Bishop, $16; Diocesan Fund, $9; Fund for Aged and Infirm Clergymen, $3; The Child's Hospital, $10.56; Diocesan Missionary, $5; Ladies' Auxiliary, $1. Total, $68.92.

General.—For the Jews, $1.00.

Total amount of Offerings, $565.32.

Property.

Church and lot (estimated worth), $3,000.

Parsonage and lot (estimated worth), $2,000.

Other property, about $700.

Condition of property, good.

Amount of salary pledged Rector, $300.

Number of sittings in the Church, 200; all free.

ST. PAUL'S CHURCH, KEESEVILLE.

Rector. The Rev. John W. Gill.

Wardens. Asa Pierce Hammond, Francis Cassidy.

Vestrymen. Henry Dundas, Philip Harrison, James Dundas, Elias J. Champlin.

Parochial.

Families, 38; Individuals (adults, 73, children, 24), 97; Baptisms infants, 4; Confirmed, since last report, 7; Present number of confirmed persons, 59: Marriages, 5; Burials, 3; Communicants, last reported, 52, died 1, removed 1, present number, 59; Public Services (Sundays, 52, Holy days, 3, other days, 52), 107; Holy Communion (public, 12, private, 4), 16; Sunday School, teachers, 5, pupils, 27; Catechizing, number of children, 27, number of times, weekly.

Offerings.

Parochial.— Current expenses, including salaries, $535; Sunday School, $15. Total, $550.

Diocesan.— Diocesan Missions, $15; Salary of the Bishop, $10.; Fund for Aged and Infirm Clergymen, $5.40; Society for Promoting Religion and Learning, $4.50. Total, $34.90.

Total amount of Offerings, $584.90.

Property.

Church and lot (estimated worth), $2,000.

Parish room (estimated worth), $1,250.

Condition of property, good.

Amount of salary pledged Rector, $400.

Number of sittings in the Church, 180; all free.

CHRIST CHURCH, PORT HENRY.

Rector. The Rev. William Ball Wright, M. A.

Wardens. Theodore Tromblee, Jr., William M. J. Botham.

Vestrymen. Frank S. Atwell, George Hoy, Charles W. ████████ ██████ ██ Foote, Jr., Charles P. Parker.

Parochial.

Families, 39; Individuals (adults, 82, children, 74), 156; Baptisms, infants, 7; Confirmed, since last report, 2; Present number of confirmed persons, 64; Marriages, 11; Burials, 6; Communicants, last reported, 52, admitted, 2, received, 1, died, 1, removed, 2, present number, 52; Public Services (Sundays, 77, Holy days, 18, other days, 57), 152; Holy Communion (public, 12, private, 1), 13; Sunday School, teachers, 5, pupils, 60; Catechizing, number of children, 14, number of times, 5; Services at Crown Point Mission, 7.

Offerings.

Parochial.—Current expenses, including salary, $948.90.

Diocesan.—Diocesan Missions, $11.80; Salary of the Bishop, $10; Diocesan Fund, $30.32; Bible and Common Prayer Book Society of Albany, $10.10; Orphan House of the Holy Saviour, $20.08; The Child's Hospital, $4.70; Society for Promoting Religion and Learning, $8.86; assessment on Rector's salary, 3 per cent, $15.60 — Total, $111.46.

General.—General Theological Seminary, $7.10; Domestic Missions, $8.11; Church Temperance Society, $3.50; Russian Famine Relief, $4; Jewish Missions, $5.12; Home of the Friendless, Plattsburgh, N. Y., $1.88; General Missions, $1. Total, $30.71.

Total amount of Offerings, $1,091.07.

Property.

Church and lot (estimated worth), $5,000.

Condition of property, good.

Amount of salary pledged Rector, $520.

Number of sittings in the Church, 180; all free.

Remarks.

The Rev. W. R. Woodbridge, late Rector of Christ Church, resigned August 1, 1892, after a Rectorship of twenty years. No services were held until November 6, when the Rev. William Ball Wright officiated, and on November 9, he received and accepted a call to be Rector, on the recommendation of Bishop Doane.

The house used as Rectory being the property of the late Rector and occupied, there is no Rectory at present, nor any allowance for house rent. There is a vacant lot for sale next to the Church, which could be obtained for $500.

EMMANUEL CHURCH, MINEVILLE.

Missionary. The Rev. W. Ball Wright, M. A.

Parochial.

Families, 24; Individuals (adults, 80, children, 53), 133; Baptisms (adult, 1, infants, 7), 8; Confirmed, since last report, 3; Present number of confirmed persons, 30; Burials, 4; Communicants, last reported, 12, admitted, 3, received, 1, died, 2, present number, 14; Public Services (Sundays, 38, Holy days, 3, other days, 16), 57; Holy Communion, public, 4; Catechizing, number of children, 10, number of times, 6.

Offerings.

Parochial.— Current expenses, including salaries, $47.96.

Diocesan.— Theological education, $5.60.

General.— Children's Lent offering for Missions, $7.86.

Total amount of Offerings, $61.42.

Property.

Church and lot (estimated worth), $1,000.
Condition of property, good.
Number of sittings in the Church, 125 ; all free.

Remarks.

After the resignation of Rev. W. R. Woodbridge, August 1, Rev. C. E. Cragg, Deacon, conducted Morning Services until November 6. The Rev. W. Ball Wright took charge on Sunday, November 13, and held services on the afternoon of same day.

ST. JAMES' CHURCH, AU SABLE FORKS.

Priest in charge. The Rev. John W. Gill.
Lay Reader. James Rogers.
Warden. James Rogers.

Parochial.

Families, 26; Individuals (adults, 74, children, 55), 129; Baptisms (adults, 15, infants, 6), 21; Confirmed, since last report, 14; Present number of confirmed persons, 46; Marriages, 1; Communicants, last reported, 47, removed, 1, present number, 46; Public Services (Sundays, 52, Holy days, 1, other days, 12), 65; Holy Communion, public, 13; Sunday School, teachers, 6, pupils, 36; Catechizing, number of children, 36, number of times, weekly.

Offerings.

Parochial.— Current expenses, including salaries, $378.16; Increase and Improvement of Church Property, $47.80. Total, $425.96.
Diocesan.— Diocesan Missions, $25; Salary of the Bishop, $16; Diocesan Fund, $6. Total, $47.
Total amount of Offerings, $472.96.

Property.

Church and lot (estimated worth), $12,000.
Parsonage and lot (estimated worth). $3,000.
Condition of property, good.
Amount of salary pledged Priest in charge, $200.
Number of sittings in the Church, 200; all free.

CHURCH OF THE REDEEMER, BLOOMINGDALE.

Missionary. The Rev. Walter H. Larom.

Parochial.

Families, 13; Individuals (adults, 26, children, 24), 50; Present number of confirmed persons, 14; Communicants, last reported, 14; Public Services, Sundays, 10; Holy Communion, public, 1; Sunday School, teachers, 3, pupils, 35.

Offerings.

All included in report of St. Luke the Beloved Physician, Saranac Lake, Franklin county.

Property.

Church and lot (estimated worth), $2,500.
Condition of property, good.
Number of sittings in the Church, 150; all free.

Remarks.

The constantly increasing work at Saranac Lake makes it more and more difficult for the Missionary to maintain regular services at this point.

22

ST. EUSTACE'S CHURCH, LAKE PLACID.

Missionary. The Rev. Walter H. Larom.
Treasurer of Building Fund. Henry B. Auchincloss.

Parochial.

Families, 5; Individuals] (adults, 9, children, 6), 15; Communicants, 6; Public Services, Sundays, 9.

Offerings.

All included in report for Church of St. Luke, Saranac Lake, Franklin county.

Remarks.

Services are held in the parlor of the Stevens House by the courtesy of the Messrs. Stevens, and in the parlor of the Union Lake House by the courtesy of the proprietor, Mr. William Martin.

ST. ANDREW'S CHURCH, SCHROON LAKE.

(See Report of the Diocesan Missionary, p. 118.)

Franklin County.

ST. MARK'S CHURCH, MALONE.

Rector. The Rev. Charles Temple.
Wardens. Hon. H. A. Taylor, Dr. R. J. Wilding.
Vestrymen. J. O. Ballard, John Fay, A. C. Hadley, Hon. Albert Hobbs, Samuel Greene, E. W. Knowlton, M. S. Mallon, A. H. Merritt.

Parochial.

Families, 103 ; Individuals (adults, 240, children, 60), 300 ; Baptisms (adults, 5, infants, 7), 12 ; Confirmed, since last report, 16 ; Present number of confirmed persons, 199 ; Marriages, 14 ; Burials, 5 ; Communicants, admitted, 16, died, 1, removed 4, present number, 162 ; Holy Communion, public, weekly ; Sunday School, teachers, 10, pupils, 50 ; Catechizing, number of children, whole school, number of times, every Sunday.

Offerings.

Parochial.— Alms at Holy Communion, $40.85 ; Current expenses, including salaries, $1,882.14 ; Sunday School, $75 ; Increase and Improvement of Church Property, $550. Total, $2,547.99.

Diocesan.— Diocesan Missions, $120 ; Salary of the Bishop, $36 ; Diocesan Fund, $36 ; Bible and Common Prayer Book Society of Albany, $5 ; Fund for Aged and Infirm Clergymen, $10 ; Fund for Widows and Orphans of Clergymen, $10 ; Orphan House of the Holy Saviour, $30 ; Society for Promoting Religion and Learning, $10. Total, $257.

General.— Domestic Missions, $27 ; Foreign Missions, $15 ; Indian Missions, $10 : Home Missions to Coloured Persons, $10 ; Mission to Jews, $8. Total, $70.

Total amount of Offerings, $2,874.99.

Property.

Church and lot (estimated worth), $20,000.
Parsonage and lot (estimated worth), $6,000.
Condition of property, excellent.
Amount of salary pledged Rector. $1,200.
Number of sittings in the Church, 270 ; rented, 250 ; free, 20.

ST. PETER'S CHURCH BRUSHTON.

Rector. The Rev. Alfred Louis Fortin.
Warden. W. S. Lawrence.
Vestrymen. W. C. Brush, J. C. Farnsworth, W. H. Smith, Robert Dunlap, G. W. Harris, James E. Brady, James Pickering.

Parochial.

Families, 13; Individuals (adults, 36, children, 16), 52; Confirmed, since last report, 2; Present number of confirmed persons, 26; Marriages, 1; Burials, 2; Communicants, last reported, 13, admitted 1, present number 20; Public Services, Sundays, 28 times, since the 12th of June to the 16th of October; Holy Communion, public, 4, for the same period; Sunday School, teachers, 4, pupils, 19; Catechizing, number of children, 15, number of times, 6, since the 12th of June.

Offerings.

Parochial.— Current expenses, including salaries, $410; Sunday School, $1.85, since June 12th to October 1st; Last mortgage on Parsonage, $111.75; Improvement on Parsonage, $14.40; Ladies' Aid have on hand, $89.19; Furnace for Parsonage, $115. Total, $742.19.

Diocesan.— Diocesan Missions, $10; Salary of the Bishop, $8; Diocesan Fund, $8.40. Total, $26.40.

Total amount of Offerings, $788.59.

Property.

Church and lot (estimated worth), $3,000.
Parsonage and lot (estimated worth), $1,600.
Condition of property, good.
Amount of salary pledged Rector, $280.
Number of sittings in the Church, 150; all free.

ST. MARK'S CHURCH, WEST BANGOR.

Missionary. The Rev. Alfred Louis Fortin.
Warden. C. A. Crooks.

Parochial.

Families, 11 ; Individuals (adults, 17, children, 8), 25 ; Present number of confirmed persons, 16 ; Marriages, 1 ; Communicants, received, 1, present number, 15 ; Public Services, Sundays, fortnightly ; Holy Communion, public, monthly ; Sunday School, teachers, 3, pupils, 14.

Offerings.

Parochial. — Current expenses, including salaries, $150 ; Sunday School, $6. Total, $156.

Diocesan.— Salary of the Bishop, $4 ; Diocesan Fund, $2.25. Total, $6.25.

Total amount of Offerings, $162.25.

Property.

Church and lot (estimated worth), $1,200.
Condition of property, good.
Amount of salary pledged Missionary, $75.
Number of sittings in the Church, 200 ; all free.

ST. JAMES' CHURCH, HOGANSBURGH.

Missionary. The Rev. David Jenkins.
Warden. Alfred Fulton.

Parochial.

Families, 13; Individuals (adults, 31, children, 14), 45; Present number of con—firmed persons, 38; Communicants, present number, 20; Public Services, on each Sunday, 1; Holy Communion, public, monthly; Sunday School, teachers, 2, pupils, 18.

Offerings.

Parochial.—Current expenses, including salaries, $172.74; Sunday School, $3.70; Increase and Improvement of Church Property, $4. Total, $180.44.

Diocesan.—Diocesan Missions, $25; Salary of the Bishop, $8; Diocesan Fund, $7.50; Other offerings for objects within the Diocese, $10.60. Total, $51.10.

Total amount of Offerings, $231.54.

Property.

Church and lot (estimated worth), $3,000.
Parsonage and lot (estimated worth), $2,500.
Other property, $100.
Amount of salary pledged Missionary, $250.
Number of sittings in the Church, 120; all free.

CHURCH OF ST. LUKE THE BELOVED PHYSICIAN, SARANAC LAKE.

Missionary. The Rev. Walter H. Larom.
Lay Reader. Mr. W. W. Godard.
Warden. E. L. Trudeau, M. D.
Treasurer. W. W. McAlpine.

Parochial.

Families, 70; Individuals (adults, 155, children, 60), 215; Baptisms (adults, 5, infants, 10), 15; Present number of confirmed persons, 82; Marriages, 3; Communicants, last reported, 75, admitted, 2, received, 4, died, 2, removed, 1, present number, 78; Public Services (Sundays, 80, Holy days, 19, other days, 40), 139, approximate; Holy Communion (public, 45, private, 1), 46; Sunday School, teachers, 11, pupils, 90.

Offerings.

Parochial.— Current expenses, including salaries, $2,159.52; Sunday School, $50; Increase and Improvement of Church Property, $3,756.03; Current expenses of Adirondack Library, $369.80. Total, $6,335.35.

Diocesan.— Diocesan Missions, $20; Salary of the Bishop, $6; Diocesan Fund, $45. Total, $71.

General.— Domestic Missions, $10; Foreign Missions, $30. Total, $40.

Total amount of Offerings, $6,446.35.

Property.

Church and lot (estimated worth), $4,000.
Lot for Rectory (estimated worth), $500.
Other property, Adirondack Library, $4,000.
Condition of property, excellent.
Indebtedness, on Library, $577.15.
Number of sittings in the Church, 200; all free.

CHURCH OF ST. JOHN IN THE WILDERNESS, PAUL SMITH'S.

Missionary. The Rev. Walter H. Larom.
Warden. E. L. Trudeau, M. D.

Parochial.

Summer Church for camp and guests at the hotel; Burials, 2; Public Services, Sundays, 12; Holy Communion, public, 3.

Offerings.

All included in Church of St. Luke the Beloved Physician, Saranac Lake, Franklin county.

Property.

Church and lot (estimated worth), $5,000.
Condition of property, excellent.
Number of sittings in the Church, 200; all free.

FORT COVINGTON MISSION.

Missionary. The Rev. David Jenkins.
Warden. M. M. Smith.

Parochial.

Families, 10; Individuals (adults, 20, children, 5), 25; Baptisms, infants, 1; Confirmed, since last report, 2; Present number of confirmed persons, 16; Communicants, admitted, 2, removed, 2, present number, 11; Public services, Sundays, weekly; Holy Communion, public, monthly.

Offerings.

Parochial.—Current expenses, including salaries, $153.59.
Diocesan.—Diocesan Missions, $4.12.
Total amount of Offerings, $157.71.

Property.

Amount of salary pledged Missionary, $175.

Fulton County.

ST. JOHN'S CHURCH, JOHNSTOWN.

Rector. The Rev. J. N. Marvin.
Lay Reader. Edward T. Carroll.
Wardens. Abiram S. Van Voast, Thomas E. Ricketts.
Vestrymen. Hon. J. M. Carroll, Isaiah Yanney, James I. Younglove, Charles Prindle, Robert J. Evans, John Chetwynde, John W. Uhlinger, Jonathan Ricketts.

Parochial.

Families, 206, parts of, 40; Baptisms (adults, 2, infants, 20), 22; Confirmed, since last report, 23; Marriages, 6; Burials, 21; Communicants, last reported, 308, admitted, 16, received, 11, died, 6, removed, 5, present number, 319; Public Services (Sundays, 159, Holy days, 46, other days, 163), 368; Holy Communion (public, 85, private, 4), 89; Sunday School, teachers, 22, pupils, 175; Catechizing, number of children, 150, number of times, weekly.

Offerings.

Parochial.—Alms at Holy Communion, $59.30; Current expenses, including salaries, $2,076.98; Sunday School, $251.93; Parish Room, $126.79; Increase and Improvement of Church Property, $171.57; Other Parochial objects, $81; Parochial Alms, $45; Altar Decoration, $35; St. John's Register, $30.76. Total, $2,878.33.

Diocesan.—Diocesan Missions, $75; Salary of the Bishop, $50; Diocesan Fund, $33; Archdeaconry of Albany, $4.88; Orphan House of the Holy Saviour, $42.51; St. Margaret's House, $11.25; Other offerings for objects within the Diocese, $9.10 ; Cathedral Debt, $22.25; Diocesan Missionary, $20; 2 boxes to Orphan House Holy Saviour, $47; 2 boxes to St. Margaret's House, $15.20; boxes and books to Diocesan Missions, $37. Total, $367.19.

General.—Foreign and Domestic Missions, $34.59; Indian Missions, $10; Home Missions to Coloured Persons, $10; Conversion of Jews, $4.25; box to Coloured Mission, $25; box to Oil City, $20; books to Western Missions, $4. Total, $107.84.

Total amount of Offerings, $3,353.36.

Property.

Church and lot (estimated worth), $20,000.
Parsonage and lot (estimated worth), $5,000.
Other property, $1,000.
Condition of property, good.
Number of sittings in the Church, 850.

CHRIST CHURCH, GLOVERSVILLE.

Missionary. The Rev. Henry Mason Smyth.
Warden. Henry Marshall.
Treasurer. David S. Thompson.
Clerk. Frank Lawrence.

Parochial.

Families, 90; Individuals (adults, 208, children, 152), 360; Baptisms (adult, 1, infants, 8), 9; Confirmed, since last report, 6; Marriages, 4; Burials, 2; Churchings, 4; Communicants, last reported, 101, admitted, 3, received, 58, died, 2, removed, 6, present number, 154; Public services, Sundays, 8 and 10: 30 A. M., 7: 30 P. M., Holy days, 10 A. M. or 7: 30 P. M., other days, Fridays; Holy Communion, public, every Sunday and on great festivals, private, 1; Sunday School, teachers, 11, pupils, 80.

Offerings.

Parochial.—Current expenses, including salaries, $1,089.91; Sunday School, $25; Charities, $74.85; Building Fund, $100; Choir Vestments, $79.56; from Churchings, $101. Total, $1,469.82.

Diocesan —Diocesan Missions, $25; Salary of [the Bishop, $10; Diocesan Fund, $12; Orphan House of the Holy Saviour, $103.04. Total, $150.04.

General.—Conversion of the Jews, $2.15.

Total amount of Offerings, $1,622.01.

Property.

Church and lot (estimated worth), $8,000.
Condition of property, fair.
Indebtedness, mortgage, $2,000.
Number of sittings in the Church, 300; all free.

Remarks.

The present incumbent took charge on the 7th of January; parts of the report cover only the time subsequent to that date.

Greene County.

ST. LUKE'S CHURCH, CATSKILL.

Rector. The Rev. Elmer P. Miller.

Wardens. William L. Du Bois, Henry T. Jones.

Vestrymen. Manly B. Mattice, Theodore A. Cole, Charles Trowbridge, Charles E. Willard, Robert Selden, W. H. H. Schofield, William S. C. Wiley, Frederic E. Craigie.

Parochial.

Families, 287 ; Baptisms (adults 6, infants, 19), 25; Confirmed, since last report, 19; Present number of confirmed persons, 355; Marriages, 8; Burials, 21; Communicants, last reported, 347, admitted, 19, received, 10, died, 3, removed 18, present number, 355; Actually communicating, 292; Public Services (Sundays, 155, Holy days, 40, other days, 146), 341; Holy Communion (public, 82, private, 13), 95; Sunday School, teachers, 21, pupils, 160.

Offerings.

Parochial.— Alms at Holy Communion, $143.16; Current expenses, including salaries, $1,833.84; Sunday School, $135.66; St. Luke's Brotherhood, $305; St. Luke's Guild Receipts, $399.79; Paid debt, $300; St. Luke's Building Fund, $282. Total, $3,399.45.

Diocesan.— Diocesan Missions, $150; Salary of the Bishop, $30; Diocesan Fund, $36; Bible and Common Prayer Book Society of Albany, $10; Fund for Aged and Infirm Clergymen, $10; Fund for Widows and Orphans of Clergymen, $10; Orphan House of the Holy Saviour, $50; The Child's Hospital (by Sunday School), $38; Diocesan Missionary (by Sunday School), $15. Total, $349.

General.— Domestic Missions, $22.50; Foreign Missions, $22.50; Missions to the Jews, $7.31; St. Mark's, Utah (by Sunday School), $40; Society for Increase of Ministry, $15; Russian Peasants, $25; Mrs. Buford and Dr. Briggs, $5. Total, $137.31.

Total amount of Offerings, $3,885.76.

Property.

Amount of salary pledged Rector, $1,200.

CHRIST CHURCH, COXSACKIE.

Rector. The Rev. E. S. De G. Tompkins.

Warden. Henry J. Hahn.

Vestrymen. R. J Washbon, N. A. Calkins, N. H. Vosburgh, J. E. Brown, Jr., Wm. Farmer, M. H. Green, G. H. Scott, Harry Jordan.

Parochial.

Families, 20; Individuals (adults, 21, children, 30), 51; Burials, 2; Communicants, present number, 44; Public Services (Sundays, 104, Holy days, 3), 107; Holy Communion, public, 14; Sunday School, teachers, 4, pupils, 27.

Offerings.

Diocesan.— Salary of the Bishop, $18.

Remarks.

This Parish has been working during the past year to build a Rectory and Parish house. So far their efforts have met with success, and it is hoped that the buildings can be erected in the spring.

TRINITY CHURCH, ATHENS

Rector. The Rev. James Wilkins Stewart.
Wardens. S. H. Nichols, H. C. Van Loan.
Vestrymen. G. S. Nichols, Robert Cleete, Wm. Cook, F. Beardsley, F. Van Schaick, Frank Nichols, George Nedtwick, M. Davenport.

Parochial.

Families, 37; Individuals (adults, 109, children, 46), 155; Baptisms (adults, 4, infants, 5), 9; Confirmed, since last report, 8; Marriages, 2; Burials, 7; Communicants, last reported, 72, admitted, 8, received, 1, died, 1, present number, 80; Public Services (Sundays, 96, Holy days, 10, other days, 34), 140; Holy Communion, public, 15; Sunday School, teachers, 8, pupils, 60; Catechising, number of children all, number of times, weekly.

Offerings.

Parochial.—Alms at Holy Communion, $16.16; Current expenses, including salaries, $700; Sunday School, $23.62. Total, $739.78.

Diocesan.—Diocesan Missions, $6.30; Salary of the Bishop, $10; Bible and Common Prayer Book Society of Albany, $3; Fund for Aged and Infirm Clergymen, $3; Orphan House of the Holy Saviour, $5.89; The Child's Hospital, $5.89. Total, $34.08.

General.—Russian Relief Fund, $6.04; Jewish Missions, $1.50. Total, $7.54.
Total amount of Offerings, $781.40.

Property.

Church and lot (estimated worth), $5,000.
Parsonage and lot (estimated worth), $3,000.
Other property, Endowment Fund, $6,000.
Condition of property, good.
Amount of salary pledged Rector, $600.
Number of sittings in the Church, 250; all free.

ST. PAUL'S CHURCH, OAK HILL.

Rector. The Rev. T. A. Snyder.
Wardens. W. S. Cheritree, C. A. Hall.
Vestrymen. Byron Hall, Theodore L. Cheritree, Ambrose H. Flower, Charles E. Graham, Hyram Snyder.

Parochial.

Burials, 1; Communicants, last reported, 36, admitted, 3, died, 1, removed, 5, present number, 33; Public Services (Sundays, 47, Holy days. 10, other days, 10), 67; Holy Communion (public, 35, private, 1), 36.

Offerings.

Parochial.— Alms at Holy Communion, $8.04; Current expenses, including salaries, $140.54. Total, $148.58.

Diocesan.— Diocesan Missions, $7.57; Diocesan Fund, $3.75. Total, $11.32.

General.— Domestic and Foreign Missions, $10.20; Jewish Missions, $1.85. Total, $12.05.
Total amount of Offerings, $171.95.

Indebtedness.

Floating debt, $130.
Amount of salary pledged Rector, $125 and rent of Rectory.

Remarks.

One hundred and thirty-six dollars have been spent, from moneys left by Miss Austin, in repairing Church.

CHRIST CHURCH, GREENVILLE.

Rector. The Rev. T. A. Snyder.
Wardens. E. N. Palmer, W. S. Rundle.
Vestrymen. Byron Waldron, W. S. Vanderbilt, L. D. Stewart, R. R. Palmer, James Ponsonby, E. A. Galation, John Galation, Herlbert Sanford.

Parochial.

Baptisms (adult, 1, infants, 2), 3; Confirmed, since last report, 8; Burials, 2; Communicants, last reported, 39, admitted, 3, received, 1, removed, 2, present number, 41; Public Services (Sundays, 47, Holy days, 8, other days, 13), 68; Holy Communion, public, 28.

Offerings,

Parochial.— Alms at Holy Communion, $4.12; Current expenses, including salaries, $115.45. Total, $119.57.

Diocesan.— Diocesan Missions, $10.05; Salary of the Bishop, $6; Diocesan Fund, $3.75. Total, $19.70.

General.— Domestic and Foreign Missions, $8.36; Jewish Missions, $2.13. Total, $10.49.

Total amount of Offerings, $149.76.

Property.

Indebtedness on repairing Rectory, $300.
Floating debt, $60.
Amount of salary pledged Rector, $125.

TRINITY CHURCH, ASHLAND.

Wardens. Darius B. Prout, Willis Chatfield.
Vestrymen. Addison Steele, George S. Smith, Henry P. Smith, Merritt McLean.

Parochial.

Families, 16; Baptisms, infants, 3; Burials, 1; Communicants, last reported, 35, died, 1, removed, 3, present number, 31; Public Services, Sundays, 11; Holy Communion, public, 3.

Offerings.

Diocesan —Salary of the Bishop, $4.

Property.

Church and lot (estimated worth), $3,000.
Parsonage and lot (estimated worth), $1,000.
Number of sittings in the Church, 150; all free.

Remarks.

Services were held on eleven Sundays in the summer, by the Rev. Watson B. Hall, of Racine, Wis.

CALVARY CHURCH, CAIRO.

Rector. The Rev. J. T. Zorn.
Lay Reader. Webster W Jennings.
Wardens. Lucius Byington, Levi K. Byington.

Vestrymen. Edwin E. Darby, John C. Lennon, George H. Noble, M. D., Selden H. Hine, Alfred Bennett, John K. Palen, Nelson Carman, Frank C. Burnham.

Parochial.

Families, 39; Individuals (adults, 75, children, 35), 110; Baptisms, infants, 6; Confirmed, since last report, 5; Present number of confirmed persons, 64; Marriages, 1; Burials, 1; Communicants, last reported, 51, admitted, 5, present number, 56; Holy Communion, public, weekly; Sunday School, teachers, 5, pupils, 35.

Offerings.

Parochial.— Alms at Holy Communion, $24.82; Current expenses, including salaries, $426.07; Sunday School, $13. Total, $463.89.

Diocesan.— Diocesan Missions, $11.60; Salary of the Bishop, $6; Orphan House of the Holy Saviour, $4.02. Total, $21.62.

General.— Domestic and Foreign Missions, $15.72; Mission to Jews, $1.30. Total, $17.92.

Total amount of Offerings, $502.53.

Property.

Church and lot (estimated worth), $4,000.
Parsonage and lot (estimated worth), $1,000.
Condition of property, good.
Amount of salary pledged Rector, $250.
Number of sittings in the Church, 150; all free.

Remarks.

The present incumbent entered upon his duties October 14th. The absence of sufficient record must account for deficiencies in the above report. Of the sum contributed for Domestic and Foreign Missions, $12.55 was the children's Easter Offering. A very considerable portion of the amount reported under the head of Current Expenses, including Salaries, was furnished by the Women's Guild, a most devoted, alert and energetic body of workers for the advancement of Parish interests.

GLORIA DEI CHURCH, PALENVILLE.

Rector. The Rev. William Charles Grubbe.
Warden. Walter Lasher.
Treasurer. Charles H. Chubb, M. D.
Clerk. Rufus T. Smith.

Parochial.

Families, 13; Individuals (adults, 40, children, 11), 51; Baptisms, infants, 3; Present number of confirmed persons, 29; Burials, 2; Communicants, last reported, 28, received, 3, removed, 2, present number, 29; Public services (Sundays, 96, Holy days, 21, other days, 32), 149; Holy Communion (public, 67, private, 3), 70.

Offerings.

Parochial.—Current expenses, including salaries, $427.23; Increase and Improvement of Church Property, $84.68. Total, $511.91.

Diocesan.—Diocesan Missions, $15; Salary of the Bishop, $8; Diocesan Fund, $9. Total, $32.

General.—Domestic and Foreign Missions, $9.23; Indian Missions, $2; American Church Building Fund, $2; Church Mission to the Jews, $2. Total, $15.23.

Total amount of Offerings, $559.14.

Property.

Church and lot (estimated worth), $6,000.
Parsonage and lot (estimated worth), $1,500.
Condition of property, good.
Amount of salary pledged Rector, $300.
Number of sittings in the Church, 150; all free.

Remarks.

From October, 1891, to July, 1892, I held services in Tannersville (West), every two weeks, at residence of Mrs. Rose. Services held, 17; Holy Communion, 17.
Total attendance at services, 241; Total Communions made, 154; Marriages, 1.

Herkimer County.

TRINITY CHURCH, FAIRFIELD.

Rector. The Rev. Clarence M. Conant, M. D.
Wardens. Reuben Neely, C. W. Nichols, M. D.
Vestrymen. Jairus Mather, John P. Todd, A. C. Wilson, D. D. Warne, F. L. Warne.

Parochial.

Families, 11; Individuals (adults, 30, children, 9), 39; Baptisms, adults, 2; Confirmed, since last report, 3; Present number of confirmed persons, 21; Communicants, last reported, 18, admitted, 3, received, 1, removed, 1, present number, 21; Public Services, last Sunday in month, Holy Communion at 10:30 A. M., service also at 3 p. M.; Holy Communion, public, 11; Sunday School, teachers, 3, pupils, 9; Catechizing, number of children, 9, number of times, every Sunday.

Offerings.

Parochial.— Alms at Holy Communion, since February 1, 1892, $8.75; Current expenses, including salaries, $147; Increase and Improvement of Church Property (personal), $50; a set of solid Holy Communion vessels (personal), $85; a new Altar (personal), $41. Total, $331.75.

Diocesan. — Diocesan Missions, $5; Salary of the Bishop, $4; Diocesan Fund, $3.12; Orphan House of the Holy Saviour, $1.30; Theological education, $1.71. Total, $15.13.

Total amount of Offerings, $346.88.

Property.

Church and lot (estimated worth), $1,000.
Parsonage and lot (estimated worth), $500.
Condition of property, Rectory, fair; Church, very bad.
Amount of salary pledged Rector, $2 per Sunday.
Number of sittings in the Church, 200; all free.

Remarks.

During the year the appointments of this old Church have been enriched by two noteworthy gifts. The first, a chestnut wood Altar, the gift of Miss H. E. Buell, of Utica. The second, a set of Eucharistic vessels, in solid silver, consisting of Chalice, Paten, Bread-box, two silver-mounted Cruets and a Spoon, the gift of Mr. A. C. Mather, of Chicago.

The importance of the work here is emphasized by the fact that the small confirmation class consisted of students of the Seminary, and that some half dozen or more of the present residents at the Seminary are Communicants of the Church.

GRACE CHURCH, NORWAY.

(No Report.)

EMMANUEL CHURCH, LITTLE FALLS.

Rector. The Rev. Ernest Mariett.
Wardens. R. S. Whitman, E. B. Waite.
Vestrymen. George W. Searles, Albert Storey, Hadley Jones, A. M. Mills, Judge G. A. Hardin, H. W. Houghton, J. D. Feeter, Charles Bailey.

Parochial.

Families, about 150; Individuals (adults, 250, children, 80), 330; Baptisms (adult, 1, infants, 14), 15; Confirmed, since last report, 14; Present number of confirmed persons, about 165; Marriages, 6; Burials, 12; Communicants, last reported, 156, admitted, 14, received, 5, died, 4, removed, 18, present number, 153; Public Services (Sundays, 102, Holy days, Holy Communion, other days, Daily Morning Prayer and Evening Prayer 3 days in week); Holy Communion (public, every Sunday and Holy day, private, 4); Sunday School, teachers, 12, pupils, 75; Catechizing, number of children, all, number of times, every Sunday.

Offerings.

Parochial.— Alms at Holy Communion, $50.25 ; Current expenses, including salaries, $3,181.94; By Young Ladies' Mission Society, $87.69. Total, $3,319.88.

Diocesan.—Diocesan Missions, $23.68; Salary of the Bishop, $40; Diocesan Fund, $36; Bible and Common Prayer Book Society of Albany, $5.02; Fund for Aged and Infirm Clergymen, $5.29; Orphan House of the Holy Saviour, $14.68; The Child's Hospital, $14.30. Diocesan Missionary's salary, $24.87. Total, $163.84

General.—Domestic Missions, $9.38; Foreign Missions, $11; Home Missions to Coloured Persons, $6.09; Jewish Mission, $4.15. Total, $30.62.

Total amount of Offerings, $3,514.34.

CHRIST CHURCH, HERKIMER.

Rector. The Rev. Charles Carroll Edmunds, Jr.
Wardens. Geo. W. Pine, Robert Earl
Vestrymen. J. P. Henderson, G. H. Kelsey, Levi A. Lawton, Clark A. Miller, H. G. Munger, C. W. Palmer, W. C. Prescott, C. C. Witherstine.

Parochial.

Baptisms (adults, 7, infants, 16), 23; Confirmed, since last report, 13; Marriages, 7; Burials, 8; Communicants, last reported, 178, admitted, 13, received, 5, died, 2, present number, 192; Public Services (Sundays, 169, Holy days, 48, other days, 140), 357; Holy Communion (public, 105, private, 3), 108 ; Sunday School, teachers, 10, pupils, 90; Catechizing, number of children, Sunday School, number of times, nearly every Sunday.

Offerings.

Parochial.—Current expenses, including salaries, $1,683.59, Sunday School, $90; Increase and Improvement of Church Property, $5,201.55; For the poor, $43.81, Choir Fund, $28.24; Altar Guild, $8. Total, $7,055.19.

Diocesan.— Diocesan Missions, $71.60 ; Salary of the Bishop, $16; Diocesan Fund, $30; Bible and Common Prayer Book Society of Albany, $5; Fund for Aged and

Infirm Clergymen, $9.17; Fund for Widows and Orphans of Clergymen, $9.17; Orphan House of the Holy Saviour (from Sunday School), $13.62; Clergy Reserve Fund, $4 50; Theological education, $7; Diocesan Missionary, $10. Total, $176.06.

General.— Domestic Missions, $21.88; Foreign Missions, $21.87; Church Missions to Jews, $6; American Church Building Fund, $7; China Mission, $3. Total, $59.75. Total amount of Offerings, $7,291.

Property.

Church and lot (estimated worth), $25,000.
Parsonage and lot (estimated worth), $4,500.
Other property, Parish Building, $4,000.
Condition of property, excellent.
Amount of salary pledged Rector, $1,000 and Rectory.
Number of sittings in the Church, 250; all free.

Remarks.

We are very thankful to be able to record the payment during the past year of the debt resting upon the Rectory and Parish house.

ST. AUGUSTINE'S CHURCH, ILION.

Rector. The Rev. William Mason Cook.
Wardens. F. C. Shepard, R. L. Winegar.
Vestrymen. Geo. P. Rix, T J. Behan, Geo. H. Barlow, Geo. H. Dyett, Alfred Williamson, N. A. Hanchett, Walter C. Rix, Walter S. Baker.

Parochial.

Families, 128; Individuals (adults, 353, children, 136), 489; Baptisms (adults, 7, infants, 13), 20; Confirmed, since last report, 15; Present number of confirmed persons, 187; Marriages, 6; Burials, 10; Churchings, 1; Communicants, last reported, 134, admitted, 15, received, 1, died, 2, removed, 15, renewed, 3, present number, 186; Public services (Sundays, 140, Holy days, 52, other days, 84), 276; Holy Communion (public, 84, private, 5), 89; Sunday School, teachers, 9, pupils, 85; Catechizing, number of children, school, number of times, as a rule, every Sunday; Industrial School, teachers, 6, pupils, 30.

Offerings.

Parochial.—Current expenses, including salaries, $1,290.14; By the Sunday School, $158.16; For the Sunday School, $46 45; Increase and Improvement of Church Property, $60; Work of the Altar Guild, $22.50; Paid on mortgage, $250. Total, $1,827.25.

Diocesan.—Diocesan Missions, $30.55; Salary of the Bishop, $12; Diocesan Fund, $18; Fund for Aged and Infirm Clergymen, $3.81; Fund for Widows and Orphans of Clergymen, $8.18; Orphan House of the Holy Saviour, $1.63; Society for Promoting Religion and Learning, $3; Salary of the Diocesan Missionary, by the Sunday School, $5.51. Total, $82.67.

General.—General Theological Seminary, $1.63; Domestic Missions, $15.82; Foreign Missions ($11.04 by the Sunday School), $26.86; Russian Famine Sufferers, $4; Church Society for Promoting Christianity Among the Jews, $2.16; Church Mission to Deaf-Mutes, $1.28. Total, $51.75.
Total amount of Offerings, $1,961.67.

Property.

Church and lot (estimated worth), $6,000.
Parsonage and lot (estimated worth), $3,000.

Condition of property, good.
Indebtedness, on mortgage, $2,000; floating, $150.
Amount of salary pledged Rector, $600.
Number of sittings in the Church, 232; all free.

Remarks.

Our loss of communicants by removal during the last year is almost unprecedented. Among these were eight heads of families, including Mr. R. L. Winegar, our Junior Warden for many years. Two communicants have died. In spite of these losses, however, the list of "actual communicants" has slightly increased.

GRACE CHURCH, MOHAWK.

Wardens. A. W. Haslehurst, E. C. Elwood.
Vestrymen. H. D. Alexander, James B. Rafter, F. L. Van Dusen, Charles Spencer, J. D. Fitch, M. D., E. H. Doolittle.

Parochial.

Communicants, present number, 61.

Property.

Church and lot (estimated worth), $3,500.
Condition of property, good.

Remarks.

The Parish has been vacant since October, 1891, when the Rev. Alfred Taylor resigned. The Vestry have been so far unable to secure a Rector.

ST. ALBAN'S CHURCH, FRANKFORT.

Priest in charge. The Rev. Wm. Mason Cook.
Wardens. Wm. J. Bennett, Frank Williams.
Vestrymen. S. S. Richards, M. D., C. B. Cleland, Edward J. Gilligan, Ernest A. Bennett, R. Rose.

Parochial.

Families, 32; Individuals (adults, 87, children, 42), 139; Baptisms (adults, 2, infants, 2), 4; Confirmed, since last report, 6; Present number of confirmed persons, 49; Burials, 3; Communicants, admitted, 7, died, 1, removed, 8, present number, 31; Public Services (Sundays, 45, Holy days, 8, other days, 22), 75; Holy Communions public, 16; Sunday School, teachers and officers, 4, pupils, 20; Catechizing, number of children, the Sunday School, number of times, every Sunday.

Offerings.

Parochial.—Alms at Holy Communion, $6.75; Current expenses, including salaries, $200; Sunday School, $5.13; Expenses of the "Mission," $21. Total, $232.88.
Diocesan. - Diocesan Missions, $5; Orphan House of the Holy Saviour, $1. Total, $6.
Total amount of Offerings, $238.88.

Property.

Church and lot (estimated worth), $2,500.
Condition of property, excellent.
Amount of salary pledged Rector, $100.
Number of sittings in the Church, 125; all free.

Remarks.

The above report is for eleven months, as the present incumbent took charge of the Parish December 1, 1891.

A " Mission " was held in the Parish in June, with excellent results. The Rev. Chas. C. Edmunds, Jr., of Christ Church, Herkimer, was the Missioner.

St. Alban's Guild, a society of women, has done much good work, contributing largely to the current expenses, and also acting as a branch of the Woman's Auxiliary.

CHURCH OF THE MEMORIAL, MIDDLEVILLE.

Rector. The Rev. Clarence M. Conant, M. D.
Warden. John Molineux.
Treasurer. C. W. Hamlin, M. D.
Secretary, George W. Griswold.

Parochial.

Families, 41; Individuals (adults, 98, children, 82), 180; Baptisms (adult, 1, infants, 3), 4; Confirmed, since last report, 4; Present number of confirmed persons, 67; Marriages, 5; Burials, 5; Communicants, last reported, 59, admitted 4, received, 5, removed, 1, present number, 67; Public Services (Sundays, 8 and 11 A. M., 7:80 P. M., Holy days, 8 and 9:30 A. M., 4:30 P. M., other days, Fridays and Saturdays, 7:30 P. M.); Holy Communion, public, 89; Sunday School, teachers, 6, pupils, 25; Catechising, number of children, 15 to 20, number of times, every Sunday.

Offerings.

Parochial.— Alms at Holy Communion (since Feb. 1, 1892), $38.81; Current expenses, including salaries, $578.31; Sunday School, $18.74; Altar hangings (Easter offering), $75; Venetian blinds for Rectory (a personal offering), $24. Total, $729.36.

Diocesan.— Diocesan Missions, $20; Salary of the Bishop, $6; Diocesan Fund, $12; Bible and Common Prayer Book Society of Albany, $5; Theological education, $3.21. Total, $46.21.

General.— Indian Missions, $2; Home Missions to Coloured Persons, $2; Russian Relief Fund, $5. Total, $9.

Total amount of Offerings, $784.57.

Property.

Church and lot (estimated worth), $10,000.
Parsonage and lot (estimated worth), $2,000.
Condition of property, excellent, except deficient heating apparatus in the Church.
Amount of salary pledged Rector, $400.
Number of sittings in the Church, 200; all free.

CHURCH OF THE GOOD SHEPHERD, CULLEN.

(See Report of the Diocesan Missionary, page 116.)

Montgomery County.

ST. ANN'S CHURCH, AMSTERDAM.

Rector. The Rev. David Sprague.
Wardens. W. Max Reid, Jno. J. Hand.
Vestrymen. Cyrus B. Chase, Thos. Mansfield, Chas. S. Nisbet. Wm. Le Grand S. Strang, Jas. T. Sugden, Hicks B. Waldron, Jno. K.

Parochial.

Families, 400; Individuals, adults and children, 1120; Baptisms (adults, 6, infants, 27), 33; Confirmed, since last report, 23; Present number of confirmed persons, 461; Marriages, 18; Burials, 26; Communicants, last reported, 328, admitted and received, 29, died, 7, removed, 10, present number, 340; Public services (Sundays, 126, Holy days, 50, other days, 38), 214; Holy Communion (public, 50, private, 3), 53; Sunday School, teachers, 15, pupils, 200; Catechizing, number of children, whole school, number of times, 10.

Offerings.

Parochial.—Alms at Holy Communion, $40.87; Current expenses, including salaries, $3,070.76; Sunday School, $130; Reduction of debt, $507.38; Amsterdam City Hospital, $26.46; Children's Home, $3.20; Benevolent Society Fund, $5; Extra, $1. Total, $3,789.67.

Diocesan.—Diocesan Missions, $56.05; Salary of the Bishop, $20; Diocesan Fund, $37.50; On salary of Missionary, $15. Total, $128.55.

General.—Domestic and Foreign Missions, $20; Russian Sufferers, $25.22; Grant Monument (G. A. R.), $14.53. Total, $59.75.

Total amount of Offerings, $3,977.97.

Property.

Church and lot (estimated worth), $50,000.
Other property, three building lots, $1,500.
Condition of property, good.
Indebtedness, $12,500.
Amount of salary pledged Rector, $1,250.
Number of sittings in the Church, 600; rented, 500; free, 100.

ZION CHURCH, FONDA.

Missionary. The Rev. C. C. Edmunds.

Wardens. Richard H. Cushney, Henry T. E. Brower.

Vestrymen. Henry B. Cushney, Giles H. Van Horne, Edward B Cushney, Richard N. Casler, William Fonda, Robert Agnew, John S. Van Horne, Henry Siver.

Parochial.

Families, 23; Individuals (adults, 65, children, 14), 79; Baptisms, infant, 1; Present number of confirmed persons, 46; Marriages, 1; Burials, 1; Communicants, last reported, 47, died, 1, removed, 4, present number, 42; Public services (Sundays, 52, Holy days, 2), 54; Sunday School, teachers, 5, pupils, 25.

Offerings.

Parochial.—Alms at Holy Communion, $29.03; Current expenses, including salaries, $323.96; Sunday School, $5.08. Total, $358.07.

Diocesan.— Diocesan Missions, $18; Salary of the Bishop, $12; Diocesan Fund, $9. Total, $39.

General.— Domestic Missions, $5.

Total amount of Offerings, $402.07.

Property.

Church and lot (estimated worth), $8,000.
Amount of salary pledged Rector, $300.
Number of sittings in the Church, 150; all free.

Remarks.

The condition of the Mission continues very much the same from year to year. Little more can be expected than to hold our own, as our people are very few in number, and there seems to be no material from which to make much increase. The religious element in the town is largely Dutch Reformed and Roman Catholic. Still something is accomplished by the continuance of the Church Services here.

THE CHURCH OF THE GOOD SHEPHERD, CANAJOHARIE.

Missionary.   The Rev. Clarence Ernest Ball.
Warden.   Arza Canfield.
Treasurer.   Randolph Spraker.

Parochial.

Families, 7; Parts of families and individuals. 29; Individuals (adults, 49, children, 17), 66; Baptisms, adult, 1; Confirmed, since last report, 1; Present number of confirmed persons, 49; Marriages. 5; Burials, 4; Communicants, last reported, 64, died, 2, removed, 1, present number enrolled. 44, Public Services (Sundays, 82, Holy days, 13, other days, 90), 185; Holy Communion (public, 38, private, 7), 45; Sunday School, teachers, 3, pupils, 33.

Offerings.

Parochial.— Alms at Holy Communion, $22.23; Current expenses, including salaries, $532.19; For Sunday School, $11.39, Increase and Improvement of Church Property, $33.50; Wass Monument, $18.   Total, $617.31.

Diocesan.— Diocesan Missions, $10; Salary of the Bishop, $6; Diocesan Fund, $10.50; Orphan House of the Holy Saviour, $14.77.   Total, $41.27.

General.— General Missions, $9.63 ; Church Society to Promote Christianity Among Jews, $5.57; Russian Famine Relief, $5.48.   Total, $20.68.

Total amount of Offerings. $679.26.

Property.

Condition of property, good.
Amount of salary pledged Rector, $350.
Number of sittings in the Church, 130; all free.

Remarks.

Item reported: Increase Church Property, estimated value of Altar Vestments, Surplice and Stole.

Other objects : Value of monument reared by the Sunday School to one of their number, deceased.

St. Agnes Guild has raised and paid out during the year for objects within and without the Mission, in cash, $215.87; besides much unestimated labor.

The Sunday School is composed for the most part of children from families not otherwise connected with the Mission.   It numbered Nov. 1, 1891, 23.   Lost during year, 4, gained, 14, present number, 33.   Balance in its treasury Nov. 1, 1891, $16.54. By Sunday Offerings to Nov. 1, 1892, $23 28.   In Mite boxes by Offerings at Children's Lenten Services and from other sources, $20.69.   Total, $60.51.

Its disbursements to Parochial and other objects are included in the foregoing general report.

THE CHURCH OF THE HOLY CROSS, FORT PLAIN.

Missionary.   The Rev. Clarence Ernest Ball.
Lay Reader.   Mr. Theo. S. Waters.
Warden.   Douglas Ayres, M. D.

24

' Clerk. Theo. S. Waters.
Treasurer. James Goble.

Parochial.

Families, 12; Parts of families and individuals, 19; Individuals (adults, 61, infants, 17), 78; Burials, 6; Present number of confirmed persons, 50; Communicants, last reported, 69, received, 1, died, 2, removed, 1, present number registered, 42; Public Services (Sundays, 48, all other days, 35), 83; Holy Communion (public, 21, private, 4), 25.

Offerings.

Parochial.—Alms at Holy Communion, $5.66; Current expenses, including salaries estimated, $235.92. Total, $241.58.

Diocesan.—Diocesan Missions, $23.65; Salary of Bishop, $6; Diocesan Fund, $3 : Orphan House of the Holy Saviour, $5. Total, $37.65.

General.—General Missions, $6.23; Russian Famine Relief, $1.98; Mission Among Jews, $2.05. Total, $10.26.

Total amount of Offerings, $289.49.

Property.

Church property (estimated worth), $7,000.
Condition, excellent.
Indebtedness on Church property, $1,600.

ST. COLUMBA'S MISSION, ST. JOHNSVILLE.

Missionary. The Rev. Clarence Ernest Ball.
Warden. Mr. Chas. Buckingham.

Parochial.

Individuals, adults, 9; Confirmed persons, 7; Burial, 1; Baptized, adult, 1; Communicants, admitted, 1, died, 1, removed, 2, present number, 5.

Offerings.

Total amount of Offerings, $10.47.

Remarks.

This Mission is at grave disadvantage, not being so situated as to have a Sunday Service. The present Missionary took charge of the work last Lent, after it had been without service over a year.

Otsego County.

ZION CHURCH, MORRIS.

Rector. The Rev. R. H. Gesner, B. D.
Wardens. Isaac Mansfield, John Smith.
Vestrymen. J. Rutherford Morris, G. Clayton Peck, George A. Yates, 2d, C. J. Smith, George A. Sanderson, R. H. Harris.
Treasurer. T. O. Duroe.
Clerk. A. E. Yates.

Parochial.

Families, about 140; Individuals (adults, about 350, children, about 150), 500, Baptisms (adults, 12, infants, 17), 29; Confirmed, since last report, 45; Present number of confirmed persons, 250, Marriages, 2; Burials, 12; Communicants, last reported, 207, admitted, 45, received, 23, died, 12, removed, 13, present number, 250; Public Services (Sundays, 188, Holy days, 25, other days, 77), 240; Holy Communion (public, 19, private, 2), 21; Sunday School, teachers, 14, pupils, 144; Catechizing, number of times, bi-monthly.

Offerings.

Parochial.—Alms at Holy Communion, $43.79; Current expenses, including salaries, $1,438.05; Sunday School, $57; Building Fund for new Rectory, $899.92; Repairs to Church, $347.75. Total, $2,786.51.

Diocesan.—Diocesan Missions, $60; Salary of the Bishop, $24; Diocesan Fund, $30; Orphan House of the Holy Saviour, $19.44; Archdeaconry of the Susquehanna, $2.57. Total, $136.01.

General.— Foreign Missions, $5; Indian Missions, $22.29; St. Stephen's College, $5.04; Mission at Cape Henlopen City, Diocese of Delaware, $15.25. Total, $47.58.

Total amount of Offerings, $2,970.10.

Property.

Church and lot (estimated worth), $20,000.

Parsonage and lot (estimated worth), $3,000.

Other property, $10,000.

Condition of property, good.

Amount of salary pledged Rector, $1,000.

Number of sittings in the Church, 500; New Lisbon Chapel, 150; Morris Memorial Chapel, 75; all free.

Remarks.

The Parish suffered the loss of its faithful and beloved Senior Warden, Mr. Nelson B. Pearsall, in May last. Mr. Pearsall's place as Lay Reader has been filled by the appointment of Mr. Willard D. Johnson, Principal of the Morris Union School.

On December 4th the Church was stripped of one-half its roof in a furious gale. Within a few days the Rector and Vestry had raised enough not only to repair the damage, but to leave a balance of $140 for any other needs or emergencies.

The Rectory fund above the cash on hand as above reported is further increased by pledges and subscriptions which make the available resources of this fund about $1,700. It is hoped that the new Rectory may be built during the coming spring and summer.

Boxes have been sent by the Parish societies to Orphanage of the Holy Saviour, Child's Hospital and Coloured Mission in the South.

The St. Nicholas Club, organized nearly a year ago, is exercising a helpful influence on the boys of the Parish.

ST. LUKE'S CHURCH, RICHFIELD.

Lay Reader. C. A. Howells.

Wardens. Burton L. Woodbury, Clarence B. Colwell.

Vestrymen. Jonas A. Lidell, Fred. A. Woodbury, John S. Curtiss, John L. Colwell.

Parochial.

Families, 7; Individuals (adults, 18, children, 4), 22; Confirmed, since last report, 3; Present number of confirmed persons, 12; Communicants, last reported, 9, admitted, 3, present number, 12; Public Services, Sundays, 10; Holy Communion, public, 2; Sunday School, teachers, 2, pupils, 7.

Offerings.

Parochial.— Alms at Holy Communion, $20.15 ; Current aries, $22.28 ; Sunday School, $35.58. Total, $78.01.

Diocesan.— Diocesan Missions, $3.15.
Total amount of Offerings, $81.16.

Property.

Church and lot (estimated worth), $2,000.
Condition of property, good.
Amount of salary pledged Rector, $150.
Number of sittings in Church, 200; all free.

Remarks.

Since our last report the Parish has put a new roof on the Church and made other needed repairs. Robert W. Tailer, of New York city, has, at his own and unsolicited expense, done a great deal toward restoring the old Church, by painting the outside, and painting and kalsomining the interior and carpeting the floor, furnishing new cushions for all the seats and making many other repairs. The Parish desires to thank Mr. Tailer for the good work done.

ST. MATTHEW'S CHURCH, UNADILLA.

Rector. The Rev. Robert N. Parke, D. D.
Wardens. Lloyd L. Woodruff, Bennitt W. Morse.
Vestrymen. Andrew J. Lewis, Milo B. Gregory, Clark I. Hayes, Paris G. Clark, M. D., William H. Heslop, J. Fred. Sands, S. Horace Chapin, Samuel S. North.

Parochial.

Families, 96; Individuals (adults, 226, children, 55), 281; Baptisms (adults, 2, infants, 3), 5; Confirmed, since last report, 9; Present number of confirmed persons, 159; Marriages, 3; Burials, 7; Communicants, last reported, 139, admitted, 9, received, 5, died, 2, removed, 2, present number, 149; Public Services (Sundays, 107, Holy days, 14, other days, 42), 163; Holy Communion, public, 31; Sunday School, teachers, 5, pupils, 46; Catechizing, number of times, 14.

Offerings.

Parochial.—Alms at Holy Communion, $28.61; Current expenses, including salaries, $1,070.32.   Total, $1,098.93.

Diocesan.—Diocesan Missions, $44.76; Diocesan Fund, $11.40; Fund for Aged and Infirm Clergymen, $9.29; Orphan House of the Holy Saviour, $28.16; Society for Promoting Religion and Learning, $4.41; Archdeaconry of the Susquehanna, $8.70; Salary of Diocesan Missionary, $10. Total, $116.72.

General.—Domestic Missions, $9.05; Foreign Missions, $6.22; Christianity Among Jews, $3.39; Russian Relief Fund, $5; New York Bible and Prayer Book Society, $4.48; Sunday School Lenten Offerings for Missions, $16.50. Total, $44.64.

Total amount of Offerings, $1,260.29.

Property.

Church and lot (estimated worth), $6,500.
Parsonage and lot (estimated worth), $4,500.
Other property, $600.
Condition of property, pretty good.
Amount of salary pledged Rector, $800.
Number of sittings in the Church, 330.

CHRIST CHURCH, COOPERSTOWN.

Rector. The Rev. Charles S. Olmsted.
Wardens. W. T. Bassett, M. D., H. M. Hooker.

Vestrymen. G. Pomeroy Keese, H. M. Merchant, Lee B. Crttenden, R. H. White, Charles J. Tuttle, William D. Boden, S. E. Crittenden.

Parochial.

Baptisms (adults, 2, infants, 21), 23; Confirmed, since last report, 17; Present number of confirmed persons, 305; Marriages, 10; Burials, 21; Communicants, present number, 253; Public Services (Sundays, all, Holy days, all, other days, Litany days); Holy Communion, public, every Sunday and Holy day; Sunday School, teachers, 14, pupils, 140; Catechizing, number of children, Sunday School, number of times, 30.

Offerings.

Parochial.—Alms at Holy Communion, $180.48; Current expenses, including salaries, $2,799.44; Sunday School, for St. Mark's School, Salt Lake, $40; Sunday School, for Missions, in Lent, $21.65; Increase and Improvement of Church Property, $1,000; Mite Society, $28.94; Father Nash Memorial Window Fund, $62.27; Extra for music, $55.50; Girls Friendly Society, $135; Altar Guild, $108.62; For Sunday School, $10.36. Total, $4,442.26.

Diocesan.— Diocesan Missions, $150 ; Salary of the Bishop, $80 ; Diocesan Fund, $45; Bible and Common Prayer Book Society of Albany, $4; Fund for Aged and Infirm Clergymen, $17.02; Orphan House of the Holy Saviour, $89.58; Salary of Diocesan Missionary, $45.53; St. Jude's Mission, Worcester, $8; Books for a Missionary, $2. Total, $441.13.

General.— Domestic Missions, $27; Foreign Missions, $27; Bishop Johnston's work in Western Texas, $1,325; Russian Famine Relief Fund, $18.79; Woman's Lenten Work, $308.85. Total, $1,706.64.

Total amount of Offerings, $6,509.03.

Remarks.

By invitation from the Rev. Mr. Hartmann I have officiated this year five times in St. John's Church, Portlandville, where there are six candidates for Baptism, and a better outlook for successful work than there has been for several years past.

CHRIST CHURCH, GILBERTSVILLE.

Rector. The Rev. David F. MacDonald.

Wardens. Ira L. Ward, Charles V. Daniels.

Vestrymen. William F. Ward, Thomas Swinyard, E. R. Clinton, J. R. Woodlands, J. G. MacCulloch, R. M. Stenson, B F. Marvin, Wm. R. Kinne.

Parochial.

Families, 43; Individuals (adults, 92, children, 28), 120; Baptisms (adults, 2, infants, 2), 4; Confirmed, since last report, 9; Present number of confirmed persons, 67; Marriages, 1; Burials, 5; Communicants, admitted, 9, received, 3, died, 2, present number, 68; Public Services (Sundays, 103, other days [Lenten], 18), 121 ; Holy Communion (public, 26, private, 1), 27; Sunday School, teachers, 6, pupils, 28; Catechizing, number of times, 4.

Offerings.

Parochial.—Alms at Holy Communion, $26.76; Rector's salary, $475; Sunday School, $8; Increase and Improvement of Church Property, $175; Other Parochial objects, $51.55; Guild charities, $18; Sexton's salary, $40; Light and fuel, $30. Total, $824.31.

Diocesan.— Diocesan Missions, $25; Salary of the Bishop, $6; For Infirm Clergymen, $2.36; Orphan House of the Holy Sav* pital, $25; for Salary of Diocesan Missionary (by Woman's Auxiliary, $5), $11.60; for Church in Sidney, $5. Total, $80.96.

General.— Domestic Missions, $8.55; Foreign Missions, $8; Enrolment Fund (by Woman's Auxiliary), $40; Orphanage in Japan (by Woman's Auxiliary), $16; Sunday School, Easter offering, $13.75; Collection (for Altar Society, $3.60, Altar desk, $3.50), $7.10; Collection for Conversion of Jews, $2. Total, $95.40.

Total amount of Offerings, $1,000.67.

Property.

Church and lot (estimated worth), $3,000.
Parsonage and lot (estimated worth), $1,800.
Other property, $2,500.
Condition of property, very good.
Amount of salary pledged Rector, $475.
Number of sittings in the Church, 200; all free.

Remarks.

In giving the number of services, I merely gave those by myself personally, especially in Maple Grove. Whenever I am not present at Maple Grove, the Lay Reader, Mr. Hull, and frequently Rev. D. Washburn, read the services. The Rev. Canon Stewart, assisted by Rev. Mr. Cook, of New York city, and myself, held a mission at this point, lasting three days. The congregations were large and appreciative. Week before last I alone held a Mission during [four days. During that time the "Ladies' Guild" was reorganized, and various other matters put, we believe, on a wholesome footing. Nor did I include in my report the services I have given in Morris Chapel. I have given in this Chapel a service once a month during the summer. I may mention here that the Rev. Mr. Gates, of Missouri, holds $50, with two years' interest, to help pay the debt on Maple Grove Chapel. This sum shall be forthcoming when the last payment is made on the debt.

IMMANUEL CHURCH, OTEGO.

Rector. The Rev. William G. W. Lewis.
Wardens. Charles Blake, George W. Sherman. Jr.
Vestrymen   C. B. Woodruff, J. H. Cossaart, M. D., J. H. Martin, M. D., F. D. Shumway, W. Parker, G. H. Goodman.

Parochial.

Families, 26; Individuals (adults, 60, children, 17), 57: Baptisms, adults, 1; Present number of confirmed persons, 39; Communicants, last reported, 87, present number, 37; Public Services (Sundays, 93, Holy days, 4, other days, 20), 117; Holy Communion, public, 22; Sunday School, teachers, 3, pupils, 14; Catechizing, number of times, 5.

Offerings.

Parochial.—Current expenses, including salaries, $475; Sunday School, $6. Total, $481.

Diocesan.—Diocesan Missions, $5; Salary of the Bishop, $6; Fund for Aged and Infirm Clergymen, $1; Fund for Widows and Orphans of Clergymen, $1; Orphan House of the Holy Saviour, $2; The Child's Hospital, $1; Clergy Reserve Fund, $1, Archdeaconry, $2.25. Total, $19.25.

General.— General Missions, $5.43; American Church Building Fund Commission, $1. Total, $6.43.

Total amount of Offerings, $506.68.

Property.

Church and lot (estimated worth), $5,000.
Condition of property, good.
Amount of salary pledged Rector, $400.
Number of sittings in the Church, 200; all free.

ST. TIMOTHY'S CHURCH, WESTFORD.

(See "Remarks," Report of Grace Church, Cherry Valley.)

GRACE CHURCH, CHERRY VALLEY.

Rector. The Rev. James E. Hall.
Wardens. A. B. Cox, J. M. Phelan.
Vestrymen. George Neal, J. A. Fonda, F. P. Harriott, C. Brooks, W. C. Roseboom, A. Brown, A. J. Thompson, George Streeter.

Parochial.

Families, 60; Individuals (adults, 145, children, 60), 205; Baptisms (adult, 1 infants, 7), 8; Confirmed, since last report, 11; Present number of confirmed persons, 114; Marriages, 3; Burials, 11; Communicants, last reported, 109, admitted, 11, died 7, present number, 113; Public Services (Sundays, 100, Holy days, 30, other days 96), 226; Holy Communion (public, 54, private, 2), 56; Sunday School, teachers, 5, pupils, 40.

Offerings.

Parochial.—Alms at Holy Communion, $393.42; Current expenses, including salaries, $1,147.28; Sunday School, $18.38. Total, $1,160.66.

Diocesan.— Diocesan Missions, $75; Salary of the Bishop, $24.50; Diocesan Fund $24; Bible and Common Prayer Book Society of Albany, $3.86; Fund for Aged and Infirm Clergymen, $5.56; Fund for Widows and Orphans of Clergymen, $5.56; Orphan House of the Holy Saviour, $54.64; The Child's Hospital, $8; Clergy Relief Fund, $20; Theological Education, $7.10. Total, $228.22.

General. — Domestic Missions, $30; Foreign Missions, $30; Church Mission to Deaf-Mutes, $8.04; Rev. E. Gay, $10; Mrs. Buford, $20. Total, $98.04.

Total amount of Offerings, $1,486.42.

Property.

Church and lot and Parsonage and lot, insured for $5,000.
Other property, Fund, $6,600.
Condition of property, good.
Amount of salary pledged Rector, $800.
Number of sittings in the Church, 250; all free.

Remarks.

I said Evening Prayer once in St. Timothy's Church, Westford; and celebrated the Holy Communion once there. The Rev. Theodore A. Snyder officiated on four Sundays at St. Timothy's, Westford, and celebrated the Holy Communion once there.

ST. JOHN'S CHURCH, RICHFIELD SPRINGS.

Rector. The Rev. Robert Granger.
Wardens. N. D. Jewell, J. A. Storer.
Vestrymen. W. B. Ward, Henry Greenman, M. D. Jewell, W. ᵀ
J. F. Getman, J. D. Carey, D. W. Harrington, G. B. Neely. .

Parochial.

Families, 122, Individuals (adults, 319, children, 105), 424; Baptisms (adults, 22, infants, 21), 43; Confirmed, since last report, 44; Present number of confirmed persons, 252; Marriages, 3; Burials 8; Communicants, last reported, 213, admitted, 16, died, 3, present number, 226; Public Services (Sundays, 94, Holy days, 17, other days, 56), 167; Holy Communion (public, 21, private, 5), 26; Sunday School, teachers, 8, pupils, 94; Catechizing, number of children, all, number of times, 12.

Offerings.

Parochial.—Current expenses, including salaries, $1,649.83; Sunday School, $122.42; Increase and Improvement of Church Property, $97.40; Ladies' Guild, $38.61; Gift to Rector, $200; for the Poor, $113.35; Parish Herald, $131.92; Ladies' Sewing Society, $515.59. Total, $2,869.12.

Diocesan.— Diocesan Missions and Missionary, $58.44; Salary of the Bishop, $16; Diocesan Fund, $12; Orphan House of the Holy Saviour, $103.25. Total, $189.69.

General.— Domestic and Foreign Missions, $14.25; Bishop Johnston for Western Texas, $135.78; one box Missionary Society for Seamen, New York city, $14; one box to Ontonagon, North Michigan. Total, $177.03.

Total amount of Offerings, $3,235.84.

Property.

Church and lot (estimated worth), with Chapel, $15,700.
Parsonage and lot (estimated worth), $6,000.
Other property, lot in Cemetery, $40.
Condition of property, perfect.
Amount of salary pledged Rector, $900 and Rectory.
Number of sittings in the Church, 400; all free.

ST. JOHN'S CHURCH, PORTLANDVILLE.

(See " Remarks," Reports Christ Church, Cooperstown, and St. James', Oneonta.)

CHRIST CHURCH, WEST BURLINGTON.

Lay Reader. C. A. Howells.
Wardens. Stephen I. Pope, John Priest.
Vestrymen. Elias C. Mather, Lewis Spencer, William Holdridge, Stephen Olive, C. G. Pierson, Burton Bailey, Clark Clark, Albert Austin.

Parochial.

' Families, 31 ; Individuals (adults, 73, children, 29), 102; Baptisms, adult, 1; Confirmed, since last report, 2 ; Present number of confirmed persons, 33; Communicants, last reported, 34, admitted, 2, removed, 4, present number, 32; Public Services (Sundays, 30, other days, 1), 31, Holy Communion, public, 4; Sunday School, teachers, 4, pupils, 34 ; Catechizing, number of times, 10.

Offerings.

Parochial— Increase and Improvement of Church Property, $13.
Diocesan.— Diocesan Missions, $5; Salary of the Bishop, $6 ; Diocesan Fund, $4.50; Salary of Diocesan Missionary, $3. Total, $18.50.
Total amount of Offerings, $31.50.

Property.

Church and lot (estimated worth), $4,000.
Parsonage and lot (estimated worth), $500.

Condition of property, fair.

Amount of salary pledged Rector, $150.

Number of sittings in the Church, 150 ; all free.

Remarks.

I have, since Trinity Sunday, supplied St. Luke's at Monticello, and the Good Shepherd at Cullen on alternate Sundays with West Burlington. Considering all circumstances the Congregations have been good at all three points. There is only a list of ten communicants at St. Luke's and none whatever at Cullen. The Good Shepherd is a new and beautiful Memorial Chapel, built by Mr. D. Jones Crain, of New York, and it is hoped that in the future there may be gathered a devout and loyal band of worshippers who will delight to toil for the Church.

The little hamlet of Cullen is deeply indebted to Mr. Crain for the true Christian interest he has shown in their welfare.

ST. PAUL'S CHURCH, EAST SPRINGFIELD.

Rector. The Rev. John Prout.

Wardens. James H. Cooke, Leslie Pell-Clarke.

Vestrymen. S. A. Young, John Scollard, G. Hyde Clarke, Daniel Gilchrist, R. L. Walrath.

Parochial.

Baptisms (adults, 13, infants, 5), 18; Confirmed, since last report, 7; Burials, 1; Churchings, 1; Communicants, last reported, 38, admitted, 8, died, 1, present number, 45; Public Services (Sundays, 93, Holy days, 40, other days, 2), 135; Holy Communion (public, 62, private, 1), 63; Sunday School, teachers, 4, pupils, 30.

Offerings.

Parochial.— Current expenses, including salaries, $534.07; Sunday School, $19.80; Increase and Improvement of Church Property, $113.00. Total, $666.87.

Diocesan.— Diocesan Missions, $30; Salary of the Bishop, $10; Diocesan Fund, $15; Bible and Common Prayer Book Society of Albany, $4; Orphan House of the Holy Saviour, $2; Theological Education, $11.08. Total, $72.08.

General.— General Missions (from Sunday School, $11.27), $22.44.

Total amount of Offerings, $761.39.

Property.

Church and lot (estimated worth), $4,350.

Rectory and lot (estimated worth), $3,050.

Condition of property, good.

Amount of salary pledged Rector, $500.

Number of sittings in the Church, 120; all free.

Remarks.

A Communion Service, presented as a memorial of Harry David Platner, was used for the first time on last Christmas day, and about the same time the Girls' Guild purchased for the Sunday School a library and book case, and the Woman's Auxiliary procured carpet and furniture for the Sacristy.

ST. MARY'S (MISSION) CHURCH, SPRINGFIELD CENTRE.

Missionary. The Rev John Prout.

Warden of the Mission. Leslie Pell-Clarke.

Clerk. G. W. Vandeveer

Treasurer. A. A. Van Horne

Parochial.

Baptisms (adults, 3, infants, 2), 5; Confirmed, since last report, 1; Marriages, 1; Burials, 2; Communicants, last reported, 22, died, 1, present number, 21; Public Services (Sundays, 33, Holy days, 5), 38; Holy Communion (public, 13, private, 1), 14; Sunday School, teachers, 4, pupils, 25.

Offerings.

Parochial.—Current expenses, including salaries, $56.81; Increase and Improvement of Church Property, $8.85. Total, $65.66.

Diocesan.— Diocesan Missions, $20; Orphan House of the Holy Saviour, $7.01. Total, $27.01.

General.—General Missions (from Sunday School, $4.50), $10.06.

Total amount of Offerings, $102.73.

Property.

Church and lot (estimated worth), $8,000.

Condition of property, good.

Number of sittings in the Church, 120; all free.

Remarks.

It should be stated that one-half of the amount pledged to the Rector of St. Paul's Church, East Springfield, is from members of the Congregation of St. Mary's, but being paid through the Treasurer of the former, does not appear on this report.

ST. JAMES' CHURCH, ONEONTA.

Rector. The Rev. E. A. Hartman (to Oct. 1st). The Rev. John E. Bold (from Nov. 1st).

Wardens. John Cope, John D. Rhode.

Vestrymen. Jas. O. Beach, Alfred N. Carr, Richard Downes, Silas Matteson, Frank Sisson, Hobart B. Somers, James Stewart, Robert M. Townsend.

Parochial.

Baptisms (adults, 5, infants, 7), 13; Confirmed, since last report, 15; Present number of confirmed persons, 248; Marriages, 6; Burials, 9; Communicants, last reported, 221, admitted, 15, received, 10, died, 3, removed, 19, present number, 224; Public Services (Sundays, 113, Holy days, 18, other days, 60), 191; Holy Communion (public, 49, private, 3), 52; Sunday School, teachers, 9, pupils, 90; Catechizing, number of times, frequently.

Offerings.

Parochial.—Alms at Holy Communion, $50.81; Current expenses, including salaries, $950.74; Street paving debt, $93. Total, $1,094.05.

Diocesan.—Diocesan Missions, $30; Salary of the Bishop, $10; Orphan House of the Holy Saviour, $26; Society for Promoting Religion and Learning, $5; Salary of General Missionary, through the Sunday School, $16.50. Total, $87.50.

General—Russian Relief Fund, $24.46.

Total amount of Offerings, $1,206.01.

Property.

Church and lot (estimated worth), $12,000.

Indebtedness, $410.

Insurance on Church, $2,000.

Number of sittings in the Church, 225; all free.

Remarks.

The Rev. E. A. Hartman resigned the Rectorship October 1st. During the summer he officiated in St. John's, Portlandville, six times. The offerings at these services amounted to $12.58.

The Archdeacon officiated at the same place five times.

The Rev. E. Ball Wright took charge of the Parish during the month of October, the Rev. John E. Bold having accepted the Rectorship from November 1st.

ST. STEPHEN'S CHURCH, MAPLE GROVE.

Missionary. The Rev. David F. MacDonald.
Lay Reader. C. B. Hull.
Wardens. Henry A. Star, C. B. Hull.
Vestrymen. W. J. Aylsworth, L. W. Davis, Frank C. Hull.

Parochial.

Families, 8; Individuals (adults, 18, children, 21), 39; Baptisms, infants, 4; Present number of confirmed persons, 21; Burials, 1; Communicants, last reported, 22, died, 1, present number, 21; Public Services, Sundays, 46; Holy Communion, public, 12; Sunday School, teachers, 2, pupils, 20; Catechizing, number of times, 4.

Offerings.

Parochial.—Alms at Holy Communion, and Sunday School offerings, $13.25; Increase and Improvement of Church Property, $136.19. Total, $149.44.

Diocesan.—Salary of the Bishop, $2; Children's Easter offering, $5. Total, $7.

General.—Domestic Missions, 50 cents; Foreign Missions, 50 cents. Total, $1.

Total amount of Offerings, $157.44.

Property.

Church and lot (estimated worth), $1,000.
Condition of property, good.
Indebtedness, $128.81.
Number of sittings in the Church, 150; all free.

THE CHURCH OF THE HOLY SPIRIT, SCHENEVUS.

Rector. The Rev. H. E. Gilchrist.
Wardens. William Cook, R. C. Mills.
Vestrymen. John Mills, G. Chas. Bowles, Fred. Page, M. E. Baldwin.

Parochial.

Families and parts of families, 24; Individuals (adults, 42, children, 20), 62; Baptisms, infants, 10; Confirmed, since last report, 2; Present number of confirmed persons, 18; Marriages, 4; Burials, 1; Communicants, last reported, 25, died, 1, removed, 6, present number, 18; Public Services (Sundays, 72, Holy days, 19, other days, 23), 114; Holy Communion, public, 7; Sunday School, teachers, 4, pupils, 15.

Offerings.

Parochial.—Current expenses, including salaries, $559.49.

Diocesan.— Diocesan Missions, $5.40; Salary of the Bishop, $4; Diocesan Fund, $1.50; Expense of Archdeaconry, 77c. Total, $11.67.

Total amount of Offerings, $561.16.

Property.

Church and lot (estimated worth), $3,000.
Condition of property, good.
Amount of salary pledged Rector, $360, and rent of a house.
Number of sittings in the Church, 100; all free.

Remarks.

The Church was consecrated on December 22, 1891.

MISSION OF ST. SIMON AND ST. JUDE, WORCESTER.

Missionary. The Rev. H. E. Gilchrist.
Warden. Chas. Fredenburgh.
Clerk. David S. Smith.
Treasurer. Richard Colbeck.

Parochial.

Families, 8; Individuals, adults, 29; Baptisms, adults, 3; Confirmed, since last report, 3; Present number of confirmed persons, 11; Communicants, admitted, 5, received, 6, present number, 11; Public Services (Sundays, 31, Holy days, 4, other days, 13), 48; Holy Communion, public, 5.

Property.

Indebtedness, $50.

Remarks.

Mission organized November 1, 1891.

Rensselaer County.

ST. PAUL'S CHURCH, TROY.

Rector. The Rev. Edgar A. Enos, D. D.
Wardens. Joseph M. Warren, Joseph J. Tillinghast.
Vestrymen. Stephen W. Barker, James H. Caldwell, John Clatworthy, Derick Lane, William W. Morrill, Charles E. Patterson, John I. Thompson, M. Edgar Wendell.

Parochial.

Baptisms (adults, 13, infants, 39), 52; Confirmed, since last report, 37; Marriages, 4; Burials, 24; Communicants, last reported, 654, admitted, 37, received, 11, died, 6, removed, 7, present number, 689 ; Public Services (Sundays, 192, Holy days, 138, other days, 560), 890; Holy Communion (public, 170, private, 26), 196; Sunday School, teachers, 18, pupils, 250; Catechizing, every Sunday; Parish School, teachers, 1, pupils, 10; Sewing School, teachers, 20, pupils, 173.

Offerings.

Parochial.— Alms at Holy Communion, not elsewhere reported, $439.94 ; Current expenses, including salaries, $9,665 ; Sunday School, $239.04; Parish School, $450 ; Increase and Improvement of Church Property, $450; Friends of the Sisterhood, $1,030 65; Altar Guild, $235.50; Miscellaneous, $72; Cash subscriptions toward Fund for Rebuilding Interior of Church, $40,550. Total, $53,132.13.

Diocesan.— Diocesan Missions (to S. E. Marvin, $1,232, Salary of the Diocesan Missionary, $200, Through Archdeaconry, $32.50, All Saints' Mission, Round Lake, $25, Raymertown, $18.25, Bath-on-Hudson, Rectory and Choir, $30.27, Miscellaneous, $61, Missionary boxes [estimated], $301.15), $1,950.17; Salary of the Bishop, $200;

Diocesan Fund, $90; Bible and Common Prayer Book Society of Albany, $15.47; Fund for Aged and Infirm Clergymen, $31.50; Fund for Widows and Orphans of Clergymen, $31.50; Orphan House of the Holy Saviour, $167; The Child's Hospital, $25; Society for Promoting Religion and Learning, $10; Clergy Reserve Fund, $70; Church Home, Troy, $500; The same, toward permanent fund, $500, Young Woman's Association, Troy, $50; St. Christina Home, $79.91; Miscellaneous, $45.25. Total, $3,765.80.

General.— Domestic Missions ($190, Bishop of Montana, $90, South Carolina, $50, Missionary box, $48), $378; Foreign Missions ($50, Persia, $13.51), $63.51; Home Missions to Coloured Persons, $20; Jews, $15. Total, $476.51.

Total amount of Offerings, $57,374.44.

Remarks.

The interior of the Church is being rebuilt by the Tiffany Glass and Decorating Company, of New York. It is hoped that the renovated building will be ready for occupancy on, or shortly after, Easter day, 1893. Since June all services have been held in the Chapel, on State street.

ST. JOHN'S CHURCH, TROY.

Rector. The Rev. Henry R. Freeman.

Wardens. Norman B. Squires, Chas. W. Tillinghast.

Vestrymen. Edward G. Gilbert, James M. Ide, C. A. McLeod, Francis N. Mann, Wm. P. Mason, Wm. M. Sanford, Charles E. Hanaman, George A. Wells.

Parochial.

Families, 210; Baptisms (adult, 1, infants, 23), 24; Confirmed, since last report, 18; Present number of confirmed persons, 441; Marriages, 7; Burials, 26; Communicants, last reported, 400, admitted, 18, received, 1, died, 7, removed, 8, present number, 404; Sunday School, teachers, 17, pupils, 200; Catechizing, number of times, every Sunday; Sewing School, 140; Woman's Guild, 60; Employment Society, 65; Mothers' Meeting, 30.

Offerings.

Parochial.—Alms at Holy Communion, $310; Current expenses, including salaries (estimated), $7,500; Sunday School, $300; Increase and Improvement of Church Property, $200; Parish Visitors' Work, $200; Altar Society, $100; Employment Society, $320; Sewing School, $75; Miscellaneous, $200. Total, $9,205.

Diocesan.— Diocesan Missions, $600; Salary of the Bishop, $175; Diocesan Fund, $90; Bible and Common Prayer Book Society of Albany, $300; Fund for Aged and Infirm Clergymen, $25; Fund for Widows and Orphans of Clergymen, $25; Orphan House of the Holy Saviour, $40; The Child's Hospital, $150; Rexleigh School, Salem, $1,100. Total, $2,505.

General.— Domestic and Foreign Missions, $230; Theological Education, $200; Other objects, $200. Total, $630.

Total amount of Offerings, $12,340.

Property.

Church and lot (estimated worth), $50,000.

Parsonage and lot (estimated worth), $25,000

Other property, Parish House, $15,000.

Condition of property, good.

Indebtedness, $8,000.

· Amount of salary pledged Rector, $2,500.

Number of sittings in Church, 600; free, 50.

Remarks.

The Rev. Thaddeus A. Snively resigned the Rectorship on Trinity Sunday, June 15, 1892.

The Rev. Henry R. Freeman accepted the Rectorship in September, and assumed charge of the Parish on the 21st Sunday after Trinity, November 6, 1892.

Owing to this vacancy, the report of the Offerings is necessarily somewhat incomplete.

CHRIST CHURCH, TROY.

Rector. The Rev. Eaton W. Maxcy, S. T. D.

Wardens. Hon. William Kemp, S. C. Tappin.

Vestrymen. Washington Akin, M. D., Peter Black, Charles Cleminshaw, J. W. A. Cluett, George Churchill, Frank W. Edmunds, Charles A. Nimmo.

Parochial.

Families, 130; Individuals (adults, 450, children, 250), 700; Baptisms (adults, 3, infants, 12), 15; Confirmed, since last report, 18; Marriages, 11; Burials, 23; Churchings, 1; Communicants, admitted, 18, received, 12, died, 6, removed, 5, present number, 269; Public Services (Sundays, 96, Holy days, 10, other days, 60), 166; Holy Communion, public, 15; Catechizing, number of times, 40.

Offerings.

Parochial.—Alms at Holy Communion, $61.66; Current expenses, including salaries, $4,721.21; Sunday School, $202.92; Increase and Improvement of Church Property, $1,000; Church Home, $225. Total, $6,210.79.

Diocesan.—Diocesan Missions, $265.23; Salary of the Bishop, $62; Fund for Widows and Orphans of Clergymen, $29.86; Orphan House of the Holy Saviour. $112.08. Total, $469.17.

General.—Foreign Missions, $15.05.

Total amount of Offerings, $6,695.01.

Property.

Church and lot (estimated worth), $35,000.

Other property, $4,000.

Amount of salary pledged Rector, $2,500.

Number of sittings in the Church, 600.

ST. LUKE'S CHURCH, TROY.

Rector. The Rev. William Brevoort Bolmer.

Wardens. James Wood, John W. Babcock.

Vestrymen. Henry E. Darby, Thomas Marles, P. Harry Mitchell, Daniel Founcks, George Haite, Edmund Adams, Thomas B. Iler, James Evans.

Parochial.

Families, 150; Individuals (adults, 320, children, 240), 560; Baptisms, infants, 28; Confirmed, since last report, 20; Present number of confirmed persons, 280; Marriages, 5; Burials, 18; Churchings, 1; Communicants, last reported, 192, admitted, 19, received, 3, died, 3, removed, 6, present number, 215; Public Services (Sundays, 169, Holy days, 87, other days, 39), 295; Holy Communion (public, 76, private, 3), 79; Sunday School, teachers, 12, pupils, 115; Catechizing, number of children, 120, number of times, 60.

Offerings.

Parochial.— Alms at Holy Communion, $51.18; Current expenses, including salaries, $1,615.45; Sunday School, $154.15; Increase and Improvement of Church Property, $354.74; Poor Women in Child-bed, 25 cents.   Total, $2,175.77.

Diocesan.— Diocesan Missions, $30.98; Salary of the Bishop, $10; Diocesan Fund, $24; Bible and Common Prayer Book Society of Albany, $4.86; Fund for Aged and Infirm Clergymen, $5.57; Fund for Widows and Orphans of Clergymen, $5.56; Orphan House of the Holy Saviour, $5.08; The Child's Hospital, $3.53; Society for Promoting Religion and Learning, $5.02.   Total, $94.60.

General. — Domestic Missions, $5.63; Foreign Missions, $4; Indian Missions, $2.53; Home Missions to Coloured Persons, $2.54; Society for Promoting Christianity among the Jews, $6.71; General Missions, $45.56; Russian Famine, $9.51; American Church Building Fund, $2.51.   Total, $78.99.

Total amount of Offerings, $2,349.36.

Property.

Church and lot (estimated worth), $25,000.
Parsonage and lot (estimated worth), $6,000.
Other property, including Chapel, $4,700.
Condition of property, tolerable.
Amount of salary pledged Rector, $800 and Rectory.
Number of sittings in the Church, 350; all free.

Remarks.

The Parish has been self-supporting since March 1st.

THE CHURCH OF THE HOLY CROSS, TROY.

Rector. The Rev. J. Ireland Tucker.

Parochial.

Baptisms (adults, 11, infants, 23), 34; Confirmed, since last report, 15; Marriages, 5; Burials, 25; Communicants, 150; Public Services (Sundays, 2, Holy days, 1, other days, 1), 4; Holy Communion, public, Sundays and Saints' days; Sunday School, teachers, 14, pupils, 135; Parish School, teachers, 5, pupils, 60.

THE FREE CHURCH OF THE ASCENSION, TROY.

Rector. The Rev. James Caird.

Trustees. William R. Bridges, James Caird, Thomas Cordwell, David Little, J. Gillespie, N. B. Squires, William A. Thompson, F. S. Lincoln.

Parochial.

Baptisms (adult, 1, infants, 16), 17; Confirmed, since last report, 10; Marriages, 5; Burials, 14; Communicants, present number, 240; Public Services (Sundays, 104, Holy days, 8, other days, 62), 174; Holy Communion (public, 14, private, 2), 16; Sunday School, teachers, 20, pupils, 185; Catechizing, every Sunday.

Offerings.

Parochial. — Current expenses, including salaries, $2,378.13; Sunday School, $553.65; Increase and Improvement of Church Property, $161.27.   Total, $2,999.05.

Diocesan.— Diocesan Missions, $44.25; Salary of the Bishop, $10; ▓▓▓▓▓ mon Prayer Book Society of Albany, $5; Orphan House of the ▓▓▓▓▓ Church Home, Troy, $10.   Total, $68.02.

General.— Domestic Missions, $45.06; Through the Woman's Auxiliary (Money, $35, Cash value four boxes, $155.16), $180.16. Total, $235.22.
Total amount of Offerings, $3,286.39.

ST. BARNABAS' CHURCH, TROY.

Rector. The Rev. George A. Holbrook.

The Corporation. Rev. Geo. A. Holbrook, President; Rev. J. Ireland Tucker, S. T. D., Vice-President; A. W. M. Moffitt, William C. Jamieson, Thomas Entwistle, Wm. W. Morrill, Wm. W. Rousseau, Chas. W. Tillinghast, 2d, Horace B. Finley, Secretary. The Local Committee: Rev. Geo. A. Holbrook, A. W. M. Moffitt, Treasurer; Thos. Entwistle, Wm. C. Jamieston, H. B. Finley.

Parochial.

Baptisms (adult, 1, infants, 23), 24; Confirmed, since last report, 18; Present number of confirmed persons, 187; Marriages, 4; Burials, 12; Churchings, 1; Communicants, last reported, 170, admitted, 22, received, 4, died, 4, removed, 5, present number, 187; Public Services (Sundays, 205, Holy and other days, 679), 884; Holy Communion (public, 205, private, 18), 223; Catechizing, number of children, all, number of times, 52.

Offerings.

Parochial.— Alms at Holy Communion, $78.93; Current expenses, including salaries, $3,481.19; S. Barnabas' Building Fund, $1,177.57; S. Barnabas' Endowment Fund, $76.72; S. Barnabas' Mortgage Fund, $13.85; For the Poor, $28.88. Total, $4,857.14.

Diocesan.—Diocesan Missions, $51.05; Salary of the Bishop, $7.50; Bible and Common Prayer Book Society of Albany, $5.76; Fund for Aged and Infirm Clergymen, $10.43; Fund for Widows and Orphans of Clergymen, $2.84; Orphan House of the Holy Saviour, $21.46: The Child's Hospital, $7.41; Church Home, Troy, $63.16, Troy Orphan Asylum, $2.70; General Missionary's Salary, $7.84. Total, $180.15.

General. — Domestic Missions, $9.58; Foreign Missions, Society of St. John the Evangelist's Kafir Mission, Capetown, $4.86; Nashotah House, $6.51; Society St. John Evangelist's New Church at Oxford, Eng., $5. Total, $25.95.
Total amount of Offerings, $5,063.24.

Property.

Church and lot (estimated worth), $4,500.
Mission House and lot (estimated worth), $3,500.
Other property (organ, chancel furniture, etc.), $1,450.
Condition of property, excellent.
Indebtedness, a mortgage of $3,600 on Mission House and lot.
The Building Fund amounts to $9,908.26.
The Mortgage Fund amounts to $805.82.
The Endowment Fund amounts to $76.72.
Amount of salary pledged Rector, $1,200 (no Rectory).
Number of sittings in the Church, 200; all free.

TRINITY CHURCH, LANSINGBURGH.

Rector. The Rev. Charles Metcalf Nickerson.

Wardens. James McQuide, Peter B. King.

Vestrymen. Eugene Hyatt, E. K. Betts, E. H. Leonard, J. M. Snyder, C. S. Holmes, E. W. Bancker, G. W. Daw.

Parochial.

Baptisms (adults, 17, infants, 26), 43 ; Confirmed, since last report, 47 ; Marriages, 7 ; Burials, 30 ; Communicants, last reported, 244, admitted, 45, received, 14, died, 5, removed, 8, present number, 290 ; Public Services (Sundays, 184, Holy days, 12, other days, 88), 284 ; Holy Communion (public, 36, private, 7), 43 ; Sunday School, teachers, 30, pupils, 229.

Offerings.

Parochial.— Alms at Holy Communion, $104 ; Current expenses, including salaries, $3,200; Increase and Improvement of Church Property, $237.50; Carpet for Church, $268.25 ; Carpet, etc., for Chapel, $239 ; Special subscription for choir, not included in salaries, $500 ; Choir vestments, $175 ; Sunday School (Mission), $72.69 ; St. Stephen's Mission, $260. Total, $5,056.44.

Diocesan. — Diocesan Missions, $200 ; Salary of the Bishop, $60 ; Diocesan Fund, $45; Fund for Widows and Orphans of Clergymen, $24.74 ; Orphan House of the Holy Saviour, $20; The Child's Hospital, $25 ; Theological Education, $17.19. Total, $391.93.

General.— Domestic Missions, $53.04 ; Foreign Missions, $26.52 ; Diocese of Indiana, $30.59 ; Church Building Fund, $23.85. Total, $134.

Total amount of Offerings, $5,582.37.

Property.

Church and lot (estimated worth), $50,000.
Parsonage and lot (estimated worth), $5,000.
Other property, $4,000.
Condition of property, good.
Amount of salary pledged Rector, $1,500.
Number of sittings in the Church, 374 ; rented, 314; free, 18.

Remarks.

The statistics of St. Stephen's Mission are included in the above. I have held service every Sunday with an average congregation of 65, and Sunday School with 10 teachers and 81 pupils. The Guilds of the Parish have done well. St. Agnes' paid for the Church carpet, and gave $30 toward refurnishing the Sunday School room. St. Cecilia's Guild gave $50 toward choir vestments, and the Guild of St. Elizabeth (Mission) helped fill a box for the Orphanage of the Holy Saviour. The will of the late Mrs. Hugh L. Rice gave $1,000 to Trinity Church and $500 to St. Stephen's Mission. The money used for the poor has been taken chiefly from the Barton fund, of which $150 has been spent.

ST. MARK'S CHURCH, HOOSICK FALLS.

Rector Emeritus. The Rev. George Huntington Nicholls, S. T. D.
Rector. The Rev. George Dent Silliman.
Wardens. J. Russell Parsons, William Shelton Nicholls.
Vestrymen. John G. Darroch, Marstin D. Greenwood, Isaac A. Allen, Charles A. Coulter, A. Danforth Geer, Nelson Gillespie, James A. Beckett, Horace H. Barnes.

Parochial.

Families and parts of families, 233; Individuals (adults, 495, children, 220), 715; Baptisms (adults, 9, infants, 28), 37 ; Confirmed, since last report, 53 ; Marriages, 10 ; Burials, 35 ; Communicants, last reported, 398, admitted, 57, died, 25, present number, 419; Public Services (Sundays, 3, Holy days,

26

2), 684 ; Holy Communion (public, 195, private, 21), 216; Sunday School, teachers, 17, pupils, 250 ; Catechizing, number of children, all, number of times, every week.

Offerings.

Parochial.— For the Poor, $49.90; Current expenses, including salaries (Treasurer's Report), $3,000; Sunday School (not elsewhere reported), $154.49; Theological Education, special, $5; General Parish expenses, $410.83. Total, $3,620.22.

Diocesan.— Diocesan Missions (special, Mrs. W. A. W. $50), $150; Salary of the Bishop, $40; Diocesan Fund, $45; Bible and Common Prayer Book Society of Albany, $7; Fund for Aged and Infirm Clergymen, $82; Orphan House of the Holy Saviour (of which King's Daughters, $5, and Sunday School League, $24.10), $35.49; The Child's Hospital, $20 ; For the Cathedral, $25; Diocesan Missionary, $25. Total, $379.49.

General.— General Theological Seminary, $9; Foreign Missions, $9.78 ; Missions to the Jews, $8; Society for the Increase of the Ministry, $82.22; Bishop Coleman, work in Delaware, $20; Sunday School Lenten offering, Domestic and Foreign Missions, $53.85; Sunday School Lenten Offering, Chinese League, $10; Sunday School, Little Samuel School, Persia, $25; Miss Emery, for Woman's Auxiliary, $10.65. Total, $178.50.

Total amount of Offerings, $4,178.21.

Property.

Church and lot (estimated worth), $35,000.
Parsonage and lot (estimated worth), $7,500.
Condition of property, good.
Amount of salary pledged Rector, $1,500.
Number of sittings in the Church, 400.

Remarks.

During the past year, the Parish has suffered an irreparable loss in the death of the Hon. Walter A. Wood, for many years Senior Warden. He was a staunch Churchman, a most liberal giver, a loyal friend, a wise counsellor, a man of great influence in the village which has been built up by the prosperity of the machine works which bear his name. That name is mentioned only in loving remembrance by the hundreds who were in his employ. He will be missed, not only here, but in the Diocese. Rarely did an appeal come to him for aid in any good work, which remained unanswered.

In the death of Mrs. Nicholls, the wife of the Rector Emeritus, the Parish has suffered another grievous loss. She was identified with her husband in the building up of the Parish, since the day of small things. A woman of rare sweetness of character, most faithful in attendance at Church services, even after her ears could not receive a word, a most patient sufferer in illness, an example to the flock — any Parish must be stronger for such a life, spent in the Master's service.

There is no man whom I so delight to honor as the Rector Emeritus. He has this year been overwhelmed with sorrow, and very near death's door, yet, now in his accustomed place, he assists at the services. It is always pleasant for me to add some words of loving gratitude to him, at the end of my yearly report.

The Woman's Auxiliary has raised during the year $270.47 for a special charity in the Parish and for Missions. Also, the Junior Auxiliary and Ministering Children League $25, both items not included in the above report.

TRINITY CHURCH, SCHAGHTICOKE.

Rector. The Rev. M. O. Smith.
Warden. Edward Searls.

Vestrymen. Charles Corbin, Joseph Parker, Frank Sigworth, Ira Askins, Robert Bartle.

Parochial.

Baptisms (adult, 1, infants, 8), 9 ; Confirmed, since last report, 14 ; Marriages, 1 ; Burials, 3 ; Communicants, last reported, 38, admitted, 14, received, 2, present number, 54.

Offerings.

Parochial.— Current expenses, including salaries, $538.67 ; Increase and Improvement of Church Property, $189.50. Total, $728.17.

Diocesan. — Diocesan Missions, $15 ; Salary of the Bishop, $6 ; Diocesan Fund; $9. Total, $30.

Total amount of Offerings, $758.17.

Amount of salary pledged Rector, $350.

Sittings in the Church, all free.

Remarks.

This report is necessarily imperfect, as the Parish has been vacant a great part of the year.

THE CHURCH OF THE MESSIAH, GREENBUSH.

Rector. The Rev. Harry A. R. Cresser.

Wardens. George Low, William H. Terrell.

Vestrymen. Richard W. Stevens, George Story, Harry E. Cole, Charles H. Smith, Theodore A. McKean, Clarence Houghton, John H. Pangburn, George P. Reisel.

Parochial.

Families, 78; Baptisms (adults, 2, infants, 4), 6; Marriages, 1; Burials, 14; Communicants, last reported, 111, received, 21, died, 7, removed, 11, present number, 114; Public Services (Sundays, 77, Holy days, 12, other days, 11), 100; Holy Communion (public, 15, private, 7), 22; Sunday School, teachers, 10, pupils, 75; Catechizing, number of children, all, number of times, once every month.

Offerings.

Parochial.—Alms at Holy Communion, $2.75; Current expenses, including salaries, $817.61 ; Sunday School, $61.50; Increase and Improvement of Church Property, $564.82; Other Parochial objects, $196.75. Total, $1,643.43.

Diocesan.— Diocesan Missions, $25; Salary of the Bishop, $10; Diocesan Fund, $24; Orphan House of the Holy Saviour, $4; The Child's Hospital, $4. Total, $67.

Total amount of Offerings, $1,710.43.

Property.

Church and lot (estimated worth), $6,000.

Other property, $1,000.

Condition of property, good.

Amount of salary pledged Rector, $900.

Number of sittings in the Church, 175, all free.

Remarks.

The present Rector took charge of the Parish in March last, after it had been vacant over four months.

During the past summer, the Church edifice has been thoroughly renovated, externally and internally, all the funds for the purpose being the people themselves.

On Easter Day, a stained glass window representing the Annunciation was dedicated.

The young people of the Parish have a fund in the bank toward the erection of a Parish House, amounting to $325.

CHURCH OF THE EPIPHANY, EAST ALBANY.

Rector. The Rev. Thomas White.

Parochial.

Families, 44; Baptisms (adults, 2, infants, 16), 18; Marriages, 6; Burials, 12; Communicants, last reported, 177, received, 2, died, 2, removed 8, present number, 170; Public Services (Sundays, 98, Holy days, 16, other days, 27), 136; Holy Communion (public, 49, private, 4), 53; Sunday School, teachers, 18, pupils, 130; Catechizing, every Sunday.

Offerings.

Parochial.— Current expenses, including salaries, $770.08; Sunday School, $69.19. Total, $839.27.

Diocesan.— Diocesan Missions (for Diocesan Missionary), $5; Salary of the Bishop, $5; Orphan House of the Holy Saviour, $2.14; The Child's Hospital, $5. Total, $17.14.

General.— Domestic Missions, $25; Foreign Missions, $25. Total, [$50.

Total amount of Offerings, $906.41.

Property.

Church and lot (estimated worth), $10,000.
Condition of property, good.
Indebtedness, $600.
Amount of salary pledged Rector, $700.
Number of sittings in the Church, 200.

Remarks.

In the report this year there has not been included the work of some of the most active societies of the Parish, or the generous gifts of friends, and especially of the Woman's Auxiliary toward the purchase of the desirable property opposite the Church for a Rectory, deeming it best to leave this latter until it should assume a more definite form.

ALL SAINTS' CHURCH, HOOSAC.

Rector. The Rev. E. D. Tibbits.
Assistants. The Rev. T. H. R. Luney, Rev. J. B. Tibbits.
Wardens. Le G. C. Tibbits, H. C. Babcock.
Vestryman. George M. Andrews, George M. Bovie, E. J. Brown, George Babcock, H. E. Hallenbeck, Henry Myers, W. J. Kellyes, D. R. Armstrong and C. E. Pierce.

Parochial.

Baptisms (adults, 11, infants, 11), 22 ; Confirmed, since last report, 27 ; Present number of confirmed persons, 188 ; Marriages, 9 ; Burials, 11 ; Communicants, last reported, 109, died, 4, present number, 134 : Public Services, every Sunday, early celebration, Matins and evenings, Holy days, early celebration, Matins and Evensong, Other days, Matins and Evensong daily ; Holy Communion (public, 124, private, 5), 129 ; Sunday School, teachers, 8, pupils, 82 ; Catechizing, every Sunday from Septuagesima to Trinity ; Parish School, teachers, 8, pupils, 18.

Offerings.

Parochial.— Current expenses, including salaries, $917.48 ; Sunday School, $21. Total, $938.48.

Diocesan.— Diocesan Missions, $30 ; Salary of the Bishop, $6 ; Orphanage at Cooperstown, $33 ; Archdeaconry of Troy, $9.40 ; Raymertown Mission Building Fund, $868.50. Total, $946.90.

General.— General Fund "Iron Cross," $4.10 ; Bishop of Delaware, for Diocesan Missions, $6. Total, $10.10.

Total amount of Offerings, $1,895.48.

Amount of salary pledged Assistant Minister, $700.

Remarks.

During the year a boy choir has been organized, which is educated in the Parish School and has daily instruction in church music. They were vested for the first time at All Saints', 1892.

CHURCH OF THE HOLY NAME, BOYNTONVILLE.

Priest in charge. The Rev. E. D. Tibbits.

Warden and Clerk. W. P. Humiston.

Parochial.

Confirmed, since last report, 2 reported as confirmed in Hoosac ; Present number of confirmed persons, 26 ; Marriages, 1 ; Burials, 1 ; Communicants, present number actually receiving, 14 ; Holy Communion, public, once a week ; Sunday School, teachers, 3, pupils, 20.

ST. GILES' MISSION, CASTLETON.

Missionary. The Rev. Canon Hatheway.

Parochial.

Families, 5 ; Individuals (adults, 18, children, 7), 25 ; Present number of confirmed persons, 15; Marriages, 1; Burials, 1; Communicants, last reported, 15, removed, 1, present number, 14; Public Services (Sundays, 58, other days, 10), 68; Holy Communion, public, 11.

Offerings.

Parochial.—Current expenses, including salaries, $370.14.

Diocesan.— Diocesan Missions, $6.

Total amount of Offerings, $376.14.

Property.

Amount of salary pledged Missionary, $200.

St. Lawrence County.

ST. JOHN'S CHURCH, OGDENSBURG.

Rector. The Rev. J. D. Morrison, D. D., LL. D.

Wardens. Charles Ashley, Louis Hasbrouck.

Vestrymen. James G. Averell, Levi Hasbrouck, J. C. Sprague, H. F. James, Egbert Burt, J. G. Knap, Thomas Lawrence.

Parochial.

Baptisms (adults, 11, infants, 49), 60; Received into the Church, 4; Confirmed, since last report, 40; Marriages, 11; Burials, 35; Holy Communion, public, every Sunday and Holy day, private, very frequent; Sunday School, teachers, 29, pupils, 270; Catechizing, number of children, whole school, number of times, frequent.

Offerings.

Parochial.—Alms at Holy Communion, $115.77; Current expenses, including salaries, $4,052.28; Sunday School, $427.24; Parish Societies, $560. Total, $5,155.29.

Diocesan.— Diocesan Missions, $500; Salary of the Bishop, $100; Diocesan Fund, $60; Bible and Common Prayer Book Society of Albany, $18.45; Fund for Aged and Infirm Clergymen, $37.68; Fund for Widows and Orphans of Clergymen, $13.79; Orphan House of the Holy Saviour, $26.40; The Child's Hospital, Box from Woman's Auxiliary, $50; Clergy Reserve Fund, $141.86; Diocesan Missionary salary, $110, of which the Sunday School gave $25, and Woman's Auxiliary $35. Total, $1,058.18.

General.— Domestic and Foreign Missions, $146.40; Home Missions to Coloured Persons (Woman's Auxiliary), $55; Woman's Auxiliary (box sent to Plymouth, Ind., $97.87; Cash for various Missions, $35), $132.89. Total, $384.29.

Total amount of Offerings, $6,547.76.

Property.

Condition of property, good.
Amount of salary pledged Rector, $2,000.
Sittings in the Church, rented and free.

ST. PAUL'S CHURCH, WADDINGTON.

Rector. The Rev. Angus C. Macdonald.
Wardens. Joseph Graves, S. J. Bower, M. D.
Vestrymen. James J. Cook, Robert Dalzel, Clarence Montgomery, John Rule, William Forsythe.

Parochial.

Families, 37; Individuals (adults, 98, children, 56), 154; Baptisms (adult, 1, infants, 7), 8; Present number of confirmed persons, 71; Marriages, 4; Burials, 6; Communicants, last reported, 70, died, 2, removed, 4, present number, 64; Public Services (Sundays, 120, Holy days, 8, other days, 40), 168; Holy Communion (public, 20, private, 2), 22; Sunday School, teachers, 6, pupils, 38; Catechizing, number of children, whole school, number of times, several.

Offerings.

Parochial.—Current expenses, including salaries, $378; Sunday School, $10; Increase and Improvement of Church Property, $50; Organist salary, $50; Value of box of clothing for Nebraska, $5; Paid Sexton's salary, $52; Interest on a loan, $12; Paid on old debt, $40. Total, $617.

Diocesan.—Diocesan Missions, $30; Salary of the Bishop, $9; Diocesan Fund, $9; Fund for Widows and Orphans of Clergymen, $3; Diocesan Missionary, $3. Total, $54.

General.—Domestic Missions, $5; Sunday School Lenten Offering, $5. Total, $10.
Total amount of Offerings, $681.

Property.

Church and lot (estimated worth), $5,000.
Parsonage and lot (estimated worth), $3,000.

Condition of property, good.
Indebtedness, money borrowed for roofing Church, $195.
Amount of salary pledged Rector, $300.
Number of sittings in Church, 200 ; all free.

Remarks.

Once more the record of a year's work, as far as that can be estimated in figures, is hereby transmitted. Altogether we are thankful for what has been achieved. Our financial statement shows a decline in the total on last year. This does not indicate a decadence of interest. A considerable portion of our invested funds has been tied up in real estate property, drawing no interest for more than a year. We hold a first mortgage which is being foreclosed as rapidly as possible. We are certain of principal and interest. This state of things has taxed ordinary resources to the utmost. I am sorry to report removal of three families during year, yet the attendance at services has not decreased and the Sunday offertory keeps well up. A successful Harvest Festival was held lately. A branch of the Junior Auxiliary is at work, and the Ladies' Guild sent forward a box of clothing to a Missionary in Nebraska, in June last.

CHRIST CHURCH, MORRISTOWN.

Missionary. The Rev. William R. Woodbridge.
Wardens. Joseph Couper, Henry A. Chapman.
Vestrymen. James A. Phillips, Thomas W. Pierce, Asa L. Palmer, George E. Pope, Henry A. Bacon, Frank B. Kingsland, Orrin P. Phillips, Edward H. Miller.

Parochial.

Families, 33; Individuals (adults, 97, children, 62), 159; Baptisms, infants, 5; Present number of confirmed persons, 73; Marriages, 1; Burials, 4; Communicants, last reported, 96, received, 3, died, 3, removed, 36, present number, 60; Public Services (Sundays, 117, Holy days, 27, other days, 20), 164; Holy Communion (public, 34, private, 2), 36; Sunday School, teachers, 5, pupils, 40; Catechizing, number of children, 40, number of times, 20.

Offerings.

Parochial.—Alms at Holy Communion, $12.99; Current expenses, including salaries, $471.08. Total, $484.07.
Diocesan.—Diocesan Missions, $50; Salary of the Bishop, $20; Diocesan Fund, $12; Fund for Aged and Infirm Clergymen, $2.96; Orphan House of the Holy Saviour, $2.04; The Child's Hospital, $10.79; Salary of Diocesan Missionary, $10. Total, $107.79.
General.—General Missions (Lent Offerings of Sunday School, $25.02), $27.29 : Jewish Missions, $1.02. Total, $28.31.
Total amount of Offerings, $620.17.

Property.

Church and lot (estimated worth), $3,000.
Parsonage and lot (estimated worth), $1,200.
Amount of salary pledged Rector, $400.
Number of sittings in the Church, 200; all free.

TRINITY CHURCH, POTSDAM.

Rector. The Rev. R. M. Kirby.
Wardens. Thomas S. Clarkson, Bloomfield Usher.

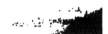

Vestrymen. E. W. Foster, T. Streatfeild Clarkson, Milton Heath, C. O. Tappan, L. Usher, H. D. Thatcher, O. G. Howe, J. G. McIntyre.

Parochial.

Baptisms (adults, 11, infants, 6), 17; Confirmed, since last report, 12; Present number of confirmed persons, 267; Marriages, 6; Burials, 11; Communicants, last reported, 218, admitted, 12, died, 5, removed, 4, present number, 221; Public Services (Sundays, 106, Holy days, 36, other days, 210), 352; Holy Communion, public, 54, private, several times; Sunday School, teachers, 15, pupils, 150; Catechising, number of children, all, number of times, often.

Offerings.

Parochial.—Alms at Holy Communion, $139.92; Current expenses, including salaries, $3,430; Sunday School, $171.85; Increase and Improvement of Church Property, $2,225; Altar Society, $144.66. Total, $5,111.43.

Diocesan.— Diocesan Missions, $1,000; Salary of the Bishop, $50; Diocesan Fund, $48; Bible and Common Prayer Book Society of Albany, $32.14; Fund for Aged and Infirm Clergymen, $46.12; Fund for Widows and Orphans of Clergymen, $42.60; Orphan House of the Holy Saviour, $117.36; The Child's Hospital, $45.35; Society for Education of Young Men for the Ministry, $58.76; General Missionary, $07; Archdeaconry of Ogdensburg, $37.33; Clergy Reserve Fund, $27; Other objects, $1,378.83. Total, $2,950.48.

General.— Domestic Missions, $235.97; Foreign Missions, $312.52; Indian Missions, $150.26; Home Missions to Jews, $26.33; St. Mark's School, Salt Lake City, $40; House of Mercy, New York, $82.61; Church Building Fund, $27; Bishop Brewer, $100. Total, $974.69.

Total amount of Offerings, $9,036.60.

GRACE CHURCH, CANTON.

Rector. The Rev. R. Wyndham Brown.

Wardens. Hon. Leslie W. Russell, Sheldon Brewer.

Vestrymen. R. B. Ellsworth, H. D. Ellsworth, J. C. Keeler, Cleland Austin, I. D. Tracey, H. H. Liotarde, Hammond B. Safford, J. C. Perkins.

Parochial.

Families, 70; Individuals (adults, 125, children, 56), 181; Baptisms, infants, 4; Marriages, 4; Burials, 5; Communicants, last reported, 97, received, 2, died, 7, removed, 11, present number, 81; Public Services (Sundays, 53, Holy days, 11), 64; Holy Communion, public, 14; Sunday School, teachers, 6, pupils, 40; Catechizing, number of times, 10.

Offerings.

Parochial.—Alms at Holy Communion, $39; Current expenses, including salaries, $550; Sunday School, $10; Increase and Improvement of Church Property, $50; To new organ for Church, $150; Harvest Festival, $17. Total, $807.

Diocesan.— Diocesan Missions, $50; Salary of the Bishop, $7; Diocesan Fund, $24. Total, $81.

Total amount of Offerings, $888.

Property.

Church and lot (estimated worth), $3,000.

Parsonage and lot (estimated worth), $5,000.

Condition of property, good.

Indebtedness on Rectory, $1,200.

Amount of salary pledged Rector, $800.

Number of sittings in the Church, 200; rented, 120; free, 80.

GRACE CHURCH, NORFOLK.

Rector. The Rev. Elmer R. Earle.
Warden. Edward H. Atwater.
Clerk. Lester Bartlett.
Treasurer. John C. O'Brien.

Parochial.

Families, 17 ; Individuals (adults, 41, children, 7), 48; Baptisms, infants, 6 ; Confirmed, since last report, 1 ; Present number of confirmed persons, 27 ; Burials, 3; Communicants, died, 2, present number, 27 ; Public Services, Sundays, 21; Holy Communion (public, 4, private, 2), 6; Sunday School, teachers, 4, pupils, 20.

Offerings.

Parochial.— Alms at Holy Communion, $1.30; Current expenses, including salaries, $78.13 ; Increase and Improvement of Church Property, $200. Total, $279.43.

Diocesan.—Diocesan Missions, $5; Salary of the Bishop, 50 cents; Diocesan Fund, $3. Total, $8.50.

Total amount of Offerings, $287.93.

Property.

Church and lot (estimated worth), $1,800.
Condition of property, good.
Amount of salary pledged Rector, $100.
Sittings in the Church, all free.

Remarks.

The present incumbent came to this Mission the third Sunday after Easter, 1892. This report covers a period of six months. Services are held on Sunday afternoons, with the exception of the third Sunday in the month, when there is morning service with a celebration of the Holy Communion. The afternoon services are well attended. The old Parish Church has been restored at a cost of $300. One hundred dollars of this was the gift of a friend of the Parish. The larger part of the remainder has been raised by the efforts of a few faithful women. The Missionary sees signs of spiritual growth in this Parish.

TRINITY CHURCH, GOUVERNEUR.

Rector. The Rev. James Alexander Dickson.
Wardens. Aaron B. Cutting, Silas A. Smith.
Vestrymen. John McCarty, Edward D. Barry, J. B. Preston, James D. Easton, Frank H. Smith.

Parochial.

Families, in part or whole, 46; Individuals (adults, 100, children, 40), 140; Baptisms (adults, 8, infants, 3), 11; Confirmed, since last report, 10; Present number of confirmed persons, 78; Marriages, 7; Burials, 11; Communicants, last reported, 66, admitted, 10, received, 2, died, 1, present number, 77; Public Services, Sundays, 88, Holy days, 20, other days, Wednesday evening and service daily during Lent; Holy Communion (public, 32, private, 1), 33; Sunday School, teachers, 5, pupils, 30; Catechizing, number of children, 30, number of times, every Sunday.

Offerings.

Parochial.—Alms at Holy Communion, $88 57; Current expenses, including salaries, $1,028; Sunday School, $18; Increase and Improvement of Church Property, $25. Total, $1,159.57.

27

Diocesan.—Diocesan Missions, $50; Salary of the Bishop, $26; Diocesan Fund, $34; Orphan House of the Holy Saviour, $5; Diocesan Missionary, $10. Total, $115.

General.—Domestic Missions, $11.25; Foreign Missions, $11.25 (Children's Lent Offerings). Total, $22.50.

Total amount of Offerings, $1,297.07.

Property.

Church and lot (estimated worth), $6,500.

Parsonage and lot (estimated worth), $3,000.

Other property, $350.

Condition of property, good.

Amount of salary pledged Rector, $800.

Number of sittings in the Church, 200; rented, 175; free, 25.

ST. JOHN'S CHURCH, MASSENA.

Rector. The Rev. F. S. Greenhalgh.

Wardens. H. T. Clark, G. A. Snaith.

Vestrymen. E. H. Pitts, E. R. Foord, J. O. Bridges, Henry Warren, L. S. Dowsing, R. H. Wilson.

Parochial.

Families, 42; Individuals (adults, 112, children, 54), 166; Baptisms (adults, 4, infants, 6), 10; Confirmed, since last report, 6; Present number of confirmed persons, 86; Marriages, 1; Burials, 2; Communicants, last reported, 60, admitted, 6, received, 4, removed, 1, present number, 69; Sunday School, teachers, 5, pupils, 53.

Offerings.

Parochial. — Current expenses, including salaries, $270.10; Sunday School, $11.83; Mortgage on Church, $55. Total, $336.93.

Diocesan.— Diocesan Missions, $25.58; Salary of the Bishop, $8. Total, $33.58.

Total amount of Offerings, $370.51.

Property.

Church and lot (estimated worth), $4,000.

Condition of property, good.

Amount of salary pledged Rector, $350.

Number of sittings in the Church, 250; all free.

Remarks.

I have only been in charge since March 1, 1892, and for four or five months preceding there had been no regular service.

ST. LUKE'S CHURCH, LISBON.

Rector. The Rev. A. C. Macdonald.

Parochial.

Families, 18; Individuals (adults, 26, children, 14), 40; Baptisms (adult, 1, infant, 1), 2; Present number of confirmed persons, 19; Burials, 1; Communicants, last reported, 14, present number, 14; Public Services (Sundays, 25, other days, 3), 28; Holy Communion (public, 2, private, 1), 3; Sunday School, teachers, 3, pupils, 14; Catechizing, number of children, all, number of times, several.

Offerings.

Parochial.—Alms at Holy Communion, $5; Increase and Improvement of Church Property, $100; Horse hire, $65; Donation to Missionary, $27. Total, $197.

Property.

Church and lot (estimated worth), $2,000.

Condition of property, good.

Amount of salary pledged Rector, $65.

Remarks.

The Missionary regrets that so many blanks appear in the returns, though it is satisfactory that there is an increase of contributions over former years. The Church has been roofed with cedar shingles, the expenditure in labor and material being $100, while the grounds have also received attention. Interior improvements of Church are contemplated. The Church was kept more comfortable in winter than hitherto, by the furnishing of an ample supply of fuel and the attendance of a faithful sexton.

ZION CHURCH, COLTON.

Rector. The Rev. George M. Irish.

Wardens. Thomas S. Clarkson, Myron E. Howard.

Vestrymen. P. Potter, J. W. Lyman, Archie Allen, S. J. Hosley, William Eacutt, Eugene Moore, A. H. Gustin, F. G. Stone.

Parochial.

Families, 74; Individuals, adults and children, 298; Baptisms (adults, 7, infants, 4), 11; Confirmed, since last report, 9; Present number of confirmed persons, 70; Marriages, 3; Burials, 7; Communicants, last reported, 54, admitted, 9, received, 1, removed, 2, present number, 62; Public Services (Sundays, 97, Holy days, 17, other days, 54), 168; Holy Communion, public, 26; Sunday School, teachers, 7, pupils, 80, Catechizing, number of children, all, number of times, frequently.

Offerings.

Parochial.—Alms at Holy Communion (not elsewhere reported), $8.75; Current expenses, including salaries, $1,155.25; Sunday School, $10.69; Increase and Improvement of Church Property, $1,033; Children's Society, $44. Total, $2,251.69.

Diocesan.— Diocesan Missions, $20; Salary of the Bishop, $4; Diocesan Fund, $4.50; Fund for Aged and Infirm Clergymen, $1.17; Orphan House of the Holy Saviour, $1.13; Salary of Diocesan Missionary, $4. Total, $34.80.

General.— Domestic Missions, $82.13; Foreign Missions, $325.05; Mary Baldwin Scholarship at Jaffa, $10.75; Box to Gobat's School, Jerusalem, $75. Total, $492.93.

Total amount of Offerings, $2,779.42.

Property.

Church and lot and Parsonage and lot, $33,400.

Condition of property, excellent.

Amount of salary pledged Rector, $900.

Number of sittings in the Church, 200; all free.

Remarks.

Through the kindness and generosity of Mr. Thomas S. Clarkson and sisters, of Potsdam, the interior of the Church has been decorated, at the cost of $1,000. The work, under the supervision of Mr. E. J. N. Stent, of New York, has been most tastefully done, and the Church is now, in every respect, a most beautiful and attractive building.

Services have been held every Sunday afternoon (with four exceptions) at Pie pont Centre. The attendance has been somewhat larger, and more interest has been shown, than for several years past.

TRINITY CHAPEL, MORLEY.

Missionary. The Rev. R. Wyndham Brown.
Warden. Thomas L. Harrison.
Treasurer. N. P. Whitney.
Clerk. H. N. Fenton.

Parochial.

Families, 45; Individuals (adults, 90, children, 30), 120; Baptisms infants, 4; Marriages, 1; Burials, 2; Communicants, last reported, 48, died, 1, removed, 2, present number, 45; Public Services, Sundays, 26; Holy Communion (public, 6, private, 2), 8. Sunday School, teachers, 3, pupils, 25.

Offerings.

Parochial.—Alms at Holy Communion, $3; Current expenses, including salaries (approximately), $60; Sunday School, $5; Other Parochial objects, $15; New furnace for Chapel, $175. Total, $258.
Diocesan.—Diocesan Missions, $25; Salary of the Bishop, $3. Total, $28.
Total amount of Offerings, $286.

Property.

Church and lot (estimated worth), $15,000.
Parsonage and lot (estimated worth), $4,000.
Condition of property, very good.
Amount of salary pledged Rector. Missionary stipend.
Number of sittings in the Church, 240; all free.

ST. THOMAS' CHURCH, LAWRENCEVILLE.

Missionary. The Rev. Alfred Louis Fortin.
Warden. William Kingston.

Parochial.

Families, 10; Individuals (adults, 23, children, 13), 36; Baptisms, infant, 1 Present number of confirmed persons, 20; Communicants, last reported, 14, present number, 19.

Offerings.

Parochial.— Current expenses, $30
Diocesan.— Diocesan Missions, $5; Diocesan Fund, $2.80. Total, $7.80.
Total amount of Offerings, $37.80.

Property.

Church and lot (estimated worth), $3,000.
Parsonage and lot (estimated worth), $1,000.
Condition of property, fairly good.
Amount of salary pledged Missionary, $93.
Number of sittings in the Church, 200; all free.

ST. ANDREW'S CHURCH, NORWOOD.

Missionary. The Rev. Elmer R. Earle.
Warden. Dr. T. A. Pease.
Clerk. F. G. Partridge.
Treasurer. W. B. Hart.

Parochial.

Families, 26; Individuals (adults, 61, children, 20), 81 ; Baptisms (adults, 3, infants, 5), 8; Confirmed, since last report, 6; Present number of confirmed persons, 35; Communicants, present number, 35; Public Services (Sundays, 44, Holy days, 3, other days, 25), 72; Holy Communion, public, 7; Sunday School, teachers, 5, pupils, 28; Catechizing, number of children, 20, number of times, 6.

Offerings.

Parochial.—Alms at Holy Communion, $4.72; Current expenses, including salaries, $145.12; Sunday School, $6.38; Increase and Improvement of Church Property, $288.68. Total, $444.90.

Diocesan. — Diocesan Missions, $5; Salary of the Bishop, $1; Diocesan Fund, $6. Total, $12.

Total amount of Offerings, $456.90.

Property.

Church and lot (estimated worth), $4,000.
Condition of property, good.
Amount of salary pledged Missionary, $200.
Number of sittings in the Church, 125; all free.

Remarks.

The present incumbent took charge of this Mission the third Sunday after Easter, 1892. From the first the Parish has been as busy as a hive of bees. The people are active in spiritual things as well as in temporal. Two services are held on Sunday, and the congregations are exceptionally good. Four hundred and seventeen dollars and sixty-eight cents have been spent in furnishing the Church and improving it inside. Of this amount, $129 were given by friends of the Parish. The outlook for this Parish seems to be bright.

A friend also paid off an indebtedness of $235.

Saratoga County.

CHRIST CHURCH, BALLSTON SPA.

Rector. The Rev. Charles Pelletreau, B. D.

Wardens. Stephen B. Medbery. John H. Westcot.

Vestrymen. Charles M. Brown, George L. Thompson, Matthew Vassar, Stephen C. Medbery, William S. Wheeler, David L. Wood, James W. Verbeck, Irving W. Wiswall.

Parochial.

Families, about 150 ; Baptisms (adult, 1, infants, 10), 11 ; Confirmed, since last report, 7 ; Marriages, 5 ; Burials, 19 ; Communicants, last reported, 250, admitted, 7, died, 8, removed, 10, present number, 239 ; Public Services, Sundays, 110, Holy days, all, Other days, 100 ; Holy Communion (public, 56, private, 3), 59 ; Sunday School, teachers, 9, pupils, 100 ; Catechizing, number of children, 100, number of times, often.

Offerings.

Parochial. — Alms at Holy Communion, $75 ; Current expenses, including salaries, $2,800 ; Sunday School, including Specials, $174 ; Increase and Improvement of Church Property, $355.25 ; Repair Fund, $207 ; Christmas Festival, $35. Total, $3,646.25.

Diocesan. — Diocesan Missions, $102.64; Salary of the Bishop, $45; Diocesan Fund, $36; Bible and Common Prayer Book Society of Albany, $2; Fund for Widows and Orphans of Clergymen, $15; Orphan House of the Holy Saviour, $20; The Child's Hospital, $24.50; For Diocesan Missionary (Sunday School), $15; Woman's Auxiliary in money and boxes, $237. Total, $405.14.

General. — Domestic Missions, $42.14; Foreign Missions, $20; Indian Missions, $20; Home Missions to Coloured Persons, $20; Babcock Scholarship, Dakota, $60; Bishop Johnston, W. Texas (special), $80; Russian Relief Fund, $37.17. Total, $279.31.

Total amount of Offerings, $4,830.70.

Property.

Church and lot (estimated worth), $18,000.
Parsonage and lot (estimated worth), $10,000.
Other property, Parish Building, $7,000.
Condition of property, good.
Amount of salary pledged Rector, $1,500.
Number of sittings in the Church, 350.

ST. JOHN'S CHURCH, STILLWATER.

Missionary. The Rev. Edward C. Hoskins.
Wardens. Joseph Moll, John Bradley.
Vestrymen. John Stringer, George Manches, Harman D. Bradt, Charles Green, George H. Lansing, John Bradley, Jr., John Taber, William Bradley.

Parochial.

Families. 15; Individuals (adults, 36, children, 3), 39; Confirmed, since last report, 2; Burial. 1; Communicants, admitted, 2, present number, 28; Public Services (Sundays, 41, Holy days, 6, other days, 7), 54; Holy Communion, public, 13.

ST. PAUL'S CHURCH, CHARLTON.

Lay Reader. John Mills Gilbert.
Wardens. William Taylor, Robert O. Davis.
Vestrymen. George C. Valentine, John Marvin, Robert Wendell, Jacob Pink.

Parochial.

Families, 19; Baptisms, infants, 4; Communicants, last reported, 28, present number, 28; Sunday School, teachers, 3, pupils, 12.

Offerings.

Parochial.— Current expenses, including salaries, $246.

Property.

Church and lot (estimated worth), $1,300.
Other property, $700.
Condition of property, fair.
Number of sittings in the Church, 125; all free.

Remarks.

Owing to the illness and death of the Rector, Rev. H. R. Timlow, the Church was without services for the greater part of the year.

Mr. John Mills Gilbert has been in charge as Lay Reader since July 22d.

GRACE CHURCH, WATERFORD.

Rector. The Rev. Samuel T. Street.

Wardens. John Higgins, Roland H. Stubbs, M. D.

Vestrymen. William Holroyd, John H. Meeker, Edw. Van Kleek, James E. Bootman, Thos. E. Clayton, Chas. H. Kavanaugh, Chas. B. Laithe, Edw. La Fay.

Parochial.

Families, 96; Individuals (adults. 213, children, 91), 304 ; Baptisms (adults, 5, infants, 3), 8; Confirmed, since last report, 15; Present number of confirmed persons, 187; Marriage, 1; Burials, 10, Communicants, last reported, 169, admitted, 7, received, 4, died, 4, removed, 5, present number, 171; Public Services (Sundays, 83, Holy days, 22, other days, 31), 136; Holy Communion, public, 54; Sunday School, teachers, 8, pupils, 75; Catechizing, number of children, school, number of times, each Sunday.

Offerings.

Parochial.—Alms at Holy Communion, $73.35; Current expenses, including salaries, $1,422.99; Sunday School, $29.70. Total, $1,526.04.

Diocesan.— Salary of the Bishop, $35; Orphan House of the Holy Saviour, $13.36. Total, $48.36.

Total amount of Offerings, $1,574.40.

Property.

Church and lot (estimated worth), $10,000.

Other property, $2,000.

Amount of salary pledged Rector, $1,000.

Number of sittings in the Church, 335; rented, 210; free, 100.

Remarks.

This Parish was without a Rector from June 1, 1892, to October 16, 1892.

ST. LUKE'S CHURCH, MECHANICVILLE.

Missionary. The Rev. Edward C. Hoskins.

Wardens. Wm. C. Tallmadge, M. W. Hart.

Vestrymen. C. W. Keefer, John E. Thomson, Wm. J. Adams, F. Longstaff, H. O. Bailey, J. H. Massey, A. J. Harvey, F. J. Collamer.

Parochial.

Families, 51; Individuals (adults, 108; children, 50), 158; Baptisms (adults, 5, infants, 6), 11; Confirmed, since last report, 11; Present number of confirmed persons, 80; Marriages, 3; Burials, 3, Communicants, admitted, 4, received, 10, removed, 4, present number, 65; Public Services (Sundays, 97, Holy days, 25, other days, 39), 161; Holy Communion (public, 41, private, 4), 45; Sunday School, teachers, 5, pupils, 37.

Offerings.

Parochial.—Current expenses, including salaries, $392.75; Sunday School, $18.44. Total, $411.19.

Diocesan.—Diocesan Missions, $15; Salary of the Bishop, $4; Diocesan Fund, $9; Orphan House of the Holy Saviour (Sunday School), $6.20. Total, $34.20.

General.—Domestic and Foreign Missions (Sunday School), $19.75.

Total amount of Offerings, $465.14.

Property.

Indebtedness, two mortgages, $1,350.
Amount of salary pledged Rector, $300.

BETHESDA CHURCH, SARATOGA SPRINGS.

Rector. The Rev. Joseph Carey, S. T. D.

Wardens. James M. Marvin, R. C. McEwen, M. D.

Vestrymen. William A. Sackett, Spencer Trask, Daniel Eddy, Walker R.
son, George R. P. Shackelford, Winsor B. French, William B. Gage, Willi
Huestis.

Parochial.

Families, 295; Individuals (adults, 649, children, 536), 1185; Baptisms (a
28, infants, 36), 64; Confirmed, since last report, 52; Present number of con
persons, 787; Marriages, 25; Burials, 72; Churchings, 3; Communicants
reported, 753, admitted, 56, received 15, died, 21, removed, 31, present numbe
Public Services (Sundays, 169, Holy days, 32, other days, 335), 536; Holy
munion (public, 102, private, 12), 114; Sunday School, teachers, 66, pupils, incl
Catharine St. Mission School, 592; Catechizing, number of children, 593, num
times, 52.

Offerings.

Parochial.—Alms at Holy Communion, $304.35; Current expenses, includir
aries, $6,349.80; Sunday School, $254.52; Parish House, $1,441.33; Home of
Shepherd, $1,026.11; Church Debt, $5,294; Altar Society, $31.92; Choir Ves
Society, $43.35. Total, $14,745.38.

Diocesan.— Diocesan Missions, $200; Salary of the Bishop, $70; Diocesan
$75; Bible and Common Prayer Book Society of Albany, $10; Fund for Age
Infirm Clergymen, $26.40; St. Christina Home, $5, The Child's Hospital
Sunday School), $20; Christ Church, Deposit, $8.32; Salary Diocesan Miss
(half from Sunday School), $50; Theological education, $25; Woman's Aux
$79. Total, $569.32.

General.— Domestic Missions, Bishop of West Texas, $67.75; Foreign Mi
Bishop of Nassau, Bahamas, $36.50, For the Jews, $12.50; Home Missi
Coloured Persons, $11.11; Bishop of Indiana, $8.43; St. Stephen's College, 1
To Rev. Dr. Langford (from Sunday School), $19 35; Home Study of Holy
tures, $25. Total, $197.56.

Total amount of Offerings, $15,512.66.

Property.

Church and lot (estimated worth), $83,000.

Parsonage and lot (estimated worth), $9,000.

Other property, Parish house, including new house, $17,000, Home of Good
herd, $6,000, Mission Chapel, $1,800.

Condition of property, good.

Indebtedness Pledges amounting to $3,150 reduce Church debt to $3,350, o
tory, $3,700, on the old Parish house, $2,700.

Amount of salary pledged Rector, $2,500, with Rectory.

Number of sittings in the Church. 1,200; part rented, part free.

Remarks.

The Rector gratefully records an increase in his salary during the year.

The Woman's Auxiliary is becoming more efficient During the year a box
at $86 has been sent to a Diocesan Missionary.

Mr. and Mrs. James A. Moore who, a year ago, so generously gave the west building of the Parish house, have furnished it throughout in a substantial manner. They also repaired and painted both buildings in June last. Here Clergymen find rooms free of charge. Mr. and Mrs. Moore have also placed in that portion of the Church known as the Morning Chapel, marble steps, an iron screen, and two stained-glass windows. A mottled, dove-colored marble tablet commemorates the names of Mr. Moore's father and mother.

ST. STEPHEN'S CHURCH, SCHUYLERVILLE.

Missionary. The Rev. W. F. Parsons.
Wardens. P. Davison, J. Hicks Smith.
Vestrymen. Thos. Bullard, T. B Aitcheson, John A. Dix.

Offerings.

Parochial.— Current expenses, including salaries, $114.98 ; Increase and Improvement of Church Property, $145. Total, $259.98.
Diocesan.— Diocesan Missions, $5 ; Diocesan Fund, $9. Total, $14.
Total amount of Offerings, $273.98.

Property.

Church and lot (estimated worth), $10,000.
Parsonage and lot (estimated worth), $3,000.
Condition of property, excellent.
Amount of salary pledged Rector, $300.
Number of sittings in the Church, 100.

Remarks.

The Church had been closed prior to July 1, when the Rev. W. F. Parsons accepted the work of both Parishes, Greenwich and Schuylerville. The Rectory has been put in excellent condition and the Rector is living in it.
The Church and grounds have been cared for and needed repairs made.
It is impossible to give a complete report for a time longer than since July 1, 1892.

CALVARY CHURCH, BURNT HILLS.

Lay Reader. John Mills Gilbert.
Wardens. Edwin Mead, Peter N. Banta.
Vestrymen. John Wheeler, John Cotton, M. D., Garret L. Cavert, Frederick E. German, Robert M. Keller, Wm. H. Larkin, Levinus Lansing, Charles H. Upham.

Parochial.

Families, 41; Individuals (adults, 91, children, 45), 136; Baptisms, infants, 2; Burials, 4; Communicants, present number, 56; Sunday School, teachers, 5, pupils, 32.

Offerings.

Parochial.—Alms at Holy Communion, $15.12; Current expenses, including salaries, $504.80. Total, $519.92.
Diocesan.—Diocesan Missions, $16.66; Salary of the Bishop, $12; Diocesan Fund, $11.70. Total, $40.36.
General.— Domestic Missions, $8.21; Foreign Missions, $7; General Missions (Sunday School Lenten Offerings), $5.24. Total, $20.45.
Total amount of Offerings, $580.73.

Property.

Church and lot (estimated worth), $3,000.
Parsonage and lot (estimated worth), $1,200.
Other property, $800.
Condition of property, fair.
Number of sittings in the Church, 200; all free.

Remarks.

Mr. John Mills Gilbert has been in charge as Lay Reader since July 22nd.

ST. JOHN'S CHURCH, EAST LINE.

Missionary.　The Rev. Thomas Boone.
Warden.　Walter Bradley.
Clerk.　Howland Fish.
Treasurer.　William Denton.

Parochial.

Families, 20; Individuals, 70; Burials, 1; Communicants, last reported, 38, re——
moved, 8, present number, 30; Public Services (Sundays, 43, other days, 9), 52 :　　:
Holy Communion, public, 11.

Offerings.

Parochial.— Current expenses, including salaries, $93.10.
Diocesan.— Diocesan Missions, $5; Salary Diocesan Missionary, $3.　Total, $8.
General.— Russian Famine Fund, $3.50.
Total amount of Offerings, $103.60.

Property.

Church and lot (estimated worth), $1,000.
Parsonage and lot (estimated worth), $1,500.
Other property, $5,000.
Condition of property, good.
Amount of salary pledged Missionary, $100.
Number of sittings in the Church, 75; all free.

GRACE CHURCH, JONESVILLE.

Missionary.　The Rev. Thomas Boone.
Warden.　William Hatlee, Sr.
Clerk.　John R. Jump.
Treasurer.　John Hatlee.

Parochial.

Families, 12; Individuals, 60; Confirmed, since last report, 6; Present number o

General.— Russian Famine Fund, $3.50; General Missions (from Sunday School), $5.37. Total, $8.87.

Total amount of Offerings, $263.93.

Property.

Church and lot (estimated worth), $1,400.
Other property, $800.
Condition of property, good.
Indebtedness, on Church property, $406.90.
Amount of salary pledged Missionary, $150.
Number of sittings in the Church, 109; all free.

ALL SAINTS' CHURCH, ROUND LAKE.

Missionary. The Rev. Thomas Boone.
Warden. W. N. Horton.
Clerk. George L. Thorne.
Treasurer. Dr. P. C. Curtis.

Parochial.

Families, 12; Individuals, 50; Baptisms (adults, 4, infants, 11), 15; Confirmed, since last report, 7; Present number of confirmed persons, 14; Communicants, last reported, 7, admitted, 7, present number, 14; Public Services (Sundays, 50, other days, 50), 100; Holy Communion, public, 24; Sunday School, teachers, 6, pupils, 50; Catechising, number of children, 40, number of times, 10.

Offerings.

Parochial.—Current expenses, including salaries, $396.98; Sunday School, $47.76; Building and furnishing new Church, $2,000. Total, $2,444.69.

Diocesan.—Diocesan Missions, $5; Salary of Diocesan Missionary, $4. Total, $9.

General.—Russian Famine Fund, $4.

Total amount of Offerings, $2,457.69.

Property.

Church and lot (estimated worth), $3,000.
Condition of property, good.
Amount of salary pledged Rector, $800.
Number of sittings in the Church, 100; all free.

Remarks.

The building of the Church in Round Lake is an event worthy of mention. The Church is a handsome one for the sum which it cost, and is universally admired. Our thanks are due to many friends in Albany and Troy for kind gifts, without which we never could have built our Church. We thank them, and assure them that we believe that the Church is now permanently established here, and that they have helped the few faithful church-people here to do a good work.

Schenectady County.

CHRIST CHURCH, DUANESBURGH.

Rector. The Rev. E. W. Flower.
Lay Reader. Edward Clarence Clark.
Wardens. Alexander McDougall, Ralph W. McDougall.

Vestrymen. James D. Featherstonhaugh, Alexander Van Pelt, George Matt George D. Matthews, Wesley Van Pelt, Ralph A. McDougall, M. D., Edwi Clark.

Parochial.

Families, 78 ; Individuals (adults, 130, children, 49), 179 ; Baptisms (adult, fant, 1), 2 ; Confirmed, since last report, 6 ; Present number of confirmed pe estimated, 115 ; Burials, 3 ; Communicants, last reported, 90, admitted, 6, rec 1, died, 3, removed, 2, present number, 92 ; Public Services (Sundays, 103, days, 28, other days, 14), 145 ; Holy Communion, public, 40 ; Sunday School, ers, 5, pupils, 42 ; Catechizing, number of times, 46.

Offerings.

Parochial.—Alms at Holy Communion, reported below ; Current expens cluding salaries, $1,347.68 ; Sunday School, $31.26 ; Increase and Improvem Church Property, $47.59 ; Local Charities, $6.85. Total, $1,433.38.

Diocesan. — Diocesan Missions, $80 ; Salary of the Bishop, $50 ; Diocesan | $30 ; Bible and Common Prayer Book Society of Albany, $4.18 ; Fund for Ag Infirm Clergymen, $6.92 ; Fund for Widows and Orphans of Clergymen, (Orphan House of the Holy Saviour, $11.13 ; The Child's Hospital, $4.90 ; The cal Education, $7.35. Total, $196.91.

General.— Domestic Missions, $33.05 ; Foreign Missions, $8.89 ; Indian Mi $2.15 ; Home Missions to Coloured Persons, $5 ; Other objects exterior to th cese, $8 ; By Woman's Auxiliary box to Coloured Mission in Virginia, $65. $92.09.

Total amount of Offerings, $1,722.38.

Property.

Church and lot (estimated worth), $2,000.
Parsonage and lot (estimated worth), $3,000.
Other property, Chapel, $1,500.
Condition of property, good.

Remarks.

I have held four services and two celebrations of the Holy Communion in th lage of Schoharie. There are seven communicants. During the past year a ber of the ladies here have met together for prayers and reading nearly every They have also purchased a silver Paten, Altar linen and other requisites for th celebration of the Holy Eucharist. They also presented the Rector at Christ valuable set of books, and have contributed money for contingent expenses.

ST. GEORGE'S CHURCH, SCHENECTADY.

Rector. The Rev. J. Philip B. Pendleton, S. T. B.
Wardens. Abram A. Van Vorst, Samuel W. Jackson.
Vestrymen. D. Cady Smith, John A. DeRemer, John Keyes Paige, Howla Barney, T. Low Barhydt, Edward D. Palmer, Charles S. Washburn.

Parochial.

Families, 350; Individuals (adults, 750, children, 440), 1190; Baptisms (adu infants, 19), 23, Confirmed, since last report, 30 ; Present number of confirme sons, 540; Marriages, 8 ; Burials, 24, Churchings, 4; Communicants, last rep 457, admitted, 28, received, 17, died, 8, removed, 12, present number, 482; 1 Services (Sundays, 230, Holy days, 91, other days, 265), 586; Holy Communion lic, 109, private, 11), 120; Sunday School, teachers, 30, pupils, 265; Catech number of children, all, number of times, weekly; Industrial School, teachers, 15, pupils, 130; Parish Agencies, St. Mary's Guild, 116 members; St. Agnes' Guild, 88 members; St. Andrew's Guild, 50 members; Industrial School, Vested Choir, Parish Paper.

Offerings.

Parochial.— Alms at Holy Communion, $352.24; Current expenses including salaries, $3,941.67; Sunday School (not reported elsewhere), $183.46; Increase and Improvement of Church Property, $241.06; St. Mary's Guild (not reported elsewhere), $435; St. Agnes' Guild, $126.57; Specials for Sunday School, Vested Choir, Parish Kalendar, Memorials, Parochial work, etc., $1,154.36. Total, $6,434.36.

Diocesan.— Diocesan Missions (including specials), $256; Salary of the Bishop, $60; Diocesan Fund, $60; Bible and Common Prayer Book Society of Albany, $19.45; Orphan House of the Holy Saviour (including box), $45.75; The Child's Hospital, $25.60; Theological Education, Schenectady Hospital, Children's Home, Woman's Diocesan League, Relief of Clergymen, $157. Total, $623.80.

General.— Domestic Missions (including boxes to Tennessee and Texas), $276; Foreign Missions, $75; Indian Missions, $23; Home Missions to Coloured Persons (including box to West Virginia), $55; Scholarship in St. John's School, Logan, Utah, Woman Worker in Utah, box to Springfield Mines, Nova Scotia, Jewish Missions, Relief of Families of Clergymen, toward building of Churches in Nebraska, Iowa and Michigan, $141.05. Total, $570.05.

Total amount of Offerings, $7,628.21.

Property.

Church and lot (estimated worth), $35,000.

Parsonage and lot (estimated worth), $8,000.

Other property, $4,000.

Condition of property, good.

Indebtedness, $2,300.

Amount of salary pledged Rector, $2,000.

Number of sittings in the Church and Chapel, 850.

CHRIST CHURCH, SCHENECTADY.

Rector. The Rev. William C. Prout.

Lay Readers. David Guy, Sidney G. Ashmore.

Wardens. James E. Curtiss, David Guy.

Vestrymen. William N. Butler, Henry C. Van Zandt, M. D., David O. Youlen, Sidney G. Ashmore, L. H. D., Edward E. Kriegsman, John H. Shaffer, Rufus W. Lampman, Robert J. English.

Parochial.

Families, 187; Individuals (adults, 290, children, 175), 465; Baptisms (adults, 2, infants, 23), 25; Confirmed, since last report, 12; Marriages, 6; Burials, 18; Communicants, present number, 175; Public Services (Sundays, 121, Holy days, 41, other days, 64), 226; Holy Communion (public, 62, private, 3), 65; Sunday School, teachers and officers, 18, pupils, 125; Catechizing, number of children, 75, number of times, 8.

Offerings.

Parochial.—Alms at Holy Communion, $64.22; Current expenses, including salaries, $1,239.67; Sunday School (not otherwise accounted for), $100.94; By the Woman's Guild (including $175 for interest on the bonded debt), $903.02; By the

King's Daughters, $113.60; By the Sunday School, for a Parish House, $100.90; For new Sunday School books, $75.75. Total, $1,898.10.

Diocesan.—Diocesan Missions, $25.37; Salary of the Bishop, $10; Diocesan Fund, $24; Bible and Common Prayer Book Society of Albany, $5.75; Clergy Reserve Fund, $1.50; Fund for Aged and Infirm Clergymen, $1.50; Fund for Widows and Orphans of Clergymen, $1.50; Orphan House of the Holy Saviour (including box from the Woman's Guild, estimated value, $25, and one from the King's Daughters, $22), $67.68; For the Cathedral Debt, $16.25. Total, $153.55.

General.—Domestic and Foreign Missions (by the Sunday School), $5.79; Church Missions to the Jews, $3.08; Box to Sunday School of Coloured Children in North Carolina, by the King's Daughters, estimated value, $15; Special Charity of the King's Daughters, $11.70. Total, $35.57.

Total amount of Offerings, $2,087.22.

Property.

Church and Lot (estimated worth), $10,000.
Parsonage and lot (estimated worth), $5,000.
Condition of property, good.
Indebtedness, mortgage, $3,500.
Amount of salary pledged Rector, $800.
Number of sittings in the Church, 180; all free.

Schoharie County.

TRINITY CHURCH, SHARON SPRINGS.

Rector. The Rev. Earnest Webster Dustan.

Trustees. Mr. A. S. Carhart, president, 126 Columbia Heights, Brooklyn, N. Y.; Mr. John H. Gardner, Secretary, Sharon Springs.

Parochial.

Families, 48; Individuals (adults, 96, children, young, 28), 124; Baptisms, infants, since July, 7; Present number of confirmed persons, 162; Burials, 2; Communicants, died, 1, present number, 85; Public Services (Sundays, 36, other days, 22), 58; Holy Communion, public, 3; Sunday School, teachers, 6, pupils, 49; Catechizing, number of times, 3.

Offerings.

Parochial.— Current expenses, including salaries, $1,050; Sunday School, since July 3, 1892, $8.44. Total, $1,058.44.

Diocesan.— Salary of the Bishop, $20.

Total amount of Offerings, $1,078.44.

Property.

Church and lot (estimated worth), $4,000.
Parsonage and lot (estimated worth), $4,000.
Condition of property, good.
Amount of salary pledged Rector, $900.
Number of sittings in the Church, 150; all free.

Remarks.

I have been in charge of this Parish since the first Sunday in July, last.

Warren County.

CHURCH OF THE MESSIAH, GLENS FALLS.

Rector. The Rev. Fenwick Mitford Cookson.

Wardens. William A. Wait, Leonard G. McDonald.

Vestrymen. Daniel Peck, George Bassinger, L. P. Juvet, W. H. Robbins, Nelson LaSalle, H. W. Coffin, M. D., H. A. Bowden, James A. Holden.

Parochial.

Families, 204; Baptisms (adults, 12, infants, 22), 34; Confirmed, since last report, 20; Marriages, 7; Burials, 17; Communicants, admitted, 20, received 8, died 1, removed, 9, present number, 334; Public Services (Sundays, 121, Holy days, 39, other days, 79), 239; Holy Communion (public, 64, private, 4), 68; Sunday School, teachers, 24, pupils, 225; Catechizing, weekly.

Offerings.

Parochial.— Alms at Holy Communion, $61.65, Current expenses, including salaries, $2,917.36; Sunday School, $158.21; Increase and Improvement of Church Property, $275.31. Total, $3,412.53.

Diocesan.— Diocesan Missions, $132.73; Salary of the Bishop, $40; Diocesan Fund, $42; Orphan House of the Holy Saviour, $33.09. Total, $247.82.

General.— Domestic Missions, $30.78 ; Foreign Missions, $13.24; Jewish Missions, $3. Total, $47.02.

Total amount of Offerings, $3,707.37.

Property.

Church and lot (estimated worth), $27,000.

Other property, Fund toward Parsonage, $4,500.

Condition of property, good.

Amount of salary pledged Rector, $1,400.

Number of sittings in the Church, 388; rented; at Harrisena, 150; free.

Remarks.

The Ladies' Aid Society continues its very valuable services.

The Altar Guild provides for the Sanctuary and cares most faithfully for all its needs.

On Easter last, Mr. James A. Holden gave to the Church a beautiful pulpit, made of brass and oak, in memory of his father, Dr. Austin W. Holden, who died July 19, 1891. Dr. Holden had been Vestryman or Warden of the Parish most of the time since its formation in 1840, and was for many years a Lay Reader, a teacher in the Sunday School, and in many ways an active worker for the Church and the poor.

The Children's Guild has done much for the poor and has sent some garments and bedding to the Orphanage and the Child's Hospital.

ST. JAMES' CHURCH, CALDWELL.

Rector. The Rev. Edwin Ruthven Armstrong.

Wardens. Henry H. Hayden, George H. Cramer.

Vestrymen. Samuel R. Archibald, Geo. W. Bates, Kleber Burlingame, James T. Crandale, Jerome N. Hubbell, H. C. Noyes, L'G. C. Cramer, F. H. Stevens, M. D.

Parochial.

Families, about 55; Individuals (adults, 130, children, 75), 205; Baptisms, since last report, to Convention, 1890 (adults, 2, infants, 3), 5; Present number of confirmed persons, about 100; Marriages, since report for 1890, 4; Burials, since report for 1890, 8; Communicants, present number, about 100; Holy Communion, public, weekly, private 1; Sunday School, teachers, 5, pupils, 45; Catechizing, number of times, weekly.

Offerings.

Parochial.—Current expenses, including salaries, $1,400; Sunday School, $7; Repairs on Church and Rectory, $500; Christmas tree, $65. Total, $1,972.

Diocesan.—Salary of the Bishop, $10; Diocesan Fund, $10. Total, $20.

Total amount of Offerings, $1,992.

Property.

Church and lot (estimated worth), $16,000.

Parsonage and lot (estimated worth), $6,000.

Condition of property, good.

Indebtedness, mortgage on Rectory, $750.

Number of sittings in the Church, 200; all free.

Remarks.

The present incumbent assumed charge on August 3, 1892, previous to which date there had been an interval (the bane of any Parish) of nearly if not quite ten months, since the departure of him who had gone in and out among his flock unwearyingly for eighteen years.

CHURCH OF THE HOLY CROSS, WARRENSBURGH.

Rector. The Rev. Hamilton Cady.

Wardens. Frederick O. Burhans, Henry Griffing.

Vestrymen. James Herrick, Emerson S. Crandall, Halsey Herrick, Thomas J. Smith, Halsey B. Hayes, Charles F. Burhans, Charles C. White, Hodges H. Hill.

Parochial.

Families, 76; Individuals (adults, 122, children, 46), 168, Baptisms (adults, 2, infants, 3), 5; Confirmed, since last report, 5; Present number of confirmed persons, 95; Burials, 2, Communicants, last reported, 81, admitted, 5, died, 1, present number, 85; Public Services, every Sunday, three times, every Holy day, three times, all other days, twice; Holy Communion (public, 52, private, 2), 54; Sunday School, teachers, 4, pupils, 32; Catechizing, number of children, all, number of times, 34

Offerings.

Parochial.—Current expenses, including salaries, $2,120.93.

Diocesan.— Diocesan Missions, $50, Salary of the Bishop, $38; Diocesan Fund, $27; Fund for Aged and Infirm Clergymen, $4.77; Orphan House of the Holy Saviour, $6.16; The Child's Hospital, $10.83; Diocesan Missionary, $5. Total, $141.76.

General. — General Theological Seminary, $5.99; Domestic Missions, $21.50. Total, $27.49.

Total amount of Offerings, $2,290.18.

Property.

Amount of salary pledged Rector, $900.

Number of sittings in the Church, 100; all free.

Remarks.

The present Rector accepted the call to this Parish on the day of his ordination to the Priesthood, March 10, 1892. Between that date and the last report services had been held on each Sunday, with but two or three exceptions.

ST. MARY'S CHURCH, LUZERNE.

Rector. The Rev. C. J. Whipple.

Wardens. John Burneson, H. J. Martine.

Vestrymen. T. H. Taylor, G. W. Beardmore, Edward Gell, J. J. Wigley, George Gell, William Gell, H. W. Underwood, W. J. Kinnear.

Parochial.

Families, 26: Individuals (adults, 67, children, 36), 103; Baptisms (adults, 4, infants, 10), 14; Confirmed, since last report, 6; Present number of confirmed persons, 53; Marriages, 2; Burials, 2; Communicants, admitted, 6, died, 1, removed, 5; Public services (Sundays, 123, Holy days, 14, other days, 92), 229; Holy Communion, public, 34; Sunday School, teachers, 5, pupils, 30; Catechizing, number of children, all, number of times, 12.

Offerings.

Parochial.—Alms at Holy Communion, $211.65; Current expenses, including salaries, $565.87; Sunday School, $45; Increase and Improvement of Church Property, $2,000; Improvement on Rectory, $850. Total, $3,672.52.

Diocesan.—Diocesan Missions, $20; Salary of the Bishop, $8; Diocesan Fund, $12. Total, $40.

General —Domestic Missions, $11.75.

Total amount of Offerings, $3,724.27.

Property.

Church and lot (estimated worth), $6,000.

Parsonage and lot (estimated worth), $1,500.

Other property, $500.

Condition of property, good.

Amount of salary pledged Rector, $400.

Number of sittings in the Church, 250; all free.

Remarks.

As not included in the above report, I wish to make mention of a new organ ($300) which has been placed in the Church during the past summer. This was purchased by the proceeds of a sale held by the ladies of St. Mary's Guild. We have also received from most generous friends two sets of hangings—green and purple—which add greatly to the beauty of our Sanctuary.

There are other improvements in progress, an account of which will appear, it is hoped, in our next report.

CHURCH OF THE GOOD SHEPHERD, CHESTERTOWN.

Rector. The Rev. Alfred Taylor.

Warden. Ralph Thurman.

Clerk. J. F. Holley.

Treasurer. S. H. Bevins.

Parochial.

Families, 29 ; Individuals (adults, 71, children, 37), 108; Baptisms (adults, infants, 2), 6; Confirmed, since last report, 5; Marriages, 1; Burials, 2; Cl cants, last reported, 58, admitted, 4, received, 1, present number, 63; Public Services, Sundays, morning and evening, Holy days, occasional, other days, Fridays; Holy Communion (public, 16, private, 1), 17; Sunday School, teachers, 3, pupils, 30.

Offerings.

Parochial.— Alms at Holy Communion, $28.62; Current expenses, including salaries, $148.41; Sunday School, $7.30; Increase and Improvement of Church Property, $6.50; Carpets for Rectory, $50. Total, $240.73.

Diocesan.— Salary of the Bishop, $6; Diocesan Fund, $15; Bible and Common Prayer Book Society of Albany, $1; Bishop's Fund for Support of Candidates for the Ministry, $4.15. Total, $26.15.

General,— Domestic Missions and Building Fund, $3.53; For Missions to the Jews, $1.25. Total, $4.78.

Total amount of Offerings, $271.66.

Property.

Church and lot (estimated worth), $4,000.
Parsonage and lot (estimated worth), $2,500.
Condition of property, good.
Amount of salary pledged Rector, $400.
Number of sittings in the Church, 100; all free.

ST. SACRAMENT CHURCH, BOLTON-ON-LAKE GEORGE.

Rector. The Rev. Clement T. Blanchet, B. D.
Warden. John B. Simpson, New York.
Clerk. Randall W. Wilson, Bolton.
Treasurer. Asa W. Dickinson, Bolton.

Parochial.

Families, 40; Individuals (adults, 60, children, 60), 120 ; Baptisms, infants, 5 : Confirmed, since last report, 6 ; Present number of confirmed persons, 61 ; Marriages, 2 ; Burials, 2 ; Communicants, last reported, 55, admitted, 6, received, 2, present number, 65 ; Public Services (Sundays, 118, Holy days, 12, other days, 104), 234 ; Holy Communion, public, 27 ; Sunday School, teachers, 5, pupils, 70 ; Catechizing, number of children, all, number of times, monthly.

Offerings.

Parochial.— Alms at Holy Communion and current expenses, including salaries, $535.54 ; Sunday School, $22.57 ; Carpeting the entire Church, $108.79 ; choir seats, cushions and railings, $50 ; Storm windows for the Rectory, $50 ; Stone walk from the gate to the Church, $150 ; Publishing illustrated historical sketch of the Church, $96.20. Total, $1,013.10.

Diocesan.— Diocesan Missions, $10 ; Salary of the Bishop, $10 ; Diocesan Fund, $27. Total, $47.

General. — Domestic Missions, $2 ; Foreign Missions, $2 ; Indian Missions, $1, Home Missions to Coloured Persons, $2 ; Among the Jews, $2 ; Russian Famine, $3.10. Total, $12.10.

Total amount of Offerings, $1,072.20.

Property.

Church and lot (estimated worth), $8,000.
Parsonage and lot (estimated worth), $3,000.
Other property, horse shed, $100.

Condition of property, good.
Amount of salary pledged Rector, $900.
Number of sittings in the Church, 150 ; all free.

Remarks.

We are again indebted to our Warden, Mr. John R. Simpson, of New York, for a new carpet for the entire Church, two choir seats, with cushions, railings and kneeling stools, and a new Parish register, and for storm windows for the Rectory.

At the suggestion of personal friends, a brief illustrated historical sketch of the Church of St. Sacrament was prepared and published by the Priest-in-charge last summer, which was well received by the many friends of our work. We are indebted to Mrs. Charles H. Meade — *née* Thieriot, and founder of the Church — for much of the information contained therein, and to Mr. Simpson, for seeing it through the Press and defraying the expenses thereof.

A neat and substantial stone-walk was laid by our own local members from the gate to the Church, without expense to the Church treasury. Further improvements of a kindred nature are contemplated for the coming year.

MISSION, SABBATH DAY POINT.

Missionary. The Rev. Clement T. Blanchet.
Lay Reader. James F. Chamberlain.

Parochial.

Families, 15; Individuals (adults, 20, children, 40), 60; Baptisms (adults, 5, infants, 3), 8; Confirmed, since last report, 7; Present number of confirmed persons, 19; Communicants, last reported, 10, admitted, 7, present number, 15; Public Services, Sundays, 8; Holy Communion, public, 1; Sunday School, teachers, 1, pupils, 15; Catechizing, number of children, all, number of times, monthly.

ST. PAUL'S CHURCH, BARTONVILLE.

Missionary. The Rev. Alfred Taylor.
Warden. John Barton.
Clerk. Alfred A. Hart.
Treasurer. Scott Barton.

Parochial.

Families, 19; Individuals (adults, 46, children, 26), 72; Baptisms, infants, 3; Confirmed, since last report, 5; Present number of confirmed persons, 40; Burial, 1; Communicants, last reported, 35, admitted, 5, present number, 40; Public Services, Sundays, all, Holy days, occasional, other days, Wednesdays; Holy Communion (public, 14, private, 1), 15; Sunday School, teachers, 4, pupils, 26.

Offerings.

Parochial.—Alms at Holy Communion, $12.54; Current expenses, including salaries, $228.58. Total, $241.12.
Diocesan.—Diocesan Fund, $8.
General.—Foreign Missions, $1.55.
Total amount of Offerings, $250.67.

Property.

Church and lot (estimated worth), $3,000.
Condition of property, new.
Amount of salary pledged Missionary, $100.
Number of sittings in the Church, $150; all free.

Washington County.

ZION CHURCH, SANDY HILL.

Rector. The Rev. Harry Elmer Gilchrist.
Lay Reader. George Arthur Ingalls.
Wardens. John William Wait, Charles T. Beach.
Vestrymen. D. Harrington, G. A. Ingalls, P. F. Langworthy, Albert Mott, M. D., John Nichols, S. H. Parks, Charles Young, O. R. Howe.

Parochial.

Families, 113; Individuals (adults, 210, children, 63), 273; Baptisms (adults, 3, infants, 13), 16; Confirmed, since last report, 12; Present number of confirmed persons, 148; Marriage, 1; Burials, 8; Communicants, admitted, 21, received, 2, died, 1, present number, 185; Public Services (Sundays, 168, Holy days, 40, other days, 201), 309; Holy Communion (public, 94, private, 2), 96; Sunday School, teachers, 5, pupils, 25; Catechising, number of times, monthly.

Offerings.

Parochial.—Alms at Holy Communion, $26.14; Current expenses, including salaries, $1,142.24; Increase and Improvement of Church Property, $29.26; Choir Books, $2.46; On indebtedness, $240.13. Total, $1,440.23.

Diocesan.—Diocesan Missions, $16.76; Salary of the Bishop, $30; Fund for Aged and Infirm Clergymen, $7.65; Orphan House of the Holy Saviour, $17.51. Total, $71.92.

General.—Church Extension, $1.55; Mission to Jews, $1.57; Order of Holy Cross, $50.51. Total, $53.63.

Total amount of Offerings, $1,565.78.

Property.

Church and lot (estimated worth), $12,000.
Parsonage and lot (estimated worth), $3,500.
Other property (Miller Fund for Literature), $300.
Condition of property, good.
Indebtedness, mortgage on Rectory, $2,000.
Bank notes outstanding, $753.
Amount of salary pledged Rector, $900 and Rectory.
Number of sittings in the Church, 300; all free.

TRINITY CHURCH, GRANVILLE.

Rector. The Rev. Chas. H. Lancaster.
Lay Reader. John S. Warren, LL. B.
Wardens. Jonathan S. Warren, Palmer D. Everts.
Vestrymen. Orville L. Goodrich, George W. Henry, Amos W. Wilcox, John S. Warren, Silas E. Everts.

Parochial.

Families, 62; Individuals (adults, 116, children, 47), 163; Baptisms (adults, 2, infants, 4), 6; Confirmed, since last report, 10; Present number of confirmed persons, 82; Marriages, 7; Burial, 1; Communicants, last reported, 60, admitted, 10, received, 9, present number, 79; Public Services (Sundays, 146, Holy days, 23, other days, 54), 223; Holy Communion, public, 64; Sunday School, teachers, 8, pupils, 45; Catechising, number of children, 45, number of times, monthly.

Offerings.

Parochial.— Current expenses, including salaries and gift to Rector, $936.93; Sunday School $36.33; Choir Fund, $16.11; Altar Guild, toward frontals, $20; St. Andrew's Brotherhood, $3.15. Total, $1,012.52.

Diocesan.— Diocesan Missions, $11.46; Salary of the Bishop, $6; Clergy Reserve Fund, $1.30. Total, $18.76.

General.— General Missions (Lenten offerings from Sunday School), $25.23; Box to coloured school children, Bedford City, Virginia, from Society of Earnest Workers, value, $35. Total, $60.23.

Total amount of Offerings, $1,091.51.

Property.

Church and lot (estimated worth), $5,000.

Parsonage and lot (estimated worth), $4,500.

Condition of property, Church, fair; Rectory, good.

Indebtedness, mortgage on Rectory, $1,800.

Amount of salary pledged Rector, $400.

Number of sittings in the Church, 200; all free.

Remarks.

Of the amounts reported above, $330.87 were secured by the efforts of the Ladies' Aid Society.

The Church received at Easter, from the Directress of the Altar Guild, the gift of a set of embroidered frontals for altar, pulpit, lectern and litany desk. Also, from the same lady, a new credence table and pair of brass vases for retable.

Trinity Chapter of St. Andrew's Brotherhood has been organized the present year, and promises good service for the Church.

During the Rector's serious illness of six months' duration, the services of the Church have been maintained both here and at North Granville by the Rev. Robert S. Locke, Priest of the Diocese of Niagara, and the efficient Lay Reader, Mr. John S. Warren.

ST. JAMES' CHURCH, FORT EDWARD.

Rector. The Rev. J. W. McIlwaine.

Wardens. James S. Kinne, Francis B. Davis.

Vestrymen. Frederick G. Tilton, Benjamin M. Tasker, George Scott, Jarvis W. Milliman, Albert H. Wicks, John J. Morgan, Robert O. Bascom, Robert A. Linendoll, M. D.

Parochial.

Families and parts of families, 102; Individuals (adults, 190, children, 93), 283; Baptisms, infants, 4; Confirmed, since last report, 3; Present number of confirmed persons, 148; Marriage, 1; Burials, 2; Communicants, admitted, 2, died, 1, removed, 8, present number, 57; Public Services, Sundays, morning and evening, Holy days, Lent, daily, except Saturday, other days, Friday evenings; Holy Communion, public, monthly and chief festivals; Sunday School, teachers, 9, pupils, 60; Catechizing, number of times, frequently.

Offerings.

Parochial.— Alms at Holy Communion, $41.40; Current expenses, including salaries, $1,050. Total, $1,091.40.

Diocesan.— Diocesan Missions (from Sunday School, $10), $30; $18; Fund for Aged and Infirm Clergymen, $7. Total, $55.

General.—General Missions (from Sunday School), $10.30 ; Mission to Deaf-Mutes, $3. Total, $13.30,
Total amount of Offerings, $1,159.70.

Property.

Church and lot (estimated worth), $7,000.
Parsonage and lot (estimated worth), $3,000.
Condition of property, very good.
Amount of salary pledged Rector, $600.
Number of sittings in the Church, 250; all free.

ST. PAUL'S CHURCH, SALEM.

Rector. The Rev. Harris C. Rush.
Wardens. Hon. James Gibson, Hon. George B. McCartee.
Vestrymen. A. K. Broughton, Frederick Keglor, David Mahaffy, Ephraim Herrick, William Alexander McNish, Frank A. Graham, George B. Martin, Joseph Hofert.

Parochial.

Families, 57 ; Baptisms (adult, 1, infants, 7), 8 ; Confirmed, since last report, 5 ; Marriages, 6 ; Burials, 10 ; Communicants, last reported, 155, admitted, 5, died, 7, removed, 3, present number, 150 ; Public Services, thrice on all Sundays, other days, four times weekly ; Holy Communion, public, each Sunday and Holy day, private, two times ; Sunday School, teachers, 6, pupils, 48 ; Catechizing, number of times, frequently.

Offerings.

Parochial.—Alms at Holy Communion, $27.08 ; Current expenses, including salaries, $1,131.15 ; Sunday School, $5 ; Parish Debt, $195.34. Total, $1,358.57.

Diocesan. — Diocesan Missions, $67.81 ; Salary of the Bishop, $30 ; Diocesan Fund, $21 ; Bible and Common Prayer Book Society of Albany, $5.04 ; Fund for Aged and Infirm Clergymen, $7.04 ; Fund for Widows and Orphans of Clergymen, $5.05 ; Orphan House of the Holy Saviour, $5.04 ; Society for Promoting Religion and Learning, $2.88 ; For promoting Christianity among the Jews, $1 07. Total, $144.93.

General.—Domestic Missions, $5.55 : Foreign Missions, $3.63. Total, $9.18.

1, received. 3, died. 8, removed, 1. present number, 178; Public Services (Sundays, 122, Holy days, 39, other days, 162), 323; Holy Communion (public, 157, private, 2), 159; Sunday School, teachers, 7, pupils, 50; Catechizing, number of children, all, number of times, occasional; Number of sermons and addresses, 117.

Offerings.

Parochial. — Current expenses, including salaries, $1,036.96 ; Sunday School, $31.53, Increase and Improvement of Church Property, $28.70; Rental of Dunson House, net, $167.20; Repair Dunson House, $24.80. Total, $1,289 19.

Diocesan. — Diocesan Missions, $50; Salary of the Bishop, $20 ; Diocesan Fund, $30. Total, $100.

Total amount of Offerings, $1,389.19.

Property.

Condition of property, good.

Indebtedness, on Parish Building, $500; Church Improvements, $130; Other Indebtedness, arrears in current expenses, etc., $320.

Amount of salary pledged Rector, $1,000 and rent of Rectory.

Number of sittings in the Church, 230; all free.

ST. LUKE'S CHURCH, CAMBRIDGE.

Rector. The Rev. Frederick H. T. Horsfield.

Wardens. Henry C. Day, Robert Davis.

Vestrymen. William J. Davis, Thomas Le Grys, Robert S. Davis, John Moneypenny, M. D., J. Fennimore Niver, M. D.

Parochial.

Families, 25; Individuals (adults, 75, children, 10), 85; Baptisms, adult, 1; Confirmed, since last report. 2; Present number of confirmed persons, 60; Burials. 2; Communicants, admitted, 2, received, 1, present number, 50; Public Services (Sundays, 110, Holy days, 15, other days, 75), 200; Holy Communion (public, 25, private, 1), 26.

Offerings.

Parochial. — Current expenses, including salaries, $1,031; Sunday School, $20; Increase and Improvement of Church Property, $1,900; Ladies' Aid, $104; Sundry expenses, $50. Total, $3,105.

Diocesan. — Diocesan Missions, $266; Salary of the Bishop, $10; Diocesan Fund, $15; Archdeaconry of Troy, $89.28. Total, $380.28.

General. — For Bishop Coleman's work, $113.

Total amount of Offerings, $3,598.28.

Property.

Church and lot (estimated worth), $6,000.

Condition of property, excellent.

Amount of salary pledged Rector, $500.

Number of sittings in the Church, 200; all free.

Remarks.

During the past year generous friends of the Parish renovated the interior of the Church — carpets, pews, walls, windows, etc. With the same kindly assistance the congregation put the exterior of the Church in perfect repair. Very beautiful white and green Altar Cloths were also presented. Handsome oak choir chairs have been given.

The twenty-fifth anniversary of the laying of the corner-stone of the Parish Church was suitably commemorated on the eve and day of St. Peter. The summer meeting of the Archdeaconry of Troy was held here at same time. Owing to the much regretted absence of our Bishop, the Right Reverend the Bishop of Delaware was with us during these services, and made them and the Benedictions most impressive.

ST. PAUL'S CHURCH, GREENWICH.

Rector. The Rev. W. F. Parsons.

Wardens. Henry L. Mowry, William R. Hobbie.

Vestrymen. B. F. Kendall, George Tucker, H. B. Bates, Thomas Emerson, S. L. Stillman, W. P. Reynolds.

Parochial.

Families, 30 ; Individuals (adults, 100, children, 45), 145 : Baptisms (adult, 1, infants, 7), 8 ; Confirmed, since last report, 13 ; Present number of confirmed persons, about 53 ; Marriages, 2 ; Burials, 2 ; Communicants, last reported, 45, admitted, 13, died, 2, removed, 3, present number, 53 ; Public Services, Sundays, two from November to June and since then, Holy days, Good Friday, other days, Fridays during August and September ; Holy Communion, public, monthly since July 1 ; Sunday School, teachers, 4, pupils, 40.

Offerings.

Parochial. — Current expenses, including salaries, $550.84 ; Sunday School, $20.18. Total, $571.02.

Diocesan. — Diocesan Missions, $25 ; Salary of the Bishop, $2 ; Diocesan Fund, $15. Total, $42.

General. — Russian Relief Fund, $15.30.

Total amount of Offerings, $628.32.

Property.

Church and lot (estimated worth), $7,000.

Condition of property, good.

Indebtedness, $400.

Amount of salary pledged Rector, $300.

Number of sittings in the Church, 230.

Remarks.

This report is necessarily incomplete and not accurate in every particular.

THE NORTH GRANVILLE MISSION, NORTH GRANVILLE.

Missionary. The Rev. Charles H. Lancaster.

Treasurer. George B. Culver.

Parochial.

Families, 8 ; Individuals (adults, 24, children, 6), 30 ; Communicants, present number, 14 ; Public Services, Sundays, 21 ; Holy Communion, public, 4.

Offerings.

Parochial. — Current expenses, including salaries, $124.03 ; Special to Rector, $21. Total, $145.03.

Diocesan. — Diocesan Missions, $10 ; Salary of the Bishop, $4 ; Diocesan Fund, $3. Total, $17.

Total amount of Offerings, $162.03.

Property.

Organ and other furniture, $177.
Amount of salary pledged Missionary, $100.
Number of sittings in the Chapel, 100; all free.

ST. JOHN'S MISSION, DOLGEVILLE, HERKIMER COUNTY.*

Missionary. The Rev. Ernest Mariett.
Warden. Albert Kuehn.
Clerk. F. M. Barney, M. D.
Treasurer. Edward A. Brown.

Parochial.

Baptisms (adults, 3, infants, 6), 9 ; Confirmed, since last report, 7; Present number of confirmed persons, 15; Communicants, admitted, 7, received, 1, removed, 1, present number, 14 ; Public Services (Sundays, 50, Holy days, 2, other days, 25), 77; Holy Communion, public, 12; Sunday School, teachers, 1, pupils, 40; Catechizing, number of children, all, number of times, every Sunday.

Offerings.

Parochial.— Current expenses, including salaries, $547.77; Increase and Improvement of Church Property, $1,450 for new Church. Total, $1,997.77.
Diocesan.— Diocesan Missions, $5.
Total amount of Offerings, $2,002.77.

Property.

Church and lot (estimated worth), $4,850.
Indebtedness, on new Church, $2,900.

Remarks.

Sunday, October 30, 1892, the corner-stone of a new Church was laid. The first service at Dolgeville was held Whitsunday, 1891. The Church will be completed about April 1, 1893. It will cost about $3,500. The lot is the gift of Mr. Alfred Dolge. About $2,000 has been pledged by the people. They will need help in raising the balance. The Church building is to seat 240.

(B.)

PERSONAL REPORTS.

69 WEST ONE HUNDRED AND FIFTH ST., NEW YORK, *November 7. 1892.*

To the Right Rev. WM. CROSWELL DOANE, D. D., LL. D., *Bishop of Albany:*

My official acts since Dec. 1, 1891, when I resigned the charge of Christ Church, Gloversville, have been as follows:

Celebrations of the Holy Communion, 272; Baptisms (adults, 2, infant, 1), 3; Candidates prepared and presented for Confirmation, 10; Burials, 4; Sermons preached, 97; Daily offices of Morning or Evening Prayer, publicly said, 104. These acts have been performed in Churches and Chapels in the Dioceses of New York, Newark, Connecticut and Long Island. The baptisms, confirmations and burials have been duly recorded in the places where such ministrations were given.

Respectfully yours,

---

*Received too late to be printed in its place under

30

To the Right Rev. W. C. DOANE, D. D., LL. D., *Bishop of Albany:*

During the past summer season I officiated three times at Indian Lake. On one Sunday I read service in a cottage in Camp Sabael; on two Sundays I read service and preached in the Locke House, enjoying the hearty cooperation of the residents and of the summer visitors.

HENRY A. DOWS.

ST. LUKE'S HOSPITAL, NEW YORK, *November* 1, 1892.

To the Right Rev. the Bishop of Albany:

I hereby report that since resigning the Rectorship of Grace Church, Waterford, on June 1, 1892, I have been performing the duties of the Chaplaincy of St. Luke's Hospital, New York city.

Respectfully submitted,

CHARLES E. FREEMAN.

ALBANY, *November* 21, 1892.

DEAR BISHOP DOANE — During the past year, besides my regular work at St. Agnes' School, I have held services twenty-four times in vacant Parishes and Missions of the Diocese; and during the months of July and August, on Little Cranberry Island, in the Diocese of Maine. I have also assisted at many services in the Cathedral of All Saints, both on Sundays and week days.

Faithfully yours,

FREDERICK M. GRAY.

OGDENSBURG, N. Y., *November* 1, 1892.

RIGHT REVEREND SIR — My health during the past year has prevented me from the regular performance of ministerial duty. In accordance with your instructions, I have held myself to be under the direction of the Rector of this Parish, viz.: St. John's, Ogdensburg. I have therefore taken such duty as has been assigned me by him, and during his absence have been in charge of the Parish. The record of my ministerial acts has consequently been by him included in his Parochial Report for the present year.

Very respectfully, Right Reverend Sir, your obedient servant,

W. H. HARISON.

To the Bishop of Albany.

Right Rev. WILLIAM C. DOANE, D. D., LL. D.:

MY DEAR BISHOP — I beg to report that my year has been spent in the work of Rexleigh School, at Salem, N. Y. The School has in it, I trust, the elements that will, in time, do the Diocese honor.

I am grateful for your ever kind advice and encouragement and for the wide-spread favor with which the Churchmen meet every appeal of mine. I hope in time to see our dream of an establishment at Rexleigh realized and the Church endowed with a noble site and School. For this we shall ever pray; remaining always,

Dutifully yours,

JOHN H. HOUGHTON, *Priest and Rector.*

SALEM, N. Y., *November* 10, 1892.

I have to report to the Bishop and Convention such religious work as offered itself and my age and state of health permitted me to perform.

W. W. LORD.

COOPERSTOWN, 1892.

LAKE WORTH, FLORIDA, *November* 7, 1892.

MY DEAR BISHOP — My ministrations at the Church of the Good Shepherd, Raquette Lake, during the past season, extended from June 22 to September 26. The same loving interest in the Services of this Mission and all that pertains to its welfare has continued. The Mission has contributed for the season $50 to the Orphan House of the Holy Saviour, Cooperstown.

Faithfully yours,
J. N. MULFORD.

Rt. Rev. WM. C. DOANE, D. D., LL. D.:

MY DEAR BISHOP — From the first of last January until June I was wholly or largely incapacitated for any pastoral work.

Since July, inclusive, the Lord being my Helper, and through the kindness of our Rector, I have had the privilege of celebrating the Lord's Supper, and of assisting in the public worship of the Church quite regularly.

Affectionately yours,
GEORGE H. NICHOLLS.

HOOSICK FALLS, *November* 14, 1892.

REPORT OF THE REV. J. LIVINGSTON REESE, D. D., REGISTRAR OF THE GENERAL CONVENTION.

My resignation of St. Paul's Church, Albany, took effect February 17, 1892. My official acts in that Parish, both before and since my resignation, are included in the Parochial Report of the Rector.

234 THIRD ST., TROY, N. Y., *November* 2, 1892.

MY DEAR BISHOP — Up to Trinity Sunday, June 15th, of this year, I was engaged as instructor in the Seabury Divinity School, Faribault, Minn., and in Mission work every Sunday, in the city of St. Paul.

On the first Sunday after Trinity I took temporary charge of St. John's Parish, Troy, N. Y., where I have remained until this date.

I go from here, as you know, to become Assistant Minister of St. Paul's Church, Albany.

Faithfully yours,
GEORGE LYNDE RICHARDSON.

To the Right Rev. WM. C. DOANE, D. D., LL. D., *Bishop of Albany.*

GLENHAM, N. Y., *November* 16, 1892.

MY DEAR BISHOP — I respectfully beg to report that during the past year I have three times officiated in the Diocese, and frequently in the Diocese of New York, and have assisted the Clergy in this and neighboring Parishes on Sundays and Holy and Saints' days.

Very truly yours in the Church,
L. H. SCHUBERT.

The Right Rev. DR. DOANE, *Bishop of Albany.*

4 WEST FORTY-EIGHTH STREET, NEW YORK, *November* 7, 1892.

MY DEAR BISHOP — I received a notice of the meeting of the Convention of the Diocese of Albany, which reminded me that I must report my whereabouts.

Last winter and spring I preached and celebrated and read the services a number of times in the English Church at Vevey, Switzerland. I also assisted in the American Chapel in Dresden, Germany.

Since my return I ministered and preached in Cherry Valley, Cambridge and Albany. I baptized seven children in All Saints' Cathedral, Albany.

DANSVILLE, N. Y., *October 2, 1892.*

RIGHT REVEREND AND DEAR SIR — Since my resignation of the Rectorship of Calvary Church, Cairo, last June, I have been unable to do any work. The following is a list of services performed from November 15, 1891, to June 15, 1892: Holy Communion (public, 34, private, 1), 35; Services (Sundays, 51, weeks days, 56), 107; Baptisms (infants, 5, adult, 1), 6; Marriages, 1; Burials, 2.

Faithfully yours,

CHAUNCEY VIBBARD.

RT. REV. AND DEAR SIR — Sojourning at Maple Grove, I continued during the first half of the past year to supplement the bi-monthly services in St. Stephen's Chapel here of the Missionary residing in another town. To my loss of voice has been added almost entire loss of sight. Some kind friends, on my completion of three score and ten years in September, proposed to mark the event by contributions toward the extinction of the Chapel debt. My friends abroad so responded that, with small remittance of interest from Rev. H. Gates, $50 were paid in October, and full discharge in January is thus secured. I had thought my seven years reviving Christ Church, W. Burlington, my concluding charity of that sort. But Providence had reserved this further pleasure for me of participating in the relief of St. Stephen's in my native hamlet.

Ever truly yours,

DANIEL WASHBURN.

CLIFTON FORGE, VA., *November 1, 1892.*

Rt. Rev. W. C. DOANE, D. D., *Bishop of Albany :*

MY DEAR BISHOP — I resigned the Parish of Rouse's Point on July 1 last; during the previous six months I had also temporary charge of Champlain, the Rev. W. D. U. Shearman having resigned that Parish last Christmas. Since then I have made a visit to England and returned and taken up work in the Diocese of Southern Virginia, as Rector of Clifton Forge and Longdale.

Yours faithfully,

H. L. WOOD.

REPORT OF THE TRUSTEES OF THE CORNING FOUNDATION FOR CHRISTIAN WORK IN THE DIOCESE OF ALBANY.

The work of the institutions under the control of the trustees has been quietly but steadily carried on. The usual meetings of the board have been held. On December 18, 1891, Mr. Oscar L. Hascy was elected a trustee to fill the place made vacant by the resignation of Mr. James G. Averell. At a special meeting of the board January 17, 1892, the death of Hon. Walter A. Wood was announced, and a minute to his memory (which will be printed elsewhere in the Journal) ordered to be entered on the records of the board. June 6, 1892, Gen. Amasa J. Parker was elected a trustee to fill the vacancy caused by the death of Mr. Wood. At the same meeting the annual charge for tuition in the school was increased from $400 to $500. Number of teachers and lecturers in the school, 44; pupils, 206.

THOMAS B. FULCHER,

November 1, 1892.   *Secretary of the Board.*

ANNUAL REPORT OF THE CHILD'S HOSPITAL.

Children received in the Child's Hospital during the year, 220; children received at St. Margaret's House, 128. Gifts from Parishes as reported in parochial reports, $1,030.70.

ANNUAL REPORT OF THE GIRLS' FRIENDLY SOCIETY FOR AMERICA, DIOCESE OF ALBANY.

Number of branches, 7: St. Paul's, Troy; St. John's, Ogdensburg; Christ, Coopers-town; St. Mark's, Hoosick Falls; Epiphany, Bath-on-the-Hudson; Emmanuel, Little Falls; Christ, Herkimer.

Number of Working Associates, 45; Honorary Associates, 25; Members, 150; Candidates, 92.

Money raised, contributed and expended, $377.

A. L. WEISE,
TROY, N. Y., *January 26, 1893.*   *Diocesan President.*

ANNUAL REPORT OF THE WOMAN'S AUXILIARY TO THE BOARD OF MISSIONS IN THE DIOCESE OF ALBANY.

Number of Parish branches reporting, 45.
Number of Junior Auxiliaries reporting, 43.
Number of boxes sent, 110.
Valuation of boxes, $5,647.42.
Money given, $1,891.02.
Total money and boxes, $7,538.44.
Balance on hand May 1, 1892, $28.43.

THE DIOCESAN LENDING LIBRARY.

Number of volumes in Library, 991.
Books loaned, 158.
Number of readers, 66.
Total amount of moneys received, $71.14.
Total amount of moneys expended, $66.38.
Balance on hand, $4.76.
The Library needs both funds and books.

THE CHURCH PERIODICAL CLUB, DIOCESE OF ALBANY.

This club receives magazines and books and distributes them for circulation among Clergymen and Mission stations. (There are branches in thirty-seven Dioceses).

Librarians, 13.
Contributors, 162.
Periodicals, 259.
Books sent to date, 393.
Sunday School books sent to date, 126.
Bibles sent to date, 4.
Prayer books sent to date, 44.
Hymnals sent to date, 11.
Sunday School papers sent regularly, 29.
Sunday School leaflets sent regularly, 190.
Christmas cards sent to date, 1446.
Easter cards sent to date, 594.
Catechisms sent to date, 150.
Christmas carols sent to date, 1111.
Easter carols sent to date, 30.
Old periodicals sent to date, 12,034.

ANNUAL REPORT OF THE CHURCH HOME IN THE CITY OF TROY.

Balance on hand at last report..	$127 95
Amount received since...	2,915 51
Total receipts..	$3,043 46
Expenditures...	3,485 37
Shortage...	$441 91

Extraordinary repairs account for the shortage.
Amount in the Permanent Fund, $30,092.70.
Average number of inmates, 11.

(C.)

LIST OF PARISHES IN UNION WITH THE CONVENTION OF THE DIOCESE
OF ALBANY, WITH THE DATES OF THEIR ADMISSION.*

ALBANY COUNTY.

St. Peter's, Albany, 1787; Trinity, Rensselaerville, 1811; St. Paul's, Albany, 1829; St. John's, Cohoes, 1831; Trinity, West Troy, 1834; Trinity, Albany, 1840; Grace, Albany, 1846; Holy Innocents, Albany, 1850; St. Mark's, Green Island, 1867; Cathedral of All Saints, Albany, 1874.

CLINTON COUNTY.

Trinity, Plattsburgh, 1830; Christ, Rouse's Point, 1853; St. John's, Champlain, 1853.

COLUMBIA COUNTY.

Christ, Hudson, 1794; St. John's, Stockport, 1845; St. Paul's, Kinderhook, 1851; Trinity, Claverack, 1856; Our Saviour, Lebanon Springs, 1882; All Saints', Hudson, 1888; St. Barnabas', Stottville, 1890; St. Mark's, Philmont, 1891.

DELAWARE COUNTY.

St. Peter's, Hobart, 1796; St. John's, Delhi, 1822; Christ, Walton, 1831; St. Paul's, Franklin, 1866; Christ, Deposit, 1871.

ESSEX COUNTY.

Church of the Cross, Ticonderoga, 1840; St. John's, Essex, 1853; St. Paul's, Keeseville, 1853; Christ, Port Henry, 1873.

FRANKLIN COUNTY.

St. Mark's, Malone, 1831; St. Peter's, Brush's Mills, 1870.

FULTON COUNTY.

St. John's, Johnstown, 1796.

GREENE COUNTY.

St. Luke's, Catskill, 1801; Christ, Coxsackie, 1806; Trinity, Athens, 1806; St. Paul's, Oak Hill, 1816; Christ, Greenville, 1825; Trinity, Ashland, 1826; Calvary, Cairo, 1832.

HERKIMER COUNTY.

Trinity, Fairfield, 1807; Grace, Norway, 1819. Emmanuel, Little Falls, 1823; Christ, Herkimer, 1854; St. Augustine's, Ilion, 1870; Grace, Mohawk, 1886.

* Dates earlier than 1868 are those of admission to union with the Convention of the Diocese of New York before the organization of the Diocese of Albany.

MONTGOMERY COUNTY.

St. Ann's, Amsterdam, 1836; Zion, Fonda, 1867.

OTSEGO COUNTY.

Zion, Morris, 1793; St. Luke's, Richfield, 1803; St. Matthew's, Unadilla, 1810; Christ, Cooperstown, 1812; Christ, Butternuts, 1834; Immanuel, Otego, 1836; St. Timothy's, Westford, 1839; Grace, Cherry Valley, 1846; St. John's, Richfield Springs, 1850; St. John's, Portlandville, 1869; Christ, West Burlington, 1871; St. Paul's, East Springfield, 1871; St. James', Oneonta, 1877.

RENSSELAER COUNTY.

St. Paul's, Troy, 1807; Trinity, Lansingburgh, 1807; St. John's, Troy, 1831; Christ, Troy, 1837; St. Mark's, Hoosick Falls, 1840; Trinity, Schaghticoke, 1846; Messiah, Greenbush, 1853; St. Luke's, Troy, 1867.

ST. LAWRENCE COUNTY.

St. John's, Ogdensburgh, 1820; St. Paul's, Waddington, 1824; Christ, Morristown, 1833; Trinity, Potsdam, 1835; Grace, Canton, 1836; Grace, Norfolk, 1844; Trinity, Bouverneur, 1869; St. John's, Massena, 1870; St. Luke's, Lisbon, 1871; Zion, Colton, 1885.

SARATOGA COUNTY.

Christ, Ballston Spa, 1787; St. John's, Stillwater, 1796; St. Paul's, Charlton, 1805; Grace, Waterford, 1810; St. Luke's, Mechanicville, 1830; Bethesda, Saratoga Springs, 1830; St. Stephen's, Schuylerville, 1846; Calvary, Burnt Hills, 1850.

SCHENECTADY COUNTY.

Christ, Duanesburgh, 1789 ; St. George's, Schenectady, 1792; Christ, Schenectady, 1869.

WARREN COUNTY.

Messiah, Glens Falls, 1840; St. James', Caldwell, 1855 ; Holy Cross, Warrensburgh, 1865 ; St. Mary's, Luzerne, 1867.

WASHINGTON COUNTY.

Zion, Sandy Hill, 1813 ; Trinity, Granville, 1815 ; St. James', Fort Edward, 1845 ; St. Paul's, Salem, 1860 : Trinity, Whitehall, 1866 ; St. Luke's, Cambridge, 1867 ; St. Paul's, Greenwich, 1875.

ORGANIZED MISSIONS.

ALBANY COUNTY.

Good Shepherd, Bethlehem ; St. Andrew's, West Troy.

CLINTON COUNTY.

St. Paul's, Mooer's Forks , St. Peter's, Ellenburgh ; St. Paul's, Ellenburgh Centre; St. Luke's, Chazy , St. John's, Salmon River ; all with consecrated buildings.

COLUMBIA COUNTY.

St. Luke's, Chatham ; St. John's in the Wilderness, Copake.

DELAWARE COUNTY.

Emmanuel, Griffin's Corners ; Grace, Stamford.

ESSEX COUNTY.

Emmanuel, Mineville; St. James', Ausable Forks, both with consecrated buildings : Good Shepherd, Bloomingdale.

FRANKLIN COUNTY.

St. Mark's, West Bangor; St. James', Hogansburgh; St. John's in the Wilderness, St. Regis Lake; St. Luke the Beloved Physician, Saranac Lake, all with consecrated buildings.

FULTON COUNTY.

Christ, Gloversville.

GREENE COUNTY.

Gloria Dei, Palenville ; St. John the Evangelist, Tannersville.

HAMILTON COUNTY.

Good Shepherd, Racquette Lake ; Of the Transfiguration, Blue Mountain Lake.

HERKIMER COUNTY.

Of the Memorial, Middleville ; Of the Good Shepherd, Cullen ; both with consecrated buildings.

MONTGOMERY COUNTY.

Holy Cross, Fort Plain; Good Shepherd, Canajoharie; St. Columba's, St. Johnsville.

OTSEGO COUNTY.

St. Mary's, Springfield Centre, with consecrated building; St. Simon and St. Jude's, Worcester.

RENSSELAER COUNTY.

St. Giles', Castleton ; Holy Name, Boyntonville, with consecrated building.

ST. LAWRENCE COUNTY.

Trinity Chapel, Morley; St. Thomas', Lawrenceville, both with consecrated buildings; Grace, Louisville Landing ; St. Joseph's, West Stockholm; All Saints', Barnhart's Island; St. Andrew's, Norwood.

SARATOGA COUNTY.

St. John's, East Line; Grace, Jonesville; All Saints', Round Lake, all with consecrated buildings.

WARREN COUNTY.

Good Shepherd, Chester; St. Paul's, Bartonville; St. Sacrament, Bolton, all with consecrated buildings.

PARISHES NOT IN UNION WITH THE CONVENTION.

ALBANY COUNTY.

Emmanuel, South Westerlo.

COLUMBIA COUNTY.

St. Luke's, Clermont, incorporated July 12, 1859.

ESSEX COUNTY.

St. Andrew's, Schroon Lake.

GREENE COUNTY.

Grace, Prattsville.

HERKIMER COUNTY.

St. Alban's, Frankfort.

OTSEGO COUNTY.

Church of the Holy Spirit, Schenevus.

RENSSELAER COUNTY.

Holy Cross, Troy; Free Church of the Ascension, Troy; Free Church of the Epiphany, East Albany; All Saints', Hoosac; St. Barnabas', Troy.

SARATOGA COUNTY.

St. John's, Conklingville.

SCHOHARIE COUNTY.

St. Luke's, Middleburgh; St. Andrew's, Schoharie; Trinity, Sharon Springs.

WARREN COUNTY.

Christ, Pottersville.

WASHINGTON COUNTY.

Grace, Crandell's Corners.

PLACES OTHER THAN PARISHES OR ORGANIZED MISSIONS, WHERE SERVICES OF THE CHURCH ARE HELD.

ALBANY COUNTY.

St. Margaret's, Menands.

CLINTON COUNTY.

Dannemora; Standish.

COLUMBIA COUNTY.

Chatham; St. James', Rossman's Mills; Canaan.

DELAWARE COUNTY.

Esperance; St. Paul's, Sidney; Bloomville; Hamden.

ESSEX COUNTY.

Crown Point; Good Shepherd, Elizabethtown; Lewis; Addison Junction; Keene Valley; Westport.

FRANKLIN COUNTY.

Good Shepherd, Santa Clara; Merciful Saviour, St. Regis Falls; Holy Innocents. Brandon; Fort Covington.

GREENE COUNTY.

Hunter.

HAMILTON COUNTY.

Locke House, Indian Lake.

HERKIMER COUNTY.

Poland; St. John's, Dolgeville.

OTSEGO COUNTY.

Morris Memorial Chapel; Noblesville; Maple Grove; Mt. Vision; Edmeston.

RENSSELAER COUNTY.

St. Stephen's, Lansingburgh; St. Paul's, Raymertown.

ST. LAWRENCE COUNTY.

Cranberry Lake; Pierpont Centre.

SARATOGA COUNTY.

St. Luke's, Milton Centre; West Charlton.

SCHOHARIE COUNTY.

Cobleskill.

WARREN COUNTY.

St. Paul's, Harrisena; Grace Memorial Chapel, Sabbath-day Point.

WASHINGTON COUNTY.

North Granville; Adamsville; Smith's Basin.

NON-REPORTING CLERGY.

The Rev. P. St. M. Podmore, The Rev. J. McC. W~~indo~~

NON-REPORTING PARISHES.

Grace, Norway.

NON-REPORTING CLERGY AND PARISHES FROM THE JOURNAL OF 1890.

In obedience to the instructions of the Convention (see Journal 1891, p. 93), letters were sent to the officers of those Parishes from whom no reports were received at the Convention of 1890. One reply was received from St. Peter's Church, Brushton, assigning absence of Missionary as the reason for failure to report. From Chateaugay and Westford, no replies were received.

(D.)

COLLECTIONS ON ACCOUNT OF BISHOP'S SALARY, 1892.

	Annual Payment.
Albany County.	
Cathedral of All Saints, Albany	$150 00
St. Peter's, Albany	150 00
St. Paul's, Albany	100 00
Trinity, Albany	20 00
Grace, Albany	24 00
Holy Innocents', Albany	30 00
St. John's, Cohoes	Bond.
Trinity, West Troy	40 00
Trinity, Rensselaerville	8 00
St. Mark's, Green Island	12 00
Columbia County.	
Christ Church, Hudson	66 00
St. John's, Stockport	26 00
St. Paul's, Kinderhook	36 00
St. John's, Copake	
Trinity, Claverack	6 00
Church of Our Saviour, Lebanon Springs	6 00
St. Luke's, Clermont	4 00
St. Barnabas', Stottville	26 00
All Saints', Hudson	6 00
St. Mark's, Philmont	6 00
St. Luke's, Chatham	1 00
Clinton County.	
Trinity, Plattsburgh	60 00
Christ Church, Rouse's Point	12 00
St. John's, Champlain	6 00
Centreville and Chateaugay	
St. Peter's, Ellenburgh	4 00
St. John's, Salmon River	
Delaware County.	
St. Peter's, Hobart	10 00
St. John's, Delhi	40 00
Christ, Walton	20 00
St. Paul's, Franklin	16 00
Christ Church, Deposit	6 00
Grace, Stamford	6 00
St. Paul's, Sidney	2 00

	Annual Payment.
Essex County.	
Of the Cross, Ticonderoga	$10 00
St. John's, Essex	16 00
Christ Church, Port Henry	10 00
Emmanuel, Mineville	
St. James', Ausable Forks	16 00
St. Andrew's, Schroon Lake	4 00
St. Paul's, Keeseville	10 00
Fulton County.	
St. John's, Johnstown	50 00
Redeemer, Northampton	
Christ Church, Gloversville	10 00
Franklin County.	
St. Mark's, Malone	36 00
St. Peter's, Brushton	8 00
St. Mark's, West Bangor	4 00
St. James', Hogansburgh	8 00
St. John's, St. Regis	
St. Luke's, Saranac	6 00
Greene County.	
St. Luke's, Catskill	30 00
Christ Church, Coxsackie	12 00
Trinity, Athens	10 00
St. Paul's, Oak Hill	
Christ Church, Greeneville	6 00
Trinity, Ashland	4 00
Calvary, Cairo	6 00
Gloria Dei, Palenville	8 00
Grace, Prattsville	
Herkimer County.	
Emmanuel, Little Falls	40 00
Christ Church, Herkimer	16 00
Grace, Mohawk	6 00
St. Augustine's, Ilion	12 00
Trinity, Fairfield	4 00
Memorial, Middleville	6 00
Grace, Norway	
Montgomery County.	
St. Ann's, Amsterdam	
Zion, Fonda	12 00
Good Shepherd, Canajoharie	6 00
Holy Cross, Fort Plain	2 00
Otsego County.	
Zion, Morris	24 00
St. Matthew's, Unadilla	16 00
Christ Church, Cooperstown	80 00
Christ Church, Gilbertsville	6 00
Immanuel, Otego	6 00
St. Timothy's, Westford	
St. John's, Portlandville	

	Annual Payment.
Otsego County — Continued.	
Grace, Cherry Valley............	$24 50
St. Paul's, East Springfield............	10 00
St. John's, Richfield Springs.....	16 00
Christ Church, West Burlington.....	6 00
St. James', Oneonta......	10 00
St. Stephen's Chapel.....	1 50
Holy Spirit, Schenevus.....	4 00
Rensselaer County.	
St. Paul's, Troy.....	200 00
St. John's, Troy.....	176 00
Christ Church, Troy.....	124 00
Holy Cross, Troy.....	50 00
Ascension, Troy.....	10 00
St. Luke's, Troy.....	10 00
St. Barnabas', Troy.....	6 00
Trinity, Lansingburgh.....	60 00
Trinity, Schaghticoke.....	6 00
Messiah, Greenbush.....	10 00
Epiphany, East Albany.....	5 00
St. Mark's, Hoosick Falls.....	40 00
All Saints', Hoosic.....	6 00
St. Lawrence County.	
St. John's, Ogdensburgh.....	100 00
St. Paul's, Waddington.....	12 00
Christ Church, Morristown.....	20 00
Trinity, Potsdam.....	50 00
Grace, Canton.....	14 00
Grace, Norfolk.....	
St. Andrew's, Norwood.....	3 50
Trinity, Gouverneur.....	26 00
St. John's, Massena.....	8 00
Trinity, Morley.....	8 00
Grace, Louisville Landing.....	
St. Thomas', Lawrenceville.....	
St. Luke's, Lisbon.....	
Zion, Colton.....	4 00
St. Philip's, Madrid.....	
All Saints', Barnhart Island.....	
Saratoga County.	
Christ Church, Ballston Spa.....	42 00
St. John's, East Line.....	
St. Paul's, Charlton.....	
Grace, Waterford.....	
Bethesda, Saratoga Springs.....	70 00
St. Stephen's, Schuylerville.....	
Calvary, Burnt Hills.....	12 00
St. John's, Conklingville.....	4 00
St. John's, Stillwater.....	4 00
St. Luke's, Mechanicville.....	4 00
Grace, Jonesville.....	2 00

	Annual Payment.
Schenectady County.	
St. George's, Schenectady	$60 00
Christ Church, Schenectady	10 00
Christ Church, Duanesburgh	50 00
Schoharie County.	
St. Luke's, Middleburgh	8 00
Trinity, Sharon Springs	20 00
Warren County.	
Messiah, Glens Falls	40 00
Harrisena	
Holy Cross, Warrensburgh	88 00
St. Mary's, Luzerne	8 00
Good Shepherd, Chestertown	6 00
St. John's, Conklingville	
St. Sacrament, Bolton	10 00
St. James', Caldwell	10 00
Washington County.	
Zion, Sandy Hill	80 00
Trinity, Granville	6 00
Mission, North Granville	5 00
St. James', Fort Edward	
St. Paul's, Salem	22 50
Trinity, Whitehall	20 00
St. Luke's, Cambridge	10 00
St. Paul's, Greenwich	4 00
Total	$2,906 00

(E.)

OFFICERS OF THE DIOCESE, TRUSTEES, ETC.

The Right Rev. William Croswell Doane, D. D., LL. D., *President.*
The Rev. William C. Prout, Schenectady, *Secretary.*
The Rev. Thomas B. Fulcher, Albany, *Assistant Secretary.*
The Rev. Frederick S. Sill, Cohoes, *Registrar.*
Mr. Selden E. Marvin, Albany, *Treasurer.*

THE STANDING COMMITTEE.

The Rev. J. Ireland Tucker, S. T. D., Troy, *President;* the Rev. Fenwick M. Cookson, Glens Falls, *Secretary;* the Rev. Wilford L. Robbins, D. D., the Rev. James Caird, Mr. Norman B. Squires, Mr. Henry S. Wynkoop, Mr. John I. Thompson, Mr. J. H. Van Antwerp.

DEPUTIES TO THE GENERAL CONVENTION.

The Rev. W. W. Battershall, D. D., the Rev. J. D. Morrison, D. D., LL. D., the Rev. Joseph Carey, S. T. D., the Rev. Charles C. Edmunds, Jr., Mr. G. Pomeroy Keese, Mr. Erastus Corning, Mr. T. Streatfeild Clarkson, Mr. John Hobart Warren.

PROVISIONAL DEPUTIES TO THE GENERAL CONVENTION.

The Rev. Edgar A. Enos, D. D., the Rev. R. M. Kirby, D. D., the Rev. C. S. Olmsted, the Rev. George D. Silliman, Mr. Leslie Pell-Clarke, Mr. Spencer Trask, Mr. Edward Sheldon, Mr. Thomas L. Harison.

DEPUTIES TO THE FEDERATE COUNCIL.

The Rev. J. Ireland Tucker, S. T. D., the Rev. Fenwick M. Cookson, the Rev. George D. Silliman, the Rev. Wilford L. Robbins, D. D., the Rev. C. C. Edmunds, Jr., the Rev. S. M. Griswold, the Rev. Wm. H. Harison, D. D., the Rev. Ernest Mariett, Mr. N. B. Warren, Mr. G. Pomeroy Keese, Mr. R. H. Cushney, Mr. Robert Earl, Mr. J. I. Thompson, Mr. F. J. Fitch, Mr. Charles E. Patterson, Mr. J. D. Henderson.

TRUSTEE OF THE GENERAL THEOLOGICAL SEMINARY UNTIL NOVEMBER 15, 1893.

The Rev. Joseph Carey, S. T. D.

MEMBERS OF THE MISSIONARY COUNCIL.

The Rev. J. Philip B. Pendleton, Mr. Benjamin H. Hall.

TRUSTEES OF THE EPISCOPAL FUND.

Mr. J. H. Van Antwerp, Albany, *Treasurer;* Mr. W. Bayard Van Rensselaer, Mr. Charles W. Tillinghast, 2d, Mr. Dean Sage, Mr. Robert C. Pruyn.

TRUSTEES OF THE FUND FOR AGED AND INFIRM CLERGYMEN.

The Right Rev. William Croswell Doane, D. D., LL. D., Mr. Selden E. Marvin, *Treasurer;* Mr. Norman B. Squires, Mr. Robert S. Oliver, Mr. J. J. Tillinghast.

TRUSTEES OF THE FUND FOR WIDOWS AND ORPHANS OF DECEASED CLERGYMEN.

The Right Rev. William Croswell Doane, D. D., LL. D., Mr. Selden E. Marvin, *Treasurer;* Mr. J. W. Tillinghast, Mr. C. W. Tillinghast, Mr. Amasa J. Parker.

TRUSTEES OF THE ORPHAN HOUSE OF THE HOLY SAVIOUR, COOPERSTOWN.

The Right Rev. William Croswell Doane, D. D., LL. D., *President.*
The Rev. Charles S. Olmsted, Cooperstown, *Secretary.*
Mr. Leslie Pell-Clarke, Springfield Centre, *Treasurer.*
Miss Susan Fenimore Cooper, Cooperstown, *Superintendent.*

TRUSTEES

The Rev. Thaddeus A. Snively, Mr. T. Streatfeild Clarkson, W. T. Bassett, M. D., until Convention, 1893.
The Rev. Walton W. Battershall, D. D., the Rev. J. Philip B. Pendleton, S. T. B., Mr. G. Pomeroy Keese, until Convention, 1894.
Mr. A. B. Cox, Mr Leslie Pell-Clarke, Mr. G Hyde Clarke, until Convention, 1895.

TRUSTEES OF THE DIOCESE OF ALBANY.

The Right Rev. William Croswell Doane, D D., LL. D., *President*
Mr. A B. Cox, Cherry Valley, *Secretary.*
Mr Benjamin H. Hall, Troy, *Treasurer.*

TRUSTEES

The Rev Charles S Olmsted, until 1893.
Mr Abram B. Cox, until 1893.
The Rev J D Morrison, D D., LL D , until 1894.

Mr. Levi Hasbrouck, until 1894.
The Rev. Frederick S. Sill, until 1895.
Mr. John H. Bagley, until 1895.
The Rev. Joseph Carey, S. T. D., until 1896.
Mr. Benjamin H. Hall, until 1896.

COMMITTEE ON THE INCORPORATION AND ADMISSION OF CHURCHES.

The Rev. J. Philip B. Pendleton, S. T. B., Mr. Richard H. Cushney, Mr. John H. Bagley.

COMMITTEE ON THE CONSTITUTION AND CANONS.

The Rev. J. W. Stewart, the Rev. R. M. Kirby, D. D., the Rev. Edgar A. Enos, D. D., the Rev. Charles M. Nickerson, D. D., Mr. James Gibson, Mr. J. D. Henderson, Mr. R. M. Townsend.

· COMMITTEE ON THE SALARY OF THE BISHOP.

The Rev. Joseph Carey, S. T. D., the Rev. W. W. Battershall, D. D., Mr. J. J. Tillinghast, Mr. Erastus Corning, Mr. J. W. Tillinghast, Mr. W. W. Rousseau, Mr. John I. Thompson, Mr. Spencer Trask. *Secretary*, Mr. W. W. Rousseau, Troy.

COMMITTEE ON THE OBSERVANCE OF THE TWENTY-FIFTH ANNIVERSARY OF THE CONSECRATION OF THE FIRST BISHOP OF ALBANY.

The Rev. J. Ireland Tucker, S. T. D., the Rev. Walton W. Battershall, D. D., the Rev. Wilford L. Robbins, D. D., the Rev. J. D. Morrison, D. D., LL. D., the Rev. Joseph Carey, S. T. D., the Rev. James Caird, the Rev. R. M. Kirby, D. D., the Rev. Fenwick M. Cookson, the Rev. Charles S. Olmsted, the Rev. Edgar A. Enos, D. D., the Rev. C. M. Nickerson, D. D., the Rev. S. M. Griswold, Mr. John I. Thompson, Mr. A. B. Cox, Mr. Erastus Corning, Mr Joseph M. Warren, Gen. Selden E. Marvin. Mr. T. Streatfeild Clarkson, Mr. L. Averill Carter, Prof. Sidney G. Ashmore, Mr John Keyes Paige, Mr. G. Pomeroy Keese, the Hon. William A. Sackett, Mr. Leslie Pell-Clarke, Mr. Nathan B. Warren.

COMMITTEE ON THE DIOCESAN FUND AND MILEAGE OF THE CLERGY.

The Rev. Sheldon M. Griswold, Mr. George Low, Mr. Charles H. Upham, Mr. James I. Younglove.

COMMISSION ON THE CLERICAL PENSION SYSTEM.

The Rt. Rev. the Bishop of the Diocese, the Rev. J. D. Morrison, D. D., LL. D., the Rev. George G. Carter, S. T. D., Mr. Selden E. Marvin, Mr. Levi Hasbrouck, Mr. Leslie Pell-Clarke.

THE BOARD OF MISSIONS.

The Right Rev. William Croswell Doane, D. D., LL. D., *President.*
The Rev. Charles Temple, *Secretary.*
Mr. Selden E. Marvin, *Treasurer.*

ARCHDEACONRY OF ALBANY.

The Rev. W. W. Battershall, D. D., Mr. J. H. Van Antwerp.

ARCHDEACONRY OF TROY.

The Rev. F. M. Cookson, Mr. George A. Walker,

ARCHDEACONRY OF THE SUSQUEHANNA.

The Rev. Robert N. Parke, D. D., Mr. Robert M. Townsend.

ARCHDEACONRY OF OGDENSBURG.

The Rev. R. M. Kirby, D. D., Mr. T. Streatfeild Clarkson,

DIOCESE AT LARGE.

The Rev. Charles Temple, Mr. William Kemp.

ARCHDEACONRIES.

FIRST. ARCHDEACONRY OF ALBANY.

Albany, Greene, Columbia, Schenectady, Montgomery, Fulton, Hamilton and
Herkimer counties.
The Rev. Frederick S. Sill, *Archdeacon.*
The Rev. Richmond Shreve, D. D., *Secretary.*
The Rev. E. Bayard Smith, *Treasurer.*

SECOND. ARCHDEACONRY OF TROY.

Rensselaer, Saratoga, Washington, Warren, Clinton and Essex counties.
The Rev. Joseph Carey, S. T. D., *Archdeacon.*
The Rev. George D. Silliman, *Secretary.*
Mr. Charles W. Tillinghast, 2d, *Treasurer.*

THIRD. ARCHDEACONRY OF THE SUSQUEHANNA.

Delaware, Otsego and Schoharie counties.
The Rev. Charles M. Olmsted, *Archdeacon.*
The Rev. Richmond H. Gesner, *Secretary and Treasurer.*

FOURTH. ARCHDEACONRY OF OGDENSBURG.

St. Lawrence and Franklin counties.
The Rev. J. D. Morrison, D. D., LL. D., *Archdeacon.*
The Rev. Charles Temple, *Secretary.*
Mr. T. Streatfeild Clarkson, *Treasurer.*

EXAMINING CHAPLAINS.

The Rev. J. Ireland Tucker, S. T. D., the Rev. Joseph Carey, S. T. D., the Rev.
J. D. Morrison, D. D., LL. D., the Rev. W. N. Irish, the Rev. Thomas B. Fulcher,
B. D., the Rev. Edgar A. Enos, D. D., the Rev. William G. W. Lewis, the Rev.
Wilford L. Robbins, D. D., the Rev. G. H. S. Walpole, the Rev. George B. Johnson,
the Rev. George G. Carter, S. T. D.

THE BIBLE AND COMMON PRAYER BOOK SOCIETY OF ALBANY AND ITS VICINITY.

The Right Rev. William Croswell Doane, D. D., LL. D., *President.*
The Rev. J. Ireland Tucker, S. T. D., *First Vice-President.*
The Rev. W. W. Battershall, D. D., *Second Vice-President.*
The Rev. J. W. Stewart, *Third Vice-President.*
The Rev. Henry R. Freeman, Troy, *Corresponding Secretary.*
The Rev. Richmond Shreve, D. D., *Recording Secretary.*
Mr. Henry B. Dauchy, Troy, *Treasurer.*

MANAGERS.

Messrs. J. H. Van Antwerp, A. A. Van Vorst, George W. Gibbons, Joseph W. Tillinghast, Francis N. Mann, George A. Wells, John H. Hulsapple, Marcus T. Hun, William C. Buell, John Horrocks, E. G. Dorlan, George B. Warren.

Applications for books may be made to the *Corresponding Secretary*, the Rev. Henry R. Freeman, Troy.

All contributions and donations should be sent to the *Treasurer*, Mr. H B. Dauchy, Troy.

(F.)

DIOCESAN BRANCHES OF GENERAL SOCIETIES.

THE DIOCESAN BRANCH OF THE WOMAN'S AUXILIARY TO THE BOARD OF MISSIONS.

President. Mrs. Melvil Dewey, 315 Madison avenue, Albany.

Vice-Presidents. Mrs. Payne, Schenectady; Mrs. McEwen, Saratoga Springs.

Recording Secretary. Miss S. B. Purdy, Troy.

Corresponding Secretary. Miss Alice Lacy, Albany.

Treasurer. Mrs. Smith S. Fine, Albany.

Managers.

For the Archdeaconry of Albany: Miss Tweddle, Menand's road, Albany, for Albany, Montgomery and Fulton counties; Mrs. A. Van Nostrand, Schenectady, for Greene, Columbia, Schenectady, Hamilton and Herkimer counties.

For the Archdeaconry of Troy: Miss Mary E. Gilbert, 189 Second street, Troy, for Rensselaer, Washington and Saratoga counties; Mrs. Wm. S. Wheeler, Ballston Spa, for Warren, Essex and Clinton counties.

For the Archdeaconry of the Susquehanna: Miss E. J. Hughes, Gilbertsville, for Otsego and Schoharie counties; Miss Laura Gay, Walton, for Delaware county.

For the Archdeaconry of Ogdensburg: . for Franklin county; Mrs. Thomas L Knap, Ogdensburg, for St. Lawrence county.

DIOCESAN LENDING LIBRARY COMMITTEE.

Mrs. Melvil Dewey, *Chairman*, 315 Madison avenue, Albany; Miss E. W. Boyd, *Treasurer*, St. Agnes' School, Albany.

CHURCH PERIODICAL CLUB, DIOCESAN CORRESPONDENT.

Miss Mary F. Burt, Rensselaerville.

THE DIOCESAN BRANCH OF THE CHURCH TEMPERANCE SOCIETY.

Delegates to the General Council. The Rev. T. A. Snively, Troy ; Mr. Henry J. Estcourt, Schenectady.

Diocesan Committee.

Clerical — The Rev. W. W. Battershall, D. D., Albany ; the Rev. Joseph N. Mulford ; the Rev. George D. Silliman, Hoosick Falls ; the Rev. Hobart Cooke, Plattsburgh.

Lay — Messrs. Smith Fine, Albany ; William Kemp, Troy ; R. C. McEwen, M. D., Saratoga ; Henry C. Day, Cambridge ; James Rogers, Ausable Forks ; Charles Ashley, Ogdensburg.

FUNDS TO WHICH OFFERINGS ARE REQUIRED BY CANON, AND THE NAMES OF THE TREASURERS TO WHOM THE SAME SHOULD BE SENT.

Diocesan Fund. Mr. S. E. Marvin, Albany.

Missions of the Diocese. Mr. S. E. Marvin, Albany.

32

For Aged and Infirm Clergymen. Mr. S. E. Marvin, Albany.

For Widows and Orphans of Deceased Clergymen. Mr. S. E. Marvin, Albany.

For the Clergy Reserve Fund. Mr. S. E. Marvin, Albany.

Bible and Common Prayer Book Society of Albany. Mr. H. B. Dauchy, Troy.

Episcopal Fund. Mr. J. H. Van Antwerp, Albany.

Salary of the Bishop. Mr. W. W. Rousseau, Troy.

For the Education of Young Men for the Ministry. The Bishop of the Diocese; Mr. Richard M. Harison, 81 Nassau street, New York.

Orphan House of the Holy Saviour. Mr. Leslie Pell-Clarke, Springfield Centre, Otsego county.

Domestic and Foreign Missions. Mr. George Bliss, 22 Bible House, New York.

Offerings for the *Child's Hospital* should be sent to Mr. Edward Bowditch, Albany.

For Missionary envelopes and Pledges apply to the *Secretary* of the Board of Missions, the Rev. Charles Temple, Malone, Franklin county.

(G.)

TRIENNIAL STATISTICS OF THE DIOCESE AS REPORTED TO THE GENERAL CONVENTION IN 1892.

PAROCHIAL.

N. B.— For the purpose of securing uniformity, the years referred to in these tables are the 'Conventional" years of each Diocese, respectively ending in the secular years named.

	1889.	1890.	1891.	Total.
DEACONS Ordained....	5	2	7	14
Received...	1	....	2	3
Transferred....	1	....	......	1
Canonically resident........	10	8	12	....
PRIESTS Ordained	3	3	3	9
Received....	11	14	6	31
Transferred	13	10	9	32
Deceased........	1		6	7
Canonically resident........	118	123	121	......
Whole number of Clergy (including Bishop).	139	132	134	......
Without cure (of whom 4 engaged in teaching)..	15	15	15	......
Receiving stipends from Diocesan Funds............	51	45	50	....
Candidates for Holy Orders admitted.....	6	8	19	33
Candidates for Holy Orders, present number.	16	18	26	......
Lay Readers....	16	18	18	....
Parishes, present number in union with Convention.	100	100	100	....
Parishes, present number not in union with Convention.	16	16	17	....
Chapels and Missions..	63	63	81	....
Church edifices..	153	153	153	......
Sittings in edifices..	42,509	42,509	42,509	......
Free Churches and Chapels........	125	125	127	....
Churches otherwise supported	28	28	36	......
Free sittings (including free seats in churches where there is a pew rental)........	30,925	30,925	30,925	....
Rectories.	73	73	76	....
Corner-stones laid	1	3	1	....
Churches consecrated	3	3	3	4
BAPTISMS: Children.	1,507	1,559	1,858	4,624
Adults.	492	419	438	1,349
Total.	1,999	1,978	1,795	5,772
Confirmed	1,568	1,401	1,166	4,135
Present number of confirmed persons	*9,491	*6,856	*8,895	....
Number of families	1,054	1,007	683	2,744
COMMUNICANTS: Added....	223	370	280	73
Lost by death.	16,507	18,428	17,662	....
Present number	476	450	464	1,413
Marriages.	974	1,060	1,138	3,172
Funerals.	1,115	1,035	1,077	....
SUNDAY-SCHOOLS: Officers and teachers........	9,872	10,685	12,455	....
Pupils............				

* Very imperfectly reported to the Convention.

OFFERINGS, CONTRIBUTIONS AND OTHER RECEIPTS.

	1889.	1890.	1891.	Total.
TAL OF RECEIPTS: Holy Communion alms	$7,553 71	$6,624 46	$6,426 69	$20,604 86
All other contributions, including stipends, etc	330,653 81	309,165 97	*383,188 18	*1,022,967 96
BURSEMENT OF SAME: Namely, to				
Foreign Missions	$2,486 13	$2,170 85	$2,250 58	$6,907 56
Domestic Missions	2,824 89	3,087 37	3,546 60	9,458 86
Indian Missions	769 57	512 68	700 85	1,983 10
Missions to coloured people	575 73	691 27	502 70	1,769 70
Education for the ministry	316 47	249 17	189 85	755 49
Aged and infirm Clergy	475 01	508 15	524 75	1,507 91
Widows and orphans of Clergymen	379 93	219 14	202 69	801 76
All other extra-diocesan objects	6,277 90	6,514 16	6,072 51	18,864 57
Assessments paid Episcopal Fund	2,711 00	2,480 00	3,185 18	8,356 18
Diocesan Convention and contingent expenses.	2,800 57	2,771 29	2,252 55	7,824 41
Diocesan Missions	11,928 86	10,559 34	9,962 31	32,450 51
Diocesan institutions (including all not general or parochial)	4,063 48	7,710 40	4,627 73	16,401 61
All other diocesan objects	5,591 68	5,410 97	*52,359 40	*63,262 05
Parochial purposes, including stipends, salaries, church improvement, charity, etc.	297,006 30	272,925 64	393,287 17	873,219 11
DOWMENTS: Capital invested for				
Episcopal Fund	$38,841 02	$36,841 02	$63,843 02	....
Aged and infirm Clergy	19,565 86	19,565 86	19,565 86	....
Widows and orphans of Clergymen	3,000 00	5,000 00	6,500 00	....
Other objects	77,785 42	80,854 95	80,854 95	....
Total	$139,192 30	$144,261 83	$170,763 83	....

TOTAL RECEIPTS FROM DIVIDENDS, INTEREST AND CONTRIBUTIONS.
(The latter as above reported.)

Episcopal Fund	$4,652 80	$5,085 14	$6,743 20	$16,481 14
Aged and infirm Clergy	1,251 26	1,349 77	1,366 37	3,967 40
Widows and orphans of Clergymen	379 93	364 14	457 69	1,201 76
Charitable institutions	6,571 43	11,145 02	8,437 76	26,154 21

CHARITABLE AND EDUCATIONAL INSTITUTIONS.

amber of Church Hospitals	1
amber of Orphan Asylums	2
amber of Homes	4
amber of Academic Institutions	3
amber of other Institutions	3

NAME AND LOCATION OF ORGANIZATION.	Nurses, Instructors, or Teachers.	Inmates, Beneficiaries, or Pupils.
he Sisterhood of the Holy Child Jesus	......	......
he Child's Hospital, Albany	12	178
he St. Margaret's House, Albany	7	79
he St. Christopher Home, East Line	4	......
he St. Christina Home, Saratoga	8	36
. Agnes' School, Albany	30	350
. Paul's Hall, Salem	6	40
he Mary Warren Free Institute, Troy	......	......
he Church Home, Troy	1	16
he Orphan House of the Holy Saviour, Cooperstown	7	130
. Peter's Orphange, Albany	1	21
he Martha Memorial House, Troy	......	......
he Bible and Common Prayer Book Society of Albany and its Vicinity	......	......

* Including $48,000 gathered from many sources for paying the debt ported to the Convention of the Diocese in the Cathedral Report,

COMPARATIVE STATEMENT OF THIS AND OF THE LAST TRIENNIAL REPORT.

	1889.	1892.	Increase.
Baptisms for three years ending......	5,199	5,763	564
Persons confirmed during three years ending..........	3,403	4,155	752
Communicants for three years ending..	15,619	17,662	2,043
Appropriations of contributions			
Objects beyond the Diocese........	$33,647 35	$68,983 79	$35,336 44
Diocesan objects..................	353,314 79	131,359 92	*221,954 87
Parochial objects...	821,468 87	873,219 11	51,750 24
Aggregate	$1,208,431 01	$1,073,562 82	*$184,868 19

(H.)
SUMMARY OF STATISTICS.

From the Bishop's Address, the Parochial, Missionary and other Reports.

Clergy (Bishop, 1, Priests, 123, Deacons, 7)......	131
Ordinations (Deacons, 3, Priests, 9)............	12
Candidates for Orders (for the Deacon's Order only, 6, for the Priest's Order, 15)............................	21
Postulants..	11
Lay Readers Licensed.......	19
Parishes in union with Convention..	101
Parishes not in union with Convention............................. ...	17
Missions (organized, 44, unorganized, 40).	84
Churches...	138
Chapels	20
Sittings in Churches and Chapels........	41,476
Free Churches and Chapels......................... ..	131
Churches otherwise supported.......	27
Free sittings (including free seats in Churches where there is a pew rental).	29,868
Rectories...	81
Corner-stone laid...	1
Churches consecrated...........	2
Buildings blessed.........	4
† Families	8,282
† Individuals (adults, 13,294, children, 6,720, not designated, 4,597)........	24,611
Baptisms (adults, 481, infants, 1,385).....	1,866
Persons confirmed.	1,470
Communicants (admitted, 1,134, received, 454, died, 295, removed, 587), present number........	19,107
Marriages...	568
Burials................................	1,289
Sunday School teachers.	1,256
Sunday School pupils...	11,028
Parish School teachers......	41
Parish School pupils...............	340

---
* Decrease.   † Many reports do not give these items.

OFFERINGS.

Parochial.

Alms	$7,263 89
Current expenses	191,873 15
Other purposes	184,939 03

$384,076 07

Diocesan.

Diocesan Missions	$13,144 75
Salary of the Bishop	3,022 17
Diocesan Fund	2,501 76
Bible and Common Prayer Book Society of Albany	283 18
Aged and Infirm Clergy Fund	499 80
Clergy Reserve Fund	318 29
Fund for Widows and Orphans of Deceased Clergymen	271 15
Orphan House of the Holy Saviour (including two bequests amounting to $4,250.59)	6,350 26
The Child's Hospital	1,030 70
Theological Education	331 69
Other purposes	6,583 00

34,336 75

General.

General Theological Seminary	$16 62
Domestic Missions	3,225 70
Foreign Missions	2,313 71
Indian Missions	530 94
Home Missions to Coloured Persons	401 05
Other purposes	6,722 44

13,210 46

Total amount of Offerings. $431,623 28

TABLE OF CONTENTS.

DIOCESE OF ALBANY.

CONSTITUTION AND CANONS.

CONSTITUTION.

ARTICLE I.

Of the Members of the Convention.

The Diocese of Albany entrusts its legislation to a Convention, to consist as follows: irst, of the Bishop, when there is one; of the Assistant Bishop, when there is one. econdly, of all Clergymen canonically resident in the Diocese for six months previ- is to the Convention, the restriction of time not to apply to Rectors duly elected or issionaries duly appointed (provided that no Clergyman suspended from the Ministry all have a seat); and, Thirdly, of the Lay Delegation from the Cathedral, and of ıy Delegations, consisting of not more than three Deputies from each other Church union with the Convention, who shall be communicants, and shall have been osen by the Vestry or Congregation of the same.

ARTICLE II.

Of the Annual Meetings of the Convention.

The Convention shall assemble on the Tuesday after the tenth day of November, in ch year, in such place as the Bishop shall appoint, giving fifteen days' notice ereof. In case of his inability to act, the Assistant Bishop, if there be one, shall ap- int the place; and, if there be no Bishop, the Standing Committee shall appoint. he place of meeting may be changed for sufficient reason after having been appointed, ovided that ten days' notice of such change shall be given.

Every Convention shall be opened with a Sermon and the Holy Communion; and e Preacher shall be appointed by the Bishop, or in case of his inability to act, or if ere be no Bishop, by the Standing Committee.

ARTICLE III.

Of Special Conventions.

The Bishop shall have power to call Special Conventions, giving thirty days' notice ereof, and shall do so when requested by a vote of three-fourths of the Standing ommittee. When there is no Bishop, the Standing Committee shall have power to ll a Special Convention, giving ninety d

ARTICLE IV.

Of the Cathedral.

"The Cathedral of All Saints in the City and Diocese of Albany" shall be the Cathedral Church of this Diocese. Three Lay Communicants shall be chosen by the Chapter as the Delegation from the Cathedral to the Convention.

ARTICLE V.

Of the Permanent Officers of the Diocese.

The permanent officers of the Diocese shall be: the Bishop of the Diocese (with right to preside, when present in Convention; and when there is an Assistant Bishop, he shall have right to preside in the absence of the Bishop), a Standing Committee, a Secretary, a Treasurer and a Registrar.

ARTICLE VI.

Of the Election of a Bishop.

When a Bishop or an Assistant Bishop is to be elected, the election shall be at the regular Annual Convention, or at a Special Convention duly called for that purpose; and such election shall require a majority of the votes of each order voting separately.

ARTICLE VII.

Of the President of the Convention.

If there be no Bishop of the Diocese, or its *ex-officio* presiding officer be absent, the Convention shall elect a President from among the Clergy, by ballot (unless the ballot be dispensed with by unanimous vote.)

ARTICLE VIII.

Of the Standing Committee.

The Standing Committee shall consist of four Clergymen and four Laymen, to be elected by ballot at each Annual Convention, by a majority of the Clergy and Lay Delegations present, and shall serve until the next Annual Convention and until a new election is made, the functions of which Committee, besides those provided for in the Canons of the General Convention, and in this Constitution, shall be determined by Canon or Resolution of the Convention. But vacancies in the Standing Committee may be filled by a majority of the votes of the remaining members until the next meeting of the Convention.

ARTICLE IX.

Of the Secretary, Treasurer and Registrar.

The Secretary shall be elected at each Annual Convention from the members thereof, by ballot, after nominations (unless the ballot be dispensed with by unanimous vote), and by a majority of the Clergy and Lay Delegations present; and he shall remain in office until his successor shall be elected. His duties shall be those required by the Canons, Resolutions and Rules of Order of the Convention.

The Treasurer and the Registrar shall be elected in a similar manner, and are not required to be members of the Convention. They shall remain in office until the next Annual Convention, and until their successors are elected.

ARTICLE X.

Of the Deliberations of the Convention and of Votes.

The Clergymen and Laymen constituting the Convention shall deliberate in one body, and each Clergyman shall have one vote, and each Lay Delegation one vote, and a majority of the aggregate votes shall be decisive except in the cases provided for in Articles VI, IX and XI.

If five votes require a division, then the voting shall be by orders separately, and the concurrence of a majority of each order shall be necessary to make a decision. But no alteration of the Constitution or Canons shall be valid without the concurrence of the Bishop and of a majority of the Clergy and of a majority of the Lay Delegations; and the Bishop's concurrence shall be presumed unless the contrary be openly expressed by him to the Convention after the vote of the Clergy and Laity and before the adjournment *sine die.*

ARTICLE XI.

Of Altering the Constitution.

The mode of altering the Constitution shall be as follows: A proposition for an amendment shall be introduced in writing and considered in the Convention; and, if approved by a majority, shall lie over till the next Convention, and, if then approved by a two-thirds vote of the Clergy and Lay Delegations present, with the Bishop's concurrence, the Constitution shall be changed accordingly.

CANONS.

CANON I.

Of the List of Clergymen in the Diocese.

SECTION 1. On the first day of each Convention, regular or special, the Ecclesiastical Authority shall present to the Convention a List of the Clergy canonically resident in the Diocese, annexing the names of their respective Parishes, Offices and residences, and the dates of their becoming resident in the Diocese.

SEC. 2. The Secretary shall record this list of names in a book to be kept by him for that purpose.

SEC. 8. From this record shall be made up by the Secretary the list of the Clergymen entitled, according to the Constitution, to seats in the Convention; which list may at any time be revised and corrected by the Convention.

CANON II.

Of the Lay Delegations.

SECTION 1. When the Lay Delegations are chosen by the Vestry, it shall be at a meeting held according to law. In case the Vestry shall not choose Deputies they may be chosen by the congregation in the manner hereinafter prescribed for Churches having no Vestries.

SEC. 2. Deputies from Churches having no Vestries shall be chosen by the Congregation at a meeting of which notice shall have been given during Divine Service on the two Sundays next previous thereto. And at such meeting the Rector or Minister shall preside, and the qualifications for voting shall be the same as those required by law for voting at an election for Churchwardens and Vestrymen.

Sec. 3. When Deputies are chosen by a Vestry, the evidence of their appointment shall be a certificate, signed by the Rector of the Church they are chosen to represent and by the Clerk of the Vestry; and if there be no Rector, then the certificate shall state that fact, and shall be signed by the Churchwarden presiding and by the Clerk of the Vestry. The certificate must state the time and place of. the election, must show upon its face that the appointment has been made in accordance with all the requirements of the Canons, and shall certify that each Deputy chosen is a Communicant of the Church and entitled to vote for Churchwardens and Vestrymen of the Church he is chosen to represent.

Sec. 4. When Deputies are chosen by the Congregation of any Church, the evidence of their appointment shall be a certificate, signed by the Rector or Minister having charge of the said Church and by the Secretary of the meeting; or if there be no such Rector or Minister, then the certificate shall state that fact, and shall be signed by the officer presiding at the meeting and by the Secretary of the same. The certificate must state the time and place of the election, must show upon its face that the appointment has been made in accordance with all the requirements of the Canons, and shall certify that each Deputy chosen is a Communicant of the Church, and, in the case of the Church having a Vestry, that he is entitled to vote for Churchwardens and Vestrymen of such Church, or, in the case of a Church having no Vestry, that he has belonged for twelve months to the Congregation he is chosen to represent. No other evidence of the appointment of Lay Deputies than such as is specified in this and the preceding section shall be received by the Convention.

Sec. 5. The Secretary of the Convention, when he shall send to any Church or Parish the required notice of the time and place of meeting of any Convention to be held, shall transmit with the same a copy of this Canon and blank printed forms of certificates of appointment of Deputies.

CANON III.

Of the Organization of the Convention.

Section 1. If the *ex-officio* presiding officer be not present at the opening of the Convention, the Secretary shall call the members present to order; and the senior Presbyter present, who is a member of the Convention, shall take the chair, and preside until a President is elected, as provided by Article VII of the Constitution.

Sec. 2. The Secretary shall then call the names of the Clergy entitled to seats in the Convention. He shall then call the names of the Churches in union with the Convention, when the Lay Deputies shall present their certificates, which shall be examined by the Secretary, and a committee of two members appointed by the presiding officer. Irregular or defective certificates, and certificates and documents referring to contested seats, shall be temporarily laid aside. The names of the Lay Deputies duly appointed shall then be called, after which the certificates and documents laid aside shall be reported to the Convention, which shall decide upon the admission of the Deputies named therein.

Sec. 3. If twenty Clergymen entitled to vote, and twenty Lay Delegations be present, they shall constitute a quorum; and the presiding officer *ex officio* shall declare the Convention duly organized. The same number of Clergymen and Lay Delegations shall, at any time, be necessary for the transaction of business, except that a smaller number may adjourn from time to time.

Sec. 4. If the presiding officer *ex officio* be not present before the convention is declared to be organized, the temporary Chairman shall direct that the members proceed to elect a President, according to Article VII of the Constitution, who, when elected, shall take the Chair and declare the Convention organized for business.

Sec. 5. The Convention shall then proceed to the election of a Secretary, a Treasurer and a Registrar, according to the Constitution. The Secretary may appoint an Assistant Secretary, also any other assistants he may require, announcing their names to the Convention.

Sec. 6. Any Rules of Order which shall have been previously adopted or sanctioned in the Convention, except such as prescribe the mode of altering the same, shall be in force until changed by the Convention, after having been duly organized.

CANON IV.

Of the Admission of a Church into Union with the Church in this Diocese, and Maintaining such Union.

Section 1. Every Church or Congregation desiring admission into union with the Church in this Diocese, shall present a written application therefor to the Convention, together with a copy of the resolution of the Vestry, or of the Congregation, authorizing such application; in which resolution the said Church, by its Vestry or Congregation, shall agree to abide by, and conform to, and observe, all the Canons of the Church, and all the rules, orders and regulations of the Convention; which copy shall be duly certified by the presiding officer of the Vestry, or of the meeting of the Congregation at which the resolution was adopted, and also by the Clerk of the Vestry or Secretary of the meeting; and shall be authenticated by the seal of the Corporation. The said application shall also be accompanied by the Certificate of Incorporation of the Church, duly recorded, or a copy thereof certified by the officer, whose duty it may be to record or file the same; and also, by a Certificate of the Ecclesiastical Authority, to the effect that he or they approve of the incorporation of such Church, and that such Church, in his or their judgment, is duly and satisfactorily established; and every Church or Congregation applying for admission shall produce satisfactory evidence that not less than twenty-five persons, members of such Church, have habitually, for at least one year preceding such application, attended Divine Service in such Church or Congregation.

Sec. 2. No application for the admission of a Church into union with the Church in this Diocese shall be considered or acted upon, at any meeting of the Convention, unless the same shall have been transmitted to the Secretary of the Convention at least thirty days before the meeting of the Convention. It shall be the duty of the Secretary of the Convention, at least twenty days before the meeting of the Convention, to deliver to a Committee, to be annually appointed (to be called the Committee on the Incorporation and Admission of Churches), all applications for admission into union which shall have been received by him, to be by such Committee examined, considered and reported upon to the Convention.

Sec. 8. Whenever hereafter any Church in union with this Convention shall neglect, for three years in succession, to make a Parochial Report, no Missionary Report being made on its behalf, and shall not, during the same period, have employed a Clergyman as its Parish Minister, nor requested of the Ecclesiastical Authority to have the services of a Missionary, such Church shall be regarded as having forfeited its connection with the Convention, and shall no longer have a right to send a Delegation to the same. The Bishop shall report such Church to the Convention in his Annual Address. Such Church, however, may be re-admitted, upon application to the Convention, accompanied by a report of its condition, and on such terms as shall appear just; such re-admission to ~~ing~~ ing of the Convention consenting to such admi

CANON V.

Of Elections.

All elections by the Convention shall be by ballot, except when the ballot is dispensed with by unanimous consent. And when an election is by ballot, a majority of the votes in each order shall be necessary to a choice.

CANON VI.

Of the Secretary of the Convention.

SECTION 1. It shall be the duty of the Secretary to take and keep the Minutes of the proceedings of the Convention, to attest its public acts, and faithfully to deliver into the hands of his successor all books and papers relating to the business and concerns of the Convention which may be in his possession or under his control. It shall also be his duty to send a printed notice to each Minister, and to each Vestry or Congregation, of the time and place appointed for the meetings of each Convention, and to publish a notice of the meeting in three of the public papers published in the Diocese of Albany, and to perform such other duties as may be required of him by the Convention.

SEC. 2. He shall transmit annually a copy of the Journal of the Convention to each of the Bishops of the Protestant Episcopal Church in the United States, to the Secretary of the House of Deputies of the General Convention, and to the Secretaries of the Diocesan Conventions; and shall ask, on behalf of the Diocese, for copies of the Diocesan Journals in exchange.

SEC. 3. He shall also transmit to every General Convention, in addition to the documents required by the Canons of the General Convention,* a certificate, signed by himself, containing a list of the Clergymen in this Diocese, and the amount of funds paid or secured to be paid (distinguishing them) to the General Theological Seminary, and also a certificate of the appointment of Clerical and Lay Deputies.

SEC. 4. Any expense incurred by a compliance with this Canon shall be paid out of the Diocesan Fund.

SEC. 5. Whenever there shall be a vacancy in the office of Secretary of the Convention, the duties thereof shall devolve upon the Assistant Secretary, if there be one, if not, upon the Secretary of the Standing Committee.

SEC. 6. Whenever, under the provisions of the Constitution, a Special Convention is called for any particular purpose, it shall be the duty of the Secretary, in the notice thereof, to specify such purpose.

CANON VII.

Of the Treasurer of the Diocese.

SECTION 1. It shall be the duty of the Treasurer of the Diocese to receive and disburse all moneys collected under the authority of the Convention, and of which the the collection and distribution shall not be otherwise regulated. He shall report, at each annual meeting of the Convention, the names of the Parishes which have failed to make the required contributions to any of the Diocesan Funds, specifying the funds to which they have failed to contribute and the amount of such deficiency.

SEC. 2 His accounts shall be rendered annually to the Convention, and shall be examined by a Committee acting under its authority.

---

* Title I, Canon 18, Sec. IV.

SEC. 3. If the Treasurer of the Convention shall die or resign his office, the Standing Committee shall appoint a Treasurer *ad interim;* to continue in office until an election be made by the Convention.

CANON VIII.

Of the Registrar.

It shall be the duty of the Registrar to collect and preserve, as the property of the Diocese, all documents and papers pertaining to the Diocese, and not in the custody of any other officer; and also the Journals and public documents of other Diocesan Conventions and of the General Convention, and other pamphlets and publications connected with the Church at large.

CANON IX.

Of Deputies to the General Convention.

SECTION 1. The Convention shall, at each regular annual meeting next preceding a stated meeting of the General Convention, elect, by the concurrent ballot of the Clerical and Lay Members, four Clergymen and four Laymen, to act as Deputies from this Diocese to the General Convention. It shall also, in like manner, elect four Clergymen and four Laymen as Provisional Deputies, to act in the case hereinafter mentioned; which Deputies and Provisional Deputies shall hold their respective offices until their successors are elected, and shall be Deputies, or Provisional Deputies, for any General Convention which may be held during their continuance in office.

SEC. 2. Should a vacancy occur by resignation, removal from the Diocese, death, or otherwise, among the Deputies or Provisional Deputies, between the stated times of election, the vacancy shall be supplied by any Convention during or prior to which such vacancy shall occur.

SEC. 3. It shall be the duty of the Deputies elect to signify to the Ecclesiastical Authority, at least ten days before the meeting of the General Convention, their acceptance of the appointment and their intention to perform its duties; in default of which the Ecclesiastical Authority shall designate, from the list of Provisional Deputies, so many as may be necessary to ensure, as far as practicable, a full representation of the Diocese. And the Ecclesiastical Authority shall, in like manner, designate, from the same list of Provisional Deputies, one or more, as the case may be, to supply any deficiency in the representation of this Diocese which may in any way occur. And the person or persons so designated by the Bishop, being furnished with a certificate thereof, shall have all the power and authority of Deputies duly elected by the Convention.

CANON X.

Of the Standing Committee.

The powers and duties of the Standing Committee over and above those given and prescribed by the Canons of the General Convention and by the Constitution of the Diocese of Albany, are further defined as follows:

SECTION 1. If there be no Bishop, or if he be unable to perform his duties, the Standing Committee shall be the Ecclesiastical Authority of the Diocese, *provided* that whenever any duty is specially imposed upon the Clerical Members of the Committee, such duty shall be performed by them only.

SEC. 2. The record of all proceedings upon a presentment of a Clergyman shall be preserved by the Standing Committee.

Sec. 8. The Standing Committee shall make a full report of all their proceedings at every Annual Convention.

CANON XI.

Of Parish Registers and Parochial Reports.

Whereas, by the Canons of the General Convention,* it is made the duty of each Clergyman of this Church to "keep a Register of Baptisms, Confirmations, Communicants, Marriages, and Funerals within his Cure, agreeably to such rules as may be provided by the Convention of the Diocese where his Cure lies;" it is hereby ordered that,

Section 1. The Record shall specify the name and the time of the birth of the child or adult baptized, with the names of the parents, sponsors or witnesses; the names of the persons confirmed; the names of the persons married, their ages and residences, also the names and residences of at least two witnesses of each marriage; the names of the persons buried, their ages, and the place of burial; and also the time when and the Minister by whom each rite was performed. The list of Communicants shall contain the names of all connected with the Parish or Mission as nearly as can be ascertained. These records shall be made by the Minister in a book provided for that purpose, belonging to each Church; which book shall be the Parish Register, and shall be preserved as a part of the records of the Church.

Sec. 2. And Whereas, by the Canons of the General Convention,† it is " ordered that every Minister of this Church, or, if the Parish be vacant, the Warden shall present, or cause to be delivered, on or before the first day of every Annual Convention, to the Bishop of the Diocese, or, where there is no Bishop, to the President of the Convention, a statement of the number of Baptisms, Confirmations, Marriages and Funerals, and of the number of Communicants in his Parish or Church; also the state and condition of the Sunday Schools in his Parish; and also the amount of the Communion alms, the contributions for 'Missions, Diocesan, Domestic and Foreign, for Parochial Schools, for Church purposes in general, and of all other matters that may throw light on the state of the same;" it is hereby further ordered that, in reporting the number of Communicants, he shall distinguish the additions, removals and deaths since the last report, and that, in reporting the contributions for Church purposes in general, he shall include the amount received for sittings in the Church and moneys raised for all Church and Parish purposes, other than those enumerated in this section.

Sec. 3. In every case where a Parish is without a Minister, the Parish Register shall be kept by some person appointed by the Vestry or Trustees; and the annual Parochial report shall be presented or forwarded to the Bishop by the Church-wardens or Trustees of the Parish.

CANON XII.

Of Vacant Parishes.

Section 1. Whenever a Parish becomes vacant, it shall be the duty of the Vestry or Trustees to give immediate notice thereof to the Bishop.

Sec. 2. The Bishop shall appoint those of the Clergy in the Diocese who can with most convenience discharge the duty, to supply such vacant Parishes as have been reported to him, at such times as may be deemed convenient and proper. And the Clergy so appointed, shall make a full report to the Bishop concerning the state of the Parishes which they have visited. It shall be the duty of the Parishes thus supplied to defray all the expenses incident to such occasional services.

---

* Title I, Canon 15, Sec 5.　† Title I, Canon 18, Sec. 1.

CANON XIII.

Of Offerings.

SECTION 1. Whereas it is the duty of all Christians, as faithful stewards of God, to set apart regularly a portion of their income as God's portion, "every one as God hath prospered him," to be used for the maintenance and extension of His Kingdom, and the relief of His poor; this Church enjoins this duty upon all her members.

SEC. 2 It shall be the duty of every Congregation of this Diocese to contribute, at least once in each year, by weekly or monthly offerings, or in some other systematic way, to the Missions of the Diocese; the Domestic and Foreign Missions and other departments of Missionary work under the control of the General Convention; the support of the Episcopate; the expenses of the Convention; the education of young men for the Holy Ministry; the distribution of the Bible and Book of Common Prayer; the support of aged and infirm Clergymen; the relief of the widows and orphans of deceased Clergymen; and the support and education of orphan children; the offerings to be sent to the Treasurers of the funds for which they are made, and the amounts of all such contributions to form distinct items in the Annual Parochial Report.

SEC. 3. "The Protestant Episcopal Society for Promoting Religion and Learning in the State of New York," in which we have an interest in common with our mother Diocese, shall be an agent of this Diocese for the education of young men for Holy Orders. A copy of its Annual report, if obtained from its Superintendent, shall be laid by the Secretary of the Convention before each Annual Convention.

SEC. 4. "The Bible and Common Prayer Book Society of Albany and its Vicinity" shall be the agent of this Diocese for the Distribution of the Bible and the Book of Common Prayer, and shall present a full report of its proceedings to each Annual Convention.

SEC. 5. The Orphan House of the Holy Saviour, at or near Cooperstown, shall be the Diocesan Orphanage, and shall make a report of its proceedings and condition to each Annual Convention.

CANON XIV.

Of the Missions of the Diocese and of Archdeaconries.

The Church in this Diocese, acknowledging her responsibility, in common with the whole Church, for the fulfilment of the charge of our Lord to preach the Gospel to every creature, and especially for the extension of the Church throughout the Diocese, declares that it is the duty of the Convention, as her representative body, to care for the Missionary work, and that every baptized Member of the Church is bound, according to his ability, to assist in carrying it on. To this end it is hereby enacted as follows:

SECTION 1. "The Board of Missions of the Protestant Episcopal Church in the Diocese of Albany," incorporated by an Act of the Legislature of the State of New York, passed February 16, 1870, shall be entrusted with the general charge and direction of the work of Missions within the Diocese, and particularly with the custody and management of all money or property given or acquired for that object, subject to the provisions of this Canon and to such written instructions as may from time to time be given to them by the Convention and entered upon the Journal thereof.

SEC. 2. The said Board of Missions shall consist of the Bishop, who shall be *ex officio* the President thereof; and of ten other members, one Clergyman and one Layman resident within the limits of each of the Archdeaconries hereinafter provided for, and nominated by said Archdeaconry, and one Clergyman and one Layman who

may be resident anywhere within the Diocese, and shall be nominated in open Convention, all of whom shall be annually chosen by the Convention, and by ballot unless the same be unanimously dispensed with. All vacancies occurring in the Board during the recess of the Convention, may be filled by the Board.

SEC. 3. The evening session of the Convention on the first day of each Annual Meeting shall be devoted to the reception and consideration of the Report of the Board of Missions and of its Treasurer, the election of the Board, and other business connected with the subject; provided that said election and other business connected with the subject may be deferred to the second day.

SEC. 4. The Board of Missions shall meet on the day after the adjournment of the Convention in each year, and elect a Secretary and a Treasurer. The Board may hold other meetings during the year, according to its own rules, and shall meet on the day preceding the Annual Convention, to audit the accounts of the Treasurer, and to adopt a report to the Convention.

SEC. 5. The Diocese shall be divided into districts called Archdeaconries, the titles and limits of which shall be as follows: The Archdeaconry of Albany shall comprise the counties of Albany, Greene, Columbia, Schenectady, Montgomery, Fulton, Hamilton and Herkimer. The Archdeaconry of Troy shall comprise the counties of Rensselaer, Saratoga, Washington, Warren, Clinton and Essex. The Archdeaconry of the Susquehanna shall comprise the counties of Delaware, Otsego and Schoharie. The Archdeaconry of Ogdensburgh shall comprise the counties of St. Lawrence and Franklin.

SEC. 6. The Bishop shall be *ex officio* the head of each Archdeaconry. He shall, however, annually appoint an Archdeacon on the nomination of each Archdeaconry, from among the Clergy thereof, who shall be the Executive Officer of the Archdeaconry. Each Archdeaconry, moreover, shall annually elect a Secretary and Treasurer, who shall make annual reports to the Convention. The Archdeacon in the absence of the Bishop shall preside at all the meetings of the Archdeaconry, and may also be present without a vote at the meetings of the Board of Missions. He shall be charged with the duty of visiting the Mission Stations and vacant Parishes, and, with the consent of the Clergy in charge, the other Parishes receiving Missionary aid within the limits of his Archdeaconry, to ascertain their condition, and to give such advice as may be required, reporting the result of his inquiries and observations to the Bishop. It shall also be his duty to stir up an increased Missionary interest and zeal, and to urge more liberal offerings for the work of Church extension. And furthermore the Archdeacon and the Clerical and Lay Members of the Board of Missions from each Archdeaconry shall be an Advisory Committee of the Board, whose duty it shall be to counsel the Board as to the amount which should be expended in, and the amount which should be raised by the Archdeaconry which they represent, and to use their best efforts to secure the required amount of Missionary offerings from their Archdeaconry.

SEC. 7. Each Archdeaconry shall hold two meetings a year at such places within its boundaries as it may designate. Other meetings may be held as the Archdeaconry may order. At all meetings of the Archdeaconry every Clergyman canonically resident within its boundaries shall be entitled to a seat; also three Laymen from each Parish or Mission Station within the limits of the Archdeaconry. Each Clergyman and each Lay Delegation shall have one vote. Any number of members present at a meeting duly called shall be competent to transact business. The meetings of Archdeaconry shall have for their main purpose the presentation of the claims of the Mission work of the Diocese and the Church. Such Missionaries as may be members shall report concerning their work, and provision may be made for especial needs of the Missionary work within the boundaries of the Archdeaconry. Contributions to

local work shall not interfere with the claims of the Diocesan Board of Missions, and shall be reported to the Treasurer thereof, and included in his Annual Report to the Convention. It shall also be the object of these Archidiaconal meetings to bring the Clergy together in fraternal intercourse and to promote their spiritual and intellectual life. Each Archdeaconry shall make its own rules as to the arrangement of services.

SEC. 8. All Missionaries shall be appointed by the Board of Missions on the nomination of the Bishop, and may be removed with his approval. But in case of a vacancy in the Episcopate, or of the absence of the Bishop from the Diocese, or of his being otherwise unable to perform his duties, the Board of Missions shall have the power of appointing and removing Missionaries.

SEC. 9. It shall be the duty of every member of the Church in the Diocese to contribute as God hath prospered him, to the funds of the Board of Missions; and every Clergyman having Parochial or Missionary charge shall impress this duty upon his people, and cause one or more Offertories to be made annually for that object.

SEC. 10. The Treasurer of the Board of Missions shall include in his Annual Report all sums certified to him as expended in local Missionary work. He shall also receive, report and pay over any special contributions from Parishes or individuals in accordance with the instructions of the contributors.

SEC. 11. The travelling expenses of the members of the Board of Missions and of the Archdeacons, attending the meetings of the Board, shall be paid out of its treasury.

SEC. 12. Any Mission Station designated by the Board of Missions may be organized by the Bishop on the application of any residents in its neighbourhood. But such station shall not be established within the Parochial Cure of any other Minister or Ministers, without either the consent of such Minister or of a majority of such Ministers, or with the advice of the Standing Committee of the Diocese. The Bishop may appoint, upon the organization of the Mission, a Churchwarden, a Clerk, and a Treasurer, which officers shall thereafter be elected by the Congregation annually in Easter week, in the same manner as provided for the choice of Deputies to Convention by section 2, of Canon II of this Diocese. They shall, as far as possible, discharge the duties which belong to their respective offices in incorporated Parishes.

SEC. 13. The title of all property, real or personal, given or purchased for the use of any Mission Station, shall be vested in "The Board of Missions of the Protestant Episcopal Church, in the Diocese of Albany," or in "The Trustees of the Diocese of Albany."

CANON XV.

Of the Episcopal Fund.

SECTION 1. The fund for the support of the Episcopate in this Diocese, now provided, together with that which may be hereafter contributed or acquired, and any accumulation accruing from the investment thereof, shall be entrusted to the Corporation, entitled "The Trustees of the Episcopal Fund of the Diocese of Albany," incorporated by an Act of the Legislature of the State of New York, passed April 28, 1869. The Trustees composing said Corporation shall be five in number, who shall be appointed by the Convention, and shall hold their offices during the pleasure thereof.

SEC. 2. All moneys belonging to the said fund shall be loaned by the said Trustees upon security of real estate, or invested in stock of the United States, or of this State, or of the city of New York, at their discretion; and all securities and investments shall be taken or made in their corporate name above mentioned; and they shall have power, from time to time, to ▓▓▓▓▓▓ ▓▓▓▓ investments. A statement, signed by the Trustees or a majo▓▓▓▓▓▓▓▓▓▓▓▓▓▓▓▓▓▓▓▓▓▓ of said fund

and securities, together with the receipts and disbursements during the year, shall be reported to the Convention at every annual meeting thereof.

CANON XVI.

Of the Diocesan Fund.

SECTION 1. WHEREAS it is indispensable to provide a fund for defraying the necessary expenses of the Convention, including the expenses of those of the Clergy who may have to travel from a distance to the Convention, and also the cost of maintaining a suitable residence for the Bishop; it is hereby required of every Congregation in this Diocese to pay to the Treasurer of the Convention on or before the day of its annual meeting, a contribution at such a rate per cent upon the salary of its Clergyman as shall have been determined by the previous Convention to be required for the purposes above-mentioned.

SEC. 2. AND WHEREAS, by the Canons of the General Convention,* it is made "the duty of the several Diocesan Conventions to forward to the Treasurer of the General Convention, at or before any meeting of the General Convention, three dollars for each Clergyman within such Diocese;" therefore, it shall be the duty of the Treasurer to retain annually out of the Diocesan Fund, one dollar for each Clergyman in this Diocese, as a special fund, to be paid over to the Treasurer of the General Convention at each meeting of the same.

CANON XVII.

Of the Aged and Infirm Clergy Fund.

SECTION 1. The fund now existing, together with all contributions hereafter received for the support of Aged and Infirm Clergymen, shall be entrusted to the Corporation entitled "The Trustees of the Fund for the support of the Aged and Infirm Clergy of the Protestant Episcopal Church in the Diocese of Albany," incorporated by an Act of the Legislature of the State of New York, passed February 16, 1870. The said Trustees shall consist of the Bishop and the Treasurer of the Diocese, together with three Lay Trustees, who shall be appointed annually by the Convention. Vacancies occurring in the number of the Lay Trustees during the recess of the Convention may be filled by the remaining Trustees.

SEC. 2. It shall be the duty of the Trustees to receive applications for relief, and to administer it in accordance with such rules and regulations as they, with the approbation of the Convention, may from time to time adopt.

SEC. 3. The Trustees shall present a detailed report of their proceedings and of the condition of the fund to every Annual Convention.

CANON XVIII.

Of the Clergy Reserve Fund.

SECTION 1. A fund shall be established to be known as the Clergy Reserve Fund of the Diocese of Albany.

SEC. 2. It shall be the duty of each Parish and Mission station in the Diocese to contribute one offering annually in behalf of this fund.

SEC. 3. The fund thus formed shall be permitted to accumulate until it shall amount to $20,000, and the income shall then be divided into annuities of $300, which shall be paid to the beneficiaries of the fund.

SEC. 4. The beneficiaries of the fund shall be the Clergy of the Diocese according to the seniority of their canonical residence.

---

* Title III, Canon 1, Sec. 5.

SEC. 5. No Clergyman shall be a beneficiary of the fund whose salary or stipend exceeds $1,000 per annum. Nor shall any Clergyman receive the annuity who has allowed the Parish or Mission under his charge to neglect its annual contribution to the fund.

SEC. 6. The principal of the fund shall not be impaired.

SEC. 7. The trustees of the fund shall be the Bishop of the Diocese, the Rector of St. Peter's Church, Albany, the Rector of St. Paul's Church, Troy, the Archdeacons of the Diocese, and the Treasurer of the Diocese, who shall be the treasurer of the fund. And they are hereby authorized to form a corporation under the Laws of the State of New York, whose object shall be to carry into effect the provisions of this Canon, and to provide for the receipt by the corporation so to be formed, of real and personal estate by gifts, purchase, devise, bequest or otherwise, for the purposes of said corporation.

CANON XIX.

Of the Fund for the Widows and Orphans of Deceased Clergymen.

SECTION 1. The fund now existing, together with all contributions hereafter received for the relief of widows and orphans of Deceased Clergymen shall be entrusted to the Corporation entitled "The Trustees of the Fund for the Widows and Orphans of Deceased Clergymen of the Protestant Episcopal Church in the Diocese of Albany," incorporated by an Act of the Legislature of the State of New York, passed February 16, 1870. The said Trustees shall consist of the Bishop and the Treasurer of the Diocese, together with three Lay Trustees, who shall be appointed annually by the Convention. Vacancies occurring in the number of the Lay Trustees during the recess of the Convention may be filled by the remaining Trustees.

SEC. 2. It shall be the duty of the Trustees to receive applications for relief, and to administer it in accordance with such rules and regulations as they, with the approbation of the Convention, may from time to time adopt.

SEC. 3. The Trustees shall present a detailed report of their proceedings and of the condition of the fund to every Annual Convention.

CANON XX.

Of the Trial of a Clergyman not being a Bishop.

Whenever any Minister of this Diocese, not being a Bishop thereof, shall become "liable to presentment and trial" under the provisions of any Canon of the General or Diocesan Convention, the mode of proceeding in this Diocese shall be as follows:

SECTION 1. The trial shall be on a presentment in writing, addressed to the Bishop of the Diocese, specifying the offences of which the accused is alleged to be guilty, with reasonable certainty as to time, place and circumstances. Such presentment may be made by the major part in number of the members of the Vestry of any Church of which the accused is Minister, or by any three Presbyters of this Diocese entitled to seats in the Convention, or as hereinafter mentioned. Whenever, from public rumor or otherwise, the Bishop shall have reason to believe that any Clergyman is under the imputation of having been guilty of any offence or misconduct for which he is liable to be tried, and that the interest of the Church requires an investigation, it shall be his duty to appoint five persons, of whom three at least shall be Presbyters, to examine the case; a majority of whom may make such examination; and if there is, in their opinion, sufficient ground for presentment, they shall present the Clergyman accordingly.

SEC. 2. A presentment being made in any one of the modes above prescribed, the Bishop, if the facts charged shall not appear to him to be such as constitute an of-

fence, may dismiss it; or if it allege facts, some of which do and some of which do not constitute an offence, he may allow it in part and dismiss the residue, or he may permit it to be amended. When it shall be allowed in whole or in part, the Bishop shall cause a copy of it to be served on the accused; and shall also nominate twelve Presbyters of this Diocese entitled to seats in the Convention, and not being parties to the presentment, and cause a list of their names to be served on the accused, who shall, within thirty days after such service, select five of them, and notify their names in writing to the Bishop; and if he shall not give such notification to the Bishop within the said thirty days, the Bishop shall select five; and the Presbyters so selected shall form a Board for the trial of the accused, and shall meet at such time and place as the Bishop shall direct, and shall have power to adjourn from time to time, and from place to place (but always within the Diocese), as they shall think proper.

SEC. 3. A written notice of the time and place of their first meeting shall be served, at least thirty days before such meeting, on the accused, and also on one of the persons making the presentment.

SEC. 4. If, at the time appointed for the first meeting of the Board of Presbyters, the whole number of five shall not attend, then those who do attend may adjourn from time to time; and if, after one adjournment or more, it shall appear to them improbable that the whole number will attend within a reasonable time, then those who do attend, not being less than three, shall constitute the board, and proceed to the trial, and a majority of them shall decide all questions.

SEC. 5. If a Clergyman presented shall confess the truth of the facts alleged in the presentment, and shall not demur thereto, it shall be the duty of the Bishop to proceed to pass sentence; and if he shall not confess them before the appointment of a Board for his trial, as before mentioned, he shall be considered as denying them.

SEC. 6. If a Clergyman presented, after having had due notice, shall not appear before the Board of Presbyters appointed for his trial, the Board may, nevertheless, proceed as if he were present, unless for good cause they shall see fit to adjourn to another day.

SEC. 7. When the Board proceed to the trial, they shall hear such evidence as shall be produced, which evidence shall be reduced to writing and signed by the witnesses, respectively; and some officer authorized by law to administer oaths may, at the desire of either party, be requested to administer an oath or affirmation to the witnesses, that they will testify the truth, the whole truth, and nothing but the truth, concerning the facts charged in the presentment. If, on or during the trial, the accused shall confess the truth of the charges, as stated in the presentment, the Board may dispense with hearing further evidence, and may proceed at once to state their opinion to the Bishop as to the sentence that ought to be pronounced.

SEC. 8. Upon the application of either party to the Bishop, and it being made satisfactorily to appear to him that any material witness cannot be procured upon the trial, the Bishop may appoint a Commissary to take the testimony of such witness. Such Commissary may be either a Clergyman or a Layman, and the party so applying shall give to the other at least six days' notice of the time and place of taking the testimony. If the person on whom the notice shall be served shall reside more than forty miles from the place of examination, notice of an additional day shall be given for every additional twenty miles of the said distance. Both parties may attend and examine the witness; and the questions and answers shall be reduced to writing and signed by the witness, and shall be certified by the Commissary, and enclosed under his seal, and transmitted to the Board, and shall be received by them as evidence. A witness examined before such Commissary may be sworn or affirmed in manner aforesaid.

Sec. 9. The Board, having deliberately considered the evidence, shall declare in a writing signed by them, or a majority of them, their decision on the charges contained in the presentment, distinctly stating whether the accused be guilty or not guilty of such charges, respectively, and also stating the sentence (if any) which, in their opinion, should be pronounced; and a copy of such decision shall be, without delay, communicated to the accused; and the original decision, together with the evidence, shall be delivered to the Bishop, who shall pronounce such canonical sentence as shall appear to him to be proper, provided the same shall not exceed in severity the sentence recommended by the Board; and such sentence shall be final. Before pronouncing any sentence, the Bishop shall summon the accused, and any three or more of the Clergy, to meet him at such time as may, in his opinion, be most convenient, in some Church to be designated by him, which shall, for that purpose, be open at the time to all persons who may choose to attend; and the sentence shall then and there be publicly pronounced by the Bishop. But the Bishop, if he shall be satisfied that justice requires it, may grant a new trial to the accused, in which case a new Board of Presbyters shall be appointed, the proceedings before whom shall be conducted as above mentioned.

Sec. 10. All notices and papers contemplated in this Canon may be served by a summoner or summoners, to be appointed for the purpose by the Bishop, and whose certificate of such service shall be evidence thereof. In case of service by any other person, the facts shall be proved by the affidavit of such person. A written notice or paper delivered to a party, or left at his last place of residence, shall be deemed a sufficient service of such notice or paper.

Sec. 11. The defendant may have the privilege of appearing by counsel; in case of the exercise of which privilege, and not otherwise, those who present shall also have the like privilege.

Sec. 12. If the Ecclesiastical Authority of any other Diocese shall, under the provisions of the Canons of the General Convention, or otherwise, make known to the Ecclesiastical Authority of this Diocese, charges against a Presbyter or Deacon thereof, such communication shall be a sufficient presentation of him for trial; and the trial shall take place as above provided. The Bishop shall appoint some competent person as Prosecutor, who shall be considered as the party making the presentment.

CANON XXI.

Of Differences between Ministers and their Congregations.

SECTION 1. Whenever there shall be any serious difference between the Rector of any Church in this Diocese and the Congregation thereof, it shall be lawful for a majority of the Vestry or Trustees to make a representation to the Bishop, stating the facts in the case and agreeing, for themselves and for the Congregation which they represent, to submit to his decision in the matter, and to perform whatever he may require of them by any order which he may make under the provisions of this Canon, and shall at the same time serve a copy of the representation on the Rector.

Sec. 2. It shall be the duty of the Bishop, at all stages of the proceeding, to seek to bring them to an amicable conclusion; and in such case the agreement between the parties, signed by them and attested by the Bishop, shall have the same force as an order made under section 4 of this Canon.

Sec. 3. If the matter shall not be amicably settled within a reasonable time, the Bishop shall convene the Clerical Members of the Standing Committee and shall give notice to the parties to appear before him and present their proofs and arguments at such time and place as he may appoint; and he may adjourn and continue the hearing in the matter in his discretion.

Sec. 4. When the hearing is concluded, the Bishop shall make such an order in regard to the matter as he may think to be just and for the true interests of the Church; and such order may require the Rector to resign his Rectorship, and may require the Church to pay a sum of money to the Rector; and it shall be the duty of the Rector and of the Church and every member thereof to submit to and abide by such order as the final and conclusive determination of all matters of difference between them. *Provided,* that no order shall be made under this or the next succeeding section of this Canon, unless with the advice and concurrence of at least two Clerical Members of the Standing Committee, who shall have been present at the hearing.

Sec. 5. If it shall be made to appear to the Bishop that any agreement made under section 2 of this Canon, or any order made under section 4 of this Canon, or of this section, shall have been disregarded by any of the parties concerned, or if an application be made to him to modify such order, he may convene the Clerical Members of the Standing Committee, and after hearing such further proofs and arguments as may be presented to him, make such further order in the matter as he may think proper with the same effect as an order made under section 4 of this Canon.

Sec. 6. If any Church or Congregation shall persistently neglect or refuse to obey any order made under this Canon, it shall be the duty of the Bishop to exhort the members of such Congregation to submit to the authority and discipline of the Church; and if they will not do so, the Convention may proceed to dissolve the union between the Church so offending and the Convention of this Diocese, and may take such other action in the matter as it may think expedient. *Provided,* that no such action shall be held or taken to be a surrender of any right which either the Church in this Diocese, or such members of such Congregation as submit to the authority and discipline of the Church may have in the corporation of such Church, or in any property belonging thereto.

Sec. 7. Whenever the Standing Committee shall be acting as the Ecclesiastical Authority of the Diocese, the Clerical Members thereof shall perform the duties herein required of the Bishop; and they shall request the Bishop of some other Diocese to attend the hearing of the case, and shall make no order therein but with his advice and assistance.

CANON XXII.

Of Amendments of the Canons.

No new Canon or amendment of a Canon shall hereafter be adopted by the Convention, unless at least one day's previous notice thereof shall have been given in open Convention; nor, unless by unanimous consent, until the same shall have been referred to, and reported upon by a Committee of at least two Presbyters and two Laymen. All propositions to amend the Canons shall be in the form of a Canon, and such sections as shall be amended shall be re-enacted in full in their amended form.

ADMISSION OF CHURCHES.

ADVICE AND INSTRUCTIONS TO CHURCHES APPLYING FOR ADMISSION INTO UNION WITH
THE PROTESTANT EPISCOPAL CHURCH IN THE DIOCESE OF ALBANY.

Under Canon IV, in order to be admitted into union with the Church in this Diocese, the Church or congregation must (in sufficient time to allow the papers to be transmitted to, *and be received by* the Secretary of the Convention at least thirty days before the meeting of the Convention) adopt a resolution, at a legally convened and held meeting of the Vestry, or (*in the case of Churches incorporated without Vestries*), of the congregation, authorizing the application for such admission to be made, and agreeing to abide by, and conform to, and observe all the Canons of the Church, and all the rules, orders and regulations of the Convention. A copy of this resolution must be duly certified by the presiding officer of the Vestry, or of the meeting of the congregation at which the resolution was adopted, and also by the Clerk of the Vestry, or Secretary of the meeting of the congregation, and must also be authenticated by the seal of the corporation.

In Churches having Vestries, this resolution should be adopted by the Vestry. In Churches incorporated without Vestries, it should be adopted by the congregation.

The following form of resolution is recommended:

Resolved, That [*here set forth the corporate name or title by which the Church is known in law as the same is described in the Certificate of Incorporation*] desire admission into union with the Church in the Diocese of Albany, and do make application therefor to the Convention of the Church in this Diocese; and do hereby agree to abide by, and conform to, and observe all the Canons of the Church, and all the rules, orders and regulations of the Convention.

The resolution must be entered accurately and at length on the minutes of the Vestry, or of the meeting of the congregation, as the case may be.

The Canon requires an application *in writing,* to the Convention, asking admission, which must then be made out. This may be signed by the Rector (if there be one), and by one or both of the Wardens, *and* by the Clerk of the Vestry; or, in the case of Churches without Vestries, by the Minister, or by the presiding officer of the meeting at which the resolution was adopted, *and also* by the Clerk of such meeting.

The following form of application is recommended:

To the Convention of the Protestant Episcopal Church in the Diocese of Albany:

The Church or congregation duly incorporated and known in law by the name of [*here set forth the corporate name or title of the Church, as the same is described in the Certificate of Incorporation*], in pursuance, and by authority of a resolution of the [*Vestry or congregation as the case may be*] of the said Church, hereby applies for admission into union with the Church in this Diocese; and presents herewith a duly certified and authenticated copy of the resolution of the said [*Vestry or congregation, as the case may be*] adopted on the   day of   189 , authorizing such application, and agreeing to abide by, and conform to, and observe all the Canons of the Church, and all the rules, orders and regulations of the Convention. *Also,* the Certificate of Incorporation of the Church (*or in case the original certificate is not presented, then say, "a duly certified copy of the Certificate of the Incorporation of the Church*), which was duly recorded in the office of the (Clerk or Register, *as the case may be*), of the   county of   on the   : day of 189 , in Book   of Certificates of Religious I

he *official designation of the book in which such Certificates are recorded in the county
in which such Church is located*), page   . Also, a certificate of the Bishop that he
approves of the incorporation of such Church, and that such Church, in his judgment, is duly and satisfactorily established. *And also*, evidence that not less than
twenty-five persons, members of such Church, have habitually, for at least one year
preceding the date of this application, attended Divine Services in such Church or
congregation.

Dated at   in the county of   and State of New York, this
          day of   189 .
By order of the [*Vestry or congregation as the case may be*].

> A. B., *Rector*.
> C. D., *Warden*.
> E. F.,   *do*.
> G. H., *Clerk*.

Or, in case of Churches having no Vestries:

> A. B., *Minister*.
> C. D., *Presiding officer of the Meeting of
>   the Congregation*.
> E. F., *Secretary of the Meeting of the
>   Congregation*.

'The Canon also requires that the application be accompanied by the following
papers:

I. A duly certified and authenticated copy of the resolution of the Vestry or congregation authorizing the application, etc.

II. The original, or a certified copy of the Certificate of Incorporation.

III. The certificate of the Bishop's approval of the incorporation, and that, in his
judgment, the Church is duly and satisfactorily established.

IV. The evidence that not less than twenty-five persons, members of such Church,
have habitually, for at least one year preceding the date of the application, attended
Divine Service in the Church or congregation.

The following is recommended as a form for certifying the resolution of the Vestry
or of the congregation:

At a meeting of the [*Vestry or congregation, as the case may be*] of the Church or
congregation known as [*here set forth the corporate name or title of the Church, as the
same is described in the Certificate of Incorporation*], duly convened, and held according to law, at   on the   day of   18 , the following
resolution was adopted:

" *Resolved*, That [*here copy, in the precise words, and at length, and accurately, the
resolution as adopted and entered on the Minutes.*"]

Which is hereby certified by A. B., the Rector of the said Church [*or, if there be
no Rector, then* C. D., the Warden, who presided at the meeting of the Vestry at
which the resolution was adopted, there being no Rector of the said Church], and
also by E. F., the Clerk of the Vestry, and is also authenticated by the seal of the
corporation.

Dated at   in the county of   the   day of
189.

> A. B., *Rector*.

[SEAL.]   [*or*] C. D. *Warden presiding*
> E. F., *Clerk of the Vestry*.

In the case of Churches having no Vestries, the certificate may be as follows:

Which is hereby certified by A. B., Minister of the Church, *or* C. D., the Presiding officer of the meeting of the congregation at which the resolution was adopted, and also by E. F., the secretary of the said meeting, and is also authenticated by the seal of the corporation.

Dated, etc. (as above).

A. B., *Minister.*
[*or*] C. D., *Presiding officer of the Meeting*
of the Congregation.
E. F., *Secretary of the Meeting.*

[SEAL.]

The following is submitted (with the approval and authority of the Bishop) as the form for his certificate:

I do hereby certify, that I approve of the incorporation of a Church known as [*here set forth the corporate name or title of the Church as the same is described in the Certificate of Incorporation*], and that such Church, in my judgment, is duly and satisfactorily established.

Dated at   the   day of   in the year of our Lord one thousand eight hundred and

Bishop.

The following is recommended as a form for the presentation of the evidence of the number of persons habitually attending the Church:

We, the undersigned, do hereby certify and declare, that we are, and for one year last past have been connected with, or been members of, and well acquainted with the affairs and condition of, the Church or congregation known as [*here set forth the corporate name or title of the Church as the same is described in the Certificate of Incorporation*], and that we have had means of knowing, and do know, the number of persons habitually attending the said Church during one year past; and that not less than twenty-five persons, members of such Church, have habitually, for at least one year preceding this date, attended Divine Service in such Church or congregation.

Dated at   in the county of   the   day of 189 .

This certificate should be signed by the Rector, or officiating Minister, if there be one, and by one or both of the Wardens, or by two or more of the Trustees (in the case of a Church incorporated without a Vestry), or by other known and reputable parties who can certify to the fact set forth.

The application, together with the requisite papers (as before set forth), must be transmitted to the Secretary of the Convention, at least thirty days before the meeting of the Convention.

The Canon (Section 2, Canon IV.) expressly declares that "no application for the admission of a Church into union with the Church in this Diocese, shall be considered or acted upon at any meeting of the Convention, unless the same shall have been transmitted to the Secretary of the Convention at least thirty days before the meeting of the Convention."

AN ACT TO AMEND THE ACTS TO PROVIDE FOR THE INCORPORATION OF RELIG
IOUS SOCIETIES, SO FAR AS THE SAME RELATE TO CHURCHES IN CONNECTION
WITH THE PROTESTANT EPISCOPAL CHURCH

Passed May 9, 1868.

*The People of the State of New York, represented in Senate and Assembly, do enact
as follows : —*

SECTION 1. The first section of the act entitled "An act to provide for the incorporation of Religious Societies," passed April 5, 1813, is hereby amended so as to read
as follows : —

1. It shall be lawful for not less than six male persons, of full age, belonging to
any church or congregation in communion with the Protestant Episcopal Church in
this State, not already incorporated, to meet at any time at the usual place of public
worship of such church or congregation, for the purpose of incorporating themselves
under this act.

2. A notice of such meeting, specifying its object, and the time and place thereof,
shall be publicly read in the time of morning service, on two Sundays next previous
thereto, by the rector or officiating minister, or, if there be none, by any other person belonging to such church or congregation ; and shall also be posted in a conspicuous place on the outside door, near the main entrance to such place of worship.

3. The rector, or if there be none, or he be necessarily absent, then one of the
church wardens or vestrymen, or any other person, called to the chair, shall preside
at such meeting, and shall receive the votes.

4. The persons entitled to vote at such meeting shall be the male persons of full
age belonging to the church or congregation, qualified as follows, and none other : —

First. Those who have been baptized in the Protestant Episcopal Church, or who
have been received therein, either by the rite of confirmation, or by receiving the
holy communion ; or,

Second. Those who have purchased, and for not less than twelve months next
prior to such meeting have owned, a pew or seat in such church ; or who, during
the same period of time, have hired and paid for a pew or seat in such church ; or
who, during the whole period aforesaid, have been contributors in money to the
support of such church.

5. The persons so qualified shall, at such meeting, by a majority of votes,
determine :

First. The name or title by which such church or congregation shall be known
in law .

Second. On what day in Easter-week an annual election for church wardens and
vestrymen shall thereafter take place.

Third. What number of vestrymen, not less than four nor more than eight, shall
annually be elected, and shall, together with the rector (if there be one), and the
two church wardens, constitute the vestry of the church.

Fourth. And shall, by a majority of votes, elect two church wardens and the
number of vestrymen that it shall have been determined are to be annually elected,

which church wardens and vestrymen thus elected shall serve until the next regular election.

6. The polls shall continue open for one hour, and longer, in the discretion of the presiding officer, or if required, by the vote of a majority of voters present.

7. The presiding officer, together with two other persons, shall make a certificate, under their hands and seals, of —

First. The church wardens and vestrymen so elected.

Second. Of the day in Easter-week so fixed for the annual election of their successors.

Third. Of the number of vestrymen (not less than four nor more than eight) so determined upon to be annually elected to constitute part of the vestry.

Fourth. Of the name or title by which such church or congregation shall be known in law.

Which certificate being duly acknowledged, or the execution and acknowledgment thereof being duly proven before any officer authorized to take the acknowledgment or proof of deeds or conveyances of real estate, to be recorded in the county where such church or place of worship of such congregation shall be situated, shall be recorded by the clerk of such county, or by the officer whose duty it is, or may hereafter be made, to record such instruments in the county in which such church or place of worship may be situated, in a book to be by him kept for such purpose.

8. The church wardens and vestrymen so elected, and their successors in office, of themselves (but if there be a rector. then together with the rector of such church or congregation), shall form a vestry, and shall be the trustees of such church or congregation ; and they and their successors shall thereupon by virtue of this act, be a body corporate, by the name or title expressed in such certificate.

9. The male persons qualified as aforesaid, provided they shall also have belonged to such church or congregation for twelve months immediately preceding, shall, in every year thereafter, on the day in Easter-week so fixed for that purpose, elect two church wardens, and as many vestrymen (not less than four nor more than eight) as shall have been legally determined to constitute part of the vestry.

10 Notice shall be given of such election by the rector, if there be one, or if there be none, or he be absent, by the officiating minister, or by a church warden, for two Sundays next previous to the day so fixed, in the time of divine service.

11. Whenever a vacancy in the board so constituted shall happen, by death or otherwise, the vestry shall order a special election to supply such vacancy ; of which notice shall be given in the time of divine service, at least ten days previous thereto.

12. The notice of any election, stated or otherwise, shall specify the place, day, and hour of holding the same. The provisions contained in the preceding sixth clause shall apply to all elections.

13. An election to supply a vacancy, and also the stated annual election, shall be holden immediately after morning service ; and at all such elections, the rector, or if there be none, or he be absent, one of the church wardens selected for the purpose by a majority of the duly qualified voters present ; or if no warden be present, a vestryman (selected in like manner) shall preside, and receive the votes of the electors, and be the returning officer : and shall enter the proceedings in the book of the minutes of the vestry, and sign his name thereto, and offer the same to as many electors present as he shall think fit, to be by them also signed and certified.

14. The church wardens and vestrymen chosen at any of the said elections, shall hold their offices until the expiration of the year for which ▓▓▓▓▓▓▓▓▓▓▓, and until others are chosen in their stead ; and shall ▓▓▓▓

rector to such church or congregation as often as there shall be a vacancy therein, and to fix his salary or compensation.

15. No board, or meeting of such vestry shall be held, unless at least three days' notice thereof shall be given in writing, under the hand of the rector or of one of the church wardens; except that for the first meeting after an election, twenty-four hours' notice shall be sufficient; and no such board shall be competent to transact any business unless the rector, if there be one, and at least one of the church wardens, and a majority of the vestrymen be present. But if the rector be absent from the State, and shall have been so absent for over four calendar months, or if the meeting has been called by the rector, and he be absent therefrom, the board shall be competent to transact all business if there be present one church warden, and a majority of the vestrymen; except that in the absence of the rector, no measure shall be taken for effecting a sale or disposition of the real property, nor may any sale or disposition of the capital or principal of the personal estate of such corporation be made, nor any act done which shall impair the rights of such rector.

16. The rector, if there be one, and if not, then the church warden present, or if both the church wardens be present, then the church warden who shall be called to the chair by a majority of votes, shall preside and have the casting vote.

17. Whenever any corporation, organized under the provisions of this act, shall deem it for the interest of such corporation to change the number of its vestrymen it shall and may be lawful for such corporation to change the same, provided that the number of such vestrymen shall not thereby be made less than four or more than eight. And in order to effect such change, the same shall be authorized and approved by the vestry at a regular meeting thereof; and shall then at the next stated annual election for wardens and vestrymen be submitted to, and ratified by, a majority of the votes of all the qualified voters voting at such election; notice of which proposed change, and that the same will be submitted for ratification at such election, shall be given at the same time and in the same manner as is required for notice of the said election; if such change be thus ratified, a certificate shall be made setting forth the resolution of the vestry, and the proceedings to ratify the same, together with the fact of the notice being given as required, and shall be acknowledged or proved and recorded in the same manner as is required for the original certificate of organization; and thereupon the number of vestrymen to constitute a part of the vestry of such corporation, shall be such as shall be fixed by the proceedings to effect such change. But such change shall not take effect or be operative until the certificate above mentioned shall have been duly recorded.

§ 2. The provisions of the ninth, tenth, eleventh, twelfth, thirteenth, fourteenth, fifteenth, sixteenth, and seventeenth clauses of section one of this act shall apply to any church or corporation in communion with the Protestant Episcopal Church in this State heretofore incorporated under the act hereby amended, or under any of the acts amending the same, or under the several acts to provide for the incorporation of religious societies, passed April 6, 1784; March 27, 1801; or the Act for the Relief of the Protestant Episcopal Church in the State of New York, passed March 17, 1795, or by any special charter made or granted before or after July 4, 1776, whereof the vestry, at a regular meeting, shall by vote determine to adopt the same; and such vote shall, at the next ensuing stated annual election for wardens and vestrymen, be submitted to, and ratified by, a majority of the votes of all the qualified voters voting at such election, notice of such vote of the vestry, and of the proposed submission of the same for ratification, having been given at the same time and in the same manner as is required by the tenth clause of the first section of this act for notice of election. But such adoption shall not take effect, or be operative, until a certificate embodying a true copy of the resolution of the vestry, as entered upon their minutes, and the proceedings to ratify the same, together with the fact of the notice being given, as required, shall have been acknowledged or proved, and shall be recorded, as is required by the foregoing seventh clause of section one, for the certificate of incorporation.

§ 3. The first section of the act passed March 5, 1819, entitled "An Act to amend the Act entitled, 'An Act to provide for the Incorporation of Religious Societies,'" is hereby repealed.

§ 4. The third section of the act passed February 15, 1826, entitled "An Act to amend an Act entitled, 'An Act to provide for the Incorporation of Religious Societies,'" passed April 5, 1813, shall not apply to any church or congregation in connection with the Protestant Episcopal Church in this State.

§ 5. All acts and parts of acts inconsistent with the provisions of this act are hereby repealed.

MINUTES

OF THE MEETING OF

THE FEDERATE COUNCIL

OF THE

FIVE DIOCESES

IN THE

STATE OF NEW YORK,

DECEMBER 28, 1892.

MINUTES

FEDERATE COUNCIL,

DECEMBER 28, 1892.

After the Celebration of the Holy Communion at 9 A. M., on Wednesday, the 28th of December, 1892, at the Chantry of Grace Church, New York, the members of the Council met at the Diocesan House, 9 Lafayette place, in accordance with the following notice:

> DIOCESAN HOUSE,
> NEW YORK, *December* 12, 1892.
>
> *Dear Sir* — Having received from the several Bishops having jurisdiction in the State of New York a unanimous request for a meeting, to consider the proposed changes in the law for the incorporation of churches and other kindred matters of common interest to the several Dioceses, I beg to give notice that a meeting of the Federate Council will be held at the Diocesan House, 29 Lafayette place, New York City, on the Innocents' day, December 28, 1892, at ten o'clock, A. M., at which the favor of your presence is requested. And I am,
>
> Very faithfully yours,
> H. C. POTTER,
> *Bishop of New York.*
>
> T. STAFFORD DROWNE,
> *Secretary.*

The Bishop of New York presided, and opened the meeting with prayer.

The Secretary called the Roll, when the following answered to their names:

The Bishops of New York, Western New York, Long Island, Albany, and Central New York.

The Rev. Drs. Gallaudet, Mulchahey, Brooks, Seabury, Van Kleeck, Rev. Mr. Canedy, and Messrs. Calvin, Miller, Egleston and Merritt, from the Diocese of New York.

The Rev. Dr. Dunham, Rev. Mr. Wrigley, from the Diocese of Western New York.

The Rev. Drs. Drowne, Haskins, Bacchus, and Rev. Mr. Swentzel, from the Diocese of Long Island.

The Rev. Messrs. Cookson, Silliman, Edmunds, Jr., Rev. Dr. Harison, and Rev. Mr. Mariett, from the Diocese of Albany.

The Rev. Drs. Babcock and Lockwood, and Messrs. Sawyer and Van Wagenen, from the Diocese of Central New York.

A quorum of members being present, the Bishop of New York announced that the Council was ready for business; and called upon Prof. Egleston to report the present *status* of the proposed Amended Act relating to the Incorporation of Churches and Election of Vestries; which he did, stating that the Act had been submitted to the Annual Conventions of the several Dioceses, and was approved by Long Island and Albany, but not approved by New York, Western New York and Central New York. He also pointed out some of the defects of the Amended Act.

The following Preamble and Resolution were proposed by the Bishop of Albany, which on motion were adopted:

At a meeting held in the Diocesan House in the City of New York, on Wednesday, December 28, 1892, at which were present the Bishops of the five Dioceses in the State of New York and a number of Clergymen and laymen from each of the five Dioceses duly accredited to represent their Dioceses, it was unanimously

Resolved, That the Legislature of the State of New York be respectfully requested, in acting upon the draft of the Religious Corporations Law presented by the Statutory Revision Committee, to substitute for all reference to the Protestant Episcopal Church in the codification recommended, the provisions of the existing statutes of 1813 and 1868 unchanged; to remain in force until the Dioceses in the State, or a majority of them, shall memorialize the Legislature for a change.

On motion of Bishop Littlejohn, it was

Resolved, That a representative, clerical or lay, be appointed from each Diocese as a Committee to present this preamble and resolution to the Legislature at Albany.

The Chairman appointed the following as this Committee: The Bishop of Albany, the Rev. Mr. Canedy of New York, the Rev. Dr. Potter of Western New York, the Rev. Dr. Alsop of Long Island, and the Rev. Dr. Brainard of Central New York.

On motion of the Rev. Mr. Cookson, it was

Resolved, That a Commission be elected by this Council to consider all matters relating to changes in the Act of Incorporating Churches of our Communion, and be asked to report amendments at a following meeting of the Council; said Commission to be nominated by the Bishop of each Diocese, and elected by the Council, the Bishops being *ex-officio* members of said Commission.

On motion of the Rev. Dr. Seabury, it was

Resolved, That one clerical and one lay member in each Diocese be nominated, to act in connection with the Bishops.

The Bishop of New York nominated the Rev. William J. Seabury, D. D., and Prof. Thomas Eccleston.

The Bishop of Western New York nominated the Rev. Charles Wells Hayes, D. D., and Judge J. M. Smith.

The Bishop of Long Island nominated the Rev. T. Stafford Drowne, D. D., and Hon. Augustus Van Wyck.

The Bishop of Albany nominated the Rev. Fenwick M. Cookson and Judge Charles E. Patterson.

The Bishop of Central New York nominated the Rev. William T. Gibson, D. D., LL. D., and Mr. A. H. Sawyer.

On motion, these several nominations were approved and announced as the Commission to act with the Bishops.

On motion of the Rev. Dr. Brooks, it was

Resolved, That a Committee be appointed to consider the subject of petitioning the Legislature of the State, so to amend the laws of the State, as to require all persons seeking marriage to obtain from a Civil Court a license, and to report to this body, if considered desirable by them, a bill providing for such a purpose.

Resolved, That this body proceed to elect the Commission, after a nomination of a clergyman and a layman by each of the five Bishops present.

The persons nominated were as follows: The Rev. Arthur Brooks, D D., and Mr. G. Macculloch Miller, from New York; the Rev. Henry Anstice, D. D., and Judge J. C. Smith, from Western New York; the Rev. Henry C. Swentzel and Mr. William S. Cogswell, from Long Island; the Rev. Charles C. Edmunds, Jr., and Hon. Robert Earl, from Albany; the Rev. Henry B. Lockwood, D. D., and Mr. John R. Van Wagenen, from Central New York.

On motion, the foregoing were elected as members of this Commission.

On motion, the Bishops of the five Dioceses were united to this Commission, with the Bishop of New York as Chairman.

On motion of the Bishop of Albany, it was

Resolved, That when this body adjourns, it adjourn to meet at the call of a majority of the Bishops of the five Dioceses.

On motion of the Bishop of New York, it was

Resolved, That a Committee be appointed to obtain, if possible, reduced railroad rates for missionaries in the State.

The following were appointed as this Committee: The Bishop of New York, the Hon. John A. King, of Long Island, and Mr. J. R. Van Wagenen, of Central New York.

On motion, it was

Resolved, That after the reading and approval of the minutes, and the usual devotions, this Council adjourn.

The minutes of this day's proceedings were read and approved.

The Chairman said appropriate collects, and gave the Blessing of Peace; and the Council stood adjourned.

Attest: T. STAFFORD DROWNE,
Secretary.

DIOCESAN INSTITUTIONS.

THE SISTERHOOD OF THE HOLY CHILD JESUS.

ST AGNES' SCHOOL, ALBANY.

THE CHILD'S HOSPITAL, ALBANY.

THE ST. MARGARET'S HOUSE, ALBANY.

THE CHURCH HOME, TROY.

THE ST. CHRISTINA HOME, SARATOGA.

THE ST. CHRISTOPHER HOME, EAST LINE.

THE ORPHAN HOUSE OF THE HOLY SAVIOUR, COOPERSTOWN.

THE BIBLE AND COMMON PRAYER BOOK SOCIETY OF ALBANY AND VICINITY.

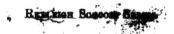

PAROCHIAL INSTITUTIONS.

ST. PETER'S ORPHANAGE, ALBANY.

THE MARTHA MEMORIAL HOUSE, TROY.

THE MARY WARREN FREE INSTITUTE, TROY.

Diocese of Albany.

Convention Journal,

A. D., 1893.

TOGETHER WITH A

REPORT OF THE PROCEEDINGS

AT THE

TWENTY-FIFTH ANNIVERSARY

OF THE

CONSECRATION OF THE BISHOP,

AND THE

MINUTES OF THE MEETING

OF THE

FEDERATE COUNCIL,

WHICH ASSEMBLED IN

NEW YORK CITY,

January 24, 1894.

JOURNAL OF THE PROCEEDINGS

OF THE

Twenty-Fifth Annual Convention

OF THE

Protestant Episcopal Church

IN THE

DIOCESE OF ALBANY,

WHICH WAS HELD IN

ALL SAINTS' CATHEDRAL, ALBANY, N. Y.,

TUESDAY, NOVEMBER 14,

A. D., 1893.

ALBANY, N. Y.:
WEED-PARSONS PRINTING CO., PRINTERS.
1894.

LIST OF THE CLERGY

IN THE

DIOCESE OF ALBANY

IN THE ORDER OF CANONICAL RESIDENCE

NOVEMBER 14, 1893.

Showing the dates of becoming resident, and, in case of those not gaining residence by Ordination, the name of the Diocese from which each was received.

Date of Reception.	Diocese from which received.	Name.
1868. Nov. 15.	At Primary Convention.	The Rt. Rev. WILLIAM CROSWELL DOANE, D. D. *Oxon.*, LL. D. *Cantab.*, Bishop.
" "	" "	The Rev. JOSEPH CAREY, S. T. D.
" "	" "	The Rev. EDGAR T. CHAPMAN.
" "	" "	The Rev. JOSEPH N. MULFORD.
" "	" "	The Rev. GEORGE H. NICHOLLS, S. T. D.
" "	" "	The Rev. J. LIVINGSTON REESE, D. D.
" "	" "	The Rev. JOHN B. TIBBITS, Deacon.
" "	" "	The Rev. J. IRELAND TUCKER, S. T. D.
" Dec. 1.	" "	The Rev. JAMES WILKINS STEWART.
1870. Mar. 7.	Massachusetts - -	The Rev. FENWICK M. COOKSON.
" June 12.	- - - - - -	The Rev. WILLIAM CURTIS PROUT.
" Dec. 6.	Pennsylvania - -	The Rev. JAMES CAIRD.
1871. April 12.	Montreal - - -	The Rev. J. D. MORRISON, D. D., LL. D.
" July 12.	Vermont - - -	The Rev. J. W. McILWAINE.
1874. May 12.	New York - -	The Rev. WILLIAM CHARLES GRUBBE.
" Aug. 3.	Western New York	The Rev. WALTON W. BATTERSHALL, D. D.
" Sept. 17.	- - - - - -	The Rev. THEODORE A. SNYDER.
" Sept. 29.	Central New York -	The Rev. MOSES E. WILSON.
" Oct. 7.	Pennsylvania -	The Rev. R. J. ADLER.
" Nov. 1.	- - - - - -	The Rev. HENRY M. SMYTH.
1875. Nov. 5.	New York - -	The Rev. CHARLES C. EDMUNDS.
1876. Mar. 12.	- - - - -	The Rev. WILLIAM B. REYNOLDS, Deacon.
" Aug. 22.	Central New York -	The Rev. WILLIAM N. IRISH.
" Sept. 26.	North Carolina - -	The Rev. WILLIAM W. LORD, D.
" Dec. 11.	New York - -	The Rev. CHARLES S. OLM
1877. Jan. 24.	- - - - -	The Rev. CHARLES EDWA

Date of Reception.	Diocese from which received.	Name.
1878. Feb. 27.	Montana - - -	- The Rev. EUGENE L. TOY.
1879. Jan. 1.	Long Island - -	- The Rev. THOMAS B. FULCHER, B. D.
" July 13.	- - - - - -	- The Rev. JOHN N. MARVIN.
" July 15.	Massachusetts -	- The Rev. SILAS M. ROGERS.
1880. May 28.	- - - - - -	- The Rev. JOHN PROUT.
" June 1.	- - - - - -	- The Rev. CHARLES C. EDMUNDS, Jr.
" Oct. 18.	Massachusetts -	- The Rev. FREDERICK H. T. HORSFIELD.
1881. Jan. 8.	Western New York	The Rev. CHARLES M. NICKERSON, D. D.
" Dec. 19.	New York - -	- The Rev. GEORGE DENT SILLIMAN, D. D.
1882. Jan. 9.	Newark - -	- The Rev. WILLIAM HENRY HARISON, D. D
" Feb. 28.	Utah - - -	- The Rev. R. M. KIRBY D. D.
" Nov. 7.	Connecticut -	- The Rev. HOBART COOKE.
" Dec. 28.	Rhode Island	- The Rev. CLEMENT J. WHIPPLE.
1883. Feb. 12.	Central New York -	The Rev. E. BAYARD SMITH.
" May 5.	Delaware - - -	- The Rev. W. G. W. LEWIS.
1884. Jan. 20.	- - - - - -	- The Rev. JAMES A. DICKSON.
" Feb. 18.	Fredericton - -	- The Rev. FREDERICK S. SILL, S. T. B.
" Mar. 4.	Ohio - - -	- The Rev. SAMUEL T. STREET.
" May 27.	Newark - -	- The Rev. CHARLES PELLETREAU.
" June 3.	- - - - -	- The Rev. EDWARD S. DEG. TOMPKINS.
" July 12.	- - - - -	- The Rev. RUSSELL WOODMAN.
1885. Jan. 10.	Springfield - - -	- The Rev. JAMES E. HALL.
" Mar. 16.	Exeter, England -	- The Rev. THOMAS H. R. LUNEY
" May 1.	Central Pennsylvania	The Rev. J. PHILIP B. PENDLETON, S. T. B
" May 30.	- - - - -	- The Rev. CHARLES TEMPLE.
" May 31.	- - - - -	- The Rev. SHELDON M. GRISWOLD.
" Aug. 6.	Maine - - -	- The Rev. RICHMOND SHREVE, D. D.
" Oct. 10.	- - - - -	- The Rev. EDWARD DUDLEY TIBBITS.
" Nov. 5.	Wisconsin - -	- The Rev. LOUIS HECTOR SCHUBERT.
" Dec. 18.	Connecticut - - -	The Rev. EATON W MAXCY D. D.
1886. Mar. 8.	Western New York	- The Rev. WILLIAM B. BOLMER.
" Sept. 24.	Yedo - - -	The Rev. CLEMENT THEOPHILUS BLANCHET
" Nov. 13.	Central Pennsylvania	The Rev. DANIEL WASHBURN.
1887. Feb. 12.	- - - - -	The Rev. JOSEPH T ZORN.
" May 19.	Connecticut - -	- The Rev. EDGAR A. ENOS, D. D.
" Nov. 5.	Massachusetts -	- The Rev. WILFORD LASH ROBBINS, D. D.
1888. Jan. 20.	Southern Ohio -	- The Rev. HENRY T. GREGORY.
" Jan. 23.	New Hampshire -	The Rev. FREDERICK MORLAND GRAY.
" May 18.	Pittsburgh - -	- The Rev WILLIAM MASON COOK, S. T. B.
" May 20.	- - - - -	The Rev. GEORGE MERIWETHER IRISH.
" May 22.	Springfield - -	- The Rev. THOMAS WHITE.
" Sept. 3.	Tennessee - -	- The Rev. ALFRED TAYLOR.
" Oct. 7.	- - - - -	- The Rev. WALTER CHARLES STEWART.
" Nov. 20.	Nova Scotia - -	- The Rev. ANGUS C. MACDONALD.
1889. April 15.	Maine - - -	- The Rev. ROBERT N PARKE, D. D.
" June 16.	- - - - -	- The Rev. ELMER PLINY MILLER.
" Sept. 23.	Springfield - -	- The Rev. oward McDOUGALL.
" Oct. 31.	Missouri - - -	The Rev. E. W FLOWER.
" Nov. 1.	New York - -	- The Rev. WALTER HASKINS LAROM.
1890. Feb. 3.	Western New York	The Rev E. RUTHVEN ARMSTRONG.
" Mar. 14.	Massachusetts - -	- The Rev. ERNEST MARIETT.
" April 25.	New Jersey - -	The Rev. HARRIS COX RUSH.
" May 8.	Rochester, England	- The Rev. S. C. THOMPSON.
" July 20.	Fredericton - -	- The Rev. CHARLES H. HATHEWAY.
" Sept. 24.	Vermont - -	- The Rev. FREDERICK SHUBALL FISHER.
1891. Jan. 22.	Quebec - - -	- The Rev. ROBERT WYNDHAM BROWN.
" Feb. 12.	Ohio - - -	- The Rev. GEORGE A. HOLBROOK.
" May 5.	New Jersey - -	- The Rev. ARTHUR LOWNDES.
" May 8.	Minnesota - -	- The Rev. RICHMOND H. GESNER.
" June 3.	- - - - -	- The Rev. FREEBORN GARRETTSON JEWET, Jr.
" June 14.	- - - - -	- The Rev. JAMES FREDERIC OLMSTED.
" July 9.	Vermont - - -	- The Rev. CLARENCE MORTIMER CONANT.

Date of Reception.	Diocese from which received.	Name.
1891. Sept. 10.	- - - - - -	The Rev. GEORGE LYNDE RICHARDSON.
" Oct. 15.	Milwaukee - -	The Rev. GEORGE GALEN CARTER, S. T. D.
" Oct. 19.	Connecticut - -	The Rev. GEORGE BRINCKERHOFF RICHARDS.
" Oct. 28.	- - - - - -	The Rev. HARRY ELMER GILCHRIST.
" Nov. 15.	New York - -	The Rev. GEORGE B. JOHNSON.
" Dec. 8.	Long Island - -	The Rev. JOHN WILLIAM GILL.
" Dec. 17.	- - - - - -	The Rev. WILLIAM FRANCIS PARSONS.
1892. Jan. 4.	Georgia - -	The Rev. THOMAS BOONE.
" Mar. 5.	New York - -	The Rev. HAMILTON CADY.
" Mar. 26.	Ontario - - -	The Rev. FRANK SLADEN GREENHALGH.
" April 11.	Springfield - -	The Rev. JOHN H. MOLINEUX.
" April 11.	Springfield - -	The Rev. PERCY ST. MICHAEL PODMORE.
" May 23.	Central New York	The Rev. ELMER R. EARLE.
" June 29.	Rupert's Land -	The Rev. ALFRED L. FORTIN.
" July 12.	Ontario - - -	The Rev. DAVID JENKINS.
" Aug. 3.	New York - -	The Rev. EDWARD CARLTON HOSKINS.
" Sept. 24.	New York - -	The Rev. EARNEST WEBSTER DUSTAN.
" Oct. 11.	Long Island - -	The Rev. HENRY R. FREEMAN.
" Nov. 14.	Pittsburgh - -	The Rev. JOHN E. BOLD.
" Nov. 16.	- - - - - -	The Rev. JOHN MILLS GILBERT, Deacon.
" Nov. 16.	- - - - - -	The Rev. CHARLES ALBERT HOWELLS, Deacon.
" Nov. 21.	Michigan - - -	The Rev. WILLIAM BALL WRIGHT.
" Dec. 22.	Tennessee - -	The Rev. MEREDITH O. SMITH.
1893. Jan. 17.	Arkansas - -	The Rev. DAVID F. McDONALD, D. D.
" Feb. 20.	Newark - -	The Rev. WILLIAM H. A. HALL.
" Feb. 20.	Tennessee - -	The Rev. CALBRAITH B. PERRY.
" May 31.	Delaware - -	The Rev. JOHN HOLWELL GEARE.
" June 7.	- - - - - -	The Rev. WILLIAM ANDERSON STIRLING, Deacon.
" June 11.	- - - - - -	The Rev. MARVIN HILL DANA, Deacon.
" June 11.	- - - - - -	The Rev. FRANK N. BOUCK, Deacon.
" June 11.	Pennsylvania - -	The Rev. THOMAS BURROWS.
" July 24.	New Jersey - -	The Rev. JAMES W. SMITH.
" July 31.	Ontario - - -	The Rev. CHARLES ELLIOTT MACKENZIE.
" Sept. 7.	Vermont - - -	The Rev. RICHARD C. SEARING.
" Sept. 21.	- - - - - -	The Rev. EDWARD T. CARROLL, Deacon.
" Oct. 16.	Quincy - - - -	The Rev HENRY CORNELIUS DYER.
" Oct. 17.	Newark - - -	The Rev. SAMUEL D. VAN LOAN.
" Oct. 27.	Milwaukee - -	The Rev WATSON B. HALL.
" Nov. 7.	Milwaukee - -	The Rev. WILLIAM STONE HAYWARD.
" Nov. 13.	New York - -	The Rev. CHURCHILL SATTERLEE.

AN ALPHABETICAL LIST OF THE CLERGY.

This mark * designates the Alumni of the General Theological Seminary.

The Right Rev. WILLIAM CROSWELL DOANE, D. D. *Oxon.*, LL. D. *Cantab.*, Bishop, Albany.

The Rev. R. J. ADLER, Rector, St. Mark's Church, Green Island, Albany county.

The Rev. E. RUTHVEN ARMSTRONG, Rector, St. James' Church, Caldwell, Warren county. P. O., Lake George.

* The Rev. WALTON W. BATTERSHALL, D. D., Rector, St. Peter's Church, Albany, Albany county.

The Rev. CLEMENT T. BLANCHET, Missionary, St. Sacrament Church, Bolton, Warren county.

The Rev. JOHN E. BOLD, Missionary, St. James' Church, Oneonta, Otsego county.

* The Rev. W. B. BOLMER, Rector, St. Luke's Church, Troy, Rensselaer county.

The Rev. THOMAS BOONE, Missionary, All Saints' Church, Round Lake, Grace Mission, Jonesville, and St. John's Church, East Line, Saratoga county.

* The Rev. FRANK N. BOUCK, Missionary, St. Luke's Church, Mechanicville, Saratoga county.

The Rev. ROBERT WYNDHAM BROWN, Rector, Grace Church, Canton, and Missionary, Trinity Chapel, Morley, St. Lawrence county.

The Rev. THOMAS BURROWS, Rector, St. Peter's Church, Hobart, Delaware county.

* The Rev. HAMILTON CADY, Rector, Church of the Holy Cross, Warrensburgh, Warren county.

The Rev. JAMES CAIRD, Rector, Free Church of the Ascension, Troy, Rensselaer county.

* The Rev. JOSEPH CAREY, S. T. D., Rector, Bethesda Church, Saratoga Springs, Saratoga county.

The Rev. EDWARD T. CARROLL. Fitchburg, Mass.

The Rev. GEORGE GALEN CARTER, S. T. D., Rector. All Saints' Church, Hudson, and Trinity Church, Claverack, and Missionary, Columbia county.

* The Rev. EDGAR T. CHAPMAN, Canon and Treasurer, Cathedral of All Saints, Priest in charge, St. Margaret's Mission, Menands Station. P. O., Troy road, Albany.

The Rev. CLARENCE MORTIMER CONANT, Missionary, Church of the Memorial, Middleville, and Trinity Church, Fairfield, Herkimer county.

* The Rev. WILLIAM MASON COOK, S. T. B., Rector, St. Augustine's Church, Ilion, and Missionary, St. Alban's Church, Frankfort, Herkimer county.

The Rev. HOBART COOKE, Rector, Trinity Church, Plattsburgh, Clinton county.

* The Rev. FENWICK M. COOKSON, Rector, Church of the Messiah, Glen's Falls, Warren county.

The Rev. CHARLES EDWARD CRAGG, Port Henry, Essex county.

* The Rev. MARVIN H. DANA, Missionary, St. John's Church, Stillwater, Saratoga county.

The Rev. JAMES A. DICKSON, Rector, Trinity Church, Gouverneur, and Missionary, St. Lawrence county.

* The Rev. EARNEST WEBSTER DUSTAN, Rector, Trinity Church, Sharon Springs, Schoharie county.

The Rev. HENRY CORNELIUS DYER, Assistant Minister, All Saints' Church, Hoosac, Rensselaer county.

The Rev. ELMER R. EARLE, Missionary, Grace Church, Norfolk, and St. Andrew's, Norwood, St. Lawrence county.

* The Rev. CHARLES C. EDMUNDS, Missionary, Zion Church, Fonda, Montgomery county. P. O., Johnston, Fulton county.

* The Rev. CHARLES C. EDMUNDS, Jr., Rector, St. Mark's Church, Hoosick Falls, Rensselaer county.

The Rev. EDGAR A. ENOS, D. D., Rector, St. Paul's Church, Troy, Rensselaer county.

* The Rev. FREDERICK S. FISHER, Rector, Christ Church, Deposit, and Missionary, Delaware county.

The Rev. E. W. FLOWER, Rector, Christ Church, Duanesburgh, Schenectady county.

The Rev. ALFRED L. FORTIN, Rector, St. Peter's Church, Brushton, and St. Mark's, West Bangor, Franklin county, and Missionary, St. Thomas' Church, Lawrenceville, St. Lawrence county.

The Rev. HENRY R. FREEMAN, Rector, St. John's Church, Troy, Rensselaer county.

* The Rev. THOMAS B. FULCHER, B. D., Canon and Precentor, Cathedral of All Saints, Albany, Albany county.

The Rev. J. HOLWELL GEARE, Rector, Trinity Church, Granville, and Missionary, North Granville, Washington county.

* The Rev. RICHMOND H. GESNER, Rector, Zion Church, Morris, Otsego county.

The Rev. JOHN MILLS GILBERT, Missionary, Calvary Church, Burnt Hills, and St. Paul's, Charlton, Saratoga county.

The Rev. HARRY ELMER GILCHRIST, Rector, Zion Church, Sandy Hill, Washington county.

The Rev. JOHN WILLIAM GILL, Rector, St. Paul's Church, Keeseville, and Missionary, St. James', Ausable Forks, Essex county.

The Rev. FREDERICK MORLAND GRAY, Honorary Canon, Cathedral of All Saints, and Chaplain, St. Agnes' School, Albany, Albany county.

The Rev. FRANK SLADEN GREENHALGH.

The Rev. HENRY T. GREGORY, Rector, Church of the Cross, Ticonderoga, and Missionary, Essex county.

* The Rev. SHELDON M. GRISWOLD, Rector, Christ Church, Hudson, Columbia county.

The Rev. WILLIAM CHARLES GRUBBE, Rector, Gloria Dei Church, Palenville, and Missionary, Greene county.

* The Rev JAMES E. HALL, Rector, Grace Church, Cherry Valley, Otsego county.

The Rev. WATSON B. HALL, Missionary, Trinity Church, Ashland, Greene county. P. O., Jewett Heights.

The Rev. WILLIAM H. A. HALL, Rector, St. Barnabas' Church, Stottville, Columbia county.

* The Rev. WILLIAM HENRY HARISON, D. D., Ogdensburgh, N. Y.

The Rev. CHARLES H. HATHEWAY, Honorary Canon, Cathedral of All Saints, Albany, also Missionary, St. Andrew's Church, West Troy, Albany county, and St. Giles', Castleton, Rensselaer county.

The Rev. WILLIAM STONE HAYWARD, Missionary, Christ Church, Morristown, St. Lawrence county.

The Rev. GEORGE A. HOLBROOK, Rector, St. Barnabas' Church, Troy, Rensselaer county.

* The Rev. FREDERICK H. T. HORSFIELD, Rector, St. Luke's Church, Cambridge, Washington county.

* The Rev. EDWARD CARLTON HOSKINS, Missionary, Church of the Good Shepherd, Canajoharie, and Church of the Holy Cross, Fort Plain, Montgomery county.

The Rev. CHARLES ALBERT HOWELLS, Missionary, Mission of the Good Shepherd, Santa Clara, Franklin county.

* The Rev. GEORGE M. IRISH, Rector, Zion Church, Colton, St. Lawrence county.

The Rev. WILLIAM N. IRISH, Rector, St. John's Church, Essex, and Missionary, Essex county.

The Rev. DAVID JENKINS, Missionary, St. James' Church, Hogansburgh, and at Fort Covington, St. Lawrence county.

The Rev. FREEBORN GARRETTSON JEWETT, Jr., Rector, St. Paul's Church, Albany, Albany county.

The Rev. GEORGE B. JOHNSON, Rector, Church of Our Saviour, Lebanon Springs, and Missionary, Columbia county.

* The Rev. R. M. KIRBY, D. D., Rector, Trinity Church, Potsdam, St. Lawrence county.

The Rev. WALTER HASKINS LAROM, Missionary, Church of St. Luke the Beloved Physician, Saranac Lake, and St. John's in the Wilderness, St. Regis Lake, Franklin county, and Good Shepherd, Bloomingdale, Essex county.

The Rev. WILLIAM G. W. LEWIS, Rector, Immanuel Church, Otego, and Missionary, Otsego county.

The Rev. WILLIAM W. LORD, D. D., Cooperstown, Otsego county.

The Rev. ARTHUR LOWNDES, Rector, St. Mark's Church, Philmont, and Missionary, Church of St. John in the Wilderness, Copake, Columbia county.

The Rev. THOMAS H. R. LUNEY, Missionary, St. Luke's Church, Chatham, Columbia county.

The Rev. ANGUS C. MACDONALD. Rector, St. Paul's Church, Waddington, and Missionary, St Luke's Church, Lisbon, St. Lawrence county.

The Rev. DAVID F. McDONALD, D. D., Rector, Christ Church, Gilbertsville, and St. Stephen's, Maple Grove, Otsego county.

*The Rev. HOWARD McDOUGALL, Missionary, Grace Mission, Stamford, Delaware county.

The Rev. J. W. McILWAINE, Rector, St. James' Church, Fort Edward, Washington county.

The Rev. CHARLES ELLIOTT MACKENZIE, Missionary, St John's Church, Massena, St. Lawrence county.

The Rev. ERNEST MARIETT, Rector, Emmanuel Church, Little Falls, Herkimer county.

The Rev. JOHN N. MARVIN, Rector, St. John's Church, Johnstown, Fulton county.

The Rev. EATON W. MAXCY, D. D., Rector, Christ Church, Troy, Rensselaer county.

*The Rev. ELMER P. MILLER, Rector, St. Luke's Church, Catskill, Greene county.

The Rev. JOHN H. MOLINEUX, Rector, Trinity Church, Whitehall, Washington county.

The Rev. J. D MORRISON, D. D., LL. D., Rector, St. John's Church, Ogdensburgh, St. Lawrence county.

The Rev. JOSEPH N MULFORD, Missionary, Church of the Good Shepherd, Raquette Lake, Hamilton county.

The Rev GEORGE H. NICHOLLS, S. T. D., Rector Emeritus, St. Mark's Church, Hoosick Falls, Rensselaer county.

* The Rev. CHARLES M. NICKERSON, D.D., Rector, Trinity Church, Lansingburgh, Rensselaer county.

*The Rev. CHARLES S. OLMSTED, Rector, Christ Church, Cooperstown, Otsego county.

The Rev JAMES FREDERIC OLMSTED, Rector, Christ Church, Schenectady, Schenectady county.

*The Rev. ROBERT N. PARKE, D D., Rector. St. Matthew's Church, Unadilla, Otsego county

The Rev WILLIAM FRANCIS PARSONS, Rector. St. Stephen's Church, Schuylerville, Saratoga county.

* The Rev CHARLES PELLETREAU, Rector, Christ Church, Ballston Spa, Saratoga county.

* The Rev J. PHILIP B. PENDLETON, S. T. B., Rector, St George's Church, Schenectady, Schenectady county

* The Rev CALBRAITH B PERRY, Rector, St. Andrew's Church, Schroon Lake, Essex county, and Priest in charge, Christ Church, Pottersville, Warren county.

The Rev PERCY ST. MICHAEL PODMORE.

* The Rev JOHN PROUT, Rector, St Paul's Church, East Springfield, and Missionary, St. Mary's Church, Springfield Centre, Otsego county

* The Rev WILLIAM C. PROUT, Rector, Christ Church, Herkimer, Herkimer county

The Rev J. LIVINGSTON REESE, D D., New York city

The Rev WILLIAM B REYNOLDS, Assistant Minister, Church of St John in the Wilderness, Copake Iron Works, Columbia county.

The Rev GEORGE BRINCKERHOFF RICHARDS, Rector, St John's Church, Richfield Springs, Otsego county.

The Rev GEORGE LYNDE RICHARDSON, Assistant Minister, St. Paul's Church, Albany, Albany county.

The Rev WILFORD LASH ROBBINS, D. D., Dean, Cathedral of All Saints, Albany, Albany county.

The Rev. SILAS M ROGERS, Rector, St Peter's Church, Ellenburgh, and St. Paul's Church, Ellenburgh Centre, and Missionary, Clinton county.

* The Rev. HARRIS COX RUSH, Rector, St. Paul's Church, Salem, Washington county.

* The Rev. CHURCHILL SATTERLEE, Assistant Minister, St. Peter's Church, Albany, Albany county.

The Rev. LOUIS H. SCHUBERT, Glenham, N. Y.

*The Rev. RICHARD C. SEARING, Rector, Christ Church, Walton, Delaware county.

The Rev. RICHMOND SHREVE, D. D., Rector, Church of the Holy Innocents, Albany, Albany county.

* The Rev. FREDERICK S. SILL, Rector, St. John's Church, Cohoes, Albany county.

* The Rev. GEORGE D. SILLIMAN, D. D., Rector, Grace Church, Albany, Albany county.

* The Rev. E. BAYARD SMITH, Rector, Trinity Church, West Troy, Albany county.

* The Rev. JAMES W. SMITH, Rector, St. Paul's Church, Kinderhook, Columbia county.

* The Rev. MEREDITH OGDEN SMITH, Missionary, Trinity Church, Schaghticoke, Rensselaer county.

The Rev. HENRY M. SMYTH, Missionary, Christ Church, Gloversville, Fulton county.

The Rev. THEODORE A. SNYDER, Rector, Christ Church, Greenville, and St. Paul's Church, Oak Hill, Greene county.

* The Rev. JAMES WILKINS STEWART, Poughkeepsie, N. Y.

The Rev. WALTER CHARLES STEWART, Honorary Canon, Cathedral of All Saints, Diocesan Missionary. P. O. Albany.

The Rev. WILLIAM ANDERSON STIRLING, Rector, Grace Church, Mohawk, and Missionary, Herkimer county.

The Rev. SAMUEL T. STREET, Rector, Grace Church, Waterford, Saratoga county.

The Rev. ALFRED TAYLOR, Missionary, Church of the Good Shepherd, Chestertown, and St. Paul's, Bartonville, Warren county.

* The Rev. CHARLES TEMPLE, S. T. B., Rector, St. Mark's Church, Malone, Franklin county.

The Rev. S. C. THOMPSON, Missionary, Trinity Church, Rensselaerville, Albany county.

* The Rev. EDWARD DUDLEY TIBBITS, Rector, All Saints' Church, Hoosac, Priest in charge, Church of the Holy Name, Boyntonville, Rensselaer county, Honorary Canon, Cathedral of All Saints.

The Rev. JOHN B. TIBBITS, Officiating, All Saints' Church, Hoosac, Rensselaer county.

The Rev. EDWARD S. DeG. TOMPKINS, Missionary, Christ Church, Coxsackie, Greene county. P. O. Kinderhook, N. Y.

* The Rev. EUGENE L. TOY, Rector, Church of St. John the Evangelist, Stockport, Columbia county.

* The Rev. JOHN IRELAND TUCKER, S. T. D., Pastor, Church of the Holy Cross, and Principal of the Warren Free Institute, Troy, Rensselaer county.

The Rev. SAMUEL D. VAN LOAN, Missionary, Emmanuel Church, Griffin's Corners, Delaware county. P. O. Pine Hill, N. Y.

The Rev. DANIEL WASHBURN, Maple Grove, Otsego county.

* The Rev. CLEMENT J. WHIPPLE, Rector, St. Mary's Church, Luzerne, Warren county, and Missionary, St. John's Church, Conklingville, Saratoga county.

* The Rev. THOMAS WHITE, Missionary, Church of the Epiphany, Bath, Rensselaer county.

The Rev. MOSES E WILSON, Rector, St. Luke's Church, Clermont, and Missionary, Columbia county.

The Rev. RUSSELL WOODMAN, Rector, Trinity Church, Albany, Albany county.

The Rev. W. BALL WRIGHT, Rector, Christ Church, Rouse's Point, and St. John's Church, Champlain, and Missionary, Clinton county.

The Rev. JOSEPH T. ZORN, Missionary, Calvary Church, Cairo, Greene county.

I certify the above to be a correct list of the clergy canonically resident in the Diocese of Albany.

ALBANY, *November* 14, 1893.

WM. CROSWELL DOANE,
Bishop.

2

SUPPLEMENT TO THE CLERGY LIST, FEBRUARY 1, 1894.

* ADDITIONS.

The Rev. C. GRAHAM ADAMS, D. D. (received from the Diocese of Indiana), Rector, Church of the Messiah, Greenbush, Rensselaer county.

The Rev. D. A. BONNAR (received from the Diocese of Pittsburgh), Missionary, St. John's Church, Dolgeville, Fulton county.

The Rev. JOHN G. FAWCETT (received from the Diocese of East Carolina), Rector, Trinity Church, Athens, Greene county.

* The Rev. WILLIAM WHITE HANCE (received from the Missionary Jurisdiction of Wyoming and Idaho), Assistant Minister, St. John's Church, Ogdensburgh, St. Lawrence county.

* The Rev. ARTHUR B. LIVERMORE (received from the Diocese of Chicago), Rector, St. John's Church, Delhi, Delaware county.

The Rev. BENJAMIN F. MILLER (received from the Diocese of Minnesota), Missionary, Church of the Holy Spirit, Schenevus, Otsego county.

REMOVAL.

The Rev. EDWARD T. CARROLL, to the Diocese of Massachusetts.

CLERGY IN CHARGE OF THE CHURCHES ON THE CONTINENT OF EUROPE, UNDER THE JURISDICTION OF THE BISHOP OF ALBANY, AS BISHOP IN CHARGE.

The Rev. J. B. MORGAN, D. D., Rector, Church of the Holy Trinity, Paris, France.

The Rev. E. F. H J. MASSÉ, Assistant, Church of the Holy Trinity, Paris, France.

The Rev. W. W. NEWELL, Assistant, Church of the Holy Trinity, in charge of St. Luke's Chapel, Paris, France.

The Rev. JOHN CORNELL, Rector, Church of the Holy Spirit, Nice, France.

The Rev. L. M. BLODGETT, Assistant, Church of the Holy Spirit, Nice, France.

The Rev. T. F. CASKEY, Rector, St. James' Church, Dresden, Germany.

The Rev. R. J. NEVIN, D. D , Rector, St. Paul's Church, Rome, Italy.

The Rev. H. A VENABLES, in charge of St James' Church, Florence, Italy.

The Rev. W S ADAMSON, Rector, Emmanuel Church, Geneva, Switzerland.

The Rev. F K MILLER, in charge of American Church, Lucerne, Switzerland.

* The names of the Clergy on this list were reported to the Convention by the Bishop. Those of them who were present are recorded in the list of Clergy in attendance at the Convention on the second day   W. C. P.

LIST OF LAY DEPUTIES.

County.	Church.	Deputies.
Albany	Cathedral of All Saints, Albany.	Gen. Selden E. Marvin.
		Charles Westlake Abrams.
		George Porter Hilton.
	St. Peter's, Albany............	Joseph W. Tillinghast.
		Theodore Townsend.
		William G. Rice.
	Trinity, Rensselaerville..... ..	John L. Rice.
		David D. L. McCulloch.
		Nathaniel Teed.
	St. Paul's, Albany.....	Andrew B. Jones.
		John W. Robe.
		John Bell.
	St. John's, Cohoes.....	Michael Andrae.
		John Horrocks.
		Luke Kavanaugh.
	Trinity, West Troy.....	William Hollands.
		John H. Hulsapple.
		Robert Trimble.
	Trinity, Albany....	George F. Granger.
		Charles E. Fairchild.
		J. Henry Marlow.
	Grace, Albany.	Benjamin F. Hinman.
		Charles W. White.
		Frank J. Smith.
	Holy Innocents', Albany	Samuel M. Van Santvoord.
		James Oswald.
		Henry S. McCall.
	St. Mark's, Green Island.......	Richard Leonard.
		James H. Ecklor.
		Robert W. Porter.
Clinton............	Christ, Rouse's Point.....	David White.
		John Philips.
		Charles Randall.
	St. John's, Champlain..... ...	Jehiel C. White.
		James M. Hackett, M. D.
		James DeF. Burroughs.
Columbia	Christ, Hudson................	Clarence Crofts.
		James M. Eisenmann.
		Samuel B. Coffin.
	St. John's, Stockport...... ...	William H. Van de Carr.
		Joshua Reynolds.
		Robert B. Reynolds.
	St. Paul's, Kinderhook........	Henry S. Wynkoop.
		Edward P. Van Alstyne.
		T. Floyd Woodworth, M. D.
	Trinity, Claverack....	John A. Nichols.
		R. Fulton Ludlow.
		Cornelius Shaw.
	All Saints,' Hudson............	William H. Cookson.
		Alex........

County.	Church.	Deputies.
Columbia..	Our Saviour, Lebanon Springs..	John G. Field.
		Charles E. Wackerhagen.
	St. Barnabas' Stottville	John J. Plass.
		Richard H. Harder, Jr.
		Charles B. Van Rensselaer.
Delaware......	St. Peter's, Hobart.............	A. H. Grant.
		Robert McNaught.
		William J. Calhoun.
	Christ, Walton................	George C. Seeley.
		Horace E. North.
		John H. Townsend.
	Christ, Deposit................	W. H. Gregory.
		Charles Pinkney.
		John M. Kerr.
Essex ....,...... ...	St. Paul's, Keeseville..........	Henry Dundas.
		Elias J. Champlin.
		Francis Cassidy.
	Christ, Port Henry............	William M. J. Botham.
		Theodore Tromblee, Jr.
		Charles W. Woodford.
Fulton	St. John's, Johnstown	Abiram S. Van Voast.
		James I. Younglove.
		Isaiah Yanney.
Greene	St. Luke's, Catskill..........	William L. DuBois.
		Henry T. Jones.
		Frederic E. Craigie.
	Trinity, Athens................	George S. Nichols.
		Henry C. Van Loan.
		Samuel H. Nichols.
	St. Paul's, Oak Hill............	Walter S. Cheritree.
		Ambrose H. Flower.
		Byron Hall.
	Christ, Greenville............	Winfield S. Rundle.
		W. S. Vanderbilt.
		Byron Waldron.
	Trinity, Ashland..............	Darius B. Prout.
		Addison Steele.
	Calvary, Cairo................	Levi K. Byington.
		Edwin E. Darby.
		John C. Lennon.
Herkimer..........	Trinity, Fairfield.............	Reuben Neely.
		Charles W. Nichols, M. D.
		Frederick Shaver.
	Emmanuel, Little Falls..	Rodney S Whitman.
		George W. Searles.
		Harry Houghton.
	Christ, Herkimer.............	George W. Pine.
		Chester W. Palmer.
		John D. Henderson.
	S. Augustine's, Ilion	Nelson A. Hanchett.
		George H. Barlow.
		Alfred Williamson.
	Grace, Mohawk.......	Alexander W. Haslehurst.
		Edward C. Elwood.
		Jasper D. Fitch, M. D.
Montgomery.........	St. Ann's, Amsterdam...... ..	Le Grand S. Strang.
		William Perry.
		H. B. Waldron.
	Zion, Fonda............	Hon. Richard H. Cushney.
		Henry T. E. Brower.
		Giles H. F. Van Horne.
Otsego.............	Zion, Morris	Isaac Mansfield.
		G. Clayton Peck.
		T. Octavius Duroe.

List of Lay Deputies.

County.	Church.	Deputies.
Otsego	St. Matthew's, Unadilla	Lloyd L. Woodruff.
		George B. Fellows.
		Frederick H. Meeker.
	Christ, Cooperstown	G. Pomeroy Keese.
		William H. Merchant.
		Horace M. Hooker.
	Christ, Butternuts.	Charles V. Daniels.
		Ira L. Ward.
	Grace, Cherry Valley	A. B. Cox.
		W. C. Roseboom.
		C. W. Brooks.
	St. John's, Richfield Springs	William B. Ward.
		John D. Cary.
		George B. Neely.
	Christ, West Burlington	Albert Austin.
		William Holdridge.
		John Priest.
	St. Paul's, E. Springfield	James H. Cooke.
		John Scollard.
		John J. Walrath.
	St. James', Oneonta	Robert M. Townsend.
		Alfred W. Carr.
		James Stewart.
Rensselaer	St. Paul's, Troy	Joseph J. Tillinghast.
		John I. Thompson.
		William W. Morrill.
	Trinity, Lansingburgh	James McQuide.
		Peter B. King.
		George W. Daw.
	St. John's, Troy	Norman B. Squires.
		Charles W. Tillinghast.
		Francis N. Mann.
	Christ, Troy	J. W. A. Cluett.
		Washington Akin, M. D.
		Hon. William Kemp.
	St. Mark's, Hoosick Falls	J. Russell Parsons, Jr.
		Charles F. W. Smith.
		A. Danforth Geer.
	Trinity, Schaghticoke	Edward Searls.
		Thomas L. Doremus.
		Almadus Wilkinson.
	Messiah, Greenbush	G. Philip Reisel.
		Clarence Houghton.
		Charles H. Smith.
	St. Luke's, Troy	James Wood.
		Thomas B. Iler.
		Henry E. Darby.
St. Lawrence	St. John's, Ogdensburgh	Louis Hasbrouck.
		Henry F. James.
		Levi Hasbrouck.
	St. Paul's, Waddington	William W. Lockwood.
	Christ, Morristown	Joseph Couper.
	Trinity, Potsdam	T. Streatfeild Clarkson.
		Edward W. Foster.
		Frederic M. Heath.
	Grace, Canton	Cleland Austin.
		Hammond B. Safford.
	Trinity, Gouverneur	Frank H. Smith.
		John H. Elliott.
	Zion, Colton	Thomas S. Clarkson.
		Myron E. Howard.
Saratoga	Christ, Ballston Spa	Irving W. Wiswall.
		Stephen B. Medbery.
		David L. Wood.

County.	Church.	Deputies.
Saratoga............	St. John's, Stillwater..........	Joseph Moll.
		John Stringer.
		Charles Green.
	St. Paul's, Charlton	George C. Valentine.
		John Cregg.
		William Taylor.
	Grace, Waterford	Edward La Fay.
		Charles Higgins Cole.
		Henry Stoughton Tracy.
	St. Luke's, Mechanicville	William C. Tallmadge.
		M. W. Hart.
		Herbert O. Bailey.
	Bethesda, Saratoga Springs	Hon. William A. Sackett.
		Winsor B. French.
		William B. Huestis.
	St. Stephen's, Schuylerville ...	Peter Davison.
		John Hicks Smith.
		Isaac Blandy.
	Calvary, Burnt Hills.........	John Cotton, M. D.
		Robert J. Wendell.
		Charles H. Upham.
Schenectady........	Christ, Duanesburgh	Ralph W. McDougall.
		Edward C. Clark.
		George Matthews.
	St. George's, Schenectady	Abram A Van Vorst.
		Samuel W. Jackson.
		John Keyes Paige.
	Christ, Schenectady	David Guy.
		Sidney G. Ashmore, L. H D.
		John H. Shaffer.
Warren............	Messiah, Glen's Falls	William A. Wait.
		Henry W. Coffin, M. D.
		Orange Ferriss
	Holy Cross, Warrensburgh ...	Henry Griffing
		Charles F Burhans
		Joseph A. Woodward
	St Mary's, Luzerne	John S Burneson.
		Thomas H. Taylor.
		Joseph Wigley
Washington........ ...	Zion, Sandy Hill	Charles T. Beach
		S H Parks
		George A Ingalls
	Trinity, Granville	Orville L Goodrich
		John S Warren.
		Silas E Everts.
	St. James', Fort Edward.	Francis B. Davis.
		John J. Morgan
		Jarvis W. Williams.
	St. Paul's, Salem	Hon James Gibson.
		George B McCartee.
		William L. Campbell
	Trinity, Whitehall	Fred H McFarran.
		Edward P Newcomb.
		Jeremiah Adams
	St Luke's, Cambridge	Henry C Day.
		John Moneypenny, M. D.
		Thomas Le Grys.
	St. Paul's, Greenwich	Henry L. Mowry.
		W. R. Hobbie.
		B. F. Kendall.

DIOCESE OF ALBANY.

RULES OF ORDER.

1. After the administration of the Holy Communion, the President shall take the chair, and call the Convention to order.

2. If the President *ex officio* is not present at the opening of the Convention, the Secretary of the last Convention shall call the Convention to order, when the Presbyter, senior by ordination, present, shall take the chair; and in such case, immediately after the organization of the Convention, a President shall be elected from among the clergy.

3. When the President takes the chair, no member shall continue standing, or shall afterward stand, unless to address the Chair.

ORDER OF BUSINESS.
FIRST DAY.

4. After the Convention is called to order, the roll of the clergy and of the parishes entitled to representation shall be called by the Secretary of the last Convention; the certificates of the lay deputies, as presented, being referred to a committee consisting of the Secretary and two members appointed by the President. If a quorum of twenty clergy and a representation of twenty parishes be present, the President shall declare the Convention duly organized.

5. The first business shall be the election of a Secretary, a Treasurer, and a Registrar. The Secretary may appoint one or more Assistant Secretaries, announcing their names to the Convention

6. Notices, resolutions, motions and other miscellaneous business shall then be in order.

7. The following committees shall be appointed by the President:
   A. On the Admission of Parishes into Union with the Convention.
   B. On the Constitution and Canons.
   C. On the Treasurer's Accounts.
   D. On the Diocesan Fund and Mileage of the Clergy.
   E. On Diocesan Missions
   F. On the Bishop's Salary and the Episcopal Fund.
   G. On the Fund for the Widows and Orphans of Deceased Clergymen.
   H. On the Aged and Infirm Clergy Fund.
   I. On the General Theological Seminary.
   J. On the Society for Promoting Religion and Learning.
   K. On unfinished business.
   L. On non-reporting Clergy and Parishes.

8. Business for these committees shall be received in the following order:
   A. Report of the Treasurer.
   B. Report of the Board of Diocesan Missions.
   C. Report of the Trustees of the Episcopal Fund and of the Bishop's Salary.

D. Report of the Trustees of the Fund for the Widows and Orphans of Deceased Clergymen, and the Treasurer of the same.

E. Report of the Trustees of the Aged and Infirm Clergy Fund, and the Treasurer of the same.

F. Report of the Society for Promoting Religion and Learning.

These reports, and those mentioned in the next rule, shall be referred to the appropriate committees, and shall not be read until such committees be ready to report upon them.

9. A. Report of the Committee on Applications of Parishes for Admission.

B. Report of the Secretary of the Convention.

C. Report of the Standing Committee of the Diocese.

D. Report of the Registrar of the Diocese.

E. Report of the Secretary and Treasurer of the Bible and Prayer Book Society of Albany and its Vicinity.

F. Reports from the Orphan House of the Holy Saviour, Cooperstown.

G. Reports of Special Committees appointed at the last Convention.

H. Miscellaneous business.

SECOND DAY.

10. On the second and each succeeding day of the session, after Daily Morning Prayer, the order of business, which shall not be departed from without the consent of two-thirds of the members present, or a special order of the day previously voted, shall be as follows:

A. Reading, correcting and approving the minutes of the previous day.

B. Calling the roll of members absent on the previous day.

C. Reports from the Regular Committees of the House, in the order of their appointment.

D. Reports from Special Committees, in the order of their appointment.

E. Unfinished business.

F. Miscellaneous business.

11. The Bishop's Address is in order at any time.

12. The annual election shall be held at noon on the second day, and continued at the order of the House until completed.

13. All reports embodying long statements of accounts shall be accompanied with a brief abstract of them, and such abstracts only shall be printed in the Journal.

GENERAL

14. When any member is about to speak, he shall rise from his seat, and shall, with due respect, address himself in an audible tone of voice to the President, confining himself strictly to the point in debate.

15. No member shall speak more than twice in the same debate without leave of the House; nor more than once, until every other member wishing to speak shall have spoken.

16. No motion shall be considered as before the House unless it be seconded, and reduced to writing when required, and announced by the Chair.

17. The mover may withdraw a motion or resolution at any time before amendment or decision, with the consent of the Convention; in which case it shall not be entered upon the minutes.

18. When a question is under consideration it shall be in order to move to lay it upon the table, to postpone it indefinitely, to postpone it to a time certain, to commit it, to amend it, or to divide it, and motions for any of these purposes shall have precedence in the order here named.

19. If the question under debate contains several distinct propositions, the same

shall be divided at the request of any member, and a vote taken separately; except that a motion to strike out and insert shall be indivisible.

20. All amendments shall be considered in the order in which they are moved. When a proposed amendment is under consideration, a motion to amend the same may be made. No after amendment to such second amendment, shall be in order; but a substitute for such second amendment, or a substitute for the whole matter, may be received. No proposition on a subject different from that under consideration shall be received under colour of a substitute.

21. A motion to lay upon the table shall be decided without debate.

22. A motion to adjourn shall always be in order when no member is speaking; and, if unqualified, shall be decided without debate. If negatived, it shall not be renewed until some other business has intervened.

23. When a question is put by the President, it shall be determined by the sound of voices, for or against it; but any three members may require a count of the votes, and tellers for that purpose shall then be appointed by the Chair; or any five votes may require that the decision be by yeas and nays and by orders, which shall be done by calling the roll of the clerical members and parishes represented, and the votes shall be entered on the Journal.

24. When the President is putting any question, the members shall continue in their seats, and shall not hold any private discourse.

25. Every member present shall vote when a question is put, unless excused by a vote of the House.

26. A motion once determined, whether in the affirmative or the negative, shall stand as the judgment of the Convention, and shall not again be considered during the same session, unless the motion to reconsider be made by one of the majority on the first decision, and be carried by a vote of two-thirds of the members present.

27. All questions of order shall be decided by the President, subject to an appeal to the House; and on such appeal no member shall speak more than once, without leave of the Convention.

28. All committees shall be appointed by the President, unless otherwise ordered by the Convention.

29. The reports of all committees shall be in writing; and unless recommitted, shall be received of course, without motion for acceptance. They shall be entered on the minutes, unless otherwise ordered. If recommending or requiring any action or expression of opinion by the Convention, they shall be accompanied by a resolution or resolutions for its consideration.

30. No rule of order shall be suspended, unless by a vote of two-thirds of the members present; nor shall any be changed or rescinded without one day's previous notice.

31. No member shall absent himself from the session of the Convention without leave of the President.

32. Before the final adjournment of the Convention, the minutes of the last day's proceedings shall be read, corrected and approved.

33. When the Convention is about to rise, every member shall keep his seat until the President leaves the chair.

STANDING ORDER.

Of the Conduct of Elections.

WHEREAS, it is expedient to provide by a standing order, for the manner of con. ducting all elections by ballot in the Convention of the Diocese of Albany, it is hereby ordered as follows :

1. The President of the Convention shall appoint one clergyman and one layman to be tellers of the clerical vote, and one clergyman and one layman to be tellers of the lay vote, for each office that is to be filled except that all the members of any committee, board or delegation shall be voted for upon one ticket, and only one set of tellers shall be appointed therefor. Vacancies, arising from temporary absence or otherwise, shall be supplied by the President.

2. When the election is to be held, the tellers for the clerical vote shall take their places, together, on one side of the house or place of meeting, and the tellers for the lay vote, together, upon the other side; and the Secretary shall supply them with the necessary boxes, and also with lists of the clergy entitled to seats in the Convention, and of the parishes entitled to representation, on which lists, as each vote is deposited, they shall make a mark against the name of the clergyman or parish voting; and these lists, signed by the tellers, shall be returned with their reports to the Convention. The names of the clergy and of the parishes shall be called by the Secretaries, and the votes shall be received by the tellers.

3. So soon as voting shall appear to have ceased, the President shall announce that the polls are about to be closed, and not less than ten minutes after such announce. ment, he may direct the tellers to count the votes, for which purpose they shall have leave to retire. The tellers shall then proceed to count the votes, and shall make written reports, stating the whole number of votes cast, and the number cast for each person, except that when less than five votes are cast for any one person, it shall suffice to include all such votes under the head of scattering. These reports shall be signed by the tellers respectively, and shall be entered upon the Journal, and the President shall announce the result

4. In case of any contest arising as to the right of any person to cast a vote, the tellers shall submit the question to the Convention before the closing of the polls.

5 If in regard to any office there shall not be a majority of votes, either in the clerical or in the lay order, for any one person, or if there shall not be a concurrence of the two orders, the Convention shall forthwith proceed to another ballot, for such and so many offices as have not been filled at the first ballot; and such second and all other ballots shall be conducted in the same manner as above provided. In case there shall still remain any vacancy to be supplied after such second ballot, further ballots may be held at the order of the Convention

6. Immediately before any ballot, it shall be in order for the nomination of any person to be made and seconded. But nominations for members of the Standing Committee and for Deputies and Provisional Deputies to the General Convention shall be made on the first day of the Convention, at the call of the President, under the order of "Miscellaneous Business," and it shall be the duty of the Secretary of the Convention to prepare, for the use of the Convention on the second day, ballots for these several offices, containing the names of all persons nominated for each office, respectively, with a note indicating the whole number to be chosen. No speech or debate shall be allowed upon such nomination, or while the Convention is *holding* an election.

JOURNAL.

All Saints' Cathedral Church, Albany, N. Y.
Tuesday, November 14, A. D., 1893.

This being the day appointed by the Constitution for the meeting of the Twenty-fifth Annual Convention of the Diocese of Albany, and the Bishop of the Diocese having designated the Cathedral of All Saints as the place of its meeting, a number of Clergy and Lay Deputies assembled in the Cathedral at half past ten o'clock in the morning.

The Holy Communion was administered, the Rev. Canon Fulcher being Celebrant, Archdeacon Sill, Epistoler, and Archdeacon Carey, Gospeler.

The Sermon was preached by the Rev. Dean Robbins, from the text:

"*And with many such parables spake He the word unto them, as they were able to bear it. But without a parable spake He not unto them.*"
ST. MARK iv, 33, 34.

After the service the Convention was called to order, in the Crypt of the Cathedral, by the Secretary of the last Convention, the Bishop of the Diocese not being present. The Rev. Robert N. Parke, D. D., being the Presbyter, senior by ordination, present, took the chair.

The following letter from the Bishop of the Diocese was presented:

ALBANY, N. Y., *Nov.* 10, 1893.
My dear Brethren of the Clergy and Laity:

I find myself compelled, with great regret, to be absent from this meeting of the Convention of the Diocese, being summoned to New York to attend to duties connected with the missionary work and the conventional commissions of the Church.

Acting with the consent and advice of the Standing Committee, I have instructed the Secretary to notify you of our desire that the Convention shall merely meet to fulfil the directions of the Constitution, organize, and, after the organization, adjourn to meet again at half-past ten o'clock on the 1st of February.

Supposing that this plan will be carried into effect, I simply address this word of greeting to those of you who shall assemble to discharge the canonical duty, with the expression of my earnest hope that, so far as possible, there may be a full representation of the Diocese at the adjourned

may be able to keep together the solemn anniversary of my consecration to the Episcopate.

With the assurance of my entire devotion, and my very earnest prayer for God's blessing upon our common work, I am,

Very faithfully your Bishop and friend,

WM. CROSWELL DOANE.

The Secretary reported having received from the Bishop a certified *List of the Clergy canonically resident in the Diocese, and called the roll of those entitled to seats in the Convention, and twenty-one were found to be present: The Rev. Messrs. Walton W. Battershall, D. D., James Caird, Joseph Carey, S. T. D., Fenwick M. Cookson, Thomas B. Fulcher, B. D., Charles H. Hatheway, Freeborn G. Jewett, Jr., Charles S. Olmsted, Robert N. Parke, D. D., William C. Prout, George L. Richardson, Wilford L. Robbins, D. D., Churchill Satterlee, Richmond Shreve, D. D., Frederick S. Sill, B. D., George D. Silliman, D. D., Meredith O. Smith, Walter C. Stewart, Charles Temple, Thomas White and Russell Woodman.

The roll of Churches in union with the Convention was called and certificates of Lay Deputies were presented. The Rev. Chairman appointed as Committee on Credentials of Lay Deputies the Rev. Fenwick M. Cookson and Mr. John Bell, of St. Paul's Church, Albany, with the Secretary.

The committee reported the credentials from forty-one Parishes as correct.†

The Secretary called the names of the Deputies, and four Deputies, representing four Churches, were found to be present: Gen. Selden E. Marvin, from the Cathedral of All Saints, Albany, Mr. John Bell, from St. Paul's Church, Albany, Mr. Frank J. Smith, from Grace Church, Albany, and Mr. James Oswald, from the Church of the Holy Innocents, Albany.

A constitutional quorum not being present, on motion of the Rev. W. C. Prout, it was

Resolved, That this Convention do now adjourn to meet in the Gymnasium of St. Agnes' School, Albany, on Thursday, February 1, 1894, at half-past ten o'clock in the morning.

The Rev. Chairman declared the Convention adjourned to the date and place fixed by the resolution.

---

* See List of Clergy, pp. 6-10.   † See List of Lay Deputies, pp. 11-14.

SECOND DAY.

THE GYMNASIUM OF ST. AGNES' SCHOOL, }
ALBANY, N. Y., *February* 1, 1894.   }

The Convention met pursuant to adjournment.

The Right Rev. the Bishop of the Diocese took the chair and called the Convention to order, and said the "Prayer to be used at the meetings of Convention."

The roll of Clergy entitled to seats in the Convention was called by the Secretary of the last Convention, and one hundred and one were found to be present, as follows:

The Right Rev. William Croswell Doane, D. D., LL. D., Bishop of the Diocese.

The Reverend.

C. Graham Adams, D. D.,	E. W. Flower,
E. R. Armstrong,	A. L. Fortin,
W. W. Battershall, D. D.,	H. R. Freeman,
C. T. Blanchet,	T. B. Fulcher. B. D.,
J. E. Bold,	J. H. Geare,
W. B. Bolmer,	R. H. Gesner,
D. A. Bonnar,	J. M. Gilbert,
Thomas Boone,	H. E. Gilchrist,
Frank N. Bouck,	J. W. Gill,
Thomas Burrows,	F. M. Gray,
Hamilton Cady,	S. M. Griswold,
James Caird,	J. E. Hall,
Joseph Carey, S. T. D.,	W. H. A. Hall,
G. G. Carter, S. T. D.,	W. W. Hance,
E. T. Chapman,	C. H. Hatheway,
C. M. Conant,	W. S. Hayward,
W. M. Cook, S. T. B.,	G. A. Holbrook,
Hobart Cooke,	F. H. T. Horsfield,
Fenwick M. Cookson,	E. C. Hoskins,
Charles E. Cragg,	C. A. Howells,
Marvin H. Dana,	G. M. Irish,
James A. Dickson.	David Jenkins,
Earnest W. Dustan,	F. G. Jewett, Jr.,
Henry C. Dyer,	G. B. Johnson,
Elmer R. Earle,	R. M. Kirby, D. D.,
C. C. Edmunds, Jr.,	W. H. Larom,
E. A. Enos, D. D..	A. B. Livermore,
J. G. Fawcett,	T. H. R. Luney,

The Reverend.

D. F. McDonald, D. D.,
C. E. Mackenzie,
J. W. McIlwaine,
Ernest Mariett,
J. N. Marvin,
E. W. Maxcy, D. D.,
B. F. Miller,
E. P. Miller,
J. H. Molineux,
J. D. Morrison, D. D., LL. D.,
C. M. Nickerson, D. D.,
C. S. Olmsted,
J. F. Olmsted,
R. N. Parke, D. D.,
W. F. Parsons,
Charles Pelletreau,
J. P. B. Pendleton, S. T. B.,
C. B. Perry, D. D.,
W. C. Prout,
W. B. Reynolds,
G. B. Richards,
G. L. Richardson,

The Reverend.

W. L. Robbins, D. D.,
H. C. Rush,
R. C. Searing,
Richmond Shreve, D. D.,
Frederick S. Sill, S. T. B.,
G. D. Silliman, D. D.,
E. B. Smith,
J. W. Smith,
M. O. Smith,
H. M. Smyth,
W. C. Stewart,
W. A. Stirling,
Alfred Taylor,
E. D. Tibbits,
E. S. DeG. Tompkins,
E. L. Toy,
Daniel Washburn,
C. J. Whipple,
Thomas White,
Russell Woodman,
W. B. Wright,
J. T. Zorn.

The Committee on Credentials of Lay Deputies reported the certificates from forty-two additional Churches as correct.*

The Secretary called the names of Deputies entitled to seats in the Convention, and eighty-six Deputies were found to be present, representing forty-nine Churches, as follows:

County	Church	Deputies.
Albany	Cathedral of All Saints	Gen Selden E Marvin.
		Charles W. Abrams.
	St. Peter's, Albany	Joseph W Tillinghast.
		Theodore Townsend.
		William G Rice.
	Trinity, Rensselaerville	Nathaniel Teed
	St. Paul's, Albany	Andrew B. Jones.
		John W. Robe.
	St. John's, Cohoes	Michael Andrae
		John Horrocks
		Luke Kavanaugh
	Trinity, Albany	George F. Granger.
		Charles E. Fairchild.
		J. Henry Marlow.
	Grace, Albany	Benjamin F Hinman.
		Charles W. White.
	Holy Innocents', Albany	S M Van Santvoord.
		James Oswald
Columbia	Christ, Hudson	Clarence Crofts.

* See List of Lay Deputies, pp 11-14

County.	Church.	Deputies.
Columbia	Christ, Hudson...........	James M. Eisenmann.
		Samuel B. Coffin.
	St. Paul's, Kinderhook	Henry S. Wynkoop.
		T. Floyd Woodworth, M. D.
	All Saints', Hudson.	William H. Cookson.
		Alexander R. Benson.
	Our Saviour, Lebanon Springs..	Charles E. Wackerhagen.
	St. Barnabas', Stottville.... ...	Charles B. Van Rensselaer.
Delaware	St. Peter's, Hobart	William J. Calhoun.
	Christ, Walton...............	Horace E. North.
		John H. Townsend.
Essex	Christ, Port Henry............	Charles W. Woodford.
Fulton..	St. John's, Johnstown	Abiram S. Van Voast.
		James I. Younglove.
Greene	St. Luke's, Catskill	William L. Du Bois.
		Henry T. Jones.
	Trinity, Athens	George S. Nichols.
Herkimer..........	Trinity, Fairfield....	Reuben Neely.
	Christ, Herkimer.............	George W. Pine.
		John D. Henderson.
	Grace, Mohawk..	Jasper D. Fitch, M. D.
Montgomery	St Ann's, Amsterdam	Le Grand S. Strang.
	Zion, Fonda......	Hon. Richard H. Cushney.
		Giles H. F. Van Horne.
Otsego	Zion, Morris	G. Clayton Peck.
		T. Octavius Duroe.
	St Matthew's, Unadilla	George B. Fellows.
	Christ, Cooperstown...	G. Pomeroy Keese.
		William H. Merchant.
		Horace M. Hooker.
	Grace, Cherry Valley..	A. B. Cox.
	St. James', Oneonta...........	Robert M. Townsend.
Rensselaer	St. Paul's, Troy.	Joseph J. Tillinghast.
		John I. Thompson.
		William W. Morrill.
	Trinity, Lansingburgh........	James McQuide.
		Peter B. King.
	St. John's, Troy......	Norman B. Squires.
		Francis N. Mann.
	Christ, Troy....	Hon. William Kemp.
	St. Mark's, Hoosick Falls	Charles F. W. Smith.
		J. Russell Parsons, Jr.
	Trinity, Schaghticoke.....	Almadus Wilkinson.
St. Lawrence........	St Paul's, Waddington... ...	William W. Lockwood.
Saratoga......	Grace, Waterford.....	Charles H. Cole.
		Henry S. Tracy.
	Bethesda, Saratoga Springs	Winsor B. French.
		William B. Huestis.
	Calvary, Burnt Hills..........	Charles H. Upham.
Schenectady..	Christ, Duanesburgh	Ralph W. McDougall.
		George Matthews.

County.	Church.	Deputies.
Schenectady........	St. George's, Schenectady......	Hon. Abram A. Van Vorst.
		Samuel W. Jackson.
		John Keyes Paige.
	Christ, Schenectady	David Guy.
		John H. Shaffer.
		Sidney G. Ashmore, L. H. D.
Warren.............	Messiah, Glens Falls....	William A. Wait.
		Henry W. Coffin, M. D.
	Holy Cross, Warrensburgh.....	Henry Griffing,
		Charles F. Burhans.
Washington........	Trinity, Granville.............	John S. Warren.
	St. James', Fort Edward.......	Francis B. Davis.
	St. Paul's, Salem.............	Hon. James Gibson.
	Trinity, Whitehall............	Fred. H. McFarran.
		Jeremiah Abrams.
	St. Luke's, Cambridge........	Henry C. Day.

A constitutional quorum being present, the Rt. Rev. President declared the Convention organized and ready for business.

The election of officers being in order, on motion of the Rev. F. M. Cookson, the ballot was unanimously dispensed with.

The Rev. William C. Prout was elected Secretary, Mr. Selden E. Marvin, Treasurer, and the Rev. Frederick S. Sill, Registrar.

The Secretary appointed the Rev. Thomas B. Fulcher as the Assistant Secretary.

On motion of the Rev. W. C. Prout, it was

Resolved, That Clergymen of other Dioceses, Professors and Students of Theology in this Church, and all persons holding any office or trust under the Convention, if not members thereof, being present, be invited to seats in the Convention.

The Rt. Rev. President having announced the invitation, the Rev. George H. Fenwick, Missionary at Sidney; the Rev. John Keller, of the Diocese of Newark; the Rev. William O. Jarvis, of Western New York; the Rev. L. C. Morgan, of Ohio (Missionary at Greenwich); the Rev. Henry W. Nelson, D. D., of Western New York; the Rev. Frederick G. Rainey, of Massachusetts; the Rev. G. Monroe Royce, of St. Peter's Church, Albany; the Rev. George M. Stanley, of Connecticut; the Rev. David L. Schwartz, of New Jersey; the Rev. Arthur Whitaker, of Newark; the Rev. John Brainard, D. D., of Central New York; the Rev. Osgood E. Herrick, D. D., of Central New York; the Rev. William R. Huntington, D. D., of New York; the Rev. Joseph Hooper, of Connecticut; the Rev. Theodosius S. Tyng, of Osaka, Japan; Mr. E. B. M. Harraden, Lay Reader at West Burlington, and Mr. G. M. Davidson, of the General Theological Seminary, *took seats* in the Convention.

On motion of the Rev. William C. Prout, it was

Ordered, 1st. That the first business in order this morning shall be the appointing of regular committees of the House, followed by the receiving and reading of Reports, of the Treasurer of the Diocese, of the Trustees of the various Funds, of the Officers of the Convention and of Committees of the last Convention.

2d. The Annual Elections shall be the order of the day at twelve o'clock, noon, followed by Miscellaneous Business.

3d. The Reports of the Board of Missions and of the Committee on the same, and the Apportionment for Missions shall be the Order of the Day at three P. M.

4th. The Evening Session shall be held in the Cathedral at eight o'clock, to hear the Annual Address of the Bishop of the Diocese.

5th. Rule of order No. 10 is hereby suspended, also section 6, of the Standing Order of the Conduct of Elections.

6th. There shall be usual recesses from half-past one to half-past two o'clock, and from half-past five to eight.

The Right Rev. President announced the regular committees.

ON THE INCORPORATION AND ADMISSION OF CHURCHES.

The Rev. J. Philip B. Pendleton.   Mr. Richard H. Cushney.
     Mr. John H. Bagley.

ON THE CONSTITUTION AND CANONS.

The Rev. R. M. Kirby, D. D.,   Mr. James Gibson,
The Rev. Edgar A. Enos, D. D.,   Mr. J. D. Henderson,
The Rev. Charles M. Nickerson, D. D.,   Mr. R. M. Townsend.
The Rev. George G. Carter, S. T. D.

ON THE ACCOUNTS OF THE TREASURER.

Mr. C. W. Palmer.   Mr. A. W. Haslehurst.

ON THE DIOCESAN FUND AND MILEAGE OF THE CLERGY.

The Rev. George D. Silliman, D. D.   Mr. J. Russell Parsons, Jr.,
     Mr. S. M. Van Santvoord,
     Mr. Benjamin F. Hinman.

ON DIOCESAN MISSIONS.

The Rev. Henry R. Freeman,   Mr. Benjamin F. Hinman,
The Rev. Richmond H. Gesner.   Mr. Charles W. Woodford.

ON THE BISHOP'S SALARY AND THE EPISCOPAL FUND.

The Rev. Charles C. Edmunds, Jr.,   Mr. Herbert O. Bailey,
The Rev. Edward Dudley Tibbits.   Mr. Henry C. Day,
     Mr. Charles T. Beach.

ON THE FUND FOR THE WIDOWS AND ORPHANS OF DECEASED CLERGYMEN.

The Rev. F. G. Jewett, Jr.   Mr. Andrew B. Jones,
     Mr. Alexander R. Benson,

ON THE AGED AND INFIRM CLERGY FUND.

The Rev. George M. Irish.   Mr. Thomas S. Clarkson,
     Mr. Frederic M. Heath.

4

On the General Theological Seminary.

The Rev. Sheldon M. Griswold,　　　Mr. William L. Du Bois,
The Rev. Elmer P. Miller,　　　　　Mr. George S. Nichols.
The Rev. Marvin H. Dana.

On the Society for Promoting Religion and Learning.

The Rev. Ernest Mariett.　　　　　Mr. William H. Cookson,
　　　　　　　　　　　　　　　　Mr. Nelson A. Hanchett.

On Unfinished Business.

The Rev. James E. Hall.　　　　　Mr. W. C. Roseboom,
　　　　　　　　　　　　　　　　Mr. T. O. Duroe.

On Non-Reporting Clergy and Parishes.

The Rev. C. M. Nickerson, D. D.　　Mr. John Horrocks,
　　　　　　　　　　　　　　　　Mr. James McQuide.

On the Registrar's Report.

The Rev. E. R. Armstrong.　　　　Mr. Charles F. Burhans,
　　　　　　　　　　　　　　　　Mr. Orange Ferriss.

On the Orphan House at Cooperstown.

The Rev. John E. Bold,　　　　　　Mr. James H. Cooke,
The Rev. Richmond H. Gesner.　　　Mr. George B. Neely.

On the Salary of the Bishop.

The Rev. Joseph Carey, S. T. D.,　　Mr. J. J. Tillinghast,
·The Rev. W. W. Battershall, D. D.　Mr. Erastus Corning,
　　　　　　　　　　　　　　　　Mr. J. W. Tillinghast,
　　　　　　　　　　　　　　　　Mr. W. W. Rousseau,
　　　　　　　　　　　　　　　　Mr. John I. Thompson,
　　　　　　　　　　　　　　　　Mr. Spencer Trask,
　　　　　　　　　　　　　　　　Mr. William G. Rice.

On the Society for the Home Study of Holy Scripture.

The Rev. W. Ball Wright,　　　　　Mr. Charles W. Woodford,
The Rev. Hobart Cooke.　　　　　　Mr. Louis Hasbrouck,
　　　　　　　　　　　　　　　　Mr. James DeF. Burroughs.

On the Bible and Prayer Book Society.

The Rev. Henry M. Smyth,　　　　Mr. Samuel W. Jackson,
The Rev. John N. Marvin,　　　　　Mr. James I. Younglove,
The Rev. James F. Olmsted.　　　　Mr. Reuben Neely.

The reports of the Treasurer of the Diocese; of the Board of Diocesan Missions; of the Trustees of the Episcopal Fund and of the Committee on the Salary of the Bishop; of the Trustees of the Fund for the Widows and Orphans of Deceased Clergymen, and of the Treasurer of the same; of the Trustees of the Aged and Infirm Clergy Fund, and of the Treasurer of the same; of the Registrar of the Diocese; of the Superintendent and of the Treasurer of the Orphan House of the Holy Saviour, Cooperstown; of the Society for Promoting Religion and Learning, and of the Treasurer of the Diocese, of Moneys received for Theological Education; of the Bible and Common Prayer Book Society; of the Society for the Home Study of Holy Scripture and Church History, were received and referred to the appropriate committees. The report of the Trustees of the Clergy Reserve Fund was received and referred to the Committee on the Aged and Infirm Clergy Fund.

The Secretary of the Convention read the reports of the Treasurer of the Diocese and of the Committee on the Accounts of the Treasurer.

REPORT OF THE TREASURER OF THE DIOCESE.

ALBANY, *November* 14, A. D., 1898.

Herewith find statement of Receipts and Disbursements for the year showing as follows:

RECEIPTS.

Balance on hand as reported to last Convention	$823 32
From Parishes	1,963 17
Total	$2,786 49

DISBURSEMENTS.

For mileage	$302 29
For Secretary's expenses	125 00
For Secretary's salary	250 00
For Bishop's traveling expenses	300 00
For sundries	72 16
For taxes, insurance and repairs, Bishop's house	521 88
For Registrar	10 00
For printing	698 60
For one-third dues, General Convention	130 00
Total	$2,409 81
Balance	376 68

It will be necessary for the Convention at this meeting to provide for the following objects: Mileage to Clergymen in attendance upon Convention; printing the Journal of the Convention; taxes and repairs, Bishop's house; sundry current expenses; one-third dues to General Convention; salary of the Secretary; traveling expenses of the Bishop.

For the above purposes I submit the following estimate of the sums that will be required:

For mileage	$300 00
For printing	700 00
For taxes and repairs Bishop's house	600 00
For sundry current expenses	150 00

For one-third dues General Convention.... .... $130 00
For salary of the Secretary.................... .... 250 00
For Bishop's traveling expenses................................ .... 300 00

To provide the above amount I recommend the Convention order an assessment of three (3) per centum upon the salaries paid or pledged the Clergymen by the Parishes and Mission Stations; one-half payable April 1, and one-half payable October 1, 1894.

I further recommend that the Treasurer be directed to pay to each Clergymen in attendance upon the Convention and belonging to this Diocese, residing a distance of twenty miles from Albany, his actual traveling expenses, provided that in no case shall he pay to exceed seven cents a mile one way.

SELDEN E. MARVIN,
Treasurer.

Amount received for clerical insurance....... .... $198 37
Amount disbursed for clerical insurance..... .... 126 80

Balance on hand........ . ... $66 57

REPORT OF THE COMMITTEE ON THE ACCOUNTS OF THE TREASURER.

The committee, to whom was referred the Report of the Treasurer of the Diocese, have examined the same, together with the vouchers for expenditure, and find the same correct.

ALEX. W. HASLEHURST,
HERKIMER, *Jan.* 29, 1894.   C. W. PALMER.

The Rev. George D. Silliman, D. D., read the report of the Committee on the Diocesan Fund and Mileage of the Clergy, and the resolutions recommended in it were adopted.

REPORT OF THE COMMITTEE ON THE DIOCESAN FUND AND THE MILE-AGE OF THE CLERGY

The Committee on the Diocesan Fund and the Mileage of the Clergy, having considered the estimates of the Treasurer of the Diocese, recommend the adoption of the following resolutions :

Resolved, That an assessment of three per centum be levied upon Parishes and Mission Stations of the Diocese, on amounts pledged to Rectors and Missionaries as salaries in each Parish and Mission Station. The amount thus levied shall be paid to the Diocesan Treasurer, one-half April 1 and one half October 1, 1894

Resolved, That the Treasurer be authorized to pay mileage to the Clergy attending Convention and residing twenty or more miles from Albany, their actual traveling expenses, provided that in no case shall it exceed seven cents a mile one way.

Resolved, That the Treasurer be authorized to pay out such other sums as are contained in his estimate of expenses

Resolved, That the Secretary be instructed to print 1,500 copies of the Bishop's Address, together with the various proceedings and addresses delivered at the Anniversary services, the same to be printed apart from the Journal of Convention, and also to be bound up with the Journals of Convention ; and that he be authorized to print 1,250 Journals of the Convention and distribute the same to the various Parishes and elsewhere at the pleasure of the Bishop.

GEO. D. SILLIMAN,
S. M VAN SANTVOORD,
BENJAMIN F. HINMAN.

On motion of the Rev. George D. Silliman, D. D., it was

Resolved, That the Secretary be instructed to ask the Presiding Bishop for a copy of his sermon to be delivered at the Anniversary Services to-morrow, for the purpose of having it printed.

Resolved, That the Secretary be instructed to ask for copies of the addresses to be made at the Anniversary Service to-morrow and of the Bishop's Reply, for the purpose of publication.

The Secretary of the Convention read the Reports of the Trustees of the Episcopal Fund and of the Treasurer of the same, and the Rev. Charles C. Edmunds, Jr., read the Report of the Committee on the Bishop's Salary and the Episcopal Fund.

REPORT OF THE TRUSTEES OF THE EPISCOPAL FUND.

To the Convention :

The undersigned, Trustees of the Episcopal Fund, respectfully report that they hold the following securities for the Fund:

Bond and Mortgage of J. Judge, 6 per cent	$1,500 00
Bond and Mortgage of D. McElveny, 5 per cent	5,000 00
Bond and Mortgage of L. Sautter, 6 per cent..................	6,000 00
Bond and Mortgage of J. Kennah, 6 per cent.....	6,000 00
Bond and Mortgage of J. E. Birdsall, 5 per cent................... ...	20,000 00
Bond and Mortgage of Smead & Northcott, 5 per cent.	8,500 00
Bond and Mortgage of L. Hasbrouck, 5 per cent................	5,000 00
Bond and Mortgage of Harriet Martin, 5 per cent........	2,500 00
Bond and Mortgage of Alma Davey, 4½ per cent	8,000 00
Bond of Grace Church, Waterford.	500 00
Bond of St. John's Church, Cohoes....	800 00
Balance of deposits in Savings Bank.	51 22
Total..	$63,851 22

St. Mark's Church, Green Island, contributed $4.15 to the principal of the Fund, April 20.

In consequence of default in payment of interest due in May on the Kennah (now Coleman Bro's) Mortgage of $6,000, it has been placed in the hands of Marcus T. Hun, Esq., for foreclosure and collection.

ALBANY, *November* 13, 1893.

Respectfully submitted.

JOHN H. VAN ANTWERP,
ROBERT C. PRUYN,
DEAN SAGE,
WM. BAYARD VAN RENSSELAER,
C. WHITNEY TILLINGHAST, 2ND.

REPORT OF THE TREASURER OF THE EPISCOPAL INCOME FUND.

J. H. Van Antwerp, Treasurer, in account with the Episcopal Income Fund:

1893.   DR.

Nov. 14. To balance November 14, 1892	**$99** 19
To 1 year's interest, Sautter Mortgage.	**380** 00
To 1 year's interest, Hasbrouck Mortgage	**250** 00
To 1 year's interest, Birdsall Mortgage..............	1,000 00
To 1 year's interest, Northcott Mortgage	425 00
To 1 year's interest, McElveny Mortgage......................	250 00
To 1 year's interest, Judge Mortgage	90 00
To 1 year's interest, Martin Mortgage...........	125 00
To 11 months, 8 days interest, Davey Mortgage	338 00
To bank interest on $8,000, invested in Davey Mortgage.......	15 78
To 1 year's interest, Grace Church, Waterford, Bond.	35 00
To 1 year's interest, St. John's Church, Cohoes, Bond.........	56 00
To interest on balance, National Savings Bank	1 98
To remittances from Mr. Rousseau, Secretary of Bishop's Salary Committee......	2,850 00
To balance due me as Treasurer......................	104 05
Total......................	**$6,000** 00

CR.

By salary paid Bishop, 1 year ending November 1, 1893........   6,000 00

ALBANY, E. & O. E., *December 5*, 1893.

Respectfully submitted.

JOHN H. VAN ANTWERP,
Treasurer of the Episcopal Fund, Diocese of Albany.

REPORT OF THE COMMITTEE ON THE REPORTS OF THE TRUSTEES OF THE EPISCOPAL FUND, OF THE TREASURER OF THE EPISCOPAL FUND, AND OF THE COMMITTEE ON THE SALARY OF THE BISHOP.*

The Committee to whom have been referred the reports of the Trustees of the Episcopal Fund, of the Treasurer of the Episcopal Fund, and of the Committee on the Salary of the Bishop, respectfully report : That the papers submitted to them have been examined and appear to be correct.

ALBANY, N. Y., *Feb.* 1, 1894.   CHAS. C. EDMUNDS, JR.,
CHAS. T. BEACH,
HENRY C. DAY.

The Secretary of the Convention read the Reports of the Trustees of the Aged and Infirm Clergy Fund and that of the Clergy Reserve Fund, and the Rev. George M. Irish read the Reports of the Committee on the Aged and Infirm Clergy Fund

REPORT OF THE TRUSTEES OF THE FUND FOR AGED AND INFIRM CLERGYMEN.

DIOCESE OF ALBANY,   }
ALBANY, *November* 14, A. D., 1893. }

The undersigned Trustees of the Fund for the Support of Aged and Infirm Clergymen, respectfully report that the receipts and disbursements for the year have been *as reported* in detail by the Treasurer, and are as follows:

---

* For the Report of the Committee on the Salary of the Bishop, see Appendix D.

RECEIPTS.

Balance on hand, as reported to last Convention	$538 68
From Parishes	634 16
From interest on investments	931 62
Total......................................	$2,104 46

DISBURSEMENTS.

For stipends.	1,125 00
Balance	$979 46

The Trustees have the following securities, which constitute the Permanent Fund:

Bond and Mortgage, Bishop's House.................	$3,600 00
Perry Judgment, Bishop's House....................	6,315 86
Learned Bond and Mortgage........................	4,000 00
Burnett Bond and Mortgage........................	1,700 00
Troy City R. R. Bond.............................	1,000 00
United States registered 4 per cent Bond..........	1,000 00
New York, Lake Erie and Western R. R. second convertible Bond.....	1,000 00
Wabash Railway Bonds............................	3,000 00
Loan on demand..................................	700 00
Cash on hand....................................	500 00
Total	$22,815 86

which represent the following receipts:

Diocese of New York.............................	$10,000 00
St. Paul's Church, Albany.........................	5,000 00
Miss Burr Legacy, Diocese of New York............	2,000 00
Leonard G. Hun Bequest..........................	250 00
From Parishes....................................	5,565 86
Total......................................	$22,815 86

During the year the Treasurer received one $1,000 Wabash Railway Bond from St. Paul's Church, Albany, for addition to the Permanent Fund.

WM. CROSWELL DOANE, President.
SELDEN E. MARVIN, Treasurer.

REPORT OF THE TREASURER OF THE CLERGY RESERVE FUND.

RECEIPTS.

Balance on hand, as reported last Convention		$381 77
St. Augustine's, Ilion............................	$1 63	
Christ, Hudson	8 85	
All Saints', Hudson	4 23	
Trinity, Claverack	1 22	
Emmanuel, Otego	1 34	
St. John's, Ogdensburgh	125 86	
Trinity, Potsdam.................................	15 55	
St. Luke's, Troy		

St. Paul's, Troy..	$30 00	
Church of the Cross, Ticonderoga.................	5 53	
Holy Innocents', Albany....	5 00	
St. Peter's, Albany.........................	14 34	
	——	$216 02
Amount on hand....................		$597 79

SELDEN E. MARVIN, *Treasurer.*

REPORT NO. 1 OF THE COMMITTEE ON THE AGED AND INFIRM CLERGY FUND.

Your Committee on the report of the Trustees of the Aged and Infirm Clergy Fund find that there has been a slight increase in the number of Parishes contributing to the Fund, and in the total amount contributed; also that there has been an increase in the amount of the permanent investments. The fact remains, however, that only about one-third of the entire number of Parishes has contributed.

The Committee would, therefore, call the attention of the Convention to the resolution offered at the last Convention and adopted, to the effect that an offering for this purpose should be taken up each year in every Parish and organized Mission.

The Committee has also examined the report of the Treasurer of the Fund and found the same to be correct.

GEORGE M. IRISH,
THOMAS S. CLARKSON,
FREDERIC M. HEATH.

REPORT NO. 2 OF THE COMMITTEE ON THE AGED AND INFIRM CLERGY FUND.

The Committee to which was referred the report of the Treasurer of the Clergy Reserve Fund would report that they find a decrease of over $100 in the amount contributed to the Fund by Parishes during the past year, as compared with the preceding year, and also a decrease of three in the number of Parishes contributing Only twelve Parishes have taken up an offering for the Fund, being only one in thirteen The Committee would call the attention of the Clergy to Canon XVIII, section 2, and because they are convinced that the failure of the Parishes in general to take up an offering for this purpose is owing to the recent date of the Fund, and to its importance not being impressed upon their attention, they would, therefore, offer the following resolution.

Resolved, That the Commission on the Clerical Pension System, appointed at the last Convention, or such members thereof as the Bishop may appoint, send out during the coming year, to each Parish and organized Mission, a circular letter explaining the working of the system and calling the attention of the Clergy to the importance of the Fund, and to the duty of the Parishes as indicated in Canon XVIII, section 2

GEORGE M. IRISH,
THOMAS S. CLARKSON,
FREDERIC M. HEATH.

The resolution recommended in Report No. 2 of the Committee on the Aged and Infirm clergy Fund was adopted.

The Secretary of the Convention read the report of the Society for Promoting Religion and Learning in the State of New York, and that of the Treasurer of the Diocese, of receipts and disbursements for theological education, and the Rev. Ernest Mariett that of the Committee on the same.

REPORT OF SOCIETY FOR PROMOTING RELIGION AND LEARNING IN THE STATE OF NEW YORK.

List of contributions received from Churches in the Diocese of Albany, from November 1, 1892, to October, 1893, and sent to the Treasurer of the Society for Promoting Religion and Learning.

1892.

Nov.	2. St. Luke's Church, Troy	$5 02
	4. St. Peter's Church, Albany	19 65
	9. Christ Church, Hudson	7 50
	21. Church of Our Saviour, Lebanon Springs	13 87
Dec. 12	St. Paul's Church, Troy	14 00

1893.

March 1.	Christ Church, Hudson	5 00
June 2.	Christ Church, Hudson	1 00
Aug. 30.	St. Paul's Church, Salem	4 78
Oct. 3.	St. Luke's Church, Troy	5 51
		$76 58

The above sum has been added to the much larger sum approriated by the Society for the benefit of students preparing for Holy Orders in the Diocese of Albany, and expended in their behalf during the past conventional year.

NEW YORK, *November,* 1893.

All of which is respectfully submitted.

ANDREW OLIVER,
Superintendent of the Society for Promoting Religion and Learning.

REPORT OF THE TREASURER OF THE DIOCESE OF RECEIPTS AND DISBURSEMENTS FOR THEOLOGICAL EDUCATION.

RECEIPTS.

Christ, Herkimer	$7 26
St. John's, Johnstown	6 39
St. John's, Cohoes	52 25
Bethesda, Saratoga Springs	25 00
Trinity, Lansingburgh	2 32
St. James', Caldwell	4 27
Trinity, Potsdam	35 83
Trinity, Sharon Springs	10 48
Grace, Canton	5 06
Christ, Morristown	5 00
Christ, Cooperstown	5 00
St. Paul's, Albany	20 15
	$178 96

DISBURSEMENTS.

For stipends	175 00
Balance on hand	$3 96

5

REPORT OF THE COMMITTEE ON THE SOCIETY FOR PROMOTING RE-LIGION AND LEARNING.

Your Committee to whom was referred the report of the Society for Promoting Religion and Learning, respectfully report that they have examined the report, which is simply a statement of sums received from certain Parishes of the Diocese. No information as to whom these sums were paid is given. The report of the Treasurer of the Diocese of sums received by him for theological education has been examined by the Committee and found correct. Vouchers for all sums paid out accompany this report.

The Committee advise that all Parishes send their contributions for theological education to the Treasurer of the Diocese, to be paid out under the sanction of the Bishop.

ERNEST MARIETT,
W. H. COOKSON,

The Rev. Sheldon M. Griswold read the following:

REPORT OF THE COMMITTEE ON THE GENERAL THEOLOGICAL SEMINARY.

The Committee on the General Theological Seminary begs leave to report that seven students from the Diocese of Albany are now pursuing their studies in this institution.

There should be one Trustee elected to succeed the Archdeacon of Troy, whose term of office expired November 15, 1893.

Your Committee, therefore, recommend the following:

Resolved, That the Rev. Joseph Carey, S. T. D., be and is hereby elected as Trustee of the General Theological Seminary for the Diocese of Albany, to hold office until November 15, 1896.

SHELDON MUNSELL GRISWOLD, Chairman.
ELMER P. MILLER,
MARVIN HILL DANA,
WM. L. DUBOIS,
GEO. S. NICHOLS.

On motion, the resolution recommended by the Committee was adopted, and the Rev. Joseph Carey, S. T. D., was elected a Trustee of the General Theological Seminary until November 15, 1896.

The Secretary of the last Convention presented and read the following

REPORT OF THE SECRETARY OF THE CONVENTION.

ALBANY, November 14, 1893.

To the Convention of the Diocese of Albany:

The Secretary of the Diocese respectfully presents the following report:

One thousand copies of the Bishop's Address and 1,250 copies of the Journal of the Convention were printed and distributed.

Letters were sent to the Clergy and Parishes that failed to report to the Convention of 1891. Replies were received from all except Grace Church, Norway, and St. Luke's, Mechanicville.

The Convention will need to elect this year the Standing Committee, the Trustees of the several funds, two Trustees of the Diocese to supply the places of two whose terms of office now expire, and one in place of Mr. Benjamin H. Hall, deceased;

three Trustees of the Orphan House of the Holy Saviour at Cooperstown, in place of three whose terms of office now expire, and one lay member of the Missionary Council, in place of Mr. Benjamin H. Hall, deceased.

Reports are to be made by the Commission on the Clerical Pension System, the Committee on the Observance of the Twenty-fifth Anniversary of the Consecration of the First Bishop of Albany, and the Committee on the Diocesan Fund and Mileage of the Clergy, to whom was referred the question of the entertainment of Clergy attending the Convention.

Nominations for members of the Board of Missions have been received : For the Convocation of Albany, the Rev. Walton W. Battershall, D. D., and Mr. John H. Van Antwerp ; for the Convocation of Troy, the Rev. Fenwick M. Cookson and Mr. George A. Wells ; for the Convocation of the Susquehanna, the Rev. Robert N. Parke, D. D., and Mr. R. M. Townsend ; for the Convocation of Ogdensburgh, the Rev. R. M. Kirby, D. D., and Mr. T. Streatfeild Clarkson.

A large number of Journals of other Dioceses and other documents have been received and forwarded to the Registrar.

Respectfully submitted,
WM. C. PROUT,
Secretary of the Convention.

The Rev. Fenwick M. Cookson presented and read the

REPORT OF THE STANDING COMMITTEE.

The Standing Committee of the Diocese of Albany presents its annual report.

At its first meeting, on December 12, 1892, the Committee organized by the election of the Rev. J. Ireland Tucker, S. T. D., President, and the Rev. Fenwick M. Cookson, Secretary.

During the year ending November 14, 1893, it has held six meetings.

It has recommended as candidates for Holy Orders : Mr. George Dort Ashley, Mr. William Wallace Lockwood, Mr. E. B. M. Harradan, Mr. H. D. MacNeil.

It has recommended for ordination to the Diaconate : Mr. William Anderson Stirling, Mr. Frank N. Bouck, Mr. Marvin Hill Dana and Mr. Edward Tourtellot Carroll.

It has recommended for ordination to the Priesthood: the Rev. Earnest Webster Dustan, the Rev. William W. Newell, and the Rev. Charles A. Howells.

The Committee has given canonical consent to the consecration of : the Rev. Frederick R. Graves as Bishop of the Missionary Jurisdiction of Shanghai, China; the Rev. John McKim as Bishop of the Missionary Jurisdiction of Yeddo, Japan; the Rev. William Lawrence, S. T. D., as Bishop of the Diocese of Massachusetts; the Rev. Thomas F. Gailor, S. T. D., as Coadjutor Bishop of the Diocese of Tennessee; the Rev. Ellison Capers, D. D., as Assistant Bishop of the Diocese of South Carolina; the Rev. A. C. A. Hall, as Bishop of the Diocese of Vermont.

Acting as " ecclesiastical authority " of the Diocese, by the Bishop's appointment, during his absence in foreign lands, from January 28, 1893, to June 6, 1893, the Committee report as follows:

February 20, 1893, granted a letter dimissory to Rev. Robert Granger to the Diocese of Southern Ohio; accepted a letter dimissory of Rev. W. H. A. Hall, from the Diocese of Newark; accepted a letter dimissory of Rev. Calbraith B. Perry from the Diocese of Tennessee.

March 18, 1893, granted a letter dimissory to Rev. W. H. Bown to the Diocese of Central New York; granted a letter of transfer to ███████████████████, candidate for Priest's Orders, to the Diocese of New███████████████████████

March 30, 1893, received a letter of acceptance of Rev. W. H. Bown from the Bishop of Central New York.

April 3, 1893, received a letter of acceptance of Mr. Thurston W. Challen, candidate for Priest's Orders, from the Bishop of Newark.

April 6, 1893, appointed officers for the St. Giles' Mission at Castleton.

April 7, 1893, granted a letter dimissory to Rev. P. St. M. Podmore to the Diocese of Chichester, England.

May 31, 1893, received a letter dimissory of Rev. J. Holwell Geare, from the Diocese of Delaware.

The Committee would urge that all persons preparing certificates or other papers for any action on the part of the Standing Committee will carefully consult the canonical forms. Much trouble would be saved applicants and the Committee, if the forms were always literally followed.

ALBANY, *February* 1, 1894.

Respectfully submitted.

J. IRELAND TUCKER,
President.

FENWICK M. COOKSON,
Secretary.

The Rev. Frederick S. Sill presented and read the

REPORT OF THE REGISTRAR, 1893.

The Registrar would respectfully report that the file of Diocesan Journals for the year 1892 is complete with the exception of Texas. The Journal of the General Convention of 1892 has been received. Of the Diocesan Journals for 1893, those of forty-three Dioceses have come to hand, leaving ten to be heard from.

Of the eighteen Missionary Jurisdictions we have received the Journals of New Mexico, Arizona, South Dakota, and Washington. The Journal of Tennessee, 1882, is still missing. Pamphlets, including sermons, addresses, charges, etc., have been presented by the Bishop, the Secretary of the Convention, and the Rev. Dr. Battershall. Several bound books on various historical and controversial subjects have been placed in the library by the Bishop. We are indebted to the Rev. Canon Fulcher for eleven complete volumes of the Church Eclectic. To these the Registrar has added three volumes, and Canon Fulcher has given part of another volume; the set at present is as follows. Vols. 2, 3, 4 [No. 12 missing], 8 [Nos. 7 and 8 missing], 9, 10, 11, 12, 13, 14, 15, 16, 17, 18, 19. Also parts of 20 and 21. The Registrar would like to receive the missing Volumes 1, 5, 6, 7, the missing No. 12 of Vol. 4, and Nos. 7 and 8 of Vol. 8, and the full numbers from Vol. 20 to date. The Bishop and many of the Clergy of this Diocese have contributed articles to this magazine, and the Registrar would suggest that the volumes in hand, and others as they are received and filled up, be bound for better preservation. The cost would be the same as for Journals, 35 cents a volume.

The Registrar acknowledges the receipt of $10 from the Treasurer of the Diocesan Fund. Cash overdrawn for binding as per last report, $6.74. Postage, 82 cents. Sundry fares, $2.25. Balance, 69 cents. Total, $10.

The Registrar is still engaged on an Alphabetical Index to the Items of his Historical Index for the first Twenty-one years of the Diocese.

The Registrar would request that when books or pamphlets are sent to the Cathedral for his office, he be notified by postal card, so that due credit may be given the donors.

For the expenses of his office during 1894 the Registrar would respectfully ask an appropriation of $10.

FREDERICK S. SILL,
Registrar.

The Secretary of the Convention read the Report of the Committee on the Registrar's Report, and on his motion the recommendation of the Committee was adopted.

REPORT OF THE COMMITTEE ON THE REGISTRAR'S REPORT.

Your Committee on the Registrar's Report respectfully would say that report is a showing of good work, well and faithfully done.

The value of the Registrar's Office as a depository for Church Literature other than Diocesan Journals is recognized and appreciated, and it is deemed that hearty thanks are due those who have the past year intrusted to its safe-keeping so large a number of volumes of the Church Eclectic, that most able and judicious champion of the truth.

Your Committee cordially indorse the Registrar's appeal for those numbers and volumes he lacks in order to complete his files, and recommend that his very modest request for an appropriation of $10 be granted him for the expenses of his office the ensuing year as stated.

ALBANY, *January* 31, 1894.

E. R. ARMSTRONG,
C. F. BURHANS.

The Rev. Richmond Shreve, D. D., presented and read the

REPORT OF THE BIBLE AND COMMON PRAYER BOOK SOCIETY OF ALBANY AND ITS VICINITY.

The anticipations expressed in the Society's Report of last year have been more than realized. It was expected that large demands would be made for the Revised Prayer Book. During the Conventional year, November, 1892, to November, 1893, the number of volumes granted was almost twice as many as were sent out in any previous year.

The interesting statement of the Corresponding Secretary, the Rev. Henry R. Freeman, summarized, is as follows:

Total number of grants made during year, 120.

Volumes distributed :

Bibles..	61
Revised Prayer Books (pew)................................	10,841
Revised Prayer Books (Chancel)............................	6
Revised Service Books (Altar).............................	5
Hymnals (old issue)......................................	217
Total number of volumes............................	11,180

It may save the Parishes disappointment and unnecessary correspondence if it be here announced that the Society is unable any longer, under its charter, to make any grants of Hymn Books for gratuitous distribution.

The Treasurer's Report is herewith summarized :

Balance on hand last report...........................	$670 24

RECEIPTS.

Special Prayer Book Fund................................	300 00
Income Permanent Fund..................................	897 00
From forty Parishes...................................	387 66
	$2,254 90

EXPENDITURES, ETC.

Added to Permanent Fund................................	$14 58	
Printing and Express Account	24 80	
For Books distributed	1,720 47	
		$1,759 85
Balance to new account.............................		$495 05

It is to be regretted that the disparity is so great between the number of grants (120), and the number of contributing Parishes (40), three to one.

If the Resolution of the Society [passed in 1878 ("That no grants of Books be made by the Secretary to non-contributing Parishes"), were still enforced, the larger proportion of the Parishes of the Diocese would still be using the Prayer Book of the last century.

Every report must in its very nature be retrospective; this — because of the grateful spirit which will animate the approaching Convention — may be permitted to extend its glance beyond the scope of a single year.

The existence of the Bible and Prayer Book Society ante-dates that of the Diocese by forty-eight years, its Charter bearing date Feb. 20, 1820.

In the report presented to the Convention of 1872 by a Committee appointed to consider the relation of the Society to the Diocese, there occurs this interesting statement: "They find that the Society became the means of forming the Northern Convocation of the Diocese of New York, which resulted later in the Diocese of Albany."

But the real growth of the Society has been attained, and its telling and permanent work has been done in the last twenty-five years.

Invested funds, 1869.............................	$4,100 00
Invested funds, 1893.........	13,400 00

VOLUMES DISTRIBUTED (1869–93).

Bibles: whole or in parts: O. T. and N. T., Psalters, etc., in English, German, French, Greek and Swedish.....	7,060
Prayer Books, Hymnals and Office Books.	67,707
Total volumes	74,767

Moneys received by Treasurers from the Parishes	$8,743 85
Amount paid for Distribution of Books.............	26,286 28

"Statistics," says Bishop Whittingham, "may be in themselves a very small thing: spiritually estimated, nothing." And yet there may be found few who will assert that many better investments have been made of the parochial funds than in placing these nigh $9,000 The voice of the living missionary has proclaimed the truth, but these nearly 75,000 silent preachers, unwearied in the passing years, have been at once a factor and an index of the growth of the Church in this Diocese, for which, with our Bishop and President, we "thank God, and take courage."

ALBANY, *November*, 1893.

RICHMOND SHREVE,
Recording Secretary.

The Secretary of the Convention read the

REPORT OF THE COMMITTEE ON THE BIBLE AND PRAYER BOOK SOCIETY.

The Committee on the Bible and Common Prayer Book Society of Albany and Vicinity, after reading with much interest the very admirable report of the Recording Secretary of the Society, commends a thoughtful consideration of it to the Church throughout the Diocese.

The facts that only forty of the Parishes have contributed to the funds of the Society during the past year, and that the small sum of $387.66 is all that has been received from this source, seem to indicate a misunderstanding on the part of both the Clergy and Laity of the needs of the Society, or some measure of indifference to its work. It may be that the *importance* of its work is not sufficiently understood. It would be a grave misfortune to many of the weaker Churches, especially in the newer fields of labor, in their need of Bibles and Prayer Books, to be cut off from this source of supply. We cannot afford to allow an association so wisely managed, and so useful as it has proved to be, to suffer through lack of means which the Church is abundantly able to provide.

The Committee respectfully recommends the adoption of the Recording Secretary's report; and, furthermore, that it be read by the Clergy of the Diocese in the Churches, and the duty of sustaining the Society, as set forth in the Canons, be enjoined upon the people.

> HENRY M. SMYTH, *Chairman.*
> J. N. MARVIN,
> J. I. YOUNGLOVE,
> J. F. OLMSTED,
> R. NEELY,
> S. W. JACKSON.

The Secretary of the Convention read the report of the Superintendent, and that of the Treasurer of the Orphan House of the Holy Saviour, at Cooperstown; and the Rev. John E. Bold, that of the Committee on the same.

REPORT OF THE SUPERINTENDENT OF THE ORPHAN HOUSE OF THE HOLY SAVIOUR.

October 1, 1893.

The number of children in the House during the past year has been 109; Church children, 47; County children, 62; remaining to-day, 75. Six boys have been taken by their friends very recently.

The work of the Orphan House of the Holy Saviour has been carried on during the past year with regularity and earnest steadiness. The House and family have been in good condition. Three contagious diseases, prevailing in the neighborhood, were introduced in succession into the family, and placed us in quarantine during some months. But while necessarily causing a great increase of labour and expense, we very thankfully record the fact that both scarlet fever and whooping-cough appeared in a very mild form. The grippe attacked several children more severely, but, thanks be to God, all were brought safely through. Though a trial to those in charge of the family, yet we should be thankful that these children are now protected from any future dangers to which they may be exposed from two diseases often very dangerous — scarlet fever and whooping-cough.

Our funds are still inadequate. An increase of our very small endowment, $3,500, is greatly to be desired. Free scholarships of $1,000 are very much needed to cover the expenses of fatherless and motherless children. A number of such children, connected with our Church, would have received at the Orphan House of the Holy Saviour sound moral and religious instruction, with very careful industrial training. But the present charges for board, required for current expenses, exceeded what their friends could afford to pay, and those children were taken to Orphanages of the Church of Rome, where they were received for fifty cents a week. A sad case of this kind has recently occurred here; two fatherless boys, in a promising state of improvement, were withdrawn from this Orphanage, because their mother, a widow, declared she could not afford to pay their board at the Diocesan Orphan House. If we could have offered some assistance from a free scholarship, those boys would have remained several years longer in hopeful conditions of improvement. Similar cases of poor widows unable to pay the expenses of their children at this Orphanage, without assistance, are of frequent occurrence, and it not unfrequently happens that fathers also, honestly struggling with poverty, withdraw their motherless children from the same cause.

With great earnestness would we repeat to-day the petition already respectfully offered in previous years to the consideration of the Diocesan Convention, for the *Endowment of Free Scholarships of* $1,000, memorial or parochial, in behalf of the poor widows and orphans of the Church, in the Diocese of Albany.

The school at the Orphan House is declared by the Commissioner for this district to be in excellent condition. At a recent examination by the Regents, held at the large union school, several of the older pupils at the Orphanage were sent down for examination in two studies, Spelling and Geography. Great was the gratification of our teachers when the result was reported. The Orphanage pupils passed with credit.   Respectfully submitted,

SUSAN FENIMORE COOPER,
Superintendent Orphan House of the Holy Saviour.

REPORT OF THE TREASURER OF THE ORPHAN HOUSE OF THE HOLY SAVIOUR AT COOPERSTOWN, FOR YEAR ENDING SEPTEMBER 30, 1893.

RECEIPTS.

Balance on hand	$23 45
County Treasurer	4,372 01
Sixty-one Churches	1,571 13
Individuals for Board	1,046 04
Personal Subscriptions	93 25
Interest on Investments	207 61
School Money	323 87
One Bequest	500 00
From Endowment Fund	1,000 00
	$9,137 36

EXPENSES.

Wages	$2,471 43
Groceries	1,185 89
Meat	596 61
Milk	1,044 81
Clothing	1,021 26
Fuel	661 41
Light	281 28
Furniture	

House Stores...	$931 87
Medicines..	85 60
Repairs..	236 82
Water...	50 00
Flour...	361 38
Miscellaneous..	133 12
	$9,133 10
Cash on hand..	4 26
	$9,137 36

STATEMENT OF CONDITION OF ORPHAN-HOUSE ENDOWMENT FUND, SEPTEMBER 30, 1893.

On hand, last report	$4,500 00
Carried to current account..............................	1,000 00
On hand..	$3,500 00

Respectfully submitted.

LESLIE PELL-CLARKE,
Treasurer.

LIST OF THE CHURCHES AND MISSION STATIONS CONTRIBUTING TO
THE SUPPORT OF THE ORPHAN HOUSE OF THE HOLY SAVIOUR AT
COOPERSTOWN FOR YEAR ENDING SEPTEMBER 30, 1893.

ARCHDEACONRY OF ALBANY.

All Saints' Cathedral	$41 37
St. Peter's, Albany......................................	106 25
Holy Innocents', Albany	7 92
Trinity, West Troy.......................................	15 00
St. Mark's, Green Island.................................	19 73
St. John's, Cohoes.......................................	11 00
Trinity, Athens..	5 92
St. Luke's, Catskill......................................	40 00
Christ Church, Duanesburg...............................	10 06
Christ Church, Schenectady...............................	17 67
Good Shepherd, Canajoharie..............................	8 09
St. John's, Johnstown....................................	31 54
Christ Church, Herkimer.................................	11 50
Our Saviour, Lebanon....................................	4 00
St. John's, Stockport....................................	10 45
St. Barnabas', Stottville.................................	12 50
All Saints', Hudson......................................	6 08
Christ Church, Gloversville..............................	90 00
Trinity, Fairfield	1 30
Trinity, Claverack	6 25
St. Augustine's, Ilion....................................	4 63
Memorial, Middleville....................................	2 00
Zion, Fonda...	3 00
St. Paul's, Kinderhook...................................	10 97
Emmanuel, Little Falls...................................	14 68
	$486 86

ARCHDEACONRY OF TROY.

St. Paul's, Troy	$117 00
St. John's, Troy	66 35
Christ Church, Troy	123 03
Ascension, Troy	8 77
St. Luke's, Troy	5 08
St. Barnabas', Troy	9 00
Trinity, Lansingburg	25 00
St. Mark's, Hoosick Falls	12 00
All Saints', Hoosac	22 66
Christ Church, Ballston Spa	10 00
St. Paul's, Salem	9 76
Zion, Sandy Hill	7 59
Holy Cross, Warrensburg	14 76
Church of the Cross, Ticonderoga	7 47
Christ Church, Port Henry	7 00
Trinity, Plattsburg	44 00
Christ Church, Rouse's Point	9 87
St. Luke's, Mechanicville	5 62
Messiah, Greenbush	4 00
St. John's, Champlain	20 55
Trinity, Schaghticoke	3 00
Epiphany, East Albany	2 14
St. James', Caldwell	2 14
Raquette Lake Mission	50 00
	$586 79

ARCHDEACONRY OF THE SUSQUEHANNA.

Christ Church, Gilbertsville	$5 00
St. John's, Delhi	18 50
Christ Church, Walton	6 97
Grace, Stamford	10 43
Christ Church, Cooperstown	103 74
Grace, Cherry Valley	27 00
St. Mary's, Springfield Centre	5 00
St. Matthew's, Unadilla	4 30
St. John's, Richfield Springs	150 00
Emmanuel, Otego	2 00
	$332 94

ARCHDEACONRY OF OGDENSBURGH.

Trinity, Potsdam	$159 25
Christ Church, Morristown	5 29
	$164 54

RECAPITULATION.

Archdeaconry of Albany...	$486 86
Archdeaconry of Troy	586 79
Archdeaconry of Susquehanna....	332 94
Archdeaconry of Ogdensburgh.	164 54
	$1,571 13

Respectfully submitted.

LESLIE PELL-CLARKE,
Treasurer.

REPORT OF THE COMMITTEE ON THE REPORTS FROM THE ORPHAN HOUSE OF THE HOLY SAVIOUR.

The Committee on the Reports of the Superintendent and Treasurer of the Orphan House of the Holy Saviour is glad to see that this excellent institution has closed out its accounts for the year without debt. We regret to learn that this has been accomplished only by withdrawing from the small endowment fund the sum of $1,000.

The number of Parishes contributing to the support of the Orphanage this year is 61, as against 70 last year, while the amount contributed is $1,571.13, as against $1,818.59.

Your Committee would call attention to the fact that the cost of maintaining a child at the Diocesan Orphanage, $2 per week, is less than at any similar Church Institution in the State, and yet the Superintendent is constantly obliged to reject worthy applicants for lack of means to support them.

We would, therefore, recommend to the kind consideration of the Convention of the Diocese, the appeal of the Superintendent for endowment — and we would urge upon the Parishes the great need of liberal contributions for this important and worthy charity.

Respectfully submitted.

JOHN E. BOLD,
Chairman.

The Secretary of the Convention read the report of the Committee on Unfinished Business; and, on his motion, the preamble and resolutions reported by the Committee were adopted.

REPORT OF THE COMMITTEE ON UNFINISHED BUSINESS.

The Committee on Unfinished Business respectfully report, that the only unfinished business before this Convention is that of the Preamble and Resolutions of the Trustees of the Diocese in their last report — accompanied by a recommendation of their adoption. to-wit.

WHEREAS, Grace Church at Norway, in Herkimer county, N. Y., has abandoned its organization, and no religious services have been held therein for more than two years past, therefore

Resolved, That, in pursuance of chapter 110 of the Laws of 1876, and section 3 of chapter 23 of the Laws of 1882, the Parish and Church of Grace Church of Norway, in Herkimer county, N. Y., aforesaid, have become and are extinct.

Resolved, That the Trustees of the Diocese of Albany be directed to take possession of the real and personal property and temporalities of said extinct Church and manage the same in such manner as warranted by law.

JAMES E. HALL,
W. C. ROSEBOOM,
T. O. DUROE.

The Rev. C. M. Nickerson, D. D., presented the report of the Committee on Non-Reporting Parishes; and, on his motion, the resolutions recommended by the Committee were adopted.

REPORT OF THE COMMITTEE ON NON-REPORTING CLERGY AND PARISHES.

The Committee on Non-Reporting Clergy and Parishes respectfully report, that in accordance with a resolution of the Convention, the Secretary wrote to the Clergy and Parishes failing to report in 1891. Replies were received from the Rev. Percy St. M. Podmore, from Grace Church, Canton, from St. John's Church, Stillwater, and from St. James' Church, Caldwell. The Rev. Percy St. M. Podmore writes that he is acting as Curate for the Rector of Crofield, England, and that his failure to reply to the Secretary's request for a report from him last year was owing to the miscarriage of the Secretary's letter. The Rev. Marvin H. Dana, in reply to the letter sent to St. John's, Stillwater, writes he is unable to say why a report was not made, and suggests that the proper person to give the desired information is the Priest who had charge of the Parish at the time. The Rev. Edwin R. Armstrong writes that the failure of St. James', Caldwell, to make a report was probably due to the fact that there was no one there to whom it was known the duty of so reporting belonged, the Parish being vacant at the time. The Rector of Grace Church, Canton, makes a similar explanation.

The Secretary's letter failed to elicit replies from St. Luke's, Mechanicville, and from Grace Church, Norway. His letter to the latter Parish was returned to him.

The Rev. J. McC. Windsor, whose name appears among the non-reporting Clergy, has taken out letters dimissory and been transferred to the Diocese of New York.

Your Committee recommend the passage of the following resolutions:

Resolved, That the Secretary of the Convention be and is hereby directed to insert in the Journal, under a separate head, a list of the names of those non-reporting Clergy and Parishes that have failed to return answer to his letter of inquiry, also a record of answers received, and the general character of the excuses offered.

Resolved, That the Secretary of the Convention be and is hereby directed to ask of the Parishes from which no report was received at the last Convention, and the Clergy, still canonically resident in the Diocese, who failed to report at the last Convention, their reasons for not complying with the requirements of the canon; and that a minute of the same be entered in the Appendix to the Journal against the names under the head of Non-reporting Clergy and Parishes; and in any case where the Secretary's request is not complied with, the fact be recorded.

Respectfully submitted.

C. M. NICKERSON.
JOHN HORROCKS.
JAMES McQUIDE.

The Rev. William Ball Wright read the Reports of the Society for the Home Study of Holy Scripture and Church History, and of the Committee on the same.

REPORT OF THE SOCIETY FOR THE HOME STUDY OF HOLY SCRIPTURE.

The objects and the methods of our work have been so fully set forth in our six previous reports that for our seventh little more seems called for than a simple summary of the work accomplished.

The past year has given us richer results than any which preceded. Our list of *students* rose from 230 to 251. The number taking the June Examination also rose from 58 to 80, which was an excess of 10 over any preceding year. Of these 80 students, 69 passed with honour. It is very noticeable that 10 of the 11 who did not reach so high a standard were students in their first year. Yet all passed with credit — not a single one failing — and many very nearly reaching the honour line.

The marked event of the year was our large class of graduates — 19 in number — who were thus entitled to wear the Jerusalem Cross.

Since none of our students could complete their four years' course until 1890, we have had but four classes in all — yet these now number 57, distributed thus — 46 in graduates in Holy Scripture, 12 in Church History, one student having graduated in both. During these seven years of our work there have been 458 Testimonials signed by the Bishop. It should be borne in mind that these are given only to those who take the June Examinations, or about one-third of our members, and that much faithful study and careful teaching can be reported on behalf of the others. And to these should also be added the students who carry on post-graduate work, there being at present 13 of them engaged upon the Psalms, some of them sending in very remarkable papers. A class in the Minor Prophets is expecting soon to begin work.

It must be admitted that there are some who, attempting little, accomplish less, but year after year the proportion is smaller. It must be admitted, also, that much of this work is done with difficulty, amidst many pressing and conflicting claims. One cause, above all others, is an ever-recurring hindrance. We carry along with our little army of students a *Hospital*, and the most of our members, sooner or later, are found upon the list of the sick or the list of household nurses. Few days ever pass without letters telling of deep anxiety or of bereavement. More than ten of our students have been left widows, and have still gone on with the work which proved such a stay and comfort. Many more have lost a parent — some a child — and very many a brother or sister, or some one near and dear.

During this last year Death has also removed from us some of our chief helpers. The Rev. Charles M. Stewart, our examiner in Church History, was first taken — a very serious loss to us. With Easter there came a blow that was almost paralyzing. A few months before our beloved friend, Miss Letitia Townsend, had come to make her home at Saint Anna's. As Student, Correspondent and Trustee she filled a large space in our Society. Her coming brought that help and cheer which scarcely any other could have supplied. Days of deep shadow were those in which she was taken from us, first to St. Luke's Hospital, and there upon the development of that most fearful of fevers, far away from our sight and care, it was a comfort to know that she was alike unconscious of the removal and of the presence of strangers, and that to herself it was but passing from loving eyes on earth into the bliss of Paradise For us held in strict quarantine in the desolated house, waiting from hour to hour till the crisis came, it was a complicated trial such as rarely comes to any household. But the memory of all her strength and sweetness rests now like the rainbow over the heavy cloud.

A few months later there came another blow. Mrs. Sarah Cleveland, the beloved sister of Bishop Doane, was taken from us almost in the act of completing a great benefaction to this Society. Her daughter, Miss Cleveland, had been one of our most devoted correspondents. A week spent by me in 1801 in their restful summer home "Parva Domus" in Bethlehem, New Hampshire, had knit strong personal ties, and during the last year Mrs. Cleveland undertook the task of securing subscriptions for an Assistant Secretary. The work was done chiefly by letters, and the loving letter in which she announced to me that this work was almost accomplished was scarcely written before the faithful hands were folded for their final rest. It is right that our many members who little knew who was caring fo oving devotion, should learn this little of these beloved friends and cherish gratefully their memories.

There is one result of our work which merits the strongest emphasis as it is one which has ever been hoped for. Our graduates are I believe all now teaching in some way, putting their knowledge and their training at once into use for others. Some of them have been formally intrusted by their Bishop with important work in religious instruction. Almost all are teaching Bible Classes. They have become our correspondents also in Holy Scripture and Church History. They look largely to us for books to help them in their special preparation in teaching. All of their letters dwell with delight upon the difference that their study has made in their teaching. Some of them speak with profound gratitude of the help it has brought to them as mothers teaching their own children.

The growth of our library work has been very marked. Four years ago we reported our first loans from this newly established work as 100 for the year. In last year's report our loans had reached 500. But in the year covered by this report, they have advanced as by a sudden bound to almost 1,000, and this out of a collection a little less than 2,000. This is exclusive of the frequent and most important use of the books made by the ladies who come to the house to examine works upon special subjects. Of course, to purchase and put in order and select and wrap and mail so many volumes and to guard against the proverbial perils of misuse and detention, is a great addition to other work, but also one of the utmost value. This Autumn the long desired card catalogue has been completed and arranged in a convenient case of drawers. The Dewey system, with some slight modifications required by our work, has been adopted, and, the execution not being my own, I may be allowed to say that I have never seen in any library a collection of cards so beautifully written and so easy to consult. The additions to the library have included some very real treasures. The next work before us is the preparation of a printed catalogue for the use of our readers. Such are the results of the past year, and I think that very few in reading them can so much as imagine the work and care and anxiety that are involved in thus providing for our large school on paper. All who come to give a helping hand in the office work are astonished at the countless details and the exceeding accuracy required to avoid hopeless confusion. Much of this work it is quite true *might* be spared if all our regulations were followed. But that will probably never be done. It is trying in the extreme when those who direct this study must give up their own hours of study to do something which a little care might have spared them. But as of the ten virgins, "five were wise and five were foolish," so we are thankful for the five, or with us, the *one hundred and twenty-five* that are careful and considerate, and seek to have patience with the five, alas for us, too often the one hundred and twenty-five that are otherwise.

If such could but see the trouble thus caused, we think they would study carefulness as a part of their Christian duty.

One other solemn charge I may be allowed, in closing this report, to extend to our students. Of the intellectual and spiritual gains of your study, there can be no doubt, but will you not seek also to perfect that *moral* training for which the Bible is the unchanging text-book?

In vain does one study the Acts of the Apostles if that lesson be not learned, so solemnly taught to the infant Church, the deadliness of all manner of falsehood and deceit. And in vain is the study of the Gospel of St. John if the very object for which he tells us it was written, be missed, and the student of the Life of Jesus Christ has not after all learned how *she* may *have* life through His name. All study is imperfect till it is wrought out in doing, and, therefore, above all things, dear fellow-students, of these Scriptures of truth, let us see to it that we *live* what we *learn*.

A final word of very real thanks is due upon these pages to the many kind friends of this Society. To our own students first, a number of whom have sent us small donations which, when combined, really exceeded the entire amount received from dues. Also in this city very kindly and generous help has come from the Clergy and a few others. Without this aid the work must have fallen to the ground. The one thing to be desired next to the devotion of some true and well-trained life to this work, is a more secure financial basis. I believe the work to have been conducted as economically as possible, and far more so than its interests really demanded. The rent of the house has been indeed subjected to criticism, but apart from a portion of it being assumed by others, much more of it should not fairly be reckoned as rent. The house, in giving rooms to those who have otherwise worked at their own charges and in supplementing the salary of a secretary, has saved expense in other directions. The most generous offer of a room in the Parish House of St. Agnes' Chapel, for the library and office, will probably be accepted.

But much of blessed possibility will pass away with this surrender of a Home, nor will the necessity of more assured support be greatly lessened. With this change I must myself relinquish even the oversight of office work and limit my care to the general direction of the work and the guidance of our students. I must own that while this work itself was never more prosperous the support of it was never such a matter of anxiety — much misapprehension has prevailed as to our resources. We have never had but one gift which exceeded one hundred dollars, and but very few to that amount. It must be I fear because it is not considered after all so very important that our women should be well instructed in such studies, and my most earnest prayer is that more women may be aroused to study the Bible, and more hearts made willing to help them — that gifts as generous as are given to all other studies may be given to these. And I appeal finally to all our students to do what lies in their power to extend to others their own deep interest.

SARAH F. SMILEY,
Director and Organizing Secretary.

REPORT OF THE COMMITTEE ON THE REPORT OF THE SOCIETY FOR THE HOME STUDY OF HOLY SCRIPTURE AND CHURCH HISTORY.

Your Committee on the Seventh Report of the Society for the Home Study of Holy Scripture and Church History have not been able to peruse the report without a mingled feeling of the deepest admiration for the work, and for the results accomplished, and also for the enthusiasm and loving service of the pious and accomplished organizing Secretary. It must be matter of sincere rejoicing that there has again been quite an increase in the number of students, and of those taking the June examination, and that while of these latter, seven-eighths passed with honour, none failed.

The hand of death has not spared some admirable and beloved friends and helpers, and by the lamented decease of Miss Letitia Townsend and Mrs. Sarah Cleveland the Society has suffered a heavy loss in more ways than one.

Your Committee notes with pleasure that the seed sown is now bearing fruit, in the increased power of many Bible Class teachers to impart knowledge of the word of God and the History of the Church.

It must be a subject of deep regret that St. Anna's Home is likely to be given up and that the devoted Secretary has to limit her efforts in the future to a merely general oversight of the work.

Your Committee presents the following resolutions:

Resolved, That subject to the discretion of the Bishop, the Secretary of the Convention be instructed to have printed in the Journal the Report of the Society for the Home Study of Holy Script

Resolved, That the Bishop be thanked for his earnest Pastoral on the restoration of
the daily Service, and that the laity be urged to take this into consideration.

Resolved, That this Convention sympathizes heartily with the aims and hopes of
the Society, and prays that earnest and loving helpers may be moved to offer themselves for carrying on the important increase of the work.

Resolved, That those whom God has prospered are respectfully advised that they
may with confidence foster and aid the blessed undertaking which this Society has
in hand.

WM. BALL WRIGHT,
HOBART COOKE,
C. W. WOODFORD,
JAMES DEF BORROUGHS.

The resolutions recommended in the Report of the Committee on
the Society for the Home Study of Holy Scripture were adopted.

The Secretary of the Convention read the

REPORT OF THE TRUSTEES OF THE FUND FOR THE SUPPORT OF WIDOWS AND ORPHANS OF DECEASED CLERGYMEN.

DIOCESE OF ALBANY,
ALBANY, *November* 14, A. D., 1893.

The Trustees for the Fund for the Support of Widows and Orphans of Deceased
Clergymen present herewith the Report of the Treasurer, showing the Receipts and
Disbursements for the year:

RECEIPTS.

Balance on hand as reported to last Convention	$1,243 90
From Parishes	239 34
From Investments	310 00
Total	$1,793 24

DISBURSEMENTS.

For Special Stipends	575 00
Balance	$1,218 24

The Trustees hold the following securities presented by St. Paul's Church, Albany:

One U. S. Registered 4 per cent Bond	$1,000 00
Two Chicago, Burlington & Quincy, Nebraska extension, 4 per cent Bonds	2,000 00
One Chicago, Burlington & Quincy 4 per cent Bond	1,000 00
One Wabash Railway 5 per cent Bond	1,000 00
Total	$5,000 00
Also 3 Bonds, $500 each	1,500 00
Making permanent investment	$6,500 00

WM. CROSWELL DOANE, *President.*
SELDEN E. MARVIN, *Treasurer.*

The Rev. Freeborn G. Jewett, Jr., presented and read the

REPORT OF THE COMMITTEE ON THE FUND FOR THE WIDOWS AND ORPHANS OF DECEASED CLERGYMEN.

The Committee on the Report of the Trustees of the Fund for the Support of the Widows and Orphans of Deceased Clergymen have examined the accounts and vouchers and find them correct. The Committee would earnestly urge the Rectors of Parishes to induce their people to more liberal contributions to this Fund. It seems hard that Clergymen who have given their life's work to the Church, with very little remuneration, should have no hope that at their death their wives and children would receive at least a reasonable care at the hands of the Church.

All of which is respectfully submitted.

FREEBORN G. JEWETT, JR.,
ANDREW B. JONES,
ALEX. R. BENSON.

The Rev. George G. Carter, S. T. D., for the Commission on the Clerical Pension System, presented a verbal report, asking to be continued; which request was granted.

The Rev. Charles S. Olmsted presented the following report, and on motion the Committee was continued.

REPORT OF THE COMMITTEE ON THE TWENTY-FIFTH ANNIVERSARY OF THE CONSECRATION OF THE FIRST BISHOP OF ALBANY.

The Committee on the Observance of the Twenty-fifth Anniversary of the Bishop of Albany's Consecration begs leave to report that there will be placed on the altar of the Cathedral, on the date of the anniversary, a very large amount in gifts and pledges toward the Chapter House Building Fund; so large as to give the Committee the timely encouragement it greatly needs. Owing to the straitness of the times, an amount sufficient to build a Chapter House has not yet been promised, and the Committee asks to be continued another year.

On the Festival of the Presentation of Christ in the Temple, to-morrow, the service arranged by a Sub-Committee of this Committee will attest the value put upon our Bishop's eminent labors of a quarter of a century by the Clergy and Laity of the Diocese.

CHARLES S. OLMSTED,
Secretary of the Committee.

The Rev. Sheldon M. Griswold presented and read the

REPORT OF THE COMMITTEE ON THE DIOCESAN FUND, APPOINTED AT THE CONVENTION OF 1892.

Your Committee on the Diocesan Fund and Mileage of the Clergy, appointed at the last Convention, begs leave to report that the following resolution was referred to them with instructions to report upon the same to the present Convention:

"*Resolved*, That the expense of entertaining the clerical members of the Diocese in attendance on the sessions of the Convention is properly a charge on the whole Diocese of Albany, and the Committee on the Diocesan Fund is requested to take the subject under consideration, and report thereon to the

6

Your Committee has carefully considered all of the conditions involved in the foregoing resolution; and respectfully reports, that the provision of the resolution seems inexpedient; and recommends, that no addition be made to the Diocesan Fund for the entertainment of the Clergy in attendance on the sessions of the Convention.

SHELDON MUNSON GRISWOLD, *Chairman*
CHARLES PELLETREAU,
CHAS. H. UPHAM,
JAS. I. YOUNGLOVE.

The hour for the annual elections having arrived, on motion, it was

Resolved, That the Secretary of the Convention be instructed to cast the ballot of the Convention for the members of the Standing Committee as elected last year.

The ballot was cast accordingly, and the Right Rev. President declared elected as members of

THE STANDING COMMITTEE.

The Rev. J. Ireland Tucker, S. T. D., the Rev. Fenwick Mitford Cookson, the Rev. Wilford Lash Robbins, D. D., the Rev. James Caird, Mr. Norman B. Squires, Mr. Henry S. Wynkoop, Mr. John I. Thompson and Mr. John H. Van Antwerp.

On motion of the Secretary of the Convention, the ballot was dispensed with, and the following elections were made:

MEMBER OF THE MISSIONARY COUNCIL.

Col. William G. Rice.

TRUSTEES OF THE EPISCOPAL FUND.

Mr. J. H. Van Antwerp, Mr. W. Bayard Van Rensselaer, Mr. Charles W. Tillinghast, 2nd, Mr. Dean Sage, Mr. Robert C. Pruyn.

TRUSTEES OF THE FUND FOR AGED AND INFIRM CLERGYMEN.

Mr. Norman B. Squires, Mr. Robert S. Oliver, and Mr. J. J. Tillinghast.

TRUSTEES OF THE FUND FOR WIDOWS AND ORPHANS OF DECEASED CLERGYMEN.

Mr. J. W. Tillinghast, Mr. C. W. Tillinghast, and Mr. Amasa J. Parker.

TRUSTEES OF THE ORPHAN HOUSE OF THE HOLY SAVIOUR AT COOPERSTOWN UNTIL CONVENTION, 1896.

The Rev. Richmond H. Gesner, Mr. T. Streatfeild Clarkson, W. T. Bassett, M. D.

TRUSTEE OF THE DIOCESE OF ALBANY UNTIL CONVENTION, 1896.
Mr. John Hudson Peck.

TRUSTEES OF THE DIOCESE UNTIL CONVENTION, 1897.
The Rev. Charles S. Olmsted, Mr. A. B. Cox.

The election of the Board of Missions being in order, nominations were received for the Archdeaconries as presented in the Report of the Secretary of the Convention; and, on motion of Gen. Selden E. Marvin, the Rev. Charles Temple and Mr. William Kemp were nominated for the Diocese at large.

On motion of the Secretary of the Convention, the ballot was unanimously dispensed with, and the following named persons were elected as the Board of Missions until the next Convention.

BOARD OF MISSIONS.

ARCHDEACONRY OF ALBANY.

The Rev. W. W. Battershall, D. D.   Mr. J. H. Van Antwerp.

ARCHDEACONRY OF TROY.

The Rev. F. M. Cookson.   Mr. George A. Wells.

ARCHDEACONRY OF THE SUSQUEHANNA.

The Rev. Robert N. Parke, D. D.   Mr. Robert M. Townsend.

ARCHDEACONRY OF OGDENSBURGH.

The Rev. R. M. Kirby, D. D.   Mr. T. Streatfeild Clarkson.

DIOCESE AT LARGE.

The Rev. Charles Temple.   Mr. William Kemp.

On motion of the Rev. Richmond Shreve, D. D., it was

Resolved, That the Parishes and Mission Stations are requested to send to the Treasurer of the Diocese, for the current Conventional year, the offering for Clerical Insurance, at the rate of one-half of one per centum on the assessment for the Diocesan Fund.

On motion of the Rev. William C. Prout, it was

Resolved, That the Bishop of the Diocese be requested to send to the Rev. Arthur C. A. Hall, D. D., who is to be to-morrow consecrated Bishop of Vermont, and to the Bishops and Clergy assembled for the service of that Consecration, a despatch conveying the cordial greetings and congratulation of this Convention.

The Right Rev. John Williams, D. D., LL. D., Bishop of Connecticut, Presiding Bishop of the Church in the United States, entering the House, was received by the Convention standing, and made a brief address.

The Right Rev. the Bishop of the Diocese read the portions of his Annual Address which refer to Diocesan Missions and the Diocesan

Missionary; and, on motion of the Rev. Walton W. Battershall, D. D., it was

Resolved, That the portions of the Bishop's Address which refer to Diocesan Missions and the Diocesan Missionary be referred to the Committee on Diocesan Missions.

Unanimous consent was given the Secretary to print in its place in the Journal the Report of the Trustees of the Diocese.

REPORT OF THE TRUSTEES OF THE DIOCESE OF ALBANY.

A meeting of the Trustees of the Diocese of Albany was held in the Crypt of the Cathedral of All Saints, Albany, on the 15th day of February, 1894.

The Secretary presented the deed of Alexander Hemsley, of Tannersville, to the Trustees of the Diocese of Albany, of the property in Tannersville, Greene county, " being the Church and land connected therewith, known as the Church of St. John the Evangelist," dated November 7, 1892, and recorded in Greene county, June 21, 1893, in book No. 132 of Deeds, at page 211.

It was voted that the Trustees of the Diocese of Albany take and accept the property described in the above-mentioned deed.

The Secretary presented the deed of David White, of Rouse's Point, to the Trustees of the Diocese of Albany, of a tract of land in Rouse's Point, Clinton county, on the south side of White avenue, fifty feet wide and one hundred feet deep, for a Rectory lot for Christ Church, with certain restrictions as to occupation.

It was voted that the Trustees of the Diocese of Albany take and accept the property described in the above-mentioned deed.

The Trustees were informed that the Vestry of Christ Church are building a Rectory on the piece of land described in this deed from David White, the estimated cost of which is $2,800. That they have raised and expended on the building $1,700, and they request the trustees to borrow the sum of $600 on bond and mortgage on this property, to complete the building. David White also offers to release his reserved rights to enable the Trustees to mortgage the property.

It was voted to borrow on bond and mortgage on the Rectory and Rectory lot of Christ Church, Rouse's Point, the sum of $600, as requested by the Vestry of that Church.

The Secretary presented the deed of Catherine J. Weir, of Sidney, to the Trustees of the Diocese of Albany, of a tract of land in the village of Sidney, Delaware county, on the south-west corner of River and Clinton streets, and recorded in Delaware county, December 7, 1892, in liber 116 of Deeds, at page 352. On this lot is built the Mission Chapel of St. Paul's, Sidney.

It was voted that the Trustees of the Diocese of Albany take and accept the property described in the above-mentioned deed.

The Trustees were informed that the building committee of St. Paul's Chapel, Sidney, had borrowed the sum of $1,000 on their joint note, for the purpose of completing the Chapel, which note would fall due very soon. And they requested the Trustees to borrow the sum of $1,000 on bond and mortgage on this property for the purpose of paying this note.

It was voted to borrow on bond and mortgage on the property of St. Paul's Chapel, Sidney, the sum of $1,000, for the purpose of paying the note of the building committee, provided they would give to the Trustees a paid-up policy of insurance of $1,000, for three years, on St. Paul's Chapel, and also furnish a bond indemnifying the Trustees against the payment of interest on the mortgage.

The Bishop and Mr. Peck were appointed a committee to consider the appointment of a clerk for this board, to keep systematic records of property committed to its care and business in relation thereto, with power to appoint said clerk.

It was voted to accept the charge of the bequest of the late Mrs. Augustus Chapman, of a trust fund for the benefit of Christ Church, Morristown, St. Lawrence county, and that the Secretary be empowered to receive the same and invest it temporarily, subject to the direction of the Trustees.

The whole question of the care and investment of trust funds was referred to the Bishop and Mr. Peck, with the request that they report at a future meeting of the Trustees.

The Rev. Mr. Sill and Mr. Bagley were requested to consider the request of the Church of the Holy Cross, Fort Plain, to move their Church down into the lower portion of the village, with the request that they report at a future meeting of the Trustees.

The following minute was adopted in regard to the death of Mr. Hall, at the suggestion of the Bishop:

The Trustees of the Diocese of Albany, meeting for the first time since the death of Mr. Benjamin H. Hall, put on record their grateful recognition of the invaluable services which Mr. Hall rendered to the Trustees, not only by his constant and careful attendance at their meetings, but also by the wisdom of his counsel, always freely given in all questions of importance; by his deep interest in the important matters intrusted to the Board; by the example of his devoted life with its entire consecration to the service of the Master.

The matter of St. Luke's Church, Middleburgh, Schoharie county, declared extinct by a resolution of the last convention, was referred to the Rev. Mr. Olmsted and the Secretary.

All of which is respectfully submitted,

A. B. Cox,
Secretary.

The following preamble and resolutions, offered by the Rev. W. C. Stewart, were, on motion of the Secretary of the Convention, referred to the Trustees of the Diocese of Albany:

WHEREAS, The Church of St. Luke, at Middleburgh, has ceased to maintain religious services for more than two consecutive years prior to November 1, 1893, according to the customs and usages of the Protestant Episcopal Church in the Diocese of Albany; and for other sufficient causes;

Resolved, That the Church and Society of the Church of St. Luke, in the town of Middleburgh, in the county of Schoharie, be, and the same is hereby, declared to be extinct.

Resolved, That the Trustees of the Diocese of Albany be directed to take possession of the temporalities belonging to the said extinct Church and manage the same in such manner as is warranted by law.

The Convention took a recess until half-past 2 o'clock.

———

HALF-PAST TWO O'CLOCK IN THE AFTERNOON.

The Convention reassembled.

The Right Rev. President took the chair and called the Convention to order.

On motion of the Rev. William M. Cook the following resolution was referred to a special committee to report to the next Convention:

Resolved, That section 5 of Canon XIV be amended so as to read as follows:

Sec. 5. The Diocese shall be divided into 'districts called Archdeaconries, the titles and limits of which shall be as follows: The Archdeaconry of Albany shall comprise the counties of Albany, Columbia and Greene. The Archdeaconry of the Mohawk shall comprise the counties of Schenectady, Montgomery, Fulton, Hamilton and Herkimer. The Archdeaconry of Troy shall comprise the counties of Rensselaer, Saratoga, Washington, Warren, Essex and Clinton. The Archdeaconry of the Susquehanna shall comprise the counties of Delaware, Otsego and Schoharie. The Archdeaconry of Ogdensburgh shall comprise the counties of St. Lawrence and Franklin.

By unanimous expression of the Convention the Bishop of the Diocese was requested to act as a member and chairman of the said Committee; and the Right Rev. President appointed other members of the Committee, one from each Archdeaconry; so that the Committee became: The Right Rev. the Bishop of the Diocese, the Rev. William Mason Cook, the Rev. Fenwick M. Cookson, Mr. G. Pomeroy Keese and Mr. Louis Hasbrouck.

The hour of three o'clock having arrived, the order of the day was taken up, being the reports from the Board of Missions.

The Rev. Henry R. Freeman presented and read the

REPORT OF THE COMMITTEE ON DIOCESAN MISSIONS.

The report of the Board of Missions indicates to no small degree the tidal-sweep of your Diocesan agencies. The missionary spirit quickens the flood-beat of the Church's life, missionary apathy marks its ebb tide. Hence with eager interest we listen to the record of Missions at these yearly gatherings of our dear Church, the messages from lips that burn with love for Christ, and that witness for Him in the wilderness and the waste places, the burden of whose tale is borne upon us as a noble record of sacrifice, of heroism and of love — the record of Missions is the year's epic

The review of such a ministry we may in no wise set at naught. It must be of no inconsiderable pride to the Diocese, and yet the glory of it is not unmixed with dishonour, the success of it not unshadowed by failure A step backward is not an evidence of defeat, but it is an admission of weakness We have receded, but not retreated. The onward movement has been arrested, but not abandoned. The history of this Diocese in her support of Missions is a long record of honour, and no temporary shadow of misfortune shall diminish aught from it, but not of honour dare we think, when, were it not for the supplementary report of our Treasurer, we should write a deficit across the balance-sheet of the year Your Committee would face such a problem with courage, if it be possible.

A deficit of faith is far more deplorable than a depleted treasury, and yet to the latter are attributed the causes of such shortcomings as have marred the year's work. Moreover, are we altogether honest in placing the *times,* rather than ourselves on the defensive; is it a depression financial, or moral, that confronts us, has there not been a shrinkage of spiritual values?

Let us look at this matter squarely and fairly, think you that retrenchment could not have begun elsewhere than at the door of our Missionary board? Unfortunately the Missionary feels the pressure of hard times before the merchant, and missionary enterprise languishes at the least sign of financial stringency It is sad indeed to think that the question of maintenance and support is so largely affected by the fluctuation of the markets; we have so much necessarily to do with money that somehow even our faith has a metallic ring in it. It is not a question of missionary extravagance, nor of any inconsiderable increase of missionary agencies, but rather the question of the honourable obligation of a Diocese to support its own Missions, to bear its own burdens, to develop its own resources. And no claim is more just than that which holds us to these obligations, to the faithful support and furtherance of which we are sacredly pledged.

These *men* that go forth are sent by us, and is it at all unreasonable that they should be fully and richly sustained by the Church that is honoured by their service?

Statistics do not inflame us, figures do not inflate us, especially in this year of grace; the mere recital of facts and the grouping of results will not appeal to us, save as we respond to the deep-stirrings of faith and the conscious thrill of honourable obligation that lead us, dear brethren, to face this great difficulty with a courage born of God, and inspired by personal duty. Your Committee would therefore urge with all earnestness a determination to advance, and not to recede — to make possible a *forward movement* all along the line, and to overcome all difficulties by a faith undaunted and undiminished.

As concerning your newly-created office of Diocesan Missionary, there can be but little question of its value at this period of its usefulness. It is no longer in the tentative or experimental stage. It has proved its utility; its efficiency has been most surely and thoroughly tested. Three years of use are not to be slightly disregarded, and yet it is not unattended by difficulties, nor undisturbed by serious questions of limitation, and still more serious problems of maintenance. Your Committee would heartily recommend its continuance, and further urge the necessity of such action as will give more definiteness to its scope and powers, and make specific provision for its support.

Your Committee would respectfully suggest that the quarterly offerings for Diocesan Missions be promptly forwarded, and would renew the proposition made several years ago, that one Sunday or more be known as the Children's Missionary Sunday or Season — such time to call for missionary contributions from the Sunday Schools of the Diocese.

Further your Committee would accentuate the need, as embodied in the call of the Bishop, for an appropriation of $11,550 for the work of the coming year. Such a pledge should be most fitting in this hour of joyous congratulations, and of memories and ministrations most truly hallowed and enshrined; our loyalty and love will meet in no higher task as a memorial to our beloved and honoured Bishop, in whose wisdom and affection we are, dear brethren, such rich sharers to-day.

All of which is respectfully submitted.

HENRY R. FREEMAN,
R. H. GESNER,
BENJAMIN F. HINMAN,
C. W. WOODFORD.

MISSIONS IN THE DIOCESE OF ALBANY.

ARCHDEACONRY OF ALBANY.

County.	Church.	Place.	Missionary.	Stipend.
Albany......	Trinity	Rensselaerville.....	Rev. S.C. Thompson,	$150
	St. Andrew's...	West Troy.........	Rev. C. H. Hatheway.	200
Greene	Gloria Dei	Palenville	Rev. W. C. Grubbe.	250
	Grace	Prattsville ......)	Rev. W. R. Hall ...	200
	Trinity	Ashland ....)		
	Trinity	Athens...!......	Rev. J. G. Fawcett.	100
	Christ.........	Coxsackie	Rev. E. S. De G. Tompkins	300
	Calvary	Cairo.............	Rev. J. T. Zorn	100
Herkimer ...	Trinity	Fairfield..... --)	Rev. C. M. Conant..	400
	Memorial	Middleville .....)		
	Grace	Mohawk.......	Rev. W. A. Stirling.	200
	St. Augustine's.	Ilion ....)	Rev. W. M. Cook ..	250
	St. Alban's.....	Frankfort.........)		
	St. John's	Dolgeville	Rev. D. A. Bonnar..	400
Fulton	Christ.........	Gloversville	Rev. H. M. Smyth..	200
Montgomery.	Zion	Fonda	Rev. C. C. Edmunds.	200
	Good Shepherd.	Canajoharie......)	Rev. E. C. Hoskins.	250
	Holy Cross.....	Fort Plain ......)		
Columbia ..	St. Luke's. ...	Clermont	Rev. M. E. Wilson.	
	All Saints'.....	Hudson ....)	Rev. G. G. Carter, S. T. D.........	250
	Trinity	Claverack ....)		
	St. Luke's.....	Chatham	Rev. T. H. R. Luney.	250
	St John-in-the-Wilderness ..	Copake............	Rev. W. B. Reynolds.	100
	St. Mark's	Philmont	Rev. A. Lowndes...	300
	Our Saviour ...	Lebanon Springs...	Rev. Geo. B. Johnson.	250

ARCHDEACONRY OF TROY.

County.	Church.	Place.	Missionary.	Stipend.
Rensselaer ..	St. Giles' ..	Castleton	Rev C. H. Hatheway.	$200
	Trinity	Schaghticoke	Rev. M. O. Smith .	300
	St. Paul's......	Raymertown.....)	Rev. H. C. Dyer ...	300
	Holy Name	Boyntonville ....)		
Saratoga	St. Stephen's ..	Schuylerville	Rev. W. F. Parsons.	250
	St. John's	Stillwater	Rev. M. H. Dana...	
	St. Luke's	Mechanicville	Rev. F. N. Bouck ..	150
	St. Paul's. ...	Charlton ... .)	Rev. J. M. Gilbert..	100
		West Charlton...)		
	St. John's	East Line..... ...)		
	Grace	Jonesville ...... }	Rev. Thos. Boone ..	200
	All Saints'	Round Lake .....)		
	St. John's	Conklingville....)	Rev. C. J. Whipple.	300
	St. Mary's	Luzerne . ...)		
	St. Andrew's ..	Schroon Lake.. ..	Rev. C. B. Perry ...	350
Warren	Good Shepherd.	Chestertown ....)	Rev. A. Taylor	250
	St. Paul's......	Bartonville .....)		
	St. Sacrament..	Bolton	Rev. C. T. Blanchet.	
Washington..	St. Luke's	Cambridge.........	Rev. F. H. T. Horsfield	100
	St. Paul's......	Greenwich........	Rev. L. C. Morgan..	250
	Trinity	Granville ... .)	Rev. J. H. Geare...	250
		North Granville..)		
	St. Paul's......	Salem	Rev. H. C. Rush ...	100
Essex	Of the Cross ...	Ticonderoga	Rev. W. R. Harris..	250
	Christ.........	Port Henry ......)	....	350
	Emmanuel ...	Mineville........)		

County.	Church.	Place.	Missionary.	Stipend.
Essex	St. John's	Essex	Rev. W. N. Irish ..	
	Good Shepherd.	Bloomingdale	Rev. W. H. Larom.	
	St. Paul's	Keeseville	Rev. J. W. Gill....	$400
	St. James'. ...	Ausable Forks ...		
Clinton	Christ..........	Rouse's Point....	Rev. W, Ball Wright	300
	St. John's . ..	Champlain......		
	St. Peter's	Ellenburgh	Rev. S. M. Rogers..	100
	St. Paul's......	Ellenburgh Centre		
	St. John's	Salmon River	Rev. Hobart Cooke.	

ARCHDEACONRY OF THE SUSQUEHANNA.

Delaware....	Christ	Deposit.	Rev. F. S. Fisher...	$250
	St. Peter's......	Hobart...........	Rev. Thos. Burrows.	300
		Bloomville.......		
	St. Paul's......	Franklin...	Rev. Grenville Rath-	
			bun	250
	Grace.........	Stamford	Rev. H. McDougall.	200
	St. Paul's......	Sidney............	Rev. G. H. Fenwick.	250
	Emmanuel.....	Fleischman's..	Rev. S. D. Van Loan	
Otsego.......	Christ	West Burlington. .	Mr. E. B. M. Harra-	
			den.............	100
	Good Shepherd.	Cullen...........	Rev. G. B. Richards.	100
	St. Luke's.. ..	Monticello		
	Immanuel......	Otego.............	Rev. W. G. W. Lewis.	200
	Holy Spirit....	Schenevus.......		
	Sts. Simon &		Rev. B. F. Miller. .	250
	Jude.........	Worcester		
	St. James'.....	Oneonta	Rev. J. E. Bold	200
	St. John's......	Portlandville		
	Christ	Gilbertsville	Rev. D. F. MacDon-	
	St. Stephen's...	Maple Grove ...	ald, D. D.........	250
	St. Paul's......	East Springfield..	Rev. John Prout....	200
	St. Mary's......	Springfield Centre		

ARCHDEACONRY OF OGDENSBURGH.

Franklin	St. John's.	St. Regis Lake. .	Rev. W. H. Larom..	
	St. Luke's.. ..	Saranac Lake		
		Santa Clara		
		St. Regis Falls...	Rev. C. A. Howells.	$300
		Paul Smith's Sta..		
	St. Mark's.. ..	West Bangor ...		
	St. Peter's.. ...	Brushton	Rev. A. L. Fortin...	300
St. Lawrence.	St. Thomas'...	Lawrenceville....		
Franklin	St. James'.....	Hogansburgh	Rev. David Jenkins.	300
		Fort Covington...		
St. Lawrence.	St. John's	Massena	Rev. C. E. Mackenzie.	325
	Grace.........	Norfolk..... ...	Rev. E. R. Earle ...	150
	St. Andrew's...	Norwood.........		
	St. Paul's......	Waddington	Rev. A. C. Macdonald	400
	St. Luke's.....	Lisbon		
	Christ	Morristown	Rev. W. S. Hayward,	300
	Trinity	Gouverneur........	Rev. J. A. Dickson..	200
	Trinity Chapel.	Morley............	Rev. R. Wyndham	
			Brown...........	200

Gen. Selden E. Marvin presented and read the

SUMMARY.

	Stations.	Missionaries.	Stipends.
In the Archdeaconry of Albany..............	25	20	$4,350
In the Archdeaconry of Troy...	35	22	4,500
In the Archdeaconry of Susquehanna........	19	13	3,550
In the Archdeaconry of Ogdensburgh........	18	10	2,475
	97	65	$13,875

Gen. Selden E. Marvin presented and read the

REPORT OF THE TREASURER OF THE BOARD OF MISSIONS.

RECEIPTS.	Salary Diocesan Missionary.	Missions.
Balance on hand as reported at last Convention...........	... ...	$228 85
Archdeaconry of Albany.		
Cathedral of All Saints.............	$50 00	$1,268 20
St. Peter's, Albany	50 00	1,002 16
St. Paul's, Albany	....	400 00
Grace, Albany ....,.............	10 00	58 36
Holy Innocents', Albany ....,...	15 00	55 58
Trinity, Albany..........	....	20 00
St. Andrew's Mission, Albany..........................	1 83	5 00
Trinity, Rensselaerville	5 25	18 04
St. John's, Cohoes	15 00	267 60
Trinity, West Troy	2 29	45 00
St. Gabriel's, West Troy....................	1 85	....
St. Andrew's, West Troy	....	9 28
St. Margaret's, Menands	4 00	9 59
St. Mark's, Green Island	9 94	37 52
Christ, Schenectady......	1 00	20 00
St. George's, Schenectady .... -	....	150 00
Christ, Duanesburgh.	20 71	64 69
St. Ann's, Amsterdam	....	8 54
Zion, Fonda	... ...	10 00
Good Shepherd, Canajoharie	2 00	23 00
Holy Cross, Fort Plain	....	10 37
St. Columba's, St. Johnsville	....	....
Emmanuel, Little Falls	3 46	19 98
St. John's, Dolgeville	....	14 50
Christ, Herkimer	10 00	74 19
St. Augustine's, Ilion	... .	37 43
Grace, Mohawk....	... .	17 37
St. Alban's, Frankfort.....................	1 00	....
Memorial, Middleville....	1 00	20 00
Trinity, Fairfield..... .... -	.. ....	5 00
St. John's, Johnstown........	30 85	81 12
Christ, Gloversville	5 00	25 00
Christ, Coxsackie	....	5 00
St. Luke's, Catskill	15 00	130 00
Trinity, Athens.............................. ...	....	25 00

	Salary Diocesan Missionary.	Missions.
St. Paul's, Oak Hill.........................	....	$5 00
Christ, Greenville..........................	....	5 00
Mission, Tannersville.......................	....	5 00
Trinity, Ashland...........................	....	5 00
Calvary, Cairo.............................	....	10 00
Gloria Dei, Palenville......................	....	15 10
Christ, Hudson.............................	$14 10	104 95
All Saints', Hudson.........................	15 00	19 68
Evangelist, Stockport.......................	11 14	25 00
St. Barnabas', Stottville....................	10 00	25 00
St. James', Rossman's Mills.................	5 57	5 00
St. Paul's, Kinderhook......................	6 68	75 00
Trinity, Claverack.........................	15 00	17 64
Our Saviour, Lebanon Springs...............	5 54	24 27
St. Luke's, Clermont.......................	....	10 00
St. John's, Copake.........................	....	6 17
St. Luke's, Chatham.......................	5 00	14 50
St. Mark's, Philmont.......................	5 00	20 00
Archdeaconry of Albany....................	....	6 17

Archdeaconry of Troy.

St. Paul's, Troy...........................	$50 00	$1,354 00
St. John's, Troy...........................	30 00	657 08
Christ, Troy..............................	....	274 12
Holy Cross, Troy..........................	....	200 00
Ascension, Troy...........................	....	50 00
St. Luke's, Troy...........................	....	20 00
St. Barnabas', Troy........................	9 84	53 42
Trinity, Lansingburgh......................	20 00	200 00
Epiphany, East Albany......................	....	....
St. Giles', Castleton.......................	....	19 00
St. Giles' Sunday-school, Castleton..........	....	2 00
St. Mark's, Hoosick Falls...................	17 00	167 50
Trinity, Schaghticoke......................	....	15 00
Messiah, Greenbush........................	....	25 00
All Saints', Hoosac........................	....	30 00
Holy Name, Boyntonville...................	3 00	5 00
Mission, Raymertown......................	5 50	....
Grace, Waterford..........................	....	5 00
St. Stephen's, Schuylerville.................	2 00	6 40
Christ, Ballston Spa........................	15 00	105 01
St. Luke's, Mechanicville...................	5 00	23 61
St. John's, Stillwater......................	....	....
St. John's, East Line.......................	3 00	5 00
Grace, Jonesville..........................	3 00	11 07
All Saints', Round Lake....................	4 00	8 38
Calvary, Burnt Hills.......................	2 40	28 04
St. Paul's, Charlton.......................	....	9 53
Bethesda, Saratoga Springs.................	50 00	219 62
St. John's, Conklingville...................		5 00

	Salary Diocesan Missionary.	Missions.
St. James', Caldwell	$12 00	$10 86
Messiah, Glens Falls	20 00	100 28
Holy Cross, Warrensburgh		50 00
St. Mary's, Luzerne	10 00	20 00
St. Sacrament, Bolton		10 00
Good Shepherd, Chestertown	3 20	15 00
St. Paul's, Bartonville		8 00
St. James', Fort Edward	5 00	20 00
St. Paul's, Salem		64 89
St. Luke's, Cambridge	10 00	185 00
St. Paul's, Greenwich		(92) 25 00
St. Paul's, Greenwich		25 00
Zion, Sandy Hill	71	33 37
Trinity, Granville		25 00
Mission, North Granville		10 00
Trinity, Whitehall		46 61
Cross, Ticonderoga	4 00	41 08
Christ, Port Henry		31 25
Emmanuel, Mineville		5 00
St. Andrew's, Schroon Lake	3 55	10 91
Good Shepherd, Elizabethtown		10 00
St. James', Ausable Forks		15 00
St. Paul's, Keeseville		15 00
St. John's, Essex		38 00
Trinity, Plattsburgh		100 00
Christ, Rouse's Point		28 05
St. John's, Champlain		23 19
St. Peter's, Ellenburgh		10 00

Archdeaconry of Susquehanna.

Christ, Cooperstown	16 71	152 92
Grace, Cherry Valley		77 90
St. James', Oneonta		53 61
St. Mary's, Springfield Centre	6 75	20 00
St. Paul's, East Springfield	6 00	30 00
Zion, Morris		55 00
Emmanuel, Otego		10 00
Christ, Gilbertsville	5 25	32 50
St. Matthew's, Unadilla		25 00
St John's, Richfield Springs		50 00
Christ, West Burlington	4 25	2 00
St. John's, Delhi		125 00
St. Peter's, Hobart		35 00
Grace, Stamford	5 00	28 06
Christ, Walton		30 00
St. Paul's, Franklin		(92) 8 40
St. Paul's, Franklin		20 00
Christ, Deposit		25 00
St. Paul's, Sidney	1 75	5 00

	Salary Diocesan Missionary.	Missions.
St. Simon and St. Jude, Worcester.......................	....	....
Holy Spirit, Schenevus.	....	$10 00
Mission, Cobleskill................	$5 00	....
Trinity, Sharon Springs	....	3 50

Archdeaconry of Ogdensburgh.

St. John's, Ogdensburgh......	25 00	523 19
Trinity, Potsdam	30 00	1,031 00
Grace, Canton	....	31 00
Trinity, Morley........	....	25 00
St. Paul's, Waddington	....	30 00
St. Luke's, Lisbon	....	5 00
Christ, Morristown.....	2 04	45 27
Trinity, Gouverneur	5 00	55 80
Grace, Norfolk	... .	5 00
St. John's, Massena	....	50 00
Zion, Colton	....	20 00
St. Thomas', Lawrenceville................................	....	9 00
St. Andrew's, Norwood.....	....	10 00
St. Mark's, Malone....	23 50	100 00
St. Peter's, Brushton	....	13 55
St. Mark's, West Bangor	....	8 00
St. James', Hogansburgh	....	25 00
St. Luke's, Saranac Lake	....	20 00
St. Paul's, Fort Covington....	....	....

Sundry sources.

Offertories at Convention...........	$89 51	
Income Miss Austin Fund	1,605 00	
Income Parochial Fund.............	40 00	
Income Gilchrist Bond....	15 00	
Income Walker Bond and Mortgage.....................	125 00	
Income Vandenburgh Bond	30 00	
Income Starr and Others Bond	39 82	
Income Tibbits Fund.....	120 00	
Income Troy and West Troy Bridge Bond................	35 00	
Income Cornell Steamboat Bond........	70 00	
Income Houghton Bonds.............................	50 00	
Income Sundry Notes	26 11	
A Friend of Missions	100 00	
G. H. N	5 00	
Robert C. Pruyn	100 00	
Mrs. Mary E. Hart.....	100 00	
Charles W. Tillinghast........	100 00	
Mrs. Mary P. Averill....................	100 00	
George H. Cramer	100 00	
Julia N. and Walter Wood	100 00	
William Kemp	100 00	
A. B. Cox ....◄........	100 00	

Nathan B. Warren...	$50 00	
Mrs. C C. Lansing	25 00	
William H. Weaver............................	100 00	
		$3,325 4
Income Miss Austin Fund for Cairo, Oak Hill and Greenville........		1,370 0
		$17,354 8
By balance		$109 2

DISBURSEMENTS.

STIPENDS.

Archdeaconry of Albany.

Rev. Samuel C. Thompson, Rensselaerville	$150 00	
Rev. C. H. Hatheway, West Troy	200 00	
Rev. Wm. Chas. Grubbe, Palenville	250 00	
Rev. E. S. DeG. Tompkins, Coxsackie....................	300 00	
Rev. W. C. Stewart, Tannersville........................	100 00	
Rev. C. M. Conant, Fairfield and Middleville	400 00	
Rev. Wm. M. Cook, Frankfort and Ilion............	300 00	
Rev. Wm. A. Stirling, Mohawk.	33 33	
Rev. Ernest Marlett, Dolgeville........	150 00	
Rev. D. A. Bonnar, Dolgeville	100 00	
Rev. H. M. Smyth, Gloversville.......	500 00	
Rev. C. C. Edmunds, Fonda	200 00	
Rev. C. E. Ball, Fort Plain and Canajoharie..............	87 50	
Rev. E. C. Hoskins, Canajoharie and Fort Plain..........	175 00	
Rev. G. G. Carter, D. D., Hudson and Claverack	300 00	
Rev. G. H. Fenwick, Chatham	225 00	
Rev. T. H. R. Luney, Chatham...........................	75 00	
Rev. Arthur Lowndes, Copake and Philmont.....	575 00	
Rev. Geo. B. Johnson, Lebanon Springs	300 00	
Rev. M. E. Wilson, Clermont........	75 00	
		$4,545 8

Archdeaconry of Troy.

Rev. Thomas White, special, East Albany..............	$100 00	
Rev. M. O. Smith, Raymertown and Schaghticoke........	340 26	
Rev. E. D. Tibbits, Boyntonville	200 00	
Rev. C. H. Hatheway, Castleton........................	200 00	
Rev. John M. Gilbert, Charlton	133 33	
Rev. E. C. Hoskins, Mechanicville	62 50	
Rev. F. N. Bouck, Mechanicville	50 00	
Rev. Thomas Boone, Jonesville, East Line and Round Lake	250 00	
Rev. W. F. Parsons, Schuylerville and Greenwich........	400 00	
Rev. F. H. T. Horsfield, Cambridge	100 00	
Rev. C. H. Lancaster, Granville	75 00	
Rev. J. Holwell Geare, Granville.....................	130 80	
Rev. H. C. Rush, Salem	100 00	
Rev. C. J. Whipple, Conklingville and Luzerne..........	300 00	
Rev. Alfred Taylor, Bartonville and Chestertown	300 00	

Rev. C. T. Blanchet, Bolton...........	$100 00	
Rev. W. Ball Wright, Mineville and Port Henry.........	350 00	
Rev. Calbraith B. Perry, D. D., Schroon Lake	216 66	
Rev. H. T. Gregory, Ticonderoga..	200 00	
Rev. J. Wm. Gill, Ausable Forks and Keeseville..	500 00	
Rev. J. F. Olmsted, Rouse's Point and Champlain.... ...	300 00	
Rev. S. M. Rogers, Ellenburgh...........................	100 00	
		$4,508 55

Archdeaconry of Susquehanna.

Rev. John E. Bold, Oneonta.	$325 00	
Rev. Howard McDougall, Stamford.......................	200 00	
Rev. F. S. Fisher, Deposit...	300 00	
Rev. Grenville Rathbun, Franklin	300 00	
Rev. C. A. Howells, Sidney	250 00	
Rev. Geo. H. Fenwick, Sidney	50 00	
Rev. W. C. W. Lewis, Otego	200 00	
Rev. Eugene Griggs, Schenevus.	208 33	
Rev. David F. McDonald, D. D., Gilbertsville............	275 00	
Rev. John Prout, East Springfield....	200 00	
Rev. Thomas Burrows, Hobart.........................	125 00	
		2,433 33

Archdeaconry of Ogdensburgh.

Rev. E. R. Earle, Norfolk and Norwood	$700 00	
Rev. F. S. Greenhalgh, Massena	135 42	
Rev. C. E. Mackenzie, Massena	121 87	
Rev. A. C. Macdonald, Waddington	400 00	
Rev. W. R. Woodbridge, Morristown	275 00	
Rev. James A. Dickson, Gouverneur	250 00	
Rev. R. Wyndham Brown, Morley	200 00	
Rev. A. L. Fortin, West Bangor and Brushton	340 00	
Rev. David Jenkins, Hogansburgh and Ft. Covington.....	325 00	
Rev. C. A. Howells, Santa Clara.......................	33 33	
		2,780 62

Diocesan Missionary.

Rev. Walter C. Stewart.		1,500 00

Sundry.

Post-office envelopes	$30 52	
Henry Stowell, printing	3 76	
		34 28
Rev. W. C. Stewart, expenses, Hunter		18 00
Rev. T. A. Snyder, one year's interest Miss Austin Fund for St. Paul's, Oak Hill...		60 00

Miss Austin Fund for Cairo, Greenville and Oak Hill.

Calvary Church, Cairo.....................	$456 68	
Christ Church, Greenville	456 65	
St. Paul's Church, Oak Hill..........	456 67	
		1,370 00
		$17,245 61
Balance		109 21
		$17,354 82

We, the undersigned, a Committee appointed to examine the accounts of the Treasurer, respectfully report we have made said examination, and find same to be correct, vouchers having been furnished for the disbursements made.

ALBANY, *November* 13, 1893.

R. M. TOWNSEND,
GEO. A. WELLS,
Committee.

DIOCESE OF ALBANY,
ALBANY, *November* 13, A. D., 1893.

Herewith find statement of receipts and disbursements for the year, showing as follows:

RECEIPTS.

Balance on hand, as reported to last Convention		$228 85
Offertories at Convention		89 51
Income from securities		2,155 93
Sundry sources		1,080 00
Income Miss Austin Fund, for Cairo, Greenville and Oak Hill		1,870 00
For salary of the Diocesan Missionary		792 66
Archdeaconry of Albany	$4,356 95	
Archdeaconry of Troy	4,475 22	
Archdeaconry of Susquehanna	798 89	
Archdeaconry of Ogdensburgh	2,006 81	
		11,637 87
		$17,354 82

DISBURSEMENTS.

Stipends

Archdeaconry of Albany	$4,545 83	
Archdeaconry of Troy	4,508 55	
Archdeaconry of the Susquehanna	2,433 33	
Archdeaconry of Ogdensburgh	2,780 62	
		$14,268 33
Salary of the General Missionary		1,500 00
Sundry purposes		47 28
Miss Austin Fund for Cairo, Greenville and Oak Hill		1,370 00
Rev. T. A. Snyder, 1 year's interest, Miss Austin Fund, St. Paul's, Oak Hill		60 00
Balance		109 21
		$17,354 82
Balance on hand		$109 21

The Permanent Fund represents the following amounts:

Misses Austin	$1,500 00
Elizabeth Sherers	750 00
Mrs. De Witt	5,000 00
Diocese of New York	2,000 00
Diocese of New York, Parochial Fund	1,000 00
Dr. William Tibbits	2,000 00
L. H. Sears	400 00

Mrs. Hannibal Green	$4,750 00
Miss Charlotte Austin	29,069 53
Total	$46,469 53

The Board holds in trust $19,000, received from the executors of Charlotte Austin, deceased, the income from which is to be paid one-third each to the Rectors, Wardens and Vestrymen of the following Parishes : Calvary Church, Cairo; Christ Church, Greenville; St. Paul's Church, Oak Hill.

The Board also holds in trust $2,000 of the bonds of the Rensselaer and Saratoga Railroad Company, the income from which is to be paid one-half each to St. Luke's Church, Mechanicville, and St. John's Church, Stillwater.

The Board has received from the Church of Our Saviour, Lebanon Springs, $500, which amount is to be invested and the income paid to said Church.

SELDEN E. MARVIN,

Treasurer.

MONEYS REPORTED BY THE DIOCESAN MISSIONARY.

Receipts from all sources	$204 22
Expenditures	192 54
Balance on hand	$11 68

The Rev. Walter Charles Stewart, Diocesan Missionary, presented the

REPORT OF THE DIOCESAN MISSIONARY.

The work of the Diocesan Missionary during the last year has been of such a routine character that a summary of statistics would almost answer all the requirements of a report. It may be as well, however, to mention a few places and record the progress made. I begin by alluding to some places referred to in my last report. It may be remembered that I spoke of having laid the cornerstone of St. Luke's Church, Chatham (24th August). By the beginning of the year (1893) the building was completed. In October the first confirmation was held; and the Mission may now be regarded as on a fair way to prosperous life. Thus ceases the connection between the Diocesan Missionary and a Mission whose reorganized and more efficient condition found its beginnings in his office.

The hope I ventured to express regarding Tannersville has been realized and services were held regularly all the year round. The Rector at Palenville very kindly fell in with my suggestions and gave services during the winter and spring, while the summer services were supplied by the Rev. J. Dows Hills, of Philadelphia. The Rev. W. C. Grubbe reports 15 services, 15 celebrations of the Holy Eucharist, and 1 marriage. The Rev. J. D. Hills reports 20 services, 14 celebrations, catechizing publicly 11 times The Rev. A. L. Wood, of Stapleton, L. I., reports 7 services, 4 celebrations, and catechizing once. The Sunday School consists of 15 scholars and 1 teacher. During the summer, through the liberality of some friends, the grounds of the church have been much improved. Three services were held in Onteora Park. On the Feast of the Transfiguration the Bishop of New York officiated in the morning, assisted by Dionysius Lattas, Archbishop of Zante, and his Deacon. In the afternoon the Archbishop sang the Greek evensong, and Bishop Potter baptized his grandson, Henry Potter Russell. Five services were also held at Hunter by Mr. Hills. For the future, reports from Tannersville will occupy places among the regular reports from Parishes and Missions.

7

Following up the plan instituted last year, I arranged for services to be held at
Westport. The Rev. Richmond Shreve, D. D., officiated there during the month of
August, holding service and preaching each Sunday evening. I quote from his
report : " All the offertories were placed in the hands of a Treasurer, Mrs. H. R.
Baremore, of Elizabeth, N. J., as a nucleus for the building of a church in the
village. Mrs. Baremore also gave a piece of land on which the church building can
be erected. When the formal transfer is made, this property will be deeded to the
Trustees of the Diocese. The size of the village of Westport, and the number of
visitors belonging to the Church, who are to be found there every year, point to it
as a promising centre of Church work during the summer months." Incidentally,
and in connection with this, I may mention the services at Elizabethtown. These
were supplied during July by the Rev. S. de L. Townsend of New York, who had
early celebration, matins and evensong, with sermons, each Sunday. During
August Dr. Shreve was in charge, and there was a celebration of the Holy Communion at 8 o'clock, and morning prayer, litany and sermon at 11 o'clock each Sunday.
There were received a pair of candelabra for altar lights; an altar, book of offices
and a Prayer-book for the desk, both of the new standard, and a glass cruet for
water. The grounds and property of the Mission were put in good order.

Last year I spoke of Ashland and parts adjacent as being left without any of the
services of the Church, except such intermittent ones as I could give. It is with
great pleasure that I am now able to report a better and more promising state of
affairs. The Rev. Watson B. Hall, late of Racine, Wis., who is well known in the
neighborhood by reason of his summer residence near Ashland, has undertaken the
work here with every prospect of gratifying success.

On the 25th of August last, acting for the Bishop, I laid the corner-stone of St.
Paul's Church, Sidney, and on the 10th of January was privileged to take part in
the opening services of the new Church. This is the realization of many hopes and
prayers, the consummation of that which was needed to add strength to the life of
the Church in this community. It may be as well to state that, until very recently,
this point was worked in connection with one in the Central New York Diocese.
With the prospect of a building, the good people promptly raised the amount
pledged to the Missionary so that he might be free from the double tie and at
liberty to concentrate his energies on the one place.

On the way to Schroon Lake one passes through Pottersville. Here, perched on a
hill, could be seen an old and almost ruined Church. For years and years no services had been held here, and the old deserted Church was left to its fate. While
I was up at Schroon Lake I commenced proceedings with a view to restoring the
Church and its services The Rev C. B. Perry, who was shortly afterward ap
pointed Missionary at Schroon Lake, took up the work, with the result that on the
9th of August the Church was formally reopened, and on the Sunday following I
held services and celebrated. Up to this time I had gone there occasionally to
officiate, Mr. Perry also going from time to time. While there is room for improve
ment in the condition of the property, it has at least been saved from absolute ruin

The Mission of SS Simon and Jude at Worcester, which, owing to various circumstances, has been in abeyance for two years, has been reorganized and put in
charge of the Missionary at Schenevus. There seems now to be every prospect for
encouraging work. A piece of land for the erection of a Church has been offered.
The Mission at St. Johnsville, which also for a long time has been in abeyance, has
been again started under what appear to be very advantageous circumstances. At
Dolgeville the new Church has been opened It was my privilege to take part in the
opening services, and also to conduct a ten days' " mission of instruction." Since
then a resident Missionary has been appointed. Some four miles from Sharon

Springs is a hamlet called Argusville. A silk mill located here gave employment to quite a goodly number of people, the majority being English. I had been there two or three times, and had completed arrangements whereby services were to be carried on, partly by myself and partly by the Rector at Sharon Springs, when the mill was burned to the ground. If the proprietor decides to build again here, the services will be carried on according to existing arrangements.

The Adirondack and St. Lawrence railroad, running from Herkimer to Malone, is opening up country which ought to be looked after. Tupper Lake two years ago contained six families, but now has a population of about 2,000. I held services here last summer, having found some church people among the inhabitants. Its distance from any point with which it can be conveniently worked makes it difficult to do any thing regular, while its importance as a center in a comparatively new field renders it desirable that something more or less regular should be done.

The Mission at Santa Clara had been vacant for a long time, and I went there frequently during the year. The reported failure of a man who has hitherto contributed largely to the support of the Mission may make a change here, though it is to be hoped arrangements can be made for the continuance of the work. A few miles back of Santa Clara, on what is known as the Blue Mountain Road, a number of people have cleared land, built houses, and commenced to farm. They are pioneers of what seems to me the opening up of a new region. From year's end to year's end they had no religious services of any kind till I started work in a little log-hut school-house. Between this region and Santa Clara, I baptized forty-nine persons— a large proportion of them being adults. A class of fourteen was ready for presentation to the Bishop for confirmation. Work was started on the building of a Church, and the foundations were laid and every thing ready for the laying of the corner-stone by the Bishop. Unfortunately circumstances arose which compelled the postponement of the visitation till next spring. There are several places in this region where a few church families are to be found, and it would be a great pity if all work here had to be abandoned except for occasional and infrequent visits.

Fort Ann presents possibilities as a center for work radiating out to several neighboring hamlets. Services have been held in three places and visits made in two others. Four children have been baptized, and three persons are prepared for confirmation. It may be possible later to arrange for somewhat regular services looking to the organization of a Mission.

For nearly two years West Burlington has had only such occasional services as I could give. Its distance from any other missionary point makes it impossible to work it in connection with another Mission. I am glad to be able to report that there is now a lay-reader (a candidate for Holy Orders), at work there under my directions. The benefit of having regular services is shown in the revived interest and growing congregations. The Sunday School has been reorganized and everything is going well. I have baptized here three adults and four children, and there are four candidates awaiting confirmation. The mother of one of the children baptized can neither read nor write, had never been inside a Church till then, did not know who God was. A bell, memorial to "Priest Hughes," has lately been put in the belfry, and was blessed by me.

Other places have been visited, but it is unnecessary to burden this report with minor details. The financial statement has been handed to the Treasurer. The statistics are as follows: Services, 152 — exclusive of occasional services in the Cathedral; sermons, 127; addresses, 12; celebrations of the Holy Communion, 51; baptisms (adults, 23, children 40), 63; prepared for confirmation, 31; marriage, 1; funerals, 2; corner-stone laid, 1.

On motion of Mr. J. D. Henderson, Lay Deputy from Christ Church, Herkimer, it was

Resolved, That the amount to be raised for Diocesan Missions be at least $11,50(for this year.

Certain changes having been announced, the apportionment of last year as so modified was adopted, as follows:

DIOCESE OF ALBANY.

PLAN OF APPORTIONMENT TO RAISE MISSIONARY FUND.

Archdeaconry of Albany.

The Cathedral of All Saints	$1,380 00
St. Peter's, Albany	1,000 00
St. Paul's, Albany	300 00
Grace, Albany	60 00
Holy Innocents', Albany	60 00
Trinity, Albany	25 00
Trinity, Rensselaerville	15 00
Trinity, West Troy	45 00
St. Andrew's, West Troy	10 00
St. Mark's, Green Island	30 00
St. John's, Cohoes	260 00
Trinity, Athens	25 00
Calvary, Cairo	10 00
Gloria Dei, Palenville	10 00
St Luke's, Catskill	150 00
Christ, Greenville	5 00
St. Paul's, Oak Hill	5 00
Christ, Duanesburgh	60 00
St. George's, Schenectady	200 00
Christ, Schenectady	25 00
St. Ann's, Amsterdam	60 00
Good Shepherd, Canajoharie	15 00
St. Columba's, St. Johnsville	2 50
Zion, Fonda	10 00
St. John's, Johnstown	75 00
Trinity, Fairfield	5 00
Christ, Herkimer	75 00
Emmanuel, Little Falls	50 00
St. Augustine's, Ilion	35 00
St. John's, Dolgeville	12 50
Good Shepherd, Cullen	5 00
Trinity, Claverack	20 00
St. Luke's, Clermont	10 00
Our Saviour, Lebanon Springs	20 00
St. John's, Stockport	25 00
St Barnabas', Stottville	40 00
St James', Rossman's Mills	5 00
St Mark's, Philmont	20 00
St Luke's Chatham	5 00
St. John's, Copake	7 50

St. Paul's, Kinderhook.	$75 00	
Christ, Hudson	115 00	
All Saints', Hudson	15 00	
Christ, Gloversville	25 00	
Grace, Mohawk	15 00	
St. Alban's, Frankfort.	5 00	
Holy Cross, Fort Plain	5 00	
Of the Memorial, Middleville	25 00	
Christ, Coxsackie	5 00	
Trinity, Ashland	5 00	
——, Tannersville	5 00	
St. Margaret's, Menands Station	5 00	
		$4,472 50

Archdeaconry of Troy.

St. Paul's, Troy	$750 00
St. Paul's, Troy, special for this year	150 00
St. John's, Troy	700 00
Christ, Troy	250 00
Holy Cross, Troy	200 00
Ascension, Troy	50 00
St. Luke's, Troy	20 00
St. Barnabas' Troy	50 00
Epiphany East Albany	5 00
Messiah, Greenbush	25 00
Trinity, Lansingburgh	175 00
Trinity, Schaghticoke	15 00
St. Mark's, Hoosick Falls	150 00
All Saints', Hoosac	30 00
Holy Name, Boyntonville	5 00
St. Giles' Castleton	11 00
Grace, Waterford	35 00
Christ, Ballston	100 00
St. John's, East Line	5 00
Grace, Jonesville	10 00
All Saints', Round Lake	10 00
Calvary, Burnt Hills	12 00
St. Paul's, Charlton	10 00
Bethesda, Saratoga	210 00
St. Stephen's, Schuylerville	7 50
St. John's, Conklingville	5 00
St. Paul's, Salem	60 00
St. John's, Stillwater	15 00
St. Luke's, Cambridge	175 00
Trinity, Granville	25 00
North Granville	10 00
St. Paul's, Greenwich	25 00
St. James', Fort Edward	25 00
Zion, Sandy Hill	20 00
Trinity, Whitehall	60 00
St. James', Caldwell	25 00
St. Mary's, Luzerne	20 00
Holy Cross, Warrensburgh	60 00

Messiah, Glens Falls	$150 00	
Good Shepherd, Chestertown..............................	15 00	
St. Paul's, Bartonville......	8 00	
St. Sacrament, Bolton................................	10 00	
Church of the Cross, Ticonderoga	30 00	
Christ, Port Henry	31 25	
Emmanuel, Mineville..	5 00	
St. James', Ausable Forks................................ ...	15 00	
St. John's, Essex......	30 00	
St. Paul's, Keeseville................................	15 00	
St. Andrew's, Schroon Lake......	10 00	
Trinity, Plattsburgh...........................	100 00	
Christ, Rouse's Point	15 00	
St. John's, Champlain...............	20 00	
St. Peter's, Ellenburgh.................................	10 00	
Good Shepherd, Elizabethtown..................	10 00	
St. Luke's, Mechanicville	30 00.	$4,014 75

Archdeaconry of the Susquehanna.

St. Peter's, Hobart..........................	$40 00	
Christ, Walton................................	40 00	
St. John's, Delhi	100 00	
Grace, Stamford...	20 00	
St. Paul's, Franklin	20 00	
St. Paul's, Sidney........	5 00	
————, Bloomville.............	5 00	
Christ, Gilbertsville`.......	25 00	
Christ, Cooperstown....	150 00	
Grace, Cherry Valley.....................................	75 00	
Zion, Morris	25 00	
St. James' Oneonta	75 00	
St. Matthew's, Unadilla.............................	50 00	
Christ, West Burlington...................................	5 00	
St. Paul's, East Springfield	50 00	
St. John's, Richfield Springs...	75 00	
Immanuel, Otego..............................	5 00	
Of the Holy Spirit, Schenevus.....	10 00	
St. Simon and St. Jude's, Worcester	5 00	
St. Luke's, Monticello....................................	5 00	
St. John's, Portlandville	5 00	790 00

Archdeaconry of Ogdensburgh.

St. John's, Ogdensburgh	$600 00
Trinity, Potsdam........	450 00
Trinity, Gouverneur.......................	50 00
St. John's, Massena.	50 00
Christ, Morristown	40 00
Grace, Norfolk..	5 00
St. Paul's, Waddington.......	30 00
Grace, Canton	50 00
Trinity Morley	25 00
St. Luke's, Lisbon	5 00
St. Andrew's, Norwood	10 00

St. Mark's, Malone.......	$100 00	
St. Peter's, Brushton.....................	10 00	
St. Thomas', Lawrenceville...........................	5 00	
Zion, Colton.........	20 00	
St. Luke's, Saranac Lake...........	40 00	
St. James', Hogansburgh..........................	25 00	
St. Mark's, West Bangor.........	5 00	
		$1,520 00
Total.........		$10,797 25

RECAPITULATION.

Archdeaconry of Albany	$4,472 50
Archdeaconry of Troy	4,014 75
Archdeaconry of the Susquehanna...........	790 00
Archdeaconry of Ogdensburgh......................	1,520 00
	$10,797 25

The following resolution was offered by the Rev. Frederick S. Sill:

Resolved, That a Committee of five, three clergymen and two laymen, be appointed to interest the children of the Diocese in the work of Diocesan Missions; to secure from them offerings for this work between the present time and the next Convention; which offerings shall be retained by the Treasurer of the Board of Missions as a fund for aggressive work in the following year, except that the expenses of the Committee may be paid out of it.

The Rev. J. Philip B. Pendleton moved to amend the resolution to read as follows:

Resolved, That a Committee of five, three clergymen and two laymen, shall be appointed to interest the children of the Diocese in the work of Diocesan Missions; to secure from them offerings for this work between the present time and the next Convention, which offerings shall be used for the payment of the salary of the Diocesan Missionary for the current year.

The amendment was adopted, and the resolution as amended was adopted.

The Right Rev. President appointed as such Committee, the Rev. J. Philip B. Pendleton, the Rev. Calbraith B. Perry, the Rev. Fenwick M. Cookson, Mr. Sidney G. Ashmore, and Mr. Francis N. Mann.

On motion of the Rev. George G. Carter, S. T. D., it was

Resolved, That the thanks of this Convention are due and are now gratefully tendered to the Clergy and Members of the Cathedral Chapter, to the authorities of St. Agnes' School, and to the Clergy and Church people of the city of Albany, for the great courtesy and kindness with which they have made the members of the Convention welcome and at home at this gathering of special joy in the Cathedral city.

The following resolution offered by the Rev. Charles S. Olmsted was unanimously adopted by a rising vote:

Resolved, That this Convention, mindful of the honour which it has enjoyed by the presence in our Cathedral city of the Presiding Bishop of the American Church, desires to record its sense of gratitude for his coming to preach at the Twenty-fifth Anniversary of our own Bishop's Consecration.

On motion of the Rev. Fenwick M. Cookson it was

Resolved, The Convention instructs the Board of Missions to continue the services of the Diocesan Missionary for the ensuing year, at the salary of last year.

Resolved, That a special effort be made to secure pledges through the Archdeaconries from the Sunday-schools and the Parochial branches of the Woman's Auxiliary for the support of the Diocesan Missionary.

On motion of the Secretary of the Convention, it was

Resolved, That when the Convention adjourn this afternoon, it be to reassemble in the Cathedral at eight o'clock this evening for hearing the Bishop's Address, and that at the conclusion of the Address the Convention adjourn *sine die* without further formality.

The following preamble and resolutions were recalled from the Trustees of the Diocese, and on motion of the Rev. W. C. Stewart they were adopted :

WHEREAS, The Church of St. Luke at Middleburgh has ceased to maintain religious services for more than two consecutive years prior to November 1, 1893, according to the customs and usages of the Protestant Episcopal Church in the Diocese of Albany; and for other sufficient causes ;

Resolved, That the Church and Society of the Church of St. Luke, in the town of Middleburgh, in the county of Schoharie, be and the same is hereby declared to be extinct.

Resolved, That the Trustees of the Diocese of Albany be directed to take possession of the temporalities belonging to the said extinct Church, and manage the same in such manner as is warranted by law.

The minutes of the Convention were read and adopted.

The Convention took a recess until 8 o'clock in the evening.

EIGHT O'CLOCK IN THE EVENING.

The Convention reassembled in the Cathedral. After the singing of a hymn, the Right Rev. The Bishop of the Diocese delivered his Annual Address.

THE BISHOP'S ADDRESS.

My well beloved, You will remember that I announced my purpose last year, of following, in this Diocese, the example set by the two Houses of General Convention in making our memorial of the dead, by mentioning, for the last time, their beloved names, and offering the commemorative prayer when the list is ended. Let us remember first the Bishops who have died this year, and next the clergy once associated with us in our work : *

The Rt. Rev. Wm. Henry Augustus Bissell, D. D., second Bishop of Vermont.

The Rt. Rev. Phillips Brooks, D. D., sixth Bishop of Massachusetts.

The Rt. Rev. Alexander Gregg, D. D., first Bishop of Texas.

The Rt. Rev. Wm. Ingraham Kip, D. D., LL. D., first Bishop of California.

The Rt. Rev. Theodore Benedict Lyman, D. D., LL. D., D. C. L., fourth Bishop of North Carolina.

---

* This record was closed before the November meeting of the Convention.

The Rev. D. Hillhouse Buel, D. D.

The Rev. Russell A. Olin.

The Rev. J. William Paige.

The Rev. John Francis Potter.

The Rev. Floridus A. Steele.

And then those of our own immediate household :

The Rev. Charles H. Lancaster, Rector of Trinity Church, Granville.

The Rev. W. S. Rowe, sometime missionary at Clermont.

The Rev. Chauncey Vibbard, Jr., Rector of Calvary Church, Cairo.

Mr. Derick Lane, Vestryman of St. Paul's Church, Troy.

Mr. Benjamin H. Hall, Vestryman of St. John's Church, Troy.

Mr. Edward G. Gilbert, Vestryman of St. John's Church, Troy.

Mr. David H. Gay, Warden of Christ Church, Walton.

Mr. Wm. Henry Weeks, Vestryman of Emmanuel Church, Little Falls.

Mr. Jairus Mather, Warden of Trinity Church, Fairfield.

Hon. Robert B. Monell, long Warden of Christ Church, Hudson.

Mr. Simeon E. Crittenden, Vestryman of Christ Church, Cooperstown.

Mr. Bloomfield Usher, Vestryman of Trinity Church, Potsdam.

Dr. R. C. McEwan, Vestrymen of Bethesda Church, Saratoga.

Dr. W. S. Gregory, Warden of Christ Church, Deposit.

Mr. Egbert N. Palmer, Warden of Christ Church, Greenville.

Mr. Jonathan S. Warren, Warden of Trinity Church, Granville.

Mr. Erastus Corning, Jr., Trustee of St. Agnes' School.

Mr. John Gregory, Sexton of Holy Innocents, Albany.

Mr. George Griswold, of the Church of the Memorial, Middleville.

Mr. David Lowrey Seymour Patterson, of St. Paul's Church, Troy.

Mrs. Edgar T. Chapman, wife of the Treasurer of All Saints' Cathedral.

Mrs. George Dent Silliman, wife of the Rector of Grace Church, Albany.

Mrs. Isaac McConihe, widow of Judge McConihe of St. Paul's Church, Troy.

Mrs. Elizabeth Nicholls Wood of Hoosick Falls.

Lydia Luscombe, child and servant of the Orphan House of the Holy Saviour, in Cooperstown.

Charlotte Trudeau, daughter of the Warden of the Church of St. Luke the Beloved Physician, Saranac Lake.

Mrs. W. A. Dart, of Trinity Church, Potsdam.

Let us pray :

Almighty and everlasting God, we yield unto thee most high praise and hearty thanks for the wonderful grace and virtue declared in all thy saints, who have been the choice vessels of thy grace and the lights of the world in their several generations; most humbly beseeching thee to give us grace so to follow the example of their stedfastness in thy faith, and obedience to thy holy commandments, that at the day of the general Resurrection, we, with all those who are of the mystical body of thy Son, may be set on his right hand; and hear that his most joyful voice: Come, ye blessed of my Father, inherit the kingdom prepared for you from the foundation of the world. Grant this, O Father, for Jesus Christ's sake, our only Mediator and Advocate. Amen.

The last Convention of the Diocese met on Tuesday, the 15th of November, in All Saints' Cathedral church, with ninety-eight clergy present, and laymen representing sixty parishes. I delivered my Charge, dealing specially with the two points of the work of the General Convention which had recently closed; and with the story of the final payment of all indebtedness upon the Cathedral building. I celebrated the Holy Communion, assisted in the service by the four Archdeacons. We had our usual missionary meeting at night, at which reports of the Missionary Society were read and an address made by the Rev. Canon Tibbits. The next morning I ordained Deacons Mr. John Mills Gilbert and Mr. Charles Albert Howells, presented by the Rev. Canon Fulcher and the Rev. Mr. Conant, and celebrated the Holy Communion. After a busy morning of work the Convention adjourned at half-past one.

On Thursday, the 17th of November, in the First Presbyterian Church in Albany, I made an address, before a large gathering of people, on the subject of the Sunday closing of the World's Fair.

On Saturday, November 19th, I instituted as Rector of the Church of Our Saviour in Lebanon Springs, the Rev. George Barent Johnson, Canon Stewart and the Rev. Messrs White and Fenwick being present. I confirmed one person; and the newly instituted Rector celebrated the Holy Communion.

On Saturday, November 26th, at the Church of the Holy Communion in New York I gave three instructions to Sunday-school teachers, and on Sunday, the 27th, I preached morning and evening in All Souls' Church, New York.

On Tuesday, November 29th, I celebrated the Holy Communion in the Church of the Heavenly Rest, New York, and gave three meditations to women in the Church during the day.

On Monday evening, December 5th, at Trinity Church, Whitehall, I preached and confirmed fourteen persons.

On Tuesday, December 6th, in the evening, in the Church of St. Luke the Beloved Physician, Saranac Lake, I preached and confirmed twenty-nine persons. The journey home, one hundred miles of which was really through the forest primeval, in a parlour car, was a strong and striking contrast to the old ways of travelling through the wilderness. It was very extraordinary, to be rushing through the wooded waste of snow, with fresh deer-tracks visible alongside of the road.

On Sunday, December 11th, in the evening, in the Church of the Messiah, Greenbush, I preached and confirmed nine persons.

On Tuesday, December 13th, in New York, I presided at a meeting of the Board of Managers and was present at a meeting of the Trustees of the Prayer-Book Distribution Society.

On Thursday, December 15th, I confirmed two persons in the Cathedral, one from St. Barnabas', Troy, and one from Mechanicville.

On Tuesday, the 27th of December, I made the Address at the laying of the Corner Stone of the Cathedral of St. John the Divine in New York; in the most entire sympathy with the Bishop, and with the great work, so auspiciously begun. It was a very perfect service, in appointment and management.

On the 28th of December I was present at a meeting of the Federate Council, which was absolutely abortive in results.

On the 31st, in the Cathedral, I confirmed one person for Trinity Church, Albany.

On Thursday, the 5th of January, in Emmanuel Church, Otego, I preached, confirmed four persons and celebrated the Holy Communion, and on Friday, January 6th, in the evening, in the Church of the Holy Innocents, Albany, I preached and confirmed eight persons.

On Tuesday, January 10th, I presided in New York at the meeting of the Board of Managers, and was present at a meeting of the Trustees of the Prayer-book Distribution Society, and of the Commission of the General Convention on Archives.

On Monday, the 16th of January, I was present at a meeting of the Archdeaconry of Albany, in St. John's Church, Cohoes.

On Tuesday, the 17th, in the Church of the Holy Cross, Troy, I took part in the burial service of the Rev. D. Hillhouse Buel, D. D., one of the old and most venerated Priests of this Diocese.

On the 24th of January I was present at a meeting of the Archdeaconry of Troy, in St. John's Church, where I celebrated the Holy Communion and made an address. On the 25th of January, in St. Peter's Church, Albany, I celebrated the Holy Communion and baptized a little child.

On Thursday, the 26th of January, I left Albany for New York, to take my passage for Europe, whither I went in discharge of my duty as Bishop in charge of the Foreign Churches.

There were many things that saddened and shadowed our parting, beside the sense of leaving the people and the work that are so dear to me. The deaths of Bishop Brooks, and of my dear friend, Mrs. Wood, whose burials I was not even able to attend, were very great personal sorrows and losses. After a very beautiful ██████████████████ its interest by a glimpse of Gibraltar, of the Balearic Islands, and of the whole coast of the Riviera, we landed at Genoa on the 8th of February, in the early evening. I had service and preached on Sunday, the 5th of February, on board the *Kaiser Wilhelm I,* having spent at sea the twenty-fourth anniversary of my consecration, with many longing desires to be among my own people.

I insert the journal record of my European visitations, because it is a part of the story of my year's work which you have the right to know, and also because I think there is need to emphasize the fact that this American Church work in Europe is and ought to be of interest to all Americans, and that they ought to know where the Church is established and what it is doing. And I am glad to bear my witness to the fact that I find among the resident Church people in these American colonies abroad, the same earnest devotion, the same true spirituality of living, and the same active energy and interest in the services and the parochial work, that characterize our best people in our best Parishes at home.

But I regret to say, that there seems to be a tendency on the part of some American men and women, travelling on the Continent, to pick up all the poorest fashions of continental people, and lend themselves to what is really, from our standpoint, a desecration of the Lord's Day. I have had a good deal to say this year about the matter of the observance of Sunday, in connection with which certain phrases have passed into common speech, which I consider very misleading and dangerous. What is commonly known as the "continental Sunday" is a day that carries with it two facts, which are inseparable from it. In the first place, the Roman Catholic in his own country, if he has any religion at all, is sure to attend, even if he does not receive, at the early Mass; and in the next place, while there is a recognition of the rightfulness of all sorts of sports, horse races and theatres and concerts, there is also the recognition of the fact, that the day is a day of labour and not of rest. Until we are willing to accept the fact that men are to *work* seven days in the week, we have no right to deal with Sunday as a day on which people have a right to give themselves to merely secular amusements. The condition of things in Chicago this year must, I hope, have abundantly satisfied people who urged the opening of the Fair, on the ground of its interest and importance for the working classes of people, that the working classes of people in America do not desire the secularizing of the Lord's Day. They have had sense enough, it seems to me, to see that it involved the possibility of taking away from them their day of rest, under the pretense of giving them a day of amusement. The whole series of public changes of plan and purpose, which left the question to be decided, not by any principle whatever, either of reverence for God or of regard for the working people, but merely by the lowest and basest sentiment of pecuniary advantage, should have taught a lesson which we shall not, in our generation at least, I think, forget. Feeling as strongly as I do and have always done about it, I take no comfort myself in the way in which the question has been muddled. But I should think that the mere Sabbatarian, who looked at it from a narrow and partisan point of view, would greatly rejoice in the way in which the managers have been "overthrown in stony places." If from the beginning, there had been any kindly and settled purpose to open the fair grounds freely on Sunday, the exhibits being closed, and give the people the rest and pleasure of the beautiful park, the solution of the question would have been both more dignified and more assured.

I began my visitation of the Foreign Churches, in Florence, on Sunday, the 12th day of February, where I preached and celebrated the Holy Communion in the morning; and on Ash Wednesday, the 15th of February, at the service of Evensong, I preached and confirmed four persons. The vestry had secured the temporary services of the Rev. Mr. Venables, a clergyman in English Orders, long resident in Florence, who had constantly assisted in the services there before. And I am very glad to say that he has so entirely commended himself, both to the members of the parish and to me, that he has been nominated to me, and appointed by me, Rector of the Parish, having been transferred to my jurisdiction. Both what I saw and what I have heard since, lead me to feel that nothing better could have been done, for the interests of the Church.

On Sunday, the 19th of February, in St. Paul's Church, Rome, I preached and celebrated the Holy Communion in the morning and took part in the Evensong service in the afternoon; and on the following Sunday, February 26th, I made my formal visitation to the Church, preaching, confirming four persons, and celebrating the Holy Communion. I confirmed afterward one person in private for the Parish; and celebrated the Holy Communion in the Church on St. Matthias' Day. The Parish has gained in many ways, since my last visitation, conspicuously in the completion of the Parish House and Rectory, which are very great and valuable additions, not only to the comfort of the clergymen, but to the working power of the Parish. I noted with thankfulness the daily Morning Prayer and the weekly celebration on Thursday in the Church, which enabled me to make my Communion on my 61st birthday; and was rejoiced greatly, here as everywhere else in the course of my visitations, to find not only a cordial welcome by old friends, but an increasing interest and appreciation of the Church's Services and work, and a prosperous condition of the congregations generally.

On Sunday, the 5th of March, in the Church of the Holy Spirit, Nice, I preached and celebrated the Holy Communion, and confirmed ten persons, and in the evening I preached again. On Wednesday, the 8th of March, I preached at one of the Lenten services in the Church, and later on confirmed two persons in the Rectory, who had been prevented from being present at the public service. Here, too, I found the Church in a very admirable condition, with a large and interested congregation, and a most beautiful piece of property.

On Sunday, the 12th of March, in Emmanuel Church, Geneva, I preached, confirmed six persons and celebrated the Holy Communion. The Parish is in most healthy condition, with a congregation that fills the Church, and I find the effort, making successfully here, as well as at Nice, which seems to me most wise, to provide a definite, not large, endowment for the maintenance of the services; because this must depend, otherwise, upon the more or less uncertain fact of the number of resident Americans connected with and interested in the Church. I went on Saturday with Mr. Adamson, the Rector, to the burial of the Vicar of the old Catholic Church; and had the pleasure of a good deal of interesting talk with several of the clergy and lay people, about the progress of their work in Switzerland, which they think is, on the whole, encouraging.

On the 15th of March, I went to Lucerne, not for a service, because our chaplain is there only for the summer months, but to see the very beautiful Church which we helped the old Catholics to build, and which we occupy in combination with them. The Church is really a most satisfactory and admirable building, and from a short conversation I had with our consul, Mr. Williams, who is the treasurer of our mission, and with one of the laymen of the old Catholic congregation, I should think the arrangement was working extremely well. The Rev. Mr. Miller, who was in charge of our part of the work during the Summer, reports good congregations and much interest in the services.

On Sunday, the 19th of March, in St. John's Church, Dresden, I celebrated the Holy Communion at the early service, preached at the 11 o'clock service, and at Evensong I preached and confirmed eight persons. On the afternoon of the 21st, I had a service of benediction for the new Rectory of the Parish, which had made me welcome within its delightful and hospitable walls; and which nowhere, more than here, is a valuable addition, not only to the comfort, but to the usefulness of the Rector and to the whole working power of the Parish. We had a very large reception after the service; and I have never seen a religious house used with more entire and unreserved thought of the best interests of the Church than this Rectory. Everybody in the parish feels it to be a home and a hive, and all the members of the household are as busy as bees, doing something with a will that promotes the good of the people and the growth of the Church. The next evening we had a meeting of the St. Andrew's brotherhood in the Rectory, of which they did me the honour to elect me a member, and which has done very good service in Dresden during the winter. Nothing is more helpful, in these foreign cities where young Americans are gathered together, than to be able to put into the mass the leaven of a little earnest Christian living and good example and work.

On Saturday, March 25th, the Feast of the Annunciation, I celebrated the Holy Communion in the Church of the Holy Trinity in Paris; and again on Sunday I celebrated at the early service there, preached at the morning service, and also at Evensong, when I confirmed twenty-nine persons, four of whom came from St. Luke's Chapel, and were presented by the Rev. Mr. Newell. The Holy Week services in the Church, daily, were a great help and comfort, and I was more than thankful that I had decided to spend that week in Paris. I celebrated the Holy Communion at St. Luke's Chapel on Maundy Thursday morning, and spent the greater part of three days with Dr. Morgan and Dr. Tuttle Smith in the examination of Mr. Newell for his ordination to the Priesthood. On Good Friday I celebrated the Holy Communion in the Church of the Holy Trinity early; and preached the three hours' Service in the Church; a very large and devout congregation of people taking their part in the worship and meditations. On Sunday, April 2d, an incomparable Easter day, I preached and celebrated the Holy Communion in the morning, and preached again at Evensong. On Easter Monday, I baptized a little child, and celebrated the Holy Communion in the Church; and on Easter Tuesday, the 4th of April, I celebrated the Holy Communion and ordered Priest the Rev. William Whiting Newell. I preached the sermon. The candidate was presented by Dr. Morgan, and the Rev. Dr. Tuttle Smith and Mr. Massé joined in the laying on of hands. The Parish is strong, alive, earnest and abounding in good works, and the service is reverent and beautiful.

Mr. Newell's ordination enables him to make more complete his most interesting and important work among the American students who live across the Seine. I was truly thankful to find a very tasteful and attractive Chapel built and occupied, where the regular services are now held, and which makes the religious centre for, and gives its consecration to, the devoted service which Mr. and Mrs. Newell render to a class of young people, greatly needing just such sympathy and interest as they find from these wise and earnest friends.

On Sunday evening, the 9th of April, I preached in St. Paul's Cathedral in London, deeply stirred by the vast and very reverent congregation.

On the afternoon of Friday we started on what proved to be a most fascinating journey to Athens and Constantinople. I had been commissioned by the Board of Missions in Baltimore, to visit the American Mission School in Athens, so that I had a duty to do there: and never duty in the world was divided and made delightful by so much pleasure. I have already made my report to the Board of Missions, as to the condition both of our Mission School itself, under the care of Miss Muir, where about three hundred children, chiefly of the ~~poorer classes~~ are most admirably taught; and about the Hill Memorial School, which is intended more for children of a higher class, and in which excellent work is done for them by Miss Masson, who is a niece of Mrs. Hill. Not the least admirable element in all these schools is the carrying out and on of Dr. Hill's wise method, which was impressed upon him by the Church in this country when he undertook the mission, of simply striving to deepen and increase the religious life of the children, *in* the Church to which by birth and Baptism they belong. The Archbishop himself is very warmly interested in them, and the religious teaching in both of them is in strict accordance with the doctrinal standards of the Orthodox Church of Greece. I found on every hand, both from the clergy and the lay people with whom I talked, the warmest expression of gratitude for the service which had been rendered to the cause both of religion and of education, by the schools during their existence in Athens. It is of course understood that our only official connection is with the Mission School under Miss Muir.

On Thursday, the 27th of April, in the Chapel of the English Embassy in Constantinople, I had the pleasure of giving Confirmation to an American gentleman living in Constantinople, and was greatly refreshed by the little touch of Christianity in the midst of so much that is antagonistic. On Tuesday, the 2d of May, I confirmed two persons in the Church of the Holy Trinity in Paris. On Sunday, May 14th, I preached in the morning in the Royal Chapel of Savoy ; and in the evening at St. Margaret's, Westminster. On the 15th, in the Church House in London, I made a speech before the Anglo-continental society. On the 16th I was present at the most solemn and impressive service of supplication, in St. Paul's Cathedral in London, in connection with the protest against the Welsh suspensory bill. And I had the pleasure, in the afternoon, of listening to some very noble speeches on that subject, by some of the strong churchmen of England. On Sunday morning, May 21st, I preached in Westminster Abbey, and on the 4th of June, on Sunday, I said the morning prayer on the good ship *Majestic*, the Captain reading the Lessons, and Bishop Barry preaching the sermon.

Landing in New York, about three in the afternoon of the 7th of June, I reached Albany in time to go into the great Schoolroom of St. Agnes, where the closing musical was going on, and where I had a most loving reception from the gathered girls and friends. On the 8th of June I made the Address and gave the Diplomas to the graduating class of St. Agnes ; and was present at the School reception in the afternoon. In the evening, in the Cathedral Church, I preached and confirmed eighty persons, of whom six were presented from West Troy by the Rev. Canon Hatheway.

On Friday evening, June 9th, in Bethesda Church, Saratoga, I preached and confirmed fifty-four persons; and on the morning of the 10th of June, in the St. Christina Home, I made an address to the children and gave the certificates to those who had earned them, Mrs. Trask as usual giving them their medals. The good work here goes gradually and graciously on. I believe it is the foundation of something of very true value and importance; and I hope another year that a fuller notice of the service will bring more people to appreciate what we are doing.

In the afternoon I was present at a missionary service in St. Paul's Church, Albany, at which the two Bishops-elect of China and Japan replied, to the great interest of all who heard them, to the address of welcome which I was glad to make.

On Sunday, the 11th of June, in the Cathedral, I preached and celebrated the Holy Communion, and ordered Deacons Mr. Marvin Hill Dana and Mr. Frank N. Bouck, presented by the Rev. Canon Fulcher. In the afternoon, in St. George's Church, Schenectady, I preached and confirmed eighteen persons. On the 13th of June, I presided at the meeting of the Board of Managers in New York, and on the 14th at meetings of the managers of the Child's Hospital and St. Margaret's House; at a chapter of the Sisterhood, and at a meeting of the Rexleigh Trustees; and in the evening, in Trinity Church, Gloversville, I preached and confirmed twenty-one persons.

On Thursday, June 15th, in the morning, in St. John's Church, Johnstown, I preached and celebrated the Holy Communion and confirmed twenty persons, two of whom came from Fonda. In the afternoon, in Christ Church, Herkimer. I preached and confirmed thirty persons, with one afterward in private at Mohawk, making thirty-one in all. It was a very beautiful service, with abundant tokens of the great success of Mr. Edmunds' faithful ministry; and while I shared fully in the sorrow of the people in regard to the going away of their Rector, I had a sense of thankfulness, that in leaving the Parish, the Diocese was not to lose him. In the evening, in St. Augustine's Church, Ilion, I preached and confirmed twenty-six persons, two of whom came from the Mission at Frankfort. On Friday, June 16th, in Emmanuel Church, Little Falls, I preached, celebrated the Holy Communion and confirmed thirty-four persons, of whom six were presented from Dolgeville. On Saturday, June 17th, in the afternoon, in St. Barnabas' Church, Stottville, I preached and confirmed twenty-one persons; and in the evening, in Christ Church, Hudson, I preached and confirmed twenty-five persons.

On Sunday, June 18, I consecrated St. John's Church, Cohoes, the Rector reading the sentence of consecration. I preached the sermon and celebrated the Holy Communion, assisted by the Rev. Charles T. Olmsted and the Rev. Dr. Babcock, who had once been Rector of the Parish. It was a day full of very sacred memories. The figure that stood most prominently before me was that of my dear brother, Bishop Brown, of Fond du Lac, whose ██████████████ at the service, and

8

Thursday, October 26th, in the morning, in Christ Church, Port Henry, I preached, celebrated the Holy Communion and confirmed six persons.

Sunday, October 29th, in St. John's Church, Cohoes, I preached, celebrated the Holy Communion and confirmed eighteen persons; and in the afternoon, in the Church of the Holy Cross, Troy, I preached and confirmed thirteen persons.

On Monday, October 30th, in the evening, in St. Luke's Church, Chatham, I preached and confirmed twenty-three persons. It was my first sight of the new building, with which I was greatly pleased, both for its beauty and for the admirable convenience of its arrangement for worship and for work. As I look back upon the story of our mission in Chatham, and realize after how many years of patience we have at last secured an attractive building there, I feel most thankful that the faith and perseverance of a few people have overcome many obstacles, and given a start to the Church, of which the large number confirmed is not only abundant evidence, but a pledge, I think, of what can be accomplished in the future in this important village.

On the 31st of October, I lighted the Halloween fire on the hearth of St. Agnes' School with great thankfulness for the long series of mercies which have blessed our work, and for the promise of the years to come. We kept our dedication festival the next day in the Cathedral, and at the Evensong, under the direction of the Men's Association of the Cathedral, we had a service of song, with the two choirs of the Cathedral and St. Peter's rendering the music, and the Rector of St. Peter's preaching. The Cathedral was thronged with a reverent and interested congregation, which filled every space in it, and the service was rendered with great beauty and precision, and gave the Cathedral the opportunity of displaying and discharging one of its legitimate uses, in advancing the musical portion of the Church's service.

On Thursday, the 2d of November, in Christ Church, Herkimer, I celebrated the Holy Communion, and made the opening address at the semi-annual meeting of the Albany branch of the Woman's Auxiliary. The Bishop of Spokane and the Rev. Mr. Forrester made most interesting addresses about the work in the West and in Mexico. I was very glad to meet my Connecticut brother again, and to recognize in the new western Bishop a friend of my younger days in the old eastern Diocese; and I was glad also to be able to renew the earnest expression of my feeling about the work which we are doing in Mexico. In spite of the discouragements and difficulties, there is good reason to believe that there never was greater promise than now, of usefulness and service both in the clear-headed and capable character of our representative, and in the great outcome, due largely to him, of the adoption of the Offices to be used in the Mexican Church. We have reason to thank God and take courage.

In the evening, in the new Church in Dolgeville, which is a very attractive and admirable building, beautiful as a Church and most convenient in its arrangement for the parochial work, I preached and confirmed six persons.

On Sunday, November 5th, in the evening, in St. Paul's Church, Albany, I preached and confirmed twenty-nine persons, making in all, fifty confirmed in the Parish this year.

On Wednesday, November 8th, in the Cathedral, I celebrated the Holy Communion and admitted Mary Grace Reynolds a full sister in the Sisterhood of the Holy Child Jesus.

On Sunday, November 12th, in the evening, in St. John's Church, Troy, I preached and confirmed twenty-five persons.

On Monday, November 13th, I confirmed one person in private, for the Cathedral.

I am thankful to be able to add among the notes of growth and gain in the Diocese during the year, the lifting of the long burthen of debt from St. John's, Cohoes, by Archdeacon Sill's devoted and persistent energy; the building of new Churches at Raymertown and Chatham and Sidney; the very great additions and enlargements made at Philmont by the building of a new Guild Hall and Rectory, connected with the Church by the Choir Room; the addition to the Church of St. John in the Wilderness, St. Regis Lake, by the building of a Sanctuary, a memorial, as the new organ is also, to the beloved daughter of the beloved Dr. Trudeau, and of a new transept as a memorial of the son of my dear old friend and brother, the Dean of the General Theological Seminary. The Church at Saranac Lake has been also improved; the Rectory built and the Library rebuilt, increasing the attractiveness and working power of this unique and valuable Mission; and all the work has been well done under the competent and generous direction of Mr. J. Lawrence Aspinwall. A new Rectory has been added in its one hundredth year to Zion Church, Morris. And last, but not least, the restoration and enrichment of the venerable Parish Church of St. Paul's in Troy, not yet quite completed, is to be dedicated to the service of God before Christmas. The work has been done by a master hand, Mr. Holzer, of Messrs. Lewis Tiffany & Co., under most careful oversight of the Rector and vestry, with a large and generous expenditure of money. It is a somewhat daring venture in the use of methods not much known among us, but the result is very rich and very beautiful. The wealth of colour has no garish effect, but the whole tone, in the very highest key, is so harmonious, and the various details of treatment have been wrought into such unity of effect, that the impression is full of dignity and beauty. And while the old walls still remain as enshrining the memories of generations of worshippers, the interior is absolutely new, and ranks, in my judgment, as a piece of perfect architectural treatment and decoration, among the

The old parish of Christ Church, Duanesburgh, celebrated with dignity and fitting ceremony the one hundredth anniversary of its consecration on the 25th of August. The building was consecrated in 1793 by Bishop Provoost. Its history is associated with names that are dear to churchmen and patriots in this State; and while from its situation it naturally cannot influence any very large number of people, it carries on, never more efficiently than under its present Rector, the gracious work of folding and feeding the Master's sheep in what is almost a wilderness, and caring for the somewhat scattered families of most faithful and true-hearted churchmen, among the staunchest laymen of this Diocese. Zion Church, Morris, kept its centennial also during the past year. A noble old Parish, mother of Bishops and the best sort of Bishops, and reaching out to care for the adjoining towns and villages, the Parish to-day brings forth more fruit in her age; and although weakened by losses as always our country Parishes are apt to be, there was never fuller evidence of life and energy than in the present rectorship. It is interesting to note that of our incorporated parishes only three are older than this: St. Peter's, Albany, the mother of us all in the Diocese, and Christ Church, Ballston, both incorporated in 1787; dear old St. George's, Schenectady, in 1792; and closely following them are Christ Church, Hudson and St. Peter's, Hobart, A. D. 1794; and St. John's, Johnstown, in 1796. Only these seven date from the last century.

I feel that it is wise for me to call the attention of the Diocese to the question of the services and support of the Diocesan Missionary. I confess, that in my long experience of the care of the Missions of the Diocese, which is by far the most interesting and important part of the Bishop's work, I have never had so much real help and comfort as I have had from this office, which the Diocese created three years ago.

The resolution, under which the office was formed, never having been put in the form of a canon, had rather passed out of my mind so far as its statement of detailed duty is concerned. I find that, not unreasonably, perhaps, there has appeared to be a conflict of duty between the office of the Archdeacon and the office of the Diocesan Missionary.

There has, moreover, been a difficulty in providing, in addition to the demands for the payment of salaries of the missionaries themselves, money enough to meet the expense of the office. I beg the Convention to face this fact fairly, because it means that we must either discontinue the office, which, I confess, I should greatly regret; or limit its duties, which, it seems to me, would be a great mistake; or make special provision for its support, which, I believe, can be done; but I think it may be necessary for the Committee on Canons to look into the definition of the duties of Archdeacons, in the sixth section of canon 14.

I do not believe, myself, that there is any conflict between the two Offices, or that we can well administer the Diocese on its missionary side, without the maintenance of both; but I am very clear that both in name, in intention and in value, a Diocesan Missionary ought to be, under the Bishop, the second chief missionary of the Diocese, doing whatever in him lies, and whatever the Bishop may direct him to do, which will help on the new or vacant missions, will tend to maintain as well as to extend the services of the Church in places where they either are not held at all, or where they are in danger of discontinuance or irregularity.

I am perfectly ready to accept the decision of the Diocese about it. I should think it wise to recognize the relation of the Diocesan Missionary to the Board, and to prescribe his duties by canon, if you will; but I am very sure that the office, if it is maintained, must be supported, and that it is worse than idle to limit and confine the sphere and character of his work.

I hope the subject may be referred to a special committee, after sufficient discussion in the Convention.

I have made the most close, careful, painful shearing down of the stipends of our missionaries, for the coming year; and I find that it is utterly impossible for the Board of Missions, to carry on even its present work, without taking a step in advance, without any attention to the places that cry out for help, unless you will appropriate and *collect* and *send* to the Treasurer $11,850 this year. The whole amount will then be only $14,350, the balance coming from our invested funds; and this makes no provision for the salary of the Diocesan Missionary. It is useless for me to waste words on this statement. It is one of those facts by which we are to be judged at the last day. It is *your* work, which you called me to do *for you*, twenty-five years ago, and I cannot do it unless you will give the means. I have but one practical suggestion to make in regard to it; and it relates to a bad habit, which is evidently as old as Christianity. When St. Paul begged the Christians at Corinth to do their duty of giving, on the simple, easy, practical plan, of setting apart a weekly offering, according as God had blessed them, he ended his exhortation with the words "that there be no gatherings when I come." These *gatherings* are the bane of our giving. The clergy put off the provision, and the Parish puts off the payment; everybody puts it off, except the Treasurer, who, to and beyond his measure, has for years saved us from discredit and the missionaries from suffering. And then comes the end of the conventional year; and the gatherings begin, the effort to get together in a month what the eleven months before ought to have done; and then the humbling process, which I hoped had been forever banished from the Diocese, of appeals made in Convention, or made by me personally, to a few people, who have already given more than their share, to come and give what other people could, should and would have given if the clergy had attended to ████████████████████rty. It is not hard times. It is not unwillingness on the part of the people. It is simply the neglect of duty on the part of the clergy. I know of what I speak. The Treasurer and I, who are in constant communication about this matter, have noticed over and over again, that a Parish, utterly negligent under one Rector, becomes prompt and generous, under a new clergyman; and that Parishes, which had been in the habit of giving regularly and generously, lapse into delays and failure when a new Rector takes the place of the old. I am absolutely certain, that if the clergy would see to it *when they go from Convention*, that, either by pledges or subscription-books or offerings, the money was collected for the first quarter *in* the first quarter, and so for each quarter of the year, the needed amount would be secured in season and, there would be no " gatherings " at the end of the year. Behind this lies another serious evil. The Diocese has never done its duty toward the general missions of the Church. We have all said what is true, that ours is a missionary Diocese, and we must take care of it, because nobody else will; and that is true too. But it is true also, that if we felt, and believed, and trained our people to feel and believe, that the missionary spirit is not measured by lines; that the same commission which began with Jerusalem, ended with "the uttermost parts of the earth;" if we would kindle our zeal for missions, at the fire of the Saviour's love for souls, we should learn the *principle* of giving; and the very effort to reach out to the farthest point, and care for Africa (both at home and abroad), for Alaska, for *Missions*, would make easy the care for what lies nearest home. As I said the other day, to the Albany Archdeaconry, if one has force enough in a fire plug to reach the topmost story of the highest house, he can easily put out a fire in the front parlour; but with hardly water enough to cover the first story, it is useless to try to put a fire out at all. And the spiritual illustration is stronger still. When the Lord wrought the miracle at Cana, to satisfy the need of a few guests at the marriage feast, He did not count numbers and create the exact amount; but He made the servants, who were to draw the water, first fill the big vessels *to the brim*. Ask God to fill us to the brim, with the mere humanity of love, and He will turn it into the richness of His own Divine Love for souls.

The summary of my acts is as follows :

Confirmations, 920; *Celebrations of Holy Communion, 53 ; *Sermons, 57; Addresses, 9; Clergy dismissed, 18; Deposed, 1 ; Died, 3; Received, 17; Added by Ordination, 4; Present number of Clergy : .Bishop, 1 ; Priests, 118 ; Deacons, 8; Total, 127. Priests ordained, 2; Deacons ordained, 6; Total, 8. Postulants admitted, 3 ; Total Postulants, 12 ; Candidates for Deacon's order admitted, 4; Total Candidates for Deacon's order, 19; Candidates for Priest's order admitted, 3 ; Total Candidates

---

* Not including those in the Cathedral.

for Priest's order, 14; Total Candidates for Holy Orders, 22. Lay-Readers licensed, 17; Total Lay-Readers, 17. Sisters admitted, 1. Churches consecrated, 4; Corner-Stones laid, 1; Benedictions, 1; Institution, 1. *Baptisms: Infants, 1. Notices of deposition, 9. Deposition, 1.

I have attended the regular meetings of the Board of Missions; the Cathedral Chapter; the Trustees of the Corning Foundation; the Managers of the Child's Hospital; and of St. Margaret's House; the Chapter of the Sisterhood; the Trustees of the Orphan House of the Holy Saviour; the Diocesan Branch of the Woman's Auxiliary; the Woman's Diocesan League; the Trustees of Rexleigh School; the Trustees of the various Diocesan Funds; the Bible and Prayer Book Society; and three of the four Archdeaconries. I have also attended meetings of the Board of Managers of the Missionary Society; of the Trustees of the Prayer Book Distribution Society; of the Federate Council; of the Commission of the General Convention on Archives; of the Church University Board of Regents; the Commission on the Revision of the Constitution and Canons. I have also made the entire visitation of the Foreign Churches.

And so, my brethren, I close the story of my last year's work, with the statement of such facts and the suggestion of such counsels as seem to me wise and well to put before you. And as we turn from Vigil to Feast, from the work of the Convention to the words of commemoration, from recent records to old recollections, I beg you to bring to our Celebration, to-morrow, not merely the loving thoughts and fervent prayers about my Consecration day, with such thanksgivings as befit you and me; but the thought and prayer of the Presentation Collect, that in the day of God " we may be presented unto Him with pure and clean hearts, by His dear Son Jesus Christ our Lord." †

ORDINATIONS.

November 16, 1892. John Mills Gilbert, to the Diaconate, in the Cathedral.

November 16, 1892. Charles Albert Howells, to the Diaconate, in the Cathedral.

April 4, 1893. The Rev. William Whiting Newell, to the Priesthood, in the Church of the Holy Trinity, Paris, France.

June 7, 1893. William Anderson Stirling, to the Diaconate, in Trinity Church, Middletown, Conn, by the Bishop of Connecticut, acting for me.

June 11, 1893. Marvin Hill Dana, to the Diaconate, in the Cathedral

June 11, 1893. Frank Norwood Bouck, to the Diaconate, in the Cathedral.

* Not including those in the Cathedral.

† For the portion of the Address containing the Bishop's reflections on the history of the Diocese for the past twenty-five years, see the Anniversary Services, etc., printed at the end of the Minutes of the Convention.

July 8, 1893. The Rev. Earnest Webster Dustan, to the Priesthood, in Trinity Church, Sharon Springs.

September 21, 1893. Edward T. Carroll, to the Diaconate, in the Cathedral.

CLERGYMEN RECEIVED FROM OTHER DIOCESES.

1891.

November 21. The Rev. William Ball Wright, from the Diocese of Michigan.

December 22. The Rev. Meredith O. Smith, from the Diocese of Tennessee.

1893.

January 17. The Rev. David F. McDonald, D. D., from the Diocese of Arkansas.

February 20. The Rev. William H. A. Hall, from the Diocese of Newark.

February 20. The Rev. Calbraith B. Perry, from the Diocese of Tennessee.

May 31. The Rev. J. Holwell Geare, from the Diocese of Delaware.

June 11. The Rev. Thomas Burrows, from the Diocese of Pennsylvania.

July 7. The Rev. Herbert A. Venables, from the Diocese of Gibraltar.

July 24. The Rev. James W. Smith, from the Diocese of New Jersey.

July 31. The Rev. C. E. Mackenzie, from the Diocese of Ontario.

September 7. The Rev. Richard C. Searing, from the Diocese of Vermont.

September 28. The Rev. Joseph M. Hayman, from the Diocese of Central New York.

October 16. The Rev. Henry C. Dyer, from the Diocese of Quincy.

October 17. The Rev. Samuel D. Van Loan, from the Diocese of Newark.

October 27. The Rev. Watson B. Hall, from the Diocese of Milwaukee.

November 7. The Rev. William Stone Hayward, from the Diocese of Milwaukee.

November 13. The Rev. Churchill Satterlee, from the Diocese of New York.

CLERGYMEN DISMISSED TO OTHER DIOCESES.

1892.

December 1. The Rev. John H. Houghton, to the Diocese of Colorado,

December 7. The Rev. Herbert Luther Wood, to the Diocese of Southern Virginia.

January 7. The Rev. Frederick G. Rainey, to the Diocese of Massachusetts.

January 9. The Rev. David L. Schwartz, to the Diocese of New Jersey.

January 30. The Rev. Ernest A. Hartmann, to the Diocese of California.

February 9. The Rev. Thaddeus A. Snively, to the Diocese of Chicago.

March 3. The Rev. Robert Granger, to the Diocese of Southern Ohio.

March 30. The Rev. William H. Bown, to the Diocese of Central New York.

April 1. The Rev. Charles E. Freeman, to the Diocese of New York.

June 23. The Rev. Clarence E. Ball, to the Diocese of Virginia.

July 12. The Rev. Creighton Spencer, to the Diocese of Long Island.

August 18. The Rev. Harry A. R. Cresser, to the Diocese of Central New York.

September 8. The Rev. Eugene Griggs, to the Diocese of Delaware.

October 4. The Rev. C. P. A. Burnett, to the Diocese of Long Island.

October 6. The Rev. David Sprague, to the Diocese of Massachusetts.

October 9. The Rev. James R. L. Nisbett, to the Diocese of Long Island.

October 14. The Rev. J. M. Windsor, to the Diocese of New York.

October 30. The Rev. Joseph M. Hayman, to the Diocese of Pennsylvania.

CANDIDATES FOR PRIEST'S ORDERS.

May 19, 1888. Mr. John C. Woodworth.

January 12, 1891. The Rev. Frank N. Bouck.

October 1, 1891. Mr. Harry Sherman Longley.

October 18, 1891. Mr. Keble Dean.

November 6, 1891. Mr. George William Farrar.

November 6, 1891. Mr. Frederic Henry Farrar.

January 28, 1892. Mr. Frederick St. George McLean.

February 11, 1892. The Rev. William Anderson Stirling.

September 29, 1892. Mr. Alexander Haswell Grant, Jr.

September 29, 1892. Mr. Lewis Gouverneur Morris.

September 29, 1892. Mr. Robert Perine.

December 22, 1892. The Rev. Charles A. Howells.

October 28, 1893. Mr. Hamilton Douglass Bentley MacNeil.

November 6, 1893. Mr. John S. Warren.

CANDIDATES FOR DEACON'S ORDER.

April 26, 1883. Mr. Gulian V. P. Lansing.

October 3, 1887. Mr. George K. Rhames.

October 3, 1887. Mr. Charles H. Moore.

December 1, 1887. Mr. John C. Woodworth.

November 19, 1888. Mr. Keble Dean.

March 9, 1891.   Mr. Harry Sherman Longley.
April 13, 1891.   Mr. Gouverneur Frank Mosher.
October 5, 1891.   Mr. George William Farrar.
October 5, 1891.   Mr. Frederic Henry Farrar.
November 18, 1891.   Mr. Robert Perine.
November 18, 1891.   Mr. Frederick St. George McLean.
March 5, 1892.   Mr. Lewis Gouverneur Morris.
June 6, 1892.   Mr. John S. Warren.
September 19, 1892.   Mr. Alexander Haswell Grant, Jr.
October 17, 1892.   Mr. George Ward Bushnell.
December 12, 1892.   Mr. George Dart Ashley.
April 4, 1893.   Mr. William Wallace Lockwood.
September 18, 1893.   Mr. Edward Buckley Monroe Harraden.
October 21, 1893.   Mr. Hamilton Douglass Bentley MacNeil.

POSTULANTS.

May 12, 1885.   Isaac Borts, M. D.
March 22, 1887.   Charles Hegamin, Jr.
March 3, 1887.   E. Townsend Jones, M. D.
May 1, 1889.   George Henry Chase.
May 27, 1889.   William Croswell Doane Willson.
July 1, 1891.   William Robert Golden.
July 1, 1892.   Albert L. Longley.
September 29, 1892.   Edmund Norman Curry.
October 1, 1892.   James Lewis Lasher.
December 16, 1892.   Joseph Henry Seebergan.
July 7, 1893.   Frank Thurber Cady.
September 21, 1893.   George Hewson Wilson.

CORNER STONE LAID.

October 18, 1893.   St. Luke's Church, Catskill.

CHURCHES CONSECRATED.

June 10, 1893.   St. John's Church, Cohoes.
July 9, 1893.   St. Paul's Church, Raymertown.
October 12, 1893.   Christ Church, Deposit.
October 17, 1893.   St. Mark's Church, Philmont.

BENEDICTION.

October 24, 1893.   New window and chancel furniture of St. Paul'
Church, Keeseville.

LAY READERS LICENSED.

1892.

November 17. W. W. Godard, St. Luke's Church, Saranac Lake.
November 18. Fred. S. Lincoln, Church of the Ascension, Troy.
November 21. George R. P. Shackelford, Bethesda Church, Saratoga Springs.

1893.

January 3. Edward Lilly, Christ Church, Gilbertsville.
January 19. Walter C. Rix, St. Augustine's Church, Ilion.
January 19. H. W. Myers, St. Paul's Church, Albany.
January 21. Silas E. Everts, Trinity Church, Granville.
January 21. Keble Dean, All Saints' Church, Hoosac.
July 6. Edward B. M. Harraden, for the Diocese.
July 7. James M. Hackett, St. John's Church, Champlain.
July 7. David White, Christ Church, Rouse's Point.
July 7. Frank Thurber Cady, St. Paul's Church, Albany.
August 29. Albert L. Longley, for the Diocese.
September 25. Harry S. Longley, for the Diocese.
September 25. Capt. Geo. E. Pond, Trinity Church, Plattsburgh.
September 29. H. A. Chapman, Christ Church, Morristown.
November 8. Robert Perine, for the Diocese. (Renewal.)

CLERGY DEPOSED.

September 28, 1893. William R. Woodbridge, Priest.

NOTICES OF CLERGY DEPOSED.

1892.

November 24. Timothy O'Connell, Priest, by the Bishop of Missouri.
December 8. R. C. E. Lockhart, Deacon, by the Assistant Bishop of Minnesota.

1893.

February 27. Elmer Ellsworth Shoemaker, ——, by the Bishop of Vermont.
March 6. Wilbur F. Watkins, Priest, by the Bishop of Pennsylvania.
March 19. Jesse Albert Locke, Priest, by the Bishop of New York.
April 11. Edwin B. Russell, Priest, by the Bishop of New Jersey.
April 28. Pliny Brett Morgan, Priest, by the Bishop of California.
July 16. Henry A. Adams, Priest, by the Bishop of New York.
November 9. William Howland, Priest, by the Bishop of Newark.

APPENDIX TO THE BISHOP'S ADDRESS.

My visitations in Europe made impossible my presence at the burials of those of whom I simply print such commemorative notices as come under my eye, only adding my deep and true sense of the loss to the Diocese and to me of two most active and faithful Priests, and of earnest and loyal laymen, my friends through all my Episcopate. We shall especially miss the kindly presence, the wise counsels and the unfailing devotion of Mr. Benjamin H. Hall, of Troy, from the Convention and the various administrative Boards of the Diocese.

REV. CHARLES H. LANCASTER.

"The Rev. Charles H. Lancaster, rector of the Episcopal Church in this village, and in charge of the Missionary Station at North Granville, quietly passed to his reward at four o'clock this afternoon, death resulting from a stroke of paralysis with which he was prostrated last Wednesday evening while engaged with a number of ladies planning parish work. He remained unconscious from the stroke until his final breath. Mr. Lancaster was born in Bristol, England, in 1833, and was educated in that place. He came to Canada in 1862, and two years later he was ordained Deacon by Bishop Fulford, of Montreal. In 1867 he was advanced to the Priesthood by the same Prelate, who dimitted him to the American Church and the Diocese of New York, he having accepted a call to the rectorate of the Parish in Ilion. He became a Presbyter of the Diocese of Albany, with its creation, and remained in its membership until his death. In 1889 he succeeded the Rev. Joseph Carey as rector at Waterford, and about two and a half years later he accepted a call to Lake George, where he served the Church eighteen years. About one year ago he accepted the call from the Church in this village, and, during his brief work here, was very successful. He was a man of deep sentiment, refinement, earnestness and zeal in his sacred calling. A widow and a foster daughter survive him."

This is the brief, public record of the village newspaper to a most brave, devoted, earnest Priest, a most uncompromising Churchman, a most untiring worker, the kindest and most loyal of friends, the cheerful courage of whose sunny nature shone out only more brightly in the patience with which he bore the great trial of the illness which laid him aside from work. And this is the minute adopted by the clergy after his burial:

At the end of a long and faithful service in the ministry, and after a patient and brave struggle of many months trying to fully serve his Parish, in spite of great bodily infirmity, our brother has finally been taken to the rest which remaineth to the people of God.

In the summer of 1891 he lost the sight of one eye by hemorrhage; in May of this year a shock of paralysis fell upon him while in the midst of active duty. A few days ago another stroke ended his life, and now to-day we come to bury him.

Endeared to his parishioners by many qualities of mind and heart he will not lie in the grave of a stranger, although but a little more than a year at work where his lot was last cast.

He has gone in and out among those to whom God gave him oversight in this Diocese for something more than twenty-three years, with cheerfulness and devotion, first in Ilion, than in Waterford, after that for eighteen years in Lake George, and finally in Granville.

Loyal to the Church and its truth, to his Bishop, his Diocese, and moved by a high sense of responsibility, he will be long remembered by the Bishop and Clergy of the Diocese and those to whom he ministered.

Born in Bristol, England, in 1833, he removed to Canada in 1862. He was ordained Deacon by Bishop Fulford in 1864, and advanced to the Priesthood by the same Bishop in 1867, and in 1869 was transferred by letter dimissory to this Diocese, where he has since lived and labored.

We shall mourn his loss as that of a faithful brother and friend, and would express our deep sympathy to his bereaved wife.

ERASTUS CORNING, JR.

At a meeting of the Trustees of the Corning Foundation, held April 11, A. D., 1893, the following minute on the death of Mr. Erastus Corning, Jr., was adopted :

In the death of Mr. Erastus Corning, Jr., which occurred on Low Sunday, April 9, A. D., 1893, the Trustees of the Corning Foundation mourn the loss of a most devoted and honoured member.

Mr. Corning was appointed a trustee of this Corporation on June 9, A. D., 1874, to fill the vacancy occasioned by the death of his grandfather, Hon. Erastus Corning, the founder of the important trust with which we are charged ; and although afflicted with a deafness which made it impossible for him, without assistance, to follow the proceedings of the Board, he was rarely absent from its meetings ; and, when, finally, long illness prevented his attendance, his interest in the work of the foundation did not cease. This was shown by his constant inquiries about the Cathedral and the institutions clustering about it, and his manifestation of pleasure in any success or advancement of the work of this Board.

It is most fitting that we enter on the records of this Corporation our estimate of his character. Loving nature in all her forms with an intensity which only those who knew him best could fully appreciate, he longed to live ; but, when God had " taught him to number his days," he resolutely set himself to face the inevitable. Bravely and with unselfish cheerfulness enduring whatever of pain was laid upon him ; greeting his friends with all his accustomed courtesy ; taking a keen interest in every thing going on about him, he patiently endured unto the end. It was granted him to receive his Lord, in the blessed Sacrament on Easter-day, at the Cathedral ; to hold converse with his most intimate friends during the ensuing week, and very early in the morning on the octave of Easter, amid the scenes he best loved, to be " saved from any more pain." He has entered into his rest. There remains to us the example of a brave, unselfish, gentle, patient spirit.

Attest :   T. B. FULCHER,
Secretary.

THE HON. R. B. MONELL.

NORTH EAST HARBOR, ME., *August* 12, 1893.

News comes to me here of the death of Hon. R. B. Monell in Albany, and it recalls, so vividly, the earlier years of my Episcopate, that I desire to put on record a small tribute of my very real reverence for his memory.

When I came to the Diocese, in 1869, Mr. Monell was among its very leading laymen. He had been, for years, an active officer in his own Church in Hudson. He was promptly elected a member of the Standing Committee at the primary Convention of the Diocese, and, from the first moment that we met and in all our constant associations, parochial and diocesan, he was always a wise counsellor, a kindly and sympathetic friend, a loyal Churchman, a humble, simple, earnest Christian man.

The later years of his life have been withdrawn from public and active service but they have never lessened or diminished his keen and in matters that pertain to the best interests of the Church, a

G

and his heart, to its last beat, was true to his Master, Whom he had served so faithfully and well, to the Church, to his Bishop and his Pastor, to his family and friends. He had come to a ripe old age with the loss of certain faculties and a failing of physical strength; but there was no dimness of the spiritual eye, and no clouding of the mind; and the end was peace. "Am I going to die?" he asked the doctor at the very end. "I am ready, and I should be so glad to go." It was a true "*Nunc dimittis.*" of one who had "seen the salvation of God."

I recall, years and years ago, an evening in his house, when I went down with him after the evening service, to see that wonderful flower of the night — the Night-blooming Cereus. His great delight and pleasure in the flower and in showing it to me, his association of its blooming with the very day of my visitation, and the unearthly scent and beauty of the flower have come back to me to-day, and are the symbol and the figure to me of the way in which his soul, having come to the fulness of its earthly years, blooms out now in a fragrance and a beauty that is really unearthly, because it is tinged and touched with a glory of paradise.

W. C. D.

MRS. WALTER A. WOOD.

Dead in her prime, when a new life of holy service seemed opening to her as in trust with the carrying on of her husband's large purposes and plans, and seeking to fill the double place to their children, Mrs. Walter A. Wood has passed away from earthly labours.

She was a woman nobly planned, whose dignified beauty of face simply expressed the nobility of nature of which it was the outward sign. Holy influences had ripened her soul, from early childhood, into the fulfilment of her birthright as "the Child of God." The inheritance of her father's character and of her mother's lineage had been nurtured, in an atmosphere of refinement and abounding generosity, into a rich completeness; and when the earthly light of her home went out in Mr. Wood's death, she sought, in the quiet of her shadowed life, to be trained to take up the new duties that devolved upon her, waiting for the strength of heart to take them up and do them, in the fear of God. And just when the physical strength seemed returning, and the ability to take her place in "the state of life to which God called her," came the other call, sudden and most strange to us. And with the confidence and composure of a child, she heard the voice, "not frightened," as she said to me, though wondering at its suddenness. And she has gone from those she loved intensely, and who returned that love, to the beloved who had gone before her.

It was my great privilege to minister to her in the last moments of her life, and the mingled humbleness and confidence, the surprise that it was "not hard to die," and the simple surrender of her will to God's, the calm clearness of her thoughtful care for those whom she most loved, the over and over repetition with a separate distinctness upon each word, "In Thee only, O Lord, do I put my trust;" and the triumph of her voice in the last words of the Tersanctus, have crowned with a halo of most holy, helpful memories this beautiful and blessed life.

Truly she so lived that "sinking in her last long sleep" "she smiled when all around her wept." Blessed she is, as one who "died in the Lord." May His peace and light refresh her soul!

W. C. D.

MR. DAVID HYDE GAY.

Fell asleep in Jesus, on Saturday night, October 14, 1893, Mr. David Gay, senior warden of Christ Church, Walton, N. Y., aged 79 years.

At a meeting of the rector, junior warden and vestrymen of Christ Church, Walton,

N. Y., holden in the vestry on Sunday evening, October 29, 1893, the following minute was unanimously adopted :

WHEREAS, It has pleased our Heavenly Father, in His wise providence, to remove from our midst our well-beloved associate, Mr. David Hyde Gay, senior warden of this parish, it is our earnest desire to place upon record the following minute :

That we remember, with deep gratitude, his noble and upright character, his Christian walk and conversation among men, and his exact and loving faithfulness to all the duties that were laid upon him.

That we record our thankfulness to Almighty God for the loving and faithful ser. vice wrought by this servant of the Lord in the Master's vineyard, extending over a period of fifty-nine years.

That we desire to remind ourselves of his many virtues, his meekness and noble Christian piety, his pure spirituality, which responded so easily and so eagerly to the motions of the Holy Spirit ; and

That we, the rector, junior warden and vestrymen of Christ Parish, Walton, order this testimony, to his worth, to be sent to his daughter, and to be published in *The Churchman* and the papers of his native place.

RICHARD C. SEARING,

JOHN G. EELLS,
    Clerk of the Vestry.

Rector.

This means the removal of a landmark. Mr. Gay was not only never absent from his place of service, in Walton, but he has been in almost every one of the Conventions of this Diocese from the first. Simple, sincere, strong in his faith, and unwithholding in his duty, he had the respect and confidence and affection of us all. I was in Walton on the evening before he died, and at his bedside, for a moment, though he did not know it, but it was a privilege to me to commend his true soul into the hands of his Merciful Saviour, to be presented pure and without spot before Him.

WILLIAM HENRY WEEKS.

MIDDLEVILLE, N. Y., *June* 8, 1893,

Mr. William H. Weeks, for many years a communicant and vestryman of Emmanuel Church, Little Falls, and its junior warden when he came to live in this village in 1891, a year prior to my taking charge here, died of paralysis on Septuagesima Sunday, January 29, 1893. He was the leading man in this work, in a spiritual sense, and a liberal contributor to its support. As a reader, his acquaintance with the most profound and sound theological writers often surprised and delighted me. His love for all that is truly churchly, and his invariable attendance at the early celebration, were proverbial in the Parish. He endured a long, trying, and, at times, painful illness with sweet and gentle patience and fortitude. I assisted Mr. Mariett to bury him on the Purification of the B. V. M., feeling deeply that I had been bereaved of a pillar of our Church in this village.

MR. GEORGE GRISWOLD.

Mr. George Griswold died Tuesday in Holy Week. On Good Friday afternoon, immediately after the solemnities of our vigil at the foot of the cross, we laid him to rest. Few men die with so utterly unsullied and sweet a reputation. I do not think he ever had an enemy.

Mr. Jairus Mather.

Mr. Jairus Mather, vestryman and treasurer of Trinity Church, Fairfield, died on Good Friday, and I buried him on Easter Monday. I enclose you a paper expressing the sentiments of his fellow vestrymen regarding him. He was not a communicant of the Church, but his whole sympathy, however, was with the Church in Fairfield, and his removal leaves a gap which will probably never be filled. He was a Christian gentleman of the old school. I have met few men who, more fully, commanded my entire respect.

I make these three extracts from Mr. Conant's letter because it touches, so admirably, the characters of these three laymen, who will be sorely missed and mourned.

PREAMBLE AND RESOLUTIONS.

Mr. Jairus Mather.

At a meeting of the wardens and vestrymen of Trinity Church, Fairfield, N. Y., held on Saturday evening, April 8, 1893, the following preamble and resolutions were unanimously adopted:

WHEREAS, It hath pleased Almighty God. In His wise Providence, to take out of this world our fellow Christian and associate, Mr. Jairus Mather, for about twenty years a vestryman of this Church, for the past three years its treasurer and ever its staunch friend and supporter, therefore,

Resolved, That while we would fain obey the apostolic injunction and "sorrow not even as others which have no hope" for those who sleep in the Lord Jesus, nevertheless we cannot but feel keenly that this Church and community share, in no inconsiderable measure, with Mr. Mather's family, a very crushing and irremediable loss in his transition to Paradise.

Resolved, That we desire to place upon record our high sense and appreciation of the Christian manliness, unfailing courtesy, unsullied integrity and rare discretion of the late Mr. Jairus Mather, whose counsel, often sought, was always freely given and has pointed not a few among us to successes which remain as monuments to his high character, ripe judgment and unfailing sagacity.

Resolved, That the clerk of this vestry is hereby instructed to cause the publication of these resolutions in the county newspapers, and to procure a copy of them, suitably engrossed, and to present the same to the widow and children of the late Mr. Jairus Mather, with the assurance of our most deep and abiding sympathy with them in this their great bereavement, which we cannot but regard as shared with them by this entire community.

(Signed)   CLARENCE M. CONANT, M. D.,
Rector in Charge.
REUBEN NEELY,
Senior Warden.
DR. C. W. NICHOLS,
Junior Warden and Clerk.

Mr. Benjamin H. Hall.

Adopted by the vestrymen of St. John's Church upon the death of Benjamin H. Hall, Esq.

WHEREAS, We are called to record, with profound sorrow, the death of our beloved brother, Benjamin H. Hall, who, for many years, has been a most devout and loyal member of St. John's Parish:

Resolved, That in the death of Mr. Hall the Church at large has lost a defender, most loyal, a servant, most wise, a son, most loving.

Resolved, That the Parish to which he devoted the best years of his life, serving it with all fidelity in varied official and personal relations, makes grateful and loving recognition of the wisdom which he ever brought to counsel, touching all things with a broad and generous culture, of the zeal and energy of a consecrated service, and of the many graces of character which ever adorned him, whilst they ever enriched others in the sweet fellowship of Christian walk and worship.

Resolved, That we tender to the bereaved family of our dear brother our tenderest sympathy, and that a copy of these resolutions be sent to them.

MR. EDWARD GRANGER GILBERT.

Adopted by the vestrymen of of St. John's Church upon the death of Edward Granger Gilbert, Esq.

WHEREAS, In the Providence of God, Mr. Edward Granger Gilbert, a faithful and devoted member of this body, has been called to depart this life:

Resolved, That we unite in an expression of profoundest sorrow in the loss of one whose active and efficient service was marked with a gracious and kindly sympathy for all. His life has borne rich and enduring testimony to those unfailing traits of heart and mind that shall ever hallow the memory of our intimacy with him. Wise and just in counsel ; earnest and sincere in helpfulness ; in spirit most generous ; in life most simple, he laboured and wrought with untiring energy.

Resolved, That this body extend to his bereaved family its most profound sympathy, and that a copy of these resolutions be sent to them.

At a special meeting of the Vestry of St. Paul's Church, Troy, held December 16, 1892, the following Minute was adopted and ordered to be spread upon the Parish Records :

MINUTE

In the death of Derick Lane, who passed to his reward on the morning of the 14th of December, 1892, we have sustained a loss which words cannot measure. As in the case of the Master, when the hem of His robe was touched, we feel that virtue has gone out of us. Not merely as a Vestryman of St. Paul's, but as a Christian man in the diversified relations of life — as husband, father, brother, Christian yoke-fellow, he seemed ever to meet the requirements of "pure and undefiled religion." The very children in the street loved him. His mere going out and coming in amongst us was a benediction. To sum up the character of such a man and fitly in-dicate our sense of loss when bereaved of him, is a task beyond our reach. Though never formally set apart as an official minister and steward of the Church's Mys-teries, yet by his life and death he preached the Gospel of *Jesus Christ,* and his ex-ample remains an abiding witness with us to the truths of revealed religion. To depart and be with *Christ* was doubtless far better for him; but for us, that he should have remained seemed needful.

Those of us who were present when his end drew on will never forget the lesson which he then taught us. It was a lesson which he himself had learned in the school of suffering and through the ministrations of pain. We saw in him one whose life had been so ordered that when the summons came to leave it, that summons found him ready, without surprise or regret, with░░░░░░░░░░░░░hurry. His pass-ing was not with resignation, but with triu░░░░░░░░░░░░░░░░░░░░░░░

ant dreams," but as one who girds himself for larger work on higher, holier ground. Of Derick Lane it may be truthfully said that "nothing in his life became him like the leaving it. He died as one that had been studied in his death."

MR. JOHN GREGORY.

John Gregory, sexton of Holy Innocents' Church for forty-three years, died Tuesday, October 24, 1893.

Extract from a memorial sermon, preached by the rector, on Sunday, October 29.

Text: Psalm 84:10. "I had rather be a door-keeper in the house of my God, than to dwell in the tents of wickedness."

This Psalm breathes the Spirit of one whose chief joy, in life, was to be found in the services of the sanctuary; whose ruling passion was love for the house of God, and whose soul shrank from wrong-doing: rather the humblest office of usefulness in the Church's service than contact with sin!

And such as these were marked traits in the character of one who was known to all those who attended the services at this Church, since the inception of the Parish, who has just been taken from us.

Through a long period of years which passes the average length of life of those present to-day, from the older members of this Church, as well as from the young, John Gregory had unquestioning confidence and unstinted affection. Ask me why this was and I will answer in words which are but echoes of your own thoughts. Because his work here was the dear work of his life; because of the unimpeachable honesty of the man, and the simple, transparent integrity of his character.

His love for this sacred house had grown only deeper with increasing years, until he watched over it, as a doting father might care for his child. So fully had this feeling taken hold of him that, for a long time past, he would not sleep unless the keys were within reach of his hand. A life of such plain uprightness is best commemorated in words of rugged simplicity.

The story of half his life is closely interwoven with the entire history of our Parish Beginning the duties of his humble office with the first rector, he has faithfully fulfilled them through all the various changes down to now. Lives have passed here which he has watched from their coming until their "passing on," and the same hand which poured the water into the font for their baptism, chimed, also, the bell at their marriage, and tolled the requiem at their burial. For the last five years he has made here, with devout regularity, his weekly Communion; he died as he lived, in the "faith and fear" of God.

There have been others who have left us legacies of financial value. *His* legacy is that of the memory of a life well-spent, of duty done, of a manly example, of an unsullied name.

"That good gray head which all men knew"— we shall see in *this* house no more.

"Father in Thy gracious keeping,
Leave we now Thy servant sleeping"

To this loving tribute, richly earned, I only add my own word of reverence for a good and gracious memory Gregory's warm welcome, his pleasant smile, his hearty hand-shake always greeted me first when I visited this Church. And the example of his service is a lesson to us all.—W. C. D

At the conclusion of the Address, prayers were said and the Benediction pronounced by the Bishop.

The Convention adjourned *sine die.*

WM. CROSWELL DOANE,
Bishop of Albany and President of the Convention.

WILLIAM C. PROUT, *Secretary.*

THOMAS B. FULCHER, *Assistant Secretary.*

TWENTY-FIFTH ANNIVERSARY

OF THE

CONSECRATION

OF THE

Right Rev. William Croswell Doane,

D. D. (Oxon) LL. D. (Cantab.),

FIRST BISHOP OF ALBANY.

SERVICES, SERMON AND ADDRESSES.

SERVICES.

The Twenty-fifth Anniversary of the Consecration of the Right Rev. William Croswell Doane, D. D., LL. D., first Bishop of Albany, was observed in the Cathedral Church of All Saints, Albany, N. Y., on Friday, the Feast of the Purification of the Blessed Virgin Mary, February 2, A. D. 1894.

The Holy Eucharist was celebrated at 7.30 o'clock in the morning, the Rev. Dean Robbins celebrating.

There was a second celebration at 9.30 o'clock, the Right Rev. William Croswell Doane, D. D., LL. D., celebrating, the Right Rev. Henry C. Potter, D. D., LL. D., Bishop of New York, reading the Epistle, and the Right Rev. John Scarborough, D. D., Bishop of New Jersey, the Gospel. The Sermon was preached by the Right Rev. John Williams, D. D., LL. D., Bishop of Connecticut, Presiding Bishop.

Other Bishops present were the Right Rev. William Hobart Hare, D. D., Missionary Bishop of South Dakota, the Right Rev. Ethelbert Talbot, D. D., LL. D., Missionary Bishop of Wyoming and Idaho, the Right Rev. William A. Leonard, D. D., Bishop of Ohio, and the Right Rev. Lemuel H. Wells, D. D., Missionary Bishop of Spokane.

One hundred and thirty clergy in surplices were in procession, besides many others on the floor of the Cathedral not vested. Lay Deputies from fifty parishes, who had come to Albany for the annual Convention of the Diocese on the previous day, were in attendance, and a large congregation of laymen from Albany, and from other parts of the Diocese, filled the Cathedral full. Amongst the distinguished visitors from abroad were the Rev. Dr. Hoffman, Dean of the General Theological Seminary, the Rev. Dr. Fairbairn, Warden of St. Stephen's College, the Rev. Dr. Potter, President of Hobart College, the Rev. Dr. Huntington of Grace Church, New York, the Rev. Dr. Satterlee of Calvary Church, New York, the Rev. Dr. Nelson of Trinity Church, Geneva, N. Y., the Rev. Dr. Brainard of St. Peter's Church, Auburn, N. Y., the Rev. John Townsend of Middletown, Conn., the Rev. Dr. Shackelford of Saratoga Springs, the Rev. Theodosius S. Tyng, of Osaka, Japan, Mr. J. Pie

Trask and Mr. George C. Clarke of New York, Mr. Edward L. Davis of Worcester, Hon. Martin I. Townsend of Troy, Mr. Douglass Merritt of Rhinebeck and many others. A very large number of communicants received the Holy Communion.

After the conclusion of the Eucharistic office, a festival Te Deum service was held, at which congratulatory addresses were presented by the Standing Committee and the Board of Missions of the Diocese, the Memorial Committee of the Diocesan Convention, the Church University Board of Regents, the General Chapter and the Chapter of the Cathedral of All Saints, the Trustees of the Corning Foundation for Christian Work in the Diocese of Albany, the Teachers and others in charge of St. Agnes' School, the Trustees of the Orphan House of the Holy Saviour, and the Sisters and Children of the Child's Hospital, St. Christina Home, and St. Margaret's House, the Graduates and the Undergraduates of St. Agnes' School.

The Bishop made an address in reply. At the conclusion of the addresses, the Bishop read some prayers and pronounced the Benediction.

Later in the day a reception was given the Bishop and Mrs. Doane in the Fort Orange Club-House, at which large numbers of persons attended to pay their respects and extend congratulations.

Following are the sermon of the Presiding Bishop, the congratulatory addresses presented at the Te Deum service, and the Bishop's reply, and also so much of the Bishop's Annual Convention Address as relates to the history of the Diocese for the past twenty-five years.

ANNIVERSARY SERMON.

DIOCESE OF ALBANY, OFFICE OF THE
SECRETARY OF THE CONVENTION,
HERKIMER, N. Y., *Feb.* 2, 1894.

The Right Rev. JOHN WILLIAMS, *D. D., LL. D.*:

Reverend Father in God—It gives me pleasure to transmit to you this resolution, adopted by the Convention of the Diocese of Albany, Feb. 1, 1894, requesting you to grant the petition of the Convention.

·*Resolved*, That the Secretary be instructed to ask the presiding Bishop for a copy of his sermon to be delivered at the anniversary services to-morrow, for the purpose of having it printed.

I am, Right Rev. Sir, respectfully and obediently your servant in Christ,

WM. C. PROUT,
Secretary of Convention, Diocese of Albany.

———

MIDDLETOWN, CONN., *Feb.* 5, 1894.

My Dear Mr. Secretary :

In reply to your note communicating the very kind resolution of the Convention of the Diocese of Albany, I can only say that I place my sermon in your hands, solely because it does, necessarily, form a part of the services of the anniversary, and for that reason alone.

With many thanks for the kind confidence of the Convention,

I am faithfully yours,

J. WILLIAMS.

The Rev. The Secretary of the Diocese of Albany.

"Thus saith the Lord God, the Holy One of Israel, In returning and rest shall ye be saved: in quietness and in confidence shall be your strength."

Isaiah xxx: 15.

It was a day of doubt and trial and impending danger in Jerusalem. Men's hearts were failing them, their minds were tossed with anxious forebodings, their counsels were perplexed and various. The future was all uncertainty, the present was all confusion. Without there were threatenings, within there were fears and discords.

Then over all the tumult and the clamor there came in its simple, and because simple, most impressive utterance, the message of the Holy One the Lord of Hosts, "In returning and rest ye shall be saved, in quietness and confidence shall be your strength;" words which seem as they fall upon the ear or meet the eye, to issue from the calm, unmoved, unchanging centre of all being, life and power; the very voice of Him who is the same "yesterday, to-day and forever."

Let us consider for a moment, just how they came to those to whom the Prophet spake them, just what counsel and encouragement they brought. We shall, then, be better able to see how and why we may take them to ourselves in this age and period; nay even on this very day of joyful thanksgiving.

They contain two promises, one of safety amid perils, and the other of strength in that assured safety. And are not these promises echoed and re-echoed throughout the word of God? Safety which mounts upward till it reaches its consummation in salvation, and strength which, renewed in those that wait upon the Lord, causes them to soar with wings as eagles, and enables them to run and not be weary, to walk and not faint.

But then, God's promises are never unconditional, though men have often tried to make them so. Wherefore, to each of these two great promises, two conditions are annexed. The promised safety is conditioned on returning and rest; the promised strength on quietness and confidence.

We have not far to seek for the character and bearing of the conditions that underlie the promises. The returning that is counselled and commanded, is a return to those old laws under which Israel had been constituted a peculiar people, and especially to that vital truth, the central one for the faith of every Israelite — a truth which I venture to believe, in the face of all denial, was given to His people from the Lord their God, by the great law-giver, amid the thunders and the lightnings of Sinai —"Thou shalt have none other gods but me."

And, then, what are the rest, the quietness, the confidence, that are enjoined? Are they, and do they end in, that sullen submission to a resistless fate, arbitrary and unreasonable, which shadowed the life of the Greek and sank the Oriental in a dreary apathy? Far, far, from that. The God of Israel, and our God, is not without moral character. Behind His power and its exercise, there lie His perfect righteousness and wisdom. And it is because these are ever and always revealed to us, that in rest and confidence and quietness, we accept His will. Says Richard Hooker, "They err, therefore, who think that of the will of God, to do this or that, there is no reason beside His will. Many times no reason known to us. But that there is no reason thereof, I judge it most unreasonable to imagine, inasmuch as He worketh all things not only according to His own will, but according to the '*counsel* of His own will.'" Let me sum all this up in the well-chosen words of another. "Where Isaiah said, 'In returning and rest ye shall be saved; in quietness and confidence shall be your strength,' he did not ask his restless countrymen to yield sullenly to an infinite force, or to bow in stupidity beneath the inscrutable will of an arbitrary despot; but to bring their conduct into harmony with a reasonable and gracious plan, which might be read in the historical events of the time, and was vindicated by the loftiest religious convictions. Isaiah preached no submission to fate, but reverence for an all-wise Ruler." We may add, that the Divine methods were all shaped in illimitable wisdom, and all illuminated by an immeasurable love.

Do not those great words as they come, in their calm majesty, ever increasing in their progress down the ages, bring lessons to the spiritual Israel, the living Church of God? Are there no special counsels to those whose lot is cast in a restless age, an age in which it may almost seem "that all the foundations of the earth are out of course?" I suppose that even those who now approach the Holy Scriptures from the assumed postulate — and it involves an enormous assumption — that prophecies and miracles are simple impossibilities, will admit as much as this; while those — in this place and presence I surely may say *we* — who believe that in old time, "holy men of God spake as they were moved by the Holy Ghost," we, who believe that in every age God has borne witness to the coming or the present Gospel of His Incarnate Son, whether by physical "signs and wonders and powers," or by those grander spiritual miracles wrought in human souls by the "gifts of the Holy Ghost," we, I say, in no spirit of complacent self-approval, but in deep and reverent humility shall be ready to declare with the great Apostle, that all these things are written for our "learning and admonition," and so to receive the lesson not as discovered by ourselves, but as revealed from God. There is, believe me, all the difference in the world between those two intellectual and spiritual tempers and their several results.

The one ends in that never settled, always disturbed condition, in which Nature and Revelation become,

> " No more than as a mirror that reflects
> To proud self-love her own intelligence,
> The one poor finite object in the abyss
> Of infinite being, twinkling restlessly."

The other ends in that quietness and confidence, safety and strength which finds in Jesus Christ "the power of God and the wisdom of God," Him first, Him last, Him midst and without end.

Has the Church in the long course of its life and work given heed to this great truth, one might well say this solemn command of our Heavenly Father? Looking at that long course with only a hasty glance, our instant answer will probably be No! We run back in thought to the earliest days. We think of the "much disputing" at the Council in Jerusalem. We remember the "envying and strife and divisions" at Corinth; the Judaizers in Galatia; "the philosophy and vain deceit" at Colosse; the denials of the resurrection; the confusions in the seven Asiatic Churches. And then, as we advance, the din and the tumult seem ever on the increase, voices wax louder and multiply indefinitely, and in the midst of their cries and clamor we are fain to ask, with bated breath, where are the returning and the rest, the quietness and the confidence, the safety and the strength?

Nay! but let us take a wider, and at the same time, a deeper view. These distractions and disturbances have all one common root and origin. They all come from individual speculations, theories and fancies adding to or taking from "the faith once for all delivered to the saints." Said the great Apostle, "There must be heresies among you " — must be, not by the ordinance of God, but the pravity of man — "that they which are approved may be made manifest." I do not undervalue, God forbid! the labors of those who have earnestly contended for the faith. But I do mean to say that it is well at times to turn away from individual assault and individual defense, and look at the attitude and position of the Church herself. And surely there is something not only reassuring but even majestic in it. All down the line of the Church's history we find her meeting error by the calm, distinct, unfaltering assertion of the truth itself. Some said that God the Father was not almighty nor yet the creator of heaven and earth, and day by day, through all the centuries, the Church replies, " I believe in God, the Father Almighty, Maker of heaven and earth." Some said the Son was not God, and the Church simply answers, "God of God, Light of Light, very God of very God, Being of one substance with the Father." Some deny the Incarnation and the answer comes, "Incarnate by the Holy Ghost of the Virgin Mary." Some deny His resurrection, and the Church _____ the third day He rose again from the dead," and so all the ____

10

the very ideal of an *Ecclesia Docens* — a teaching Church — an ideal tenfold more real than that which dreams of a Church that in fussy activities, setting herself to do what God never laid upon her, instead of holding aloft this body of salvific truth, busies herself with tearing off something from it, or with sewing on it "purple patches glittering from afar," of individual fancies and all newfangledness? Is there not something here of "that calm dignity, that regal port that marks Agamemnon the king of men?" And mark this: How such a quiet, continuous, persistent witness brings the assurance of safety and strength to troubled, anxious souls. How that truth seems to loom up under such a witness, far above all strife, discussions, controversy:

> "As some tall cliff that lifts its awful form,
> Swells from the vale and midway meets the storm;
> Though round its base the rolling clouds are spread,
> Eternal sunshine settles on its head."

Yes! Eternal sunshine, the sunshine of God's truth, and grace, and love!

And now I turn from these more general thoughts, on which, perhaps, too much time has been spent, to the special considerations of this thrice joyful anniversary. Our Blessed Lord Himself has taught us, that "of the abundance of the heart the mouth speaketh." And yet, there are and there must be in every life, times and occasions, when because of the very abundance of the heart the lips are almost sealed; when because of personal relations not to be brought into the light of "garish day," the loving thought, the earnest prayer, even the 'strong conviction, take refuge in the inmost shrine of one's own being, and in "expressive silence muse the praise" that the tongue scarce dares to trust itself to utter. Need I tell you, dear Brethren, how this presses upon me to-day? Need I say that this very thing makes it harder for me to speak to you fit words, than it might be to many another?

May I venture just here to say, that as I stand here, thoughts and memories of many years come back to me, memories of far distant days when I was numbered among the clergy of this favored region; memories, shadowed indeed, but still always bright, of the "green pastures" and the "waters of quietness," in and beside which my lot was cast in my first and only parish. Of all the brethren who in those days — fifty years ago — dwelt here in good and joyful unity, one only, I think, remains among you, the honoured and beloved President of the Standing Committee of this Diocese — long may he be spared to you! Of the five who from this city and its immediate neighbourhood were called from time to time to the Episcopate, all but one are gone; gone

> "Like clouds that rake the mountain summits,
> Or waves that own no curbing hand;"

and that one cannot but say, what doubtless others are saying for him, "Superfluous lags the veteran on the stage." But enough, more than enough, of this. Your Diocese, brethren, and that Episcopate of a quarter of a century for which, to-day, we give God hearty thanks, and offer well-won congratulations to him who holds it, claim thought and word alike. Let that first word be what comes at once to mind and heart, " *Si monumentum quæris, circumspice.* "

One might almost have prophesied that the son of that great prelate whose name must be forever identified with the inception and prosecution of the work of Christian education for the daughters of the Church, would inaugurate his own Episcopate by following in such footsteps. And thus began those institutions, the crown of which is here in this Cathedral, lifting its "high piled mass" in its majesty and beauty, upon this "sovran hill ; " standing over against those halls of legislation, to bear continuous and unchanging witness to the great law of God, that "Righteousness exalteth a nation, but sin is a reproach to any people."

Shall I speak of other homes for the poor, the aged and the orphan elsewhere ? Of your vigorous missionary work, your communicants more than doubled, of all in short that not only tells of material progress, but how much more of that without which all material progress is less than nothing, growth in spiritual life and consecration to the Lord's great work for men? You know all this ; nay, more than this, you have shared in it ; you have helped it on — no man feels that this day more deeply than your Bishop — and on it God has poured out His blessing "like the dew of Hermon which fell upon the hill of Sion."

Nor need I, nor can I speak at length of work in other lands, or here at home outside your own Diocese, which enters into the story of the Church's life, and must ever find its record there. Of two things, however, I must make mention, brief and inadequate though it be ; first, of labours given to the Prayer Book and Hymnal of this Church, which the whole Church gratefully acknowledges ; and next, of that Chapel by the sea in a distant Diocese, which, consecrated by holiest memories of the departed and deepest benedictions of the living, stands like a lighthouse on a rock-bound shore, with its story of many a soul brought to safe anchorage in the peaceful haven of the one faith, and tells how rest and refreshment were found, not in idle days, but in ministries for our Lord and Master.

There are, however, things which have no record upon earth, and of which neither you nor I can ever know. Some one has well said that a Bishop's life is the loneliest life of any that are lived. Men are slow to understand this. They see a Bishop passing around his Diocese in the work of his visitations, always in the public eye; they see him in Synod surrounded by his clergy and his laity, and he seems to them never to be alone, always to be living in the full. ble̶a̶s̶i̶n̶g̶ .:"Right that

beats upon a throne," so that loneliness seems to them the one thing that
cannot be asserted of his life. And yet, as there is no loneliness like
that of a stranger in the throng of a crowded city, so it is here; the loneliness of a responsibility which none can share; of a knowledge which
must rest with him alone; of arriving at decisions in regard to which no
counsel can be sought but that which he seeks on his knees in the soli-
tude of his closet; of anxieties which must be kept in his own bosom; of
sleepless hours around which gather, in thick array, doubts and difficulties that crush him to the earth. "Who is weak and he is not weak?
Who is offended and he burns not?" Think of these things, dear brethren, and let them enter into your prayers, to-day and ever; for him who
is set over you in the Lord to be your servant for his Master's sake.

And now, were I asked to sum up in fewest words the brilliant record
of the quarter of a century for which we here and now thank Him to
whom all such thanksgivings should ascend, do I need, or can I find,
better words than those which form my text: "In returning and rest ye
shall be saved, in quietness and confidence shall be your strength?" Have
you not seen, ever, the "returning" in the proclamation of the one
Catholic and apostolic faith, and in the recurrence to the "old paths" trod
by the feet of saints and martyrs, the "rest" that is not the rest of sloth
and ·inactivity, but of patient continuance in well-doing; the "quietness" that is not the slumber of self-indulgent ease, but of calm and persistent labour; the confidence "that is not the confidence of self-sufficient
reliance, but of trust in Him, by whom and in whom we can accomplish
all things; and have not all these brought to you a "safety" that can
come only from Him who "maketh us to dwell in safety," and a "strength"
that can only enable us to be "strong in the Lord and in the power of
His might." I take you, brethren, to record this day that herein you
have found "safety" and "strength," the "safety" of the rock that cannot be shaken, the "strength" of Him without whom "nothing is strong,
nothing is holy." And I pray God to grant that these blessings may
abound to you more and more; that your honoured Bishop may be spared
to witness the jubilee year of his consecration, and that then those of
you who may see, what I and many who are here to-day shall not see,
may say with hearts as full as are ours to-day: "This shall be my rest
forever; here will I dwell, for I have a delight therein; I will deck her
priests with health, and her saints shall rejoice and sing, there shall I
make the horn of David to flourish; I have ordained a lantern for mine
anointed."

ANNIVERSARY ADDRESSES.

CONGRATULATORY ADDRESSES.

To the Right Reverend WM. CROSWELL DOANE, *D. D., LL. D., Bishop of Albany :*

Reverend Father in God — It is much to be regretted that the honoured President of our Standing Committee could not speak to you to-day in person; but his words are from his full heart and are the adopted words of the whole committee.

On the celebration of the Twenty-fifth Anniversary of your Consecration to the Episcopate, the Standing Committee of the Diocese of Albany, with reverence and love, offer their hearty congratulations, joined with the devout wish, that God may continue to bless, for years to come as in years past, your zealous and active endeavours to feed and tend the flock committed to your spiritual charge.

We would forego the words of eulogy as unfitted to the time and place and refer to the public documents of the Church to attest the wisdom, vigour and efficiency with which you have administered the affairs of this Diocese. You have founded St. Agnes's School — a school established not simply for the mental and æsthetic training of girls, but for the culture of the nobler elements of Christian character and virtuous womanhood. You have founded the Child's Hospital, St. Margaret's Home for Babies, the St. Christina Home at Saratoga, the Sisterhood of the Holy Child Jesus, and fostered from its beginning the Orphan House of the Holy Saviour in Cooperstown. To devise such peculiar institutions of education and of charity needs a man of wise forethought, generous feelings, delicate sensibility, and keen sympathy with acute and helpless suffering, and moved, by the principle of obedience and the impulse of love, to feed the lambs of the flock.

One of the distinguishing features which mark, Reverend Father in God, your supervision and care of this Diocese, is the missionary spirit, which is shown in the zealous and liberal efforts to preach the Gospel and administer the Holy Sacraments in every part of the territory belonging to your spiritual charge. Our missionary enterprise and success must be attributed, under God's blessing, in a great measure to your own faithful efforts, labours and importunity in the cause of the *Divine Master* and *His Church*. The number of our communicants in 1869 was less than eight thousand, and now is close to twenty tho▓▓▓▓▓▓▓▓▓▓▓▓

symbolize the strength of the missionary activity among Clergy and
Laity, which has been fostered and maintained through your own personal
influence and the prudent appropriation of funds placed at the disposal
of our Board of Missions.

By a wise and vigorous yet liberal policy, and with your unwearied
and patient efforts "to maintain and set forward quietness, love and
peace among all men," you have protected this Diocese against the mis-
chiefs of factious partisanship. A spirit of good will pervades the
Diocese and secures unity of will and action in our counsels and plans,
and this agreeably to the Divine promise: "In quietness and confidence
has been our strength."

The Cathedral of All Saints with its Chapter-House will be the lasting
memorial of your own zealous devotion to the interests of our blessed
Lord's glory and truth, and the evidence of the love and reverence of
"the faithful," who have helped to carry out your pious wishes and bold
plans. The idea of building a Cathedral was the bright and glorious
conception of genius, inspired by a holy faith, and accomplished by fervent, earnest prayer and patient labours. Here we may recall to mind
the incident that happened at Capernaum and is recorded by St. Luke :
"A certain centurion's servant who was dear unto him, was sick and
ready to die. And when he heard of Jesus he sent unto Him the elders
of the Jews, beseeching Him that He would come and heal his servant.
And when they came to Jesus, they besought Him instantly, saying,
That he was worthy for whom He should do this; for he loveth our
nation and he hath built us a synagogue. Then went Jesus with them —
And they that were sent, returning to the house, found the servant whole
that had been sick."

And now, much loved and revered Bishop, we add our sincere wish
and earnest prayer that the Diocese of Albany for years to come may
reap the benefits of your faithful pastoral care, that as your days so may
your strength be, that with those that wait upon the Lord you may renew
your strength, and when human labours are finished and "the Chief Shepherd shall appear, you may receive a crown of glory that fadeth not
away," and then with all the blessed Saints, Confessors and Martyrs may
take forever your part in the active service of praise and adoration before
the throne of God and of the Lamb.

J. IRELAND TUCKER, *President,*

F. M. COOKSON, *Secretary,*

W. L. ROBBINS,

JAMES CAIRD,

N. B. SQUIRES,

HENRY S. WYNKOOP,

JOHN I. THOMPSON,

J. H. VAN ANTWERP,

Standing Committee of the Diocese of Albany.

CONGRATULATORY ADDRESS IN BEHALF OF THE BOARD OF MISSIONS.
By the Rev. WALTON W. BATTERSHALL, D. D., Rector of St. Peter's Church,
Albany.

Reverend Father in God — In behalf of the Board of Missions of the Diocese of Albany, I have the honour to present you congratulations on this Twenty-fifth Anniversary of your Consecration to the Episcopate.

The congratulations of a beloved child have a peculiar warmth and tenderness. They touch the heart of a father like the stroke of a musician who knows and loves his instrument. I am persuaded that no words of affection and gratitude uttered in this high solemnity can be dearer to you than those which come from the organization which represents the most distinctive and important work in the Diocese; a work which, amid the manifold cares and labours of your Episcopate, has claimed and received a large share of your anxiety and prayer and toil.

When, twenty-five years ago, the Missionary Convocation of Northern New York was created the Diocese of Albany, the chief fact that suggested and justified the creation was the vast area and the large enterprise of the mission work within the territory that was then severed from the mother Diocese. The fact, like all facts, became a force. It defined at once the necessity of the creation and the distinctive character of the new Diocese.

It was a bold step, a venture of faith, to cut out of the great Diocese of New York its chief missionary field, and make it an independent jurisdiction, which must henceforth find within itself its sources of organic life and development. But the Faith was the child as well as the mother of works ; and the result justified the venture. The Northern Convocation, under the fostering care of the illustrious Bishop which it had given to the Diocese, had been trained to missionary zeal and sacrifice, and the first act of its diocesan life was to enlarge and organize the missionary work within its borders.

In the Second Convention of the Diocese of Albany, held September 29, 1869, the committee, which was the precursor of the present Board of Missions, reported that one-half of the eighty clergymen belonging to the Diocese were in part dependent on the Missionary Fund, and announced for the next conventional year appropriations to the diocesan missions on the scale of $10,000. At the very start, the new Diocese struck a high note in its missionary work, so high that, until recently, it has served as the keynote of its missionary history. For all this there was required a certain audacity of faith, which by God's grace, the Diocese caught from him who, for the first time, presided at its councils.

With no discounted phrases, the Board of Missions, in its congratulation, recognizes the wisdom and energy of organization with which you have conducted the mission work of the Diocese. But there are more

intimate and sacred aspects of that work, which must needs lie closer to
the heart of one who, like yourself, feels the spiritual fatherhood of the
office which he bears in the Church of God.   I speak for the sixty-five
missionaries who are toiling in the ninety-five mission stations of the
Diocese to-day.   They would not thank me, and I would represent them
untruly, if I should try to exploit the peculiar hardship of their work.
Some of them have the honours and the trained power which the veteran
wins, but most of them are in the flush of young life, with its high
visions and ardent consecrations, and they feel 'with the prophet that
"it is good for a man that he bear the yoke in his youth."   They understand that the yoke means the putting forth of strength and the discipline of strength.   The grace of the dear Name for whom it is borne
makes it easy.   But it is something to a missionary that he feels between
his neck and the yoke the strong hand of his Bishop.   These twenty-five
years I do not think that you have ever withheld that hand.   As chief
missionary of the Diocese you have come in close and sympathetic contact with its mission clergy.   You have celebrated at their altars, you
have sat with them at their firesides, you have entered into their cares,
you have advised with them in their perplexities, you have known what
it means when a deacon or priest tries to build up the Church, or keep it
from decay, in a scattered community, where the tides of life move slug-
gishly, where resources are slender and friends are few, where the Church
with no historic or social prestige, with no splendor of shrine or ritual,
must make and maintain its foothold amid prejudice and indifference,
and with naked hands do its spiritual errand.

Those to whom the Church has intrusted this service (and they are
the majority of the clergy of your Diocese), have been held close to your
heart.   From the nature of the case, the personnel changes,— changes
only too rapidly ; but whatever the enlistments or the promotions, the
mission corps of your clergy have felt your sympathy, your leadership,
and have caught the contagion of your faith and courage.

In behalf of them, as in behalf of the organization which is charged
with the maintenance of their work, I tender you affectionate congratulations on this completion of a quarter of a century of Episcopal toil and
fruitage.

May God continue to prosper you, give you joy in your work, and
multiply its immortal fruitions.

FROM THE MEMORIAL COMMITTEE OF THE DIOCESAN CONVENTION.

By the Rev. CHARLES S. OLMSTED.

Reverend Father in God—The Committee on the Due Observance of the Twenty-fifth Anniversary of your Episcopal Consecration, salute you in the Kingdom and Patience of Jesus Christ.

We share with you in the memories; we rejoice with you in the hopes of this day. We gather with you the blossoms that these full and plenteous years so richly show.

A fitting symbol of this day would be a mirror, which should retain all the forms that ever passed before it in these twenty-five years, and show them at one glance to every beholder. The past is beautiful; much more may the future be!

Long may you live to enjoy the fruits of your labours here! Great may your recompense be when the bird of time shall fold her wings, and perch upon the rock eternity.

CHARLES S. OLMSTED,
For the Committee.

FEAST OF THE PURIFICATION, B. V. M., A. D., 1894. DIOCESE OF ALBANY.

FROM THE CHURCH UNIVERSITY BOARD OF REGENTS.

By the Rev. ELIPHALET NOTT POTTER, D. D., LL. D.. D. C. L.

To the Rt. Rev. Dr. WILLIAM CROSWELL DOANE, *Bishop of Albany:*
THE FEAST OF THE PURIFICATION, *Feb.* 2, A. D. 1894.

Reverend Father in God— On this auspicious day, and as connected with the College and University work of the Church, we feel that the anniversary would be indeed incomplete without cordial reference (though necessarily brief and inadequate) to your services for the cause of education; not only as a Regent and Vice-Chancellor of the University of the State of New York, not only as the founder, the life and the soul of St. Agnes' School, and the President of the Society for the Home Study of the Holy Scriptures; but also as an Honorary Chancellor and Visitor of Hobart College, and as the Chairman of the Church University Board of Regents.

In the words of the Hebrew Poet :

Blessed is the man that walketh not in the counsel of the ungodly, nor standeth in the way of sinners, nor sitteth in the seat of the scornful.*

---

* This is written in the Address and was read by Dr. Pott

If this Divine Beatitude (Ps. 1: 1) is appropriate, so in view of your exaltation of the Churchly home as the foundation of Christian Education, and of your inscription of Gladstone's words on duty over the great fire-place of your school, the lines of the modern bard seem no less applicable to you as one who is

> " The gladdener of ten thousand hearths,
>   The idol of his own."

For the educational cause, then, as well as for your Diocesan and other duties, we of the Church College and University, pray that there may be granted unto you length of days with all the good gifts of God.

Faithfully yours,

ELIPHALET NOTT POTTER,

*President of Hobart College, Geneva, N. Y., and Advocate-Regent
of the Church University Board of Regents.*

{ SEAL OF }
{ HOBART }
{ COLLEGE. }

FROM THE GENERAL CHAPTER OF THE CATHEDRAL OF ALL SAINTS, ALBANY.

By the Rev. J. D. MORRISON, D. D., LL. D.

Reverend Father in God—I have the honour to present to you the greeting of the General Chapter of the Cathedral of the Diocese of Albany on this Twenty-fifth Anniversary of your Consecration as Bishop of Albany. A quarter of a century is a long span in the life of man. If taken from our prime it necessarily represents the period, humanly speaking, of most fruitful activity, when hope, courage and energy have been at their best, and the longing and ambition to accomplish great things have been accompanied by powers capable of grand achievements. It is such a period in your career that we look back upon to-day with sympathetic interest, and loving appreciation. The General Chapter of this Cathedral occupies a position which enables it to know your record intimately, and to measure with some degree of accuracy the results of those incessant labours which have marked your fruitful Episcopate, for it is composed of elements which represent very widely the Church life of this Diocese, and it stands in corporate relation to this great Cathedral Institution in which it has been your aim to sum up the powers and energies of the Diocese in the sense in which the heart may be said to sum up the life of the human frame. Many of the members of this Chapter have been labouring under your direction and have been associated with you in our Diocesan work during the whole or the greater part of those twenty-five years that you have stood here in your lot as the Watchman and Ruler of the Church. They have watched with sympathetic eye your arduous endeavours, they have known something of your burdens although carried always with severe and uncomplaining patience, they have admired and wondered at your invincible courage and unflagging perseverance, and have rejoiced as they saw you steadily attaining step by step to that high mark which your devotion to the Church had set before you.

Time would not permit me even to mention that long honour roll of good deeds which you have so happily accomplished in your career as Bishop of Albany, much less to dwell on the circumstances which have attended these achievements; and therefore of your labours as a Christian student, or as a man of affairs battling in the front rank of good citizens for the highest interests of the commonwealth, your service as the most zealous of missionaries, your record as a Bishop, whether wisely and faithfully administering the weighty, delicate and most difficult duties of the Diocese, or serving the Church at large with a statesman-like grasp of principles, with intense sympathy for every progressive movement, yet with a loyal conservatism to Catholic traditions, of these things I cannot speak. And of the great work with which this General Chapter is connected, the crown of your many labours, what need I say but this: *Si queris monumentum circumspice.* Yes, let the great educational establishment, the noble works of mercy, the grand temple of worship, the foundations of theological learning and of evangelical activity, here planted by your wisdom, your sacrifice and toil, attest with a silent eloquence more impressive than any living voice how wonderfully you have carried out the principle of the conservation of energy, not permitting it to evaporate in splendid but idle dreams, or to spend itself in fervid but fruitless enthusiasms, but compelling it to crystallize in noble and enduring forms, which shall testify from generation to generation for the comfort of the faithful and to the confusion of the infidel, that the Church of God is here and has come to stay. If we are right when we count them worthy of honour who have dared to attempt great things for the glory of God and the good of their fellow men, even when their efforts have been failures, how great should be our felicitation when we can point to one who has not only toiled manfully but triumphed gloriously, one whose bitter self-denial and unflinching effort have borne abundant fruit.

It is, sir, with that knowledge that the General Chapter of this Cathedral tenders to you to-day its sympathetic congratulations.

Because during these twenty-five years you have magnified your office as a Bishop in the Church of God, using to the full your splendid energies and endowments, at whatever personal cost, to   then and to set forward the Church, both within and beyond this Diocese; because your example has been always a stimulus and an encouragement to every willing worker, and a silent but stinging reproach to every selfish, slothful soul; because you have been a wise master-builder, laying, with statesmanlike sagacity, foundations of Church life which will endure for many generations; because of your labours as a Christian scholar; because of your record as one of the foremost citizens of the State; and lastly, because of your character as a man, a man whose heart harbours no malice, a man always most generous to the bitterest opponent, a man with a tender heart and an open hand for any one in trouble, a man whose fault it is to possess a charity which can believe evil of nobody, and a magnanimity which instinctively defends the party which seems weak and forlorn; we salute you with glad heart, Bishop, statesman, scholar, friend. We wish you many coming years of happy usefulness and fruitful administration. We invoke on you that blessing which maketh truly rich and addeth no sorrow thereto, and for this great Cathedral with the institutions clustered about it we turn to our Psalter for a benediction:

"O pray for the peace of Jerusalem; they shall prosper that love thee. Peace be within thy walls, and plenteousness within thy palaces."

"For my brethren and companions' sakes I will wish thee prosperity. Yea, because of the house of the Lord our God I will seek to do thee good."

FROM THE CHAPTER OF THE CATHEDRAL OF ALL SAINTS, ALBANY.

By the Rev. WILFORD L. ROBBINS, D. D., DEAN.

Reverend Father in God—The closer and more intimate relations of life refuse to lend themselves readily to exigencies of public speech. In standing here to-day, as representative of the Cathedral Chapter, to convey to you our heartfelt congratulation on this the Twenty-fifth Anniversary of your Consecration, I feel that it were easier for me to touch upon any other aspect of your great work for the Church than that which centres more exclusively in the Cathedral. Something of the sacredness of the family inheres in the confidence, the affection, the absolute unanimity of purpose, which has always characterized the relation subsisting between the Cathedral Chapter and you, its Bishop and Presiding Officer. What words, then, can adequately express the sentiment of the Chapter when you are honoured, and receive in some slight degree the acknowledgment of all that your Episcopate has meant to the American Church? Truly, congratulation signifies to us all that the derivation of the word suggests. We *rejoice with you,* for your joys are ours.

In one special regard the Chapter is perhaps better fitted than others to bear testimony to-day. Through the searching test of more than twenty years' experience, its own life and work have demonstrated the far-seeing wisdom which laid the foundations of the Cathedral and framed its Constitution. This work certainly cannot be deemed among the less important accomplishments of the first Bishop of Albany. At a time when the American Church is confronting those problems which always arise, as an organization passes from the simpler methods of its initial work to the greater complexity involved in larger borders and more manifold activities, the question of the Cathedral system must become of most practical import. The dignity of the Episcopal office, after the first barren appointments of a missionary outpost have given place to the usages of an established institution, demands a central Church, rising above mere parochial obligation, which shall be the ecclesiastical home of the Bishop. Diocesan interests, as the differentiation of growth becomes more marked, require the centralizing agency of a Cathedral foundation.

But who shall solve the difficulty of a sympathetic adaptation of venerable traditions to modern needs? Who shall guard us against those crude essays at novelty inspired by the very youth and inexperience of the land in which we live? Who shall balance with nice discrimination the prerogatives which safeguard the Bishop's due influence, with that scope for free and independent work requisite if we expect fruitful results from those holding subordinate positions? We might well have asked these questions in a spirit nigh unto despair, had not the Cathedral legislation, of which we have had experience, answered them for us beyond a peradventure. The influence thus exerted upon the Church at large will become increasingly evident as the years roll on. The irresistible argument of *success* puts a stop to all possible cavil.

Nor can one resist reference to that quality which has brightened the darkest day, and surmounted the most threatening obstacles, namely, the unfailing hopefulness and courage of him who took the great task in hand. Thankful for confidence and sympathy, yet if these ever seemed for a moment to fail, then one man could bear the burden of responsibility, and that without a tremor. Those who are privileged to come into contact with so rare and beautiful an assurance of hope, ought to be strengthened and bettered their life through, by the example.

We do not live in an era of great architecture. Men build in these days rather with the head than with the heart. However exquisite the finish, however stately the proportions, there is commonly an absence in our churches of that subtle spirit of devotion which makes the shrines of another time redolent with every prayerful impulse. The Cathedral of All Saints, even in its present unfinished state, stands as one of the few instances in this country of a great and truly religious building. All praise to the technical skill of the architect, and to the generosity of numerous benefactors — a vast sum of self-denial on the part of humble folk, as well as munificence on the part of others, is enwrought in the structure. But above all else it bears the impress of one man's devotion. If its memorials render it even now in its youth venerable with sweet associations; if its rugged honesty puts to shame the shallow pretentiousness which disfigures too much of our art; if the rich symbolism of its pictured glass and carving turn the thought heavenward; these all with one voice bear record that this is no product of a committee's brain or of the mechanical skill of the handicraftsman, but rather the emanation of a great man's heart, enriched by sympathy with what is noblest and best in the past as well as the present.

To be the builder of the first American Cathedral worthy the name is no slight claim on the gratitude of coming generations.

But while thus recognizing the wide bearing of the Bishop's work on the American Church in its larger relations; while rendering him all honour in that he has instituted within the Diocese that which shall in years to come be its pride and glory — the Chapter of the Cathedral must e red tesunru at the last with lingering fondness to the thought of him who is in an especial way its own pastor and guide — and as such, with full heart, tender him its devotion, its respect and love.

FROM THE TRUSTEES OF THE CORNING FOUNDATION FOR CHRISTIAN WORK IN THE DIOCESE OF ALBANY.

By GEN. SELDEN E. MARVIN.

Dearly Beloved Bishop — The Trustees of the Corning Foundation desire to express their congratulations to you, upon this occasion of deep interest to all the varied interests and institutions of this great Diocese, and to bespeak for you all the honour, all the happiness that the accomplishment of such a work as is to-day presented throughout the Diocese can bring to any man.

It was certainly a most worthy choice of the Convention that elected you to the distinguished office of a Bishop in the Church of God — a choice that no one, we assume, would now wish to recall after a period of a quarter of a century of trial. The results following your administration of the Diocese of Albany are startling in their measure of importance and success, and beneficent in their relation and results to the Church. You have used your powers for the upbuilding of the Diocese in all the various means for Christian work and service. You fitly portrayed, in a few words, uttered in one of your Convention Addresses in the early years of the existence of the Diocese, the basis upon which success was to be built, when you said, "Work to me is not the necessity but the luxury of my life."

Our chief concern upon this occasion is with the institutions of learning and mercy which have grown up amongst us. The Corning Foundation for Christian Work in the Diocese of Albany was incorporated by an act of the Legislature in 1873. Through your clear and wise presentation of the need of a school for the Christian education of girls to Mr. Erastus Corning, his intelligent and comprehensive mind appreciating the benefits, purchased the land upon which the buildings of St. Agnes' School, the Child's Hospital and St. Margaret's Home now stand, upon which the foundation is laid for the Graduates' Hall, and upon which a Sisters' House for the Sisterhood of the Holy Child Jesus, will in time be built. The name of Mr. Corning will be indissolubly associated with all this work through the years to come, as will that of his son, in the magnificent gift of the land upon which this Cathedral stands. All honour to such men who in their life-time give such gifts and are enabled to enjoy the fruits and benefits of their giving.

St. Agnes' School, on the Corning foundation, was opened in 1870 Although it had its birth in a small house on Columbia Place, it started with the evidences of a future success, and we assume that you have not been disappointed in the results that have come from its administration during the years of its existence. It has sent out 340 graduates, while a still larger number have been added to those who have gone out from its precincts and are now fulfilling the obligations of womanhood in their respective homes. Its corps of teachers has always been of the very best, and every personal care and moral control has been exercised with clear and constant religious teaching and influence to mould the characters and shape the natures of the girls. Its commencements have been marked by an attractiveness of form and ceremonial which make a strong impression upon those fortunate in their ability to be present, and the addresses made on these occasions by yourself have left an impress upon all connected with the school that time will not efface; even more than this, upon the whole community who have been stirred by the grandeur and beauty of their composition, and the dignity and worth of their golden influence. They may properly be called the Mosaics of Fatherly Admonition and Advice.

The Child's Hospital was organized in 1876 and has supplied a greatly needed source of comfort and relief to afflicted and disabled children, who, without such treatment and care as are here given, might have grown up in a condition of deformity, weakness and incapacity for any active work. Now through the kind administration of the sisters

11

in charge, the skill of the physicians and surgeons, they are, in so far as is possible, relieved of their bodily ailments and disabilities, and fitted to go out into the world and take their share in its duties and responsibilities. The government of this institution reflects much credit upon all having to do with its management. It is a sweet and blessed charity and stirs the most sensitive and generous instincts of a common humanity in its favour and support. St. Margaret's Home is typical, in all its methods and ways, of the Child's Hospital, caring for much younger children, having its own governing body, and working to bring about the most favourable results through the kindly offices of the sisters in charge. St. Christina Home in Saratoga Springs is not only a rendezvous for the children during the summer season and a resort that furnishes them with a much needed change of air and scene, but is established as an Industrial School for girls, where, winter and summer, they are most carefully taught and trained. The beneficent results that have followed the labours of the faithful sisters of the Sisterhood of the Holy Child Jesus are the strongest attestation of the wisdom of the establishment of the Sisterhood as an auxiliary for the educational, spiritual, practical and parochial work of the Diocese. The outcome of their service is the highest testimonial to their value.

The teachers, the graduates and undergraduates of St. Agnes' School — those that have gone out from its doors without having taken the full course, the former inmates of the Child's Hospital, St. Margaret's and St. Christina Homes — the present inmates of these institutions — the sisters of the Sisterhood will ever hold in grateful and loving memory your noble, intelligent, sympathetic efforts in their behalf. It was your wise and sagacious judgment, your tender and loving nature, the highest and best of humanity's gifts as usurping so large a part of your being, that gave them birth and have carried them so successfully through all adversity to their present successful relation to the affairs of the world. These teachers, these girls, these children, these sisters will never fail to do you honour, to crown you with their rich blessings, and offer up their daily petitions to the throne on high for an increase of the abundant gifts conferred upon you, and for many years of a life of activity, the harvest of which shall be as fruitful as that which the records of a quarter of a century attest and which has won the approval of your fellow-workers.

FROM THE TEACHERS OF ST. AGNES' SCHOOL.
By the Rev. FREDERICK M. GRAY.

Reverend Father in God—It has been given to me to speak a word of loving congratulation in behalf of the teachers and others engaged in the work of St. Agnes' School. It has been already said here to-day, and fitly said, that words are too poor to express what is in our hearts on this happy anniversary. But, although words cannot express what is in our hearts to-day, we do desire to say how deeply and gratefully we appreciate the care and the wisdom which have guided us in our work, so often filled with perplexity and trial; the words of instruction and counsel which have been our support and inspiration; the courtesy, sympathy and kindness, which have been never-failing. We regard it a high privilege and honour to have a share with you, under your direction, in educating the children of the Church and of the school, in sound learning, in the ways of gracious, refined and high-minded womanhood, and in the wisdom which maketh wise unto salvation.

And we hope and trust that the years to come may be filled with the joy of success in all your undertakings, until the day when you shall be called to the light and the joy of the Life eternal.

CONGRATULATORY ADDRESS OF THE TRUSTEES OF THE ORPHAN HOUSE OF THE HOLY SAVIOUR, TO THE RIGHT REVEREND WILLIAM CROSWELL DOANE, D. D., (Oxon.), LL. D., (Cantab.), BISHOP OF ALBANY, ON THE TWENTY-FIFTH ANNIVERSARY OF HIS EPISCOPAL CONSECRATION.
By Mr. G. POMEROY KEESE.

Reverend Father in God — We, the Trustees of the Orphan House of the Holy Saviour, in Cooperstown, on this auspicious day of the Twenty-fifth Anniversary of your Episcopal Consecration, desire to extend to you our sincere and hearty congratulations.

We are grateful to you, Right Reverend Sir, for the kind interest you have shown toward the work of this Institution from the date of its foundation, early in your Episcopate; and for your fatherly sympathy with us in the many hours of anxiety which, from time to time, have shadowed our path.

We recall the many instances where you have come to our rescue, with gracious appeals to the faithful in our behalf, that have always brought to us the evident blessing of our Heavenly Father.

The two hands with which you have builded are Faith and Patience, by which, not the Orphan House of the Holy Saviour alone, but the work in general of this, your Diocese, has been supported.

Long may you be permitted to work with these hands of blessing!
Higher yet and higher, by your happy labours, with God's grace, may the
towers of our gladness rise! Long may it be ere the now purpling hues
of your life's golden daylight change to the tints of the Eventide!
February 2d.   Feast of the Purif. B. V. M., A. D. 1894.

> Susan Fenimore Cooper,
> Leslie Pell-Clarke,
> G. Pomeroy Keese,
> Wilson T. Bassett,
> A. Beekman Cox,
> J. Philip B. Pendleton,
> Walton W. Battershall,
> R. Herbert Gesner,
> Charles S. Olmsted.

From the Sisterhood of the Holy Child Jesus.
Read by the Rev. Thomas B. Fulcher.

Reverend Father in God — To the many tributes of reverent affection that have come to you to-day, the Sisters add a loving greeting
on behalf of themselves, their fellow-workers and the many children in
The Child's Hospital, St. Christina Home and St. Margaret's House.

It is with thankful hearts that on this Twenty-fifth Anniversary of your
Consecration, we realize how God has blessed the work that we have been
permitted to share with you. We acknowledge most gratefully for
nearly twenty-five hundred children, who during these years have been
committed to your fostering care, the benefits and blessings which they
have received through your untiring zeal, in upholding and sustaining,
by your godly counsel and influence, the various works of charity
through which these mercies have come to them.

The children who have already gone out from us to take their places
in the world would gladly come back, if it were possible, to express
again to-day as they have often done before, their grateful recognition of
all that they owe to you.

As in the past you have always been remembered in the daily prayers
of all our households, so will you be in the future, and may God grant
you a double portion of His Spirit in many more years of faithful labour
in His service.

The Rev. Canon Fulcher presented from the Faculty, the Graduates and Undergraduates of St. Agnes' School, a silver casket, in which were the following Addresses:

FROM THE GRADUATES OF ST. AGNES' SCHOOL.

Reverend Father in God — It is a great pleasure to me that I am called to be the voice through which on this day of days in your calendar, are to be uttered words of loving greeting by the children of St. Agnes School.

* Like the sunshine that warms many waters,
And gladdens them all on their way,
Is the love in the hearts of your daughters,
Who rise and salute you to-day.

We speak — there are hundreds of voices —
Yet one is the word on each tongue,
A word that loves, blesses, rejoices,
And crowns you with honours unsung.

We bless you, for lives deepened, brightened,
For strength, that *your* strength has made great,
For the darkness that *your* words have lightened,
And the crooked *your* hands have made straight.

And we pray that long years and unbroken
Their pages of life may unfold;
And the past be but promise and token
Of all that the future shall hold.

Fresh laurels be yours — honours newer —
And tributes and fame, by the way,
Yet Fortune can send nothing truer,
Than the love that we bear you to-day.

FROM THE UNDERGRADUATES OF ST. AGNES' SCHOOL.

OUR BISHOP.

† It seems but a fitting greeting,
On this anniversary year,
That a little gift of silver
Should come from your children here,
To you who so long have led us,
Tenderly on our way,
Whose love has ever been with us,
Helping us, day by day.

---

* Written by Mrs. Bessie Chandler Parker
† Written by Mary Chahoon, a pupil

'Twas a custom, quaint and poetic,
  They had in the olden time,
To add just a bit of silver
  In the casting of every chime,
Which, mixed with the baser metal,
  Gave a sweet tone to the bell,
A grander, fuller music,
  That listening hearts loved well.

We can wish you no honour greater
  Than comes with the work of your life,
Like Antaeus of old, you have risen
  Thrice stronger from every strife.
And in the years of the future,
  As in the years that are past,
May strength sufficient be given
  To labour to the last.

Our fondest love is but little,
  In that wealth which is yours, we know,
Yet the silver was never lost sight of
  In the chimes of long ago.
And from out the hearts of your children,
  Who know you and love you so well,
May there come to your life a sweetness
  As from silver once cast in each bell.

THE BISHOP'S REPLY.

At the close of the last address, the Bishop rising from his chair, under the evident pressure of intense feeling, walked hurriedly into the pulpit with the silver casket, and the printed order of services, and said, in substance:

And, after all this, it is printed here " that the Bishop is to reply," and what can he say, unless it be " Pity me, O my friends!"

There are moments which come into every man's life when the deepest feelings of his heart and the highest reasonings of his mind come together and accept as absolutely true that sublime statement of the Preacher in the Book Ecclesiastes, "God is in heaven, and thou upon earth; therefore let thy words be few." And because I stand here to-day before God in Heaven, in the presence of Him who is my Father and my Saviour and is to be my Judge, and because I know how much of me is on the earth; it must be that my words shall be few, asking first of all, of Him who has honoured and permitted me to be His servant now for five and twenty years, who knows the service of my Bishopric better even than I know it, in all its shallowness and shortcomings,— that He will forgive it for His dear Love's sake, that He will accept it for my Master's sake, and that He will pardon His servant in it all.

You, dear friends who are here to-day, know *something* at least, of what lays itself upon my heart to crush the fragrance out, of its most inmost love and feelings. Yet even *you* do not know it all,— that my beloved brother Bishops are here to-day, coming at such a time and from such distances, just to be gracious and generous and kind to me; that I have been privileged to have before my eyes the sight, and in my ears the sound, of the form and the voice of the man who is more to me than any other man in all the world, my more than brother, my father, my beloved Presiding Bishop; that my own dear brethren, clerical and lay, have come to me in such goodly numbers; that such words have been spoken, as you know perfectly well, dear brothers, no man *can* deserve, just as well as I know that I *do* not deserve them; that messages have come to me by letter and by telegram and by word of mouth from little children,— I do not know what is in here (indicating the silver casket from St. Agnes' School), and I do ̶̶̶̶̶̶̶̶̶̶̶̶̶̶̶̶̶̶̶̶̶̶̶̶ that have been spoken here,—but in other ways, from little children in Sunday Schools, from my own dear daughters of St. Agnes scattered far away, (one, dear Bishop Hare, from Rosebud in South Dakota only yesterday); that messages have come from a young coloured girl in Troy, dead since, and dying with a kindly word of blessing and of interest upon her lips for me; that all this has come to me, besides what you have heard and seen; greetings from those who are my associates not merely in Church work, and in Diocesan work, and in things that lie under our heart and eye, but from my associates in work outside the Diocese, in the Church and in the State:—surely you will realize that I must be well-nigh speechless!

Well, I cannot say, dear friends, that you have made me believe the words that have been spoken, because I know they are *not* true, but you have made me willing gratefully and humbly to accept them, because the dear friends who have written and spoken them believe them to be true.

And so, humbled and lifted up at once, I stand here with infinite thankfulness for the one thing which, everybody must know, has been the single secret and spring of whatsoever success Almighty God has wrought out through me, namely, the wonderful and unutterable graciousness and generosity of the loyalty and the love that have been about me, at every turn. Perhaps the gift of leadership in me, certainly the gift of love from you; this is the whole story.

As I look back to-day and recall the dear names of the old priests and the old laymen — so few of them are left — so freshly is the memory of every one of them left in my own heart and mind—as I recall, not merely those who bore with me the first burden and brunt of the Episcopate, but as I look about me here and see the priests and the laymen, yes, and the women and children, who have been the makers of this Diocese — I know, dear friends, that if it had not been for all the loyalty and all the love and all the patience which have borne with the impatience and the impetuosity, that years of discipline have somewhat chastened and controlled, I should long since have broken my head against stone walls of impossibility, and my heart against stonier walls of failure. "*Non mihi, Domine,*" and you will want me also to say "*Non nobis, Domine,*" neither to me, nor to us, but to God only, be the praise.

For when the whole is fully revealed, the very men that have told a part of the story to-day have borne witness, in the words that they have spoken, and the works that they have helped me to do, that neither I, nor any other man on earth, single-handed and alone, nay, not I nor any other man on earth, who was not hundred-handed, like Briareus of old, could have even touched the work that Almighty God has permitted you and me, *together*, to do.

And so, as I said to you at first, humbly and all unworthily, I am ready, dear friends, because of the truthfulness of the hearts of the men and the women who have written and spoken all these words, and of the men and the women that are gathered about me now, to accept all the graciousness and kindliness and devotion, even though it be without measure and beyond merit.   And I take it all, dear friends, only as the stimulus and the pledge for better services and richer sacrifices, in whatever days of work there may be left to us; and in the humble consciousness that under all and after all and through all, there is but One Who is the Cornerstone and the Master Builder and the Temple and the Capstone all in one, and that is He, whom you and I are set to love and serve, the Lord and Saviour Jesus Christ.

And unto Him, One with the Father and the Holy Spirit, Three sacred Persons and One only and Eternal God, be evermore ascribed all Glory and all Praise.   Amen.

FROM THE BISHOP'S ANNUAL CONVENTION ADDRESS.*

There is a certain element of likeness to the old god Janus, in my position here to-day, two-faced, that he might look two ways. I must, without the advantage of his facial construction, imitate his attitude. The future I am ready to face, with eye that looks both up and on; but my thoughts look chiefly backward, because at any twenty-fifth anniversary the past tense is so much longer than the future.

Naturally and almost necessarily then, what I have to say this year takes the past tense and the historical tone. The very changes that have taken place remind me, that there are few in the Convention now, to whom the story of the earlier years of our Diocesan life is in the least familiar. And this anniversary makes the fit time for gathering, in a shape that may be preserved, some of the salient points. I should be glad enough to leave the duty to other hands, but no one knows the facts as I do, and they are of interest to us in this great reunion, when we are thinking, as people do round the home-hearth at family gatherings, about the mercies and the memories of the household.

As I came to make ready for the solemnities of our commemoration, I opened instinctively the journal of our Primary Convention in which I sat, as you are sitting now, to share the counsels and help in the organization of the Diocese, with little idea that I was to be set as leader in the work which lay before us then. I had as little thought of the event, as desire for it. And when it came — the news brought to me in my library (where I had gone during the counting of the last ballot) by my father's old and faithful servant Michael — I took the service up with the purpose in my heart to love it and to cherish it "till death us should part."

I leave others to say what He has wrought, through labours abundant though unworthy, with just the single correction, needful when we stand, living or dead, before the partial judgment of too generous friends, that I am more concerned to-day with confessions than with congratulations, with gratitude than with praise; that I pray God to avert the reversal of your estimate; to make me humble and to pardon

---

* This portion of the Bishop's Address which was delivered on the eve of the festival, being the night of the meeting of the adjourned Convention, is printed here as part of the recollections of the twenty-five years of his Episcopate.

the shortcomings; to bless the host of brethren and friends who have been so loyal and so loving to me ; to forgive the secret sins known only to me and to Him; to pledge us for whatever time of work remains, to greater sacrifices and truer service : and, — as I prayed that night when I stood before the Primary Convention of the Diocese,— to give us and to give to those who have passed from labour to rest, some part of the "crown of glory that fadeth not away," in the day when "the chief Shepherd shall appear."

As I read down the list of the one hundred and thirty names which signed the solemn testimonial that night in St. Peter's Church, I am struck with the fact that of the fifty-five clerical signers (out of sixty-eight who were present) thirty-two are still living, only nine of whom are in the Diocese: Carey, Chapman, Tucker, Reese, Nichols, Mulford, Tibbits, Stewart and myself; a strong reminder of the changes and chances of this mortal life, and a still sadder reminder of the changes in the life of the clergy.

Of the seventy-five laymen (out of one hundred and twenty-five present) who signed the testimonial, twenty-seven are still living, and in the Diocese; of whom at least fourteen are either members of this Convention to-day, or are still actively connected with the work of the Diocese: Van Antwerp, Earle, Keese, Clarkson, Gibson, Higgins, Gibbons, Burhans, Wade, Bagley, Van Voast, Cushney and Taylor. Of the older laymen of the Convention, beside those who signed the testimonial, there are also still living and still in active relations to the Church in the Diocese: Messrs. Van Vorst and Jackson, of Schenectady ; W. Maxwell Reid, of Amsterdam; Fitch, of Prattsville; W. J. Thompson, of Unadilla; George S. Weaver, of Albany; Kemp and Squires, of Troy ; Nichols, of Athens; Pine, of Herkimer; Darby, of Cairo ; Birdsall, of Otego; Averell, of Ogdensburgh; Finch, of Glens Falls ; Williams, of Salem; Wynkoop, of Kinderhook ; while the good names are still good in the second generation, of Tillinghast, Burhans, Chadwick, Kellogg, McNeil, Prout, Snyder, Mann, Booth, McDougall, Rockwell, Houghton and Beach. And we have given to the Episcopate of the American Church five Bishops, of whom Robertson and Brown are dead, and Tuttle, Rulison and myself still working in the Office.

Of my six consecrators, only two are living, the two who presented me to the Bishop that day, the Bishops of Maine and Long Island.

The problem which confronted the Bishop of this Diocese at the beginning was not an easy one ; a large missionary district, with no colouring in it of romance, and with only two strong central cities from which means could be had for the sinews of war; not a penny of endowment, except, in small part, for the Episcopate itself; and an utter absence anywhere of that large energy and ⬛⬛⬛⬛⬛⬛ prise, which the great cities give to men and ⬛⬛⬛⬛

rush and whirl of worldliness having in it an impulse, when it is caught and consecrated — like the water power of Niagara turned into electric dynamos — which gives such splendid impetus to Christian work. And there was the kind of pride in traditional uses, and of contentment with the general condition of things, which it is not pleasant to stir up, and which is not always pleasant when it is waked up. Perhaps God put the problem before me, because enthusiasm and sanguineness are more likely to try to solve such difficulties, than experience and caution.

I prefer to let the aim and the idea of the Episcopate as I have held them speak for themselves in the outcome of these five and twenty years of mutual work. I only ask you to interpret them in the light of these two thoughts which seem to me essentially connected with the office of a Bishop: First, in its outward bearing, the building up of a strong centre for unity and work; and next the strengthening and extending of the Church, within the borders of the Diocese for which we are first responsible to God. Both of these are subordinate, and in my judgment they ought to be, to the duty which a Bishop owes to the Church of God. To keep the proper balance among these three demanding duties must be the most difficult effort of a Bishop's life, and naturally must be the point of it, where he is most exposed to criticism and misunderstanding.

It is quite natural, and one of the things which we are set to bear, that somebody will think in each of these relations that too much thought and time are given to the other two. I only ask, not for myself but for those who are working with me in the great brotherhood of the Episcopate and for whosoever shall come after me, that with whatever kindly judgment may be made of many human failures and shortcomings and misjudgments, it will not be forgotten, that, perhaps, what seems neglect in one department, may only mean the effort, which exceeds all human strength, to do the duties of the other two.

The history of this Diocese antedates its diocesan existence. Years ago, long before I ever came to be a worker in this part of the Church of Christ, the men who were at work here were forced, by their own earnest spirit of service, by their longing to extend the Church, and by their remoteness from the See City, to organize what was known as "the Missionary Convocation of Northern New York." It came very near doing us the bad turn of fastening its admirable, descriptive, Convocational title, as our geographical Diocesan name. Under God, we owe our happy escape from that, to the brightness and the Churchly spirit of the Hon. F. James Fitch, a deputy from Catskill in the Primary Convention, whose "argument to the absurd" proposing for accuracy's sake, the name of "the Diocese of Rouse's Point and Catskill," turned the scale. But the character of the Diocese was really fixed and set, by the tone and temper of the men who began and carried on the work of the Convocation of

Northern New York. It had taken its stamp of Churchmanship, from its Bishop when he was Rector of St. Peter's, Albany, from my beloved friend and more than brother, the Bishop of Connecticut, when he was Rector of St. George's, Schenectady, from Payne, Brown, Tucker, Bostwick, Nicholls, Carey, Hughes and the other noble Priests, who loved the Church, and believed in it, as men ought to, who say the Creed. And the Diocese grew out of it, "after *its* kind." I thank God, that since it pleased Him to call me to the labours and cares of the Episcopate, He let me "enter upon their labours," and gave me such men as they were, as some of them, thank God, still are, to be "my fellow workers unto the Kingdom of God."

As I re-read the sermons preached by the venerable Bishop of New York, and by the venerable Rector of St. Paul's Church, Troy, at the Primary Convention which elected me, and at the first Convention over which I presided, I am struck with the similarity of their insistence upon the great duty of upholding the Church as a Divine Institution duly organized, and of the positive teaching of doctrine.

Listen to the old Bishop's earnest words :

"Positive teaching and positive work, organized work, systematic work, permanent institutions, associated labour on the principle of absolute self-consecration for Christ's sake, in a Body having corporate life, capable of much extension and wide ramification, fitted for all works of piety and charity; among others, for Christian education on sound principles. These means, steadily and faithfully employed, in humble dependence upon the assistance of the Blessed Spirit, in pure, loving devotion to our dear Lord and Saviour, will make you and your Church ' strong in the Lord and in the power of His might.'" And again : "The faith of God standeth sure. It is not matter of opinion. It is not left to cunning argumentation. By this appeal to the unquestionable facts of primitive faith and practice, the truth of God in Holy Scripture is effectually protected from modern glosses and false interpretations. Every great and vital truth is taken out of the province of mere opinion, and carried over into the domain of absolute fact. There remains not a shadow of uncertainty as to what we are to believe or what we are to do." So far the Bishop.

And Dr. Coit, in his own racy way, speaking of doctrine, says : "Christianity is something or it is nothing. If it is something, it is an immense and indispensable something ; and if it be, then it has doctrines,—such doctrines as go to the very essence of medicine, and law, and politics, and government, and trade, and human practical life all over, and all through. And if it have such doctrines, then those doctrines must be preached, as an imperative necessity. And if they are mysterious, recondite, summoning man to implicit faith, in spite of the pride of reason and the pratings of

my brethren, men are worse than fools, to intrust the preaching of such doctrines to word-painters, to sentimentalists, to the votaries of cant and rant and popular admiration. Such pulpiteers will run religion down, and the Church down with it, till none are so poor as to do them reverence; and infidels will speak out loudly, what they now mutter in whispers, that the pulpit had better be treated as the English Parliament has been treating the Church of Ireland, and disendowed as an incumbrance." And he adds, in connection with the polity of the Church: "One of the best educated lawyers I ever knew, once told me, that long-continued and undisputed precedent was law. "Law, sir," continued he, "why, such precedent is absolute law." "Well," was my remark in consequence, "then episcopacy is the absolute law of Christendom; for Gibbon himself acknowledged that it had a string of precedents to appeal to, of fourteen hundred years' standing (from A. D. 100 to A. D. 1500)." And I might have added to Gibbons' testimony, that of David Blondel, the ablest and most candid Presbyterian, who ever commented on the Church History of ancient times. Both these men admit that as soon as the agitations of its settlement had taken place, and Christianity appeared as a polity, and as an extended organization, then Episcopacy appeared, *universally*, as a fixed fact in it, and continued so to the times of Zuingle and Calvin. And well they might; for Episcopacy has left a record along the great causeways of Church History which has not been left by the observance of the Lord's Day, by Infant Baptism, by the Trinity, by the Canon of the New Testament itself. When Chrysostom began in, say A. D. 400, to preach Homilies on the Acts of the Apostles, he told his hearers he was going to preach about a book which many of them had never so much as heard of. He could say this, in Constantinople, the new capital of the great Roman Empire, the topmost point of politics and civilization for the outspread world. He could not have said as much about Episcopacy in the remotest corner of Christendom without being laughed to scorn. My brethren, if men would be as deferential to precedents *out of* courts of law, as they are *in* them, there would be no difficulty in finding a Christian platform for all Christendom to stand on. Let them take the dogmatic decisions of the first six Ecumenical Councils, which our homilies have acknowledged (or even the first four to which, so far as doctrine only was concerned, the Cambridge platform of 1680 did signal honor), and there would be an " end of controversy," about all genuinely catholic points of Christian *doctrine.* Let them take the testimony of those Councils, about Episcopacy, as millions upon millions have done about the proper day for celebrating the festival of Easter, and there would be an " end of controversy " about all genuinely catholic points of Christian *discipline.* Let them take this testimony about liturgical ceremonies and a sufficient uniformity about Christian *worship* might be determined and established, for the terraqueous globe."

These are both sermons which might well be reprinted to-day as " Tracts for the Times."

I am somewhat amused at two other coincidences in these two sermons, both of which had reference to me. The old Bishop told me, long years after, that he had in his hopes my election as Bishop of Albany, when he urged my acceptance of the Rectorship of St. Peter's in 1867; the very thing, in my judgment, as I told him, which was likely to make that election impossible. But this is how the Bishop betrayed what was in his heart, though nobody knew it then. "No one needs to be told that the Church is by no means going to change her policy of ages, the policy, I mean, of looking, as a general thing, to persons of middle age for well-tried and well-trained labourers meet to be elevated to the Episcopal Office. Yet, when Divine Providence shall seem to point to a faithful servant of Christ, who is somewhat younger, though of full canonical age, as a person of peculiar qualifications for the peculiar work, we may be sure that the Church will no more refuse in the future than she has refused in the past, to call such a one to the forefront of her great warfare." And the old Rector of St. Paul's, suspicious of the youth which I had then, strange as it may seem now, closed his sermon in this way: " We are on the verge of a new era for our own ecclesiastical localities. Let us leave the future to its natural and orderly development. 'Sufficient unto the day is the evil thereof.' Let us rally around our young Bishop and hold his hands up — finding as little fault as may be, and awarding all the credit possible. And let us do this (as I am sure he would prefer to have us do), on the solid ground of principle, and not on the slippery and shifting ground of personal partiality. Let us kindly remember the testimony of the most competent witness St. Chrysostom. " The soul of a Bishop," said he, " is for all the world like a vessel in a storm, lashed upon every side, by friends, by foes, by one's own people, by strangers."

I have no intention of reviewing at length my own work for these twenty-five years. That I must do rather on my knees before God, in Retreats, in an Ember season, preparing for the Judgment Day. But as illustrating what I have said of my ideas of a Bishop's work from the outset, and as indicating God's great goodness in enabling us to turn these hopes and prophecies into realization and history, I may be allowed to quote two passages, from my first Address to the second Convention of the Diocese, speaking of the offer which the Vestry of St. Peter's Church made to me, that I would use it as my Cathedral Church, I said : "I am not one of those who feel that the headship of a Parish interferes with the administration of a Diocese. On the contrary I think no episcopate complete, that has not a centre, the Cathedral, as well as a circumference, the Diocese. But I have no ambition to ~~plant the Cathedral~~,(or anything

else) which is a mere unreality, unless the seats are free and the administration of the parish legally, formally and finally committed to a management, of which the Bishop and his Clergy form an integral part, with the
Laity.   What the future has in store I do not know.   God helping me,
if I live long enough, the Diocese of Albany will have the reality of a
Cathedral, with all that it involves, of work and worship, in frequent
services, in schools and houses of mercy of every kind."   And, in laying
out, in the same Address, "the matters of special importance which demand of the Churchmen of this Diocese prompt and liberal efforts and
attention," I said: "A Church School for girls to be founded near the
City, and cared for by Christian women, devoted for the love of Christ to
their great work; houses of mercy for the sick, for the fallen, for orphan,
and for the aged, to be established, where the best openings may occur t
or developed out of existing institutions, such as the Church Home in
Troy, and the Orphanage beginning now at Cooperstown."

Go back with me to the story of these openings; "a study of origins," it
might be called.

The story of the Church Home in Troy is this: In 1854 a House
of Mercy had been established by the Brotherhood of St. Barnabas, called
the "Church Asylum," for the relief of the aged, the sick, the infirm
and the destitute.   It was twice temporarily housed, and the name
was changed to "the Church Home" when it was incorporated by the
Legislature.   The present new building, which stands on its attractive
and commanding position, was completed and occupied in 1874, and was
blessed on the 15th of April in that year.   It has gone quietly on in its
gracious service and always recalls to me, in its ministry to the servants
of God in their declining years, the cry of the two at Emmaus, "Abide
with us, for it is towards evening and the day is far spent."   In 1881, the
beautiful Chapel built by her children in dutiful memory of their aged
and beloved mother Mrs. Caroline Elizabeth Tibbits Lane, was dedicated
during the Easter octave, to the worship of God and for the spiritual care
of the inmates of the Home.   My yearly Lenten visitation there is
among the satisfactions of my Episcopal life ; and the sunny, quiet,
simple refinement of the rooms in the Home is beautiful to see, and full
of the thought of, and the preparation for, rest and peace.   Mrs. Howard
Hart has added to her previous benefactions the gift of the house and
land adjoining the Chapel on the north.

The story of the Orphan House of the Holy Saviour, in Cooperstown,
is this.   It began in the true and tender heart of a woman, touched with
the pity which the Saviour felt for little children, for a little child orphaned
by her widowed mother's death, in the Thanksgiving Hospital at
Cooperstown.   Her life, for more than a quarter of a century, has been
consecrated to this beneficent and blessed work.   Gathering to herself
in humble quarters first, some like-minded helpers, she began the

actual service. The first building was dedicated by Bishop Tuttle in the autumn of 1869. What *we* have done has only been to hold up her hands, and that not strongly as we should have; and to give legal existence and material shape to what is the outgrowth of the love and faith and devotion of Miss Susan Fenimore Cooper. The Board of Trustee, was organized in 1870. Some years later on, a reorganization was effected, to bring the Institution into closer relations with the Dioceses and, after much anxious thought and planning, the building was finally finished and blessed in September, 1883. It has gone on in the discharge of its gracious service, caring for a large number of children who otherwise would have been left to the questionable associations of the poor-house, or to the neglect of headless homes. In many ways there are abundant tokens, of the untold value and blessing of what it has done. And, thank God, dear Miss Cooper still survives to give the unstinted service of her undiminished love and faith to all the details of the administration.

The story of St. Agnes' School is this. First and foremost, it is born in me, from my father, and was reborn in my Baptism to believe in Christian Education, as the only real and thorough training in the world. There is no Roman Catholic on earth, who believes more absolutely than I do, that we ought to train every one of our children, in all the parts of their nature, *side by side*, so that the development may be complete and not partial; spiritually, intellectually and physically; in religion and morals, in secular learning and in athletics. I am equally satisfied that the Churches ought to do this, in America, with their own means, given as an offering to God, and not gotten by taxation or legislation, or from the State, in any way. And I am equally clear, that for such children as the Churches cannot and do not educate, in schools which they found and support and control, the Common School system is a necessity, is a most wise provision, is first rate so far as it goes; and may not be interfered with in the interests of any religious body whatever. It must, of course, be *un*religious, which is a very different thing from *ir*religious; and Christian parents and Christian bodies must supplement this teaching of the mind and body, of intelligence, morality and health, with the implanting of the principles of the Faith. So we began, a few of us, quietly, but with very clear purpose, gathering a small number of children in a small house in Columbia Place. When the present Bishop's house was bought, all that lay west of it was waste territory, with a disused foundry, some small houses and stables, and a large dumping ground. My envious eye coveted the land, which, by a curious combination of circumstances, came, almost unexpectedly, within my reach. The promise of the first Mr. Erastus Corning to give the land, when $50,000 were secured for the building, gave impulse to the effort, which God blessed with success. It ▆▆▆▆▆▆▆▆▆▆▆▆ to most

12

people, as some other things seemed dreams; but if I was the dreamer it was dreamed with some pretty hard stones under my head. After two years of school work in the little house, which even then ran over into a second house around the corner, we moved into the new building on the eve of All Saints' Day, A. D., 1872. Two years had founded the School and attained the building. The fire we lighted that night on the hearth has been relighted now twenty-one times; and it flashes out and gets an answer back, as hilltop used to answer hilltop with the old beacon fires, from hundreds of homes, where our children keep the memory alive of their school associations. St. Agnes' has educated many hundred women, who honour her as we honour them. And while I carry in one hand the weight of anxious and responsible care, I carry in the other a balancing weight of satisfaction and comfort, which makes the load easy to bear; as I am sometimes told, by kindly people who *will* take both of my travelling-bags out of my hand, that it is easier to carry two than one, because they balance better. The School has been three times enlarged since its first building. There are still with us, thank God, some of those who almost began the work, and some of our own graduates are teachers there. You have the right to count it among the honours of the Diocese.

The story of the Sisterhood is this: From the very first it was evident that we needed the help of women with ability to teach and work, whose lives should be absolutely set apart to the service of the Master in this way. I thoroughly recognize the consecration of other lives *without* the vows. But I believe in the blessing of the *vowed* life. And from time to time, such women have been given to us, until now we number sixteen, with others looking toward the Sisterhood. Only sixteen, I grieve to say, but sixteen, I am glad to say, of such Sisters as are invaluable in their devoted helpfulness. There have been, as there must always be in such difficult and delicate relations, siftings and losses, but the residuum is transparently pure. I have felt it the Bishop's place to direct and control this organization myself in its Constitution, and in the Rules and Services of the religious life of the Sisters. It would have been easier to increase the number, if freer scope had been given to the kind of extremes which attract women of emotional natures by their permitted extravagances; or if the important so-called practical side of work were allowed to displace the religious regulation of their lives. But measured by spirit and character, and by results, both personal and in the work, I believe that ours is the wiser, and in the end the richer way. The Sisters do teaching work in St. Agnes' School, parochial work in the Cathedral and in St. Paul's Parish, Troy, nursing in the Child's Hospital and in St. Margaret's House here, and training work in the St. Christina Home in Saratoga.

The story of the Child's Hospital and its affiliated houses, is this : It was born, as every thing has been here, and as I think every thing ought to be, not out of a theory, but out of a pressing necessity. We had established a day-nursery in a little house on LaFayette street, and among the first of very few children sent to us was a little girl suffering from hip disease. After much persuasion she was intrusted to us for continuous care and treatment. To-day she is a well woman, earning her livelihood. From this the work changed its purpose, and other children came. It grew first into the picturesque building which was completed in 1877, after the pattern of "the God's Providence House" in Chester, which is used now, in part, for the Sisters' home, and in part for St. Margaret's House. And then for the sake of larger and better accommodation the present building was erected and blessed on "The Angels' Day," in 1891. It stands almost on the foundation of the old Cathedral Chapel, upon ground consecrated by twenty years of constant worship, like the ashes that made even "Santa Croce's sacred precincts holier."

St. Margaret's House rose up, in 1884, in like manner to supply a felt need in the care of forsaken and forlorn babies. It needs a better housing than it has. It must get one. And the St. Christina Home in Saratoga grew out of the most blessed and beautiful memory of a child, whose motto, alike in life and in death, it fairly illustrates, to

"Make life long, by good works and deeds."

Beginning in 1882 as a Convalescent Home, the building and land were given in 1886, and the Industrial School was opened the next year. It is destined, I believe, to prove a blessing in two ways : First, in the provision of Christian servants who recognize the principle of service; and then in giving masters and mistresses a sense of their real responsibility and relation to those whom they employ.

This is the story of the Cathedral. It was in my prayers and purposes from the very first. But the first step toward it was not taken until provision actually had to be made for a place where the teachers and children of St Agnes' School could worship. The choice lay between the smallness of an Oratory for the Sisters or a Chapel for the School, and the largeness of the idea of a Bishop's Church, which could provide for these necessities and more besides. With the long established evidence of the almost universality of the Cathedral idea, from time immemorial; with the fact that these old reservoirs of spiritual power, all over England, had been proving their value in the last century, by filling up and overflowing with the refreshing forces of the awakened religious life of the Church; and with my own clear convictions that a Bishop, every Bishop, ought to have his place of special central service and overseeing; there seemed to be *no* choice. The difficul-

ties, which seemed to most people impossibilities, were easy to see and
hard to face. And it was a long while before the idea could worry
and worm and work itself into the minds of others. But that very slow-
ness was our safety, as it led to the establishment of the *work* at the
start, while the place of worship was left poor and bare, rich only in its
services and sacrifices. Then it let the thought permeate the Diocese,
without any irritating element in it of a demand for money. And best of
all, it gave me years of loving care and planning, in which the details of
the building ripened themselves into the most minute points of pillar
and window, of carving and colour, so that "when the fulness of the
time was come" the plan was ready, in its harmonious unity, to be put
into lasting shape, and the live soul of it was ready to become incarnate.
Our original purpose of building at the east end of the School was abandoned, for lack of room and insecurity of foundation: and when the site
was finally chosen, the purchase of it was made possible by the gift of
my good friend, Mr. Corning, just as his father had given the ground for
St. Agnes' School. There is no need to tell how after that the accomplished building was secured. The tide of its success ebbed and flowed,
but the flowing got the better of the ebbing. Its highest water
marks were reached, on the 29th of June, A. D., 1882, when Mr.
Marcus Hun telegraphed me that the land was secured and the
title completed ; on the third of June, A. D., 1884, when, amid
a great gathering of gracious friends, the cornerstone was laid:
on the 16th of February, A. D., 1886, when the women put their hearts
and hands to it in the organization of the Diocesan League, which
I count always as the chief minister in its success; on the 23d of October,
A. D. 1887, when the Chapter decided to borrow and the New York
Mutual Life Insurance Company agreed to lend the money needed to
complete the building for use; on the 20th of November, A. D., 1888,
when, with fourteen Bishops gathering about me and before a great congregation of the Diocese and the City, and of friends from outside, the
building was blessed and set apart to the worship of God; on the 22nd
of February, A. D., 1892, when a most dear friend and generous benefactor inaugurated the movement which led to the payment of the
debt; and on "Refreshment Sunday," A. D., 1892, when with solemn
thanksgiving the whole sum was offered on the Altar; and the Cathedral stood, as it stands now, free from debt. The building, materially
speaking, has in it an element of life. Something or other in it is continually growing, a capital or a doorway breaks into bloom, or a window
glows with the glory of new colour. That I am content and satisfied, I
cannot say; but neither can I say how infinitely thankful I am for the
outcome, and for the widespread interest and generous love *out* of which it
has *come*. I hope, though I do not expect, to see the building finished. I
cannot ask for this, except of God. But I do ask and expect, as well as

hope for its current support, for the provision of a small endowment; enough for instance to support the music, *or* (perhaps *and*) a Missionary Stall. And while there is not time left for very great accomplishment *by me*, I venture to say again, with a prophetic spirit that is limited by the narrow horizon of my advanced years, that if I live long enough, this will be done; and two crying needs of our work here will be satisfied as well; a decent home for the Sisters where they can have room enough to live and grow; and a proper house for St. Margaret's.

There are many tokens of growth in life and power in the city of Troy and, I thank God, of growth in unity and sympathy with its sister city. St. Paul's has gathered about itself its Chapel with rooms for the Parochial School and Parish work; the Martha Memorial House beautiful not only for its beautiful memory, but in the abundant measure of its work; "cumbered," it really is, with much serving by the Sisters and the faithful "friends of the Sisterhood," who have, besides this, also, chosen the better part" of Mary; and just now, in its old age, the Church has clothed itself inside with "a clothing really of wrought gold," like "the King's daughter." St. John's has as beautiful a property, in its new Parish House and Rectory close to the Church, as I know anywhere. Christ Church has been admirably decorated, and has added a most complete and convenient building for its practical service. The Free Church of the Ascension crowns its commanding situation, with a building which will always keep alive the name and life of Mr. Farnham. St. Barnabas' still worships in its little Chapel, but has gathered a goodly fund for the new building. And the Church of the Holy Cross, with no marring of its unique and rare charm, offers its exquisite service of song, in the old Building enlarged and beautified by the addition of a Sanctuary, which fitly crowns the whole. It is a matter of just pride and pleasure to me that we shall use for the first time in the Cathedral tomorrow the musical edition of the Revised Hymnal, which the Church owes to the "chief musician" of this Diocese, our revered and beloved Dr. Tucker. It will in the future as before, both for its intrinsic value and for its association with the author, whose name and character are among the treasures of the Diocese of Albany, become the Hymnal of our chief use. Its publication makes inexcusable the non-using of the new Hymnal, which I beg to say is the only Hymnal of authority in this Church, the old Hymnal being merely permitted for economy's sake until the copies in use be worn out, and no other Hymnal having any standing whatever in the Church. May I venture to say in this connection, that I wish the experiment might be tried, which I understand to be the habit in almost all other religious bodies, of securing the purchase of musical editions of the Hymnal by the people, so that they may be in the pews. It would be a suggestion, to say the least of it, and possibly a help, to break up the dull silence and the proxy worship of our public services and make "the people, yea *all* the people, praise God."

It is the weak point of this Diocese that it has only these two large centres of Albany and Troy; but the Church is strong and growing stronger in them both. Albany, besides the Cathedral and its group of buildings added within these five-and-twenty years, can tell the same story; of St. Peter's with its new tower, its beautifully renewed interior and with its Parish House and new Orphan Home; St. Paul's redecorated, and with its Parish House and Rectory; Grace Church, moved and increased in size and beauty and efficiency and with its Rectory; and Trinity and the Holy Innocents' each with its own Rectory. And the Diocese feels and owns most gratefully the strength that goes out from its two central Cities, which give considerably more than one-third of all the missionary offerings in the Diocese.

Troy and Albany are of course the only large cities, which can be called Diocesan centres. But I have no right to ignore the central sources of strength in two cities at least, without which the great northern section of this Diocese would be a waste. I mean Ogdensburgh and Potsdam, in both which places I am impressed always with a sense of the power and influence of the Church. St. John's, Ogdensburgh, has every outward and inward token of the real energy that is there and that makes the Archdeacon eye and hand to me. Its noble Church, its large and admirable Chapel and Parish House and its Rectory, are all in my day. I may say the same of Potsdam, whose Church is virtually new, and keeps on renewing its beauty year by year. The Chapel is a gem, and the Parish has gained hold more and more on the strong men of the place, and sits like a beautiful mother in the dignity of matronhood, with Churches and Chapels nestling about her, Colton and Norwood and Lawrence, owing their birth and life to the missionary zeal and the large liberality of the Rector and lay people of Trinity Church.

But while our special growth has been in bringing small hamlets within the blessed influence of the Church, good gains have been made of strength and beauty otherwise; in Cooperstown, with its lovely added Chancel and Chapel and Rectory; in Saratoga, with its old Church made new with great richness and beauty; in Lansingburgh, where the splendid old elms still wave over the new and noble Church and the Chapel adjoining; in Malone, where a most dignified Church building replaces the old wooden Church; in Delhi, where the exquisite stone Chapel and the beautiful Rectory have been added by the gifts, or in the memory of Mr. Edwin Sheldon; in Richfield Springs, with its new and fine Church and Chapel, besides the new building at Cullen and the restored old Church at Monticello; in old St. George's, Schenectady, the best instance I know of, an old Church renewed in complete harmony with *its former self*; in Glens Falls, with its fair Chancel, its fine tower and its choir rooms; in Warrensburgh, with its most admirable Rectory and Library, with reading and working rooms attached; and so on —

There is one other growth in this Diocese which is very near and dear to me, I mean our work in the Adirondack wilderness. We have now there thirteen Churches and Chapels with one Rectory and one Library. In 1876 Dr. Hopkins and I agreed one day to go to Whiteface, for a climb and the view. When we came as far as Plattsburgh on our way, we found the forest fires had so filled the air with smoke, that the ascent would be difficult and the view destroyed. So, telegraphing Paul Smith to expect us for the night and to arrange for a service in the hotel, we went on. It was late in the day when we came there. We had service in the big parlour that night, ruddy with a great wood fire, and all aglow with a mixture that I had never seen before, of autumn leaves and water lilies in full bloom. Early the next morning, at a Celebration in one of the smaller rooms, I took an offertory, which I gave to Dr. Trudeau, as a nest egg for a building fund. And out of that providential leading has grown the system of Chapels which, like the chain of the Adirondack lakes, are linked in one after another, and carry refreshment and consolation to the sick people who are there, winter and summer now, and to not a few of the residents and guides. I have great joy in the Church's step-by-step progress, in the wilderness of this Diocese.

I could go on so with the garrulousness of an old man, and tire you out with my talking, as I find I can still tire out most of the clergy with my work. But the time would fail me to tell of other advances, in the beauty of Church buildings elsewhere, in the added Churches, Rectories and Parish Houses, in the elevation of the character of Public Worship, in the increased frequency of Celebrations of the Holy Communion. In 1869, in my first Address, I asked of the Diocese the building of churches at Ticonderoga, Ilion, Middleville, Springfield, Esperance, Morley, Gloversville, Lawrenceville, Schenevus, Mohawk, Oneonta, Canajoharie, Conklingville, Ausable Forks and Massena; and they have been built, and others too. The points where nothing has been done, of which I spoke then, and where I should not advise it to be done to-day, were Garrattsville, Schoharie, Madrid, Exeter, Newport and Chateaugay. And as I look over the map, which always hangs where I can see it in the Cathedral, I find, that of places which were marked empty then, either missions have been established or churches built, at Bangor, Elizabethtown, Port Henry, Raymertown, Philmont, Chatham, Castleton, Dolgeville, Boyntonville, Frankfort, Schenectady, Sidney, Stamford, Esperance, Mineville, Springfield Centre and Springfield. These are but some of the outward and visible signs, to which are not wanting, I believe, the inward and spiritual grace of deepening earnestness and more devout service, and larger consecration in the service of our Lord.

The figures of religious growth, symbols I pray God of real and eternal value, are as follows, in the last twenty-five years: Baptisms, 43,430; confirmations, 27,203; ordinations to the Diaconate, 111; ordinations to the Priesthood, 124; Churches and Chapels consecrated, 78; increase in communicants, 12,000. Over against which, I must add the dying out of missionary work, inevitable I believe much as I regret it, at Centreville, Boquet, Willsboro, Whallonsburgh, Wadhams, and Hampton ; and the entire failure, very sad to me, of two attempts to establish a Boys' School, at Cooperstown and at Salem.

As I end this outline sketch, and look out from the close of this period of work, I desire above all things to stand in my place here and say, before God, that the element of most intense gratitude to me is the *one-heartedness* of the Diocese of Albany. We are not all of one mind; there is no dead level of unnatural uniformity of opinion or practice; there are usages and utterances among us widely differing in their character; there has been no human pressure brought to bear, to lift, or lower anybody's views; there has been no system of natural or unnatural selection to pick out men who should be of one particular standard of churchmanship. I can say honestly, and call you all to witness, that I have never interfered · except by way of counsel, with the selection of a Rector, and that I have never been governed by theological opinions in my appointment of missionaries. And yet there are no divisions, no party lines, no hot discussions, no disputed elections, no burning questions in the Diocese; and there have not been for years. The Diocese has its own atmosphere in which we all breathe freely and it is the atmosphere of the high lands. It attracts men who like its environment. It holds men, not seldom at real cost of sacrifice. It brings men back who go away. And its influence is felt and recognized by our own lay people, upon the clergy who come to us and in the church at large. It is a Diocese where episcopal authority, presbyterian parity and lay independence are illustrated in absolute harmony. I know no better word for it than one-heartedness. And I recognize it as God's choice gift to us, growing and deepening through all these years, coming from the presence of the Holy Spirit, Who alone "maketh men to be of one mind in an House."

APPENDIX.

(A.)

PAROCHIAL REPORTS.

Albany County.

CATHEDRAL OF ALL SAINTS, ALBANY.

THE CATHEDRAL CHAPTER.

Bishop. The Right Rev. William Croswell Doane, D. D., LL. D.

Dean. The Rev. Wilford L. Robbins, D. D.

Precentor. The Rev. Thomas B. Fulcher, B. D.

Treasurer. The Rev. Edgar T. Chapman.

Honorary Canons. The Revs. F. M. Gray, Edward D. Tibbits, Charles H. Hatheway, Walter C. Stewart.

Lay Members. A. Bleecker Banks, Thomas Hun, M. D., Erastus Corning, Selden E. Marvin, Assistant Treasurer, Marcus T. Hun, Vice-Chancellor, Robert S. Oliver·

Parochial.

Families, 233; Individuals, 1,172; Baptisms (adults, 10, infants, 83), 93; Confirmed, since last report, 74; Marriages, 8; Burials, 52; Churchings, 3; Communicants, last reported, 632, present number, 679 ; Public Services, Daily Celebration of Holy Communion throughout the year, Sundays and Holy days, two Celebrations, Daily Matins and Evensong; Holy Communion, private, 37; Sunday School, teachers, 19, pupils, 170; Catechizing, number of times, 25; St. Agnes' School, teachers, 38, pupils, 208.

Offerings.

Parochial.— Alms at Holy Communion, $561.75; Current expenses, including salaries, $14,223.09; Sunday School, $74.95; Increase and Improvement of Church Property, endowment, $500; Choir Endowment Fund, $25.26; Guild House, $1,400.06; Sisters' House, $5; Woman's Cathedral League, $113.50. Total, $16,903.61.

Diocesan.— Diocesan Missions, $1,200; Woman's Auxiliary Board of Missions, $75.32 ; Salary of the Bishop, $150; Diocesan Fund, $150; Fund for Aged and Infirm Clergymen, $5, Fund for Widows and Orphans of Clergymen, $5; Orphan House of the Holy Saviour, $41.37; The Child's Hospital, $262.37; St. Margaret's House, $10. Total, $1,899.06.

General.— Domestic Missions, $325.33; Foreign Missions (Sunday School), $103; Jewish Missions, $33.03; Miss Emery's School, $45.15; Orphanage for Coloured People at Lynchburgh, Va., $173.51. Total, $680.02.

Total amount of Offerings, $19,482.69.

Property.

Church and lot (estimated worth), $350,000.
Other property, $12,000.
Insurance, $52,000.
Amount of salary pledged Dean, $5,000.
Amount of salary pledged Precentor, $1,300.
Number of sittings in the Church, 2,375, all free.

ST. PETER'S CHURCH, ALBANY.

Rector. The Rev. Walton W. Battershall, D. D.
Assistant. The Rev. Churchill Satterlee.
Wardens. George H. Weaver, Joseph W. Tillinghast.
Vestrymen. Henry |T. Martin, Luther H. Tucker, Theodore Townsend, F. E. Griswold, Robert C. Pruyn, Thomas S. Wiles, Abraham Lansing, William G. Rice.

Parochial.

Individuals, 1,260; Baptisms (adults, 4, infants, 22), 26; Present number of Confirmed Persons, 732; Marriages, 21; Burials, 28; Communicants, last reported, 730, received, 25, died, 8, removed, 15, present number, 732; Public Services (Sundays, 140, Holy days, 30, other days, 190), 360; Holy Communion (public, 90, private 18), 108; Sunday School, teachers, 34, pupils, 300; Parish School, teachers, 5, pupils, 16.

Offerings.

Parochial.—Alms at Holy Communion, $1,100.91; Current expenses, including salaries, $13,460.41; Sunday School, $143.42; St. Peter's Orphanage, $1,531.52; Increase and Improvement of Church Property, $2,291.73; Chancel Guild, $185.35; Parish Aid Society, $855.36; Christmas Tree, $282.56; Sunday School Library and Seats, $1,153.77; Endowment Fund, $134.08. Total, $21,139.11.

Diocesan.— Diocesan Missions, $1,003; Salary of the Bishop, $150; Diocesan Fund, $140; Bible and Common Prayer Book Society of Albany, $51.66; Diocesan Missionary, $100; Orphan House of the Holy Saviour, $106.26; The Child's Hospital, from Sunday School, $24.65; Society for Promoting Religion and Learning, $12.71; St. Christina Home, from Sunday School, $10; Clergy Reserve Fund, $14.34; Fireman's Fund, from Sunday School, $60. Total, $1,672.62.

General.—Domestic Missions, $304.77; Foreign Missions, $177.85; Indian Missions, $126.05; Home Missions to Coloured Persons, $120.97; Bishop of Montana, $255.42; Bishop of Montana, Mite Chests, $130; St. John's College, Shanghai, $100; Church Building Fund, $19.35; St. Helena, Beaufort, $18.45; St. Thomas', Ravenswood, $20; Rectory, East Albany, $25; Church, Woodstock, $10; Woman's Auxiliary, $977.25. Total, $2,285.11.

Total amount of Offerings, $25,096.84.

Property.

Church and lot (estimated worth), $210,000.
Parsonage and lot (estimated worth), $5,000.
Other property, Parish House Orphanage, $40,000.
Condition of property, good.
Amount of salary pledged Rector, $4,500.
Amount of salary pledged Assistant Minister, $1,000.
Number of sittings in the Church and Chapel, 1,250.

Remarks.

Last Christmas a Bronze Angel Lectern was placed in the Church by Mrs. Macdonald, to the memory of her late husband, John Macdonald, for several years a Vestryman of the Parish.

Decorated glass was placed in the four lancets over the porch of the Church, by Mrs. Charles L. Pruyn, to the memory of her father and mother, Sebastian Vischer and Olivia Sherman Talcott.

ST. PAUL'S CHURCH, ALBANY.

Rector. The Rev. Freeborn G. Jewett, Jr.

Assistant. The Rev. George L. Richardson.

Wardens. John H. Van Antwerp, John Woodward.

Vestrymen. George P. Wilson, Robert Geer, Matthew H. Robertson, Eugene Burlingame, Henry A. Dwight, Wallace N. Horton, James H. Manning, Edgar B. Holden.

Parochial.

Families, 336; Individuals, 1,244; Baptisms (adults, 8, infants, 17), 25; Confirmed, since last report, 50; Present number of Confirmed Persons, 767; Marriages, 10; Burials, 31; Communicants, last reported, 752, admitted, 50, received, 24, died, 16, removed, 43, present number, 767; Public Services (Sundays, 204, other days, 105), 309; Holy Communion (public, 38, private, 18), 56.

Offerings.

Parochial.— Alms at Holy Communion, $460.34; Current expenses, including salaries, $8,183.58; Sunday School, $623.72;* other parochial objects, $850.77. Total, $10,118.41.

Diocesan.— Diocesan Missions, $400; Salary of the Bishop, $100; Diocesan Fund, $60; Fund for Aged and Infirm Clergyman, $1,000. Total, $1,560.

General.— Domestic Missions, $253.27; Foreign Missions, $363.72; Other objects exterior to the Diocese, $109.92. Total, $726.91.

Total amount of Offerings, $12,405.32.

TRINITY CHURCH, ALBANY.

Rector. The Rev. Russell Woodman.

Wardens. William Little (died in June), John A. Howe.

Vestrymen. John Pritchard, Richard Norris, George Granger, Henry Marlow, Norden Johnston, Charles Fairchild, Edward Johnston, John Harder.

Parochial.

Baptisms (adults, 2, infants, 24), 26; Confirmed, since last report, 2; Marriages, 26; Burials, 26; Communicants, last reported, 210, actually receiving, 175, received, 2, died, 6, removed, 14, present number, 192; Public Services, Sundays, morning and evening; Holy Communion, public, weekly and Holy days, private, 18; Sunday School, teachers, 20, pupils, 167; Catechizing, school, monthly.

Offerings.

Parochial.—Alms at Holy Communion, $48.51; Current ~~expenses, including~~ salaries, $1,991; Sunday School $64; Increase and Improv~~ement~~ $478.94. Total, $2,582.45.

Diocesan.—Diocesan Missions, $20; Salary of the Bishop, $20; Diocesan Fund, $10; Bible and Common Prayer Book Society of Albany, $7; Fund for Aged and Infirm Clergymen, $4.35; Orphan House of the Holy Saviour, $3.60; The Child's Hospital (J. A. Howe), $5. Total, $69.95.

General.— Domestic Missions, $5; Foreign Missions, $2.61; Indian Missions, $5; Other objects exterior to the Diocese, $5. Total, $17.61.

Total amount of Offerings, $2,670.01.

Property.

Church and lot (estimated worth), $40,000.
Parsonage and lot (estimated worth), $8,000.
Condition of property, good.
Indebtedness, $12,000, $300 of which has been paid off the past year.

GRACE CHURCH, ALBANY.

Rector. The Rev. George Dent Silliman, S. T. D.
Wardens. Benjamin F. Hinman, Charles W. White.
Vestrymen. Frank J. Smith, James C. Sewell, Henry Burn, George B. Longleway, Edward Sewell, Frederick Gilliland, James Beauman, William Rankin.

Parochial.

Baptism (adults, 1, infants, 41), 42; Marriages, 20; Burials, 33; Communicants, last reported, 412, received, 3, died, 10, removed, 4, present number, 401; Public Services. Sundays, 3, Holy days, 2, other days, daily since September Ember days; Holy Communion, public, every Sunday and Holy days, private, 6; Sunday School, teachers, 36, pupils, 353; Catechizing, every Sunday.

Offerings.

Parochial.— Current expenses, including salaries, $2,688.52; Sunday School, not included elsewhere, $294.43; Repairs on Parsonage, $538.20; Sinking Fund for debt, $75. Total, $3,596.15.

Diocesan.— Diocesan Missions, $50; Salary of the Bishop, $24; Diocesan Fund, $36; Bible and Common Prayer Book Society of Albany, $20; Fund for Aged and Infirm Clergymen, $10.56; The Child's Hospital, $15; Diocesan Missionary, $10. Clerical Insurance, $6. Total, $171.56.

General. — Domestic and Foreign Missions, $99.45; Missions to Jews, $8.55. Total, $108.

Total amount of Offerings, $3,875.71.

Property.

Church and lot (estimated worth), $15,000.
Parsonage and lot (estimated worth), $5,000.
Condition of property, good.
Indebtedness (mortgage), $2,000.
Amount of salary pledged Rector, $1,200.
Number of sittings in the Church, 500; all free.

Remarks.

The Rev. Wm. Henry Bown resigned the rectorship April 4th. The present Rector took charge Monday in Whitsun week.

HOLY INNOCENTS' CHURCH, ALBANY.

Rector. The Rev. Richmond Shreve, D. D.

Wardens. S. M. Van Santvoord, W. H. Weaver.

Vestrymen. B. Lodge, Jr., James Oswald, H. S. McCall, Robert Parker, Thos. J. Tobin, W. H. Riley, Thomas Kyle, George C. Bishop.

Parochial.

Baptisms (adults 3, infants, 13), 16; Confirmed, since last report, 8; Marriages, 12; Burials, 23; Communicants, last reported, 191, admitted, 8, received, 4, died, 10, removed, 8, present number, 185; Public Services (Sundays, 145, Holy days, 25, other days, 62), 232; Holy Communion (public, 58, private, 10), 68; Sunday School, teachers and officers, 18, pupils, 135; Catechizing, number of children, school, number of times, 17.

Offerings.

Parochial.— Alms at Holy Communion, $67.72; Current expenses, including salaries, $2,750.85; Sunday School, $171.87; Increase and Improvement of Church Property, $257.87. Total, $3,247.31.

Diocesan — Diocesan Missions, $50; Salary of the Bishop, $30; Diocesan Fund, $52 50; Bible and Common Prayer Book Society of Albany, $5; Fund for Aged and Infirm Clergymen, $6.13; Fund for Widows and Orphans of Clergymen, $6.17; Orphan House of the Holy Saviour, $7.92; Salary Diocesan Missionary, $15; Clergy Reserve Fund, $5; Clerical Insurance, $7.50. Total, $185.22.

General.— Foreign Missions, $19; Indian Missions, $60. Total, $79.

Total amount of Offerings, $3,511.53.

Property.

Church and lot (estimated worth), $20,000.

Parsonage and lot (estimated worth), $5,000.

Condition of property, good.

Indebtedness, on Rectory, $1,500.

Insurance, Church, Parish House and Rectory, $14,500.

Number of sittings in the Church, 340; all free.

Remarks.

Our Communicant list has been reduced this year by the numbers — larger than usual — of deaths and removals. One name in particular must needs be recorded here, with a single, loving word "In Memoriam."

JOHN GREGORY, the Sexton of the Church for over forty-three years, died October 24, 1893. He had served continuously from the foundation of the Parish, with the exception of three months.

He was a "good and faithful servant," and has entered, we believe, into the (partial) joy of his Lord.

TRINITY CHURCH, RENSSELAERVILLE.

Missionary. The Rev. S. C. Thompson.

Wardens. John L. Rice, Nathaniel Teed.

Vestrymen. C. B. Cross, Frank Rice, Dewey Bell, James Rider, Luther Fox, Henry Sweet, Frank Frisbee, David D'L. McCulloch.

Parochial.

Families, 24; Individuals (adults, 75, children, 30), 105; Baptisms (adults, 5, infants, 5), 10; Present number of Confirmed Persons, ▮▮▮▮▮▮▮▮▮▮▮▮▮▮▮ 2; Communicants, last reported, 50; received, 1, removed, 7, present number, 43; Public Services (Sundays, 100, Holy days, 5, other days, 18), 123; Holy Communion (public, 13, private, 7), 20; Sunday School, teachers, 6, pupils, 25; Catechizing, number of times, 12.

Offerings.

Parochial.—Alms at Holy Communion, $29.51; Current expenses, including salaries, $378.96. Total, $408.47.

Diocesan.—Diocesan Missions, $13.99; Salary of the Bishop, $8; Diocesan Fund, $9; Thanksgiving day for poor, $1.77. Total, $32.76.

General.—Good Friday for Jews, $1.50.

Total amount of Offerings, $442.73.

Property.

Church and lot (estimated worth), $4,000.

Parsonage and lot (estimated worth), $500.

Other property, $175.

Insurance, $2,000.

Amount of salary pledged Missionary, $350.

ST. JOHN'S CHURCH, COHOES.

Rector. The Rev. Frederick S. Sill, B. D.

Wardens. Michael Andrae, John Horrocks.

Vestrymen. George Campbell, Reuben Lee, William S. Shipley, Luke Kavanaugh, Harry J. P. Green, Robert R. Chadwick, Charles H. Disbrow, William T. Ford.

Parochial.

Families, 358; Individuals not included, 96; Individuals (adults, 1,015, children 465), 1,480; Baptisms (adults, 3, infants, 45), 48; Confirmed, since last report, 18; Marriages, 20; Burials, 33; Churchings, 2; Communicants, last reported, 544, admitted, 2, received, 18, died, 6, removed, 8, present number, 550; Public Services (Sundays, 142, Holy days, 48, other days, 120), 310; Holy Communion (public, 76, private, 5), 81; Sunday School, teachers and officers, 25, pupils, 300; Catechizing, number of times, 52.

Offerings.

Parochial.—Alms at Holy Communion, $54.21; Current expenses, including salaries, $3,099.76; Sunday School, $126.97 ($110.96 included elsewhere); Increase and Improvement of Church Property, $443.74; Removal of Debt, $2,700; Introduction of Vested Choir, $256.69; Howe Fund for Poor, $57; King's Daughters, $11.60, Church Home, increase, $64.41; Chancel Committee, $15.83. Total, $6,830.21.

Diocesan.— Diocesan Missions, $250; Salary of the Bishop, $56; Diocesan Fund, $52.50; Bible and Common Prayer Book Society of Albany, $10; Fund for Aged and Infirm Clergymen, $13; Orphan House of the Holy Saviour, $16; The Child's Hospital (Wom. Aux.), $16; Theological Education, $52.25; Diocesan Missionary, $10, Archdeaconry of Albany. $26.51. Total, $502.26.

General.— Domestic Missions, $35.11; Foreign Missions, $35.10; Indian Missions (Wom. Aux.), $10; Home Missions to Coloured Persons (Wom. Aux.), $10; Jewish Missions, $9.17; Alaska Mission (Wom. Aux.), $5; Bishop Leonard's Work (Wom. Aux.), $5; St. John's College, China Mission (Wom. Aux.), $10; Woman's Auxiliary, $261.33 (Total, $317.33); Annandale, $2.50. Total, $383.21.

Total amount of Offerings, $7,715.68.

Property.

Church and lot (estimated worth), $40,000.

Parsonage and lot (estimated worth), $10,000.

Other property, Howe Fund, $1,500; Church Home Fund, $2,902.08.

Condition of property, very good.

Insurance, $28,000.

Amount of salary pledged Rector, $1,500.

Number of sittings in the Church, 800; all free, but assigned.

Remarks.

On Christmas Day, 1892, a vested choir was introduced, consisting of 8 men, 10 boys and 20 women. There are now 22 women singers.

On the 18th of June, 1893, the Church was consecrated by the Bishop of the Diocese, the balance of the debt having been paid off on June 1. The Rev. Dr. Theodore Babcock, a former Rector, and the Rev. C. Tyler Olmsted of Utica, N. Y., a former parishioner, were present.

TRINITY CHURCH, WEST TROY.

Rector. The Rev. E. Bayard Smith.

Wardens. William Hollands, John H. Hulsapple.

Vestrymen. William E. Baxter, Charles H. Crabbe, William Doring, Edmund S. Hollands, Thomas Rath, Bertram F. Stewart, Robert Trimble, William C. Baxter.

Parochial.

Families, 200; Individuals (adults, 400, children, 300), 700; Baptisms (adults, 1, infants, 28), 29; Present number of confirmed persons, 270; Marriages, 6; Burials, 26; Communicants, last reported, 272, received, 14, died, 8, removed, 11, present number, 267; Public Services (Sundays, 96, Holy days, 18, other days, 118), 232; Holy Communion (public, 50, private, 3), 53; Trinity Sunday School, teachers, 18, pupils, 129; St. Gabriel's Sunday School, teachers, 9, pupils, 90. Total, 246. Catechizing every session.

Offerings.

Parochial.— Alms at Holy Communion, $96.75; Current expenses, including salaries, $2,233.02; Sunday School, Trinity, $58.83, St. Gabriel's, $49.83, Chapel, $27.54; Daughters of the Cross, $121.23. Total, $2,586.70.

Diocesan.— Diocesan Missions, $45; Salary of the Bishop, $40; Diocesan Fund, $24; Bible and Common Prayer Book Society of Albany, $9; Fund for Aged and Infirm Clergymen, $17.41; Fund for Widows and Orphans of Clergymen, $6.18; Orphan House of the Holy Saviour, $15; The Child's Hospital, $18.28; Diocesan Missionary, Trinity Sunday School, $2.29, St. Gabriel's Sunday School, $1.85; St. Paul's, Sidney, $11.30. Total, $190.31.

General.— Domestic Missions, $11.16; Foreign Missions, $5.73; Fairview Home, $10; Humane Society, $3; Mission to Jews, $3.83; St. Gabriel's for Missions, $12.44; Woman's Auxiliary, $13.90; Woman's Auxiliary Box, valued, $25. Total, $84.56.

Total amount of Offerings, $2,861.57.

Property.

Church and lot (estimated worth), $24,000.

Parsonage and lot (estimated worth), $8,000.

Other property, $4,000.

Condition of property, excellent.

Number of sittings in the Church, 377, apportioned; Trinity Chapel, 150, free; St. Gabriel's Chapel, 150, free.

Fully insured.

Remarks.

The Daughters of the Cross have purchased an excellent piano for the Guild Room.

ST. ANDREW'S MISSION, WEST TROY.

Missionary. The Rev. Canon Hatheway.
Warden. H. C. Williamson.

Parochial.

Families, 18; Individuals (adults, 50, children, 55), 105; Baptisms (children, 4, infants, 3), 7; Confirmed, since last report, 9; Present number of Confirmed Persons, 45; Marriages, 2; Burials, 2; Communicants, last reported, 45, admitted, 3, received, 1, removed, 9, present number, 40; Public Services (Sundays, 50, Holy days, 2, other days, 14), 66; Holy Communion (public), 12; Sunday School, teachers, 7, pupils, 45; Catechizing, number of children, 40, number of times, 12.

Offerings.

Parochial.— Current expenses, including salaries, $561.78.
General.— Domestic Missions, $5; Indian Missions, $2.75. Total, $7.75.
Total amount of Offerings, $569.53.

Property.

Condition of property, good.
Amount of salary pledged Missionary, $450.
Sittings in the Church, all free.

Remarks.

The work is very encouraging. Notwithstanding the general depression and our many losses, the results are gratifying. We thank God and take courage.

ST. MARK'S CHURCH, GREEN ISLAND.

Rector. The Rev. R. J. Adler.
Wardens. Richard Leonard, William E. Gilbert.
Vestrymen. Henry Stowell, Harry Farmer, William W. Butler, James H. Eckler, Louis Harter, Jr., Robert W. Porter, J. Andrew Best, John Watson.

Parochial.

Families, 151; Individuals (adults, 217, children, 230), 447; Baptisms (adults, 2, infants, 11), 13; Confirmed, since last report, 11; Present number of Confirmed Persons, 213; Marriages, 9; Burials, 13; Churchings, 1; Communicants, present number, 183; Public Services (Sundays, 116, other days, 63), 179; Holy Communion (public, 19, private, 2), 21: Sunday School, teachers, 13, pupils, 141; Catechizing, the whole school, weekly.

Offerings.

Parochial.— Alms at Holy Communion, $16.64; Current expenses, including salaries, $1,592.48; Improvement of Church property, $623; Special, for Chalice and Altar Linen, $90. Total, $2,322.12.

Parochial.— Diocesan Missions ($9.94 of which is from Sunday School for Diocesan Missionary), $47 46; Salary of the Bishop, $12; Diocesan Fund, $17.50; Bible and Common Prayer Book Society of Albany, $5.42; Increase of the Episcopate Fund, $7; Fund for Aged and Infirm Clergymen, $5.57; Orphan House of the Holy Saviour ($3.37 of which is from Sunday School), $19 73; The Child's Hospital, for St. Christina Home, from Sunday School, $10. Total, $124.68.

General.— General Missions, from Sunday School, $38.09; Domestic Missions, $12.30; Foreign Missions, $11.85; Home Missions to Coloured Persons, through Woman's Auxiliary (in goods), $40; Home Mission to Jews, $5.55; American Church Building Fund, $5.10. Total, $112.89.

Total amount of Offerings, $2,539.69.

Property.

Church, Chapel and lots (estimated worth), $20,000.
Rectory and lot (estimated worth), $7,000.
Condition of property, good.
Insurance, $9,000.
Sittings in the Church and Chapel, all free.

Remarks.

Of the above amount contributed for improvement of Church property, $100 (from the Ladies Society) was expended upon stone for the south porch of the Church; and the balance upon a clere-story of six gothic windows piercing the roof of the Church on either side, adding an harmonious dignity and airiness that admits a flood of light into the architectural beauties of the structure. Over the openings canvas is now stretched while the Cathedral glass is being manufactured. A duplicate of our solid-silver chalice, and a beautifully-worked set of altar linen was provided by the special contribution of the Misses Gilbert "in loving memory of their parents."

The " Permanent Fund " is undergoing a slow but natural increase.

ST. MARGARET'S CHURCH, MENANDS.

Priest in charge The Rev. Edgar T. Chapman.

Parochial.

Families, 22, Individuals (adults, 78, children, 39), 117; Baptisms (infants), 4. Marriages, 4; Burials, 6, Communicants, last reported, 62, present number, 62; Public Services, Sundays, 2 each, Holy days, 1 each; Holy Communion (public), all Sundays and Holy days. Sunday School, teachers, 5, pupils, 30; Catechizing, monthly.

Offerings.

Diocesan.—Diocesan Missions $.3 59. Orphan House of the Holy Saviour, $5; The Child's Hospital, $5.

Total amount of Offerings, $23 59.

Clinton County.

TRINITY CHURCH, PLATTSBURGH

Rector. The Rev. Hobart Cooke
Lay Readers. Hon John H. Booth, Capt George E. Pond, U. S. A.
Wardens. George F. Nichols, Wm. T. Ketcham.
Vestrymen. Hon S. A. Kellogg, Hon John M. Weaver, Alvah L. Inman, Albert M. Warren Hon. George S. Weed, John Ross, Millard F. Parkhurst, Edward T. Gilliland.

13

Parochial.

Baptisms (adults, 3, infants, 7), 10; Confirmed, since last report, 17; Marriages, 9; Burials, 14; Communicants, 247; Public Services (Sundays, Holy days and other days), 261; Holy Communion (public, 70, private, 3), 73; Sunday School, teachers, 12, pupils, 105.

Offerings.

Parochial.—Alms at Holy Communion, $97.72; Current expenses, including salaries, $3,497.94; Sunday School, $200.60; Home of the Friendless, $36; Other parochial objects, $150. Total, $2,982.26.

Diocesan.—Diocesan Missions, $100; Salary of the Bishop, $60; Diocesan Fund and Clerical Insurance, $52.50; Orphan House of the Holy Saviour, $44; The Child's Hospital, $25. Total, $281.50.

General.—Domestic and Foreign Missions, $45; Jewish Missions, $8. Total, $53.

Total amount of Offerings, $3,316.76.

Property.

Church and lot (estimated worth), $20,000.
Parsonage and lot (estimated worth), $6,000.
Condition of property, excellent.
Amount of salary pledged Rector, $1,500.
Number of sittings in the Church, 450; rented.

CHRIST CHURCH, ROUSE'S POINT.

Rector. The Rev. James F. Olmsted.
Wardens. William Crook, David White.
Vestrymen. J. R. Sperry, J. R. Myers, Alexander Wood, H. L. Clarke, J. H. Van Buskirk.

Parochial.

Families, 70; Individuals (adults, 140, children, 50), 190; Baptisms, infants, 5; Present number of Confirmed Persons, about 100; Marriages, 1; Burials, 7; Communicants, last reported, 59, admitted, 2, died, 3, removed, 2, present number (corrected), 62; Public Services (Sundays, 52, Holy days, 2, other days, 17), 71; Holy Communion (public, 13, private, 2), 15; Sunday School, teachers, 6, pupils, 46; Catechizing, number of children, school, number of times, fortnightly.

Offerings.

Parochial.— Alms at Holy Communion, $23.04, Current expenses, including salaries, $727.31, Sunday School, $11. Total, $761.35.

Diocesan.— Diocesan Missions, $17.88; Salary of the Bishop, $12 ; Diocesan Fund, $14, Orphan House of the Holy Saviour, $9 87; Chapter House Fund, $12.03. Total, $54.78.

General.—General Theological Seminary, Domestic and Foreign Missions, $8.16; for the Jews, $6.07; Foreign and Domestic Missions from Sunday School, $6.61. Total, $20.84.

Total amount of Offerings, $847.97.

Property.

Church and lot (estimated worth), $3,000.
Condition of property, poor.
Indebtedness, note, $75.
Amount of salary pledged Rector, $400.
Number of sittings in the Church, 215; rented, 144; free, 71.

Remarks.

The Rev. James F. Olmsted resigned this parish November 1, 1893, and the Rev. W. Ball Wright succeeded to the Rectorship.

ST. JOHN'S, CHAMPLAIN.

Rector. The Rev. James F. Olmsted.

Wardens. James Averill, Jr., Jehiel C. White.

Vestrymen. Henry Hoyle, James De F. Burroughs, James M. Hackett, M. D., John H. Crook.

Parochial.

Families, 28; Individuals (adults, 48, children, 32), 80; Baptisms, infants, 4; Present number of Confirmed Persons, 47; Marriages, 4, Burials, 2; Communicants, last reported, 45, present number, 45; Public Services (Sundays, 77, Holy days, 24, other days, 50), 151; Holy Communion (public, 65, private, 3), 68; Sunday School, teachers, 4, pupils, 21; Catechizing, number of children, school, number of times, Sundays.

Offerings.

Parochial.— Alms at Holy Communion, $25.30, Current expenses, including salaries, $535.20; Sunday School, $5.65; Increase and Improvement of Church Property, $75; Paid interest and part of principal of debt, $63.50. Total, $703.65.

Diocesan.— Diocesan Missions, $20; Salary of the Bishop, $6; Diocesan Fund, $14; Orphan House of the Holy Saviour, $12.55; Chapter House Fund, $8.98. Total, $61.53.

General.— Domestic and Foreign Missions, $10.85; Domestic and Foreign Missions, from Sunday School, $18.80; for the Jews, $2.66. Total, $32.31.

Total amount of Offerings, $797.49.

Property.

Church and lot (estimated worth), $3,000.

Parsonage and lot (estimated worth), $1,600.

Condition of property, good.

Indebtedness, note, $200.

Amount of salary pledged Rector, $400.

Number of sittings in the Church, 200; all free.

Remarks.

The Rev. James F Olmsted resigned this parish, Nov. 1, 1893, and the Rev. W. Ball Wright succeeded to the Rectorship.

ST. PETER'S CHURCH, ELLENBURGH.

Rector. The Rev Silas M. Rogers, A. M.

Wardens. William H. Sawyer and Giles H. Carew.

Vestrymen. George Higgins, Edwin Sawyer, Herman Allen, Allen Sargent, Bryan Emerson, Millard Emerson and William Shutts.

Parochial.

Baptisms (adults, 2, infants, 3), 5; Marriages, 4; Burials, 4; Communicants, died, 12, removed, 4, present number, 38; Public Services (Sundays), 51; Sunday School, teachers, 2, pupils, 20.

Offerings.

Parochial.—Alms at Holy Communion, $17.05; Sunday School, $9. Total, $26.05.
Diocesan.— Diocesan Missions, $5; Salary of the Bishop, $4; Diocesan Fund, $3; Fund for Aged and Infirm Clergymen, $2. Total, $14.
General.— Foreign Missions, $4.
Total amount of Offerings, $44.05.

Property.

Church and lot (estimated worth), $2,000.
Condition of property, good.
Number of sittings in the Church, 150.

ST. PAUL'S CHURCH, ELLENBURGH CENTRE.

Rector. The Rev. Silas M. Rogers, A. M,
Wardens. Orson Hoff and George W. Carpenter.
Vestrymen. Alfred Harris, Lyman Carpenter, Thomas Harris, Samuel Gilmore, Alden Hazzletine, Stephen Goodspeed and Ryland Holt.

Parochial.

Baptisms, infants, 8; Marriages, 1; Burials, 2; Communicants, removed, 1, present number, 25; Public Services, Sundays, 50.

Offerings.

Parochial.—Alms at Holy Communion, $5; Increase and Improvement of Church Property, $24. Total, $29.
Diocesan.— Diocesan Missions, $5.
Total amount of Offerings, $34.

Property.

Church and lot (estimated worth), $2,000.
Condition of property, good.

Columbia County.

CHRIST CHURCH, HUDSON.

Rector. The Rev. Sheldon Munson Griswold.
Lay Readers. Mr. A. E. Heard, Mr. D. B. MacNeil.
Wardens W. B. Skinner, H. J. Baringer
Vestrymen. J. P. Wheeler, M. D., John M. Pearson, A. C. Stott, C. W. Bostwick, Clarence L. Crofts, F. T. Punderson, James Eisenmann and Samuel B. Coffin.

Parochial.

Families (about), 250; Baptisms (adults, 10, infants, 45), 55; Confirmed, since last report, 25. Present number of Confirmed Persons, 495, Marriages, 9, Burials, 28. Churchings, 1; Communicants, last reported, 483, admitted, 25, died, 7, removed, 11, present number (recorded), 491; Public Services (Sundays, 149, Holy days, 92, other days, 353), 594, Holy Communion (public, 105, private 9), 114; Sunday School, teachers, 24, pupils, 263, Catechizing, whole school, weekly.

Offerings.

Parochial.—Alms at Holy Communion. $117.70; Current expenses, including salaries, $3,336.24; Sunday School, $168.75; Increase and Improvement of Church Property, $1,241.19; Other parochial objects, $308. Total, $5,171.88.

Diocesan —Diocesan Missions, $100; Salary of the Bishop, $66; Diocesan Fund, $97.50; Bible and Common Prayer Book Society of Albany, $11.20; Fund for Aged and Infirm Clergymen, $9.19; Fund for Widows and Orphans of Clergymen, $10.85; Orphan House of the Holy Saviour, $6.03; The Child's Hospital (from Sunday School), $17.10; Society for Promoting Religion and Learning, $7.84; Clergy Reserve Fund, $9.18; Diocesan Missionary (from Sunday School), $14.10; Canon Stewart, for work in Cobleskill, $10. Total, $359.99.

General.—Domestic Missions, $25.50; Foreign Missions, $12.60; Home Missions to Coloured Persons, $4.26; for Rev. Mr. Pott in China, $22; for Missions to the Jews, $9.39; American Church Building Fund, $15. Total, $88.75.

Total amount of Offerings. $5,619.63.

Property.

Church and lot (estimated worth), $40,000
Parsonage and lot (estimated worth), $7,000.
Other property, $3,000.
Condition of property, thoroughly good.
Indebtedness, floating (about), $2,000.
Insurance, $23,000.
Amount of salary pledged Rector, $1,500.
Number of sittings in the Church, 500; number rented, about three-fourths.

Remarks.

The Rector held eleven services at the House of Refuge for Women, at one of which the Bishop of the Diocese preached. At 6 the Rector preached, and 4 were celebrations of the Holy Communion. The Rev. Dr. Carter also conducted several services at the same place.

ALL SAINTS' CHURCH, HUDSON.

Rector. The Rev. George G. Carter.
Wardens William H. Cookson, Richard A. Aitken.
Vestrymen. Alexander R. Benson, George H. Palmer, Robert Storm, Benjamin Thompson.

Parochial.

Families, 39, Baptisms (infants), 10, Present number of Confirmed Persons, 100; Marriages, 2, Burials, 5; Communicants, last reported, 89, admitted, 1, received, 2, died, 2, removed, 4, present number, 86; Public Services (Sundays, 110, Holy days, 38, other days, 140), 288, Holy Communion (public, 110, private, 6), 116; Sunday School, teachers, 16, pupils, 144; Catechizing, number of children, all, number of times, 54.

Offerings.

Parochial — Current expenses, including salaries, $503.63; Sunday School, $72.46. Total, $576.09

Diocesan.— Diocesan Missions, $32.68, Salary of the Bishop, $6; Diocesan Fund, $10.50; Fund for Aged and Infirm Clergymen, $4.22, Fund for Widows and Orphans of Clergymen, $4.22; Orphan House of the Holy Saviour (Woman's Auxiliary), 1 box; The Child's Hospital, $8.50 (besides materials and work, Woman's Auxiliary); For St. Luke's, Chatham, $7.37; Clergy Reserve Fund, $4.23. Total, $77.72.

General.—Home Missions to Coloured Persons, $53.24 (from Sunday School, $14.16); General Missions, $7.28; Missions to Deaf Mutes, $7. Total, $67.52.

Total amount of Offerings, $720.33.

Property.

Condition of property, good.

Insurance, $3,000.

Amount of salary pledged Rector, $800.

Sittings in the Church, all free.

CHURCH OF ST. JOHN THE EVANGELIST, STOCKPORT.

Rector. The Rev. Eugene L. Toy.

Assistant. The Rev. William B. Reynolds.

Wardens. William H. Van de Carr, Jacob H. Pultz.

Vestrymen. F. H. Scott, G. Byron Reynolds, John H. Wild, Frank M. Snyder, Fred W. Buss, Robert B. Reynolds, Frank Steuerwald, Ormerod Hanson.

Parochial.

Baptisms, infants, 12; Present number of Confirmed Persons, about 150; Marriages, 1; Burials, 14; Communicants, last reported, 149, admitted, 2, received, 1, died, 6, removed, 6, present number, 140; Public Services (Sundays, 182, Holy days, 102), 284; Holy Communion (public, 85, private, 3), 88; Sunday School, teachers, 20, pupils, 172; Catechizing, number of children, all, number of times, every Sunday; Sewing School, teachers, 5, pupils, 40.

Offerings.

Parochial.—Current expenses, including salaries, $1,484.86; For King's Daughters, $2.60. Total, $1,487.46.

Diocesan.—Diocesan Missions, $25; Salary of the Bishop, $26, Diocesan Fund, $16.72; Orphan House of the Holy Saviour, $10.28; Diocesan Missionary, $15; St. Paul's, Sidney, N. Y., $5, St. Luke's, Chatham, N. Y., $5. Total, $103.

General.—General Missions, $35.24; Church Society for the Jews, $2.45; To a King's Daughter in Vermont, $15.78. Total, $53.47.

Total amount of Offerings, $1,643.93.

Property.

Church and lot (estimated worth), $15,000.

Parsonage and lot (estimated worth), $4,000.

Other property, Parish school-house, $3,000, Organ, $1,500.

Condition of property, very good.

Insurance, $4,000.

Amount of salary pledged Rector, $900, and Rectory.

Amount of salary pledged Assistant Minister, none.

Number of sittings in the Church and Chapel, 330, all free.

Remarks.

Communion Alms and Sunday School offerings are included in report as offerings for Missions, Diocesan Missionary, etc. Service and Sunday School are held every Sunday at St. James' Mission, Rossman's Mills.

Not included in the above, is the sending by the Women's Guild, of two boxes, one of Christmas tree presents to the Crow Creek Agency, South Dakota, and one of clothing, to Salt Lake City, Utah, (estimated value, including freight charges, $90.44,); and a present to the Parish Church of a set of new Altar Service and Prayer Books. Total receipts of Guild, $122.49.

The King's Daughters gave to the Church a full set of white hangings, Altar cloth, etc., and a closet for them, costing in all, $88.13. Total receipts, $184.79.

In Oct., 1892, the Women's Guild of St. James' Mission was organized, and it has given to the Mission Chapel a new Altar cloth, window shades, a surplice, and has had a vestry room built in the old porch. Total receipts, $51.32.

ST. PAUL'S CHURCH, KINDERHOOK.

Rector. The Rev. James Wessell Smith.

Wardens. Henry T. Wynkoop, Edward P. Van Alstyne.

Vestrymen. Francis Silvester, T. Floyd Woodworth, M. D., Franklin B. Van Alstyne, Tunis Devoe, Andrew Ketterson, James M. Hawley, William Heeney, Elbridge T. Howard.

Parochial.

Families, 68; Individuals (adults, 155, children, 59), 214; Baptisms (adults, 2, infants, 13), 15; Present number of Confirmed Persons, 113; Burials, 3; Communicants, last reported, 133, received, 6, died, 2, removed, 25, present number, 112; Public Services (Sundays, 132, Holy days, 23, other days, 57), 212; Holy Communion (public, 44, private, 2), 46, Sunday School, teachers, 7, pupils, 54; Catechizing, number of children, whole school, number of times, 5.

Offerings.

Parochial.— Alms at Holy Communion, $10.23; Current expenses, including salaries, $1,098.58; Increase and Improvement of Church Property, $25. Total, $1,133.81.

Diocesan.— Diocesan Missions, $31; Salary of the Bishop, $36; Diocesan Fund, $; Bible and Common Prayer Book Society of Albany, $9; Orphan House of the Holy Saviour (from Sunday School), $6.41; The Child's Hospital (from Sunday School), $6.41. Total, $109.82.

General.— Domestic and Foreign Missions (from Sunday School, $15.75, included), $41.80.

Total amount of Offerings, $1,285.43

Property.

Church and lot (estimated worth), $5,000.

Parsonage and lot (estimated worth), $3,000.

Condition of property, very good.

Insurance, $3,500.

Amount of salary pledged Rector, $900.

Sittings in the Church, all free.

Remarks.

The present Rector, the Rev. James W. Smith, began June 18, 1893, to which time the Rectorship had been vacant since June 25, 1892, but the services on Sundays and the greater feasts have been held regularly (including the Holy Communion), by invited Clergy, and the Senior Warden, Henry S. Wynkoop, Esq., as lay-reader, whose devoted services and care have been gratefully appreciated and acknowledged by a cordial resolution of the Vestry in meeting.

TRINITY CHURCH, CLAVERACK.

Rector, The Rev. George G. Carter.
Wardens. Robert Fulton Ludlow, Richard M. Ludlow.
Vestrymen. Cornelius Shaw, Arthur Rowley, James J. Studley, Franklin P. Studley.

Parochial.

Families, 26; Present number of Confirmed Persons, 60; Marriage, 1; Communicants, last reported, 50, admitted, 2, received, 2, removed, 3, present number, 51; Public Services (Sundays, 52, Holy days, 8, other days, 25), 85, Holy Communion (public, 30, private, 1), 31; Sunday School, teachers, 6, pupils, 50; Catechizing, number of children, all, number of times, 15.

Offerings.

Parochial.—Current expenses, including salaries, $316.21; Sunday School, $28.90; Increase and Improvement of Church Property, $34.50. Total, $379.61.

Diocesan.—Diocesan Missions, $27.66; Salary of the Bishop, $6; Diocesan Fund, $7; Fund for Aged and Infirm Clergymen, $3.66; The Child's Hospital, $3.74; Chapter House, $25. Total, $73.06.

General.—General Missions (Domestic, Foreign and Indian), $7.

Total amount of Offerings, $459.67.

Property.

Condition of property, good.
Insurance, $2,950.
Amount of salary pledged Rector, $200.

CHURCH OF OUR SAVIOUR, LEBANON SPRINGS.

Rector. The Rev. George B. Johnson.
Wardens. Silas G. Owen, John G. Field.
Vestrymen. Francis Myers, J. Harry Cox, George A. Temple, Judah R. Jones, Charles E. Wackerhagen.

Parochial.

Families, 19; Individuals (adults, 46, children, 19), 65; Confirmed, since last report, 1; Present number of Confirmed Persons, 37; Communicants, last reported, 31, admitted, 1, died, 2, present number, 30; Public Services (Sundays, 104, Holy days, 66, other days, 478), 648, Holy Communion, public, 63.

Offerings

Parochial —Alms at Holy Communion, $22.33, Current expenses, including salaries, $310 87 Total, $333.20.

Diocesan.— Diocesan Missions, $22 54, Salary of the Bishop, $6; Diocesan Fund, $9; Diocesan Missionary, $5; Orphan House of the Holy Saviour, $4; Society for Promoting Religion and Learning, $12.87; Clergy Insurance Fund, $1.50. Total, $60 91.

General.— Domestic Missions, $4 21; Foreign Missions, $4.21; Home Missions to Coloured Persons, $2 80 Total, $11.22

Total amount of Offerings, $405 33.

Property.

Church and lot (estimated worth), $3,000.
Parsonage lot (estimated worth), $275.

Other property, money in hand for Rectory, $1,243.67.
Amount of salary pledged Rector, $300.
Number of sittings in the Church, 150; all free.

Remarks.

The $500 bequeathed to the Church by the late Merriman M. Field have been intrusted for investment to the Treasurer of the Diocesan Board of Missions, so that the interest only will be at the disposal of the Vestry. The death of Mr. William Henry Babcock removes from the Parish one who from its first organization in 1870 has been one of its Wardens.

ST. BARNABAS' CHURCH, STOTTVILLE.

Rector. The Rev. Wm. H. A. Hall.
Wardens. Frank H. Stott, John J. Plass.
Vestrymen. Levi Plass, Charles H. Stott, Fred. A. Welch, R. H. Harder, Jr., Fred. H. Palmer, James Shortell, David Cooper, Charles B. Van Rensselaer.

Parochial.

Families, 80, Individuals (adults, 240, children. 200), 440; Baptisms (adults, 5, infants, 9), 14; Confirmed, since last report, 21, Present number of Confirmed Persons, 182; Marriages, 5; Burials, 6; Communicants, last reported, 189, admitted, 21, received, 3, died, 2, removed, 3, present number, 182, who have communicated during the last year, 128; Public Services (Sundays, 130, Holy days, 36, other days, 226), 392; Holy Communion (public, 56, private, 5), 61; Sunday School, teachers, 81, pupils, 176; Catechizing, number of children, all, number of times, 37.

Offerings.

Parochial.— Alms at Holy Communion, $84.43; Current expenses, including salaries, $1,120.82; Sunday School, $58.91: Increase and Improvement of Church Property, $55.30; Ladies' Aid Society, $138.94; Rector's Library Fund, $10; Altar Guild, $123.68. Total, $1,592.08.

Diocesan.— Diocesan Missions, $25; Salary of the Bishop, $26; Fund for Aged and Infirm Clergymen, $17; Orphan House of the Holy Saviour, $12.50; Home for the Aged, Hudson, $42.92; Mission at Cobleskill, $25; Mission at Sidney, $12.07; Salary of Diocesan Missionary, $10. Total, $170.49.

General.— Home Missions to Coloured Persons, $8.30; Sisters of St. Margaret, $6.50; General Missions (S. S.), $39   Total, $53.80.

Total amount of Offerings, $1,816 37

Property.

Church and lot (estimated worth), $10,000.
Condition of property, good
Insurance, $9,000.
Amount of salary pledged Rector, $1,000.
Number of sittings in the Church, 325; all free.

Remarks.

There is now in hand about $1,200, toward the erection of a much needed Rectory. A careful revision of the roll of communicants results in an apparent discrepancy between this and last year's report.

ST. MARK'S CHURCH, PHILMONT.

Rector. The Rev. Arthur Lowndes.
Wardens. George Baker, Henry Kroosz.
Vestrymen. George Edward Clum, S. W. Richardson, Richard Allen Woodruff.
M. D., F. W. Herington, Dean Best, Charles Pitcher.
Vestry Clerk. F. W. Herington.

Parochial.

Families, 45; Individuals (adults, 70, children, 30), 100; Baptisms (adults, 2, infants, 4), 6; Marriages, 1; Burials, 1; Communicants, last reported, 80, received, 1, died, 1, removed, 6, present number, 74; Public Services (Sundays, 212, Holy days, 54, other days, 22), 288; Holy Communion (public, 88, private, 1), 89; Sunday School, teachers, 5, pupils, 40; Catechizing, number of children, the Sunday School, number of times, monthly.

Offerings.

Parochial.— Current expenses, including salaries, $968.52; Sunday School, $30.59; Increase and Improvement of Church Property, Guild Hall, Study and Rectory, $13,015; Furnace in Church, $50; Frescoing Church, $200; Roodscreen, Altar candlesticks and additions to Sanctuary, $800. Total, $15,064.11.

Diocesan.—Diocesan Missions, $38.97; Salary of the Bishop, $6; Fund for Aged and Infirm Clergymen, $3; Fund for Widows and Orphans of Clergymen, $3; Orphan House of the Holy Saviour, box, value, $10; Education of Young Men for the Ministry, $3; Diocesan Missionary, $5. Total, $68.97.

General — Domestic Missions, $5; Foreign Missions, $5; Clergymen's Retiring Fund, $12. Total, $22.

Total amount of Offerings, $15,155.08.

Property.

Church and lot (estimated worth), $10,000
Parsonage and lot (estimated worth), $8,500
Guild Hall, $6,500
Church ornaments, $1,000
Condition of property, excellent
Indebtedness, bond and mortgage on Rectory, $4,500
Floating debt on repairs and improvements, $275.
Insurance, $4,775.
Amount of salary pledged Rector, $700
Number of sittings in the Church, 300, all free.

Remarks.

The Guild Hall and Rectory are completed through the munificence of Mr James Aken, who has during the past year added from time to time to his original gift. We are indebted to him not only for the land, the Guild Hall, the Choir Room and the Study, and for the loan of the money to build the Rectory, but also for many practical and ornamental additions to the buildings. His generosity has been surpassed only by his unostentatious and simple manner of giving. To him must belong the reward of the " cheerful giver."

To friends far and near, rich and poor, the Rector is indebted for numerous gifts for the adornment of the Sanctuary and for the erection of the Roodscreen. The Church has been frescoed throughout by Mr E. J N Stent in a manner that reflects credit both to his loyal churchmanship and to his artistic taste. The women of the Parish have undertaken to meet this expense.

A chapter of the Brotherhood of St Andrew has been formed.

ST. LUKE'S CHURCH, CLERMONT.

Rector. The Rev. M. E. Wilson.

Trustees. Robert Dibble, Harold Wilson, M E. Wilson, Geo. Z. Foland, W. C. Doane, H. J. Rivenburgh.

Parochial.

Baptisms (infants), 6; Marriages, 1; Communicants, last reported, 18, removed, 2, present number, 16; Public Services (Sundays, 47, Holy days, 5), 52; Holy Communion (public), 10.

Offerings.

Parochial.— Alms at Holy Communion, $13.60; Parochial objects, $8.40. Total, $22.

Diocesan.— Diocesan Missions, $10; Salary of the Bishop, $4; Diocesan Fund. $2. Total, $16.

Total amount of Offerings, $38.

CHURCH OF ST. JOHN IN THE WILDERNESS, COPAKE IRON WORKS.

Rector. The Rev. Arthur Lowndes.

Assistant. The Rev. William Benjamin Reynolds

Warden. Charles Ridgeley Elliott.

Parochial.

Families, 18; Individuals (adults, 21, infants, 9). 30. Baptisms (infants), 1; Present number of Confirmed Persons. 13; Burials, 1; Communicants, last reported, 8, received, 3, died, 1, removed 1, present number, 9; Public Services (Sundays, 22. other days, 2), 24; Holy Communion (public, 3, private, 2), 5.

Offerings.

Parochial.— Current expenses, including salaries. $108.70; Increase and Improvement of Church Property, $26. Total, $134.70.

Diocesan.— Diocesan Missions, $5.

Total amount of Offerings, $139.70.

Property.

Church and lot (estimated worth), $2,500.

Parsonage and lot (estimated worth), $2,000.

Condition of Property, good.

Indebtedness, floating debt ($200 loan to repair Rectory, $55.40 on current expenses), $255.40.

Insurance on Church, $1,000, on Rectory, $1,000, on Church furniture, $250. Total, $2,250.

Amount of salary pledged Rector, ——.

Amount of salary pledged the Assistant Minister, $450.

Number of sittings in the Church, 150; all free.

Remarks.

By the assistance of the Rev. F. Thompson, of Cannan, Conn., and of a lay-reader, I have been able to keep the Church open with some regularity this year since spring. The Rev. W B. Reynolds has accepted the position of deacon-in-charge, and will take up his residence in the Parish in November. The establishment of the Summer

Home at Copake, of the Parish of the Heavenly Rest, New York, in the coming year will, I hope, tend to strengthen the Parish. Between here and Copake, at Hillsdale, Craigville, Martindale, and the surrounding farming country, are scattered Church people who, now that there is a resident clergyman at Copake, will be visited, and it is hoped to open up a Mission at Hillsdale before very long.

ST. LUKE'S CHURCH, CHATHAM.

Missionary. The Rev. H. R. Luney.

Parochial.

Families and parts of families, 19; Individuals (adults, 50, children, 20), 70; Baptisms (adults), 5; Confirmed, since last report, 23; Present number of Confirmed Persons, 35; Burials, 1; Communicants, last reported, 10, admitted, 25, present number, 35; Public Services (Sundays), 99; Holy Communion (public), 27; Sunday School, teachers, 4, pupils, 30; Catechizing, number of persons, 30, number of times, every Sunday.

Offerings.

Parochial.—Current expenses, including salaries, $568.83; Sunday School, $5.63. Total, $574.46.

Diocesan.—Diocesan Missions, $14.50; Salary of the Bishop, $2; Fund for Aged and Infirm Clergymen, $8.75. Total, $25.25.

Total amount of Offerings, $599.71.

Property.

Church and lot (estimated worth), $12,000.
Condition of property, excellent.
Indebtedness, mortgages, $3,000; loan, $1,850.
Insurance, $3,000.
Amount of salary pledged Rector, $500.
Number of sittings in the Church, 200; all free.

Delaware County.

ST. PETER'S CHURCH, HOBART.

Rector. The Rev. Thomas Burrows.
Wardens. A. H. Grant, George Barlow
Vestrymen. William. J. Calhoun, George Moore, Robert McNaught, Roswell Barlow, George M. Sturges, James Porteus, O B. Foote

Parochial.

Families, 53, Baptisms (adults, 10, infant, 1), 11; Confirmed, since last report, 10; Burials, 8, Communicants, last reported, 52, admitted, 9, received, 1, died, 7, present number about 105. Public Services (Sundays, 43, Holy days, 3, other days, 17), 63; Holy Communion (public), 5; Sunday School, teachers, 6, pupils, 85; Catechizing, number of times, 5.

Offerings.

Parochial.—Alms at Holy Communion, $15; Current expenses, including salaries, $283 37; Increase and Improvement of Church Property, $350; Other Parochial objects: For Choir Music, $15.49, Surplice, Cassock and Stole, $22.80. Total, $686.66.

Diocesan —Diocesan Missions, $26.45; Salary of the Bishop, $20. Total, $46.45.

Total amount of Offerings, $733.11.

Property.

Church and lot (estimated worth), $5,000.
Parsonage and lot (estimated worth), $1,500.
Other property, cemetery.
Condition of property, good.
Indebtedness, $100.
Insurance on Church, $5,000; on Rectory, $1,500.
Amount of salary pledged Rector, $500.
Number of sittings in the Church, 350; rented, 144; free, 206.

Remarks.

This report covers the five months of my Rectorship, from June 1 to November 1. Before that time six of the eight funerals reported had taken place, and most of the improvements to the Church property.

The number of communicants here given (103) is from the record. The actua participants would not equal more than about half that number.

A Chapter of the Brotherhood of St. Andrew, with twenty-five members, and one of the Daughters of the King, with twenty-four members, have been organized. These and a Parish Guild afford scope for the activities of the people, and promise good results.

An encouraging work is under way at Bloomville, nine miles distant. Services are held on alternate Sunday afternoons, with an average attendance of 45.

ST. JOHN'S CHURCH, DELHI.

Wardens. Charles E. Hitt, R. G. Hughston.
Vestrymen. Alex. Shaw, G. M. Harley, G. A. Paine, John W. Woodruff, H. A. Pitcher, John A. Kemp, S. E. Smith.

Parochial.

Families, 98; Individuals, 301; Baptisms (adults, 4, infants, 6), 10; Present number of Confirmed Persons, 218; Marriages, 4; Burials, 11; Communicants, present number, about 170; Public Services (Sundays, 144, Holy days, 19, other days, 58), 221; Holy Communion (public, 75, private, 3), 78; Sunday School, teachers, 8, pupils, 72.

Offerings.

Parochial.— Alms at Holy Communion, $99.49; Current expenses, including salaries, $1,973.53; Other Parochial objects, $5.11. Total, $2,078.13.
Diocesan.— Diocesan Missions, $7.50; Fund for Aged and Infirm Clergymen, $20; Orphan House of the Holy Saviour, $18 50; For Archdeaconry of Susquehanna, $15.32. Total, $63 32
General.— Domestic and Foreign Missions, $47; For Society Conversion of Jews, $4.10. Total, $51.10.
Total amount of Offerings, $2,191.21.

Property.

Church and lot (estimated worth), $10,000.
Parsonage and lot (estimated worth), $8,000.
Other property, Memorial Chapel, $25,000.
Condition of property, good.
Indebtedness, Parochial, $125; Missions, $117.50; Di

Amount of salary pledged Rector, $1,200.
Number of sittings in the Church, 288; free, 36.

Remarks.

Chapel sittings, all free, 125.

CHRIST CHURCH, WALTON.

Rector. The Rev. Richard C. Searing.
Warden. George C. Seeley.
Vestrymen. John S. Eells, Samuel H. Fancher, Julius W. St. John, Joseph Harby, Horace E. North, Edwin W. Pond, John H. Townsend, Thomas A. Pine.

Parochial.

Families, 110; Individuals (adults, 260, children, 90), 350; Baptisms (adults, 6, infants, 13), 19; Confirmed, since last report, 18; Marriages, 4; Burials, 11 ; Communicants, revised list for last year, 128, admitted, 17, received, 2, died, 4; removed, 1, present number, 147; Public Services (Sundays, 184, Holy days, 30, other days, 80), 234; Holy Communion (public), 69; Sunday School, teachers, 16, pupils, 110; Catechizing, number of children, all, number of times, 20.

Offerings.

Parochial.—Alms at Holy Communion, $22.29; Current expenses, including salaries, $2,205.04; Sunday School, $48.39; Increase and Improvement of Church Property, $82.77; Young Men's Christian Association, $4.32; Town Sunday School Association, $1.68; Work of Sanctuary Guild, $23.93 ; From Woman's Auxiliary for box for Orphan House at Cooperstown, $35. Total, $2,423.42.

Diocesan.—Diocesan Missions, $17.35; Salary of the Bishop, $20; Diocesan Fund, $30; Orphan House of the Holy Saviour, $6.97; For Archdeaconry of the Susquehanna, $5.23; Choir Festival at Cooperstown, $5. Total, $84.55.

General.— General Missions (from Sunday School), $24.88 ; Promoting Christianity among the Jews, $5 ; From the Woman's Auxiliary for Missions also, $38; Value of Missionary box, $50. Total, $117.88.

Total amount of Offerings, $2,615.85.

Property.

Church and lot (estimated worth), $10,000.
Parsonage and lot (estimated worth), $4,000.
Other property, $2,400, and legacy of $20,000, not yet secured.
Condition of property, good.
Indebtedness, deficit in current expenses for about three years, $1,500.
Amount of salary pledged Rector, $1,000
Number of sittings in the Church, 300; rented, 240; free, 60.

Remarks.

The Rector took charge of the Parish July 21, 1893. The present report is, therefore, more or less imperfect, in so far as some items must be estimated and not stated with accuracy.

One most severe loss our Parish has suffered this year in the decease of Mr. David Hyde Gay, confirmed in 1834 and made Clerk of the Vestry, made a Vestryman in 1837, Junior Warden in 1848 and Senior Warden in 1869, and retaining this position to the end of his life. "He was a good man and full of the Holy Ghost."

ST. PAUL'S, FRANKLIN.

Missionary. The Rev. G. A. Rathbun.

Wardens. Henry S. Edwards, E. P. Howe.

Vestrymen. George Copeland, Edward Naragon, Alfred Barnes, Herbert Baldwin, Levi Stilson.

Parochial.

Families, 50; Baptisms (adults, 1, infants, 7), 8; Present number of Confirmed Persons, 74; Communicants, last reported, 64, died, 1, present number, 63; Public Services (Sundays, 52, Holy days, 4, other days, 48), 104; Holy Communion (public), 2; Sunday School, teachers, 4, pupils, 20.

Offerings.

Parochial.— Current expenses, including salaries, $655.61; Sunday School, $17.33; Altar Society, $25; Dorcas Society, $5.85. Total, $703.79.

Diocesan.— Diocesan Missions, $20; Salary of the Bishop, $16; Diocesan Fund, $7; Orphan House of the Holy Saviour, $23. Total, $43.

Total amount of Offerings, $746.79.

Property

Church and lot (estimated worth), $6,500.

Parsonage and lot (estimated worth), $1,500.

Condition of property, good.

Insurance, $3,800.

Amount of salary pledged Rector, $200.

Number of sittings in the Church, 400; all free.

CHRIST CHURCH, DEPOSIT.

Rector. The Rev. Frederick S. Fisher.

Wardens. Dr. William H. Gregory, died October 8, 1893; Titus M. Bixby.

Vestrymen.—C. Onderdonk. John M. Kerr, Philip Munson, Charles Pinkney, James McDonald.

Parochial.

Families, 50; Individuals (adults, 105, children, 46), 151; Baptisms (adults, 2, infants, 11), 13; Confirmed, since last report, 11; Present number of Confirmed Persons, 95; Marriages, 1; Burials, 2; Communicants, last reported, 88, admitted, 11, died, 1, removed, 4, present number, 89; Public Services, Sundays, all, Holy days, most, other days, Fridays; Holy Communion (public), Monthly and on Holy days; Sunday School, teachers 5, pupils, 50; Catechizing, each Sunday.

Offerings.

- Sunday School, to credence, $29.20; Increase and Improvement of Church Property, not known, for Sunday School, $16.87; Easter for New Church, $26.20. Total, $72.07.

Diocesan.—Diocesan Missions, $18; Salary of the Bishop, $6. Total, $24.

General.—Domestic Missions, $5.66.

Total amount of Offerings, $101.73.

Property.

Church and lot (estimated worth), $8,000.

Other property, old church, $1,200.

Condition of property, good.

Indebtedness, none, save the result of a change in the cellar, which was not according to previous specification, $150.

Insurance, $4,000.

Amount of salary pledged Rector, $600.

Number of sittings in the Church, $250.

Remarks.

The new Church of the Parish, a well-built stone building, was consecrated by the Bishop of the Diocese, Thursday, October 12, 1893.

GRACE CHURCH, STAMFORD.

Missionary. The Rev. Howard McDougall.

Warden. Albert Clist.

Trustees. Brundage Handford Foote, John Elliott.

Parochial.

Families, 20; Individuals (adults, 39, children, 26), 65; Present number of Confirmed Persons, 32; Burials, 3; Communicants, last reported, 30, removed, 4, present number, 29; Public Services (Sundays, 153, Holy days, 13, other days, 17), 183; Holy Communion (public), 56; Sunday School, teachers, 5, pupils, 28; Catechizing, 40.

Offerings.

Parochial.— Alms at Holy Communion, at early services, $10.30, at late services, $35.55; Current expenses, including salaries, $595; Sunday School, $30; Increase and Improvement of Church Property, $100. Total, $770.85.

Diocesan.— Diocesan Missions, $20; Salary of the Bishop, $6; Diocesan Fund, $9; Orphan House of the Holy Saviour, Lenten Offerings of S. S. children, $10.53, and two barrels of clothing, estimated at $25 each, from Parish. Total, $95.53.

Total amount of Offerings, $866.38

Property.

Church and lot (estimated worth), $2,500.

Condition of property, good.

Insurance, $1,000.

Amount of salary pledged Rector, $450.

Number of sittings in the Church, 200; all free.

Remarks.

A fair was held in August at which $500 was realized. There is also $425 belonging to this Parish in two Kingston banks.

ST. PAUL'S CHURCH, SIDNEY.

Priest-in-charge. The Rev. George H. Fenwick.

Warden. E. Winsor.

Parochial.

Communicants, last reported, 47, Sunday School, teachers, 6, pupils, 26; Catechizing, every Sunday.

Property.

Church and lot (estimated worth), $5,000

Amount of salary pledged Rector, $500.

Remarks.

By appointment of the Bishop I took charge of this Mission on the 1st day of September, 1893. Just a week before my appointment the laying of the corner-stone of the new Church took place; the building is well under way, and we hope to hold our first service in the new Church early in Advent. The value of the Church property will be about $5,000. A large portion of this amount has been already gathered, and we hope next year to report the building completed and out of debt.

EMMANUEL CHURCH, GRIFFIN'S CORNERS.
Missionary. The Rev. Samuel D. Van Loan.

Parochial.

Individuals, 35; Baptisms (adults, 2, infants, 1), 3; Confirmed, since last report, 11; Marriages, 1; Communicants, last reported, 5, admitted, 6, received, 1, present number, 12; Public Services (Sundays), 15; Holy Communion (public), 3; Sunday School, teachers, 2, pupils, 12.

Offerings.
Current expenses, including salaries, $323.60.

Remarks.
Services will be held (D. V.) throughout the winter and coming summer. A more detailed report will be made in 1894.

Essex County.
THE CHURCH OF THE CROSS, TICONDEROGA.

Rector. The Rev. Henry T. Gregory.
Wardens. John C. Fenton, D. C. Bascom.
Vestrymen. George B. Bascom, Henry C. Burnet, W. T. Bryan, J. H. Bryan, Frederick Higgins, Lyman Malcolm, William C. Noyes, R. M. Wilbur.

Parochial.

Families, 70; Baptisms (infants), 4; Confirmed, since last report, 1; Marriages, 3; Burials, 4; Communicants, last reported, 90, received, 2, died, 4, removed, 4, present number, 84; Public Services (Sundays, 88, Holy days, 14, other days, 34), 136; Holy Communion (public), 21; Sunday School, teachers, 3, pupils, 70; Catechizing, Sunday School, frequently.

Offerings.

Parochial -- Current expenses, including salaries, $536.45; Sunday School, $61.71; Increase and Improvement of Church Property, $370.27; Insurance, $16 50. Total, $984.93.

Diocesan — Diocesan Missions, $30, Salary of the Bishop, $7.50; Bible and Common Prayer Book Society of Albany, $6.88. Fund for Aged and Infirm Clergymen, and Fund for Widows and Orphans of Clergymen, $6.83; Orphan House of the Holy Saviour, $7 42, Clergy Reserve Fund, $5.53; Salary of Diocesan Missionary, $4. Total, $68.16.

General.—General Missions, $30.50; Pine Ridge Agency, $5, Jewish Missions, $2.50. Total, $38.

Total amount of Offerings, $1,091.09.

Property.
Church and lot (estimated worth), $9,000.
Parsonage and lot (estimated worth), $2,500.
Condition of property, good.

Insurance on Church and Rectory, $7,450.
Amount of salary pledged Rector, $500.
Number of sittings in the Church, 270; all free.

Remarks.

A Circle of the King's Daughters, besides contributing the within amount reported for Indian Missions, sent to the Pine Ridge Agency a Sunday School Christmasbox, worth $33. A Memorial Window to a faithful communicant has been placed over the Altar, adding much to the beauty of the Chancel.

ST. JOHN'S CHURCH, ESSEX.

Rector. The Rev. William Norman Irish.
Wardens. Stephen D. Derby, Andrew J. Tucker.
Vestrymen. Anthony J. B. Ross, Robert Fortune, Moses A. Knowlton, Edward W. Richardson, Ervin G. Lyon, Henry H. Knapp.

Parochial.

Families, 50; Individuals (adults, 70, children, 15). 85; Baptisms (infants), 3; Communicants, last reported, 88, admitted, 3, received, 1, died, 2, removed, 2, present number, 88; Public Services (Sundays, 100, Holy days, 10, other days, 60), 170; Holy Communion (public, 23, private, 2), 24; Sunday School, teachers, 4, public, 13; Catechizing, frequently.

Offerings.

Parochial.—Alms at Holy Communion, $42.83; Current expenses, including salaries, $305.09; Sunday School, $17.67; Revised Prayer Books, $5. Total, $400.59.

Diocesan.—Diocesan Missions, $30; Salary of the Bishop, $16; Diocesan Fund, $9; Bible and Common Prayer Book Society of Albany, $5; Fund for Aged and Infirm Clergymen, $3.17; Fund for Widows and Orphans of Clergymen, $3. Total, $66.17.

General.—Domestic and Foreign Missions (from Sunday School, $9.25, from Congregation, $5), $14.25, for the Jews, $2. Total, $16.25.

Total amount of Offerings, $483.01.

Property.

Church and lot (estimated worth), $3,000.
Parsonage and lot (estimated worth), $2,000.
Other property, $700.
Condition of property, good.
Insurance, Rectory, $1,600, Church, $1,000.
Amount of salary pledged Rector, $300.
Sittings in the Church, 150; all free.

Remarks.

The Parish is virtually without children, and those in the village are nearly all French Canadian, or descendants, and are connected with the Roman Communion. During the past year the Senior Warden, Mr. S. D. Derby, has conducted a Bible Class with excellent results.

ST. PAUL'S CHURCH, KEESEVILLE.

Rector. The Rev John W. Gill.
Wardens. Henry Dundas, Frances Cassidy.
Vestrymen.— James Dundas, Elias J. Champlin, Philip Harrison, Frank Rice.

Parochial.

Families, 38; Individuals (adults, 70, children, 26), 96; Baptisms (adults, 1, infants, 5), 6; Confirmed, since last report, 1; Present number of Confirmed Persons, 56; Marriages, 1; Burials, 5; Communicants, last reported, 59, received, 1, died, 5, removed, 1, present number, 53; Public Services (Sundays, 48, Holy days, 3, other days, 48), 99; Holy Communion (public), 15; Sunday School, teachers, 5, pupils, 27; Catechizing, number of children, 27, number of times, weekly. ·

Offerings.

Parochial.—Current expenses, including salaries, $677; Sunday School, $2. Total, $679.

Diocesan.—Salary of the Bishop, $10; Diocesan Fund, $15. Total, $25.

General. —Domestic Missions, $2.

Total amount of Offerings, $706.

Property.

Church and lot (estimated worth), $2,000.

Parish Rooms (estimated worth), $1,250.

Condition of property, good.

Insurance, $1,500.

Amount of salary pledged Rector, $400.

Number of sittings in the Church, 180; all free.

Remarks.

On Easter Sunday the Sunday School presented to the Church a stained-glass window, representing the Good Shepherd. There were also presented on the same day an Eagle Lectern, and a pair of Brass Candlesticks, as Memorials to two of the faithful departed. I rejoice to say that Mrs. Hammond, a faithful communicant of this Church, now in paradise, has left in her will $1,000 to St. Paul's Church.

CHRIST CHURCH, PORT HENRY.

Rector. The Rev. W. Ball Wright, M. A.

Wardens. Theodore Tromblee, Jr., W. M. J. Botham.

Vestrymen. F. S. Atwell, George Hoy, W. F. Foote, Jr., C. P. Parker, C. W. Woodford.

Parochial.

Families, 39. Individuals (adults, 78, children, 70), 148; Baptisms (adults, 9, infants, 5), 14; Confirmed, since last report. 5; Present number of Confirmed Persons, 63; Marriages, 1; Burials, 8; Churchings, 1; Communicants, last reported, 52, admitted, 5, received, 1, died, 1, removed, 4, present number, 53; Public Services (Sundays, 104, Holy days, 20, other days, 102), 226; Holy Communion (public, 58, private, 1), 59; Sunday School, teachers, 4, pupils, 25; Catechizing, number of children, 2, number of times, 8; Services at Crown Point Mission, 13.

Offerings.

Parochial.—For current expenses, Sunday School and Increase and Improvement of Church Property, $434.59 ; Paid Rector, $520. Total, $954.59.

Diocesan.—Diocesan Missions, $31.25; Salary of the Bishop, $10; Diocesan Fund, $7.80; Increase of the Episcopate Fund, $1.30; Orphan House of the Holy Saviour, $7. Total, $57.35.

General.— Domestic Missions, $5.05; Foreign Missions, $3.10. Total, $8.15.

Total amount of Offerings, $1,020.09.

Property.

Church and lot (estimated worth), $5,000.
Condition of property, good.
Insurance, $1,500.
Amount of salary pledged Rector, from November 1, 1892, to 1893, $520; from November 1, 1893, to 1894, $300.
Number of sittings in the Church, 180; all free.

EMMANUEL CHURCH, MINEVILLE.

Missionary. The Rev. Wm. Ball Wright, M. A.

Parochial.

Families, 28; Individuals (adults, 84, children, 56) 140; Baptisms, 4; Present number of Confirmed Persons, 34; Burials, 1; Communicants, last reported, 12, received, 4, removed, 2, present number, 14; Public Services (Sundays, 32, Holy days, 1, other days, 6), 39; Holy Communion (public), 4; Sunday School, teachers, 4, pupils, 20; Catechizing, number of children, 10, number of times, 12.

Offerings.

Parochial,— Current expenses, including salaries, $19.60.
Diocesan,— Diocesan Missions, $5.
Total amount of Offerings, $24.60.

Property.

Church and lot (estimated worth), $1,000.
Condition of property, good.
Insurance, paid to December, 1894.
Number of sittings in the Church, 125; all free.

Remarks.

The Rev. W. Ball Wright held services with very sparse attendance till the end of January, every Sunday, then on alternate Sundays, going the other Sundays to Crown Point. In October, 1893, some new members came to live, including two ladies, who have taken hold, and so the Sunday School, after being discontinued for two years, has been re-established and has already twenty scholars and four teachers.

ST. JAMES' CHURCH, AUSABLE FORKS.

Priest in charge. Rev. Jno. W. Gill.
Lay Reader. James Rogers.
Warden. James Rogers.

Parochial.

Families, 27; Individuals (adults, 78, children, 56), 134; Baptisms (infants), 1; Confirmed, since last report, 4, Present number of Confirmed Persons, 50; Marriages, 2, Burials, 2; Communicants, last reported, 47, present number, 51, Public Services (Sundays, 48, other days, 3), 51, Holy Communion (public), 13; Sunday School. teachers, 5, pupils, 47; Catechizing, number of children, 47, number of times, weekly.

Offerings.

Parochial.— Current expenses, including salaries, $430; Increase and Improvement of Church Property, $186.33. Total, $616.33.
Diocesan — Diocesan Missions, $15, Salary of the Bishop, $16. Total, $31.
Total amount of Offerings, $647.33.

Property.

Church and lot (estimated worth), $8,000.
Condition of property, good.
Insurance, $5,000.
Amount of salary pledged Rector, $200.
Number of sittings in the Church, 200; free.

Remarks.

During the past year the outside of the Church has been painted. and the St. James' Guild, composed of the ladies of the congregation, have recarpeted the Church.

CHURCH OF THE REDEEMER, BLOOMINGDALE.

Rector. The Rev. Walter H. Larom.

Parochial.

Families, 15; Individuals (adults, 27, children, 40), 67; Baptisms (infants), 3; Present number of Confirmed Persons, 15; Marriages, 2; Communicants, last reported, 12, present number, 15; Public Services (Sundays), 12; Holy Communion (public), 1; Sunday School, teachers, 4, pupils, 50.

Offerings.

See St. Luke's Church, Saranac Lake.

Property.

Church and lot (estimated worth), $2,500.
Condition of property, good.
Sittings in the Church all free.

ST. ANDREW'S CHURCH, SCHROON LAKE.

Rector. The Rev. Calbraith Bourne Perry.
Wardens. Effingham Nichols, Bayard Clark.
Vestrymen. Jacob Bohrman, Robert Taylor, Oren Taylor, Aug. Boyle, Bradford Squires.

Parochial.

Families, 47; Individuals (adults, 102, children, 63), 165: Baptisms (adults, 3, infants, 8), 11; Confirmed, since last report, 12; Marriages, 2; Burials, 4; Churchings, 1, Communicants, admitted, 14, died, 3, present number, 53; Public Services (Sundays, 129, Holy days, 38, other days, 16), 183, Holy Communion (public, 56, private, 3), 59; Sunday School, teachers, 6, pupils, 50.

Offerings.

Parochial.— Current expenses, including salaries, $839.08.
Diocesan.— Diocesan Missions, $8.39; Salary of the Bishop, $4. Total, $12.39.
General.— Domestic Missions, $7.
Total amount of Offerings, $858.47.

Property.

Condition of property, in thorough repair.

Remarks.

For several years St. Andrew's had been supplied with services only in the summer, but by the energy of the Diocesan Missionary money was raised to keep the Church open throughout the year, and there was a good attendance all through the winter months. Provision has been made for the coming winter also; besides a number of gifts from summer visitors and from members of the congregation, Altar, Litany-desk, Altar cloths and other hangings and embroideries, a valuable lot of land, seventy-five feet front by three hundred feet deep, has been given by Mr. James D. Platt for the erection of a Parish building and Hall.

ST. EUSTACE'S CHURCH, LAKE PLACID.

Missionary.   The Rev. Walter H. Larom.
Treasurer of Building Fund.   Henry B. Auchincloss.

Parochial.

Public Services (Sundays), 18.

Offerings.

All included in report for Church of St. Luke, Saranac Lake, Franklin county.

Remarks.

No Church building.   Summer services are held in the Stevens House and in the Mirror Lake House.

Franklin County.

ST. MARK'S CHURCH, MALONE.

Rector.   The Rev. Charles Temple.
Wardens.   Dr. R. J. Wilding, M. S. Mallon.
Vestrymen.   J. O. Ballard, John Fay, A. C. Hadley, Hon. Albert Hobbs, Samuel Greene, E. W. Knowlton, A. H. Merritt, C. W. Allen.

Parochial.

Families, 100; Individuals (adults, 220, children, 55), 275; Baptisms (infants), 7; Present number of Confirmed Persons, 180; Marriages, 6; Burials, 7; Communicants, last reported, 162, died, 5, removed, 14, present number, 143; Public Services (Sundays, 125, other days, 55), 180; Holy Communion, public, weekly, private, frequent; Sunday School, teachers, 10, pupils, 50, Catechizing, number of children, all, number of times, weekly.

Offerings.

Parochial.—Alms at Holy Communion, $48.88; Current expenses, including salaries, $1,951.95; Sunday School, $70, Increase and Improvement of Church Property, $220.33; Other Parochial Objects, $15.66.   Total, $2,306.82.

Diocesan.— Diocesan Missions, $100; Salary of the Bishop, $36; Diocesan Fund, $36.   Total, $172.

General — Domestic Missions, $10; Foreign Missions, $10; Indian Missions, $10; Home Missions to Coloured Persons, $10; Missions to Jews, $8.   Total, $48.

Total amount of Offerings, $2,526.82.

Property.

Church and lot (estimated worth), $20,000.
Parsonage and lot (estimated worth), $6,000.

Condition of property, excellent.
Insurance, $15,000.
Amount of salary pledged Rector, $1,300.
Number of sittings in the Church, 270; rented, 250; free, 20.

ST. PETER'S CHURCH, BRUSHTON.

Rector. The Rev. A. L. Fortin.
Wardens. W. S. Lawrence, H. C. Brush.
Vestrymen. James Consworth, James Sargent, W. H. Smith, J. E. Brady, George Harris, James Pickering, Robert Dunlap.

Parochial.

Families, 15; Individuals (adults, 60, children, 13), 73; Baptisms (adults, 2, infants, 2), 4; Present number of Confirmed Persons, 26; Burials, 3; Communicants, last reported, 20, admitted, 1, removed, 1, present number, 20; Public Services (Sundays), 117; Holy Communion (public), 12; Sunday School, teachers, 3, pupils, 19; Catechizing, number of times, 12.

Offerings.

Parochial.— Current expenses, including salaries, $356; Sunday School, $21; Increase and Improvement of Church Property, $165; Other Parochial Objects, $174.20. Total, $716.20.

Diocesan.— Diocesan Missions, $10; Salary of the Bishop, $8; Diocesan Fund, $9.80. Total, $27.80.

General.— Domestic and Foreign Missions, per Sunday School, $8.19.
Total amount of Offerings, $752.19.

Property.

Church and lot (estimated worth), $3,000.
Parsonage and lot (estimated worth), $1,600.
Condition of property, excellent.
Amount of salary pledged Rector, $280.
Number of sittings in the Church, 150; all free.

ST. MARK'S CHURCH, WEST BANGOR.

Rector. The Rev. A. L. Fortin.
Warden. C. A. Crooks.

Parochial.

Families, 14; Individuals (adults, 21, children, 12), 33; Confirmed, since last report, 16; Present number of Confirmed Persons, 16; Burials, 1; Communicants, last reported, 15, present number, 15; Public Services, fortnightly; Holy Communion (public), 12, monthly; Sunday School, teachers, 3, pupils, 17.

Offerings.

Parochial.— Current expenses, including salaries, $75; Sunday School, $4.50. Total, $79.50.

Diocesan.— Diocesan Missions, $5; Diocesan Fund, $2.63. Total, $7.63.
General.— Foreign Missions, $3.20.
Total amount of Offerings, $90.33.

Property.

Church and lot (estimated worth), $1,200.
Condition of property, good.
Insurance, $1,000.
Amount of salary pledged Rector $75.
Number of sittings in the Church, 200; all free.

Remarks.

A Ladies' Aid has been organized a few weeks ago, and already good work has been accomplished. The Sunday School is in a good state of efficiency under the fostering care of Mrs. Darling and Miss Winslow. The congregations have increased during the past year, but we have had no addition to our membership.

ST. JAMES' CHURCH, HOGANSBURGH.

Missionary. The Rev. David Jenkins.
Warden. A. A. Fulton.

Parochial.

Families, 17; Individuals (adults, 38, children, 14), 52; Baptisms (infants), 1; Present number of Confirmed Persons, 35; Marriages, 1; Burials, 2; Communicants, present number, 23; Public Services, one each Sunday; Holy Communion (public), monthly; Sunday School, teachers, 2, pupils, 9.

Offerings.

Parochial.— Current expenses, including salaries, $250; Increase and Improvement of Church Property, $9.55. Total, $259.55.

Diocesan.— Diocesan Missions, $25; Salary of the Bishop, $8; Diocesan Fund, $7.50; Insurance Fund for Clergymen, $1.25. Total, $41.75.

Total amount of Offerings, $301.30.

Property.

Church and lot (estimated worth), $3,000.
Parsonage and lot (estimated worth), $700.
Other property, $150.
Condition of property, good.
Insurance on Parsonage, $700.
Amount of salary pledged Rector. $250.
Number of sittings in the Church, 140; all free.

Remarks.

The Parsonage is being put in thorough repair by the Warden, A. A. Fulton, and all at his expense; could not get the amount expended by him up to date.

CHURCH OF ST. LUKE THE BELOVED PHYSICIAN, SARANAC LAKE.

Rector The Rev. Walter H. Larom.
Warden Dr. E. L. Trudeau.

Parochial.

Families, 80; Individuals (adults, 150, children, 100), 250; Baptisms (adults, 4, infants, 15), 19; Confirmed, since last report, 29, Marriages, 3; Burials, 5; Communicants, last reported, 86, admitted, 14, received, 4, died, 1, removed, 5, present number, 100. Public Services (Sundays, 76, Holy days, 18, other days, 53), 147; Holy Communion (public, 40, private, 6), 46; Sunday School, teachers. 10, pupils, 110.

Offerings.

Parochial.—Current expenses, including salaries, $2,963 57; Parish School, $75 75; Total, $3,039.32.

Diocesan.—Diocesan Missions, $20; Salary of the Bishop, $6; Diocesan Fund, $25; Other offerings for objects within the Diocese, $100; Total, $151.

Total amount of offerings, $3,190.32.

Property.

Church and lot (estimated worth), $4,000.
Other property, library, $7,000.
Condition of property, excellent.
Amount of salary pledged Rector, no stated amount.

Remarks.

Many of the Church Records were burnt up at a recent fire, together with a portion of the Rector's library. The above records are correct as nearly as can be ascertained.

THE CHURCH OF ST. JOHN IN THE WILDERNESS, PAUL SMITH'S.

Rector. The Rev. Walter H. Larom.
Warden. Dr. E. L. Trudeau.

Parochial.

Families (Summer Church), 1; Burials, 2; Public Services, Sundays, 14; Holy Communion, public, 8.

Offerings.

Vide St. Luke's Church, Saranac Lake.

Property.

Church and lot (estimated worth), $8,000.
Condition of property, excellent.
Number of sittings in the Church, 275; all free.

FORT COVINGTON MISSION.

Missionary. The Rev. David Jenkins.
Warden. M. M. Smith.

Parochial.

Families, 10; Individuals (adults, 22, children, 6), 28; Baptisms, infants, 2; Present number of Confirmed Persons, 17; Marriages, 2; Communicants, present number, 13; Public Services, one each Sunday; Holy Communion, public, monthly.

Offerings.

Parochial.—Current expenses, including salaries, $200.
Diocesan.—Diocesan fund, $6.13.
Total amount of Offerings, $206.13.

Property.

Amount of salary pledged Rector, $175.

GOOD SHEPHERD CHURCH, SANTA CLARA.

Missionary. The Rev. Charles A. Howells.
Warden. John Hurd.

Parochial.

Baptisms (adults, 2, infants, 6), 8; Burials, 2; Communicants, present number, 7; Public Services, Sundays, 18; Holy Communion, public, 1; Sunday Schools, teachers, 3, pupils, 25.

Offerings.

Parochial.—Current expenses, including salaries, $120.66.

Property.

Amount of salary pledged Rector, $700.

Fulton County.

ST. JOHN'S CHURCH, JOHNSTOWN.

Rector. The Rev. J. N. Marvin.
Wardens. Abiram S. Van Voast, Thomas E. Ricketts.
Vestrymen. Hon. J. M. Carroll, Isaiah Yanney, Jonathan Ricketts, James I. Younglove, Charles Prindle, Robert J. Evans, John Chetwynde, John W. Uhlinger.

Parochial.

Families, 221, parts of, 51; Baptisms (adults, 5, infants, 19), 24; Confirmed, since last report, 17; Marriages, 5; Burials, 14; Communicants, last reported, 303, admitted, 21, received, 13, died, 9, removed, 10, present number, 318; Public Services (Sundays, 152, Holy days, 31, other days,* 146), 329; Holy Communion (public, 91, private, 6), 97; Sunday School, teachers, 26, pupils, 175; Catechizing, number of children, 145.

Offerings.

Parochial.— Alms at Holy Communion, $45.63; Current expenses, including salaries, $2,258.03; Sunday School, $267.59; Increase and Improvement of Church Property, $20.25; Parish Charities, $150; St. John's Register, $75; Other Parochial Objects, $100. Total, $2,916.50.

Diocesan.— Diocesan Missions, $75;, Salary of the Bishop, $50; Diocesan Fund, $38.50; Orphan House of the Holy Saviour, $31.50, The Child's Hospital, St. Margaret's House, $13; Theological Education, $6.39; Diocesan Missionary, $20; boxes, Cooperstown Orphanage, $35; 1 box, Child's Hospital, $4.75; 1 box, St. Margaret's House, $4 Total, $277.64.

General.— Domestic Missions, $23.93; Foreign and Domestic Missions, $29.86; Indian Missions, $7.50; Jewish Missions, $2.89; box to Bishop Whipple's Hospital (value), $65; the Church Temperance Society, $10. Total, $139.18.

Total amount of Offerings, $3,333.32.

Property.

Church and lot (estimated worth), $20,000.
Parsonage and lot (estimated worth), $5,000.
Other property, $1,000.
Number of sittings in the Church, 350; all free.

CHRIST CHURCH, GLOVERSVILLE.

Missionary The Rev. Henry Mason Smyth.
Warden. Henry Marshall.
Treasurer. David S. Thompson.
Clerk. Frank Lawrence.

---

* Daily prayers are said in the Rector's study when not said in the Church.

Parochial.

Families, 103; Individuals (adults, 252, children, 162), 414; Baptisms (adults, 3, infants, 18), 21; Confirmed, since last report, 21; Marriages, 4; Burials, 9; Communicants, last reported, 154, admitted, 22, received, 26, died, 3, removed, 9, present number, 190; Public Services, Sundays, 8 A. M. (excepting first of the month), 10:30 A. M., and 7:30 P. M., Holy days, 10 A. M. or 7:30 P. M., other days, Fridays; Holy Communion, Sundays and great festivals, private, 2; Sunday School, teachers, 10, pupils, 100; Catechizing, frequently.

Offerings.

Parochial.— Current expenses, including salaries, $951.47; Sunday School, $15.06; Increase and Improvement of Church Property, $751.76; Other Parochial Objects, $96.78. Total, $1,815.07.

Diocesan.— Diocesan Missions, $25; Salary of Bishop, $10; The Child's Hospital, $10; Diocesan Missionary, $5. Total, $54.73.

General.— Conversion of the Jews, $4.73.

Total amount of Offerings, $1,869.80.

Property.

Church and lot (estimated worth), $8,000.

Condition of property, excellent.

Indebtedness, mortgage, $2,000.

Amount of salary pledged Missionary, $700.

Number of sittings in the Church, 300; all free.

ST. JOHN'S CHURCH, DOLGEVILLE.

Missionary. The Rev. D. A. Bonnar, since August 1.

Warden. Albert Kuehn.

Treasurer. D. R. Fowler.

Parochial.

Baptisms (adults, 6, infants, 3), 9; Confirmed, since last report (two occasions), 13; Present number of Confirmed Persons, 31; Churchings, 1; Communicants, last reported, 14, admitted, 6, received, 2, present number, 22; Public Services (Sundays, 65, Holy days, 2, other days, 20), 87; Holy Communion, public, 25.

Offerings.

Parochial.—Alms at Holy Communion, $4.58; Current expenses, including salaries, $200.68; Rent of rooms, $59.50; Rent of organ, $16; Increase and Improvement of Church Property, $61.69; Church building, $143.02; Altar silver, $7.14; Font fund, $1; Altar guild, $2.50; Insurance, $14. Total, $510.11

Diocesan.—Diocesan Missions, $10.

Total amount of Offerings, $520.11.

Property.

Church and lot (estimated worth), $5,000.

Condition of property, good.

Indebtedness, on account of Church building, $2,638.52; on account current expenses, $50.

Insurance, $2,000.

Amount of salary pledged Rector, $400.

Number of sittings in the Church, 240; all free.

The Church was finished, so far as to be used and opened for services on Sunday, June 18 last, Canon Stewart and the Rev. Mr. Mariett holding a week's Mission for Instruction at that time.   August 1, the present Priest in charge entered on his duties.   This report, therefore, includes a large amount of work done by Mr. Mariett, who was in charge the first nine months of the Convention year.   The Ladies' Society has continued to render very efficient help, as in the past.   The conditions have changed since the last report, Presbyterians, Universalists and German Methodists having all entered on the field to contend for the ascendency.   Many who had given their support to the Church's Mission have been attracted to these other centers for one or other reason — and we are thrown, as is likely to be the case generally, upon our own strength for carrying on the work.   Financial straitness has crippled to a large degree the power of the few Church people, and in consequence we are hardly able to do one-half of what should be done here to carry on the work — and have been unable to do any thing whatever toward completing the building or paying a portion of the debt.   We shall hope for assistance from the faithful in our Diocese — when the present hardness has been removed from the money and labour interests.   Of the money reported above, $245.35 have come from the Ladies' Society.

Greene County.

ST. LUKE'S CHURCH, CATSKILL.

Rector.   The Rev. Elmer P. Miller.
Lay Reader.   Frederic E. Craigie.
Wardens.   Wm. L. Du Bois and Henry T. Jones.
Vestrymen.   M. B. Mattice, Theo. A. Cole, W. H. H. Schofield, Charles S. Willard, Charles Trowbridge, Robert Selden, Wm. S. C. Wiley and Frederic E. Craigie.

Parochial.

Families, 225; Baptisms (adults, 5, infants, 15), 20; Confirmed, since last report, 16; Present number of Confirmed Persons, 389; Marriages, 7; Burials, 25; Communicants, last reported, 355, admitted, 28, received, 20, died, 6, removed, 8, present number, 389; Public Services (Sundays, 151, Holy days, 44, other days, 147), 342, Holy Communion (public, 78, private, 10), 88; Sunday School, teachers, 18, pupils, 160.

Offerings.

Parochial.—Alms at Holy Communion, $142.21; Current expenses, including salaries, $2,131.61; Sunday School, $102.20; Reading room and record, $190 00; New Church Fund, $5,584.20.   Total, $8,150.22.

Diocesan.—Diocesan Missions, $150, Salary of the Bishop, $30; Diocesan Fund, $36, Bible and Common Prayer Book Society of Albany, $10; Fund for Aged and Infirm Clergymen, $10, Orphan House of the Holy Saviour, $40; The Child's Hospital (by Sunday School), $48; Diocesan Missionary (by Sunday School), $15; Missionary insurance, $6.   Total, $345.

General.—Domestic Missions, $20; Foreign Missions, $15; For Church, Muskogee, I. T , $5; Missions to the Jews, $6.07; Bishop Leonard, Utah, $9 31; St. Mark's School, Utah (by Sunday School), $40; Miss Buford, $2.50; Dr. Briggs, $2.50.   Total, $100 38.

Total amount of Offerings, $8,595.60.

Property.

Church and lot (estimated worth), $8,000.
Parsonage and lot (estimated worth), $4,500.
Other property, $9,000.
Insurance, $7,000.
Amount of salary pledged Rector, $1,200.

CHRIST CHURCH, COXSACKIE.

Rector. The Rev. E. S. De G. Tompkins.
Wardens. H. J. Hahn, N. H. Vosburg.
Vestrymen. N. A. Calkins, J. E. Brown, Jr., Wm. Farmer, M. H. Green, H. Jordan, E. Moorley, G. H. Scott, L. Van Bergen.

Parochial.

Families, 23; Burials, 2; Communicants, present number, 45; Public Services (Sundays, 104, Holy days, 3), 107; Holy Communion, public, 15; Sunday School, teachers, 3, pupils, 25.

Offerings.

Parochial.—Alms at Holy Communion, $700; Current expenses, including salaries, $725. Total, $1,425.
Diocesan.—Diocesan Missions, $5; Salary of the Bishop, $12. Total, $17.
Total amount of Offerings, $1,442.

Remarks.

During the year a rectory and parish room have been erected and nearly completed. By spring it is hoped the whole Church property will be in a complete and attractive condition.

TRINITY CHURCH, ATHENS.

Wardens. Samuel H. Nichols, Henry C. Van Loan.
Vestrymen. Geo. S. Nichols, Frank Beardsley, Wm. Cook, Frank Nichols, Geo. Nedtwick, M. Davenport.

Property.

Church and lot (estimated worth), $5,000.
Parsonage and lot (estimated worth), $2,000.
Other property, $6,000.
Condition of property, good.
Number of sittings in the Church, 250; all free.

Remarks.

Our late Rector, Rev. J. W. Stewart, having resigned and removed, we have no information from which a complete report can be made.

ST. PAUL'S CHURCH, OAK HILL.

Rector. The Rev. T. A. Snyder.
Wardens. Walter S. Cheritree, Charles A. Hall.
Vestrymen. Byron Hall, Theodore L. Cheritree, Ambrose H. Flower, Charles E. Graham, Hyram Snyder.

Parochial.

Families, 19; Marriages, 1; Communicants, last reported, 33, received, 1, present number, 34; Public Services (Sundays, 47, Holy days, 8, other days, 6), 61; Holy Communion, public, 32.

Offerings.

Parochial.—Alms at Holy Communion, $5.87; Current expenses, including salaries, $162.53; Increase and Improvement of Church Property, $293.71. Total, $463.11.

Diocesan.—Diocesan Missions, $5; Salary of the Bishop, $6; Bible and Common Prayer Book Society of Albany, $2; Chapter House Fund, $5. Total, $18.

General.— Domestic and Foreign Missions, 87 cts.

Total amount of Offerings, $480.98.

Property.

Condition of property, improved.

Amount of salary pledged Rector, $125, and rent of rectory.

Remarks.

The repairs on Church were made from the income of the Miss Austin fund.

CHRIST CHURCH, GREENVILLE.

Rector. The Rev. T. A. Snyder.

Warden. Winfield S. Rundle.

Vestrymen. Byron Waldron, W. S. Vanderbilt, James Ponsonby, John Galatian, E. A. Galatian, Reuben R. Palmer, L. D. Stewart, Herbert Sanford.

Parochial.

Families, 20; Baptisms, adults, 1; Marriages, 1; Burials, 2; Communicants, last reported, 41, died 2, removed, 6, present number, 33; Public Services (Sundays, 48, Holy days, 6), 54; Holy Communion (public, 26, private, 3), 29.

Offerings.

Parochial.—Alms at Holy Communion, $6.39; Current expenses, including salaries, $113.10; Increase and Improvement of Church Property, $32.82. Total, $152.31.

Diocesan.—Diocesan Missions, $5; Salary of the Bishop, $6; Diocesan Fund, $2; Bible and Common Prayer Book Society of Albany, $2; 25th Anniversary Consecration Bishop Doane, $5. Total, $20.

General.—Domestic and Foreign Missions, $4.09.

Total amount of Offerings, $176.40.

Property.

Condition of property, Rectory needs painting.

Indebtedness, on repairs of Rectory, $315.14.

Remarks.

I wish to put on record the great loss to the parish by the death of Egbert N. Palmer, who was for many years a faithful warden, and also a careful and efficient Treasurer of the parish. He left $400 to the parish, which is to be used to put a new roof on the Church. Faithful unto death, he awaits the crown of eternal life.

TRINITY CHURCH, ASHLAND.

Missionary. The Rev. Watson B. Hall

Wardens. Darius B. Prout, Willis Chatfield.

Vestrymen. Addison Steele, George S. Smith, Henry P. Smith, Merritt McLean.

Parochial.

Families, 16; Baptisms, adults, 1; Burials, 2; Communicants, last reported, 31, died, 1, present number, 30; Public Services, Sundays, 20; Holy Communion, public, 5.

CALVARY CHURCH, CAIRO.

Rector. The Rev. J. T. Zorn.
Lay Reader. Webster W. Jennings
Wardens. Lucius W. Byington, Levi K. Byington.
Vestrymen. Edwin E. Darby, John C. Lennon, George H. Noble, M. D., Selden H. Hine, Alfred Bennett, John K. Palen, Nelson Carman, F. C. Burnham.

Parochial.

Families, 36; Individuals (adults, 70, children, 15), 85; Baptisms (adults 2, infants, 3), 5; Present number of Confirmed Persons, 52; Marriages, 1; Burials, 6; Communicants, last reported, 56, died, 1, removed, 3, present number, 52; Public Services (Sundays, 116, Holy days, 61, other days, 364), 541; Holy Communion (public, 78, private, 1), 79; Sunday School, teachers, 3, pupils, 15; Catechizing, number of children, 15, number of times, 20.

Offerings.

Parochial.—Alms at Holy Communion, $19.01; Current expenses, including salaries, $203.74; Increase and Improvement of Church Property, $110. Total, $362.75.

Diocesan.—Salary of Bishop, $6; Diocesan Fund, $7.50; Fund for Aged and Infirm Clergymen, $1.15; Orphan House of the Holy Saviour, $1.27. Total, $15.92.

General.— Domestic and Foreign Missions, $14.35; Church Temperance Society, $1.11. Total, $15.46.

Total amount of Offerings, $394.13.

Property.

Church and lot (estimated worth), $4,000.
Parsonage and lot (estimated worth), $1,000.
Condition of property, Church, good; Rectory, fair.
Insurance (Church, $2,000, Furniture, $500, Rectory, $1,000), $3,500.
Amount of salary pledged Rector, $250.
Number of sittings in the Church, 150; all free.

Remarks.

One hundred and ten dollars expended upon a new roof for the Church was contributed by the Women's Guild. Two of the Burials reported, and two of the Baptisms, were of inmates of the County Alms-house. Twelve Sunday afternoon services were held at the Alms-house. Beginning with Lent, and continuing until November 1st, Matins and Evensong were said daily in the Church, with but few exceptions, when the Offices were said in the Rectory. Throughout the winter they will be said daily at the Rectory, and the people are invited to attend them.

GLORIA DEI CHURCH, PALENVILLE.

Rector. The Rev. Wm. C. Grubbe.
Wardens. Walter Lasher.
Treasurer. Charles H. Chubb, M. D.
Clerk. Rufus T. Smith.

Parochial.

Families, 11; Individuals (adults, 38, children, 10), 48; Baptisms (adults, 1, infants, 1), 2; Present number of Confirmed Persons, 28; Burials, 3; Communicants, last reported, 29, admitted, 3, received, 5, died, 1, removed, 4, present number 32; Public Services (Sundays, 96, Holy days, 15, other days, 63), 174; Holy Communion (public, 118, private, 3), 121.

Offerings.

Parochial.—Current expenses, including salaries, $458.52; Increase and Improvement of Church Property, $181.75. Total, $640.27.

Diocesan.—Diocesan Missions, $12.10; Salary of the Bishop, $8; Diocesan Fund, $9. Total, $29.10.

General.—Domestic and Foreign Missions, $5; Church Mission to the Jews, $1. Total, $6.

Total amount of Offerings, $675.37.

Property.

Church and lot (estimated worth), $6,000.
Parsonage and lot (estimated worth), $1,500.
Condition of property, good.
Insurance, on Church, $2,200, on Rectory, $1,200.
Amount of salary pledged Rector, $800.
Number of sittings in Church, 150; all free.

Remarks.

Through the efforts of the Ladies Aid Society and of L. A. Holcomb, M. D., a coal furnace has been placed in the Church, to the comfort and satisfaction of the congregation.

From November, 1892, to July, 1893, I held services in Tannersville, every two weeks, at the residence of Mrs. Rose. Services held, 14; Holy Communion, 14, Marriages, 1.

Herkimer County.

TRINITY CHURCH, FAIRFIELD.

Priest in charge. The Rev. Clarence M. Conant.
Wardens. Reuben Neely, C. W. Nichols, M. D.
Vestrymen. John P. Todd, A. C Wilson, D. D. Warne, F. L. Warne and John Whitney.

Parochial.

Families, 10; Individuals (adults, 27, children, 9), 36; Present number of Confirmed Persons, 19, Burials, 1; Communicants, last reported, 21, removed, 2, present number, 19, Public Services, last Sunday in month, 10:30 A. M., other Sundays, 3 P. M.; Holy Communion, public, 11.

Offerings.

Parochial —Alms at Holy Communion, about $5, Current expenses, including salaries, about $135; Repairs to Church, $15; Repairs to Rectory, $61.21, set of coloured Stoles (personal), $10; set of Eucharistic vestments linen (personal), $15; white, silk Burse and Veil (personal), $8 Total, $249.21.

Diocesan —Fund for Aged and Infirm Clergymen, $1.

General —Foreign Missions, $1, Home Missions to Coloured Persons, $1; Missions to Jews, 50 cents. Total, $2.50 .

Total amount of Offerings, $252.71.

Property.

Church and lot (estimated worth), $1,000.

Parsonage and lot (estimated worth), $500.

Condition of property, Church, very bad; Rectory, good.

Amount of salary pledged Rector, $2 per Sunday.

Number of sittings in the Church, 200; all free.

During the year past, the Parish has had three very useful gifts. A beautifully embroidered white silk Burse and Veil from the Sisters of the Holy Nativity, Providence, R. I.; a set of linen Eucharistic vestments, from the Massachusetts Altar Society; and a set of handsome coloured Stoles from the Sisters of St. Margaret, Boston.

EMMANUEL CHURCH, LITTLE FALLS.

Rector. The Rev. Ernest Mariett.

Wardens. Rodney S. Whitman, Eben B. Waite.

Vestrymen. Hon. Geo. A. Hardin, Albert Storey, Geo. W. Searles, James D. Feeter, Hadley Jones, Harry Houghton, William Kingston, Charles Bailey.

Parochial.

Families, about 150; Individuals (adults, 250, children, 80), 330; Baptisms (adults, 3, infants, 26), 29; Confirmed, since last report, 27; Present number of Confirmed Persons, 175; Marriages, 3; Burials, 5; Communicants, last reported, 153, admitted, 27, received, 1, died, 1, removed, 8, present number, 170; Public Services Sundays, 3, Holy days, 1, other days, daily Morning Prayer and Friday Evening Prayer; Holy Communion, public, every Sunday and Holy day, private, 4; Sunday School, teachers, 12, pupils, 80; Catechizing, number of children, all, number of times, every Sunday; Parish School, teacher, the Rector, pupils, 5.

Offerings.

Parochial.—Alms at Holy Communion, $44.83; Current expenses, including salaries, $2,468.22; Increase and Improvement of Church Property, $2,726.18; Other Parochial objects, $26. Total, $5,264.73.

Diocesan.—Diocesan Missions, $20.38; Salary of the Bishop, $30; Diocesan Fund, $67; Bible and Common Prayer Book Society of Albany, $6.06; Fund for Aged and Infirm Clergymen, $2; Fund for Widows and Orphans of Clergymen, $2.62; Orphan House of the Holy Saviour, $14.04; The Child's Hospital, $31.02; Theological education, $2.81; For St. John's Mission, Dolgeville, From Sunday School, $60.82. Total, $250.05.

General.—Domestic Missions, $2.25; Foreign Missions, $4.53; Home Missions to Coloured Persons, $1 60; Jewish Missions, $7.66. Total, $16.04.

Total amount of Offerings, $5,530.82.

Property.

Church and lot (estimated worth), $20,000.

Parsonage and lot (estimated worth), $7,000.

Other property (Chapel, $2,000, House and lots, $4,000), $6,000.

Condition of property, good.

Insurance, $14,500.

Amount of salary pledged Rector, $1,200.

Number of sittings in the Church (and Chapel), 500; all free.

15

Remarks.

The Parish has added to the Church property a beautiful new organ, costing about $3,500. The total offering for the last year is larger than any previous year since 1870. The number confirmed (27), is the largest in the history of the Parish, which dates from 1835.

CHRIST CHURCH, HERKIMER.

Rector. The Rev. William C. Prout.

Wardens. George W. Pine, Robert Earl.

Vestrymen. J. D. Henderson, G. H. Kelsey, Levi A. Lawton, Clark A. Miller, H. G. Munger, C. W. Palmer, W. C. Prescott, C. C. Witherstine.

Parochial.

Families, 115; Individuals (adults, 316, children, 138), 454; Baptisms (adults, 6, infants, 21), 27; Confirmed, since last report, 31; Marriages, 6; Burials, 7; Communicants, last reported, 193, admitted, 27, received, 13, died, 1, removed, 2, present number, 229; Public Services, Sundays, 3 each Sunday, Holy days, Holy Communion, other days, Morning Prayer, daily, Evening Prayer, twice a week; Holy Communion, every Sunday and Holy day; Sunday School, teachers, 10, pupils, 90; Catechizing, number of children, Sunday School, number of times, every Sunday.

Offerings.

Parochial.—Current expenses, including salaries, $1,591.36; Sunday School, $95.96; Increase and Improvement of Church Property, $61.33; Missionary Guild (by clothing and money), $188.50; Choir Fund, $50.10; Altar Fund, $23.11; Poor Fund, $40. Total, $2,050.36.

Diocesan.—Diocesan Missions, $74.19; Salary of the Bishop, $16; Diocesan Fund, $35; Fund for Aged and Infirm Clergymen, $14.23; Fund for Widows and Orphans of Clergymen, $14.28; Orphan House of the Holy Saviour, $11.50; Diocesan Missionary, $10; Theological Education, $7.26. Total, $182.41.

General.—Jewish Missions, $6.50.

Total amount of Offerings, $2,239.26.

Property.

Church and lot (estimated worth), $25,000.

Parsonage and lot (estimated worth), $4,500.

Parish House, $4.000,

Condition of property, excellent.

Insurance, $13,000.

Amount of salary pledged Rector, $1,000 and use of Rectory.

Number of sittings in the Church, 250; all free.

ST. AUGUSTINE'S CHURCH, ILION.

Rector. The Rev. Wm. Mason Cook.

Wardens. F. C. Shepard, Geo. P. Rix.

Vestrymen. T. J. Behan, Geo. H. Barlow, Geo. H. Dyett, Alfred Williamson, N. A. Hanchett, Walter C. Rix, Walter S. Baker, John M. Weller.

Parochial.

Families, 134; Individuals (adults, 401, children, 142), 543; Baptisms (adults, 9, infants, 16), 25; Confirmed, since last report, 24; Present number of Confirmed Persons, 202; Marriages, 6; Burials, 9; Communicants, last reported, 136, admitted, 25, received, 13, died, 2, removed, 6, present number, 166; Public Services (Sundays, 143, Holy days, 50, other days, 104, cottage service, 1), 298; Holy Communion (public, 85, private, 6), 91; Sunday School, officers, 5, teachers, 12, pupils, 92; Catechizing, number of children, the school, number of times, weekly; Industrial School, teachers, 8, pupils, 75.

Offerings.

Parochial.-- Current expenses, including salaries, $1,382.52: By the Sunday School, $43.78; For the Sunday School, $35.50; Work of the Altar Guild, $12.82; Paid on Mortgage, $260.41. Total, $1,735.03.

Diocesan.—Diocesan Missions, $35; Salary of Bishop, $12; Diocesan Fund and Clergy Insurance, $21; Orphan House of the Holy Saviour, $4.63; Diocesan Missionary's Salary, by the Sunday School, $5; Clerical Reserve Fund, $1.63. Total, $79.26.

General.—General Theological Seminary, $1.63; Domestic and Foreign Mission ($14.89 by the Sunday School), $24.99; Church Mission to Deaf Mutes, $1.65; Bible and Prayer Book Society, $1.16 Total, $29.43.

Total amount of Offerings, $1,843.72.

Property.

Church and lot (estimated worth), $6,000.
Parsonage and lot (estimated worth), $3,000.
Condition of property, somewhat in need of repairs.
Indebtedness, on mortgage, $1,739.59; floating, $164.61.
Insurance, $5,000.
Amount of salary pledged Rector, $600.
Number of sittings in the Church, 232; all free.

Remarks.

Handsome red book markers for the Bible have been presented to the Parish. A small package of clothing was sent to the Orphan House of the Holy Saviour, Cooperstown.

GRACE CHURCH, MOHAWK.

Rector. The Rev. Wm. A. Stirling.
Wardens. Alex. W. Haslehurst, Edward C. Elwood.
Vestrymen. H. D. Alexander, James B. Rafter, Frank L. Van Dusen, Charles Spencer, J. D. Fitch, M. D., E. H. Doolittle.

Parochial.

Families, 40, Individuals (adults, 125, children, 53), 178; Baptisms (adults, 5, infants, 8), 13; Marriages, 2; Burials, 5; Communicants, last reported, 61, admitted, 1, present number, 62; Public Services (Sundays, 34, Holy days, 7, other days, 6), 47; Holy Communion, public, 3; Sunday School, teachers, 7, pupils, 48; Catechizing, number of children, whole Sunday School, number of times, 7.

Offerings.

Parochial — Alms at Holy Communion, $5.78; Current expenses, including salaries, $297.90; Sunday School, $10.20. Total, $313.88.
Diocesan.— Diocesan Missions, $15; Salary of the Bishop, $3. Total, $18.
Total amount of Offerings, $331.88.

Property.

Church and lot (estimated worth), $3,500.
Condition of property, excellent, and out of debt.
Insurance, $2,000.
Amount of salary pledged Rector, $600.
Number of sittings in the Church, 160: all free.

Remarks.

The above report is for less than five months, as the present incumbent took charge of the Parish, June 15, 1898. The Church was closed twenty months prior to this date.

ST. ALBAN'S CHURCH, FRANKFORT.

Rector. The Rev. Wm. Mason Cook.
Wardens. Wm. J. Bennett, Frank Williams.
Vestrymen. C. B. Cleland, Edward J. Gilligan, Ernest A. Bennett, R. Rose, Geo. W. Dyson.

Parochial.

Families, 33; Individuals (adults, 98, children, 47), 145; Baptisms, infants, 4. Confirmed, since last report, 2; Present number of Confirmed Persons, 30; Burials, 2; Communicants, last reported, 31, admitted, 1, removed, 3, present number, 29; Public Services (Sundays, 62, Holy days, 4, other days, 5), 71; Holy Communion, public, 12; Sunday School, teachers, 3, pupils, 25; Catechizing, number of children, school, number of times, weekly.

Offerings.

Parochial.— Alms at Holy Communion, $9.83; Current expenses, including salaries, $148 13, By the Sunday School, $8 70. For the Sunday School, $5 50: Increase and Improvements of Church Property, $50, Work of St Alban's Guild, $69 19, To Balance Offerings, $3 94. Total, $295.29

Diocesan.— Diocesan Missions, $5; Salary of the Diocesan Missionary (by the Sunday School), $1. Total, $6.

General — Domestic and Foreign Missions (by the Sunday School), $6.56.

Total amount of Offerings, $307 85.

Property

Church and lot (estimated worth), $3,000.
Condition of property, good.
Insurance, $2 000.
Amount of salary pledged Rector, $100
Number of sittings in the Church, 125, all free

Remarks

A new chancel window of pleasing design, made of cathedral glass, was put in the Church during the year.

A box of clothing worth $10 was sent to the Orphan House of the Holy Saviour by the St. Alban's Guild

THE CHURCH OF THE MEMORIAL, MIDDLEVILLE

Priest in charge. The Rev Clarence M Conant.
Warden. Mr John Molineux
Treasurer. C. W Hamlin, M. D.
Secretary. Edward W Yuirru

Parochial.

Families, 40; Individuals (adults, 96, children, 33), 129; Baptisms, infants, 1; Present number of Confirmed Persons, 65; Marriages, 1; Burials, 8; Communicants, last reported, 67. received, 2, died, 1, removed, 3, present number, 65; Public Services, Sundays, 8 and 10:30 A. M., 7:30 P. M. (except last Sunday in month, no forenoon service), Holy days. 8 and 9 A. M., 5 P. M., other days, daily, 9 A. M., 5 P. M. (except Fridays, 7:30 P. M. instead of 5). Holy Communion, public, 97; Sunday School, teachers, 3, pupils, 20; Catechizing. number of children, 10 to 15, number of times, every Sunday.

Offerings.

Parochial.— Alms at Holy Communion, $254.50; Current expenses, including salaries, $700.77; Sunday School, $9.62; Increase and Improvement of Church Property, $92. Total, $1,056.89.

Diocesan.— Diocesan Missions, $3; Salary of the Bishop, $6; Diocesan Fund, $14; Bible and Common Prayer Book Society of Albany, $5; Fund for Aged and Infirm Clergymen, $5; Orphan House of the Holy Saviour, $2. Total, $35.

General.— Domestic Missions, $2; Foreign Missions, $2; Indian Missions, $6.83; Home Missions to Coloured Persons, $1; Missions to Jews, $2.25. Total, $13.58.

·Total amount of Offerings, $1,105.47.

Property.

Church and lot (estimated worth), $10,000.
Parsonage and lot (estimated worth), $2,000.
Condition of property, excellent, except deficient heating apparatus in Church.
Amount of salary pledged Rector, $400.
Number of sittings in the Church, 200; all free.

Remarks.

On Easter day, 1893, an effort was made to pay the debt on the Rectory, which was so successful that nearly $100 was upon the Altar at the offertory. On hearing of the result, a gentleman, in times past a financial pillar of this Mission, at once added his check for nearly $50, entirely relieving the Parish from debt.

CHURCH OF THE GOOD SHEPHERD, CULLEN.

Services have been conducted by the Rector of St. John's, Richfield Springs, on every other Sunday afternoon, and during the mild weather, every other Friday evening. Offerings since July, $49.31. The attendance has been good, a choir started, and interest on the increase.

Montgomery County.

ST. ANN'S CHURCH, AMSTERDAM.

Wardens. W. Max Reid, John J. Hand.
Vestrymen. Cyrus W. Chase, Thos. Mansfield, Chas. S. Nisbet, Wm. Ryland, Jas. T. Sugden, Le Grand S. Strang, Jno. K. Warnick, Hicks B. Waldron.

Parochial.

Families, 400; Individuals, 1,120; Baptisms (adults, 3, infants, 28), 31; Marriages, 13; Burials, 22; Communicants, last reported, 329, received, 8, died, 5, removed, 14, present number; 317; Public Services (Sundays, 88, not including Holy Communion Holy days, 49, other days, 15), 152; Holy Communion (public, 45, private, 4), 49; Sunday School, teachers, 13, pupils, 200.

Offerings.

Parochial.—Alms at Holy Communion, $41.04; Current expenses, including salaries, $2,835.86; Increase and Improvement of Church Property, $273.45; Reduction of debt, $1,035; Children's Home, $7.36; City Hospital, $7.40; Albany City Hospital, $7.87. Total, $4,207.48.

Diocesan.—Diocesan Missions, $8.54.

General.—Domestic and Foreign Missions, $20; Church Temperance Society, $25.48. Total, $45.48.

Total amount of Offerings, $4,261.50.

Property.

Church and lot (estimated worth), $50,000.
Other property, three building lots, $1,500.
Condition of property, good.
Indebtedness, $13,800.
Insurance, $10,000.
Amount of salary pledged Rector, $1,250.
Number of sittings in Church, 600; rented, 500; free, 100.

Remarks.

The Aid Society and St. Ann's Guild have, as heretofore, worked for the reduction of the debt, which is noticed in the above report.

The Altar Society has furnished the Vestry Room with a new desk and carpet.

The Chapter of St. Andrew's Brotherhood has done much good work in drawing the men closer together. They have formed a branch of the Young Crusaders to interest the boys of the Church, and have helped very materially in relieving the distress caused by the closing of so many of the industries in our city.

A very small branch of the Woman's Auxiliary exists, which has done its " mite " the past year, not included in above report.

ZION CHURCH, FONDA.

Missionary. The Rev. C. C. Edmunds.
Wardens. R. H. Cushney, Henry T. E. Brower.
Vestrymen. Henry B. Cushney, Giles H. F. Van Horne, Edward B. Cushney, Richard N. Casler, William Fonda, Robert Agnew, John S. Van Horne, Henry Siver.

Parochial.

Families, 24; Individuals (adults, 76, children, 20), 96; Baptisms, infants, 3, Confirmed, since last report, 2; Present number of Confirmed Persons, 52; Burials, 3, Communicants, last reported, 47, admitted, 2, received, 4, died, 2, present number, 51, Public Services (Sundays, 52, Holy days, 2), 54; Holy Communion, public, 13.

Offerings.

Parochial.—Alms at Holy Communion, $23.35; Current expenses, including salaries, $412.26. Total, $485.61

Diocesan.— Diocesan Missions, $10; Salary of the Bishop, $12; Diocesan Fund, $9; Orphan House of the Holy Saviour, $3; Clergyman Insurance Fund, $1.50. Total, $35.50.

General.— Domestic Missions, $24.46.

Total amount of Offerings, $495.57.

Property.

Church and lot (estimated worth), $8.000.
Condition of property, good.
Amount of salary pledged Rector, $300.
Number of sittings in the Church, 150, all free.

Remarks.

The services of the Church have been kept up during the past year on Sunday mornings. There is no great change of any kind to report, but we are thankful to be able to say that we appear to be holding our own with some little addition. We can only trust that the services, as held steadily, are themselves a seed-sowing that, in God's Providence, will bring some harvest, at least, to His glory.

THE CHURCH OF THE GOOD SHEPHERD, CANAJOHARIE.

Rector. The Rev. Edward C. Hoskins.

Parochial.

Families, 12; Individuals (adults, 59, children, 33), 92; Baptisms, infants, 1; Present number of Confirmed Persons, 37; Burials, 2; Communicants, last reported, 44, died, 2, present number enrolled, 37; Public Services (Sundays, 73, Holy days, 10, other days, 42), 130 (including 15 held at Palatine Bridge); Holy Communion (public, 37, private, 5), 42; Sunday School, teachers, 3, pupils, 33; Catechizing, number of children, 33, number of times, once a month.

Offerings.

Parochial.— Alms at Holy Communion, April 9, to November 1, $140.58; Current expenses, salaries, April 9, to November 1, $204.16; Sunday School, November 1, 1892, to November 1, 1893, $10.90. Total, $355.64.

Diocesan.— Salary of the Bishop, $6; Diocesan Fund, $10; The Child's Hospital, by Sunday School, $2 64. Total, $18.64.

General.— General Missions, by Sunday School, $16.01.

Total amount of Offerings, $390.29.

Property

Church and lot (cost to build), $10,000.
Condition of property, good.
Amount of salary pledged Rector, $350.
Number of sittings in the Church, 130; all free.

THE CHURCH OF THE HOLY CROSS, FORT PLAIN.

Missionary. The Rev. Edward C. Hoskins.

Parochial.

Families, 18; Parts of families, 14; Individuals (adults, 61, children, 20), 81; Baptisms (adults, 3, infants, 1), 4; Present number of Confirmed Persons, 50;

Burials, 3; Communicants, last reported, 42, died, 1, removed, 1, present number registered, 45; Public Services (Sundays, 35, including two held in the seqool-house in Nelliston, Holy days, 1, other days, 13, held in private houses and in school-house in Nelliston), 49; Holy Communion (public, 8, private, 2), 10; it is impracticable to maintain the Sunday School at present, owing to the location of the Church building; Catechizing, number of children, 7.

Offerings.

Parochial.— Alms at Holy Communion, $137.15; Current expenses, including salaries, $137.15.

Diocesan.— Salary of Bishop, $6; Diocesan Fund, $5. Total, $11.

Total amount of Offerings, $148.15.

Property.

Church and lot (estimated worth), $7,000.

Condition of property, good.

Indebtedness, $1,600.

Otsego County.

ZION CHURCH, MORRIS.

Rector. The Rev. R. H. Gesner, B. D.

Wardens. Isaac Mansfield, John Smith.

Vestrymen. G. Clayton Peck, George A. Yates, 2d, C. J. Smith, George A. Sanderson, R. H. Harris, Willard D. Johnson. Treasurer, T. O. Duroe; Clerk, A. E. Yates.

Parochial.

Families, about 140; Individuals (adults, about 350, children, about 150), about 500; Baptisms (adults, 2, infants, 12), 14; Present number of Confirmed Persons, 250; Marriages, 6; Burials, 2; Communicants, last reported, 250, received, 1, died, 1, present number, 250; Public Services (Sundays, 139, Holy days, 25, other days, 88), 252; Holy Communion, public, 20; Sunday School, teachers, 13, pupils, 130; Catechizing, monthly.

Offerings.

Parochial.—Alms at Holy Communion, $31.31; Current expenses, including salaries, $1,191.82; Sunday School, $147.01; Rectory Fund, $1,163.77. Total, $2,533.91.

Diocesan.— Diocesan Missions, $40; Orphan House of the Holy Saviour, $7.59; The Child's Hospital, $5.58; Archdeaconry of the Susquehanna, $5.58; Diocesan Missionary, $10. Total, $68.75.

General. — Domestic Missions, $30; Jewish Missions, $5. Total, $35.

Total amount of Offerings, $2,637.66.

Property.

Church and lot (estimated worth), $20,000.

Parsonage and lot (estimated worth), $4,000.

Other property, $10,000.

Condition of property, excellent.

Indebtedness, $300 on new Rectory.

Insurance, $8,000.

Amount of salary pledged Rector, $1,000.

Number of sittings in the Church, 500; in chapel, 225; all free.

Remarks.

Very valuable boxes have been sent to the needy in different places. The last one, valued at $102, was sent to Beaufort, S. C., to relieve the sufferers from the great storm of August. Since the above report was prepared the new rectory has been entirely paid for; cost about $3,000, complete.

ST. LUKE'S CHURCH, RICHFIELD.

Minister in charge. The Rev. George Brinckerhoff Richards.
Warden. Clarence B. Colwell.
Vestrymen. Fred. A. Woodbury, John S. Curtiss, John L. Colwell.

Parochial.

Families, 7; Individuals (adults, 16, children, 4), 20; Present number of Confirmed Persons, 10; Burials, 3; Communicants, last reported, 12, died, 2, present number, 10; Public Services (Sundays, 25, other days, 10), 35; Sunday School, teachers, 2, pupils, 30.

Offerings.

Parochial.— Current expenses, including salaries, $38.36; Sunday School, $33. Total, $71.36.

Property.

Church and lot (estimated worth), $2,000.
Condition of property, good.
Amount of salary pledged Rector, $150.
Number of sittings in the Church, 200; all free.

Remarks.

Services have been held on alternate Sunday afternoons, and in mild weather every other Friday evening. A Sunday School has been started and promises to be successful. The condition of the Church and the possibility for any work is entirely due to the kind interest of Mr. Robert W. Tailer, of New York. He has placed beautiful and adequate stoves in the Church, that the services may continue throughout the winter. He has given us lamps and hymnals and furnished a conveyance for the minister in charge.

ST. MATTHEW'S CHURCH, UNADILLA.

Rector. The Rev. Robert N. Parke, D. D.
Wardens. L. L. Woodruff, B. W. Morse.
Vestrymen. Andrew J. Lewis, Milo B. Gregory, William H. Heslop, J. Fred Sands, S. Horace Chapin, Samuel S. North, Frederick H. Meeker.

Parochial.

Families, 96; Individuals (adults, 234, children, 59), 293; Baptisms, infants, 1; Confirmed, since last report, 6; Present number of Confirmed Persons, 159; Marriages, 2; Burials, 7; Communicants, last reported, 149, admitted, 6, received, 7, died, 3, removed, 8, present number, 151; Public Services (Sundays, 123, Holy days, 5, other days, 55), 183; Holy Communion (public, 31, private, 3), 34; Sunday School, teachers, 6, pupils, 45; Catechizing, number of times, 15.

Offerings.

Parochial.— Alms at Holy Communion, $54.65; Current expenses, including salaries, about $1,100; Sunday School, $18.75; Increase and Improvement of Church Property, $98.13; St. Margaret's Guild, $8.45. Total, $1,274.98.

Diocesan.— Diocesan Missions, $25; Salary of the Bishop, $16; Diocesan Fund, $7.87; Bible and Common Prayer Book Society of Albany, $4.64; Fund for Aged and Infirm Clergymen, $10.40; Orphan House of the Holy Saviour, $1.30; The Child's Hospital, $5.58; Clergy Insurance, $4. Total, $86.79.

General.— Domestic Missions, $14.18; Foreign Missions, $8.13; Sunday School for Missions, $21; Promoting Christianity Among Jews, $4.51. Total, $47.82.

Total amount of Offerings, $1,409.59.

Property.

Church and lot (estimated worth), $6,500.
Parsonage and lot (estimated worth), $4,500.
Other property, $600.
Condition of property, medium.
Amount of salary pledged Rector, $800.
Number of sittings in the Church, 330.

CHRIST CHURCH, COOPERSTOWN.

Rector. The Rev. Charles S. Olmsted.
Wardens. Wilson T. Bassett, M. D., H. M. Horten.
Vestrymen. G. Pomeroy Keese, Wm. H. Merchant, Leo B. Cruttenden, R. H. White, Charles J. Tuttle, Wm. D. Boden, Wm. Constable.

Parochial.

Baptisms (adults, 2, infants, 21), 23; Confirmed, since last report, 15; Burials, 14; Communicants, present number, 270; Public Services, Sundays, all, Holy days, all, other days, Wednesdays and Fridays, daily in Lent; Holy Communion, public, every Sunday, private, 5; Sunday School, teachers, 14, pupils, 140; Catechizing, number of children, Sunday School, number of times, 32.

Offerings.

Parochial.— Alms at Holy Communion, $182.29; Current expenses, including salaries, $3,269.30; Sunday School, $65.42; Girls' Friendly Society, $50; Extra for music, $8.50; Gifts for Father Nash window, $19.79, Special gift to the poor, $11.50; Sundry gifts, $18; Woman's Auxiliary, $300.60; for Sunday School, $9.82; Mite Society, $37.27; other objects, $141. Total, $4,108.49.

Diocesan — Diocesan Missions, $152.92; Salary of the Bishop, $80; Diocesan Fund, $45; Bible and Common Prayer Book Society of Albany, $2.65; Fund for Aged and Infirm Clergymen, $24.08; Fund for Widows and Orphans of Clergymen, $10; Orphan House of the Holy Saviour, $103.74, Deposit, $3; Otego, $20; Salary of Diocesan Missionary, $16.71, Theological Education, $5; Cobleskill, $25; Sidney, $2.40. Total, $490.50.

General.— Domestic Missions, $27.85; Foreign Missions, $18.80; Indian Missions, $7.50, Home Missions to Coloured Persons, $7.50, St. Matthew's Cathedral, Laramie, Wy., $6.52. Total, $68.17.

Total amount of Offerings, $4,667.16.

CHRIST CHURCH, GILBERTSVILLE.

Rector. The Rev. David F. MacDonald.
Wardens. Ira L. Ward, Charles V. Daniels.
Vestrymen. Frank Ward, Richard Stenson, E. R. Clinton, Edward Lillie, Thomas Swinyard, Benjamin Mervin.

Parochial.

Families, 43; Individuals (adults, 95, children, 30), 125; Baptisms (adults, 1, infants, 2), 3; Present number of Confirmed Persons, 70; Burials, 4; Communicants, received, 3, present number, 70; Public Services (Sundays, 104, Holy days, 6, other days, 19, Lenten), 129; Holy Communion, public, 18; Sunday School, teachers, 7, pupils, 25; Catechizing, number of times, 3.

Offerings.

Parochial —Alms at Holy Communion, $40; Current expenses, including salaries, $515; Sunday School, $8; Increase and Improvement of Church Property, $120.16; Cost of Insurance, $27; Expenses of Choir to Cooperstown, $12.50; Solid brass Lectern, $200; Solid brass Altar Cross, $65. Total, $987.66.

Diocesan.—Diocesan Missions, $25; Salary of the Bishop, $6; Diocesan Fund, $3; Orphan House of the Holy Saviour, $6; Diocesan Missionary, $5; Special Offering, by appeal, for Diocesan Missions, $7.50. Total, $52.50.

General. — Domestic Missions, $5; Foreign Missions, $5; Offering for Jews, $1.30; Easter Offering by Sunday School Children, $17; Easter Offering by Congregation for General Missions, $7.50; " Woman's Auxiliary in boxes and money to Cooperstown Orphanage, Child's Hospital and Collinsville, California, $50. Total, $86.30.

Total amount of Offerings, $1,126.46.

Property.

Church and lot (estimated worth), $3,000.
Parsonage and lot (estimated worth), $1,800.
Other property, $2,500.
Condition of property, very good.
Church building and bell insured for $1,800.
Parsonage and barn insured for $1,000.
Amount of salary pledged Rector, $475.
Number of sittings in the Church, 200; all free.

Remarks.

The very handsome brass Lectern and Altar Cross are memorial gifts by Mrs. Marion Murray Swinyard, who takes a deep interest in whatever pertains to the well-being of our little Parish.

I did not include in the number of " Public Services " those I rendered in " Morris Memorial Chapel." The Rev. Mr. Gesner, of Morris, no doubt, will report them.

IMMANUEL CHURCH, OTEGO.

Rector. The Rev. W. G. W. Lewis.

Wardens. Charles Blake, George W. Sherman, Jr.

Vestrymen. C. B. Woodruff, J. H. Cossaart, M. D., J. H. Martin, M. D., F. D. Shumway, W. Parker, G. H. Goodman.

Parochial.

Families, 27; Individuals (adults, 59, children, 18), 77; Baptisms, infants, 1; Confirmed, since last report, 4; Present number of Confirmed Persons, 42; Marriages, 1; Burials, 1; Communicants, last reported, 37, admitted, 4, died, 1, removed, 3, present number, 37; Public Services (Sundays, 64, Holy days, 16, other days, 8), 88; Holy Communion, public, 29, Sunday School, teachers, 1, pupils, 8; Catechizing, number of times, 15.

Offerings.

Parochial.— Current expenses, including salaries, $460; Sunday School, $3.50 Total, $463.50.

Diocesan.— Diocesan Missions, $10; Salary of the Bishop, $6; Fund for Aged and Infirm Clergymen, $1; Fund for Widows and Orphans of Clergymen, $1; Orphan House of the Holy Saviour, $2; The Child's Hospital, $6; Clergy Reserve Fund. $1.34.   Total, $27.34.

General.— General Missions, $5.39; Church Building Fund, $1.50.   Total. $6.89 Total amount of Offerings, $497.73.

Property.

Church and lot (estimated worth), $5,000.
Condition of property, good.
Amount of salary pledged Rector, $200.
Number of sittings in the Church, 200; all free.

ST. TIMOTHY'S CHURCH, WESTFORD.

(See "Remarks," Report of Grace Church, Cherry Valley.)

GRACE CHURCH, CHERRY VALLEY.

Rector. The Rev. James E. Hall.
Wardens. A. B. Cox, J. M. Phelan.
Vestrymen. George Neal, J. A. Fonda, F. P. Harriott, A. J. Thompson, W. C. Roseboom, George Streeter, C. W. Brooks, N. F. Yates, M. D.

Parochial.

Families, 58, Individuals (adults, 150, children, 50), 200; Baptisms, infants, 5. Present number of Confirmed Persons, 112, Marriages, 3. Burials, 8, Communicants. last reported, 113, admitted, 2, died, 2. removed, 4, present number, 109; Public Services (Sundays, 98, Holy days, 30, other days, 96), 224, Holy Communion (public, 52, private, 3), 55; Sunday School, teachers, 5, pupils, 40

Offerings.

Parochial.— Alms at Holy Communion, $403 07; Current expenses, including salaries, $917.92; Sunday School, $18 03   Total, $1,339.02.

Diocesan — Diocesan Missions, $75; Salary of the Bishop, $26; Diocesan Fund, $24, Bible and Common Prayer Book Society of Albany, $4.03, Fund for Aged and Infirm Clergymen, $17.50; Fund for Widows and Orphans of Clergymen, $7.50, Orphan House of the Holy Saviour, $27. The Child's Hospital, $9.30, Clergy Insurance Premiums, $4; Archdeaconry of the Susquehanna, $6.59   Total, $200.92.

General.— Domestic Missions, $40, Foreign Missions, $40, Society for Promoting Christianity Among the Jews, $2 15. Miss Buford's work. $13. House of the Good Shepherd, $10; Church Mission to Deaf-Mutes $8.08   Total, $113.23.

Total amount of Offerings, $1,653.17

Property.

Church and lot, and Parsonage and lot (estimated worth), $6,000.
Other property, fund, $6,500.
Insurance, $5,000.
Amount of salary pledged Rector, $800
Number of sittings in the Church, 250; all free.

Remarks.

The Rector said Evening Prayer twice, and Morning Prayer and Litany twice, and celebrated the Holy Communion twice, at St. Timothy's, Westford.

ST. JOHN'S CHURCH, RICHFIELD SPRINGS.

Rector. The Rev. George Brinckerhoff Richards.
Wardens. N. D. Jewell, J. A. Storer.
Vestrymen. W. B. Ward, Henry Greenman, M. D. Jewell, W. B. Crain, M. D., J. F. Getman, J. D. Carey, D. W. Harrington, G. B. Neely.

Parochial.

Families, 122; Individuals (adults, 319, children, 105), 424; Baptisms (adults, 5, infants, 28), 33; Present number of Confirmed Persons, 252; Marriages, 4; Burials, 10; Communicants, last reported, 226, removed, 20, present number, 206; Public Services (Sundays, 118, Holy days, 17, other days, 56), 191; Holy Communion (public, 21, private, 3), 24; Sunday School, teachers, 8, pupils, 94; Catechizing, number of children, all, number of times, each Sunday.

Offerings.

Parochial.— Alms at Holy Communion (June to November), $72.09; Current expenses, including salaries, $1,832.22; Sunday School, $85.11; Ladies Guild, $31.41; box to Sailors' Mission, N. Y. city, $35; Village charities, $15.85; box to Newport, Del., $16. Total, $2,087.68.

Diocesan.— Diocesan Missions, $59; Salary of the Bishop, $20; Diocesan Fund, $12; Orphan House of the Holy Saviour, $150. Total, $241.

Total amount of Offerings, $2,328.68.

Property.

Church and lot with Chapel (estimated worth), $15,700.
Parsonage and lot (estimated worth), $6,000.
Other property, lot in cemetery, $40.
Condition of property, good.
Insurance, $11,675.
Amount of salary pledged Rector, $1,100.
Number of sittings in the Church, 400; all free.

Remarks.

The present Rector took charge on the fifteenth of June. For obvious reasons this report is in parts incomplete.

ST. JOHN'S CHURCH, PORTLANDVILLE.

See " Remarks," Report, St. James' Church, Oneonta.

CHRIST CHURCH, WEST BURLINGTON.

Lay Reader. Edward B. M. Harraden.
Wardens. Stephen I. Pope, John Priest.
Vestrymen. Elias C. Mather, Lewis Spencer, William Holdridge, Stephen Olive, C. G. Pierson, Burton Bailey, Clark Clark, Albert Austin.

Parochial.

Families, 40; Individuals (adults, 88, children, 87), 130; Present number of Confirmed Persons, 33; Communicants, present number, 88; Public Services (Sundays, three (3) times, Holy days, each, other days, Wednesday and Friday; Holy Communion, public, 4; Sunday School, teachers, 4, pupils, 35; Catechizing, school, monthly.

Offerings.

Parochial.— Current expenses, $12.50; Increase and Improvement of Church property, $11.50; Insurance, $22. Total, $46.

Diocesan.— Diocesan Missions, $3; Salary of the Bishop, $6. Total, $9.

Total amount of Offerings, $55.

Property.

Church and lot (estimated worth), $4,000.

Parsonage and lot (estimated worth), $500.

Condition of property, fair.

Insurance, $1,500.

Amount of salary pledged Rector, $150.

Number of sittings in the Church, 150; all free.

Remarks.

I have only had charge since October 22, 1893, the Church having only occasional services for about a year. The services are well attended and there seems a great revival of interest in this old Parish.

ST. PAUL'S CHURCH, EAST SPRINGFIELD.

Rector. The Rev. John Prout.

Wardens. James H. Cooke, Leslie Pell-Clarke.

Vestrymen. John Scollard, Robert Walrath, G. Hyde Clarke, Daniel Gilchrist, Sheldon A. Young.

Parochial.

Baptisms, infants, 5; Marriages, 3, Burials, 2; Communicants, last reported, 45, admitted, 1, died, 1, present number, 45; Public Services (Sundays, 72, Holy days, 109, other days, 220), 401; Holy Communion (public, 57, private, 1), 58, Sunday School, teachers, 5, pupils, 30.

Offerings.

Parochial.— Current expenses, including salaries, $527.21; Sunday School, $9.05; Increase and Improvement of Church Property, $75, Insurance, $52. Total, $663.26.

Diocesan. — Diocesan Missions, $30; Salary of Bishop, $10; Diocesan Fund, $17.50. Total, $57.50.

General.— General Missions (from S. S. $9.25), $29 60.

Total amount of Offerings, $760.36.

Property.

Church and lot (estimated worth), $4,350.

Parsonage and lot (estimated worth), $3,050.

Condition of property, good

Insurance (on Church, $2,000, on Rectory, $2,000, on organ, $500), $4,500.

Amount of salary pledged Rector, $500.

Number of sittings in the Church, 120, all free.

ST MARY'S MISSION CHURCH, SPRINGFIELD CENTRE.

Missionary. The Rev. John Prout.

Warden of the Mission Leslie Pell-Clarke.

Parochial.

Baptisms (adults, 1, infants, 4), 5: Burials, 3; Communicants, last reported, 22, removed, 1, present number, 21; Public Services (Sundays, 27, Holy days, 1), 28; Holy Communion, public, 6: Sunday School, teachers, 4, pupils, 30.

Offerings.

Parochial.— Alms at Holy Communion, $60.

Diocesan.— Diocesan Missions, $20; Salary of the Bishop (through treasurer of St. Paul's, East Springfield), $4; Diocesan Fund (through treasurer of St. Paul's, East Springfield), $6. Total, $30.

General and Foreign Missions (from S. S. $3.50), $15.75.

Total amount of Offerings, $105.75.

Property.

Church and lot (estimated worth), $8,000.

Condition of property, good.

Number of sittings in the Church, 120, all free.

Remarks.

It should be stated that half of the amount pledged to the Rector of St. Paul's Church, East Springfield, is from members of the congregation of St. Mary's, but, being paid through the treasurer of St. Paul's, does not appear on this report.

ST. JAMES' CHURCH, ONEONTA.

Rector. The Rev. John E. Bold.

Wardens. John Cope, John D. Rohde.

Vestrymen. Jas. O. Beach, A. W. Carr, Richard Downes, Benj. F. Sisson, Hobart B. Somers, Jas. M. Stewart, Robert M. Townsend.

Parochial.

Families, 112, Baptisms (adults, 9, infants, 18), 27; Confirmed, since last report, 14; Present number of Confirmed Persons, 260; Marriages, 6; Burials, 9; Communicants, last reported, 224, admitted, 12, received, 16, died, 4, removed, 13. present number, 235; Public Services (Sundays, 142, Holy days, 20, other days, 77), 239; Holy Communion, public, 63; Sunday School, teachers, 10, pupils, 88; Catechizing, number of children, whole school, number of times, every Sunday.

Offerings.

Parochial.— Alms at Holy Communion, $76.39; Current expenses, including salaries, $1,005.47; Sunday School, $46 16; Increase and Improvement of Church Property, $1,905.63 Total, $3,033.65.

Diocesan.— Diocesan Missions, $50, Salary of the Bishop, $10; Diocesan Fund, $24; Orphan House of the Holy Saviour, $10; Society for Promoting Religion and Learning, $5.25. Total, $99 25.

General.— Domestic Missions, $25, Foreign Missions, $25. Total, $50.

Total amount of Offerings, $3,182.90.

Property.

Church and lot (estimated worth), $12,000.

Parsonage and lot (estimated worth

Condition of property, excellent.
Indebtedness, mortgage on Parsonage, $2,000.
Other debts, $650.
Insurance on the Church, $4,000.
Insurance on the Parsonage, $2,000.
Amount of salary pledged Rector, $900.
Number of sittings in the Church, 225; all free.

Remarks.

During the summer and until the middle of October, services were held twice a month in St. John's Church, Portlandville. As the few Church people who attend the services are mostly farmers who have to come long distances, it was decided to discontinue the services during the winter.

There are about six families and the same number of communicants connected with the Mission, but the services in the summer are usually well attended, the number varying from twenty to forty. Five persons, a father, mother and three children, were baptized in St. John's Church, October 15th, but these, as also the families and communicants above mentioned, are included in the report of St. James', Oneonta.

ST. STEPHEN'S CHAPEL, MAPLE GROVE.

Rector. The Rev. David F. MacDonald.

Parochial.

Families, 8; Individuals (adults, 15, children, 16), 31; Baptisms, adult, 1; Present number of Confirmed Persons, 24; Marriages, 2; Burials, 1; Communicants, removed 2; Public Services (Sundays, 30, Holy days, 3), 33; Holy Communion (public, 12, private, 1), 13; Sunday School, teachers, 3, pupils, 16; Catechizing, number of times, 1.

Offerings.

Parochial.— Alms at Holy Communion, $4.42; Sunday School, $11.14, Increase and Improvement of Church Property, $128.81, Cost of Insurance, $11.25.   Total, $155.62.

Diocesan.— Salary of Bishop, $2.

General.— Foreign Missions, $2.44.

Total amount of Offerings, $160.06.

Property

Church and lot (estimated worth), $1,000.
Condition of property, good.
Insurance, $600.
Number of sittings in the Church, 120; all free.

HOLY SPIRIT CHURCH, SCHENEVUS.

Missionary. The Rev. Benjamin F. Miller.
Wardens. R. C. Mills, B. F Bennett.
Vestrymen   F. E. Page, John Mills, M. E. Baldwin, C. G. Bowles, A. W. Johnson.

Parochial.

Families, 27; Baptisms (adults, 3, infants, 2), 5: Confirmed, since last report, 2; Present number of confirmed persons, 21; Marriages, 1; Communicants, last reported,

18; Public Services (Sundays, 60, other days, 8), 68; Holy Communion, public, 10; Sunday School, teachers, 5, pupils, 26; Catechizing, number of children, 26, number of times, frequently.

Offerings.

Parochial.— Alms at Holy Communion, $9.29; Current expenses, including salaries, $409.49; Sunday School, $16.50; Rectory Fund, $8.81; Baptismal Font, $20.63. Total, $464.72.

Diocesan.— Diocesan Missions, $10; Salary of the Bishop, $4; Diocesan Fund, $1.50; Bible and Common Prayer Book Society of Albany, $1; Chapter House, $5; Expense of Convention, $1. Total, $22.50.

General.— Domestic Missions, $3.25.

Total amount of Offerings, $490.47.

Property.

Church and lot (estimated worth), $3,000.

Condition of property, good.

Amount of salary pledged Rector, $360, and house.

Number of sittings in the Church, 100; all free.

CHURCH OF ST. SIMON AND ST. JUDE, WORCESTER.

See Report of the Diocesan Missionary, p. 66.

Rensselaer County.

ST. PAUL'S CHURCH, TROY, N. Y.

Rector. The Rev. Edgar A. Enos, D. D.

Wardens. Joseph M. Warren, Joseph J. Tillinghast.

Vestrymen. Stephen W. Barker, James H. Caldwell, John Clatworthy, Geo. T. Lane, William W. Morrill, Charles E. Patterson, John I. Thompson, M. Edgar Wendell.

Parochial.

Baptisms (adults, 8, infants, 26), 34; Marriages, 7; Burials, 31; Communicants, last reported, 689, received, 15, died, 13, removed, 1, present number, 690; Public Services, Sundays, Celebration of the Holy Communion on all Sundays and Holy days, also Matins and Evensong; on all Holy days and first Sunday in each month a second Celebration; private, 20; matins daily throughout the year; Sunday School, teachers, 21, pupils, 250; Catechizing, every Sunday; Parish School, teachers, 3, pupils, 17; Sewing School, teachers, 23, pupils, 162; Girls' Friendly Society, associates, 10, members, 127.

Offerings.

Parochial.— Alms at Holy Communion, not elsewhere reported, $203.25; Current expenses, including salaries, $9,093.70; Sunday School, $364.43; Parish School, $486.60; Friends of the Sisterhood, $1,098.21; Altar Guild, $200.80; Miscellaneous, $179.16; Rebuilding Interior of Church (balance of expenses), $29,450. Total, $41,076.15.

Diocesan.—Diocesan Missions (through Offertory, $1,354, through Woman's Auxiliary and Junior Auxiliaries, money, $471.63, boxes, $350.73), $2,176.36; Salary of Bishop, $200; Diocesan Fund, $90; Bible and Common Prayer ~~~~~~~~~~~~~~, Albany, $21; Fund for Aged and Infirm Clergymen, $9~~~~~~~~~~~~~~~~~~~~~~~~~~~~~~

men, $30; Orphan House of the Holy Saviour, $117; The Child's Hospital, $10; So-. ciety for Promoting Religion and Learning, $45; Clergy Reserve Fund, $30; S. Christina Home, $329; Church Home, Troy, $500; Tuition of Divinity Student, $130. Total, $3,706.66.

General.— Domestic Missions, $386; Foreign Missions, $51; Indian Missions, $15; Home Missions to Coloured Persons, $15; Deaf-Mutes in New York, $10. Total, $477. Total amount of Offerings, $45,261.81.

Remarks.

The new interior of the Church is completed, with the exception of the Chancel Window, and has been blessed by the Bishop. The cost of the work, so far, is about $70,000, including Memorials.

ST. JOHN'S CHURCH, TROY.

Rector. The Rev. Henry Raymond Freeman.
Wardens. N. B. Squires, Charles W. Tillinghast.
Vestrymen. Francis N. Mann, Wm. P. Mason, Chas. A. McLeod, Wm. M. Sanford, George A. Wells, Jas. M. Ide, Chas. E. Hanaman, Wm. A. Thompson.

Parochial.

Families, 220; Baptisms (adults, 2, infants, 21), 23; Confirmed, since last report, 26; Present number of Confirmed Persons, 467; Marriages, 9; Burials, 27; Communicants, last reported, 404, admitted, 26, received, 10, died, 5, removed, 5, present number, 420; Public Services (Sundays, 125, Holy days, 30, other days 150), 305; Holy Communion (public, 60, private, 10), 70; Sunday School, teachers, 23, pupils, 200; Catechizing, every Sunday.

Offerings.

Parochial.— Alms at Holy Communion, $344.69; Current expenses including salaries, $6,274.92; Sunday School, $350; Employment Society, $268.82; Special Poor Fund, $150; Sewing School, $75; Special Offerings, $2,920.05; Subscriptions, etc., $3,750. Total, $14,133.48.

Diocesan.— Diocesan Missions, $732.28; Salary of the Bishop, $132; Diocesan Fund, $90; Bible and Common Prayer Book Society of Albany, $25; Fund for Aged and Infirm Clergymen, $30; Fund for Widows and Orphans of Clergymen, $31.28; The Child's Hospital, $75; The Orphan House of the Holy Saviour, $50; The St. Christina Home, $20; Woman's Auxiliary, $55; The Church Home, Troy, $500. Total, $1,740.56.

General.— Domestic Missions, $150; Foreign Missions, $150; Foreign and Domestic Missions (Sunday School Lenten offerings), $200; Theological Education, $50; Missionary boxes, Domestic Missions, $612.88; American Church Building Fund, $15; Church Mission to Deaf-Mutes, $10; Troy Orphan Asylum, $35. Total, $1,222.88.

Total amount of Offerings, $17,096.92.

Property.

Church and lot (estimated worth), $50,000.
Parsonage and lot (estimated worth), $25,000.
Other property, Parish House, $15,000.
Condition of property, good.

Indebtedness, $8,000.
Amount of salary pledged Rector, $2,500.
Number of sittings in the Church, 600; free, 50.

CHRIST CHURCH, TROY.

Rector. The Rev. Eaton W. Maxcy, D. D.
Wardens. Hon. William Kemp, Samuel C. Tappin.
Vestrymen. Washington Akin, M. D., Peter Black, Charles Cleminshaw, J. W. A. Cluett, George Churchill, Frank W. Edmunds, William Kemp, Jr., Charles A. Nimmo.

Parochial.

Families, 130; Individuals (adults, 450, children, 250), 700; Baptisms (adults, 8, infants, 7), 15; Marriages, 5; Burials, 18; Communicants, last reported, 269, received, 10, died, 3, removed, 6, present number, 270; Public Services (Sundays, 96, Holy days, 10, other days, 60), 166; Holy Communion, public, 25; Sunday School, teachers 15; pupils, 150; Catechizing, number of times, 40.

Offerings.

Parochial.— Alms at Holy Communion, $72; Current expenses, including salaries, $5,307.84; Sunday School, $50; Increase and Improvement of Church Property, $75; Church Home, $225. Total, $5,729.84.

Diocesan.— Diocesan Missions, $275; Salary of the Bishop, $62; Diocesan Fund, $75; Fund for Aged and Infirm Clergymen, $33.91; Clergy insurance premium, $12.50. Total, $458.41.

Total amount of Offerings, $6,188.25.

Property.

Church and lot (estimated worth), $35,000.
Other property, $4,000.
Insurance, $31,500.
Amount of salary pledged Rector, $2,500.
Number of sittings in the Church, 600.

CHURCH OF THE HOLY CROSS, TROY.

Pastor. The Rev. J. Ireland Tucker.

Parochial.

Confirmed, since last report, 13; Communicants, 150; Public Services, Sundays, 2 each, Holy days, 1 each, other days, 1 each; Holy Communion, public, Sundays and Saints days; Sunday School, teachers, 14, pupils, 135; Parish School, teachers, 4, pupils, 60.

Offerings.

Diocesan.— Diocesan Missions, $200; Salary of the Bishop, $50; Diocesan Fund, $20; Fund for Widows and Orphans of Clergymen, $27.88. Total, $297.88.

ST. LUKE'S CHURCH, TROY.

Rector. The Rev. Wm. Brevoort Bolmer.
Wardens. James Wood, John W. Babcock.
Vestrymen. Thomas B. Iler,* Thomas Marles, Henry E. Darby, P. Harry Mitchell, Daniel Founcks, George Haite, Edmund Adams, James Evans.

Parochial.

Families, 159; Individuals (adults, 320, children, 240), 560; Baptisms, infants, 21; Present number of Confirmed Persons, 280; Marriages, 7; Burials, 16; Churchings, 3, Communicants, last reported, 215, received, 3, died, 4, removed, 6, present number, 208; Public Services (Sundays, 168, Holy days, 140, other days, 378), 686; Holy Communion (public, 83, private, 1), 84; Sunday School, teachers, 12, pupils, 150; Catechizing, number of children, 70, number of times, 64.

Offerings.

Parochial.—Alms at Holy Communion, $42.24; Current expenses, including salaries, $1,505.62; Sunday School, $85.80; Increase and Improvement of Church Property, $88.66; Poor Women in Child-bed, $1.25. Total, $1,723.57.

Diocesan.— Diocesan Missions, $20; Salary of the Bishop, $10; Diocesan Fund, $38; Bible and Common Prayer Book Society of Albany, $4.50; Fund for Aged and Infirm Clergymen, $7.63; Fund for Widows and Orphans of Clergymen, $7.63; Orphan House of the Holy Saviour, $4.16; Society for Promoting Religion and Learning, $5.51; Clergy Reserve Fund, $3.97. Total, $90.40.

General.— Domestic Missions, $5.31; Foreign Missions, $4.96; Indian Missions, $3.44; Home Missions to Coloured Persons, $3.85; General Missions, $29.47; American Church Building Fund, $1.92; Promoting Christianity Among Jews, $4.67. Total, $52.62.

Total amount of Offerings, $1,866.59.

Property.

Church and lot (estimated worth), $35,000.
Parsonage and lot (estimated worth), $6,000.
Other property, $4,700.
Condition of property, tolerable.
Insurance, $10,600.
Amount of salary pledged Rector, $800 and Rectory.
Number of sittings in the Church, 850; all free.

FREE CHURCH OF THE ASCENSION, TROY.

Rector. The Rev. James Caird.
Trustees. Wm. R. Bridges, James Caird, Thomas Cordwell, J. J. Gillespie, David Little, Fred. S. Lincoln, N. B. Squires, W. A. Thompson.

Parochial.

Baptisms (adults, 1, infants, 19), 20; Marriages, 4; Burials, 15; Communicants, present number, 240; Public Services (Sundays, 104, Holy days, 10, other days, 65), 179; Holy Communion, public, 14; Sunday School, teachers, 20, pupils, 185; Catechizing, number of times, every Sunday.

Offerings.

Parochial.— Current expenses, including salaries, $2,070.74; Sunday School, $332.81; Increase and Improvement of Church Property, $67.67; City Assessment, $158.86. Total, $2,630.08.

Diocesan. — Diocesan Missions, $50; Salary of the Bishop, $10; Bible and Common Prayer Book Society of Albany, $5; Church Home, $10. Total, $75.

General.— Indian Missions, $5; Home Missions to Coloured Persons, $5; By the Woman's Auxiliary, four boxes of clothing, estimated value, $135.19. Total, $145.19.

Total amount of Offerings, $2,850.27.

ST. BARNABAS', TROY.

Rector. The Rev. Geo. A. Holbrook.

The Corporation. Rev. Geo. A. Holbrook, President; Rev. J. Ireland Tucker, S. T. D., Vice-President; A. W. M. Moffitt, Wm. C. Jamieson, Thos. Entwistle, Wm. W. Morrill, Wm. W. Rousseau, C. W. Tillinghast, 2d, Horace B. Finley.

The Local Committee. Rev. Geo. A. Holbrook, A. W. M. Moffit, Treasurer; Thos. Entwistle, Wm. C. Jamieson, H. B. Finley.

Parochial.

Baptisms (adults, 2, infants, 25), 27; Confirmed, since last report, 15; Present number of Confirmed Persons, 199; Marriages, 5; Burials, 13; Churchings, 1; Communicants, last reported, 187, admitted, 18, received, 3, died, 3, removed, 6, present number, 199; Public Services (Sundays, 208, other days, 821), 1,029; Holy Communion (public, 244, private, 11), 255; Catechizing, number of children, all, number of times, 52.

Offerings.

Parochial.—Alms at Holy Communion, $88.30; Current expenses, including salaries, $3,515.41; Increase and Improvement of Church Property, $296.02; Charities, $28.33: Building Fund, $2,020.35; Mortgage Fund, $28.42; Endowment Fund, $3.51. Total, $6 486.74.

Diocesan.— Diocesan Missions, $53.42; Salary of the Bishop, $6; Bible and Common Prayer Book Society of Albany, $3.11; Fund for Aged and Infirm Clergymen, $13.73; Fund for Widows and Orphans of Clergymen, $3.54; Orphan House of the Holy Saviour, $27.44; The Child's Hospital, $5.22; Church Home, Troy, $63.98; Troy Orphan Asylum, $2.42. Total, $177.86.

General.— Domestic Missions, $48.91; Foreign Missions (S. S. J. E.'s, Capetown, Kafir Mission), $3.32; Nashotah House, $5.35; Ch. Mission to the Jews, $7.93; Society of S. John, Evangelist, $25.28. Total, $90.79.

Total amount of Offerings, $6,755.39.

Property.

Church and lot (estimated worth), $4,500.

Mission House and lot (estimated worth), $3,500.

Other Property (organ, chancel furniture. etc.), $1,508.

Condition of property, excellent.

Indebtedness, a mortgage of $3,500 on Mission House and lot.

Insurance, $6,950.

The Building Fund amounts to $11,928.61.

The Endowment Fund amounts to $80.23.

The Mortgage Fund amounts to $34.24.

Amount of salary pledged Rector, $1,200; (no Rectory).

Number of sittings in the Church, 200; number free, all.

Remarks.

During the Convention year, $1,100 have been paid upon the mortgage on the Mission House. Of this sum, $800 were from the Mortgage Fund, and the balance from the treasury. A very beautiful sanctuary lamp has been given by the congregation, and placed in the church in memory of a late Rector — Rev. Wm. D. Martin.

TRINITY CHURCH, LANSINGBURGH.

Rector. The Rev. Charles Metcalf Nickerson.

Wardens. James McQueide, Peter B. King.

Vestrymen. James Snyder, Charles Holmes, Charles Wills, Geo. W. Daw, Edward Leonard, E. Warren Banker, Eugene Hunt, Geo. P. Nichols.

Parochial.

Baptisms (adults, 3, infants, 16), 19; Confirmed, since last report, 10; Marriages, 1; Burials, 21; Communicants, last reported, 290, admitted, 10, recieved, 2, died, 5, removed, 14, present number, 283; Public Services (Sundays, 166, other days, 94), 260; Holy Communion (public, 54, private, 7), 61; Sunday School, teachers, 28, pupils, 257.

Offerings.

Parochial.—Alms at Holy Communion, $164.09; Current expenses, including salaries, $3,200; Sunday School, $144; Litany Desk, $80; Sunday School books, $60; Choir (special), $500; Choir vestments, $34.49. Total, $4,182.58.

Diocesan.— Diocesan Missions, $200; Salary of the Bishop, $60; Diocesan Fund, $45; Fund for Aged and Infirm Clergymen, $39.68; Fund for Widows and Orphans of Clergymen, $35; Orphan House of the Holy Saviour, $20; Society for Promoting Religion and Learning, $2.32; Diocesan Missionary, $20. Total, $452.

General.— Domestic Missions, $66.96; Foreign Missions, $33.48. Total, $100.44. Total amount of Offerings, $4,735.02.

Property.

Church and lot (estimated worth), $50,000.
Parsonage and lot (estimated worth), $5,000.
Other Property, chapel, $4,000.
Condition of property, good.
Indebtedness, $700.
Insurance, $17,000.
Amount of salary pledged Rector, $1,500.
Number of sittings in the Church, 374; number rented, 314; number free, 18.

ST. MARK'S CHURCH, HOOSICK FALLS.

Rector. The Rev. Chas. C. Edmunds.
Rector Emeritus. The Rev. Geo. H. Nicholls, D. D.
Wardens. J. Russell Parsons, W. S. Nicholls.
Vestrymen. Isaac A. Allen, H. H. Barnes, Chas. A. Coulter, John G. Darroch, A. Danforth Geer, Nelson Gillespie, Hinsdill Parsons, C. F. W. Smith.

Parochial.

Baptisms, (adults, 5, infants, 24), 29; Marriages, 4; Burials, 19; Communicants, last reported, 418; Public Services (Sundays, 3, Holy days, 2, other days, 2), about 600 in all; Holy Communion (public), about 200; Sunday School, teachers, 18; pupils, 185; Catechizing, number of children, all, number of times, weekly.

Offerings.

Parochial.— Current expenses, including salaries, [$2,632.20 ; Sunday School, $247.84, for the Poor, $66.10. Total, $2,916.14.

Diocesan.—Diocesan Missions, $150.50; Salary of the Bishop, $40; Diocesan Fund, $52.50; Bible and Common Prayer Book Society of Albany, $15; Fund for Aged and Infirm Clergymen, $24.62; Orphan House of the Holy Saviour, $12; The Child's Hospital, $33.77. Total, $328.39.

General.— Foreign Missions, $10.87; Mission to Jews, $10.00 ; Bishop Talbot's School (from S. S.), $50; China Mission, $23.30. Total, $94.17.

Total amount of Offerings, $3,338.70.

Property.

Church and lot (estimated worth), $25,000.
Parsonage and lot (estimated worth), $7,500.
Condition of property, good.
Indebtedness, $2,900.
Insurance (Church), $22,500; (Rectory), $5.000.
Amount of salary pledged Rector, $1,500.
Number of sittings in the Church, 400; number rented, almost all.

Remarks.

It is impossible for the present Rector as a new-comer to the Parish to present a fuller report. In particular no accurate report of Communicants can be made, a large number of these on the list having removed from the town on account of the depression in business, whether permanently or not remains to be seen. In addition to the amounts reported above, the Woman's Auxiliary raised $495.45, and the Junior Auxiliary, $75.80, during the conventional year, of which sum the greater part has been expended for charitable and Missionary purposes within and without the parish.

TRINITY CHURCH, SCHAGHTICOKE.

Rector. The Rev. M. O. Smith.
Wardens. Edward Searls, Frank Sigwarth.
Vestrymen. Chas. Corbin, Robt. Barth, Ira E. Askins, Jos. W. Parker, Almadus Wilkinson.

Parochial.

Families, 35; Baptisms (infants), 4; Marriages, 1; Burials, 4; Communicants, admitted, 1, received, 2, died, 3, removed, 7, present number, 38; Public Services (Sundays, 90, Holy days, 32, other days, 31), 153; Holy Communion (public, 62, private, 5), 67.

Offerings.

Parochial.— Current expenses, including salaries, $449.23
Diocesan.— Diocesan Missions, $15; Salary of the Bishop, $6; Diocesan Fund, $9; Orphan House of the Holy Saviour, $3; Clergy Insurance, $1.50. Total, $34.50.
Total amount of Offerings, $483.73.

Property.

Church and lot (estimated worth), $4,000.
Parsonage and lot (estimated worth), $3,750.
Indebtedness, $2,300.
Insurance, $6,450.
Amount of salary pledged Rector, $300.
Number of sittings in the Church, 200; all free.

Remarks.

The Parish has been presented with a Solid Silver Chalice and Paten by some of the members of the congregation, and with a pair of brass vases for the Altar.

CHURCH OF THE MESSIAH, GREENBUSH.

Wardens. Charles H. Smith, Wm. H. Terrell.
Vestrymen. Richard W. Stevens, Theodore A. McKean, Clarence Houghton, Geo. P. Reisel, Geo. Johnston, Alfred Wilson, Henry Morris, Charles A. McClean.

Parochial.

Families, 74; Baptisms (adults, 1, infants, 13), 14; Confirmed, since last report, 9: Marriages 1; Burials, 11; Communicants, last reported, 124, received, 9, died, 6, removed, 7, present number, 111; Public Services (Sundays, 83, Holy days, 16), 99; Holy Communion (public, 14, private, 6), 20; Sunday School, teachers, 9, pupils, 60; Catechizing, number of children, all, number of times, once every month.

Offerings.

Parochial.— Alms at Holy Communion, $13.62; Current expenses, including salaries, $1,071.76; Sunday School, $35.42; Increase and Improvement of Church Property, $375. Total, $1,495.80.

Diocesan.—Diocesan Missions, $25; Salary of the Bishop, $10; Fund for Aged and Infirm Clergymen, $1.50; Fund for Widows and Orphans of Clergymen, $1.50; the Child's Hospital, $5. Total, $43.

General.— General Missions, $10.75.

Total amount of Offerings, $1,549.55.

Property.

Church and lot (estimated worth), $10,000.

Other property, $1,000.

Condition of property, good.

Insurance, $2,750.

Number of sittings in the Church, 175; all free.

Remarks.

This report is necessarily imperfect, as the parish has been vacant a great part of the year, having no Rector since July 23.

On the nineteenth Sunday after Trinity a stained glass window representing Praise and Gratitude was dedicated.

The young people of the parish have a fund in the bank toward the erection of a parish house, amounting to $388.

The Ladies' Aid Society has raised during the year $210 for current expenses and missions.

EPIPHANY CHURCH, EAST ALBANY.

Rector. The Rev. Thomas White.

Parochial.

Families, 49; Individuals (adults, 109, children, 47), 156; Baptisms, infants, 16; Marriages, 7; Burials, 21; Communicants, last reported, 177, received, 6, died, 3, removed, 7, present number, 173; Public Services (Sundays, 86, Holy days, 21, other days, 44), 151; Holy Communion (public), 36; Sunday School, teachers, 14, pupils, 120; Catechizing, number of children, 120, number of times, every Sunday; Parish School, teachers, 1, pupils, 26.

Offerings.

Parochial.— Current expenses, including salaries, $942.68; Sunday School, $78.15; Parish School, $60. Total, $1,080.83.

Diocesan.— The Child's Hospital, $5.

General.— General Missions, $35.10.

Total amount of Offerings, $1,120.93.

Property.

Church and lot (estimated worth), $5,000.
Parsonage and lot (estimated worth), $4,000.
Other Property, $500.
Condition of property, good.
Indebtedness, mortgage on Rectory, $4,000, mortgage on Parish School, $400.
Amount of salary pledged Rector, $700.
Number of sittings in the Church, 200; all free.

Remarks.

The "Mite Society" of the Church has received during the past year, in sums of five cents, collected weekly, for the Rector's salary, $130.

The "Ladies' Aid Society" has raised toward the same, and for repairing the sidewalk, nearly $150.

The Woman's Auxiliary have aided in the general work of the Church in sewing for the Child's Hospital and in working for a box for Diocesan Missions.

The Woman's Guild have taken upon themselves the task of raising funds for the liquidation of the debt upon the Rectory and School; in this they have been greatly encouraged by the generous gifts of friends in Albany and Troy.

It is to be hoped that when the Parish is looking toward its own needs it will be able to see the lamentable lack of zeal for what is required of them in the diocesan and domestic field.

ALL SAINTS' CHURCH, HOOSAC.

Rector. The Rev. Edward Dudley Tibbits.
Assistant. The Rev. John B. Tibbits.
Wardens. Le Grand C. Tibbits, George M. Bovie.
Vestrymen. Henry C. Babcock, George E. Babcock, Isaac W. Bovie, Paul Breese, Jonathan Cottrell, Henry Myers, Charles E. Pierce.

Parochial.

Baptisms (adults, 5, infants, 8), 13; Marriages, 4; Burials, 9; Communicants, present number, 130; Public Services, daily Matins and Evensong; Holy Communion (public, 106, private, 1), 107; Sunday School, teachers, 7, pupils, 100.

Offerings.

Parochial.— Alms at Holy Communion, $257.15; Current expenses, including salaries, $566.83; Sunday School Christmas tree, $19.46; Expenses of choir to Albany on Ascension Day, $16.16; Choir festival, $8.38. Total, $867.98.

Diocesan.— Diocesan Missions, $30; Salary of the Bishop, $6; Orphan House of the Holy Saviour (Thanksgiving Offering, $5.66, Sunday School, $17), $22.66; The Child's Hospital, $13.49. Total, $72.15.

General.— Domestic and Foreign Missions, $30.94; St. Augustine's Mission, Boston, $8.13; The General Fund of the Iron Cross, $4.28. Total, $43.35.

Total amount of Offerings, $983.48.

CHURCH OF THE HOLY NAME, BOYNTONVILLE.

Rector. The Rev. Henry Cornelius Dyer.
Warden. Willis Humiston.

Parochial.

Communicants, present number, 25; Holy Communion (public, 11, private, 5), 16; Sunday School, teachers, 1, pupils, 9.

Offerings.

Diocesan.— Diocesan Missions, $5.

ST. PAUL'S CHURCH, RAYMERTOWN.

Rector. The Rev. Henry Cornelius Dyer.
Warden: Frederick Mitchell.

Parochial.

Confirmed, since last report, 13; Present number of Confirmed Persons, 19; Burials, 1; Communicants, last reported, 4, present number, 19; Holy Communion, public, 16; Sunday School, teachers, 1, pupils, 30.

Offerings.

Parochial.— Alms at Holy Communion, $40.

ST. GILES' MISSION, CASTLETON.

Missionary. The Rev. Canon Hatheway.
Warden. C. P. Woodworth.

Parochial.

Families, 7; Individuals (adults, 26, children, 17), 43; Baptisms, infants, 12; Present number of Confirmed Persons, 18; Burials, 1; Communicants, last reported, 15, admitted 3, removed, 2, present number, 18; Public Services (Sundays, 52, Holy days, 2, other days, 6), 60; Holy Communion, public, 11; Sunday School, teachers, 5, pupils, 20; Catechizing, number of children, 20, number of times, once a month.

Offerings.

Parochial.— Current expenses, including salaries, $413.53.
Diocesan.— Diocesan Missions, $10.
General.— Domestic Missions, $2.
Total amount of Offerings, $425.53.

Property.

Amount of salary pledged Rector, $200.

Remarks.

The last year is the best that the Mission has seen. A lot for a Church has been purchased for $1,100. We gave a mortgage for $760, but as there is a building on rear of the lot that rents for $136, this takes care of the interest and will in time clear off the mortgage. We are collecting for a church building fund and have on hand $224.51. With the sanction of our Bishop, and the good will in a substantial manner from our friends, we hope to commence building in the spring.

St. Lawrence County.

ST. JOHN'S CHURCH, OGDENSBURG.

Rector. The Rev. J. D. Morrison.
Wardens. Charles Ashley, Louis Hasbrouck.
Vestrymen. J. G. Averell, J. C. Sprague, Levi Hasbrouck, J. G. Knapp, E. N. Burt, S. F. Palmer, Henry F. James.

Parochial.

Families, 300; Baptisms (adults, 3, infants, 47), 50; Confirmed since last report, 20; Marriages, 16; Burials, 24; Holy Communion public, Sundays and Holy days, private, frequent; Sunday School, teachers, 26, pupils, 340; Catechizing, number of children, whole school, number of times, frequently.

Offerings.

Parochial.— Alms at Holy Communion, $108.51; Current Expenses, including salaries, $5,019.65; Sunday School, $200; Parish Societies, $433.01; other Parochial objects, $300. Total, $6,061.17.

Diocesan.— Diocesan Missions, $500; Salary of the Bishop, $100; Diocesan Fund, $60; Bible and Common Prayer Book Society of Albany, $18.22; Fund for Aged and Infirm Clergymen, $29.40; Clergy Reserve Fund, $125.36; Woman's Auxiliary for Diocesan Missionary Salary, $25. Total, $857.98.

General.— Domestic and Foreign Missions, $116.67; * Woman's Auxiliary Box to Montana, $110; Cash, Contributions for Beaufort, S. C., and other objects, $42. Total, $268.67.

Total amount of Offerings, $7,187.82.

Property.

Condition of property, good.
Insurance, $57,000.

ST. PAUL'S CHURCH, WADDINGTON.

Rector. The Rev. A. C. Macdonald.
Wardens. Joseph Graves, S. J. Bower, M. D.
Vestrymen. James I. Cook, Robert Dalzel, Clarence Montgomery, John Rule, William Forsythe.

Parochial.

Families, 38; Individuals (adults, 96, children, 60), 156; Baptisms (adults, 2, infants, 12), 14; Present Number of Confirmed Persons, 71; Marriages, 5; Burials, 9; Communicants, last reported, 64, received, 1, present number, 65; Public Services (Sundays, 150, Holy days, 10, other days, 54), 214; Holy Communion (public), 21; Sunday School, teachers, 6, pupils, 39; Catechizing, number of children, all, number of times, several.

Offerings.

Parochial.— Current Expenses, including salaries, $325; Sunday School, $12; Increase and Improvement of Church Property, $121; Organist's Salary, $50; Sexton's Salary, $50; Interest on loan, $12; Offertory, Archdeaconry meeting, $11; Junior Auxiliary work box, $4. Total, $585.

Diocesan.—Diocesan Missions, $30; Salary of the Bishop, $9; Diocesan Fund, $9; Bible and Common Prayer Book Society of Albany, $3. Total, $51.

General.— Domestic Missions, $5; Foreign Missions, $3; Sunday School Lenten Offering, $5. Total, $13.

Total amount of Offerings, $649.

Property.

Church and lot (estimated worth), $5,000.
Parsonage and lot (estimated worth), $3,000.
Condition of property, good.
Amount of salary pledged Rector, $300.
Number of sittings in the Church, 200; all free.

* In addition to the above the above Woman's Auxiliary report a box, but do not state to whom sent; value, $123.19.

Remarks.

A notable event, commemorative of founding Churches in these regions, occurred during the year — the seventy-fifth anniversary, and its celebration, of St. Paul's Church. This occurred on the 9th of October, services being held on four days· Advantage of Fall Meeting of Archdeaconry was taken for the purpose — the combination having proved most satisfactory in a number of ways. A good attendance, Clerical and Lay, Holy Eucharists, Memorial Service of great interest, hearty services, discussion of important questions, with charming weather, contributed to this end. The Historical Address of Rector will likely be printed. The work of Parish continues much as heretofore, one healthy sign being the increased number of baptisms. Financial depression, with the usual quiet character of business, has had its effect. Still, none of our people have lost heart in the work of the Holy Catholic Church.

CHRIST CHURCH, MORRISTOWN.

Rector. The Rev. William Stone Hayward, from Nov. 1, 1893.

Wardens. Joseph Couper, Henry A. Chapman.

Vestrymen. T. W. Pierce, E. H. Miller, A. L. Palmer, —— Miller, E. Kingsland, F. B. Kingsland, Henry A. Bacon, G. E. Pope.

Parochial.

Families, 35; Individuals (adults, 98, children, 67), 165; Baptisms (adults, 5, infants, 7), 12; Confirmed, since last report, 10; Present number of Confirmed Persons, 88; Marriages, 4; Burials, 5; Communicants, last reported, 96, admitted, 10: received, 4, died, 5, removed, 6, present number, 76; Public Services (Sundays, 131, Holy days, 43, other days, 202), 376; Holy Communion (public, 41, private, 1), 42; Sunday School, teachers, 7, pupils, 52; Catechizing, number of times, 9.

Offerings.

Parochial.—Alms at Holy Communion, $8.38; Current expenses, including salaries, $445 29; Sunday School, $34.14. Total, $487.81.

Diocesan.— Diocesan Missions, $40; Salary of the Bishop, $20; Bible and Common Prayer Book Society of Albany. $4; Orphan House of the Holy Saviour, $1.18; The Child's Hospital, $5. Total, $70.18.

General.— Children's Lenten offering for General Missions, $12.89.

Total amount of Offerings, $570.88

Property.

Church and lot (estimated worth), $2,000.

Parsonage and lot (estimated worth), $2,000.

Condition of Property, fairly good.

TRINITY CHURCH, POTSDAM.

Rector. The Rev. R. M. Kirby.

Wardens. Thomas S. Clarkson, Bloomfield Usher.

Vestrymen. T Streatfeild Clarkson. E. W Foster, C. O. Tappan, Luke Usher. H. D Thatcher, O G Howe, J. G. McIntyre, F. M. Heath.

Parochial.

Baptisms, (adults, 11, infants, 21), 32; Confirmed, since last report, 16; Present number of Confirmed Persons, 276. Marriages, 5; Burials, 10; Communicants, last reported, 218, admitted, 16. received, 4, died, 3, removed, 8, present number, 227; Public Services (Sundays, 104, Holy days, 39, other days, 223), 366, Holy Communion, public, 66, Sunday School, teachers, 15, pupils, 161; Catechizing, number of children, all, number of times, often.

Offerings.

Parochial.— Alms at Holy Communion, $234.54; Current expenses, including sala-ries, $2,927.77; Sunday School, $205.22; Increase and Improvement of Church Property, $283; Altar Society, $248.30. Total, $3,898.83.

Diocesan.— Diocesan Missions, $1,031; Salary of the Bishop, $50; Diocesan Fund, $50; Bible and Common Prayer Book Society of Albany, $22; Fund for Aged and Infirm Clergymen, $70.38; Fund for Widows and Orphans of Clergymen, $47.46; Orphan House of the Holy Saviour, $159.25; The Child's Hospital, $50; Society for Promoting Religion and Learning, $85.83; General Missionary, $50; Clergy Relief Fund, $15.55; Archdeaconry of Ogdensburg, $5.50; Other objects, $160. Total, $1,752.97.

General.— Domestic Missions from Sunday School, $88; Domestic Missions, $235; Foreign Missions, $297.50; Indian Missions, $264.50; Home Missions to Jews, $29; Sunday School for Bp. Leonard, Utah, $40; St. Helena's Church, Beaufort, S. C., $150.76; Woman's Auxiliary, cash for Indians, $70. Total, $1,174.76.

Total amount of Offerings, $6,826.56

Property.

Church and lot (estimated worth), $60,000.
Parsonage and lot (estimated worth), $4,000.
Condition of property, excellent.
Insurance, Church and Parsonage, $47,500.
Amount of salary pledged Rector, $1,600.
Number of sittings in the Church, 350; Chapel,150; all free.

Remarks.

In addition to the above, boxes of money, value of $185, have been sent away by the Woman's Auxiliary.

GRACE CHURCH, CANTON.

Rector. The Rev. R. Wyndham Brown.
Wardens. Hon. Leslie W. Russell, Sheldon Brewer
Vestrymen. Hon. J. C. Keeler, R. R. Ellsworth, H. D. Ellsworth, Cleland Austin, J. D. Tracey, H. H. Liotarde, H. B. Safford, J. C. Perkins.

Parochial.

Families, 80; Individuals, (adults, 153, children, 60), 213; Baptisms (infants), 11; Confirmed, since last report, 10; Present number of Confirmed Persons, 130; Mar-riages, 3; Burials, 6; Communicants, last reported, 81, admitted, 7, received, 6, removed, 2, present number, 92; Public Services (Sundays, 96, Holy days, 10, other days, 22), 128; Holy Communion (public), 25, Sunday School, teachers, 6, pupils, 40; Catechizing, number of times, frequently.

Offerings.

Parochial.— Alms at Holy Communion, $60; Current expenses, including sala-ries, $1,150; Sunday School, $30; Increase and Improvement of Church Property, $60; Ladies' Aid Society, $100; Parsonage Improvements, $125; Church Furnishing, $25; Interest on Mortgage, $72; Insurance premiums, $60. Total, $1,682.

Diocesan.— Diocesan Missions, $31; Salary of Bishop, $14 ; Diocesan Fund, $24, Education of Young Men for the Ministry, $5. Total, $74.

General.— Domestic Missions, $11.50.

Total amount of Offerings, $1,4━━━━━━━━━.

Property.

Church and lot (estimated worth), $3,000.
Parsonage and lot (estimated worth), $5,000.
Condition of property, good.
Indebtedness, Mortgage on Rectory, $1,200; Insurance, $2,500.
Amount of salary pledged Rector, $800.
Number of sittings in the Church, 200; rented, 120; free, 80.

GRACE CHURCH, NORFOLK.

Rector. The Rev. Elmer R. Earle.
Warden. E. H. Atwater.
Treasurer. H. F. Allen.
Clerk. John C. O'Brien.

Parochial.

Families, 18; Individuals, 50; Baptisms (infants), 6; Confirmed, since last report, 3; Present number of Confirmed Persons, 30; Burials, 2; Communicants, last reported, 27, admitted, 3, present number, 30; Public Services (Sundays, 48, Holy days, 2), 50; Holy Communion (public, 10, private, 1), 11; Sunday School, teachers, 4, pupils, 25.

Offerings.

Parochial. — Alms at Holy Communion, $1.14; Current expenses, including salaries, $100.09; Sunday School, $40.48; Increase and Improvement of Church Property, $124.62. Total, $266.26.

Diocesan.—Diocesan Missions, $5; Salary of Bishop, $2; Diocesan Fund, $3; Auxiliary boxes for the Child's Hospital, $15.30. Total, $25.30.

General.— Children's Lenten Boxes for Domestic Missions, $3.58.

Total amount of Offerings, $298.14.

Property.

Church and lot (estimated worth), $2,000.
Condition of property, good.
Amount of salary pledged Rector, $100.
Sittings in the Church all free.

Remarks.

The Missionary holds Sunday afternoon service in Norfolk, except on the third Sunday in the month, when there is morning service with a celebration of the Holy Communion. There is no numerical growth to the Church in this place. Were it not for a few faithful Church families nothing could be done.

TRINITY CHURCH, GOUVERNEUR.

Rector. The Rev. James Alexander Dickson.
Wardens. Aaron B. Cutting and Frank H. Smith.
Vestrymen. John McCarty, Edward D. Barry, J. B. Preston, James D. Easton, Gerrit S. Conger.

Parochial.

Families, in part or whole, 49; Individuals (adults, 109, children, 50), 159; Baptisms, infants, 3; Present number of Confirmed Persons, 83; Marriages, 6; Burials, 7; Communicants, last reported, 77, received, 2, present number, 79; Public Services (Sundays, 88, Holy Days, 20), 108, Other Days, Wednesday evening and daily during Lent; Holy Communion (public), 32; Sunday School, teachers, 5, pupils, 40; Catechising, number of children, 40, number of times, every Sunday.

Offerings.

Parochial.—Alms at Holy Communion, $90; Current expenses, including salaries, $1,062, Sunday School, $20; Increase and Improvement of Church Property, $1,248 95. Total, $2,420.95.

Diocesan.—Diocesan Missions, $55; Salary of the Bishop, $26; Diocesan Fund, $28. Total, $109.

General.—Domestic Missions (Lent Offering of Sunday School), $9.80; Foreign Missions (Lent Offering of Sunday School), $9.80. Total, $19.60.

Total amount of Offerings, $2,549.55.

Property.

Church and lot (estimated worth), $6,500.

Parsonage and lot (estimated worth), $3,000.

Other property, $250.

Condition of property, good.

Insurance, $3,000.

Amount of salary pledged Rector, $800.

Number of sittings in the Church, 200; part rented and part free.

ST. JOHN'S CHURCH, MASSENA.

Rector. The Rev. Charles Elliott Mackenzie.

Wardens. H. T. Clark, G. A. Snaith.

Vestrymen. E. H. Pitts, E. R. Foord, L. S. Doming, J. O. Bridges, H. H. Warren, James Webb.

Parochial.

Families, 89; Individuals (adults, 239, children, 131), 370; Baptisms (adults, 2, infants, 14), 16; Confirmed, since last report, 1; Present number of Confirmed Persons, 105; Marriage, 1; Burials, 6; Communicants, present number, 62; Public Services (Sundays, 53, Holy days, 4, other days, 26), 83, Holy Communion (public), 11; Sunday School, teachers, 5, pupils, 60; Catechizing, number of children, 48, number of times, 2.

Offerings.

Parochial.—Current expenses, including salaries, $516.15; Sunday School, $30; Mortgage (principal, $250, interest, $83), $333. Total, $879.15.

Diocesan.—Diocesan Missions, $30; Salary of the Bishop, $8; Diocesan Fund, $9.75. Total, $47.75.

Total amount of Offerings, $926.90.

Property.

Church and Lot (estimated worth) $7,000.

Condition of property, good as far as finished.

Indebtedness, $3,500.

Insurance, $3,000.

Amount of salary pledged Rector, $325.

Number of sittings in the church, 250; all free,

Remarks.

I took charge on June 16, so the returns for services above are only since that date. I regret that the returns this time are necessarily incomplete. Families and services in Long Sault Island are included above. All the work is much behind hand, but the prospects are good. The Woman's Aid has done noble service and a branch of the Daughters of the █████████████████████████

ST. LUKE'S CHURCH, LISBON.

Rector. The Rev. A. C. Macdonald.
Warden. Andrew O'Neil.

Parochial.

Families, 13; Individuals (adults, 26, children, 14), 40; Baptisms (infants), 2; Present number of Confirmed Persons, 19; Burials, 1; Communicants, last reported, 14, admitted, 1, died, 1, present number, 14; Public Services (Sundays, 36, other days, 4), 40; Holy Communion (public), 2; Sunday School, teachers, 3, pupils, 12.

Offerings.

Parochial.— Alms at Holy Communion, $1; Current expenses, including salaries, $45; Expenses for livery, $50; Bought Horse for Rector, $45. Total, $141.
Diocesan.— Diocesan Missions, $5.
Total amount of Offerings, $146.

Property.

Church and lot (estimated worth), $2,000.
Parsonage and lot (estimated worth), $50.
Condition of property, good.
Amount of salary pledged Rector, $60.

Remarks.

The little flock here has made a great stride in advance in purchasing a horse for the Missionary. The people here, without distinction, attend the services of the Church. The "dissidence of dissent" dies hard in these regions though.

ZION CHURCH, COLTON.

Rector. The Rev. George M. Irish.
Wardens. Thomas S. Clarkson, Myron E. Howard.
Vestrymen. P. Potter, J. W. Lyman, Archie Allen, S. J. Hosley, Wm. Eacutt, Eugene Moore, A. H. Gustin, F. G. Stone.

Parochial.

Families, 72; Individuals (adults and children), 286; Baptisms, (adults, 4, infants, 3), 7; Present number of Confirmed Persons, 71; Marriages, 3; Burials, 10; Communicants, last reported, 62, received, 1, removed, 1, present number, 62; Public Services (Sundays, 99, Holy days, 20, other days, 58), 177; Holy communion (public) 30; Sunday School, teachers, 7, pupils, 82; Catechizing, number of children, all number of times, frequently.

Offerings.

Parochial.— Alms of Holy Communion (not elsewhere reported), $9.70; Current expenses, including salaries, $1,190.32; Sunday School, $7.43; Increase and Improvement to Church Property, $99; Reading room, $50. Total, $1,356.45.
Diocesan.— Diocesan Missions, $11.10; Salary of the Bishop, $4; Diocesan Fund, $4.50; Fund for Aged and Infirm Clergymen, $1.72. Total, $21.32.
General.— Domestic Missions, $82.35; Foreign Missions, $321.72; Missionary Box (estimated value), $75. Total, $479.07.
Total amount of Offerings, $1,856.84.

Remarks.

Services were held at Pierpont every Sunday afternoon, except during July and August.

TRINITY CHAPEL, MORLEY.

Rector. The Rev. B. Wyndham Brown.
Warden. Hon. Thomas L. Harison.
Treasurer. N. P. Whitney.
Clerk. H. N. Fenton.

Parochial.

Families, 45; Individuals (adults, 90, children, 30), 120; Baptisms (adults, 1, infants, 3), 4; Confirmed, since last report, 8; Marriages, 1; Communicants, last reported, 45, admitted, 6, present number, 51; Public Services (Sundays, 48, Holy days, 3, other days, 6), 57; Holy Communion (public 16, private, 4), 20; Sunday School, teachers, 3, pupils, 25.

Offerings.

Parochial.—Alms at Holy Communion, $2.57; Current expenses, including salaries, $75; Increase and Improvement of Church Property, $20; Balance paid on new furnace for Church, $8.15; To Missionary, $64. Total, $169.72.

Diocesan.— Diocesan Missions, $25; Salary of the Bishop, $6. Total, $31.
Total amount of Offerings, $200.72.

Property.

Church and lot (estimated worth), $15,000.
Parsonage and lot (estimated worth), $4,000.
Condition of property, very good.
Amount of salary pledged Rector, missionary stipend.
Number of sittings in the Church, 240; all free.

ST. THOMAS' CHURCH, LAWRENCEVILLE.

Rector. The Rev. A. L. Fortin.
Warden. William Kingston.

Parochial.

Families, 13; Individuals (adults, 30, children, 14), 44; Present number of Confirmed Persons, 23; Communicants, last reported, 19, received, 1, present number, 20; Public Services, Sundays, fortnightly; Holy Communion, public, monthly; Sunday School, teachers, 1, pupils, 12.

Offerings.

Parochial.— Current expenses, including salaries, $110.70; Increase and Improvement of Church Property, $30.75; Fuel, etc., $7. Total, $148.45.

Diocesan.— Diocesan Missions, $5; Diocesan Fund, $3.25. Total, $8.25.
Total amount of Offerings, $156.70.

Property.

Church and lot (estimated worth), $2,500.
Parsonage and lot (estimated worth), $1,000.
Condition of property, the Church needs repairing.
Insurance, on Parsonage, $1,000.
Amount of salary pledged Rector, $93.
Number of sittings in the Church, 200; all free.

Remarks.

A Sunday School has been organized a short time ago. Miss Frances Kingston, who is a most faithful Church worker, carries it on. We are greatly indebted to Miss Clarkson of Potsdam, for ~~books~~

17

ST. ANDREW'S CHURCH, NORWOOD.

Rector. The Rev. Elmer R. Earle.
Warden. M. Valley.
Clerk. F. G. Partridge.
Treasurer. J. A. Valley.

Parochial.

Families, 24; Individuals (adults, 60, children, 20), 80; Baptisms (adults, 1, infants, 3), 4; Confirmed, since last report, 6; Present number of Confirmed Persons, 40; Marriages, 2; Burials, 5; Communicants, last reported, 35, admitted, 6, died, 1, present number, 40; Public Services (Sundays, 98, Holy days, 5, other days, 45), 148; Holy Communion, public, 12; Sunday School, teachers, 3, pupils, 20; Catechizing, number of children, 20, number of times, 12.

Offerings.

Parochial.—Alms at Holy Communion, $2.84; Current expenses, including salaries, $293.47; Sunday School, $12.38; Increase and Improvement of Church Property, $250.05; Altar cloths (gift of a communicant), $20. Total, $578.74.
Diocesan.— Diocesan Missions, $10; Salary of the Bishop, $4; Diocesan Fund, $6; For the Diocesan Chapter-house, $3. Total, $23.
General.— Sunday School Lenten Offering for Domestic Missions, $5.78.
Total amount of Offerings, $607.52.

Property.

Church and lot (estimated worth), $4,000.
Condition of property, good.
Insurance, $2,000.
Amount of salary pledged Missionary, $200.
Number of sittings in the Church, 150; all free.

Remarks.

In this Mission things have gone along quite smoothly during the past year. The services have been well attended. The Missionary has a Parish Guild which has done good service. The larger part of the money spent upon Church improvement was earned by the Guild. Friends of the Parish have placed in the Church a handsome font and prayer-desk.

GRACE MISSION, LOUISVILLE LANDING.

Missionary. Rev. C. E. Mackenzie.
Warden. R. B. Matthews.
Clerk. Otis Wells.
Treasurer. Benj. Nicholls.

Parochial.

Families, 27; Individuals (adults, 70, children, 27), 97; Baptisms (infants), 8; Present number of Confirmed Persons, 22; Marriages, 1; Burials, 1; Public Services (week days), 11 (three months).

Offerings.

Current expenses, $15.

Remarks.

This Mission has been practically dormant for five years, but it has lately been revived under very hopeful conditions.

Saratoga County.

CHRIST CHURCH, BALLSTON SPA.

Rector. The Rev. Charles Pelletreau, B. D.
Wardens. Stephen B. Medbery, John H. Wescot.
Vestrymen. Charles M. Brown, Geo. L. Thompson, Matthew Vassar, Stephen C. Medbery, William S. Wheeler, David L. Wood, James W. Verbeck, Irving W. Wiswall.

Parochial.

Families, and parts of families, 150; Baptisms (adults, 1, infants, 11), 12; Marriages, 4; Burials, 10; Communicants, present number, 250; Public Services, Sundays, 104, Holy days, all, other days, 96, Holy Communion (public), 53; Sunday School, teachers, 9, pupils, 100 ; Catechizing, number of children, 75, number of times, often.

Offerings.

Parochial.—Alms at Holy Communion, $60 ; Current expenses, including salaries, $3,057.78; Sunday School Collections, $36; New Memorial Altar (special), $450; Christmas Tree, $37 ; Easter Offering and proceeds of Sunday School Entertainment for New Doors, $130; Evening collections, $57.86; Special for the Poor, $25. Total, $3,853.64.

Diocesan.— Diocesan Missions, $105.01; Salary of the Bishop, $42; Diocesan Fund, and Clergy Insurance, $42; Bible and Common Prayer Book Society of Albany, $4.30; Fund for Aged and Infirm Clergymen, $14.25; Orphan House of the Holy Saviour, $10; The Child's Hospital, $34.50; Diocesan Missionary, $15; Woman's Auxiliary in cash and boxes, $159.97. Total, $427.03.

General.— Domestic Missions, $20.50; Foreign Missions, $20.50; Indian Missions, $20.50; Home Missions to Coloured Persons, $20.50; Missions in Indiana (special), $5; Babcock Scholarship, S Dakota, $60; Junior Auxiliary box to Coloured School in Virginia, $20. Total, $167.

Total amount of Offerings, $4,417.67.

Property.

Church and lot (estimated worth), $18,000.
Parsonage and lot (estimated worth), $10,000.
Other Property, Parish House, $7,000.
Condition of property, excellent.
Insurance, $14,000.
Amount of salary pledged Rector, $1,500.
Number of sittings in the Church, 350.

ST. JOHN'S CHURCH, STILLWATER.

Deacon in charge. The Rev. Marvin Hill Dana, M. A., LL. B.
Wardens. John Stringer, John Bradley.
Vestrymen. Wm. Bradley, John Bradley, Jr., Charles Green, John Tabor, Joseph Moll, George Lansing,
Clerk. H. D. Bradt.

Parochial.

Families, 15; Individuals (adults, 29, children, 8), 89; ent number of Confirmed Persons, 80; Communicant received, 1, removed, 1, present number, 80 : Public Services, Sundays, Matins, Litany, Children's Vespers, Vespers ; Holy days, Matins ; Other days, Compline and Lecture, Wednesday evenings; Holy Communion (public), monthly as Priest can be secured; Sunday School, pupils, 23 ; Catechizing, number of children, the whole school, number of times, weekly.

Property.

Church and lot, New Wooden Church.
Other property, Endowment, $6,500.
Indebtedness, none.
Insurance, $1,800.
Amount of salary pledged Rector, $600.

Remarks.

It is impossible to make a full and perfect report from the records discoverable in the Parish. The Parish is small, but with a certain limited chance for growth. It has a good working spirit, though rather of a domestic taste as concerns the direction of its efforts. The financial status is excellent.

ST. PAUL'S CHURCH, CHARLTON.

Minister in charge. The Rev. John Mills Gilbert.
Wardens. William Taylor, Robert O. Davis.
Vestrymen. George C. Valentine, John Marvin, John Craig, John Taylor.

Parochial.

Families, 19; Burials, 2; Communicants, last reported, 28, died, 2, present number, 26; Public Services (Sundays, 46, other days, 9), 55; Holy Communion (public), 3; Sunday School, teachers, 3, pupils, 14; Catechizing, number of times, 3.

Offerings.

Parochial. — Current expenses, including salaries, $245; Sunday School, $8. Total, $253.
General.—General Missions, $18.40.
Total amount of Offerings, $271.40.

Property.

Church and lot (estimated worth), $1,300.
Other property, $700.
Condition of property, fair.
Insurance, $1,950.
Number of sittings in the Church, 125; all free.

Remarks.

It is much to be regretted that the occasions for the celebration of the Holy Eucharist have been so few, owing to the fact that the Minister in charge is but in deacon's orders, and the extreme difficulty of securing the services of a Priest at such a distance from the city.

We extend our hearty thanks to Rev. W. C. Prout and Rev. Canon Stewart for their kind assistance.

GRACE CHURCH, WATERFORD.

(No report.)

ST. LUKE'S CHURCH, MECHANICVILLE.

Missionary. The Rev. Frank N. Bouck.
Wardens. Wm. C. Tallmadge, M. W. Hart.
Vestrymen. H. O. Bailey, Isaac Richardson, John Todd, C. W. Keefer, Francis Longstaff, A. J. Harvey, John E. Thomson, Geo. W. Clark.

Parochial.

Families, 60; Individuals (adults, 110, children, 50), 160; Baptisms (adults, 1, infants, 6), 7; Present number of Confirmed Persons, 80; Burials, 3; Communicants, last reported, 65, present number, 40; Public Services (Sundays, 28, Holy Days, 3, other days, 13), 44; Sunday School, teachers, 5, pupils, 34; Catechizing, number of children, 34, number of times, weekly.

Offerings.

Parochial.—Current expenses, including salaries, $484.28; Sunday School, $15.10. Total, $499.38.

Diocesan.—Diocesan Missions, $16.62; Salary of the Bishop, $4; Orphan House of the Holy Saviour (Sunday School), $5.62. Total, $26.24.

General.—Domestic Missions (Sunday School), $6.92; Foreign Missions (Sunday School), $6.92. Total, $13.84.

Total amount of Offerings, $539.46.

Property.

Church and lot, and Parsonage and lot (estimated worth), $5,000.
Other property (Mancius endowment), $1,000.
Condition of property, good.
Indebtedness, mortgage on Church property, $850.
Insurance (Church, $2,200, Rectory, $1,500), $3,700.
Amount of salary pledged Rector, $500.
Number of sittings in the Church, 175; all free.

Remarks.

Church without Rector from April 1 to August 1.
The incompleteness of the report on the first page is owing to my having been in charge of the Parish but three months.
The present number of actual Communicants in the Parish is very small.

BETHESDA CHURCH, SARATOGA SPRINGS.

Rector. The Rev. Joseph Carey, S. T. D.
Wardens. James M. Marvin, Robert Charles McEwen, M. D.
Vestrymen. William A. Sackett, Spencer Trask, Daniel Eddy, Walter R. Johnson, George R. P. Shackelford, Winsor B. French, William B. Gage, William B. Huestis.

Parochial.

Families, 325; Individuals (adults, 652, children, 537), 1189; Baptisms (adults, 23, infants, 33), 56; Confirmed, since last report, 54; Present number of Confirmed Persons, 790; Marriages, 33; Burials, 64; Churchings, 2; Communicants, last reported, 772, admitted, 54, received, 2, died, 17, removed, 25, present number, 786; Public Services (Sundays, 168, Holy days, 33, other days, 336), 537; Holy Communion (public, 105, private, 10), 115; Sunday School, teachers, 67, pupils (including Catharine Street Mission Sunday School), 597; Catechizing, number of children, 597, number of times, 52.

Offerings.

Parochial.—Alms at Holy Communion for charitable work, $293.64: Current expenses, including salaries, $5,412.55; Sunday School, $813.62; Parish House, $944.47; Home of Good Shepherd, $766.57; Choir Vestment Society, $32.24; Choir Music, $20.42; Church debt, $1,505; Altar Society, $58.17. Total, $9,846.68.

Diocesan.—Diocesan Missions, $200; Salary of Bishop, $70; Diocesan Fund, $75; Bible and Common Prayer Book Society of Albany, $27; Theological Education, $25; Fund for Aged and Infirm Clergymen, $30.16; Orphan House of the Holy Saviour, box (value), $40; The Child's Hospital, $23.39; Woman's Auxiliary, $68; Archdeaconry of Troy, $36 26; St. Stephen's Church, Schuylerville, $5.25; Salary Diocesan Missionary, $50; Clerical Insurance, $12.50; Box to a Missionary of the Diocese, value, $76. Total, $743.56.

General.—Domestic Missions, $25; Society, Increase of Ministry, $9.70; Rev. P. D. Hay, Beaufort Sufferers, $33.60; St. Stephen's College, $12.50; St. Augustine's School, Raleigh, $5.13. Total, $84.95.

Total amount of Offerings, $10,675.19.

Property.

Church, and lot (estimated worth), $83,000.
Parsonage and lot (estimated worth), $9,000.
Other property, Parish House, $17,000.
House of Good Shepherd, $6,000.
Mission Chapel, $1,800.
Condition of property, good.
Indebtedness, on Church, $4,000; on Rectory, $3,700; on Old Section of Parish House, $2,400.
Insurance, $25,000.
Amount of salary pledged Rector, with Rectory, $2,500.
Number of sittings in the Church, 1,200.
Number rented, part; number free, part.

Remarks.

The year has been marked by the gift of two Candelabras, of fifteen lights each, from Mrs. Christian von Spiegel, for the Sanctuary, greatly enhancing its beauty. It is with gratitude that record is also made of gifts from Mr. and Mrs. James A. Moore, who have already done so much for the Parish. They gave a richly-carved Litany Desk, with proper "Cloths" for the Church Seasons, in February last; and in October they put in the Church Porch two beautiful stained-glass windows,—"The Raising of the Daughter of Jairus" and "Christ Healing the Sick."

ST. STEPHEN'S CHURCH, SCHUYLERVILLE.

Rector. The Rev. W. F. Parsons.
Wardens. Mr. Peter Davison, Mr. J. Hicks Smith.
Vestrymen. Messrs. M. J. H. Lowber, John A. Dix, Fred McNaughton, Alvin R. Carpenter, Theo. B. Aitcheson, J. I. C. Blandy.

Parochial.

Families, 46; Individuals (adults, 84, children, 65), 149; Baptisms (adults, 1, infants, 16) 17; Confirmed, since last report, 15; Present number of Confirmed Persons, 84; Marriages, 6; Burials, 1; Communicants, admitted, 15, died, 1, present number, 84; Public Services, Sundays, 72, Holy days, 13, other days, 56), 141 ; Holy Communion (public). 22; Sunday School, teachers, 6, pupils, 43 ; Catechizing, number of children, all, number of times, nearly every Sunday since July 1st, when it was organized.

Offerings.

Parochial.— Alms at Holy Communion, $14.42; Current expenses, including salaries, $408.44 ; Sunday School, $12.46; Increase and Improvement of Church Property, $220; Raised by Ladies' Aid Society, $120. Total, $775.82.

Diocesan.— Salary of Bishop, $9; Diocesan Fund, $5. Total, $14.

General.— Foreign and Indian Missions, $3.

Total amount of Offerings, $792.32.

Property.

Church and lot (estimated worth), $10,000.

Parsonage and lot (estimated worth), $3,000.

Condition of property, excellent.

Insurance on Rectory, $1,500.

Amount of salary pledged Rector, $500.

Number of sittings in the Church, 230; number free, all.

CALVARY CHURCH, BURNT HILLS.

Minister in charge. The Rev. John Mills Gilbert.

Wardens. Edwin Mead, Charles H. Upham.

Vestrymen. John Cotton, M. D., Garret L. Cavert, Robert M. Keller, Robert J. Wendell, Jacob H. Pink, Levinus Lansing, Frederic E. German, William H. Larkin.

Parochial.

Families, 41 ; Individuals (adults, 88, children, 45), 133 ; Baptisms (infants), 4; Burials, 6; Communicants, last reported, 56, received, 1, died, 2, removed, 1, present number, 54; Public Services (Sundays, 99, Holy days, 39, other days, 185), 323; Holy Communion (public), 6 ; Sunday School, teachers, 5, pupils, 33 ; Catechizing, number of times, 5.

Offerings.

Parochial.— Alms at Holy Communion, $8.02 : Current expenses, including salaries, $545.27; Sunday School, $4.49. Total, $557.78.

Diocesan.— Diocesan Missions, $33.34; Salary of Bishop, $12; Diocesan Fund, $14. Total, $59.34.

General.— Domestic Missions, $5 ; Foreign Missions, $5.65 ; General Missions, (Sunday School, Lenten), $9.02. Total, $19.67.

Total amount of Offerings, $636.79.

Property.

Church and lot (estimated worth), $3,000.

Parsonage and lot (estimated worth), $1,200.

Other property, $800.

Condition of property, good.

Insurance, $4,200.

Amount of salary pledged Rector, $400.

Number of sittings in the Church, 200; all free.

Remarks.

During the year the Rectory has been repaired at an ex

ST. JOHN'S CHURCH, EAST LINE.

Missionary. The Rev. Thomas Boone.
Warden. Howland Fish.
Secretary. Walter Bradley.
Treasurer. Wm. Denton.

Parochial.

Families, 20; Individuals, 60; Communicants, last reported, 36, present number, 36; Public Services (Sundays, 50, Holy days, 4, other days, 3), 57; Holy Communion, (public), 10.

Offerings.

Parochial.—Current expenses, including salaries, $104.25. Total, $104.25.

Diocesan.—Diocesan Missions, $5; Diocesan Fund, $3; Bible and Common Prayer Book Society of Albany, $2.50; Diocesan Evangelist, $3; Clerical Insurance, 50 cents. Total, $14.

Total amount of Offerings, $118.25.

Property.

Church and lot (estimated worth), $1,000
Parsonage and lot (estimated worth), $1,500.
Other property, $5,000.
Condition of property, good.
Amount of salary pledged Rector, $100.
Number of sittings in the Church, 75; all free.

GRACE CHURCH, JONESVILLE.

Missionary. The Rev. Thomas Boone.
Warden. James Jump.
Treasurer. Wm. Hatlee, Jr.
Secretary. John R. Jump.

Parochial.

Families, 14; Individuals, 65; Baptisms (infants), 3; Present number of Confirmed Persons, 50; Marriages, 1; Communicants, last reported, 29, present number, 29; Public Services (Sundays, 52, Holy Days, 4, other days, 6), 62; Holy Communion (public), 13; Sunday School, teachers, 4, pupils, 40.

Offerings.

Parochial.—Current expenses, including salaries, $192.63; Sunday School, $10; Improvement of Church Property, $3; Interest on debt, $24.36. Total, $229.99.

Diocesan.—Diocesan Missions, $10; Salary of the Bishop, 4; Diocesan Fund, $4.50; Bible and Common Prayer Book Society of Albany, $3.30; Diocesan Evangelist, $3. Total, $24.80.

Total amount of Offerings, $254.79.

Property.

Church and lot (estimated worth), $1,400.
Other property, $800.
Condition of property, good.
Indebtedness, $406.90.
Insurance, $800.
Amount of salary pledged Rector, $150.
Number of sittings in the Church, 109; all free.

ALL SAINTS' CHURCH, ROUND LAKE.

Missionary. The Rev. Thomas Boone.
Warden. W. N. Horton.
Treasurer. P. C. Curtis.
Clerk. G. L. Thorne.

Parochial.

Families, 15; Individuals, 50: Baptisms (adults, 7, infants, 3), 10; Present number of Confirmed Persons, 13; Marriages, 1; Burials, 1; Communicants, last reported, 14, died, 1, present number, 13; Public Services (Sundays, 52, Holy Days, 5, other days, 60), 117; Holy Communion (public, 19, private, 1), 20; Sunday School, teachers, 4, pupils, 38.

Offerings.

Parochial.—Current expenses, including salaries, $385.45; Increase and Improvement of Church Property, $359.81. Sunday School, $17.29. Total, $762.55.

Diocesan.—Diocesan Missions, $5; Diocesan Fund, $9; Bible and Common Prayer Book Society of Albany, $3; Diocesan Evangelist, $4; Clerical Insurance, $1.50. Total, $22.50.

Total amount of Offerings, $785.05.

Property.

Church and lot (estimated worth), $3,000.
Condition of property, good.
Insurance, $1,500.
Amount of salary pledged Rector, $300.
Number of sittings in the Church, 100: all free.

Schenectady County.

CHRIST CHURCH, DUANESBURGH.

Rector. The Rev. E. W. Flower.
Lay Reader. Mr. Edward Clarence Clark.
Wardens. Alexander McDougall. Ralph W. McDougall.
Vestrymen. James D. Featherstonhaugh, Alexander Van Pelt, George Matthews, George D. Matthews, Wesley Van Pelt, Edward C. Clark, R. A. McDougall, M. D., Charles Gilchrist.

Parochial.

Families, 79: Individuals (adults, 132, children, 50), 182; Baptisms (adults 2, infants, 6), 8; Present number of Confirmed Persons, estimated, 117; Marriages, 2; Burials, 1; Communicants, last reported, 92, admitted, 1, received, 2, removed, 1, present number, 94; Public Services (Sundays, 97, Holy days, 23, other days, 18), 138; Holy Communion (public), 31; Sunday School, teachers, 7, pupils, 48; Catechizing, number of times, 42.

Offerings.

Parochial.—Alms at Holy Communion (not otherwise reported), $6.33; Current expenses, including salaries, $1,299.25; Increase and Improvement of Church Property, $344.60. Total, $1,650.18

Diocesan.—Diocesan Missions and General Missionary, $80; Salary of the Bishop, $50; Diocesan Fund, $35; Bible and Common Prayer Book Society of Albany, $6.63; Fund for Aged and Infirm Clergymen, $3.65; Fund for Widows and Orphans of

Clergymen, $2.04; Orphan House of the Holy Saviour, $10.06; The Child's Hospital, $5.64; Box to a Diocesan Missionary (value), $30; To Missions in the Diocese, $5.84. Total, $228.86.

General.—Domestic and Foreign Missions, $35.82; Foreign Missions, $9.35; Indian Missions, $2; Home Missions to Coloured Persons, $2; Aged and Infirm Clergy (general), $3.65; Missions to the Jews, $3.50; American Church Building Fund, $4.20; S. John's College, Shanghai, $3; Work in Nevada and Utah, $5; Work in West Missouri, $1. Total, $68.52.

Total amount of Offerings, $1,947.56.

Property.

Church and lot (estimated worth), $3,000.
Parsonage and lot (estimated worth), $3,000.
Other property, Chapel and lot, $2,000.
Condition of property, good.
Insurance, $5,000.

Remarks.

On the 25th day of August, the Church celebrated the one hundreth anniversary of its consecration. Appropriate services were held. The congregation placed, by their gifts, an excellent bell in the tower. There was presented, by members of the Duane family, a marble font, with cover, and an ewer, in memory of the Hon. James Duane, founder of the Parish; also a brass memorial altar cross, brass vases, altar service book, glass cruets and other gifts for the Sanctuary, from present and former parishioners.

ST. GEORGE'S CHURCH, SCHENECTADY.

Rector. The Rev J. Philip B. Pendleton, S. T. B.
Wardens. Abram A. Van Vorst, Samuel W. Jackson.
Vestrymen. D. Cady Smith, John A. De Remer, John Keyes Paige, Howland S. Barney, T. Low Barhydt, Edward D. Palmer, Charles S. Washburn, De Lancey W. Watkins.

Parochial.

Families, 354; Individuals (adults, 760, children, 450), 1210; Baptisms (adults, 5, infants, 23), 28; Confirmed, since last report, 18; Present number of Confirmed Persons, 560; Marriages, 9; Burials, 36; Churchings, 6; Communicants, last reported, 482, admitted, 19, received, 15, died, 12, removed, 10, present number, 494; Public Services (Sundays, 220, Holy days, 99, other days, 210), 529; Holy Communion (public, 102, private, 11), 113; Sunday School, teachers, 29, pupils, 251; Catechizing, number of children, all, number of times, weekly; Industrial School, teachers, 19, pupils, 151. *Parish Agencies:* St. Mary's Guild, 110 members; St. Agnes' Guild, 40 members; St. Andrew's Guild, 52 members; Industrial School; Vested Choir; Parish paper.

Offerings.

Parochial.—Alms at Holy Communion, $446.46; Current expenses, including salaries, $3,654; Sunday School (not reported elsewhere), $163.02; Increase and Improvement of Church Property, $495; St. Mary's Guild (not reported elsewhere), $247.45; St. Agnes' Guild, $103.14; Reduction of Indebtedness, $1,285; Special for Sunday School, Vested Choir, Memorials, Parish Kalendar, etc., $376. Total, $6,772.07.

Diocesan.—Diocesan Missions (including specials), $170.10; Salary of the Bishop, $60; Diocesan Fund, $60; Clerical Insurance, $10; Theological Education, $50; Orphan House of the Holy Saviour, $21.25; The Child's Hospital, $32.01; The Chapter House of All Saints' Cathedral, $45.40; Ellis Hospital, $100. Total, $548.76.

General.—Domestic Missions (including boxes to Iowa, Virginia and Pittsburg), $230.62; Foreign Missions, $85; Indian Missions, $30; Home Missions to Coloured Persons, $20; Scholarship in St. John's School, Logan, Utah, daughter of a deceased Missionary in Virginia, Jewish Missions, Woman Missionary in Alaska, Enrolment Fund, $149.59. Total, $515.30.

Total amount of Offerings, $7,836.13.

Property.

Church and lot (estimated worth), $35,000.

Parsonage and lot (estimated worth), $8,000.

Other property, $4,000.

Condition of property, good.

Indebtedness, $1,500.

Amount of salary pledged Rector, $2,000, with Rectory.

Number of sittings in the Church and Chapel, 850.

Remarks.

For a number of years past there has been an indebtedness of about $3,000 resting upon the Parish, and we are glad to report that of this amount nearly $2,300 have been pledged during the past year, $1,285 of which have already been paid in. In connection with the observance of the twenty-fifth anniversary of the consecration of the Bishop of Albany, it is an interesting coincidence that two of our delegates to the present Convention, Messrs Abram A. Van Vorst and Samuel W. Jackson, were also Deputies to the Primary Convention of the Diocese.

CHRIST CHURCH, SCHENECTADY.

Rector. The Rev. James F. Olmsted.

Wardens. James E. Curtiss, David Guy.

Vestrymen. William N. Butler, Henry C. Van Zandt, M. D., David O. Youlen, Sidney G. Ashmore, L. H. D., Edward E. Kriegsman, John H. Shaffer, Rufus W. Lampman, Robert J. English.

Parochial.

Families, 187; Individuals (adults, 290, children, 175), 465; Baptisms (adults, 1, infants, 17), 18; Marriages, 3; Burials, 19 , Communicants, last reported, 175, died, 9, present number, 166 ; Public Services (Sundays, 146, Holy days, 38, other days, 70), 254; Holy Communion (public, 69, private, 3), 72; Sunday School, teachers, 15, pupils, 121; Catechizing, number of children, School, number of times, every Sunday.

Offerings.

Parochial — Alms at Holy Communion, $46.22; Current expenses, including salaries, $1,102.88, Sunday School (not otherwise accounted for), $108.45; By the King's Daughters, $19.52, S. S Christmas Tree, $68.79; For a Parish House, $97.71; Special for Music, $45; On Bonded Debt, $800 ; By the Woman's Guild, (including $161.25 interest on bonded debt), $315.22. Total $2,603.79.

Diocesan — Diocesan Missions, $20; Salary of the Bishop, $7.50; Diocesan Fund, $12; Bible and Common Prayer Book Society of Albany, $6.59 ; Orphan House of the Holy Saviour, $17.67; Diocesan Missionary, $1. Total, $64.76.

General.— Sunday School Offerings to Domestic and Foreign Missions, $5.25, to the Jews, $4.30; Box for Coloured Children in N. Carolina by King's Daughters, $16.75; Special Charity of King's Daughters, $23. Total, $49.30.

Total amount of Offerings, $2,707.85.

Property.

Church and lot (estimated worth), $10,000.
Parsonage and lot (estimated worth), $5,000.
Other property, Parish House Fund, $1,126.37.
Condition of property, good.
Indebtedness, Mortgage, $2,700.
Insurance on Church and furniture, $3,500; on Rectory, $2,500.
Amount of salary pledged Rector, $800.
Number of sittings in the Church, 180; all free.

Remarks.

The Rev. Wm. C. Prout resigned the Rectorship of this Parish on September 1, 1893, and the present Rector entered on his Rectorship on All Saints' Day, 1893.

Schoharie County.

TRINITY CHURCH, SHARON SPRINGS.

Rector. The Rev. Earnest Webster Dustan.

The Church is vested under a board of trustees, composed as follows : Dr. A. W. Gardner, President; John H. Gardner, Treasurer; Seth Parsons, Secretary; J. F. Lehman, N. W. Stratton (all of Sharon Springs), and Captain Taylor, The Armory, Springfield, Mass.

Parochial.

Families, 48; Individuals (adults, 84, children, 4), 88; Baptisms, infants, 1; Confirmed, since last report, 4; Present Number of Confirmed Persons, 88; Marriages, 2; Communicants, last reported, 85, admitted, 4, died, 1, present number, 88; Public Services (Sundays, 98, Holy days, 2, other days, 38), 138; Holy Communion, public, 10; Sunday School, teachers, 7, pupils, 77; Catechizing, number of Children, not recorded, number of times, 3.

Offerings.

Parochial.— Current expenses, including salaries, $1,300; Sunday School, $12; Increase and improvement of church property, $50; Trinity Guild and the Woman's Auxiliary, raised by entertainments, $112. Total, $1,474.*

Diocesan.— Salary of the Bishop, $20; The Woman's Auxiliary and St. Agnes' Guild sent a box to the Cooperstown Orphanage worth, about $30. Total, $50.

General.— Foreign Missions, $16, The Sunday School offerings during Lent were sent to the Society for Promoting Christianity Among the Jews, amounting to $4. Total, $20.

Total amount of Offerings, $1,544.

Property.

Church and lot (estimated worth), $4,000.
Parsonage and lot (estimated worth), $4,000.

---

* With this the interior of the Church was completely and appropriately redecorated.

Other property, $100
Condition of property, good.
Insurance, the triennial premium, $75.
Amount of salary pledged Rector, $900.
Number of sittings in the Church, 200; all free.

Remarks.

The Church has received, during the past year, a black walnut Credence Table from St. Agnes' Guild; also, a silver and glass water cruet from Mrs. Francis Rawle, a pair of brass altar candlesticks from Mr. G. Heatley Dulles, and a set of green altar cloths from Miss Bartholow, all of Philadelphia.

Warren County.

THE CHURCH OF THE MESSIAH, GLENS FALLS.

Rector. The Rev. Fenwick Mitford Cookson.
Wardens. William A. Walt, L. P. Juvet.
Vestrymen. W. H. Robbins, Nelson La Salle, H. W. Coffin, M. D., H. A. Bowden, James A. Holden, D. J. Finch, Orange Ferriss, John E. Parry.

Parochial.

Families, 250; Individuals 776; Baptisms (adults, 7, infants, 29), 36; Confirmed, since last report, 24; Marriages, 6; Burials, 27; Communicants, admitted, 24, died, 10, present number, 385; Public Services (Sundays, 131, Holy days, 39, other days, 79), 249; Holy Communion (public, 64, private, 5), 69; Sunday School, teachers, 18, officers, 5, pupils, 220; Catechizing, weekly.

Offerings.

Parochial.—Alms at Holy Communion, $79.48; Current expenses, including salaries, $2,737.60; Sunday School, $171.70; Increase and Improvement of Church property, $183.25; Other Parochial objects, $152.61. Total, $3,323.64;

Diocesan.—Diocesan Missions, $117.50; Salary of the Bishop, $40; Diocesan Fund, $42; The Child's Hospital, $42.52; Salary Diocesan Missionary, $20; Chapter House, $20. Total, $282.02.

General.— Domestic Missions, $26.19; Foreign Missions, $25; Jewish Missions, $2.29. Total, $53.48.

Total amount of Offerings, $3,659.14.

Property.

Church and lot (estimated worth), $20,000.
Parsonage lot (estimated worth), $2,800.
Other property, $2,082.
Condition of property, good.
Insurance, $15,500.
Amount of salary pledged Rector, $1,400.
Number of sittings in the Church, 888 rented; at Harrisena, 150 free.

Remarks.

The Ladies' Aid Society pledges $500 towards the ~~music fund, and does~~ much charitable work.

Two Chapters of a Sunday School Guild engage in charitable work.

The Altar Guild takes full care of the altar and chancel and has earned $152.61

Services are held every Sunday afternoon at a public hall, belonging to a parishioner, Mr. J. W. Stewart, in South Glens Falls.

ST. JAMES' CHURCH, LAKE GEORGE.

Rector. The Rev. Edwin Ruthven Armstrong.

Wardens. H. H. Hayden, George H. Cramer.

Vestrymen. S. R. Archibald, G. W. Bates, K. Burlingame, A. P. Cooke (capt. U. S. N.), Le Grand C. Cramer, J. T. Crandale, J. N. Hubbell. H. C. Noyes.

Parochial.

Families, about 55; Individuals (adults, 126, children, 75), 201; Baptisms (adults 3, infants 14), 17; Confirmed, since last report, 5; Present number of Confirmed Persons, about 102; Marriages, 6; Burials, 4; Communicants, last reported, about 100, admitted, 5, received, 1, died, 2, removed, 1, present number, about 103; Public Services, all Sundays and other Holy days, all Fridays throughout the year and Wednesdays in Lent; Holy Communion (public, 80, private, 1), 81; Sunday School, teachers, 5, pupils, 63; Catechizing, number of children, about 25, number of times, weekly.

Offerings.

Parochial.—Alms at Holy Communion, $62.18; Current expenses, including salaries, less assessments for Bishop's stipend and for Diocesan Fund, $1,370; Sunday School, $7.47; Increase and improvement of Church Property, $83; Sunday School Library, $48.43; Offerings for Easter flowers, $3.92; Offerings for Christmas tree, $9.92; Further contributed for same by outside friends, $42; Special for Rectory water rate, $10, Lamp for Church entrance, $11.25. Total, $1,648.17.

Diocesan.— Diocesan Missions, $9.38; * Salary of the Bishop $10; * Diocesan Fund, $10; Bible and Common Prayer Book Society of Albany, $5.71; Fund for Aged and Infirm Clergy, and Fund for Widows and Orphans of Clergymen, $3.16; Orphan House of the Holy Saviour, $2.14; Aid for Postulants, $4.34. Total, $44.73.

General.-- Domestic and Foreign Missions (from congregation, $9.40, children's Lenten offerings, $20.32), $29.72; Society for Promoting Christianity among Jews, $1.16; American Church Building Fund, $1.07. Total, $31.95.

Total amount of Offerings, $1,724.85.

Property.

Church and lot (estimated worth), $16,000.

Parsonage and lot (estimated worth), $6,000.

Condition of property, good.

Indebtedness, mortgage on Rectory, $750.

Number of sittings in the Church, 200; all free.

Remarks.

At Easter this Church was the recipient of a neat and substantial Altar Rail in oak on burnished brass standards, as a thank offering for recovery from severe illness by the junior Church Warden. At the same time a handsome Lectern in black walnut was presented it by Wm. Matthews of Croton, who bears ever a warm interest in the welfare of St. James'.

---

* These two met out of "Current Expenses" above.

About the same time the Rector, Wardens, and Vestrymen of Trinity Church, Sing Sing, N. Y., generously sent this Church a handsome black walnut altar, decorated with brass, burnished, and colours. A retable to correspond accompanied it.

HOLY CROSS CHURCH, WARRENSBURGH.

Rector The Rev. Hamilton Cady.

Wardens. Frederick O. Burhans, Henry Griffing.

Vestrymen. James Herrick, Emerson S. Crandall, Halsey Herrick, Thomas J. Smith, Moses Sutton, Charles F. Burhans, Joseph A. Woodward, Hodges H. Hill.

Parochial.

Families, 82; Individuals (adults, 165, children, 59), 224; Baptisms (adults, 1, infants, 3), 4; Present number of Confirmed Persons, 99; Burials; 6; Communicants, last reported, 85, received, 9, died, 3, removed, 2, present number, 89; Public Services, Sundays, 3, Holy days, 8, other days, 2; Holy Communion (public, 84, private, 2), 86; Sunday School, teachers, 4, pupils, 52; Catechizing, number of children, all, number of times, every Sunday.

Offerings.

Parochial.— Current expenses, including salaries, $1,762.38.

Diocesan.— Diocesan Missions, $50; Salary of the Bishop, $38; Diocesan Fund, $27; Bible and Common Prayer Book Society of Albany, $4.82; Orphan House of the Holy Saviour, $14.76; The Child's Hospital, $9; Insurance of Clergymen, $4. Total, $147.58.

General.— General Theological Seminary, $8.60; Domestic Missions, $9.55; Indian Missions (Sunday School), $20. Total, $38.15.

Total amount of Offerings, $1,948.11

Remarks.

Offering for the Orphan House of the Holy Saviour, Child's Hospital and Indian Mission, $35.58, was from the Sunday School offerings.

ST. MARY'S CHURCH, LUZERNE.

Rector. The Rev. C. J. Whipple.

Wardens. John S. Burneson, J. B. Wigley.

Vestrymen. Edward Gell, T. H. Taylor, J. T. Stebbins, George Gell, J. J. Wigley, C. E. Gillespie, H. J. Martine, C. H. McMaster.

Parochial.

Families, 25; Individuals (adults, 58, children, 35), 93; Baptisms, infants, 3; Present number of Confirmed Persons, 48; Burials, 5; Communicants, received, 1, removed, 5; Public Services (Sundays, 114, Holy days, 8, other days, 75), 197; Holy Communion (public, 27, private, 1), 28; Sunday School, teachers, 4, pupils, 25; Catechizing, number of children, all, number of times, 20.

Offerings.

Parochial.—Alms at Holy Communion, $205.87; Current expenses, including salaries, $536.37; Sunday School, $45; Increase and Improvement of Church Property, $200. Total, $987.24.

Diocesan.—Diocesan Missions, $20; Salary of the Bishop, $8; Diocesan Fund, $12; Diocesan Missionary, $10. Total, $50.

Total amount of Offerings, $1,087.24.

Property.

Church and lot (estimated worth), $7,000.
Parsonage and lot (estimated worth), $2,000.
Other property, $500.
Condition of property, good.
Insurance, $5,700.
Amount of salary pledged Rector, $400.
Number of sittings in the Church, 250; all free.

Remarks.

Since my last report, we have been able to build a small Chapel, which we find a great convenience, especially during the winter. It will seat 125, and cost nearly $2,500. It is with great thankfulness that I can report the completion of this building without any debt resting on it. It is furnished in a very churchly manner. Beside the Chapel, we have a large and very pleasant Parish-room. Nearly $1,000 have been expended in improvements on the Rectory. In a material way, we have, during the past year, been abundantly blessed.

All the Diocesan assessments against St. John's, Conklingville, for the year, have been fully paid, which, however, are not included in the above report.

CHURCH OF THE GOOD SHEPHERD, CHESTERTOWN.

Rector. The Rev. Alfred Taylor.
Warden. Ralph Thurman.
Clerk. J. F. Holley.
Treasurer. S. H. Bevins.

Parochial.

Families, 30; Individuals (adults, 73, children, 37), 110; Baptisms (infants), 2; Marriages, 1; Communicants, last reported, 63, removed, 3, present number, 60. Public Services, Sundays, 100, Holy Days, occasional, other days, Fridays; Holy Communion (public), 14: Sunday School, teachers, 2, pupils, 9.

Offerings.

Parochial.— Alms at Holy Communion, $5.60; Current expenses, including salaries, $483.64; Carpet for rectory, $50. Total, $539.24.

Diocesan.— Diocesan Missions,$15; Salary of the Bishop, $6; Diocesan Fund, $12; Clergy Insurance, $3; Special Offertory for Diocesan Missions, $3.20. Total, $39.20. Total amount of Offerings, $578.44.

Property.

Church and lot (estimated worth), $4,000.
Parsonage and lot (estimated worth), $2,500.
Condition of property, very good.
Insurance on Church, $3,500.
Insurance on Rectory, $2,000.
Amount of salary pledged Rector, $400.
Number of sittings in the Church, 100; all free.

ST. PAUL'S CHURCH, BARTONVILLE.

Rector. The Rev. Alfred Taylor.
Warden. L Gregory.
Treasurer. Scott Barton.
Clerk. H. C. Robbins.

Parochial.

Families, 19; Individuals (adults, 46, children, 28), 74; Baptisms (adults, 2, infants, 2), 4; Present number of Confirmed Persons, 40; Marriages, 1; Communicants, last reported, 40, present number, 40; Public Services, Sundays, every Sunday, Holy days, 2, other days, Wednesdays, part of the year; Holy Communion (public), 12; Sunday School, teachers, 4, pupils, 26.

Offerings.

Alms at Holy Communion, $11.65; Current expenses, including salaries, $253.20. Total, $264.85.

Diocesan.—Diocesan Missions, 30 cents; Diocesan Fund, $8. Total, $8.30. Total amount of offerings, $273.15.

Property.

Church and lot (estimated worth), $3,000.
Condition of property, very good.
Insurance on Church, $2,500.
Amount of salary pledged Rector, $100.
Number of sittings in the Church, 150; all free.

ST. SACRAMENT CHURCH, BOLTON-ON-LAKE GEORGE.

Rector. The Rev. Clement T. Blanchet, B. D.
Wardens. John B. Simpson, Clarence R. Conger.
Vestrymen. Asa W. Dickinson, James Fowden, Randall W. Wilson, L. W. Boyce, Elias Taylor, Hiram F. Seaman.

Parochial.

Families, 45; Individuals (adults, 72, children, 72), 144; Baptisms (adults, 12, infants, 26), 38; Confirmed, since last report, 4; Present number of Confirmed Persons, 70; Marriages, 3; Burials, 2; Communicants, last reported, 65, admitted, 4, received, 1, present number, 70; Public Services (Sundays, 118, Holy days, 12, other days, 104), 234; Holy Communion (public, 24, private, 1), 25; Sunday School, teachers, 6, pupils, 80; Catechizing, number of children, all, number of times, monthly.

Offerings.

Parochial.—Alms at Holy Communion and Current expenses, including salaries, $384.65; Sunday School, $29.63; Stone door steps, etc., $75; Steel sheeting roof for the Rectory, $150; Iron fence for Rectory front, $100, Prayer books and hymnals for chancel and pews, $100. Total, $839.28.

Diocesan.—Diocesan Missions, $10; Salary of the Bishop, $10; Diocesan Fund, $27. Fund for Aged and Infirm Clergymen, $2. Total, $49.

General.—Domestic Missions, $2, Foreign Missions, $2; Indian Missions, $2; Home Missions to Coloured Persons, $2; Missions to the Jews, $2; Clergy Retiring Fund, $3. Total, $13.

Total amount of Offerings, $901.28.

Property.

Church and lot (estimated worth), $8,000.
Parsonage and lot (estimated worth), $3,000.
Other property, horse shed, $100.
Condition of property, good.

18

Amount of salary pledged Rector, $900.
Number of sittings in Church, 150; all free.

Remarks.

The Rector is under obligations to Mr. Clarence R. Conger, Deacon and Junior Warden, for very efficient and acceptable assistance in the chancel and in the pulpit; and to Rev. Dr. Van DeWater of New York, for holding services at different points on the Lake, at a distance from Bolton, at which offerings were made for the benefit of our work, amounting to $200.

The Parish is indebted to Mr. Simpson for the gift of an iron fence for the front of the Rectory grounds and for an annual gift to the Sunday School at Christmas; and to Mr. Conger for supplying the altar and chancel with appropriate prayer books and hymnals, the choir and pews with hymnals, and the Sunday School with Catechisms, and the Rector with vestments. Acting on the advice of the Bishop a vestry of eight members was duly elected in Easter week and it is hoped that the new organization will be productive of much good, as it will tend to develop and sustain a spirit of interest in the welfare of the Parish, and in its relations to the Diocese and to the Church at large.

The completion of the stone walk and steps at the main entrance of the Church was done by our local members.

The work at Sabbath-Day Point is reported separately and the apparent falling off of Communicants at Bolton is accounted for by the number reported there, who were before this reported here.

GRACE MEMORIAL CHAPEL, SABBATH-DAY POINT, LAKE GEORGE.

Priest in charge. The Rev. Clement T. Blanchet, B. D,
Lay Reader. James F. Chamberlain, Esq.

Parochial.

Families, 22; Individuals (adults, 44, children, 47), 91 ; Baptisms (adults, 1, infants, 9), 10; Present number of Confirmed Persons, 20 ; Communicants, last reported, 15, admitted, 6, present number, 21; Public Services (Sundays, 8, other days, 1), 9 ; Holy Communion (public), 1; Sunday School, teachers, 1, pupils, 20 ; Catechizing, number of children, all, number of times, bi-monthly.

Remarks.

The work here has, as heretofore, been carried on mainly by our devoted Lay Reader, the venerable James F. Chamberlain, now fully eighty years of age, who, as a trustee of Grace Memorial Chapel, avails himself of the presence of visiting clergy, and of an occasional visit of the Rector of the Church of St. Sacrament at Bolton, for the administration of the Holy Sacraments, and reports the same regularly to him to be entered upon his Parish register, from which it appears that since 1889 nearly 100 persons have been baptized: by Rt. Rev. Geo. F. Seymour, children, 1 ; Rev. Dr. T. M. Peters of New York, adults, 14, children, 21; Rev. John F. Steen of New York, adults, 10, children, 36; Rev. C. T. Blanchet of Bolton, adults, 4, children, 4. Total number, adults, 28, Children, 62.

CHRIST CHURCH, POTTERSVILLE.

Rector. The Rev. Calbraith B. Perry in temporary charge.
Wardens. John Agard, Edward Rawlins.
Vestrymen. H. C. Talbot, John Wells, Joseph Mills, Nicolas Bibby, Philander Griswold, Frank Griswold, Henry Thompson.

Parochial.

Baptisms (adults, 3, infants, 4), 7; Confirmed, since last report, 1; Marriages, 1; Communicants, Present number, 12; Public Services (Sundays, 10, other days, 4), 14; Holy Communion, public, 1.

Offerings.

Parochial.— Current expenses, including salaries, $172.82.

Property.

Church and lot, and parsonage and lot (estimated worth), $600.

Remarks.

There had been no services held at Pottersville for many years, the church being in ruins, roofless and otherwise unfit for services, until during the last winter, urged by the people of the place, I held occasional services in the Masonic Hall. In the spring the people, on their own motion, undertook to repair the church. Though far from restored to the " beauty of holiness," which it evidently once possessed, it has been sufficiently rebuilt to hold services. On the 8th of August the Archdeacon of Troy, by the authority of the Bishop, formally reopened it in the presence of a number of clergy and a very large congregation, Canon Stewart remaining over the following Sunday and administering Holy Communion. On the 24th of September the Rt. Rev. the Bishop of the Diocese visited the church and administered Confirmation.

Washington County.

ZION CHURCH, SANDY HILL.

Rector. The Rev. H. Elmer Gilchrist.

Lay Reader. Geo. A. Ingalls.

Wardens. Charles T. Beach. S. H. Parks.

Vestrymen. P. F. Langworthy, John Nichols, Geo. A. Ingalls, D. Harrington, Charles A. Young, O. R. Howe, L. Sherrill, Geo. Thurman.

Parochial.

Families, 108; Individuals (adults, 206, children, 60), 266; Baptisms (infants), 5; Present number of Confirmed Persons, 145; Marriages, 2; Burials, 6; Communicants, last reported, 185, admitted, 2, died, 3, removed, 4, present number, 189; Public Services (Sundays, 157, Holy days, 44, other days, 141), 342; Holy Communion (public, 58, private, 4), 62; Sunday School, teachers, 7, pupils, 85; Catechizing, number of children, 30, number of times, monthly.

Offerings.

Parochial.— Alms at Holy Communion, $19.71; Current expenses, including salaries, $1,394.57, Sunday School, $11 09; Increase and Improvement of Church Property, $8. From Communion alms for sundries, $14.59; Reduction of debt, $118. Total, $1,565.96.

Diocesan.— Diocesan Missions, $18.70; Salary of the Bishop, $30; Diocesan Fund, $30; Fund for Aged and Infirm Clergymen, $5.50; Orphan House of the Holy Saviour, estimated value, $5; The Child's Hospital, $14.83. Total, $104.03.

General.— Domestic Missions, estimated value, $5; Foreign Missions, $11 Total, $16.

Total amount of Offerings, $1,685.99

Property.

Church and lot (estimated worth), $8,000.
Parsonage and lot (estimated worth), $3,500.
Other property, Miller fund for literature, $300.
Condition of property, fair.
Indebtedness, mortgage on Rectory, $2,000.
Bank notes outstanding, $685.
Insurance, all property insured.
Amount of salary pledged Rector, $900, and Rectory.
Number of sittings in the Church, 300; all free.

TRINITY CHURCH, GRANVILLE.

Rector. The Rev. J. Holwell Geare, M. A.
Wardens. Palmer D. Everts, Orville L. Goodrich.
Vestrymen. Byron H. Sykes, Silas E. Everts, George W. Henry, Amos W. Wilcox, George Tobey.

Parochial.

Families, 70; Individuals (adults, 127, children, 58), 185; Baptisms (adults, 1, infants, 3), 4; Present number of Confirmed Persons, 94; Marriages, 1; Burials, 3; Churchings, 1; Communicants, last reported, 79, received, 5, died, 2, present number, 82; Public Services, Sundays, every Sunday, three times, Holy Days, every Holy Day, twice, other days, daily Matins and Evensong; Holy Communion public, every Sunday, every Holy Day, and every Thursday; Sunday School, teachers, 8, pupils, 58; Catechizing, number of children, 58, number of times, frequently.

Offerings.

Parochial.— Alms at Holy Communion, and Current expenses, including salaries, $644.17; Sunday School, $17.50; Increase and Improvement of Church Property, $150; other Parochial objects, including $300 paid on mortgage on Rectory, $355. Total, $1,166.67.

Diocesan.— Diocesan Missions, $15; Salary of the Bishop, $4.50. Total, $19.50.
General.—General Missions, Sunday School, $15.
Total amount of Offerings, $1,201.17.

Property.

Church and lot (estimated worth), $5,000.
Parsonage and lot (estimated worth), $4,500.
Condition of property, Church, fair; Rectory, good.
Indebtedness, mortgage on Rectory, $1,500.
Amount of salary pledged Rector, $450.
Number of sittings in the Church, 200; all free.

ST. JAMES' CHURCH, FORT EDWARD.

Rector. The Rev. J. W. McIlwaine.
Wardens. James G. Kinne, Francis B. Davis.
Vestrymen. Frederick G. Tilton, Benj. M. Tasker, George Scott, Jarvis W. Milliman, Albert H. Wicks, John J. Morgan, Robert O. Bascom, Robert A. Linendoll, M. D.

Parochial.

Families, and parts of families, 100 ; Individuals (adults, 168, children, 72), 240 ; Baptisms (infants), 4 ; Present number of Confirmed Persons, 139 ; Marriages, 2;

Burials, 4; Communicants, received, 2, died, 2. removed, 13, present number, 188; Communicating more or less frequently, 60; Public Services, Sundays, morning and evening, Holy days, Lent, daily, other days, Friday evenings; Holy Communion (public), monthly; Lent, weekly; Sunday School, teachers, 8, pupils, 40; Catechizing, number of times, weekly.

Offerings.

Parochial.—Alms at Holy Communion, $23; Current expenses, including salaries, $1,150; For the Sunday School, $70; From the Sunday School for Sunday School purposes, $14.85. Total, $1,257.85.

Diocesan.— Diocesan Missions, $20; Diocesan Fund, $18; Fund for Aged and Infirm Clergymen, $4; Diocesan Missionary (from Sunday School), $5. Total, $47.

General.— General Missions (from Sunday School), $7.

Total amount of Offerings, $1,311.85.

Property.

Church and lot (estimated worth), $7,000.
Parsonage and lot (estimated worth), $3,000.
Condition of property, good.
Insurance, $9,000.
Amount of salary pledged Rector, $600.
Number of sittings in the Church, 250; all free.

ST. PAUL'S CHURCH, SALEM.

Rector. The Rev. Harris C. Rush.
Wardens. Hon. James Gibson, Hon. George B. McCartee.
Vestrymen. A. K. Broughton, Frederick Kegler, Ephraim Harrick, Wm. Alexander McNish, George B. Martin, Joseph Hofert, Moses Johnson, Wm. L. Campbell.

Parochial.

Families, 56; Baptisms (adults, 1, infants, 5), 6; Marriages, 1; Burials, 5; Communicants, last reported, 150, died, 1, removed, 4, present number, 145; Public Services, thrice on all Sundays, other days, twice weekly; Holy Communion, public, each Sunday and Holy Day, private, 1; Sunday School, teachers, 5, pupils, 44; Catechizing, number of times, frequently.

Offerings.

Parochial.—Alms at Holy Communion, $54.81; Current expenses, including salaries, $1,022.80; Christmas tree, $13.50; Organ, $187.50. Total, $1,278.61.

Diocesan.— Diocesan Missions, $44.18; Salary of the Bishop, $30; Diocesan Fund, $24.50; Bible and Common Prayer Book Society of Albany, $4.73; Fund for Aged and Infirm Clergymen, $5, Fund for Widows and Orphans of Clergymen, $4.73; Orphan House of the Holy Saviour, $4.72, Society for Promoting Religion and Learning, $4.73 Total, $122.59.

General.— Domestic Missions, $5.79, Foreign Missions, $4.87; Society for the Promotion of Christianity among the Jews, $2.23. Total, $12.89.

Total amount of Offerings, $1,414.09.

Property.

Church and lot (estimated worth), $6,000.
Rectory and additions thereto (estimated w...

Parish House (estimated worth), $2,500.
Condition of property, good.
Insurance on Church building, $2,500.
Insurance on Rectory and additions thereto, $5,000.
Insurance on Parish House, $2,500.
Amount of salary pledged Rector, $700.
Number of sittings in the Church, 250; all free.

Remarks.

The Rectory and additions thereto, together with Parish House, above reported, were occupied until June last by Rexleigh School. These buildings are vacant and yield the parish no pecuniary income.

TRINITY CHURCH, WHITEHALL.

Rector. The Rev. John Henry Molineux.
Wardens. F. H. McFerran, E. P. Newcomb.
Vestrymen. Messrs. Jeremiah Adams, George Brett, Chauncey Bates, Tracy Cowen, Robert Hall, John C. Hopson, Fred Cowen, H. B. Skeels.

Parochial.

Families, 121; Individuals (adults, 260, children, 94), 354; Baptisms (adults, 9, infants, 10), 19; Confirmed, since last report, 14; Present number of Confirmed Persons (estimated), 218; Marriages, 3; Burials, 5; Communicants, last reported, 178, admitted, 14, received, 3, died, 2, removed, 3, present number, 190; Public Services (Sundays, 139, Holy days, 39, other days, 151), 329; Holy Communion (public, 153, private, 19), 172; Sunday School, teachers, 7, pupils, 70; Catechizing, number of children, all, number of times, frequently.

Offerings.

Parochial.— Current Expenses, including salaries, $1,337.17; Sunday School, $28.30; Increase and Improvement of Church Property, $19.36; Music, $200. Total, $1,584.83.
Diocesan.— Diocesan Missions, $46.61; Salary of the Bishop, $20. Total, $66.61.
Total amount of Offerings, $1,651.44.

Property.

Condition of Property, good.
Indebtedness on parish building, $450; arrears, insurance, current expenses previous to '92.
Amount of salary pledged Rector, $1,000, and Rectory.
Number of sittings in the church, 230; all free.

ST. LUKE'S CHURCH, CAMBRIDGE.

Rector. The Rev. Frederick H. T. Horsfield.
Wardens. Henry C. Day, Robert Davis.
Vestrymen. William J. Davis, Thomas Le Grys, Robert S. Davis, John Money-penny, M. D., J. Fenimore Niver, M. D.

Parochial.

Families, 25; Individuals (adults, 70, children, 8), 78; Baptisms (adults, 1, infants, 3), 4; Present number of Confirmed Persons, 50; Marriages, 2; Burials, 1; Communicants, present number, 50; Public Services (Sundays, 100, Holy days, 15, other days, 75), 190; Holy Communion (public), 40; Sunday School, teachers. 1, pupils, 8.

Offerings.

Parochial.—Current expenses, including salaries, $907.92; Sunday School, $25; Increase and Improvement of Church Property, $100; Ladies' Aid Society, $104; For Rectory Fund, $263.15. Total, $1,400.07.

Diocesan.— Diocesan Missions, $185; Salary of the Bishop, $10; Diocesan Fund, $15; Diocesan Missionary, $10. Total, $220.

General.— General Missions, $27. Total, $27.

Total amount of Offerings, $1,647.07.

Property.

Church and lot (estimated worth), $7,000.

Condition of property, excellent.

Insurance, $7,000.

Amount of salary pledged Rector. $500.

Number of sittings in the Church, 200; all free.

Remarks.

Handsome Eucharistic lights were presented to the Parish at Easter; also, vases, etc.

At Christmas the same kind friends presented a beautiful red silk Altar Antependium, embroidered in pomegranates, pulpit hangings to match. book-marks; also, richly wrought stole.

ST. PAUL'S CHURCH, GREENWICH.

Wardens. H. L. Mowry, W. R. Hobbie.

Vestrymen. B. F. Kendall, Geo. Tucker, H. B. Bates, Thos. Emerson, S. L. Stillman, W. P. Reynolds.

Parochial.

Families, 80; Individuals (adults, 100, children, 50), 150; Present number of Confirmed Persons, about 50, Marriages, 1; Burials, 2; Communicants, last reported, 45, died, 1. removed, 3, present number, 50; Public Services, Sundays, morning service, to July 1, Holy Days, Good Friday, Holy Communion, public, monthly, to July 1, private, 1; Sunday School, teachers, 4, pupils, 40.

Offerings.

Parochial.—Current expenses, including salaries, $316.33; Sunday School, $9.13; Ladies' Aid Society, gifts, etc., $394.16. Total, $719.62.

Diocesan.— Diocesan Missions, $25; Salary of the Bishop, $4. Total, $29.

Total amount of Offerings, $748.62.

Property.

Church and lot (estimated worth), $7,000.

Condition of property, good.

Insurance, $6,500.

Amount of salary pledged Rector, $300.

Number of sittings in the Church, 240; all free.

Remarks.

We have had services but once on Sunday for eight months, the Parish being united with Schuylerville. Since J.

The balance of debt reported last year as nearly $400, has been paid, and mortgage discharged.

NORTH GRANVILLE MISSION, NORTH GRANVILLE.

Priest in charge. The Rev. J. H. Geare.
Treasurer. George B. Culver.

Parochial.

Families, 8 ; Individuals (adults, 24, children, 6), 30 ; Communicants, present number, 14; Public Services (Sundays), 29; Holy Communion (public), 7.

Offerings.

Parochial.— Current expenses, including salaries, $96.10.
Diocesan.— Diocesan Missions, $10 ; Salary of Bishop, $4 ; Diocesan Fund. $3·
Total, $17.
Total amount of Offerings, $113.10.

Property.

Organ and other furniture, $177.
Amount of salary pledged Rector, $100.
Number of sittings in the Chapel, 100; all free.

(B.)

PERSONAL REPORTS AND REPORTS OF INSTITUTIONS.

PORT HENRY, N. Y., *January* 6, 1894.

To the Right Rev. WM. CROSWELL DOANE, S. T. D.:

MY DEAR BISHOP — I beg leave to report that during the past year I have assisted the Rev. W. Ball Wright at Port Henry, and at Mineville, at the celebrations of the Holy Communion. and in occasional services. I have also officiated at one funeral. Since Rev. Mr. Wright's removal to Rouse's Point, I have held Service at Emmanuel Church, Mineville, every Sunday afternoon.

Your servant in Christ,
CHAS. E. CRAGG.

To the Right Rev. W. C. DOANE, D. D., *Bishop of Albany.*

Last summer I officiated at Indian Lake for the fourth successive season. A service was held on each Sunday morning during the last two weeks in July, and the first two weeks in August. On one Sunday I officiated in a cottage in Camp Sabael, and on three Sundays at the Locke House, on the opposite side of the lake At each of the services the attendance was excellent, and I invariably enjoyed the kind cooperation of residents as well as of summer visitors.

HENRY A. DOWS.

ALBANY, *February* 11, 1894.

DEAR BISHOP DOANE — During the Conventional year, besides my other duties at St. Agnes' School, I have said the daily morning office of devotion during the school year. On Sundays I have been engaged the greater part of the time in occasional services in vacant Parishes and Missions of the Diocese, and at Little Cranberry

Island, in the Diocese of Maine, in the summer vacation. I have also assisted frequently both on Sundays and week days at the Services in the Cathedral. I have celebrated at the Holy Communion 15 times, have said the Morning or Evening Prayer 76 times, and have preached 45 sermons. I have officiated at one burial, and have baptised one infant.

FEDERICK M. GRAY.

OGDENSBURG, N. Y., *December* 30, 1893.

The Right Reverend WILLIAM CROSWELL DOANE. S. T. D., LL. D.:

Right Reverend Sir — During the past year I have been prevented, by ill-health, from the performance of regular Parish duty. I have, however, officiated occasionally for the Rev. Dr. Morrison, Rector of St. John's Church, Ogdensburg, and taken such clerical work as he assigned me. My ministerial acts are, therefore, included in his Parochial report.   Very respectfully, etc.,

W. H. HARISON.

COOPERSTOWN, N. Y., *November* 1, 1893.

I have to report to the Bishop an occasional service and sermon outside the Diocese, and a public religious address within it.   Respectfully,

W. W. LORD.

LAKE WORTH, FLORIDA, *November* 14, 1893.

MY DEAR BISHOP — My summer ministrations at the Church of the Good Shepherd, Raquette Lake, extended from June 22 to October 10.

The work of the Church there is confined almost entirely to summer visitors, as there are very few "all year" residents on the lake. Although this Mission receives no aid from the Board of Missions, it has succeeded, for a few years past, in contributing $50 a year to some Diocesan object. But during the past summer, so few visitors were at Raquette Lake, this contribution had to be omitted.

Faithfully yours,

J. N. MULFORD.

HOOSICK FALLS, *November* 14, 1893.

Right Reverend WILLIAM C. DOANE, D. D., LL. D.:

MY DEAR BISHOP — Within the Conventional year last past, by the blessing of Almighty God and the brotherly kindness and courtesy of our excellent Rectors, I have had the privilege of baptising, celebrating the Holy Eucharist, preaching, and in the Lord's Day services assisting with a good degree of regularity.

Loyally and affectionately yours,

GEO. HUNTINGTON NICHOLS.

To the Rt. Rev. W. C. DOANE, D. D.:   *November* 17, 1893.

I respectfully report that during the last Conventional year I have attended to my duties as Registrar of the General Convention, and have officiated and preached many times in different Parishes.

J. LIVINGSTON REESE.

GLENHAM, N. Y., *January* 10, 1894.

The Rt. Rev. DR. DOANE, *Bishop of Albany, Albany, N. Y.:*

The Rev. L. H. Schubert respectfully begs to report that during the
has occasionally officiated in the Diocese of New York.

POUGHKEEPSIE, *December 7, 1893.*

MY DEAR BISHOP — Owing to failing health I resigned the Rectorship of Trinity Church, Athens, to take effect the 1st of July, 1893. I regret to say that I am at present wholly unable to undertake any pastoral work.

Affectionately yours,

J. W. STEWART.

RT. REV. AND DEAR SIR — As opportunities offered I have occasionally officiated during the past year, though physically disabled.

Very truly yours,

DANIEL WASHBURN.

REPORT OF THE TRUSTEES OF THE CORNING FOUNDATION FOR CHRISTIAN WORK IN THE DIOCESE OF ALBANY.

At a special meeting of the Trustees, held on the 11th day of April, A. D., 1893, a minute on the death of Erastus Corning, Jr., was read and ordered to be entered on the record of the proceedings of the Board. (This minute will be found printed in the appendix to the Bishop's Address.)

On June 8th the Board ordered the usual diploma to be given to fourteen members of the graduating class of St. Agnes' School.

On June 12th Mr. Edward Bowditch was elected a Trustee' of the Corporation, to fill the place made vacant by the death of Erastus Corning, Jr.

During the past summer an entirely new heating apparatus has been placed in the school buildings.

Number of teachers in the school during the year ending November 1st, 39. Number of pupils, 264.

November 1, 1893.

THOMAS B. FULCHER,

Secretary of the Board.

ANNUAL REPORT OF THE CHILD'S HOSPITAL.

The eighteenth year has closed, and the Child's Hospital begins a new year, with hopes that as time rolls on, the lives of many more children can be made brighter and their sufferings relieved. We feel more encouraged this year, as the decrease in gifts spoken of last year has been made up, and the Treasurer's report is most gratifying. It is only through the continued interest of friends that the work can be successfully carried on, therefore, we earnestly trust the same kind help will be given this year. As in the past, we have much to be thankful for in the way of special gifts, for all of which we heartily return thanks.

The summer is eagerly looked forward to and heartily enjoyed. Thanks are specially due to the many kind friends in Troy and Saratoga, who do so much for the comfort and support of the children while at the St. Christina Home.

The Treasurer of St. Margaret's House also sends us a most encouraging report of increased interest in this part of the work. The children in St. Margaret's House, being very young, require special and more care than in an orphanage or hospital, and the question has arisen, can we give them this care? It is, therefore, with pleasure we learn of any increase of gifts, but we ask for still further aid to let us supply the necessary nurses and assistants for the satisfactory carrying on of the work of taking care of young babies.

We heartily thank Mr. Bowditch, Treasurer of the Child's Hospital, and his able assistant, Mr. Blanchard, for their kind and efficient services.

Thanks, too, are gladly given to Mr. C. L. Pruyn, for his kindness in acting as Treasurer for St. Margaret's House. We cannot fully express our deep sense of obligation to the physicians and surgeons for their untiring interest in the work, both of the Hospital and of St. Margaret's House.

The Managers hope that the nineteenth year will show increased good done to suffering children and greater interest in the two charities, whose reports we now give to our friends.

This report cannot be closed without special and most grateful mention of the fact that Mrs. Harriet Cramer Porter sent, last June, $5,000 to The Child's Hospital and $2,000 to St. Margaret's House; a benefaction not only most cheering and helpful to us, but securing to the generous giver the pleasure of realizing the benefit of her gift to us, and the blessing of giving to the relief of the little children.

CAROLINE G. HUN,
Secretary.

TREASURER'S REPORT FOR THE YEAR ENDING SEPTEMBER 30, 1893.

Edward Bowditch, Treasurer, in Account with the Child's Hospital.

Receipts.

Amount on hand September 30, 1892	$360 26
Annual subscriptions	879 50
Private gifts	635 51
Donations for beds	781 00
In memoriam	101 00
Churches, Sunday-schools, etc.	702 06
Board	6,341 86
Sundry	769 55
	$10,520 74

Expenditures.

Provisions	$3,361 88
Fuel	1,295 66
Clothing	460 37
Wages	2,970 46
Dispensary	502 97
Furniture	117 39
Repairs and improvements	270 44
Telephone	46 50
Gas	347 20
Water tax	86 00
Printing annual report	85 00
D. Morey, Co. Treas.	95 91
Sundries	185 48
	$9,825 26
Balance on hand September 30, 1893	695 48
	$10,520 74

SUMMARY OF THE REPORT OF THE MEDICAL STAFF.

| | Admitted. | | Discharged. | | | Remaining in Hospital. | Total. |
	Male.	Female.	Cured.	Improved.	Died.		
Medical Division..........	23	34	28	10	4	15	57
Ophthalmic and Aural Division...	32	42	47	17	....	10	74
Surgical Division.............. ...	56	57	45	27	3	38	113
Total......................	111	133	120	54	7	63	244

ANNUAL REPORT OF ST. MARGARET'S HOUSE FOR THE YEAR ENDING SEPTEMBER 30, 1898.

Charles L. Pruyn in Account with St. Margaret's House.

Receipts.

Cash on hand October 1, 1892.................................	$63 84
Annual subscriptions...................	265 00
Special subscriptions..................	319 20
Special subscriptions for nurse.......................	96 00
Board........... ;	3,779 92
Income from invested funds, J. H. Brooks, treasurer....	101 60
Loan at bank...........	300 00
	$4,925 56

Expenditures.

Provisions	$1,394 69
Fuel..	419 00
Clothing..	216 40
Wages	961 80
Dispensary.	61 29
Furniture.	57 71
Repairs and improvements..........	160 51
Sundries.........	379 61
Gas...	210 60
Water tax.......................	37 00
Repaid loan and interest	303 20
Balance cash on hand October 1, 1893.......	723 75
	$4,925 56

NUMBER OF CHILDREN CARED FOR.

At the Child's Hospital..................................	170
At St. Margaret's House......	120
At the St. Christina Home Industrial School..	35

REPORT OF THE GIRLS' FRIENDLY SOCIETY IN AMERICA
IN THE DIOCESE OF ALBANY.

BRANCHES.	Number of working associates.	Number of honorary associates.	Number of members.	Number of candidates.
Troy :				
St. Paul's	12	16	66	48
Cooperstown:				
Christ Church.	12	7	25	9
Hoosick Falls:				
St. Mark's	2	....	10	11
Bath-on-the-Hudson:				
Epiphany	4	....	21	35
Johnstown :				
St. John's.	6	3	20	....
Cohoes:				
St. John's	3	....	40	....
Total	39	26	182	103

RECAPITULATION.

Number of branches.. 6
Number of working associates 39
Number of honorary associates.... 26
Number of members. 182
Number of candidates... 103
Amount of money raised and expended, $500.35.

MRS. C. W. PALMER,
Diocesan Secretary.

ANNUAL REPORT OF THE WOMAN'S AUXILIARY TO THE BOARD OF MISSIONS IN THE DIOCESE OF ALBANY.

Number of Parish branches reporting, 51.
Number of boxes sent, 100.
Valuation of boxes, $4,919.61.
Money given, $2,284.45.
Total money and boxes, $7,204.05.
Balance on hand May 1, 1893, $137.36.

THE JUNIOR AUXILIARY.

Number of branches reporting, 21.
Value of work done, $960.30.

THE DIOCESAN LENDING LIBRARY.

Number of volumes in Library, 1024.
Books loaned, 137.
Number of readers, 88.
Total amount of moneys received, $104.76.
Total amount of moneys expended, $91.94,
Balance on hand, $12.82.
The Library needs both funds and books.

THE CHURCH PERIODICAL CLUB, DIOCESE OF ALBANY.

This club receives magazines and books and distributes them for circulation among Clergymen and Mission stations. (There are branches in thirty-seven Dioceses.)

Librarians, 14.
Contributors, 168.
Periodicals, 291.
Books sent to date, 118.
Sunday School books sent to date, 126.
Bibles sent to date, 13.
Prayer books sent to date, 205.
Hymnals sent to date, 9.
Sunday School papers sent regularly, 92.
Sunday School leaflets sent regularly, 40.
Christmas cards sent to date, 143.
Easter cards sent to date, 235.
Catechisms sent to date, 171.
Christmas carols sent to date, 598.
Easter carols sent to date, 769.
Old periodicals sent to date, 10193.

ANNUAL REPORT OF THE CHURCH HOME IN THE CITY OF TROY.

Receipts for the year..	$3,886 30
Expenses for the year	3,541 77
Shortage for the year......................................	$155 47

Property.

Real estate	$37,000 00
Personal (permanent fund)..................................	30,092 00
Total...	$67,092 00

Debts, none, except shortage of current expenses.
Aaverage number of inmates, 10.
Present number of inmates, 10.

(C.)

LIST OF PARISHES IN UNION WITH THE CONVENTION OF THE DIOCESE OF ALBANY, WITH THE DATES OF THEIR ADMISSION.*

ALBANY COUNTY.

St. Peter's, Albany, 1787; Trinity, Rensselaerville, 1811; St. Paul's, Albany, 1829; St. John's Cohoes, 1831; Trinity, West Troy, 1834; Trinity, Albany, 1840; Grace, Albany, 1846; Holy Innocents, Albany, 1850; St. Mark's, Green Island, 1867; Cathedral of All Saints, Albany, 1874.

CLINTON COUNTY.

Trinity, Plattsburgh, 1830; Christ, Rouse's Point, 1853; St. John's, Champlain, 1853.

---

* Dates earlier than 1868 are those of admission to Union with the Convention of the Diocese of New York before the organization of the Diocese of Albany.

COLUMBIA COUNTY.

Christ, Hudson, 1794 ; St. John's, Stockport, 1845 ; St. Paul's, Kinderhook, 1851 ; Trinity, Claverack, 1856 ; Our Saviour, Lebanon Springs, 1882 ; All Saints', Hudson, 1888; St. Barnabas', Stottville, 1890; St. Mark's, Philmont, 1891.

DELAWARE COUNTY.

St. Peter's, Hobart, 1796; St. John's, Delhi, 1822; Christ, Walton, 1831; St. Paul's, Franklin, 1866; Christ, Deposit, 1871.

ESSEX COUNTY.

Church of the Cross, Ticonderoga, 1840; St. John's, Essex, 1853; St. Paul's, Keeseville, 1853; Christ, Port Henry, 1873.

FRANKLIN COUNTY.

St. Mark's, Malone, 1831; St. Peter's, Brush's Mills, 1870.

FULTON COUNTY.

St. John's, Johnstown, 1796.

GREENE COUNTY.

St. Luke's, Catskill, 1801 ; Christ, Coxsackie, 1806 ; Trinity, Athens, 1806 ; St. Paul's, Oak Hill, 1816 ; Christ, Greenville, 1825 ; Trinity, Ashland, 1826 ; Calvary, Cairo, 1832.

HERKIMER COUNTY.

Trinity, Fairfield, 1807 ; Emmanuel, Little Falls, 1823 ; Christ, Herkimer, 1854 ; St. Augustine's, Ilion, 1870; Grace, Mohawk, 1886.

MONTGOMERY COUNTY.

St. Ann's, Amsterdam, 1836; Zion, Fonda, 1867.

OTSEGO COUNTY.

Zion, Morris, 1793; St. Luke's, Richfield, 1803; St. Matthew's, Unadilla, 1810; Christ, Cooperstown, 1812; Christ, Butternuts, 1834; Immanuel, Otego, 1836; St. Timothy's, Westford, 1839; Grace, Cherry Valley, 1846; St. John's, Richfield Springs, 1850; St. John's, Portlandville, 1869; Christ, West Burlington, 1871; St. Paul's East Springfield, 1871; St. James', Oneonta, 1877.

RENSSELAER COUNTY.

St. Paul's, Troy, 1807; Trinity, Lansingburgh 1807; St. John's, Troy, 1831; Christ, Troy, 1837; St. Mark's, Hoosick Falls, 1840; Trinity, Schaghticoke, 1846; Messiah, Greenbush, 1853; St. Luke's, Troy, 1867.

ST. LAWRENCE COUNTY.

St. John's, Ogdensburg, 1820; St. Paul's, Waddington, 1824; Christ, Morristown, 1833; Trinity, Potsdam, 1835; Grace, Canton, 1836; Grace, Norfolk, 1844; Trinity, Gouverneur, 1869; St. John's, Massena, 1870; St Luke's, Lisbon, 1871; Zion, Colton, 1885.

SARATOGA COUNTY.

Christ, Ballston Spa, 1787; St. John's, Stillwater, 1796; St. Paul's, Charlton, 1805; Grace, Waterford, 1810; St. Luke's, Mechanicville, 1830; Bethesda, Saratoga Springs, 1830; St. Stephen's, Schuylerville, 1846; Calvary, Burnt Hills, 1850.

SCHENECTADY COUNTY.

Christ, Duanesburgh, 1789; St. George's, Schenectady, 1799; Christ, 1869.

WARREN COUNTY.

Messiah, Glens Falls, 1840; St. James', Caldwell, 1855; Holy Cross, Warrensburgh, 1865; St. Mary's, Luzerne, 1867.

WASHINGTON COUNTY.

Zion, Sandy Hill, 1813; Trinity, Granville, 1815; St. James', Fort Edward, 1845; St. Paul's, Salem, 1860; Trinity, Whitehall, 1866; St. Luke's, Cambridge, 1867; St. Paul's, Greenwich, 1875.

ORGANIZED MISSIONS.

ALBANY COUNTY.

Good Shepherd, Bethlehem; St. Andrew's, West Troy.

CLINTON COUNTY.

St. Paul's, Mooor's Forks; St. Peter's, Ellenburgh; St. Paul's, Ellenburgh Centre; St. Luke's, Chazy; St. John's, Salmon River; all with consecrated buildings.

COLUMBIA COUNTY.

St. Luke's, Chatham; St. John's-in-the-Wilderness, Copake.

DELAWARE COUNTY.

Emmanuel, Fleischman's; Grace, Stamford.

ESSEX COUNTY.

Emmanuel, Mineville; St. James', Ausable Forks, both with consecrated buildings; Good Shepherd, Bloomingdale.

FRANKLIN COUNTY.

St. Mark's, West Bangor; St. James', Hogansburgh; St. John's-in-the-Wilderness, St. Regis Lake; St. Luke the Beloved Physician, Saranac Lake, all with consecrated buildings.

FULTON COUNTY.

Christ, Gloversville; St. John's, Dolgeville.

GREENE COUNTY.

Gloria Dei, Palenville; St. John the Evangelist, Tannersville.

HAMILTON COUNTY.

Good Shepherd, Raquette Lake; Of the Transfiguration, Blue Mountain Lake.

HERKIMER COUNTY.

Of the Memorial, Middleville; Of the Good Shepherd, Cullen; both with consecrated buildings.

MONTGOMERY COUNTY.

Holy Cross, Fort Plain; Good Shepherd, Canajoharie; St. Columbia's, St. Johnsville.

OTSEGO COUNTY.

St. Mary's, Springfield Centre, with consecrated building; St. Simon and St. Jude's, Worcester.

RENSSELAER COUNTY.

St. Giles', Castleton; Holy Name, Boyntonville, with consecrated building.

ST. LAWRENCE COUNTY.

Trinity Chapel, Morley; St. Thomas', Lawrenceville, both with consecrated buildings; Grace, Louisville Landing; St. Joseph's, West Stockholm; All Saints', Barnhart's Island; St. Andrew's, Norwood.

SARATOGA COUNTY.

St. John's, East Line; Grace, Jonesville; All Saints', Round Lake, all with consecrated buildings.

WARREN COUNTY.

Good Shepherd, Chester; St. Paul's, Bartonville; St. Sacrament, Bolton, all with consecrated buildings.

PARISHES NOT IN UNION WITH THE CONVENTION.

ALBANY COUNTY.

Emmanuel, South Westerlo.

COLUMBIA COUNTY.

St. Luke's, Clermont, incorporated July 12, 1859.

ESSEX COUNTY.

St. Andrew's, Schroon Lake.

GREENE COUNTY.

Grace, Prattsville.

HERKIMER COUNTY.

St. Alban's, Frankfort.

OTSEGO COUNTY.

Church of the Holy Spirit, Schenevus.

RENSSELAER COUNTY.

Holy Cross, Troy; Free Church of the Ascension, Troy; Free Church of the Epiphany, East Albany; All Saints', Hoosac; St. Barnabas', Troy.

SARATOGA COUNTY.

St. John's, Conklingville.

SCHOHARIE COUNTY.

St. Andrew's, Schoharie; Trinity, Sharon Springs.

WARREN COUNTY.

Christ, Pottersville.

WASHINGTON COUNTY.

Grace, Crandell's Corners.

PLACES OTHER THAN PARISHES OR ORGANIZED MISSIONS, WHERE SERVICES OF THE CHURCH ARE HELD.

ALBANY COUNTY.

St. Margaret's, Menands.

CLINTON COUNTY.

Dannemora; Standish.

COLUMBIA COUNTY.

Chatham; St. James', Rossman's Mills; Canaan.

DELAWARE COUNTY.

Esperance; St. Paul's, Sidney; Bloomville; Hamden.

ESSEX COUNTY.

Crown Point; Good Shepherd, Elizabethtown; Lewis; Addison Junction; Keene Valley; Westport.

FRANKLIN COUNTY.

Good Shepherd, Santa Clara; Merciful Saviour, St. Regis Falls; Holy Innocents, Brandon; Fort Covington.

GREENE COUNTY.

Hunter; Onteora Park.

HAMILTON COUNTY.

Locke House, Indian Lake.

HERKIMER COUNTY.

Poland.

MONTGOMERY COUNTY.

Nelliston.

OTSEGO COUNTY.

Morris Memorial Chapel; Nobleaville; Maple Grove; Mt. Vision; Edmeston.

RENSSELAER COUNTY.

St. Stephen's, Lansingburgh; St. Paul's, Raymertown.

ST. LAWRENCE COUNTY.

Cranberry Lake ; Pierpont Centre.

SARATOGA COUNTY.

St. Luke's, Milton Centre; West Charlton ; South Glens Falls.

SCHOHARIE COUNTY.

Cobleskill.

WARREN COUNTY.

St. Paul's Harrisena; Grace Memorial Chapel, Sabbath-Day Point.

WASHINGTON COUNTY.

North Granville; Adamsville; Smith's Basin; Fort Ann.

NON–REPORTING CLERGY.

The Rev. F. S. Greenhalgh, The Rev. S. T. Street,

NON-REPORTING PARISHES.

Grace, Waterford.

NON-REPORTING CLERGY AND PARISHES FROM THE JOURNAL OF 1890.

In obedience to the instructions of the Convention (see Journal 1891, p. 93), letters were sent to the Clergy, and to the officers of the Parishes, from whom no reports were received at the Convention of 1891. Replies were received from the Rev. Mr. Podmore ; Grace Church, Canton ; St. John's, Stillwater ; and St. James', Caldwell ; assigning as reasons for not reporting in 1891, miscarriage of the Secretary's letter, and that there was no one in the Parishes at the time to whom it was known that a report should be made. No replies were received from St. Luke's Church, Mechanicville, and Grace Church, Norway.

(D)

COLLECTION ON ACCOUNT OF BISHOP'S SALARY, 1893.

Those marked with Asterisk (*) have paid balance for annual assessment, but received too late to appear in this account Some Parishes appear to have paid more than their regular assessment. This occurs from part of assessment for 1892 received too late, appearing account of 1893.

Albany County.	Annual Payment.
Cathedral of All Saints, Albany	$150 00
St. Peter's, Albany	150 00
St. Paul's, Albany	100 00
Trinity, Albany*	......
Grace, Albany	16 00

	Annual Payment.
Albany County — Continued.	
Holy Innocents, Albany	$30 00
St. John's, Cohoes	......
Trinity, West Troy	40 00
Trinity, Rensselaerville*	6 00
St. Mark's, Green Island	12 00
Columbia County.	
Christ Church, Hudson	66 00
St. John's, Stockport	26 00
St. Paul's, Kinderhook	36 00
St. John's, Copake	
Trinity, Claverack	6 00
Church of Our Saviour, Lebanon Springs	6 00
St. Luke's, Clermont	4 00
St. Barnabas', Stottville	26 00
All Saints', Hudson	6 00
St. Mark's, Philmont	6 00
St. Luke's, Chatham	2 00
Clinton County.	
Trinity, Plattsburgh*	45 00
Christ, Rouse's Point	12 00
St. John's, Champlain	4 50
Centreville and Chateaugay	......
St. Peter's, Ellenburgh	4 00
St. John's, Salmon River	......
Delaware County.	
St. Peter's, Hobart*	15 00
St. John's, Delhi	40 00
Christ, Walton	20 00
St. Paul's, Franklin	20 00
Christ, Deposit	6 00
Grace, Stamford	6 00
St. Paul's, Sidney	3 00
Essex County.	
Of the Cross, Ticonderoga	10 00
St. John's, Essex	16 00
Christ Church, Port Henry	10 00
Emmanuel, Mineville	......
St. James', Ausable Forks	12 00
St. Andrew's, Schroon Lake	4 00
St. Paul's, Keeseville	10 00
Fulton County.	
St. John's, Johnstown	50 00
Redeemer, Northampton	......
Christ Church, Gloversville	10 00
Franklin County.	
St. Mark's, Malone*	......
St. Peter's, Brushton	8 00
St. Mark's, West Bangor	4 00

	Annual Payment.
Franklin County — Continued	
St. James', Hogansburgh	$8 00
St. John's, St. Regis	......
St. Luke's, Saranac	6 00
Greene County.	
St. Luke's, Catskill	22 50
Christ Church, Coxsackie	6 00
Trinity, Athens	......
St. Paul's, Oak Hill	......
Christ Church, Greenville	6 00
Trinity, Ashland	4 00
Calvary, Cairo	6 00
Gloria Dei, Palenville	8 00
Grace, Prattsville	......
Herkimer County.	
Emmanuel, Little Falls	20 00
Christ Church, Herkimer	16 00
Grace, Mohawk	6 00
St. Augustine's, Ilion	21 00
Trinity, Fairfield*	......
Memorial, Middleville	6 00
Grace, Norway	......
Montgomery County.	
St. Ann's, Amsterdam	......
Zion, Fonda	12 00
Good Shepherd, Canajoharie	8 00
Holy Cross, Fort Plain	......
Otsego County.	
Zion, Morris	......
St. Matthew's, Unadilla	16 00
Christ Church, Cooperstown	80 00
Christ Church, Gilbertsville	6 00
Immanuel, Otego	4 50
St. Timothy's, Westford	......
St. John's, Portlandville	......
Grace, Cherry Valley	25 00
St. Paul's, East Springfield	10 00
St. John's, Richfield Springs	16 00
Christ Church, West Burlington	4 50
St. James', Oneonta	10 00
St. Stephen's Chapel, Maple Grove	2 00
Holy Spirit, Schenevus	4 00
Rensselaer County.	
St. Paul's, Troy	200 00
St. John's, Troy	176 00
Christ Church, Troy	186 00
Holy Cross, Troy	50 00
Ascension, Troy	10 00
St. Luke's, Troy	10 00

	Annual Payment.
Rensselaer County — Continued.	
St. Barnabas', Troy	$6 00
Trinity, Lansingburgh	60 00
Trinity, Schaghticoke	6 00
Messiah, Greenbush	10 00
Epiphany, E. Albany	1 00
St. Mark's, Hoosick Falls	40 00
All Saints', Hoosac	6 00
St. Lawrence County.	
St. John's, Ogdensburg	100 00
St. Paul's, Waddington	12 00
Christ Church, Morristown	20 00
Trinity, Potsdam	50 00
Grace, Canton	14 00
Grace, Norfolk	2 00
St. Andrew's, Norwood	4 00
Trinity, Gouverneur	26 00
St. John's Massena	8 00
Trinity, Morley	5 00
Grace, Louisville Landing	......
St. Thomas', Lawrenceville	......
St. Luke's, Lisbon	......
Zion, Colton	4 00
St. Phillip's Madrid	......
All Saints', Barnhardt's Island	......
Saratoga County.	
Christ Church, Ballston Spa	84 00
St. John's, East Line	......
St. Paul's, Charlton	......
Grace, Waterford	......
Bethesda, Saratoga Springs	105 00
St. Stephen's, Schuylerville	6 00
Calvary, Burnt Hills	12 00
St. John's, Conklingville	6 00
St. John's, Stillwater	3 00
St. Luke's, Mechanicville	4 00
Grace, Jonesville	4 00
Schenectady County.	
St. George's, Schenectady	60 00
Christ Church, Schenectady	10 00
Christ Church, Duanesburgh	50 00
Schoharie County.	
St. Luke's, Middleburgh	1 00
Trinity, Sharon Springs	15 00
Warren County.	
Messiah, Glens Falls	......
—— Harrisena	......
Holy Cross, Warrensburgh	38 00
St. Mary's, Luzerne	8 00

	Annual Payment.
Warren County — Continued.	
Good Shepherd, Chestertown	$7 50
St. John's, Conklingville..........	......
St. Sacrament, Bolton	16 00
St. James, Caldwell*	5 00
Washington County.	
Zion, Sandy Hill	37 50
Trinity, Granville	4 50
Mission, North Granville	4 00
St. James, Fort Edward	.....
St. Paul's, Salem	37 50
Trinity, Whitehall	40 00
St. Luke's, Cambridge..............	10 00
St. Paul's, Greenwich	6 00
Total for 1893	$2,905 00

(E.)

OFFICERS OF THE DIOCESE, TRUSTEES, ETC.

The Right Rev. William Croswell Doane, D. D., Ll. D., *President.*
The Rev. William C. Prout, Herkimer, *Secretary.*
The Rev. Thomas B. Fulcher, Albany, *Assistant Secretary.*
The Rev. Frederick S. Sill, Cohoes, *Registrar.*
Gen. Selden E. Marvin, Albany, *Treasurer.*

THE STANDING COMMITTEE.

The Rev. J. Ireland Tucker, S. T. D., Troy, *President;* the Rev. Fenwick M. Cookson, Glens Falls, *Secretary;* the Rev. Wilford L. Robbins, D. D., the Rev. James Caird, Mr. Norman B. Squires, Mr. Henry S. Wynkoop, Mr. John I. Thompson, Mr. J. H. Van Antwerp.

DEPUTIES TO THE GENERAL CONVENTION.

The Rev. Walton W. Battershall, D. D., the Rev. J. D. Morrison, D. D., Ll. D., the Rev. Joseph Carey, S. T. D., the Rev. Charles C. Edmunds, Jr., Mr. G. Pomeroy Keese, Mr. Erastus Corning, Mr. T. Streatfeild Clarkson, Mr. John Hobart Warren.

PROVISIONAL DEPUTIES TO THE GENERAL CONVENTION.

The Rev. Edgar A. Enos, D. D., the Rev. R. M. Kirby, D. D., the Rev. C. S. Olmsted, the Rev. George D. Silliman, D. D., Mr. Leslie Pell-Clarke, Mr. Spencer Trask, Mr. Edward Sheldon, Mr. Thomas L. Harison.

DEPUTIES TO THE FEDERATE COUNCIL.

The Rev. J. Ireland Tucker, S. T. D., the Rev. Fenwick M. Cookson, the Rev. George D. Silliman, D. D., the Rev. Wilford L. Robbins, D. D., the Rev. C. C. Edmunds, Jr, the Rev. S. M. Griswold, the Rev. William H. Harison, D. D., the Rev. Ernest Mariett, Mr. N. B. Warren, Mr. G. Pomeroy Keese, Mr. R. H. Cushney, Mr. Robert Earl, Mr. J. I. Thompson, Mr. F. J. Fitch, Mr. Charles E. Patterson, Mr. J. D. Henderson.

TRUSTEE OF THE GENERAL THEOLOGICAL SEMINARY UNTIL NOVEM-
BER 15, 1896.

The Rev. Joseph Carey, S. T. D.

MEMBERS OF THE MISSIONARY COUNCIL.

ELECTED BY THE GENERAL CONVENTION.

The Rev. Walton W. Battershall, D. D., the Rev. Sheldon M. Griswold, Mr. G.
Hyde Clarke.

ELECTED BY THE CONVENTION OF THE DIOCESE.

The Rev. J. Philip B. Pendleton, S. T. B., Col. William G. Rice.

TRUSTEES OF THE EPISCOPAL FUND.

Mr. J. H. Van Antwerp, Albany, *Treasurer;* Mr. W. Bayard Van Rensselaer, Mr.
Charles W. Tillinghast, 2d, Mr. Dean Sage, Mr. Robert C. Pruyn.

TRUSTEES OF THE FUND FOR AGED AND INFIRM CLERGYMEN.

The Right Rev. William Croswell Doane, D. D., LL. D., Mr. Selden E. Marvin,
Treasurer; Mr. Norman B. Squires, Mr. Robert S. Oliver, Mr. J. J. Tillinghast.

TRUSTEES OF THE FUND FOR WIDOWS AND ORPHANS OF DECEASED CLERGYMEN.

The Right Rev. William Croswell Doane, D. D., LL. D., Mr. Selden E. Marvin,
Treasurer, Mr. J. W. Tillinghast, Mr. C. W. Tillinghast, Mr. Amasa J. Parker.

TRUSTEES OF THE ORPHAN HOUSE OF THE HOLY SAVIOUR, COOPERS-TOWN.

The Right Rev. William Croswell Doane, D. D., LL. D., *President.*

The Rev. Charles S. Olmsted, Cooperstown, *Secretary.*

Mr. Leslie Pell-Clarke, Springfield Centre, *Treasurer.*

Miss Susan Fenimore Cooper, Cooperstown, *Superintendent.*

TRUSTEES.

The Rev. Walton W. Battershall, D. D., the Rev. J. Philip B. Pendleton, S. T.
B., Mr. G. Pomeroy Keese, until Convention, 1894.

Mr. A. B. Cox, Mr. Leslie Pell-Clarke, Mr. G. Hyde Clarke, until Convention, 1895.

The Rev. Richmond H. Gesner, Mr. T. Streatfeild Clarkson, W. T. Bassett, M. D.,
until Convention, 1896

TRUSTEES OF THE DIOCESE OF ALBANY.

The Right Rev. William Croswell Doane, D D., LL. D., *President.*

Mr. A. B. Cox, Cherry Valley, *Secretary.*

Mr. John Hudson Peck, Troy, *Treasurer.*

TRUSTEES.

The Rev. J. D. Morrison, D. D., LL D., until Convention, 1894.

Mr. Levi Hasbrouck, until Convention, 1894.

The Rev. Frederick S. Sill, until Convention, 1895.

Mr. John H. Bagley, until Convention, 1895.

The Rev. Joseph Carey, S. T. D., until Convention, 1896.

Mr. John Hudson Peck, until Convention, 1896.

The Rev. Charles S. Olmsted, until Convention, 1897.

Mr. Abram B. Cox, until Convention, 1897.

COMMITTEE ON THE INCORPORATION AND ADMISSION OF CHURCHES.

The Rev. J. Philip B. Pendleton, S. T. B., Mr. Richard H. Cushney, Mr. John H. Bagley.

COMMITTEE ON THE CONSTITUTION AND CANONS.

The Rev. R. M. Kirby, D. D., the Rev. Edgar A. Enos, D. D., the Rev. Charles M. Nickerson, D. D., the Rev. George G. Carter, S. T. D., Mr. James Gibson, Mr. J. D. Henderson, R. M. Townsend.

COMMITTEE ON THE SALARY OF THE BISHOP.

The Rev. Joseph Carey, S. T. D., the Rev. W. W. Battershall, D. D., Mr. J. J. Tillinghast, Mr. Erastus Corning, Mr. J. W. Tillinghast, Mr. W. W. Rousseau, Mr. John I. Thompson, Mr. Spencer Trask. *Secretary*, Mr. W. W. Rousseau, Troy.

COMMITTEE ON THE OBSERVANCE OF THE TWENTY-FIFTH ANNIVERSARY OF THE CONSECRATION OF THE FIRST BISHOP OF ALBANY.

The Rev. J. Ireland Tucker, S. T. D., the Rev. Walton W. Battershall, D. D., the Rev. Wilford L. Robbins, D. D., the Rev. J. D. Morrison, D. D., LL. D., the Rev. Joseph Carey, S. T. D., the Rev. James Caird, the Rev. R. M. Kirby, D. D., the Rev. Fenwick M. Cookson, the Rev. Charles S. Olmsted, the Rev. Edgar A. Enos, D. D., the Rev. C. M. Nickerson, D. D., the Rev. S. M. Griswold, Mr. John I. Thompson, Mr. A. B. Cox, Mr. Erastus Corning, Mr. Joseph M. Warren, Gen. Selden E. Marvin, Mr. T. Streatfeild Clarkson, Mr. L. Averill Carter, Prof. Sidney G. Ashmore, Mr. John Keyes Paige, Mr. G. Pomeroy Keese, the Hon. William A. Sackett, Mr. Leslie Pell-Clarke, Mr. Nathan B. Warren.

COMMITTEE ON THE BOUNDARIES OF ARCHDEACONRIES.

The Right Rev. the Bishop of the Diocese, the Rev. William M. Cook, the Rev. Fenwick M. Cookson, Mr. G. Pomeroy Keese, Mr. Louis Hasbrouck.

COMMITTEE TO INTEREST THE CHILDREN OF THE DIOCESE IN DIOCESAN MISSIONS.

The Rev. J. Philip B. Pendleton, the Rev. Calbraith B. Perry, the Rev. Fenwick M. Cookson, Mr. Sidney G. Ashmore, Mr. Francis N. Mann.

COMMISSION ON THE CLERICAL PENSION SYSTEM.

The Right Rev. the Bishop of the Diocese, the Rev. J. D. Morrison, D. D., LL. D., the Rev. George G. Carter, S. T. D., Mr. Selden E. Marvin, Mr. Levi Hasbrouck, Mr. Leslie Pell-Clarke.

THE BOARD OF MISSIONS.

The Right Rev. William Croswell Doane, D. D., LL. D., *President.*
The Rev. Sheldon M. Griswold, Hudson, *Secretary.*
Mr. Selden E. Marvin, Albany, *Treasurer.*

ARCHDEACONRY OF ALBANY.

The Rev. Walton W. Battershall, D. D., Mr. J. H. Van Antwerp.

ARCHDEACONRY OF TROY.

The Rev. Fenwick M. Cookson, Mr. George A. Wells.

ARCHDEACONRY OF THE SUSQUEHANNA.

The Rev. Robert N. Parke, D. D., Mr. Robert M. Townsend.

ARCHDEACONRY OF OGDENSBURGH.
The Rev. R. M. Kirby, D. D., Mr. T. Streatfeild Clarkson.

DIOCESE AT LARGE.
*The Rev. Sheldon M. Griswold, Mr. William Kemp.

ARCHDEACONRIES.
FIRST. ARCHDEACONRY OF ALBANY.
Albany, Greene, Columbia, Schenectady, Montgomery, Fulton, Hamilton and Herkimer counties.
The Rev. Frederick S. Sill, S. T. B., *Archdeacon.*
The Rev. Richmond Shreve, D. D., *Secretary.*
The Rev. E. Bayard Smith, *Treasurer.*

SECOND. ARCHDEACONRY OF TROY.
Rensselaer, Saratoga, Washington, Warren, Clinton and Essex counties.
The Rev. Joseph Carey, S. T. D., *Archdeacon.*
The Rev. Clement T. Blanchet, *Secretary.*
Mr. Charles W. Tillinghast, 2d, *Treasurer.*

THIRD. ARCHDEACONRY OF THE SUSQUEHANNA.
Delaware, Otsego and Schoharie counties.
The Rev. Charles S. Olmsted, *Archdeacon.*
The Rev. Richmond H. Gesner, *Secretary and Treasurer.*

FOURTH. ARCHDEACONRY OF OGDENSBURGH.
St. Lawrence and Franklin counties.
The Rev. J. D. Morrison, D. D., LL. D., *Archdeacon.*
The Rev. Charles Temple, *Secretary.*
Mr. T. Streatfeild Clarkson, *Treasurer.*

EXAMINING CHAPLAINS.
The Rev. J. Ireland Tucker, S. T. D., the Rev. Joseph Carey, S. T. D., the Rev. J. D. Morrison, D. D., LL. D., the Rev. W. N. Irish, the Rev. Thomas B. Fulcher, B. D., the Rev. Edgar A. Enos, D. D., the Rev. William G. W. Lewis, the Rev. Wilford L. Robbins, D. D., the Rev. G. H. S. Walpole, the Rev. George B. Johnson, the Rev. George G. Carter, S. T. D., the Rev. J. Philip B. Pendleton, S. T. B., the Rev. Eaton W. Maxcy, D. D.

THE BIBLE AND COMMON PRAYER BOOK SOCIETY OF ALBANY AND ITS VICINITY.
The Right Rev. William Croswell Doane, D. D., LL. D., *President.*
The Rev. J. Ireland Tucker, S. T. D., *First Vice-President.*
The Rev. W. W. Battershall, D. D., *Second Vice-President.*
The Rev. J. W. Stewart, *Third Vice-President.*
The Rev. Henry R. Freeman, Troy, *Corresponding Secretary.*
The Rev. Richmond Shreve, D. D., *Recording Secretary.*
Mr. Henry B. Dauchy, Troy, *Treasurer.*

MANAGERS.
Messrs. J. H. Van Antwerp, A. A. Van Vorst, George W. Gibbons, Joseph W. Tillinghast, Francis N. Mann, George A. Wells, John H. Hulsapple, Marcus T. Hun, William C. Buell, John Horrocks, E. G. Dorlan, George B. Warren.

---

*Elected by the Board of Missions, Feb. 15, 1894, to fill the vacancy occasioned by the resignation of the Rev. Charles Temple.

Applications for books may be made to the *Corresponding Secretary*, the Rev. Henry R. Freeman, Troy.

All contributions and donations should be sent to the *Treasurer*, Mr. H. B. Dauchy, Troy.

(F.)

DIOCESAN BRANCHES OF GENERAL SOCIETIES.

THE DIOCESAN BRANCH OF THE WOMAN'S AUXILIARY TO THE BOARD OF MISSIONS.

President. Mrs. Melvil Dewey, 315 Madison avenue, Albany.
Vice-Presidents. Mrs. Payne, Schenectady ; Mrs. McEwen, Saratoga Springs.
Recording Secretary. Miss S. B. Purdy, 80 First street, Troy.
Corresponding Secretary. Miss Alice Lacy, 74 Chapel street, Albany.
Treasurer. Mrs. Smith S. Fine, 40 South Hawk street, Albany.

Managers.

For the Archdeaconry of Albany: Miss Tweddle, Menand's road, Albany, for Albany, Montgomery and Fulton counties ; Mrs. Van Nostrand, Schenectady, for Greene, Columbia, Schenectady, Hamilton and Herkimer counties.

For the Archdeaconry of Troy: Miss Ella F. Cusack, 58 Second street, Troy, for Rensselaer, Washington and Saratoga counties; Mrs. Wm. S. Wheeler, Ballston Spa, for Warren, Essex and Clinton counties.

For the Archdeaconry of the Susquehanna : Miss E. J. Hughes, Gilbertsville, for Otsego and Schoharie counties ; Miss Laura Gay, Walton, for Delaware county.

For the Archdeaconry of Ogdensburgh : Miss Josephine S. Kirby, Potsdam, for Franklin and St. Lawrence counties.

DIOCESAN LENDING LIBRARY COMMITTEE.

Mrs. Melvil Dewey, *Chairman*, 315 Madison avenue, Albany ; Miss E. W. Boyd, *Treasurer*, St. Agnes' School, Albany.

CHURCH PERIODICAL CLUB, DIOCESAN CORRESPONDENT.

Miss Mary F. Burt, Rensselaerville.

THE DIOCESAN BRANCH OF THE CHURCH TEMPERANCE SOCIETY.

Delegates to the General Council. The Rev. William M. Cook, Ilion; Mr. Henry J. Estcourt, Schenectady.

Diocesan Committee.

Clerical — The Rev. W. W. Battershall, D. D., Albany; the Rev. Joseph N. Mulford; the Rev. George D. Silliman, D. D., Albany; the Rev. Hobart Cooke, Plattsburgh.

Lay — Messrs Smith S. Fine, Albany; William Kemp; Troy; Thomas R. Wade, Albany; Henry C. Day, Cambridge; James Rogers, Ausable Forks; Charles Ashley, Ogdensburgh.

FUNDS TO WHICH OFFERINGS ARE REQUIRED BY CANON, AND THE NAMES OF THE TREASURERS TO WHOM THE SAME SHOULD BE SENT.

Diocesan Fund. Mr. S. E. Marvin, Albany.
Missions of the Diocese. Mr. S. E. Marvin, Albany.
For Aged and Infirm Clergymen. Mr. S. E. Marvin, Albany.
For Widows and Orphans of Deceased Clergymen. Mr. S. E. Marvin, Albany.

For the Clergy Reserve Fund. Mr. S. E. Marvin, Albany.
Bible and Common Prayer Book Society of Albany. Mr. H. B. Dauchy, Troy.
Episcopal Fund. Mr. J. H. Van Antwerp, Albany.
Salary of the Bishop. Mr. W. W. Rousseau, Troy.
For the Education of Young Men for the Ministry. The Treasurer of the Diocese,
or Mr. Richard M. Harison, 31 Nassau street, New York.
Orphan House of the Holy Saviour. Mr. Leslie Pell-Clarke, Springfield Centre,
Otsego county.
Domestic and Foreign Missions. Mr. George Bliss, Church Missions House, Fourth
avenue and Twenty-second street, New York.
Offerings for the *Child's Hospital* should be sent to Mr. Edward Bowditch, Albany.
For Missionary Envelopes and Pledges apply to the *Secretary* of the Board of Missions, the Rev. Sheldon M. Griswold, Hudson, Columbia county.

(G.)

SUMMARY OF STATISTICS.

From the Bishop's Address, the Parochial, Missionary and other Reports.

Clergy (Bishop, 1, Priests, 118, Deacons, 8).	127
Ordinations (Deacons, 6, Priests, 2)	8
Candidates for Orders (for the Deacon's Order only, 8, for the Priest's Order, 14)	22
Postulants	12
Lay Readers Licensed	17
Parishes in union with Convention	100
Parishes not in union with Convention	18
Missions (organized, 44, unorganized, 40)	84
Churches	144
Chapels	20
Sittings in Churches and Chapels	41,483
Free Churches and Chapels	134
Churches otherwise supported	30
Free sittings (including free seats in Churches where there is a pew rental).	29,899
Rectories	83
Corner-stone laid	1
Churches consecrated	4
Buildings blessed	1
* Families	9,179
* Individuals (adults, 12,863, children, 6,566, not designated, 6,384)	25,813
Baptisms (adults, 338, infants, 1,393)	1,731
Persons confirmed	920
Communicants (admitted, 642, received, 407, died, 312, removed, 495), present number	19,470
Marriages	479
Burials	1,146
Sunday School teachers	1,284
Sunday School pupils	10,707
Parish School teachers	47
Parish School pupils	

---

* Many reports do not give these items.

Total amount of Offerings.......... ....

(H.)
TABULAR STATEMENT OF THE CHIEF STATISTICS OF THE DIOCESE FOR THE TWENTY-FIVE YEARS OF ITS HISTORY.

YEAR	BAPTISMS				Deacons ordained	Priests ordained	Churches consecrated	Persons confirmed	Communicants	OFFERINGS AND CONTRIBUTIONS			
	Adult	Infant	Undesignated	Total						Parochial	Diocesan	General	Total
1869	338	1,052	35	1,420	...	5	11	938	7,887	$133,958 68	$36,310 72	$14,546 28	$188,715 58
1870	434	1,174	45	1,653	9	4	8	994	7,724	191,405 15	24,120 08	16,712 65	239,297 88
1871	358	1,199	4	1,561	2	3	7	1,006	8,240	191,956 58	13,818 97	7,885 96	213,660 81
1872	430	1,310	77	1,817	10	8	1	1,005	8,645	288,938 73	24,384 37	15,306 89	288,604 49
1873	364	1,344		1,606	3	4		925	9,130	270,929 15	22,500 13	12,579 08	306,008 36
1874	314	1,280		1,594	9	5	4	1,041	9,944	298,750 45	24,071 47	8,618 25	336,635 17
1875	415	1,267		1,682	9	8	1	1,077	9,818	283,792 54	21,847 96	4,889 45	309,979 95
1876	490	1,236		1,726	2	5		1,149	10,663	208,966 88	28,506 96	6,014 94	293,890 18
1877	447	1,378		1,825	8	10	3	1,356	10,176	197,004 90	16,510 40	7,668 73	221,909 08
1878	378	1,094	49	1,472	5	4		857	11,877	191,053 41	15,985 07	8,649 08	216,996 56
1879	407	1,497		1,953	1	6	8	1,087	13,226	206,368 14	20,786 16	7,985 28	296,489 58
1880	350	1,306		1,556	4	4	1	866	12,776	223,306 75	28,028 12	6,505 64	251,843 80
1881	271	1,194	88	1,465	8	7	4	1,017	13,044	212,164 86	26,383 88	11,281 54	249,780 28
1882	365	1,434		1,888	5	8	3	939	13,018	259,870 89	31,749 98	6,906 49	298,928 53
1883	351	1,388		1,739	7	5	8	1,100	14,340	226,438 68	33,904 99	9,034 40	269,863 70
1884	364	1,360		1,738	2	5	4	890	13,750	248,743 63	33,260 04	10,138 40	291,181 07
1885	349	1,385		1,634	3	9	4	1,135	13,907	243,294 08	24,696 97	8,197 06	275,190 11
1886	415	1,401		1,816	5	2		1,049	15,455	245,399 97	24,189 11	10,142 21	279,681 21
1887	434	1,299		1,728	9	1	3	1,296	15,702	294,124 14	26,880 63	11,802 09	382,756 85
1888	353	1,307		1,660	1	1	3	1,058	15,619	283,044 34	39,059 02	11,708 05	382,806 91
1889	493	1,507		1,999	2	8	3	1,598	16,507	297,006 80	28,267 00	12,984 22	388,207 53
1890	419	1,559		1,978	5	3	2	1,401	16,498	273,925 64	29,988 46	12,976 33	316,790 48
1891	438	1,538		1,786	2	9	3	1,166	17,662	208,387 17	25,304 46	13,078 24	341,564 87
1892	481	1,385		1,866	7	3	2	1,470	19,107	384,075 07	34,336 75	13,210 46	481,623 28
1893	388	1,393		1,731	6	3	4	920	19,470	317,906 04	35,983 34	11,773 44	355,612 88
Total	9,750	32,808	293	42,881	113	124	77	27,383	......	$6,159,142 21	$689,007 91	$319,356 79	$7,110,506 91

TABLE OF CONTENTS.

DIOCESE OF ALBANY.

CONSTITUTION AND CANONS.

CONSTITUTION.

ARTICLE I.

Of the Members of the Convention.

The Diocese of Albany entrusts its legislation to a Convention, to consist as follows: First, of the Bishop, when there is one; of the Assistant Bishop, when there is one. Secondly, of all Clergymen canonically resident in the Diocese for six months previous to the Convention, the restriction of time not to apply to Rectors duly elected or Missionaries duly appointed (provided that no Clergyman suspended from the Ministry shall have a seat); and, Thirdly, of the Lay Delegation from the Cathedral, and of Lay Delegations, consisting of not more than three Deputies from each other Church in union with the Convention, who shall be communicants, and shall have been chosen by the Vestry or Congregation of the same.

ARTICLE II.

Of the Annual Meetings of the Convention.

The Convention shall assemble on the Tuesday after the tenth day of November, in each year, in such place as the Bishop shall appoint, giving fifteen days' notice thereof. In case of his inability to act, the Assistant Bishop, if there be one, shall appoint the place; and, if there be no Bishop, the Standing Committee shall appoint. The place of meeting may be changed for sufficient reason after having been appointed, provided that ten days' notice of such change shall be given.

Every Convention shall be opened with a Sermon and the Holy Communion: and the Preacher shall be appointed by the Bishop, or in case of his inability to act, or if there be no Bishop, by the Standing Committee.

ARTICLE III.

Of Special Conventions.

The Bishop shall have power to call Special Conventions, giving thirty days' notice thereof, and shall do so when requested by a vote of three-fourths of the Standing Committee. When there is no Bishop, the Standing Committee shall have power to call a Special Convention, giving ninety days' notice thereof.

ARTICLE IV.

Of the Cathedral.

"The Cathedral of All Saints in the City and Diocese of Albany" shall be the Cathedral Church of this Diocese. Three Lay Communicants shall be chosen by the Chapter as the Delegation from the Cathedral to the Convention.

ARTICLE V.

Of the Permanent Officers of the Diocese.

The permanent officers of the Diocese shall be: the Bishop of the Diocese (with right to preside, when present in Convention; and when there is an Assistant Bishop, he shall have right to preside in the absence of the Bishop), a Standing Committee, a Secretary, a Treasurer and a Registrar.

ARTICLE VI.

Of the Election of a Bishop.

When a Bishop or an Assistant Bishop is to be elected, the election shall be at the regular Annual Convention, or at a Special Convention duly called for that purpose; and such election shall require a majority of the votes of each order voting separately.

ARTICLE VII.

Of the President of the Convention.

If there be no Bishop of the Diocese, or its *ex-officio* presiding officer be absent, the Convention shall elect a President from among the Clergy, by ballot (unless the ballot be dispensed with by unanimous vote.)

ARTICLE VIII.

Of the Standing Committee.

The Standing Committee shall consist of four Clergymen and four Laymen, to be elected by ballot at each Annual Convention, by a majority of the Clergy and Lay Delegations present, and shall serve until the next Annual Convention and until a new election is made, the functions of which Committee, besides those provided for in the Canons of the General Convention, and in this Constitution, shall be determined by Canon or Resolution of the Convention. But vacancies in the Standing Committee may be filled by a majority of the votes of the remaining members until the next meeting of the Convention.

ARTICLE IX.

Of the Secretary, Treasurer and Registrar.

The Secretary shall be elected at each Annual Convention from the members thereof, by ballot, after nominations (unless the ballot be dispensed with by unanimous vote), and by a majority of the Clergy and Lay Delegations present; and he shall remain in office until his successor shall be elected. His duties shall be those required by the Canons, Resolutions and Rules of Order of the Convention.

The Treasurer and the Registrar shall be elected in a similar manner, and are not required to be members of the Convention. They shall remain in office until the next Annual Convention, and until their successors are elected.

ARTICLE X.

Of the Deliberations of the Convention and of Votes.

The Clergymen and Laymen constituting the Convention shall deliberate in one body, and each Clergyman shall have one vote, and each Lay Delegation one vote, and a majority of the aggregate votes shall be decisive except in the cases provided for in Articles VI, IX and XI.

If five votes require a division, then the voting shall be by orders separately, and the concurrence of a majority of each order shall be necessary to make a decision. But no alteration of the Constitution or Canons shall be valid without the concurrence of the Bishop and of a majority of the Clergy and of a majority of the Lay Delegations; and the Bishop's concurrence shall be presumed unless the contrary be openly expressed by him to the Convention after the vote of the Clergy and Laity and before the adjournment *sine die.*

ARTICLE XI.

Of Altering the Constitution.

The mode of altering the Constitution shall be as follows: A proposition for an amendment shall be introduced in writing and considered in the Convention; and, if approved by a majority, shall lie over till the next Convention, and, if then approved by a two-thirds vote of the Clergy and Lay Delegations present, with the Bishop's concurrence, the Constitution shall be changed accordingly.

CANONS.

CANON I.

Of the List of Clergymen in the Diocese.

SECTION 1. On the first day of each Convention, regular or special, the Ecclesiastical Authority shall present to the Convention a List of the Clergy canonically resident in the Diocese, annexing the names of their respective Parishes, Offices and residences, and the dates of their becoming resident in the Diocese.

SEC. 2. The Secretary shall record this list of names in a book to be kept by him for that purpose.

SEC. 3. From this record shall be made up by the Secretary the list of the Clergymen entitled, according to the Constitution, to seats in the Convention; which list may at any time be revised and corrected by the Convention.

CANON II.

Of the Lay Delegations.

SECTION 1. When the Lay Delegations are chosen by the Vestry, it shall be at a meeting held according to law. In case the Vestry shall not choose Deputies they may be chosen by the congregation in the manner hereinafter prescribed for Churches having no Vestries.

SEC. 2. Deputies from Churches having no Vestries shall be chosen by the Congregation at a meeting of which notice shall have been given during Divine Service on the two Sundays next previous thereto. And at such meeting the Rector or Minister shall preside, and the qualifications for voting shall be the same as those required by law for voting at an election for Churchwardens and Vestrymen.

SEC. 3. When Deputies are chosen by a Vestry, the evidence of their appointment shall be a certificate, signed by the Rector of the Church they are chosen to represent and by the Clerk of the Vestry; and if there be no Rector, then the certificate shall state that fact, and shall be signed by the Churchwarden presiding and by the Clerk of the Vestry. The certificate must state the time and place of the election, must show upon its face that the appointment has been made in accordance with all the requirements of the Canons, and shall certify that each Deputy chosen is a Communicant of the Church and entitled to vote for Churchwardens and Vestrymen of the Church he is chosen to represent.

SEC. 4. When Deputies are chosen by the Congregation of any Church, the evidence of their appointment shall be a certificate, signed by the Rector or Minister having charge of the said Church and by the Secretary of the meeting; or if there be no such Rector or Minister, then the certificate shall state that fact, and shall be signed by the officer presiding at the meeting and by the Secretary of the same. The certificate must state the time and place of the election, must show upon its face that the appointment has been made in accordance with all the requirements of the Canons, and shall certify that each Deputy chosen is a Communicant of the Church, and, in the case of the Church having a Vestry, that he is entitled to vote for Churchwardens and Vestrymen of such Church, or, in the case of a Church having no Vestry, that he has belonged for twelve months to the Congregation he is chosen to represent. No other evidence of the appointment of Lay Deputies than such as is specified in this and the preceding section shall be received by the Convention.

SEC. 5. The Secretary of the Convention, when he shall send to any Church or Parish the required notice of the time and place of meeting of any Convention to be held, shall transmit with the same a copy of this Canon and blank printed forms of certificates of appointment of Deputies.

CANON III.

Of the Organization of the Convention.

SECTION 1. If the *ex-officio* presiding officer be not present at the opening of the Convention, the Secretary shall call the members present to order; and the senior Presbyter present, who is a member of the Convention, shall take the chair, and preside until a President is elected, as provided by Article VII of the Constitution.

SEC. 2. The Secretary shall then call the names of the Clergy entitled to seats in the Convention. He shall then call the names of the Churches in union with the Convention, when the Lay Deputies shall present their certificates, which shall be examined by the Secretary, and a committee of two members appointed by the presiding officer. Irregular or defective certificates, and certificates and documents referring to contested seats, shall be temporarily laid aside. The names of the Lay Deputies duly appointed shall then be called, after which the certificates and documents laid aside shall be reported to the Convention, which shall decide upon the admission of the Deputies named therein.

SEC. 3. If twenty Clergymen entitled to vote, and twenty Lay Delegations be present, they shall constitute a quorum; and the presiding officer *ex officio* shall declare the Convention duly organized. The same number of Clergymen and Lay Delegations shall, at any time, be necessary for the transaction of business, except that a smaller number may adjourn from time to time.

SEC. 4. If the presiding officer *ex officio* be not present before the convention is declared *to be* organized, the temporary Chairman shall direct that the members proceed *to elect* a President, according to Article VII of the Constitution, who, when -1, shall take the Chair and declare the Convention organized for business.

SEC. 5. The Convention shall then proceed to the election of a Secretary, a Treasurer and a Registrar, according to the Constitution. The Secretary may appoint an Assistant Secretary, also any other assistants he may require, announcing their names to the Convention.

SEC. 6. Any Rules of Order which shall have been previously adopted or sanctioned in the Convention, except such as prescribe the mode of altering the same, shall be in force until changed by the Convention, after having been duly organized.

CANON IV.

Of the Admission of a Church into Union with the Church in this Diocese, and Maintaining such Union.

SECTION 1. Every Church or Congregation desiring admission into union with the Church in this Diocese, shall present a written application therefor to the Convention, together with a copy of the resolution of the Vestry, or of the Congregation, authorizing such application; in which resolution the said Church, by its Vestry or Congregation, shall agree to abide by, and conform to, and observe, all the Canons of the Church, and all the rules, orders and regulations of the Convention; which copy shall be duly certified by the presiding officer of the Vestry, or of the meeting of the Congregation at which the resolution was adopted, and also by the Clerk of the Vestry or Secretary of the meeting; and shall be authenticated by the seal of the Corporation. The said application shall also be accompanied by the Certificate of Incorporation of the Church, duly recorded, or a copy thereof certified by the officer, whose duty it may be to record or file the same; and also, by a Certificate of the Ecclesiastical Authority, to the effect that he or they approve of the incorporation of such Church, and that such Church, in his or their judgment, is duly and satisfactorily established; and every Church or Congregation applying for admission shall produce satisfactory evidence that not less than twenty-five persons, members of such Church, have habitually, for at least one year preceding such application, attended Divine Service in such Church or Congregation.

SEC. 2. No application for the admission of a Church into union with the Church in this Diocese shall be considered or acted upon, at any meeting of the Convention, unless the same shall have been transmitted to the Secretary of the Convention at least thirty days before the meeting of the Convention. It shall be the duty of the Secretary of the Convention, at least twenty days before the meeting of the Convention, to deliver to a Committee, to be annually appointed (to be called the Committee on the Incorporation and Admission of Churches), all applications for admission into union which shall have been received by him, to be by such Committee examined, considered and reported upon to the Convention.

SEC. 3. Whenever hereafter any Church in union with this Convention shall neglect, for three years in succession, to make a Parochial Report, no Missionary Report being made on its behalf, and shall not, during the same period, have employed a Clergyman as its Parish Minister, nor requested of the Ecclesiastical Authority to have the services of a Missionary, such Church shall be regarded as having forfeited its connection with the Convention, and shall no longer have a right to send a Delegation to the same. The Bishop shall report such Church to the Convention in his Annual Address. Such Church, however, may be re-admitted, upon application to the Convention, accompanied by a report of its condition, and on such terms as shall appear just; such re-admission to take effect from and after the rising of the Convention consenting to such admission.

CANON V.

Of Elections.

All elections by the Convention shall be by ballot, except when the ballot is dispensed with by unanimous consent. And when an election is by ballot, a majority of the votes in each order shall be necessary to a choice.

CANON VI.

Of the Secretary of the Convention.

SECTION 1. It shall be the duty of the Secretary to take and keep the Minutes of the proceedings of the Convention, to attest its public acts, and faithfully to deliver into the hands of his successor all books and papers relating to the business and concerns of the Convention which may be in his possession or under his control. It shall also be his duty to send a printed notice to each Minister, and to each Vestry or Congregation, of the time and place appointed for the meetings of each Convention, and to publish a notice of the meeting in three of the public papers published in the Diocese of Albany, and to perform such other duties as may be required of him by the Convention.

SEC. 2. He shall transmit annually a copy of the Journal of the Convention to each of the Bishops of the Protestant Episcopal Church in the United States, to the Secretary of the House of Deputies of the General Convention, and to the Secretaries of the Diocesan Conventions; and shall ask, on behalf of the Diocese, for copies of the Diocesan Journals in exchange.

SEC. 3. He shall also transmit to every General Convention, in addition to the documents required by the Canons of the General Convention,* a certificate, signed by himself, containing a list of the Clergymen in this Diocese, and the amount of funds paid or secured to be paid (distinguishing them) to the General Theological Seminary, and also a certificate of the appointment of Clerical and Lay Deputies.

SEC. 4. Any expense incurred by a compliance with this Canon shall be paid out of the Diocesan Fund.

SEC. 5. Whenever there shall be a vacancy in the office of Secretary of the Convention, the duties thereof shall devolve upon the Assistant Secretary, if there be one; if not, upon the Secretary of the Standing Committee.

SEC. 6. Whenever, under the provisions of the Constitution, a Special Convention is called for any particular purpose, it shall be the duty of the Secretary, in the notice thereof, to specify such purpose.

CANON VII.

Of the Treasurer of the Diocese.

SECTION 1. It shall be the duty of the Treasurer of the Diocese to receive and disburse all moneys collected under the authority of the Convention, and of which the the collection and distribution shall not be otherwise regulated. He shall report, at each annual meeting of the Convention, names of the Parishes which have failed to make the required contributions to any of the Diocesan Funds, specifying the funds to which they have failed to contribute and the amount of such deficiency.

SEC. 2. His accounts shall be rendered annually to the Convention, and shall be examined by a Committee acting under its authority.

---

* Title I, Canon 18, Sec IV.

Sec. 3. If the Treasurer of the Convention shall die or resign his office, the Standing Committee shall appoint a Treasurer *ad interim;* to continue in office until an election be made by the Convention.

CANON VIII.

Of the Registrar.

It shall be the duty of the Registrar to collect and preserve, as the property of the Diocese, all documents and papers pertaining to the Diocese, and not in the custody of any other officer; and also the Journals and public documents of other Diocesan Conventions and of the General Convention, and other pamphlets and publications connected with the Church at large.

CANON IX.

Of Deputies to the General Convention.

SECTION 1. The Convention shall, at each regular annual meeting next preceding a stated meeting of the General Convention, elect, by the concurrent ballot of the Clerical and Lay Members, four Clergymen and four Laymen, to act as Deputies from this Diocese to the General Convention. It shall also, in like manner, elect four Clergymen and four Laymen as Provisional Deputies, to act in the case hereinafter mentioned; which Deputies and Provisional Deputies shall hold their respective offices until their successors are elected, and shall be Deputies, or Provisional Deputies, for any General Convention which may be held during their continuance in office.

Sec. 2. Should a vacancy occur by resignation, removal from the Diocese, death, or otherwise, among the Deputies or Provisional Deputies, between the stated times of election, the vacancy shall be supplied by any Convention during or prior to which such vacancy shall occur.

Sec. 3. It shall be the duty of the Deputies elect to signify to the Ecclesiastical Authority, at least ten days before the meeting of the General Convention, their acceptance of the appointment and their intention to perform its duties; in default of which the Ecclesiastical Authority shall designate, from the list of Provisional Deputies, so many as may be necessary to ensure, as far as practicable, a full representation of the Diocese. And the Ecclesiastical Authority shall, in like manner, designate, from the same list of Provisional Deputies, one or more, as the case may be, to supply any deficiency in the representation of this Diocese which may in any way occur. And the person or persons so designated by the Bishop, being furnished with a certificate thereof, shall have all the power and authority of Deputies duly elected by the Convention.

CANON X.

Of the Standing Committee.

The powers and duties of the Standing Committee over and above those given and prescribed by the Canons of the General Convention and by the Constitution of the Diocese of Albany, are further defined as follows:

SECTION 1. If there be no Bishop, or if he be unable to perform his duties, the Standing Committee shall be the Ecclesiastical Authority of the Diocese, *provided* that whenever any duty is specially imposed upon the Clerical Members of the Committee, such duty shall be performed by them only.

Sec. 2. The record of all proceedings upon a presentment of a Clergyman shall be preserved by the Standing Committee.

SEC. 3. The Standing Committee shall make a full report of all their proceedings at every Annual Convention.

CANON XI.

Of Parish Registers and Parochial Reports.

WHEREAS, by the Canons of the General Convention,* it is made the duty of each Clergyman of this Church to "keep a Register of Baptisms, Confirmations, Communicants, Marriages, and Funerals within his Cure, agreeably to such rules as may be provided by the Convention of the Diocese where his Cure lies;" it is hereby ordered that,

SECTION 1. The Record shall specify the name and the time of the birth of the child or adult baptized, with the names of the parents, sponsors or witnesses; the names of the persons confirmed; the names of the persons married, their ages and residences, also the names and residences of at least two witnesses of each marriage; the names of the persons buried, their ages, and the place of burial; and also the time when and the Minister by whom each rite was performed. The list of Communicants shall contain the names of all connected with the Parish or Mission as nearly as can be ascertained. These records shall be made by the Minister in a book provided for that purpose, belonging to each Church; which book shall be the Parish Register, and shall be preserved as a part of the records of the Church.

SEC. 2. AND WHEREAS, by the Canons of the General Convention,† it is " ordered that every Minister of this Church, or, if the Parish be vacant, the Warden shall present, or cause to be delivered, on or before the first day of every Annual Convention, to the Bishop of the Diocese, or, where there is no Bishop, to the President of the Convention, a statement of the number of Baptisms, Confirmations, Marriages and Funerals, and of the number of Communicants in his Parish or Church; also the state and condition'of the Sunday Schools in his Parish; and also the amount of the Communion alms, the contributions for 'Missions, Diocesan, Domestic and Foreign, for Parochial Schools, for Church purposes in general, and of all other matters that may throw light on the state of the same;" it is hereby further ordered that, in reporting the number of Communicants, he shall distinguish the additions, removals and deaths since the last report, and that, in reporting the contributions for Church purposes in general, he shall include the amount received for sittings in the Church and moneys raised for all Church and Parish purposes, other than those enumerated in this section.

SEC. 3. In every case where a Parish is without a Minister, the Parish Register shall be kept by some person appointed by the Vestry or Trustees; and the annual Parochial report shall be presented or forwarded to the Bishop by the Churchwardens or Trustees of the Parish.

CANON XII.

Of Vacant Parishes.

SECTION 1. Whenever a Parish becomes vacant, it shall be the duty of the Vestry or Trustees to give immediate notice thereof to the Bishop.

SEC. 2. The Bishop shall appoint those of the Clergy in the Diocese who can with most convenience discharge the duty, to supply such vacant Parishes as have been reported to him, at such times as may be deemed convenient and proper. And the Clergy so appointed, shall make a full report to the Bishop concerning the state of the Parishes which they have visited. It shall be the duty of the Parishes thus supplied to defray all the expenses incident to such occasional services.

---

* Title I, Canon 15, Sec. 5.   † Title I, Canon 18, Sec. 1.

CANON XIII.

Of Offerings.

SECTION 1. Whereas it is the duty of all Christians, as faithful stewards of God, to set apart regularly a portion of their income as God's portion, "every one as God hath prospered him," to be used for the maintenance and extension of His kingdom, and the relief of His poor; this Church enjoins this duty upon all her members.

SEC. 2 It shall be the duty of every Congregation of this Diocese to contribute, at least once in each year, by weekly or monthly offerings, or in some other systematic way, to the Missions of the Diocese; the Domestic and Foreign Missions and other departments of Missionary work under the control of the General Convention; the support of the Episcopate; the expenses of the Convention; the education of young men for the Holy Ministry; the distribution of the Bible and Book of Common Prayer; the support of aged and infirm Clergymen; the relief of the widows and orphans of deceased Clergymen; and the support and education of orphan children; the offer-ings to be sent to the Treasurers of the funds for which they are made, and the amounts of all such contributions to form distinct items in the Annual Parochial Report.

SEC. 3. "The Protestant Episcopal Society for Promoting Religion and Learning in the State of New York," in which we have an interest in common with our mother Diocese, shall be an agent of this Diocese for the education of young men for Holy Orders. A copy of its Annual report, if obtained from its Superintendent, shall be laid by the Secretary of the Convention before each Annual Convention.

SEC. 4. "The Bible and Common Prayer Book Society of Albany and its Vicinity" shall be the agent of this Diocese for the Distribution of the Bible and the Book of Common Prayer, and shall present a full report of its proceedings to each Annual Convention.

SEC. 5. The Orphan House of the Holy Saviour, at or near Cooperstown, shall be the Diocesan Orphanage, and shall make a report of its proceedings and condition to each Annual Convention.

CANON XIV.

Of the Missions of the Diocese and of Archdeaconries.

The Church in this Diocese, acknowledging her responsibility, in common with the whole Church, for the fulfilment of the charge of our Lord to preach the Gospel to every creature, and especially for the extension of the Church throughout the Diocese, declares that it is the duty of the Convention, as her representative body, to care for the Missionary work, and that every baptized Member of the Church is bound, according to his ability, to assist in carrying it on. To this end it is hereby enacted as follows:

SECTION 1. "The Board of Missions of the Protestant Episcopal Church in the Diocese of Albany," incorporated by an Act of the Legislature of the State of New York, passed February 16, 1870, shall be entrusted with the general charge and direction of the work of Missions within the Diocese, and particularly with the custody and management of all money or property given or acquired for that object, subject to the provisions of this Canon and to such written instructions as may from time to time be given to them by the Convention and entered upon the Journal thereof.

SEC. 2. The said Board of Missions shall consist of the Bishop, who shall be *ex officio* the President thereof; and of ten other members, one Clergyman and one Lay-man resident within the limits of each of the Archdeaconries hereinafter provided for, and nominated by said Archdeaconry, and one Clergyman and one Layman who

may be resident anywhere within the Diocese, and shall be nominated in open Convention, all of whom shall be annually chosen by the Convention, and by ballot unless the same be unanimously dispensed with. All vacancies occurring in the Board during the recess of the Convention, may be filled by the Board.

SEC. 3. The evening session of the Convention on the first day of each Annual Meeting shall be devoted to the reception and consideration of the Report of the Board of Missions and of its Treasurer, the election of the Board, and other business connected with the subject; provided that said election and other business connected with the subject may be deferred to the second day.

SEC. 4. The Board of Missions shall meet on the day after the adjournment of the Convention in each year, and elect a Secretary and a Treasurer. The Board may hold other meetings during the year, according to its own rules, and shall meet on the day preceding the Annual Convention, to audit the accounts of the Treasurer, and to adopt a report to the Convention.

SEC. 5. The Diocese shall be divided into districts called Archdeaconries, the titles and limits of which shall be as follows: The Archdeaconry of Albany shall comprise the counties of Albany, Greene, Columbia, Schenectady, Montgomery, Fulton, Hamilton and Herkimer. The Archdeaconry of Troy shall comprise the counties of Rensselaer, Saratoga, Washington, Warren, Clinton and Essex. The Archdeaconry of the Susquehanna shall comprise the counties of Delaware, Otsego and Schoharie. The Archdeaconry of Ogdensburgh shall comprise the counties of St. Lawrence and Franklin.

SEC. 6. The Bishop shall be *ex officio* the head of each Archdeaconry. He shall, however, annually appoint an Archdeacon on the nomination of each Archdeaconry, from among the Clergy thereof, who shall be the Executive Officer of the Archdeaconry. Each Archdeaconry, moreover, shall annually elect a Secretary and Treasurer, who shall make annual reports to the Convention. The Archdeacon in the absence of the Bishop shall preside at all the meetings of the Archdeaconry, and may also be present without a vote at the meetings of the Board of Missions. He shall be charged with the duty of visiting the Mission Stations and vacant Parishes, and, with the consent of the Clergy in charge, the other Parishes receiving Missionary aid within the limits of his Archdeaconry, to ascertain their condition, and to give such advice as may be required, reporting the result of his inquiries and observations to the Bishop. It shall also be his duty to stir up an increased Missionary interest and zeal, and to urge more liberal offerings for the work of Church extension. And furthermore the Archdeacon and the Clerical and Lay Members of the Board of Missions from each Archdeaconry shall be an Advisory Committee of the Board, whose duty it shall be to counsel the Board as to the amount which should be expended in, and the amount which should be raised by the Archdeaconry which they represent, and to use their best efforts to secure the required amount of Missionary offerings from their Archdeaconry

SEC. 7 Each Archdeaconry shall hold two meetings a year at such places within its boundaries as it may designate. Other meetings may be held as the Archdeaconry may order. At all meetings of the Archdeaconry every Clergyman canonically resident within its boundaries shall be entitled to a seat; also three Laymen from each Parish or Mission Station within the limits of the Archdeaconry Each Clergyman and each Lay Delegation shall have one vote. Any number of members present at a meeting duly called shall be competent to transact business. The meetings of Archdeaconry shall have for their main purpose the presentation of the claims of the Mission work of the Diocese and the Church Such Missionaries as may be members shall report concerning their work, and provision may be made for especial needs of Missionary work within the boundaries of the Archdeaconry. Contributions to

local work shall not interfere with the claims of the Diocesan Board of Missions, and shall be reported to the Treasurer thereof, and included in his Annual Report to the Convention. It shall also be the object of these Archidiaconal meetings to bring the Clergy together in fraternal intercourse and to promote their spiritual and intellectual life. Each Archdeaconry shall make its own rules as to the arrangement of services.

Sec. 8. All Missionaries shall be appointed by the Board of Missions on the nomination of the Bishop, and may be removed with his approval. But in case of a vacancy in the Episcopate, or of the absence of the Bishop from the Diocese, or of his being otherwise unable to perform his duties, the Board of Missions shall have the power of appointing and removing Missionaries.

Sec. 9. It shall be the duty of every member of the Church in the Diocese to contribute as God hath prospered him, to the funds of the Board of Missions; and every Clergyman having Parochial or Missionary charge shall impress this duty upon his people, and cause one or more Offertories to be made annually for that object.

Sec. 10. The Treasurer of the Board of Missions shall include in his Annual Report all sums certified to him as expended in local Missionary work. He shall also receive, report and pay over any special contributions from Parishes or individuals in accordance with the instructions of the contributors.

Sec. 11. The travelling expenses of the members of the Board of Missions and of the Archdeacons, attending the meetings of the Board, shall be paid out of its treasury.

Sec. 12. Any Mission Station designated by the Board of Missions may be organized by the Bishop on the application of any residents in its neighbourhood. But such station shall not be established within the Parochial Cure of any other Minister or Ministers, without either the consent of such Minister or of a majority of such Ministers, or with the advice of the Standing Committee of the Diocese. The Bishop may appoint, upon the organization of the Mission, a Churchwarden, a Clerk, and a Treasurer, which officers shall thereafter be elected by the Congregation annually in Easter week, in the same manner as provided for the choice of Deputies to Convention by section 2, of Canon II of this Diocese. They shall, as far as possible, discharge the duties which belong to their respective offices in incorporated Parishes.

Sec. 13. The title of all property, real or personal, given or purchased for the use of any Mission Station, shall be vested in "The Board of Missions of the Protestant Episcopal Church, in the Diocese of Albany," or in "The Trustees of the Diocese of Albany."

Canon XV.

Of the Episcopal Fund.

Section 1. The fund for the support of the Episcopate in this Diocese, now provided, together with that which may be hereafter contributed or acquired, and any accumulation accruing from the investment thereof, shall be entrusted to the Corporation, entitled "The Trustees of the Episcopal Fund of the Diocese of Albany," incorporated by an Act of the Legislature of the State of New York, passed April 28, 1869. The Trustees composing said Corporation shall be five in number, who shall be appointed by the Convention, and shall hold their offices during the pleasure thereof.

Sec. 2. All moneys belonging to the said fund shall be loaned by the said Trustees upon security of real estate, or invested in stock of the United States, or of this State, or of the city of New York, at their discretion; and all securities and investments shall be taken or made in their corporate name above mentioned; and they shall have power, from time to time, to change such investments. A statement, signed by the Trustees or a majority of them, exhibiting the condition of said fund

and securities, together with the receipts and disbursements during the year, shall be reported to the Convention at every annual meeting thereof.

CANON XVI.

Of the Diocesan Fund.

SECTION 1. WHEREAS it is indispensable to provide a fund for defraying the necessary expenses of the Convention, including the expenses of those of the Clergy who may have to travel from a distance to the Convention, and also the cost of maintaining a suitable residence for the Bishop; it is hereby required of every Congregation in this Diocese to pay to the Treasurer of the Convention on or before the day of its annual meeting, a contribution at such a rate per cent upon the salary of its Clergyman as shall have been determined by the previous Convention to be required for the purposes above-mentioned.

SEC. 2. AND WHEREAS, by the Canons of the General Convention,* it is made "the duty of the several Diocesan Conventions to forward to the Treasurer of the General Convention, at or before any meeting of the General Convention, three dollars for each Clergyman within such Diocese;" therefore, it shall be the duty of the Treasurer to retain annually out of the Diocesan Fund, one dollar for each Clergyman in this Diocese, as a special fund, to be paid over to the Treasurer of the General Convention at each meeting of the same.

CANON XVII.

Of the Aged and Infirm Clergy Fund.

SECTION 1. The fund now existing, together with all contributions hereafter received for the support of Aged and Infirm Clergymen, shall be entrusted to the Corporation entitled "The Trustees of the Fund for the support of the Aged and Infirm Clergy of the Protestant Episcopal Church in the Diocese of Albany," incorporated by an Act of the Legislature of the State of New York, passed February 16, 1870. The said Trustees shall consist of the Bishop and the Treasurer of the Diocese, together with three Lay Trustees, who shall be appointed annually by the Convention. Vacancies occurring in the number of the Lay Trustees during the recess of the Convention may be filled by the remaining Trustees.

SEC. 2. It shall be the duty of the Trustees to receive applications for relief, and to administer it in accordance with such rules and regulations as they, with the approbation of the Convention, may from time to time adopt.

SEC. 3. The Trustees shall present a detailed report of their proceedings and of the condition of the fund to every Annual Convention.

CANON XVIII.

Of the Clergy Reserve Fund.

SECTION 1. A fund shall be established to be known as the Clergy Reserve Fund of the Diocese of Albany.

SEC. 2. It shall be the duty of each Parish and Mission station in the Diocese to contribute one offering annually in behalf of this fund.

SEC. 3. The fund thus formed shall be permitted to accumulate until it shall amount to $20,000, and the income shall then be divided into annuities of $300, which shall be paid to the beneficiaries of the fund.

SEC. 4. The beneficiaries of the fund shall be the Clergy of the Diocese according to the seniority of their canonical residence.

---

* Title III, Canon 1, Sec. 5.

SEC. 5. No Clergyman shall be a beneficiary of the fund whose salary or stipend exceeds $1,000 per annum. Nor shall any Clergyman receive the annuity who has allowed the Parish or Mission under his charge to neglect its annual contribution to the fund.

SEC. 6. The principal of the fund shall not be impaired.

SEC. 7. The trustees of the fund shall be the Bishop of the Diocese, the Rector of St. Peter's Church, Albany, the Rector of St. Paul's Church, Troy, the Archdeacons of the Diocese, and the Treasurer of the Diocese, who shall be the treasurer of the fund. And they are hereby authorized to form a corporation under the Laws of the State of New York, whose object shall be to carry into effect the provisions of this Canon, and to provide for the receipt by the corporation so to be formed, of real and personal estate by gifts, purchase, devise, bequest or otherwise, for the purposes of said corporation.

CANON XIX.

Of the Fund for the Widows and Orphans of Deceased Clergymen.

SECTION 1. The fund now existing, together with all contributions hereafter received for the relief of widows and orphans of Deceased Clergymen shall be entrusted to the Corporation entitled "The Trustees of the Fund for the Widows and Orphans of Deceased Clergymen of the Protestant Episcopal Church in the Diocese of Albany," incorporated by an Act of the Legislature of the State of New York, passed February 16, 1870. The said Trustees shall consist of the Bishop and the Treasurer of the Diocese, together with three Lay Trustees, who shall be appointed annually by the Convention. Vacancies occurring in the number of the Lay Trustees during the recess of the Convention may be filled by the remaining Trustees.

SEC. 2. It shall be the duty of the Trustees to receive applications for relief, and to administer it in accordance with such rules and regulations as they, with the approbation of the Convention, may from time to time adopt.

SEC. 3. The Trustees shall present a detailed report of their proceedings and of the condition of the fund to every Annual Convention.

CANON XX.

Of the Trial of a Clergyman not being a Bishop.

Whenever any Minister of this Diocese, not being a Bishop thereof, shall become "liable to presentment and trial" under the provisions of any Canon of the General or Diocesan Convention, the mode of proceeding in this Diocese shall be as follows:

SECTION 1. The trial shall be on a presentment in writing, addressed to the Bishop of the Diocese, specifying the offences of which the accused is alleged to be guilty, with reasonable certainty as to time, place and circumstances. Such presentment may be made by the major part in number of the members of the Vestry of any Church of which the accused is Minister, or by any three Presbyters of this Diocese entitled to seats in the Convention, or as hereinafter mentioned. Whenever, from public rumor or otherwise, the Bishop shall have reason to believe that any Clergyman is under the imputation of having been guilty of any offence or misconduct for which he is liable to be tried, and that the interest of the Church requires an investigation, it shall be his duty to appoint five persons, of whom three at least shall be Presbyters, to examine the case; a majority of whom may make such examination; and if there is, in their opinion, sufficient ground for presentment, they shall present the Clergyman accordingly.

SEC. 2. A presentment being made in any one of the modes above prescribed, the Bishop, if the facts charged shall not appear to him to be such as constitute an of-

fence, may dismiss it; or if it allege facts, some of which do and some of which do not constitute an offence, he may allow it in part and dismiss the residue, or he may permit it to be amended. When it shall be allowed in whole or in part, the Bishop shall cause a copy of it to be served on the accused; and shall also nominate twelve Presbyters of this Diocese entitled to seats in the Convention, and not being parties to the presentment, and cause a list of their names to be served on the accused, who shall, within thirty days after such service, select five of them, and notify their names in writing to the Bishop; and if he shall not give such notification to the Bishop within the said thirty days, the Bishop shall select five; and the Presbyters so selected shall form a Board for the trial of the accused, and shall meet at such time and place as the Bishop shall direct, and shall have power to adjourn from time to time, and from place to place (but always within the Diocese), as they shall think proper.

Sec. 3. A written notice of the time and place of their first meeting shall be served, at least thirty days before such meeting, on the accused, and also on one of the persons making the presentment.

Sec. 4. If, at the time appointed for the first meeting of the Board of Presbyters, the whole number of five shall not attend, then those who do attend may adjourn from time to time; and if, after one adjournment or more, it shall appear to them improbable that the whole number will attend within a reasonable time, then those who do attend, not being less than three, shall constitute the board, and proceed to the trial, and a majority of them shall decide all questions.

Sec. 5. If a Clergyman presented shall confess the truth of the facts alleged in the presentment, and shall not demur thereto, it shall be the duty of the Bishop to proceed to pass sentence; and if he shall not confess them before the appointment of a Board for his trial, as before mentioned, he shall be considered as denying them.

Sec. 6. If a Clergyman presented, after having had due notice, shall not appear before the Board of Presbyters appointed for his trial, the Board may, nevertheless, proceed as if he were present, unless for good cause they shall see fit to adjourn to another day.

Sec. 7. When the Board proceed to the trial, they shall hear such evidence as shall be produced, which evidence shall be reduced to writing and signed by the witnesses, respectively, and some officer authorized by law to administer oaths may, at the desire of either party, be requested to administer an oath or affirmation to the witnesses, that they will testify the truth, the whole truth, and nothing but the truth, concerning the facts charged in the presentment If, on or during the trial, the accused shall confess the truth of the charges, as stated in the presentment, the Board may dispense with hearing further evidence, and may proceed at once to state their opinion to the Bishop as to the sentence that ought to be pronounced.

Sec. 8. Upon the application of either party to the Bishop, and it being made satisfactorily to appear to him that any material witness cannot be procured upon the trial, the Bishop may appoint a Commissary to take the testimony of such witness. Such Commissary may be either a Clergyman or a Layman, and the party so applying shall give to the other at least six days' notice of the time and place of taking the testimony. If the person on whom the notice shall be served shall reside more than forty miles from the place of examination, notice of an additional day shall be given for every additional twenty miles of the said distance. Both parties may attend and examine the witness; and the questions and answers shall be reduced to writing and signed by the witness, and shall be certified by the Commissary, and enclosed under his seal, and transmitted to the Board, and shall be received by them as evidence. A witness examined before such Commissary may be sworn or affirmed in manner aforesaid.

SEC. 9. The Board, having deliberately considered the evidence, shall declare in a writing signed by them, or a majority of them, their decision on the charges contained in the presentment, distinctly stating whether the accused be guilty or not guilty of such charges, respectively, and also stating the sentence (if any) which, in their opinion, should be pronounced; and a copy of such decision shall be, without delay, communicated to the accused; and the original decision, together with the evidence, shall be delivered to the Bishop, who shall pronounce such canonical sentence as shall appear to him to be proper, provided the same shall not exceed in severity the sentence recommended by the Board; and such sentence shall be final. Before pronouncing any sentence, the Bishop shall summon the accused, and any three or more of the Clergy, to meet him at such time as may, in his opinion, be most convenient, in some Church to be designated by him, which shall, for that purpose, be open at the time to all persons who may choose to attend; and the sentence shall then and there be publicly pronounced by the Bishop. But the Bishop, if he shall be satisfied that justice requires it, may grant a new trial to the accused, in which case a new Board of Presbyters shall be appointed, the proceedings before whom shall be conducted as above mentioned.

SEC. 10. All notices and papers contemplated in this Canon may be served by a summoner or summoners, to be appointed for the purpose by the Bishop, and whose certificate of such service shall be evidence thereof. In case of service by any other person, the facts shall be proved by the affidavit of such person. A written notice or paper delivered to a party, or left at his last place of residence, shall be deemed a sufficient service of such notice or paper.

SEC. 11. The defendant may have the privilege of appearing by counsel; in case of the exercise of which privilege, and not otherwise, those who present shall also have the like privilege.

SEC. 12. If the Ecclesiastical Authority of any other Diocese shall, under the provisions of the Canons of the General Convention, or otherwise, make known to the Ecclesiastical Authority of this Diocese, charges against a Presbyter or Deacon thereof, such communication shall be a sufficient presentation of him for trial; and the trial shall take place as above provided. The Bishop shall appoint some competent person as Prosecutor, who shall be considered as the party making the presentment.

CANON XXI.

Of Differences between Ministers and their Congregations.

SECTION 1. Whenever there shall be any serious difference between the Rector of any Church in this Diocese and the Congregation thereof, it shall be lawful for a majority of the Vestry or Trustees to make a representation to the Bishop, stating the facts in the case and agreeing, for themselves and for the Congregation which they represent, to submit to his decision in the matter, and to perform whatever he may require of them by any order which he may make under the provisions of this Canon, and shall at the same time serve a copy of the representation on the Rector.

SEC. 2. It shall be the duty of the Bishop, at all stages of the proceeding, to seek to bring them to an amicable conclusion; and in such case the agreement between the parties, signed by them and attested by the Bishop, shall have the same force as an order made under section 4 of this Canon.

SEC. 3. If the matter shall not be amicably settled within a reasonable time, the Bishop shall convene the Clerical Members of the Standing Committee and shall give notice to the parties to appear before him and present their proofs and arguments at such time and place as he may appoint; and he may adjourn and continue the hearing in the matter in his discretion.

SEC. 4. When the hearing is concluded, the Bishop shall make such an order in regard to the matter as he may think to be just and for the true interests of the Church; and such order may require the Rector to resign his Rectorship, and may require the Church to pay a sum of money to the Rector; and it shall be the duty of the Rector and of the Church and every member thereof to submit to and abide by such order as the final and conclusive determination of all matters of dif. ference between them. *Provided*, that no order shall be made under this or the next succeeding section of this Canon, unless with the advice and concurrence of at least two Clerical Members of the Standing Committee, who shall have been present at the hearing.

SEC. 5. If it shall be made to appear to the Bishop that any agreement made under section 2 of this Canon, or any order made under section 4 of this Canon, or of this section, shall have been disregarded by any of the parties concerned, or if an appli- cation be made to him to modify such order, he may convene the Clerical Members of the Standing Committee, and after hearing such further proofs and arguments as may be presented to him, make such further order in the matter as he may think proper with the same effect as an order made under section 4 of this Canon.

SEC. 6. If any Church or Congregation shall persistently neglect or refuse to obey any order made under this Canon, it shall be the duty of the Bishop to exhort the members of such Congregation to submit to the authority and discipline of the Church; and if they will not do so, the Convention may proceed to dissolve the union between the Church so offending and the Convention of this Diocese, and may take such other action in the matter as it may think expedient. *Provided*, that no such action shall be held or taken to be a surrender of any right which either the Church in this Diocese, or such members of such Congregation as submit to the authority and discipline of the Church may have in the corporation of such Church, or in any property belonging thereto.

SEC. 7. Whenever the Standing Committee shall be acting as the Ecclesiastical Authority of the Diocese, the Clerical Members thereof shall perform the duties herein required of the Bishop; and they shall request the Bishop of some other Diocese to attend the hearing of the case, and shall make no order therein but with his advice and assistance.

CANON XXII.

Of Amendments of the Canons.

No new Canon or amendment of a Canon shall hereafter be adopted by the Con- vention, unless at least one day's previous notice thereof shall have been given in open Convention; nor, unless by unanimous consent, until the same shall have been referred to, and reported upon by a Committee of at least two Presbyters and two Laymen. All propositions to amend the Canons shall be in the form of a Canon, and such sections as shall be amended shall be re-enacted in full in their amended form.

ADMISSION OF CHURCHES.

Under Canon IV, in order to be admitted into union with the Church in this Diocese, the Church or congregation must (in sufficient time to allow the papers to be transmitted to, *and be received by* the Secretary of the Convention at least thirty days before the meeting of the Convention) adopt a resolution, at a legally convened and held meeting of the Vestry, or (*in the case of Churches incorporated without Vestries*), of the congregation, authorizing the application for such admission to be made, and agreeing to abide by, and conform to, and observe all the Canons of the Church, and all the rules, orders and regulations of the Convention. A copy of this resolution must be duly certified by the presiding officer of the Vestry, or of the meeting of the congregation at which the resolution was adopted, and also by the Clerk of the Vestry, or Secretary of the meeting of the congregation, and must also be authenticated by the seal of the corporation.

In Churches having Vestries, this resolution should be adopted by the Vestry. In Churches incorporated without Vestries, it should be adopted by the congregation.

The following form of resolution is recommended:

Resolved, That [*here set forth the corporate name or title by which the Church is known in law as the same is described in the Certificate of Incorporation*] desire admission into union with the Church in the Diocese of Albany, and do make application therefor to the Convention of the Church in this Diocese; and do hereby agree to abide by, and conform to, and observe all the Canons of the Church, and all the rules, orders and regulations of the Convention.

The resolution must be entered accurately and at length on the minutes of the Vestry, or of the meeting of the congregation, as the case may be.

The Canon requires an application *in writing,* to the Convention, asking admission, which must then be made out. This may be signed by the Rector (if there be one), and by one or both of the Wardens, *and* by the Clerk of the Vestry; or, in the case of Churches without Vestries, by the Minister, or by the presiding officer of the meeting at which the resolution was adopted, *and also* by the Clerk of such meeting.

The following form of application is recommended:

To the Convention of the Protestant Episcopal Church in the Diocese of Albany:

The Church or congregation duly incorporated and known in law by the name of [*here set forth the corporate name or title of the Church, as the same is described in the Certificate of Incorporation*], in pursuance, and by authority of a resolution of the [*Vestry or congregation as the case may be*] of the said Church, hereby applies for admission into union with the Church in this Diocese; and presents herewith a duly certified and authenticated copy of the resolution of the said [*Vestry or congregation, as the case may be*] adopted on the   day of   189 , authorizing such application, and agreeing to abide by, and conform to, and observe all the Canons of the Church, and all the rules, orders and regulations of the Convention. *Also,* the Certificate of Incorporation of the Church (*or in case the original certificate is not presented, then say, "a duly certified copy of the Certificate of the Incorporation of the Church*), which was duly recorded in the office of the (Clerk or Register, *as the case may be*), of the   county of   on the   day of 189 , in Book   of Certificates of Religious Incorporations, (*or whatever may be*

the *official designation of the book in which such Certificates are recorded in the county
in which such Church is located*), page   . Also, a certificate of the Bishop that he
approves of the incorporation of such Church, and that such Church, in his judgment, is duly and satisfactorily established. *And also*, evidence that not less than
twenty-five persons, members of such Church, have habitually, for at least one year
preceding the date of this application, attended Divine Services in such Church or
congregation.

Dated at   in the county of   and State of New York, this
         day of   189 .

By order of the [*Vestry or congregation as the case may be*].

                               A. B., *Rector.*
                               C. D., *Warden.*
                               E. F.,   *do.*
                               G. H., *Clerk.*

Or, in case of Churches having no Vestries:

                        A. B., *Minister.*
                        C. D., *Presiding officer of the Meeting of
                                 the Congregation.*
                        E. F., *Secretary of the Meeting of the
                                 Congregation.*

The Canon also requires that the application be accompanied by the following
papers:

I. A duly certified and authenticated copy of the resolution of the Vestry or congregation authorizing the application, etc.

II. The original, or a certified copy of the Certificate of Incorporation.

III. The certificate of the Bishop's approval of the incorporation, and that, in his
judgment, the Church is duly and satisfactorily established.

IV. The evidence that not less than twenty-five persons, members of such Church,
have habitually, for at least one year preceding the date of the application, attended
Divine Service in the Church or congregation.

The following is recommended as a form for certifying the resolution of the Vestry
or of the congregation:

At a meeting of the [*Vestry or congregation, as the case may be*] of the Church or
congregation known as [*here set forth the corporate name or title of the Church, as the
same is described in the Certificate of Incorporation*], duly convened, and held according to law, at   on the   day of   18 , the following
resolution was adopted:

"*Resolved*, That [*here copy, in the precise words, and at length, and accurately, the
resolution as adopted and entered on the Minutes.*"]

Which is hereby certified by A. B., the Rector of the said Church [*or, if there be
no Rector, then* C. D., the Warden, who presided at the meeting of the Vestry at
which the resolution was adopted, there being no Rector of the said Church], and
also by E. F., the Clerk of the Vestry, and is also authenticated by the seal of the
corporation.

Dated at   in the county of   the   day of
189.

    [SEAL.]   A. B., *Rector.*
                                  [*or*] C. D. *Warden presiding*
                                    E. F., *Clerk of the Vestry.*

In the case of Churches having no Vestries, the certificate may be as follows:

Which is hereby certified by A. B., Minister of the Church, *or* C. D., the Presiding officer of the meeting of the congregation at which the resolution was adopted, and also by E. F., the secretary of the said meeting, and is also authenticated by the seal of the corporation.

Dated, etc. (as above).

A. B., *Minister.*

[*or*] C. D., *Presiding officer of the Meeting of the Congregation.*

E. F., *Secretary of the Meeting.*

[SEAL.]

The following is submitted (with the approval and authority of the Bishop) as the form for his certificate:

I do hereby certify, that I approve of the incorporation of a Church known as [*here set forth the corporate name or title of the Church as the same is described in the Certificate of Incorporation*], and that such Church, in my judgment, is duly and satisfactorily established.

Dated at   the   day of   in the year of our Lord one thousand eight hundred and

Bishop.

The following is recommended as a form for the presentation of the evidence of the number of persons habitually attending the Church:

We, the undersigned, do hereby certify and declare, that we are, and for one year last past have been connected with, or been members of, and well acquainted with the affairs and condition of, the Church or congregation known as [*here set forth the corporate name or title of the Church as the same is described in the Certificate of Incorporation*], and that we have had means of knowing, and do know, the number of persons habitually attending the said Church during one year past; and that not less than twenty-five persons, members of such Church, have habitually, for at least one year preceding this date, attended Divine Service in such Church or congregation.

Dated at   in the county of   the   day of 189 .

This certificate should be signed by the Rector, or officiating Minister, if there be one, and by one or both of the Wardens, or by two or more of the Trustees (in the case of a Church incorporated without a Vestry), or by other known and reputable parties who can certify to the fact set forth.

The application, together with the requisite papers (as before set forth), must be transmitted to the Secretary of the Convention, at least thirty days before the meeting of the Convention.

The Canon (Section 2, Canon IV.) expressly declares that "no application for the admission of a Church into union with the Church in this Diocese, shall be considered or acted upon at any meeting of the Convention, unless the same shall have been transmitted to the Secretary of the Convention at least thirty days before the meeting of the Convention."

ACT OF THE LEGISLATURE OF THE STATE OF NEW YORK, MAY 9, 1868,
CHAPTER 803.

An Act to amend the Acts to provide for the Incorporation of Religious Societies, so far as the same relate to Churches in Connection
with the Protestant Episcopal Church

Passed May 9, 1868.

*The People of the State of New York, represented in Senate and Assembly, do enact
as follows : —*

Section 1. The first section of the act entitled "An act to provide for the incorporation of Religious Societies," passed April 5, 1813, is hereby amended so as to read
as follows : —

1. It shall be lawful for not less than six male persons, of full age, belonging to
any church or congregation in communion with the Protestant Episcopal Church in
this State, not already incorporated, to meet at any time at the usual place of public
worship of such church or congregation, for the purpose of incorporating themselves
under this act.

2. A notice of such meeting, specifying its object, and the time and place thereof,
shall be publicly read in the time of morning service, on two Sundays next previous
thereto, by the rector or officiating minister, or, if there be none, by any other person belonging to such church or congregation ; and shall also be posted in a conspicuous place on the outside door, near the main entrance to such place of worship.

3. The rector, or if there be none, or he be necessarily absent, then one of the
church wardens or vestrymen, or any other person, called to the chair, shall preside
at such meeting, and shall receive the votes.

4. The persons entitled to vote at such meeting shall be the male persons of full
age belonging to the church or congregation, qualified as follows, and none other : —

First. Those who have been baptized in the Protestant Episcopal Church, or who
have been received therein, either by the rite of confirmation, or by receiving the
holy communion ; or,

Second. Those who have purchased, and for not less than twelve months next
prior to such meeting have owned, a pew or seat in such church ; or who, during
the same period of time, have hired and paid for a pew or seat in such church ; or
who, during the whole period aforesaid, have been contributors in money to the
support of such church.

5. The persons so qualified shall, at such meeting, by a majority of votes,
determine :

First. The name or title by which such church or congregation shall be known
in law.

Second. On what day in Easter-week an annual election for church wardens and
vestrymen shall thereafter take place.

Third. What number of vestrymen, not less than four nor more than eight, shall
annually be elected, and shall, together with the rector (if there be one), and the
two church wardens, constitute the vestry of the church.

Fourth. And shall, by a majority of votes, elect two church wardens and the
number of vestrymen that it shall have been determined are to be annually elected,

which church wardens and vestrymen thus elected shall serve until the next regular election.

6. The polls shall continue open for one hour, and longer, in the discretion of the presiding officer, or if required, by the vote of a majority of voters present.

7. The presiding officer, together with two other persons, shall make a certificate, under their hands and seals, of —

First. The church wardens and vestrymen so elected.

Second. Of the day in Easter-week so fixed for the annual election of their successors.

Third. Of the number of vestrymen (not less than four nor more than eight) so determined upon to be annually elected to constitute part of the vestry.

Fourth. Of the name or title by which such church or congregation shall be known in law.

Which certificate being duly acknowledged, or the execution and acknowledgment thereof being duly proven before any officer authorized to take the acknowledgment or proof of deeds or conveyances of real estate, to be recorded in the county where such church or place of worship of such congregation shall be situated, shall be recorded by the clerk of such county, or by the officer whose duty it is, or may hereafter be made, to record such instruments in the county in which such church or place of worship may be situated, in a book to be by him kept for such purpose.

8. The church wardens and vestrymen so elected, and their successors in office, of themselves (but if there be a rector, then together with the rector of such church or congregation), shall form a vestry, and shall be the trustees of such church or congregation ; and they and their successors shall thereupon by virtue of this act, be a body corporate, by the name or title expressed in such certificate.

9. The male persons qualified as aforesaid, provided they shall also have belonged to such church or congregation for twelve months immediately preceding, shall, in every year thereafter, on the day in Easter-week so fixed for that purpose, elect two church wardens, and as many vestrymen (not less than four nor more than eight) as shall have been legally determined to constitute part of the vestry.

10. Notice shall be given of such election by the rector, if there be one, or if there be none, or he be absent, by the officiating minister, or by a church warden, for two Sundays next previous to the day so fixed, in the time of divine service.

11. Whenever a vacancy in the board so constituted shall happen, by death or otherwise, the vestry shall order a special election to supply such vacancy ; of which notice shall be given in the time of divine service, at least ten days previous thereto.

12. The notice of any election, stated or otherwise, shall specify the place, day, and hour of holding the same. The provisions contained in the preceding sixth clause shall apply to all elections.

13. An election to supply a vacancy, and also the stated annual election, shall be holden immediately after morning service ; and at all such elections, the rector, or if there be none, or he be absent, one of the church wardens selected for the purpose by a majority of the duly qualified voters present ; or if no warden be present, a vestryman (selected in like manner) shall preside, and receive the votes of the electors, and be the returning officer ; and shall enter the proceedings in the book of the minutes of the vestry, and sign his name thereto, and offer the same to as many electors present as he shall think fit, to be by them also signed and certified.

14. The church wardens and vestrymen chosen at any of the said elections, shall hold their offices until the expiration of the year for which they shall be chosen, and until others are chosen in their stead : and shall have power to call and induct a

rector to such church or congregation as often as there shall be a vacancy therein, and to fix his salary or compensation.

15. No board, or meeting of such vestry shall be held, unless at least three days' notice thereof shall be given in writing, under the hand of the rector or of one of the church wardens; except that for the first meeting after an election, twenty-four hours' notice shall be sufficient; and no such board shall be competent to transact any business unless the rector, if there be one, and at least one of the church wardens, and a majority of the vestrymen be present. But if the rector be absent from the State, and shall have been so absent for over four calendar months, or if the meeting has been called by the rector, and he be absent therefrom, the board shall be competent to transact all business if there be present one church warden, and a majority of the vestrymen; except that in the absence of the rector, no measure shall be taken for effecting a sale or disposition of the real property, nor may any sale or disposition of the capital or principal of the personal estate of such corporation be made, nor any act done which shall impair the rights of such rector.

16. The rector, if there be one, and if not, then the church warden present, or if both the church wardens be present, then the church warden who shall be called to the chair by a majority of votes, shall preside and have the casting vote.

17 Whenever any corporation, organized under the provisions of this act, shall deem it for the interest of such corporation to change the number of its vestrymen, it shall and may be lawful for such corporation to change the same, provided that the number of such vestrymen shall not thereby be made less than four or more than eight. And in order to effect such change, the same shall be authorized and approved by the vestry at a regular meeting thereof; and shall then at the next stated annual election for wardens and vestrymen be submitted to, and ratified by, a majority of the votes of all the qualified voters voting at such election; notice of which proposed change, and that the same will be submitted for ratification at such election, shall be given at the same time, and in the same manner as is required for notice of the said election; if such change be thus ratified, a certificate shall be made setting forth the resolution of the vestry, and the proceedings to ratify the same, together with the fact of the notice being given as required, and shall be acknowledged or proved and recorded in the same manner as is required for the original certificate of organization; and thereupon the number of vestrymen to constitute a part of the vestry of such corporation, shall be such as shall be fixed by the proceedings to effect such change. But such change shall not take effect or be operative until the certificate above mentioned shall have been duly recorded.

§ 2. The provisions of the ninth, tenth, eleventh, twelfth, thirteenth, fourteenth, fifteenth, sixteenth, and seventeenth clauses of section one of this act shall apply to any church or corporation in communion with the Protestant Episcopal Church in this State heretofore incorporated under the act hereby amended, or under any of the acts amending the same, or under the several acts to provide for the incorporation of religious societies, passed April 6, 1784; March 27, 1801; or the Act for the Relief of the Protestant Episcopal Church in the State of New York, passed March 17, 1795; or by any special charter made or granted before or after July 4, 1776, whereof the vestry, at a regular meeting, shall by vote determine to adopt the same; and such vote shall, at the next ensuing stated annual election for wardens and vestrymen, be submitted to, and ratified by, a majority of the votes of all the qualified voters voting at such election, notice of such vote of the vestry, and of the proposed submission of the same for ratification, having been given at the same time and in the same manner as is required by the tenth clause of the first section of this act for notice of election. But such adoption shall not take effect, or be operative, until a certificate embodying a true copy of the resolution of the vestry, as entered upon their minutes, and the proceedings to ratify the same, together with the fact of the notice being given, as required, shall have been acknowledged or proved, and shall be recorded, as is required by the foregoing seventh clause of section one, for the certificate of incorporation.

§ 3. The first section of the act passed March 5, 1819, entitled "An Act to amend the Act entitled, 'An Act to provide for the Incorporation of Religious Societies,'" is hereby repealed.

§ 4. The third section of the act passed February 15, 1826, entitled "An Act to amend an Act entitled, 'An Act to provide for the Incorporation of Religious Societies,'" passed April 5, 1813, shall not apply to any church or congregation in connection with the Protestant Episcopal Church in this State.

§ 5. All acts and parts of acts inconsistent with the provisions of this act are hereby repealed.

MINUTES

OF THE MEETING OF

THE FEDERATE COUNCIL

OF THE

FIVE DIOCESES

IN THE

STATE OF NEW YORK,

JANUARY 24, 1894.

MINUTES

FEDERATE COUNCIL.

———

NEW YORK, *January* 24, 1894.

The Holy Communion was celebrated in the Chantry of Grace Church, on the 24th of January, 1894, at 9 A. M., after which the members of the Federate Council met at 10 A. M., at the Diocesan House, 29 Lafayette Place, in accordance with the following notice :

NEW YORK, *January* 5, 1894.

A majority of the Bishops having so requested, a meeting of the Federate Council of the State of New York will be held at the Diocesan House, 29 Lafayette Place, New York, on *Wednesday*, A. M., *January* 24, *A. D.* 1894, at ten o'clock. There will be a celebration of the Holy Communion in the Chantry of Grace Church at 9 A. M.

H. C. POTTER,

Bishop of New York.

The Bishop of New York took the Chair and opened the meeting with prayers.

The Secretary proceeded to call the Roll, when the following answered to their names and took their seats as members :

The Bishop of New York, the Bishop of Albany, and the Bishop of Western New York.

From the Diocese of New York, the Rev. Drs. Gallaudet, Mulchahey, Brooks, Seabury, Van Kleeck, Rev. Messrs. Canedy and Brown, and Messrs. Calvin, Miller, and Merritt.

From the Diocese of Western New York, the Rev. Drs. Rankine, Hayes, and Lobdell.

From the Diocese of Long Island, the Rev. Drs. Drowne, Haskins, Cox, Cooper, Rev. Messrs. Baker and Swentzel, and Mr. Cogswell.

From the Diocese of Albany, the Rev. Messrs. Cookson, Edmunds, Jr., Griswold, and Mariett.

From the Diocese of Central New York, the Rev. Drs. Brainard, Lockwood, and Babcock, and Messrs. Sawyer, Van Wagenen, and Dunning.

The Rev. Mr. Cookson moved the adoption of certain Rules of Order, which he had adapted from the Rules of Order of the Diocese of New York, as the Rules of this Body.

The Rev. Mr. Canedy moved that Article IV of the Constitution, which had been proposed for this Body, but had not been adopted by the Dioceses, be made a Rule of Order in place of part of Rule XIX.

On motion, these Rules were referred to a special Committee for consideration.

The Bishop of New York appointed the Rev. Mr. Cookson, Dr. Brainard, Rev. Messrs. Canedy and Baker, and Judge Calvin as this Committee.

The Bishop of Albany stated, at length, the purpose of this Special Session of the Federate Council; the desirability of finishing the work upon the new Act on the Organization of Parishes and the Election of Vestries, proposed to be submitted to the State Legislature; and read a communication from Mr. Collin, one of the Commissioners of Statutory Revision.

The Bishop of New York read a communication from Prof. Eggleston, regretting that his illness would prevent him from attending the Council, and suggesting certain important amendments which he deemed it desirable to adopt, before the proposed Act should be presented to the Legislature, and which he intended to propose to the Commission appointed last year, had it been practicable to call it together.

It having been considered competent for this Body, in the absence of any Report from the Commission, to amend and complete the legislation proposed in 1889;

On motion of the Rev. Dr. Hayes, it was

Resolved, That we go into a Committee of the Whole for the purpose of considering the changes that may be desirable in the Act.

On motion, the Bishop of Western New York was requested to act as Chairman of the Committee of the Whole.

The Secretary was requested to read the whole Act as formulated in 1889, by the Federate Council.

On motion of the Rev. Dr. Van Kleeck, it was

Resolved, That the several Sub-Sections which it is proposed to amend in the Act, be taken up singly, and the amendments be considered and adopted.

On motion of the Bishop of New York, it was

Resolved, That in all places in this Act, the words " male person or persons " shall be changed to " man " or " men."

On motion, it was

Ordered, That sub-section 3 be altered so as to read: "The officiating Minister, or if there be none, or he shall be necessarily absent, any other person called to the Chair shall preside at such meeting, and shall receive the votes.

On motion, it was

Ordered, That sub-section 4 shall read: "The persons entitled to vote at each meeting shall be men of full age, etc.," and in the latter clause, "those who have been baptized, or who have been regular contributors, etc."

On motion, it was

Ordered, That sub-section 5, clause *third*, shall read in the place of "the Monday," as follows: "On such day in the week after the first Sunday in Advent, as may be designated in the Act of Incorporation, and until others are elected in their stead."

On motion, it was

Ordered, That sub-sections 8 and 9 be adopted with the word "parish" substituted for "Church" in the latter, and elsewhere when preferable.

On motion, it was

Ordered, That sub-section 10 be altered so as to read instead of "On the Monday," as follows: "On such day in the week after the first Sunday in Advent in each year, as may be designated in the Act of Incorporation, the men qualified to vote in every congregation, etc."

On motion of the Bishop of Albany, sub-section 11 was amended so as to read, and with this amendment, it was adopted.

"The persons entitled to vote at such annual election shall be men of full age belonging to the church or congregation, who have been regular attendants and contributors to the support of the parish or congregation for not less than twelve months next prior to such meeting," and on motion it was adopted as amended.

On motion, sub-section 12 was amended and adopted so as to read as follows:

"No person shall be eligible for office as warden who is not a man of full age and a communicant, or as vestryman who is not a man of full age and baptized."

On motion, sub-sections 13, 14, 15, 16, 17 and 18 were adopted as they read.

On motion of the Rev. Dr. Hayes, it was

Ordered, That sub-section 19 be adopted with the substitution of "parish" for "corporation," and sub-section 20, after dropping the words "or corporation."

On motion of the Rev. Dr. Van Kleeck, it was

Ordered, That when this Committee of the Whole shall rise, they recommend the foregoing amendments and action to the Council for adoption.

The Committee then rose.

On motion of the Rev. Dr. Hayes, it was

Resolved, That the action taken by the committee be adopted as the action of the Federate Council.[1]

On motion of the Rev. Dr. Gallaudet, amended by the Bishop of New York, it was

Resolved, That it is the judgment of this body that a separate article embodying the law of this Church be requested of the Statutory Committee of the Legislature, similar to the plan followed for the Roman and Greek churches.

The Bishop of New York, having an engagement elsewhere, begged leave to present the following resolutions, which would require no discussion :

Resolved, That the Secretary be instructed to convey to the Right Rev., the Bishop of Central New York, the respectful and affectionate salutations of this Council, and to assure him of its hearty sympathy in his large and arduous work, and in his efforts for the extension of Christ's Kingdom and the due guardianship of the flock committed to his charge.

On motion, this Resolution was adopted unanimously by a rising vote.

On the further motion of the Bishop of New York, it was

Resolved, That a Committee be appointed consisting of the Bishops of the State, five Presbyters, and five Laymen, to consider and report to a future meeting of this Council, as to the expediency and practicability of such a re-distribution of the territory of the State of New York into six or more dioceses, as shall most effectually promote the work of the Church and the continued usefulness and efficiency of its Episcopate.

The Bishop of Albany stated that he would appoint this Committee after obtaining from each of the other Bishops the nomination of a presbyter and a layman. He subsequently reported

For the Diocese of New York: Rev. Brady E. Backus, D. D., and Mr. Douglas Merritt.

For the Diocese of Western New York: Rev. James W. Ashton, D. D., and Judge J. M. Smith.

For the Diocese of Long Island: Rev. Henry C. Swentzel, and Hon. John A. King.

For the Diocese of Albany: Rev. C. C. Edmunds, Jr., and Mr. Selden E. Marvin.

And for the Diocese of Central New York: Rev. A. B. Goodrich, D. D., and Judge Charles Andrews.

On motion of the Rev. Mr. Cookson, it was

Resolved, That a Committee consisting of one Bishop, one Presbyter, and one Layman, be appointed to carefully consider the amended Act of Incorporation of the Church in this State, decided upon this day by this Council, and make any needed correction of clerical errors, and report the Act, as thus perfected, to the Secretary of this Council.

The Bishop of Albany appointed Bishop Littlejohn, Rev. Dr. Seabury, and Judge Sawyer as this Committee.

On motion of Judge Calvin, it was

Resolved, That the same Committee take into consideration the condition of parishes already organized in case this law should be enacted.

On motion of Judge Calvin, it was

Resolved, That the Secretary print the perfected Act and send it to the members of the Council and to the Secretaries of the five Dioceses.

On motion of the Bishop of Albany, it was

Resolved, That under the powers assured to this Body by the Canon of the General Convention, the Federate Council is competent to take such action as it may deem necessary to secure any legislative enactments which the common interests of the Church in the State may require.

Resolved, That having due regard to the relations of the Dioceses to the Federate Council and to the history of the discussion in regard to the proposed changes in the Act of Incorporation the Secretary be instructed to notify the action of the Federate Council to the Convention of each Diocese in the State of New York, with the earnest request that each Convention will take final action in regard to that subject at its next session.

On motion of the Bishop of Albany, in behalf of the Bishop of Western New York, it was

Resolved, That the five Dioceses of the Protestant Episcopal Church in the State of New York as represented in this Federate Council, recognize the necessity of sundry amendments in the Act as now existing, and are substantially agreed as to the amendments which have been under their consideration; and while they are not prepared as yet to present this body of amendments as their final decision, they ask when the Commission of Statutory Revision shall meet the point in their work, that the existing laws relating to the Protestant Episcopal Church in this State shall be for the present incorporated as a separate section in the statute, to which the five Dioceses will formulate amendments at their earliest ability, to be communicated to the Commission.

The Rev. Dr. Brooks reported, in behalf of the Commission to consider the subject of a Marriage License, that the matter was deemed inexpedient and impracticable.

On motion of the Rev. Dr. Cooper, it was

Resolved, That the thanks of this Council are returned to the Bishop of New York for his courtesy and hospitality.

On motion, the Council adjourned.

Attest: T. STAFFORD DROWNE,
                                                          Secretary.

Institutions Within the Diocese.

Diocesan.

THE SISTERHOOD OF THE HOLY CHILD JESUS.

ST. AGNES' SCHOOL, ALBANY.

THE CHILD'S HOSPITAL, ALBANY.

ST. MARGARET'S HOUSE, ALBANY.

THE CHURCH HOME, TROY.

THE ST. CHRISTINA HOME, SARATOGA SPRINGS.

THE ST. CHRISTOPHER HOME, EAST LINE.

THE ORPHAN HOUSE OF THE HOLY SAVIOUR, COOPERSTOWN.

THE BIBLE AND COMMON PRAYER BOOK SOCIETY OF ALBANY AND VICINITY.

ST. FAITH'S SCHOOL FOR GIRLS, SARATOGA SPRINGS.

Parochial.

ST. PETER'S ORPHANAGE, ALBANY.

THE MARTHA MEMORIAL HOUSE, TROY.

THE MARY WARREN FREE INSTITUTE, TROY.

Canonical and Other Offerings

WITH

NAMES OF TREASURERS.

— — —

DIOCESAN FUND.

> Gen. Selden E. Marvin, Albany.

MISSIONS OF THE DIOCESE.

> Gen. Selden E. Marvin, Albany.

FUND FOR AGED AND INFIRM CLERGYMEN.

> Gen. Selden E. Marvin, Albany.

FUND FOR WIDOWS AND ORPHANS OF DECEASED CLERGYMEN.

> Gen. Selden E. Marvin, Albany.

CLERGY RESERVE FUND.

> Gen. Selden E. Marvin, Albany.

BIBLE AND COMMON PRAYER BOOK SOCIETY OF ALBANY.

> Mr. H. B. Dauchy, Troy.

EPISCOPAL FUND.

> Mr. J. H. Van Antwerp, Albany.

SALARY OF THE BISHOP.

> Mr. W. W. Rousseau, Troy.

EDUCATION OF YOUNG MEN FOR THE MINISTRY.

> The Treasurer of the Diocese, or Mr. Richard M. Harison, 31 Nassau street, New York.

ORPHAN HOUSE OF THE HOLY SAVIOUR.

> Mr. Leslie Pell-Clarke, Springfield Centre, Otsego county.

DOMESTIC AND FOREIGN MISSIONS.

> Mr. George Bliss, Church Missions House, Fourth avenue and Twenty-second Street, New York.

Lightning Source UK Ltd.
Milton Keynes UK
UKHW012121180219
337529UK00012B/1483/P

ISBN 978-0-331-67210-7
PIBN 11068534

Forgotten Books is a registered trademark of FB &c Ltd.
Copyright © 2018 FB &c Ltd.
FB &c Ltd, Dalton House, 60 Windsor Avenue, London, SW19 2RR.
Company number 08720141. Registered in England and Wales.

For support please visit www.forgottenbooks.com